BUSINESSES AND ORGANIZATIONS CITED IN THIS BOOK

3M Dental Products Division

Accenture
ADAC Laboratories
Advanced Circuits
Advocate Good Samaritan Hospital (GSAM)
Airbus
Alcoa
Alliance for Work-Life Progress
Allied Signal
Amalgamated Clothing and Textile Workers
Amazon.com
American College of Surgeons
American Electric Power
American Express
American Honda Motor Co.
American Management Association
American National Standards Institute (ANSI)
American Productivity and Quality Center
American Quality Foundation
American Red Cross
American Society for Quality (ASQ)
Ames Rubber Corporation
AMR Research, Inc.
Apple
Armstrong Building Products Operations
Artesyn Technologies
AT&T
Avis

Bama Companies, Inc.
Bank of Montreal
Baptist Hospital Inc.
Baxter Healthcare International
Bell System
Bell Telephone Laboratories
Best Buy
Bethesda Hospital, Inc.
BI
BMW
Boeing
Boeing Aerospace Support
Boeing Airlift and Tanker
Branch-Smith Printing Division
British Airways
Bronson Methodist Hospital

Cadillac Motor Car Company
Cal-Poly State University
Caterpillar Financial Services Corporation (CFSC)
Caterpillar Inc.
Center for Creative Leadership

Centers for Medicare and Medicaid Services
Chick-fil-A
Chrysler Corporation
Chugach School District
Cigna Corp.
Cincinnati Fiberglass
Citibank
Clarke American Checks
Clifton Metal Works
CNH Capital
Coca-Cola Company
Compaq
Computer Associates
Consolidated School District 15 (D15)
Continental Airlines
Coors Brewing Company
Corning Telecommunications Products
    Division (TPD)
CSN Stores
Cummins Engine Company
Custom Research Inc.

Daimler-Chrysler
Dana Corporation-Spicer Driveshaft Division
Datsun
Deere & Company
Delcor Homes
Dell Inc.
Delta Group
Domino's Pizza
Don Simon Homes
Douglas Aircraft
Doylestown Hospital
DuPont
DynMcDermott Petroleum Operations

Eastman Chemical Company
eBay
Economic Club of Chicago
ENBI Corporation
Enterprise Resource Planning
Environmental Protection Agency
European Foundation for Quality Management
European Organization for Quality Control

Federal Trade Commission
FedEx
Fidelity Investments
First National Bank of Chicago
Florida Power and Light
Ford Motor Company
Froedtert Memorial Lutheran Hospital, Milwaukee

continued in back of book

Managing for Quality *and* Performance Excellence

NINTH EDITION

JAMES R. EVANS
University of Cincinnati

WILLIAM M. LINDSAY
Professor Emeritus of Management
Northern Kentucky University

SOUTH-WESTERN
CENGAGE Learning

Australia • Brazil • Japan • Korea • Mexico • Singapore • Spain • United Kingdom • United States

SOUTH-WESTERN
CENGAGE Learning·

Managing for Quality and Performance Excellence, Ninth Edition
James R. Evans and William M. Lindsay

Senior Vice President, LRS/Acquisitions & Solutions Planning: Jack W. Calhoun

Editorial Director, Business & Economics: Erin Joyner

Editor-in-Chief: Joe Sabatino

Senior Acquisition Editor: Charles McCormick, Jr.

Developmental Editor: Conor Allen

Editorial Assistant: Anne Merrill

Senior Brand Manager: Kristen Hurd

Art and Cover Direction, Production Management, and Composition: PreMediaGlobal

Media Editor: Chris Valentine

Rights Acquisition Director: Audrey Pettengill

Rights Acquisition Specialist, Text and Image: John Hill

Manufacturing Planner: Ron Montgomery

Cover Image(s): © Datacraft Co Ltd/ Getty Images

For product information and technology assistance, contact us at
Cengage Learning Customer & Sales Support, 1-800-354-9706

For permission to use material from this text or product,
submit all requests online at **www.cengage.com/permissions**
Further permissions questions can be emailed to
permissionrequest@cengage.com

Library of Congress Control Number: 2012952324

ISBN-13: 978-1-285-06946-3

ISBN-10: 1-285-06946-3

South-Western
5191 Natorp Boulevard
Mason, OH 45040
USA

Cengage Learning is a leading provider of customized learning solutions with office locations around the globe, including Singapore, the United Kingdom, Australia, Mexico, Brazil, and Japan. Locate your local office at: **www.cengage.com/global**

Cengage Learning products are represented in Canada by Nelson Education, Ltd.

For your course and learning solutions, visit **www.cengage.com**

Purchase any of our products at your local college store or at our preferred online store **www.cengagebrain.com**

Printed in the United States of America
1 2 3 4 5 6 7 16 15 14 13 12

Brief Contents

Contents

PART 3   BEYOND QUALITY MANAGEMENT: MANAGING FOR PERFORMANCE EXCELLENCE   519

Chapter 10   The Baldrige Framework for Performance Excellence   521

APPENDICES

Preface

Continuous and breakthrough improvement are two of the most important concepts in quality. With each new edition of this book, we practice continuous improvement by updating the content to reflect current trends and practices in quality management and performance excellence approaches. Every so often, however, some breakthrough improvement is needed. While this edition contains the same essential content as previous editions, we have made substantial changes in the organization and presentation of the material. In reflecting on the title "Managing for Quality *and* (emphasis added) Performance Excellence," along with current quality initiatives in many organizations to "get back to the basics," we came to the conclusion that students and future managers need a solid foundation in the principles of quality management before they can fully appreciate the concept of performance excellence from an organizational perspective (i.e. the Baldrige Criteria). Thus, we have reorganized the material to focus on three main concepts: the foundation principles of quality management; tools and techniques to drive and support design, control, and improvement of quality; followed by an organizational view of performance excellence as reflected by the Malcolm Baldrige Criteria. Along with this reorganization, we have made numerous pedagogical improvements by streamlining much of the content, removing dated material, adding new and current perspectives, clearly illustrating numerical examples, and strengthening the use of Excel for numerical calculations. And Cengage Learning has designed a new look and format!

So why is quality still vital to America and the world? The American Society for Quality (ASQ) monitors news items reported in the press. What types of stories do we find? Food safety and toy recalls, health care, the automotive industry, and various product glitches dominate. Indeed, quality—or lack of quality—is a vital issue in everyone's life. Quality is relevant and important for today's students and future business leaders, as well as those already in the workforce. Today's business and nonprofit organizations need to capitalize on the knowledge and "lessons learned" that excellent organizations have acquired.

Sadly, in 2012 the U.S. Congress eliminated federal funding for the Baldrige Award Program. While the future of Baldrige is in transition to the private sector, we remain firmly committed to its principles and practices as "the leading edge of validated management practices," as described by a former chair of the Baldrige Panel of Judges. We feel that one of the best ways of obtaining such knowledge is from the national role models that have emerged from the Baldrige program in the United States and similar programs throughout the world. We continue to use Baldrige as the fundamental framework for organizing and presenting key issues of performance excellence.

CHANGES IN THE NINTH EDITION

- The ninth edition of *Managing for Quality and Performance Excellence* continues to embrace the fundamental principles, criteria, and historical foundations of total quality, while providing a foundation for understanding and applying technical tools and performance excellence from an enterprise perspective. All chapters have been updated to provide the most current coverage available.

- We have updated and strengthened the quantitative material in this book, particularly in Chapter 6 on statistical methods. We have developed new and updated Excel templates to facilitate problem solving and incorporated them into numerous examples.
- We have also developed new and interesting *Quality Profiles* and *Quality in Practice* cases and a wide variety of examples from organizations around the world. These profiles and QIP cases emphasize the importance of quality in the global economy. We also added new cases and revised many end-of-chapter problems from the previous edition.

Some highlights that continue from the previous edition include:

- Student-friendly layout highlighting important concepts
- Student Companion Website materials that include summaries of key points and terminology, data files, Excel templates and examples, and various materials relating to the Baldrige Award Program
- Text coverage of most of the body of knowledge (BOK) required for ASQ certification as a Certified Quality Manager

ORGANIZATION

Part I focuses on the principles of quality; Part II concentrates on technical tools and techniques, and Part III focuses on performance excellence and the Baldrige Criteria. This organization provides the instructor with considerable flexibility by focusing on both managerial and technical topics for audiences ranging from undergraduate students to MBA students or executives.

Part I provides an introduction to quality management principles.

- Chapter 1 introduces the notion of quality, definitions, its history and importance, the role of quality in manufacturing and service, and its impact on competitive advantage and financial return.
- Chapter 2 explores the foundations of modern quality management from the perspectives of Deming, Juran, and Crosby, and summarizes the fundamental principles of quality management. This chapter also discusses variation and statistical thinking, quality management systems, and ISO 9000.
- Chapters 3, 4, and 5 focus on the three core principles of quality: customers, the workforce, and processes. Each of these chapters builds on key concepts that are reflected in the quality management literature and the Baldrige Criteria, but does so independently from Baldrige, which is addressed in Part III.

Part II focuses on the technical issues underlying quality design, control, and improvement.

- Chapter 6 focuses on statistical tools and methods.
- In Chapter 7 we focus on quality in product design and the variety of tools and techniques that support it.
- Chapter 8 introduces process measurement provides a basic coverage of statistical process control (SPC).

- Chapter 9 focuses on process improvement and introduces Six Sigma in a unified fashion.

  Part III is all about organizational quality, Baldrige, and implementation.

- Chapter 10 introduces the Baldrige framework and criteria, as well as international quality and performance excellence programs.
- In Chapter 11, we provide a strategic focus on quality, and discuss strategic planning, organizational design, and strategic work system design.
- Chapter 12 focuses on the use of data and information to measure and manage organizational performance. This chapter includes discussion of balanced scorecards and modern approaches to knowledge management.
- Chapter 13 discusses leadership for quality, both from a practical and theoretical perspective, and also includes an updated section on governance and societal responsibilities.
- The final chapter, Chapter 14, deals with building and sustaining high-performance organizations.

Features and Pedagogy to Enhance Learning

Each chapter begins with featured Quality Profiles of two role-model organizations. Most of these organizations are Baldrige recipients. Quality Spotlight boxes identify examples of unique organizational practices, and icons in the margin indicate that extensive supplementary materials may be found on the accompanying Student Companion website.

In each chapter, *Quality in Practice* case studies describe real applications of the chapter material. They reinforce the chapter concepts and provide opportunities for discussion and more practical understanding. Many of the case studies are drawn from real, published, or personal experiences of the authors.

End-of-chapter materials for each chapter include Review Questions, which are designed to help students check their understanding of the key concepts presented in the chapter. Chapters in Parts I and II also have Discussion Questions that are open-ended or experiential in nature, and designed to help students expand their thinking or tie practical experiences to abstract concepts. As appropriate, Problems are designed to help students develop and practice quantitative skills. Most chapters have a section entitled Projects, Etc. that provides projects involving field investigation or other types of research. Finally, each chapter includes several cases, which encourage critical thinking through application of quality concepts to unstructured or comprehensive situations.

Flexibility for Teaching

The text is designed to support different types of courses. For example, an undergraduate course in quality management might focus on basic quality principles, tools, and techniques covered in Chapters 1 through 9, with perhaps an introduction to performance excellence and the Baldrige Criteria in Chapter 10 and a brief discussion of material in Chapters 11 through 14. An MBA course focusing on the managerial aspects of quality might begin with Chapters 1 and 2, introduce the Baldrige framework in Chapter 10, and then cover chapters 3, 4, 5, and 11 through 14 with perhaps some brief discussions of tools and techniques in Chapters 6 through 9.

Student Companion Site

The student companion site for this book contains summaries of key points and terminology for each chapter, Excel templates, datasets, and more. To get free access to these materials, go to www.cengagebrain.com, and search for this book by its title.

Instructor Resources

Instructor's Resource CD (978-1-285-18406-7): Place all of the key teaching resources you need conveniently at your fingertips with this all-in-one source for planning, teaching, grading and assessing student understanding and progress. This CD now includes the full Instructor's Manual/Solutions Manual with teaching suggestions and answers to all cases and problems in the text, Test Bank in Word and Exam-View® computerized format, and PowerPoint® presentation slides.

PowerPoint® Slides: Created by text coauthor, James Evans, these clear presentation slides help bring your lectures to life, clarify difficult concepts, and provide guides for student note-taking and study. The slides are also available for download on the instructor resource website.

Instructor Resource Website: To access the instructor resource website, visit www.cengagebrain.com and search for this book by its title. In addition to the quality management strengths, insights into the Baldrige Award, Six Sigma, and ISO 9000 found within this edition, you can access a rich array of teaching and learning resources at the interactive companion website. You can easily download password-protected teaching resources, including brief videos highlighting winning practices of Baldrige award winners, the PowerPoints, Instructor's Manual/Solutions Manual, and Test Bank whenever you need them to support your course. A new feature in this edition is a set of Instructor Reserve problems from the problem-solving chapters, which instructors can use for in-class demonstrations of problem-solving techniques or for student "workshop" sessions. For chapters with numerical problems, PowerPoint versions of selected problems from the end-of-chapter and Instructor Reserve sets are also provided.

Instructor's Manual/Solutions Manual: Prepared by text coauthor, William Lindsay, this critical teaching tool contains insightful teaching suggestions and notes as well as answers to all end-of-chapter questions, exercises, problems, and cases for your convenience. Available on both the IRCD and the instructor resource website.

Note on Company References and Citations

In today's ever-changing business environment, many companies and divisions are sold, merged, or divested, whereas others have declared bankruptcy, resulting in name changes. For example, Texas Instruments Defense Systems & Electronics Group was sold to Raytheon and is now part of Thales Raytheon Systems Company, and AT&T Universal Card Services was bought by CitiBank (which is now CitiGroup). Although we have made efforts to note these changes in the book, others will undoubtedly occur after publication. In citing applications of quality management in these companies, we have generally preserved their original names to clarify that the practices and results cited occurred under their original corporate identities.

ACKNOWLEDGMENTS

We are extremely grateful to all the quality professionals, professors, reviewers, and students who have provided valuable ideas and comments during the development of this and previous editions.

Many people deserve special thanks for their contributions to development and production of the book. Our regards go to our senior acquisitions editor Charles McCormick, Jr., who we regard as a close and valuable friend, developmental editor Conor Allen, senior content production manager Kim Kusnerak, technology project manager Chris Valentine, and John Hill of the Permissions Coordination Group at Cengage Learning, and Richard Fenton, Mary Schiller, and Esther Craig, our previous editors at West Educational Publishing, and our long-time, now-retired developmental editor at Thomson Higher Education Division, Alice Denny.

Quality expert Joseph Juran was asked in an interview in 2002 what advice he would give to someone just starting out in quality today. He replied, "I would start out by saying 'Are you lucky!' Because I think the best is yet to be. In this current century, we are going to see a lot of growth in quality because the scope has expanded so much … away from manufacturing to all the other industries, including the giants: health care, education, and government." We will continue to do our best to improve this book in our quest for quality and to spread what we truly believe is a fundamentally important message to current and future generations of business leaders. We appreciate any and all feedback about the book. Feel free to contact us at the email addresses below.

James R. Evans (james.evans@uc.edu)
William M. Lindsay (lindsay@nku.edu)

PART 1

Principles of Quality

H. James Harrington, columnist for *Quality Digest* magazine and one of the leading quality management consultants in the world, lamented the lack of a true quality focus in the United States and around the world, from both organizational and personal perspectives. He observed

> *From where I stand, CEOs around the world have lost much of their interest in quality … we are more interested in reducing cost, removing waste, and reducing cycle time … Maybe it's time we got back to basic quality measurements. We talk about getting to the root cause of problems. Well, I think we need to get to the root results of our actions by measuring the level of customer satisfaction improvement, the increase in mean time to failure, reducing percent defective during the first 90 days of usage, stopping product recalls, and lowering return rates—not dollars saved, inventory turns, or output per hour. We are trying to do everything for everybody, and as a result we are missing the real quality objective—better and better products and services.*
>
> *We need to take pride in what we do. When you go home at night and look in the mirror, will you able to smile and say, "I did my very best"? Too many of us stop short of being our best. We say, "That's good enough," never knowing how good we could be … To make up for these sloppy work habits, we are using information technology to offset the lack of interest in the job and the lack of commitment to the organization … What we need to do is get back to basics. The things that made us great in the first place are hard work, pride in accomplishment, technical education, and strong family values.*[1]

Does quality matter to you personally as a consumer and future employee or manager? We certainly hope so, because that is what this book is about. While poor quality can be a source of irritation and frustration to you as a consumer, it can be costly to businesses (and investors) in the form of product recalls or lost customers. Poor quality can be lethal—on April 20, 2010, BP's Deepwater Horizon drilling rig exploded due to poor quality cement around the well that contractors failed to test in order to save time and money. The explosion killed 11 people, led to the largest environmental disaster in U.S. history, and cost BP $10 billion. It would have taken only 10 hours and cost only $128,000 to check the cement. The economic welfare and survival of businesses and nations depends on the quality of the goods and services they produce, which depend fundamentally on the quality of the workforce and management practices that define their organization.

Quality has become a vital component of every modern organization and will remain an important part of a continual quest for improving performance across the globe. Joseph Juran, one of the most respected leaders of quality in the twentieth century, suggested that the past century will be defined by historians as the century of productivity, and the current century has to be the century of quality. "We've made dependence on the quality of our technology a part of life."[2]

Building and maintaining quality into an organization's goods and services, and more importantly, into the infrastructure of the organization itself is not an easy task. If it were, there would be little need for this book. As a member of the emerging generation of business leaders, you have an opportunity and a responsibility to improve the quality of your organization and society at large, not just for products and services, but in everything you say and do.

Part 1 introduces the basic concepts of quality. Chapter 1 discusses the definition and history of quality, and the impact of quality on competitive advantage and business results. Chapter 2 describes the foundations of modern quality management—the philosophies on which modern concepts of quality are based, the key principles of quality management, and ISO 9000, which provides a basis for a solid quality management system. Chapters 3, 4, and 5 focus on each of the three core principles of quality: customer focus, workforce focus, and process focus.

NOTES

1. H. James Harrington, "Are We Going Astray?" *Quality Digest*, Feb. 2008; "The Decline of U.S. Dominance—Part 1," *Quality Digest*, April 2008; "The Decline of U.S. Dominance—Part 2," *Quality Digest*, May 2008. www.qualitydigest.com. Reprinted with permission.

2. Thomas A. Stewart, "A Conversation with Joseph Juran," *Fortune*, January 11, 1999, 168–169.

Introduction to Quality

Quality is by no means a new concept in modern business. In October 1887, William Cooper Procter, grandson of the founder of Procter & Gamble, told his employees, "The first job we have is to turn out quality merchandise that consumers will buy and keep on buying. If we produce it efficiently and economically, we will earn a profit, in which you will share." Procter's statement addresses three issues that are critical to managers of manufacturing and service organizations: *productivity*, *cost*, and *quality*. Productivity (the measure of efficiency defined as the amount of output achieved per unit of input), the cost of operations, and the quality of the goods and services that create customer satisfaction all contribute to profitability. Of these three determinants of profitability, the most significant factor in determining the long-run success or failure of any organization is quality. Some 125 years later, this sentiment was echoed by the Conference Board, which concluded from a survey of more than 700 CEOs and executives from around the world that quality is uniquely positioned to accelerate organizational growth through better execution and alignment, and it also provides the voice of the customer critical to developing innovative products and services.[1]

High-quality goods and services can provide an organization with a competitive edge. A reputation for high quality generates satisfied and loyal customers who reward the organization with continued patronage and favorable word-of-mouth advertising, often resulting in new customers. In contrast, the consequences of failing to adequately address quality can be devastating. Consider Toyota Motor Company: Toyota developed an impeccable reputation for high quality and low cost through relentless attention and continuous improvement of its production processes. The Camry became the best-selling car in America, and by 2008 Toyota overtook General Motors in global sales. But in 2009, a series of "unintended acceleration" incidents, including one involving a Lexus ES 350, led to $2 billion in recalls to replace floor mats and gas pedal assemblies. Other defects involving antilock braking systems, the wire cables holding spare tires, and vehicle software were soon uncovered, resulting in additional recalls and even suspended sales of eight popular models. As one columnist noted, "No matter how rigorous an automaker's development process might be, there's still potential for problems with quality or reliability."[2] The problem extended beyond engineering into the underlying management processes of the company. Newspaper articles accused the company of hiding defects that they knew about for many years. Toyota quickly lost its credibility and trustworthiness. Despite the fact that the company was later exonerated, with no finding of design flaws in their braking systems, the damage was done. Akio Toyoda, grandson of the company's founder, stated, "We maybe slacked in some of our core principles [like] attention to the basics of manufacturing…. We're working hard to fill those gaps … and secure the confidence of our customers."[3] To refocus on quality, Toyota appointed a chief quality officer and an advisory panel on safety, and restructured its reporting system to better communicate defect issues. As this case suggests, quality is vital to products (goods and/or services) as well as the management processes and systems that produce and deliver them.

At the beginning of each chapter we profile two "role-model" organizations, most of which are recipients of the Baldrige Award (also known as the Malcolm Baldrige National Quality Award). The Baldrige Award recognizes outstanding U.S. organizations that have highly effective management practices that lead to superior business results; we will learn more about it in Part III of this book. These examples will help you understand some of the approaches and cultural factors that are characteristic of organizations that have pursued a strategy of quality and performance excellence.

The mandate for focusing on quality is clear and simple. In working with Chrysler Corporation to improve quality several decades ago, a vice president of the United Auto Workers (UAW) succinctly stated the importance of quality: "No quality, no sales. No sales, no profit. No profit, no jobs." The role of quality is recognized in many organizations with senior executives in charge of quality at the highest levels of management. For instance, Apple created a new position— Senior Vice President of Operations Dedicated to Product Quality—whose responsibility is to ensure that Apple's products meet "the highest standards of quality."[4]

In this chapter, we introduce the notion of quality. We discuss how it is defined, historical developments, its importance in business and in building and sustaining competitive advantage, and the role of quality in manufacturing, service, and business systems.

quality**profiles**

Motorola, Inc. and MidwayUSA

Motorola, Inc. was a household name and a recognized leader in quality for a long time. Like many other companies, Motorola has had its share of difficulties in tough competitive technology markets and economic environments, and as a result, has made many changes in its business operations, existing today as two divisions: Motorola Mobility, which provides communication products for the consumer market, and Motorola Solutions, which provides mission-critical communications products and services to enterprises and governments.

Motorola was a leader in the U.S. quality revolution during the 1980s and was one of the first organizations to receive the Baldrige Award in 1988. It built its culture on two key beliefs: respect for people and uncompromising integrity. Motorola was a pioneer in continual reduction of defects and cycle times in all the company's processes, from design, order entry, manufacturing, and marketing, to administrative functions. Employees in every function of the business measure defects and use statistical techniques to analyze the results. Products that once took weeks to make are now completed in less than an hour. Even the time needed for closing the financial books has been reduced; what used to take a month was shortened to only four days by applying quality principles.

Throughout its history, Motorola's maintained a focus on quality. In 2002, the Commercial, Government, and Industrial Solutions Sector (CGISS) also received a Baldrige Award. CGISS was recognized around the world for its environmental, health, and safety efforts. Customers reported high levels of satisfaction, and the division demonstrated strong financial, product quality, cycle time, and productivity performance. These results came from exceptional practices in managing human assets, sharing data and information with employees, customers, and suppliers, and aligning all its business processes with key organizational objectives.

MidwayUSA is a family-owned catalog and Internet retailer offering "Just About Everything (SM)" for shooters, reloaders, gunsmiths, and hunters. Based in Columbia, Missouri, MidwayUSA has 243 fulltime and 100 part-time employees. MidwayUSA's vision is both simple and challenging: "To be the best-run business in America for the benefit of our Customers." Many in the company's workforce have a deep passion for shooting, hunting, and outdoor sports, allowing them to use personal knowledge and insight to better serve their customers. All salaried employees (including senior leaders) spend one hour each week on the phone taking orders and answering customer requests. Employees are selected for leadership development based on their support of the company's core value of "Customer-driven excellence" in addition to other performance-based criteria. Through its website, MidwayUSA directly solicits customer input on improving operations by regularly featuring online surveys, posting customer reviews of the products the company offers, and providing an "I'm Having Trouble Finding" option so customers can suggest additions to the product line.

This focus on customers has yielded impressive results. MidwayUSA's customer satisfaction rating is 93 percent, and customer retention is at an all-time high of 98 percent. Overall customer loyalty, measured as "likelihood to shop again," is 94 percent. Performance results for gross sales, net income as a percentage of net sales, earnings distribution, and inventory turns all exceed MidwayUSA's number one competitor, with MidwayUSA's 2008 sales growth rate nearly three times higher.

Source: Adapted from Baldrige Award Recipient Profiles, National Institute of Standards and Technology, U.S. Department of Commerce.

DEFINING QUALITY

Quality can be a confusing concept, partly because people view quality subjectively and in relation to differing criteria based on their individual roles in the production-marketing value chain. In addition, the meaning of quality continues to evolve as the quality profession grows and matures. Neither consultants nor business professionals agree on a universal definition. For example, one study that asked managers of 86 firms in the eastern United States to define quality produced several dozen different responses, including the following:

1. Perfection
2. Consistency
3. Eliminating waste
4. Speed of delivery
5. Compliance with policies and procedures
6. Providing a good, usable product
7. Doing it right the first time
8. Delighting or pleasing customers
9. Total customer service and satisfaction[5]

Thus, it is important to understand the various perspectives from which quality is viewed in order to fully appreciate the role it plays in the many parts of a business organization. Quality can be defined from six different perspectives: *transcendent, product, value, user, manufacturing*, and *customer*.[6]

Transcendent (Judgmental) Perspective

One common notion of quality, often used by consumers, is that it is synonymous with superiority or excellence. In 1931, Walter Shewhart, who was one of the pioneers of quality control, first defined quality as the goodness of a product. This view is referred to as the *transcendent* (*transcend*, "to rise above or extend notably beyond ordinary limits"), or judgmental, definition of quality. In this sense, quality is "both absolute and universally recognizable, a mark of uncompromising standards and high achievement."[7] Common examples of products associated with an image of excellence are Rolex watches, Ritz-Carlton hotels, and Lexus automobiles. From this perspective, quality cannot be defined precisely—you just know it when you see it. It is often loosely related to the aesthetic characteristics of products that are promoted by marketing and advertising. Product excellence is also often associated with higher prices. However, high quality is not necessarily correlated with price. Just consider the case of a Florida man who purchased a $262,000 Lamborghini only to find a leaky roof, a battery that quit without notice, a sunroof that detached when the car hit a bump, and doors that jammed![8]

Excellence is abstract and subjective, and standards of excellence may vary considerably among individuals. Hence, the transcendent definition is of little practical value to managers. It does not provide a means by which quality can be measured or assessed as a basis for practical business decisions.

Product Perspective

Another definition of quality is that it is related to the *quantity* of some product attribute, such as the thread count of a shirt or bed sheet, or the number of different features in an automobile or a cell phone. This assessment implies that larger numbers of product attributes are equivalent to higher quality, so designers often try to incorporate more features into products, whether the customers want them or not. As with the transcendent notion of quality, the assessment of product attributes may vary considerably among individuals. Thus, good marketing research is needed to understand what features customers want in a product.

User Perspective

Individuals have different wants and needs and, hence, different expectations of a product. This leads to a user-based definition of quality—*fitness for intended use*, or how well the product performs its intended function. Both a Cadillac CTS and a Honda Civic are fit for use; they simply serve different needs and different groups of customers. If you want a highway-touring vehicle with luxury amenities, then a Cadillac may better satisfy your needs. If you want a vehicle for commuting in a congested urban environment, a Civic might be preferable.

Nissan Motor Company Ltd.'s early experience in the U.S. market provides an example of applying the fitness-for-use concept.[9] Nissan tested the U.S. market in 1960. Not wanting to put the Nissan name on a very risky venture, they decided to use the name Datsun on all cars and trucks sold in North America. Although the car was economical to own, U.S. drivers found it to be slow, hard to drive, low-powered, and not very comfortable. In essence, it lacked most of the qualities that North American drivers expected and was not "fit for use." The U.S. representative, Mr. Katayama, kept trying to understand customer needs and providing feedback to the designers. For some time, his company refused to believe that U.S. tastes were different from its own. After many years of nagging, Mr. Katayama finally got a product that Americans liked, the sporty 1970 240Z. Eventually, the Nissan brand name replaced Datsun. Car enthusiasts will know that Nissan in 2002 reintroduced a modern version of this classic vehicle, currently the 370Z.

A second example comes from a U.S. appliance company whose stoves and refrigerators were admired by Japanese buyers. Unfortunately, the smaller living quarters of the typical Japanese home lack enough space to accommodate the U.S. models. Some could not even pass through the narrow doors of Japanese kitchens. Although the products' performance characteristics were high, the products were simply not fit for use in Japan.

Value Perspective

A fourth approach to defining quality is based on *value*; that is, the relationship of product benefits to price. Consumers no longer buy solely on the basis of price. They compare the quality of the total package of goods and services that a business offers (sometimes called the *customer benefit package*) with price and with competitive offerings. The customer benefit package includes the physical product and its quality dimensions; presale support, such as ease of ordering; rapid, on-time, and accurate delivery; and postsale support, such as field service, warranties, and technical support. If competitors offer better choices for a similar price, consumers will rationally select the package with the highest perceived quality. If a competitor offers the same quality package of goods and services at a lower price, customers would generally choose the one having the lower price. From this perspective, a quality product is one that provides similar benefits as competing products a lower price, or one that offers greater benefits at a comparable price. A good example is generic pharmaceuticals, which usually provide the same medical benefits at a lower price.

Competing on the basis of value became a key business strategy in the early 1990s. Procter & Gamble, for example, instituted a concept it called *value pricing*—offering products at "everyday" low prices in an attempt to counter the common consumer practice of buying whatever brand happens to be on special. In this way, P&G hoped to attain consumer brand loyalty and more consistent sales, which also provided significant advantages for its manufacturing and distribution systems.

Competition demands that businesses continually seek to satisfy consumers' needs at lower prices. The ability to keep prices low requires a strong internal focus on efficiency and quality, as quality improvements in operations generally reduce costs by reducing scrap and rework. Thus, organizations must focus on continually improving both the consumer benefit package and the quality and efficiency of their internal operations.

Manufacturing Perspective

Consumers and organizations want consistency in goods and services. When you frequent a Chipotle restaurant, you expect the same amount of ingredients and taste in every burrito. For the Coca-Cola Company, quality is "about manufacturing a product that people can depend on every time they reach for it," according to Donald R. Keough, former president and chief operations officer. Through rigorous quality and packaging standards, Coca-Cola strives to ensure that its products will taste the same anywhere in the world a consumer might buy them. Service organizations likewise strive for consistency in performance; The Ritz-Carlton Hotel Company, for example, seeks to ensure that its customers will have the same quality experience at any of their properties around the world.

Having standards for goods and services and meeting these standards leads to the fifth definition of quality: *conformance to specifications*. **Specifications** are targets and tolerances determined by designers of goods and services. Targets (formally called *nominal specifications*) are the ideal values for which production is to strive; tolerances are necessary because it is impossible to meet targets all of the time. In manufacturing, for example, a part dimension might be specified as "0.236 $\pm$ 0.003 cm." These measurements would mean that the target, or ideal value, is 0.236 centimeters, and that the allowable variation (tolerance) is 0.003 centimeters from the target. Thus, any dimension in the range 0.233 to 0.239 centimeters would conform to specifications. Likewise, in services, "on-time arrival" for an airplane is typically defined as being within 15 minutes of the scheduled arrival time. The target is the scheduled time, and the tolerance is specified to be 15 minutes. Specifications are meaningless, however, if they do not reflect attributes that are deemed important to the consumer. This definition provides an unambiguous way to measure quality and determine if a good is manufactured or a service is delivered as it was designed.

Customer Perspective

The American National Standards Institute (ANSI) and the American Society for Quality (ASQ) standardized official definitions of quality terminology in 1978.[10] They defined quality as *the totality of features and characteristics of a product or service that bears on its ability to satisfy given needs*. This definition draws heavily on the product and user definitions and is driven by the need to create satisfied customers. By the end of the 1980s, many organizations had begun using a simpler, yet powerful, customer-based definition of quality that remains popular today: *meeting or exceeding customer expectations.*

To understand this definition, one must first understand the meanings of "customer." Most people think of a customer as the ultimate purchaser of a product or service; for instance, the person who buys an automobile for personal use or the guest who registers at a hotel is considered an ultimate purchaser. These customers are more precisely referred to as **consumers**. Clearly, meeting the expectations of consumers is the ultimate goal of any business. Before a product reaches consumers, however, it may flow through a chain of many firms or departments, each of which adds some value to the product. For example, an automobile engine plant may purchase steel from a steel company, produce engines, and then transport the engines to an assembly plant. The steel company is a supplier to the engine plant; the engine plant is a supplier to the assembly plant. The engine plant is thus a customer of the steel company, and the assembly plant is a customer of the engine plant. These customers are called **external customers**.

Every employee in an organization also has **internal customers** who receive goods or services from suppliers within the organization. An assembly department, for example, is an internal customer of the machining department, and a person on an assembly line is an internal customer of the person who performs the previous task. Most businesses consist of many such "chains of customers." Thus, the job of any employee is to satisfy the needs of their internal customers, or the entire system can fail. This focus is a radical departure from traditional ways of thinking in a functionally oriented organization. It allows workers to understand their role in the larger system and their contribution to the final product. (Who are the customers of a university, its instructors, and its students?)

Customer-driven quality is fundamental to high-performing organizations. For instance, Hilton Hotels Corp. implemented its Ultimate Service program, which trains employees to anticipate guest needs, personalize service, and if necessary, deal with complaints quickly and seamlessly in an effort to ensure high levels of customer satisfaction. Hilton also uses rigorous inspections and satisfaction loyalty tracking surveys.[11]

Integrating Quality Perspectives in the Value Chain

Individuals in different business functions—for example, the designer, manufacturer or service provider, distributor, or customer—speak different "languages." Thus, different quality perspectives at different points in the value chain are important to ultimately create and deliver goods and services that will satisfy customers' needs and expectations. To understand this more clearly, examine Figure 1.1, which shows the essential elements of a value chain in manufacturing for developing, producing, and distributing goods to customers. The customer is the driving force for the production of goods and services, and customers generally view quality from either the *transcendent* or the *product perspective*. The goods and services produced should meet customers' needs and expectations. It is the role of the marketing function to determine these. Hence, the *user perspective* of quality is meaningful to people who work in marketing.

The manufacturer must translate customer requirements into detailed product and process specifications. Making this translation is the role of research and development, product design, and engineering. Product specifications might address such attributes as size, form, finish, taste, dimensions, tolerances, materials, operational characteristics, and safety features. Process specifications indicate the types of equipment, tools, and facilities to be used in production. Product designers must balance performance and cost to meet

FIGURE 1.1
Quality Perspectives
in the Value Chain

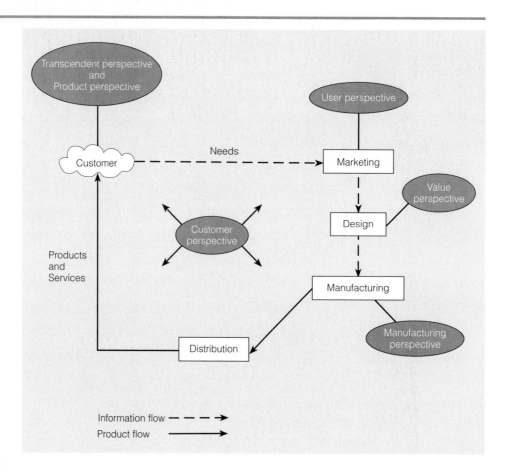

financial and marketing objectives; thus, the *value perspective* of quality is most useful at this stage.

The manufacturing function is responsible for guaranteeing that design specifications are met during production and that the final product performs as intended. Thus, for production workers, quality is defined by the *manufacturing perspective*.

Throughout the value chain, each function is an internal customer of others, and the firm itself may be an external customer or supplier to other firms. Thus, the *customer perspective* provides the basis for coordinating the entire value chain.

HISTORY OF QUALITY MANAGEMENT

As the philosopher George Santayana once said, "Those who cannot remember the past are condemned to repeat it." Thus, an understanding of the history of quality can be quite insightful. Quality has been an important aspect of production operations throughout history.[12] For instance, Egyptian wall paintings circa 1450 BC show evidence of measurement and inspection. Stones for the pyramids were cut so precisely that even today it is impossible to put a knife blade between the blocks. The Egyptians' success was due to good design, the consistent use of well-developed building methods and procedures, and precise measuring devices.

Modern quality assurance methods actually began millennia ago in China during the Zhou Dynasty. Specific governmental departments were created and given responsibility for:

- Production, inventory, and product distribution of raw material (what we now call supply chain management)
- Production and manufacturing
- Formulating and executing quality standards
- Supervision and inspection

These departments were well organized and helped establish China's central control over production processes. The system even included an independent quality organization responsible for end-to-end oversight that reported directly to the highest level of government.

The central government issued policies and procedures to control production across China—including production of utensils, carts, cotton, and silk—and prohibited the sale of nonconforming, inferior, and substandard products. An example of one of the decrees of the Zhou Dynasty is: "Utensils under standards are not allowed to be sold on the market; carts under standards are not allowed to be sold on the market; cottons and silks of which the quality and size are not up to the standards are not allowed to be sold on the market." In ancient China, inspection at various stages by the workers themselves was important in establishing responsibility for quality. When a product was found to be nonconforming, the responsible worker was identified and the root causes for the failure evaluated.

A Quality in Practice feature at the end of this chapter examines the role of quality in modern China.

The Age of Craftsmanship

During the Middle Ages in Europe, the skilled craftsperson served both as manufacturer and inspector. "Manufacturers" who dealt directly with the customer took considerable pride in workmanship. Craft guilds, consisting of masters, journeymen, and apprentices, emerged to ensure that craftspeople were adequately trained. Quality assurance was informal; every effort was made to ensure that quality was built into products by the people who produced them. These themes, which were lost with the advent of the Industrial Revolution, are important foundations of modern quality management.

In the middle of the eighteenth century, a French gunsmith named Honoré Blanc developed a system for manufacturing muskets to a standard pattern using interchangeable parts. Thomas Jefferson brought the idea to America, and in 1798, the new U.S. government awarded Eli Whitney a two-year contract to supply 10,000 muskets to its armed forces. The use of interchangeable parts necessitated careful control of quality. Whereas a customized product built by a craftsperson can be tweaked and hammered to fit and work correctly, random matching of mating parts provides no such assurance. The parts must be produced according to a carefully designed standard. Whitney designed special machine tools and trained unskilled workers to make parts following a fixed design, which were then measured and compared to a model. He underestimated the effect of variation in production processes, however (an obstacle that continues to plague many companies to this day). Because of the resulting problems, Whitney needed more than 10 years to complete the project. Nonetheless, the value of the concept of interchangeable parts was recognized, making quality assurance a critical component of the production process during the Industrial Revolution.

The Early Twentieth Century

In the early 1900s, the work of Frederick W. Taylor, often called the "father of scientific management," led to a new philosophy of production. Taylor's innovation was to separate the planning function from the execution function. Managers and engineers were given the task of planning; supervisors and workers took on the task of execution. This approach worked well at the turn of the century, when workers lacked the education needed for doing planning. By segmenting a job into specific work tasks and focusing on increasing efficiency, quality assurance fell into the hands of inspectors. Manufacturers were able to ship good-quality products, but at great costs. Defects were present, but were removed by inspection. Plants employed hundreds, even thousands, of inspectors. Inspection was thus the primary means of quality control during the first half of the twentieth century.

Eventually, manufacturing companies created separate quality departments. This artificial separation of production workers from responsibility for quality assurance led to indifference to quality among both workers and their managers. Concluding that quality was the responsibility of the quality department, many upper managers turned their attention to output quantity and efficiency. Because they had delegated so much responsibility for quality to others, upper managers gained little knowledge about quality, and when the quality crisis hit, they were ill-prepared to deal with it.

Ironically, one of the leaders of the second Industrial Revolution, Henry Ford, Sr., developed many of the fundamentals of what we now call "total quality practices" in the early 1900s. This piece of history was not discovered until Ford executives visited Japan in 1982 to study Japanese management practices. As the story goes, one Japanese executive referred repeatedly to "the book," which the Ford people learned was a Japanese translation of *My Life and Work*, written by Henry Ford and Samuel Crowther in 1926 (New York: Garden City Publishing Co.). "The book" had become Japan's industrial bible and helped Ford Motor Company realize how it had strayed from its principles over the years. Quality historians noted that Ford executives had to go to a used bookstore to find a copy when they returned to the United States.

The Bell System was the leader in the early modern history of industrial quality management.[13] It created an inspection department in its Western Electric Company in the early 1900s to support the Bell operating companies. Although the Bell System achieved its noteworthy quality through massive inspection efforts, the importance of quality in providing telephone service across the nation led it to research and develop new approaches. In the 1920s, employees of Western Electric's inspection department were transferred to Bell Telephone Laboratories. The duties of this group included the development of new theories and methods of inspection for improving and maintaining quality. The early pioneers of quality—Walter Shewhart, Harold Dodge, George Edwards, and others such as Joseph Juran and W. Edwards Deming—were members of this group. These pioneers coined the term **quality assurance**—which refers to any planned and systematic activity directed toward providing consumers with products (goods and services) of appropriate quality, along with the confidence that products meet consumers' requirements—and developed many useful techniques for measuring, controlling, and improving quality. Thus, quality became a technical discipline.

The Western Electric group, led by Walter Shewhart, ushered in the era of **statistical quality control (SQC)**, the application of statistical methods for controlling quality. Shewhart is credited with developing control charts, which became a popular means of identifying quality problems in production processes and ensuring consistency of output. Others in the group developed many other useful statistical techniques and approaches.

During World War II the U.S. military began using statistical sampling procedures and imposing stringent standards on suppliers. The War Production Board offered free training courses in the statistical methods developed within the Bell System. The impact on wartime production was minimal, but the effort developed quality specialists, who began to use and extend these tools within their organizations. Thus, statistical quality control became widely known and gradually adopted throughout manufacturing industries. Sampling tables labeled MIL-STD, for military standard, were developed and are still widely used today. The discipline's first professional journal, *Industrial Quality Control*, was published in 1944, and professional societies—notably the American Society for Quality Control (now called the American Society for Quality, www.asq.org)—were founded soon after to develop, promote, and apply quality concepts. ASQ is recognized as the leading international society for quality.

Post–World War II

After the war, during the late 1940s and early 1950s, the shortage of civilian goods in the United States made production a top priority. In most companies, quality remained the province of the specialist. Quality was not a priority of top managers, who delegated this responsibility to quality managers. Top management showed little interest in quality improvement or the prevention of defects and errors, relying instead on mass inspection.

During this time, two U.S. consultants, Dr. Joseph Juran and Dr. W. Edwards Deming, introduced statistical quality control techniques to the Japanese to aid them in their rebuilding efforts. A significant part of their educational activity was focused on upper management, rather than quality specialists alone. With the support of top managers, the Japanese integrated quality throughout their organizations and developed a culture of continuous improvement (sometimes referred to by the Japanese term *kaizen*, pronounced kī-zen). Back in 1951, the Union of Japanese Scientists and Engineers (JUSE) instituted the Deming Prize (see Chapter 2) to reward individuals and organizations who meet stringent criteria for quality management practice.

Improvements in Japanese quality were slow and steady; some 20 years passed before the quality of Japanese products exceeded that of Western manufacturers. By the 1970s, primarily because of the higher quality levels of their products, Japanese companies' penetration into Western markets was significant. Hewlett-Packard reported one of the more startling facts in 1980. In testing 300,000 16K RAM chips from three U.S. and three Japanese manufacturers, Hewlett-Packard found that the Japanese chips had an incoming failure rate of *zero* failures per thousand compared to rates of 11 and 19 for the U.S. chips. After a thousand hours of use, the failure rate of the U.S. chips was up to 27 times higher. In a few short years, the Japanese made major inroads into a market previously dominated by American companies. Likewise, the number of quality problems reported by consumers for Japanese cars was significantly lower than for domestic models. In the 1980s the U.S. steel, consumer electronics, and even banking industries also were suffering from global competition. U.S. business recognized the crisis.

The U.S. "Quality Revolution"

The decade of the 1980s was a period of remarkable change and growing awareness of quality by consumers, industry, and government. During the 1950s and 1960s, when "made in Japan" was associated with inferior products, U.S. consumers purchased domestic goods and accepted their quality without question. During the 1970s, however, increased global competition and the availability of higher-quality foreign products led U.S. consumers, armed with increased access to information, to consider their purchasing decisions more carefully and to demand high quality and reliability in goods and services at a fair price.

As technology advanced and products became more complex, the likelihood of a quality problem increased. Government safety regulations, product recalls, and the rapid increase in product-liability judgments changed society's attitude from "let the buyer beware" to "let the producer beware." Businesses began to recognize that quality was vital to their survival. A Westinghouse vice president of corporate productivity and quality summed up the situation with the quote often attributed to Dr. Samuel Johnson: "Nothing concentrates a man's mind so wonderfully as the prospect of being hanged in the morning."

One of the most influential individuals in the quality revolution was W. Edwards Deming. In 1980, NBC televised a special program entitled "If Japan Can … Why Can't We?" The widely-viewed program revealed Deming's key role in the development of Japanese quality, and his name was soon a household word among corporate executives. Although Deming had helped to transform Japanese industry three decades earlier, it was only after the television program that U.S. manufacturers asked for his help. From 1980 until his death in 1993, his leadership and expertise helped many U.S. organizations to revolutionize their approach to quality.

Quality became recognized as a key to worldwide competitiveness and was heavily promoted throughout industry.[14] Most major U.S. firms instituted extensive quality improvement campaigns, directed not only at improving internal operations, but also toward satisfying external customers. Xerox, for instance, discovered that its Japanese competitors were selling small copiers for what it cost Xerox to make them at the time, and as a consequence, initiated a corporate-wide quality improvement focus to meet the challenge. Xerox, and its former CEO David Kearns, who led their "Leadership Through Quality" initiative, had a major influence in the promotion of quality among U.S. corporations. In the five years of continuous improvement culminating in the firm's receiving the Baldrige Award in 1989, defects per 100 machines were decreased by 78 percent, unscheduled maintenance was decreased by 40 percent, manufacturing costs dropped 20 percent, product development time decreased by 60 percent, overall product quality improved 93 percent, service response time was improved by 27 percent, and the company recaptured much of the market it had lost. The company experienced strong growth during the 1990s. However, Xerox lost focus on quality as a key business driver, much of it due to short-sightedness on the part of former top management. Fortunately, better corporate leadership recognized the crisis and renewed its focus and commitment to quality (see the Quality in Practice case at the end of this chapter).

Early Successes

As business and industry began to focus on quality, the government recognized how critical quality is to the nation's economic health. In 1984, the U.S. government designated October as National Quality Month. In 1985, NASA announced an Excellence Award for Quality and Productivity. In 1987, the Baldrige Award, a statement of national intent to provide quality leadership, was established by an act of Congress. The Baldrige Award became the most influential instrument for creating quality awareness among U.S. businesses, and has also had significant global impact. In 1988, President Reagan established the Federal Quality Prototype Award and the President's Award for governmental agencies.

From the late 1980s and through the mid-1990s, interest in quality grew at an unprecedented rate. Manufacturers as well as service organizations made significant strides in improving quality. In the automobile industry, for example, improvement efforts by U.S. automakers reduced the number of problems reported per 100 domestic cars in the first 60 to 90 days of ownership from about 170 in 1987 to 136 in 1991. The gaps between Japanese and U.S. quality began to narrow, and U.S. firms regained much of the ground they had lost. (The rate has continued to improve, and many domestic models now rank among the top in recent J. D. Power and Associates' Initial Quality surveys.)

In 1989, Florida Power and Light was the first non-Japanese company to be awarded Japan's coveted Deming Prize for quality; AT&T Power Systems was the second in 1994. Quality practices expanded into the service sector and into such nonprofit organizations as schools and hospitals. By 1990, quality drove nearly every organization's quest for success. By the mid-1990s, thousands of professional books had been written, and quality-related consulting and training had blossomed into a thriving industry. Organizations began to share their knowledge and experience through formal and informal networking. The majority of states in the United States developed award programs for recognizing quality achievements in business, education, not-for-profits, and government. In 1999, Congress added nonprofit education and health care sectors to the Baldrige Award, and all other nonprofit organizations became eligible in 2007.

From Product Quality to Total Quality Management

In the 1970s, a General Electric task force studied consumer perceptions of the quality of various GE product lines.[15] Lines with relatively poor reputations for quality were found to deemphasize the customer's viewpoint, regard quality as synonymous with tight tolerance and conformance to specifications, tie quality objectives to manufacturing flow, express quality objectives as the number of defects per unit, and use formal quality control systems only in manufacturing. In contrast, product lines that received customer praise were found to emphasize satisfying customer expectations, determine customer needs through market research, use customer-based quality performance measures, and have formalized quality control systems in place for all business functions, not just for manufacturing. The task force concluded that quality must not be viewed solely as a technical discipline, but rather as a management discipline. That is, quality issues permeate all aspects of business enterprise: design, marketing, manufacturing, human resource management, supplier relations, and financial management, to name just a few.

Managers began to realize that the approaches they use to listen to customers and develop long-term relationships, develop strategy, measure performance and analyze data, reward and train employees, design and deliver products and services, and act as leaders in their organizations are the true enablers of quality, customer satisfaction, and business results. In other words, they recognized that the "quality of management" is as important as the "management of quality." In this fashion, quality assurance gave way to *quality management*. Many began to use the term **Big Q** to contrast the difference between managing for quality in all organizational processes as opposed to focusing solely on manufacturing quality (**Little q**).

As organizations came to recognize the broad scope of quality, the concept of **total quality management (TQM)**, or simply **total quality (TQ)**, emerged. A definition of total quality was endorsed in 1992 by the chairs and CEOs of nine major U.S.

corporations in cooperation with deans of business and engineering departments of major universities, and recognized consultants:

> *Total Quality (TQ) is a people-focused management system that aims at continual increase in customer satisfaction at continually lower real cost. TQ is a total system approach (not a separate area or program) and an integral part of high-level strategy; it works horizontally across functions and departments, involves all employees, top to bottom, and extends backward and forward to include the supply chain and the customer chain. TQ stresses learning and adaptation to continual change as keys to organizational success.*
>
> *The foundation of total quality is philosophical: the scientific method. TQ includes systems, methods, and tools. The systems permit change; the philosophy stays the same. TQ is anchored in values that stress the dignity of the individual and the power of community action.*[16]

Procter & Gamble proposed a more concise definition: Total quality is the unyielding and continually improving effort by everyone in an organization to understand, meet, and exceed the expectations of customers.

Actually, the concept of TQ had been around for some time. A. V. Feigenbaum recognized the importance of a comprehensive organizational approach to quality in the 1950s and coined the term *total quality control*.[17] The Japanese adopted Feigenbaum's concept and renamed it *companywide quality control*. The term *total quality management* was developed by the U.S. Naval Air Systems Command to describe its Japanese-style approach to quality improvement that is based on participation of all members of an organization in improving goods, services, and the organizational culture.

Management Failures

With all the hype and rhetoric (and the unfortunate three-letter-acronym, TQM), organizations scrambled to institute quality programs in the early 1990s. In their haste, many failed, leading to very disappointing results. Consequently, TQM met some harsh criticism. In reference to Douglas Aircraft, a troubled subsidiary of McDonnell Douglas Corporation (since merged with the Boeing Corporation), *Newsweek* stated, "The aircraft maker three years ago embraced 'Total Quality Management,' a Japanese import that had become the American business cult of the 1980s … At Douglas, TQM appeared to be just one more hothouse Japanese flower never meant to grow on rocky ground."[18] Other articles suggested that total quality approaches were passing fads and inherently flawed. However, reasons for TQM failures were most-often rooted in flawed organizational approaches and management systems, such as poor quality strategies or good strategies that were poorly executed, and not because of the underlying principles of quality management. As the editor of *Quality Digest* put it: "No, TQM isn't dead. TQM failures just prove that bad management is still alive and kicking." Although quality can drive business success, it cannot guarantee it, and one must not infer that business failures or stock price drops are the result of poor quality. Today, quality is a requirement just to play the game.

Performance Excellence

As TQM changed the way that organizations thought about customers, human resources, and manufacturing and service processes, many top executives began to recognize that *all* fundamental business activities—such as the role of leadership in guiding an organization, how an organization creates strategic plans for the future, how data and information are used to make business decisions, and so on—needed to be based on quality principles, work together as a system, and be continuously improved as environmental conditions and business directions change. From this perspective, the product-focused notion of quality evolved into a new concept, called performance excellence. **Performance excellence** can be defined as an integrated approach to organizational performance management that results in

1. delivery of ever-improving value to customers and stakeholders, contributing to organizational sustainability,
2. improvement of overall organizational effectiveness and capabilities, and
3. organizational and personal learning.

We will focus on performance excellence in Part III of this book after we have studied the basic practices, tools, and techniques of quality management.

Emergence of Six Sigma

In the quest to remain competitive, and after learning from the failures of TQM, a new approach to quality improvement emerged in the late 1990s, called *Six Sigma*. Six Sigma is a customer-focused, results-oriented approach to business improvement that integrates many traditional quality improvement tools and techniques that have been tested and validated over the years, with a bottom-line and strategic orientation that appeals to senior managers, thus gaining their support. Many organizations have adopted Six Sigma as a way of revitalizing their quality efforts. Recently, Six Sigma tools have been integrated with lean tools from the Toyota production system to address not only quality problems, but other key business problems involving cost reduction and efficiency. We will discuss Six Sigma in depth in Chapter 9.

Current and Future Challenges

The real challenge today is to ensure that managers continue to focus on quality management and performance excellence throughout their organizations. An executive at Texas Instruments observed that "Quality will have to be everywhere, integrated into all aspects of a winning organization." Unfortunately, a survey sponsored by ASQ found significant gaps between executives' awareness of quality improvement processes and implementation, suggesting that many organizations either are not using these proven approaches or simply don't realize that approaches they do use are rooted in the quality discipline (and may miss key opportunities to improve them).[19] As former Xerox president David Kearns observed, quality is "a race without a finish line."

The global marketplace and domestic and international competition have made organizations around the world realize that their survival depends on high quality.[20] Many countries, such as Korea and India, have mounted national efforts to increase quality awareness, including conferences, seminars, radio shows, school essay contests, and pamphlet distribution. Spain and Brazil have encouraged the publication of quality books in their native language to make them more accessible (this book has been translated into Spanish and Chinese). Several professional groups united to form the Middle East Quality Association. Hamdan Bin Mohammed e-University (HBMeU) was established by the government of the United Arab Emirates in Dubai in 2009. It initiated its e-School of Business & Quality Management, which offers undergraduate and master's degree programs in various facets of quality management, as well as continuing education classes and conferences in the region through its e-TQM Institute.[21]

These trends will only increase the level of business competition in the future. Approaches such as Six Sigma require increased levels of training and education for managers and front-line employees alike, as well as the development of technical staff. Thus, a key challenge is to allocate the necessary resources to maintain a focus on quality, particularly in times of economic downturns. However, businesses will require an economic justification for quality initiatives: Quality must deliver bottom-line results. But as we noted earlier, the process is not easy; quality requires persistence, discipline, and steadfast leadership committed to excellence.

In 2011, the American Society for Quality identified eight key forces that will influence the future of quality:[22]

1. *Global Responsibility*: An organization must be fully aware of the global impact of its local decisions and realize that as demand grows for the planet's finite resources, waste is increasingly unacceptable. Global responsibility also involves human rights, labor practices, fair operating practices, consumer interests and contributions to society. In an increasingly connected and informed world, responsible efforts are being rewarded by consumers, making it more important than ever to maintain a reputation as an organization driven by global concern.

2. *Consumer Awareness*: With today's technology such as the Internet, Twitter, and Facebook, consumers have access to a wealth of information on which to make purchasing decisions. As a result, organizations must be quick when responding to their customers' concerns and match their products to customers' wants and needs, or risk having their customers defect to a competitor. Many service providers maintain electronic databases that capture customer preferences, allowing them to customize the customer experience. Manufacturing technologies will need to provide similar levels of customization, allowing for economic order quantities of one, along with zero wait times.

3. *Globalization*: Globalization no longer means just an opportunity for organizations to enter new markets. Today, firms have to contend with a growing number of competitors and sources of lower-cost labor and assume the risks associated with global supply chains.

4. *Increasing Rate of Change*: Technology has shifted the rate of change into an entirely new gear, which brings with it opportunities and threats. The threat lies in the possibility that humanity won't be able to adapt to the disruptions that accompany technological advances. But, if it can, the opportunities are nearly limitless. Product life cycles are getting shorter, and industries come into existence, thrive, and die within our lifetimes. As a result, being first to market means more now than ever before, as does the ability to anticipate and respond quickly to consumer demand.

5. *Workforce of the Future*: Competition for talent will increase, and along with technological advances, will change how and where work is done. As a result, organizations will need to become more flexible with how and where their workforces operate. Organizations will need to make a greater investment in training and education, and place a greater emphasis on professional certifications, which will evolve based on organizations' demands for demonstrated competency from its employees.

6. *Aging Population*: As people live longer, organizations face higher costs for healthcare and social welfare programs. Retirement becomes "a short-lived artifact of the latter half of the twentieth century." Demographers predict that by 2025, the majority of the population will be over the age of 65. The result is a growing market for organizations to consider as the aging lifestyle becomes more prevalent.

7. *Twenty-first Century Quality*: Quality isn't the same as it was 50 years ago, or even five years ago. Quality is moving beyond the organization's walls to encompass a

customer's entire experience with the organization rather than just the quality of the product or service. This provides more opportunities for quality professionals to apply their skills; we may soon see quality applied to social problems, proving that "quality is exerting itself in new ways—in hopeful ways."

8. *Innovation*: According to the study, innovation is "the pursuit of something different and exciting." Innovation lies at the heart of organizational survival. As the study states, "If innovation means the ability of a company to anticipate customer needs—expressed or unexpressed, known or unknown—and bring products or services to the marketplace that excite customers, then clearly innovation is the fuel of growth in today's changing world, and more so tomorrow."

These eight forces will impact how organizations configure themselves, how managers plan and lead, and how all workers will perform to achieve quality. As ASQ noted, "Quality should shape society. Ultimately, quality methodology will be used to build a better world."

QUALITY IN MANUFACTURING

Manufacturing Systems

Quality management is rooted in manufacturing; therefore, that's where we will begin. Figure 1.2 illustrates a typical manufacturing system and the key relationships among its functions. The quality concerns of each component of the system are described next.

FIGURE 1.2
Functional Relationships in a Typical Manufacturing System

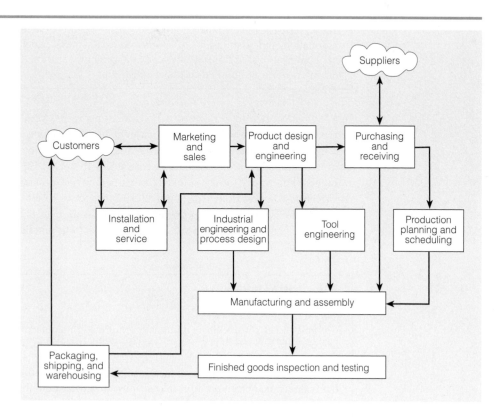

Marketing and Sales   Milton Hershey, the founder of Hershey Foods Corporation, understood the relationship between quality and sales. He used to say, "Give them quality. That's the best advertising in the world." For the first 68 years it was in business, Hershey Foods did not see a need to advertise its products in the mass media.[23] Marketing and sales involve much more than advertising and selling. Today, marketing and sales employees have important responsibilities for quality, such as learning the products and product features that consumers want and knowing the prices that consumers are willing to pay for them. This information enables a firm to define products that are fit for use and capable of being produced within the technological and budgetary constraints of the organization. Salespeople can help to obtain feedback on product performance from customers and convey this information to product designers and engineers for further improvements. They should also help to ensure that customers receive adequate assistance and are completely satisfied.

 QUALITYSPOTLIGHT

Ames Rubber Corporation

Ames Rubber Corporation, based in Hamburg, New Jersey, produces rubber rollers used to feed paper, transfer toner, and fuse toner to paper in office machines such as copiers, printers, and typewriters. All products are made to order to customer design and specification. Its warranties are among the best in the industry and include a refund of the customer's portion of development costs for prototype parts if Ames fails to achieve the specifications. Sales representatives take special note of such things as the volume of work a customer or prospective customer expects, the product features the customer seeks, and the customer's cost, service, and delivery requirements. Ames's sales department also conducts quarterly customer satisfaction surveys and monthly customer contact surveys. Customer satisfaction surveys collect data in the areas of products, service, information, and relationships. Customer contact surveys, which take the form of informal conversations, explore quality, cost, delivery, and service. The company uses all of this information to improve customer satisfaction.

Product Design and Engineering   Under-engineered products will fail in the marketplace because they will not meet customer needs. Products that are over-engineered, that is, those that exceed the customer requirements, may not find a profitable market. Japanese automakers, for instance, discovered in the early 1990s that many consumers were unwilling to pay for some luxury features they had designed into their cars as standard features. Poorly designed manufacturing processes result in poor quality or higher costs. Good design can help to prevent manufacturing defects and service errors and to reduce the need for the non-value-adding inspection practices that have dominated much of U.S. industry.

 QUALITYSPOTLIGHT

Motorola

Motorola places considerable emphasis on improving manufacturing quality by reducing defects through its product and process design activities. Motorola sets an ambitious goal of *six sigma quality*—a level of quality representing no more than 3.4 defects per million opportunities—for every process in the company. To reach this goal, Motorola knows that before it manufactures a product it must first determine the product characteristics that will satisfy customers (marketing's role); decide whether these characteristics can be achieved through the product's design, the manufacturing process, or the materials used; develop design tolerances that will assure successful product performance; conduct measurements to determine process variations from existing specifications; and then hone the product design, manufacturing process, or both, in order to achieve the desired results.

Purchasing and Receiving   The quality of purchased parts and services and the timeliness of their delivery are critical. The purchasing department can help a firm achieve quality by:

- Selecting quality-conscious suppliers
- Ensuring that purchase orders clearly define the quality requirements specified by product design and engineering
- Bringing together technical staffs from both the buyer's and suppliers' companies to design products and solve technical problems
- Establishing long-term supplier relationships based on trust
- Providing quality-improvement training to suppliers
- Informing suppliers of any problems encountered with their goods
- Maintaining good communication with suppliers as quality requirements and design changes occur

The receiving department is the link between purchasing and production. It must ensure that the delivered items are of the quality specified by the purchase contract, which it does through various inspection and testing policies. If the incoming material is of high quality, extensive inspection and testing is not necessary. Many companies now require that their suppliers provide proof that their processes can consistently turn out products of specified quality and give preferential treatment to those that can.

Production Planning and Scheduling   A production plan specifies long-term and short-term production requirements for filling customer orders and meeting anticipated demand. The correct materials, tools, and equipment must be available at the proper time and in the proper places in order to maintain a smooth flow of production. Modern concepts of production planning and scheduling, such as small batch and single piece flow, have been shown to lead to quality improvements and cost savings.

Manufacturing and Assembly   The role of manufacturing and assembly in producing quality is to ensure that the product is made correctly. The linkage to design and process engineering, as noted earlier, is obvious; manufacturing cannot do its job without a good product design and good process technology. Once in production, however, no defects should be acceptable. If and when they do occur, every effort must be made to identify their causes and eliminate them. Inspecting-out already defective items is costly and wasteful.

QUALITYSPOTLIGHT

Ames Rubber Corporation

Ames Rubber Corporation produces more than 17,000 custom parts by means of a wide range of manufacturing operations such as casting, extrusion, spraying, and molding. Each operation requires appropriate measuring methods and devices that can closely monitor the manufacturing process. Sophisticated measuring and testing equipment, such as laser-measuring devices, ensure in-line process control. All Ames manufacturing staff must understand the importance and use of statistics in controlling processes. At each production step, operators, inspectors, and supervisors collect and evaluate performance data. This practice allows Ames to detect deviations from the processes immediately and to make the necessary adjustments.

Tool Engineering   The tool engineering function is responsible for designing and maintaining the tools used in manufacturing and inspection. Worn manufacturing tools result in defective parts, and improperly calibrated inspection gauges give misleading information. These and other tool problems lead to poor quality and inefficiency. Engineers at Ames Rubber use statistical techniques to evaluate tooling and equipment and conduct periodic studies to ensure that Ames continues to meet or exceed product requirements. If they cannot, the result is excessive scrap, waste, and higher costs.

Industrial Engineering and Process Design   The job of industrial engineers and process designers is to work with product design engineers to develop realistic specifications. In addition, they must select appropriate technologies, equipment, and work methods for producing quality products. For example, Nissan Motor Manufacturing has a fully automated paint system in which robots are programmed to move along with cars. Because the robots always know where the body is, the robot will stop if the line stops but continue the paint cycle until finished as a means of keeping paint quality consistent.[24] Industrial engineers also work on designing facilities and arranging equipment to achieve a smooth production flow and to reduce the opportunities for product damage. Recently, industrial engineering as a profession has been incorporating the types of activities more often taught in business schools.

Finished Goods Inspection and Testing   If quality is built into the product properly, inspection should be unnecessary except for auditing purposes and functional testing. Electronic components, for example, are subjected to extensive "burn-in" tests that ensure proper operation and eliminate short-life items. In any case, inspection should be used as a means of gathering information that can be used to improve quality, not simply to remove defective items.

Packaging, Shipping, and Warehousing   Even good-quality items that leave the plant floor can be incorrectly labeled or damaged in transit. Packaging, shipping, and warehousing—often termed logistics activities—are the functions that protect quality after goods are produced. Accurate coding and expiration dating of products is important for traceability (often for legal requirements) and for customers.

Installation and Service   Products must be used correctly in order to benefit the customer. Users must understand a product and have adequate instructions for proper installation and operation. Should any problem occur, customer satisfaction depends on good after-the-sale service. At one company, truck drivers saw the opportunity to do more than merely deliver materials to receiving docks. Where labor relations permit, they make deliveries to specific locations within plants and assist with unloading, stocking, and inventory counts. Many companies specify standards for customer service similar to the dimensions and tolerances prescribed for manufactured goods. For example, associates are expected to arrive for all appointments on time and to return customer phone calls within a prescribed time period. They are also responsible for knowing and observing their respective customers' rules and regulations, especially those that concern safety procedures.

QUALITY IN SERVICE ORGANIZATIONS

Service organizations include all nonmanufacturing organizations such as hotels, restaurants, financial and legal services, and transportation, except such industries as agriculture, mining, and construction. The service sector grew rapidly in the second half of the twentieth century. Today more than 80 percent of the nonfarm employees in the United States are working in services, and more than half the jobs in manufacturing industries are service-related.

Service organizations were probably a good 10 years behind manufacturing in implementing quality approaches. This lag can be attributed to the fact that service industries had not confronted the same aggressive foreign competition that manufacturing faced. Another factor is the high turnover rate in service industry jobs, which typically pay less than manufacturing jobs. Constantly changing personnel makes establishing a culture for quality more difficult. Also, the very nature of quality is significantly different in services than in manufacturing. However, the importance of quality in services cannot be overestimated. Studies show that companies can boost their profits by almost 100 percent by retaining just 5 percent more of their customers than their competitors retain.[25] This drastic difference is because the cost of acquiring new customers is much higher than the costs associated with retaining customers. Companies with loyal, long-time customers— even with higher unit costs and smaller market share—can financially outperform competitors with higher customer turnover.

Pure service businesses deliver intangible products. Examples would include a law firm, whose product is legal advice, and a health care facility, whose product is comfort and better health. Service is also a key element for many traditional manufacturing companies. For instance, manufacturers such as Xerox provide extensive maintenance and consulting services, which may be more important to the customer than its tangible products. When you buy an automobile, you are also buying the manufacturer and dealer services. A columnist for *Autoweek* noted that most automakers "have the quality and design thing down pat." However, he also noted: "None of this matters if a customer walks into the dealership and isn't treated like a king. Ditto if you have to call the automaker's customer-service line. You'd better be taken care of, and the experience has to be hassle-free."[26]

Contrasts with Manufacturing

The production of services differs from manufacturing in many ways, and these differences carry important implications for quality management. The most critical differences between services and manufacturing are:

1. Customer needs and performance standards are often difficult to identify and measure, primarily because the customers define what they are, and each customer is different.
2. The production of services typically requires a higher degree of customization than does manufacturing. Doctors, lawyers, insurance salespeople, and food-service employees must tailor their services to individual customers. In manufacturing, the goal is uniformity.
3. The output of many service systems is intangible, whereas manufacturing produces tangible, visible products. Manufacturing quality can be assessed against firm design specifications (for example, the depth of cut should be 0.125 inch), but service quality can only be assessed against customers' subjective, nebulous expectations, and

past experiences. (What is a "good" sales experience?) Also, the customer can "have and hold" a manufactured product, but can only remember a service. Manufactured goods can be recalled or replaced by the manufacturer, but poor service can only be followed up by apologies and reparations.

4. Services are produced and consumed simultaneously, whereas manufactured goods are produced prior to consumption. In addition, many services must be performed at the convenience of the customer. Therefore, services cannot be stored, inventoried, or inspected prior to delivery as manufactured goods are. Much more attention must therefore be paid to training and building quality into the service as a means of quality assurance.

5. Customers often are involved in the service process and are present while it is being performed, whereas manufacturing is performed away from the customer. For example, customers of a quick-service restaurant place their own orders, carry their food to the table, and are expected to clear the table when they have finished eating.

6. Services are generally labor intensive, whereas manufacturing is more capital intensive. The quality of human interaction is a vital factor for services that involve human contact. For example, the quality of hospital care depends heavily on interactions among the patients, nurses, doctors, and other medical staff. Banks have found that tellers' friendliness is a key factor in retaining depositors. Hence, the behavior and morale of service employees is critical in delivering a quality service experience.

7. Many service organizations must handle large numbers of customer transactions. For example, on a given business day, the Royal Bank of Canada might process more than 5.5 million transactions for 7.5 million customers through 1,600 branches and more than 3,500 banking machines, and FedEx might handle several million shipments across the globe each day. Such large volumes increase the opportunity for error.

Components of Service Quality

Many service organizations such as airlines, banks, and hotels have well-developed quality systems. These systems begin with a commitment to the customer. For example, Amazon.com has pioneered a number of innovative approaches to improve customer satisfaction, ranging from easy-to-use website design to fast order fulfillment.

Service quality may be viewed from a manufacturing analogy, for instance, technical standards such as the components of a properly made-up guest room for a hotel, service transaction speed, or accuracy of information. However, managing intangible quality characteristics is more difficult, because they usually depend on employee performance and behavior. This dependence does not imply that these factors are not important in manufacturing, of course, but they have special significance in services—just as engineering technology might have in manufacturing.

The two most important drivers of service quality are *people* and *technology*. Many organizations rely on call centers as their primary means of customer contact. Call centers can be a means of competitive advantage by serving customers more efficiently and personalizing transactions to build relationships; however, they can also be a source of frustration if not designed and managed correctly. Customer-contact employees need access to the right technology and company information to do their jobs. FedEx, for example, furnishes employees with the information and technology they need to continually improve their performance. The Digitally Assisted Dispatch System (DADS) communicates to all couriers through screens in their vans, enabling quick response to pickup and delivery dispatches; it allows couriers to manage their time and routes with high efficiency. Information technology improves productivity, increases communication, and allows customer contact employees to handle almost any customer issue.

Customers evaluate a service primarily by the quality of the human contact. A *Wall Street Journal* survey found that Americans' biggest complaints about service workers are of delivery people or salespeople who fail to show up when you have stayed home at a scheduled time for them; salespeople who are poorly informed; and salesclerks who talk on the phone while waiting on you, say "It's not my department," talk down to you, or cannot describe how a product works.

Many service organizations act on the motto "If we take care of our people, they will take care of our customers." FedEx, for example, has numerous policies and practices to take care of its people, including a "no layoff" philosophy, a "guaranteed fair treatment procedure" for handling grievances, and a well-developed recognition program for team and individual contributions to company performance. The company credo—*People, Service, Profits*—demonstrates the importance of people. All potential decisions in the company are evaluated first on their impact on the employees (people), and then on customers (service) and the company's financial performance (profits).

In many companies, unfortunately, the front-line workers—salesclerks, receptionists, delivery personnel, and so on, who have the most contact with customers—receive the lowest pay, minimal training, little decision-making authority, and little responsibility (when workers receive authority and responsibility, that is termed *empowerment*, which we discuss further in Chapter 4). Recruiting and selecting the right types of individuals and training them are particularly important, because service workers need to be skilled in handling every customer interaction, from greeting customers to asking the right questions. High-quality service workers also require effective reward systems that recognize customer satisfaction results and customer-focused behaviors, appropriate skills and abilities for performing the job, and supervisors who act more as coaches and mentors than as administrators.

 QUALITYSPOTLIGHT

The Ritz Carlton-Hotel Company

The Ritz-Carlton Hotel Company, LLC is one service company with an exemplary focus on its people.[27] The Ritz-Carlton is widely-recognized for its exemplary human resource practices. They train employees to know what they are supposed to do, how well they are doing, and have the authority to make changes as necessary. For example, the role of the housekeeper is not simply to make beds, but to create a memorable experience for the customer. Each hotel has a director of human resources and a training manager, who are assisted by the hotel's quality leader. Each work area has a departmental trainer who is responsible for training and certifying new employees in his or her unit. New employees receive two days' orientation in which senior executives personally demonstrate Ritz-Carlton methods and instill Ritz-Carlton values. Three weeks later, managers monitor the effectiveness of the instruction and then conduct a follow-up training session. Later, they must pass written and skill-demonstration tests in order to become certified in their work areas. Every day, in each work area, each shift supervisor conducts a quality line-up meeting and briefing session. The workforce receives continuous teaching and coaching to refresh skills and improve performance, reinforce the purpose of the job, and to provide recognition for achievements. Through these and other mechanisms, workers receive more than 100 hours of quality education aimed at fostering a commitment to premium service, solving problems, setting goals, and generating new ideas. Workers are empowered to enlist the aid of others to resolve a problem swiftly, to spend up to $2,000 to satisfy a guest, to decide the business terms of a sale, to be involved in setting plans for their particular work area, and to speak with anyone in the company regarding any problem. The Ritz-Carlton has improved the turnover rate of the workforce steadily to well below industry averages.

Many service industries exploit information technology to achieve high customer service. Restaurants, for example, use handheld order-entry computer terminals to speed up the ordering process. An order is instantaneously transmitted to the kitchen or bar, where it is displayed and the guest check is printed. In addition to saving time, such systems improve accuracy by standardizing the order-taking, billing, and inventory procedures and reducing the need for handwriting. Credit authorizations, which once took several minutes by telephone, are now accomplished in seconds through computerized authorization systems. FedEx's handheld "SuperTracker" scans packages' bar codes every time packages change hands between pickup and delivery. The Ritz-Carlton Hotel Company exploits information technology to remember each of its 800,000+ customers. Knowledge of individual customer preferences, previous difficulties, family and personal interests, and preferred credit cards is stored in a database accessible to every hotel. This guest-profiling system allows each customer to be treated individually by giving front-desk employees immediate access to such information as whether the guest smokes, whether he or she prefers scented or unscented soap, and what kind of pillow he or she prefers.

Without a doubt, the largest impact of information technology for service has been in e-commerce. Customers can shop for almost any product; configure, price, and order computer systems; and take virtual test drives of automobiles and select from thousands of possible combinations of options on the Internet in the convenience of their homes. Information technology can be used to develop and enhance customer relationships. Amazon.com, from which many readers have probably ordered, has been extremely successful at this. They provide extensive information about products, such as reader reviews to help customers evaluate books, search used bookstores for out-of-print books, and even provide e-mail thank you letters a month or so after purchase. However, while information technology reduces labor intensity and increases the speed of service, it can have adverse effects on other dimensions of quality. Some people, including some customers, will argue that customer satisfaction is decreased when less personal interaction takes place. (Have you ever gotten irritated when wading through multiple menus on an automated telephone answering system?) Thus, service providers must balance conflicting quality concerns.

QUALITY IN BUSINESS SUPPORT FUNCTIONS

In addition to manufacturing and service activities, other business support activities are necessary for achieving quality. Some of these activities are discussed here.

Finance and Accounting   The finance function is responsible for obtaining funds, controlling their use, analyzing investment opportunities, and ensuring that the firm operates cost-effectively and—ideally—profitably. Financial decisions affect manufacturing equipment purchases, cost-control policies, price-volume decisions, and nearly all facets of the organization. Finance must authorize sufficient budgeting for equipment, training, and other means of assuring quality. Financial studies can help to expose the costs of poor quality and opportunities for reducing it. Accounting data are useful in identifying areas for quality improvement and tracking the progress of quality improvement programs. Furthermore, inappropriate accounting approaches can hide poor quality.

Financial and accounting personnel who have contacts with customers can directly influence the service their company provides. At many companies, for example, employees chart invoice accuracy, the time needed to process invoices, and the time needed to pay bills. In addition, they can apply quality improvement techniques to improve their own operations. Financial personnel at Motorola, for example, were able to reduce the time needed to close the books from one month to four days.

Legal Services   A firm's legal department attempts to guarantee that the firm complies with laws and regulations regarding such things as product labeling, packaging, safety, and transportation; designs and words its warranties properly; satisfies its contractual requirements; and has proper procedures and documentation in place in the event of liability claims against it. The rapid increase in liability suits has made legal services an important aspect of quality assurance.

Quality Assurance   Because some managers lack the technical expertise required for performing needed statistical tests or data analyses, technical specialists—usually in the "quality assurance department"—assist the managers in these tasks. Quality assurance specialists perform special statistical studies and analyses and may be assigned to work with any of the manufacturing or business support functions. It must be remembered that a firm's quality assurance department cannot guarantee quality. Its proper role is to provide guidance and support to everyone in the organization in order to achieve this goal.

A customer-driven quality focus must involve every function in the organization, including manufacturing, service, and business support functions. Quality is indeed everyone's responsibility.

QUALITY AND COMPETITIVE ADVANTAGE

Competitive advantage denotes a firm's ability to achieve market superiority. A strong competitive advantage provides customer value, leads to financial success and business sustainability, and is difficult for competitors to copy. High quality is itself an important source of competitive advantage. This was demonstrated by several research studies during the 1980s. PIMS Associates, Inc., a subsidiary of the Strategic Planning Institute, maintains a database of 1,200 companies and studies the impact of product quality on corporate performance.[28] PIMS researchers found the following:

- Product quality is an important determinant of business profitability.
- Businesses that offer premium-quality products and services usually have large market shares and were early entrants into their markets.
- Quality is positively and significantly related to a higher return on investment for almost all kinds of products and market situations. (PIMS studies showed that firms whose products were perceived as having superior quality earned more than three times the return on sales of firms whose products were perceived as having inferior quality.)

- Instituting a strategy of quality improvement usually leads to increased market share, but at the cost of reduced short-run profitability.
- High-quality producers can usually charge premium prices.

These findings are summarized in Figure 1.3. Profitability is driven by both the quality of design and conformance. Improvements in design will differentiate the product from its competitors, improve a firm's quality reputation, and improve the perceived value of the product. These factors allow the firm to command higher prices as well as to achieve a greater market share, which in turn leads to increased revenues that offset the costs of improving the design. Improved conformance in production or service delivery leads to lower costs through savings in rework, scrap, resolution of errors, and warranty expenses. Philip Crosby popularized this viewpoint in his book *Quality Is Free.*[29] Crosby states:

> *Quality is not only free, it is an honest-to-everything profit maker. Every penny you don't spend on doing things wrong, over, or instead of, becomes half a penny right on the bottom line. In these days of "who knows what is going to happen to our business tomorrow," there aren't many ways left to make a profit improvement. If you concentrate on making quality certain, you can probably increase your profit by an amount equal to 5 percent to 10 percent of your sales. That is a lot of money for free. The net effect of improved quality of design and conformance is increased profits.*

Many organizations focus only on one of these quality dimensions; for example, they might focus on defect elimination but fail to design products that customers really want, or they design great products that are plagued with defects and service errors. A case in point is the auto industry. For example, a new model of the Buick Regal beat out the Toyota Camry and Honda Accord in *Consumer Reports'* reliability rankings, but did not make the recommended list because of ho-hum design compared to its competition. In response to such criticism, U.S. automakers have recruited European designers to improve interior amenities and create more exciting exterior styling.[30] On the flip side of the coin is Nissan, which designed and launched many new hot-selling vehicles in the United States, but fell dramatically in J. D. Power & Associates' Initial Quality Survey, resulting in part from using cheaper materials at the expense of manufacturing precision and lacking the engineering resources to check thoroughly for defects during manufacturing.[31]

FIGURE 1.3
Quality and
Profitability

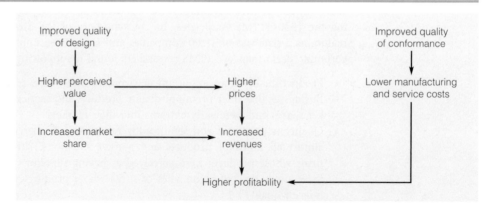

Quality and Business Results

As an old saying goes, "The proof is in the pudding." Various research studies have shown that quality-focused companies achieved better employee participation and relations, improved product and service quality, higher productivity, greater customer satisfaction, increased market share, and improved profitability.[32]

Considerable evidence also exists that quality initiatives positively impact the bottom line. Kevin Hendricks and Vinod Singhal published one of the most celebrated studies in 1997.[33] Based on objective data and rigorous statistical analysis, the study showed that when implemented effectively, total quality management approaches improve financial performance dramatically. Using a sample of about 600 publicly traded companies that received quality awards either from their customers (such as automotive manufacturers) or through Baldrige and state and local quality award programs, Hendricks and Singhal examined performance results from six years before to four years after receiving their first quality award. The primary performance measure tracked was the percent change in operating income and a variety of measures that might affect operating income: percent change in sales, total assets, number of employees, return on sales, and return on assets. These results were compared to a set of control firms that were similar in size to the award recipients and in the same industry. The analysis revealed significant differences between the sample and the control group. Specifically, the growth in operating income averaged 91 percent versus 43 percent for the control group. Award recipients also experienced a 69 percent jump in sales (compared to 32 percent for the control group), a 79 percent increase in total assets (compared to 37 percent), a 23 percent increase in the number of employees (compared to 7 percent), an 8 percent improvement in return on sales (compared to zero percent), and a 9 percent improvement in return on assets (compared to 6 percent). Small companies actually outperformed large companies, and over a five-year period, the portfolio of award recipients beat the S&P 500 index by 34 percent.

One may also look at the exceptional performance of Baldrige Award recipients to show that a focus on quality breeds success. A sample of some operational and financial results are highlighted below.

1. Nestlé Purina PetCare Co. (NPPC) has had sustained revenue growth and met its sales goal during the nation's economic downturn and when the U.S. pet population grew only marginally.

2. Business satisfaction with the city of Coral Springs, Florida, rose from 76 percent to 97 percent over a four-year period. *Money* magazine named Coral Springs as one of the Best Places to Live. The city was named as one of the 100 best communities for young people by America's Promise Alliance for multiple years.

3. PRO-TEC Coating Company consistently achieves the quality expectations of its customers by delivering products with a defect rate of less than 0.12 percent and has scored better than its competition on product quality, on-time delivery, service, and product development. Its return on assets, a measure of long-term viability, has had a sustained upward trend.

4. The overall Net Promoter (NP) scores (a loyalty metric defined by the level of repeat sales and referrals) for MEDRAD, a manufacturer of medical imaging devices, were consistently 60 percent or higher compared to the 50 percent or higher marks for other organizations nationwide. MEDRAD's global customer satisfaction ratings using the NP system steadily increased from 50 percent to 63 percent, surpassing the best-in-class benchmark of 50 percent.

5. AtlantiCare, a nonprofit health system in southeastern New Jersey, saw its system revenues grew from $280 million to $651 million over an eight-year period, reflecting an 11 percent compound annual growth rate, compared to a state average of 5.6 percent. During this time period, AtlantiCare's medical center volume increased from about 34,000 to over 56,000 discharges—also more than twice the state average.

6. Although its per-pupil operations expenditures are among the lowest in North Carolina, Iredell-Statesville Schools is ranked academically in the state's top 10 school systems. Additionally, its SAT scores rose steadily over five years with the state rank rising from 57th (out of 115 school districts) to seventh during that time.

7. Poudre Valley Health System's market share rose to 62.3 percent in the system's primary service area, 42 percent higher than that of the closest competitor.

QUALITY AND PERSONAL VALUES

Today, organizations are asking employees to take more responsibility for acting as the point of contact between the organization and the customer, to be team players, and to provide better customer service. Rath & Strong, a Lexington, Massachusetts-based management consulting firm, polled almost 200 executives from Fortune 500 companies about activities that foster superior performance results for an organization.[34] The survey revealed that *personal initiative*, when combined with a customer orientation, resulted in a positive impact on business success and sales growth rate.

Quality begins with individual attitudes and behavior. Robert Galvin, former CEO of Motorola, once told the Economic Club of Chicago, "Quality is a very personal obligation. If you can't talk about quality in the first person… then you have not moved to the level of involvement of quality that is absolutely essential." Employees who embrace quality as a personal value often go beyond what they're asked or normally expected to do in order to reach a difficult goal or provide extraordinary service to a customer. Nordstrom's customer service stories are legendary, and include employees who have ironed a new shirt for a customer who needed it that afternoon, one who warmed customers' cars in winter while they shopped, and even one who refunded money for a set of tire chains, even though Nordstrom does not sell them![35]

Personal quality is an essential ingredient to make quality happen in the workplace, yet most organizations have neglected it for a long time. Perhaps management, in particular, operates under the idea that promoting quality is something that organizations do *to* employees, rather than something they do *with* employees.

Unless quality is internalized at the personal level, it will never become rooted in the culture of an organization. Thus, quality must begin at a personal level (and that means *you*!) and practiced in all activities of daily life.

SUMMARY OF KEY POINTS AND TERMINOLOGY

The Student Companion Site provides a summary of key concepts and terminology introduced in this chapter.

QUALITY *in* PRACTICE

The Evolution of Quality at Xerox[36]

The Xerox 914, the first plain-paper copier, was introduced in 1959. Regarded by many people as the most successful business product ever introduced, it created a new industry. During the 1960s Xerox grew rapidly, selling all it could produce, and reached $1 billion in revenue in record-setting time. By the mid-1970s its return on assets was in the low 20 percent range. Its competitive advantage was due to strong patents, a growing market, and little competition. In such an environment, management was not pressed to focus on customers.

Facing a Competitive Crisis

During the 1970s, however, IBM and Kodak entered the high-volume copier business—Xerox's principal market. Several Japanese companies introduced high-quality low-volume copiers, a market that Xerox had virtually ignored, and established a foundation for moving into the high-volume market. In addition, the Federal Trade Commission accused Xerox of illegally monopolizing the copier business. After negotiations, Xerox agreed to open approximately 1,700 patents to competitors. Xerox was soon losing market share to Japanese competitors, and by the early 1980s it faced a serious competitive threat from copy machine manufacturers in Japan; Xerox's market share had fallen to less than 50 percent. Some people even predicted that the company would not survive. Rework, scrap, excessive inspection, lost business, and other problems were estimated to be costing Xerox more than 20 percent of revenue, which in 1983 amounted to nearly $2 billion. Both the company and its primary union, the Amalgamated Clothing and Textile Workers, were concerned. In comparing itself with its competition, Xerox discovered that it had nine times as many suppliers, twice as many employees, cycle times that were twice as long, 10 times as many rejects, and seven times as many manufacturing defects in finished products. It was clear that radical changes were required.

Leadership Through Quality

In 1983, company president David T. Kearns became convinced that Xerox needed a long-range, comprehensive quality strategy as well as a change in its traditional management culture (see Figure 1.4). Kearns was aware of Japanese subsidiary Fuji Xerox's success in implementing quality management practices and was approached by several Xerox employees about instituting total quality management. He commissioned a team to outline a quality strategy for Xerox. The team's report stated that instituting it would require changes in behaviors and attitudes throughout the company as well as operational changes in the company's business practices. Kearns determined that Xerox would initiate a total quality management approach, that they would take the time to "design it right the first time," and that the effort would involve all employees. Kearns and the company's top 25 managers wrote the Xerox Quality Policy, which states:

> Xerox is a quality company. Quality is the basic business principle for Xerox. Quality means providing our external and internal customers with innovative products and services that fully satisfy their requirements. Quality improvement is the job of every Xerox employee.

This policy led to a process called Leadership Through Quality, which had three objectives:

1. To instill quality as the basic business principle in Xerox, and to ensure that quality improvement becomes the job of every Xerox person.
2. To ensure that Xerox people, individually and collectively, provide our external and internal customers with innovative products and services that fully satisfies their existing and latent requirements.
3. To establish, as a way of life, management and work processes that enable all Xerox people to continuously pursue quality improvement in meeting customer requirements.

In addition, Leadership Through Quality was directed at achieving four goals in all Xerox activities:

- Customer Goal: To become an organization with whom customers are eager to do business.
- Employee Goal: To create an environment where everyone can take pride in the organization and feel responsible for its success.

FIGURE 1.4   Origin of the 1983 Xerox Quality Imperative

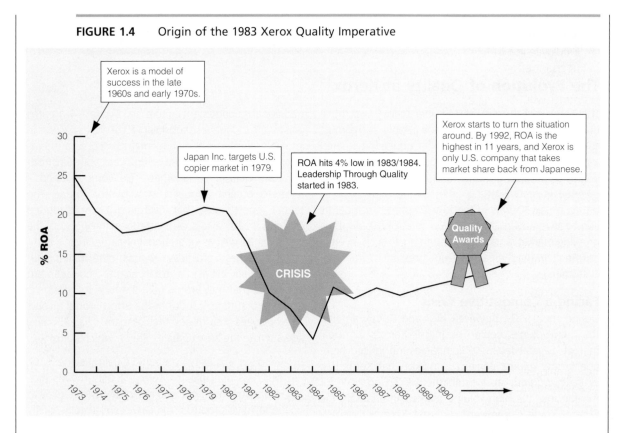

- Business Goal: To increase profits and presence at a rate faster than the markets in which Xerox competes.
- Process Goal: To use Leadership Through Quality principles in all Xerox does.

Leadership Through Quality radically changed the way Xerox did business. All activities, such as product planning, distribution, and establishing unit objectives, began with a focus on customer requirements. Benchmarking—identifying and studying the companies and organizations that best perform critical business functions and then incorporating those organizations' ideas into the firm's operations—became an important component of Xerox's quality efforts. Xerox benchmarked more than 200 processes with those of noncompetitive companies. For instance, ideas for improving production scheduling came from Cummins Engine Company, ideas for improving the distribution system came from L. L. Bean, and ideas for improving billing processes came from American Express.

Measuring customer satisfaction and training were important components of the program. Every month, 40,000 surveys were mailed to customers, seeking feedback on equipment performance, sales, service, and administrative support. Any reported dissatisfaction was dealt with immediately and was usually resolved in a matter of days. When the program was instituted, every Xerox employee worldwide, and at all levels of the company, received the same training in quality principles. This training began with top management and filtered down through each level of the firm. Five years, 4 million labor-hours, and more than $125 million later, all employees had received quality-related training. In 1988, about 79 percent of Xerox employees were involved in quality improvement teams.

Several other steps were taken. Xerox worked with suppliers to improve their processes, implement statistical methods and a total quality process, and to support a just-in-time inventory concept. Suppliers that joined in these efforts were involved in the earliest phases of new product designs and rewarded with long-term contracts.

Employee involvement and participation was also an important effort. Xerox had always had good relationships with its unions. In 1980, the company signed a contract with its principal union, the Amalgamated Clothing and Textile Workers, encouraging union members' participation in quality improvement processes. It was the first program in the company that linked managers with employees in a mutual problem-solving approach and served as a model for other corporations. A subsequent contract included the provision that "every employee shall support the concept of continuous quality improvement while reducing quality costs through teamwork."

Most important, management became the role model for the new way of doing business. Managers were required to practice quality in their daily activities and to promote Leadership Through Quality among their peers and subordinates. Reward and recognition systems were modified to focus on teamwork and quality results. Managers became coaches, involving their employees in the act of running the business on a routine basis.

From the initiation of Leadership Through Quality until the point at which Xerox's Business Products and Systems organization won the Malcolm Baldrige National Quality Award in 1989, some of the most obvious impacts of the Leadership Through Quality program included the following:

1. Reject rates on the assembly line fell from 10,000 parts per million to 300 parts per million.
2. Ninety-five percent of supplied parts no longer needed inspection; in 1989, 30 U.S. suppliers went the entire year defect-free.
3. The number of suppliers was cut from 5,000 to fewer than 500.
4. The cost of purchased parts was reduced by 45 percent.
5. Despite inflation, manufacturing costs dropped 20 percent.
6. Product development time decreased by 60 percent.
7. Overall product quality improved 93 percent.

Xerox learned that customer satisfaction plus employee motivation and satisfaction resulted in increased market share and improved return on assets. In 1989, President David Kearns observed that quality is "a race without a finish line."

Crisis and Quality Renewal

Throughout the 1990s, Xerox grew at a steady rate. However, at the turn of the century, the technology downturn, coupled with a decreased focus on quality by top corporate management, resulted in a significant stock price drop and a new crisis (see Figure 1.5). A top management shake-up, resulting in new corporate leadership, renewed the company's focus on quality, beginning with "New Quality" in 2001 and leading to the current "Lean Six Sigma" initiative.

The New Quality philosophy built on the quality legacy established in the 1983 Leadership Through Quality process. Soon afterward, as Six Sigma became more popular across the United States, this approach was refined around a structured, Six Sigma-based improvement process with more emphasis on behaviors and leadership to achieve performance excellence. The new thrust, established in 2003 and called "Lean Six Sigma" (see Chapter 9 for a detailed discussion), includes a dedicated infrastructure and resource commitment to focus on key business issues: critical customer opportunities, significant training of employees and "Black Belt" improvement specialists, a value-driven project selection process, and an increased customer focus with a clear linkage to business strategy and objectives. The basic principles support the core value "We Deliver Quality and Excellence in All We Do" and are stated as:

- Customer-focused employees, accountable for business results, are fundamental to our success.
- Our work environment enables participation, speed, and teamwork based on trust, learning, and recognition.
- Everyone at Xerox has business objectives aligned to the Xerox direction. A disciplined process is used to assess progress towards delivery of results.
- Customer-focused work processes, supported by disciplined use of quality tools, enable rapid changes and yield predictable business results.
- Everyone takes responsibility to communicate and act on benchmarks and knowledge that enable rapid change in the best interests of customers and shareholders.

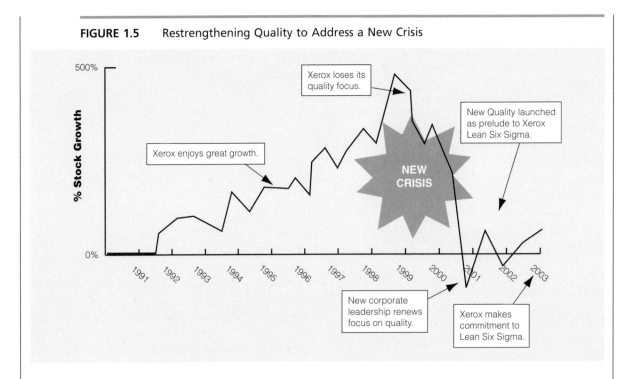

FIGURE 1.5   Restrengthening Quality to Address a New Crisis

The key components of Xerox's Lean Six Sigma are as follows:

1. Performance excellence process
   - Supports clearer, simpler alignment of corporate direction to individual objectives
   - Emphasizes ongoing inspection/assessment of business priorities
   - Clear links to market trends, benchmarking, and Lean Six Sigma
   - Supports a simplified "Baldrige-type" business assessment model
2. DMAIC (define, measure, analyze, improve, control) process
   - Based on industry-proven Six Sigma approach with speed and focus
   - Four steps support improvement projects, set goals
   - Used to proactively capture opportunities or solve problems
   - Full set of lean and Six Sigma tools
3. Market trends and benchmarking
   - Reinforces market focus and encourages external view
   - Disciplined approach to benchmarking
   - Establishes a common four-step approach to benchmarking
   - Encourages all employees to be aware of changing markets
   - Strong linkage to performance excellence process and DMAIC
4. Behaviors and leadership
   - Reinforces customer focus
   - Expands interactive skills to include more team effectiveness
   - Promotes faster decision making and introduces new meeting tool

The heart of Xerox's Lean Six Sigma is the performance excellence process, illustrated in Figure 1.6. It consists of three phases: setting direction, deploying direction, and delivering and inspecting results. It starts at the top of the organization—even the chair and CEO has an individual performance excellence plan with objectives that are aligned with organization goals and measures and targets for assessment. This approach provides clear communication of direction and accountability for objectives.

FIGURE 1.6   Xerox Performance Excellence Process

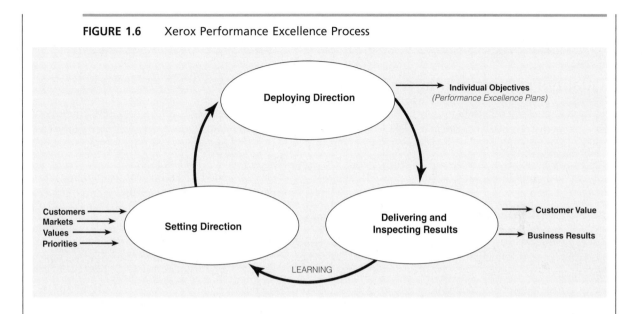

A structured approach is used to prioritize and select projects that have high benefits relative to the effort involved in accomplishing them. Statistical methods, lean work flow methods, and other process management skills are used to drive improvement from a factual, objective basis, driven by the DMAIC methodology.

Market trends and benchmarking help provide an external perspective required to lead the market with innovative products, services, and solutions and add value to the customer experience. This component encourages all people to share information and knowledge that enable changes in the best interest of customers and shareholders. Finally, behaviors and leadership reinforce customer-focused behaviors, based on the principle that "Quality is the responsibility of every Xerox employee."

In 2003, Xerox trained more than 1,000 senior leaders across the company and communicated this business approach, the key differences from their quality legacy, and expectations to every employee, and rapidly moved Lean Six Sigma concepts from manufacturing and supply chain into all business areas. After Lean Six Sigma became internalized within Xerox, the company began to leverage its

expertise through consulting services to help other companies improve. One application was at the Brooklyn Public Library. Using Lean Six Sigma, the Xerox Global Services team led library administrators through a fact-based analysis, seeking out core processes, making them controllable, and then automating them, resulting in a comprehensive Patron Access Management system that effectively merged people, processes, and technology to provide better service and free up time for the library staff.

Key Issues for Discussion

1. Contrast Leadership for Quality and Lean Six Sigma as quality initiatives for Xerox. How did their motivations differ? What differences or similarities are evident in the principles behind these initiatives and the way in which they were implemented?

2. What lessons might this experience—particularly in responding to the new crisis—have for other organizations?

3. Discuss the meaning of "Quality is a race without a finish line." What is its significance to Xerox, or to any organization?

QUALITY *in* PRACTICE

Quality Practices in Modern China

In this chapter, we noted that many of today's quality approaches evolved in ancient China. Jack Pompeo, a telecommunications professional who relocated to lead quality initiatives at Huawei Technologies, provides a first-hand look at quality in modern China.[37]

Quality processes today continue to be influenced by remnants of ancient policies and practices established 3,000 years ago. China continues to exercise strong centralized oversight over end-to-end production processes, extending from the purchase of incoming materials and in-process testing through final acceptances and customer care. Today's Chinese quality systems strongly emphasize tools, methodology and measurement, and place great importance on key quality management processes, including self-inspection, traceability, and recruiting and training of workers. However, even in light of recent and highly-publicized recalls, China's population is adapting and learning rapidly and is hungry for best practices and new challenges.

Today, China is seeking to introduce new ideas like total quality management and team empowerment, which have taken Western society decades to adapt and integrate into business management, in a fraction of the time. China is striving to improve its education, health, living standards, and, most important, its manufactured consumer products, and is embracing modern quality management philosophies. In just the past few years, Chinese manufacturers have adopted a wide array of quality tools and techniques. This has created a clash in China's desire to maintain balance between a centuries-old culture and the demands placed on the nation by technological progress.

China has an official policy to grow the economy about 8 percent annually, the rate state officials calculate would create the 15 million new jobs each year needed to absorb new entrants into the labor market and discards from the shrinking state sector. Every policy is calibrated to ensure economic output continues to expand at this rapid pace. Like businesses in the rest of the world, Chinese organizations are driven by numbers. They identify gaps in their quality management systems and are closing them quickly.

They understand that they have a narrow window of opportunity to transform themselves from low cost producers to competitive and high quality global leaders.

Huawei Technologies is one of China's largest telecommunications manufacturers, with annual sales of more than $10 billion. The company is located in Shenzhen, in the southern portion of the Guangdong Province on the eastern shore of the Pearl River Delta, neighboring Hong Kong to the south. Huawei's products provide reliable telecom services to more than 100 countries. But the company's goal is not to be just another telecom manufacturer; it is to be the quality leader in the telecommunications industry. Huawei's senior management recently declared the company's desire to be the "Toyota of the telecom industry." To achieve this, Huawei has studied Western telecom manufacturing in great detail and has invested heavily in the latest tools and technology. It is constantly looking for better tools and techniques that will make it a world leader, moving away from its current emphasis on low-cost production.

Huawei's rapid economic growth parallels the company's desire to be the world leader, and Huawei is now in the midst of understanding the critical role that quality processes play in its future expansion. The company places a strong focus on measurements, tools, and methods to enforce strict quality control of production processes. Its management systems are based on accepted worldwide processes and standards and are applied across all of Huawei's product lines in design, development, manufacturing, sales, installation, and service. Huawei also has a complete end-to-end integrated product development process that was implemented with the support of IBM in early 1998. In 2002, Huawei started Six Sigma quality initiatives in its manufacturing center and migrated them into R&D product lines. A Six Sigma steering committee oversees the deployment and reviews and approves projects to ensure they meet the launch criteria and resources are available to support the teams.

The QuEST Forum is a unique collaboration of telecommunications service providers and suppliers dedicated to telecom supply chain quality and performance. The Forum supports its member organizations to pursue performance excellence through implementing a common quality standard, emphasizing industry best practices and delivering a benchmarking measurement system. There are 11 benchmark measurements, including number of problem reports, problem report fix response time, on-time delivery, network element impact outage measurement, and field replacement unit returns. Huawei recently launched an initiative in partnership with the QuEST Forum's integrated global quality workgroup. The goal is to set up a benchmark study team to better understand causes of variability in the benchmark data and raise industry performance.

The benchmark data are a critical component of Huawei's quality management system and are integrated into top management's personal business commitments and the executive management team balanced scorecard. The balanced scorecard measures four key areas in corporation health: financial and profit, customer and quality, growth and learning, and internal business performance. The report cards and quality metrics are linked to both the executives' performance reviews and bonuses.

Huawei Technologies is just one example of the progress that Chinese companies have made in quality. Today, its automobile industry is beginning to distribute in the United States and in Europe. The government has embarked on a nation-wide program to improve product quality and safety throughout the supply chain that includes a safety tracking and accountability system and a national product quality-monitoring network.[38] However, the nation is not without its obstacles. The continued rapid growth of the Chinese economy is threatened by infrastructure limitations, pollution, logistical bottlenecks, a young banking system, and the imbalance between male and female births. Also, China cannot continue progressing by copying foreign technologies forever. China might need another decade to overcome a long list of quality manufacturing problems, such as weak design, before its companies can compete with those in Japan and America.

Key Issues for Discussion

1. Do you see any parallels between today's China and post–World War II Japan? What differences are evident?
2. What opportunities does China have to learn from the progress made in quality in Japan and the West over the past half-century?

REVIEW QUESTIONS

1. What factors have contributed to the increased awareness of quality in modern business?
2. What practices do Motorola and MidwayUSA in the Quality Profiles use to help them achieve high quality?
3. Summarize the six quality perspectives described in this chapter.
4. Distinguish among consumers, external customers, and internal customers. Illustrate how these concepts apply to a Chipotle's restaurant, a Walmart, or a similar franchise or chain store.
5. Explain why a single quality definition is not sufficient.
6. Briefly summarize the history of quality before and since the industrial revolution. What caused the most significant changes?
7. Define the following terms:
   a. quality assurance
   b. total quality

   c. performance excellence
   d. competitive advantage
8. Explain how each major function of a manufacturing system contributes to total quality.
9. Why is service quality especially important in today's business environment?
10. Discuss the differences between manufacturing and service organizations. What are the implications of these differences for quality management?
11. Explain the roles of people and information technology in providing quality service. How does The Ritz-Carlton Hotel Company, LLC use employees and information technology for quality service?
12. How can business support activities help to sustain quality in an organization? Give examples of some key business support activities and their role in quality.
13. How does quality support the achievement of competitive advantage?

14. What did Philip Crosby mean by "Quality is free"?

15. Explain the role of both design and conformance quality in improving a firm's profitability.

16. What evidence exists to counter the claim that "Quality does not pay"?

17. Why is it important to personalize quality principles?

DISCUSSION QUESTIONS

1. Discuss how either good or poor quality affects you personally as a consumer. For instance, describe experiences in which your expectations were met, exceeded, or not met when you purchased goods or services. Did your experience change your regard for the organization and/or its product? How?

2. Discuss the importance of quality to the national interest of any country in the world. Given China's emergence as a global economic power, of what importance do you believe that quality will play in their future?

3. A reader wrote to *Business Week* (July 9 & 16, 2007, p. 16) and noted: "Americans have switched from Detroit Big Three vehicles to Honda and Toyota vehicles not for visual design features but for durability, reliability, good fuel consumption, and low full cost of operation. Detroit needs to offer five-passenger, 35-mile-per-gallon vehicles with 100,000 mile bumper-to-bumper warranties over 10 years of ownership to cause satisfied Honda and Toyota buyers to switch." What definitions of quality are implied in these comments?

4. Choose a product or service to illustrate how several definitions of quality can apply simultaneously.

5. Think of a product or a service that you are considering purchasing. Develop a list of fitness-for-use criteria that are meaningful to you.

6. A top Ford executive stated "You can't have great value unless you have great quality." Comment on this statement. Do you agree? Why or why not?

7. *PCWorld Magazine* changed its method of rating new products to base scores only on product performance, design, and features, dropping price as a criterion, although it will be clearly stated. Their reasoning was "When we used price as a criterion, high-flying products often got dinged for having higher-than average prices, while budget items got a boost based on value. Now superior products—those that are well designed, easiest to use, feature rich, and power packed—get our highest rating."[39] How does this approach relate to the definitions of quality? Does it help or hinder consumers?

8. What definition of quality is implied by the following consumer advertisements? Explain your reasoning.

   a. A DirectTV ad that states "Now get over 150 channels for only $29.99 for 12 months."

   b. A deodorant ad that promises "Stay dry in sticky situations."

   c. An ad for Paul Mitchell hair care products that states: "Repair years of damage in minutes with Kera Triplex 2-step repair in-salon treatment. Reduces breakage up to 80%; improves shine up to 35%; prevents color fade up to 67%. Take home the benefits of strong, healthy hair with the complete Awapuhi hair care system. Protect and nourish hair with every wash, condition, and style."

   d. A Bulova watch add that explains "Most quartz watches are accurate to 15 seconds a month—Bulova Precisionist is accurate to 10 seconds a year. The key is Precisionist's unique three-prong quartz crystal, which produces a vibration frequency of 262.144 kilohertz, eight times greater than the usual two-prong crystal and the highest of any watch available today. And, the innovative design of the Precisionist movement reduces the effects of temperature variation without using a high maintenance thermo-regulating integrated circuit. The result is a watch that is extraordinarily precise, yet so easy to operate."

   e. Symantec, a software firm that makes antivirus software and performs e-mail storage and security services that advertises:
   - No viruses
   - No spam
   - No downtime
   - E-mail done right

f. A Samsung ad that explains, "The Samsung BD-UP5000 gives you the best of both HD worlds by bridging Blu-ray and HD DVD capabilities together in one player … at an incredible Full HD 1080 p resolution, which delivers up to six times the picture quality of standard definition DVDs."

9. What do you think are the most important lessons that managers can learn from studying the history of quality management?

10. Provide some specific examples that illustrate how any of the eight forces that will influence the future of quality are reflected in today's business news.

11. Provide specific examples of how the differences between manufacturing and service organizations are evident in a school or a hospital.

12. Select a service activity with which you are familiar. If you were the manager of this activity, what "conformance to specifications" criteria would you use to monitor it?

13. Cite some examples from your own experience in which you felt service quality was truly top-notch, and some in which it was not. What do you think might be some of the fundamental differences in the infrastructure and management practices of these organizations?

14. How are people and information technology used to improve service in your college or university?

15. What role has the Internet played in improving service quality? What barriers to service quality might it have?

16. In this chapter, we noted that much of the work performed in traditional manufacturing organizations now involve service. Provide some examples of this, drawing upon the functions illustrated in Figure 1.2.

17. Choose an organization that you have read about or with which you have personal experience and describe their sources of competitive advantage. For each, state whether you believe that quality supports their strategy or does not support it.

18. How can you internalize and practice quality at a personal level in your daily activities?

PROJECTS, ETC.

1. Develop a portfolio of advertisements from newspapers and magazines and illustrate how quality is used in promoting these products. How do the ads imply the different definitions of quality?

2. Similar to the Xerox case, another organization that reinvented itself through quality initiatives is Continental Airlines (recently merged with United Airlines). Conduct some research and write a three- to five-page paper on Continental's quality journey and practices. Comment on the potential impact of Continental's quality initiatives on the merged company.

3. Examine the annual reports of one company over a period of years. Summarize how quality is discussed or implied in the company's statements and philosophy. Are any changes in the perspectives of quality evident over time?

4. Many countries around the world have professional organizations similar to the American Society for Quality; however, each has its own unique history and offers exclusive activities to its corporate and individual members. They include Excellence Finland, Excellence Ireland, German Society for Quality, Hong Kong Society for Quality, Instituto Profesional Argentino para la Calidad y la Excelencia, Israel Society for Quality, Union of Japanese Scientists and Engineers (JUSE), National Quality Institute (Canada), Programa Gaucho da Qualidade e Produtividade (Brazil), Singapore Quality Institute, and the Spanish Association for Quality. Conduct some research on several of these societies and contrast their similarities and differences.

5. Interview some key managers at a nearby manufacturing company and construct a diagram similar to Figure 1.2 showing the company's key functions and their relationships. Summarize the major quality concerns of each function.

6. Interview some managers at a local service organization and summarize the role of people and information technology in providing quality service. How are people and information technology integrated into long-range improvement plans and strategies?

7. Develop a "personal quality checklist" that you would like to achieve each day and analyze the

results over an extended period of time. The listing of possible checklist standards might include:

- Review class notes after each class
- No text messaging during classes
- Limit phone calls to 10 minutes
- No more than 30 minutes per day spent on social networking websites
- No more than x hours of television per week
- Update schedule daily on PDA or computer calendar
- Get up promptly—no snooze alarm
- Ensure that team members are informed on project progress, each day or each week
- Complete all reading assignments as due
- Inform professor of essential absences via e-mail, text, or phone message at least 24 hours in advance
- Work in library (or other quiet place) to avoid interruptions
- No more than one "junk food" snack per day
- Exercise in gym for at least one hour, twice per week
- Turn off cell phone during classes
- Prepare or buy, and eat, breakfast every day

- E-mail or call parents at least once per week
- Ensure that bank account is never overdrawn by checking balance online at least every other day

Select around 10 items from this list, or make up your own that are more important to you. Whatever is meaningful to you may be tracked. Failure to adhere to these standards is considered a "defect." Use charts to plot and analyze results. After you have gathered data for a week or two, review the data for the purposes of analysis and improvement. You might wish to share your personal checklist items and goals with your instructor, a colleague, spouse, or friend, and discuss your progress. The focus is on improving, not being critical!

After completing the project, answer these questions:

a. What did your analysis reveal?
b. Did you find that you improved simply because you began to measure these "defects"?
c. How did you feel about discussing your progress with others?
d. How might such a process help in a work environment?[40]

CASES

SKILLED CARE PHARMACY[41]

Skilled Care Pharmacy, located in Mason, Ohio, is a $25 million privately held regional provider of pharmaceutical products delivered within the long-term care, assisted living, hospice, and group home environments. The following products are included within this service:

- Medications and related billing services
- Medical records
- Information systems
- Continuing education
- Consulting services to include pharmacy, nursing, dietary, and social services

The key customer groups that Skilled Care provides services to include the senior population housed within the extended and long-term care environments. Customers within this sector depend on Skilled Care to provide their daily pharmaceutical needs at a competitive rate. Because of the high risk

factor of its business, these needs require that the right drug be delivered to the right patient at the right time. Moreover, depending on the environment being served, different medication dispensing methods may be used such as vials, multidose packaging, or unit dose boxes. Also, depending on the customer type, specific delivery requirements may be implemented to better serve the end user.

Skilled Care's dedication and commitment to continuous quality improvement is evident throughout its internal and external operations. By reflecting on the principles needed to attain quality success across all levels of customers, Skilled Care adopted the quality policy statement shown in Figure 1.7.

Skilled Care's employee population includes 176 culturally diverse associates committed to a substance-free workplace. The team includes associates with all levels of educational training representing many of the

FIGURE 1.7 Skilled Care Quality Policy

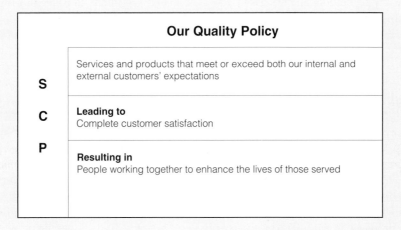

Source: Courtesy of Nancy Milnarik, VP of Quality, Skilled Care, Inc., Mason Ohio. Reprinted with permission.

following disciplines: pharmacists, pharmacy technicians, medical data entry, accountants, billing specialists, nurses, human resources, sales/marketing, purchasing, administrative and administrative assistance, delivery, customer service representatives, and IT certified personnel. At times, multifaceted work teams are formed through cross-functional approaches to complete the task(s) at hand.

Skilled Care's deliverables are generated from its sole 24,000-square foot location in Mason, Ohio. The pharmacy, which is open 24 hours a day, 365 days a year, is secured by a Honeywell alarm system. The company's primary technology rests within its pharmacy software, Rescot. This system enables Skilled Care to process, bill, and generate pertinent data critical to the overall operations of the company. Other partnerships have also been established within Skilled Care's multidosed packaging capabilities and wholesaler purchasing interface.

SCP utilizes the Internet for publishing pertinent information and news as well as hosts a web-enabled customer service application called Track-It to report specific information about customer issues for companywide resolution. Advantages of e-commerce include quicker customer service response time for all areas of service including placing the order, pharmacist's review, delivery, and billing of the product.

Skilled Care Pharmacy faces key strategic challenges from the rapidly evolving financial structure of health care, a shortage of licensed pharmacist personnel, the constant evolution of medical practice, and employee retention at all levels. These, as well as future challenges, are always balanced with the responsibility to the stakeholders.

Discussion Questions

1. How might the various definitions of quality apply to Skilled Care?
2. How are the six quality perspectives reflected in Skilled Care's policy and operations?
3. Given the nature of Skilled Care's operations and the challenges it faces, discuss how a total quality approach can help the company meet these challenges and improve its ability to provide the services its customers need.

CHELSEY'S RESTAURANT _____

Chelsey, a young entrepreneur who has worked in various restaurants throughout high school and college, has decided to develop a new type of restaurant that focuses primarily on takeout of home-cooked meals for busy professionals on their way home from work. The restaurant would also have a small dining area for customers who wish to eat the food there. Because this prospective business will have to compete with national franchises and other traditional local restaurants, Chelsey wants to ensure that this business will compete on quality and develop a strong quality reputation. She has asked you to help her understand the issues that she must address in designing and managing this restaurant.

Using the six quality perspectives and any other concepts discussed in this chapter to advise Chelsey on what she might consider to assure high quality for this venture.

DEERE & COMPANY

Deere & Company (http://www.deere.com) (also known as John Deere, after its founder) is a world-leading manufacturer, distributor, and financier of equipment for agriculture, construction, forestry, and commercial and consumer applications (lawn and grounds care). Deere's objective has consistently been to be the low-cost producer in the markets it serves. However, it seeks to do so while maintaining an image of quality and customer focus. Its company values are quality, innovation, integrity, and commitment. Because of the company's close ties to the agricultural industry, corporate performance in both sales and profits was highly variable over the last several decades due to cycles of low prices and oversupplies of many agricultural products. During that period, the company made various adjustments in its product mix and manufacturing processes to enable it to better compete and survive in the global environment.

The excerpts below come from various Deere annual reports.

1999

Highlighting our pursuit of genuine value through continuous improvement is an aggressive series of process-based initiatives targeting Six-Sigma levels of performance and customer satisfaction. During the year, some 900 projects involving the efforts of several thousand employees, were completed or in progress. Their goal: Streamlining business processes, large and small, and pursuing operational excellence throughout the company…. In support of the initiative stressing customer focus, our operating divisions are structuring their activities around the core processes of customer acquisition, order fulfillment, product development and customer support.

2003

A totally new compensation and rewards system, which began taking effect in 2003, is supporting

the attainment of our goals and promoting true alignment among the interests of customers, employees and investors. Thousands of management employees at all levels are now eligible for a bonus payable when our service to customers earns a return above the cost of capital over a multiyear period.

2005

Deere employees are tightly aligned with our business objectives and are being evaluated and compensated accordingly. Virtually all 21,000 of our salaried employees worldwide follow detailed performance plans tailored to their own responsibilities and development potential. The plans spell out how each individual's efforts contribute to meeting unit and company goals…. A prime example of how product innovation is driving higher sales, the John Deere 2500 E greens mower is the golf and turf industry's first mower that uses hybrid technology. Result: Lower noise and better fuel efficiency but plenty of power (18-hp)…. Building on a tradition of stewardship, the company has continued to develop product solutions that are less disruptive to the surrounding environment. Deere's newly introduced Tier 3-compliant PowerTech Plus engines use the latest technology to deliver better fuel economy and more power while meeting stringent emissions regulations. In another case, the company in 2005 became the first equipment manufacturer to use biodiesel as a factory fill at its U.S. manufacturing locations.

2008

Rigorous asset management lies at the heart of our strategy to achieve more consistent returns, add to our comparative advantage, and weather tough economic times…. Following rigorous processes everywhere helps address the growing scope and scale of our operations and helps achieve increased levels of consistency, simplicity, efficiency and quality. Many of our approaches are unique to Deere and hard to copy.

With respect to quality improvement, the company is aggressively implementing the Deere Product Quality System (DPQS), a set of world-class manufacturing practices designed to meet rising customer expectations for increased product reliability. Product lines responsible for most of the company's sales received advanced quality certification through 2008. DPQS is expected to make a major impact on the company's ability to further serve customers and reduce expense as the effort advances quality to a still-higher level.

As a leading corporate citizen, Deere takes its responsibilities seriously. In this regard, employee safety has always been one of John Deere's top priorities. In 2008, our facilities remained among the safest in the world with employee injury-frequency rates in line with the company's historic lows. As an environmental leader noted primarily for advanced equipment designed to treat the environment with increasing care, the company also has made sustainability an integral part of its operations. A case in point is the new biomass energy system that went into operation during the year at our German combine factory. It enables the facility to provide for much of its own heating and cooling needs, while reducing greenhouse gas emissions. Further in 2008, Deere announced plans to reduce greenhouse gas emissions from its global operations as part of participation in the U.S. Environmental Protection Agency's Climate Leaders program....

Through the aligned efforts of a dedicated workforce more than 50,000 strong worldwide, John Deere is establishing a performance-based culture that is making quite an impact on our results. Deere's team-enrichment initiative supports this emphasis on employee teaming and collaboration. By promoting a more global and inclusive work environment, team enrichment helps the company strengthen its competitive advantage through the attraction and retention of highly talented employees from all backgrounds.

2010

As our world changes, so must John Deere. With those words, the company in 2010 introduced an ambitious blueprint to guide its efforts in meeting the world's expanding needs in the years ahead... The strategy concentrates the company's focus on two growth areas—agricultural and construction equipment solutions. Other operations—turf, forestry, parts, engines, intelligent solutions, and financial services—have vital roles supporting or complementing the growth operations. Emphasizing a lineup of tightly knit operations puts Deere in a stronger position to leverage strengths, optimize investments, efficiently target leadership and employee resources, and extend its ability to compete in the global marketplace.

Further, the revised strategy sets out challenging metrics including $50 billion in mid-cycle sales by 2018 and 12 percent mid-cycle operating margins by 2014. Meeting these goals would result in a near-doubling of sales, a healthy increase in profitability, and an almost three-fold increase in economic profit, or SVA. The strategic plan targets roughly half of the company's sales coming from outside the U.S. and Canada by 2018, versus about one-third today. In addition, measures are being introduced to help assure that financial performance remains sustainable as we accelerate our growth aspirations. "Health" metrics, as they're being known, pertain to product quality, market share and employee engagement, among other areas.

Assignment

On the basis of this information, prepare a brief report discussing Deere & Company's evolution of quality. Relate your discussion to historical trends, future challenges, the various definitional perspectives of quality, and other issues discussed in this chapter, including quality perspectives. For example, how has their perspective of quality and the practices used to implement it changed over the years? Update the case by reviewing Deere's latest annual report and include any new information in your analysis.

NOTES

1. "Conference Board High on Quality Management," *Quality Progress*, August 2011, 13.

2. Angus Mackenzie, "Feet of Clay," *Motor Trend*, April 2010, 8.

3. Alex Taylor III, "How Toyota Lost Its Way," *Fortune*, July 26, 2010, 108–118.

4. http://gizmodo.com/5593194/

5. Nabil Tamimi and Rose Sebastianelli, "How Firms Define and Measure Quality," *Production and Inventory Management Journal* 37, no. 3 (Third Quarter, 1996), 34–39.

6. Four comprehensive reviews of the concept and definition of quality are: David A. Garvin, "What Does Product Quality Really Mean?" *Sloan Management Review* 26, no. 1 (1984), 25–43; Gerald F. Smith, "The Meaning of Quality," *Total Quality Management* 4, no. 3 (1993), 235–244; Carol A. Reeves and David A. Bednar, "Defining Quality: Alternatives and Implications," *Academy of Management Review* 19, no. 3 (1994), 419–445; and Kristie W. Seawright and Scott T. Young, "A Quality Definition Continuum," *Interfaces* 26, no. 3 (May–June 1996), 107–113.

7. David A. Garvin, "What Does Product Quality Really Mean?" *Sloan Management Review* 26, no. 1 (1984), 25.

8. "Lamborghini Owner Says He Got $262,000 Lemon," *Cincinnati Enquirer*, June 23, 1998, B5.

9. Gregory M. Seal, "1990s—Years of Promise, Years of Peril for U.S. Manufacturers," *Industrial Engineering* 22, no. 1 (January 1990), 18–21. We also thank Ben Valentin for providing some historical facts about Nissan and Datsun.

10. ANSI/ASQC A3-1978, *Quality Systems Terminology* (Milwaukee, WI: American Society for Quality Control, 1978).

11. "Quality Pays at Hilton Hotels," *Quality Digest*, August 2005, 9.

12. Early history is reported in Delmer C. Dague, "Quality—Historical Perspective," *Quality Control in Manufacturing* (Warrendale, PA: Society of Automotive Engineers, 1981); and L. P. Provost and C. L. Norman, "Variation through the Ages," *Quality Progress* 23, no. 12 (December 1990), 39–44. Modern events are discussed in Nancy Karabatsos, "Quality in Transition, Part One: Account of the '80s," *Quality Progress* 22, no. 12 (December 1989), 22–26; and Joseph M. Juran, "The Upcoming Century of Quality," address to the ASQC Annual Quality Congress, Las Vegas, May 24, 1994. A comprehensive historical account may be found in J. M. Juran, *A History of Managing for Quality* (Milwaukee, WI: ASQC Quality Press, 1995). Discussions of quality in China were adapted from the first chapter, "Ancient China's History of Managing for Quality," in Juran's book and from Jack Pompeo, "Living Inside China's Quality Revolution," *Quality Progress*, August 2007, 30–35.

13. M. D. Fagan (ed.), *A History of Engineering and Science in the Bell System: The Early Years, 1875–1925* (New York: Bell Telephone Laboratories, 1974).

14. "Manufacturing Tops List of Concerns Among Executives," *Industrial Engineering* 22, no. 6 (June 1990), 8.

15. Lawrence Utzig, "Quality Reputation—Precious Asset," *ASQC Technical Conference Transactions*, Atlanta: 1980, 145–154.

16. Procter & Gamble, *Report to the Total Quality Leadership Steering Committee and Working Councils* (Cincinnati, OH: Procter & Gamble, 1992).

17. A. V. Feigenbaum, *Total Quality Control*, 3rd ed., rev. (New York: McGraw-Hill, 1991), 77, 78.

18. "The Cost of Quality," *Newsweek*, September 7, 1992, 48–49.

19. Kennedy Smith, "Managers Disagree on Quality's Definition" *Quality Digest*, May 2004, 6.

20. Lori L. Silverman with Annabeth L. Propst, "Quality Today: Recognizing the Critical SHIFT," *Quality Progress*, February 1999, 53–60.

21. (http://www.hbmeu.ac.ae/our-offerings/e-school-business-quality-management)

22. *2011 Future of Quality Study*, Milwaukee, WI: American Society for Quality, http://asq.org/about-asq/how-we-do/futures-study.html, accessed January 10, 2011.

23. "A Profile of Hershey Foods Corporation," Hershey Foods Corporation, Hershey, PA, 7.

24. Jeff Sabatini, "Flawless (Nearly)," *Automotive Manufacturing & Production*, November 1999, 60–62.

25. Frederick F. Reichheld and W. Earl Sasser, Jr., "Zero Defections: Quality Comes to Services," *Harvard Business Review* 68, no. 5 (September-October 1990), 105–112.

26. Wes Raynal, "Quality Matters, but Service Is Tops," *Autoweek*, July 19, 2010, 14.

27. Adapted from the Malcolm Baldrige National Quality Award application summaries of The Ritz-Carlton Hotel Company, LLC © 1992 and 1999. All rights reserved. Reprinted with permission of The Ritz-Carlton Hotel Company, LLC; Cheri Henderson, "Putting on the Ritz," *TQM Magazine* 2, no. 5 (November–December 1992), 292–296; and remarks by various Ritz-Carlton managers at the 2000 Quest for Excellence Conference, Washington, D.C.

28. *The PIMS Letter on Business Strategy*, no. 4 (Cambridge, MA: Strategic Planning Institute, 1986).

29. Philip Crosby, *Quality Is Free* (New York: McGraw-Hill, 1979).

30. Kathleen Kerwin, "When Flawless Isn't Enough," *Business Week*, December 8, 2003.

31. David Welch, "Nissan: The Squeaks Get Louder," *Business Week*, May 17, 2004, 44.

32. U.S. General Accounting Office, "Management Practices: U.S. Companies Improve Performance Through Quality Efforts," GA/NSIAD-91-190. (May 1991); "Progress on the Quality Road," *Incentive*, April 1995, 7.

33. Kevin B. Hendricks and Vinod R. Singhal, "Does Implementing an Effective TQM Program Actually Improve Operating Performance? Empirical Evidence from Firms That Have Won Quality Awards," *Management Science* 43, 9 (September 1997), 1258–1274. The results of this study appeared in extensive business and trade publications such as *Business Week*, *Fortune*, and others.

34. Rath & Strong Executive Panel, Winter 1994 Survey on Personal Initiative, Summary of Findings.

35. Ron Zemke and Dick Schaaf, *The Service Edge* (New York: New American Library, 1989), 352–355; William Davidow and Bro Utall, Total Customer Service (New York: Harper & Row, 1989), 86–87. Other good examples at FedEx can be found at www.fedexstories.com.

36. Information for this feature was obtained from "Xerox Quest for Quality and the Malcolm Baldrige National Quality Award" presentation script; Norman E. Rickard, Jr., "The Quest for Quality: A Race without a Finish Line," Industrial Engineering, January 1991, 25–27; Howard S. Gitlow and Elvira N. Loredo, "Total Quality Management at Xerox: A Case Study," *Quality Engineering* 5, no. 3 (1993), 403–432; Xerox Quality Solutions, A World of Quality (Milwaukee, WI: ASQC QualityPress, 1993); and "Restrengthening Xerox: Our Lean Six Sigma Journey," Presentation slides, May 2003. Courtesy of Xerox Corporation. "Know What Counts. Measure What Matters. Deliver Results. Lean Six Sigma and the Quest for Continuous Improvement." (http://www.xerox.com/downloads/usa/en/x/Xerox_Lean_Six_Sigma_Brochure.pdf). Our thanks also go to George Maszleof Xerox Corporation for providing the information on Six Sigma initiatives.

37. Reprinted with permission from Jack Pompeo, "Living Inside China's Quality Revolution," *Quality Progress*, August 2007, 30–35. Copyright © 2007 American Society for Quality. No further distribution allowed without permission.

38. Scott M. Paton, "Is China Another Japan?" *Quality Digest*, January 2008, 128.

39. *PCWorld Magazine*, October 2009, p. 7.

40. Adapted from Harry V. Roberts and Bernard F. Sergesketter, *Quality Is Personal: A Foundation for Total Quality Management*, Copyright © 1993 with the permission of The Free Press, a Division of Simon & Schuster Adult Publishing Group.

41. Appreciation for materials in this case is expressed to Nancy Mlinarik, VP of Quality, Skilled Care, Inc.

Foundations of Quality Management

In the 1890s, Caesar Ritz defined the standards for a luxury hotel; these evolved into the quality responsibilities of the employees—the "Ladies and Gentlemen Serving Ladies and Gentlemen"—of today's Ritz-Carlton Hotel Company: anticipating the wishes and needs of the guests, resolving their problems, and exhibiting genuinely caring conduct toward guests and each other. The Ritz-Carlton management recognized that the key to ensuring that these responsibilities are realized was to create a "Skilled and Empowered Work Force Operating with Pride and Joy." The concept of "pride and joy" in work—and its impact on quality—is one of the foundations of the philosophy of W. Edwards Deming. Deming, along with Joseph M. Juran and Philip B. Crosby, are regarded as true "management gurus" in the quality revolution. Their insights into measuring, managing, and improving quality have had profound impacts on countless managers and entire corporations around the world.

This chapter presents the quality management philosophies of these three leaders, their similarities and differences, and also examines their individual contributions to modern practice. In addition, it discusses the contributions of other key individuals who have helped to shape current thinking in quality management. Their contributions established the principles of total quality and the implementation of quality management systems, such as ISO 9000, which we also introduce in this chapter.

quality**profiles**

Texas Nameplate Company, Inc. and MEDRAD

Founded in 1946, Texas Nameplate Company, Inc. (TNC), with only 43 employees, manufactures and sells identification and information labels that are affixed to refrigerators, oil-field equipment, high-pressure valves, trucks, computer equipment, and other products made by more than 1,000 customers throughout the United States and in nine foreign countries. TNC has honed the raw attributes inherent to its small size—from streamlined communications and rapid decision-making to shared goals and accessible leaders—into competitive advantages. It started by changing the traditional, hierarchical leadership structure into a flatter, team-based structure built on mutual respect and guided by the philosophy that "Fear is useless; what is needed is trust." The result is a close-knit organization that is finely tuned to the requirements of its customers. TNC aims to create a continuous learning environment that enables empowered teams of workers to take charge of processes and to deliver products and services with a "star quality." Customer contact employees are empowered to resolve customer complaints without consulting management, and production workers are responsible for tailoring processes to optimize contributions to company goals and to meet team-set standards. TNC reduced its defects from 3.65 percent to about 1 percent in four years. Customers consistently give the company an "excellent" rating (5 to 6 on a scale of 6) in 12 key business areas, including product quality, reliable performance, on-time delivery, and overall satisfaction, and in its employee survey, satisfaction rates in five areas employees say are the most important: fair pay, job content satisfaction, recognition, fairness/respect, and career development, exceed national norms by a significant margin.

For more than 40 years, MEDRAD has been committed to improving patient outcomes by developing, marketing, and servicing innovative, cost-efficient medical imaging and other devices for diagnosing and treating diseases. MEDRAD has created an environment of distributed decision making in support of a culture of high performance. Decision making is done at the point of customer interaction, where the customer can be a client, an employee, or any other stakeholder of MEDRAD. This model allows the organization to respond with agility and speed to the needs of the business units, clients, and employees. The company uses systematic approaches to capture customers' expectations and preferences through various listening posts, trade associations, and other mechanisms and communicates them to the appropriate sales team for analysis. The Customer Complaint Process focuses on timely response and successful resolution of customer issues and ensures that the organization determines causes and completes corrective actions. Because of its customer-focused practices, MEDRAD's overall Net Promoter (NP) scores (a loyalty metric defined by the level of repeat sales and referrals) have been consistently 60 percent or higher, compared to the 50 percent or higher marks for other organizations over the same time periods. In the area of service support, MEDRAD consistently scored 80 percent or higher compared to 50 percent for the best-in-class benchmark.

Sources: Malcolm Baldrige National Quality Award, Profiles of Winners, and 2002 Quest for Excellence video script, National Institute of Standards and Technology, Department of Commerce.

THE DEMING PHILOSOPHY

No individual has had more influence on quality management than Dr. W. Edwards Deming (1900–1993). Deming received a Ph.D. in physics and was trained as a statistician, so much of his philosophy can be traced to these roots. He worked for Western Electric during its pioneering era of statistical quality control in the 1920s and 1930s. Deming recognized the importance of viewing management processes statistically. During World War II he taught quality control courses as part of the U.S. national defense effort, but he realized that teaching statistics only to engineers and factory workers would never solve the fundamental quality problems that manufacturing needed to address. Despite numerous efforts, his attempts to convey the message of quality to upper-level managers in the United States were ignored.

Shortly after World War II, Deming was invited to Japan to help the country take a census. The Japanese had heard about his theories and their usefulness to U.S. companies during the war. Consequently, he soon began to teach them statistical quality control. His thinking went beyond mere statistics, however. Deming preached the importance of top management leadership, customer/supplier partnerships, and continuous improvement in product development and manufacturing processes. Japanese managers embraced these ideas, and the rest, as they say, is history. Deming's influence on Japanese industry was so great that the Union of Japanese Scientists and Engineers established the Deming Application Prize in 1951 to recognize companies that show a high level of achievement in quality practices. Deming also received Japan's highest honor, the Royal Order of the Sacred Treasure, from the emperor. The former chairman of NEC Electronics once said, "There is not a day I don't think about what Dr. Deming meant to us."

Although Deming lived in Washington, D.C., he remained virtually unknown in the United States until 1980, when NBC telecast a program entitled "If Japan Can ... Why Can't We?" The documentary highlighted Deming's contributions in Japan and his later work with Nashua Corporation. Shortly afterward, his name was frequently on the lips of U.S. corporate executives. Companies such as Ford, GM, and Procter & Gamble invited him to work with them to improve their quality. To their surprise, Deming did not lay out "a quality improvement program" for them. His goal was to plant the seeds of quality knowledge from which managers could learn, allowing them to develop effective quality management systems. Deming worked with passion until his death in December 1993 at the age of 93, knowing he had little time left to make a difference in his home country. When asked how he would like to be remembered, Deming replied, "I probably won't even be remembered." Then after a long pause, he added, "Well, maybe ... as someone who spent his life trying to keep America from committing suicide."[1]

Just how influential was Deming? The 60th anniversary issue of Motor Trend *magazine listed eight "automotive events that changed the world."[2] One of them was "1950: W. Edwards Deming lectures the Japanese Union of Scientists and Engineers." The magazine observed that Toyota, Honda, Nissan "all owe their success to the sage America ignored."*

Unlike other management gurus and consultants, Deming never defined or described quality precisely. In his last book, he stated, "A product or a service possesses quality if it helps somebody and enjoys a good and sustainable market."[3] In Deming's view, variation is the chief culprit of poor quality. In mechanical assemblies, for example, variations from specifications for part dimensions lead to inconsistent performance and premature wear and failure. Likewise, inconsistencies in human behavior in service frustrate customers and damage companies' reputations. To reduce variation, Deming advocated a never-ending cycle of continuous improvement supported by statistical analysis.

FIGURE 2.1
The Deming Chain
Reaction

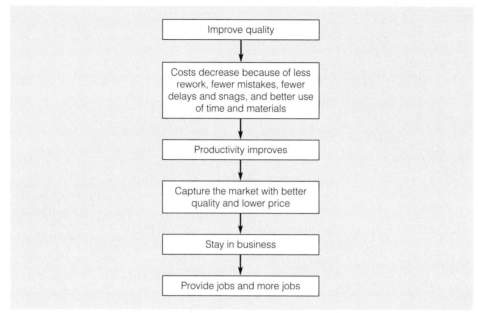

Source: Deming, W. Edwards, Out of the Crisis, © 2000 Massachusetts Institute of Technology, by permission of The MIT Press.

The Deming philosophy focuses on continuous improvements in product and service quality by reducing uncertainty and variability in design, manufacturing, and service processes, driven by the leadership of top management. Deming also postulated that higher quality leads to higher productivity, which in turn leads to long-term competitive strength. The **Deming Chain Reaction** theory (see Figure 2.1) summarizes this view. The theory is that improvements in quality lead to lower costs because they result in less rework, fewer mistakes, fewer delays and snags, and better use of time and materials. Lower costs, in turn, lead to productivity improvements. With better quality and lower prices, a firm can achieve a higher market share and thus stay in business, providing more and more jobs. Deming stressed that top management must assume the overriding responsibility for quality improvement.

Deming's 14 Points

In his early work in the United States, he preached the **14 Points** (see Table 2.1), which represented a radical departure from management thinking and practice. At that time (in the 1960s and 1970s), manufacturing was driven by quotas and strict work measurement, with adversarial relationships between labor and management. Many organizations were ruled by autocratic managers who had little interest in listening to customers, engaging the workforce, or improving quality. Deming believed that companies could not prosper and grow with this type of management, and proposed the 14 Points for achieving quality excellence. Although management practices today are vastly different from when Deming first began to preach his philosophy, the 14 Points still convey important insights and provide guidance for managing effective organizations. We will briefly consider the key lessons of each.

TABLE 2.1 Deming's 14 Points	1. Create and publish to all employees a statement of the aims and purposes of the company or other organization. The management must demonstrate constantly their commitment to this statement. 2. Learn the new philosophy, top management and everybody. 3. Understand the purpose of inspection, for improvement of processes and reduction of cost. 4. End the practice of awarding business on the basis of price tag alone. 5. Improve constantly and forever the system of production and service. 6. Institute training. 7. Teach and institute leadership. 8. Drive out fear. Create trust. Create a climate for innovation. 9. Optimize toward the aims and purposes of the company the efforts of teams, groups, staff areas. 10. Eliminate exhortations for the workforce. 11. (a) Eliminate numerical quotas for production. Instead, learn and institute methods for improvement. (b) Eliminate MBO [management by objective]. Instead, learn the capabilities of processes and how to improve them. 12. Remove barriers that rob people of pride of workmanship. 13. Encourage education and self-improvement for everyone. 14. Take action to accomplish the transformation.

Source: Deming, W. Edwards, Out of the Crisis, figures: Fourteen Points, condensed and expanded versions, pages 23–24, © 2000 Massachusetts Institute of Technology, by permission of The MIT Press.

Point 1: Create a Vision and Demonstrate Commitment   An organization must define its values, mission, and vision of the future to provide long-term direction for its management and employees. Deming believed that businesses should not exist simply for profit; they are social entities whose basic purpose is to serve their customers and employees. To fulfill this purpose, they must take a long-term view, invest in innovation, education, and training, and take responsibility for providing jobs and improving a firm's competitive position. This responsibility lies with top management. Effective leadership begins with commitment, but making a commitment to quality and performance excellence is still difficult for managers. Even when managers have conducted a thorough assessment of their organization and know what they need to change, many do not effectively follow up on opportunities.[4] Reasons range from denial ("We can't be that bad!") to excuses ("We have a lot of irons on the fire right now.").

Point 2: Learn the New Philosophy   Historical ways of managing built on outdated twentieth century practices such as numerical quotas or motivational slogans will not work in today's global business environment. Nevertheless, some organizations, such as call centers, are still managed like this. To survive in today's competitive environment, companies must take a customer-driven approach to quality. To accomplish this, everyone, from the boardroom to the stockroom, must learn and understand the principles of quality and performance excellence. However, people change jobs and organizations generally have a short memory—both need to continually renew themselves to learn new approaches and relearn many older ones. This is often called "organizational learning," and will be addressed in a later chapter.

Point 3: Understand Inspection   In the twentieth century, inspection had been the principal means for quality control; companies employed dozens or even hundreds of inspectors, sometimes as many as regular production workers. Routine inspection acknowledges that defects are present, encourages a lack of attention to quality by production workers, and does not add value to the product. The rework and disposition of defective material decreases productivity and increases costs. Deming encouraged workers to take responsibility for their work, rather than leave the problems for someone else down the production line. He advocated more in-process inspection and the use of statistical tools that would help to eliminate post-production inspection. Thus, inspection should be used as an information-gathering tool for improvement, not as a means of "assuring" quality. Today, this new role of inspection has been integrated into the quality management practices of most companies. However, few managers truly understand variation in production and how to leverage in-process data for improvement. By understanding and seeking to reduce variation, managers can eliminate many sources of unnecessary inspection, thus reducing non-value-added costs associated with operations.

Point 4: Stop Making Decisions Purely on the Basis of Cost   Purchasing departments have long been driven by cost minimization and competition among suppliers without regard for quality. In 1931, Walter Shewhart noted that price has no meaning without quality.[5] (Think about the value based definition of quality from Chapter 1.) Yet purchasing managers have typically been evaluated by the amount of money they spend. Deming recognized that the direct costs associated with poor quality materials that arise during production or during warranty periods, as well as the loss of customer goodwill, can far exceed the cost "savings" perceived by purchasing. Thus, purchasing must understand its role as a supplier to production and its impact on the system.

Deming also urged businesses to establish long-term relationships with fewer suppliers, leading to loyalty and opportunities for mutual improvement. Management previously justified multiple suppliers for reasons such as providing protection against strikes or natural disasters, while ignoring "hidden" costs such as increased travel to visit suppliers, loss of volume discounts, increased setup charges resulting in higher unit costs, and increased inventory and administrative expense. Most importantly, constantly changing suppliers solely on the basis of price increases the variation in the material supplied to production, because each supplier's process is different. In contrast, a reduced supply base decreases the variation coming into the process, thus reducing scrap, rework, and the need for adjustment to accommodate this variation. A long-term relationship strengthens the supplier–customer bond, allows the supplier to produce in greater quantity, improves communication with the customer, and therefore enhances opportunities for process improvement. Today's emphasis on supply chain management (SCM) reflects the achievement of Point 4. SCM focuses heavily on a system's view of the supply chain with the objective of minimizing total supply chain costs and developing stronger partnerships with suppliers.

Point 5: Improve Constantly and Forever   Improvements are necessary in both design and operations. Improved design of goods and services comes from understanding customer needs and continual market surveys and other sources of feedback, and from understanding the manufacturing and service delivery process. Improvements in operations are achieved by reducing the causes and impacts of variation, and engaging all employees to innovate and seek ways of doing their jobs more efficiently and effectively. When quality improves, productivity improves and costs decrease, as the Deming chain reaction (Figure 2.1) suggests. Today, continuous improvement is recognized as a necessary means for survival in a highly competitive and global business environment. The tools for improvement are constantly evolving, and organizations need to ensure that their employees understand and apply them effectively, which requires training, the focus of the next Point.

Point 6: Institute Training   People are an organization's most valuable resource; they want to do a good job and require training to do it well. Not only does training improve quality and productivity, but it adds to worker morale, and demonstrates to workers that the company is dedicated to investing in their future. Training must transcend such basic job skills as running a machine or following the script when talking to customers. Training should include tools for diagnosing, analyzing, and solving quality problems and identifying improvement opportunities. Today, many companies have excellent training programs for technology related to direct production, but still fail to enrich the ancillary skills of their workforce. Here is where some of the most lucrative opportunities exist to make an impact on key business results.

Point 7: Institute Leadership   Deming recognized that one of biggest impediments to improvement was a lack of leadership. The job of management is leadership, not supervision. Supervision is simply overseeing and directing work; leadership means providing guidance to help employees perform better. Leadership can help to eliminate the element of fear from the job and encourage teamwork. Leadership was, is, and will continue to be, a challenging issue in every organization, particularly as new generations of managers replace those who have learned to lead. Thus, this Point of Deming's will always be relevant to organizations.

Point 8: Drive Out Fear   Fear is manifested in many ways: fear of reprisal, fear of failure, fear of the unknown, fear of relinquishing control, and fear of change. No system can work without the mutual respect of managers and workers. Workers are often afraid to report quality problems because they might not meet their quotas, their incentive pay might be reduced, or they might be blamed for problems in the system. Managers are also afraid to cooperate with other departments, because the other managers might receive higher performance ratings and bonuses, or because they fear takeovers or reorganizations. Creating a culture without fear is a slow process but can be destroyed in an instant with a transition of leadership and a change in corporate policies. Therefore, today's managers need to continue to be sensitive to the impact that fear can have on their organizations.

Point 9: Optimize the Efforts of Teams   Teamwork helps to break down barriers between departments and individuals. Barriers between functional areas occur when managers fear they might lose power. Internal competition for raises and performance ratings inhibits teamwork and cooperation. This leads to poor quality because other departments cannot understand what their internal customers want and do not get what they need from their internal suppliers. Training and employee involvement are important means of removing such barriers.

Point 10: Eliminate Exhortations   Many early attempts to improve quality focused solely on behavioral change. However, posters, slogans, and motivational programs are directed at the wrong people. They assume that all quality problems are due to the workforce and overlook the major source of problems—the systems that management designs.

A well-designed system that provides workers with the right tools and environment will lead to higher levels of trust and motivation than slogans and goals can achieve.

Point 11: Eliminate Numerical Quotas and Management by Objective (MBO)

Many organizations manage by goals and arbitrary objectives. Standards and quotas do not encourage improvement, particularly if rewards or performance appraisals are tied to meeting quotas. Workers may short-cut quality to reach the goal, and this still happens more than you might think. Then once a goal is reached, little incentive remains for workers to continue; they will often do no more than they are asked to do. Arbitrary goals, such as increasing sales by 5 percent next year or decreasing costs next quarter by 10 percent, have no meaning without a method to achieve them. Deming acknowledged that goals are useful, but numerical goals set for others without incorporating a method to reach the goal generate frustration and resentment. Management must understand the system and continually try to improve it, rather than focus on short-term goals.

Point 12: Remove Barriers to Pride in Workmanship   People on the factory floor
and even in management were often treated as, in Deming's words, "a commodity." Factory workers are often given monotonous tasks; provided with inferior machines, tools, or materials; told to run defective items to meet sales pressures; and report to supervisors who know little about the job—and then are blamed when problems occur. Effective organizations need to understand the factors that motivate and engage workers and build an environment in which workers take pride in what they do, understand the meaning of their work, and are rewarded for their accomplishments.

Point 13: Encourage Education and Self-Improvement   The difference between
this Point and Point 6 is subtle. Point 6 refers to training in specific job skills; Point 13 refers to continuing, broad education for self-development. Organizations must invest in their people at all levels to ensure success in the long term. A fundamental mission of business is to provide jobs as stated in Point 1, but business and society also have the responsibility to improve the value of the individual. Developing the worth of the individual is a powerful motivation method. Today, many companies understand that elevating the general knowledge base of their workforce—outside of specific job skills—returns many benefits. However, others still view this task as a cost that can be easily cut when financial trade-offs must be made.

Point 14: Take Action   Any cultural change begins with top management and includes
everyone. Changing an organizational culture generally meets with skepticism and resistance that many firms find difficult to deal with, particularly when many of the traditional management practices Deming felt must be eliminated are deeply ingrained in the organization's culture.

Many firms have used Deming's principles and organized their quality approaches around his philosophy. Some companies, such as 1991 Baldrige Award winner Zytec Corporation, now a part of Artesyn Technologies, and Hillerich & Bradsby used Deming's principles with great success.

Many people criticized Deming because his philosophy is just that: a philosophy. It lacked specific directions and approaches that told managers "how to do it," and it did not fit into the traditional American business culture. But as Deming often stated, "There is no instant pudding." Quality excellence takes learning, hard work, and dedication, and many are unwilling to make the commitment.

QUALITYSPOTLIGHT

Hilllerich & Bradsby

Hillerich & Bradsby Co. (H&B) has been making the Louisville Slugger brand of baseball bat since 1884.[6] In the mid-1980s, the company faced significant challenges from market changes and competition. CEO Jack Hillerich attended a four-day Deming seminar, which provided the basis for the company's current quality efforts. Returning from the seminar, Hillerich decided to see what changes that Deming advocated were possible in an old company with an old union and a history of labor/management problems. Hillerich persuaded union officials to attend another Deming seminar with five senior managers. Following the seminar, a core group of union and management people developed a strategy to change the company. They talked about building trust and changing to system "to make it something you want to work in." Employees were interested, but skeptical. To demonstrate their commitment, managers examined Deming's 14 Points, and picked several they believed they could make progress on through actions that would demonstrate a serious intention to change. One of the first changes was the elimination of work quotas that were tied to hourly salaries and a schedule of warnings and penalties for failures to meet quotas. Instead, a team-based approach was initiated. Although only a few workers took advantage of the change, overall productivity actually improved as rework decreased because workers were taking pride in their work to produce things the right way first. H&B also eliminated performance appraisals and commission-based pay in sales. The company also focused its efforts on training and education, resulting in an openness to change and capacity for teamwork. Today, the Deming philosophy is still the core of H&B's guiding principles.

Profound Knowledge

The 14 Points caused some confusion and misunderstanding among businesspeople, because Deming did not provide a clear rationale for them. Near the end of his life, however, he synthesized the underlying foundations of the 14 Points into four simple elements that he called a **System of Profound Knowledge**:

1. Appreciation for a system
2. Understanding variation
3. Theory of knowledge
4. Psychology

Systems   A **system** is a set of functions or activities within an organization that work together for the aim of the organization. A system is composed of many smaller, interacting subsystems. For example, a McDonald's restaurant is a system that includes the order-taker/cashier subsystem, grill and food preparation subsystem, drive-through subsystem, and order fulfillment subsystem. These subsystems are linked together as internal customers and suppliers. Likewise, every organization is composed of many individual functions, which are often seen as separate units on an organization chart. However, as we noted in Chapter 1, most processes are cross-functional. Thus, managers should focus on the interactions of parts and of the system with other systems, rather than the actions of parts taken separately.

The aim of any system should be for all stakeholders—stockholders, employees, customers, community, and the environment—to benefit over the long term. To manage any system, managers must understand the interrelationships among the systems' components and among the stakeholders who are involved. Russell Ackoff, a noted authority in systems thinking, explained the importance of systems thinking in the following way:

> … a combination of the best practices by each part of a system taken separately does not yield the best system. We may not even get a good one. A company that has 12 facilities, each producing the same variations of the same type of beverage, had broken the production process down into 15 steps. It produced a table showing each factory (a column) and each of the 15 steps (rows). The company then carried out a study to determine the cost of each step at each factory (a costly study), which identified for each step the factory with the lowest cost. At each factory, the company tried to replace each of its steps that was not the lowest cost with the one used in the factory that had the lowest cost. Had this succeeded, each factory would be producing with steps that had each attained the lowest cost in any factory. It did not work! The lowest-cost steps did not fit together. The result was only a few insignificant cosmetic changes that did not justify the cost of the exercise.[7]

Suboptimization (doing the best for individual components) results in losses to everybody in the system. For example, to purchase materials at the lowest price will often result in excessive costs in scrap and repair during manufacturing and increase overall costs; minimizing the cost of manufacturing alone might result in products that do not meet designers' specifications and customer needs. Such situations lead to a win–lose effect. Purchasing wins, manufacturing loses; manufacturing wins, customers lose; and so on.

Systems thinking applies also to managing people. Pitting individuals or departments against each other for resources is self-destructive to an organization. The individuals or departments will perform to maximize their own expected gain, not that of the entire firm. Therefore, optimizing the system requires internal cooperation. Likewise, traditional performance appraisals do not consider interactions within the system. Many factors affect an individual employee's performance, including the following:

- The training received
- The information and resources provided
- The leadership of supervisors and managers
- Disruptions on the job
- Management policies and practices

Few performance appraisals recognize such factors and often place blame on individuals who have little ability to control their environment.

Variation The second part of Profound Knowledge is a basic understanding of statistical theory and variation. We see variation everywhere, from hitting golf balls to the meals and service in a restaurant. A device called a *quincunx* illustrates a natural process of variation. In a quincunx, small balls are dropped from a hole in the top and hit a series of pins as they fall toward collection boxes. The pins cause each ball to move randomly to the left or right as it strikes each pin on its way down. (If you have ever watched the television show *The Price is Right*, you have seen a quincunx in the plinko game! If not, Google "plinko.")

A computer-simulated quincunx is shown in Figure 2.2.[8] Figure 2.3 shows the frequency distribution of where the balls landed in one simulation. Note that most balls end up toward the middle of the box, resulting in a symmetrical bell-shaped distribution similar to a normal distribution. Even though all balls are dropped from the same position, the end result shows variation.

FIGURE 2.2   A Quincunx in Action

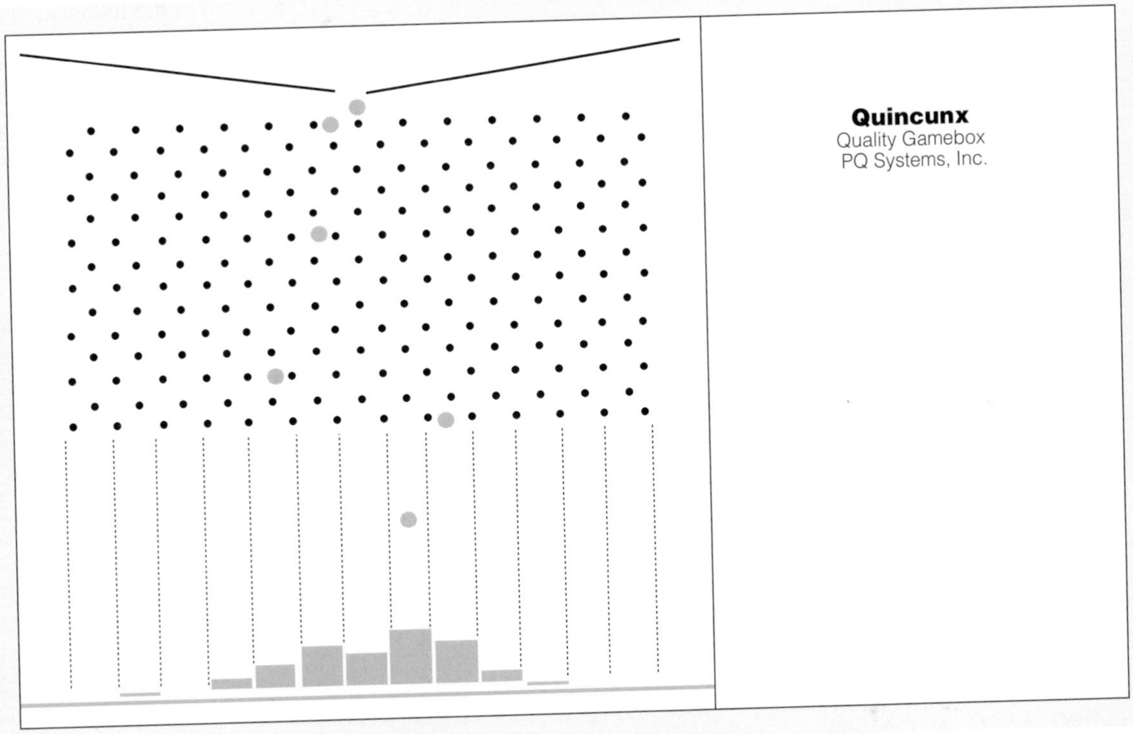

Source: From Quality Gamebox, a registered trademark of Productivity–Quality Systems, Inc. Copyright PQ Systems, www.pqsystems.com

The same kind of variation exists in any production and service process, generally due to factors inherent in the design of the system, which cannot easily be controlled. Excessive variation results in products that fail or perform erratically and inconsistent service that does not meet customers' expectations. Statistical methods are the primary tools used to identify and quantify variation. Deming proposed that every employee in the firm be familiar with statistical techniques and other problem-solving tools. Statistics is a common language that every employee—from top executives to line workers—can use to communicate with one another. Its value lies in its objectivity; statistics leaves little room for ambiguity or misunderstanding.

Today, modern technology has improved our ability to produce many physical parts with very little variation; however, the variation that stems from human behavior and performance continues to hamper quality efforts. Deming suggested that management first understand, and then work to reduce variation through improvements in technology, process design, and training. With less variation, both the producer and consumer benefit. The producer benefits by needing less inspection, experiencing less scrap and rework, and having more consistent human performance, resulting in higher productivity and customer satisfaction. The consumer has the advantage of knowing that all products and services have similar quality characteristics and will perform or be delivered consistently. This advantage can be especially critical when the consumer is another firm using large quantities of the product in its own manufacturing or service operations.

FIGURE 2.3   Results from a Quincunx Experiment

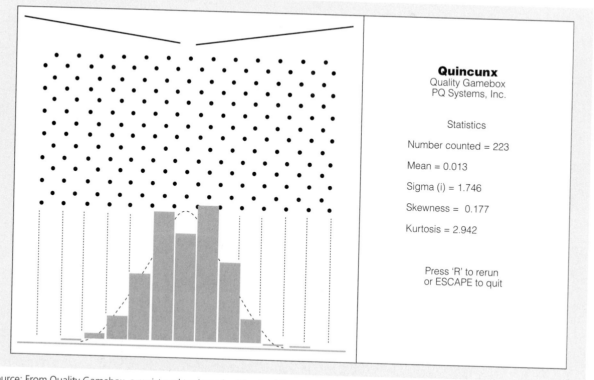

Source: From Quality Gamebox, a registered trademark of Productivity–Quality Systems, Inc. Copyright PQ Systems, www.pqsystems.com

Theory of Knowledge   The third part of Profound Knowledge is the **theory of knowledge**, the branch of philosophy concerned with the nature and scope of knowledge, its presuppositions and basis, and the general reliability of claims to knowledge. Basically, managers need to understand how things work and why decisions that affect the future should be effective. Any rational plan, however simple, requires prediction concerning conditions, behavior, and comparison of performance, and such predictions should be grounded in theory.

For example, it is easy to learn a "cookbook" approach to applying a statistical formula, or using a Microsoft Excel Data Analysis tool. Doing so, however, runs the risk of using the tools inappropriately. Understanding the assumptions and theory behind statistical tools and techniques is vital to applying them correctly. Countless managers use a similar cookbook approach to managing by reading the latest self-help book and blindly following the author's recommendations. Many companies jump on popular approaches advocated by business consultants, only to see the approach fail. Copying an example of success, without understanding it with theory, may lead to disaster.

Deming emphasized that knowledge is not possible without theory, and experience alone does not establish a theory. Experience only describes—it cannot be tested or validated—and

Deming was influenced greatly by Clarence Irving Lewis, author of Mind and the World, *who stated, "There is no knowledge without interpretation. If interpretation, which represents an activity of the mind, is always subject to the check of further experience, how is knowledge possible at all?... An argument from past to future at best is probable only, and even this probability must rest upon principles which are themselves more than probable."[9]*

alone it is of no help in management. Theory, on the other hand, helps one to understand cause-and-effect relationships that can be used for prediction and rational management decisions. It is one reason why Deming never gave managers any "solutions" or prescriptions for achieving quality. He wanted them to learn and discover what works and what is appropriate for their individual organizations and to rationalize their decisions, rather than simply copying others.

Psychology   Psychology helps us understand people, interactions between people and circumstances, interactions between leaders and employees, and any system of management. It is critical to designing a work environment that promotes employee satisfaction and well-being. Much of Deming's philosophy is based on understanding human behavior and treating people fairly. Most managers operate under the assumption that all people are alike. However, people differ from one another. A true leader must be aware of these differences and work toward optimizing everybody's abilities and preferences.

People can be motivated intrinsically and extrinsically; however, the most powerful motivators are intrinsic. People are born with a need for love and esteem in their relationships with other people. Some circumstances provide people with dignity and self-esteem. Conversely, circumstances that deny people these advantages will smother intrinsic motivation. Fear does not motivate people; instead, it prevents the system from reaching its full potential. If people cannot enjoy their work, they will not be productive and focused on quality principles. Psychology helps us to nurture and preserve these positive innate attributes of people; otherwise, we resort to carrots and sticks that offer no long-term values.

One of Deming's more controversial beliefs is that pay is not a motivator, which industrial psychologists have been saying for decades. The chairman of General Motors once stated if GM doubled the salary of every employee, nothing would change. Monetary rewards are a way out for managers who do not understand how to manage intrinsic motivation. When joy in work becomes secondary to getting good ratings, employees are ruled by external forces and must act to protect what they have and avoid punishment.

Impacts of Profound Knowledge   Peter Scholtes, a noted consultant, makes some salient observations about the failure to understand the components of Profound Knowledge:[10]

When people don't understand systems:

- They see events as individual incidents rather than the net result of many interactions and interdependent forces.
- They see the symptoms but not the deep causes of problems.
- They don't understand how an intervention in one part of [an organization] can cause havoc in another place or at another time.
- They blame individuals for problems even when those individuals have little or no ability to control the events around them.
- They don't understand the ancient African saying, "It takes a whole village to raise a child."

When people don't understand variation:

- They don't see trends that are occurring.
- They see trends where there are none.
- They don't know when expectations are realistic.
- They don't understand past performance so they can't predict future performance.
- They don't know the difference between prediction, forecasting, and guesswork.

- They give others credit or blame when those people are simply either lucky or unlucky, which usually occurs because people tend to attribute everything to human effort, heroics, frailty, error, or deliberate sabotage, no matter what the systemic cause.
- They are less likely to distinguish between fact and opinion.

When people don't understand psychology:

- They don't understand motivation or why people do what they do.
- They resort to carrots and sticks and other forms of induced motivation that offer no positive effect and impair the relationship between the motivator and the one being motivated.
- They don't understand the process of change and the resistance to it.
- They revert to coercive and paternalistic approaches when dealing with people.
- They create cynicism, demoralization, demotivation, guilt, resentment, burnout, craziness, and turnover.

When people don't understand the theory of knowledge:

- They don't know how to plan and accomplish learning and improvement.
- They don't understand the difference between improvement and change.
- Problems will remain unsolved, despite their best efforts.

Little of Deming's system of Profound Knowledge is original. Walter Shewhart developed the distinction between common and special causes of variation in the 1920s; business schools began to teach many of the behavioral theories to which Deming subscribed in the 1960s; management scientists refined systems theory in the 1950s through the 1970s; and scientists in all fields have long understood the relationships among prediction, observation, and theory. Deming's major contribution was to tie these concepts together in the context of business. He recognized their synergy and developed them into a unified universal theory of management.

> *Deming's legacy lives on through the W. Edwards Deming Institute (http://deming.org).*

THE JURAN PHILOSOPHY

Joseph Juran (1904–2008) was born in Romania and came to the United States in 1912. He joined Western Electric in the 1920s as it pioneered in the development of statistical methods for quality. He spent much of his time as a corporate industrial engineer and, in 1951, did most of the writing, editing, and publishing of the *Quality Control Handbook*. This book, one of the most comprehensive quality manuals ever written, has been revised several times and continues to be a popular reference.

Like Deming, Juran taught quality principles to the Japanese in the 1950s and was a principal force in their quality reorganization. Among the steps taken by Japanese organizations as a result of Juran's leadership were:

- Directing quality from the senior management level
- Training the entire management hierarchy in quality principles
- Striving to improve quality at a revolutionary rate
- Reporting progress on quality goals to executive levels
- Involving the workforce in quality
- Revising the reward and recognition structure to include quality[11]

During the quality revolution in the second half of the twentieth century, Juran echoed Deming's conclusion that U.S. businesses faced a major crisis in quality due to the huge costs of poor quality and the loss of sales to foreign competition. Both men felt that the solution to this crisis depends on new thinking about quality that includes all levels of the managerial hierarchy. Upper management in particular requires training and experience in managing for quality. Even into this century, Juran continued to warn the United States that it faces losing its status as an economic superpower unless it improves the quality of its goods and services.

Unlike Deming, however, Juran did not propose a major cultural change in the organization, but rather sought to improve quality by working within the system familiar to managers. Thus, his programs were designed to fit into a company's strategic business planning process with minimal risk of rejection. He argued that employees at different levels of an organization speak in their own "languages." (Deming, on the other hand, believed statistics should be the common language.) Juran stated that top management speaks in the language of dollars; workers speak in the language of things; and middle management must be able to speak both languages and translate between dollars and things. Thus, to get top management's attention, quality issues must be cast in the language they understand—dollars. Hence, Juran advocated the use of quality cost accounting and analysis to focus attention on quality problems. At the operational level, Juran focused on increasing conformance to specifications through elimination of defects, supported extensively by statistical tools for analysis. Thus, his philosophy fit well into existing management systems.

Juran suggested that quality should be viewed from both external and internal perspectives; that is, quality is related to (1) product performance that results in customer satisfaction, and (2) freedom from product deficiencies, which avoids customer dissatisfaction. Juran proposed the user-based definition of quality we introduced in Chapter 1: "fitness for use." How products and services are designed, manufactured and delivered, and serviced in the field all contribute to fitness for use. Thus, the pursuit of quality is viewed on two levels: (1) the mission of the firm as a whole is to achieve high design quality; and (2) the mission of each department in the firm is to achieve high-conformance quality. Like Deming, Juran advocated a never-ending spiral of activities that includes market research, product development, design, planning for manufacture, purchasing, production process control, inspection and testing, and sales, followed by customer feedback. The interdependency of these functions emphasizes the need for competent companywide quality management. Senior management must play an active and enthusiastic leadership role in the quality management process.

Juran's prescriptions focus on three major quality processes, called the **Quality Trilogy**: (1) *quality planning*—the process of preparing to meet quality goals; (2) *quality control*—the process of meeting quality goals during operations; and (3) *quality improvement*—the process of breaking through to unprecedented levels of performance. At the time he proposed this structure, few companies were engaging in any significant planning or improvement activities. Thus, Juran was promoting a major cultural shift in management thinking.

Quality planning begins with identifying customers, both external and internal, determining their needs, translating customer needs into specifications, developing product features that respond to those needs, and developing the processes capable of producing the product or delivering the service. Thus, like Deming, Juran wanted employees to know who uses their products, whether in the next department or in another organization. Quality goals based on meeting the needs of customers and suppliers alike at a minimum combined cost are then established. Next, the process that can produce the product to satisfy customers' needs and meet quality goals under operating conditions must be designed. Strategic planning for quality—similar to the firm's financial planning process—determines short-term and long-term goals, sets priorities, compares results with previous plans, and meshes the plans with other corporate strategic objectives.

As a parallel to Deming's emphasis on identifying and reducing sources of variation, Juran stated that quality control involves determining what to control, establishing units of measurement to evaluate data objectively, establishing standards of performance, measuring actual performance, interpreting the difference between actual performance and the standard, and taking action on the difference.

Unlike Deming, however, Juran specified a detailed program for quality improvement. According to Juran, all breakthroughs follow a commonsense sequence of discovery, organization, diagnosis, corrective action, and control, which he formalized as the **breakthrough sequence**, and which can be summarized as follows:

- *Proof of the Need*: Managers, especially top managers, need to be convinced that quality improvements are simply good economics. Through data collection efforts, information on poor quality, low productivity, or poor service can be translated into the language of money—the universal language of top management—to justify a request for resources to implement a quality improvement program.
- *Project Identification*: All breakthroughs are achieved project-by-project, and in no other way. By taking a project approach, management provides a forum for converting an atmosphere of defensiveness or blame into one of constructive action. Participation in a project increases the likelihood that the participant will act on the results.
- *Organization for Breakthrough*: Organization for improvement requires a clear responsibility for guiding the project. The responsibility for the project may be as broad as an entire division with formal committee structures or as narrow as a small group of workers at one production operation. These groups provide the definition and agreement as to the specific aims of the project, the authority to conduct experiments, and implementation strategies. The path from problem to solution consists of two journeys: one from symptom to cause (the diagnostic journey) and the other from cause to remedy (the remedial journey), which must be performed by different individuals with the appropriate skills.
- *Diagnostic Journey*: Diagnosticians skilled in data collection, statistics, and other problem-solving tools are needed at this stage. Some projects will require full-time, specialized experts (such as Six Sigma Black Belts) while the workforce can perform others. Management-controllable and operator-controllable problems require different methods of diagnosis and remedy.
- *Remedial Journey*: The remedial journey consists of several phases: choosing an alternative that optimizes total cost (similar to one of Deming's points), implementing remedial action, and dealing with resistance to change.
- *Holding the Gains*: This final step involves establishing the new standards and procedures, training the workforce, and instituting controls to make sure that the breakthrough does not die over time.

Juran's approaches are reflected in the practices of a wide variety of organizations today.

The Juran Institute, founded by Dr. Juran, provides substantial training in the form of seminars, videos, and other materials (http://www.juran.com).

Many aspects of the Juran and Deming philosophies are similar. The focus on top management commitment, the need for improvement, the use of quality control techniques, and the importance of training are fundamental to both philosophies. However, they did not agree on all points. For instance, Juran believed that Deming was wrong to tell management to drive out fear; he noted: "Fear can bring out the best in people."[12]

THE CROSBY PHILOSOPHY

Philip B. Crosby (1926–2001) was corporate vice president for quality at International Telephone and Telegraph (ITT) for 14 years after working his way up from line inspector. After leaving ITT, he established Philip Crosby Associates in 1979 to develop and offer training programs. He also authored several popular books. His first book, *Quality Is Free*, sold about one million copies and was largely responsible for bringing quality to the attention of top corporate managers in the United States. The essence of Crosby's quality philosophy is embodied in what he calls the **Absolutes of Quality Management** and the **Basic Elements of Improvement**. Crosby's Absolutes of Quality Management include the following points:

- *Quality means conformance to requirements, not elegance.* Crosby's definition of quality is similar to the manufacturing perspective that we discussed in Chapter 1. Quality is judged solely on whether requirements have been met; nonconformance is the absence of quality. Requirements are ironclad and must be clearly stated so that they cannot be misunderstood. Requirements act as communication devices. Setting requirements is the responsibility of management. Once requirements are established, then one can take measurements to determine conformance to those requirements.

- *There is no such thing as a quality problem.* Problems originate in functional departments. Thus, a firm may experience accounting problems, manufacturing problems, design problems, technical support problems, and so on. In Crosby's view, these are all quality problems, but the burden of responsibility for solving them falls on these functional departments and not in the quality department. The role of the quality department should be to measure conformance, report results, and provide leadership and support to drive quality improvement. This Absolute is similar to Deming's third Point.

- *There is no such thing as the economics of quality; doing the job right the first time is always cheaper.* Crosby supports the premise that "economics of quality" has no meaning. Quality is free; what costs money are all actions that involve not doing jobs right the first time. The Deming chain reaction sends a similar message.

- *The only performance measurement is the cost of quality, which is the expense of nonconformance.* Crosby noted that most companies spend 15 percent to 20 percent of their sales dollars on quality costs. A company with a well-run quality management program can achieve a cost of quality that is less than 2.5 percent of sales, primarily in the prevention and appraisal categories. Crosby suggested that organizations measure and publicize the cost of poor quality. This helps to call problems to management's attention, to select opportunities for corrective action, and to track quality improvement over time. Juran also supported this concept.

- *The only performance standard is "Zero Defects (ZD)."* He explained it as follows:

Zero Defects is a performance standard. It is the standard of the craftsperson regardless of his or her assignment ... The theme of ZD is do it right the first time. That means concentrating on preventing defects rather than just finding and fixing them.

People are conditioned to believe that error is inevitable; thus they not only accept error, they anticipate it. It does not bother us to make a few errors in our work ... to err is human. We all have our own standards in business or academic life—our own points at which errors begin to bother us. It is good to get an A in school, but it may be OK to pass with a C.

We do not maintain these standards, however, when it comes to our personal life. If we did, we should expect to be shortchanged every now and then when we cash our paycheck; we should expect hospital nurses to drop a constant percentage of newborn babies … We as individuals do not tolerate these things. We have a dual standard: one for ourselves and one for our work.

Most human error is caused by lack of attention rather than lack of knowledge. Lack of attention is created when we assume that error is inevitable. If we consider this condition carefully, and pledge ourselves to make a constant conscious effort to do our jobs right the first time, we will take a giant step toward eliminating the waste of rework, scrap, and repair that increases cost and reduces individual opportunity.[13]

Juran and Deming, on the other hand, would point out that despite workers' good intentions, the overwhelming majority of quality problems stem not from human error, but from poorly designed systems that are the responsibility of management.

Crosby's Basic Elements of Improvement were *determination, education,* and *implementation.* Determination means that top management must take quality improvement seriously. Everyone should understand the Absolutes, which can be accomplished only through education. Finally, every member of the management team must understand the implementation process.

> *Philip Crosby Associates (http:// www.philipcrosby.com) continues Crosby's legacy and consults with numerous organizations in quality implementation and training.*

Crosby's approach to quality was primarily behavioral, and emphasized management and organizational processes to change corporate culture and attitudes rather than statistical techniques and improvement methodologies. Like Juran, his approach fit well within existing organizational structures.

Comparing Deming, Juran, and Crosby

Despite their significant differences to implementing organizational change, the philosophies of Deming, Juran, and Crosby are more alike than different. Each views quality as imperative in the future competitiveness in global markets; makes top management commitment an absolute necessity; demonstrates that quality management practices will save, not cost money; places responsibility for quality on management, not the workers; stresses the need for continuous, never-ending improvement; acknowledges the importance of the customer and strong management/worker partnerships; and recognizes the need for and difficulties associated with changing the organizational culture.

Although each of these philosophies can be highly effective by itself, the choice is not always clear. An organization must understand the nature and differences of the philosophies and how they fit into their own unique culture. More often than not, organizations develop an approach specifically tailored to their own culture and management style, which incorporates many of the ideas from all three philosophies.

OTHER QUALITY PHILOSOPHERS

Two other notable figures in the quality arena include A. V. Feigenbaum and Kaoru Ishikawa. In this section we briefly review the accomplishments of these individuals.[14]

A. V. Feigenbaum

A. V. Feigenbaum's career in quality began over a half century ago. For 10 years, he was the manager of worldwide manufacturing and quality control at General Electric. In 1968, he founded General Systems Company of Pittsfield, Massachusetts, and still serves as its president and CEO. Feigenbaum has traveled and spoken to various audiences and groups around the world over the years. He was elected as the founding chairman of the board of the International Academy of Quality, which has attracted active participation from the European Organization for Quality Control, the Union of Japanese Scientists and Engineers (JUSE), as well as the American Society for Quality.

Feigenbaum is best known for coining the phrase *total quality control*, which he defined as "an effective system for integrating the quality development, quality mainte-nance, and quality improvement efforts of the various groups in an organization so as to enable production and service at the most economical levels which allow full customer satisfaction," and explained in his book *Total Quality Control*, which was first published in 1951 under the title *Quality Control: Principles, Practice, and Administration*. He viewed quality as a strategic business tool that requires involvement from everyone in the organization, and promoted the use of quality costs as a measurement and evaluation tool.

Feigenbaum's philosophy is summarized in his **Three Steps to Quality**:

1. *Quality Leadership*: A continuous management emphasis is grounded on sound planning rather than reaction to failures. Management must maintain a constant focus and lead the quality effort.
2. *Modern Quality Technology*: The traditional quality department cannot resolve 80 percent to 90 percent of quality problems. This task requires the integration of office staff as well as engineers and shop-floor workers in the process who continually evaluate and implement new techniques to satisfy customers in the future.
3. *Organizational Commitment*: Continuous training and motivation of the entire work-force as well as an integration of quality in business planning indicate the importance of quality and provide the means for including it in all aspects of the firm's activities.

Feigenbaum also popularized the term *hidden factory*, which described the portion of plant capacity wasted due to poor quality. Many of his ideas remain embedded in con-temporary thinking, and have become important elements of the Malcolm Baldrige National Quality Award criteria. These aspects include the principles that the customer is the judge of quality; quality and innovation are interrelated and mutually beneficial; managing quality is the same as managing the business; quality is a continuous process of improvement; and customers and suppliers should be involved the process. In 2008, he received the prestigious National Medal of Technology and Innovation.[15]

> *Feigenbaum and Ishikawa were both awarded the title of Honor-ary Members of the American Society for Quality in 1986. At that time, the society had only four living honorary members, two of whom were W. Edwards Deming and Joseph M. Juran.*

Kaoru Ishikawa

An early pioneer in the quality revolution in Japan, Kaoru Ishi-kawa was the foremost figure in Japanese quality until his death in 1989. He was instrumental in the development of the broad outlines of Japanese quality strategy, and without his leadership, the Japanese quality movement would not enjoy the worldwide acclaim and success that it has today. Dr. Ishikawa was a professor of engineering at Tokyo University for many years. As a member of the editorial review board for the Japanese journal *Quality Control for Foremen*, founded in 1962, and later as the chief executive director of the QC Circle Headquarters at the Union of Japanese Scientists and Engineers (JUSE), Dr. Ishikawa influenced the development of a participative, bottom-up view of quality, which became the trademark of the Japanese approach to quality management. However, Ishikawa was also able to get the attention of top management and persuade them that a companywide approach to quality control was necessary for total success.

Ishikawa built on Feigenbaum's concept of total quality and promoted greater involvement by all employees, from the top management to the front-line staff, by reducing reliance on quality professionals and quality departments. He advocated collecting and analyzing factual data using simple visual tools, statistical techniques, and teamwork as the foundations for implementing total quality. Like others, Ishikawa believed that quality begins with the customer and therefore, understanding customers' needs is the basis for improvement, and that complaints should be actively sought. Some key elements of his philosophy are summarized here.

1. Quality begins with education and ends with education.
2. The first step in quality is to know the requirements of customers.
3. The ideal state of quality control occurs when inspection is no longer necessary.
4. Remove the root cause, not the symptoms.
5. Quality control is the responsibility of all workers and all divisions.
6. Do not confuse the means with the objectives.
7. Put quality first and set your sights on long-term profits.
8. Marketing is the entrance and exit of quality.
9. Top management must not show anger when facts are presented by subordinates.
10. Ninety-five percent of problems in a company can be solved with simple tools for analysis and problem solving.
11. Data without dispersion information (i.e., variability) are false data.

Dr. Ishikawa is best known for developing a popular quality improvement tool called a cause-and-effect diagram, which often bears his name (see Chapter 9).

PRINCIPLES, PRACTICES, AND TECHNIQUES OF QUALITY MANAGEMENT

In a classic research article, James W. Dean, Jr. and David E. Bowen characterize total quality by its principles, practices, and techniques.[16] **Principles** are the foundation of the philosophy, **practices** are activities by which the principles are implemented, and **techniques** are tools and approaches that help managers and workers make the practices effective. All are vital for achieving high quality and performance excellence.

Quality Management Principles

The TQ philosophy was based initially on three core principles: *customer focus, teamwork*, and *continuous improvement*. Despite their obvious simplicity, these principles represented a significant departure from traditional management practices. Historically, firms did little to understand external customer requirements, much less those of internal customers. Products were designed from a "market out" perspective (build it and they will come) rather than from a "market in" perspective that seeks to meet customer expectations and requirements. Managers and specialists controlled and directed production systems; workers were told what to do and how to do it, and rarely were asked for their input. Teamwork and the soliciting of ideas from the workforce were virtually nonexistent. A certain amount of waste and error was tolerable and was controlled by post-production inspection. Improvements in quality generally resulted from technological breakthroughs instead of a relentless mindset of continuous improvement. With TQ, organizations began to actively identify customer needs and expectations, build quality into the organization by tapping the knowledge and experience of the workforce, and continually improve its processes and systems.

The quality management principles underlying ISO 9000:2000 were derived from the collective experience and knowledge of international experts who participate in ISO Technical Committee ISO/TC 176, Quality Management and Quality Assurance, which is responsible for developing and maintaining the ISO 9000 standards.

As the discipline evolved, the principles that define modern quality management have also naturally evolved as we have learned more about what it takes to build and sustain quality in an organization. Table 2.2 is a list of the quality management principles that underlie the international quality standards known as ISO 9000:2000, which we describe later in this chapter. These are "comprehensive and fundamental rules or beliefs for leading and operating an organization" that better reflect the basic principles and practices of total quality. In addition to customer focus, involvement of people (teamwork), and continual improvement, important principles of quality management are leadership, process approach, a system approach to management, a factual approach to decision making, and mutually beneficial supplier relationships. These principles are evident within the philosophies of Deming, Juran, and Crosby, and will be reflected in our discussions, examples, and cases throughout the rest of this book.

Quality Management Practices

The Quality Profile features at the beginning of each chapter show how many of the quality management practices in Table 2.3 are used to achieve exceptional results in many organizations.

Quality management practices represent the approaches that organizations use to achieve the principles. Table 2.3 summarizes representative practices associated with each of the principles in Table 2.2. Again, we will be discussing and illustrating these throughout the rest of this book.

Quality Management Techniques

Techniques include a wide variety of tools to plan work activities, collect data, analyze results, monitor progress, and solve problems. For instance, an Excel chart showing trends in manufacturing defects as workers progress through a training program is a simple tool to monitor the effectiveness of the training; the statistical technique of experimental design can be used to optimize process settings to reduce scrap or increase yield. Throughout this book, and particularly in Part II, we will introduce many techniques that are useful in quality planning, control, and improvement activities.

One of the most important techniques is basic statistics. As we have discussed, Deming emphasized the importance of using statistical methods for quality. Although we formally discuss statistical tools and methods in Chapter 6, the ability to view data and information from a statistical perspective is a vital skill. We introduce this next, as it also relates closely to the Deming philosophy and experiments that he used in his teaching activities.

TABLE 2.2   Quality Management Principles

Principle 1: Customer Focus

Organizations depend on their customers and therefore should understand current and future customer needs, should meet customer requirements, and strive to exceed customer expectations.

Principle 2: Leadership

Leaders establish unity of purpose and direction of the organization. They should create and maintain the internal environment in which people can become fully involved in achieving the organization's objectives.

Principle 3: Involvement of People

People at all levels are the essence of an organization and their full involvement enables their abilities to be used for the organization's benefit.

Principle 4: Process Approach

A desired result is achieved more efficiently when activities and related resources are managed as a process.

Principle 5: System Approach to Management

Identifying, understanding, and managing interrelated processes as a system contributes to the organization's effectiveness and efficiency in achieving its objectives.

Principle 6: Continual Improvement

Continual improvement of the organization's overall performance should be a permanent objective of the organization.

Principle 7: Factual Approach to Decision Making

Effective decisions are based on the analysis of data and information.

Principle 8: Mutually Beneficial Supplier Relationships

An organization and its suppliers are interdependent and a mutually beneficial relationship enhances the ability of both to create value.

Source: http://www.iso.org/iso/qmp. Reprinted with permission.

TABLE 2.3   Practices for Implementing Quality Management Principles[17]

Principle 1: Customer Focus

- Researching and understanding customer needs and expectations.
- Ensuring that the objectives of the organization are linked to customer needs and expectations.
- Communicating customer needs and expectations throughout the organization.
- Measuring customer satisfaction and acting on the results.
- Systematically managing customer relationships.
- Ensuring a balanced approach between satisfying customers and other interested parties (such as owners, employees, suppliers, financiers, local communities and society as a whole).

Principle 2: Leadership

- Considering the needs of all interested parties including customers, owners, employees, suppliers, financiers, local communities and society as a whole.
- Establishing a clear vision of the organization's future.
- Setting challenging goals and targets.
- Creating and sustaining shared values, fairness and ethical role models at all levels of the organization.
- Establishing trust and eliminating fear.
- Providing people with the required resources, training and freedom to act with responsibility and accountability.
- Inspiring, encouraging, and recognizing people's contributions.

(continued)

TABLE 2.3   Practices for Implementing Quality Management Principles (*Continued*)

Principle 3: Involvement of People
- People understanding the importance of their contribution and role in the organization.
- People identifying constraints to their performance.
- People accepting ownership of problems and their responsibility for solving them.
- People evaluating their performance against their personal goals and objectives.
- People actively seeking opportunities to enhance their competence, knowledge, and experience.
- People freely sharing knowledge and experience.
- People openly discussing problems and issues.

Principle 4: Process Approach
- Systematically defining the activities necessary to obtain a desired result.
- Establishing clear responsibility and accountability for managing key activities.
- Analyzing and measuring of the capability of key activities.
- Identifying the interfaces of key activities within and between the functions of the organization.
- Focusing on the factors such as resources, methods, and materials that will improve key activities of the organization.
- Evaluating risks, consequences, and impacts of activities on customers, suppliers, and other interested parties.

Principle 5: System Approach to Management
- Structuring a system to achieve the organization's objectives in the most effective and efficient way.
- Understanding the interdependencies between the processes of the system.
- Structured approaches that harmonize and integrate processes.
- Providing a better understanding of the roles and responsibilities necessary for achieving common objectives and thereby reducing cross-functional barriers.
- Understanding organizational capabilities and establishing resource constraints prior to action.
- Targeting and defining how specific activities within a system should operate.
- Continually improving the system through measurement and evaluation.

Principle 6: Continual Improvement
- Employing a consistent organization-wide approach to continual improvement of the organization's performance.
- Providing people with training in the methods and tools of continual improvement.
- Making continual improvement of products, processes, and systems an objective for every individual in the organization.
- Establishing goals to guide, and measures to track, continual improvement.
- Recognizing and acknowledging improvements.

Principle 7: Factual Approach to Decision Making
- Ensuring that data and information are sufficiently accurate and reliable.
- Making data accessible to those who need it.
- Analyzing data and information using valid methods.
- Making decisions and taking action based on factual analysis, balanced with experience and intuition.

Principle 8: Mutually Beneficial Supplier Relationships
- Establishing relationships that balance short-term gains with long-term considerations.
- Pooling of expertise and resources with partners.
- Identifying and selecting key suppliers.

(*continued*)

TABLE 2.3 Practices for Implementing Quality Management Principles *(Continued)*

- Clear and open communication.
- Sharing information and future plans.
- Establishing joint development and improvement activities.
- Inspiring, encouraging, and recognizing improvements and achievements by suppliers.

VARIATION AND STATISTICAL THINKING

Brian Joiner, a noted quality management consultant, relates the following scenario:[18]

> *Ed was a regional VP for a service company that had facilities around the world. He was determined that the facilities in his region would get the highest customer satisfaction ratings in the company. If he noticed that a facility had a major drop in satisfaction ratings in one month or had "below average" ratings for three months in a row, he would call the manager and ask what had happened—and make it clear that next month's rating had better improve. And most of the time, it did!*

As the average satisfaction score dropped from 65 to 60 between February and March, Ed's memo to his managers read:

> *Bad news! We dropped five points! We should all focus on improving these scores right away! I realize that our usage rates have increased faster than anticipated, so you've really got to hustle to give our customers great service. I know you can do it!*

As Joiner observed, "Do you look at data this way? This month versus last month? This month versus the same month last year? Do you sometimes look at the latest data point? The last two data points? I couldn't understand why people would only want to look at two data points. Finally, it became clear to me. With any two data points, it's easy to compute a trend: 'Things are down 2 percent this month from last month. This month is 30 percent above the same month last year.' Unfortunately, we learn nothing of importance by comparing two results when they both come from a stable process . . . and most data of importance to management are from stable processes."

Brian Joiner's scenario points to the need for managers to think statistically. Unfortunately, most do not, and often make decisions based on a single data point or two, see trends when they don't exist, or try to manipulate financial or operational results they cannot truly control.

Statistical thinking is a philosophy of learning and action based on these principles:

1. All work occurs in a system of interconnected processes.
2. Variation exists in all processes.
3. Understanding and reducing variation are keys to success.[19]

With the enormous wealth of information that is available to organizations today, being able to understand variability in data and to think statistically are vital to managing modern enterprises.

Understanding Variation

Figure 2.4 shows the sources of variation that affect most manufacturing processes. Different lots of material may vary in strength, thickness, or moisture content, for example. Cutting tools have inherent variation in their strength and composition. During

FIGURE 2.4
Sources of Variation
in a Production
Process

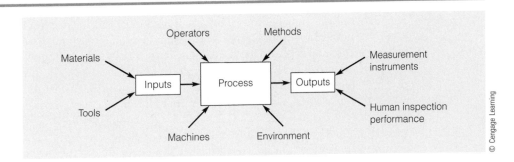

manufacturing, tools experience wear, vibrations cause changes in machine settings, and electrical fluctuations cause variations in power. Operators may not position parts on fixtures consistently, and physical and emotional stress affect operators' consistency. In addition, measurement gauges and human inspection capabilities are not uniform. Even when measurements of several items by the same instrument are the same, it is due to a lack of precision in the measurement instrument; extremely precise instruments always reveal slight differences.

Some of the operational problems created by variation include the following:[20]

- *Variation Increases Unpredictability*: If we don't understand the variation in a system, we cannot predict its future performance.
- *Variation Reduces Capacity Utilization*: If a process has little variability, then managers can increase the load on the process because they do not have to incorporate slack into their production plans.
- *Variation Contributes to a "Bullwhip" Effect*: This well-known phenomenon occurs in supply chains; when small changes in demand occur, the variation in production and inventory levels becomes increasingly amplified upstream at distribution centers, factories, and suppliers, resulting in unnecessary costs and difficulties in managing material flow.
- *Variation Makes It Difficult to Find Root Causes*: Process variation makes it difficult to determine whether problems are due to external factors such as raw materials or reside within the processes themselves.
- *Variation Makes It Difficult to Detect Potential Problems Early*: Unusual variation is a signal that problems exist; if a process has little inherent variation, then it is easier to detect when a problem actually does occur.

The complex interactions of these variations in materials, tools, machines, operators, and the environment are not easily understood. Variation due to any of these individual sources appears at random; individual sources cannot be identified or explained. However their combined effect is stable and can usually be predicted statistically. These factors are present as a natural part of a process and are referred to as **common causes of variation**. Common causes are a result of the design of the product and production system and generally account for about 80 to 95 percent of the observed variation in the output of a production process. Therefore, common cause variation can only be reduced if the product is redesigned, or if better technology or training is provided for the production process. For example, Wilson Sporting Goods Company acknowledged that small irregularities in golf balls can cause the heavier core of golf balls to be off center, resulting in balls that don't roll straight, with up to 1 in 12 high-end balls having this problem. To solve the problem, Wilson introduced a new ball design, with a lighter core and heavier cover.[21]

The remaining variation in a production process is the result of **special causes**, often called **assignable causes of variation**. Special causes arise from external sources that are not inherent in the process. They appear sporadically and disrupt the random pattern of common causes. Hence, they tend to be easily detectable using statistical methods and are usually economical to correct. Common factors that lead to special causes could be a bad batch of material from a supplier, a poorly trained substitute machine operator, a broken or worn tool, or a miscalibration of measuring instruments. Unusual variation that results from such isolated incidents can be explained or corrected.

The failure to distinguish between these two types of variation can lead to two fundamental management mistakes in attempting to improve a process:

1. To treat as a special cause any fault, complaint, mistake, breakdown, accident, or shortage when it actually is due to common causes.
2. To attribute to common causes any fault, complaint, mistake, breakdown, accident, or shortage when it actually is due to a special cause.

In the first case, tampering with a stable system can increase the variation in the system. In the second case, the opportunity to reduce variation is missed because the amount of variation is mistakenly assumed to be uncontrollable.

Deming's Red Bead and Funnel Experiments[22]

Statistical thinking lies at the heart of the Deming philosophy and his principles of Profound Knowledge. In his four-day management seminars, Deming used two simple yet powerful experiments to educate his audience about statistical thinking. The first is the **Red Bead experiment**, which proceeds as follows. A Foreman (usually Deming) selects several volunteers from the audience: Six Willing Workers, a Recorder, two Inspectors, and a Chief Inspector. The materials for the experiment include 4,000 wooden beads—800 red and 3,200 white—and two Tupperware boxes, one slightly smaller than the other. Also, a paddle with 50 holes or depressions is used to scoop up 50 beads, which is the prescribed workload. In this experiment, the company is "producing" beads for a new customer who needs only white beads and will not take red beads. The Foreman explains that everyone will be an apprentice for three days to learn the job. During apprenticeship, the workers may ask questions. Once production starts, however, no questions are allowed. The procedures are rigid; no departures from procedures are permitted so that no variation in performance will occur. The Foreman explains to the Willing Workers that their jobs depend on their performance and if they are dismissed, many others are willing to replace them. Furthermore, no resignations are allowed.

> *Deming has been credited with keeping statistics in the forefront of the worldwide quality improvement movement: "The triumph of statistics is the triumph of Dr. Deming. When others have wavered or been lukewarm in their support for statistics, Dr. Deming has stood firm in his conviction that statistics is the heart of quality control. Indeed, he goes further and makes statistical principles central to the whole production process."[23]*

The company's work standard, the Foreman explains, is 50 beads per day. The production process is simple: Mix the raw material and pour it into the smaller box. Repeat this procedure, returning the beads from the smaller box to the larger one. Grasp the paddle and insert it into the bead mixture. Raise the paddle at a 44-degree angle so that every depression will hold a bead. The two Inspectors count the beads independently and record

FIGURE 2.5   First Day's Production (The paddle shows the result of the last Willing Worker, Ann)

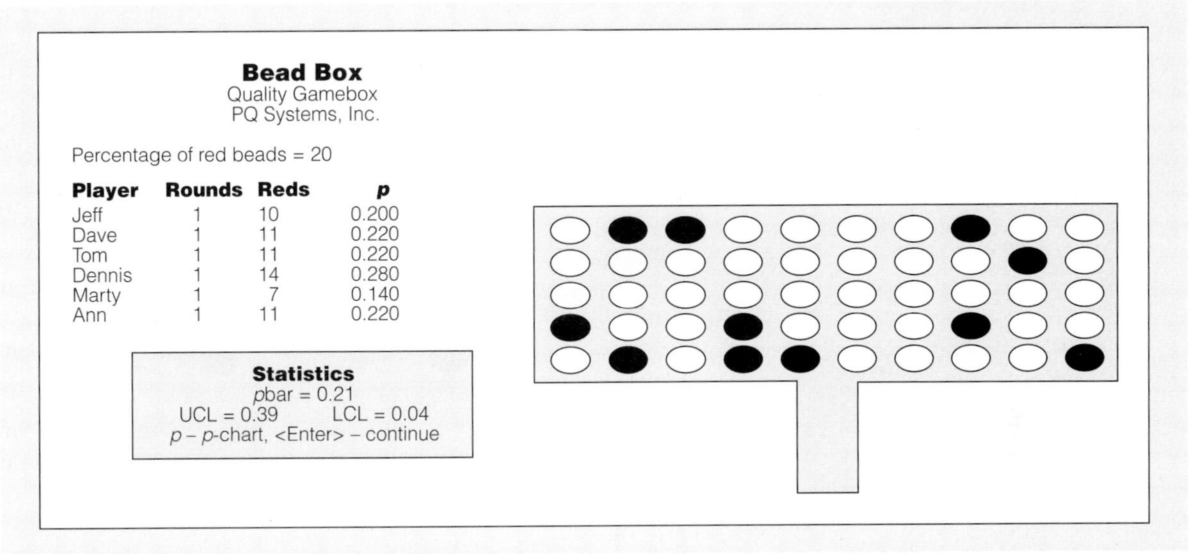

Bead Box
Quality Gamebox
PQ Systems, Inc.

Percentage of red beads = 20

Player	Rounds	Reds	*p*
Jeff	1	10	0.200
Dave	1	11	0.220
Tom	1	11	0.220
Dennis	1	14	0.280
Marty	1	7	0.140
Ann	1	11	0.220

Statistics
*p*bar = 0.21
UCL = 0.39   LCL = 0.04
p – *p*-chart, <Enter> – continue

Source: Copyright PQ Systems, www.pqsystems.com

the counts. The Chief Inspector checks the counts and announces the results, which are written down by the Recorder. The Chief Inspector then dismisses the worker. When all six Willing Workers have produced the day's quota, the Foreman evaluates the results.

Figure 2.5 shows the results of the first day's production generated with the Quality Gamebox computer simulation software. The Foreman is disappointed. He reminds the Willing Workers that their job is to make white beads, not red ones. The company is on a merit system, and it rewards only good performance. Marty only made 7 red beads and deserves a pay increase. The data do not lie; he is the best worker. Dennis made 14 red beads. Everyone likes him, but he must be placed on probation. The Foreman announces that management has set a goal of no more than 7 red beads per day per worker, and sees no reason why everyone cannot be as good as Marty.

Figure 2.6 shows the cumulative results for the second day. We see that after two days, Jeff had produced 23 red beads, Dave 24, Tom 20, Dennis 21, Marty 17, and Ann 23. (The second day's results can be found by subtraction: Jeff produces 13 beads, Dave 13, Tom 9, Dennis 7, Marty 10, and Ann 12.) The overall performance was not good. Management is watching carefully. The Foreman reminds them again that their jobs depend on performance. Marty is a big disappointment. The merit increase obviously went to his head. The Foreman chastises him in front of the other workers. Dennis, on the other hand, showed remarkable improvement; probation and the threat of losing his job made him a better worker—only 7 red beads—a 50 percent reduction in defects! He met the goal; if he can do it, anyone can. Dennis gets a special commendation from the plant manager.

At the beginning of the third day, management announces a Zero Defects Day. Everyone will do their best on this last day of the apprenticeship program. The Foreman is desperate and he tells the Willing Workers again that their jobs are their own responsibility. From Figure 2.7, production figures can be determined (by computing the difference between the cumulative output of day 3 and day 2), and show that Jeff produces 12 red beads, Dave 18, Tom 17, Dennis 9, Marty 6, and Ann 11. Clearly, Marty learned a lesson the day before, but the group's overall performance is not good. Management is

FIGURE 2.6   Second Day's Cumulative Results

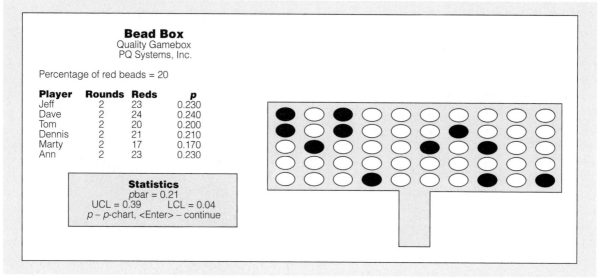

Source: Copyright PQ Systems, www.pqsystems.com

FIGURE 2.7   Third Day's Cumulative Results

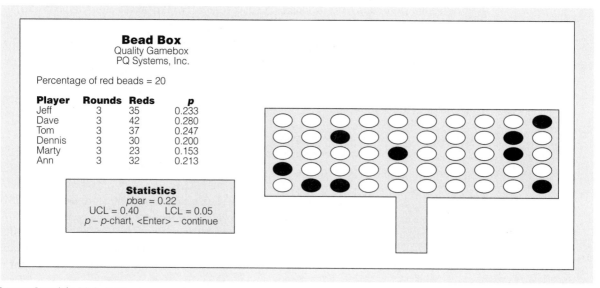

Source: Copyright PQ Systems, www.pqsystems.com

bitterly disappointed at the results. The Zero Defect Day program did not improve quality substantially; in fact, more red beads were produced today than ever before. Costs are getting out of control, and there is talk of shutting down the entire plant. Dave and Tom receive pink slips informing them that tomorrow will be their last day; their work is clearly much worse than the others. But the Foreman is optimistic. He puts up a poster saying "Be a Quality Worker!" to encourage the others to reach the goal.

FIGURE 2.8   Fourth Day's Cumulative Results

Bead Box
Quality Gamebox
PQ Systems, Inc.

Percentage of red beads = 20

Player	Rounds	Reds	p
Jeff	4	43	0.215
Dave	4	53	0.265
Tom	4	45	0.225
Dennis	4	39	0.195
Marty	4	31	0.155
Ann	4	41	0.205

Statistics
$p$bar = 0.21
UCL = 0.38   LCL = 0.04
p – p-chart, <Enter> – continue

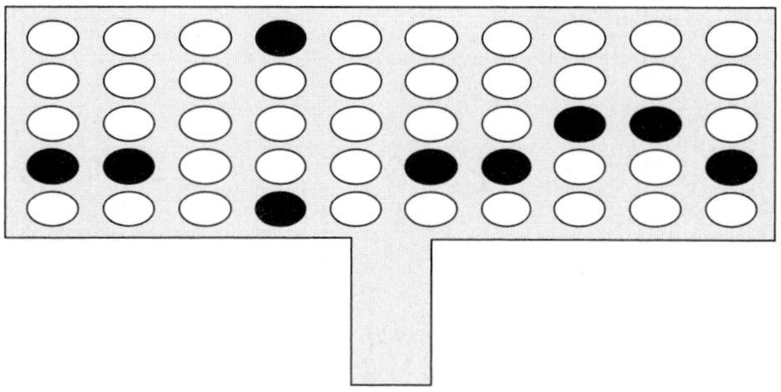

Source: Copyright PQ Systems, www.pqsystems.com

On the fourth day (see Figure 2.8), we find that the number of red beads produced by the six Willing Workers is 8, 11, 8, 9, 8, and 9. The production is still not good enough. The Foreman announces that management has decided to close the plant after all.

The Red Bead experiment offers several important lessons for managers:

- *Variation exists in systems and, if stable, can be predicted.* If we plot the fraction of red beads produced by each worker each day, we can observe this variation easily. Figure 2.9 is a plot of the fraction of red beads produced over time. All points fluctuate about the overall average, which is 0.21, falling roughly between 0.10 and 0.40. In Chapter 8, we will learn to calculate *statistical limits of variation* (0.04 and 0.38)—limits between which we would expect results from a stable system to fall. This variation shows that that the system of production is indeed stable; that is, the variation arises from common causes. Although the exact number of red beads in any particular paddle is not predictable, we can describe statistically what we expect from the system.

- *All the variation in the production of red beads, and the variation from day to day of any Willing Worker, came entirely from the process itself.* In this experiment, Deming deliberately eliminated the source of variability that managers usually believe is the most significant: people. Each worker was basically identical, and no evidence showed that any one of them was better than another. They could not control the number of red beads produced and could do no better than the system would allow. Neither motivation nor threats had any influence. Unfortunately, many managers believe that all variation is controllable and place blame on those who cannot do anything about it.

- *Numerical goals are often meaningless.* A Foreman who gives out merit pay and puts people on probation, supposedly as rewards and punishment of performance, actually rewards and punishes the performance of the process, not the Willing Workers. To rank or appraise people arbitrarily is demoralizing, especially when workers cannot influence the outcomes. No matter what the goal is, it has no effect on the actual number of red beads produced. Exhorting workers to "Do their best" only leads to

FIGURE 2.9 Run Chart of Fraction of Red Beads Produced

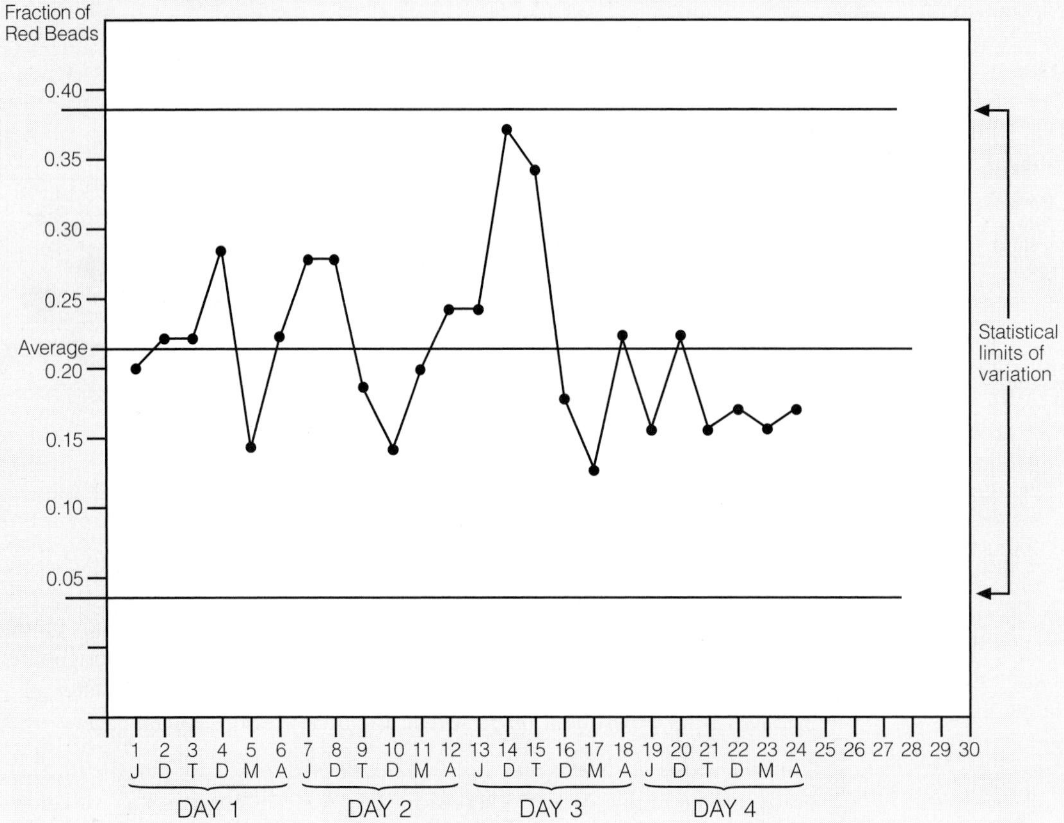

frustration. Management has no basis to assume that the best Willing Workers of the past will be the best in the future.

- *Management is responsible for the system.* The experiment shows bad management. Procedures are rigid. The Willing Workers have no say in improving the process. Management is responsible for the incoming material, but does not work with the supplier to improve the inputs to the system. Management designed the production system and decided to rely on inspection to control the process. These decisions have far more influence on the outcomes than the efforts of the workers. Three inspectors are probably as costly as the six workers and add practically no value to the output.

Deming's second experiment is the **Funnel Experiment**. Its purpose is to show that people can and do affect the outcomes of many processes and create unwanted variation by "tampering" with the process, or indiscriminately trying to remove common causes of variation. In this experiment, a funnel is suspended above a table with a target drawn on a tablecloth. The goal is to hit the target. Participants drop a marble through the funnel and mark the place where the marble eventually lands. Rarely will the marble rest on the target. This variation is due to common causes in the process. One strategy is to simply leave the funnel alone, which creates some variation of points around the target. This

FIGURE 2.10
Two Rules for Adjusting the Funnel

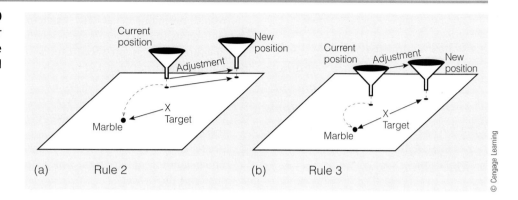

may be called *Rule 1*. However, many people believe they can improve the results by adjusting the location of the funnel. Three possible rules for adjusting the funnel are:

Rule 2. Measure the deviation from the point at which the marble comes to rest and the target. Move the funnel an equal distance in the opposite direction from its current position [Figure 2.10(a)].

Rule 3. Measure the deviation from the point at which the marble comes to rest and the target. Set the funnel an equal distance in the opposite direction of the error from the target [Figure 2.10(b)].

Rule 4. Place the funnel over the spot where the marble last came to rest.

Figure 2.11 shows a computer simulation of these strategies using the Quality Gamebox. Clearly the first rule—leave the funnel alone—results in the least variation.

FIGURE 2.11
Results of the Funnel Experiment

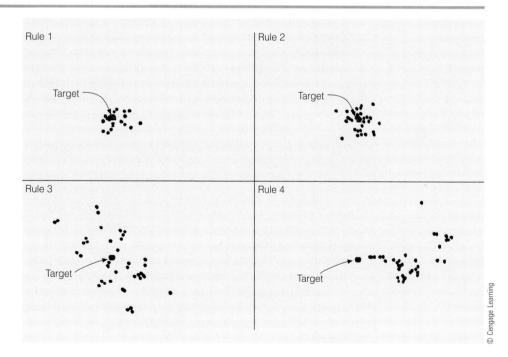

Formal statistical methods are vital to modern quality management; we will review important statistical concepts and methods in Chapter 6, and use them in various applications of quality in other chapters.

People use these rules inappropriately all the time, causing more variation than would normally occur. An amateur golfer who hits a bad shot tends to make an immediate adjustment. If the last manufactured part is off-specification, adjust the machine. If a schedule was not met last month, change the process. If the last quarter's earnings report was less than expected, dump the stock. If an employee's performance last week was subpar (or exceptional), punish (or reward) the employee. In all of these cases, the error is usually compounded by an inappropriate reaction. All of these policies stem from a lack of understanding of variation, which originates from not understanding the process.

QUALITY MANAGEMENT SYSTEMS

Organizations need a structured and systematic approach to implement the principles, practices, and techniques of total quality.[24] According to the ASQ online glossary, a **quality management system (QMS)** can be considered a mechanism for managing and continuously improving core processes to "achieve maximum customer satisfaction at the lowest overall cost to the organization." It applies and synthesizes standards, methods, and tools to achieve quality-related goals. Thus a quality management system represents a specific implementation of quality concepts, standards, methods, and tools, and is unique to an organization. A QMS provides a basis for documenting processes used to control and improve operations, drive innovation, and achieve the following objectives:

- Higher product conformity and less variation.
- Fewer defects, waste, rework, and human error.
- Improved productivity, efficiency, and effectiveness.

One of the first things to do is to establish a **quality policy**—a formal document that demonstrates a commitment to achieving high quality and meeting customer expectations. Next, management must establish an organizational structure for its QMS that includes responsibilities, methods of communication, maintenance of essential records and documentation, and procedures for reviewing performance. Management must also identify and provide appropriate resources to achieve the objectives set forth in their quality policy. These resources might include people with special skills, training, workspaces, manufacturing equipment, inspection technology, computer software, and the supporting work environment. Individuals must be given the responsibility to initiate actions to prevent the occurrence of defects and errors, to identify and solve quality-related problems, and to verify the implementation of solutions.

The core of a QMS is focused on creating the goods and services that customers want. Therefore, a QMS should include processes for identifying customer requirements, product planning and design processes, purchasing procedures, methods and technology for controlling the production of goods and services throughout the supply chain, inspection and/or testing, disposition of nonconforming product, and maintenance and validation of measuring and test equipment.

Understanding performance requires measurement and data analysis processes to evaluate the conformity of goods and services, customer satisfaction, and the integrity of the QMS itself. Such measurement should provide the basis for corrective action and continuous improvement, as well as prevention of future problems.

A **quality manual** serves as a permanent reference for implementing and maintaining the system. A quality manual need not be complex; a small company might need only a dozen pages while a large organization might need manuals for all key functions. Sufficient records should be maintained to demonstrate conformance to requirements and verify that the quality system is operating effectively. Typical records that might be maintained are inspection reports, test data, audit reports, and calibration data. They should be readily retrievable for analysis to identify trends and monitor the effectiveness of corrective actions. Other documents, such as drawings, specifications, inspection procedures and instructions, work instructions, and operation sheets are vital to achieving quality and should likewise be controlled.

Finally, the system needs to be maintained and kept up to date. This maintenance can be facilitated through **internal audits**, which focus on identifying whether documented procedures are being followed and are effective, and reporting the issues to management for corrective action. Internal audits generally include a review of process records, training records, complaints, corrective actions, and previous audit reports. A typical internal audit begins by asking those who perform a process regularly to explain how it works.[25] Their statements are compared to written procedures, and compliance and deviations are noted. Next, the trail of paperwork or other data are examined to determine whether the process is consistent with the intent of the written procedure and the worker's explanation. Internal auditors also need to analyze whether the process is meeting its intent and objectives, thus focusing on continuous improvement.

Although many ways exist to structure a QMS, many organizations start with the **ISO 9000 family of standards**, which are a set of standards and guidelines for quality management systems that represents an international consensus on good quality management practices.[26] They provide a comprehensive framework for designing and managing a quality management system and help organizations establish a process orientation and the discipline to document and control key processes.

ISO 9000 Family of Standards

As quality became a major focus of businesses throughout the world, various organizations developed standards and guidelines. Terms such as quality management, quality control, quality system, and quality assurance acquired different, sometimes conflicting meanings from country to country, within a country, and even within an industry.[27] To standardize quality requirements for European countries within the Common Market and those wishing to do business with those countries, a specialized agency for standardization, the International Organization for Standardization (IOS), founded in 1946 and composed of representatives from the national standards bodies of 91 nations, adopted a series of written quality standards in 1987. The IOS took a unique approach in adopting the "ISO" prefix in naming the standards. *ISO* is a scientific term for equal (as in isotherm lines on a weather map, which show equal temperatures). Thus, the intent was to ensure that organizations certified under the ISO 9000 standards have quality equal to their peers. The standards have been adopted in the United States by the American National Standards Institute (ANSI) with the endorsement and cooperation of the American Society for Quality (ASQ). The standards are recognized throughout the world.

The standards required documentation for all processes affecting quality and suggest that compliance through auditing leads to continuous improvement. In some foreign markets, companies will not buy from suppliers who are not certified to the standards. For example, many products sold in Europe, such as telecommunication terminal equipment, medical devices, gas appliances, toys, and construction products require product certifications to assure safety. Often, ISO certification is necessary to obtain product certification. Thus, meeting these standards became a requirement for international business.

The standards became especially important when the Treaty on European Union was signed at Maastricht, the Netherlands in 1992, establishing free trade between member countries and making quality a key strategic objective. Consequently, the standards were revised in 1994. The ISO 9000:1994 series standards consisted of 20 fundamental elements of a basic quality system that included such things as management responsibility, design control, purchasing, product identification and traceability, process control, inspection and testing, corrective and preventive action, internal quality audits, training, and statistical techniques. The standards were intended to meet five objectives:

1. Achieve, maintain, and seek to continuously improve product quality (including services) in relationship to requirements.
2. Improve the quality of operations to continually meet customers' and stakeholders' stated and implied needs.
3. Provide confidence to internal management and other employees that quality requirements are being fulfilled and that improvement is taking place.
4. Provide confidence to customers and other stakeholders that quality requirements are being achieved in the delivered product.
5. Provide confidence that quality system requirements are fulfilled.

While these objectives were certainly in line with a TQ philosophy, the original standards and the 1994 revision met with considerable controversy.[28] The standards only required that the organization have a documented, verifiable process in place to ensure that it consistently produces what it says it will produce. A company could comply with the standards and still produce a poor-quality product—as long as it did so consistently! The European Union called for a deemphasis on ISO 9000 registration, citing the fact that companies were more concerned with "passing a test" than on focusing their energies on quality processes and improvement. In response, the IOS revised the standards in 2000. ISO 9000:2000 reflected a completely new structure, based on the eight quality management principles in Table 2.2. These eight principles were voted on and overwhelmingly approved at a conference in 1997 attended by 36 representatives of countries.[29]

In 2008, an amendment to the standards was released, designed to clarify some of the language and concepts, and improve compatibility with ISO 14001:2004, the popular environmental standard. It focused on clarifying legal standards, outsourcing, internal audits, the concept of competence, design and development processes, monitoring and measuring processes, and controlling non-conforming products.[30] However, the main focus of the standards were not substantially changed.

The ISO 9000 family standards focus on developing, documenting, and implementing procedures to ensure consistency of operations and performance in production and service delivery processes, with the aim of continual improvement, and supported by fundamental principles of total quality. The standards are generic and intended to apply to any organization, regardless of type, size, or products provided.

The standards consist of three documents:

1. *ISO 9000:2005—Fundamentals and vocabulary*: This document provides fundamental background information and establishes definitions of key terms used in the standards.

2. *ISO 9001:2008—Requirements*: This is the core document that provides the specific requirements for a quality management system to help organizations consistently provide products that meet customer and other regulatory requirements. The standard specifies the requirements that a quality system must meet, but does not dictate how they should be achieved, allowing them to be interpreted and applied to meet the unique needs of different types of businesses or national cultures. The standard does require that the organization audit its quality system to verify that it is managing its processes effectively. This standard can also be also used for customer audits or third-party certification. Many organizations pursue this to provide independent credibility and recognition of their quality management systems.

3. *ISO 9004:2009—Guidelines for Performance Improvements*: This document provides guidelines to assist organizations in improving and sustaining their quality management systems.

The ISO 9001:2008 requirements provide a structure for a basic quality assurance system. It consists of four major areas: Management Responsibility, Resource Management, Product Realization, and Measurement, Analysis, and Improvement.

- *Management Responsibility* addresses what top management must do to ensure an effective quality system, such as promoting the importance of quality throughout the organization, developing and implementing the quality management system, identifying and meeting customer requirements, defining an organizational quality policy and quality objectives, clearly defining responsibilities for quality, and controlling documents and records.
- *Resource Management* ensures that an organization provides sufficient people, facilities, and training resources.
- *Product Realization* refers to controlling the production/service process from receipt of an order or quote through design, materials procurement, manufacturing or service delivery, distribution, and subsequent field service.
- *Measurement, Analysis, and Improvement* focuses on control procedures for assuring quality in products and processes, analysis of quality-related data, and correction, prevention, and improvement planning activities.

The requirements are stated as a set of numbered "clauses" that state precisely what the organization should do. For example, clause 6.4, called "Work Environment," is: "The organization shall determine and manage the work environment needed to achieve conformity to product requirement. Note: The term 'work environment' relates to those conditions under which work is performed including physical, environmental, and other factors (such as noise, temperature, humidity, lighting, or weather)."[31] This clause requires the organization to identify aspects of the work environment that may impact the quality of the good or service produced, and have an approach for managing people-related factors such as work methods and ergonomics as well as the physical work environment. In addition, the standard requires 20 different types of documentation to be maintained. This provides the ability to audit conformance to the standards and can also provide due diligence and protect against liability. The standards can be rather difficult to understand, but numerous resources are available to help managers interpret and use them.[32]

Although manufacturing is the largest adopter of ISO 9000, the standards are intended to apply to all types of businesses, including electronics and chemicals, and to services such as healthcare, banking, and transportation. The evolution of the standard has shed its manufacturing roots and made it easier for service companies to apply. For example, a software developer, Computer Associates of Islandia, New York, employs over 14,000 people in more than 40 countries. They used ISO 9001 to build a strong framework throughout all its sites (many of which were obtained through acquisitions of other software companies) to help standardize product development and support. Sears, Roebuck and Co. has registered almost 400 product repair centers and in-home services. As another example, in 1998, the Centers for Medicare and Medicaid Services began requiring ISO 9001 certification for all its new business contracts with claims processors.[33] Some professionals have argued that ISO 9000 can provide more effective management of public school systems.[34]

The ISO 9000 standards originally were intended to be advisory in nature and to be used for two-party contractual situations (between a customer and supplier) and for internal auditing. However, they quickly evolved into criteria for companies who wished to "certify" their quality management or achieve "registration" through a third-party auditor, usually a laboratory or some other accreditation agency (called a registrar). This process began in the United Kingdom. Rather than a supplier being audited for compliance to the standards by each customer, the registrar certifies the company, and this certification is accepted by all of the supplier's customers.

Implementing ISO 9000 is not an easy task.[35] Meeting the registration standards can be a painstaking and costly undertaking, often requiring organizations to develop and institute many new procedures and train many people. Individual sites—not entire companies—must achieve registration individually. All costs are borne by the applicant, so the process can be quite expensive. A registration audit may cost anywhere from $10,000 to more than $40,000, while the internal cost for documentation and training may exceed $100,000. Recertification is required every three years. Successful implementation of ISO 9000 requires the resources and support of top management, but the details fall mainly within the province of operating managers, supervisors, and employees to identify, develop, and document critical work processes.

ISO 9000 has three principal benefits:[36]

- *It provides discipline.* The ISO 9001 requirement for audits forces an organization to review its quality system on a routine basis. If it fails to maintain the quality system, audits should recognize this and call for corrective action.
- *It contains the basics of a good quality system.* ISO 9001 includes basic requirements for any sound quality system, such as understanding customer requirements, ensuring the ability to meet them, ensuring people resources capable of doing the work that affects quality, ensuring physical resources and support services needed to meet product requirements, and ensuring that problems are identified and corrected.
- *It offers a marketing program.* ISO certified organizations can use their status to differentiate themselves in the eyes of customers.

Many diverse organizations have realized significant benefits from ISO 9000 that range from higher customer satisfaction and retention, better quality products, and improved productivity. At DuPont, for example, ISO 9000 has been credited with increasing on-time delivery from 70 percent to 90 percent, decreasing cycle time from 15 days to 1.5 days, increasing first-pass yields from 72 percent to 92 percent, and reducing the number of test procedures by one-third. Sun Microsystems' Milpitas plant was certified in 1992, and managers believe that it helped deliver improved quality and service to customers.[37]

In Canada, Toronto Plastics, Ltd. reduced defects from 150,000 per million to 15,000 per million after one year of ISO implementation.[38] The first home builder to achieve registration, Michigan-based Delcor Homes, reduced its rate for correctable defects from 27.4 to 1.7 in two years and improved its building experience approval rating from the mid-60s to the mid-90s on a 100-point scale.[39] Thus, using ISO 9000 as a basis for a quality system can improve productivity, decrease costs, and increase customer satisfaction. In addition, organizations have found that using ISO 9000 resulted in increased use of data as a business management tool, increased management commitment, more efficient management reviews, and improved customer communication.[40]

> *A recent survey by the IOS has shown that China and Italy lead the world in ISO 9001 certifications. Current information can be obtained from the ISO website (http://www.iso.org).*

Building Effective Quality Management Systems

One practitioner has observed them many quality management systems focus more on compliance rather than improving quality. This is an easy trap to fall into, particularly when applying ISO 9000 or other compliance processes such as those in life-science manufacturing, which are regulated by the Food and Drug Administration.[41] The goals of the quality department can easily become disconnected from the quality processes across the organization if the focus evolves toward simply maintaining data and documentation to display an ISO certificate or meet regulatory requirements. For example, studies in the life-sciences industry have shown that less than 40 percent of organizations have integrated their QMS with enterprise resource planning (ERP), less than 30 percent with manufacturing execution systems (MES), and only about 25 percent with supply chain management (SCM).[42]

An effective QMS needs to be integrated with enterprise systems such as ERP, MES, and SCM, and should focus on actionable decision making, seeking the root causes of problems, and improving processes and systems. It should drive the principles of quality management throughout the organization by fostering effective practices to implement the principles, as we described in Table 2.3. Again, as Deming, Juran, and Crosby so often pointed out, these responsibilities lie with an organization's leadership. In ISO 9000:2000, the entire section on Management Responsibility is concerned with the role of leadership in driving a quality system. For example, the standards require that "Top management shall provide evidence of its commitment to the development and implementation of the quality management system and continually improving its effectiveness by (a) communicating to the organization the importance of meeting customer as well as statutory and regulatory requirements, (b) establishing the quality policy, (c) ensuring that quality objectives are established, (d) conducting management reviews, and (e) ensuring the availability of resources." More specific responsibilities are spelled out in detail in other clauses of the standards.

SUMMARY OF KEY POINTS AND TERMINOLOGY

The Student Companion Site provides a summary of key concepts and terminology introduced in this chapter.

QUALITY *in* PRACTICE

Bringing Quality Principles to Life at KARLEE[43]

KARLEE is a contract manufacturer of precision sheet metal and machined components for telecommunications, semiconductor, and medical equipment industries, located in Garland, Texas. KARLEE provides a vertically integrated range of services that support customers from initial component design to a finished, assembled product. Their services include:

- Advanced design engineering support
- Prototype production
- Manufacture and assembly of precision machined and sheet metal fabricated products
- Product finishing (painting, silk screening, plating)
- Value-added assembly integration (cabling, power supply and back plane installation, and electrical testing)

Throughout its business, KARLEE exemplifies the principles of total quality in its business practices. Some of these are described below.

Customer Focus. KARLEE made a strategic decision to carefully select customers that support its values—particularly a systematic approach to business and performance management, desire for long-term partnerships, and global leadership. Management and Team Leaders work with each customer to establish current requirements and future needs, and each customer is assigned a three-person Customer Service team that is on call 24 hours a day for day-to-day production issues.

Leadership. Senior Executive Leaders (SELs) and the KARLEE Leadership Committee (KLC) set the strategic direction of the company, and communicate and reinforce values and expectations through performance reviews, participation in improvement or strategic projects, regular interactions with customers and team members, and recognition of team member achievements.

Involvement of People. Production and delivery processes are designed around cell manufacturing. Teams are responsible for knowing their customer's requirements and producing according to those requirements. Teams are empowered to change targets recommended during strategic planning if they believe it will help them achieve higher performance, as well as to schedule work, manage inventory, and design the layout of their work areas.

Process Approach. Processes such as prototype development, scheduling, production setup, fabrication, assembly, and delivery require process owners to be responsible for maintaining the process to customer requirements. A Quality Assurance team member works with manufacturing teams to create process documentation.

System Approach to Management. KARLEE'S strategic planning approach includes a strategic assessment of the entire company, and aligns corporate objectives and goals with its key business drivers. KARLEE uses information and data to set goals, align organizational directions and manage resource at the operating, process, and organizational levels.

Continual Improvement. Teams use a structured approach to evaluate and improve their processes, documenting them and presenting a status report of improvements to senior leaders and the KARLEE Steering Committee. Teams benchmark competitors, "best practice" companies, and customers to learn from others.

Factual Approach to Decision Making. Teams analyze defect data, customer-reported problems, and control charts generated during production to identify problems and opportunities for improvement. Every business goal and project has defined methods for measurement, and senior leaders meet weekly to review company performance and ensure alignment with directions and plans.

Mutually Beneficial Supplier Relationships. KARLEE selects and develops suppliers that share their commitment to customer satisfaction to ensure they have the materials and services needed to support their customers. Supplier performance issues and expectations are discussed with individual suppliers and presented at the annual Supplier Symposium.

All this has contributed to an increased sales growth, and high levels of customer and employee satisfaction, and quality and operational performance,

resulting in KARLEE receiving a Baldrige Award in 2000.

Key Issues for Discussion

1. From the information presented here, how would you say that KARLEE defines quality, drawing upon the definitions in Chapter 1?
2. Discuss how KARLEE's practices reflect the philosophies of Deming, Juran, and Crosby.

QUALITY *in* PRACTICE

ISO 9000 and Sears' Quality Management System[44]

Sears, Roebuck and Co., a wholly owned subsidiary of Sears Holdings Corp., is one of the largest retailers in North America. Sears offers a range of home merchandise, apparel, and automotive products and services through more than 2,400 Sears-branded and affiliated stores in the United States and Canada, which includes about 926 full-line and 1,100 specialty stores in the United States alone. Sears is the largest national provider of product repair services, with more than 14 million repairs performed annually.

After an eight-year effort, the company registered its product repair centers' and in-home service's quality management systems (QMS) to ISO 9001. Sears has always maintained a strong commitment to quality in its products and services. In keeping with this commitment, in 1998 the company decided to register all of its product repair centers to the ISO 9002:1994 quality management system standard (which was subsequently replaced by ISO 9001:2000). By the end of 2002, all of the 32 carry-in service centers were registered to ISO 9001. Once the repair centers were registered, Sears turned to the in-home service side of its business. About 10,000 Sears' technicians repair one of every five appliances in America. By the end of 2005, Sears had 383 locations under the scope of its ISO 9001 registration, including all six in-home regions. The company's 48 districts have their own certificates.

Recognizing that ISO 9001 provides a framework for large organizations to implement a consistent,

cohesive program across geographic lines and throughout a multifaceted business, Sears sought registration to enhance its organizational process compliance. The company wanted a consistent process for improving customer satisfaction and enhancing service capabilities. ISO 9001 implementation played a large role in assisting with process standardization across the company. ISO 9001 is often associated with the manufacturing industry, and one major hurdle Sears had to overcome was communicating the value of a QMS within a retail and service environment.

ISO 9001 became a fundamental tool that provides the company a safe base for continued improvements. For example, Sears has made dramatic improvements in calibrating the tools used for repairs and service calls. Although the company had calibrated some of its tools prior to implementing ISO 9001, the standard requires 100-percent tool calibration for safety purposes. Not only does Sears have an expansive program for calibrating its tools, but it has also opened and registered its own calibration lab to ISO/IEC 17025. This move minimizes calibration costs and expands third-party business opportunities.

Another significant benefit of ISO 9001 involves the company's handling of refrigerant. Sears works with Freon and other hazardous materials, which could pose a serious environmental violation if not handled properly. As part of its ISO 9001 efforts, Sears improved its existing hazardous-materials program by implementing a comprehensive program on refrigerant handling.

The standard also helped Sears' efficiency in completing repairs. For instance, in the Chattanooga, Tennessee, carry-in facility, the average daily completion rate for repairing lawn mowers or other items doubled from four or five to eight or nine per repairman as a result of ISO 9001 implementation.

Sears' district office in Houston has improved its technician recall rate because of the QMS. The recall rate is the percentage of times service technicians must return to customers' homes for a second time within 30 days. Before the SST, the recall rate in Houston was about 12 percent. In 2004, Houston service technicians made more than a quarter of a million service calls, with a 9.3-percent recall rate. In 2005, the rate dropped to 7.9 percent.

ISO 9001 has been instrumental in helping to standardize the manner in which technicians record field observations. This is important for solving certain types of problems, such as an appliance or part malfunction, customer abuse or an accident. To ensure consistency, technicians use a special tool kit for recording the event, including a disposable camera and standardized forms.

Key Issues for Discussion

1. What issues do you think that a large company such as Sears had to face in implementing ISO 9000 across its vast organization?
2. How are the ISO 9000:2000 Quality Management Principles reflected in this example? How might these principles have helped Sears address the issues you identified in the first question?

REVIEW QUESTIONS

1. How does Deming's definition of quality—"A product or a service possesses quality if it helps somebody and enjoys a good and sustainable market"—compare with the definitions discussed in Chapter 1?
2. Explain the Deming chain reaction.
3. Summarize Deming's 14 Points. How does each point relate to the four components of Profound Knowledge?
4. Summarize the four components of Profound Knowledge. How do they mutually support each other?
5. What is a system? Why is "systems thinking" important to quality management?
6. Why is it important to understand variation from a statistical perspective?
7. Explain the implications of not understanding the components of Profound Knowledge as suggested by Peter Scholtes.
8. Explain Juran's Quality Trilogy.
9. Summarize the breakthrough sequence that Juran advocated for quality improvement.
10. How is Juran's philosophy similar to or different from Deming's?
11. What are Crosby's Absolutes of Quality Management and Basic Elements of Improvement? How

are they similar to or different from Deming's 14 Points?
12. Summarize the key contributions of Feigenbaum and Ishikawa to modern quality thinking.
13. Explain the differences among quality principles, practices, and techniques.
14. List and briefly explain the eight principles of quality management.
15. State two or three practices associated with each principle of quality management.
16. What is statistical thinking? Why is it important to managers and workers at all levels of an organization?
17. What are the operational problems created by excessive variation?
18. Explain the difference between common and special causes of variation.
19. Explain the two fundamental mistakes that managers make when attempting to improve a process. Can you cite any examples in your personal experience in which such mistakes were made?
20. What are the lessons of the red bead and funnel experiments? Can you cite any examples in your experience where someone acted counter to these lessons?

21. What is a quality management system (QMS)? Describe the features that a good QMS should have.
22. Briefly summarize the rationale behind ISO 9000. What are the objectives of the standards?
23. What are the three principal benefits of ISO 9000?
24. Why are all quality management systems not effective? What can be done to make them effective?

DISCUSSION QUESTIONS

1. Compare the Deming Chain Reaction (Figure 2.1) with Figure 1.3, which suggests the relationships between quality and profitability. Discuss the similarities and differences. Which do you think is the better model, if you had to choose one to present to a senior manager? Can you suggest a different model that captures both?
2. Discuss the interrelationships among Deming's 14 Points. How do they support each other? Why must they be viewed as a whole rather than separately?
3. The following themes form the basis for Deming's philosophy. Classify the 14 Points into these categories and discuss the commonalties within each category.
   a. Organizational purpose and mission
   b. Quantitative goals
   c. Revolution of management philosophy
   d. Elimination of seat-of-the-pants decisions
   e. Cooperation building
   f. Improvement of manager/worker relations
4. The original version of Deming's 14 Points (developed in the early 1980s) is given in Table 2.4. Contrast each of these with the revised version in Table 2.1 given in the chapter. Explain the implications of the changes. Why might Deming have made these changes?
5. Suggest ways that management can recognize the existence of fear in an organization. What strategies might managers use to deal with and eliminate fear?
6. Discuss how Deming's 14 Points can apply to an academic environment. How can learning and classroom performance be improved by applying Deming's philosophy?
7. In a videotape made in 1993, Deming related a story of an executive who spent an entire day flying from city to city, changing planes several times, because her company's travel department received a cheaper fare than if she had taken a direct flight.

How does this example violate the concepts of Profound Knowledge and the 14 Points, and what should the company do about it?

8. Melissa Clare works for a software company as a technical support representative. Her duties include answering the telephone, providing information to customers, and troubleshooting technical problems. Her supervisor told her to be courteous and not to rush callers. However, the supervisor also told her that she must answer an average of 15 calls per hour so that the department's account manager can meet his or her budget. Melissa comes home each day frustrated because the computer is slow in delivering information that she needs and sometimes provides the wrong information, causing her to search for the information in complex manuals. When she is pressed for time, she often cuts the call off prematurely or provides only the minimal information necessary. What might Deming say about this situation? Explain which of the 14 Points might be violated. Drawing upon Deming's principles, outline a plan to improve this situation.
9. What implications might Deming's Profound Knowledge have for Wall Street traders whose buying and selling behavior reacts somewhat wildly to daily news and government economic reports?
10. Think of a system with which you are familiar, such as your college, fraternity, or a student organization. What is the purpose of that system? What would it mean to optimize that system?
11. Whose philosophy—Deming, Juran, or Crosby—resonates most with your thinking and experience? Explain why.
12. Review the Quality Profiles presented at the beginning of Chapter 1 and this chapter. List specific practices cited in these examples and how they support the quality management principles in Table 2.2.

TABLE 2.4   Original Version of Deming's 14 Points

1. Create constancy of purpose toward improvement of product and service, with the aim of becoming competitive and to stay in business and to provide jobs.

2. Adopt the new philosophy. We are in a new economic age. Western management must awaken to the challenge, must learn their responsibilities, and take on leadership for change.

3. Cease dependence on inspection to achieve quality. Eliminate the need for inspection on a mass basis by building quality into the product in the first place.

4. End the practice of awarding business on the basis of price tag alone. Instead, minimize total cost. Move toward a single supplier for any one item, on a long-term relationship of loyalty and trust.

5. Improve constantly and forever the system of production and service to improve quality and productivity, and thus constantly decrease costs.

6. Institute training on the job.

7. Institute leadership. The aim of supervision should be to help people and machines and gadgets do a better job. Supervision of management is in need of overhaul, as well as the supervision of production workers.

8. Drive out fear so everyone can work effectively for the company.

9. Break down barriers between departments. People in research, design, sales, and production must work as a team, to foresee problems of production and those that may be encountered with the product or service.

10. Eliminate slogans, exhortations, and targets for the work force that ask for zero defects or new levels of productivity. Such exhortations only create adversarial relationships, as the bulk of the causes of low quality and low productivity belong to the system and thus lie beyond the power of the work force.

11a. Eliminate work standards (quotas) on the factory floor. Substitute leadership.

11b. Eliminate management by objective. Eliminate management by numbers, numerical goals. Substitute leadership.

12a. Remove barriers that rob hourly workers of their right to pride of workmanship. The responsibility of supervisors must be changed from sheer numbers to quality.

12b. Remove barriers that rob people in management and engineering of their right to pride in workmanship. This means, inter alia, abolishment of the annual or merit rating and of management by objective.

13. Institute a vigorous program of education and self-improvement.

14. Put everybody in the company to work to accomplish the transformation. The transformation is everybody's job.

13. Thinking of your experiences in a job that you have held. How might the principles and practices of quality management listed in Tables 2.2 and 2.3 be applied to improve this organization?

14. List some examples of variation that you observe in your daily life. Would they be classified as common or special causes? How might they be reduced?

15. One of our former students who sews as a hobby observed that it's often difficult to control thread tension (tightness versus slackness of the stitch) as the tension normally exhibits variation. She learned from experience that if she adjusts the tension every time a stitch comes out too tight or loose, it generally makes matters worse. However, other times, the stitching is clearly bad and

requires an adjustment. Explain how her observations relate to statistical thinking. Can you think of other situations in your life that illustrate these concepts?

16. Examine the following requirements from ISO 9000. Which directly help control or improve quality, and which do not? For those that do not, why do you think that they are part of the standard?

    a. "The organization shall determine requirements specified by the customer."

    b. "Records from management reviews shall be maintained."

    c. "… documentation shall include … documents needed … to ensure the effective planning, operation and control of its processes … "

    d. "… shall determine the monitoring and measurement to be undertaken … to provide evidence of conformity of product to determined requirements."

    e. "The quality management system … shall include a quality manual."

    f. "… establish and implement the inspection or other activities necessary for ensuring that purchased product meets specified requirements."

PROJECTS, ETC.

1. Study the annual reports of some major companies issued over a period of several years. Do you see evidence of implementation of the quality philosophies discussed in this chapter?

2. Design a questionnaire or survey instrument to determine the degree to which an organization is "Demingized." Explain how you developed the questions.

3. Interview a quality professional at a local company about their quality management system. Consider questions such as: Do they have a quality manual?

Is their QMS integrated with other enterprise business systems?

4. Interview some managers at a local company that is pursuing or has pursued ISO 9000 registration. Report on the reasons for achieving registration, the perceived benefits, and the problems the company encountered during the process.

5. Search the Internet to find information about current registration trends for ISO 9000. How widespread is ISO 9000 in the United States as compared to Europe and other global regions?

CASES

THE DISCIPLINARY CITATION[45]

A local delivery service has 40 drivers who deliver packages throughout the metropolitan area. Occasionally, drivers make mistakes, such as entering the wrong package number on a shipping document, failing to get a signature, and so on. A total of 280 mistakes were made in one year as shown in the Excel file *C02-CaseData* in the *Student Companion Site* for this chapter. The manager in charge of this operation has issued disciplinary citations to drivers for each mistake.

Discussion Questions

1. What is your opinion of the manager's approach? How does it compare with the Deming philosophy?

2. How might the analysis of these data help the manager to understand the variation in the system? (Plot the data to obtain some insight.) How can the data help the manager to improve the performance of this system?

SANTA CRUZ GUITAR COMPANY[46]

Santa Cruz Guitar Company (SCGC) is a small-scale manufacturing operation, producing fewer than 800 instruments a year. The company does not have a formal quality department nor has it consciously tried to apply the principles of TQM. Nevertheless, a tour of its facilities and operations suggest that many of the principles of TQM and Deming's 14 Points are evident.

Although modern computer numerical controlled (CNC) equipment is used to manufacture minor parts of the guitar, the secret of SCGC's success lies in the small staff of 14 craftsmen, known as luthiers, who apply care and attention to detail while hand-crafting the major components of each instrument. The shop floor is divided into six workstations at which the guitars are progressively assembled as they move from station to station. Experienced luthiers, who are empowered to make their own quality decisions, staff each station. The guitar does not move to the next station until the luthier and another more senior luthier are satisfied with the quality of the work. The manufacturing department inspects what it produces. The company recruits only those who desire to work in a team environment and have a passion for guitar making.

There are seven major steps in the process of making a guitar:

1. *Selecting and Drying the Wood:* The guitar-making process starts with the selection of the highest grades of tonewoods. The wood is treated in an evaporative dehumidifying kiln that slowly and carefully removes bound cellular moisture from the wood. The target moisture level is 3 percent, but when exposed to the temperature/humidity conditions of the shop floor, the moisture content stabilizes at 6 percent. The shop floor is kept at a constant 47 percent humidity, which is optimum for maintaining the equilibrium of moisture conditions.
2. *Rough Cutting the Wood:* Once dried, the wood is worked down to rough usable forms using traditional woodworking tools. However, SCGC uses a CNC machine for creating the necks.
3. *Bending the Sides:* To create the desired shapes, the guitar sides are first dipped into water for 10 minutes to condition the wood and then placed under gradual hand pressure on a hot bending template. At that point, the tension in the wood has been relaxed, and the wood eventually takes the shape of the template. This process is best performed by human hands because sides that are shaped by machines have a tendency to spring back when they are being forced into molds.
4. *Cutting the Top and Back:* The top and back of the guitars then are cut to shape, and braces are applied to each surface. The thicknesses of the top and braces have the most influence on the final sound of the guitar. As the luthier shaves off ribbons of wood from the top and braces, he will tap the top to hear the tone that results from each series of shavings until the tone is perfect. Since the true sound of the instruments will not be fully realized until they are assembled, the luthiers write down what they did while building the top. After final assembly, if a guitar produces a sound so special it knocks the player's socks off, the luthier who built the top will immediately be notified and asked to check his notes to see how this was accomplished so the sound can be duplicated in the future.
5. *Cutting the Neck:* About 60 percent of the SCGC guitar necks are cut on the CNC machine. It is the only major part that is not hand-made. It is critical that the dimensions of the neck be consistent, and the CNC machine does that better than human hands. The 40 percent of necks that are hand-made are done that way because of a customer's specifications. Ebony fret boards, which are inlaid with mother-of-pearl, are then glued to the necks.
6. *Applying the Finish:* The guitar body is finished with 12 protective layers of a specially formulated lacquer composed primarily of nitrocellulose and plasticizers to preserve the wood surfaces. The lacquer is thin enough that the sound is not dampened.
7. *Completing Final Assembly and Setup:* The neck is fitted to the body using a dovetail joint and glued in place. Then the bridge is glued to the body. In the next step, called the setup, the saddle and nut, which suspend the strings over the instrument and are made from bovine bones, are installed. Finally, the strings are placed on the guitar, and it is played for the first time. A technician then adjusts the neck or string height to optimize the feel and playability of the instrument.

SCGC has a web page where guitar owners can have questions about their guitars answered. At SCGC, workers are encouraged to further enhance their skills either by taking external courses or by a practice that allows them to build two instruments a year for personal use. These opportunities allow the craftsmen to explore new techniques in guitar building and become familiar with the entire guitar building

process. SCGC workers are even encouraged to go out on their own to open a luthier business someday.

Based on this tour of SCGC, can you identify how the operations and quality practices reflect Deming's 14 points?

WALKER AUTO SALES AND SERVICE

Walker Auto Sales and Service (WASS) is a full service dealership for a major domestic automobile brand. Essentially, WASS provides three main services: new car sales, used car sales, and repair and maintenance service. Because of the competitive nature of the market, the firm's owner, Darren Walker, wants to take a more systematic approach to improving service and providing a high level of customer satisfaction. Through surveys, focus groups, and analysis of complaint data and information, he identified some important requirements for these services. Customers expect a favorable impression when they arrive at the dealership—a wide range of vehicles and options to evaluate, available salespeople, to be greeted promptly, and to feel comfortable and not pressured. They also expect salespersons to be courteous, knowledgeable about the cars, respect their time, and honor verbal promises. For repair and maintenance service, customers want to have the work explained appropriately, to be fully informed of any additional necessary work, and to have all work reviewed upon completion. They

want good time estimates and communications with the service department.

Suppliers play an important role in the business and the entire value chain. The dealership needs quality parts, product availability when needed, timely delivery, and fair prices. WASS also receives corporate support for its employee benefits and certain training programs, information technology planning and intranet/Internet development, marketing and advertising, and strategic planning direction. WASS is facing increasing competition for skilled employee talent, changing customer demographics that are leading to growing demand, and more competition as a result of new foreign dealerships that are locating in its market area. Darren recognizes the need to "become the dealership of choice" in its market.

Drawing upon the principles of quality management and the unique nature of services addressed in Chapter 1, describe some of the issues that Darren must consider in achieving his vision. Develop a list of action plans that he might consider.

THE QUARTERLY SALES REPORT[47]

Ron Hagler, the vice president of sales for Selit Corp., had just received a report on the past five years of quarterly sales data for the regions under his authority (see sales data shown in the Excel worksheet *C02-CaseData.xlsx* on the Student Companion Site). Not happy with the results, he got on the phone to his secretary. "Marsha, tell the regional managers I need to speak with them this afternoon. Everyone must attend."

Marsha had been Hagler's secretary for almost a decade. She knew by the tone in his voice that he meant business, so she contacted the regional managers about the impromptu meeting at 2 P.M. At 1:55 P.M., the regional managers filed into the room. The only time

they were called into a meeting together was when Hagler was unhappy.

Hagler wasted no time. "I just received the quarterly sales report. Northeast sales were fantastic. Steve, you not only improved 17.6 percent in the fourth quarter, but you also increased sales a whopping 20.6 percent over the previous year. I don't know how you do it!" Steve smiled. His philosophy to end the year with a bang by getting customers to stockpile units had paid off again. Hagler had failed to notice that Steve's first quarter sales were always sluggish.

Hagler continued: "Terry, Southwest sales were also superb. You showed an 11.7 percent increase in the fourth quarter and an 11.8 percent increase over the previous year." Terry also smiled. She wasn't sure how she did so well, but she sure wasn't going to change anything.

"Jan, Northwest sales were up 17.2 percent in the fourth quarter, but down 8.2 percent from the previous year," said Hagler. "You need to find out what you did previously to make your sales go through the roof. Even so, your performance in the fourth quarter was good." Jan tried to hide his puzzlement. Although he had received a big order in November, it was the first big order he had received in a long time. Overall, sales for the Northwest were declining.

Hagler was now ready to deal with the "problem" regions. "Leslie, North Central sales were down 5.5 percent in the fourth quarter, but up 4.7 percent from the previous year. I don't understand how your sales vary so much. Do you need more incentive?" Leslie looked down. She had been working very hard the past five years and had acquired numerous new accounts. In fact, she received a bonus for acquiring the most new business in 2009.

"Kim, Mid-Atlantic sales were down 3.2 percent in the fourth quarter and down 2.6 percent from the previous year. I'm very disappointed in your performance. You were once my best sales representative. I had high expectations for you. Now, I can only hope that your first quarter results show some sign of life." Kim felt her face get red. She knew she had sold more units in 2011 than in 2010. "What does Hagler know anyway," she thought to herself. "He's just an empty suit."

Hagler turned to Dave, who felt a surge of adrenaline. "Dave, South Central sales were the worst of all! Sales were down 19.7 percent in the fourth quarter and down 22.3 percent from the previous year. How can you explain this? Do you value your job? I want to see a dramatic improvement in this quarter's results or else!" Dave felt numb. It was a tough region, with a lot of competition. Sure, accounts were lost over the years, but those lost were always replaced with new ones. How could he be doing so badly?

How can Hagler improve his approach by applying principles of statistical thinking? Use any analyses of the data that you feel are appropriate, such as construction of Excel charts or computing summary statistics to fully explain your thinking and help him.

NOTES

1. John Hillkirk, "World-Famous Quality Expert Dead at 93," *USA Today*, December 21, 1993.
2. *Motor Trend*, November 2009, p. 86
3. W. Edwards Deming, The New Economics for Industry, Government, Education (Cambridge, MA: MIT Center for Advanced Engineering Study, 1993).
4. Matthew W. Ford and James R. Evans, "The Role of Follow-Up in Achieving Results from Self-Assessment Processes, *International Journal of Quality and Reliability Management*, Vol. 23, Issue 6, 2006.
5. Walter A. Shewhart, *Economic Control of Quality of a Manufactured Product* (New York: Van Nostrand, 1931).
6. Adapted from March Laree Jacques, "Big League Quality," *Quality Progress*, August 2001, 27–34.
7. Russell L. Ackoff, Recreating the Corporation: A Design of Organizations for the 21st Century, Oxford, 1999.
8. The quincunx simulator is contained in the Quality Gamebox, a registered trademark of P-Q Systems, Inc., 10468 Miamisburg-Springboro Road, Miamisburg, OH 45342; 937-885-2255; 800-777-3020. It can be purchased and downloaded at: http://www.pqsystems.com/products /sixsigma/QualityGamebox/QualityGamebox.php.
9. Clarence Irving Lewis, Mind and the World (Mineola, NY: Dover, 1929).
10. Reprinted with permission from Peter Scholtes, "Communities as Systems," *Quality Progress*, July 1997, 49–53. Copyright © 1997 American Society for Quality. No further distribution allowed without permission.
11. "Juran Honors Japanese Quality at His 100th Birthday Event," *Quality Digest*, June 2004, 6.
12. Jeremy Main, "Under the Spell of the Quality Gurus," *Fortune*, August 18, 1986, 30–34.
13. Philip B. Crosby, Quality Is Free (New York: McGraw-Hill, 1979), 200–201.
14. Facts in this section were obtained from "Profile: the ASQC Honorary Members A. V. Feigenbaum and Kaoru Ishikawa," *Quality Progress* 19, no. 8 (August 1986), 43–45; and Bruce Brocka and M. Suzanne Brocka, *Quality Management: Implementing the Best Ideas of the Masters* (Homewood, IL: Business One Irwin, 1992). A related article that summarizes the contributions of these individuals as well as others is "Guru Guide: Six Thought Leaders Who Changed the Quality World Forever," *Quality Progress*, November 2010, p. 14–21.

15. More about Feigenbaum can be found in Gregory H. Watson, "Feigenbaum's Enduring Influence," *Quality Progress*, November 2005, pp. 51–55, and on the General Systems Company website at http://www.gensysco.com/.

16. James W. Dean, Jr. and David E. Bowen, "Management Theory and Total Quality: Improving Research and Practice Through Theory Development," *Academy of Management Review*, vol. 19, no. 3 (1994), pp. 392–418.

17. Source: International Organization for Standardization, http://www.iso.org/iso/iso_catalogue/management_and _leadership_standards/quality_management/qmp.htm

18. Adapted from Brian L. Joiner, *Fourth Generation Management* (New York: McGraw-Hill, 1994), 129.

19. Reprinted with permission from Galen Britz, Don Emerling, Lynne Hare, Roger Hoerl, and Janice Shade, "How to Teach Others to Apply Statistical Thinking," *Quality Progress*, June 1997, 67–79. © 1997, American Society for Quality. No further distribution allowed without permission.

20. Steven A. Melnyk and R. T. Christensen, "Variance is Evil," *APICS The Performance Advantage*, June 2002, 19.

21. Kimberly Weisul, "So Your Lie May Always Be True," *BusinessWeek*, February 25, 2002, 16.

22. Based on descriptions given in W. Edwards Deming, *The New Economics For Industry, Government, Education* (Cambridge, MA: MIT Center for Advanced Engineering Study, 1993).

23. Frank H. Squires, "The Triumph of Statistics," Quality, February 1982, 75.

24. Nicole Radziwill, Diane Olson, Andrew Vollmar, Ted Lippert, Ted Mattis, Kevin Van Dewark, and John W. Sinn, "Starting from Scratch, Roadmap and Toolkit: Recipe for a New Quality System," *Quality Progress* 40 (2008), pp. 40–47, http://asq.org/quality-progress/2008/09/basic-quality/starting-from-scratch.html.

25. Tom Taormina, "Conducting Successful Internal Audits," Quality Digest, June 1998, 44–47.

26. International Organization for Standardization, "ISO 9000 essentials," http://www.iso.org/iso/iso_catalogue/management_and_leadership_standards/quality_management/iso_9000_essentials.htm

27. Michael J. Timbers, "ISO 9000 and Europe's Attempts to Mandate Quality," *Journal of European Business*, March–April 1992, 14–25.

28. Amy Zuckerman, "ISO/QS-9000 Registration Issues Heating Up Worldwide," *The Quality Observer*, June 1997, 21–23.

29. Amy Zuckerman and Rosalind McClymont, "Tracking the Ongoing ISO 9000 Revisions," *Business Standards*, 2, no. 2 (March–April 2000), 13–15; Jack West, with Charles A. Cianfrani and Joseph J. Tsiakals, "A Breeze or a Breakthough? Conforming to ISO 9000:2000," *Quality Progress*, March 2000, 41–44. See also by West et al., "Quality Management Principles: Foundation of ISO 9000:2000 Family, Part 5," *Quality Progress*, February 2000, 113–116; and "Quality Management Principles: Foundation of ISO 9000:2000 Family, Part 6," *Quality Progress*, March 2000, 79–81.

30. Dirk Dusharme, "ISO 9001: The Shift to Service," *Quality Digest*, July 2005, 33–36; John Scott, "ISO 9000 in Service: The Good, the Bad, and the Ugly," *Quality Progress*, September 2005, 42–48.

31. ANSI/ISO/ASQ Q9001-2008.

32. For example, one excellent book is C. A. Cianfrani, J. J. Tsiakals, and J. E. West, *ISO 9001:2008 Explained, 3rd ed.*, Milwaukee, WI: ASQ Quality Press (2009).

33. John E. "Jack" West, "Small Change, Big Payoff," *Quality Progress*, April 2009, 47–52.

34. William A. Stimson, "Better Public Schools With ISO 9000:2000," *Quality Progress*, September 2003, 38–45.

35. Implementation guidelines are suggested in the case study by Steven E. Webster, "ISO 9000 Certification, A Success Story at Nu Visions Manufacturing," *IIE Solutions*, April 1997, 18–21.

36. Jack Dearing, "ISO 9001: Could It Be Better?" *Quality Progress*, February 2007, 23–27.

37. ISO 9000 Update, *Fortune*, September 30, 1996, 134[J].

38. Astrid L. H. Eckstein and Jaydeep Balakrishnan, "The ISO 9000 Series: Quality Management Systems for the Global Economy," *Production and Inventory Management Journal* 34, no. 4 (Fourth Quarter 1993), 66–71.

39. "Home Builder Constructs Quality with ISO 9000," *Quality Digest*, February 2000, 13.

40. Sandford Liebesman and James Mroz, "ISO 9000:2000 Experiences: First Results Are In," *Quality Progress*, April 2002, 52–59.

41. Karim Lokas, "Why Your QMS Should Concentrate on the Product Instead of Compliance," *Quality Progress*, August 2011, 47–52.

42. Lokas, *ibid*.

43. Adapted from KARLEE 2000 Malcolm Baldrige Application Summary, National Institute of Standards and Technology, U.S. Department of Commerce.

44. Adapted from Pam Parry, "Sears Delivers a Better QMS," *Quality Digest*, January 10, 2007.

45. Based on an anecdote in W. Edwards Deming, Out of the Crisis (Cambridge, MA: MIT Center for Advanced Engineering Study, 1986).

46. Reprinted with permission from Luke T. Foo, "Good Vibrations: Ingrained Quality Practices Mirror Deming's 14 points," *Quality Progress*, February 2008, pp. 25–30. Copyright © 2008 American Society for Quality. No further distribution allowed without permission.

47. Reprinted with permission from Galen Britz, Don Emerling, Lynn Hare, Roger Hoerl, and Janice Shade, "How to Teach Others to Apply Statistical Thinking," *Quality Progress*, June 1997, pp. 67–79. Copyright © 1997 American Society for Quality. No further distribution allowed without permission.

Customer Focus

Customer focus might be the most important principle of quality management. The customer is the ultimate judge of the quality of goods and services, and, as has been eloquently stated, "Without customers, you don't have a business."[1] In Japanese, a single word, *okyakusama*, means both "customer" and "honorable guest." World-class organizations are obsessed with meeting and exceeding customer expectations. Many organizations such as the Ritz-Carlton Hotel Company, Disney, and Toyota's Lexus division were built on the notion of satisfying the customer.

Perceptions of value and satisfaction are influenced by many factors throughout the customer's overall purchase, ownership, and service experiences. The Executive Director of Global Quality Strategy at General Motors noted "If the customer is satisfied with the whole experience with the product, then you have a quality product."[2] The key phrase is "the whole experience." To meet or exceed customer expectations, organizations must fully understand all product and service attributes that contribute to customer value and lead to satisfaction and loyalty. To accomplish this task, an organization's efforts need to extend well beyond merely meeting specifications, reducing defects and errors, or resolving complaints. They must include both designing new products that truly delight the customer and responding rapidly to changing consumer and market demands. An organization that is close to its customer knows what the customer wants, how the customer uses its products, and anticipates needs that the customer may not even be able to express. It also continually develops new ways of enhancing customer relationships.

Customer focus is a key requirement of ISO 9000:2000. For example, in the Management Responsibility section, one requirement is "Top management shall ensure that customer requirements are determined and are met with the aim of enhancing customer satisfaction." This puts the responsibility for customer focus on senior leadership. In the Product Realization section, the standards require that the organization determine customer requirements, including delivery and postdelivery activities, and any requirements not stated by the customer but necessary for specified or intended use. In addition, the organization must establish procedures for communicating with customers about product information and other inquiries, and for obtaining feedback, including complaints. In the Measurement, Analysis, and Improvement sections, the standards require that the organization monitor customer perceptions as to whether the organization has met customer requirements; that is, customer satisfaction.

This chapter focuses on customer-driven excellence. Table 3.1 summarizes the key quality management practices for focusing on customers, which we will elaborate on in the remainder of the chapter. The Quality Profiles provide two examples of organizations that focus considerable attention on their customers.

TABLE 3.1   Key Customer-Focused Practices for Quality Management

- Identify the most important customer groups and markets, considering competitors and other potential customers, and segment the customer base to better meet differing needs.
- Understand both near-term and longer-term customer needs and expectations (the "voice of the customer") and employ systematic processes for listening and learning from customers, potential customers, and customers of competitors to obtain actionable information about products and customer support.
- Understand the linkages between the voice of the customer and design, production, and delivery processes; and use voice-of-the-customer information to identify and innovate product offerings and customer support processes to meet and exceed customer requirements and expectations, to expand relationships, and to identify and attract new customers and markets.
- Create an organizational culture and support framework that allows customers to easily contact an organization to conduct business, receive a consistently positive customer experience, provide feedback, obtain assistance, receive prompt resolution of their concerns, and facilitate improvement.
- Manage customer relationships that build loyalty, enhance satisfaction and engagement, and lead to the acquisition of new customers.
- Measure customer satisfaction, engagement, and dissatisfaction; compare the results relative to competitors and industry benchmarks; and use the information to evaluate and improve organizational processes.

quality**profiles**

Park Place Lexus and K&N Management

With two locations in the Dallas, Texas area, Park Place Lexus (PPL) sells new Lexus vehicles and pre-owned luxury vehicles, services Lexus and other vehicles, and sells Lexus parts to the wholesale and retail markets. PPL has committed substantial resources to ensuring that client relationships, once established, can be maintained in a way that contributes value to both parties. This includes the development and deployment of a client-relationship management database that tracks all aspects of the PPL-Client interaction and provides the resulting information to members (the term used by PPL to refer to company employees). PPL uses its Client Concern Resolution (CCR) process to address any problems that might occur in any area of the client experience. CCR empowers the individual member to resolve client complaints on the spot by allowing each member to spend up to $250 to resolve a complaint, or up to $2,000 by committee.

PPL has identified eight key value creation processes that have direct interface with clients, significantly contribute to the delivery of service to its clients, or provide opportunity for business growth. For all of these key processes, PPL has identified process requirements as well as process measures to help them track progress toward meeting these requirements. PPL has extensive training programs and career development planning for its workforce. A focus on personal and organizational learning is the key to PPL's efforts to motivate members, which then results in exceptional understanding of client's needs and the ability to deliver service to meet those needs.

As a result of these focused efforts, Park Place Lexus Grapevine location had a New Car Client Satisfaction Index (CSI) of 99.8 percent in 2004, making it the highest rated Lexus dealership in the nation. PPL's continued client focus has reduced the number of complaints that promises were not met from 130 in 2002 to 3 in 2005, that clients were misled by staff from 22 in 2002 to 1 in 2005, and about discourteous treatment from 28 in 2002 to 1 in 2005.

K&N Management is the licensed Austin, Texas-area developer for Rudy's "Country Store" & Bar-B-Q and the creator of Mighty Fine Burgers, Fries and Shakes, two fast-casual restaurant concepts. The company's culture is based on quality and excellence; strong relationships with its customers, referred to as "guests"; and a vision "to become world famous by delighting one guest at a time." K&N Management builds and maintains a focus on "guest delight," relying on innovation and technology to create product offerings that meet or exceed guest requirements. Guests can access store information and events via websites and social media, as well as through innovative approaches such as EyeClick, an interactive system at each Mighty Fine location. Feedback is collected with an iPad that administers short surveys around the main meal periods and uploads the information to a third-party host for aggregation. Takeout guests are directed to a web-based survey.

All leaders carry a personal digital assistant (PDA) that alerts them of guest comments and complaints and daily performance results. Ongoing listening and learning approaches are used to maintain a list of key guest requirements (KGRs) that are aligned with key business drivers. The company's performance against its KGRs is systematically measured and communicated throughout the workforce. Performance gaps and opportunities are funneled into appropriate planning approaches, ranging from problem solving to strategic planning.

In sales, K&N Management's restaurants significantly outperform local competitors and national chains. For both K&N restaurant concepts, guests rate their satisfaction with food quality, hospitality, cleanliness, speed of service, and value at least 4.7 on a 5-point scale, outperforming the best competitor. Overall guest satisfaction ratings are over 4.7 for both, also beating the best competitor.

Source: Adapted from Malcolm Baldrige National Quality Award, Profiles of Winners, National Institute of Standards and Technology, Department of Commerce.

CUSTOMER SATISFACTION AND ENGAGEMENT

The ASQ Quality Glossary defines **customer satisfaction** as "the result of delivering a product or service that meets customer requirements." Customer satisfaction is vital to keeping customers and growing a business. For example, Avis long ago recognized that there are two ways to increase market share in the rental car business: (1) by buying large volumes of corporate business with extremely low rates and (2) by improving customer satisfaction levels, thereby increasing repurchase intent and repeat business. However, Avis stated that it would not buy business at low rates for the sole purpose of increasing market share; rather, it focuses on improving customer satisfaction. Avis's marketing department uses a full range of research and analysis to keep pace with changing market trends and develops programs that respond to customers' needs. Avis also monitors trends and levels of customer satisfaction, and calls numerous customers each month to assess in detail satisfaction levels.[3]

Customer satisfaction drives profitability. The typical company gets 65 percent of its business from existing customers, and it costs five times more to find a new customer than to keep an existing one happy.[4] Statistics show that growth in market share and financial success are strongly correlated with customer satisfaction. One study found that businesses with a 98 percent customer retention rate are twice as profitable as those at 94 percent. Johnson Controls, Inc. (JCI) discovered that 91 percent of contract renewals came from customers who were either satisfied or very satisfied. A percentage point increase in the overall satisfaction score was worth $13 million in service contract renewals annually. JCI also learned that those customers who gave a "not satisfied" rating had a much higher defection rate. After seeing the financial impact of customer satisfaction, JCI made improving customer satisfaction a key initiative.[5]

Although satisfaction is important, organizations need to look further. First, they must avoid creating dissatisfied customers because of product or service failures. Studies have shown that dissatisfied customers tell at least twice as many friends about bad experiences than they tell about good ones. For example, customers of mass merchandisers shared negative experiences with an average of six people during one Christmas shopping season, and people told about the experiences were up to five times as likely to avoid the store as the original unhappy customer.[6] Second, they must try to develop *loyal* customers—those who stay with a company and make positive referrals. Satisfaction and loyalty are very different concepts. To quote Patrick Mehne, former chief quality officer at The Ritz-Carlton Hotel Company: "Satisfaction is an attitude; loyalty is a behavior." Customers who are merely satisfied may often purchase from competitors because of convenience, promotions, or other factors. Loyal customers place a priority on doing business with a particular organization, and will often go out of their way or pay a premium to stay with the company. Loyal customers spend more, are willing to pay higher prices, refer new clients, and are less costly to do business with. As an example, many years ago Carl Sewell recognized that the average lifetime value of a loyal customer for his Cadillac dealership was over $300,000, providing a clear mandate for developing customer loyalty.[7]

Customer satisfaction and loyalty have evolved into a new concept: **customer engagement** refers to customers' investment in or commitment to a brand and product offerings. Customer engagement is an important outcome of a customer-focused culture and the organization's listening, learning, and performance-excellence strategy. Characteristics of customer engagement include:

Customer engagement was introduced in the 2009–2010 Baldrige Criteria for Performance Excellence as a recognition of its increasing importance to organizations that compete in a global marketplace and in competitive local markets. We will discuss the Baldrige Criteria in Chapter 10.

- customer retention and loyalty,
- customers' willingness to make an effort to do business with the organization, and
- customers' willingness to actively advocate for and recommend the brand and product offerings.

Customer engagement is influenced by an organization's integrity and the relationships it builds with its customers.[8] As one small business owner stated, "We build customer loyalty by telling our customers the truth, whether it is good or bad news."[9]

The American Customer Satisfaction Index[10]

In 1994, the University of Michigan Business School and the American Society for Quality (ASQ) released the first American Customer Satisfaction Index (ACSI), an economic indicator that measures customer satisfaction at the national level. It was the first cross-industry benchmark in the United States to measure customer satisfaction. Similar indexes previously existed in Sweden and Germany. One of the goals of the ACSI is to raise the public's perception and understanding of quality, as do the consumer price index and other economic indicators. This increased awareness will help to interpret price and productivity measures and promote customer-driven quality.

The ACSI is based on customer evaluations of the quality of goods and services purchased in the United States and produced by both domestic firms and foreign firms with a substantial U.S. market share. It uses data from telephone interviews conducted in a national sample of 46,000 consumers who recently bought or used a company's product or service in a tested, multiequation econometric model (see Figure 3.1) that links customer satisfaction to its determinants: customer expectations, perceived quality, and perceived value. Customer satisfaction, in turn, is linked to customer loyalty, which has an impact on profitability. The model is used to compute four levels of indexes: a national customer satisfaction index and indexes for seven industrial sectors, 40 specific industries, and 203 organizations and agencies within those industries.

The 1994 ACSI results provided a baseline against which customer satisfaction levels can be tracked over time. This enables researchers to answer the questions: Are customer satisfaction and evaluations improving or declining for the nation's output of goods and services? Are they improving or declining for particular organizations, sectors of industry, or specific industries? The initial 1994 results showed that nondurable manufacturing scored relatively high in customer satisfaction, whereas public administration and government services scored relatively low. The overall national index declined continually until 1997 but has generally improved overall since. Some of the largest improvements occurred in the retail, finance, and e-commerce sectors.

Magazines and newspapers such as Fortune *and* The Wall Street Journal *generally report current ACSI results. Results and other information are available from the ACSI website, http://www. theacsi.org.*

The index quantifies the value that customers place on products, and thus drives quality improvement. Organizations can use the data to assess customer loyalty, identify potential barriers to entry within markets, predict return on investments, and pinpoint areas in which customer expectations are not being satisfied. The ACSI is updated on a rolling basis with one to three sectors of the economy measured each quarter.

FIGURE 3.1
ACSI Model

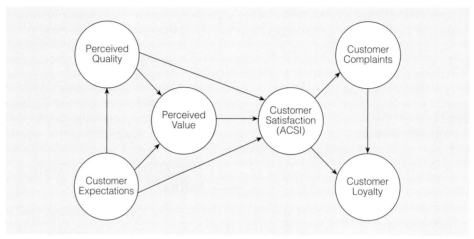

Source: Courtesy of National Quality Research Center (see endnote 11).

IDENTIFYING CUSTOMERS

The first step in being customer focused is to understand who your customers are. While this sounds obvious, the concept of "customer" may mean many different things. Most employees think that "customers" are those people who ultimately purchase and use a company's products. These end users, or **consumers**, certainly are an important group. However, consumers are not the only customer group of concern. The easiest way to identify customers is to think in terms of customer–supplier relationships.

AT&T uses a customer–supplier model as shown in Figure 3.2. Every process receives inputs from suppliers and creates outputs for customers. The feedback loops suggest that suppliers must also be considered as customers. They need appropriate information about the requirements they must meet. Within an organization, the recipient of another's output (which could be a product, service or information) is called an **internal customer**. Internal customers could be other departments or processes within the organization or individual workers. For instance, manufacturing is a customer of purchasing, a nursing unit is a customer of the hospital laundry, and the reservations department is a customer of the information systems department for an airline or hotel. Figure 1.2 in Chapter 1 is a good example of the internal customer–supplier relationships within a typical manufacturing firm. In addition, individual workers receive inputs from others and produce outputs for other internal customers. Some examples

FIGURE 3.2
AT&T's Customer–
Supplier Model

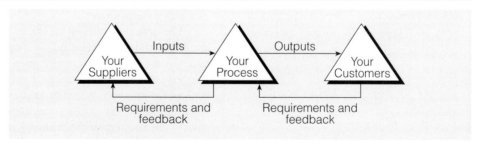

Source: Courtesy of AT&T Archives and History Center.

of these internal customers are the assembly line worker at the next station, an executive's administrative assistant, the order taker who passes along orders to the kitchen staff at McDonald's, or an radiologic technologist who must meet a physician's timely request. Internal customer–supplier relationships help process owners and workers understand how their work links to the final product.

An organization may also have **external customers**—those who fall between the organization and the consumer, but are not part of the organization. External customers have needs and expectations different from consumers. An example is a manufacturer of consumer products that distributes to retail stores such as Walmart and grocery stores. The retail stores are external customers of the manufacturer. They have specific needs for timely delivery, appropriate product displays, accurate invoicing, and so forth.

Identifying customer–supplier relationships begins with asking some fundamental questions:

1. What goods or services are produced by my work?
2. Who uses these products and services?
3. Who do I call, write to, or answer questions for?
4. Who supplies the inputs to my process?

Eventually, everyone can better understand their role in satisfying not only their internal customers, but also the external customers. The natural customer–supplier linkages among individuals, departments, and functions build up the "chain of customers" throughout an organization that connect every individual and function to the external customers and consumers, thus characterizing the organization's value chain.

It is also important to recognize that employees and the public at large are important customers of an organization. Viewing employees as customers, an organization then must consciously strive to build and maintain a work environment conducive to the well-being and growth of all employees by paying attention to health, safety, and ergonomics (the study of physical capabilities of people in the design of workplaces, tools, instruments) issues. An organization must also anticipate public concerns and assess the possible impacts on society of its products, services, and operations, such as safety and the environment. These issues will be addressed in other chapters.

Customer Segmentation

Customers generally have different requirements and expectations. For example, Macy's department stores defines four lifestyles of its core customers: "Katherine"—traditional, classic dresser who doesn't take a lot of risks and likes quality; "Julie"—neo-traditional and slightly more edgy but still classic; "Erin"—a contemporary customer who loves newness and shops by brand; and "Alex"—the fashion customer who wants only the latest and greatest (there's a male version too!).[11] A company usually cannot satisfy all customers with the same products or services. This issue is particularly important for those that do business globally (just think of the differences in regulations for automobiles in various countries or the differences in electrical power systems in the United States versus Europe). Therefore, organizations that segment customers into natural groups and customize the products or services are better able to respond to customers' needs. Segmentation allows a company to prioritize customer groups, for instance by considering for each group the benefits of satisfying their requirements and the consequences of failing to satisfy their requirements.

There are many different ways to approach customer segmentation. Customer segmentation might be based on geography, demographic factors, ways in which products are used, volumes, or expected levels of service. For example, Motorola's Commercial, Government, and Industrial Solutions Sector segments its customers in two ways, first by world region, and second by sales distribution channel (direct and indirect). The Ritz-Carlton Hotel Company ranks potential and current customers by volume, geography, and profit. The Royal Bank of Canada (RBC) identified a key customer segment, "snowbirds," Canadians who spend the winter in Florida or Arizona. These individuals want to borrow in the United States for condos or houses and want to be served by employees who know Canada as well as the United States and even speak French when necessary. So, RBC opened a branch in Florida, which achieved exceptional results.[12]

Juran suggested classifying customers into two main groups: the *vital few* and the *useful many*.[13] For example, organizers of conventions and meetings book large blocks of hotel rooms and have large catering needs. They represent the vital few and deserve special attention on an individual basis. Individual travelers and families are the useful many and typically need only standardized attention as a group.

Another way of segmenting customers with an eye toward business results is by profitability. Many businesses spend a lot of money trying to acquire customers who are not profitable and probably will never be. Profit potential can be measured by the **net present value of the customer (NPVC)**.[14] NPVC is the total profits (revenues associated with a customer minus expenses needed to serve a customer) discounted over time. For instance, the profits associated with customers at an automobile dealer consist of the profit from the sale of a car plus the profit from service visits. The number of transactions associated with repeat customers can easily be estimated. As another example, frequent fliers represent high NPVC customers to an airline. By segmenting them according to their frequency, an airline can determine the net value of offering increasing levels of benefits to fliers at higher frequency levels as a means of retaining current customers or enticing potential customers. Firms can also use NPVC to eliminate customers with low or negative values that represent a financial liability. For example, the Fleet Financial Group dropped its basic savings account interest rate, hoping to lose customers who had only savings accounts.[15]

Segmentation helps an organization to align its internal processes according to the most important customer expectations or their impact on shareholder value. For instance, Fidelity Investments realized that some customers who were doing limited business with Fidelity were using costly resources of service representatives too frequently. They began teaching those customers how to use the company's lowest cost channels: its automated phone lines and its website, which was made friendlier and easier to use. They could still talk to service reps, but the phone system identified their calls and routed them into longer queues as a disincentive to call, so the most profitable customers could be served more quickly. Fidelity was willing to lose some of these customers, because their profitability would increase; however, 96 percent of them stayed and most switched to lower-cost channels.[16]

UNDERSTANDING CUSTOMER NEEDS

At Ideo, one of the world's leading design firms (which designed Apple's first mouse, standup toothpaste tubes, and many other innovative products), design doesn't begin with a far-out concept or a cool drawing. It begins with a deep understanding of the people who might use whatever product or service that eventually emerges from its work, drawing from anthropology, psychology, biomechanics, and other disciplines.[17] Organizations first need to understand the drivers of customer satisfaction—what do customers want or expect from our goods and services? For example, credit card users might have the following expectations for four key business activities associated with the card:

1. *Applying for an Account*: Accessible, responsive, accurate, and professional
2. *Using the Card*: Easy to use and hassle free, features, reasonable fees, and credit limits
3. *Billing*: Accurate, timely, and easy to understand
4. *Customer Service*: Accessible, responsive, and professional

Perhaps one of the best examples of understanding customer needs and using this information effectively is Frank Perdue's chicken business.[18] Perdue learned what customers' key purchase criteria were; these criteria included a yellow bird, high meat-to-bone ratio, no pinfeathers, freshness, availability, and brand image. He also determined the relative importance of each criterion, and how well the company and its competitors were meeting each one. By systematically improving his ability to exceed customers' expectations relative to the competition, Perdue gained market share even though his chickens were premium-priced. Among Perdue's innovations was using a jet engine that dried the chickens after plucking, allowing the pinfeathers to be singed off.

Considerable marketing efforts go into correctly identifying customer needs. Ford, for instance, identified about 90 features that customers want in sales and service, including a ride to their next stop when they drop off a car for service and appointments within one day of a desired date. Ford then trimmed the list to seven service standards and six sales standards against which dealers have begun to measure themselves.[19]

Quality Dimensions of Goods and Services

David A. Garvin suggested that products have multiple dimensions of quality:[20]

1. *Performance*: A product's primary operating characteristics. Using an automobile as an example, characteristics would include such things as acceleration, braking distance, steering, and handling.
2. *Features*: The "bells and whistles" of a product. A car may have power options, a CD player, iPod® connections, satellite radio, and antilock brakes.
3. *Reliability*: The probability of a product's surviving over a specified period of time under stated conditions of use. A car's ability to start on cold days and frequency of failures are reliability factors.
4. *Conformance*: The degree to which physical and performance characteristics of a product match pre-established standards. A car's fit and finish and freedom from noises and squeaks can reflect this dimension.
5. *Durability*: The amount of use one gets from a product before it physically deteriorates or until replacement is preferable. For a car it might include corrosion resistance and the long wear of upholstery fabric.
6. *Serviceability*: The speed, courtesy, and competence of repair work. An automobile owner might be concerned with access to spare parts, the number of miles between major maintenance services, and the expense of service.
7. *Aesthetics*: How a product looks, feels, sounds, tastes, or smells. A car's color, instrument panel design, control placement, and "feel of the road," for example, may make it aesthetically pleasing.

Table 3.2 gives some examples of these dimensions for both a manufactured product and a service product.

Quality Dimension	Manufactured Product (Guitar Amplifier)	Service Product (Checking Account)
Performance	Signal-to-noise ratio; power (wattage)	Speed of online transactions
Features	SD card; drum kits	Automatic bill paying
Conformance	Accurate tuner	Accuracy
Reliability	Mean time to failure	Receiving statements on time every month
Durability	Not damaged with frequent handling and transportation	Keeping pace with industry trends and product offerings
Serviceability	Ease of repair	Prompt resolution of errors
Aesthetics	Location and size of knobs and controls	Appearance of bank lobby

Source: Adapted and modified from Paul E. Pisek, "Defining Quality at the Marketing/Development Interface," Quality Progress, Vol. 20, No. 6, pp. 28–36. Copyright © 1987 American Society for Quality. Reprinted with permission.

Customers today pay more attention to service issues than to the physical goods themselves. One study found that customers are five times more likely to switch because of perceived service problems than for price concerns or product quality issues. Another estimated that the average company loses as many as 35 percent of its customers each year, and that about two-thirds of these are lost because of poor customer service. Thus, an understanding of service-related needs and expectations is important. For services, research has identified five principal dimensions that contribute to customer perceptions of quality:

1. *Reliability*: The ability to provide what was promised, dependably and accurately. Examples include customer service representatives responding in the promised time, following customer instructions, providing error-free invoices and statements, and making repairs correctly the first time.
2. *Assurance*: The knowledge and courtesy of employees, and their ability to convey trust and confidence. Examples include the ability to answer questions, having the capabilities to do the necessary work, monitoring credit card transactions to avoid possible fraud, and being polite and pleasant during customer transactions.
3. *Tangibles*: The physical facilities and equipment, and the appearance of personnel. Tangibles include attractive facilities, appropriately dressed employees, and well-designed forms that are easy to read and interpret.
4. *Empathy*: The degree of caring and individual attention provided to customers. Some examples might be the willingness to schedule deliveries at the customer's convenience, explaining technical jargon in a layperson's language, and recognizing regular customers and calling them by name.
5. *Responsiveness*: The willingness to help customers and provide prompt service. Examples include acting quickly to resolve problems, promptly crediting returned merchandise, and rapidly replacing defective products.

| **EXAMPLE 3.1** | Classifying Customer Needs on Dimensions of Service Quality |

A car rental agency surveys its customers on the following dimensions.

- Cleanliness of the rental facility
- Courtesy of staff
- Efficiency of vehicle pickup/return
- Cleanliness of vehicle
- Professionalism of staff in explaining the contract and options

We may classify each of these according to the five service quality dimensions as follows:

1. Cleanliness of the rental facility: *tangibles*
2. Courtesy of staff: *assurance*
3. Efficiency of vehicle pickup/return: *reliability*
4. Cleanliness of vehicle: *tangibles*
5. Professionalism of staff in explaining the contract and options: *assurance*

Note that none of these dimensions address empathy or responsiveness. Later in this chapter we will discuss how to design good customer surveys.

The Kano Model of Customer Requirements

Noriaki Kano, professor emeritus of the Tokyo University of Science. suggested segmenting customer requirements into three groups:

1. *Dissatisfiers ("must haves")*: Basic requirements that customers expected in a product or service. In an automobile, a radio, heater, and basic safety features are examples, which are generally not stated by customers but assumed as given. If these features are *not* present, the customer is dissatisfied.
2. *Satisfiers ("wants")*: Requirements that customers expressly say they want. Many car buyers want a sunroof, satellite radio, or navigation system. Although these requirements are generally not expected, fulfilling them creates satisfaction.
3. *Exciters/delighters ("never thought of")*: New or innovative features that customers do not expect or even anticipate, such as separate rear-seat video controls that allow children to watch DVD movies, or wi-fi capabilities in a car, but love once they have them.

Providing dissatisfiers and satisfiers is often considered the minimum required to stay in business. These can usually be identified from surveys, complaints, and interviews with lost customers. To be truly competitive, however, organizations must surprise and delight customers by going beyond basic requirements and expressed desires. Hospitals, for example, are introducing numerous innovations in patient care services that are designed to change traditions. These not only include significant improvements in food services—Doylestown Hospital in Philadelphia started an "At Your Request" program offering gourmet selections—as well as other amenities such as in-room massages, video-on-demand, wireless access, and even champagne in maternity wards.[21] To innovate, organizations can exploit the creativity of its leaders (think of Steve Jobs at Apple) and employees, opinions and suggestions from outside expert advisors and customer focus groups, and ideas captured from new technology forums.

Innovations, however, are not exciters/delighters for long. As customers become familiar with them, exciters/delighters become satisfiers over time. For instance, antilock brakes and traction control certainly were exciters/delighters when they were first introduced, but now many car buyers expect them when buying a new car. Likewise, navigation systems, which were originally exciters/delighters, are probably viewed as satisfiers today. As technology evolves, consumer expectations continually increase. Eventually, satisfiers become dissatisfiers.

In the Kano classification system, dissatisfiers and satisfiers are relatively easy to determine through routine marketing research. For example, the hot-selling Ford F-150 pickup truck relied on extensive consumer research at the beginning of the redesign process. However, traditional market research efforts may not be effective in understanding exciters/delighters, and may even backfire. Ford listened to a sample of customers and asked whether they wanted a fourth door on one of its minivans. Only about one-third thought it was a great idea, so Ford scrapped the idea. Chrysler, on the other hand, spent a lot more time living with owners of vans and observing their behavior, watching them wrestle to get things in and out, noting all the occasions where a fourth door would really be convenient, and was very successful after introducing a fourth door.[22]

Gathering the Voice of the Customer

Customer requirements, as expressed in the customer's own terms, are called the **voice of the customer**. However, the customer's meaning is the crucial part of the message. As the vice president of marketing at Whirlpool stated, "The consumer speaks in code."[23] Whirlpool's research showed that consumers wanted clean refrigerators, which could be interpreted to mean that they wanted easy-to-clean refrigerators. After analyzing the data and asking more questions, Whirlpool found out what most consumers actually wanted was refrigerators that looked clean with minimum fuss. As a result, Whirlpool designed new models to have stucco-like fronts and sides that hide fingerprints.

When former Disney executive Paul Pressler assumed the CEO position at Gap, he met with each of Gap's top 50 executives, asking them such standard questions as "What about Gap do you want to preserve and why?" "What about Gap do you want to change and why?" and so on. But he also added one of his own: "What is your most important tool for figuring out what the consumer wants?"[24] Organizations use a variety of methods, or "listening posts," to collect information about customer needs and expectations, their importance, and customer satisfaction with the company's performance on these measures. Some of these approaches for gathering customer information include comment cards and formal surveys, focus groups, direct customer contact, field intelligence, complaint analysis, and monitoring the Internet and social media. Each has various advantages and disadvantages.

- *Comment Cards and Formal Surveys*: Comment cards and formal surveys are easy ways to solicit customer information. These approaches typically concentrate on measuring customer satisfaction, which is discussed later in this chapter, and often include questions pertaining to the customers' perception of the importance of particular quality dimensions as well as open-ended questions. However, few customers generally will respond to comment cards placed at restaurant tables or in hotel rooms, and those who do may not represent the typical customer. Formal surveys can be designed to scientifically sample a customer base, but can also suffer from nonresponse bias. However, some organizations find that they work well.
- *Focus Groups*: A focus group is a panel of individuals (customers or non-customers) who answer questions about a company's products and services as well as those of competitors. This interview approach allows a company to carefully select the composition of the panel and probe panel members about important issues, such as

comparing experiences with expectations, in depth. Key questions that one might ask include: What do you like about the product or service? What pleases or delights you? What do you dislike? What problems have you encountered? If you had the ability, how would you change the product or service? Binney & Smith, maker of Crayolas, conducts focus groups with the ultimate customer: young children. Focus groups offer a substantial advantage by providing the direct voice of the customer to an organization. A disadvantage of focus groups is their higher cost of implementation compared to other approaches.

- *Direct Customer Contact*: In customer-driven organizations, top executives commonly visit with customers personally. Hearing issues and complaints firsthand is often an eye-opening experience. For example, Black & Decker executives have gone to homeowners' workshops to watch how customers used their tools, asked why they liked or disliked certain ones, and even observed how they cleaned up their work space when they finished.

- *Field Intelligence*: Any employee who comes in direct contact with customers, such as salespeople, repair technicians, telephone operators, and receptionists, can obtain useful information simply by engaging in conversation and listening to customers. The effectiveness of this method depends upon a culture that encourages open communication with superiors. As another approach, employees simply observe customer behavior. One hotel noticed that customers did not use the complimentary bath crystals, so they eliminated the crystals (saving costs) and added other features that customers wanted. Field intelligence is perhaps one of the least-exploited approaches to listening and learning.[25] To do it well, organizations need to build awareness of the need to gather information, develop a system to feed information to a central collecting place for analysis and dissemination, train employees who have frequent direct customer contact to actively listen to the voice of the customer and feed information back through the system, make review of the information a standard part of the company's management review process, and ensure that the right individuals take action and follow up.

- *Complaints*: Complaints, although undesirable from a service point of view, can be a key source of customer information. Complaints allow an organization to learn about product failures and service problems, particularly the gaps between expectations and performance. Hewlett-Packard, for example, assigns every piece of customer feedback to an "owner" in the company who must act on the information and report back to the person who called. If a customer complains about a printer, someone will check the company's database to see if the complaint is widespread and what the company is doing about it.

- *Internet and Social Media Monitoring*: The Internet and social media such as Facebook offer organizations a fertile arena for finding out what consumers think of their products. Internet users frequently seek advice from other users on strengths and weaknesses of products, share experiences on service quality, or pose specific problems they need to resolve.[26] By monitoring the conversations on discussion groups and blogs, for example, managers can obtain valuable insights on customer perceptions and product or service quality problems. In open forums, customer comments can often be translated into creative product improvements. In addition, the Internet can be a good source of information about competitors' products. The cost of monitoring Internet conversations is minimal compared to the costs of other types of survey approaches, and customers are not biased by any questions that may be asked. However, the conversations may be considerably less structured and unfocused, and thus may contain less usable information. Also, unlike a focus group or telephone interview, inaccurate perceptions or factual errors cannot be corrected. Social media such as Facebook and Twitter can also provide a wealth of information. K&N Management, for example, monitors social media activity using an analytical marketing tool to measure guest engagement.

Many leading organizations use a combination of multiple listening posts to gather customer information, and then cross-check the results for validity and synthesize the information. Figure 3.3 shows the wide variety of listening and learning approaches for different customer segments used by Nestlé Purina PetCare Company, which makes a variety of dog and cat food products. In this figure, "consumer" refers to the pet owners who purchase their products, while "customer" refers to the retailers (external customers) that stock and sell the products in their stores. Of course, pets are important customers also!

Some organizations use unconventional and innovative approaches to understand customers. Texas Instruments created a simulated classroom to understand how mathematics teachers use calculators; and a manager at Levi Strauss used to talk with teens who were lined up to buy rock concert tickets. The president of Chick-fil-A, and all other corporate employees, spend at least one day each year behind the counter. The president has camped out overnight with customers at over a dozen store openings in just one year. At Whirlpool, when customers rate a competitor's product higher in satisfaction surveys, engineers take it apart to find out why. They also have hundreds of consumers fiddle with computer-simulated products while engineers record the users' reactions on videotape.[27]

Besides consumers, organizations must also pay attention to the needs of external customers. In designing its Icy Rider sled, Rubbermaid used a combination of field research, competitive product analysis, and consumer focus groups. It also listened to major

FIGURE 3.3   Customer Listening Posts at Nestlé Purina PetCare Company

Customer Listening Method	Purpose
Consumer	
Millward Brown Surveys	Determine brand awareness/image
Nielsen Data	Monitor consumer product usage
Panel Data	Monitor consumer behavior
Advertising score	Measure TV ad effectiveness
Consumer complaints/feedback	Obtain consumer feedback
Focus groups	Get detailed feedback on products
New product testing	Evaluate extended usage/feedback
Customer	
"Top-to-Top" meetings with each key customer	Understand unique goals/strategies and high-level issues/concerns
Joint volume planning meetings	Align tactical execution
Monthly business meetings with each key account	Review tactical execution; make necessary adjustments
Customer Advisory Councils	Learn about industry trends
Meetings with NPPC CDG VP at each key account	Assess quality of account management & execution; learn about key strategic issues

Source: Malcolm Baldrige Award Application Summary

retailers, such as Walmart, who wanted such products to be stackable and save space.[28] Sometimes, attention to the needs of external customers offers opportunities to provide exciters/delighters. General Electric (which makes aircraft engines for the airline industry) provided Six Sigma specialists to Southwest Airlines at no cost to work on problems that had nothing to do with GE products. GE also offers training in its management techniques, shares its expertise in working globally, and allows customers to tap into market information and basic research developed by its business units. As one GE executive noted, "The more successful our customers are, the more successful we will be."[29]

Understanding the needs of internal customers is as important as understanding those of consumers and external customers. This point is reflected in the AT&T customer–supplier model in Figure 3.2. For example, in many service industries, customer-contact employees depend on a variety of information and support from internal suppliers, such as the information systems department, warehousing and production scheduling, and engineering and design functions. Failure to meet the needs of customer-contact employees will have a detrimental effect on external customers. A division of the former General Telephone and Electronics Corporation (now Verizon), GTE Supply, negotiated contracts, purchased products, and distributed goods for internal telephone operations customer groups at each GTE local telephone company. In response to complaints from its internal customers, GTE Supply began to survey its internal customers to identify needs and information for improvement. This approach dramatically improved satisfaction levels, reduced costs, and decreased cycle times.[30]

Analyzing Voice of the Customer Data

Because voice of the customer data typically consists of a large number of verbal comments or other textual information, it needs to be sorted and consolidated into logical groups so that managers can understand the key issues. One useful tool for organizing large volumes of information efficiently and identifying natural patterns or groupings in the information is the **affinity diagram**. An affinity diagram is a main ingredient of the KJ method, developed in the 1960s by Kawakita Jiro, a Japanese anthropologist. The affinity diagram is a technique for gathering and organizing a large number of ideas or facts.[31]

EXAMPLE 3.2

Creating an Affinity Diagram for Customer Needs

Suppose that a banking team determined that the most important requirement for mortgage customers is timely closings.[32] Through focus groups and other customer interviews, customers listed the following as key elements of timely closings:

1. Expeditious processes
2. Reliability
3. Consistent and accurate information
4. Competitive rates
5. Notification of industry changes
6. Prior approvals
7. Innovation
8. Modem link between computers
9. Buyer orientation
10. Diversity of programs
11. Mutual job understanding
12. Flexibility
13. Professionalism
14. Timely and accurate status reports

The company's team would group these items into logical categories (Post-It® notes are often used because they can be easily moved around on a wall) and provide a descriptive title for each category. The result is an affinity diagram, shown in Figure 3.4, which indicates that the key customer requirements for timely closings are communication, effective service, and loan products.

FIGURE 3.4
Affinity Diagram

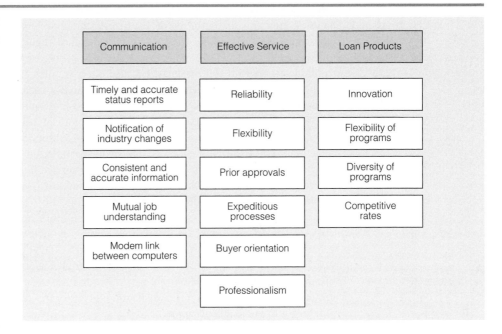

Through organization of an affinity diagram, information can be used to better design a company's products and processes to meet customer requirements. Affinity diagrams can be used for many other applications. For example, they can be used to organize any large group of complex ideas or issues, such as potential reasons for quality problems, or things a company must do to successfully market a product.

Modern methods of business analytics, such as text mining and text analytics, can automate the process of capturing and analyzing huge amounts of textual data, and are emerging as important tools for understanding customers. Text analytics allows users to break down sentences linguistically and extract meaningful data that can be searched, summed, counted, and otherwise statistically analyzed.

 **QUALITY**SPOTLIGHT
JetBlue

JetBlue Airways receives nearly 500 e-mails from passengers every day and more than 40,000 survey responses per month.[33] Additional feedback is obtained from an online customer survey of thousands of "TrueBlue" members. Half the data are written responses to open-ended questions in unstructured text. It simply was not cost efficient or even possible to read or analyze all the comments. Nevertheless, customer relationship managers wanted to understand and analyze customer sentiment and be able to drill down into issues and requests. As a result, JetBlue decided to implement text analytics software to help automate the process of tracking and analyzing the customer feedback. The software automatically extracts relevant data from survey responses, e-mail messages, web forums, blog entries, news articles, and other customer communications to provide analysts and managers with deeper insights into customer satisfaction, sentiment, and loyalty. In addition to active daily, weekly, and monthly analysis of customer feedback, managers at JetBlue receive customized reports that summarize the customer feedback, allowing executives and managers to make informed decisions about the company's long-term strategic activities.

LINKING CUSTOMER NEEDS TO DESIGN, PRODUCTION, AND SERVICE DELIVERY

VOC information must be linked to design, production, and delivery processes. Consider e-commerce, for example. A study of Internet bank service found that customers perceived quality along three broad categories: customer service quality, banking service product quality, and online systems quality.[34] The quality dimensions that were important to customers included:

- *Customer Service Quality:* reliability, responsiveness, competence, courtesy, credibility, access, communication, understanding the customer, collaboration, and continuous improvement;
- *Banking Service Product Quality:* product variety/diverse features; and
- *Online Systems Quality:* content, accuracy, ease of use, timeliness, aesthetics, and security.

However, the research suggested that Internet banks have been doing a poor job in meeting these needs. There was a clear disconnect between the customer requirements and the processes that were supposed to meet those requirements. While banks have been incorporating more technology into their service processes, a study by Accenture found that few customers believed that technology has improved the quality of service; in fact, 62 percent did not think that technology has helped at all.[35]

 QUALITYSPOTLIGHT

Advanced Circuits

A good example of one company that understands the linkage between customer needs and its processes is Advanced Circuits, a small Denver manufacturer of printed circuit boards.[36] In struggling to compete with offshore competitors, Advanced Circuits took a close look at its customers and their needs, and redesigned their processes enabling them to cut prices by 50 percent, triple production capacity, and double profitability. They began with a clear customer segmentation strategy: while they couldn't compete for production orders with long lead times, they could compete successfully where delivery time was critical—generally three days or fewer—or when orders were too small to interest big manufacturers with large production setup costs. They combined different jobs in the same production run, thus minimizing the material used in each batch, reducing production costs, and increasing capacity. They also discovered that customers need prototypes for boards quickly during the design process, often in two or three days, they need only a very small quantity, and they often need to communicate directly with the fabricator about design specifications.

To support this strategy, they mailed brochures describing a fixed pricing matrix. This in itself was revolutionary in the industry. Prior to that time, all quotes were individually requested and delivered. They also added credit card capability and the promise that prototype orders would be delivered on time or they'd be free. The Internet was used to provide better and faster service, such as enabling engineers to enter design parameters online, which allowed them to return quotes instantly. (Even today, many competitors take up to a week to return a quote.) Customers began to use the quote engine as a design tool. Because they could get quotes so fast, they were able to experiment with different board designs, densities, and geometries. As the company founder noted, "Customer focus is a great device for motivating employees because it removes all ambiguity from the decision-making process. Our view is, if it's good for our customers, it's probably good for us."

One way of understanding the linkage of the VOC to internal process is what is often called the **gap model**. Figure 3.5 provides a view of the process in which customer needs and expectations are translated into design, production, and delivery processes. True customer needs and expectations are called *expected quality*. Expected quality is what the customer assumes will be received from the product. The producer identifies these needs and expectations and translates them into specifications for products and services. *Actual quality* is the outcome of the production process and what is delivered to the customer. Customers will assess quality and develop perceptions (*perceived quality*) by comparing their expectations (expected quality) with what they receive (actual quality). If expected quality is higher than actual quality, then the customer will probably be dissatisfied. On the other hand, if actual quality exceeds expectations, then the customer will be satisfied or even surprised and delighted.

Actual quality may differ considerably from expected quality if information gets lost or is misinterpreted from one step to the next in Figure 3.5 (hence the "gaps"). For instance, ineffective market research efforts may incorrectly assess the true customer needs and expectations. Designers of products and services may develop specifications that inadequately reflect these needs. Manufacturing operations or customer-contact personnel may not deliver according to the specifications. Thus, producers should make every effort to ensure that actual quality conforms to expected quality and minimize the potential gaps between what customers want and what they actually get. Good internal communication among organizational functions is important.

Figure 3.5 also suggests that organizations need good communication with customers.[37] Customers may not use the product correctly or may have unreasonable expectations about what it can do, marketing sometimes makes promises it cannot keep, or advertising is misleading. Thus, organizations need to pay greater attention to overall

FIGURE 3.5
The Gap Model

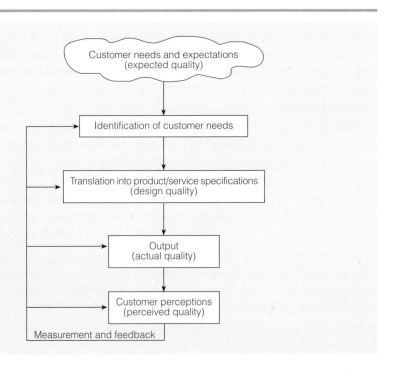

customer experiences that impact perceptions. Such attention might include better user manuals or information on product packaging as well as unambiguous advertising.

A great way of linking the voice of the customer to service delivery processes is through empowered employees (see Chapter 4 for more detailed discussion of this concept). For instance, employees at the specialty grocery chain Trader Joe's talk and listen extensively to customers and are empowered to take action to meet their needs. They can open any product a customer wants to taste and are encouraged to recommend products they like and be honest about items they don't. All store employees can e-mail buyers directly with ideas or feedback from customers. Trader Joe's store design and inventory stems directly from listening to its customers.[38]

BUILDING A CUSTOMER-FOCUSED ORGANIZATION

Creating a customer-focused organization takes hard work and discipline. It must be built on good policies, good people, and good processes. A good example of a customer-focused organization is Deer Valley Ski Resort. Everything about Deer Valley—from its facilities, services, and processes, and the interaction between employees and guests—is designed to focus on the customer. It is no wonder that Deer Valley is consistently rated as the best ski resort in North America by ski enthusiast magazines.

QUALITYSPOTLIGHT
Deer Valley Ski Resort

Deer Valley Ski Resort in Park City, Utah, is viewed by many as the premier U.S. ski resort, providing exceptional services and a superior ski vacation experience. The resort offers curbside ski valet service to take equipment from vehicles, parking lot attendants to ensure efficient parking, and a shuttle to transport guests from the lot to Snow Park Lodge. Guests walk to the slopes on heated pavers which prevent the pavement from freezing and assist in snow removal. The central gathering area by the base lifts is wide and level, allowing plenty of room to put on equipment and easy access to the lifts. At the end of the day, guests can store their skis without charge at each lodge. The resort limits the number of skiers on the mountain to reduce lines and congestion, and offers complimentary mountain tours for both expert and intermediate skiers. Everyone is committed to ensuring that each guest has a wonderful experience, from "mountain hosts" stationed at the top of the lifts to answer questions and provide directions, to the friendly workers at the cafeterias and restaurants, whose food and service is consistently highly rated. "Our goal is to make each guest feel like a winner," says Bob Wheaton, vice president and general manager. "We go the extra mile on the mountain, in our ski school, and throughout our food-service operation because we want our guests to know they come first."[39]

An organization fosters customer satisfaction and engagement by developing trust, communicating with customers, and effectively managing the interactions and relationships with customers through its processes and its people. Customer-focused organizations focus on four key processes:

1. Making sincere commitments to customers
2. Ensuring quality customer contact
3. Selecting and developing customer contact employees
4. Managing complaints and service recovery

Customer Commitments

Organizations that truly believe in the quality of their products make sincere commitments to their customers. Effective commitments address the principal concerns of customers, are free from conditions that might weaken customers' trust and confidence, and are communicated clearly and simply to customers. A customer commitment might be as simple as guaranteeing that your call or e-mail inquiry will be returned promptly. (Have you ever encountered a website with a disclaimer "We cannot always answer every question that we receive"?) Many commitments take the form of explicit guarantees and warranties. An extraordinary guarantee that promises exceptional, uncompromising quality and customer satisfaction, and backs that promise with a payout intended to fully recapture the customer's goodwill with few if any strings attached is one of the strongest actions a company can take to improve itself.[40] L.L. Bean's guarantee is a good example: "Everything we sell is backed by a 100 percent unconditional guarantee. We do not want you to have anything from L.L. Bean that is not completely satisfactory. Return anything you buy from us at any time for any reason it proves otherwise."

Customer Contact and Interaction

Customers interact with organizations in many different ways. Every interaction between a customer and the organization—whether it be face-to-face with a salesperson or customer service representative or online on a website—is called a **moment of truth**. During moments of truth, customers form perceptions about the quality of the service by comparing their expectations with the actual outcomes. Thus, customer satisfaction or dissatisfaction takes place during moments of truth.

> *The term "moment of truth" was coined by the CEO of Scandinavian Airlines System, Jan Carlzon.*

Consider an airline, for example. Moments of truth occur whenever a customer makes a reservation, buys tickets online, checks in online or at the airport, checks baggage, boards a flight, orders a beverage, requests a magazine, deplanes, and picks up baggage. Multiply these instances by the number of passengers and the number of daily flights, and it is easy to see that hundreds of thousands of moments of truth occur each day. Each occurrence influences a positive or negative image about the company.

QUALITYSPOTLIGHT

Southwest Airlines

Southwest Airlines recognizes the power of customer focus.[41] Known for its legendary service, the Southwest culture ensures that it serves the needs of its Customers (with a capital C) in a friendly, caring, and enthusiastic manner. Every one of the approximately 1,000 customers who write to the airline get a personal response (not a form letter) within four weeks, and frequent fliers get birthday cards. The airline even moved a flight up a quarter-hour when five medical students who commuted weekly to an out-of-state medical school complained that the flight got them to class 15 minutes late. To quote the CEO, "We dignify the Customer." This statement applies to internal customers also; it is not unusual to find pilots helping ground crews unload baggage. As one executive stated, "We are not an airline with great customer service. We are a great customer service organization that happens to be in the airline business." Southwest's customer commitment was apparent in the hours after the September 11 terrorist attacks. The top executives swiftly agreed to grant refunds to all customers who asked for them, regardless of ticket restrictions, despite the fact that it might have cost them several hundred million dollars. Refund claims never came; in fact, one loyal customer sent in $1,000 to support Southwest after the attacks. Southwest has consistently been the most profitable U.S. airline.

Customer-focused organizations make it easy for customers to conduct business. Procter & Gamble was the first company to install a toll-free number for its products in 1974. Today, e-mail and website access are the media of choice for many consumers. For example, Premier, Inc. provides a wide variety of avenues for customers to seek assistance, conduct business, and make complaints or suggestions. These include toll-free telephone, Internet, a Customer Solution Center, customer advisory committee meetings, product user group meetings, field staff site visits, technical assistance fax, regional performance improvement forums, and product support centers. The City of Coral Springs provides a website, CityTV, CityRadio, CityBlog, Customer Care Center, a quarterly magazine, annual report, neighborhood and business meetings, and advisory boards and committees.

Customer contact requirements are measurable performance levels or expectations that define the quality of customer contact with an organization. These expectations might include technical requirements such as response time (answering the telephone within two rings or shipping orders the same day), or behavioral requirements (using a customer's name whenever possible). St. Luke's Hospital has translated its understanding of how patients want to be treated and involved and has established a clear set of 12 Customer Contact Requirements (see Figure 3.6).

Selecting and Developing Customer Contact Employees

Customer-contact employees are particularly important in creating customer satisfaction as they often are the only means by which a customer interacts with an organization.

FIGURE 3.6   St. Luke's Hospital of Kansas City Customer–Contact Requirements

1. Greet patients/guests by introducing myself, address patients/guests by last name unless otherwise told.
2. Ask sincerely, "How may I help you?"
3. Knock, request permission to enter the room, and explain what I am going to do.
4. Complete initial assessment on all patients within eight hours.
5. Acknowledge all patient/guests requests, and be accountable for follow-up.
6. Address all complaints within 24 hours or less.
7. Introduce any replacement caregiver.
8. Promote family-centered care: listen thoughtfully to all patients/guests, and provide timely communication to the appropriate person(s) for action.
9. Respect and acknowledge diversity, culture, and values of my patients, their family, visitors, and my co-workers.
10. Maintain confidentiality of all information.
11. Know, or have access to, legal and regulatory requirements and standards of care related to my specific responsibilities.
12. Thank my customers for choosing Saint Luke's Hospital.

Source: Malcolm Baldrige National Quality Award Application Summary, 2003, National Institute of Standards and Technology, Department of Commerce, Courtesy of St. Luke's Health System.

As Jim Miller, president of Prime Performance noted about the banking industry, "For most customers tellers don't just represent the bank. They are the bank. That's why their behavior and attitudes are so important. ... Successful service depends on simple actions. These include greeting the customer immediately upon entering the lobby, smiling, using the customer's name, saying "thank you," and being helpful. Quick, accurate transactions are crucial, but most banks excel at this. So, it isn't a competitive advantage."[42]

Procter & Gamble calls its consumer relations department the "voice of the company." A staff of more than 250 employees handles in excess of three million contacts each year. Their mission is stated as "We are a world-class consumer response center. We provide superior service to consumers who contact Procter & Gamble, encourage product repurchase, and help build brand loyalty. We protect the Company's image and the reputation of our brands by resolving complaints before they are escalated to government agencies or the media. We capture and report consumer data to key Company functions, identify and share consumer insights, counsel product categories on consumer issues and trends, and manage consumer handling and interaction during crises."

Businesses must carefully select customer contact employees, train them well, and empower them to meet and exceed customer expectations. Many businesses begin with the recruiting process, selecting those employees who show the ability and desire to develop good customer relationships; for example, Procter & Gamble seeks people with excellent interpersonal and communication skills, strong problem-solving and analytical skills, assertiveness, stress tolerance, patience and empathy, accuracy and attention to detail, and computer literacy. Job applicants often go through rigorous screening processes that might include aptitude testing, customer-service role-playing exercises, background checks, credit checks, and medical evaluations.

Next, organizations must train them. For many organizations, customer relationship training involves every person who comes in contact with customers. For example, the customer contact requirements at St. Luke's Hospital are incorporated into a new patient-focused care delivery model and all health care team members are trained in these contact requirements. All employees receive a VIP (Very Important Principles) card with these requirements and they are posted throughout the hospital. Customer-contact employees must understand the products and services well enough to answer any question, develop good listening and problem recovery skills, and feel able to handle problems. Fairmont Hotels created an orientation program to help new employees understand what it feels like to be a guest, even having their cars valet-parked and staying in the hotel for a night. The Ritz-Carlton Hotel Company follows orientation training with on-the-job training and, subsequently, job certification. The company reinforces its values daily, recognizes extraordinary achievement, and appraises performance based on expectations explained during the orientation, training, and certification processes.

Service Recovery and Complaint Management

Despite all efforts to satisfy customers, every business experiences unhappy customers. Complaints can adversely affect business if not dealt with effectively. A company called TARP, formerly known as Technical Assistance Research Programs, Inc., conducted studies that revealed the following information:[43]

1. The average company never hears from 96 percent of its unhappy customers. Dissatisfied individual and business customers tend not to complain. For every complaint

received, the company has 26 more customers with problems, six of whom have problems that are serious.

2. Of the customers who make a complaint, more than half will again do business with that organization if their complaint is resolved. If the customer feels that the complaint was resolved quickly, the figure jumps to 95 percent. On the other hand, experiences of customers who remain unsatisfied after complaining result in substantial amounts of negative word of mouth.

Service recovery is a vital element to maintaining customer relationships. Studies in the service management literature suggest that customers who rated service quality highly also had the highest expectations for service recovery. Loyal customers are most likely to become dissatisfied when problems are not resolved but are most likely to increase or maintain loyalty whenever the problem is deemed to have been resolved successfully. However, non-loyal customers show the greatest likelihood of decreasing their loyalty even when a failure is resolved. This suggests that there is much to gain from responding to service failures to nonloyal customers, but it also highlights how difficult this may be to accomplish.[44] An example of the impact of service recovery on customer satisfaction was reported in a *Fortune* magazine article:

> *A global hotel chain was stunned to discover a perverse consequence of its customer-centric Six Sigma quality initiative. Apparently guests were mildly pleased by the chain's sincere efforts to provide a hassle-free stay. But what really moved the customer-satisfaction needle was how well the hotel responded when something went wrong. Guests who had experienced a problem that was quickly and politely resolved rated the hotel service higher than guests who had had no problems at all. What's more, more guests with happy resolution of their hassle said they were likely to recommend the hotel than did the trouble-free guests.[45]*

Customer-focused organizations consider complaints as opportunities for improvement. Encouraging customers to complain, making it easy for them to do so, and effectively resolving complaints increases customer loyalty and retention. A compelling story was related by a Walmart customer in a letter to *Fortune* magazine. He had telephoned Walmart's headquarters to complain about its store in La Plata, Argentina. The switchboard immediately rang the vice president of international operations, who thanked him for calling, asked detailed questions, and inquired whether he was willing to repeat his story to the Latin American VP, to whom he was transferred immediately. He was then asked if he would be willing to talk to the Argentinean store manager; 10 minutes later he received the call from La Plata. The customer observed, "On my next trip to Argentina, a year later, the store had been transformed. No wonder Walmart is the world's largest retailer."

Many organizations have well-defined processes for dealing with complaints. For example, at Figure 3.7 shows the process used by Cargill Corn Milling (CCM), a manufacturer of value-added corn- and sugar-based products. The basic steps are to record the incident, investigate, identify, review, and implement corrective action. Throughout the process, CCM contacts the customer to seek information and verify that the corrective action was effective. All incidents are entered in the Customer Relationship tracking (CRT) system within 24 hours of notification. The database allows the company to review data by time periods, types of nonconformances, product, customer, location, department, or functional area.

In dealing with complaints, employees need to listen carefully to determine the customer's feelings and then respond sympathetically, ensuring that the complaint is understood. They should make every effort to resolve the problem quickly. This should include

FIGURE 3.7 Complaint Management Process at Cargill Corn Milling

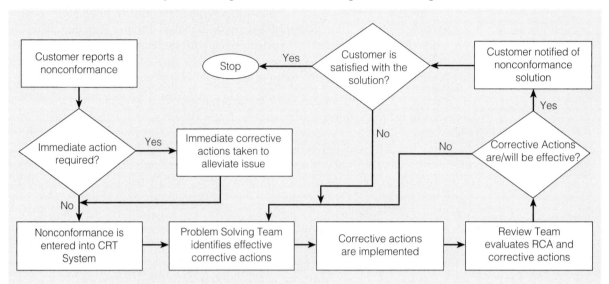

Source: Cargill Corn Milling 2008 Baldrige Award Application Summary – Public Version; www.nist.gov/baldrige.

first acknowledging that a customer had a problem ("We're sorry you had a problem") to express empathy for the inconvenience that the customer encountered; willingly accepting the complaint ("Thanks for letting us know about it"); describe corrective action concisely and clearly ("Here's what we're going to do about it"); and appealing to the customer for continued loyalty ("We'd appreciate you giving us another chance"). The objective is to leverage the complaint into long-term customer loyalty.[46]

Many organizations have meaningful acronyms to help employees remember service recovery steps. For example, Poudre Valley Health System uses CARE: *Clarify* the customer's concerns and expectations, *Apologize* and acknowledge the problem, *Resolve* the problem and *Explain* how the problem will be fixed. Starbucks' Service Recovery process is *Listen, Acknowledge, Take* action, *Thank* the person, and *Encourage* to return—appropriately known by LATTE. Regardless of the approach or name, what is important is that a process is followed and everyone is trained to apply it.

Customer-focused organizations empower their front-line people to do whatever is necessary to satisfy a customer. At The Ritz-Carlton, all employees can do whatever it takes to provide "instant pacification." No matter what their normal duties are, other employees must assist if aid is requested by a fellow worker who is responding to a guest's complaint or wish. Ritz-Carlton employees can spend up to $2,000 to resolve complaints with no questions asked. However, the actions of empowered employees should be guided by a common vision; that is, employees require a consistent understanding of what actions they may or should take.

To improve products and processes effectively, organizations must do more than simply respond to a customer's complaint. They need a systematic process for collecting and analyzing complaint data and then using that information for improvements. The Ritz-Carlton, for example, uses Guest Incident Action forms, which are aggregated on a monthly basis at each hotel, to ensure that complaints were handled effectively and steps taken to eliminate the cause of the problem.

MANAGING CUSTOMER RELATIONSHIPS

Excellent organizations foster close relationships with customers that lead to high levels of satisfaction and loyalty. For example, Lexus owners who become accustomed to the at-home pickup of their vehicles for service, free loaners, and other special dealer touches such as concierge service may find it difficult to give up these services when it is time to purchase a new car. In Bank of Montreal's Private Client Services group, bankers provide services according to the preferences of their clients who value convenience and time, not the traditions of the bank. These preferences might mean meeting in the client's home or office instead of the bank.[47]

Customer relationships can be fostered through strategic partnerships and alliances and using technology to facilitate better communication with customers and linkages to internal operations.

Strategic Partnerships and Alliances

Today's suppliers are being asked to take on greater responsibilities to help their customers. As organizations focus more on their core competencies—the things they do best—they are looking outside their organizations for assistance with noncritical support processes. **Customer–supplier partnerships**—long-term relationships characterized by teamwork and mutual confidence—represent an important strategic alliance in achieving excellence and business success. Benefits of such partnerships include access to technology or distribution channels not available internally, shared risks in new investments and product development, improved products through early design recommendations based on supplier capabilities, and reduced operations costs through better communications. For example, FedEx and Jostens formed a strategic partnership that enabled both to benefit from new sales of scholastic jewelry and yearbooks.[48] They took advantage of each other's strengths: Jostens provided a high-quality product with superior service, and FedEx provided reliable high-volume, short-interval delivery for these time-critical products.

Many organizations work closely with suppliers that share common values. This close relationship improves supplier capabilities by teaching them quality-related tools and approaches. Although many businesses have formal supplier certification programs (discussed in Chapter 5) in which they rate their suppliers, some ask suppliers to rate them as customers. Motorola established a 15-member council of suppliers to rate Motorola's practices and offer suggestions for improving, for example, the accuracy of production schedules or design layouts that Motorola provides.[49] Some typical questions that might be asked of their suppliers include:[50] What expectations do you have that are not being met? What type of technical assistance would you like from us? What type of feedback would you like from us? What benefits are you looking for in a partnership? Better two-way communication can improve both products and relationships.

Customer-Focused Technology

Technology can greatly enhance an organization's ability to leverage customer-related information and provide improved customer service. For instance, Continental Airlines' online system alerts the company when planes arrive late and assesses passengers' needs, delaying departures of other flights or sending carts to make connections easier; the BT Group revamped its self-service web portal used by customers to manage telecom accounts and linked it to the system used by the company's customer support staff to improve consistency.[51]

Another company that exploits technology in developing customer relationships is Tsutaya, Japan's largest video, book, and CD chain.[52] Using a point-of-sale system that facilitates real-time inventory tracking between headquarters and franchises and a website and wireless site called Tsutaya Online (TOL), Tsutaya tracks purchases, demographic data, spending behavior, and by implication, lifestyles and interests. This system enables them to offer personalized product recommendations. For example, if you bought a CD by a certain artist, TOL will e-mail a digital music clip when the next album debuts. Tsutaya also developed a sophisticated recommendation engine to match a customer's video rental history and mood to the ideal movie selection. Many other organizations, such as Netflix, Blockbuster, and Amazon.com, use technology in similar ways. Grocery and retail stores use loyalty cards to capture and analyze detailed data about customer purchase behavior.

Technology is a key enabler of **customer relationship management (CRM)** software, which is designed to help organizations increase customer loyalty, target their most profitable customers, and streamline customer communication processes. A typical CRM system includes market segmentation and analysis, customer service and relationship building, effective complaint resolution, cross-selling goods and services, order processing, and field service.

CRM helps firms gain and maintain competitive advantage by:

- Segmenting markets based on demographic and behavioral characteristics
- Tracking sales trends and advertising effectiveness by customer and market segment
- Identifying which customers should be the focus of targeted marketing initiatives with predicted high customer response rates
- Forecasting customer retention (and defection) rates and providing feedback as to why customers leave a company
- Studying which goods and services are purchased together, leading to good ways to bundle them
- Studying and predicting which Web characteristics are most attractive to customers and how the website might be improved

CRM systems provide a variety of useful operational data to managers, including the average time spent responding to customer questions, comments, and concerns; average order tracking (flow) time; total revenue generated by each customer (and sometimes their family or business) from all goods and services bought by the customer; and the total picture of economic value of the customer to the firm, cost per marketing campaign, and price discrepancies.

MEASURING CUSTOMER SATISFACTION AND ENGAGEMENT

Customer feedback is vital to a business. Through feedback, a company learns how satisfied its customers are with its products and services and sometimes about competitors' products and services. Measurement of customer satisfaction and engagement completes the loop shown in Figure 3.5. For example, BI uses three approaches to track customer satisfaction: a Transactional Customer Satisfaction Index for immediate feedback, an annual Relationship Customer Satisfaction Index to learn about specific attributes of satisfaction and intent for repeat business, and a competitive study to see how it performs relative to competitors. SSM Health Care uses standardized surveys that are customized to its five major patient segments, informal discussions with patients and families, and focus groups to understand satisfaction and dissatisfaction. They use online analytical processing software to drill down to a particular nursing unit, for example, to examine inpatient loyalty and compare those to other units within a hospital or across the corporation. Then, they distribute results electronically that identify specific improvements that will give the greatest gains in patient satisfaction to executives and patient satisfaction coordinators.

An effective customer satisfaction measurement system results in reliable information about customer ratings of specific product and service features and about the relationship between these ratings and the customer's likely future market behavior. Customer satisfaction and engagement measurement allows an organization to do the following:

1. Discover customer perceptions of how well the organization is doing in meeting customer needs, and compare performance relative to competitors.
2. Identify causes of dissatisfaction and failed expectations as well as drivers of delight to understand the reasons why customers are loyal or not loyal to the company.
3. Identify internal work process that drive satisfaction and loyalty and discover areas for improvement in the design and delivery of products and services, as well as for training and coaching of employees.
4. Track trends to determine whether changes actually result in improvements.

Customer satisfaction measures may include product attributes such as product quality, product performance, usability, and maintainability; service attributes such as attitude, service time, on-time delivery, exception handling, accountability, and technical support; image attributes such as reliability and price; and overall satisfaction measures. Comparisons with key competitors can be especially insightful. Businesses often rely on third parties to conduct blind surveys to determine who key competitors are and how their products and services compare. Competitive comparisons often clarify how improvements in quality can translate into better customer satisfaction or whether key quality characteristics are being overlooked. For example, the city of Portland, Oregon, mails a survey annually to about 10,000 of its citizens, asking them to rate the performance of the police department, water bureau, environmental services, and public transportation. The city also asks them if they feel safe walking at night in their neighborhoods, parks, and downtown; whether the streets are clean enough, how they feel about recreation services offered, and how they rate the livability of the city. The results are benchmarked against six other cities, and if Portland is not doing as well, the mayor tries to find out why.[53]

It is important to understand that customer satisfaction is a psychological attitude. It is not easy to measure, and can only be observed indirectly. The ACSI model in Figure 3.1 shows that customer satisfaction is influenced by customer expectations and perceptions of quality and value. Thus, it is difficult to reduce these complex relationships into a single measure.

Designing Satisfaction Surveys

The first step in developing a customer satisfaction survey is to determine its purpose. Surveys should be designed to clearly provide the users of the survey results with the information they need to make decisions. A critical question to consider is "Who is the customer?" Managers, purchasing agents, end users, and others all may be affected by a company's products and services. Xerox, for instance, sends specific surveys to buyers, managers, and users. Buyers provide feedback on their perceptions of the sales processes, managers provide input on billing and other administrative processes, and users provide feedback on product performance and technical support.

Customer satisfaction measurement should not be confined to external customers. Information from internal customers also contributes to the assessment of the organization's strengths and weaknesses. Often the problems that cause employee dissatisfaction are the same issues that cause dissatisfaction in external customers. Many organizations use employee opinion surveys or similar vehicles to seek employee feedback on the work environment, benefits, compensation, management, team activities, rewards and recognition, and company plans and values. However, other indicators of employee satisfaction are absenteeism, turnover, grievances, and strikes, which can often supply better information than surveys that many employees may not take seriously.

The next issue to address is who should conduct the survey. Independent third-party organizations often have more credibility to respondents and can ensure objectivity in the results. After these preliminary steps are completed, it is necessary to define the sample frame; that is, the target group from which a sample is chosen. Depending on the purpose of the survey, the frame might be the entire customer base or a specific segment. For example, a manufacturer of commercial lawn tractors might design one survey for golf course superintendents who purchase the tractors and another for end users who ride them daily.

Next, we must select the appropriate survey instrument. Formal written surveys by mail or e-mail are the most common means of measuring customer satisfaction, although other techniques, such as face-to-face interviews, telephone interviews, and focus groups are used. Written surveys have the advantage of low data collection costs, self-administration, and ease of analysis; when used, they should be kept short and simple. In addition, they can probe deeply into the issues. However, they suffer from high nonresponse bias, require large sample sizes, and generally measure predetermined perceptions of what is important to customers, thus reducing the scope of qualitative information that can be obtained. Face-to-face interviews and focus groups, on the other hand, require much smaller sample sizes and can generate a significant amount of qualitative information, but incur high costs and participant time commitments. Telephone interviews fall somewhere in between these extremes. Telephone interviews appear to be the preferred approach for companies with a limited number of business customers; mail-based surveys are used to track routine transactions, where key attributes are stable over time. For example, Toyota uses mail surveys to identify unhappy customers and then telephones them for more details. This approach is cost-effective when the majority of customers are satisfied.[54]

Customer satisfaction surveys are difficult to design properly, and you can find many examples of poor and ineffective surveys at many restaurants and retailers. Some surveys are too long; others are too short. It is important to choose carefully the questions that matter the most to customers. One should avoid leading questions, compound questions that address more than one issue or idea, ambiguous questions, acronyms and jargon that the respondent may not understand, and double negatives.

The types of questions to ask in a survey must be properly worded to achieve actionable results. By **actionable**, we mean that responses are tied directly to key business processes, so that what needs to be improved is clear; and information can be translated into cost/revenue implications to support the setting of improvement priorities. Many survey questions lack reliability—that is, they often do not reflect the attribute being measured, or different customers interpret the questions differently. For example, the question "How would you rate the quality of service?" for a restaurant is too ambiguous and provides little actionable information. Some people might interpret service quality as the amount of attention the server provided; others might interpret the question as whether the server could answer questions about the menu or whether food was delivered too quickly or too slowly. Better questions would be: "How attentive was the server to your needs?"; "Was the server able to answer your questions about the menu?"; and "How was the pace of your meal?" More specific questions allow the user to identify the source of any dissatisfaction. Open-ended questions such as "What one thing did you like most about your visit?" or "What one thing could we do to improve your experience?" often provide useful information. Most surveys also ask for basic demographic information to stratify the data.

A "Likert" scale is commonly used to measure the response (see Table 3.3). Likert scales allow customers to express their degree of opinion. Five-point scales have been shown to have good reliability and are often used, although 7- and even 10-point scales are common. Responses of "5" tell a company what it is doing very well. Responses of "4" suggest that customer expectations are being met, but that the company may be vulnerable to competitors. Responses of "3" mean that the product or service barely meets customer expectations and that much room for improvement exists. Responses of "1" or "2" indicate serious problems. However, most scales like these exhibit response bias; that is, people tend to give either high or low values. If responses are clustered on the high side, it is difficult to discriminate among responses, and the resulting skewness in the distribution causes the mean value to be misleading.

One example of a simple satisfaction survey from a local restaurant is shown in Figure 3.8. The survey seeks feedback about not only their food, but potential dissatisfiers such as cleanliness, service, and employee attitude. It also includes space for open-ended comments. Questions that are missing, however, are the likelihood of returning and referring others, which studies have shown are closely linked to customer loyalty.

The final task is to design the reporting format and the data entry methods. Modern technology, such as computer databases in conjunction with a variety of statistical analysis tools, assists in tracking customer satisfaction and provides information for continuous improvement. As a final note, surveys should always be pretested to: determine whether instructions are understandable, identify questions that may be misunderstood or poorly worded, determine how long it takes to complete the survey, and determine the level of customer interest.

Graniterock Company is a California manufacturer of high-quality construction materials for road and highway construction and maintenance and for residential and commercial building construction. Its major product lines include rock, sand, and gravel aggregates, ready-mix concrete, blacktop, and other products. Surveying its principal customer groups is one of the key approaches Graniterock uses to improve customer satisfaction. The surveys ask respondents to rate factors in buying concrete, not

TABLE 3.3 Examples of Likert Scales Used for Customer Satisfaction Measurement	Very Poor	Poor	Neither Poor nor Good	Good	Very Good
	1	2	3	4	5
	Strongly Disagree	Disagree	Neither Agree nor Disagree	Agree	Strongly Agree
	1	2	3	4	5
	Very Dissatisfied	Dissatisfied	Neither Satisfied nor Dissatisfied	Satisfied	Very Satisfied
	1	2	3	4	5

FIGURE 3.8
Hilton Hotel Guest
Survey

IZZY'S CARES!

Pleasing you is our objective. We want our customers to enjoy the food and experience of Izzy's - your comments will help us in maintaining our high standards for service, quality, value & enjoyment. Kindly take a minute to complete this card. Please drop off at cash register, place in mail, or comment online at www.izzys.com. Thanks for your help and hurry back!

John Geisen - President

_____ _____ _____ AM/PM
Location   Date   Time

☐ Take-Out   ☐ Breakfast ☐ Lunch   ☐ Dinner
☐ Eat-In   ☐ PLATTERS/PARTY TRAY

Please rate the following:	Excellent	Good	Fair	Poor
Cleanliness	☐	☐	☐	☐
Service	☐	☐	☐	☐
Employee attitude	☐	☐	☐	☐
Portions	☐	☐	☐	☐
Taste	☐	☐	☐	☐
Value	☐	☐	☐	☐
Atmosphere	☐	☐	☐	☐

Are you a: Travel time to IZZY'S:
☐ First time person   ☐ 1 to 10 minutes
☐ Occasional patron   ☐ 11 to 20 minutes
☐ Regular patron   ☐ More than 20 minutes

WAS THE SERVICE PROMPT? _____
RESTROOMS CLEAN & SUPPLIED? _____
DINING AREA & UTENSILS CLEAN? _____

WHAT DID YOU HAVE TO EAT? _____
_____
_____

COMMENTS: _____
_____
_____
_____
_____
_____

MORE QUESTIONS:
Do you have any suggestions for new menu items?
_____
_____

Please send: Catering Info.☐ Take-out Menu☐ Party Tray Info.☐

Optional:
Name: _____
Address: _____
City _____ State _____ Zip _____
Phone: _____
E-mail: _____

Source: www.izzys.com

FIGURE 3.9
Graniterock
Customer Impor-
tance Survey

What is important to YOU?

Please rate each of the following on a scale from 1 to 5 with 5 being most important in your decision to purchase from a supplier.

Importance	Concrete Least . . . Most	Building Materials Least . . . Most
Responsive to special needs	1 2 3 4 5	1 2 3 4 5
Easy to place orders	1 2 3 4 5	1 2 3 4 5
Consistent product quality	1 2 3 4 5	1 2 3 4 5
On-time delivery	1 2 3 4 5	1 2 3 4 5
Accurate invoices	1 2 3 4 5	1 2 3 4 5
Lowest prices	1 2 3 4 5	1 2 3 4 5
Attractive credit terms	1 2 3 4 5	1 2 3 4 5
Salespeople's skills	1 2 3 4 5	1 2 3 4 5
Helpful dispatchers	1 2 3 4 5	1 2 3 4 5
Courteous drivers	1 2 3 4 5	1 2 3 4 5
Supplier resolves problems fairly and quickly	1 2 3 4 5	1 2 3 4 5

Please write in any other items not listed above which are very important to you in making your purchase decision:

_____

_____

Source: Reprinted with permission of Graniterock.

only from Graniterock, but from competitors as well. (Figure 3.9 shows such a survey.) Through information obtained from the surveys, Graniterock determined that the most important factors to customers in order of importance are on-time delivery, product quality, scheduling (ability to deliver products on short notice), problem resolution, price, credit terms, and salespeople's skills. Annually, the company surveys customers and noncustomers to obtain a "report card" on their service (see Figure 3.10). Graniterock repeats the survey every three or four years as priorities change, particularly if the economy changes. The surveys also ask open-ended questions about what customers like and dislike.[55]

Analyzing and Using Customer Feedback

Deming stressed the importance of using customer feedback to improve a company's products and processes (refer to Figure 1.3 in Chapter 1). By examining trends in customer satisfaction measures and linking satisfaction data to its internal processes, a business can see its progress and areas for improvement. Someone must have the responsibility and accountability for developing improvement plans based on customer satisfaction results. Many businesses, for example, tie managers' annual bonuses to customer satisfaction results. This practice acts as an incentive for managers and a direction for their efforts.

Good customer satisfaction measurement identifies processes that have high impact on satisfaction and distinguishes between low performing processes low performance and those that are performing well. One way to evaluate customer satisfaction and use it effectively is to collect information on both the importance and the performance of key quality characteristics. For example, a hotel might ask how important check-in speed, check-out speed, staff attitude, and so on, are, as well as how the customer rates the

FIGURE 3.10
Graniterock Cus-
tomer Report Card

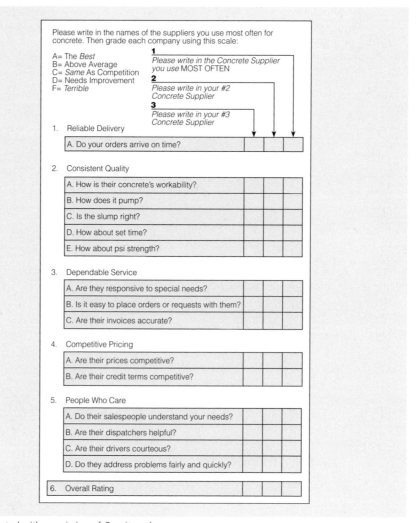

Source: Reprinted with permission of Graniterock.

hotel on these attributes. Evaluation of such data can be accomplished using a grid similar to the one shown in Figure 3.11, on which mean performance and importance scores
for individual attributes are plotted.[56] Results in the diagonal quadrants (the shaded
areas) are good. A firm ideally wants to achieve high performance on important characteristics, and not to waste resources on characteristics of low importance. Results off the
diagonal indicate that the firm either is wasting resources to achieve high performance
on unimportant customer attributes (overkill), or is not performing acceptably on important customer attributes, leaving the firm vulnerable to competition. The results of such
an analysis can help target areas for improvement and cost savings, as well as provide
useful input for strategic planning. Often, competitor data are also plotted, providing a
comparison against the competition. Graniterock Company, featured in the last section,
uses this approach. The results of their importance survey and competitive performance
survey are summarized and plotted on an importance/performance graph to assess the
strengths and vulnerabilities of the company and its competitors. The scales are chosen

FIGURE 3.11
Performance-
Importance
Comparison

Importance	Performance	
	Low	High
High	Vulnerable	Strengths
Low	Who cares?	Overkill

so that each axis represents the industry average. Graniterock looks at the distance between its ratings and those of the competitors. If the ratings are close, customers cannot differentiate Graniterock from its competitors on that particular measure. By posting these graphs on bulletin boards at each plant, the company ensures that all employees, particularly salespeople, are fully informed of the survey results.

EXAMPLE 3.3

Analyzing Customer Satisfaction Data

Analyze the following customer satisfaction results (measured on a 5-point scale) for a fast-food restaurant. What recommendations would you make to the managers?

Attribute	Importance	Performance
Fresh buns	4.83	4.80
Cheese is melted	4.26	4.82
Drink is not watery	4.88	4.64
Fries are crisp	4.85	4.80
Fries are seasoned	4.12	4.48
Service is fast	4.93	4.61
Open 24 hours	3.91	4.81
Good variety of food	4.46	3.87
Nutritional data displayed	3.76	4.65
Children's menu available	4.80	3.97
Tables kept clean	4.91	4.89
Low-fat items available	3.62	4.55

Figure 3.12 shows the performance-importance grid. The means are shown by the solid lines and the data labels correspond to the performance measures. The attributes in each quadrant are:

- *Who Cares?*: fries are seasoned, low-fat items available
- *Overkill*: cheese is melted, open 24 hours, nutritional data displayed
- *Vulnerable*: Good variety of food, children's menu available,
- *Strengths*: fries are crisp, service is fast, drink is not watery, tables kept clean, fresh buns

This analysis suggests that efforts should be made to increase food variety and have a children's menu in order to compete in this market. Also, the restaurant may save significant money by not being open 24 hours. Few resources are probably spent on ensuring that cheese is melted or that nutritional data are displayed, so it probably does not make any difference to changes these attributes. The restaurant should maintain its focus on the strengths that are identified.

FIGURE 3.12
Performance-
Importance Com-
parison Example

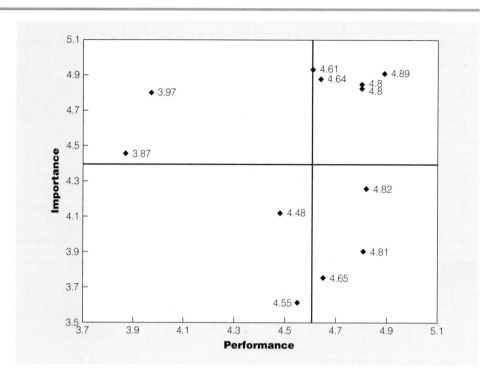

Many organizations have integrated customer feedback into their continuous improvement activities and in redesigning products and services. For example, Skilled Care Pharmacy (see Case Study in Chapter 1), located in Mason, Ohio, is a $25 million privately held regional provider of pharmaceutical products delivered within the long-term care, assisted living, hospice, and group home environments. Skilled Care developed a Customer Grade Card, benchmarked from Baldrige winner Wainwright Industries, to measure customer satisfaction. The Grade Card uses a school-like A-through-D scoring system shown in Figure 3.13. The scores from the four questions covering Quality, Responsiveness, Delivery, and Communication are converted from letters to numbers and averaged. Any questions that were graded C or below generate an immediate phone call or personal visit to the customer by the Customer Care Team to investigate and resolve the issue. An example of how the feedback was used for improvement involved some low scores received for "Delivery." Management determined there was potential risk of losing valuable customers. Upon investigation, it became evident that the issue was not timely delivery, but their system of cut-off times for ordering

FIGURE 3.13   Skilled Care's Customer Grade Card Scoring System

A = Customer Totally Satisfied	100 points
B = Customer Generally Satisfied	90 points
C = Customer Generally Dissatisfied	50 points
D = Customer Totally Dissatisfied	0 points

Source: Reprinted with permission of Skilled Care Pharmacy, Inc.

medications for same-day delivery. If the customer missed the cut-off time, then they did not receive their order until the next day, and, Skilled Care was considered to be "late." Their response to this customer need was to extend pharmacy ordering hours and to aggressively modify staff schedules for the order processing and pharmacy departments. In turn, they were able to offer an additional five hours for customers to phone or fax medication orders for receipt the same day. As a result, satisfaction scores for "Delivery" rose dramatically.

Why Many Customer Satisfaction Efforts Fail[57]

Determining and using customer satisfaction information should be viewed as a key business process. Just going through the motions can often lead to failure. A. Blanton Godfrey suggests several reasons why customer satisfaction efforts fail to produce useful results.

1. *Poor measurement schemes.* Just tracking the percentage of "satisfied and very satisfied" customers on a five-point Likert scale provides little actionable information. Many surveys provide biased results because few dissatisfied customers respond, or the surveys lack adequate sample sizes or randomization. Survey designers need appropriate understanding of statistical concepts.
2. *Failure to identify appropriate quality dimensions.* Many surveys address issues the company thinks are important, not what customers think. This error results from a lack of capturing reliable information about customer needs and expectations.
3. *Failure to weight dimensions appropriately.* Even if organizations measure the right things, they may not understand which dimensions are important. As a result, they spend too much effort on dimensions with the lowest scores that may not be important to the customers. Use of techniques such as importance/performance analysis can help focus attention toward the key dimensions.
4. *Lack of comparison with leading competitors.* Quality and perception of quality is relative. Without appropriate comparative data, competitors may be improving much faster than an organization realizes.
5. *Failure to measure potential and former customers.* Without an understanding of why non-customers do not do business with a company, or more importantly, why customers leave, an organization risks losing market share to competitors and may be headed for demise.
6. *Confusing loyalty with satisfaction.* Customer retention and loyalty provide an indication of the organization's future; satisfaction only relates to the present. The next section addresses this issue.

Measuring Customer Loyalty

We noted earlier in this chapter that satisfaction is different from loyalty. Commonly used factors to measure customer loyalty are:[58]

- Overall satisfaction
- Likelihood of a first-time purchaser to repurchase
- Likelihood to recommend
- Likelihood to continue purchasing the same products or services
- Likelihood to purchase different products or services

- Likelihood to increase frequency of purchasing
- Likelihood to switch to a different provider

Today, many firms use a metric called the **net promoter score (NPS)**, which was developed by (and is a registered trademark of) Fred Reichheld, Bain & Company, and Satmetrix. NPS is claimed to correlate strongly with market and revenue growth. The metric is based on one simple question, "What is the likelihood that you would recommend us?" evaluated on a scale from 0 to 10. Scores of 9 or 10 are usually associated with loyal customers who will typically be repeat customers ("promoters"); scores of 7 or 8 are associated with customers who are satisfied but may switch to competitors ("passives"); and scores of 6 or below represent unhappy customers who may spread negative comments ("detractors"). Promoters are less price-sensitive and are more profitable, while detractors are more-price sensitive, defect at higher rates, and consequently are less profitable. NPS is the difference in the percentage of promoters and detractors.

EXAMPLE 3.4

Calculating a Net Promoter Score

A sample of 300 customers who responded to the question "What is the likelihood that you would recommend us?" resulted in the following:

Score	Frequency
10	63
9	82
8	64
7	41
6	21
5	12
4	6
3	7
2	3
1	0
0	1

The total number of promoters is $63 + 82 = 145$; the total number of detractors is $21 + 12 + 6 + 7 + 3 + 0 + 1 = 50$. As a percentage of the total, these are 48.3 percent and 16.7 percent, so the net promoter score is $48.3\% - 16.7\% = 31.6\%$.

Successful companies such as Trader Joe's, Costco, and Apple may have NPS scores in the 70- to 90-percent range, but scores over 50 percent are good.[59] However, some criticism of the research underlying NPS has been raised, which concluded that NPS is not linked strongly to customer loyalty-based behaviors, and alone does not provide a complete picture of customer intentions.[60] It should be supported by other relevant metrics and approaches to better understand customer behavior.

An alternative to traditional customer satisfaction measurement that focuses more on customer loyalty than on satisfaction is **customer perceived value (CPV)**.[61] CPV measures how customers assess benefits—such as product performance, ease of use, or time savings—against costs, such as purchase price, installation cost or time, and so on, in making purchase decisions. Sellers that provide the greatest CPV at the time of the purchasing decision always win the sale. CPV measurement includes potential buyers rather than just existing customers, is forward-looking rather than retrospective, and examines choices relative to alternatives rather than relative to expectations. Typical questions that are asked include "What benefits are important to you?" and

"How well do you believe that each product or supplier will deliver those benefits?" and focus on perceptions of future value rather than past experiences.

CPV methodology identifies the most important product attributes that prospective customers use to compare one offering against another and their relative importance and performance. One approach for assessing importance is to ask the customer to place a percentage value of importance on each attribute so the total sums to 100 percent, thus eliminating the common problem of giving high ratings to each factor. Asking customers to rate the performance of different offerings on each attribute on a 10-point scale can assess relative performance; the difference in ratings is the relative performance.

EXAMPLE 3.5

Assessing Competitive Performance

In assessing the relative importance of four attributes of a casual restaurant, a customer might assign 30 percent to menu variety, 20 percent to food quality, 10 percent to atmosphere, and 40 percent to value. This essentially provides a ranking of these attributes as value, menu variety, food quality, and atmosphere. In rating the performance of comparing two restaurants, A and B, we might find the following:

Attribute	Relative Importance	Restaurant A	Restaurant B	Relative Performance
Menu variety	30%	8	10	−2
Foot quality	20%	7	4	3
Atmosphere	10%	8	8	0
Value	40%	7	6	1

By multiplying the relative importance values by the performance ratings and summing, we see that restaurant A has a weighted value of 7.4 while restaurant B has a weighted value of 7.0. Therefore, the weighted difference is 0.4. Overall, restaurant A has a higher perceived value but could improve its perceived value by improving its menu variety. Such information becomes the basis for strategic decisions.

SUMMARY OF KEY POINTS AND TERMINOLOGY

The Student Companion Site provides a summary of key concepts and terminology introduced in this chapter.

QUALITY *in* PRACTICE

Harley-Davidson[62]

Harley-Davidson, Inc. was originally founded in 1903 by William S. Harley and brothers Arthur and Walter Davidson. The company is well-known for its high-end cruiser and touring motorcycles, which it designs, manufactures, and sells in North America, Europe/ Middle East/Africa (EMEA), Asia/Pacific, and Latin America. It also offers other products and services:

- Parts & Accessories: replacement parts and mechanical and cosmetic accessories.

- General Merchandise MotorClothes: apparel and riding gear.
- Licensed Products: t-shirts, vehicle accessories, jewelry, small leather goods, toys, and numerous other products.
- Harley-Davidson Museum: In 2008, the Harley-Davidson Museum was opened in Milwaukee, Wisconsin. The 130,000 square foot facility houses the Harley-Davidson Museum and Archives, a restaurant, café, retail store, and special event space. The museum strives to provide a unique experience that the company believes builds and strengthens bonds between the brand and riders as well as the general public.
- Other Services: Harley-Davison also provides a variety of services to its independent dealers including service and business management training programs, customized dealer software packages and delivery of its motorcycles.

Products are marketed to retail customers worldwide primarily through advertising and promotional activities via television, print, radio, direct mailings, as well as electronic advertising and social networks. Additionally, local marketing efforts are accomplished through a cooperative program with the Harley's independent dealers.

Competition in the heavyweight motorcycle market is based upon a number of factors, including price, quality, reliability, styling, product features, customer preference, warranties, and availability of financing (the company also has a Financial Services division). The company builds its competitive advantage in two ways: (1) by supporting the motorcycling lifestyle across a wide demographic range through events, rides, and rallies and (2) by making available the other products and services described above and financing.

Since the 1980s, the company has struggled as it attempted to retain market share, keep unionized workers satisfied, and develop healthy financial results. Its most recent financial report shows both progress and another round of reinventing itself in a tough global economy. Harley-Davidson has long been aware of the vital link between marketing and manufacturing. It has also worked for decades to build brand awareness and customer loyalty.

U.S. retail purchasers of new Harley-Davidson motorcycles include both core and outreach customers and are diverse in terms of age, gender and ethnicity. The company defines its U.S. core customer base as men over the age of 35 and its U.S. outreach customers as women, young adults, and ethnically diverse adults. Harley-Davidson is the market share leader in U.S. new motorcycle registrations in terms of heavyweight (street legal 651cc+) registrations within all its customer definitions including men over the age of 35, women, young adults and ethnically diverse adults.[63] The average U.S. retail purchaser of a new Harley-Davidson motorcycle has a median household income of approximately $85,000. More than three-quarters of the U.S. retail sales of new Harley-Davidson motorcycles are to purchasers with at least one year of education beyond high school and 34 percent of the buyers have college/graduate degrees.[64]

Harley defines its customer segments for heavyweight (651+ cc) motorcycles as:

- Traditional (a basic motorcycle which usually features upright seating for one or two passengers);
- Sportbike (incorporates racing technology, aerodynamic styling, low handlebars with a "sport" riding position and high performance tires);
- Cruiser (emphasizes styling and individual owner customization);
- Touring (incorporates features such as saddlebags, fairings, or large luggage compartments and emphasizes rider comfort and load capacity); and
- Dual (designed with the capability for use on public roads as well as for off-highway recreational use).

The company is also implementing a multigenerational and multicultural customer marketing strategy outside of the United States. As a result, it is establishing definitions for core and outreach customer segments outside of the United States.

Customer focus is one of the key areas of importance in the company. This is clearly reflected in Harley-Davidson's vision:

We fulfill dreams inspired by the many roads of the world by providing remarkable motorcycles and extraordinary customer experiences. We fuel the passion for freedom in our customers to express their own individuality.[65]

Customer experiences have traditionally been at the center of much of the company's marketing. To attract customers and achieve its goals, the company not only participates in motorcycle rallies, both large and small, around the world, but also in major motorcycle consumer shows, racing activities, music festivals, mixed martial arts activities and other special promotional and charitable events. In 1983 they established the Harley Owners Group® concept. Fondly referred to as H.O.G.®, it quickly became the largest factory-sponsored motorcycle club in the world. H.O.G. now has approximately one million members worldwide. This group promotes Harley-Davidson products and the related lifestyle and also sponsors many motorcycle events, including rallies and rides for Harley-Davidson motorcycle enthusiasts throughout the world. In 2010, the company established what it calls a "Creativity Model," whereby it uses web-based crowd-sourcing as a source for its main marketing creative development. Crowd-sourcing draws on the ideas of passionate brand fans around the world to help guide the creative direction of the brand. Harley-Davidson also works closely with outside experts in media, digital marketing, and product placement to expand its marketing impact.

The company's manufacturing strategy is designed to continuously improve product quality and productivity while reducing costs and increasing flexibility to respond to ongoing changes in the marketplace. Flexible manufacturing processes and flexible supply chains, combined with cost-competitive and flexible labor agreements, are the key enablers to respond to customers in a cost-effective manner. The ongoing restructuring of the company's U.S. manufacturing plants, which commenced in 2009, supports the company's efforts to become more flexible and cost competitive allowing it to get the right product at the right time to the customer. To support its international growth initiatives, the company has built CKD (Complete Knock Down) assembly plants in Brazil and India. The CKD plants assemble motorcycles for local markets from component kits produced at U.S. plants and by suppliers.

Key Issues for Discussion

1. How do various dimensions of quality introduced in this chapter align with the quality characteristics that are important to Harley-Davidson and its customers?
2. Discuss how Harley-Davidson's approaches help it to maintain a focus on its customers and enhance customer satisfaction, loyalty, and engagement? You may want to research and include information from recent annual reports.

QUALITY in PRACTICE

Unique Online Furniture, Inc.[66]

Unique Online Furniture, Inc. sells a variety of home furnishings, including bathroom vanities, vessel sinks, faucets, mirrors, light fixtures, and curtain rods, to individual retail clients in the contiguous United States and Canada via several e-commerce websites (UniqueVanities.com, UniqueMirrorsOnline.com, UniqueLightFixture.com, UniqueEcoFurniture.com, and UniqueIronCurtainRods.com).

The company faces competition from a number of competitors, including CSN Stores, eBay, and Amazon. While these competitors offer brand names and low pricing, they lack close, personal customer relationships and communication. Unique Online Furniture exploits these competitive weaknesses in their business model, which is based on the key customer requirements they identified:

1. *Affordability*: Customers want unique items at affordable prices.
2. *Variety*: Customers in our market are looking for variety in home furnishing products that they cannot necessarily find in their local brick and mortar stores.
3. *Online Purchase Security*: When purchasing large ticket items online, our customers want to feel safe and secure during the transaction.
4. *Guarantees or Low Risk*: Customers want the risks of buying sight unseen minimized.

5. *Free or Low Cost Shipping*: Customers want large items delivered to their front door at no additional cost.

Unique Online Furniture offers over two thousand unique products across their websites. Their websites offer a secure online buying experience, and the company is registered with the Better Business Bureau. They also have a satisfaction guarantee return policy, by which clients can return their item for any reason and are only responsible for the cost to ship it back. If there are any problems with an order, they go above and beyond what the average retailer would do. They handle difficult situations in a timely fashion, specific to the client's needs, and with sincerity and integrity.

But it's the personal attention to individual customers that sets them apart. They provide a very high level of client service throughout the buying process. They have a formal client experience process that client service team members follow (see Figure 3.13), and use multiple communication mechanisms—phone, e-mail, and live chat—to meet client's communication needs. This includes a video e-mail from the president thanking them for their order and setting expectations, a personal phone call within 24 hours after an order has been received to confirm all details, a shipping video e-mail to provide detailed instructions on how to properly receive their large item, a video on eco-friendly solutions on how

to dispose of the large amount of packing materials, a gift certificate that can be used on future orders, and a thank-you gift that is wrapped and mailed to every client.

Perhaps more surprisingly, they also treat their suppliers just like their customers, and recognize the people (many of whom are not recognized within their own organizations) that help them in providing a great client experience. For example, they have sent Christmas gifts to the people they work directly with at each manufacturer. Another innovation is a "You Totally Rock" certificate and a small gift that is sent to one person from their manufacturers that went above and beyond expectations in helping them out.

Through these customer-focused approaches, Unique Online Furniture, Inc. has created a large clientele base and a reputation built upon customer service and quality that sets them apart from competitors. And would you be surprised to learn that it's only a four-person organization?

Questions for Discussion

1. How does Unique Online Furniture, Inc.'s key customer requirements compare with the Key Customer-Focused Practices in Table 3.1?

2. Can you suggest other ways to use the Client Experience Checklist (Figure 3.14) to gauge customer satisfaction levels and/or enhance the customer's positive experience with Unique Online Furniture?

FIGURE 3.14   Unique Online Furniture, Inc. Client Experience Checklist

Client Experience Checklist		
Mission	Unique Online Furniture, Inc. will be recognized as the e-commerce shopping experience that has the look and feel of a brick-and-mortar store. We will treat our clients with personal touch points that feel like we shook their hand or gave them a hug. Our clients will feel confident buying from us sight unseen because we will take care of them. We will accomplish this through a focus on the personal and professional development of the people within our organization.	Everyday
Processing Orders Who's responsible: Sales Specialist		
All Orders are to be processed within 24 hours if received by 4pm CST on a business day (M-F), same day; after 4pm CST, next business day		
Client Places Order via Phone/ Internet	All phone orders are processed thru website UNLESS unusual circumstances require thru authorize.net; if processed thru authorize.net, detailed order info needs to be included in notes for clients e-mail reference including initials of processor.	NA

(continued)

FIGURE 3.14   Unique Online Furniture, Inc. Client Experience Checklist (*Continued*)

Client Confirmation E-mail (Automated)	Client Receives Confirmation E-mail from us; Includes Order Status Link, Shipping Info and Return Policy.	Immediate
Thank You E-mail (Automated)	Client Receives Thank You for Your Order E-mail with Video Link http://www.uniquevanities.com/thank-you.html	Immediate
Order Received	Order Received via Internet	Immediate
If Client Confirm Returned Undeliverable	If no-reply e-mail comes thru, forward the confirmation e-mail to the client again.	Immediate
Confirm Availability with Manufacturer	Print Order & Check Availability with Manufacturer via Phone	24 Hours
Client Touch Point: Confirm Order with Client via Phone	Call Client to Confirm Availability & Upsell Other Website Offerings	24 Hours
Client Touch Point: Confirm Order with Client via E-mail	Update Order Status Module with Availability and E-mail Client. If out of stock or DC, prepare a few similar alternatives that are in stock (same size, style and pricing). Use Client Communication Text Templates, personalize based on client communications.	24 Hours
Submit Order	E-mail PO to Manufacturer	24 Hours
Capture Payment	Capture Payment Authorize.net or Paypal	24 Hours
Manufacturer Confirmation	Confirmations received within timelines below	See Timelines (1-3 Bus days)
Schedule Transportation	Schedule Transportation According to Manufacturer Guidelines	Immediate After Mfgr. Confirmation Received
Client Touch Point: E-mail Tracking Info	Check tracking info each evening for all daily pickups, and Update Order Status Module and E-mail Client. Client tracking e-mail includes link to video on shipping and receiving instructions and eco-friendly ways to reuse or recycle packaging materials (website specific) http://www.uniquevanities.com/shipping-receiving-instructions.html http://www.uniquevanities.com/eco-friendly-package-disposal.html Use Client Communication Text Templates, personalize based on client communications.	Same Day as Freight Pick Up
Client Touch Point: Mail GC	Gift Certificates Created at Same Time tracking information e-mails sent, and mailed next day	Same Day as Freight Pick Up
Client Touch Point: Mail Thank You Gift	Mail Thank You Gift (website specific)	Every 2 Weeks
Client Service Follow Up Who's responsible: Operations		
Client Touch Point: E-mail Product Review (Automated)	E-mail Product Review (Automated thru Order Status Module)	Automated 3 Weeks After Order Status Changed to Shipped

(*continued*)

FIGURE 3.14   Unique Online Furniture, Inc. Client Experience Checklist (*Continued*)

Client Touch Point: E-mail Survey	E-mail Survey	Monthly
Read Product Reviews/Surveys	All product reviews and surveys are to be read. Follow up on any concerns presented by clients via phone (primary) e-mail (secondary). Provide solutions to any concerns. Follow up with a note of thanks to any specific comments of praise. Review in Monthly Team Conference Call.	Monthly
Update Testimonials Page	Post authorized testimonials to website, send e-mail to team with a link for all to read. Review in Monthly Team Conference Call.	Monthly
Back Order Follow Up Guidelines		
Back Orders	If accepting orders that are on backorder, then client must be told that you will follow up with them in intervals as follows: if backorder for a month, then will follow up in 2 weeks with an update; if back order for more than a month, then follow up monthly; create a backup order follow up list documenting when you followed up. E-mail is OK; phone call is preferred. Document all communication.	Schedule

REVIEW QUESTIONS

1. What factors influence customer value and satisfaction?
2. What specific issues of customer focus are addressed in the ISO 9000:2000 framework?
3. Summarize the key customer focused practices for performance excellence. Which of these are reflected in Park Place Lexus and K&N Management?
4. Explain the difference between satisfaction and loyalty. Why is loyalty more important?
5. What is customer engagement? How does it differ from satisfaction?
6. Describe the model used in computing the American Customer Satisfaction Index. How might a business use the information from the ACSI database?
7. Explain the difference between consumers, internal customers, and external customers.
8. Explain the AT&T customer–supplier model. Why would it be an important component in training new employees?
9. Why is it important to segment customers? Describe some ways of defining customer segments.
10. Explain the two classifications of quality dimensions for goods and services. Contrast the similarities and differences between the two classifications for services.
11. What is the Kano model, and what are its implications for quality management?
12. What is the voice of the customer? List the major listening and learning approaches used to gather voice of the customer information. What are the advantages and disadvantages of each?
13. Describe how affinity diagrams are used to organize and work with customer-related information.
14. Explain the gap model shown in Figure 3.5. What do expected quality, actual quality, and perceived quality mean, and how do they relate with one another?
15. What is a moment of truth, and how can this concept be used to improve quality?
16. Explain the importance of commitments to building customer relationships.
17. Who are customer contact employees? Why are they critical to an organization?
18. Explain the role of training and empowerment of customer-contact employees in achieving customer satisfaction.

19. What are customer contact requirements? Provide some examples different from those in the book.
20. Why should a company make it easy for customers to complain? Describe the features of an effective complaint management process.
21. List the key factors that should be included in a good service recovery.
22. Why are strategic partnerships and alliances useful to an organization?
23. How can customer relationship management (CRM) software help organizations develop and improve a focus on customers?
24. Why should an organization measure customer satisfaction? Describe the key steps that must be addressed in designing customer satisfaction surveys.
25. What types of questions should be included in customer satisfaction surveys?
26. Explain the concept of importance-performance analysis and its benefit to an organization.
27. Why do many customer satisfaction efforts fail?
28. How is the net promoter score measured? What insights does the score provide to management?
29. What is customer perceived value, and how can an organization benefit from measuring it?

DISCUSSION QUESTIONS

1. Can you describe a customer-focused organization similar to Avis or K&N Management's restaurants with which you have had personal experience? What aspects of the organization impressed you the most?
2. Thinking about organizations that you encounter in your daily life (your college, bookstores, restaurants, and so on), identify examples of customer-focused practices from Table 3.1 that are evident in these organizations.
3. Are you loyal to any particular businesses? Why or why not?
4. Many organizations, such as banks, offer significant incentives to attract new customers, such as $150 to open a new checking account. However, existing customers rarely receive incentives to stay. What do you think of such practices? What are the implications—pro or con—of them?
5. A service representative of a major U.S. airline told a customer about an internal memo that had been circulated called "No Waivers, No Favors," which promises significant and negative consequences to any employee giving a customer special treatment outside of the airline's strict policies. As the employee noted, "Now, nobody is doing anything until we find out what happens to us if we are a little lenient about enforcing a rule. People are scared." Why do you think that management adopted this policy? What implications will it probably have for customers?
6. Construct a list of at least 10 different names for a "customer," for example, buyer, client, and so on.
7. Think about the "supply chain" for filling a doctor's prescription. Describe the different types of customers involved in the process.
8. Recall the AT&T customer–supplier model in Figure 3.2. For each of the following departments in a typical company, discuss who are their internal or external customers and suppliers.
   a. Operations
   b. Information Systems
   c. Human Resources
   d. Mailroom
   e. Payroll
9. How might a college or university segment its customers? What specific needs might each of these customer groups have?
10. You might be familiar with the electronics superstore Best Buy. Like the Macy's example in the chapter, Best Buy has segmented its customer base into fictitious people: Barry—an affluent tech enthusiast, Jill—a busy suburban mom, Buzz—a young gadget fiend, Ray—a price-conscious family guy, and Mr. Storefront—a small business owner.[67] How might this segmentation help the company to better design its stores and train its employees? Suggest some things that the company might do to customize its stores and service to these customer segments.
11. The five dimensions of service quality are important to such retail stores as Walmart and Target. Assuming that these represent key customer requirements, what things might these companies

do in designing their stores and operations to ensure that they meet these requirements?

12. In the context of a fast-food restaurant, make a list of different characteristics that might describe "freshness." Classify them by means of an affinity diagram. What does your response mean for measuring satisfaction of this attribute?

13. How might your school use the gap model in Figure 3.5?

14. Prepare a list of moments of truth that you encounter during a typical quarter or semester at your college or university.

15. Write a generic customer satisfaction policy that a firm might use to convey trust to its customers and as a means of determining employee values, policies, and training initiatives.

16. Discuss the lessons that organizations can learn about customer relationships and customer contact employees from the following experiences:[68]
   a. In shopping for a cell phone, a customer met a salesperson who introduced herself, asked her name, went through the features that related to her needs, and didn't try to sell her the most expensive phone.
   b. A woman encountered a sales person in a home improvement store who commented "Oh, shopping for your husband?"
   c. A couple stranded in a restaurant booth with no waiter or silverware made eye contact with a waitress who quickly replied, "Your waiter is late. I can't take your order because this isn't my station."
   d. While shopping for a TV antenna, a customer asked the difference between various models. The salesperson replied "Some cost more because they look better."

17. If you were the manager of a small pizza restaurant (dine-in and limited delivery), what customer contact requirements might you specify for your employees who take phone orders, work the cash register, and serve as waiters? How would you train them?

18. A manager at a franchise of casual restaurant observed that there are three types of customers who complain: those who feel they should receive exceptional service because of the price they pay; "regulars" who become accustomed to a certain level of food and service quality but perceive some difference; and customers in large groups who often complain about longer waiting times. How might the restaurant address these types of customers?

19. Choose some e-commerce site with which you are familiar. Analyze how "customer-focused" the organization appears to be and provide specific examples to justify your opinions.

20. An article in the *Harvard Business Review* (Matthew Dixon, Karen Freeman and Nicholas Toman, "Stop Trying to Delight Your Customers," July-August 2010, pp. 116–122) suggests that delighting customers by exceeding service expectations does not build loyalty, but that reducing the effort customers must do to get a satisfactory resolution to a service issue does. Do you agree or disagree with these findings and why? Are they necessarily at odds with one another?

21. One of our former students discovered a way to receive great service: Ask for a satisfaction survey before the end of the transaction. In one experience, the student observed an instant change in how she was treated. What does such an experience tell you about the company?

22. A customer survey for a pharmacy asks customers to rate the pharmacy according to the following:
   • Friendly pharmacist
   • Knowledgeable pharmacist
   • Friendly pharmacy technician
   • Knowledgeable pharmacy technician
   • Quick checkout

   They use a 1-5 Likert scale ranging from Disappointed to Excellent. Comment on how actionable this survey is to measure performance and enable the pharmacy to improve. Are there any other things you can suggest to improve the survey?

PROBLEMS

1. *Ski* magazine conducts and annual survey of readers to rate ski resorts. They used the following attributes as the basis for the survey: snow, grooming, terrain variety, challenge, value, lifts, service, weather, access, on-mountain food, lodging, dining, après-ski, off-hill activities, family programs, scenery, terrain parks, and overall satisfaction. Classify each of these attributes using the eight

dimensions of quality (that is, performance, features, etc.).

2. Classify the following customer requirements for a hotel using the five key dimensions of service quality—reliability, assurance, tangibles, empathy, or responsiveness.[69]
   - Hotel equipment is always functioning
   - Hotel staff is knowledgeable to answer guest's questions
   - Hotel has comfortable beds, furniture, and fittings
   - Guests feel safe as services are delivered to their rooms
   - Hotel services are provided as promised
   - Hotel has well-dressed staff
   - Hotel staff is always willing to help guests
   - Hotel furnishings appear to be clean and shiny
   - Guests receive individual attention
   - Guests feel that hotel services are provided at a competitive and affordable price

3. Consider the following customer expectations for a fast-food (quick-service) restaurant. Classify them as dissatisfiers, satisfiers, or exciters/delighters. Justify your reasoning.
   a. Special prices on certain days
   b. Food is safe to eat
   c. Hot food is served hot
   d. Service is friendly
   e. Background music
   f. Playland for children
   g. Restaurant is clean inside
   h. Food is fresh
   i. A "one-bite" money-back guarantee
   j. Orders can be phoned in for pickup at a separate window

4. Table 3.4 is a hypothetical list of customer requirements as determined through a focus group conducted by an airline. Develop an affinity diagram, classify these requirements into appropriate categories, and design a questionnaire to survey customers. Be sure to address any other pertinent issues/questions as well as customer information that would be appropriate to include in the questionnaire.

5. A local franchise of a national car rental firm conducted a survey of customers to determine their perceptions of the importance of key product and service attributes as well as their perceptions of the company's performance.[70] The results are given in Tables 3.5 and 3.6. In Table 3.5, importance was measured on a five-point scale ranging from "not at all important" to "extremely important." Note that Table 3.6 is segmented by personal and business use, and that two different scales were used (the percentage values are based on the percentage of "yes" responses; all others are on a five-point scale from "poor" to "excellent"). What conclusions might you make from these data? What possible improvements can you suggest?

6. Versele Sporting Goods is a family-owned regional sporting goods store located in a small Midwestern town, and competes with a larger national sporting goods chain in a larger city about 40 miles away, as well as major national retail "superstore" with generally lower prices. Versele's specializes is athletic equipment, accessories, and clothing and it seeks to create a competitive advantage through high-quality customer service. Their vision is to be the "best-run sporting goods store in America." They hire people who are passionate about sports, engage in sporting activities so that they can better relate to the products and customers, and cross-train associates so that they are a good knowledge of all product lines, no matter what their personal interests are.

   To better understand what customers value and how they perform relative to their competition, they conducted a survey to rate customers' perceptions for their store and their two main competitors on the following attributes (using a 1–7 Likert scale):
   1. Friendliness of employees
   2. Knowledge of products
   3. Helpfulness in selecting the right product
   4. Store layout
   5. Product availability
   6. Product quality
   7. Ease of checkout
   8. Overall customer satisfaction
   9. Willingness to recommend to others.
      a. Results from the survey, taken from a random sample of 50 customers per month for 12 months, can be found in the Excel file *C03Data.xlsx* on the Student Companion Site. Analyze the data in groups relating to employee attributes, store characteristics and customer attitudes. From your analysis, what might Versele's do to create "exciters/delighters" that would help them compete with the larger national chain and local superstore?

TABLE 3.4
Airline Customer Requirements

- Quality food
- Ability to solve problems and answer questions during flight
- Efficient boarding procedures
- Appealing interior appearance
- Well-maintained seats
- Reservation calls answered promptly
- Timely and accurate communication of information prior to boarding
- Good selection of magazines and newspapers
- Efficient and attentive flight attendants
- Good beverage selection
- Clean lavatories
- Efficient ticket line and waiting procedures
- Convenient ground transportation
- Courteous reservations personnel
- Good-quality audio/visual system
- Sufficient quantity of food
- Interesting in-flight magazine
- Courteous and efficient gate personnel
- In-flight telephone access
- Good variety of audio/visual programming
- Flight attendants knowledgeable of airline programs and policies
- Correct explanation of fares and schedules
- Efficient seat-selection process
- Courteous and efficient sky cap
- Timely and accurate communication of flight information (in-flight)
- Convenient baggage check-in
- Timely baggage check-in
- Comfortable seating and leg room
- Assistance for passengers with special needs
- Courteous ticket counter personnel
- Convenient parking close to terminal
- Ability to solve baggage claim problems
- Ability of reservation agents to answer questions

TABLE 3.5
Importance Ratings of Product/Service Attributes

Mechanical condition of car	4.50
Check-out speed/efficiency	4.35
Cleanliness of vehicle	3.98
Getting reserved car or better	3.85
Friendliness of staff	3.80
Check-in speed/efficiency	3.75
Cleanliness of facility	3.60
Employee appearance	3.52
Getting nonsmoking car	3.50
Speed of coach service	3.29

Source: Adapted from Ralph F. Altman and Marilyn M. Helms, "Quantifying Service Quality: A Case Study of a Rental Car Agency," Production and Inventory Management 36, no. 2 (Second Quarter 1995), 45–50. Reprinted with permission of APICS—The Educational Society for Resource Management, Falls Church, VA.

TABLE 3.6 Customer Ratings of Performance	Personal use	Business use
Mechanical condition of car	4.515	4.710
Check-out speed/efficiency	4.853	4.163
Cleanliness of vehicle	4.929	4.688
Getting reserved car or better	4.259	4.888
Friendliness of staff	96%	91%
Check-in speed/efficiency	4.315	4.105
Cleanliness of facility	4.193	3.500
Employee appearance	100%	100%
Getting nonsmoking car	86%	100%
Speed of coach service	90%	85%

b. Using the five dimensions of service quality, what other attributes might the store include in the survey?

7. Ramsey's Radical Reservations (RRR.com) takes and processes reservations on land, sea, air, and even space travel and prides itself in being a "one-stop" service for adventure travel. Data in spreadsheet *C03Data.xlsx* on the Student Companion Site shows results from 200 customers who were sampled during one representative week. Count the number of responses at each level (10 through 1) and determine the number and percentage of customers at the promoter, passive, and detractor levels. Then calculate net promoter score (NPS). Is it at a high, medium, or low level? What should Ramsey do, considering that this is a typical week's score?

8. Angelina's Beauty Emporium started out with a mission of providing hair care, beauty treatment, and spa services to middle-income women. Angelina would like to move to a more upscale clientele, if possible. She has collected weekly data for the past two years (104 weeks) by asking over 200 clients per week to answer the question: "What is the likelihood that you would recommend us?" evaluated on a scale from 0 to 10. Data can be found in C03-Data.xlsx in the Premium Online Content website. Compute the percentage of respondents who are promoters, passives, and detractors, and then compute the NPS score. (a) Plot these scores on several graphs and give an explanation for possible causes of any trends that you see in the data. (b) Angelina tried a promotion for upscale clients for eight weeks (from week 41 to 49) and four weeks (between weeks 92 and 95). What do the results show?

9. Premier Computer Designs is trying to design a powerful, portable computer targeted toward quality managers. They have surveyed a panel of quality managers and have found that the characteristics that are important to such managers are: speed, active memory, portability, reliability, and price. Premier has two different models that they had the panel to rate. The relative importance percentages and ratings are shown in the table in spreadsheet *C03-Data.xlsx* on the Student Companion Site. Calculate the relative performance and weighted customer perceived value (CPV) of each pilot computer product. Which one should Premier scale up for full production? If they wanted to produce the other design as a "backup," which one characteristic of the second best computer should they try to enhance?

PROJECTS, ETC.

1. Perform some research to examine recent trends in the American Customer Satisfaction Index. What economic sectors show improvement? Which don't? How has the overall index changed?

2. Based on the information in this chapter, propose new approaches for measuring customer satisfaction for your faculty and instructors that go beyond the traditional course evaluation processes that your school may use.

3. You may have visited or purchased items from large computer and software retail stores. In a group brainstorming session, identify those characteristics of such a store that would be most important to you, and design a customer survey to evaluate customers' importance and the store's performance.

4. Interview some managers of small businesses to determine how they respond to complaints and use complaint information in their organizations.

5. Describe some ways that organizations can improve websites and make them more customer-focused. You might consider examining a variety of websites and identifying "best practices."

6. Gather several customer satisfaction surveys or comment cards from local establishments. Analyze them as to their ability to lead to actionable information that will help the organization, and propose any improvements or redesign you deem appropriate.

7. You have undoubtedly made numerous purchases in retail clothing stores such as the Gap, Banana Republic, Old Navy, and so on. Develop a customer satisfaction survey based upon the five service quality dimensions discussed in this chapter. You should have at least two questions for each dimension.

8. This exercise provides an experience with developing an affinity diagram for analyzing complaints and would best be performed by the class as a whole.[71] Each student writes one or more descriptions of personal experiences of frustration and dissatisfaction with products and services. Two examples might be: "Every time I purchase a CD, the seal is difficult and time-consuming to remove. I have even cracked the case a few times while trying to remove it." "I purchased a new pair of running shoes, and the laces were too long." These experiences should be written on large sticky notes and posted on the classroom wall. Students then group the responses into logical categories and develop descriptive headers for each group that explain the causes of dissatisfaction and then create the affinity diagram. For instance, the shoe example might fall into a group titled "Product components are incompatible." An alternative project is to use positive comments about products and services.

9. A number of pizza chains or restaurants are probably located around your college campus. Using a focus group of students, conduct an interview to determine what factors are important in selecting a traditional or pizza restaurant. Once you have identified these factors, design a satisfaction survey to compare perceptions among the most popular restaurants in your area. Ask a sample of students who visited at least to two of them to complete the survey. Analyze the results and draw conclusions in a written report.

10. Design customer satisfaction questionnaires for high school students and their parents who take a campus visit and are considering applying to your school.

11. Find an example of a highly publicized service or product failure in the news (such as unreasonable waiting on a plane on a runway or the poor reception on the first release of the iPhone 4). Research and write a short paper on how the company addressed the problem to recover customer confidence and loyalty.

CASES

ROSIE'S PIZZERIA[72]

Rosie's Pizzeria is a privately-held chain of neighborhood pizzerias with over 50 locations in the Midwest that offers full-service dine-in, carryout, and home delivery. Rosie's competes against such national chains as Pizza Hut, Papa John's, and other local restaurants, yet holds a 45 to 50 percent share in its market area. As part of a new strategic planning process, Rosie's identified growth as a key strategic goal. Because the local market was essentially saturated, however, the executive management team worked on strategies for growing the company for three years and produced no tangible results. One of the reasons for the impasse was the lack of sound, factual data. The executive management team had developed three growth strategies, but could not agree on which one to follow because of a lack of a fact-based foundation for the decision.

A project team was formed to tackle this issue, and was given complete latitude to make any recommendation for an Italian/pizzeria concept based on customer needs and expectations. The team consisted of the marketing director (team leader), two executive vice presidents, the director of operations, two franchise owners, an external strategic business partner, and the CEO, who was the team sponsor. The team felt it was necessary to fully understand the voice of the customer. To do this, they ventured out into the community to ask consumers to express their needs and expectations through their experiences. The team completed numerous in-depth, one-on-one interviews with consumers both inside and outside of their current market area to provide examples of dining incidents these individuals had experienced, seeking "the good, the bad, and the ugly." Here are some responses from customers of current competitors and potential competitors in other markets.

1. "So there I was, like herded cattle, standing on the hard concrete floor, cold wind blasting my ankles every time the door opened, waiting and waiting for our name to be called."
2. "And then I saw a dirty rag being slopped around a dirty table!"
3. "The manager said, 'That's not a gnat, that's black pepper,' so I said I know the difference between black pepper and a gnat, black pepper doesn't have little wings on it!"
4. "When they're that age, going to the bathroom is a full-contact sport—they're reaching and grabbing at everything, and you're trying to keep them from touching anything because the bathroom is so dirty."

Questions for Discussion

1. What were the customers actually saying in the four responses given in this case? Translate them into customer requirements using actionable business language.
2. In addition to your responses to question 1, the voice of the customer process identified the following customer requirements: food and drinks at their proper temperature, fresh food, meeting the unique needs of adult guests as well as families, exceeding service expectations, an easy to read and understand menu, and caring staff. Suggest how these customer requirements can be translated into production and service delivery processes and activities.
3. Conduct a similar mock voice of the customer process for your school or college. What did you learn?

PAULI'S RESTAURANT AND MICROBREWERY

You have been appointed General Manager of Pauli's Restaurant and Microbrewery, a popular downtown pub in a major city, after working there for several years as a waiter and recently a shift manager. Pauli's has locations in six regional cities and operates a corporate website. One of the features of the website is a customer feedback section that is sent directly to the corporate VP and to the appropriate General Manager. After your first weekend on the job, you received the following comment:

We had a lousy service experience last Saturday at your restaurant. We eat there several times a year before the theater and had 6:15 reservations, with which we are usually done eating—including dessert—by 7:30 or 7:40 at the latest to get to the theater in time. Service was ridiculously slow. We finally ordered dessert around 7:20–7:25 and it took at least 10 minutes for the waitress to come back and tell us they didn't have the coconut key lime pie that was listed on special; we ordered something else and waited and waited. Eventually, we had to find the waitress and tell her to forget it because we didn't have time. My wife tried to flag her down for half an hour to get her coffee refilled. To top it off, we didn't even receive an apology; the only thing she did quickly was to process the check. She was clearly over-committed to too many tables to provide us with adequate service. Very disappointing for what we considered one of our favorite places, especially as we were bringing friends with us who had never been there before.

Draft a response to this customer. Analyze the responses of your classmates. What makes a good "service recovery" response? Develop some general guidelines.

FIRST INTERNET RELIABLE BANK

First Internet Reliable (FIR) Bank was started in 1994 by Mimi Livingstone, the daughter of a prominent banker in Redmond, Washington, and two men. Livingstone had worked for five years at Washington Mutual Bank and then quit to earn her MBA at the University of Washington. She teamed up with two "techies"—Marvin Arbol and Nick Sistemas—who had gone to the same Seattle suburban high school as Bill Gates, who graduated from there some ten years earlier. Arbol and Sistemas worked at Microsoft in the late 1980s after they had graduated from prestigious universities with degrees in software engineering, and had led teams that pioneered in the development of some of Microsoft's most popular products. Having accumulated a substantial amount in Microsoft stock options, they decided to leave Microsoft and do something different by helping Livingstone start her bank.

With their combination of skills and excellent insights into technology, Livingstone, Abol, and Sistemas foresaw that the Internet could be used to deliver innovative banking services, beginning at the local level, and expanding regionally, nationally, and internationally as growth and technological maturity permitted.

The goals of FIR Bank were:

- To pioneer banking over the Internet, locally, nationally, and internationally
- To develop a network to initially provide loan services and stock trading, but later to add additional products such as individual and commercial accounts, as the business growth warranted
- To provide customer service that reached or exceeded service found at a "bricks and mortar" bank at a lower cost than was traditionally expected
- To make financial information about loans, investing and financial services available online through such downloadable materials as a quarterly newsletter, booklets, audio-visual and other "state of the art" media, as web technology permitted
- To avoid the temptation that was becoming evident among other Internet companies to "grow like crazy," burn through the cash of venture capitalists and other investors, take the company public, and sell out

Internet Banking 1995–2000

At the time that Livingstone, Arbol, and Sistemas started FIR, they were both visionary and practical. They understood that, initially, customers of Internet banks come from innovation-minded, busy people who are technologically advanced. They also knew that there were many limitations to this form of enterprise that included:

- Internet banks don't have "bricks and mortar" offices and branches open to customers
- The "product" is intangible, unlike books or flowers
- Security is a major concern
- Customer expectations vary widely
- Regulation is heavy in the banking industry
- Profit margins are narrow

However, many advantages existed for starting an Internet bank in 1995, including:

- There is no direct competition in the banking sector
- The costs of "bricks and mortar" can be avoided
- Many of the transactions that bank clerks and tellers do can be automated
- Electronic infrastructure available at reasonable costs is rapidly being built
- If volumes can be "ramped up" costs per transaction will rapidly decrease
- Reliable operations can be built electronically for high volumes of transactions

FIR Bank grew and prospered in the last years of the twentieth century and survived growing competition from copycat Internet banks and later from the "bricks and mortar" banks that saw the growing threat and promise of Internet banking. Many banks got in too late to make it a profitable business, but it became something that a bank had to do because of competition. FIR Bank stuck to their strategy, and Livingstone, Arbol, and Sistemas matured in their ability to grow with a constant eye on customer and market needs.

Internet Banking 2001–Present

After the September 11, 2001 attack on the World Trade Center and the Dot.Com Internet bust that occurred almost simultaneously, there were fewer banks of every variety, but the Internet banking competition got tougher.

A nationwide survey, done in 2004, showed the team at FIR that some of the key characteristics of online bank customers were:[73] *Broadband and online experience.* Sixty-three percent of those with broadband Internet capability at home have tried online banking, compared with 32 percent of those with dial-up connections. And 51 percent of those who have more than six years of internet experience have tried banking online, compared to 27 percent of those with three years or less of online experience.

- *The rise of GenX*. People with Internet connections between the ages of 28 and 39 to have tried online banking. Some 60 percent have done so, compared to 38 percent of wired GenY members (those 18–27) and 25 percent of those with Internet connections over the age of 60.
- *Men*. In the past two years, online men are notably more likely to perform online banking activities than online women. Half of men with Internet connections (49 percent) have tried online banking, compared to 39 percent of online women. This is a change from the situation two years ago when internet-connected men and women were equally as likely to be banking online.
- *Higher socio-economic status*. Online banking, like many other Internet activities, is most likely to be performed by those living in well-off households (households with more than $75,000 in income), those who have college and graduate degrees, and those who live in suburbs. It is important to note, though, that there has been an across-the-board increase in online banking that has brought more of those who are working class, those who don't have college degrees, and those in rural areas into the online banking population.

By 2005, there were fewer than 20 viable autonomous Internet banks (those without traditional bank facilities and operations). FIR found that their Internet customers were more profitable than "ordinary" banking customers, were more likely to remain loyal to their bank if treated well, and provided excellent "word-of-mouth" advertising to friends, family members, and acquaintances. In short, they were worth competing for.

FIR did a customer survey over the Internet in 2010 consisting of a random sample of 1,000 customers. Responses showed that there were a number of things that customers liked about the online banking experience, but a number of things that they did not like. The survey provided for both closed-ended and open-ended responses.

One of the most important questions involved customer service perceptions. Customers were asked to name the dimension of customer service that gave them the most satisfaction. Interestingly, these responses centered around personal contact with customer service representatives. The top responses included: the accessibility provided by FIR to discuss problems with customer service representatives (CSR's) (16 percent); the relatively short time it takes to resolve most problems (15 percent); the quality of the response provided by CSR's (14 percent); and the manner and approach of CSR's (11 percent).

The closed-ended responses, when matched with customer demographics, confirmed that FIR customers were generally "typical" of Internet banking customers, as suggested by the Pew survey. Most had high-speed Internet connections, were men, and were in medium to high socio-economic categories. As might be expected, because of their location in the northwest United States, approximately 50 percent of their customers were in technical occupations.

The open-ended questions showed other areas, some of which were unexpected. Some typical responses included:

- *Respondent 13*: I relly luv the convience of being abl to bank online 24/7. The Web page is EZ to use.
- *Respondent 889*: I can easily check my balance and pay bills from my FIR account. It's a little inconvenient to have to mail my deposits. However, I have recently requested that my company direct-deposit my paycheck, so that will make things easier.
- *Respondent 557*: When I looked around to determine where I could get the best deal on a home equity loan, FIR beat the competition by a mile! Not only did they have the best interest rate, but my CSR, Veena, was really helpful. She used the online application information that I submitted to get preliminary approval the same day. Then she "locked in" the rate. By the end of the week, she had the appraisal done by a local appraiser, and had e-mailed the forms to me to sign. I printed them, signed, and had my signature notarized the same day. All the signed forms were sent and returned in three days, via package express. Total elapsed time was 6 working days. GREAT WORK!!
- *Respondent 235*: I really like your website, where I frequently pay bills, check my balances, and transfer money between my accounts. Since I do some business overseas, your recent addition of the capability to transfer funds electronically has been a Godsend.

That's why I'm frustrated and puzzled. Why can't you add one OBVIOUS capability—the ability to get my money from an ATM? I have to keep a local account open, just for that!

- *Respondent 3*: I've been satisfied with my FIR account, but I'm considering closing my account and opening a traditional account with my local bank. I've received three PHISHING-type e-mails that used the FIR Bank name and looked just like those that you send out, right down to your logo! The first time, I actually went to the website in the e-mail, but when it asked for my social security number, as well as my account number, I got suspicious. I logged off and called your security office. They told me that you'd never send out an e-mail asking for the social security number. They were very nice and took down the information about the PHISH'er. They followed up with an e-mail, saying that they were getting close to finding and "closing down" the crook. Still, I'm very concerned about identity theft. What are you doing to increase security and guard my information against hackers?
- *Respondent 137*: I have been delighted with the features and functionality of my commercial FIR account until now. However, I'm forced to close my account and open one with one of the traditional "bricks and mortar" banks that has become more competitive in Internet and commercial

customer service. As you know, businesses don't have the protection that retail customers have, when it comes to identity theft/hackers. Individuals are protected, so if anyone steals their credit card, they bear a maximum risk of $50. We businesspeople are open to any kind of bank fraud, and must bear all the risk if someone swipes our card number. However, XYA Bank has now set a policy to protect small businesses in the same way as individual clients. I'm going with them.

After reviewing the survey results, Livingstone, Abol, and Sistemas wondered if their business model simply needed tweaking or a major overhaul, which might even require building brick and mortar offices to meet customer needs.

Discussion Questions

1. Even though the complete survey is not included in the case, summarize how the closed-ended and open-ended questions provided valuable customer insights for FIR.
2. What customer segments are targeted by FIR? On what issues should FIR focus in order to build relationships with its varied customer segments?
3. Can you recommend specific activities and practices in which they might engage, in order to improve customer service quality and retain customers such as Respondents 3 and 137?

GOLD STAR CHILI: CUSTOMER AND MARKET KNOWLEDGE[74]

Gold Star Chili, Inc., based in Cincinnati, Ohio, was founded in 1965 as a family-owned system of franchised and company-owned restaurants. Gold Star operates over 100 regional locations (most of which are franchised, with a few being company restaurants or are co-owned). The Gold Star menu is based on a unique, "Cincinnati-style" chili recipe, flavored with a proprietary blend of spices from around the world. The chili is prepared in a central commissary, designed to reduce equipment needs at individual restaurants, promote consistency, and reduce labor costs. Most locations have both in-store dining and a drive-through. Gold Star operates in a highly competitive market against other multilocation chili firms and traditional fast-food competitors such as McDonald's, Taco Bell, and Kentucky Fried Chicken. It trails its major

competitor, Skyline, which has a larger advertising budget, in market share. Gold Star Chili is an active participant with the Cincinnati Restaurant Association and the National Restaurant Association. These connections help maintain awareness of business trends, and advances in new technology. Changing business needs are assessed by reviewing the annual reports of competing restaurants, and an annual market research study that permits benchmarking against the restaurant/convenience food industry in general.

Gold Star Chili defines two key customer groups: direct customers who use Gold Star products and services, and indirect customers with whom Gold Star has other relationships. Direct customers are divided into six customer segments, determined by product use: restaurant customers, franchisees, franchise applicants, retail customers, retail wholesalers, and mail-order customers. Indirect customers include product suppliers, service suppliers, co-packers, brokers/consultants, shareholders, and regulatory agencies.

Gold Star's mission is to create lasting relationships based upon respect, trust, and support given to customers. More than 70 percent of customers eat in a Gold Star restaurant at least once a month, and 20 to 30 percent eat at least once per week. The loyalty of the customer base permits servers and store managers to get to know customers personally and learn much about consumer needs.

Franchisees are attracted by the relatively low investment required to join the Gold Star family of restaurants, the opportunity to operate a profitable business, and to benefit from the strong brand equity built into the Gold Star name. All department heads treat franchisees as internal customers, and have signed a pledge guaranteeing to return calls within 24 hours. If a franchisee reports a problem with product quality, Gold Star often hand-delivers replacement product the same day. Many franchisees build relationships through local store marketing. Many owner/managers are active in the community with

sponsorships of teams or school programs. Gold Star provides owners with school achievement awards they can distribute to local schools.

Visit the company's website at www.goldstarchili.com to gain a perspective about the company, its menu, activities, and culture. Click the "About Us" link to read about the history and mission of the company. Using the information provided in the case and concepts developed in this chapter, answer the following:

1. What would be some moments of truth in Gold Star's environment?
2. What implications would the segmentation of Gold Star's customers have on their customer-focused practices?
3. What types of approaches should Gold Star consider to listen and learn from different customer segments?
4. How would you design customer satisfaction surveys for Gold Star consumers and for franchisee (who are customers of the corporation)? What types of questions would you ask?

NOTES

1. Don Peppers & Martha Rogers, "Customers Don't Grow on Trees," *Fast Company*, July 2005, pp. 19–20.
2. "GM's New Approach to Quality," *Automotive Design and Production*, June/July 2012, p. 24.
3. Avis 1992 Annual Report and *Quality Review*.
4. Jane Norman, "Royal Treatment Keeps Customers Loyal," *The Cincinnati Enquirer*, May 31, 1998, E3, E5.
5. Steve Hoisington and Earl Naumann, "The Loyalty Elephant," *Quality Progress*, February 2003, 33–41.
6. "Revenge of the Irate Shopper," *Business Week*, April 17, 2006, 14.
7. Carl Sewell and Paul B. Brown, *Customers for Life* (New York: Doubleday-Currency, 1990).
8. J. M. Juran, *Juran on Quality by Design* (New York: The Free Press, 1992), 7.
9. The Forum Corporation, "Customer Focus Research," executive briefing, Boston, 1988.
10. Model developed by National Quality Research Center, University of Michigan Business School for the American Customer Satisfaction Index, (ACSI). Cosponsored with American Society for Quality Control, 1994.
11. "Here's Mr. Macy," *Fortune*, November 28, 2005, 139–142.
12. Larry Selden and Geoffrey Colvin, "5 Rules for Finding the Next Dell," *Fortune*, July 12, 2004, 103–107.
13. J. M. Juran, *Juran on Quality by Design* (New York: The Free Press, 1992), Chapter 3.
14. Michael J. Stahl, William K. Barnes, Sarah F. Gardial, William C. Parr, and Robert B. Woodruff, "Customer-Value Analysis Helps Hone Strategy," *Quality Progress*, April 1999, 53–58.
15. "Time to Put Away the Checkbook: Now Fleet Needs to Bring Order to Its Furious Expansion," *Business Week*, June 10, 1996, 100.
16. Larry Selden and Geoffrey Colvin, "Will This Customer Sink Your Stock?" *Fortune*, September 30, 2002, 127–132.
17. Daniel H. Pink, "Out of the Box," *Fast Company*, October 2003, 104–106.
18. Robert D. Buzzell and Bradley T. Gale, *The PIMS Principles: Linking Strategy to Performance* (New York: The Free Press, 1987).
19. Rahul Jacob, "Why Some Customers Are More Equal Than Others," *Fortune*, September 19, 1994, 215–224.

20. David A. Garvin, "What Does Product Quality Really Mean?" *Sloan Management Review* 26, no. 1 (1984), 25–43.

21. Dawn Fallik, "Hospitals Try to Woo Patients with Amenities," *Cincinnati Enquirer*, October 9, 2005, A28.

22. "Getting an Edge," *Across the Board*, February 2000, 43–48.

23. "How to Listen to Consumers," *Fortune*, 11 January, 1993, 77.

24. Patricia Sellers, "Gap's New Guy Upstairs," *Fortune*, April 14, 2003, 110–116.

25. Russ Westcott "Your Customers Are Talking, But Are You Listening?" *Quality Progress*, February 2006, 22–27.

26. Byron J. Finch, "A New Way to Listen to the Customer," *Quality Progress* 30, no. 5 (May 1997), 73–76.

27. "How to Listen to Consumers," *Fortune*, January 11, 1993, 77.

28. Bruce Nussbaum, "Designs for Living," *Business Week*, June 2, 1997, 99.

29. Diane Brady, "Will Jeff Immelt's New Push Pay Off for GE?" *Business Week*, October 13, 2003, 94–98.

30. James H. Drew and Tye R. Fussell, "Becoming Partners with Internal Customers," *Quality Progress* 29, no. 10 (October 1996), 51–54.

31. "KJ" is a registered trademark of the Kawayoshida Research Center.

32. This example is adapted from Donald L. McLaurin and Shareen Bell, "Making Customer Service More Than Just a Slogan," *Quality Progress* 26, no. 11 (November 1993), 35–39.

33. Adapted from Bryan Jeppsen, "Safe Landing: Thanks to Text Analytics, JetBlue Ensures Customers Are Heard," *Quality Progress*, February 2010.

34. Minjoon Jun and Shaohan Cai, "The Key Determinants of Internet Banking Service Quality: A Content Analysis," *International Journal of Bank Marketing* 19, no. 7 (2001), 276–291.

35. Robert Wollan. "CIOs and the Battle for Consumers," *Bank Systems & Technology*, January 31, 2006, http://www.banktech.com/news/showArticle.jhtml?articleID=177103806&pgno=2.

36. Ron Huston, "Made in the U.S.A," *Quality Digest*, December 2004, 22–25.

37. John A Goodman, Dianne Ward, and Scott Broetzmann, "It Might Not Be Your Product," *Quality Progress*, April 2002, 73–78.

38. "2004 Fast Company Customers First Awards," *Fast Company*, October 2004, 79–88.

39. Courtesy of Deer Valley Resort.

40. Christopher Hart, "What Is an Extraordinary Guarantee?" *The Quality Observer* 3, no. 5 (March 1994), 15.

41. Richard S. Teitelbaum, "Where Service Flies Right," *Fortune*, August 24, 1992, 117–118; Southwest Airlines, available at http://iflyswa.com; Kevin Freiberg and Jackie Freiberg, *NUTS! Southwest Airlines' Crazy Recipe for*

Business and Personal Success (Austin, TX: Bard Press, 1996); "Holding Steady," *Business Week*, February 3, 2003, 86.

42. "Bank Tellers Have Huge Impact on Customer Satisfaction," http://www.prweb.com/releases/2011/2/prweb8205782.htm.

43. Karl Albrecht and Ronald E. Zemke, *Service America* (Homewood, IL: Dow Jones-Irwin, 1985), and John Goodman and Steve Newman, "Understanding customer behavior and complaints," *Quality Progress*, January 2003, 51–55.

44. Christopher W. Craighead, Kirk R. Karwan, and Janis L. Miller. "The Effects of Severity of Failure and Customer Loyalty on Service Recovery Strategies," *Production and Operations Management*, Vol. 13, No. 4, Winter 2004, pp. 307–321.

45. Michael Schrage, "Make No Mistake?" Fortune, December 11, 2001.

46. Craig Cochran, "Leveraging Customer Complaints into Customer Loyalty," *Quality Digest*, December 2004, 26–29.

47. Jane Carroll, "Mickey's Not for Everybody," *Across the Board*, February 2000, 11.

48. AT&T Corporate Quality Office, *Supplier Quality Management: Foundations* (1994).

49. Myron Magnet, "The New Golden Rule of Business," *Fortune*, February 21, 1994, 60–64.

50. Patricia C. La Londe, "Surveys As Supplier Relationship Tool," ASQ's 54th Annual Quality Congress proceedings, Indianapolis, IN, 2000, 684–686.

51. "Pacesetters – Customer Service," *Business Week*, November 21, 2005, 85.

52. Eric Almquist and Carla Heaton, "Customers Are Disappearing," *Across the Board*, July–August, 2002, 61–63.

53. Lucy McCauley, "How May I Help You?" *Fast Company*, March 2000, 93.

54. John Goodman, David DePalma, and Scott Breetzmann, "Maximizing the Value of Customer Feedback," *Quality Progress* 29, no. 12 (December 1996), 35–39.

55. Malcolm Baldrige National Quality Award Profiles of Winners, 1988–1993; and materials provided by Graniterock, including the 1992 Malcolm Baldrige Application Summary; Edward O. Welles, "How're We Doing?" *Inc.*, May 1991; Martha Heine, "Using Customer Report Cards Ups Service," undated reprint from *Concrete Trader*; and "Customer Report Cards at Graniterock," available at http://www.baldrigeplus.com.

56. Importance-performance analysis was first introduced by J. A. Martilla and J. C. James, "Importance-Performance Analysis," *Journal of Marketing* 41 (1977), 77–79.

57. A. Blanton Godfrey, "Beyond Satisfaction," *Quality Digest*, January 1996, 15.

58. Bob E. Hayes, "The True Test of Loyalty," *Quality Progress*, June 2008, 20–26.

59. More information may be found at the official website for the net promoter community, http://www.net promoter.com.

60. See Timothy L. Keiningham, Lerzan Aksoy, Bruce Cooil and Tor Wallin Andreassen, "Linking Customer Loyalty to Growth," *MIT Sloan Management Review* 29, no. 4 (Summer 2008), 50–57.

61. David C. Swaddling and Charles Miller, "Don't Measure Customer Satisfaction," *Quality Progress*, May 2002, 62–67.

62. Much of the information in this case is adapted from Harley-Davidson, Inc. SEC Form 10-K (Annual Report), 02/24/11 for the Period Ending 12/31/10.

63. Source: R. L. Polk & Co. 2009 motorcycle registrations.

64. Sources: 2010 Company Studies.

65. HarleyD_Annual Report2010.pdf, back cover. http://investor.harley-davidson.com/phoenix.zhtml?c=87981&p=irol-irhome&locale=en_US&bmLocale=en_US&locale=en_US&bmLocale=en_US (accessed 2/3/2012).

66. We are grateful to Julia Ritzenthaler, owner of Unique Online Furniture, Inc. for providing the information in this case.

67. Matthew Boyle, "Best Buy's Giant Gamble," *Fortune*, April 3, 2006, 69–75.

68. "Getting to Very Satisfied," *Fast Company*, February 2004, 32.

69. Adapted from Kioumars Paryani, Ali Masoudi, and Elizabeth A. Cudney, "QFD Application in the Hospitality Industry: A Hotel Case Study," *Quality Management Journal* 17, no. 1 (2010), pp. 7–28.

70. Adapted from Ralph F. Altman and Marilyn M. Helms, "Quantifying Service Quality: A Case Study of a Rental Car Agency," *Production and Inventory Management* 36, no. 2 (Second Quarter 1995), 45–50. Reprinted with permission of APICS—The Educational Society for Resource Management, Falls Church, VA.

71. Edna White, Ravi Behara, and Sunil Babbar, "Mine Customer Experiences," *Quality Progress*, July 2002, 63–67.

72. Our thanks go to Brian Cundiff of LaRosa's Inc. for providing the foundation for this fictionalized case.

73. Susannah Fox, "The state of online banking, Pew Internet & American Life Project," November 2004. http://www.pewinternet.org/PPF/r/149/report_display.asp (accessed 2/8/06).

74. We thank Kim Olden of Gold Star Chili for providing basic company information; and Gold Star Chili, Inc. for granting permission to use this material.

Workforce Focus

Toyota's Georgetown, Kentucky, plant has been a multiple winner of the J. D. Power Gold Plant Quality Award. When asked about the "secret" behind the superior Toyota paint finishes, one manager replied, "We've got nothing, technology-wise, that anyone else can't have. There's no secret Toyota Quality Machine out there. The quality machine is the workforce—the team members on the paint line, the suppliers, the engineers—everybody who has a hand in production here takes the attitude that we're making world-class vehicles."[1] Deming emphasized that no organization can survive without good people; people who are improving. The human resource is the only one that competitors cannot copy, and the only one that can synergize, that is, produce output whose value is greater than the sum of its parts. In the words of the late Walter Wriston, former CEO of Citibank, "The person who figures out how to harness the collective genius of the people in his or her organization is going to blow the competition away."

Organizations are learning that to satisfy customers, they must first satisfy the workforce. **Workforce** refers to everyone who is actively involved in accomplishing the work of an organization. This encompasses paid employees as well as volunteers and contract employees, and includes team leaders, supervisors, and managers at all levels. Many companies refer to their employees as "associates" or "partners" to signify the importance that people have in driving business performance. Workforce satisfaction is strongly related to customer satisfaction and, ultimately, to business performance. FedEx, for instance, has found direct statistical correlation between customer and workforce satisfaction; a drop in workforce satisfaction scores precedes a drop in customer satisfaction by about two months. Researchers in service operations in industries ranging from communications to banking to fast food, have observed similar relationships.[2] An extensive research study by the Gallup Organization of 7,939 business units in 36 companies showed that employee satisfaction and engagement were positively related to not only to customer satisfaction and loyalty, but also to productivity, profit, turnover, and safety.[3]

The workforce is an important component of a basic quality system. ISO 9000:2000 includes several workforce-focused requirements. The standards require that "Personnel performing work affecting product quality shall be competent on the basis of appropriate education, training, skills, and experience." They further require that organizations determine the level of competence that employees need, provide training or other means to ensure competency, evaluate the effectiveness of training or other actions taken, ensure that employees are aware of how their work contributes to quality objectives, and maintain appropriate records of education, training, and experience. The standards also address the work environment from the standpoint of providing buildings, workspace, utilities, equipment, and supporting services needed to achieve conformance to product requirements, as well as determining and managing the work environment, including safety, ergonomics, and environmental factors.

The ability to meet ever-changing customer needs and leverage technological innovations demands new approaches to workforce management. In this chapter, we address key issues that organizations must focus on in order to build a workforce environment conducive to high performance. Table 4.1 summarizes key workforce-related practices for achieving high quality. The Quality Profiles describe how two organizations that leverage these practices to achieve outstanding results.

TABLE 4.1 Key Workforce-Focused Practices for Quality	<ul><li>Understand the key factors that drive workforce engagement, satisfaction, and motivation.</li><li>Design and manage work and jobs to promote effective communication, cooperation, skill sharing, empowerment, innovation, and the ability to benefit from diverse ideas and thinking of employees and develop an organizational culture conducive to high performance and motivation.</li><li>Make appropriate investments in development and learning, both for the workforce and the organization's leaders.</li><li>Create an environment that ensures and improves workplace health, safety, and security, and supports the workforce via policies, services, and benefits.</li><li>Develop a performance management system based on compensation, recognition, reward, and incentives that supports high performance work and workforce engagement.</li><li>Assess workforce engagement and satisfaction and use results for improvement.</li><li>Assess workforce capability and capacity needs and use the results to capitalize on core competencies, address strategic challenges, recruit and retain skilled and competent people, and accomplish the work of the organization.</li><li>Manage career progression for the entire workforce and succession planning for management and leadership positions.</li></ul>

quality**profiles**

Veterans Affairs Cooperative Studies Program Clinical Research Pharmacy Coordinating Center and PRO-TEC Coating Company

The Veterans Affairs Cooperative Studies Program (VACSP) Clinical Research Pharmacy Coordinating Center (the Center) is a federal government organization that supports clinical trials targeting current health issues for America's veterans. The Center focuses on the pharmaceutical, safety, and regulatory aspects related to designing and implementing clinical trials conducted worldwide by the VACSP and other federal agencies and industries. The Center manufactures, packages, stores, labels, distributes, and tracks clinical trial materials (drugs and devices) and monitors patient safety.

The Center sees engagement as the single most important criterion for workforce satisfaction. Excellence in the workplace, superior customer service, and personal involvement in organizational improvement are rewarded through the Center's performance management system with visible, tangible benefits, such as time off or cash. Both management and peers can use multiple methods to recognize a job well done. The Center also encourages career and personal advancement for its workforce by providing financial and other support for education and training. In fact, application of formal and informal learning is required for employees to be eligible for the organization's highest performance rating.

The Center's ratings for workforce engagement have outperformed the Gallup Q12 75th percentile for the Professional, Scientific, and Technical Services segment, and for workforce satisfaction, results have exceeded Gallup's overall 75th percentile. Low turnover, a supportive learning environment, and leadership effectiveness are factors in the Center's recognition as a Federal Executive Board Employer of Choice for 2008 and 2009, as well as a top ten ranking in the "New Mexico Best Places to Work for 2009."

PRO-TEC Coating Company, established in 1990 as a joint venture between United States Steel Corporation and Kobe Steel Ltd. of Japan, provides coated sheet steel primarily to the U.S. automotive industry for use in manufacturing cars, trucks, and sport utility vehicles. PRO-TEC's 236 employees, called Associates, work in a state-of-the-art 730,000-square-foot facility in the small rural town of Leipsic, Ohio. With its heritage from U.S. Steel and Kobe Steel, PRO-TEC has developed its own unique culture centered around three fundamental concepts—*ownership, responsibility,* and *accountability*. From the beginning, the company incorporated numerous best-management practices, including lean manufacturing and continuous improvement, and relied on a well-trained, self-directed, empowered workforce to help the company become an industry leader. PRO-TEC routinely scores better than its competition in product quality, on-time delivery, service, product development, and overall quality.

PRO-TEC's Associates work in self-directed teams and are empowered, innovative leaders who fix problems as they are identified and use a continuous improvement process called "I-to-I" to Initiate and Implement process and product improvements. New Associates go through three weeks of orientation and training, followed by six months of mentoring. The company's commitment to Associate quality of life through safety, education and training, and an above-average compensation and "cafeteria-style" benefits package reflects the value PRO-TEC places on attracting and retaining its workforce. All Associates are salaried and participate in a profit sharing plan that has provided an average payout of approximately 15 percent of annual base pay. In a survey, Associates agreed or strongly agreed with the following statements: "The people I work with cooperate and work as a team," "I know what is expected of me at work," "I am supported when responding to customers' questions or problems," and "I am satisfied with my job." PRO-TEC has a turnover rate of less than 2 percent and has never had a layoff.

In a manufacturing environment that poses potential hazards, PRO-TEC's facility was designed with safety, health, and security in mind, along with minimizing environmental impacts. During an emergency, PRO-TEC's hierarchy of priorities are to first, preserve human life and the safety of Associates, responders, and the public; second, minimize impact to the environment; and, third, minimize property damage and disruption of operations. Since 2004,

PRO-TEC has shown a 1.65 recordable injury frequency or below per 200,000 man-hours. PRO-TEC was a 2007 Baldrige recipient.

Source: Malcolm Baldrige National Quality Award, Profiles of Winners, National Institute of Standards and Technology, Department of Commerce.

THE EVOLUTION OF WORKFORCE MANAGEMENT

The role of people at work certainly changed as business and technology evolved over the years. Prior to the Industrial Revolution, skilled craftspeople had a major stake in the quality of their products because their families' livelihoods depended on the sale of those products. They were motivated by pride in their work as well as the need for survival. Frederick W. Taylor promulgated the departure from the craftsmanship concept. Taylor concluded that a factory should be managed on a scientific basis. So he focused on work methods design, the establishment of standards for daily work, selection and training of workers, and piecework incentives. Taylor separated planning from execution, concluding that foremen and workers of those days lacked the education necessary to plan their work. The foreman's role was to ensure that the workforce met productivity standards. Other pioneers of scientific management, such as Frank and Lillian Gilbreth and Henry Gantt, further refined the Taylor system through motion study, methods improvement, ergonomics, scheduling, and wage incentive systems.

The Taylor system dramatically improved productivity. However, it also changed many manufacturing jobs into a series of mundane and mindless tasks. Without a systems perspective and a focus on the customer, the responsibility for quality shifted from workers to inspectors, and as a result, quality eroded. The Taylor philosophy also contributed to the development of labor unions and established an adversarial relationship between labor and management that has yet to be completely overcome. Nevertheless, the Taylor system was the key force behind the explosive economic development of the twentieth century.

On the other hand, the Taylor system failed to exploit an organization's most important asset—the knowledge and creativity of the workforce. As executives at The Ritz-Carlton Hotel Company have stated, human beings don't serve a function, they have a purpose, and the role of the human resources function is to unleash the power of the workforce to achieve the goals of the organization.[4] Studies show that this philosophy results in higher quality, lower costs, less waste, better utilization, increased capacity, reduced turnover and absenteeism, faster implementation of change, greater human skill development, and better individual self-esteem.[5] It also requires more attention to the psychological aspects of work—one of the key principles of the Deming philosophy.

Workforce management (which has also been widely known as **human resource management**, or **HRM**) is the function performed in organizations that facilitates the most effective use of people (employees) to achieve organizational and individual goals.[6] The objectives of an effective workforce management system are to build a high-performance workplace and maintain an environment for quality excellence to enable employees and the organization to achieve strategic objectives and adapt to change.

Many modern workforce management practices evolved from research at the Hawthorne Works of the Western Electric Company in the late 1920s. Interestingly, both Deming and Juran were working for Western Electric at the time, which may have influenced their views on quality and the workforce.

Workforce management activities include determining the organization's workforce needs; assisting in the design of work systems; recruiting, selecting, training and developing, counseling, motivating, and rewarding employees; acting as a liaison with unions and government organizations; and handling other matters of employee well-being. Human resource professionals need to foster competence and commitment among employees, develop the capabilities that allow managers to execute on strategy, help build relationships with customers, and create confidence among investors in the future value of the firm.[7]

Today, workforce management is no longer just the responsibility of the HR department. Its principles have permeated the daily job responsibilities of managers at all levels. Developing skills through training and coaching, promoting teamwork and participation, motivating and recognizing employees, and providing meaningful communication are important human resource skills that all managers must practice to achieve performance excellence. At Xerox, for instance, managers are directly accountable for the development and implementation of workforce plans that support the quality goals of the company. Thus, understanding both the theory and practice of workforce management is a vital task for all managers.

Workforce management is also beginning to assume more of a strategic role in business. For example, at BI, the importance of workforce management is reflected in the fact that a senior vice president within the Office of the President leads the human resource function. **Strategic human resource management** is concerned with the contributions HR strategies make to organizational effectiveness, and how these contributions are accomplished.[8] It involves designing and implementing a set of internally consistent policies and practices to ensure that an organization's human capital (employees' collective knowledge, skills, and abilities) contributes to overall business objectives.[9] Research shows that strategic human resource management practices are positively associated with organizational performance indicators such as share price, profits, net sales per employee, gross rate of return on assets, employee retention, employee attitudes, and customer retention rates. Despite this, evidence indicates that most organizations have not transitioned from traditional HR practices to a strategic orientation. For example, a survey conducted by the Society for Human Resource Management found that only 56 percent of respondents reported that their HR departments had a strategic plan in place.[10] A strategic perspective of HR requires a radical change in the business mindset. Table 4.2 summarizes key issues of HR management and contrasts differences between traditional and strategic HR.

HIGH PERFORMANCE WORK CULTURE

Performance simply means the extent to which an individual contributes to achieving the goals and objectives of an organization. The design, organization, and management of work and the work environment are crucial to high performance. **High-performance work** refers to work approaches used to systematically pursue ever-higher levels of overall organizational and human performance. High-performance work is characterized by flexibility, innovation, knowledge and skill sharing, alignment with organizational

TABLE 4.2 Traditional HR Versus Strategic HR[11]

Key Issues	Traditional HR	Strategic HR (SHR)
Fundamental mind-set	• Transactional • Compliance/enforcement orientation	• Transformational • Consultative orientation
View of organization	• Micro • Narrow skill application	• Macro • Broad skill application

Education and training	• Traditional human resources management (HR specialist)
	• Limited business acumen
		• Basic business competencies
		• HR education/training with emphasis on the following:
		  • Organizational theory
		  • Organizational culture
		  • Organizational change
		  • Strategic management
		  • Job design

Critical skills	• Organization • Compliance	• Strategic thinking • Planning • Diagnosis and analysis • Consultation • Managing change
View of employees	• Heads, costs • People are exploitable resources	• Minds, assets • People are critical resources
Timeframe	• Short-term, immediate needs	• Mid-to long-term, current and future needs
Process/outcome orientation	• Primary concern for process • Process control	• Primary concern for results • Process innovation
Risk	• Low risk taking • Reliance on proven approaches	• High risk taking • Experiment with new, promising approaches
Response to change	• Inflexible to change	• Flexible to change
HR systems and practices	• Routine, established programs and systems (e.g., traditional training programs)	• Adaptive, innovative programs and systems to fit future needs (e.g., Web-based, just-in-time training)
Approach to system development	• Reactive-benchmarking, best practices • Responding to stated needs	• Anticipatory-forecasting, predicting needs • Recognizing unstated needs
Primary areas of practice	• Transactions, highly repetitive in nature (eg., recruitment/selection, training, compensation, labor relations)	• Transformations, change, innovation (eg., strategy, knowledge management, culture, organizational change, talent management, leadership development)
Status in organization	• Weak	• Strong

directions, customer focus, and rapid response to changing business needs and market-place requirements.

A culture for high-performance work leads to successful results. Employees need to understand the importance of customer satisfaction, to be given the training and responsibilities to achieve it, and to feel that they do indeed make a difference. Creating such a culture begins with senior leadership's commitment to the workforce.[12] Leading organizations make a commitment to people explicit in their vision, mission, and values, and have robust systems in place to listen to their people and to understand what matters to them. They strive to be the best place to work. Rulon Stacey, president and CEO of Poudre Valley Health System located in Fort Collins, CO, says, "I love working at a place where people love working. I love going around this organization and talking to people and seeing them happy. Our first strategic objective has always been to meet the needs of our employees because so much builds off of that." And he says to his people, "We expect you're going to give the best patient care that our patients have ever received, and it's not fair for us to expect you're going to give the best care if you don't work in the best place you've ever worked."[13]

The Alliance for Work-Life Progress found that organizations that exhibit a high performance work culture as reflected by job autonomy, challenging work and continuous learning opportunities, involvement in decision-making, supervisors' support of workers' success on the job, and flexible work options have a happier and more effective workforce. One need only look at *Fortune* magazine's annual list of the "100 Best Companies to Work For" to support these findings. Although this list changes each year, Google has been at or near the top of the list for several years. As *Fortune* noted,

> *At Google you can do your laundry; drop off your dry cleaning; get an oil change, then have your car washed; work out in the gym; attend subsidized exercise classes; get a massage; study Mandarin, Japanese, Spanish, and French; and ask a personal concierge to arrange dinner reservations. Naturally you can get haircuts onsite. Want to buy a hybrid car? The company will give you $5,000 toward that environmentally friendly end.*[14] CEO and co-founder Larry Page was asked in a Fortune interview: *"How important are Google's wonderful lifestyle perks, from the free food to the messages, for the employee experience you're trying to design?"* His response (in part) was: *"I don't think it's any of those individual things. It's important that the company be a family, that people feel that they're part of the company, and the company is like a family to them. When you treat people this way, you get better productivity. Rather than caring about what hours you worked, you care about output. We should continue to innovate in our relationship with our employees and figure out the best things we can do for them."*[15]

Kay Kendall and Glenn Bodison propose five "Conditions of Collaboration" that characterize a culture of high performance: respect, aligned values, shared purpose, communication, and trust.[16]

- *Respect* means believing in the inherent worth of another person. Respect also is taking into consideration the views and desires of others. When you respect another person, you consider what is important to him or her when you are planning and making decisions.
- *Values* are the guiding principles and behaviors that embody how an organization and its people are expected to operate. Values reflect and reinforce an organization's culture. *Aligned values* create a congruency between what the organization stands for and the personal beliefs of the individual.

- *Purpose* is the fundamental reason an organization exists. It inspires an organization and guides its setting of values. Typically, individuals who share a purpose with the organization for which they work are frequently more motivated. Having a shared purpose promotes collaboration because it minimizes the focus on individual desires and elevates the focus to a greater good.
- *Communication* is often cited as one of the most important factors related to employee motivation. Communication that flows freely in all directions promotes collaboration.
- *Trust* – that management trusts the workforce and vice-versa—is vital. A survey by Annandale, Virginia-based MasteryWorks Inc. concluded that employees leave their organizations because of trust, observing that "Lack of trust was an issue with almost every person who had left an organization."[17]

These attributes are usually evident in companies that are recognized as outstanding places to work.

PRINCIPLES OF WORKFORCE ENGAGEMENT AND MOTIVATION

Joseph Juran credited Japanese managers' full use of the knowledge and creativity of the entire workforce as one of the reasons for Japan's rapid quality achievements. When managers give employees the tools to make good decisions and the freedom and encouragement to make contributions, they virtually guarantee that better quality products and production processes will result. High performance workforce management practices are built on understanding the principles of workforce engagement and motivation.

Workforce Engagement

One way is to create more satisfied employees is to engage them in their work and make them a part of the "fabric" of the organization. **Workforce engagement** refers to the extent of workforce commitment, both emotional and intellectual, to accomplishing the work, mission, and vision of the organization. Engagement is manifest in Deming's concept of "pride and joy" in work that was reflected in his 14 Points. Engagement means that workers find personal meaning and motivation in their work, have a strong emotional bond to their organization, are actively involved in and committed to their work, feel that their jobs are important, know that their opinions and ideas have value, and often go beyond their immediate job responsibilities for the good of the organization. Studies have shown that engagement leads to greater levels of satisfaction among the workforce and improves organizational performance.[18] Organizations with high levels of workforce engagement are often characterized by high-performing work environments in which people are motivated to do their utmost for the benefit of their customers and for the success of the organization.

A compelling example of workforce engagement occurred in 2002 when former Southwest Airlines CEO Herb Kelleher sent a letter concerning the current fuel cost crisis to the home of every employee. "Jet fuel costs three times what it did one year ago. Southwest uses 19 million gallons a week. Our profitability is in jeopardy," he wrote. He asked each worker to help by identifying a way to save $5 a day. That would, he explained in the letter, save Southwest $51 million annually. The response was immediate. A group of mechanics figured out how to reduce the costs of heating the aircraft. Another department offered to do its own janitorial work. Within six weeks of the letter being sent to the employees, this large organization found ways to save more than $2 million.[19]

Workforce engagement is rooted in the psychology of human needs and supported by the motivation models of Maslow, Herzberg, and McGregor that we will discuss shortly. Employees are motivated through exciting work, responsibility, and recognition. Engagement provides a powerful means of achieving the highest order individual needs of self-realization and fulfillment. Employee engagement offers many advantages over traditional management practices as it:

- Replaces the adversarial mentality with trust and cooperation
- Develops the skills and leadership capability of individuals, creating a sense of mission and fostering trust
- Increases employee morale and commitment to the organization
- Fosters creativity and innovation, the source of competitive advantage
- Helps people understand quality principles and instills these principles into the corporate culture
- Allows employees to solve problems at the source immediately
- Improves quality and productivity[20]

Every organization has a unique culture. What drives employee engagement will differ among different organizations. Thus, every organization should conduct its own research to determine the drivers of engagement. For example, at Saint Luke's Hospital in Kansas City, MO, factors that determine employee well-being, satisfaction, and motivation are uncovered through formal surveys, open forums with senior leaders, targeted focus groups, senior leader "walk rounds," "staying" and "exit" interviews, and the Peer Review Grievance Process.

QUALITYSPOTLIGHT

MEDRAD

MEDRAD uses the *Great Places to Work (GPTW)* survey used by *Fortune* magazine as the basis for understanding the key engagement factors in the company.[21] GPTW is based on 20 years of research and measures three factors and five dimensions that define the best workplaces. These dimensions—credibility, respect, fairness, pride, and camaraderie—are shown in Figure 4.1. They are highly correlated with workforce engagement and satisfaction, and business performance. MEDRAD validates these dimensions as it implements its global action planning process related to the survey results. While they are consistent across the company, survey results vary across workforce groups and segments. This process enables the organization to make specific determinations of engagement and satisfaction for different work groups and segments. Any group can access the GPTW database to learn from the Top 100 companies and best-in-class practices. The structure of the GPTW survey affords respondents the opportunity to assess engagement and satisfaction factors for both MEDRAD overall and the specific department in which the respondent works. This enables the organization to determine drivers of engagement and satisfaction for specific work groups and segments.[22]

A global benchmarking study of employee engagement conducted by Right Management identified the following as the top 10 drivers (among 26 in the survey) of workforce engagement:[23]

1. Commitment to organizational values.
2. Knowing that customers are satisfied with products and services.

FIGURE 4.1
Key Factors of
Workforce Engage-
ment for MEDRAD

Key Engagement Factors and Related Survey Dimensions

1. **Employees trust the people they work with**
   Credibility
   - Communications are open and accessible
   - Competence in coordinating human and material resources
   - Integrity in carrying out vision with consistency
   Respect
   - Supporting professional development and showing appreciation
   - Collaboration with employees on relevant decisions
   - Caring for employees as individuals with personal lives
   Fairness
   - Equity–balanced treatment for all in terms of reward
   - Impartiality–absence of favoritism in hiring and promotions
   - Justice–lack of discrimination and process for appeals

2. **Employees have pride in what they do**
   Pride
   - In personal job, individual contributions
   - In work produced by one's team and one's group
   - In the organization's products and standing in the community

3. **Employees enjoy the people they work with**
   Camaraderie
   - Ability to be oneself
   - Socially friendly and welcoming atmosphere
   - Sense of "family" or "team"

Source: MEDRAD 2010 Baldrige Application Summary, http://www.baldrige.nist.gov/Contacts_Profiles.htm.

3. Belief that opinions count.
4. Clearly understanding work expectations.
5. Understanding of how personal contributions help meet customer needs.
6. Being recognized and rewarded fairly.
7. Knowing that senior leaders value the workforce.
8. Being treated equally with respect.
9. Being able to concentrate on the job and work processes.
10. Alignment of personal work objectives to work plans.

The study found that the drivers of engagement vary by country; however, one driver was constant across all countries—Commitment to organizational values. This suggests the importance of creating and building a values-driven organization. In many non-profit organizations, employees and volunteers are drawn to and derive meaning from their work because the work is aligned with their personal values. As the president of a successful travel agency once stated, "By maintaining an enjoyable, bureaucracy-free work environment, one that encourages innovative thinking … and honest communication, people are freed to concentrate solely on the needs of the clients."[24]

Employee Involvement

Engagement begins with involvement. **Employee involvement (EI)** refers to any activity by which employees participate in work-related decisions and improvement activities, with the objectives of tapping the creative energies of all employees and improving their motivation. Tom Peters suggested involving everyone in everything, in such activities as quality and productivity improvement, measuring and monitoring results, budget development, new technology assessment, recruiting and hiring, making customer calls, and participating in customer visits.[25] Pete Coors, CEO of Coors Brewing, explained it simply, "We're moving from an environment where the supervisor says, 'This is the way it is going to be done and if you don't like it, go someplace else,' to an environment where the supervisor can grow with the changes, get his troops together and say, 'Look, you guys are operating the equipment, what do you think we ought to do?'"[26]

EI initiatives are by no means new.[27] Many programs and experiments have been implemented over more than 100 years by industrial engineers, statisticians, and behavioral scientists. Early attempts influenced modern practices considerably. Unfortunately, these approaches lacked the complementary elements of TQ, such as a customer orientation, top management leadership and support, and a common set of tools for problem solving and continuous improvement.

EI approaches can range from simple sharing of information or providing input on work-related issues and making suggestions to self-directed responsibilities such as setting goals, making business decisions, and solving problems, often in cross-functional teams.

One of the easiest ways to involve employees on an individual basis is the suggestion system. An **employee suggestion system** is a management tool for the submission, evaluation, and implementation of an employee's idea to save cost, increase quality, or improve other elements of work such as safety. At Toyota, for instance, employees generate nearly three million ideas each year—an average of 60 per employee—of which 85 percent are implemented by management. Companies typically reward employees for implemented suggestions.

Simple suggestion systems can have many benefits. Thinking about solutions to problems at work makes even routine work enjoyable; writing down the suggestions improves workers' reasoning ability and writing skills. Satisfaction is the by-product of an implemented idea and a job made easier, safer, or better. Recognition for suggestions leads to higher levels of motivation, peer recognition, and possible monetary rewards. Workers gain an increased understanding of their work, which may lead to promotions and better interpersonal relationships in the workplace.

 QUALITYSPOTLIGHT
Wainwright Industries

Suggestion systems are often tied to incentives. Wainwright Industries developed a unique and effective approach that has been benchmarked extensively.[28] Suggestion programs were viewed as neither systematic nor continuous, and not woven into the fabric of daily operations. Their approach was designed to overcome these shortcomings in the following ways:

- Focusing employees on small, incremental improvements within their own areas of responsibility and control
- Recognizing all employees for their level of participation regardless of the value of the improvement

- Scaling team-based improvement efforts in a way that minimizes downtime and provides people with the tools and techniques to produce successful outcomes
- Positioning supervisors as the catalyst for cultural change through a coaching and support role in the employee involvement and improvement process

The process contains two main components: individual implemented improvements and team-based system improvements. Rather than submitting suggestions for someone else to approve and implement, employees are provided with training and given the responsibility to take the initiative to make improvements on their own without prior approval within the scope of their main job responsibilities. Upon making improvements, they complete a form to document what they have done and present it to the supervisors, whose role is not to approve or disapprove, but to acknowledge the improvement and to point out any issues that the employee needs to understand. All forms submitted during the week are placed into a random drawing for some type of award determined by the individual unit. At the end of each quarter, every individual who met his or her goal of implemented improvements receives some type of valued recognition. The team-based approach breaks large initiatives into smaller manageable projects. Breaking down large tasks allows employees to understand how their individual jobs fit into the big picture and maximizes participation, while reducing time requirements for any particular employee. Wainwright was able to cite more than 50 implemented improvements per employee per year, far exceeding those of most American and Japanese companies.

Motivation

Understanding human behavior and motivation are major elements of Deming's Profound Knowledge discussed in Chapter 2. Deming spoke of motivation as being primarily intrinsic (internal), and was suspicious of external forms of motivation, such as incentives and bonuses. Although thousands of studies have been performed over the years on human and animal subjects in attempts to define and refine the concept of motivation, it remains an extremely complex phenomenon that still is not fully understood. As managers in a high performance environment take on the roles of coaches and facilitators, their skills in motivating employees become even more crucial.

Saul W. Gellerman defined **motivation** as "the art of creating conditions that allow every one of us, warts and all, to get his work done at his own peak level of efficiency."[29] A more formal definition of motivation is *an individual's response to a felt need*. Thus, some stimulus, or activating event, must spur the need to respond to that stimulus, generating the response itself. For example, an individual worker given the goal or quality task of achieving zero defects on the parts that he or she produces may feel a need to keep his or her job. Consequently, the worker is motivated by the stimulus of fear and responds by carefully producing parts to achieve the goal. Another less insecure worker may feel the need for approval of his or her work by peers or superiors and be motivated by the stimulus of pride. The worker then responds to that need and that stimulus by producing high-quality parts.

There is no such thing as an unmotivated employee, but the system within which people work can either seriously impede motivation or enhance it. Researchers have proposed many theories and models to describe how and why people are motivated. A theory is a way to describe, predict, and control what is observed in the world. Models graphically or symbolically show what a theory is saying in words. Often a model is so closely associated with a theory that the terms are used interchangeably. For example, Herzberg's Two-Factor theory describes two categories of factors in his model, called "maintenance" and "motivational" factors. Maintenance factors are conditions that employees have come to expect, such as a safe working environment, a reasonable level of job security, supervision, and even adequate pay. Workers in a situation with these conditions will not be dissatisfied, but maintenance factors generally do not provide any motivation to work harder. Motivational factors, such as recognition, advancement, achievement, and the nature of the work itself are less tangible, but do motivate people to be more committed to and satisfied with their work. From Herzberg's theory arose the concept of job enrichment. With job enrichment, employees gain a sense of fulfillment (satisfaction) from completion of every cycle of a task. Acquiring cross-functional skills, working in teams, and increased empowerment are forms of job enrichment.

Theories and models are often classified according to common themes. James L. Bowditch and Anthony F. Buono categorize motivation theories as *content*, *process*, and *environmentally based* theories.[30] These theories are often studied in traditional management courses and are summarized in Table 4.3. In the behavioral sciences, as well as in the pure sciences, the originator of a theory is becoming more and more difficult to determine because many researchers' ideas often overlap. Thus, the information in Table 4.3 is merely suggestive of one or more names that have been associated with the development of the theory.

Motivation theories can be applied to support high performance in any organization. For example, Herzberg's theory suggests that ignoring maintenance factors such as supervision, working conditions, salary, peer relations, status, and security will produce dissatisfaction and negatively impact the work environment, while enhancing the motivating factors will produce a positive effect. Thus, understanding and applying the theories should result in more effective designs of work systems and the work environment.

A rather puzzling situation exists in the theoretical and practical development of the concept of motivation. Very little new research has been performed on new concepts or

TABLE 4.3
A Classification of Motivation Theories

Motivation Theory	Pioneer/Developer	Type of Theory
Content Theories		
Hierarchy of Needs	Abraham Maslow	Need
Motivation and Maintenance	Douglas McGregor	Need/satisfaction
Theory X-Y	Frederick Herzberg	Managerial expectations
n-Ach, n-Aff, n-Pow	David McClelland	Acquired need
Process Theories		
Preference–Expectancy	Victor H. Vroom	Expectancy
Contingency	Porter and Lawler	Expectancy/reward
Goal Setting	Edward Locke	Goal
Path–Goal Theory of Leadership	Robert J. House	Goal
Environmentally Based Theories		
Operant Conditioning	B. F. Skinner	Reinforcement
Equity	J. Stacy Adams	Equity
Social Learning/Self-Efficacy	A. Bandura; Snyder and Williams	Social learning/self-efficacy

approaches to motivation in recent years. Yet, the workplace has been the scene of constant and chaotic change that has spawned new motivational challenges, as Steers, et al. noted:

- Companies are both downsizing and expanding (often at the same time, in different divisions or levels of the hierarchy);
- The workforce is characterized by increased diversity with highly divergent needs and demands;
- Information technology has frequently changed both the manner and location of work activities;
- New organizational forms (such as those found in e-commerce) are now commonplace;
- Teams are redefining the notion of hierarchy, as well as traditional power distributions;
- The use of contingent workers is on the rise;
- Managing knowledge workers continues to perplex experienced managers across divergent industries; and
- Globalization and the challenges of managing across borders are now the norm instead of the exception.[31]

It is apparent that the chaotic content, process, and environment of motivation will make new demands on both workers and leader/managers. To the extent that any of the factors of motivation can be controlled, it is important to tailor motivation approaches to the needs and culture of the organization as well as to individual employees. Nucor, for instance, motivates employees through its innovative compensation structure. American Express focuses on helping employees reach a development goal using an approach called "label and link" (their employee surveys indicate that learning and development is a high priority). When managers give someone an assignment, they should label what they are doing and link it to what's important to that person.[32] Thus, by allowing employees to achieve their own unique levels of excellence and valuing them for what they contribute, they will be motivated to work towards meeting common organizational goals.

DESIGNING HIGH-PERFORMANCE WORK SYSTEMS

The design of work should provide individuals with both the intrinsic and extrinsic motivation to achieve quality and operational performance objectives. Leading companies view the design of work systems in a fashion similar to the design of their key products and processes. For example, Cargill Kitchen Solutions (formerly Sunny Fresh Foods) (CKS), designs its work systems to emphasize safety, quality, compensation and recognition, and employee development in support of individual development and CKS's long-term goals. Many of its work systems are unique to the industry. Examples are a "ramp-in" schedule in which new employees are allowed to work for only a specified number of hours to learn their jobs and minimize the potential for repetitive stress injuries; and a rotation system by which employees rotate to another workstation every 20 minutes. This format ensures that workers can understand and respond to product quality issues at any stage of the process and understand their internal customers; it also fights boredom, reduces repetitive stress injuries, and promotes learning. In addition,

CKS uses a "buddy" system in which new employees are matched with high-performing experienced employees who serve as role models for operational excellence and behavioral competencies.

Work and Job Design

Work design refers to how employees are organized in formal and informal units, such as departments and teams. **Job design** refers to responsibilities and tasks assigned to individuals. Both work and job design are vital to organizational effectiveness and personal job satisfaction. Unfortunately, managers often do not understand workers' needs. One research study found that the top five employee needs in the workplace are interesting work, recognition, feeling "in" on things, security, and pay. Managers, however, believed pay to be number one. Many companies understand that the best way to influence job satisfaction and motivate workers is to make jobs more rewarding, which can entail introducing variety into work, emphasizing the importance and significance of the job, providing more autonomy and empowerment, and giving meaningful feedback.

An integrating theory that helps us understand how job design impacts motivation, satisfaction, and organizational effectiveness was proposed by Hackman and Oldham.[33] Their model has been validated in numerous organizational settings. The model proposes that five core characteristics of job design influence three critical psychological states, which in turn, drive work outcomes. These core job design characteristics are:

1. *Task significance*: The degree to which the job gives the participants the feeling that they have a substantial impact on the organization or the world, for example, solving a customer's problem rather than simply filing papers
2. *Task identity*: The degree to which the worker can perceive the task as a whole, identifiable piece of work from start to finish, for example, building an entire component rather than performing a small repetitive task
3. *Skill variety*: The degree to which the job requires the worker to use a variety of skills and talents, for example, physical skills in machining a part and mental skills in using a computer to track quality measurements
4. *Autonomy*: The degree to which the task permits freedom, independence, and personal control to be exercised over the work, for example, being able to stop a production line to solve a problem
5. *Feedback from the job*: The degree to which clear, timely information about the effectiveness of performance of the individual is available, not only from supervisors, but also from measurements that the worker might take directly

High levels of skill variety, task identity, and task significance create a psychological state of "experienced meaningfulness"—the psychological need of workers to have the feeling that their work is a significant contribution to the organization and society. High autonomy drives the psychological state of "experienced responsibility"—the need of workers to be accountable for the quality and quantity of work produced. Finally, feedback from the job creates the psychological state "knowledge of results"—the need of workers to know how their work is evaluated and the results of their evaluation. Together, these psychological states drive key work outcomes of employee motivation, growth satisfaction, overall job satisfaction, and work effectiveness. The model suggests that if managers want to improve employee motivation, satisfaction, and work effectiveness, they should strive to improve the meaningfulness of work, responsibility, and knowledge of results by improving the five core job characteristics.

Quality is related in a primary or secondary sense to all five of these core job characteristics. Quality of a product or service is undoubtedly increased by a worker's dedicated application of skills, which is enhanced by task identity and a feeling of task significance. More directly, quality of work is enhanced by a job design that incorporates autonomy and feedback relating to quality characteristics. The key outcomes of high general job satisfaction and high work effectiveness can then be seen as results that define and reinforce excellent quality.

An example illustrating the Hackman and Oldham model stems from the experiences of one of the authors' students. She was a liberal arts major in college, and had worked at the art museum in the city where she attended college.

> *After I'd been there for three years, I was able to work more autonomously, trouble-shooting problems, taking steps to resolve those problems, and taking the initiative to improve my job. Guided by the museum's mission statement and my department's mission statement, I felt empowered to make changes or take steps to achieve the museum's strategic goals. After a while, I learned that my job wasn't entirely about following strict procedures. It was a real epiphany for me to figure out that I could make decisions and think on my feet to benefit a visitor, a volunteer, a co-worker, etc. For example, every year in May, the museum experiences a rush of school tours. It's the busiest time of year with school groups touring every day, Tuesday through Friday, on the hour or half-hour. The more years I worked through this crunch, the better equipped I was to promote positive changes for the "spring rush." Two years ago, the museum had a spring exhibit of Egyptian artifacts that was expected to attract many school tours. Working with many other departments like Security and Marketing, I was able to help implement school tours on Mondays when we were normally closed to the public and relieve some of the problems associated with the high demand.[34]*

Her comments show autonomy facilitated by empowerment. Her example of benefiting customers, volunteers, and coworkers demonstrate task significance and task identity, along with evidence of skill variety. She clearly experienced meaningfulness of the work and experienced responsibility. Although feedback is not addressed directly, it can be implied that she received feedback from the stakeholders regarding their experiences and her contribution to achieving them. This example particularly shows the importance of work design in jobs that have much direct customer contact, but it also applies to other types of jobs such as manufacturing where it can be more difficult to convey the significance of the task.

Several common approaches to work design—job enlargement, job rotation, and job enrichment—are supported by this model. IBM was apparently the first user of **job enlargement**, in which workers' jobs were expanded to include several tasks rather than one single, low-level task. This approach reduced fragmentation of jobs and generally resulted in lower production costs, greater worker satisfaction, and higher quality, but it required higher wage rates and the purchase of more inspection equipment. **Job rotation** is a technique by which individual workers learn several tasks by rotating from one to another. The purpose of job rotation is to renew interest or motivation of the individual and to increase his or her complement of skills. However, several studies showed that the main benefit was to increase workers' skills but that little, if any, motivational benefit could be expected.[35] Finally, **job enrichment** entails "vertical job loading" in which workers are given more authority, responsibility, and autonomy rather than simply more or different work to do.

Garvin cited an interesting example of how Japanese managers in the air-conditioning industry view job enrichment as important to quality.[36] In Japan, newly hired workers are trained so that they can do every job on the line before eventually being assigned to only one job. Training frequently requires 6–12 months, in contrast to the standard training time of one to two days for newly hired production workers in U.S. air-conditioning companies. The advantage of this "enriched" training is that workers are better able to track a defect to its source and can frequently suggest remedies to problems because they understand the entire process from start to finish. Job enrichment has been used successfully in a number of firms, notably AT&T, which experienced better employee attitudes and performance, as well as Texas Instruments, IBM, and General Foods.

In the modern, technology-dominated era, the nature of work is constantly changing. Today's entry-level workers, accustomed to using Facebook and smartphones, are also exploiting contemporary technology such as blogs and wikis (editable websites) in their work environments. For instance, about 1,500 employees of the financial firm Dresdner Kleinwort Wasserstein use virtual workspaces to create, edit, comment, and revise projects in real time. Another example is Basecamp®, a collaborative project-management service that lets groups of people post messages and files, create to-do lists, and set milestones for a project, all on simple private web pages. One firm cut the time to complete a massive redesign project from at least two years to about eight months. New capabilities to use Basecamp® for interactive collaboration anywhere and anytime are available now via an i-Phone® app.[37] Thus, managers will constantly face new challenges to design work and jobs that are effective in meeting organizational goals and objectives as well as motivating and satisfying to the people in their organizations.

Empowerment

Empowerment simply means giving people authority—to make decisions based on what they feel is right, to have control over their work, to take risks and learn from mistakes, and to promote change. It is a shift of decision responsibility downward within an organization—from management to workers on the production floor or to service workers on the front lines. Empowerment requires employees to step outside their traditional roles and make decisions previously made by managers.[38] Moreover, empowerment requires, as the management of Wainwright Industries once stated, *a sincere belief and trust in people*.

The need to empower the entire workforce in order for quality to succeed has long been recognized. Juran wrote that "ideally, quality control should be delegated to the workforce to the maximum extent possible."[39] Five of Deming's 14 Points relate directly to the notion of empowerment:

Point 6: Institute training.

Point 7: Teach and institute leadership.

Point 8: Drive out fear. Create trust. Create a climate for innovation.

Point 10: Eliminate exhortations for the workforce.

Point 13: Encourage education and self-improvement for everyone.[40]

These points suggest that managers need to involve workers more directly in decision-making processes, thus giving them the security and confidence to make decisions, and providing them with the necessary tools and training.

Examples of empowerment abound. At AT&T, design engineers have the authority to stop a design, and line operators can stop the production line if they detect a quality problem. In Ritz-Carlton hotels, each employee can spend up to $2,000 to satisfy a customer. Because of the high level of empowerment given to individuals and teams at Texas Nameplate, the company disbanded its quality control department, assigning its activities to various people who do the work. Workers in the Coors Brewery container operation give each other performance evaluations, and even screen, interview, and hire new people for the line. A Corning Glass plant replaced 21 different jobs with one "specialist" job and gave employee teams broad authority over production scheduling and division of labor.

Empowerment can benefit customers who buy the organization's products and services. For instance, empowered employees can often reduce bureaucratic red tape that customers encounter—such as seeking a supervisor's signature—which makes customer transactions speedier and more pleasant. At Motorola, for instance, sales representatives have the authority to replace defective products up to six years after purchase, a decision that used to require top management approval. Anne Mulcahy, former CEO of Xerox, described the benefits of empowerment using an example about service representatives who handle customers' calls and take orders for supplies:

> *It's a demanding job that traditionally hasn't included much flexibility. Well, we had real issues in one of our call centers a few years ago. Effectiveness and morale were down; absenteeism and turnover were up. And when managers got tough, things only got worse. So we tried something radically different—we asked the reps to set their own schedules. After we did this, all our measures started heading in the right direction.*[41]

Empowered employees must have the wisdom to know what to do and when to do it, the motivation to do it, and the right tools to accomplish the task.[42] These requirements may mean significant changes in work systems, specifically, the following:

- Employees be provided education, resources, and encouragement
- Policies and procedures be examined for needless restrictions on the ability of employees to serve customers
- An atmosphere of trust be fostered rather than resentment and punishment for failure
- Information be shared freely rather than closely guarded as a source of control and power
- Workers feel their efforts are desired and needed for the success of the organization
- Managers be given the required support and training to adopt a "hands-off" leadership style

- Employees be trained in the amount of latitude they are allowed to take. Formulating decision rules and providing role-playing scenarios are excellent ways of teaching employees[43]

Empowerment also means that leaders and managers must relinquish some of the power that they previously held. This power shift often creates management fears that workers will abuse this privilege. However, experience shows that front-line workers generally are more conservative than managers. For example, companies that have empowered employee groups to evaluate performance and grant pay raises to their peers have found that they are much tougher than managers were.

Empowerment gives managers new responsibilities. They must hire and develop people capable of handling empowerment, encourage risk taking, and recognize achievements. Giving employees information about company finances and the financial implications of empowered decisions is also important. At DuPont's Delaware River plant, management shares cost figures with all workers.[44] By sharing this information, management believes that workers will think more for themselves and identify with company goals. To help employees make decisions on issues affecting production, a department manager at the Eastman Chemical plant in Texas supplied operators with a daily financial report that showed how their decisions affected the bottom line. As a result, department profits doubled in four months and quality improved by 50 percent as employees began suggesting cost-saving improvements.[45]

David Geisler suggests that what traditionally passes for empowerment does not allow employees to use their skills and talents to the maximum.[46] He promotes the concept of **self-determination** as an extension of empowerment and argues that individual and organizational effectiveness result when employees are allowed to achieve their own unique levels of excellence; and that personal power arises when employees are certain that the organization is free of barriers, they are valued for what they contribute, and they are allowed to express themselves.

Teamwork

Perhaps one of the most significant organizational changes that has resulted from total quality is teamwork. A single person rarely has enough knowledge or experience to understand all aspects of the most important work processes; thus, team approaches are essential for achieving quality and performance excellence. Teams, and the need for such team skills as cooperation, communication, and group decision making, represent a fundamental shift in how the work is performed in the United States and most countries in the Western world.

A **team** is a group of people who work together and cooperate to share work and responsibility.[47] Teamwork breaks down barriers among individuals, departments, and line and staff functions, an action prescribed by one of Deming's 14 Points. Teams provide opportunities to individuals to solve problems that they may not be able to solve on their own. Employees who participate in team activities feel more empowered, are more satisfied with the rate of improvement in quality in their companies, and receive better training in both job-related and problem-solving skills. Teams also help organizations to capitalize on diverse ideas, cultures, and thinking of employees.

Teams encourage free-flowing participation and interaction among its members. FedEx has thousands of Quality Action teams; Boeing Airlift and Tanker Division has more than 100 integrated product teams (IPTs) that are typically made up of engineering, work-team, customer, and supplier representatives. Granite Rock, with fewer than 400 employees, has about 100 functioning teams, ranging from 10 corporate quality teams to project teams, purchasing teams, task forces, and function teams composed of people who do the same job at different locations.

Teams often perform a variety of problem-solving activities, such as determining customer needs, developing a flowchart to study a process, brainstorming to discover opportunities for improvement, selecting projects, recommending corrective actions, and tracking the effectiveness of solutions. Teams may also assume many traditional managerial functions. For example, they might hire their own workers, approve parts from suppliers, choose equipment, and handle budgets.

Many types of teams exist in different companies and industries (see Figure 4.2 for an example of teams at Baptist Hospital, Inc.). Among the most common are the following:

- *Management Teams:* Teams consisting mainly of managers from various functions, such as sales and production that coordinate work among teams
- *Natural Work Teams:* Teams organized to perform entire jobs, rather than specialized, assembly line-type work
- *Self-Managed Teams (SMTs):* Specially empowered work teams defined as "a highly trained group of employees, from 6 to 18, on average, fully responsible for turning out a well-defined segment of finished work—also known as **self-directed work teams**. The segment could be a final product, like a refrigerator or ball bearing; or a service, like a fully processed insurance claim. It could also be a complete but intermediate product or service, like a finished refrigerator motor, an aircraft fuselage, or the circuit plans for a television set."[48]
- *Virtual Teams:* Teams in which members communicate by computer, take turns as leaders, and jump in and out as necessary.[49] These types of teams use a combination of cloud computing, e-mail, video conferencing, and shared computer screen technologies to get their jobs done.

FIGURE 4.2   Teams at Baptist Hospital, Inc.

People	Service	Quality	Financial	Growth
Baptist University Board	Patient Loyalty Teams:	Clinical Excellence Teams:	Revenue Cycle Teams:	Service Lines:
Education Planning Committee	• Culture	• Acute Myocardial	• Payment Compliance	• Oncology
Employee Benefits Team	• Communication	• Congestive Heart Failure	• Patient Registration	• Cardiology
Bright Ideas	• Customer Loyalty	• Pneumonia	• Billing and Collections	• Orthopedics
Diversity Council	• Physician Loyalty	Skin Care Integrity Team	• Managed Care Pricing	
Faith in Action	• Employee Loyalty	Medication Event Team	• Documentation & Coding	
Operation Teen		Environment of Care Committee	• Late/Lost Charges	
			• Charge Master	

Source: Malcolm Baldrige National Quality Award Application Summary. National Institue of Standards and Technology, U.S. Department of Commerce, 2003. Courtsey of Ava Abney, VP Quality & Safety, Baptist Health Care. Reprinted with permission.

- *Quality Circles:* Teams of workers and supervisors that meet regularly to address work-related problems involving quality and productivity.[50]
- *Problem-Solving Teams:* Teams whose members gather to solve a specific problem and then disband. (The difference between these and quality circles is that quality circles usually remain in existence for a much longer period of time.)
- *Project Teams:* Teams with a specific mission to develop something new or to accomplish a complex task. (Project teams have been in use since World War II, and probably before that. However, project teams recently gained a new measure of importance and respect in the context of Six Sigma.)

Management teams, natural work teams, self-managed teams, and virtual teams typically work on routine business activities—managing an organization, building a product, or designing an electronic system—and are an integral part of how work is organized and designed. Quality circles, problem-solving teams, and project teams, on the other hand, work more on an ad-hoc basis to address specific tasks or issues, often relating to quality improvement. Also, natural work teams, self-managed teams, and quality circles typically are *intraorganizational;* that is, members usually come from the same department or function. Management teams, problem-solving teams, virtual teams, and project teams, are usually *cross-functional;* they work on specific tasks or processes that cut across boundaries of several different departments regardless of their organizational home. An example of a cross-functional team is the platform team approach to automotive vehicle development introduced by Chrysler.[51] For the first time in the automotive industry, this approach brought together professionals from engineering, design, quality, manufacturing, business planning, program management, purchasing, sales, marketing, and finance to work together to get a new vehicle to market. Today, all automobile manufacturers develop products using similar cross-functional team approaches.

Virtual teams present special challenges to managers.[52] Virtual teaming requires special attention to communication, technology, sponsorship, and leadership issues. For example, the team leader needs to be able to tackle issues that he or she might not have encountered with traditional teams. One of the biggest disadvantages is the lack of experience members have working with one another. They are not aware of each other's work standards and cannot scrutinize these ethics as consistently as traditional teams. This issue can be overcome by developing operating agreements by all team members, spelling out what they commit to do or not to do. Another factor is that communication is more complex because body language, voice inflection, and other communication cues are eliminated. Thus, virtual team members must be able to excel in relating their own ideas, and also understand the information others are trying to convey.

Quality circles were one of the first types of teams to focus specifically on quality. Although quality circles were popularized and implemented on a widespread basis in Japan beginning around 1960 and are often attributed to Kaoru Ishikawa of the University of Tokyo, history suggests that the concept was first implemented by Daniel Willard at the Baltimore and Ohio Railroad as part of "The Cooperative Plan," which began from joint worker-management meetings designed to raise and evaluate service-quality-related issues and suggestions.[53] The Union of Japanese Scientists and Engineers (JUSE) estimated that registration in quality circles in Japan grew from 400 members in 1962 to 200,000 members in 1968 to more than 700,000 members in 1978. Quality circles emerged in the United States in the late 1960s, reached a pinnacle in the early 1980s, but then began to lose favor among executives.[54] Much of the feeling of disappointment in their promise resulted from management's failure to understand how to implement and manage them successfully. Still, they represented a starting point for many U.S. companies to develop and test out ideas on teamwork and participative management, and many are still active today. More importantly, they paved the way for more progressive kinds of teams. Quality control circles are still alive and well internationally, especially in Asia.[55]

[*More details about team structuring and management of Six Sigma projects can be found in Chapter 9.*]

Project teams are vital to Six Sigma because of the interdisciplinary nature of such projects. Six Sigma projects require a diversity of skills that range from technical analysis, to creative solution development, and implementation. Thus, Six Sigma teams not only address immediate problems, but also provide an environment for individual learning, management development, and career advancement.

Team leaders and team members need a variety of skills.[56] Team leaders require expertise in:

- Conflict management and resolution
- Team management
- Leadership skills
- Decision making
- Communication
- Negotiation
- Cross-cultural training

Conflict management involves dealing proactively with disagreements that may occur when two or more technical experts get together. Team management involves ensuring that project members remain focused on the goals, time frame, and costs of their part of the project. Leadership skills require that the project leader guide the work of the team, including team development, while managing upward to the project champion and outward to other project teams and team leaders. Decision making requires that good decisions be made in a timely fashion. Communication channels must be established and maintained throughout the course of the project. Negotiation is needed in order to secure the resources required for successful project completion. Cross-cultural training may involve team members of other nationalities, or it may simply involve people from different functional areas with divergent points of view. In either case, it is extremely important for team members to be able to listen and learn about different perspectives on shared project goals from team and nonteam people who may have widely differing thoughts about issues under consideration.

Compared to the technical tools for gathering and analyzing data, the "soft skills"—those that involve people, such as project management and team facilitation—are more difficult to teach and learn. Team members need skills to participate effectively in meetings and an ability to reach agreement with others. Some rules for effective meetings include:[57]

- Use agendas.
- Have a facilitator.
- Take minutes.
- Draft the next agenda.
- Evaluate the meeting.
- Adhere to the "100-mile" rule.

Also suggested are the use of detailed agendas that include topics, a sentence about the importance of each, who will present them, the estimated time for each topic, and the type of item, such as discussion, decision, or information topics. A facilitator can keep the discussion on time and on target, prevent anyone from dominating or being overlooked, and help bring the discussion to a close. A scribe who takes minutes can record subjects, decisions, and who will be responsible for actions taken. Drafting the next agenda at the end of the meeting serves to set a plan of action for going forward. Evaluating the meeting incorporates a continuous improvement step. Adhering to the "100-mile" rule requires a commitment to focus on the meeting so clearly that "no one should be called from the meeting unless it is so important that the disruption would occur even if the meeting was 100 miles away from the workplace."[58]

Reaching agreement or consensus among team members is often accomplished using the nominal group technique (NGT), developed to provide a way to prioritize and focus on important project objectives in the project definition stage.[59] One of the major advantages of the technique is that it balances the power of each individual involved in the decision process. Key steps in the process include the following:

1. Request that all participants (usually 5–10 persons) write or say which problem or issue they feel is most important.
2. Record all problems or issues.
3. Develop a master list of problems or issues.
4. Generate and distribute to each participant a form that numbers the problems or issues in no particular order.
5. Request that each participant rank the top five problems or issues by assigning five points to their most important perceived problem and one point to the least important of their top five.
6. Tally the results by adding the points for each problem or issue.
7. The problem or issue with the highest number is the most important one for the team as a whole.
8. Discuss the results and generate a final ranked list for process improvement action planning.[60]

This approach provides a more democratic way of making decisions and helps individuals to feel that they have contributed to the process.

In addition, team members must possess a shared vision and behavioral skills. A shared vision can unify a team and provide the motivation for successfully implementing a project or change initiative. Developing one generally requires team discussions early on; unfortunately, inexperienced project leaders frequently bypass these discussions in an effort to get the project underway. People who are technically oriented often neglect behavioral skills, thinking that such skills are unnecessary in order to solve technical problems.

Teams are generally formed in organizational settings by direction from a manager, leader, or governing body. They are typically given a broad objective (operate this process according to certain guidelines, put a man on the moon in this decade, design a process to make cookies using elves as workers, etc.). The team may also be given a time frame and resource limits, if it is a project team.

Self-managed teams (SMTs) represent the greatest challenge. Organizations that use SMTs typically arrive at them through one of two routes: organizational start-up with SMTs in place, or transformations from more limited team structures. The second is often a next logical step after other types of employee involvement programs reach

FIGURE 4.3   Boeing A&T Team Development Process

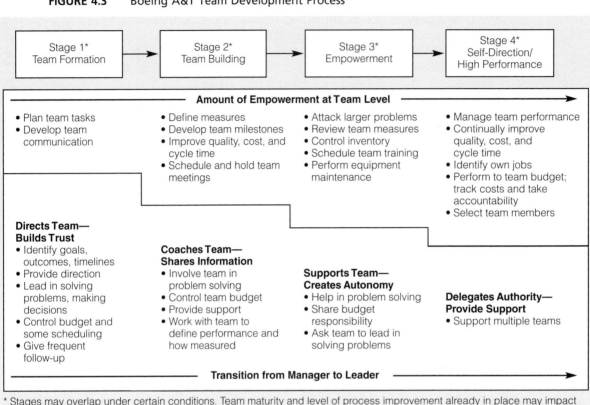

* Stages may overlap under certain conditions. Team maturity and level of process improvement already in place may impact stage application.

Source: Courtesy of Boeing Airlift and Tanker Programs.

maturity. Figure 4.3 shows the approach used by Boeing Airlift and Tanker Programs to develop self-managed teams, a result of a historic agreement between the company and union to support employee participation and empowerment. Some evidence of the effectiveness of this process is that the work of the Boeing C-17 Stuffed Tailcone team earned it a first place finish in the 2007 International Team Excellence Competition, sponsored by ASQ's Team and Workplace Excellence Forum.[61]

Teams go through a fairly predictable cycle of formation and growth, regardless of their charge and goals. The key stages of a team's life cycle are called *forming, storming, norming, performing*, and *adjourning*.[62] Forming takes place when the team is introduced, meets together, and explores issues of their new assignment. Storming occurs when team members disagree on team roles and challenge the way that the team will function. The third stage, norming, takes place when the issues of the previous stage have been worked out, and team members agree on roles, ground rules, and acceptable behavior when doing the work of the team. Stage four, performing, characterizes the productive phase of the life cycle when team members cooperate to solve problems and complete the goals of their assigned work. In the adjourning phase, the team wraps up the project, satisfactorily completes its goals, and prepares to disband or move on to another project.

Teams require various leadership and maintenance activities, especially if the team is large and the project or work assignment is complex. Typical roles that members must assume are the champion, sponsor, team leader, facilitator, timekeeper, scribe, and team member. Studies have suggested that many problems that teams encounter are due to failures in the "mechanics" of team operations.[63] Contributing factors include the lack of application of meeting skills, improper use of agendas, failure to determine team member roles and responsibilities, lack of setting and keeping ground rules, and lack of appropriate facilitative behaviors. Others have suggested that failures are rooted in organizational practices (bad policies, stupid procedures, bleary vision, ill-conceived reward system, confused goals, unresolved roles, antiteam culture); leadership (bad leadership, insufficient feedback and information, the wrong tools); and individual/team barriers (mismatched needs, hidden agendas, personality conflicts, lack of team trust, unwillingness to change).[64] Thus, managers need to carefully evaluate how teams are introduced in their organizations and address team building as a critical work process.

Peter Scholtes, a leading authority on teams for quality improvement, suggested 10 ingredients for a successful team. These items provide some guidance during the forming stage and can mitigate issues that might lead to "storming":

1. *Clarity in team goals.* As a sound basis, a team agrees on a mission, purpose, and goals.
2. *An improvement plan.* A plan guides the team in determining schedules and mileposts by helping the team decide what advice, assistance, training, materials, and other resources it may need.
3. *Clearly defined roles.* All members must understand their duties and know who is responsible for what issues and tasks.
4. *Clear communication.* Team members should speak with clarity, listen actively, and share information.
5. *Beneficial team behaviors.* Teams should encourage members to use effective skills and practices to facilitate discussions and meetings.
6. *Well-defined decision procedures.* Teams should use data as the basis for decisions and learn to reach consensus on important issues.
7. *Balanced participation.* Everyone should participate, contribute their talents, and share commitment to the team's success.
8. *Established ground rules.* The group outlines acceptable and unacceptable behaviors.
9. *Awareness of group process.* Team members exhibit sensitivity to nonverbal communication, understand group dynamics, and work on group process issues.
10. *Use of the scientific approach.* With structured problem-solving processes, teams can more easily find root causes of problems.[65]

Workplace Environment

Because employees are key stakeholders of any organization, their health, safety, and overall well-being are important factors in the work environment. Health and safety have always been priorities in most companies, but working conditions now extend beyond basic issues of keeping the work area safe and clean. For example, as we learn more about ergonomic-related disorders such as carpal tunnel syndrome and other repetitive stress injuries, employers have an even greater responsibility to incorporate health and safety factors into human resource plans. FedEx teaches employees how to handle dangerous goods, lift heavy packages correctly, and drive safely. Johnson & Johnson's Ethicon Endosurgery Division, in Blue Ash, Ohio, has a Wellness Center with exercise rooms and equipment to support employees in their manufacturing and R&D facility. Employees can use the center before or after working hours or during their breaks. In addition, those workers who are assembling products get regular, programmed "ergonomic" breaks every few hours, where they are required to do exercises designed to prevent repetitive motion injuries. At The Ritz-Carlton Hotel Company, LLC, project teams configure the best combination of technology and procedures to eliminate causes of safety and security problems. Other responsibilities include providing reasonable accommodations to workers with disabilities or ensuring that male and female employees are protected from sexual harassment from fellow workers and others.

Most companies provide many opportunities that contribute to the quality of working life. They can provide personal and career counseling, career development and employability services, recreational or cultural activities, daycare, special leave for family responsibilities or for community services, flexible work hours, outplacement services, and extended health care for retirees. Graniterock, for example, sponsors company picnics and parties at regular intervals. The best way to determine what types of programs and benefits are best for their workforce is simply to ask them. Many firms survey their employees about what benefits they enjoy and which they would like the company to offer. Not only does this increase worker satisfaction, but it also builds engagement.

 QUALITYSPOTLIGHT

SAS Institute

SAS Institute, Inc., consistently one of *Fortune*'s "100 Best Companies to Work For," is a high-tech software development company based in Cary, North Carolina. SAS has a people-focused founder and CEO in the person of James Goodnight. Perhaps the most eye-opening policy of the firm is its mandated seven-hour workday. No "all-nighters" are expected of SAS employees. The multibillionaire Goodnight sets the example by leaving the office at 5 P.M., sharp. Many of the lavish employee perks at the sprawling corporate campus are family and lifestyle-oriented, from daycare centers, lactation rooms, a Montessori school, and a college prep private high school, to a 55,000-square-foot athletic facility, free massages, free car washes, and end-of-year bonuses. The payoff? SAS has about 4 percent turnover in an industry where 20 percent is the norm.[66]

Workforce Learning and Development

Training can be one of the largest costs in an organization. Not surprisingly, it is one in which many companies are reluctant to invest. However, research indicates that companies that spend heavily on training their workers outperform companies that spend considerably less, as measured on the basis of overall stock market returns. Thus, a strong workforce development system is vital to a high performance work system.

The leaders in quality—Deming, Juran, and Crosby—actively promoted quality training and education. Two of Deming's 14 Points, for example, are devoted to these issues. Training and education should focus on both what people need to *know* as well as what things they need to know *how to do*. Training related to quality generally includes quality awareness, leadership, project management, communications, teamwork, problem solving, interpreting and using data, meeting customer requirements, process analysis, process simplification, waste reduction, cycle time reduction, error-proofing, and other issues that affect employee effectiveness, efficiency, and safety. Education needs might also include basic skills, such as reading, writing, language, mathematics, or computer skills.

It is important to ensure that training addresses key organizational needs, contributes to the organizational mission and vision, is delivered effectively, evaluated, and reinforced on the job. Customer service representatives at FedEx receive five weeks of training before they ever speak unsupervised with a customer. Before starting their job, every new employee at Stoner, Inc., a small, family-owned business with less than 50 employees, completes a two-week orientation program. In addition to ethics and safety training, new employees spend one day shadowing every job in the company including spending time with the company president. Baptist University, the internal education and training arm of Baptist Hospital, Inc. (BHI), is used as the primary source for training all employees at BHI. All BHI employees are required to receive 60 hours of learning per year.

Workforce development approaches vary by company and are delivered in a variety of ways, including on-the-job or traditional classroom environments. In some, managers train their workers directly in a top-down fashion beginning with the CEO; this approach was pioneered by Xerox during its transition to total quality. Others use classroom instruction or self-paced methods employing technology such as distance learning. Smaller companies often use outside consultants. Capitalizing on today's technology and the demographics of its younger employees, restaurants such as Pal's Sudden Service and Chuck E. Cheese have experimented with using iPods for training.[67] Identifying training opportunities and implementing them should be addressed as a key business process; Figure 4.4 shows how MEDRAD uses a systematic process to design, deliver, and evaluate education and training.

Continual reinforcement of knowledge learned is essential. Many companies send employees to courses, but then allow the knowledge to slip away. New knowledge can be reinforced in several ways. Motorola uses on-the-job coaching to reinforce training; The Ritz-Carlton has follow-up sessions to monitor instructional effectiveness. The Ritz-Carlton holds a "quality lineup" briefing session each day in every work area.

FIGURE 4.4   MEDRAD Learning and Development Process

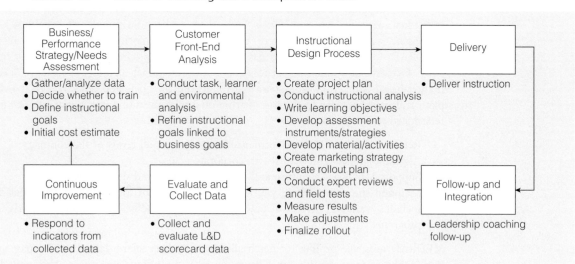

Source: MEDRAD, Malcolm Baldrige Application Summary, 2003, National Institue of Standards and Technology, U.S. Department of Commerce. Reprinted with permission.

During these sessions, employees receive instructions on achieving quality certification within the company. Work area teams set the quality certification performance standards of each position. Finally, companies need an approach for evaluating training effectiveness. The Ritz-Carlton requires employees to pass written and skill demonstration tests. Other companies use on-the-job evaluation or tests in simulated work environments. Many measure behavior and attitude changes. However, the true test of training effectiveness is results. By establishing a link between training and results, companies can show the impact on customer satisfaction and also identify gaps in training.

Compensation and Recognition

Individuals are motivated both intrinsically and extrinsically. The design of interesting work and jobs, empowerment, teamwork, and a great work environment can provide intrinsic motivation, but invariably the question "What's in it for me?" ultimately gets asked. Thus, organizations need to have effective compensation and recognition approaches.

Compensation and recognition refer to all aspects of pay and reward, including promotions, bonuses, and recognition, either monetary and nonmonetary, individual and group. Compensation is always a sticky issue, closely tied to the subject of motivation and employee satisfaction. Although money can be a motivator, it often causes employees to believe they are being treated unfairly, and forces managers to deliver negative messages. Eventually, it diminishes intrinsic motivation and creates win–lose situations. The objectives of a good compensation system should be to attract, retain, and not demotivate employees. Other objectives include reducing unexplainable variation in pay (think about Deming's principles) and encouraging internal cooperation rather than competition. Most companies still use traditional financial measures, such as revenue growth, profitability, and cost management, as a basis for compensation; more progressive organizations use quality measures such as customer satisfaction, defect prevention, and cycle time reduction to make compensation decisions.

Many progressive companies now base compensation on the market rate for an individual with proven capabilities, and then make adjustments as capabilities are increased, along with enhanced responsibilities, seniority, and business results. MEDRAD, for example, bases its pay range on market pricing rather than on an internally focused job-evaluation process. A cross-functional project team developed a market-based compensation system that reinforced the goals and objectives of the company and pays base pay in the top quartile of similar positions in the market. The team redesigned the pay structure to:

- Retain and attract high performance individuals at all levels of the company;
- Align individuals and teams with corporate goals;
- Support MEDRAD's culture and employee growth and development; and,
- Maintain the view of base pay as one component of total compensation that also includes variable incentive pay, gainsharing, benefits, and other rewards and programs.

MEDRAD uses role profiles to match all jobs to market salary data. The new pay equation combines market value for a given job with the unique qualities of the individual. Every job now has a market range with a target zone. MEDRAD's goal is to move employees to their target zone over time, based on their performance and experience.

Many companies link compensation to company track records, unit performance, team success, or individual achievement.[68] Team-based pay and **gainsharing**, an approach in which all employees share savings equally, are popular approaches. Compensation for individuals is sometimes tied to the acquisition of new skills, often within the context of a continuous improvement program in which all employees are given opportunities to broaden their work-related competencies.

 QUALITYSPOTLIGHT

Nucor

Nucor Corporation, the largest steel producer in the United States, is well-known for having succeeded in attacking quality, productivity, participation, and compensation issues through use of a unique system of gainsharing. Nucor has more than 200 operating facilities in North America and around the world, and is one of the world's largest recyclers of any kind. The company's management philosophy is clearly described in its mission statement on the company's website:

> *Nucor is made up of more than 20,000 teammates whose goal is to take care of our customers. We are accomplishing this by being the safest, highest quality, lowest cost, most productive, and most profitable steel and steel products company in the world.*
>
> *We are committed to doing this while being cultural and environmental stewards in our communities where we work. We are succeeding by working together.*
>
> *Taking care of our customers means all of our customers: our employees, our shareholders and the people who purchase and use our products.*[69]

Although Nucor is a multibillion dollar company, its headquarters staff consists of only 95 people, and it maintains a relatively simple organizational structure, with only five levels from the CEO down to the first-line employee. Nucor boasts that there is an absence of corporate perks for executives, with no special parking places, vacation plans, or first-class travel. When times are tight, executives' pay is cut before first-line employees' pay.

Nucor's compensation at all levels is based on pay for performance. In the mills, this means that pay is tied to the number of tons of steel produced each day. The company has found that this results in above industry average wages for employees and phenomenal productivity levels. By pushing decision-making to the lowest levels of the organization, employees are empowered to do such things as stop production when they see a problem, or talk directly with customers to explore ways to improve quality. Employees are given freedom to fail in order to encourage them to try new ideas.

Employee relations at Nucor are based on four clear-cut principles:

1. *Management is obligated to manage Nucor in such a way that employees will have the opportunity to earn according to their productivity.*
2. *Employees should feel confident that if they do their jobs properly, they will have a job tomorrow.*
3. *Employees have the right to be treated fairly and must believe that they will be.*
4. *Employees must have an avenue of appeal when they believe they are being treated unfairly.*

To emphasize the importance of employees as a vital part of the corporate culture and its ongoing success, the cover of the company's Annual Report contains the individual names of a segment of its employees, in alphabetical order. In past years, Nucor featured the names of each of its 20,500 employees spread over the first 14 cover pages of the report.

Despite the tough times, including the recent economic downturn of 2008–2010, Nucor has maintained their policy of no layoffs, as it has throughout the history of the current company. More about the Nucor story can be found on its website at http://www.nucor.com.

Recognition and rewards can be powerful motivators. They can be monetary or non-monetary, formal or informal, individual or group. Rewards might include trips, promotional gifts, clothing, time off, plaques and certificates, or simple recognition ceremonies. In many cases, sincere nonmonetary recognition is valued more by employees than money or gifts, which can often create resentment. Whatever the recognition, it should have symbolic value that employees can inspire employees in the future. A simple example is the "Caught Doing Good" program at Pal's Sudden Service. Any staff member or team caught making an improved or exemplary job contribution in production or customer service is recognized on the spot with written public praise for the deed. A staff member, manager, or even a customer or supplier can documents it on a special form and post it on the store bulletin board.[70]

Employees understand that their efforts make a difference, that the organization values its people and cares about their success, thus reinforcing their pride and self-esteem (remember Deming's focus on "pride and joy" in work). Organizations receive greater motivation, loyalty, and effort from recognized employees along with increased performance, thereby improving their advantages over competitors.[71] Recognition has important benefits to both employees and their organizations. It provides a visible means of promoting quality efforts and telling employees that the organization values their efforts, which stimulates their motivation to improve.

Not everyone values the same types of recognition and reward. A Conference Board study found that a combination of cash and noncash recognition works better for clerical and hourly workers than for managers and professional/technical employees; for these groups, compensation-based incentives such as stock options are more successful.[72] Thus, any recognition and reward initiative should be tailored to the specific needs and wants of the employee segment.

Certain key practices lead to effective recognition and rewards:

- *Give both individual and team awards.* At The Ritz-Carlton, individual awards include verbal and written praise and the most desirable job assignments. Team awards include bonus pools and sharing in the gratuity system.
- *Tie rewards to measurable performance.* When Custom Research, Inc. attained a specific corporate goal, the entire company is taken on a trip to destinations such as San Francisco and Disney World!
- *Involve everyone.* Recognition programs should be available to everyone in the organization, including both front-line employees and senior management, and employees should participate in their design.
- *Drive behaviors that support organizational values and high performance.* Leading companies recognize and reward behavior, not just results. Figure 4.5 shows the different types of recognition and reward mechanisms used by Premier, Inc.
- *Publicizing extensively.* Many companies recognize employees through newsletters, certificates and pins, special breakfasts or luncheons, and annual events such as competitions. Making recognition public reinforces its significance, and having top managers preside in giving recognition sends an important message that they really understand and appreciate employees' efforts.
- *Making recognition fun.* Wells Fargo Bank gives employees a choice of unusual rewards, like "a menu item named after you in the company cafeteria," or "The Chairman or President does your job for a day while you train and supervise." A dentist in Oakland, CA, instead of just giving a cash bonus to his staff, closed down his office and took them to a shopping mall. He handed them each an

FIGURE 4.5
Premier, Inc. Recognition and Reward Mechanisms Award Recognition

Award	Recognition
The Premier Award	Value-based high performance
The Premier Team Award	Team-based high performance
Cash Spot Bonus	Project/Goal achievement
Premier "Turtle" Award	Innovation "sticking your neck out"
Employee Choice Award	Spontaneous values behavior
Service Recognition (5, 10, 15, 20, 25, 30 yr)	Service years with Premier
Commission Programs	Sales objectives
Unit Recognition programs	Behaviors and achievement

Source: Premier, Inc. Recognition and Reward Mechanisms; Premier Performance Management Process, 2007 Malcolm Baldrige Application Summary, NIST, U.S. Department of Commerce.

envelope containing the money and said "You have to spend all the money on gifts for yourself. You have one hour to spend it, and you have to buy at least five different items. Any money you haven't spent in the next hour comes back to me. Go get 'em!" The employees spent the next hour dashing wildly from one store to the next, yelling back and forth to each other about the treasures they'd found. At the next staff meeting, everyone brought the presents they had purchased for themselves for a show-and-tell session with the group.[73]

Performance Management

Considerable truth can be found in the statement, "How one is evaluated determines how one performs." This reality can be dangerous. Many years ago, Analog Devices, a successful Massachusetts analog and digital equipment manufacturer, embraced TQ but found its stock price steadily declining. One of its key measures (on which managers were rewarded) was new product introduction time, with an objective of reducing it from 36 to 6 months. The product development team focused on this objective; as a result, engineers turned away from riskier new products and designed mundane derivatives of old products that no longer met customers' needs. The company subsequently scrapped that goal.[74]

Performance appraisal is a process for subjectively evaluating the quality of an employee's work. However, performance appraisal is an exceedingly difficult activity. Organizations typically use performance appraisals to provide feedback to employees who can then recognize and build on their strengths and work on their weaknesses (that is, opportunities for improvement), determine training needs, allocate compensation and rewards, identify individuals to promote, assess the pool of talent across the organization, and identify the best and worst performers. As such, they can provide a paper trail to fight wrongful-discharge suits and act as a formal warning system to marginal employees.[75] Many leading organizations use performance appraisal for changing corporate culture.

Conventional appraisal processes typically involve setting objectives for a certain period of time (typically for the year ahead), either unilaterally or jointly by the manager with his or her subordinate. Objectives might focus on development of knowledge or skills, results such as output and productivity, or behavior. Objective setting is followed by a supervisory review of accomplishments, strengths and weaknesses, or personal characteristics of the subordinate related to the job at the end of the review period. Often, the form used for performance rating has 10 to 15 tangible and intangible categories, such as quantity of work, quality of work, works well with others, takes initiative, and so on, to be rated on a five- or seven-point scale from "excellent" to "unsatisfactory" or "poor." The performance appraisal interview may be accompanied by announcements of raises, bonuses, or promotions. In some cases, company policy dictates a certain distribution of results, such as "no more than 10 percent of any department's employees may be rated as excellent" or "merit raises or bonuses will only be paid to employees who are rated as excellent or very good."

Dissatisfaction with conventional performance appraisal systems is common among both managers, who are the appraisers, and workers, who are appraised. General Motors, for example, discovered that 90 percent of its people believed they were in the top 10 percent. How discouraging is it to be rated lower? Many managers are inclined to give higher ratings because of potential negative impacts. Numerous research studies over the past several decades have pointed out the problems and pitfalls of performance appraisals.[76]

Many legitimate objections can be made:[77]

- They tend to foster mediocrity and discourage risk taking.
- They focus on short-term and measurable results, thereby discouraging long-term planning or thinking and ignoring important behaviors that are more difficult to measure.
- They focus on the individual and therefore tend to discourage or destroy teamwork within and between departments.
- The process is detection-oriented rather than prevention-oriented.
- They are often unfair, as managers frequently do not possess observational accuracy.
- They fail to distinguish between factors that are within the employees' control and system-determined factors that are beyond their control.

One approach that has overcomes many of these objections is called **360-degree feedback**. In an ideal 360-degree approach, a group of individuals who interact with the employee (or team) on a frequent basis participate in both the goal-setting process and the performance appraisal process. This group might include suppliers, clients, peers, internal customers, managers, and subordinates. The process involves two-way communication in which both parties discuss such needs as service levels, response times, accuracy of work and so on, which are often expressed as written service contracts. At the end of the performance period, selected representatives who participated in the goal setting evaluate how well the goals of the service contracts have been met, and provide feedback. The final performance appraisal consists of discussing an aggregation of the comments and ratings with the employee, and serves as a process for setting goals for the next period and for employee development. Because the approach is new, little systematic research has been performed on its effectiveness; however, user feedback has been positive.

Performance appraisals are most effective when they are based on the objectives that support the strategic directions of the organization, best practices, and continuous improvement. An effective performance management process should focus on feedback and improvement. Figure 4.6 shows a typical process that is used at Premier, Inc. It begins with a clear picture of employee expectations in Step 1. As part of the strategic

FIGURE 4.6
Premier Perfor-
mance Manage-
ment Process

Step	Process
1	Establish Expectation (Define expected outcomes & behaviors)
2	Manage Performance (Provide performance feedback and support)
3	Measure and Reward Performance (Assess performance (Performance Appraisals), Reward appropriate outcomes/behaviors)
4	Improve Performance (Provide development and growth (IDP) for continued improvement and growth)

Source: Premier Performance Management Process, 2007 Malcolm Baldrige Application Summary, NIST. U.S. Department of Commerce.

planning process, all goals and actions are cascaded to units and employees through Deployment Grids that outline employee performance goals to ensure line of sight to Corporate and BU Goal achievement. Managers meet individually with each employee to review and agree upon expectations and to identify support needed to accomplish goals. Plans are developed by managers and employees to support Unit Goal achievement. In Step 2, managers provide on-going feedback, coaching, and redirection, as appropriate, to individuals and teams to encourage goal achievement and Core Values based behaviors. Both informal and formal interaction and review takes place throughout the year, with a minimum of two formal review meetings with each employee. Step 3 takes place at the end of each fiscal year, with managers meeting each employee to provide required formal evaluation. The first part of the evaluation measures Corporate Goal achievement and individual contribution against fiscal year goals documented on the Deployment Grid. The second part is based on three dimensions: individual performance, Premier Core Values-based competencies, and leadership and team support skills.[78]

Today, many leading organizations are focusing on identifying a small number of core competencies that are critical to the organization's success.[79] These core competencies are the behaviors, skills, and attributes every member is expected to have. They also use **mastery descriptions**, narratives of behavior that one who has mastered it would likely engage in. For example, a mastery description of *Customer Focus* might be:

> *Dedicated to meeting the expectations and requirements of internal and external customers. Knows who every one of his/her customers is and can state what that individual's expectations are. Gets firsthand customer information and uses it for improvements in products and services. Speaks and acts with customers in mind. Takes the client's side in well-founded complaints. Is skilled at managing customer expectations. Establishes and maintains effective relationships with customers and gains their trust and respect. Actively seeks customers' feedback on the quality of service he/she provides.*

A behavioral frequency scale, in which appraisers indicate how frequently the appraisee does the things listed in the mastery descriptions (rarely, occasionally, frequently, or regularly, for example) is often used. This avoids numerical judgments of performance, defensive reactions, and provides a guide of what to do to improve.

In the spirit of Deming, many companies are replacing performance evaluation altogether with workforce development and learning systems that provide feedback for improvement. Graniterock, for example, does not emphasize past performance, but sets professional development goals in conjunction with the company's needs. No stigma is attached to failure; the thrust of the process is to develop each individual to the fullest.

ASSESSING WORKFORCE EFFECTIVENESS, SATISFACTION, AND ENGAGEMENT

Measurement of workforce effectiveness, satisfaction, and engagement are important to determine how work systems are performing and contributing to an organization's strategic objectives, and also to provide a foundation for improvement. In fact, research has suggested that organizations that use people measures as part of a balanced set of measures to manage the business achieve significantly higher return on investment and return on assets than those that don't. Nevertheless, few organizations have well-defined people measures or use them to predict key business outcomes.[80] Understanding the "voice of the employee," particularly with regard to employee satisfaction, management policies, and their internal customers and suppliers helps organizations improve their human resource management practices.

Both outcome and process measures provide data by which to assess workforce effectiveness. Outcome measures might include "hard" measures such as number of teams, rate of growth, percentage of employees involved, number of suggestions implemented, time taken to respond to suggestions, employee turnover, absenteeism, and grievances; as well as "soft" measures such as perceptions of teamwork and management effectiveness, engagement, satisfaction, and empowerment. Typical process measures include the number of suggestions that employees make, the numbers of participants in project teams, and participation in educational programs. Team process effectiveness can be assessed by tracking the average time it takes to complete a process improvement project, and determining whether teams are getting better, smarter, and faster at performing improvements. Organizations should also look for other indicators of performance, such as improvements in team selection and planning processes, frequency of use of quality improvement tools by employees, employee understanding of problem-solving approaches, and senior management involvement. Many companies also ask employees to rate their supervisors on leadership, communication, and support.

The most common approach to assess worker perceptions and satisfaction is through a formal survey. Questions in a typical survey might be grouped into such basic categories as satisfaction with quality of worklife, teamwork, communications, opportunities and training, facilities, leadership, compensation, benefits, and the company. For example, Marlow Industries uses a survey that addresses a broad variety of issues, including management support, the company's total quality system, organizational effectiveness, training, continuous improvement, and worker satisfaction. Table 4.4 shows most of the questions included in their survey. All responses are made on a five-item scale ranging from *totally disagree* to *very much agree*. Xerox produces its survey in 25 languages. Fifty-four questions are grouped into eight categories: Directions/communications, Valuing people, Trust, Learning, Feedback, Recognition, Participation/involvement, and Teamwork. Xerox compares results against similar companies such as Allied Signal, Honeywell, Sun Microsystems, Texas Instruments, and others. Many research-based and commercial survey instruments are available.[81]

TABLE 4.4   Employee Quality Survey—Marlow Industries

Management Support
1. The president is an active supporter of quality at Marlow Industries.
2. Senior management (VPs) are active supporters of quality at Marlow Industries.
3. My supervisor is an active supporter of quality at Marlow Industries.
4. My supervisor is concerned more about the quality of my work than the quantity of my work.
5. My supervisor can help me to do my job better.
6. My supervisor encourages good housekeeping efforts.
7. I receive recognition for a top quality job done.

Total Quality System
1. Marlow Industries' Total Quality System is not a fad. It will be active long into the future.
2. The Total Quality system has made an improvement in the performance of my work.
3. The Total Quality system has made an improvement in my ability to do my job right the first time.
4. I understand the meaning of the Quality Policy.
5. I believe in the meaning of the Quality Policy.
6. I understand the meaning of the Quality Pledge.
7. I believe in the meaning of the Quality Pledge.
8. All departments within Marlow Industries support the Total Quality system.
9. My co-workers support quality first.
10. My co-workers believe in the Quality Pledge.
11. My "supplier" co-worker treats me as his/her "customer" and meets my needs.
12. I know who my internal "customer" is.
13. I am able to meet the requirements of my internal customer.
14. I believe that improving quality is the key to maintaining Marlow Industries' success.

Organizational Effectiveness
1. I receive feedback that helps me perform my job better.
2. I am encouraged to stop and ask questions if something does not seem right.
3. There is a high level of quality in the products we ship to our external customers.
4. Marlow Industries provides reliable processes and equipment so that I can do my job right the first time.
5. I do not use defective materials.
6. I am provided proper procedures to do my job right.
7. My fellow workers have a high level of enthusiasm about Marlow Industries' quality.
8. I believe control charts will help us improve quality.
9. I believe Marlow Industries offers a high quality working environment.
10. I enjoy my job.

Training
1. I have received training to be able to do my job right the first time.
2. I have received training on how to determine if the work I do conforms to Marlow Industries' workmanship standards, and other requirements of the customer.
3. I receive adequate safety training so that I am aware of the safety and health requirements of my job.
4. My supervisor has received adequate training to be able to do his/her job right the first time.
5. My co-worker has received adequate training to be able to do his/her job right the first time.
6. I have received ongoing training.
7. The training I have received has been very helpful to me in my job.

Job Satisfaction and Morale
1. I have a high level of personal job satisfaction.
2. My morale is high.
3. The morale of my work group is high.

Involvement
1. I feel involved at Marlow Industries.
2. I would like to be more involved at Marlow Industries.

Source: Reprinted with permission of Marlow Industries.

Results provide a basis for evaluation and improvement. At Saint Luke's Hospital in Kansas City, MO, employee satisfaction results are segmented by unit level, job type, shift assignments, and ethnicity to provide hospital leadership with information that can be acted upon to enhance satisfaction and motivation. In evaluating results, trends and long-term results should be emphasized, and they should be communicated to employees. A good system should report results on a regular basis, perhaps monthly or quarterly, with a summary year-end report, using graphical aids wherever possible. Detailed reports should go to lower-level managers, showing results at their level. Summary reports should go to higher management levels. Specific action, such as training, changes in reward or recognition, or improvements to support employee well-being should be taken based on results.

Measuring Workforce Engagement

In Figure 4.1, we showed the key dimensions of employee engagement that MEDRAD uses based on the GPTW survey. Numerous other consulting organizations, such as Right Management, discussed earlier in this chapter, have proposed survey instruments to measure workforce engagement. Perhaps the most well-known instrument—called the Q12— was developed and is implemented by the Gallup Organization. The Q12 consists of 12 survey statements that Gallup found as those that best form the foundation of strong feelings of engagement. These include factors like knowing what is expected in one's work; having the right materials and equipment to do the job; receiving recognition and feedback on progress and development; having opinions that count, feeling of importance of the job; and opportunities to learn grow and develop. (Q12 is a registered trademark of the Gallup Organization and the survey questions may only be legally used with permission.)

> *The Q12 is based on more than 30 years of in-depth behavioral economic research involving more than 17 million employees, and the research underlying the instrument has been published in the* Journal of Applied Psychology, *the* Harvard Business Review, *and in two books published by* Gallup.[82]

Gallup analyzes the survey results and creates an "engagement index" that assigns people into one of three categories:

1. *Engaged employees* who work with passion and feel a profound connection to their company. They drive innovation and move the organization forward.
2. *Not-engaged employees* who are essentially "checked out." They are sleepwalking through their workday. They are putting in time, but not enough energy or passion into their work.
3. *Actively disengaged employees* who aren't just unhappy at work; they're busy acting out their unhappiness. Every day, these workers undermine what their engaged co-workers accomplish.

Gallup states that in world-class organizations, the ratio of engaged to actively disengaged employees is 9.57:1, while in average organizations, the ratio is 1.83:1. They estimate the cost of lost productivity due to actively disengaged employees to be more than $300 billion in the United States alone. These results are significant for organizations, and support the importance of building a work environment that fosters engagement and the need to understand the level of engagement in the organization.

SUSTAINING HIGH-PERFORMANCE WORK SYSTEMS

Organizations must take a long-term view of its work systems and take the necessary steps to ensure that high performance is sustained. This requires a regular assessment of workforce capability and capacity needs; hiring the right employees, and attending to career progression and succession planning.

Workforce Capability and Capacity

Workforce capability refers to an organization's ability to accomplish its work processes through the knowledge, skills, abilities, and competencies of its people. Capability may include the ability to build and sustain relationships with customers; to innovate and transition to new technologies; to develop new products, services, and work processes; and to meet changing business, market, and regulatory demands. **Workforce capacity** refers to an organization's ability to ensure sufficient staffing levels to accomplish its work processes and successfully deliver products and services to customers, including the ability to meet seasonal or varying demand levels.

Workforce capability and capacity should consider not only current needs but also future requirements based on strategic objectives and action plans. We will discuss the importance of human resource planning in conjunction with strategic planning in Chapter 10. For example, to assess its workforce capability, Consolidated District 15 school system asks its department staff a series of audit questions to clarify how they contribute to the accomplishment of the school's mission. The answers to these questions drive the development of determining the work that needs to be done and school improvement plans. To manage its workforce capacity, Saint Luke's Hospital has a workforce planning system responsive to both current and changing health care needs. The system includes a "Workforce Planning and Assessment Tool," a detailed staffing analysis for all departments supporting patient care, and human resource action plans that are created based upon the strategic plan.

Meeting and exceeding customer expectations begins with hiring the right people whose skills and attitudes will support and enhance the organization's objectives. First, one must identify what skills and competencies they need. At MEDRAD, for example, the Human Resources department, working with senior staff, came up with a list of core behavioral/management competencies through an analysis of future leadership requirements based on MEDRAD's vision and an assessment of the company's current capabilities. Then, MEDRAD hired a consulting company to help refine and expand the definition and use of core competencies. The consultants worked with the Human Resources Advisory Board and senior staff, conducted extensive interviews of high potential, high performing companies, and made recommendations based on their analysis and industry experience. Table 4.5 shows the key competencies they expect in their employees.

The next step is to identify job candidates based on the skills and competencies during the hiring process. Branch-Smith Printing specifies the set of skills required to perform a job. Candidates are screened with a set of questions designed to assess their skills to perform the job functions as defined in the job descriptions. They use behavior-based questions to assess whether candidates have the characteristics to excel in their team-based, quality-focused environment. Two additional assessments are given to candidates who meet the first criteria. One is a pre-employment screening tool for assessing the

TABLE 4.5
Key Employee
Competencies at
MEDRAD

- Performance development
- High performance orientation
- Adaptability
- Sound judgment
- Detail orientation
- Planning organizing
- Communications (written, verbal, professional)
- Motivation and empowerment
- Cross-functional teamwork and collaboration
- Customer focus

- Values driven (respect for others, integrity, etc.)
- Continuous innovation and improvement (creativity process orientation, etc.)
- Change implementation
- Persuasion and consensus building
- Medrad/market/industry knowledge
- Global perspective
- Building partnerships
- Strategic visioning
- Project management

Source: Reprinted with permission of MEDRAD.

attitudes of job candidates regarding integrity, responsibility, and work ethic. The second uses advanced technology to predict job suitability and matches people with the job for which they are applying.

Customer-contact employees make up a large segment of today's workforce. Limited availability of people with the skills to perform complex, rapidly changing jobs is forcing workforce managers to rethink their selection criteria. Traditional hiring practices have been based on cognitive or technical rather than interpersonal skills. The criterion is now shifting to attributes such as enthusiasm, resourcefulness, creativity, and the flexibility to learn new skills rapidly. The internal customer concept suggests that every employee needs good interpersonal skills. Even technical skill requirements are changing; to apply quality principles on the job, all workers must have basic mathematics and logical-thinking abilities. To ensure that job candidates have the requisite skills, new approaches, such as psychological testing and situational role playing, are now being used in the hiring process.

Some organizations are using highly innovative approaches to recruit employees. Health care, for example, has long faced severe shortages of key personnel such as nurses. North Mississippi Medical Center has a unique recruiting process that begins with Let's Pretend Hospital, a tool to educate first graders in health care careers. Other programs, such as the Summer Health Academy and the Advanced Health Academy are designed for middle school students. High school and vocational students can participate in Medical Explorers, Job Shadowing, and facility tours. High school seniors pursuing a medical career are candidates for annual medical scholarships. The Nurse Mentorship Academy provides 16 hours of lecture, guest speakers, job shadowing, and volunteering for exploring a career in nursing.

An important part of workforce capability and capacity planning for long-term sustainability is succession planning for leadership and management positions. Many companies have formal processes to identify, develop, and position future leaders to assume key responsibilities. Many managers are required to identify successors and create formal succession plans that include development objectives and activities such as mentoring and coaching, or job rotation. The City of Coral Springs, Florida, for example, formalizes succession planning through its Leadership Development Program, which proactively identifies and develops employees who have the potential to hold future leadership and key individual contributor positions. Through the program, two development paths have been created to support individual growth and guide the timing of leadership development: Senior Leadership path and Management Leadership path. Participants in the Senior Leadership path participate in designated strategic learning events including Leadership Coral Springs, the Florida International University Strategic Management Program, joint senior management team/participant meetings, quarterly Supervisory Forums, 360-degree assessments, attendance at one City Commission meeting per quarter, and attendance at all strategic planning and budget workshops. In addition to the strategic learning events, participants complete a career development profile and are paired with a mentor from the senior management team. Participants in the Management Leadership path participate in designated activities including quarterly Supervisory Forums, Request for Proposal (RFP) processes, focus groups and cross-functional teams, and a personality profile.

Career development is also changing because of a focus on quality and high performance. As managerial roles shift from directing and controlling to coaching and facilitating, managers, who must deal with cross-functional problems, benefit more from horizontal movement than from upward movement in narrow functional areas. Flatter organizations limit promotion opportunities. Thus, career development expands learning opportunities and creates more challenging assignments rather than increasing spans of managerial control. At Pal's Sudden Service, employees advance on a planned basis to fill process team roles as they learn more job skills and operational positions. The most capable team members are selected to back up assistant managers and are put on a path for advancement to assistant manager, and possibly to owner/operator succession.

SUMMARY OF KEY POINTS AND TERMINOLOGY

The Student Companion Site provides a summary of key concepts and terminology introduced in this chapter.

QUALITY *in* PRACTICE

Training for Improving Service Quality at Honda[83]

American Honda Motor Co. is part of Honda's North American operations. Based in Torrance, CA, American Honda provides information services, purchasing, financial services, leasing support, and a host of sales and marketing-related services to Honda's business and manufacturing units throughout North America. In 2001, American Honda's associate learning and organizational development group undertook a broad assessment of its approach to training, looking at what was offered, why, to whom, and how. One focus of this initiative was to deepen the emphasis on quality, which has long permeated Honda's manufacturing operations, within the internal support and service portions of the organization. "The Honda philosophy encourages every individual to continuously expand his or her ability to identify and impact both internal and supplier quality," says Lou Juneman, manager of associate learning and organizational development for American Honda. "Innovation, branding, customer satisfaction, and efficiency are central to our success; therefore, quality is at the core of everything we do."

The challenge laid out for the development group was to improve and extend the delivery of training for employees, reduce their time away from the job for training, take advantage of expanding technology capabilities and infrastructure and, above all, ensure a tangible transfer of skills that would take internal service quality to an entirely new level. Honda's approach to service quality improvement through e-learning was focused and disciplined. First, the company began to use a learning management system (LMS) to schedule, administer, and track training. The system was applied not only to instructor-led offerings but also to pure online training, blended learning (a unique mix of online and instructor-led training), and other offerings. Using a customized LMS, Honda employees and their managers learned to define and manage individual training plans as well as enroll in, complete, and track their progress in courses and curricula through a learner-specific web portal.

Decisions also had to be made about which programs to offer and which formats would best support the overall emphasis on growth and quality. Their approach, called blended learning, is to provide the best mix of electronic, instructor-led, and self-paced learning to employees. One of the programs to which the blended learning approach was applied was problem solving and decision making. This program sharpens an individual's ability to separate and clarify issues, identify those that need immediate attention, and resolve them using a systematic, rational problem-solving, decision-making or action-planning process. These rational thinking skills have been successfully taught at American Honda for many years in a purely instructor-led workshop version. The skills have been critical to establishing and sustaining quality throughout Honda, in both the manufacturing and service/support areas. American Honda worked closely with several vendors to shorten the time spent at the workshop, produce online learning elements, and document results electronically. The blended learning approach also enabled American Honda to capture and measure detailed, useful data about how the problem-solving and decision-making processes are used to impact and improve quality in critical service and support areas.

American Honda realized from the beginning that training, by itself, wouldn't lead to quality improvements. Applying the skills learned during a training experience regularly and accurately requires a great deal of practice and support. This led to American Honda's three-phase learning model (see Figure 4.7). The first phase takes place online. For two to three

FIGURE 4.7 American Honda's Three-Phase Learning Model

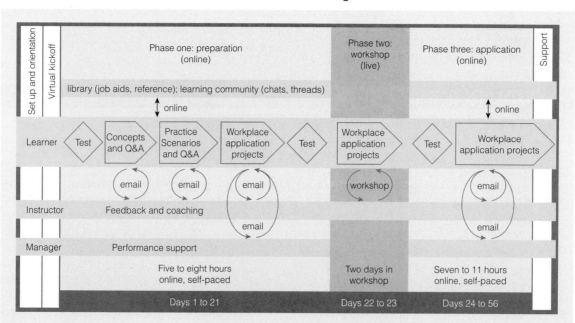

Source: Reprinted with permission from Wayne Stottler, "Improving Service Quality at Honda," *Quality Progress*, October 2004, pp. 33–38. Copyright © 2004 American Society for Quality. No further distribution allowed without permission.

weeks, learners access a series of online modules that introduce the logical processes for effective problem solving and decision making. Learner progress is essentially self-paced, but because the content is driven from a web server, the instructor can follow the progress of each learner and provide ongoing encouragement and support. During phase one, learners are also asked to identify situations to which they intend to apply the techniques so they can focus on these situations when they attend the workshop. This powerful combination of initial learning and preparation for applying the concepts to real-life issues ensures the following phase will not only be efficient but will also build deep understanding and significant motivation to use the ideas on the job after training.

The second phase takes place at the workshop. Guided by the instructor, learners spend two days deepening their understanding of the concepts, discussing best practices and additional techniques for problem solving and decision making, and practicing on detailed case scenarios. Because skill transfer—and results—occur most rapidly when one starts with the learner's on-the-job issues, a significant portion of the session is spent working on the problems, decisions and plans identified in phase one. Simultaneously, learners receive coaching and feedback from the instructor and one another. Learners leave the session ready to fully apply the concepts and with a plan in hand to move successfully from the workshop to consistent use of the concepts back on the job.

The final phase takes place back online. In the three weeks following the session, learners resolve the on-the-job issues they began to work on during the workshop. They document the specific techniques they used to resolve the issues for instructor review, feedback, and approval. During phase three, learners have access to a host of online support tools and information. They can contact the instructor with questions at any time. The goal of this phase is to ensure use of the learned concepts, build confidence, get results, and capture information about how the problem-solving and decision-making tools impact American Honda's business; how they create quality and value through their use.

Honda managers learned a lot about electronic learning. As one observed, "True online learning requires culture change, and like any change, it requires planning, communication, and persistence." While online learning displaces some workshop time—the session was pared from three days to two—learners must take time to go online and learn. This requires new behaviors on the part of learners (who have to find the time and resist distractions), managers (who have to encourage and protect the time necessary for online learning), and instructors (who become performance partners and must be available to coach and support learners).

To promote and support the success rate of online learners, American Honda now kicks off each training session with a web conference to clarify expectations and provide participants with practical tips for online learning. In addition, learners' managers are brought into the loop and asked for input into the choice of high priority problems, decisions, and plans to be tackled during the workshop. Instructors at American Honda have also received additional training to help them effectively coach online learners and act quickly to intervene with anyone experiencing difficulties. The company has also created an extensive online library of reference and support materials on which instructors can draw.

Because instructors can track phase one learning progress in real time, they can provide direct support to individual learners even before they come to the workshop. As a result, the instructor can tailor the learning experience, minimizing the one-size-fits-all approach that frustrates many people in traditional training. After the session, the instructor becomes an on-call coach—tracking progress, providing pointers, and answering questions so learners get personalized support during the critical days following the workshop, when traditional learners often stumble and give up in frustration.

This adds up to a higher quality learning experience that produces the motivation and support Juneman believes are key to setting the stage for integrating learned concepts into daily use long-term. Because learners now submit online documentation of the issues they have resolved, it is much easier to see how and where the concepts are being used and evaluate the impact of the training on the bottom line of the organization. They have identified five indicators that support the success of this initiative:

1. Increased learner readiness for workshop learning
2. Better identification of relevant application topics
3. Increased volume of completed applications
4. Increased dollar value of after-workshop applications
5. Greater ongoing use of skills

With more than 300 learners having taken advantage of the blended learning opportunity in the last couple of years, American Honda is happy with the results. Juneman offers an example: "When someone in our dealer support function uses these rational-thinking processes to systematically find and resolve the cause of a longstanding computer systems issue, I know he or she and a number of other people across the organization will be able to work more efficiently. The quality of individual output is improved, customers are happier and more efficient, and learners are very likely to use the problem-solving process again and again to achieve similar results."

Key Issues for Discussion

1. Why did Honda use a blended learning approach rather than, for example, a pure virtual online learning approach?
2. What were the benefits of the three-phase learning model? How does it support the achievement of high performance?
3. What lessons might other organizations learn from Honda's experience?

Source: Text adapted from Wayne Stottler, "Improving Service Quality at Honda," Quality Progress, October 2004, 33–38. Copyright © 2001, American Society for Quality. Reprinted with permission.

QUALITY *in* PRACTICE

Improving Employee Retention Through Six Sigma[84]

Hewitt Associates, based in Lincolnshire, IL, is a human resources (HR) outsourcing and consulting company. The customer service (CS) role at Hewitt—and many other companies that rely heavily on CS to deliver outsourced processes—requires significant training on the proprietary systems used to handle data from client organizations. The organization was losing CS talent at an annual turnover rate close to 100 percent, which is common in this line of work. When the company determined it could save millions of dollars through stronger retention of its CS representatives, senior leaders ask the HR department to make it happen. Consequently, HR embarked on a Six Sigma project.

The first step was to quantify the cost of turnover for CS representatives—to defend the required investment and realize the proposed return on investment (ROI). The cost of turnover includes both hard and soft costs: separation processing costs, replacement hiring costs, new hire training costs, and lost productivity. HR brought together the statisticians, workforce engineers, and line leaders responsible for coordinating and managing the costs of a 2,500-plus person CS center. The team focused on the hard costs of hiring and training, but spent the bulk of time on measuring lost productivity in the CS environment—the biggest cost in any turnover model. The model resulted in an average hard dollar cost savings figure of about $24,000 for each avoided separation. Based on the

annualized turnover rate for the current year, the cost of lost CS productivity for the HR outsourcing segment of Hewitt's business was estimated as approximately $14.5 million. Layering in the hard dollar costs for training and recruiting brought the total to nearly $16 million, or about 13 percent of Hewitt's overall net operating income in that year.

Based on the work Hewitt does with its HR consulting clients, the company knows there is a strong positive relationship between engagement and organizational performance. Specifically, companies with higher levels of engagement are likely to have greater sales growth and higher total shareholder return. Hewitt conducts an annual associate engagement survey that measures not only all the standard employee opinion survey components, such as satisfaction with opportunities, but also intent to display certain behaviors known to have an impact on business results (see Figure 4.8). One of those survey items asked: "How likely is it that you will be working at Hewitt one year from now?" Predictive analysis has shown that of the representatives who respond that it is unlikely they will be working at Hewitt, about half actually leave within one year, making this item an important leading indicator of retention.

Hewitt also uses regression analysis to determine the most important drivers of retention for the CS representatives. Elements of the work environment in which satisfaction is low but the relationship to

FIGURE 4.8   Hewitt's Employee Engagement Framework

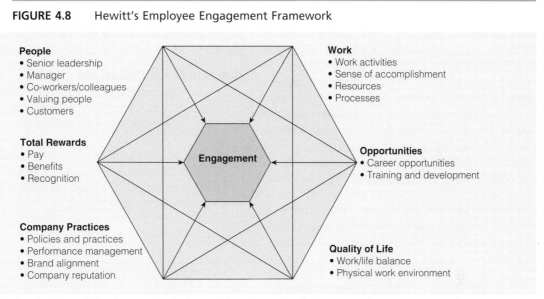

People
- Senior leadership
- Manager
- Co-workers/colleagues
- Valuing people
- Customers

Total Rewards
- Pay
- Benefits
- Recognition

Company Practices
- Policies and practices
- Performance management
- Brand alignment
- Company reputation

Engagement

Work
- Work activities
- Sense of accomplishment
- Resources
- Processes

Opportunities
- Career opportunities
- Training and development

Quality of Life
- Work/life balance
- Physical work environment

Source: Reprinted with permission from Jon Leatherbury, "Talent Show," *Quality Progress*, Vol. 41, No. 11, November 2008. Copyright © 2008 American Society for Quality. No further distribution allowed without permission.

retention is high were identified as opportunities for growth and training and rewards (pay and recognition). Elements of the work environment in which satisfaction is high but the threat to retention is high if the area is neglected were work activities and managers and leadership.

The team focused on solutions aligned to the retention driver areas, specifically rewards. A careful review of recent market data then revealed total compensation rates had dropped slightly below market average. A targeted group of proficient CS representatives received a market correction in their base pay. The retention rate for the group of representatives receiving the adjustment was significantly higher than the retention rate of those not receiving adjustments (96 percent vs. 83 percent).

Based on this intervention, the resulting analysis revealed Hewitt was able to avoid losing an additional 80 proficient CS representatives, assuming retention among these proficient CS representatives would have been on par with the overall group who did not receive the intervention. At $24,000 for each separation avoided, the benefit associated with the pay increase equaled $1.9 million—or a return on investment of 217 percent.

At first, senior leaders were reluctant to make further investments in the rewards strategy for a population of associates who historically come and go frequently. But hard data, involvement from line management and, eventually, a bold proposal from HR helped them to see the business problem differently. In the end, the annualized ROI bought credibility with senior leaders and highlighted the importance of HR being in a position to make and defend data-based decisions that yield a strong ROI.

Fixing competitive pay was only part of the solution. The company began to implement additional solutions aimed at the other top drivers of retention for the CS population. HR developed a realistic job profile targeted at explicitly showing candidates up front what the first few months of the role—when turnover is highest—entail. Additionally, HR has implemented a role-based capability assessment to measure job fit at the time of application. The data will aid in understanding how well incoming job fit is predictive of future performance. The goal is to further impact attrition within the first six months that is due to job abandonment, inability to meet basic productivity requirements, or dislike of day-to-day responsibilities.

HR redesigned technical training to ensure associates become productive more quickly and better understand the link between performance and growth opportunity, which is based on productivity results. A formal career path tool is also being constructed to help CS representatives navigate the career journey more effectively. The goal is to decrease time to proficiency and attrition in the 6–12 month timeframe—a period when CS representatives become more productive but often leave for better-perceived career and development opportunities elsewhere. Finally, HR developed a formal manager effectiveness curriculum for managers and local leaders, focusing this training on interaction management, team leading, and conflict resolution. Manager interaction sessions also will be delivered to improve one-on-one coaching opportunities between managers and CS representatives. This should lead to stronger engagement and retention of CS representatives and managers. Enhanced interactions and coaching opportunities will lead to enhanced productivity.

The Six Sigma method has helped HR professionals at Hewitt think differently about business problems, address root causes quicker and demonstrate the ROI of the talent solutions they implement.

Key Issues for Discussion

1. Explain the importance and benefit of using data-driven analytical tools, such as Six Sigma methodology, to address a human resource management issue.
2. Discuss how the solutions that the company identified support its employee engagement framework and should improve engagement and ultimately retention.

REVIEW QUESTIONS

1. Explain why there is a logical relationship between customer satisfaction and employee satisfaction.
2. Describe the impact of the Taylor system on quality, productivity, and workforce management. How do TQ principles differ from the Taylor system?
3. Summarize the key workforce-focused practices for performance excellence.
4. Define workforce management. Explain its role from a strategic perspective.
5. Explain the concept of workforce engagement. What advantages does it provide to an organization?
6. What is employee involvement? Discuss different approaches to employee involvement.
7. Define the term *motivation*. Why is motivation critical for performance excellence?
8. List the key factors that characterize high performance work.
9. Explain the difference between *work design* and *job design*. How does the Hackman and Oldham model enhance understanding of how job design affects motivation, satisfaction, and organizational effectiveness?
10. Contrast job enlargement with job enrichment. How do they support the Hackman and Oldham model?
11. What is *empowerment*? How does it benefit both the organization and employees?
12. Explain the concept of self-determination and how it differs from empowerment.
13. What is a *team*? Define the major types of teams found in organizations today.
14. Contrast the differences between quality circles and self-managed teams. What are the key characteristics of self-managed teams not found in quality circles?
15. Discuss the five phases that teams typically go through during their life cycle.
16. Explain the important issues an organization must consider in developing successful teams.
17. What issues must organizations consider with respect to health, safety, and employee well-being in the work environment?
18. List and describe the tools needed for running an effective meeting.
19. What are the steps required to perform the nominal group technique (NGT)?
20. What types of compensation practices support a performance excellence philosophy?
21. Explain the key practices that lead to effective recognition and reward approaches?
22. Briefly summarize traditional performance appraisal processes. From a performance excellence perspective, what objections have been raised concerning these processes? Describe some modern practices.

23. What is *360-degree feedback*? How does it differ from traditional performance appraisal approaches? How does it address the major criticisms of traditional performance appraisal processes and support TQ efforts?

24. Why is it important to assess workforce engagement and satisfaction? Describe some common approaches.

25. Outline the characteristics of the Gallup Q12 survey instrument for employee engagement and explain the management uses for three categories in the resulting "engagement index."

26. Why is it important to consider workforce capability and capacity in designing and sustaining high performance work systems?

27. Explain some modern practices for hiring, workforce learning, and career development.

DISCUSSION QUESTIONS

1. What is your reaction to the quote about Toyota in the opening paragraph of the chapter? Would such an observation be true of most other organizations? Is it really true that competitors cannot copy the human resources of an organization? Why or why not?

2. The late Peter Drucker, arguably one of the most respected and influential writers on management in the twentieth century, observed:

   Whatever his limitations and shortcomings—and he had many—no other American, not even Henry Ford (1863–1947), had anything like Taylor's impact. "Scientific Management" (and its successor, "Industrial Engineering") is the one American philosophy that has swept the world—more so even than the Constitution and the Federalist Papers. In the last century there has been only one worldwide philosophy that could compete with Taylor's: Marxism. And in the end Taylor has triumphed over Marx.[85]

   Comment on Drucker's observations about the Taylor system. Do you agree with his statement about Taylor versus Marx? Why or why not?

3. How can a fraternity or student organization use the workforce-focused practices in Table 4.1 to improve the organization? If you are involved in such an organization, develop a strategic "workforce" plan that supports performance excellence.

4. What things might you observe in an organization that has high levels of workforce engagement? What might you observe in one that has low levels of engagement?

5. An engineering service firm that performs repair and maintenance of laboratory equipment asks its technicians to write weekly journal entries describing their work experiences. The company owner reviews them each week and provides feedback to the technicians. What implications might this practice have for fostering employee engagement? Can you think of any other benefits?

6. What motivates *you* to study and perform in the classroom? How do motivation theories apply to you personally? Discuss how these theories might lead to new ways of teaching and learning.

7. When simple theories such as those of Maslow, Herzberg, and McGregor explain motivation, why does the search continue for more complex ones or for ones that integrate several different theories, such as Porter and Lawler's theory? What implications do they have for quality?

8. Think of a job you have had. Apply the Hackman and Oldham model to evaluate how the job design impacted your motivation and satisfaction, as well as organizational effectiveness.

9. Describe some examples of job enlargement or job enrichment that you have either seen or personally encountered in a job.

10. Cite some examples of empowerment or lack of empowerment from your own experiences.

11. How might the concept of empowerment be employed in a classroom?

12. How might a jazz quartet be viewed as a metaphor for a team in a business situation?

13. How should teams deal with "slackers"? How would you deal with them in the context of a student project team?

14. Consider the statement, "How one is evaluated determines how one performs." What does this notion mean for your classes? Would your performance change if grades were abolished (as Deming strongly advocated)?

15. Discuss the conditions under which team incentives, gainsharing, and "pay for increased skills" reward systems may work. When is it a poor idea to install such systems?

16. Students in early grades often receive many kinds of recognition: stickers, candy, and so on, for good work. As we discussed, similar forms of recognition are common in the workplace. Yet little daily recognition is given at the high school and college level. Discuss possible reasons for this difference and design a recognition program that might be appropriate in your class.

17. Discuss the controversy over performance appraisal. Do you agree with Deming's approach, or do you take the more traditional viewpoint toward performance appraisal? Why?

18. Most colleges and universities use a course/instructor evaluation system. If your school has one, how is it used? Does it support continuous improvement or is it used strictly for performance appraisal? How might the evaluation instrument or process be modified to better reflect quality principles?

19. Jack Welch, former CEO of General Electric, stated his passion for making people GE's core competency yet he used a system in which executives in the bottom 10 percent of a forced performance ranking were eliminated. What do you think of this approach? How does it fit with a total quality philosophy? How would you respond to someone who says, "I think all my people are pretty good. If I fire the bottom 10 percent, that would just give me a new bottom 10 percent. Where does it end?"

20. Recently, new "employee performance software" has been developed to track individual output. For example, British Airways uses it to ensure that customer service reps' time in the break room or on personal calls doesn't count on the clock. The technology can keep track so that extra incentive dollars are eventually directed in to the paychecks of those whose digital records merit them. It can also help managers understand how to assemble the most effective teams or who to lay off.[86] Discuss the implications of such technology from a quality and high performance perspective.

21. Many companies today seek the best available applicants and train them in quality principles. What implications does this practice have for designing college curricula and choosing elective courses in a given program?

22. Often, the preamble to one's call to a company will be a recorded message that says something like "For quality purposes, this call may be recorded." What do you think the real purpose of such an approach is? Is it to improve quality or to monitor poorly trained employees or catch them deviating from company scripts? Would an empowered organization need to use this method?

23. The training strategy that Xerox used is summarized as follows:
    a. The training is uniform—common tools and processes are taught across all of Xerox, to all employees, creating a "common language within Xerox" that fosters cohesive team functioning.
    b. Training is conducted in family groups, with all members starting and finishing training at the same time to facilitate the change process.
    c. Training starts at the top of the organization with the CEO and cascades downward to all employees.[87]

    What advantages does such strategy have? Do you see any possible disadvantages? Would this approach work in any business?

24. Labor relations between unions and management can make it difficult to establish TQ-oriented HR practices within organizations. The National Labor Relations Board (NLRB) ruled on two cases in 1993 and 1994 that complicate a company's determination of how far it can go legally to set up and use employee participation programs (EPPs) to make improvements in the workplace. The two cases involved a small, nonunion company, Electromation, and a large company, DuPont. These case decisions by a five-person board were based on interpretations of the National Labor Relations Act (NLRA, or Wagner Act), passed in the 1930's which prohibits unfair labor practices. The rulings are found in the NLRB proceedings as Electromation vs. International Brotherhood of Teamsters (309 NLRB-No. 163), and E. I. duPont de Nemours and Company vs. Chemical Workers Association, Inc. (311 NLRB-No. 88). In the Electromation case, the nonunion company's management set up five employee action committees to deal with policies concerning absenteeism, smoking, communications, pay for premium positions,

and attendance bonuses. In DuPont's case, management unilaterally (without bargaining with the union) changed the composition of safety and fitness committees to include nonmanagerial employees (where the committees had previously been composed only of management) at a unionized New Jersey plant. Stated briefly, the cases specified that "employer-dominated labor organizations" are prohibited. In both cases, the employee teams/committees were ruled to be "labor organizations" and to be "management dominated." Discuss the implications of these cases, particularly in the context of high-performing organizations. You might wish to conduct further research on these cases.

PROJECTS, ETC.

1. Review the most recent list of *Fortune's* "100 Best Companies to Work For" and summarize the best practices of these companies, classifying them into themes such as engagement, work environment, training, and so on. Have any of these companies or their business units received a Baldrige Award?
2. Search some current business periodicals (e.g., *Fortune*, *Fast Company*, *Business Week*) for articles dealing with workforce-management issues. Explain how they relate to the material in this chapter. Are any new approaches or practices emerging?
3. Interview managers at a local organization about their workforce-management practices, focusing on engagement and work and job design issues. Report on your perceptions of how well their practices support a high-performance workplace.
4. Survey local companies to determine if and how they use suggestion systems. What levels of participation do they have? Are suggestions tied to rewards and recognitions?

5. Investigate the extent of team participation at some local companies. What kinds of teams do you find? Do managers believe these teams are effective?
6. Interview some managers at a local company on their approaches to motivation. Summarize their responses and analyze them in the context of motivation theories. Can you provide any suggestions for improving their practices?
7. Research the impacts of the Internet on workforce management practices in an actual firm. One possible approach would be to interview an HR manager at a company that is building e-commerce capability. Another approach might be to visit the websites of several firms, examine practices that may be described, and compare and contrast your findings.
8. Does your school survey its faculty and staff to assess issues of engagement, satisfaction, and the work environment? If so, obtain a copy of the survey and analyze it relative to the concepts in this chapter; if not, design one that might be used.

CASES

THE DYSFUNCTIONAL MANAGER

Christina worked at a retail store in a shopping mall. Her manager made the job quite stressful. She never had the schedule for the next week completed on time, so Christina and other employees were never able to plan adequately. They would say, "Well, if the manager doesn't do her work right, why should I?" When switching shifts that required working with the manager, the manager was usually texting on the phone and paid little attention to customers, but she would not let the employees use their phones while they were working. As a result, most employees used their phones when the manager was not around and did little selling. The manager also paid little attention to inventory management, resulting in stress between employees and customers, as many items which a customer requested could not be found even though the computer indicated they were available. Work hours were often recorded incorrectly, resulting in errors in paychecks. Employee turnover was very high and sales were low. After a while, the manager was replaced. The new manager improved inventory control using frequent counts to over 99 percent accuracy; had the schedule completed two weeks ahead of time; took care of paycheck errors quickly and ensured that they were almost always correct; and showed gratitude to employees for their work. Employees were able to reach their quotas more easily and sales increased. Christina noted: "I was happy to come to work then,

which caused me to be happy, friendly, and wanting to do my job more correctly."

Discussion Questions

1. How does Christina's experience relate to the concepts in this chapter? Thoroughly explain the implications and relationships to the various theories we described.

2. How might the list of employee competencies used by MEDRAD have been applied to individuals selected as managers in order to improve the store's day-to-day operations?

GOLDEN PLAZA HOTEL

Sandra Wilford was recently promoted to General Manager of the Golden Plaza Hotel, San Francisco. She had previously been an assistant manager at the corporation's hotel in Denver. The Denver hotel was truly a team-based organization. Sandra had seen the benefits from teamwork that propelled the hotel to the top of the corporation in customer satisfaction ratings. In fact, it was one of the reasons she was asked to take over the San Francisco property. The previous general manager's policies had created large turnover among the staff and continuing loss of market share that led to his firing.

Sandra was reviewing her notes from a meeting with all the hotel's supervisors and assistant managers. The meeting tried to identify why many employees were reluctant to be "team players" or even to participate on teams that she was trying to initiate based on her experiences in Denver. Among the reasons that surfaced were the following:

- Child care obligations, classes, and other outside commitments made it difficult for some associates to meet before or after shifts.
- Many of the custodial workers who were functionally illiterate seemed to be uncomfortable in interaction with other associates.

- Several associates feel that their current jobs are simply too demanding to take on the additional meetings that would be necessary.
- One assistant manager felt that some of her people preferred to work alone and usually disrupted meetings in which they were involved.
- Because of the previous general manager, there was a lot of cynicism among the associates and many didn't trust management. They felt that teams were simply a political ploy to get support for unpopular decisions. The previous general manager had established some teams that had failed miserably and many associates were bitter and had conflicts with other departments. There seemed to be a widespread attitude of "What's in it for me?"
- Some associates thought that the expectations of team processes would be overwhelming and were afraid if the team failed, they would be held personally responsible and their careers would be in jeopardy. Others thought that their jobs might be eliminated.

Sandra stared at this list and wondered what she had gotten herself into. What recommendations would you make to her to address these issues?

THE HOPEFUL TELECOMMUTER

Jennifer Smith was pregnant, and she was happy about it. She and her husband, Jim, had been planning to start a family for some time. However, she was concerned about her job as a Northeast Zone supply chain manager for health and beauty products for Big Otter Stores. Big Otter was a large, multibillion dollar food store chain that had stores in 47 states. It was a conventionally organized retailer divided into three geographic regions (Atlantic, Mid-American, and Western) with 12 zones (4 per region).

Zone supply chain managers, such as Jennifer, were the link between the store managers and their product-line suppliers. Jennifer had been ranked number one in customer and in supplier satisfaction surveys for health and beauty product lines for the last two years. She knew that she was eligible for six months of maternity leave under the federal Family Leave Act, and that the company would have to provide a job for her upon her return. What she didn't like was the thought that they did not have to, and probably would not, give her the same job that she was now holding so well.

Jennifer had talked with Jim, at length, about what to do. They agreed that she should approach her regional manager, Sarah Strong, the Zone VP, about the possibility of "telecommuting" to her job after the baby came. Jennifer thought that she could do 85–90 percent of the job at home on her own schedule. A large part of her job consisted of verbal and fax contacts with store managers and suppliers, as well as extensive use of a computer for manipulating databases, preparing spreadsheet reports, and sending and responding to e-mail. The other 10–15 percent of the time, when she had to be in the office for face-to-face meetings or had to take brief trips, her parents and Jim could keep the baby and cover for her at home.

When Jennifer approached Sarah Strong, Sarah was interested, but would not commit herself to supporting Jennifer's request to telecommute. She said that the company had never done that before, and it might pose a number of difficulties. She did say that she would take her request forward to the two VP's who could approve or disapprove it. Both senior managers would have to approve Jennifer's request, however. Sarah asked Jennifer to prepare some "talking points" concerning the benefits versus the limitations of the arrangement that she could present to the vice president of human resources, and the senior vice president of operations, Sarah's manager. Sarah also asked Jennifer to prepare a cost estimate, in consultation with the Zone information systems manager.

The following was what Jennifer prepared for the estimated costs:

Laptop computer and docking station	$3,500.00
Setup DSL dedicated phone line	250.00
Fax machine	250.00
Computer desk and chair	375.00
Telephone line charges (6 months)	240.00
Total	$4,615.00

Discussion Questions

1. You are Jennifer. What "talking points" would you prepare to support your case? Include both the strengths and limitations of telecommuting. Keep in mind the needs of your "customers," the human resources VP, as well as Sarah, and the VP of operations.

2. What issues do you think that the VP of human resources might raise? What issues do you think the senior VP of operations might raise?

3. How does your answer demonstrate the principles of empowerment? How might it fit the components of the Hackman–Oldham Job Characteristics model?

NORDAM EUROPE, LTD.[88]

Nordam Europe, Ltd. is a joint venture between The Nordam Group, Inc. and GE. Aircraft Engine Services, Ltd. The Nordam group is an acknowledged leader in aircraft component manufacturing and repair with facilities on three continents, and is the largest privately held FAA-approved repair station in the world for composite, aircraft structures. Some of its customers include: General Electric, British Airways, FedEx, DHL, and Air France. The Blackwood, Wales facility's primary role is the overhaul and repair of jet engines.

The Blackwood division employs 180 workers, 16 of whom are aged 50 and over.

The company has a strong, though brief, history of adoption and practice of equal opportunity in its hiring and HR practices. The company's Equal Opportunities policy prohibits hiring, placement, or dismissal based on gender, race, religion, or age. The HR Department is currently in the process of reviewing most of the company's HR policies in order to develop a Staff Handbook containing all employee related policies. The policies were originally set up in 1997, when the company was formed. Approval of the revised policies will be done by the managing director and the Head of Support Services. A systematic process is also being set up to review all HR policies annually.

The company's early HR policies were developed in a period of rapid expansion. The internal promotion of the Head of Support Services as the senior HR manager has resulted in development of a new, systematic approach towards upgrading all aspects of employee relations management. With a non-discriminatory HR process, the company will continue to judge all employees on the basis of their ability, attitude, skills, commitment, and general approach to work.

Recruitment

In the past, Nordam Europe had used an employment agency for recruitment, but recently it has set a policy to place all recruitment advertising for operative staff with the local JobCentre, a government supported agency. Nordam continues to use some employment agents to fill certain positions, and at the senior management level, the company has made use of a headhunting agency. The HR department has been vigilant in avoiding the use of direct or indirect reference to age or other bias in advertising. In addition, it develops both job and person profiles, again ensuring that there are no age-related or other discriminatory descriptions.

Selection and Retention

Nordam Europe's business is heavily dependent on a high level of safety, quality, and working to precise standards in order to maintain aircraft jet engine nacelles and thrust reversers. Nordam continues to work on policies that will provide stability in its workforce. The following is a brief summary of the company's selection process.

1. Applicant's résumés are received.

2. Screening of applicants is performed by a departmental manager and a personnel officer to develop a short list of those they would like to interview. Suitability for the job is assessed by reviewing the individuals' background and relevant job or technical experience. The process avoids any consideration of race, gender, nationality, disability, religion, or age.

3. The short-listed applicants are invited for interview with the departmental manager and personnel officer. The latter is a trained, experienced interviewer who provides consistency within the interviewing process, ensuring that equal opportunity issues are taken into consideration where appropriate. The company is clear that all decisions relating to job offers are made on the basis of suitability for the post and that age, or other non-job related factors, are irrelevant.

Nordam Europe's Head of Support Services was voluntarily separated from his previous job after 30 years in the automotive industry, where he worked primarily in finance, administration, and operational areas. He sought alternative work in those areas. He circulated his résumé to numerous companies, but was concerned that his age (50) would count against him. The individual was pleased to be asked to visit Nordam Europe for an informal chat. He was later surprised to be offered a role in the production-engineering department. Although new to production engineering, Nordam felt that he would be able to make a valuable contribution to the business, because of his previous experience and administrative skills. He began in production engineering on a three-month temporary contract, but after approximately four weeks, Nordam recognized his capabilities and offered him a permanent position within the company, which he accepted.

Training and Development

Nordam Europe engages in extensive training and development. Because of the industry's need to maintain safety and precision standards in aircraft components, there are ongoing training requirements. These are related to technological advances in the context of repairs to aircraft engine nacelle and thrust reversers. All new employees receive a copy of Training and Development Policy Statement upon company induction. The annual staff appraisal system includes performance measurement and provides an opportunity to identify training and development needs in line with the company's business objectives. Shop floor workers are expected to take training, particularly where training is required to maintain their technical approvals to work on jet engines. All workers have been found to be eager to receive the training made available.

Promotion

Because of the newness of the company, a formal promotion structure has not been developed, although a few individuals have been promoted to fill key posts, when vacated. Age is never a factor in selection for promotion. The post of Head of Support Services was created in 1999. As mentioned, the individual who was hired for the position in production engineering had broad experience in finance, administration, and operational areas in the automotive industry. He was promoted to Head of Support Services. Later, the Head of Support Services was invited by the new managing director to take responsibility for the company's Human Resource Department. Despite him not being an HR specialist, the company felt that his previous experience would provide a good core competence, particularly in the area of "managing people." Thus, the previous experiences of an older worker was recognized by a company and used to good effect in filling a variety of posts. As the Head of Support Services said, "I was able to offer a range of experiences and a high degree of flexibility to an organization that was developing and growing."

Redundancy (Layoff) Policy

Recently, the company faced the situation of having to make several employees redundant (British term for layoffs). The company's redundancy policy had several options including seeking volunteers, a reduction in the scale of working and the application of objective selection criteria. The objective selection criteria were used in this situation. No worker was selected for redundancy on the basis of their age.

Discussion Questions

1. How do the approaches used by Nordam Europe seem to support high performance work, drawing upon the ideas presented in this chapter?
2. How do employee education, training, and development address the organizational needs associated with new employee orientation, diversity, ethical business practices, and management and leadership development?
3. What are some possible leadership and motivation advantages of using older workers for the type of work done by Nordam Europe?
4. How are the problems of age discrimination in hiring and layoffs in the United States and the U.K. similar and different? (You may want to research the issue on the Internet.) Why is this important, and how does it tie to the social responsibility issues that are increasingly important in today's business environment?

NOTES

1. Robin Yale Bergstrom, "People, Process, Paint," *Production*, April 1995, 48–51.
2. James L. Heskett, W. Earl Sasser, Jr., and Leonard A. Schlesinger, *The Service Profit Chain* (New York: The Free Press, 1997), 101.
3. James K. Harter, Frank L. Schmidt, and Theodore L. Hayes "Business-Unit-Level Relationship Between Employee Satisfaction, Employee Engagement, and Business Outcomes: A Meta-Analysis," *Journal of Applied Psychology*, Vol. 87, No. 2 (2002), 268–279.
4. Town Hall discussion at the Quest for Excellence Conference, Washington D.C., March 2000.
5. Richard E. Walton, "From Control to Commitment in the Workplace," *Harvard Business Review* 63, no. 2 (March/April 1985), 77–84. © by the President and Fellows of Harvard College; all rights reserved.
6. Lloyd L. Byars and Leslie W. Rue, *Human Resource Management*, 10th ed. (New York: Irwin/McGraw-Hill, 2010), 4.
7. "How to Do HR Right," *Fast Company*, August 2005, 46.
8. J. Ericksen, and L. Dyer, "Toward a Strategic Human Resource Management Model of High Reliability Organization Performance," *International Journal of Human Resource Management*, Vol. 16, No. 6 (2005) pp. 907–928.
9. J. Bret Becton and Mike Schraeder, "Strategic Human Resources Management: Are We There Yet?" *The Journal for Quality & Participation*, January 2009, pp. 11–18.

10. S. Fegley, "Strategic HR Management Survey Report," *SHR Research*, 2006.

11. J. Bret Becton and Mike Schraeder, "Strategic Human Resources Management: Are We There Yet?" *The Journal for Quality & Participation*, January 2009, pp. 11–18.

12. Kay Kendall and Glenn Bodison, "The Power of People in Achieving Performance Excellence," *Journal for Quality & Participation*, July 2010, pp. 10–14.

13. Poudre Valley Health System Baldrige Award Video, U.S. Department of Commerce, Baldrige Award Program.

14. Adam Lashinski, "Google is No. 1: Search and enjoy" Fortune, January 8, 2007. http://money.cnn.com/magazines/fortune/fortune_archive/2007/01/22/8397996/index.htm (accessed 4/9/09).

15. Adam Lashinski, "The Fortune Interview: Larry Page," Fortune, February 6, 2012, 99.

16. Kay Kendall and Glenn Bodison, "The Power of People in Achieving Performance Excellence," *Journal for Quality & Participation*, July 2010, pp. 10–14.

17. "It's My Manager, Stupid," *Across the Board,* January 2000, p. 9.

18. E. E. Lawler, S. A. Mohrman, and G. E. Ledford, Jr., *Employee Involvement and Total Quality Management: Practices and Results in Fortune 1000 Companies.*, San Francisco: Jossey-Bass, 1992, p. 60; and Linda Grant, "Happy Workers, High Returns," *Fortune,* January 12, 1998, p. 81. A formal research study of the relationship between employee engagement and business outcomes is reported in James K. Harter, Frank L. Schmidt, and Theodore L. Hayes, "Business-Unit-Level Relationship Between Employee Satisfaction, Employee Engagement, and Business Outcomes: A Meta-Analysis," *Journal of Applied Psychology* 87, no. 2 (2002), pp. 268–279.

19. The Employee Involvement Association's e-newsletter *Ideas & Inspirations*, which gave credit to: *The CEO Refresher* by Freda Turner, PhD. The Web link is no longer active.

20. Joseph J. Gufreda, Larry A. Maynard, and Lucy N. Lytle, "Employee Involvement in the Quality Process," in Ernst & Young Quality Improvement Consulting Group, *Total Quality!: An Executive's Guide for the 1990s* (Homewood, IL: Richard D. Irwin, 1990).

21. See http://www.greatplacetowork.com for details and information about the survey and services offered by this firm.

22. 2010 MEDRAD Baldrige Award Application Summary, available at http://www.nist.gov/baldrige.

23. Right Management Global Benchmarking Employee Engagement Study, December, 2008; cited in Tom Becker, "Happiness Helps: Career Development, Breeds Employee Engagement, Boosts Organizational Performance," *Quality Progress*, January 2011.

24. Hal F. Rosenbluth, "Have Quality, Will Travel," *TQM Magazine,* November/December 1992, pp. 267–270.

25. Tom J. Peters, *Thriving on Chaos: Handbook for a Management Revolution* (New York: Alfred A. Knopf, 1988).

26. Alan Wolf, "Golden Opportunities," *Beverage World*, February 1991.

27. A more comprehensive review of history and the forerunners of quality circles from the early 1900s can be found in William M. Lindsay, "Quality Circles and Participative Work Improvement: A Cross-Disciplinary History," in Dennis F. Ray (ed.), *Southern Management Association Proceedings* (New York: Mississippi State University, 1987), 220–222.

28. From materials provided by Mike Simms, former plant manager.

29. Saul W. Gellerman, *Motivation in the Real World* (Dutton, 1992).

30. James L. Bowditch and Anthony F. Buono, *A Primer on Organizational Behavior*, 2d ed. (New York: John Wiley & Sons, 1990), 52.

31. Richard M. Steers, Richard T. Mowday, and Debra L. Shapiro, "Introduction to Special Topic Forum: The Future of Work Motivation Theory," *Academy of Management Review*, 2004, Vol. 29, No. 3, 379–387.

32. "Making the Job Meaningful All the Way Down the Line," *Business Week* May 1, 2006, 60.

33. Portions adapted from Chapter 4, "Motivation Through the Design of Work," in J. R. Hackman and G. R. Oldham, *Work Redesign* (Reading, MA: Addison-Wesley, 1980).

34. Our appreciation goes to Ms. Gretchen Faulkner for providing this example.

35. Hackman and Oldham, *Work Redesign*.

36. David A Garvin, *Managing Quality* (New York: The Free Press, 1988), 202–203.

37. Robert D. Hof, "Teamwork, Supercharged," *Business Week*, November 21, 2005, 90–94.

38. Douglas K. Miscikowski and Eric W. Stein, "Empowering Employees to Pull The Quality Trigger," *Quality Progress*, October 2008, 43–48.

39. J. M. Juran, *Juran on Leadership for Quality: An Executive Handbook* (New York: The Free Press, 1989), 264.

40. Phillip A. Smith, William D. Anderson, and Stanley A. Brooking, "Employee Empowerment: A Case Study," *Production and Inventory Management* 34, no. 3 (1993), 45–50.

41. "Leader of the Pack," insert in special advertising feature "Work Life," Fortune, September 19, 2005, S4.

42. John Troyer, "Empowerment," Guest Editorial, *Quality Digest*, October 1996, 64.

43. AT&T Quality Steering Committee, *Great Performances* (AT&T Bell Laboratories, 1991), 39; and William Smitley and David Scott, "Empowerment: Unlocking the Potential of Your Work Force," *Quality Digest* 14, no. 8 (August 1994), 40–46.

44. "Changing a Culture: DuPont Tries to Make Sure That Its Research Wizardry Serves the Bottom Line," *Wall Street Journal*, March 27, 1992, A5.

45. Robert S. Kaplan, "Texas Eastman Company," Harvard Business School Case, No. 9-190-039.

46. David Geisler, "The Next Level in Employee Empowerment," *Quality Progress*, Vol. 38, No. 6 (2005), pp. 48–52. Copyright © 2001, American Society for Quality. Reprinted with permission.

47. *Source:* Dictionary of Human Resources and Personnel Management (2006), © A & C Black Publishers Ltd 2006. Retrieved from http://www.credoreference.com/entry/acb/team (accessed 2/6/12).

48. Jack D. Orsburn, Linda Moran, Ed Musselwhite, and John H. Zenger, *Self-Directed Work Teams* (Homewood, IL: Business One-Irwin, 1990), 27–34.

49. Brian Dumaine, "The Trouble with Teams," *Fortune*, September 5, 1994, 86–92.

50. For an historical perspective, see J. M. Juran, "The QC Circle Phenomenon," *Industrial Quality Control*, January 1967, 329–336.

51. "Platform Approach at Chrysler," *Quality '93: Empowering People with Technology, Fortune* Advertisement, September 20, 1993.

52. Mark R. Hagen, "Teams Expand into Cyberspace," *Quality Progress*, June 1999, 90–93.

53. David M. Vrooman, *Daniel Willard and Progressive Management on the Baltimore and Ohio Railroad*, Ohio State University Press, Columbus (1991).

54. Sidney P. Rubinstein, "QC Circles and U.S. Participative Movements," *1972 ASQC Technical Conference Transactions*, Washington, D.C., 391–396. For more about the history and impact of quality circles in the early 1980s in the United States, see William M. Lindsay, *Measurement of Quality Circle Effectiveness: A Survey and Critique*, unpublished M.S. thesis, University of Cincinnati, College of Engineering (May 1986), 72, 117–120.

55. *Quality Digest*, "Quality Circles Still Big in India," http://www.qualitydigest.com/currentmag/news.shtml#7; and http://www.cmseducation.org/icsqcc/. Flyer for Fourteenth International Convention on Students' Quality Control Circles 2011. Accessed 2/6/12.

56. James P. Lewis, *Team-Based Project Management* (New York: Amacom, 1998).

57. Peter R. Scholtes, *The Team Handbook*, 3rd ed. Madison, WI: Oriel, Inc., 2003, 42–45.

58. Scholtes, *Team Handbook*, 45.

59. Andre L. Delbecq, Andre H. Van de Ven, and David H. Gustafson, *Group Techniques for Program Planning* (Glenview, IL: Scott Foresman and Co., 1975).

60. John E. Bauer, Grace L. Duffy, and Russell T. Westcott (eds.), *The Quality Improvement Handbook* (Milwaukee, WI: ASQ Quality Press, 2002), 108–109.

61. Nicole Adrian, "A Gold Medal Solution," *Quality Progress*, March 2008, 44–50.

62. Samuel C. Certo, *Modern Management*, 9th ed. (Upper Saddle River, NJ: Prentice Hall, 2003), 389. See also Gina Abudi, "The Five Stages of Project Team Development," http://www.pmhut.com/the-five-stages-of-project-team-development, retrieved March 27, 2012.

63. George Eckes, *The Six Sigma Revolution* (New York: John Wiley & Sons, 2001), 251–254.

64. Harvey A. Robbins and Michael Finley, *Why Teams Don't Work: What Went Wrong and How to Make it Right* (Princeton, NJ: Peterson's/Pacesetter Books, 1995), 14–15.

65. Peter R. Scholtes et al., *The Team Handbook: How to Use Teams to Improve Quality* (Madison, WI: Joiner Associates, Inc., 1988), 6-10–6-22.

66. Michelle Conlin and Kathy Moore, "Photo Essay—SAS," *Business Week*, June 19, 2000, 192–202.

67. "The Boss Is Watching – So Watch Your iPod," *Business Week*, April 24, 2006, 16.

68. "Bonus Pay: Buzzword or Bonanza?" *Business Week*, November 14, 1994, 62–64.

69. http://www.nucor.com/story/chapter4. (accessed 3/27/12).

70. Pal's 2001 Malcolm Baldrige Application Summary, http://www.nist.gov/baldrige.

71. Craig Cochran, "The Sound of All Hands Clapping," *Quality Digest*, September 2003, 38–40.

72. Bruce N. Pfau and Steven E. Gross, *Innovative Reward and Recognition Strategies in TQM*, The Conference Board, Report Number 1051, 1993.

73. Cited in Matt Weinstein, "Having Fun With Reward and Recognition," #284 from *Innovative Leader* 6, no. 7 (July 1997), http://www.winstonbrill.com/bril001/html/article_index/articles/251-300/article284_body.html (accessed 3/4/12).

74. Bruce N. Pfau and Steven E. Gross, *Innovative Reward and Recognition Strategies in TQM*, The Conference Board, Report Number 1051, 1993.

75. George Eckes, "Practical Alternatives to Performance Appraisals," *Quality Progress* 27, no. 11 (November 1994), 57–60.

76. Douglas McGregor, "An Uneasy Look at Performance Appraisal," *Harvard Business Review*, September–October 1972; Herbert H. Meyer, Emanuel Kay, and John R. P. French, Jr., "Split Roles in Performance Appraisal," *Harvard Business Review*, January–February 1965; Harry Levinson, "Appraisal of What Performance?" *Harvard Business Review*, January–February 1965; A. M. Mohrman, *Deming Versus Performance Appraisal: Is There a Resolution?* (Los Angeles: Center for Effective Organizations, University of Southern California, 1989).

77. John F. Milliman and Fred R. McFadden, "Toward Changing Performance Appraisal to Address TQM Concerns: The 360-Degree Feedback Process," *Quality Management Journal* 4, no. 3 (1997), 44–64.

78. Adapted from 2007 Malcolm Baldrige Application Summary, National Institute of Standards and Technology, U.S. Department of Commerce. Reprinted with permission.

79. Dick Grote, "The Secrets of Performance Appraisal: Best Practices from the Masters," *Across the Board,* May 2000, 14–20.

80. Brian S. Morgan and William A. Schiemann, "Measuring People and Performance: Closing the Gaps," *Quality Progress,* January 1999, 47–53.

81. See John D. Cook, Susan J. Hepworth, Toby D. Wall, and Peter B. Warr, *The Experience of Work* (London, Academic Press, 1981); and Dale Henderson and Fess Green, "Measuring Self-Managed Workteams," *Journal for Quality and Participation,* January–February 1997, 52–56.

82. http://www.gallup.com/consulting/52/employee-engagement.aspx.

83. Text adapted from Wayne Stottler, "Improving Service Quality at Honda," *Quality Progress,* October 2004, 33–38. Copyright © 2001, American Society for Quality. Reprinted with permission.

84. Reprinted with permission from Jon Leatherbury, "Talent Show," *Quality Progress,* Vol. 41, No. 11, November 2008, 48–55. Copyright © 2008, American Society for Quality. No further distribution allowed without permission.

85. Peter F. Drucker, *Management Challenges for the 21st Century* (New York: HarperBusiness, 1999), 139.

86. Michelle Conlin, "The Software Says You're Just Average," *Business Week,* February 25, 2002, 126.

87. Xerox Business Products and Systems, Malcolm Baldrige National Quality Award application, 1989.

88. Adapted from http://www.dwp.gov.uk/age-positive/ by permission of Age Positive/Department for Work and Pensions.

The former president of Texas Instruments Defense Systems & Electronics Group (now part of Raytheon) had a sign in his office that read: "*Unless you change the process, why would you expect the results to change?*" Deming and Juran observed that the overwhelming majority of quality problems are associated with processes; few are caused by the workforce directly. Thus, it is vital to understand how to design, manage, and improve processes, and this responsibility belongs to management.

A **process** is a sequence of linked activities that is intended to achieve some result, such as producing a good or service for a customer within or outside the organization. Generally, processes involve combinations of people, machines, tools, techniques, materials, and improvements in a defined series of steps or actions.[1] We typically think of processes in the context of production: the collection of activities and operations involved in transforming inputs (physical facilities, materials, capital, equipment, people, and energy) into outputs (products and services). Common types of production processes include machining, mixing, assembly, filling orders, or approving loans. However, nearly every major activity within an organization involves a process that crosses traditional organizational boundaries as illustrated in Figure 5.1. For example, an order fulfillment

FIGURE 5.1   Process Versus Function

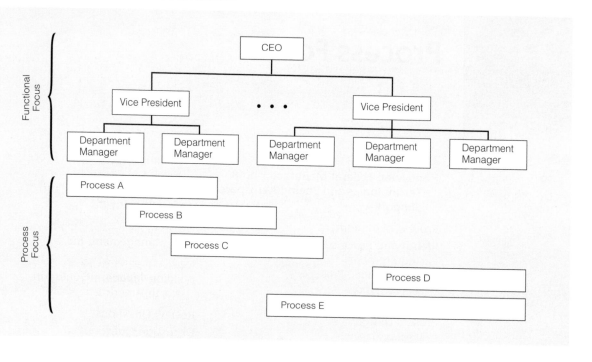

process might involve a salesperson placing the order; a marketing representative entering it on the company's computer system; a credit check by finance; picking, packaging, and shipping by distribution and logistics personnel; invoicing by finance; and installation by field service engineers. A process perspective links together all necessary activities and increases one's understanding of the entire system, rather than focusing on only a small part. Many of the greatest opportunities for improving organizational performance lie in the organizational interfaces—those spaces between the boxes on an organization chart.

TABLE 5.1   Key Process-Focused Practices for Quality Management

- Identify vital work processes that relate to core competencies and deliver customer value, profitability, organizational success, and sustainability.
- Determine key work process requirements, incorporating input from customers, suppliers, partners, and collaborators.
- Design and innovate work processes to meet all requirements, incorporating new technology, organizational knowledge, product excellence, the need for agility, cycle time reduction, productivity, cost control, and other efficiency and effectiveness factors.
- Seek ways to prevent defects, service errors, and rework and minimize costs associated with inspections, tests, and process or performance audits.
- Implement work processes and control their day-to-day operation to ensure that they meet design requirements, using appropriate performance measures along with customer, supplier, partner, and collaborator input as needed.
- Improve work processes to achieve better performance, reduce variability, improve products and services, keep processes current with business needs and directions, and share improvements with other organizational units and processes to drive organizational learning and innovation.
- Incorporate effective process management practices in the overall supply chain.

In this chapter, we focus on the importance of understanding and managing processes for quality. Table 5.1 summarizes the key practices that all organizations should use for managing its processes. The Quality Profiles in this chapter describe two organizations that leverage processes for the benefit of their customers.

quality**profiles**

Honeywell Federal Manufacturing & Technologies and Boeing Aerospace Support

Honeywell Federal Manufacturing & Technologies (FM&T), LLC is a management and operations contractor with the National Nuclear Security Administration. The facilities under its management are multidisciplinary engineering and manufacturing operations specializing in electrical, mechanical, and engineered material components for national defense systems. FM&T's vision is "to be the preferred partner with the United States Government and its allies, distinguished by our trusted relationships and recognized for our ability to deliver exceptional solutions for national and homeland security." This vision goes hand-in-hand with the organization's mission "to design and deliver products, manage operations, and provide targeted services to advance national and homeland security objectives for the United States Government and its allies." To support these goals, FM&T developed a robust, systematic governing system and planning process called the Management Assurance System. By incorporating strategic planning, checks that ensure processes align with goals, and feedback scorecards, the system identifies, implements, measures, and sustains the "critical-to-quality" needs necessary for desired performance.

FM&T uses a Six Sigma Plus Continuous Improvement Model that ensures integration of customer and business requirements into all design projects and has led to multiple cycles of learning and improvement for many of the organization's work processes. The result is a business culture that pays precise attention to detail and insists on delivering results—a culture FM&T describes as "Commitments Made, Commitments Kept." Among the results achieved are annual cost savings between $23.5 million and $27 million from increased productivity and deployed innovations; improvements of at least 20 percent each year in energy conservation; and supply-chain savings of approximately $65 million.

Boeing Aerospace Support (AS) is part of the Boeing Company, the largest aerospace company in the world.

Boeing AS provides products and services, including aircraft maintenance, modification, and repair, and training for aircrews and maintenance staff, to reduce life-cycle costs and increase the effectiveness of aircraft. Ninety-seven percent of Boeing AS's business comes from military customers. Carefully planned and well-managed processes combined with a culture that encourages knowledge sharing and working together have been essential to Boeing AS's ability to deliver high-quality products and services. Boeing AS has developed a seven-step approach for defining, managing, stabilizing, and improving processes. This process-based management, or PBM, methodology also is used to set goals and performance metrics and requires interaction and agreement among process owners, users, suppliers, and customers. Teams of employees who "own" and are responsible for the company's complex operations and processes are the core of the company's high-performance work environment. A highly structured process known as the "AS People System" helps to ensure that employees who comprise these teams understand priorities and expectations; have the knowledge, training, and tools they need to do the job and to assess performance against goals and objectives; and are rewarded and recognized for their accomplishments.

Since 1999, on-time delivery of maintenance and modification products and services, significant hardware, and other products has been between 95 and 99 percent. Quality ratings for the maintenance of C-17 aircraft have been near 100 percent since 1998, exceeding those of AS's competitors. The Supplier On-Time Delivery Rate improved from about 68 percent in 1999 to about 95 percent in 2003, matching best-in-Boeing results. Quality of Supplier Deliverables has been consistently above 99.5 percent.

Source: Malcolm Baldrige Award Profiles of Winners. National Institute of Standards and Technology, U.S. Department of Commerce.

PROCESS MANAGEMENT

Process management involves planning and administering the activities necessary to achieve a high level of performance in key organizational processes, and identifying opportunities for improving quality and operational performance, and ultimately, customer satisfaction. Process management consists of three major activities: *design, control, and improvement.*[2] *Design* focuses on ensuring that the inputs to the process, such as materials, technology, work methods, and a trained workforce are adequate; and that the process can achieve its requirements. *Control* focuses on maintaining consistency in output by assessing performance and taking corrective action when necessary. *Improvement* focuses on continually seeking to achieve higher levels of performance, such as reduced variation, higher yields, fewer defects and errors, smaller cycle times, and so on. **Cycle time** refers to the time it takes to accomplish one cycle of a process (e.g., the time from when a customer orders a product to the time that it is delivered, or the total time needed to introduce a new product). Cycle time is one of the most important metrics in process management.

Individuals or groups, known as **process owners**, are accountable for process performance and have the authority to control and improve their process. Process owners may range from high-level executives who manage cross-functional processes to workers who run a manufacturing cell or an assembly operation on the shop floor. Assigning process owners ensures that someone is responsible to manage the process and optimize its effectiveness.

Many aspects of ISO 9000:2000 deal with process management activities. (In fact, the entire set of standards is focused on an organization's ability to understand, define, document, and manage its processes.) For example, one of the requirements is that organizations plan and control the design and development of products and manage the interfaces between different groups involved in design and development to ensure effective communication and clear assignment of responsibility. The standards also address the management of inputs and outputs for design and development activities, and use of systematic reviews to evaluate the ability to meet requirements, identify any problems, and propose necessary actions; purchasing processes; control of production and service, including measurement and process validation; control of monitoring and measuring devices used to evaluate conformity; analysis and improvement; monitoring and measurement of quality management processes; and continual improvement, including preventive and corrective action. The standards require that an organization use its quality policy, objectives, audit results, data analysis, corrective and preventive actions, and management reviews to continually improve its quality management system's effectiveness.

To apply the techniques of process management, processes must be (1) repeatable and (2) measurable. Repeatability means that the process must recur over time. The cycle may be long, as with product development processes or patent applications; or it may be short, as with a manufacturing operation or an order entry process. Measurement provides the ability to capture important quality and performance indicators to reveal patterns about process performance. Meeting these two conditions ensures that sufficient data can be collected to reveal useful information for control and improvement.

Nearly every leading company views process management as a fundamental business activity. AT&T, for example, identified the following principles to guide their process management activities:

- Process improvement focuses on the end-to-end process.
- The mind-set of quality is one of prevention and continuous improvement.

- Everyone manages a process at some level and is simultaneously a customer and a supplier.
- Customer needs drive process improvement.
- Corrective action focuses on removing the root cause of the problem rather than on treating its symptoms.
- Process simplification reduces opportunities for errors and rework.
- Process improvement results from a disciplined and structured application of quality management principles.[3]

Many companies also use an integrated framework to guide process management activities. For instance, Boeing Aerospace Support developed a process-based management (PBM) framework that consists of three phases: *define the process* (design), *measure the process* (control), and *improve the process* (improvement). The framework begins with a design phase by defining the process and establishing customer-centric metrics by which to measure performance. The control phase monitors the metrics and stabilizes the process to lead to predictable performance. Finally, an improvement phase sets improvement goals, develops an implementation plan, and implements it. This phase uses Six Sigma, lean tools, and other classic methods. After improvements are implemented, the approach goes back to the control phase to monitor the new improvement. Note that all three elements of process management—design, control, and improvement—are integrated into this framework.

IDENTIFYING PROCESSES AND REQUIREMENTS

Nearly everything an organization does can be viewed as a process. Common processes include acquiring customer and market knowledge, strategic planning, research and development, purchasing, developing new products or services, manufacturing and assembly, fulfilling customer orders, managing information, measuring and analyzing performance, and training employees, to name just a few. Leading organizations identify important processes throughout the value chain that affect their ability to deliver customer value. These processes typically fall into two categories: value-creation processes and support processes.

Value-Creation Processes

According to AT&T, a process is how work creates value for customers.[4] **Value-creation processes** (sometimes called *core processes*) are those most important to "running the business" and maintaining or achieving a sustainable competitive advantage. Value-creation processes frequently align closely to an organization's core competencies and strategic objectives, which we will discuss in Chapter 10. They drive the creation of products and services, are critical to customer satisfaction, and have a major impact on the strategic goals of an organization. For example, Corning Telecommunications Products Division (TPD) identified and documented more than 800 processes in all areas of its business, of which 50 were designated as core business processes that merit special emphasis. Each core process is owned and managed by a key business leader.

Value-creation processes typically include product design and production/delivery processes. Product design processes involve all activities that are performed to incorporate customer requirements, new technology, and organizational knowledge into the functional specifications of a manufactured good or service. Production/delivery processes create or deliver the actual product; examples are manufacturing, assembly,

> *We will discuss quality in product design in depth in Chapter 7, along with various tools and techniques to support product design processes.*

dispensing medications, teaching a class, and so on. In addition, value-creation processes include other critical business processes such as research and development, technology acquisition, supply chain management, mergers and acquisitions, and project management. In nonprofit organizations, value-creation processes might include fundraising, media relations, and public policy advocacy.

In many organizations, value-creation processes take the form of **projects**—temporary work structures that start up, produce products or services, and then shut down.[5] Some organizations focus exclusively on projects because of the nature of their work. They tend to deliver unique, one-of-a-kind products or services tailored to the specific needs of an individual customer. Examples include performing clinical trials for pharmaceutical companies, market research studies, consulting, and systems installation. Thus, projects are the chief means of value creation. Projects generally cut across organizational boundaries and require the coordination of many different departments and functions. **Project management** involves all activities associated with planning, scheduling, and controlling projects. Although every project is unique, many projects have similar underlying processes; thus, viewing them from a process management perspective can be beneficial.

QUALITYSPOTLIGHT

Custom Research Incorporated

Custom Research Incorporated (CRI) conducts unique market research studies for many different organizations. A Cycle Time Task Force identified nine common processes for all marketing research studies: identification of client requirements/expectations, questionnaire design, questionnaire programming, sampling, data collection, data tabulation, report and analysis, internal communication, and client communication. A Process Task Force was formed to map and improve each process. For example, CRI developed a "one-entry system" that eliminates the need to enter data into its computer system more than once and allows questionnaires to be tested for validity and reliability, eliminating several programming steps and helping to reduce cycle time. An account team is in charge of every research project. Project-related problems anywhere in the process are recognized and reported by the team. Team members use their problem-solving skills to determine whether the variation is due to common or special causes, analyze the reasons for the occurrence, and implement changes that will prevent it from recurring. When each project is completed, the account team completes a Project Quality Recap documenting problems and solutions and rating the performance of internal departments. Teams refer to the Recaps on file when they have similar projects or subsequent projects from the same client.[6]

Support Processes

Support processes are those that are most important to an organization's value-creation processes, employees, and daily operations. They provide infrastructure for value-creation processes, but generally do not add value directly to the product or service. Support processes might include processes for finance and accounting, facilities management, legal services, human resource services, public relations, and other administrative services. In a school system, for example, support processes might include transportation, custodial, central stores, information technology, and maintenance. A process such as order entry that might be thought of as a value-creation process for one company (e.g., a direct mail distributor) may be considered a support process for another (e.g., a custom manufacturer). Value-creation processes generally require a higher level of attention than do support processes; however, failure to adequately manage support processes can certainly impede the functioning of value-creation processes.

Processes can be broken down in a hierarchical fashion. At the top level, an organization must identify the major value-creation and support processes that require attention by senior managers. Each major process consists of many subprocesses that are managed by functional managers or cross-functional teams. Finally, each subprocess consists of many specific work steps performed by individuals at the performer level. As an example, Boeing Airlift and Tanker (A&T) Programs have developed an "enterprise process model" that views the entire business as eight interconnected process families. These major groupings range from enterprise leadership and new business development to production and post-delivery product support. Each family encompasses up to 10 major processes which, in turn, are made up of several tiers of supporting subprocesses. A&T manages cross-cutting relationships as "mega-processes" that extend to suppliers and customers.

Process Requirements

Understanding the requirements that processes should meet is vital to designing them. One of the fundamental questions asked at SSM Health Care during their process design activities is "What are the customer's expected outcomes from the process?" Reviewing patient/customer feedback data, conducting specialized surveys or focus groups, and including customers on design teams help them answer this question.

Given the diverse nature of value-creation processes, the requirements and performance characteristics might vary significantly for different processes. In general, value-creation process requirements are driven by consumer or external customer needs. For example, if hotel customers expect fast, error-free check-in, then the check-in process must be designed for speed and accuracy. Support process requirements, on the other hand, are driven by internal customer needs and must be aligned with the needs of key value-creation processes. For example, information technology processes at a hotel must support the check-in process requirements of speed and accuracy; this would require real-time information on room availability.

Table 5.2 shows the value-creation processes and their requirements defined by Pal's Sudden Service, a regional chain of fast-food restaurants in the southeastern United States. Their support processes include accounting/finance, human resources, maintenance, management information systems, ordering, and stocking. Other critical support processes that lead to business success and growth might be research and development, technology acquisition, supply chain management and supplier partnering, mergers and acquisitions, project management, or sales and marketing. These processes will differ greatly among organizations, depending on the nature of products and services, customer and market requirements, global focus, and other factors. For example, a hospital might define its key value-creation processes as preadmission screening, admission and registration, assessment and diagnosis, treatment, discharge, and follow up; support services might include workforce management, medical records and information technology, financial planning, supply chain management, environmental services, and physical plant operations.

Identifying process requirements provides the basis for measuring process performance. For example, the measures used by SSM Health Care to monitor the requirements of their key processes are shown in Table 5.3. Daily, weekly, monthly, and quarterly performance assessments provide the opportunity to review and manage these measures and identify ways of preventing potential errors before they affect the patient.

We will discuss measurement issues in more detail in Chapters 8 and 12.

TABLE 5.2   Value-Creation Processes for Pal's Sudden Service

Process	Principal Requirements
Order taking	Accurate, fast, friendly
Cooking	Proper temperature
Product assembly	Proper sequence, sanitary, correct ingredients and amounts, speed, proper temperature, neat
Cash collection	Accurate, fast, friendly
Slicing	Cut/size, freshness/color
Chili preparation	Proper temperature, quantity, freshness
Ham/chicken preparation	Proper temperature, quantity, freshness
Supply chain management	Price/cost, order accuracy
Property acquisition	Sales potential, adherence to budget
Construction	On time, within budget
Marketing and advertising	Clear message, brand recognition

Source: Reprinted with permission of Pal's Sudden Service.

TABLE 5.3   SSM Health Care Process Requirements and Measures

Process	Key Requirements	Key Measures
Admit		
Admitting/registration	Timeliness	• Time to admit patients to the setting of care • Timeliness in admitting/registration rate on patient satisfaction survey questions
Assess		
Patient assessment	Timeliness	• % of histories and physicals charted within 24 hours or prior to surgery • Pain assessed at appropriate intervals, per hospital policy
Clinical laboratory and radiology services	Accuracy and Timeliness	• Quality control results/repeat rates • Turnaround time • Response rate on medical staff satisfaction survey
Care Delivery/Treatment		
Provision of clinical care	Nurse responsiveness, pain management, successful clinical, outcomes	• Response rate on patient satisfaction and medical staff survey questions • Wait time for pain medications • % CHF patients received medication instructions/weighing • % Ischemic heart patients discharged on proven therapies • Unplanned readmits/returns to ER or Operating Room • Mortality

(continued)

TABLE 5.3   SSM Health Care Process Requirements and Measures (*Continued*)

Process	Key Requirements	Key Measures
Pharmacy/medication use	Accuracy	• Use of dangerous abbreviations in medication orders • Med error rate or adverse drug events resulting from medication errors
Surgical services/anesthesia	Professional skill, competence/communication	• Clear documentation of informed surgical and anesthesia consent • Perioperative mortality • Surgical site infection rates
Discharge		
Case management	Appropriate utilization	• Average length of stay (ALOS) • Payment denials • Unplanned readmits
Discharge from setting of care	Assistance and clear directions	• Discharge instructions documented and provided to patient • Response rate on patient satisfaction survey

Source: Reprinted with permission of SSM Health Care.

PROCESS DESIGN

The goal of process design is to develop an efficient process that satisfies both internal and external customer requirements and is capable of achieving the requisite level of quality and performance. Other factors that might need to be considered in process design include safety, cost, variability, productivity, environmental impact, "green" manufacturing, measurement capability, and maintainability of equipment. Because processes generally cut across traditional organizational functions and rarely operate in isolation, process designs must be considered in relation to other processes that impact them.

Process design begins with understanding its purpose and requirements, who the customer is, and what outputs are produced. The purpose of a manufacturing process, for instance, is to produce a component or semifinished good for the next manufacturing process. Thus, process design usually starts with a detailed technical analysis of characteristics of the product, technological capabilities of machines and equipment, required operations sequences, assembly methods, and so on, which are often conducted by industrial or manufacturing engineers. The purpose of an order-taking process is to accurately identify in a friendly fashion what a customer wants. A process design might start by identifying ways that customers prefer to place orders and how long they are willing to wait, for example.

Technology is an integral part of process design that makes today's service and manufacturing processes operate productively and meet customer needs better than ever. Staples, for example, incorporates robotics into its order-fulfillment processes. Small, two-foot high, three-foot long machines travel the aisles of warehouses and read barcode stickers on the floor. After a computer sends stock location information to them, they slide under storage racks, lift them up, and bring them to stations where workers pull the products and pack them for shipping. They then return the racks to their original locations. After their introduction, productivity improved by 60 percent and customers get their orders quicker. Fast-food restaurants have carefully designed their food preparation and delivery processes for a high degree of accuracy and fast response time. New hands-free intercom systems, better microphones that reduce ambient kitchen noise, and screens that display a customer's order are all focused on these requirements.[7]

Process Mapping

Designing a process requires a systematic approach. For most processes, this includes defining the sequence of steps that need to be performed, along with formal documentation of procedures and requirements. To describe the specific steps in a process and their sequence, we generally develop a **process map** or flowchart, along with standard operating procedures and work instructions. Figure 5.2 shows a flowchart for training printing press operators. The process defines the steps and decision points required to achieve certification, and ensures that all requirements are met.

As design tools, flowcharts enable management to study and analyze processes prior to implementation in order to improve quality and operational performance. The AT&T customer–supplier model that we introduced in Chapter 3 provides a way of building a detailed process flowchart. Start with the outputs, or customer requirements, and move backward through the process to identify the key steps needed to produce each output;

FIGURE 5.2

Example of a Process Map for Training Printing Press Operators

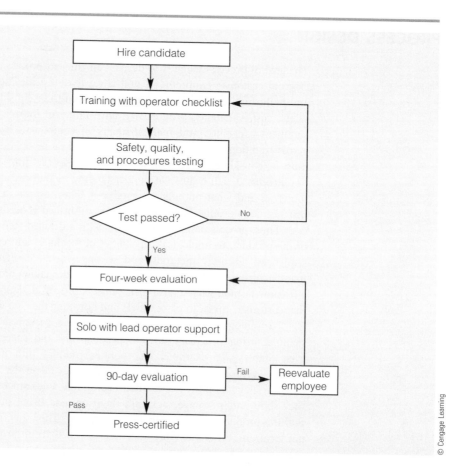

© Cengage Learning

stop when the process reaches the supplier input stage. AT&T calls this technique "backward chaining."[8] AT&T suggests the following steps:

1. Begin with the process output and ask, "What is the last essential subprocess that produces the output of the process?"
2. For that subprocess, ask, "What input does it need to produce the process output?" For each input, test its value to ensure that it is required.
3. For each input, identify its source. In many cases, the input will be the output of the previous subprocess. In some cases, the input may come from external suppliers.
4. Continue backward, one subprocess at a time, until each input comes from an external supplier.

EXAMPLE 5.1

Suppose that a hospital wants to design a process for administering medication to a patient. Clearly, the last subprocess is "patient receives medicine." The input to this subprocess is "medicine is delivered from the pharmacy." Working backwards, we identify the previous subprocess as "pharmacy fills prescription order" and "physician writes order." We may then expand each subprocess to create a more detailed process description that includes checks and reviews and more detailed steps. Figure 5.3 shows how this design might end up.

After a flowchart is developed, several fundamental questions can be asked to analyze the process and create a more effective design:

- Are the steps in the process arranged in logical sequence?

FIGURE 5.3   Medical Administration Process

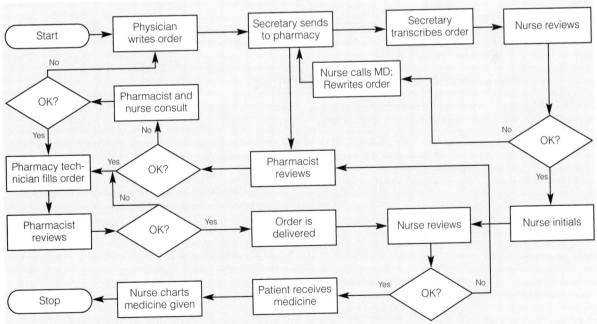

Source: Ellen Williams and Ray Tailey, "The Use of Failure Mode Effect and Criticality Analysis in a Medication Error Subcommittee," *ASQC Health Care Division Newsletter*, Winter 1996, 4. Copyright © 1996 ASQC. Reprinted with permission.

- Do all steps add value? Can some steps be eliminated and should others be added in order to improve quality or operational performance? Can some be combined? Should some be reordered?
- Are capacities of each step in balance; that is, do bottlenecks exist for which customers will incur excessive waiting time?
- What skills, equipment, and tools are required at each step of the process? Should some steps be automated?
- At which points in the system might errors occur that would result in customer dissatisfaction, and how might these errors be corrected?
- At which point or points should quality be measured?
- Where interaction with the customer occurs, what procedures and guidelines should employees follow to present a positive image?

For example, to determine if a process step has value, more detailed questions may be asked, such as:

- Would the customer notice a loss of value if this step were eliminated?
- Would the product or service be obviously incomplete without this step?
- If you were forced to complete the product or service on an emergency basis, is this step too important to skip?
- If you owned the business and could pocket the savings from skipping this step, would you include it?
- If the step is a review or inspection, is the reject rate significant? Are the consequences of an error at this step significant?

If any of these answers is no, then the value of the step is suspect and should be investigated more thoroughly.[9]

In knowledge work, such as strategic planning or research and development, process does not necessarily imply formal sequences of steps, but general understandings regarding competent performance. Thus, defining a process for knowledge rework may not rely on process maps, but rather, general descriptions of requirements.

Process Design for Services

Most cross-functional business value-creation processes and all support processes are primarily service-oriented. Thus, it is important to understand the fundamental differences between manufacturing and service processes. First, the outputs of service processes are not as well defined, as are manufactured products. For example, even though all banks offer similar tangible goods such as checking, loans, automated tellers, and so forth, the real differentiating factor among banks is the service they provide. Second, most service processes involve a greater interaction with the customer, often making it easier to identify needs and expectations. On the other hand, customers often cannot define their needs for service until after they have some point of reference or comparison.

Service processes often involve both internal and external activities, a factor that complicates design for quality. In a bank, for example, poor service can result from the way that tellers treat customers and also from poor quality of information systems and communications equipment beyond the control of the tellers. Internal activities are primarily concerned with efficiency (quality of conformance), while external activities—with direct customer interaction—require attention to effectiveness (quality of design). All too often, workers involved in internal operations do not understand how their performance affects the customers they do not see. The success of the process depends on everyone—workers involved in internal as well as external activities—understanding that they add value to the customer.

Services have three basic components:

1. physical facilities, processes, and procedures;
2. employee behavior; and
3. employee professional judgment.[10]

Designing a service essentially involves determining an effective balance among all three of these. Too much or too little emphasis on one component will lead to poor quality or inefficiency. For example, too much emphasis on procedures might result in timely and efficient service, but might also suggest insensitivity and apathy toward the customer. Too much emphasis on behavior might provide a friendly and personable environment at the expense of slow, inconsistent, or chaotic service. Too much emphasis on professional judgment might lead to good solutions to customer problems but also to slow, inconsistent, or insensitive service.

The five key service dimensions that we introduced in Chapter 3—reliability, assurance, tangibles, empathy, and responsiveness—provide a basis for designing quality into the three service components. For instance, reliability is a key aspect of processes and procedures; assurance relates to professional judgment; tangibles ties to physical facilities; and empathy and responsiveness are characteristics of employee behavior.

 QUALITYSPOTLIGHT

The City of Coral Springs

The City of Coral Springs, Florida, clearly understands its customer requirements and incorporates them into the design of its processes. The city's building permit work process is designed to be responsive, professional, consistent, and accessible; and its fleet maintenance work process is designed to be reliable, convenient, and responsive. Processes are designed to meet all key requirements through multiple phases of testing and revision before a process or significant process change is fully implemented and through involvement of customers in the design. Teams develop innovations when existing processes fail to meet changing requirements or research on best practices shows that existing approaches are inadequate to meet new requirements. New technology is incorporated into processes through Information Services staff who serve on all development teams. They research best practices, and scout and critique new technology through professional associations, user groups, and networks of local governments. Coral Springs has incorporated web-enabled applications into the building permit process, the employment process, and water bill payment.[11]

A useful approach to designing services is to recognize that services differ in three dimensions:

1. customer contact and interaction,
2. labor intensity, and
3. customization.

For example, a railroad is low in all three dimensions. On the other hand, an interior design service would be high in all three dimensions. A typical fast-food restaurant would be medium in customer contact, high in labor intensity, and low to medium in customization.

Services low in all three dimensions of this classification are more similar to manufacturing organizations. The emphasis on quality should be focused on the physical facilities and procedures; behavior and professional judgment are relatively unimportant. As contact and interaction between the customer and the service system increases, the customer's impression of physical facilities, processes, and procedures becomes more important, as does the behavior of employees. The process design might have to include information to help customers understand and follow the sequence of process steps. Such service processes also require guidance to the providers of those services on handling contingencies related to the possible actions or behaviors of customers that cannot always be predicted.

As labor intensity increases, variations between individuals become more important; however, the elements of personal behavior and professional judgment will remain relatively unimportant as long as the degrees of customization and contact and interaction remain low. As customization increases, professional judgment becomes a bigger factor in the ability to provide high quality service. In services that are high in all three dimensions, facilities, behavior, and professional judgment must be equally balanced.

In designing service processes, the following questions should be considered:[12]

- What service standards are required to be met?
- What is the final result of the service to be provided?
- At what point does the service begin, and what signals its completion?
- What is the maximum waiting time that a customer will tolerate?
- How long should it take to perform the service?
- Who must the consumer deal with in completing the service?
- What components of the service are essential? Desirable? Superfluous?
- Which components can differ from one service encounter to another while still meeting standards?

Design for Agility

As customer needs and expectations change, organizations must design processes that are increasingly agile. **Agility** is a term that is commonly used to characterize flexibility and short cycle times. Electronic commerce, for instance, requires more rapid, flexible, and customized responses than traditional market outlets. **Flexibility** refers to the ability to adapt quickly and effectively to changing requirements. It might mean rapid changeover from one product to another, rapid response to changing demands, or the ability to produce a wide range of customized services. Flexibility might demand special strategies such as modular designs, sharing components, sharing manufacturing lines, and specialized training for employees. It also involves outsourcing decisions, agreements with key suppliers, and innovative partnering arrangements. Enablers of agility include close relationships with customers to understand their emerging needs and requirements, empowering employees as decision makers, effective manufacturing and information technology, close supplier and partner relationships, and breakthrough improvement.

A good example of agility is the Stockholm-based fashion retailer, Hennes & Mauritz (H&M). While traditional clothing retailers design their products at least six months in advance of the selling season, H&M can rush items into stores in as little as three weeks. By monitoring consumer trends and identifying hot-selling items, its designers immediately start to sketch new styles, which are then developed by pattern makers, often using employees as live models. Designs are sent electronically to factories in Europe and Asia that can handle the jobs quickly, and in less than two months, most H&M stores will have the new styles in stock. One of the company's enablers is empowered employees who can dream up and produce new fashions without formal approval.[13]

Agility is crucial to such customer-focused strategies as *mass customization*— providing personalized, custom-designed products to meet individual customer preferences at prices comparable to mass-produced items. Lands' End customers can take simple shirt and pants size measurements at home and answer a series of questions on its website. Then, using a series of algorithms, Lands' End translates the information into a customized pattern that is sent to one of five contracted manufacturers in the United States and overseas, where the plants cut and sew the garment and ship it directly to the customer. The data are saved on the website, making reordering a breeze.[14] Mass customization requires significant changes to traditional manufacturing processes that focus on either customized, crafted products or mass-produced, standardized products.[15] These processes incorporate flexible manufacturing technologies, just-in-time systems, information technology, and emphasize cycle time reduction.

Mistake-Proofing Processes

Human beings tend to make mistakes inadvertently.[16] Typical mistakes in production are omitted steps in a process, setup errors, missing parts, wrong parts, or incorrect adjustments. Such errors can arise from the following factors:

- Forgetfulness due to lack of reinforcement or guidance
- Misunderstanding or incorrect identification because of the lack of familiarity with a process or procedures
- Lack of experience
- Absentmindedness and lack of attention, especially when a process is automated

Blaming workers not only discourages them and lowers morale, but usually does not address the source of the problems, which, as Deming and Juran often stated, is usually in the system.

Preventing mistakes can be done in three ways:

1. *Designing potential defects and errors out of the process.* Clearly, this approach is the best because it eliminates any possibility that the error or defect will occur and will not result in rework, scrap, or wasted time.
2. *Identifying potential defects and errors and stopping a process before they occur.* Although this approach prevents defects and errors, it does result in some non-value-added time.
3. *Identifying defects and errors soon after they occur and quickly correcting the process.* This can avoid large amounts of costly defects and errors in the future, but does result in some scrap, rework, and wasted resources.

Good design can eliminate many defects and errors, but still cannot account for the human factor.

Poka-yoke (POH-kah YOH-kay) is an approach for mistake-proofing processes using automatic devices or simple methods to avoid human error. Poka-yoke is focused on two aspects: (1) prediction, or recognizing that a defect is about to occur and providing a warning, and (2) detection, or recognizing that a defect has occurred and stopping the process. The poka-yoke concept was developed and refined in the early 1960s by the late Shigeo Shingo, a Japanese manufacturing engineer who developed the Toyota production system.[17] Shingo visited a plant and observed that the plant was not using any type of measurement or statistical process control system for tracking defects. When asked why, the manager replied that they did not make any defects to track! His investigation led to the development of a mistake-proofing approach called Zero Quality Control, or ZQC. ZQC is driven by simple and inexpensive inspection processes, such as successive checking, in which operators inspect the work of the prior operation before continuing, and self-checking, in which operators assess the quality of their own work. Poka-yokes are designed to facilitate this process or remove the human element completely.

Many applications of poka-yoke are deceptively simple, inexpensive to implement, and are often quite creative. Poka-yoke is a good way of engaging workers in continuous improvement activities. One of Shingo's first poka-yoke devices involved a process at the Yamada Electric plant in which workers assemble a switch having two push buttons supported by two springs.[18] Occasionally, the worker would forget to insert a spring under each button, which led to a costly and embarrassing repair at the customer's facility. In the old method, the worker would take two springs out of a large parts box and then assemble the switch. To prevent this mistake, the worker was instructed first to place two springs in a small dish in front of the parts box, and then assemble the switch. If a spring remains in the dish, the operator knows immediately that an error has occurred. The solution was simple, inexpensive, and provided immediate feedback to the operator. Many other examples can be cited:

- Many machines have sensors that would be activated only if the part was placed in the correct position.
- A device on a drill counts the number of holes drilled in a work piece; a buzzer sounds if the work piece is removed before the correct number of holes has been drilled.
- Computer programs display a warning message if a file that has not been saved is to be closed.
- Passwords set for web accounts are entered twice.
- Orders for critical aircraft parts use pre-fit foam forms that only allow the correct part to be placed in them, ensuring that the correct parts are shipped.
- Associates at Amazon sort products into bins that weigh them and compare the weight to the order; if there is an inconsistency, the associate is prompted to verify the items.

Richard B. Chase and Douglas M. Stewart suggest that the same concepts can be applied to services.[19] The major differences are that service mistake-proofing must account for the customers' activities as well as those of the producer, and for interactions between the customer and provider. Chase and Stewart classify service poka-yokes by the type of error they are designed to prevent: server errors and customer errors. Server errors result from the task, treatment, or tangibles of the service. Customer errors occur during preparation, the service encounter, or during resolution. The following list summarizes the typical types of service errors and related poka-yokes.

- *Task errors* include doing work incorrectly, work not requested, work on the wrong order, or working too slowly. Some examples of poka-yoke devices for task errors are computer prompts, color-coded cash register keys, measuring tools such as a French-fry scoop, and signaling devices. Hospitals use trays for surgical instruments that have indentations for each instrument, preventing the surgeon from leaving one of them in the patient. Simple checklists are often used; for example, LifeWings, a company that applies flight-tested safety lessons from the aviation industry to medicine, works with medical teams to create standardized lists of activities for every procedure.[20]
- *Treatment errors* arise in the contact between the server and the customer, such as lack of courteous behavior, and failure to acknowledge, listen, or react appropriately to the customer. A bank encourages eye contact by requiring tellers to record the customer's eye color on a checklist as they start the transaction. To promote friendliness at a fast-food restaurant, trainers provide the four specific cues for when to smile: when greeting the customer, when taking the order, when telling about the dessert special, and when giving the customer change. They encourage employees to observe whether the customer smiled back, a natural reinforcer for smiling.

- *Tangible errors* are those in physical elements of the service, such as unclean facilities, dirty uniforms, inappropriate temperature, and document errors. Hotels wrap paper strips around towels to help the housekeeping staff identify clean linen and show which ones should be replaced. Spell-checkers in word processing software help reduce document misspellings (provided they are used!).
- *Customer errors in preparation* include the failure to bring necessary materials to the encounter, to understand their role in the service transaction, and to engage the correct service. A computer manufacturer provides a flowchart to specify how to place a service call. By guiding the customers through three yes-or-no questions, the flowchart prompts them to have the necessary information before calling.
- *Customer errors during an encounter* can be due to inattention, misunderstanding, or simply a memory lapse, and include failure to remember steps in the process or to follow instructions. Poka-yoke examples include height bars at amusement rides that indicate rider size requirements, beepers that signal customers to remove cards from ATM machines, and locks on airplane lavatory doors that must be closed to turn on the lights. Some cashiers at restaurants fold back the top edge of credit card receipts, holding together the restaurant's copies while revealing the customer's copy.
- *Customer errors at the resolution stage* of a service encounter include failure to signal service inadequacies, to learn from experience, to adjust expectations, and to execute appropriate post-encounter actions. Hotels might enclose a small gift certificate to encourage guests to provide feedback. Strategically placed tray-return stands and trash receptacles remind customers to return trays in fast-food facilities.

PROCESS CONTROL

A British Airways Boeing B-777 was forced to make an emergency landing in Houston after an engine caught fire. The cause was traced to the fact that the wrong engine blade had been processed and shipped to the customer, and that inspections to prevent such an error were inadequate. GE's "quality notice" on the incident stated that employees failed to detect that the blade casting was misidentified when it arrived at the plant or after they processed and cleared it for installation. The notice recommended adding verification requirements at several stages of the process, which the company has done. The incident cost GE $8 million.[21] Although GE acted swiftly to resolve the problems, this case demonstrates the importance of process control. Process control is important for two reasons. First, process control methods are the basis for effective daily management. Second, long-term improvements cannot be made to a process unless the process is first brought under control.

Control is the activity of ensuring conformance to the requirements and taking corrective action when necessary to correct problems and maintain stable performance. The distinction between control and improvement is illustrated in Figure 5.4. Any process performance measure naturally fluctuates around some average level. Abnormal conditions or unusual events may cause a departure from this pattern. Removing the causes of such abnormalities and maintaining consistent performance is the essence of control. However, even a controlled process that has too much variation can be detrimental to customer satisfaction and financial performance. For example, research in the airline industry has shown that lack of service consistency (with respect to arrival times) has a definite impact on customer dissatisfaction. Process consistency was found to be at least as important as average performance for better-performing firms, where customer expectations are high.[22] Thus, improvement can mean changing the average performance to a

FIGURE 5.4
Control versus
Improvement

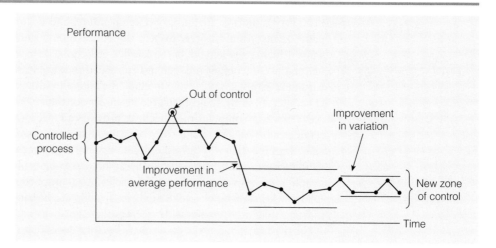

new level or reducing variation around the current average performance. Process control is the responsibility of those who directly accomplish the work, such as machine operators, order-fulfillment workers, and so on. Long-term improvement is generally the responsibility of management, with the help and engagement of the workforce.

Any control system has four elements: (1) *a standard or goal*, (2) *a means of measuring accomplishment*, (3) *comparison of results with the standard to provide feedback*, and (4) *the ability to make corrections as appropriate*. Goals and standards are defined during planning and design processes. They establish what is supposed to be accomplished. These goals and standards are reflected by measurable quality characteristics, such as product dimensions, service times, or employee behavior. For example, golf balls must meet five standards to be considered as conforming to the Rules of Golf: minimum size, maximum weight, spherical symmetry, maximum initial velocity, and overall distance.[23] In some call centers, employees must follow a specific script or ask certain questions of every customer.

Measuring quality characteristics may be accomplished through some sort of inspection activity. For instance, golf balls are measured for size by trying to drop them through a metal ring—a conforming ball sticks to the ring while a nonconforming ball falls through; digital scales measure weight to one-thousandth of a gram; and initial velocity is measured in a special machine by finding the time it takes a ball struck at 98 mph to break a ballistic screen at the end of a tube exactly 6.28 feet away. Call centers might record conversations between customers and employees. Table 5.4 shows some of the key work processes in the City of Coral Springs Florida, their requirements, and both long-term and short-term in-process measures used to control these processes.

By comparing results with the standards or goals, one can determine whether corrective action is needed. Many companies use statistical process control (see Chapter 8) as a means of signaling when deviations from standards require corrective action. Corrective action might entail adjusting machine settings or retraining call center employees.

Control should be the foundation for organizational learning. Many companies have adopted an approach that has been used in the U.S. military, called **after-action review**, or **debrief**. This review consists of asking four basic questions:

1. What was supposed to happen?
2. What actually happened?

TABLE 5.4   Work Processes in the City of Coral Springs [Adapted from City of Coral Springs Baldrige Application Summary; www.nist.gov/baldrige]

Key Work Processes	Requirements	Performance Measurement	In-Process Measures
Police Patrol	Visible, emergency response under 6 minutes, and lower crime and accident rate than other Broward cities	Response time for priority one calls Crime Rate Accidents at major intersections	Daily reports on response time, weekly GIS reports on clime patterns, and weekly GIS reports on accidents
Police Investigations	Low crime rate	Clearance rate	Monthly open case report
Fire Suppression	Response under 8 minutes, and sufficient equipment and qualified staff to minimize damage	User rating from survey % response under 8 minutes	Daily reports on response time and staff responding to calls
Emergency Medical Services	Response time under 8 minutes, appropriate response to medical situation, and professional, compassionate behavior	User rating from survey % response under 8 minutes	Daily reports on response time and transaction surveys of families using service
Parks Maintenance	Safety, aesthetics, and functionality	Maintenance rating from survey Parks safety rating	Data from quarterly point of contact surveys

3. Why was there a difference?
4. What can we learn?

Thus, rather than simply correcting unacceptable events, the focus is on preventing them from occurring again.

Process Control in Manufacturing

In manufacturing, control is usually applied to incoming materials, key processes, and final products and services. Control in manufacturing starts with purchasing and receiving processes. Clearly, if incoming materials are of poor quality, then the final product will certainly be no better. In a TQ environment, customers should not have to rely on heavy inspection of purchased items. The burden of supplying high-quality product should rest with the suppliers themselves. Occasional inspection might be used to audit compliance, but suppliers should be expected to provide documentation and statistical evidence that they are meeting specifications.

Because unwanted variation can arise during production, in-process control is needed throughout the production process. Many different mechanisms are used in manufacturing facilities to control quality. For example, DaimlerChrysler's Toluca Assembly Plant in Mexico verifies parts, processes, fit, and finish every step of the way, from stamping and body to paint and final assembly. The control practices include visual management through quality alert systems, which are designed to call immediate attention to abnormal conditions. The system provides visual and audible signals for each station for tooling, production, maintenance, and material flow.[24] When the process owner assumes the role of inspector for manual manufacturing work or assembly, the occurrence of unwanted variation can quickly be recognized and immediate adjustments to stabilize the process can be made. Done properly, this activity can eliminate the need for independent inspection after the fact. In many cases, control processes are automated. For instance, in the production of plastic sheet stock, thickness depends on temperature. Sensors monitor the sheet thickness; if it begins to go out of tolerance, the system can adjust the temperature in order to change the thickness. At Hyundai, optical sensors are used to measure tolerances to ensure tight welds and minimal gaps between panels, and cars are put through high-pressure water chambers to test the integrity of door seals.

Final inspection represents the last point in the manufacturing process at which the producer can verify that the product meets customer requirements. For many consumer products, final inspection consists of functional testing. At Hyundai, every vehicle produced at its Alabama plant is road tested on a special test track. In many industries such as electronics, computerized test equipment allows for 100 percent of the product to be tested rapidly and cost-effectively.

Effective quality control systems include documented procedures for all key processes; a clear understanding of the appropriate equipment and working environment; methods for monitoring and controlling critical quality characteristics; approval processes for equipment; criteria for workmanship, such as written standards, samples, or illustrations; and maintenance activities. Documented control procedures are usually written down in a **process control plan**. Cincinnati Fiberglass, a small manufacturer of fiberglass parts for trucks, uses a control plan for each production process that includes the process name, tool used, standard operating procedure, tolerance, inspection frequency, sample size, person responsible, reporting document, and reaction plan. Of particular importance is the ability to trace all components of a product back to process equipment, operators, and to the original material from which it was made. Process control also includes monitoring the accuracy and variability of equipment, operator knowledge and skills, the accuracy of measurement results and data used, and environmental factors such as time and temperature.

Process Control in Services

For many services, process control follows the same paradigm as in manufacturing: define a standard or goal, measure accomplishment, compare results with the standard, and make corrections as needed. An example of a structured quality control process in the service industry is the "10-Step Monitoring and Evaluation Process" set forth by the Joint Commission on Accrediting Health Care Organizations. This process, shown in Table 5.5, provides a detailed sequence of activities for monitoring and evaluating the quality of health care in an effort to identify problems and improve care. Standards and goals are defined in steps 2 through 5; measurement is accomplished in step 6; and comparison and feedback is performed in the remaining steps.

In services with high customer contact, labor intensity, and/or customization, control can be challenging. Human behavior—both the customer's and the service provider's—is more difficult to control than mechanical or automated processes. The Quality Spotlight for the The Ritz-Carlton Hotel Company describes their proactive approach to quality control that is designed for their intensive personalized service environment.

TABLE 5.5   10-Step Monitoring and Evaluation Process for Health Care Organizations

- *Step 1: Assign Responsibility.* The emergency department director is responsible for, and actively participates in, monitoring and evaluation. The director assigns responsibility for the specific duties related to monitoring and evaluation.
- *Step 2: Delineate Scope of Care.* The department considers the scope of care provided within emergency services to establish a basis for identifying important aspects of care to monitor and evaluate. The scope of care is a complete inventory of what the emergency department does.
- *Step 3: Identify Important Aspects of Care.* Important aspects of care are those that are high-risk, high-volume, and/or problem-prone. Staff identify important aspects of care so that monitoring and evaluation focuses on emergency department activities with the greatest impact on patient care.
- *Step 4: Identify Indicators.* Indicators of quality are identified for each important aspect of care. An indicator is a measurable variable related to a structure, process, or out-come of care. Examples of possible indicators (all of which would need to be further defined) include insufficient staffing for sudden surges in patient volume (structure), delays in physicians reporting to the emergency room (process), and transfusion errors (outcome).
- *Step 5: Establish Thresholds for Evaluation.* A threshold for evaluation is the level or point at which intensive evaluation of care is triggered. A threshold may be 0% or 100% or any other appropriate level. Emergency department staff should establish a threshold for each indicator.
- *Step 6: Collect and Organize Data.* Appropriate emergency department staff should collect data pertaining to the indicators. Data are organized to facilitate comparison with the thresholds for evaluation.
- *Step 7: Evaluate Care.* When the cumulative data related to an indicator reach the threshold for evaluation, appropriate emergency department staff evaluate the care provided to determine whether a problem exists. This evaluation, which in many cases will take the form of peer review, should focus on possible trends and performance patterns. The evaluation is designed to identify causes of any problems or methods by which care or performance may be improved.
- *Step 8: Take Actions to Solve Problems.* When problems are identified, action plans are developed, approved at appropriate levels, and enacted to solve the problem or take the opportunity to improve care.
- *Step 9: Assess Actions and Document Improvement.* The effectiveness of any actions taken is assessed and documented. Further actions necessary to solve a problem are taken and their effectiveness is assessed.
- *Step 10: Communicate Relevant Information to the Organization-wide Quality Assurance Program.* Findings from and conclusions of monitoring and evaluation, including actions taken to solve problems and improve care, are documented and reported monthly through the hospital's established channels of communication.

Source: "Medical Staff Monitoring and Evaluation—Departmental Review," Chicago. Copyright by the Joint Commission on Accreditation of Health Care Organizations, Oakbrook Terrace, IL. Reprinted with permission.

QUALITYSPOTLIGHT

The Ritz-Carlton Hotel Company

At The Ritz-Carlton Hotel Company, systems for collecting and using quality-related measures are widely deployed and used extensively throughout the organization.[25] Each hotel tracks service quality indicators on a daily basis. The Ritz-Carlton recognizes that many customer requirements are sensory, and thus, difficult to measure. However, by selecting, training, and certifying employees in their knowledge of The Ritz-Carlton Gold Standards of service, they are able to assess their work through appropriate sensory measurements—taste, sight, smell, sound, and touch—and take appropriate actions.

The company uses three types of control processes to deliver quality:

1. Self-control of the individual employee based on their spontaneous and learned behavior.
2. Basic control mechanisms, which are carried out by every member of the workforce. The first person who detects a problem is empowered to break away from routine duties, investigate and correct the problem immediately, document the incident, and then return to their routine.
3. Critical success factor control for critical processes. Process teams use customer and organizational requirement measurements to determine quality, speed, and cost performance. These measurements are compared against benchmarks and customer satisfaction data to determine corrective action and resource allocation. The Ritz-Carlton conducts both self-audits and outside audits. Self-audits are carried out internally at all levels, from one individual or function to an entire hotel. Process walk-throughs occur daily in hotels, while senior leaders assess field operations during formal reviews at various intervals. Outside audits are performed by independent travel and hospitality rating organizations. All audits must be documented, and any findings must be submitted to the senior leader of the unit being audited. They are responsible for action and for assessing the implementation and effectiveness of recommended corrective actions.

PROCESS IMPROVEMENT

In 1950, when W. Edwards Deming was helping Japan with its postwar rebuilding effort, he emphasized the importance of continuous improvement. While presenting to a group of Japanese industrialists (collectively representing about 80 percent of the nation's capital), he drew the diagram shown in Figure 5.5. This diagram depicts not only the relationships among inputs, processes, and outputs, but also the roles of consumers and suppliers, the interdependency of organizational processes, the usefulness of consumer research, and the importance of continuous improvement of all elements of the

FIGURE 5.5   Deming's View of a Production System

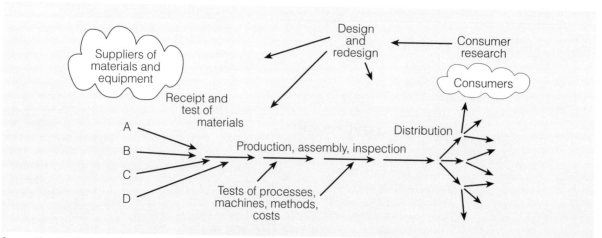

Source: Deming, W. Edwards, *Out of the Crisis*, figures: Deming's View of a Production System, page 4; The Deming Chain Reaction, page 3, © 2000 Massachusetts Institute of Technology, by permission of The MIT Press.

production system. Deming told the Japanese that understanding customers and suppliers was crucial to planning for quality. He advised them that continuous improvement of both products and production processes through better understanding of customer requirements is the key to capturing world markets. Deming predicted that within five years Japanese manufacturers would be making products of the highest quality in the world and would have gained a large share of the world market. He was wrong. By applying these ideas, the Japanese penetrated several global markets in less than four years!

Continuous improvement refers to both incremental changes, which are small and gradual, and breakthrough improvements, which are large and rapid. Continuous improvement is one of the foundation principles of total quality. It is an important business strategy in competitive markets because

- Customer loyalty is driven by delivered value.
- Delivered value is created by business processes.
- Sustained success in competitive markets requires a business to continuously improve delivered value.
- To continuously improve value-creation ability, a business must continuously improve its value-creation processes.[26]

Improvement should be a proactive task of management and be viewed as an opportunity, not simply as a reaction to problems and competitive threats.

Many opportunities for improvement exist, the most obvious being reductions in manufacturing defects or service errors. One example occurred at Dell. Although it has had some of the highest quality ratings in the PC industry, CEO Michael Dell became obsessed with finding ways to reduce machine failure rates. He concluded that failures were related to the number of times a hard drive was handled during assembly, and insisted that the number of "touches" be reduced from an existing level of more than 30 per drive. Production lines were revamped and the number was reduced to fewer than 15. Soon after, the reject rate of hard drives fell by 40 percent and the overall failure rated dropped by 20 percent.[27] Other examples of improvements include new and improved products and services, reductions in waste and cost, more efficient manufacturing systems, increased productivity and effectiveness in the use of all resources, and improved responsiveness and cycle time performance for such processes as resolving customer complaints or new product introduction. Organizations should also consider improving all managerial practices such as leadership and strategic planning, which we will address in Part III of this book.

One important area for improvement is reducing cycle time. Reductions in cycle time serve two purposes. First, they speed up work processes so that customer response is improved. Second, reductions in cycle time can only be accomplished by streamlining and simplifying processes to eliminate non-value-added steps such as rework. This approach forces improvements in quality by reducing the potential for mistakes and errors. By reducing non-value-added steps, costs are reduced as well. Thus, cycle time reductions often drive simultaneous improvements in organization, quality, cost, and productivity. Significant reductions in cycle time cannot be achieved simply by focusing on individual subprocesses; cross-functional processes must be examined all across the organization. Through these activities, the company comes to understand work at the organizational level and to engage in cooperative behaviors. Thus, cycle time reduction often drives simultaneous improvements in quality and productivity.

QUALITYSPOTLIGHT
Procter & Gamble

An example of cycle time reduction is Procter & Gamble's over-the-counter (OTC) clinical division, which conducts clinical studies that involve testing drugs, health care products, or treatments in humans.[28] Such testing follows rigorous design, conduct, analysis, and summary of the data collected. P&G had at least four different ways to perform a clinical study and needed to find the best way to meet its research and development needs. They chose to focus on cycle time reduction. Their approach built on fundamental TQ principles: focusing on the customer, fact-based decisions, continual improvement, empowerment, the right leadership structure, and an understanding of work processes. The team found that final reports took months to prepare. Only by mapping the existing process did they fully understand the causes of long production times and the amount of rework and recycling during review and sign-off. By restructuring the activities from sequential to parallel work and identifying critical measurements to monitor the process, they were able to reduce the time to less than four weeks. Figure 5.6 shows how the improvements were reflected in a process map.

Real improvement depends on *learning*, which means understanding why changes are successful through feedback between practices and results, leading to new goals and approaches. A **learning cycle** consists of four stages:

1. Planning
2. Execution of plans
3. Assessment of progress
4. Revision of plans based upon assessment findings

Peter Senge, a professor at the Massachusetts Institute of Technology (MIT), has become the major advocate of the learning organization movement. He defines the **learning organization** as

> *... an organization that is continually expanding its capacity to create its future. For such an organization, it is not enough merely to survive. "Survival learning" or what is more often termed "adaptive learning" is important—indeed it is necessary. But for a learning organization, "adaptive learning" must be joined by "generative learning," learning that enhances our capacity to create.*[29]

> *The concept of organizational learning is not new. It has its roots in general systems theory[30] and systems dynamics[31] developed in the 1950s and 1960s, as well as theories of learning from organizational psychology.*

The conceptual framework behind this definition requires an understanding and integration of many of the concepts and principles that are part of the total quality philosophy. Senge repeatedly points out, "Over the long run, superior performance depends on superior learning." Continuous improvement and learning should be a regular part of daily work, practiced at personal, work unit, and organizational levels, driven by opportunities to affect significant change, and focused on sharing throughout the organization.

Continuous Improvement

The concept of continuous improvement dates back many years. One of the earliest examples in the United States was at National Cash Register Company (NCR). After a shipment of defective cash registers was returned in 1894, the company's founder, John Patterson, discovered unpleasant and unsafe working conditions. He made many changes, including better lighting, new safety devices, ventilation, lounges, and lockers.

FIGURE 5.6   Final Report "Is" and "Should" Process Map Example

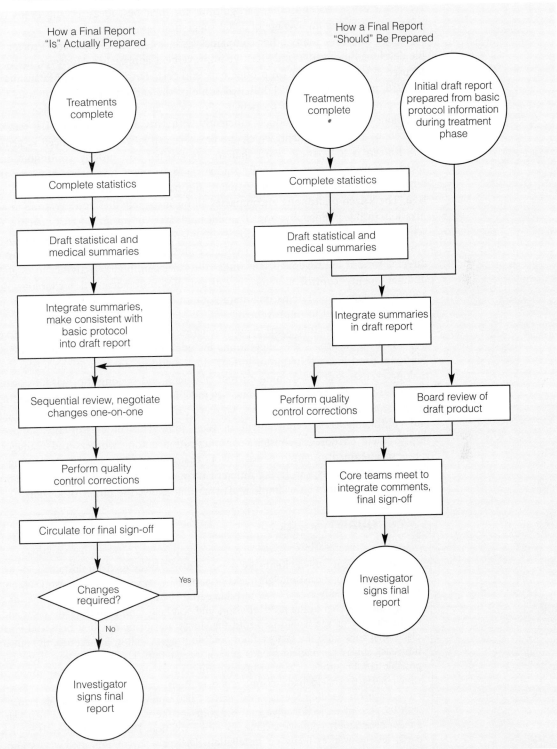

The company offered extensive evening classes to improve employees' education and skills, and instituted a program for soliciting suggestions from factory workers. Workers received cash prizes and other recognitions for their best ideas; by the 1940s the company was receiving an average of 3,000 suggestions each year.

Over the years, many other companies such as Lincoln Electric and Procter & Gamble developed innovative and effective improvement approaches. However, many of these focused almost exclusively on productivity and cost. Toshiba in 1946, Matsushita Electric in 1950, and Toyota in 1951 initiated some of the earliest formal continuous improvement programs. Toyota, in particular, pioneered just-in-time (JIT), which showed that companies could make products efficiently with virtually zero defects. JIT established a philosophy of improvement, which the Japanese call **kaizen** (pronounced kī-zen).

Kaizen is a Japanese word that means gradual and orderly continuous improvement.[32] Kaizen focuses on small, gradual, and frequent improvements over the long term with minimum financial investment, and participation by everyone in the organization. The kaizen philosophy encompasses all business activities and everyone in an organization. In this philosophy, improvement in all areas of business—cost, meeting delivery schedules, employee safety and skill development, supplier relations, new product development, or productivity—serve to enhance the quality of the firm. Thus, any activity directed toward improvement falls under the kaizen umbrella. Activities to establish traditional quality control systems, install robotics and advanced technology, institute employee suggestion systems, maintain equipment, and implement just-in-time production systems all lead to improvement.

The Kaizen Institute (http://www.kaizen-institute.com) suggests some basic tips for implementing kaizen. These suggestions include not seeking perfection; discarding conventional fixed ideas; thinking of how to do something, not why it cannot be done; not making excuses, but questioning current practices; and seeking the "wisdom of ten people rather than the knowledge of one." By instilling kaizen into people and training them in basic quality improvement tools, workers can build this philosophy into their work and continually seek improvement in their jobs. This process-oriented approach to improvement encourages constant communication among workers and managers. Kaizen is so ingrained in employees at Toyota that one manager was quoted saying "When I'm mowing the grass, I'm trying different turns to see if I can do it faster."[33] The Quality Spotlight describes an example at Toyota that shows the power of kaizen.

 QUALITYSPOTLIGHT

Toyota Georgetown

At Toyota's Georgetown, Kentucky plant, a workstation used for installing visors and seat belts used to consist of eight racks of parts. The racks crowded the workstation, giving the worker ready access to all possible parts. The operator would eyeball the car coming up the line, step to the racks of visors and seat belts, and grab the right parts and run to the car. He or she would step into the slowly advancing car, bolt belts and visors in place, step back onto the factory floor, and do it again—all in 55 seconds, the unvarying time each slowly moving car spends at each workstation. The problem was, there were 12 possible combinations of sun visors and nine variations of seat belts. So just deciding which parts to snatch had become a job in itself. In every shift, 500 cars passed the racks, each car needing four specific parts: 2,000 opportunities to make an error. Even with 99 percent perfection, five cars per shift got the wrong sun visors or seat belts. So a team of assembly employees came up with a solution. Don't make the worker pick the parts; let the worker focus on installation. Deliver a kit of presorted visors and seat belts—one kit per car, each containing exactly the right parts. The team applied the simplest technology available, a Rubbermaid caddy.

Kaizen requires a significant cultural change from everyone in the organization, from top management to front-line employees. In many organizations, this is difficult to achieve. As a result, and also because of the typical business focus on short-term results and the search for the "silver bullet" solution, kaizen is not always properly implemented.[34]

Three things are required for a successful kaizen program: operating practices, total involvement, and training.[35] First, operating practices expose new improvement opportunities. Practices such as just-in-time reveal waste and inefficiency as well as poor quality. Second, in kaizen, every employee strives for improvement. Top management, for example, views improvement as an inherent component of corporate strategy and provides support to improvement activities by allocating resources effectively and providing reward structures that are conducive to improvement. Middle management can implement top management's improvement goals by establishing, upgrading, and maintaining operating standards that reflect those goals; by improving cooperation between departments; and by making employees conscious of their responsibility for improvement and developing their problem-solving skills through training. Supervisors can direct more of their attention to improvement rather than "supervision," which, in turn, facilitates communication and offers better guidance to workers. Finally, workers can engage in improvement through suggestion systems and small group activities, self-development programs that teach practical problem-solving techniques, and enhanced job performance skills. All these improvements require significant training, both in the philosophy and in tools and techniques.

The kaizen philosophy has been widely adopted and is used by many firms in the United States and around the world. The Ritz-Carlton Hotel Company has eight mechanisms devoted solely to the improvement of process, product, and service quality:

- *New Hotel Start-Up Improvement Process:* A cross-sectional team from the entire company works together to identify and correct problem areas.
- *Comprehensive Performance Evaluation Process:* The work area team mechanism that empowers people who perform a job to develop the job procedures and performance standards.
- *Quality Network:* A mechanism of peer approval through which an individual employee can advance a good idea.
- *Standing Problem-Solving Team:* A standing work area team that addresses any problem it chooses.
- *Quality Improvement Team:* Special teams assembled to solve an assigned problem identified by an individual employee or leaders.
- *Strategic Quality Planning:* Annual work area teams identify their missions, primary supplier objectives and action plans, internal objectives and action plans, and progress reviews.
- *Streamlining Process:* The annual hotel evaluation of processes, products, or services that are no longer valuable to the customer.
- *Process Improvement:* The team mechanism for corporate leaders, managers, and employees to improve the most critical processes.

At ENBI Corporation, a New York manufacturer of precision metal shafts and roller assemblies for the printer, copier, and fax machine markets, kaizen projects have resulted in a 48 percent increase in productivity, a 30 percent reduction in cycle time, and a 73 percent reduction in inventory.[36] Kaizen has been successfully applied in the Mercedes-Benz truck factory in Brazil, resulting in reductions of 30 percent in manufacturing space, 45 percent in inventory, 70 percent in lead time, and 70 percent in set-up time over a three-year period. Sixteen employees have full-time responsibility for kaizen activities.[37]

Although kaizen is meant to be a part of daily work, many organizations are faced with quality or performance issues that require immediate attention. As a result, kaizen concepts have been incorporated into a team- and project-driven rapid improvement initiative called a *kaizen blitz*. A **kaizen blitz** is an intense and rapid improvement process in which a team or a department throws all its resources into an improvement project over a short time period, as opposed to traditional kaizen applications, which are performed on a part-time basis. Blitz teams are generally comprised of employees from all areas involved in the process who understand it and can implement changes on the spot. Improvement is immediate, exciting, and satisfying for all those involved in the process. Some examples of using kaizen blitz at Magnivision include the following:[38]

- The molded lens department ran two shifts per day, using 13 employees, and after 40 percent rework, yielded 1,300 pieces per day. The production line was unbalanced and work piled up between stations, which added to quality problems as the work-in-process was often damaged. After a three-day blitz, the team reduced the production to one shift of six employees and a balanced line, reducing rework to 10 percent and increasing yield to 3,500 pieces per day, saving more than $179,000.
- In Retail Services, a blitz team investigated problems that continually plagued employees, and discovered that many were related to the software system. Some of the same customer information had to be entered in multiple screens, sometimes the system took a long time to process information, and sometimes it was difficult to find specific information quickly. Neither the programmers nor the engineers were aware of these problems. By getting everyone together, some solutions were easily determined. Estimated savings were $125,000.

Breakthrough Improvement

Breakthrough improvement refers to discontinuous change, as opposed to the gradual, continuous improvement philosophy of kaizen. Breakthrough improvements result from innovative and creative thinking; often these are motivated by **stretch goals**, or **breakthrough objectives**. Stretch goals force an organization to think in a radically different way and to encourage major improvements as well as incremental ones. When a goal of 10 percent improvement is set, managers or engineers can usually meet it with some minor improvements. However, when the goal is 1,000 percent improvement, employees must be creative and think "outside of the box." The seemingly impossible is often achieved, yielding dramatic improvements and boosting morale. Motorola's Six Sigma thrust was driven by a goal of improving product and services quality ten times within two years, and at least 100-fold within four years. For stretch goals to be successful, they must derive unambiguously from corporate strategy. Organizations must not set goals that result in unreasonable stress to employees or punish failure. In addition, they must provide appropriate help and tools to accomplish the task. Two approaches for breakthrough improvement that help companies achieve stretch goals are *benchmarking* and *reengineering*.

The development and realization of improvement objectives, particularly stretch objectives, is often aided through the process of benchmarking. **Benchmarking** is defined as "measuring your performance against that of best-in-class companies, determining how the best-in-class achieve those performance levels, and using the information as a basis for your own company's targets, strategies, and implementation,"[39] or more simply, "the search of industry best practices that lead to superior performance."[40] The term **best**

practices refers to approaches that produce exceptional results, are usually innovative in terms of the use of technology or human resources, and are recognized by customers or industry experts. When GTE worked to improve eight core processes of its telephone operations, it examined the best practices of some 84 companies from diverse industries. By studying outside best practices, a company can identify and import new technology, skills, structures, training, and capabilities.[41]

The concept of benchmarking is not new. In the early 1800s, Francis Lowell, a New England industrialist, traveled to England to study manufacturing techniques at the best British mill factories. Henry Ford created the assembly line after taking a tour of a Chicago slaughterhouse and watching carcasses, hung on hooks mounted on a monorail, move from one workstation to another. Toyota's just-in-time production system was influenced by the replenishment practices of U.S. supermarkets. Modern benchmarking was initiated by Xerox when it wanted to improve its spare parts distribution system. Xerox identified the warehousing and distribution practices of L. L. Bean as a best practice and adopted their approaches.

An organization may decide to engage in benchmarking for several reasons. It eliminates "reinventing the wheel" along with associated wasted time and resources. It helps identify performance gaps between an organization and competitors, leading to realistic goals. It encourages employees to continuously innovate. Finally, because it is a process of continuous learning, benchmarking emphasizes sensitivity to the changing needs of customers.[42]

Many organizations start with **competitive benchmarking**—studying products or business results against competitors to compare pricing, technical quality, features, and other quality or performance characteristics. For example, a television cable company might compare its customer satisfaction rating or service response time to other cable companies; a manufacturer of TVs might compare its unit production costs or field failure rates against competitors. Significant gaps suggest key opportunities for improvement.

Process benchmarking identifies the most effective practices in key work processes in organizations that perform similar functions, no matter in what industry. For example, when Graniterock could not find any company that was measuring on-time delivery of concrete, it talked with Domino's Pizza, a worldwide leader in on-time delivery of a rapidly perishable product (a characteristic shared with freshly mixed concrete) to acquire new ideas for measuring and improving its processes. Texas Instruments studied the kitting (order preparation) practices of six companies, including Mary Kay Cosmetics, and designed a process that captured the best practices of each of them, cutting kitting cycle time in half. A General Mills plant in Lodi, California, had an average machine changeover time of three hours. Then somebody said, "From three hours to 10 minutes!" Employees went to a NASCAR track, videotaped the pit crews, and studied the process to identify how the principles could be applied to the production changeover processes. Several months later, the average time fell to 17 minutes.[43] Thus, companies should not aim benchmarking solely at direct competitors or similar organizations; in fact, they would be mistaken to do so. If a company simply benchmarks within its own industry, it may merely be competitive and have a slight edge in those areas in which it is the industry leader. However, if benchmarks are adopted from outside the industry, a company may learn ideas and processes as well as new applications that allow it to surpass the best within its own industry and to achieve distinctive superiority.

Through benchmarking, a company discovers its strengths and weaknesses and those of other industry leaders and learns how to incorporate the best practices into its own operations. Benchmarking can provide motivation to achieve stretch goals by helping employees to see what others can accomplish. For example, to meet a stretch target of reducing the time to build new 747 and 767 airplanes at Boeing from 18 months (in 1992) to 8 months, teams studied the world's best producers of everything from computers to ships. Within 4 years, the time had been reduced to 10 months.[44]

Reengineering has been defined as "the fundamental rethinking and radical redesign of business processes to achieve dramatic improvements in critical, contemporary measures of performance, such as cost, quality, service, and speed."[45] Such questioning often uncovers obsolete, erroneous, or inappropriate assumptions. Radical redesign involves tossing out existing procedures and reinventing the process, not just incrementally improving it. The goal is to achieve quantum leaps in performance. Successful reengineering requires fundamental understanding of processes, creative thinking to break away from old traditions and assumptions, and effective use of information technology. Reengineering involves asking basic questions about business processes: Why do we do it? Why is it done this way? Some good examples of reengineering are provided below:

- IBM Credit Corporation cut the process of financing IBM computers, software, and services from seven days to four hours by rethinking the process. Originally, the process was designed to handle difficult applications and required four highly trained specialists and a series of handoffs. The actual work took only about 1.5 hours; the rest of the time was spent in transit or delay. By questioning the assumption that every application was unique and difficult to process, IBM Credit Corporation was able to replace the specialists by a single individual supported by a user-friendly computer system that provided access to all the data and tools that the specialists would use.
- Intel Corporation had previously used a 91-step process costing thousands of dollars to purchase ballpoint pens—the same process used to purchase forklift trucks! The improved process was reduced to eight steps.
- In rethinking its purpose as a customer-driven, retail service company rather than a manufacturing company, Taco Bell eliminated the kitchen from its restaurants. Meat and beans are cooked outside the restaurant at central commissaries and reheated. Other food items such as diced tomatoes, onions, and olives are prepared off-site. This innovation saved about 11 million hours of work and $7 million per year over the entire chain.[46]

Benchmarking can greatly assist reengineering efforts. Reengineering without benchmarking probably will produce 5 to 10 percent improvements; benchmarking can increase this percentage to 50 or 75 percent.

MANAGING SUPPLY CHAIN PROCESSES

Today, supply chains are among the most important business processes and can be viewed as encompassing many key value-creation and support processes such as supplier selection and certification, purchasing, logistics, receiving, and performance measurement. The importance of high-quality supply chains became evident after the 2011 earthquake and tsunami in northern Japan. Toyota and Honda, as well as other companies in Asia, experienced severe supply chain disruptions in their production facilities. Toyota's global output fell by 47.8 percent in April versus the previous year, and Honda's production fell by 52.9 percent.[47] However, because of the strength of their supply chains, both companies rebounded rapidly.

Supply chains help to create competitive advantage in delivery, flexibility, and cost reduction. A report from AMR Research, Inc. suggests that companies that excel in supply chain operations also perform better in other financial measures of success. As one executive at AMR Research stated, "value chain performance translates into productivity and market-share leadership…. [S]upply chain leadership means more than just low costs and efficiency—it requires a superior ability to shape and respond to shifts in demand with innovative products and services."[48]

Suppliers include not only companies that provide materials and components, but also distributors, transportation companies, and information, health care, and education providers. Key suppliers might provide unique design, technology, integration, or marketing capabilities that are not available within the business, and therefore can be critical to achieving such strategic objectives as lower costs, faster time-to-market, and improved quality. Many companies segment suppliers into categories based on their importance to the business and manage them accordingly. For example, at Corning, Level 1 suppliers, who provide raw materials, cases, and hardware, are deemed critical to business success and are managed by teams that include representatives from engineering, materials control, purchasing, and the supplier company. Level 2 suppliers provide specialty materials, equipment, and services, and are managed by internal customers. Level 3 suppliers provide commodity items and are centrally managed by purchasing.[49]

Increasingly, suppliers are viewed as partners with customers, because there usually is a codependent relationship. A powerful example of supplier partnerships is the response that occurred when a fire destroyed the main source of a crucial $5 brake valve for Toyota.[50] Without it, Toyota had to shut down its 20 plants in Japan. Within hours of the disaster, other suppliers began taking blueprints, improvising tooling systems, and setting up makeshift production lines. Within days, the 36 suppliers, aided by more than 150 other subcontractors, had almost 50 production lines making small batches of the valve. Even a sewing-machine company that had never made car parts spent 500 person-hours refitting a milling machine to make just 40 valves a day. Toyota promised the suppliers a bonus of about $100 million "as a token of our appreciation."

Effective supply chain management is based on three guiding principles:

1. Recognizing the strategic importance of suppliers in accomplishing business objectives, particularly minimizing the total cost of ownership,
2. Developing win-win relationships through long-term partnerships rather than as adversaries, and
3. Establishing trust through openness and honesty, thus leading to mutual advantages.

For example, long-term partnerships with quality-minded suppliers enabled Texas Nameplate Company to nearly eliminate inspections of incoming materials. These "ship-direct-to-stock" suppliers are required to be defect-free for at least two years and meet all requirements specified on purchase orders. For a company such Boeing, which spent $36 billion on 17,525 suppliers in 52 countries in 2010, success hinges on partnering with the right suppliers. In 2008, Boeing created a forum in which it meets with supplier representatives every other month, with a goal of improving the supplier performance measurement process and its tools. As Dorothy Knight of Honeywell Aerospace noted, "I appreciate the opportunity to work with Boeing…. These forums show just how Boeing understands the value of true supplier collaboration."[51]

Supplier Certification

Many companies use some type of **supplier certification process** to help manage their supply chain. These processes are designed to rate and certify suppliers who provide quality materials in a cost-effective and timely manner. For example, the Pharmaceutical

Manufacturers Association defines a **certified supplier** as one that, after extensive investigation, is found to supply material of such quality that routine testing on each lot received is unnecessary. Certification provides recognition for high-quality suppliers, which motivates them to improve continuously and attract more business. Target, for instance, purchases goods from more than 3,000 factories around the world. Every factory must meet their global social compliance requirements and must pass unannounced audits. Target also evaluates the quality of the products being made, documentation, capability, and capacity of the factories. The factories are expected to address any corrective action recommendations or risk being dropped as a supplier.[52]

Supplier certification is driven by performance measurement and rating processes. For example, at Boeing, suppliers are rated on delivery—the percentage of pieces the supplier delivered on time to Boeing during a 12–month period; general performance—a comprehensive assessment of a supplier's business management performance from Boeing experts who assess supplier performance in the areas of management, scheduling, technical issues, cost and quality; and quality—either the percentage of pieces accepted, during a 12–month period, cost of product nonconformance subtracted from the price of products received during a 12–month period, or a scorecard criteria of quality indicators jointly selected by Boeing and the supplier. These ratings are translated in one of five performance categories: gold, silver, bronze, yellow, and red. Suppliers are eligible to receive the annual Boeing Performance Excellence Award if they achieve silver or gold performance ratings for the entire performance year.[53]

Supplier certification processes can be time-consuming and expensive to administer. One approach to avoiding unnecessary audit costs and helping to assure buyers that specified practices are being followed is to use a uniform set of standards such as ISO 9000. As we described in Chapter 2, ISO 9000 was motivated by the need for widespread supplier certification.

SUMMARY OF KEY POINTS AND TERMINOLOGY

The Student Companion Site provides a summary of key concepts and terminology introduced in this chapter.

QUALITY *in* PRACTICE

K&N Management, Inc.[54]

K&N Management, Inc.[55] is the developer and licensing agent for Rudy's Country Store and Bar-B-Q, as well as Mighty Fine Burgers, Fries, and Shakes outlets in the Austin, Texas market. K&N started with a limited menu driven by high quality food, speed of service, and a focus on doing a few things excellently instead of many things just average. By 2005, the company had expanded from one to four Rudy's locations. In 2009, after only two years of operation, Mighty Fine Burgers, Fries and Shakes, boasting an innovative concept in fast-casual food, demonstrated that it was one of the best start-up fast-casual concepts in the nation. That year, they added two additional stores to their rapidly growing chain.

Customers require high-quality food served quickly and accurately by friendly team members (K&N's terminology for their employees) in a clean environment. This requires well-defined processes with clearly defined requirements and measurements. K&N uses a comprehensive system for process management that incorporates design, control, and improvement (Figure 5.7). Design of work processes is linked to product offerings; as new or improved products are designed (boxes 1-3 in Figure 5.7), re-design of work processes may be necessary. First, equipment needs are analyzed, based on the equipment capability requirements and selection characteristics (boxes 4 and 5). Next, workforce needs are

FIGURE 5.7   Process Management Framework at K & N Management

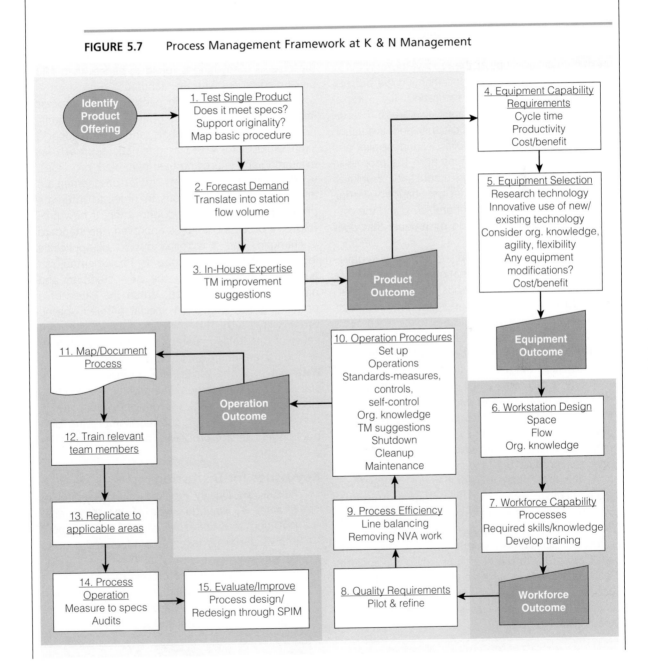

determined, including the design of workstations and the capabilities needed in the workforce (boxes 6 and 7). Design of the operations addresses quality requirements, process efficiency, and operating procedures (boxes 8, 9, and 10). Because the restaurant industry experiences seasonal fluctuations, K&N designs work processes to meet varying levels of demand. Cycle time (boxes 4, 5, 6, and 10), productivity (box 9), and cost control factors (boxes 5, 10, and 13) are considered during the design/redesign process.

Process control and improvement are addressed in the remaining steps of the process (boxes 11–15). This includes mapping and documenting the process, training team members, replicating (i.e., implementing) the process to all applicable areas, measuring and auditing to specifications, and evaluation and improvement. K&N applies lean principles and removes non-value-added steps from the process in order to improve quality and productivity. Employee training in self-management includes basic knowledge of how to identify and correct problems, and the critical importance of not passing on product that does not fully meet the standard.

Each process is designed so the process requirements are translated to operational steps, which are a set of behaviors and methods that if they are performed to standard will result in the product meeting standards. K&N uses measures to control process output using visual standards that allow team members to see if standards are being met. Following the process steps and the associated behaviors and methods, along with visual standards, provides in-process controls. In most work processes there are in-process indicators which show if the process is performing to standard. For example, prep team members check portion weights and visually compare the product to standards. If the fries do not look like the right color coming out of the fryer, team members correct or throw out the product. Various checks are used as mistake-proofing devices. For example, every burger is checked with the guest's order before wrapping; the cashier reads back the order to the guest to verify it is complete; team members use a triple-check system to verify accuracy on Group Meal orders; and the cashier checks items off of a to-go pad before placing them in the to-go bag.

Each operation is designed so the team member is in a state of self-control, meaning that they know the standards, have the skills to check to see if the process output meets the standards, and are empowered to correct it or stop the product unless it meets 100 percent of the standards. Team members are given the necessary coaching, materials, and knowledge of, and access to, equipment. They are provided with an understanding of the process, standards, and expectations for results. They are empowered with the ability to not only carry out the process, but to stop the process if anything is found to be less than 100 percent compliant with the standards.

Data that indicate the need for work process improvements come from operations inspections, process audits, team members, and guest feedback. Even senior leaders use a systematic approach for evaluating and improving their own work processes. Work process improvements and lessons learned are deployed to other locations in order to integrate organizational learning and innovation. If new process or a process change is approved, the standard is changed, and it is rolled out to all applicable locations. After the change is implemented, an audit is performed using the new standard and discrepancies are corrected. When the cause of a problem is not known, a special problem-solving process is used. This includes finding the root cause of the problem, determining the best solution, designing an improvement and implementing it, determining if the results are positive, and if so, standardizing the solution. The problem-solving process has assisted K&N in reducing variability in processes across the organization, improving production and service processes, and achieving better performance.

Key Issues for Discussion

1. Review the Quality Profile at the beginning of Chapter 3. How do some of the things that K&N does to capture the "voice of the customer" impact the steps taken in product and process design?

2. What is the purpose of process management at K&N, and how important are team members in ensuring that process management activities are implemented flawlessly and seamlessly?

QUALITY *in* PRACTICE

Building Japanese Quality in North America[56]

Lexus automobiles have consistently led the industry in quality. In 2000, Cambridge, Ontario, was chosen as the site of the first Lexus plant outside Japan, designated to build the RX 330 SUV. The assistant general manager for manufacturing observed, "We understood from the beginning that to be accepted we had to be not just as good as but better than Kyushu [the location of the Lexus plant in Japan]."

Teamwork at Cambridge starts with teaching workers about every stage of the production process, and about the duties of other team members. Not only does this reinforce the idea that each job is important, but it increases motivation: Each team member does his or her job better if he or she understands how other jobs are done and how one job affects another. This is all part of the *kaizen* philosophy, which at Cambridge is all about the many small inventions masterminded by team members on the line. Most are simple ideas that would occur only to a person doing the job—a clip to hold a part, say, or a jig or template to protect a part from damage, or the replacement of several parts by one. (These inventions are themselves called *kaizens*.)

In order to foster this mindset, engineers and managers created an environment like a clean room, brightly lit like a pharmaceutical laboratory, with a place for everything and everything in its place. Traditional automobile factories are dark and noisy places, filled with flying sparks and the pounding of metal stamping machines. The Cambridge plant, by contrast, is painted in light colors (coordinated by an interior designer) and boasts a spotless floor—the result of constant sweeping up with small brooms and dustpans. These come from "5s" stations, a key element of lean production (see Chapter 9). Cleanliness plays such a large role because at a typical automobile plant most defects are caused by the process of manufacturing itself, by bumps and scrapes from workers. That's why there are no rings or watches on the line at Cambridge, no jeans with rivets to scratch bodies, and why fragments of metal are swept up before they can infiltrate the paint system. The Lexus philosophy is based on the fundamental insight that quality must be built into each part of the production process, not applied as an afterthought through inspections or fixes. Each worker is also a quality control inspector of his or her own work and that of his or her fellow team members—entrusted with the task of eliminating defects before they move down the line.

In the service of this ideal, computer monitors high above the plant's floor display the status of production at each point. Pulling a cord allows team members to stop the line entirely, if necessary. When this happens, the news is indicated by towers of lights, and by characteristic brief musical tones unique to each station, like personal cell phone rings. At the Cambridge plant, Lexus has taken this quality control to a new level, with the introduction of "quality gates": checkpoints where items found to be of particular concern to customers (such as flawless vertical paint surfaces and the fit of headlights into the body of the vehicle) are noted and evaluated. At the welding area's quality gate, for example, welds are tested with hammer and chisel and alignments measured with jigs. Team members certify each vehicle's weld integrity by applying their initials in bright colors. These personal testimonials to care and quality will ride with the vehicles for their lifetimes, albeit under coats of paint or hidden away from the customer's eye. Then, at the end of the welding process, the bodies receive an even closer inspection, distinguished by that special human touch that makes Lexus so rare among car companies. Under an angled roof made up of light tubes, team members sweep their hands carefully across every inch of the vehicles' exteriors. With small, black abrasive squares in their gloved hands, they smooth out any remaining spots or irregularities.

Once welded, vehicle bodies move to the paint shop, more spotless than any other part of the plant. It has the air of a Silicon Valley clean room. Team members wear special antistatic suits. Two sets of doors make an airlock to the paint area. Downdrafts and grated walkways with water beneath catch particles of lint and dust. No cardboard is allowed anywhere in the area. Each vehicle body is vacuumed to remove metal shavings. And the base-coats themselves—the key paint layers that give vehicles their colors—are made of a water-soluble paint, not environmentally hazardous solvents. Spraying is carried out by robotic arms grasping cartridges of measured paint. The cartridges hold just enough paint for one vehicle and are refilled. This allows for mixing colors on the line—no longer must a batch of blue or red vehicles be run together. Finally, a machine called a Perceptron, which measures the changing reflection of light on the vehicle's surface, a rippling effect called "orange peel"—tests for gloss and smoothness.

After painting comes assembly. Here the focus is on the fit and finish of doors, windows, and other key items, such as interior accent pieces. Doors are removed early in the assembly process and make their own course through the plant before rejoining the body—always the same body, of course. This affords access to the inside of the vehicle and protects the door leather and wood from damage. To install the headliner—the large single piece in the ceiling—a team member is swung inside the vehicle in a clever little seat on an arm, called a Raku. Then there are the interior detail items, such as wood paneling. Each vehicle comes with sets of wooden parts that are cut from the same log, and then stained and finished together. If a wood component is damaged in assembly, all the other pieces from its set are replaced as well.

At the end of the line, on a typical day, one vehicle sits in a steady rainstorm, undergoing weather-proof testing. Two others are installed in bays for what are known as "shipping quality audits"—where random vehicles are chosen for an extra-close, no-holds-barred, semi-surgical inspection. The finished RX 330s then run through a test track with bumps and curves. A driver speeds, then brakes, then takes his hands off the wheel to be sure the new vehicles don't pull to one side or the other. Eventually, they'll board the railcars ready to carry them off to a distant city and a new owner. As for Cambridge surpassing Japan, so far they're on track: they're even sending kaizens back to Kyushu.

Key Issues for Discussion

1. Discuss how the processes designed into the Cambridge plant support the achievement of high product quality. What specific aspects of the process relate to design, control, and improvement?
2. What lessons or best practices might be learned and applied to other companies (outside of the automotive industry)?

REVIEW QUESTIONS

1. What is a process? Provide several examples.
2. State several key process-focused practices for quality management.
3. Define process management and its three key activities. Why is process management important to any business?
4. Discuss how process management is addressed in the ISO 9000:2000 criteria.
5. Why is it important that processes be repeatable and measurable?
6. Explain the differences between value-creation and support processes. Provide some examples of each.
7. Describe some organizations that use projects as their primary value-creation processes. How might the project management process differ in such organizations, in comparison with firms or departments that only use projects on an ad hoc or as-needed basis?
8. What is process mapping? Why is it important in process design?
9. List important questions that should be asked when analyzing process maps to create a more effective design.
10. Explain the differences between designing processes for manufactured goods and services. How should the design of service processes be approached?
11. Why is agility important for processes in today's business environment?
12. Why do people make inadvertent mistakes? How does poka-yoke help prevent such mistakes?
13. Describe the types of errors that service poka-yokes are designed to prevent.
14. Define process control and tell why it is important.

15. Describe the four elements of any control system.
16. Explain the concept of after-action review.
17. How is process control generally implemented in manufacturing and in services? Describe the similarities and differences.
18. What is continuous improvement? Provide several examples of the types of improvements on which organizations should focus.
19. List the four stages of a learning cycle. Why is organizational learning important?
20. Explain the concepts of kaizen and kaizen blitz. How are they similar? How are they different?
21. How can reductions in cycle time lead to improvements in processes?
22. What is breakthrough improvement? How does it differ from kaizen?
23. What is a stretch goal? How can stretch goals help an organization?
24. Define benchmarking and list its benefits.
25. What is reengineering? How can TQ principles assist in reengineering efforts?
26. Why is it important to establish strong relationships with suppliers? What are some good supplier management practices?
27. What is the purpose of supplier certification?
28. Explain some of the common practices for supplier certification. How does ISO 9000 support these practices?

DISCUSSION QUESTIONS

1. A. Blanton Godfrey notes that many organizations are "wired for failure"; that is, their processes are not designed effectively or aligned with each other.[57] He cites several examples. One is overscheduling at airports. During the 4:15 to 4:30 P.M. time slot, 35 arrivals are scheduled in Atlanta, even though in optimal weather conditions the airport can handle only 25 in 15 minutes; with bad weather, this number drops to 17. Another company celebrated its largest sales contract in history only to discover that all qualified suppliers for critical materials were at capacity. A third example is the unwillingness of departments to work together. When products fail in the plant or in service, it isn't because designers choose components they know will fail; they often have insufficient information about the problems that result from their choices. Such problems can be mitigated by good process management. Discuss his observations and cite examples of your own to illustrate each of the three issues.

2. Identify some of the key processes associated with the following business activities for a typical company: sales and marketing, supply chain management, managing information technology, and managing human resources.

3. Provide some examples of processes that are repeatable and measurable and some that are not.

4. List some of the common processes that you perform as a student. How can these processes be improved? What types of noneducational institutions perform similar processes and might be candidates for benchmarking?

5. Refer to Example 5.1 and Figure 5.3:
   a. Using the questions suggested in the chapter for process analysis and design following the example, suggest any improvements to the process that might be made.
   b. Discuss possible sources of errors and poka-yokes that might be used to prevent these errors.

6. How can a manager effectively balance the three key components of a service system design?

7. Legal Sea Foods operates several restaurants and fish markets in the Boston area and other East Coast locations. The company's standards of excellence mandate that it serves only the freshest, highest-quality seafood. It guarantees the quality by buying only the "top of the catch" fish daily. Although Legal Sea Foods tries to make available the widest variety every day, certain species of fish are subject to migratory patterns and are not always present in New England waters. Weather conditions may also prevent local fishermen from fishing in certain areas.

   Freshly caught fish are rushed to the company's quality control center where they are cut and filleted in an environmentally controlled state-of-the-art facility. All shellfish come from government-certified beds and are tested in an in-house microbiology laboratory for wholesomeness and purity. There are even special lobster storage tanks so that all lobsters are held under optimum conditions, in clean, pollution-free water. Every seafood item is inspected for quality eight separate times before it reaches the table.

At Legal Sea Foods' restaurants, each meal is cooked to order. Even though servers make every effort to deliver all meals within minutes of each other, they will not jeopardize the quality of an item by holding it beneath a heat lamp until the entire order is ready. The service staff is trained to work as a team for better service. More than one service person frequently delivers food to a table. When any item is ready, the closest available person serves it. Customer questions can be directed to any employee, not just the person who took the initial order.

a. What are the major processes performed by Legal Sea Foods? How does the process design support its goal of serving only the freshest, highest-quality seafood?

b. Where would Legal Sea Foods fall on the three-dimensional classification of service organizations? Is its process design consistent with this classification?

8. McDonald's used to make food to stock, storing sandwiches in a large tray used to fulfill customer orders. When sales went flat in the mid-1990s and independent market testing showed a widening gap with competition in food quality, McDonald's recognized that the make-to-stock process was not meeting customer demands. After five years of lab and market testing, McDonald's rolled out the new "Just for You" system, which began in March 1998, to create a make-to-order environment. This shift required a massive change in technology with computers to coordinate orders; food production equipment using "rapid toasters" and temperature-controlled "launching zones" to replace the old heat lamps and holding bins; new food preparation tables, and retraining efforts for the entire domestic food production organization of more than 600,000 crew members. However, this system has apparently backfired. Sales did not improve as expected and customers complained about slow service. The new system increased the average service time 2 to 3 minutes per order, and 15-minute waits were not uncommon. McDonald's stock price decreased, and rivals such as Wendy's captured additional market share.[58] What lessons does this experience suggest for process management? What might McDonald's have done differently?

9. The Cincinnati Water Works (CWW) serves approximately 1 million customers.[59] Its billing system allows customer service representatives (CSRs) to retrieve information from customer accounts quickly using almost any piece of data such as customer name, address, phone number, social security number, and so on. Besides a customer's account history, the system contains everything that was said in a call, including documentation of past problems and their resolution. An integrated voice response system provides automated phone support for bill paying and account balances, tells customers of the approximate wait time to speak to a CSR, and allows the customers to leave a message for a CSR to return a call. An information board in the department shows the number of customers waiting, average length of time waiting, and the number of CSRs that are busy and doing postcall work. A pop-up screen provides CSRs with customer data before the phone rings so that he or she will have the customer's information before they even say hello. Work orders taken by CSRs, such as a broken water main or leaking meter, are routed automatically to a field service supervisor for immediate attention.

This system is also used internally to allocate maintenance workers when a problem arises at a pumping station or treatment facility. A geographic information system is used for mapping the locations of water mains and fire hydrants, and provides field service employees, meter readers, and contractors exact information to accomplish their work. Handheld meter readers are used to locate meters and download data into computers. Touch pad devices provide exterior connections to inside meters, eliminating the necessity to enter a house or building. CWW has also installed automated meter readers and radio frequency devices that simply require a company van to drive by the building to automatically obtain readings.

Discuss how technology has affected the processes of CWW. What specific types of improvements (quality, cycle time, etc.) were these applications designed to address? Can you think of similar uses of these technologies in other service applications?

10. The president of Circle H assigned you to perform a complete investigation to determine the causes of certain quality problems and to recommend appropriate corrective action. You have authority to talk to any other person within the company.

The early stages of your investigation establish that the three reasons most often cited by customers are symptomatic of some major quality problems in the company's operations. In proceeding with the audit, you decide to review all available data, which may yield indications of the root causes of these problems.

Further investigation reveals that, over a recent four-month period, a procedural change was made in the order approval process. You wish to find out whether this change caused a significant difference in the amount of time required to process an order from field sales through shipping. You therefore decide to investigate this particular situation.

On completion of your investigation into the problems with order processing, you determine that the change in procedures for order approval led to an increase in the amount of time required restocking goods in the customers' stores. You want to recommend corrective action for this problem, but you first do additional investigation as to why the change was made. You learn that, because of large losses on delinquent accounts receivable, the change was made to require that the credit manager approve all restock orders. This approval requirement added an average of three hours to the amount of internal processing time needed for a restock order.

On review of your report, the president of Circle H takes note of administrative problems whose existence he had never suspected. To assure that corrective action will be effective and sustained, the president assigns you to take charge of the corrective action program.[60]

a. What types of data would be most useful to review for clues as to why the three major customer complaints occurred?

b. How would you investigate whether the change in the order approval process had a significant effect on order processing time?

c. Given your knowledge of problems in both order processing and accounts receivable, what should you do?

11. Are classroom examinations a means of control or improvement? What should they be?

12. The kaizen philosophy seeks to encourage suggestions, not to find excuses for failing to improve. Typical excuses are "If it's not broken, don't fix it," "I'm too busy to work on it," and "It's not in the budget." Think of at least five other excuses why people don't try to improve.

PROBLEMS

1. The process of making a batch of paint in a paint factory consists of the following steps: First the correct amount of raw materials must be mixed in the proper sequence. The operator must follow specified safety instructions. After mixing, a sample is drawn and taken to a laboratory, where it is tested to ensure conformance to customer requirements and specifications. Next, the mixing tank is taken to a filling station and verified to be the correct one prior to filling individual cans of paint. The filled cans go to the packing department where labels are printed and applied to the cans. They are inspected to ensure that the labels are correct and the proper quantity was produced for the customer's order. The cans are packed in boxes and moved to shipping.

   a. Develop a flowchart that maps out this process.

   b. Enrich the flowchart by adding detailed steps, which may not have been described in detail.

   c. Determine if any opportunities exist for improving this process using the questions posed in the chapter.

2. The process for filling a prescription at a large retail pharmacy begins when a customer's physician calls the pharmacy or the customer drops off a written prescription. Sometimes the customer needs to refill a prescription and if no refills remain, the pharmacy will call the physician for approval. The prescription information is entered into a computer, insurance information is checked or solicited from the customer, and the prescription is put in a queue for either a pharmacist or a technician to count out the number of pills or pull some other medicine from inventory. A label is prepared and printed, and affixed to the bottle. If the prescription is prepared by a technician, then a pharmacist must check and verify it. The completed prescription is placed in a basket for pickup.

   a. Develop a flowchart that maps out this process.

   b. Enrich the flowchart by adding detailed steps, which may not have been described in detail.

   c. Determine if any opportunities exist for improving this process using the questions posed in the chapter. For example, how might technology, such as an automated telephone system or the Internet, be incorporated into the process to improve customer satisfaction?

3. Maintaining accuracy of books on the shelves in a college library is an important task. Consider the following problems that are often observed:
   - Books are not placed in the correct shelf position, which includes those books that have been checked out and returned, as well as those taken off the shelves for use within the library by patrons.
   - New or returned books are not checked in, and consequently the online catalog does not show their availability.

   What procedures or poka-yokes might you suggest for mitigating these problems? You might wish to talk to some librarians or administrators at your college library to see how they address such problems.

4. You have most likely taken your car for service at an automobile dealership. Typical activities in servicing a customer's automobile include making an appointment, meeting with a service advisor to discuss the service or problem, waiting for the work to be performed, paying the bill, and receiving the vehicle. Draw a flowchart for this process with detailed activities for these steps. Identify potential failures that customers may experience and discuss possible poke-yokes that the dealership might use to prevent such failures and ensure customer satisfaction.

5. The process for depositing a check at a local bank begins with the teller determining if the customer wants to receive any cash back. If not, the teller checks to see if the payee's name is on the account, stamps the deposit slip, and gives the customer a receipt. If there is cash back, the teller adds the checks and subtracts the net deposit to verify the cash amount on the deposit slip, checks and verifies the customer's account, makes a "cash out" ticket for bank accounting, and gives the customer back the cash and receipt. Draw a flowchart for this process and identify potential sources of error and poka-yokes that might be used to mitigate these errors.

6. Global food supply chains consist of many processes. Bananas, for example, are grown on farms in South or Central America. At the farm, the growth and quality are monitored continuously, and samples are tested periodically. Once the bananas in a cluster reaches a certain size, it is cut from the tree. Workers cut the cluster into smaller clusters of five to six bananas. The bananas are rinsed, and then inspected. If the fruit is approved, the importer's sticker is placed on the bananas and the fruit is packaged to avoid bruising. Boxes of bananas are loaded into containers and shipped via cargo ships to a port in the United States. If the bananas are not ripe enough, they can be treated with a gas to hasten ripening. Bananas are sorted by color, as different customers have different requirements (for example, green, yellow, or brown). They are then boxed per customer specifications and sent to the customer (retailer, restaurant, hotel, and so on).
   a. Construct a flowchart depicting the supply chain for bananas.
   b. Describe the principal processes in this supply chain.
   c. What types of supplier management activities might the importer use to help control the quality of the bananas?

PROJECTS, ETC.

1. Interview a plant manager at a local factory to determine his or her philosophy on process management. What techniques does the company use?

2. The food industry has a process control approach called HACCP—Hazard Analysis and Critical Control Points. Conduct some research to learn about HACCP. (See article on the Student Companion website for this chapter.) Then apply the approach to the following case.

Christina Clark works at a food service operation for a large amusement park. She has been charged with developing a process control plan based on HACCP principles for meeting food safety requirements. For example, the requirements for hot dogs include:

Receiving: Refrigerated hot dogs should be between 40°F and 34°F when received.
Storage: Storage temperature should be between 40°F and 34°F.

Cooking: Hot dogs should be heated to a temperature of 145 ± 5°F within 30 minutes of placing on the grill.

Cooked Storage: Leftover hot dogs must be covered and placed in refrigeration immediately and reach a temperature of 40°F or lower within four hours.

Reheating: Hot dogs must be reheated to an internal temperature of 165°F within 20 minutes, one time only.

Develop a process control plan for ensuring that these requirements are met. Design any forms or "standard operating procedures" that you think would be helpful in implementing your plan.

3. Design a process for the following activities:
   a. Preparing for an exam
   b. Writing a term paper
   c. Planning a vacation
   d. Making breakfast for your family
   e. Washing your car
   Discuss ways in which both quality and cycle time might be improved.

4. Design an instrument for evaluating the "process focus" of an organization. For example, what characteristics would you look for in firms that have a strong process orientation?

5. Barker is a small custom producer of equipment used in various process industries such as chemicals and beverages. Each piece of equipment is customer designed from customer specifications. The process generally consists of five steps:

a. Customer quote creation
b. Preproduction planning (if awarded the contract)
c. Quality assurance plan
d. Manufacturing
e. Inspection and delivery

Develop a process manual for this company that outlines specific activities that should be performed within each of these process steps. Be sure to clearly describe how design, control, and improvement are integrated into this process, and also consider other issues discussed in this chapter, such as the project nature of this process.

6. Think of a casual dining restaurant that you frequent. The process of fulfilling customer's needs and creating a satisfying dining experience begins when the customer walks through the door and ends when the customer leaves. Using process mapping, poka-yoke, and other process management techniques described in this chapter, design the overall process and subprocesses that would create a good customer experience.

7. Identify several sources of errors as a student or in your personal life. Develop some poka-yokes that might prevent them.

8. Interview a plant manager or quality professional at one or more local companies to see whether they use any poka-yoke approaches to mistake-proof their operations.

9. Search the Internet for John Grout's Poka-Yoke website and write a report on the information you discover.

CASES

THE STATE UNIVERSITY EXPERIENCE

Wow! That State University video was really cool. It has lots of majors; it's close to home so I can keep my job; and Mom and Dad loved it when they visited. I wish I could know what it's really like to be a student at State. Hmmm, I think I'll ask Mom and Dad to take a campus tour with me …

I'm sure that we took our tour on the hottest day of the summer. The campus is huge—it took us about two hours to complete the tour and we didn't even see everything! I wasn't sure that the tour guide knew what he was doing. We went into a gigantic lecture hall and the lights weren't even on. Our tour guide couldn't find them so we had to hold the doors open so the sunlight could come in. About three-fourths of the way through the tour, our guide said, "State University isn't really a bad place to go to school; you just have to learn the system." I wonder what he meant by that?

This application is really confusing. How do I let the admissions office know that I am interested in physics, mechanical engineering, and industrial design? Even my parents can't figure it out. I guess I'll call the admissions office for some help …

I'm so excited! Mom just handed me a letter from State! Maybe they've already accepted me. What? What's this? They say I need to send my transcript. I did that when I mailed in my application two weeks ago. What's going on? I hope it won't affect my application. I'd better check with Admissions …

You can't find my file? I thought you were only missing my transcript. I asked my counselor if she had sent it in yet. She told me that she sent it last week. Oh, you'll call me back when you locate my file? O.K.…

Finally, I've been accepted! Wait a minute. I didn't apply to University College; that's a two-year program. I wanted physics, M.E., or industrial design. Well, because my only choice is U. College and I really want to go to State, I guess I'll send in the confirmation form. It really looks a lot like the application. In fact, I know I gave them a lot of the same information. I wonder why they need it again? Seems like a waste of time …

Orientation was a lot of fun. I'm glad they straightened out my acceptance at U. College. I think I will enjoy State after all. I met lots of other students. I saw my advisor and I signed up for classes. All I have left to do is pay my tuition bill. Whoops. None of my financial aid is on this bill. I know I filled out all of the forms because I got an award letter from State. There is no way my parents and I can pay for this without financial aid. It says at the bottom, I'll lose all of my classes if I don't pay the bill on time …

I'm not confirmed on the computer? I sent in my form and the fee a long time ago. What am I going to do? I don't want to lose all of my classes. I have to go to the admissions office or my college office and get a letter that says I am a confirmed student. O.K. If I do that tomorrow, will I still have all of my classes? …

I can't sleep; I'm so nervous about my first day …

Discussion Questions

1. What breakdowns in service processes has this student experienced?
2. What types of process management activities should State University administrators undertake?

GOLD STAR CHILI: PROCESS MANAGEMENT[61]

(We encourage you to review the Gold Star Chili case in Chapter 3 first for background information about the company.) Gold Star Chili is a chain of chili restaurants in the greater Cincinnati area. Figure 5.8 shows a process-based organization of the company. Three major value-creation processes link the operation of the company to its customers and other stakeholders:

1. Franchising
2. Restaurant operations
3. Manufacturing/distribution

The franchising process is designed to ensure a smooth and successful start-up that meets company objectives. Because franchise process delays are costly, the process helps to eliminate variability, reduce cycle time, and cut down on problems that might occur during development and introduction. Restaurant processes include Cash Register, Steam Table, Drive-Thru, Tables, Bussers, and Management. Chili is produced at the Gold Star Commissary and shipped to the restaurants. Sustaining these processes are various support processes, such as research and development, human resources, accounting, purchasing, operations, training, marketing, and customer satisfaction, as well as design processes for new products, menus, and facilities.

Using the information provided, develop a process management plan for this company. Be specific in your recommendations of how they should address process design, control, and improvement activities.

FIGURE 5.8   Gold Star Chili, Inc. Organization

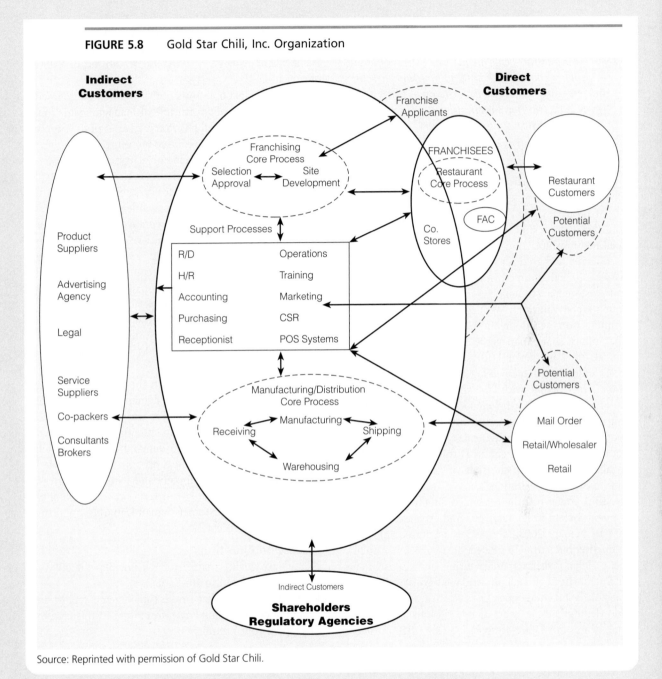

Source: Reprinted with permission of Gold Star Chili.

IBM'S INTEGRATED SUPPLY CHAIN[62]

Managing an integrated supply chain (ISC) is highly dependent on quality management practices. IBM, which considers the effective and efficient operation of its supply chain as a key factor in improving its competitiveness, has approached implementation of its integrated supply chain ("ISC") from a strategic perspective. The company began the transformation effort toward an ISC in 1999. According to the supply chain manager,

Supply chain management is definitely the key element of competitiveness at IBM. Competition is no longer between single organizations but rather

between integrated supply chains. We must not forget the other functions in the organization, such as quality, being achieved at every stage of the supply chain; marketing, finance and accounting are also a key element in our strategy. We started the transformation of logistics in 1999 with the aim of integrating the different pieces of the puzzle.

The most critical factor prior to the launch of the change program was the articulation and communication of IBM's values. The key values that IBM employees espouse are: dedication to every client's success, innovation that matters, and trust and personal responsibility in all relationships.

Having a shared set of values helps IBM to make fast decisions that directly impact supplier performance and customer satisfaction. The influence of values occurs when values are applied to personal work and in interactions with one another and the wider world. The supply chain manager made the point that it is critical for a particular leadership style to align with IBM's culture. "I have been at IBM for more than 20 years. I met people with fantastic personalities, with a lot of charisma but who could not fit into the IBM culture. I think that it is not because they were not good leaders; it is because their style of leadership did not align with the IBM culture. I think there should be an alignment between the style of the leader and the culture of the organization."

IBM established the Integrated Supply Chain Management System in January 2002 and expanded the mission in January 2003. The ISC is organized into four distinctive but strongly related areas: customer fulfillment, global logistics, manufacturing, and procurement. These functions are all underpinned by ISC business transformation and operations strategy, which provide depth. On the other hand, IBM has established core teams that are responsible for the proactive implementation of the various activities in the ISC. The three teams are: the operations team, strategy team, and talent team, which provide the breadth for the ISC organization.

The principal objectives of the ISC are underpinned by the strategic quality principle of managing variation, hence cutting costs in the various activities of the supply chain, and engaging in continuous reinvention. These principles have led to specific objectives for IBM's On-Demand Supply Chain, which are to: deliver competitive cost advantage and reduce the variability in the cost and expense structure; improve sales productivity by decreasing the time sales representatives spend on order fulfillment by 25 percent per year; accelerate the cash conversion cycle by 33 percent over two years by continuing to drive improved inventory, accounts receivable, and supplier payment terms execution; improve inventory turns by one per year, increase payables by at least one day per year, and improve receivables by one to two days per year; and deliver marked improvement in supply chain capability to contribute to IBM achieving #1 in customer satisfaction.

Much of IBM's success with the ISC management system has been due to the on-demand business model and seeing ISC as a competitive weapon. The core to the On-Demand Supply Chain system is best described by IBM's definition of its on-demand business model: "An enterprise whose business processes are integrated end-to-end across the company and with key partners, suppliers, and customers—can respond with flexibility and speed to any customer demand, market opportunity or external threat."

Discussion Questions

1. How are quality management principles directly or indirectly related to IBM's ISC?
2. Discuss the role that process management plays in supply chains, using any information in this case to support your arguments.

NOTES

1. 2011–2012 Criteria for Performance Excellence, Baldrige Performance Excellence Program, U.S. Department of Commerce.
2. In his article, "Beyond PDCA—A New Process Management Model," *Quality Progress*, July 2006, 45–52, Praveen Gupta proposes a variation of these activities: prepare, perform, perfect, and progress, as an easily understood and implementable framework for process management.
3. AT&T Quality Steering Committee, *Process Quality Management & Improvement Guidelines*, AT&T Publication Center, AT&T Bell Laboratories (1987).

4. AT&T's Total Quality Approach, AT&T Corporate Quality Office (1992), 6.

5. Paula K. Martin and Karen Tate, "Projects That Get Quality Treatment," *Journal for Quality and Participation*, November/December 1998, 58–61.

6. Custom Research Incorporated, "Highlights of CRI's Best Practices," 1996 *Baldrige Application Abstract*, 13–14.

7. Sarah Anne Wright, "Putting Fast-Food to the Test," *Cincinnati Enquirer*, July 9, 2000, F1, 2.

8. AT&T Quality Steering Committee, *Reengineering Handbook*, AT&T Bell Laboratories (1991), 45.

9. Gary Vansuch, "Improving the 'Improve' Step in Six Sigma DMAIC Projects: Lean Enterprise and Process Streamlining Tools—Part 1," *Competitive Advantage* 12, no. 2 (Spring 2004), pp. 1, 4–5.

10. John Haywood-Farmer, "A Conceptual Model of Service Quality," *International Journal of Operations and Production Management* 8, no. 6 (1988), 19–29.

11. City of Coral Springs 2007 Baldrige Application Summary.

12. Adapted and modified from Charles D. Zimmerman, III, and John W. Enell, "Service Industries," Sec. 33 in J. M. Juran (ed.), *Juran's Quality Control Handbook*, 4th ed. (New York: McGraw-Hill, 1988).

13. "It's the Latest Thing—Really," *Business Week*, March 27, 2006, 70–71.

14. Julie Schlosser, "Cashing in on the new world of me," *Fortune*, December 13, 2004, 245–250.

15. Rebecca Duray and Glenn W. Milligan, "Improving Customers Satisfaction Through Mass Customization," *Quality Progress*, August 1999, 60–66.

16. For an interesting, albeit academic discussion of the psychology of human error and its relationship to mistake-proofing, see Douglas M. Stewart and Richard B. Chase, "The Impact of Human Error on Delivering Service Quality," *Production and Operations Management* 8, no. 3 (Fall 1999), 240–263; and Douglas M. Stewart and John R. Grout, "The Human Side of Mistake Proofing," *Production and Operations Management* 10, no. 4 (Winter 2001), 440–459.

17. From *Poka-Yoke: Improving Product Quality by Preventing Defects*. Edited by NKS/Factory Magazine, English translation copyright © 1988 by Productivity Press, Inc., P.O. Box 3007, Cambridge, MA 02140, 800-394-6868. Reprinted by permission.

18. Harry Robinson, "Using Poka-Yoke Techniques for Early Defect Detection," Paper presented at the Sixth International Conference on Software Testing and Analysis and Review (STAR '97).

19. Excerpts reprinted from Richard B. Chase and Douglas M. Stewart, "Make Your Service Fail-Safe," *Sloan Management Review* 35, no. 3 (Spring 1994), 35–44.

20. Michael A. Prospero, "Top Scalpel," *Fast Company*, April 2006, 31.

21. "GE errors linked to plane fire," *Cincinnati Enquirer*, December 14, 2004, F1,2.

22. N. Tsikriktsis and J. Heineke, "The Impact of Process Variation on Customer Dissatisfaction: Evidence from the U.S. Domestic Airline Industry," *Decision Sciences* 35, no. 1, Winter 2004, 129–142.

23. "Testing for Conformity: An Inside Job," *Golf Journal*, May 1998, 20–25.

24. "DaimlerChrysler's Quality Practices Pay Off for PT Cruiser," News and Analysis, *Metrologyworld.com* (accessed 3/23/00).

25. Adapted from the Malcolm Baldrige National Quality Award Application Summaries of The Ritz-Carlton Hotel Company, LLC, 1992 and 1999.

26. Robert A. Gardner, "Resolving the Process Paradox," *Quality Progress*, March 2001, 51–59.

27. Andrew E. Serwer, "Michael Dell Turns the PC World Inside Out," *Fortune*, September 8, 1997, 76–86.

28. David A. McCamey, Robert W. Bogs, and Linda M. Bayuk, "More, Better, Faster from Total Quality Effort," *Quality Progress*, August 1999, 43–50.

29. Peter M. Senge, *The Fifth Discipline: The Art and Practice of the Learning Organization* (New York: Doubleday Currency, 1990), 14.

30. L. von Bertalanffy, "The Theory of Open Systems in Physics and Biology," *Science* 111 (1950), 23–19.

31. J. W. Forrester, *Industrial Dynamics* (New York: John Wiley & Sons, 1961).

32. Masaaki Imai, *KAIZEN—The Key to Japan's Competitive Success* (New York: McGraw-Hill, 1986).

33. "No Satisfaction at Toyota," *Fast Company*, December 2006, p. 82.

34. For a perspective on this and related issues from Japan's "Father of Continuous Improvement," see Laura Smith, "Profiles in Quality with Masaaki Imai," *Quality Digest*, October 2005, 54–56.

35. Alan Robinson (ed.), *Continuous Improvement in Operations* (Cambridge, MA: Productivity Press, 1991).

36. Lea A. P. Tonkin, "Kaizen Blitz[SM] 5: Bottleneck-Bashing Comes to Rochester, NY," *Target* 12, no. 4 (September–October 1996), 41–43.

37. Mark Oakeson, "Makes Dollars & Sense for Mercedes-Benz in Brazil," *IIE Solutions* (April 1997), 32–35.

38. Eleanor Chilson, "Kaizen Blitzes at Magnivision: $809,270 Cost Savings," *Quality Management Forum* 29, no. 1 (Winter 2003).

39. Lawrence S. Pryor, "Benchmarking: A Self-Improvement Strategy," *Journal of Business Strategy*, November/December 1989, 28–32.

40. Robert C. Camp, *Benchmarking: The Search for Industry Best Practices That Lead to Superior Performance* (Milwaukee. WI: ASQC Quality Press and UNIPUB/Quality Resources, 1989).

41. Christopher E. Bogan and Michael J. English, "Benchmarking for Best Practices: Winning Through Innovative Adaptation," *Quality Digest*, August 1994, 52–62.

42. Cathy Hill, "Benchmarking and Best Practices," The 54th Annual Quality Congress *Proceedings of the American Society for Quality*, 2000.

43. John Hackl, "New Beginnings: Change Is Here to Stay," *Quality Progress*, February 1998, 5.

44. Shawn Tully, "*Why to Go for Stretch Targets*," *Fortune*, November 14, 1994, 45–58.

45. Michael Hammer and James Champy, *Reengineering the Corporation* (New York: HarperBusiness, 1993), 177–178.

46. Hammer and Champy, *Reengineering the Corporation*.

47. "Toyota and Honda to Recover Quickly from Supply Chain Disruption," http://www.wheelsunplugged.com/ViewNews.aspx?newsid=10012 (accessed 2/6/12).

48. "Supply Chain Excellence," Special Advertising Section, *Business Week*, April 25, 2005.

49. Larry Kishpaugh, "Process Management and Business Results," presentation at the 1996 Regional Malcolm Baldrige Award Conference, Boston, Massachusetts.

50. Valerie Reitman, "Toyota's Fast Rebound After Fire at Supplier Shows Why It's Tough," *Wall Street Journal*, May 8, 1997, 1.

51. Kirsten Parks and Timothy Connor, "An Inside Look at How Boeing's Supplier Rating System Keeps the Aviation Giant Focused on Continuous Improvement," *Quality Progress*, April 2011.

52. William H. Murphy, "An Inside Look at How Target Ensures Quality in a Complex Supply Chain," *Quality Progress*, June 2010.

53. Parks and Connor, "Inside Look at Boeing's Supply Chain.".

54. Adapted from 2010 K&N Management Malcolm Baldrige National Quality Award Application summary, http://www.baldrige.nist.gov/Contacts_Profiles.htm.

55. You might wish to review the K&N Management Quality Profile at the beginning of Chapter 3 for additional information about the company.

56. Adapted from Phil Patton, "Northern Exposure," *Lexus Magazine*, Quarter 1, 2004, 39–42.

57. A. Blanton Godfrey, "Planned Failures," *Quality Digest*, March 2000, 156.

58. John E. Ettlie, "What the Auto Industry Can Learn from McDonald's," *Automotive Manufacturing & Production*, October 1999, 42; David Stires, "Fallen Arches," *Fortune*, April 29, 2002, 74–76.

59. Adapted from a student project by one of the author's students, Tim Planitz, December 2001.

60. Adapted from ASQ Quality Auditor Certification Brochure, July 1989.

61. Reprinted with permission of Gold Star Chili.

62. Adapted from Mile Terziovski and Phillipe Hermel, "The Role of Quality Management Practice in the Performance of Integrated Supply Chains: A Multiple Cross-Case Analysis," *Quality Management Journal* 18, no. 2 (2011), pp. 10–25.

PART 2

Tools and Techniques for Quality

Quality professionals require both a strong foundation in managerial practices and expertise in technical subjects. Assuring quality of products and services is accomplished primarily by the appropriate use of effective statistical tools and other analytical techniques for analyzing data; solving problems; designing, controlling and improving processes; and reducing the potential for failure. In this part of the book, we focus on tools and techniques used in quality management.

Chapter 6 reviews important statistical methods and provides numerous examples to illustrate the wide variety of applications in quality. Microsoft Excel is used as much as possible to facilitate numerical calculations, and several easy-to-use spreadsheet templates are introduced. In Chapter 7 we introduce tools that support design efforts, including quality function deployment, the Taguchi loss function, reliability, failure mode and effects analysis, and other practical techniques. Chapter 8 focuses on process measurement and control, and we provide a comprehensive introduction to statistical process control, again supported by easy-to-use Excel templates. Finally, Chapter 9 describes process improvement methodologies, introduces Six Sigma methodology as a framework for improvement, and highlights various analytic and visual tools that support process improvement and problem solving efforts. Each chapter in this section of the book provides numerous problems for practice in developing these technical skills.

Statistical Methods in Quality Management

Statistics is a science concerned with "the collection, organization, analysis, interpretation, and presentation of data."[1] Statistics is essential for quality and for implementing a continuous improvement philosophy (see the *Quality Profiles* for Graniterock and Branch-Smith). Statistical methods help managers make sense of data and gain insight about the nature of variation in the processes they manage. All managers, supervisors, and production and clerical workers should have some knowledge of basic statistical methods and applications. Technology, such as today's powerful PCs and user-friendly software for data analysis and visualization, has greatly facilitated the ability to use statistics and quality tools in daily work.

The use of statistical methods in quality dates back to 1903, when the Bell System faced a problem designing its central offices.[2] A telephone subscriber takes the phone off the hook and gets a dial tone, meaning that he is connected to a trunk line that goes to the central office. The question was, "How many of those lines do you need?" Theoretically, every subscriber could use the phone at the same time, but in reality only a few percent actually do. Analysts collected and analyzed statistical information on the demand day-by-day, hour-by-hour, and identified the peak periods to determine how many lines were required to meet a service standard (the probability of not getting a dial tone). In the 1920s, Bell Labs thought that statistical tools would have applications in the factory and began to experiment with statistical sampling, eventually leading to the development of control charts. Joseph Juran was involved in trying to sell this new technology in the factories, but had little success until World War II, when the push to improve quality in the military began with the implementation of statistical methods in factories in earnest.

In this book, we will use Microsoft Excel 2010 whenever appropriate to perform statistical calculations and create charts. The Student Companion site contains all of the spreadsheets and Excel templates used in examples; these will help you in working many end-of-chapter problems.

Since then, statistical methods have found numerous applications in quality, including product and market analysis, product and process design, process control, testing and inspection, identification and verification of process improvements, and reliability analysis. Statistical methods are fundamental to Six Sigma practice. In fact, Six Sigma has led to a renaissance of statistics in business; workers at all organizational levels are receiving statistical training that had never been done before.

Readers of this text are assumed to have prior knowledge of elementary statistics. This chapter provides a brief review of some of the more important concepts of probability and statistics that are used in quality; however, the chapter is not intended to be comprehensive. Our primary purpose is to

illustrate some typical applications in quality and provide the foundation for topics in subsequent chapters. It can also be useful for students pursuing Six Sigma Green Belt certification. In our experience, we have found that statistics is a subject for which you learn something new every time you review what you thought you had learned before!

quality**profiles**

Graniterock Company and Branch-Smith Printing Division

Founded in 1900, Graniterock produces rock, sand, and gravel aggregates; ready-mix concrete; asphalt; road treatments; and recycled road-base material. It also retails building materials made by other manufacturers and runs a highway-paving operation. It competes in a six-county area extending from San Francisco southward to Monterey. Most of its major competitors are firms owned by multinational construction-material companies.

Charts for each product line help executives assess Graniterock's performance relative to competitors on key product and service attributes, ranked according to customer priorities. After annual improvement targets are set, the executive committee

expects branches and divisions to develop their own implementation plans. Coordination across divisions is fostered by 10 Corporate Quality Teams that oversee and help align improvement efforts across the entire organization.

As part of Graniterock's effort to reduce process variability and increase product reliability, many employees are trained in statistical process control, root-cause analysis, and other quality-assurance and problem-solving methods. This workforce capability helps the company exploit the advantages afforded by investments in computer-controlled processing equipment. Its newest batch plant features a computer-controlled process for mixing batches of concrete, enabling real-time monitoring of key process indicators. With the electronically controlled system, which Graniterock helped a supplier design, the reliability of several key processes has reached the 6-sigma level.

Applying statistical process control to all product lines has helped the company reduce variable costs and produce materials that exceed customer specifications and industry- and government-set standards. For example, Graniterock's concrete products consistently exceed the industry performance specifications by 100 times.

Branch-Smith, Inc. is a fourth-generation family business. The Branch-Smith Printing Division (BSPD) specializes in creating multipage, bound materials with services ranging from design to mailing for specialty customers. The company took the time to find out precisely what niche it could most successfully fill in the ultra-competitive printing arena. Aware that more than 1,000 printing firms crowd the Dallas/Fort Worth market, Branch-Smith used a study of the industry to determine a primary customer base. This careful, data-driven approach—typical of how the company operates—pointed toward clients with printing needs too small for larger shops, but that fit well with what BSPD did best, providing expert solutions and leveraging cost advantages normally associated with web press operations while capitalizing on

its specialized sheet-fed printing capabilities. Every Branch-Smith function is geared toward providing the best possible customer service at the lowest possible cost. To that end, databases and software tools are used extensively to gather information about, and to improve, processes involving customer service, all phases of production, continuous improvement, and decision making. An important tool called the Quality Information Database, or QID, places key data dealing with suppliers, opportunities for improvement, customer complaints, and internal nonconformance in a central location. The company's Management Review Team—responsible, among other things, for establishing and monitoring the organization's direction—uses this data to document and track progress. BSPD experienced a 72 percent growth over four years and held that gain in 2002, when the industry declined 6.6 percent. Even though BSPD is a small business in a highly fragmented industry, its market share in the Dallas/Fort Worth area has almost tripled, increasing from 0.50 percent in 1997 to 1.46 percent in 2002.

Source: Adapted from Malcolm Baldrige National Quality Award, Profiles of Winners, and 2002 Quest for Excellence video script, National Institute of Standards and Technology, Department of Commerce.

BASIC PROBABILITY CONCEPTS

To apply statistics properly, you need to have a basic understanding of probability and probability distributions. In statistical terminology, an **experiment** is a process that results in some outcome. Two examples would be taking a sample of 10 parts from a production process or burning a light bulb until it fails. The **outcome** of an experiment is a result that we observe; it might be number of defective parts in the sample or the length of time until the bulb fails. The collection of all possible outcomes of an experiment is called the **sample space**. For instance, out of 10 parts, we might have 0, 1, 2, or up to 10 defectives; the life of a light bulb can be any amount of time expressed as a real number from 0 to (theoretically) infinity since we cannot establish a finite upper limit. Note that a sample space may consist of a small number of discrete outcomes or an infinite number of countable outcomes or real numbers.

Probability is the likelihood that an outcome occurs. Suppose we label the n outcomes in a sample space as O_1, O_2, ... O_n, where O_i represents the ith outcome in the sample space. Let $P(O_i)$ be the probability associated with the outcome O_i. Then:

- *The probability associated with any outcome must be between 0 and 1, or*

$$0 \leq P(O_i) \leq 1 \text{ for each outcome } O_i$$

- *The sum of the probabilities over all possible outcomes must be 1.0, or*

$$P(O_1) + P(O_2) + \ldots + P(O_n) = 1$$

An **event** is a collection of one or more outcomes from a sample space, such as finding 2 or fewer defectives in the sample of 10, or having a bulb burn for more than 1000 hours. If A is any event, the **complement** of A, denoted as A^c, consists of all outcomes in the sample space not in A. For example, if A is the event of finding 2 or fewer defectives in a sample of 10, then A^c is the event of finding 3 or more defectives.

Two events are **mutually exclusive** if they have no outcomes in common. For example, if A is the event "2 or fewer defects in a sample" and B is the event "5 or more defects," then clearly A and B are mutually exclusive.

The following rules apply to calculating probabilities of events:

Rule 1: The probability of any event is the sum of the probabilities of the outcomes that compose that event.

Rule 2: The probability of the complement of any event A is $P(A^c) = 1 - P(A)$.

Rule 3: If events A and B are mutually exclusive, then $P(A \text{ or } B) = P(A) + P(B)$.

Rule 4: If two events A and B are not mutually exclusive, then $P(A \text{ or } B) = P(A) + P(B) - P(A \text{ and } B)$.

In these rules, $(A \text{ and } B)$ represents the intersection of events A and B; that is, all outcomes belonging to both A and B.

EXAMPLE 6.1

Using Probability Rules

In testing a new personal computer after assembly, a company discovered that among a sample of 100 units, 3 failed to boot up properly because of a defect in the motherboard, 4 units had a hard drive failure, and 2 units experienced both failures. Let A be the event "failure to boot" and B be the event "hard drive failure." Then $P(A) = 3/100$ and $P(B) = 4/100$. However, these events are not mutually exclusive because both A and B occurred together; specifically, $P(A \text{ and } B) = 2/100$. Therefore, the probability that one or the other failure occurred is $P(A \text{ or } B) = P(A) + P(B) - P(A \text{ and } B) = 3/100 + 4/100 - 2/100 = 5/100$.

Conditional probability is the probability of occurrence of one event A, given that another event B is known to be true or have already occurred. In general, the conditional probability of an event A given that event B is known to have occurred, is:

$$P(A \mid B) = \frac{P(A \text{ and } B)}{P(B)} \tag{6.1}$$

We read the notation $P(A \mid B)$ as "the probability of A given B."

The conditional probability formula may be used in other ways. For example, multiplying both sides of formula (6.1) by $P(B)$, we obtain $P(A \text{ and } B) = P(A \mid B) P(B)$. Note that we may switch the roles of A and B and write $P(B \text{ and } A) = P(B \mid A) P(A)$. But $P(B \text{ and } A)$ is the same as $P(A \text{ and } B)$; thus we can express $P(A \text{ and } B)$ in two ways:

$$P(A \text{ and } B) = P(A \mid B)P(B) = P(B \mid A)P(A) \tag{6.2}$$

This is often called the **multiplication rule of probability**.

EXAMPLE 6.2

Applying Conditional Probability

Diagnostic tests on products or equipment are often unreliable. For example, if a test indicates a failure, it may be wrong some fraction of the time; similarly, a test that results in a pass may also be wrong. Suppose that if a product that is defective, a diagnostic test indicates that it is defective only 94 percent of the time, and if the product is good, the test incorrectly states that it is defective 2 percent of the time. Assume that the true percentage of product failures is 1 percent. This situation can be illustrated by a tree diagram as shown in Figure 6.1. The probability associated with any branch is conditional on what has happened before. Thus, along the top right branch, 0.94 represents the probability that the test indicates that the product is defective given that the product actually is defective.

Using the multiplication rule, the probability that the product is actually defective *and* the test indicates that it is defective can be found by multiplying the probabilities along the branches of the tree (see Figure 6.2 for the calculation of these joint probabilities). Thus,

> P(*test indicates defective* and *product is defective*)
> = P(*test indicates defective* | *product is defective*) P(*product is defective*)
> = (0.94)(0.01) = 0.0094.

Similarly,

> P(*test indicates defective* and *product is not defective*)
> = P(*test indicates defective* | *product is not defective*) P(*product is not defective*)
> = (0.02)(0.99) = 0.0198.

FIGURE 6.1

Tree Diagram and Probabilities for Diagnostic Testing

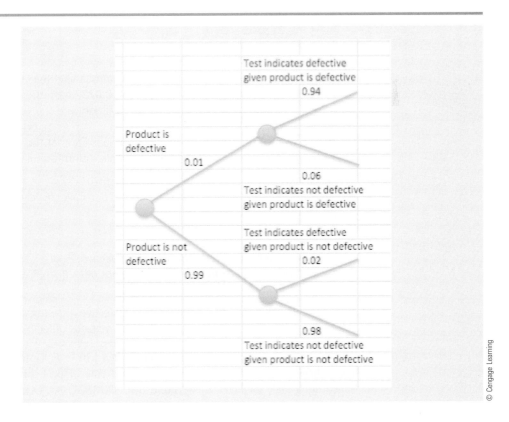

FIGURE 6.2   Calculation of Joint Probabilities

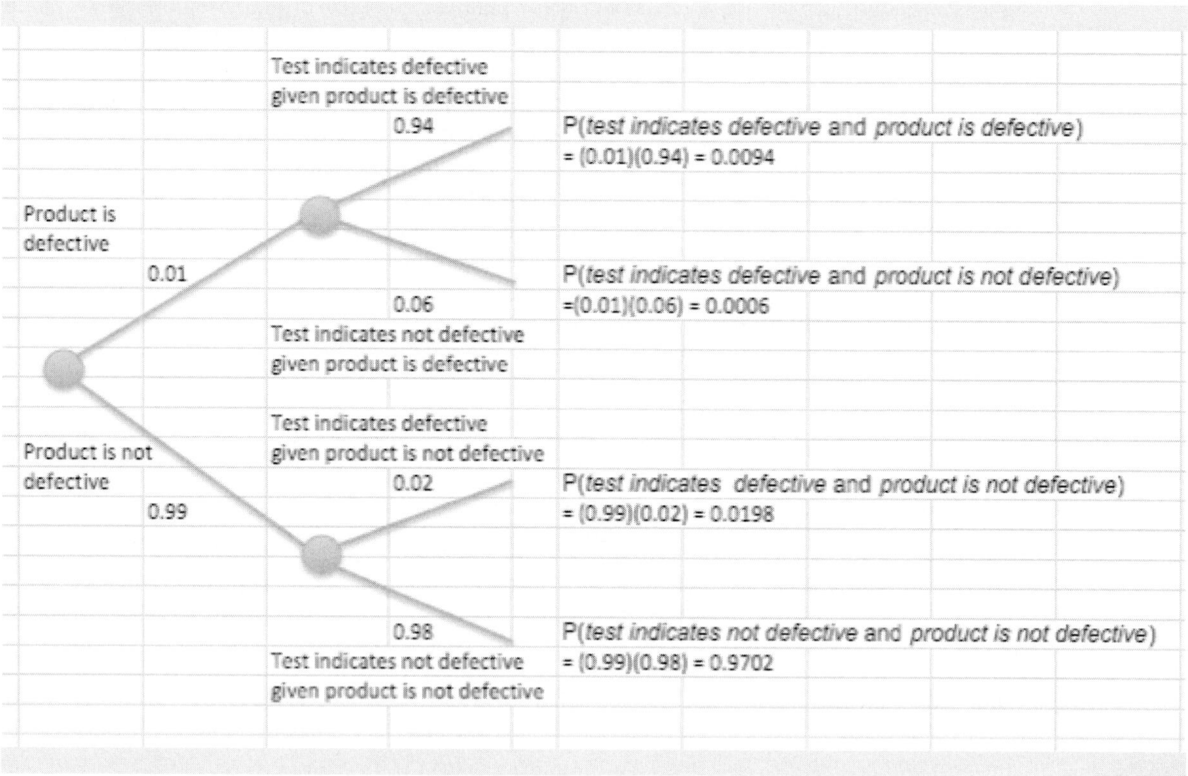

Thus, for any randomly sampled product, the probability that the test will indicate that the product is defective is $0.0094 + 0.0198 = 0.0292$ even though the true probability is 0.01. Similarly, the probability that the test will indicate the product is not defective is $0.0006 + 0.9702 = 0.9708$.

We may also compute the conditional probability that the product is truly defective after knowing the result of the test. For example, using formula (6.1) we have:

> P(product is defective | test indicates defective)
> $= P$(test indicates defective and product is defective)$/P$(test indicates defective)
> $= 0.0094/0.0292 = 0.3219.$

and

> P(product is defective | test indicates not defective)
> $= P$(test indicates defective and product is not defective)$/P$(test indicates defective)
> $= 0.0198/0.0292 = 0.6781.$

You should verify that P(product is not defective | test indicates not defective) = 0.99948, and P(product is not defective | test indicates defective) = 0.00062.

Two events A and B are **independent** if $P(A \mid B) = P(A)$. If two events are independent, then we can simplify the multiplication rule of probability in equation (6.2) by substituting $P(A)$ for $P(A \mid B)$: $P(A \text{ and } B) = P(B)P(A) = P(A)P(B)$.

EXAMPLE 6.3	Multiplication Rule for Independent Events

Suppose a process consists of two sequential steps, with the probability of a nondefective part produced in the first step (event A) being 0.95 and the probability of a nondefective part produced in the second step (event B) being 0.98. Clearly the two events are independent, so the probability of producing a nondefective part in the process is P(A and B) = P(A) P(B) = (0.95)(0.98) = 0.931. This means that if we start with 1000 parts, only 931 will be nondefective at the end of the process. In quality control terminology, this is often called the *rolled throughput yield,* which we will formally define in Chapter 8.

PROBABILITY DISTRIBUTIONS

A **random variable** is a numerical description of the outcome of an experiment. Formally, a random variable is a function that assigns a numerical value to every possible outcome in a sample space. For example, suppose an experiment consists of sampling 10 parts and counting the number of defectives. We might define the random variable X to be the number of defective parts in the sample. If the experiment consists of testing a product after final assembly, the outcomes would be pass or fail. We might define a random variable Y to be 1 if the outcome is pass, and 0 if the outcome is fail. A random variable can be either discrete or continuous, depending on the specific numerical values it may assume.

A **probability distribution** is a characterization of the possible values that a random variable may assume along with the probability of assuming these values. A probability distribution can be either discrete or continuous, depending on the nature of the random variable it models. For a random variable X, the probability distribution of X is denoted by a mathematical function $f(x)$. The symbol x_i represents the ith value of the random variable X and $f(x_i)$ its probability. The **cumulative distribution function**, $F(x)$, specifies the probability that the random variable X will assume a value *less than or equal to* a specified value, x. This is also denoted as $P(X \leq x)$, and read as "the probability that the random variable X is less than or equal to x."

Discrete Probability Distributions

We will review two important discrete probability distributions used in quality applications, the binomial and Poisson distributions.

Binomial Distribution   The **binomial distribution** describes the probability of obtaining exactly x "successes" in a sequence of n identical experiments, called trials. A *success* can be any one of two possible outcomes of each experiment. In some situations, it might represent a defective item, in others, a good item. The probability of success in each trial is a constant value p. The binomial probability function is given by the following formula:

$$f(x) = \binom{n}{x} p^x (1-p)^{n-x}$$
$$= \frac{n!}{x!(n-x)!} p^x (1-p)^{n-x} \quad x = 0, 1, 2, ..., n \tag{6.3}$$

where p is the probability of a success, n is the number of items in the sample, and x is the number of items for which the probability is desired (0, 1, 2, …, n). The expected value, variance, and standard deviation of the binomial distribution are

> *Excel 2010 provides useful functions for computing probabilities for the probability distributions we use in this book.*

$$E[X] = \mu = np \tag{6.4}$$
$$\sigma^2 = np(1 - p) \tag{6.5}$$
$$\sigma = \sqrt{np(1 - p)} \tag{6.6}$$

The formula for the probability mass function for the binomial distribution is rather complex, and binomial probabilities are tedious to compute by hand; however, they can be computed easily in Excel 2010 using the function:

BINOM.DIST(*number_s, trials, probability_s, cumulative*)

In this function, *number_s* plays the role of x, and *probability_s* is the same as p. If *cumulative* is set to TRUE, then this function will provide the cumulative probability function $F(x)$; otherwise the default is FALSE, and it provides values of the probability mass function, $f(x)$.

EXAMPLE 6.4　　Using the Binomial Distribution

If the probability that a process produces a defective part is 0.2, then the probability distribution that x parts out of a sample of 10 will be defective is described using formula (6.3) with $n = 10$ and $p = 0.2$:

$$f(x) = \begin{cases} \dbinom{10}{x}(0.2)^x(0.8)^{(10-x)} & \text{for } x = 0, 1, 2, \ldots 10 \\ 0, \textit{otherwise} \end{cases}$$

Thus, to find the probability that 3 parts among a sample of 10 will be defective, we compute

> *The Binomial worksheet shown in Figure 6.3 is available on the Student Companion Site in the Probability Distribution Templates Excel workbook.*

$$f(3) = \binom{10}{3}(0.2)^3(0.8)^{10-3} = \frac{10!}{3!7!}(0.008)(0.2097152)$$

$$= 120(0.008)(0.2097152) = 0.20133$$

The binomial probability distribution and cumulative probability distribution can be tabulated using the Excel BINOM.DIST function. Figure 6.3 shows an Excel template for calculating binomial probabilities and tabulating the distributions.

Poisson Distribution　　The second discrete distribution often used in quality control is the **Poisson distribution**. The Poisson probability distribution is given by

$$f(x) = \frac{e^{-\lambda}\lambda^x}{x!} \tag{6.7}$$

where λ = expected value or average number of occurrences, $x = 0, 1, 2, 3, \ldots$, and $e = 2.71828$, a constant.

The Poisson distribution is closely related to the binomial distribution. It is derived by allowing the sample size (n) to become very large (approaching infinity) and the probability of success or failure (p) to become very small (approaching zero) while the

FIGURE 6.3

Binomial Probability
Calculations Using
Excel

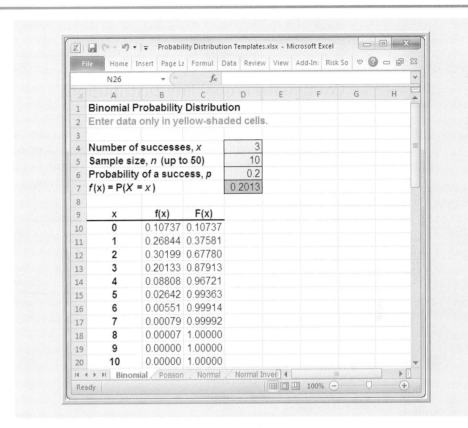

© Cengage Learning

expected value (np) remains constant. Thus, when n is large relative to p, the Poisson distribution can be used as an approximation to the binomial. A common rule of thumb is if $p \leq 0.05$ and $n \geq 20$, the Poisson will be a good approximation with $\mu = np$. It is also used to calculate the number of occurrences of an event over a specified interval of time or space, such as the number of scratches per square inch on a polished surface.

Like the binomial, Poisson probabilities are cumbersome to compute by hand. Probabilities can easily be computed in Excel using the function POISSON.DIST(x, *mean*, *cumulative*). We will use this in the next example.

An Excel template for calculating the Poisson distribution is available in the Poisson worksheet in the Probability Distributions Templates workbook on the Student Companion Site.

EXAMPLE 6.5   Using the Poisson Distribution

Suppose that, on average, the number of cosmetic defects (which can be touched up and polished) found during postpainting inspection of a product is 12. The probability that exactly x defects will be found is given by the Poisson distribution in formula (6.7) with a mean of 12, or,

$$f(x) = \begin{cases} \dfrac{e^{-12}12^x}{x!}, & \text{for } x = 0, 1, 2, \dots \\ 0, \text{ otherwise} \end{cases}$$

Substituting $x = 5$ in this formula, the probability that exactly 5 defects will be found is $f(5) = 0.01274$. Figure 6.4 shows the calculations using the *Poisson* spreadsheet template.

Continuous Probability Distributions

A continuous random variable is defined over one or more intervals of real numbers, and therefore has an infinite number of possible outcomes. A curve that characterizes outcomes of a continuous random variable is called a **probability density function,** and is described by a mathematical function *f(x)*. For continuous random variables, it does not make mathematical sense to attempt to define a probability for a specific

FIGURE 6.4 Poisson Probability Calculations Using Excel

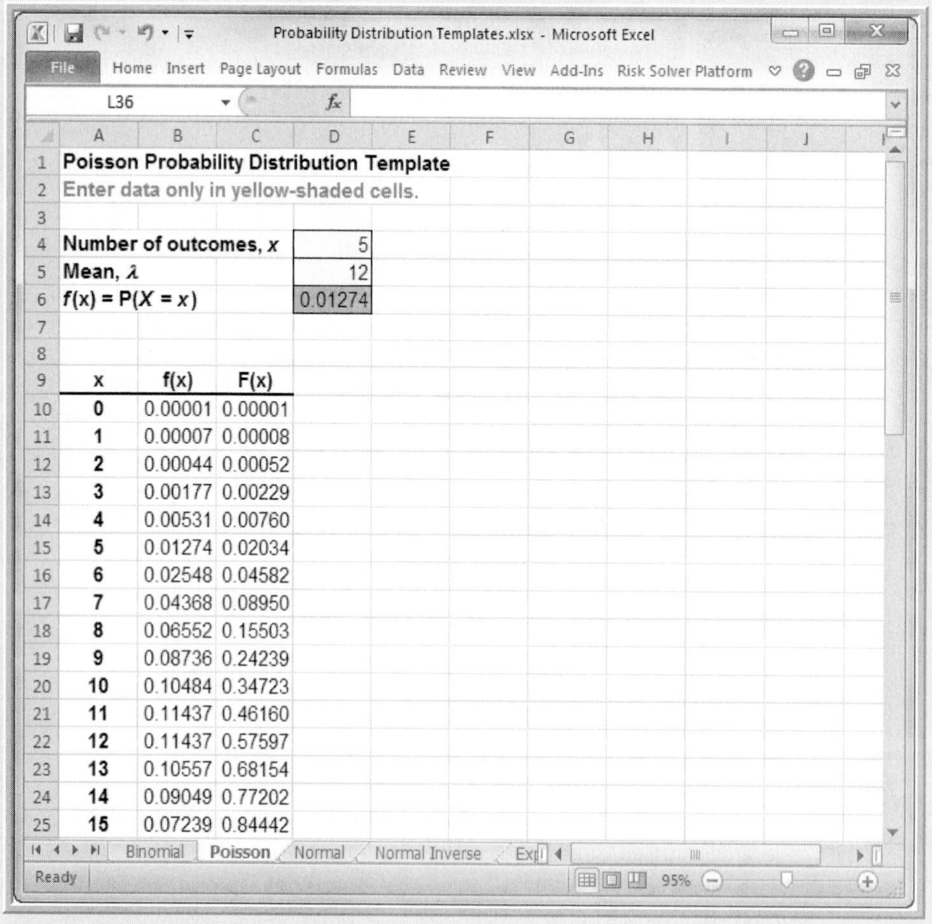

Poisson Probability Distribution Template

Enter data only in yellow-shaded cells.

Number of outcomes, *x*	5
Mean, λ	12
***f*(x) = P(*X* = *x*)**	0.01274

x	f(x)	F(x)
0	0.00001	0.00001
1	0.00007	0.00008
2	0.00044	0.00052
3	0.00177	0.00229
4	0.00531	0.00760
5	0.01274	0.02034
6	0.02548	0.04582
7	0.04368	0.08950
8	0.06552	0.15503
9	0.08736	0.24239
10	0.10484	0.34723
11	0.11437	0.46160
12	0.11437	0.57597
13	0.10557	0.68154
14	0.09049	0.77202
15	0.07239	0.84442

value of x because there are an infinite number of values. Probabilities are only defined over intervals. Thus, we may calculate probabilities between two numbers a and b, $P(a \leq X \leq b)$, or to the left or right of a number c, for example, $P(X \leq c)$ and $P(X \geq c)$. $P(a \leq X \leq b)$ is the area under the density function between a and b.

The cumulative distribution function for a continuous random variable is denoted the same way as for discrete random variables, $F(x)$, and represents the probability that the random variable X is less than or equal to x, $P(X \leq x)$. $F(x)$ represents the area under the density function to the left of x. Knowing $F(x)$ makes it easy to compute probabilities over intervals for continuous distributions. The probability that X is between a and b is equal to the difference of the cumulative distribution function evaluated at these two points; that is:

$$P(a \leq X \leq b) = P(X \leq b) - P(X \leq a) = F(b) - F(a) \tag{6.8}$$

For continuous distributions we need not be concerned about the endpoints as we were with discrete distributions because $P(a \leq X \leq b)$ is the same as $P(a < X < b)$.

Normal Distribution

The probability density function of the **normal distribution** is represented graphically by the familiar bell-shaped curve. However, not every symmetric, unimodal curve is a normal distribution, nor can all data from a sample or population be assumed to fit a normal distribution. However, data are often assumed to be normally distributed to simplify certain calculations. In most cases, this assumption makes little difference in the results but is important from a theoretical perspective.

The probability density function for the normal distribution is as follows:

$$f(x) = \frac{1}{\sqrt{2\pi\sigma^2}} e^{-(x-\mu)^2/2\sigma^2} \quad \text{for} \ -\infty < x < \infty \tag{6.9}$$

where

μ = the mean of the random variable x

σ^2 = the variance of x

$e = 2.71828 \ldots$

$\pi = 3.14159 \ldots$

If a normal random variable has a mean $\mu = 0$ and a standard deviation $\sigma = 1$, it is called a **standard normal distribution**. The letter z is usually used to represent this particular random variable. By using the constants 0 and 1 for the mean and standard deviation, respectively, the probability density function for the normal distribution can be simplified as

$$f(z) = \frac{1}{\sqrt{2\pi}} e^{-z^2/2} \tag{6.10}$$

This standard normal distribution function is shown in Figure 6.5. Because $\sigma = 1$, the scale on the z axis is given in units of standard deviations. Special tables of areas under the normal curve have been developed as an aid in computing probabilities. Such a table is given in Appendix A.

FIGURE 6.5
Standard Normal
Distribution

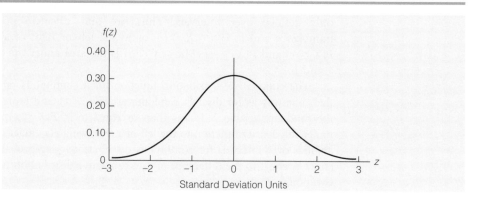

Standard Deviation Units

The Normal worksheet in the Probability Distribution Templates workbook on the Student Companion Site can be used to calculate normal probabilities and is used in the following example. This worksheet calculates the z-value and cumulative probability for any value of x and also provides a tabulation of the cumulative normal distribution within three standard deviations of the mean for any specified mean and standard deviation, as well as a chart of the cumulative distribution.

Fortunately, if x is any value from a normal distribution with mean μ and standard deviation σ, we may easily convert it to an equivalent value from a standard normal distribution using the following formula:

$$z = \frac{x - \mu}{\sigma} \qquad (6.11)$$

This is often used to compute normal probabilities using a standard normal cumulative distribution table (Appendix A in the back of the book). The Excel function NORM.DIST(x, *mean, standard deviation, TRUE*) calculates the cumulative probability $F(x) = P(X \leq x)$ for a specified mean and standard deviation. The Excel function NORM.S.DIST(z) calculates the cumulative probability for any value of z for the standard normal distribution.

This formula takes the value of the variable of interest (x), subtracts the mean value (μ), and divides by the standard deviation (σ). This calculation yields a random variable z, which has a standard normal distribution. Probabilities for this variable can then be found in the table in Appendix A.

EXAMPLE 6.6   Using the Normal Distribution

A manufacturer of MRI scanners used for medical diagnosis has data that indicates that the mean number of days (μ) between equipment malfunctions is 1020 days, with a standard deviation of 20 days. Assuming a normal distribution, what is the probability that the number of days between adjustments will be less than 1044 days? More than 980 days? Between 980 and 1044 days?

To use the table in Appendix A, first convert the value of x to a z-value. For $x = 1044$ days, we have:

$$z = \frac{x - \mu}{\sigma} = \frac{1044 - 1020}{20} = 1.2$$

This means that 1044 days is 1.2 standard deviations above the mean of 1020 days. Therefore, using Appendix A, $P(X \leq 1044) = P(z \leq 1.2) = 0.8849$. This probability can be found directly using the Excel function NORM.DIST(1044,1020,20,TRUE). Figure 6.6 shows the use of the *Normal* probability template.

To find the probability that X exceeds 980 days, first find the corresponding z-value:

$$z = \frac{x - \mu}{\sigma} = \frac{980 - 1020}{20} = -2.0$$

Note that $P(X \leq 980) = P(z \leq -2.0) = 0.02275$. Therefore, $P(X > 980) = 1 - 0.02275 = 0.97725$. This can be found using Excel as $1 - $ NORM.DIST(980,1020,20,TRUE).

Finally, to find the probability that X is between 1044 and 980 days, we use formula (6.8):

$$
\begin{aligned}
P(980 \leq X \leq 1044) &= P(X \leq 1044) - P(X \leq 980) \\
&= F(1044) - F(980) = 0.88493 - 0.02275 \\
&= 0.86218.
\end{aligned}
$$

The Excel function NORM.INV(*probability, mean, standard_dev*) can be used when we know the cumulative probability but don't know the value of x. In this function, *probability* is the cumulative probability value corresponding to the value of x we seek.

> *The Excel worksheet* Normal Inverse *in the Probability Distributions Templates workbook on the Student Companion Site uses the NORM.INV function to find the value of x for a specified cumulative probability.*

FIGURE 6.6   Normal Probability Calculations Using Excel (Portion of the Excel worksheet *Normal*)

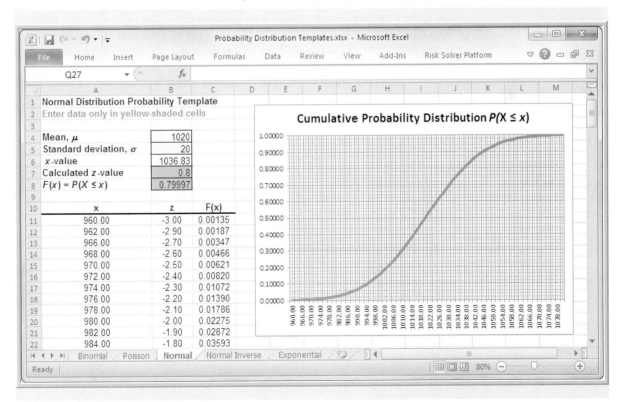

EXAMPLE 6.7

Using the Normal Inverse Function

Suppose that the manufacturer of MRI scanners wishes to determine the number of days for which the probability that the equipment would not malfunction is 0.80. In this case, we know that $P(X \leq x) = 0.8$. This is equivalent to $P(Z \leq z) = 0.8$, where $z = (x - 1044)/20$. From Appendix A, we can determine that z is approximately equal to 0.84. Therefore, solving $0.84 = (x - 1044)/20$ for x yields $x = 1060.8$. Figure 6.7 shows the application of the *Normal Inverse* Excel template to this example.

Unfortunately, most business processes do not produce normal distributions.[3] Lack of a normal distribution often results from the tendency to control processes tightly, which eliminates many sources of natural variation, as well as from human behavior, physical laws, and inspection practices. For example, data on the number of days customers take to pay bills typically show that many customers like to prepay; others send payments that arrive just after the due date. This behavior causes spikes in the distribution that do not conform to normality. In a hot-dip galvanizing process, a zinc layer forms when the base material reaches the temperature of molten zinc. However, if the part is removed before the critical temperature is reached, no zinc will adhere at all. Thus, all parts will have some minimum zinc thickness and the left side of the distribution will not tail off gradually as does a normal distribution. Other situations that lead to nonnormal data include:[4]

1. Too many extreme values resulting from measurement or data-entry errors.
2. Overlapping of two or more distributions resulting from mixing data from different processes.
3. Round-off errors in measurement or measurement devices with poor resolution that can make data look discrete rather than continuous.
4. Data that have been sorted; for example, removing samples that fall outside specification limits after inspection will cut off the tails of a normal distribution and may make it look more uniform.
5. Processes that have many values close to zero, resulting in a positively skewed distribution. Often, the data can be transformed to a normal distribution by using a mathematical transformation such as taking logarithms.

FIGURE 6.7
Normal Inverse
Distribution
Calculation
Template

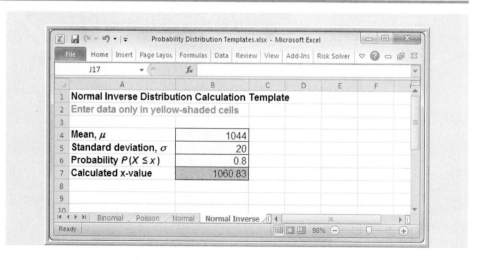

6. Data that naturally follow some other distribution, such as survival times of electronic components, extreme value data such as the longest machine downtime each day, and so on.

Therefore, it is important to fully understand the nature of your data before applying statistical theory that depends on normality assumptions.

Exponential Distribution

Another continuous distribution commonly used in quality is the **exponential distribution**. The exponential distribution models the time between randomly occurring events, such as the time to or between failures of mechanical or electrical components. Hence, it is used extensively in reliability models, as we will see in Chapter 7. The exponential distribution is related to the Poisson distribution: if the distribution of the time between events is exponential, then the number of events occurring during an interval of time is Poisson. For example, if the average time between failures of a machine is exponential with a mean of 500 hours, then the average number of failures per hour is Poisson with a mean of 1/500 failures/hour.

The probability density function is:

$$f(x) = \lambda e^{-\lambda x} \quad \text{for } x \geq 0 \tag{6.12}$$

where

$1/\lambda$ = mean of the exponential distribution (note that λ is the mean of the corresponding Poisson distribution)

x = time or distance over which the variable extends

e = 2.71828... (the base of natural logarithms)

The Excel worksheet Exponential *in the* Probability Distribution Templates *workbook on the* Student Companion Site *can be used to compute exponential probabilities.*

The cumulative distribution function is

$$F(x) = 1 - e^{-\lambda x} \tag{6.13}$$

The exponential distribution has the properties that it is bounded below by 0, it has its greatest density at 0, and the density declines as x increases. The Excel function EXPON.DIST(x, *lambda*, *TRUE*) can be used to compute cumulative exponential probabilities.

EXAMPLE 6.8

Using the Exponential Distribution

A company that makes electronic components for tablet devices tested a large number of these components. They found that the average time to failure is $1/\lambda$ = 4000 hours. What is the probability that a component will fail within 500 hours? After 4000 hours?

The mean rate of failure is λ = 1/4000 = 0.00025 failures/hour. Therefore, the probability of failure within 500 hours is

$$F(500) = 1 - e^{-(0.00025)(500)} = 0.1175$$

The Excel function EXPON.DIST(x, 0.00025, TRUE) calculates the probability of a failure within x hours. Therefore, EXPON.DIST(500, 0.00025, TRUE) will result in the same value. Figure 6.8 shows the *Exponential* spreadsheet template applied to this example.

The probability of failure after 4000 hours is

$$F(4000) = 1 - e^{-(0.00025)(4000)} = 0.6321$$

FIGURE 6.8
Exponential Probability Calculations Using Excel

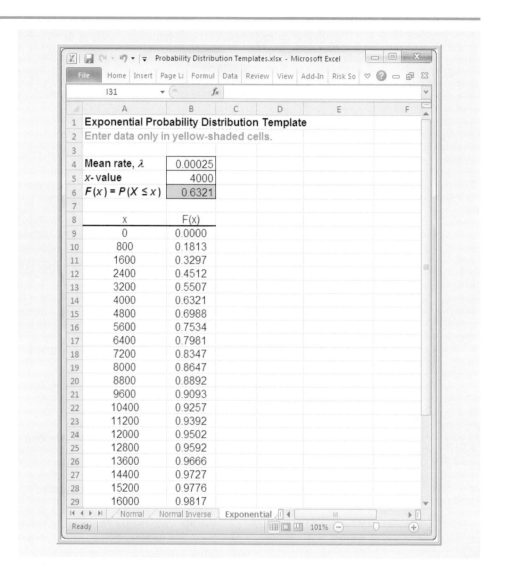

Note that 4000 hours is the average (mean) time to failure; however, the probability of failing before 4000 hours is not one half, which is a common misconception. The mean is not the same as the median, as this example clearly illustrates.

STATISTICAL METHODOLOGY

Figure 6.9 summarizes the basic elements of statistical methodology used in quality. One usually begins by describing data visually and numerically. **Descriptive statistics** are methods of presenting data visually and numerically, and includes charts (such as Excel column, line, and pie charts), frequency distributions and histograms to organize and

FIGURE 6.9   Basic Statistical Methodology for Quality

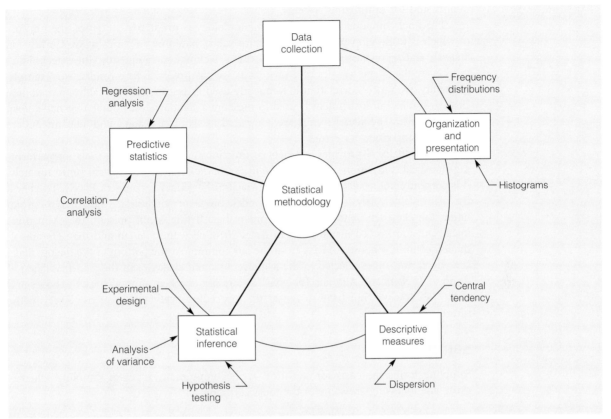

present data, measures of central tendency (means, medians, proportions), and measures of dispersion (range, standard deviation, variance). For example, an airline might investigate the problem of lost baggage and determine that the major causes of the problem are lost or damaged identification tags, incorrect tags on the bags, and misrouting to baggage claim areas. An examination of frequencies for each of these categories might show that lost or damaged bags accounted for 50 percent of the problems, incorrect tags for 30 percent, and misrouting for only 20 percent. The airline might also compute the average number of baggage errors per 1,000 passengers each month and chart the data to identify trends and determine if process improvements are effective.

The second component of statistical problem solving is statistical inference. **Statistical inference** is the process of drawing conclusions about unknown characteristics of a population from which data were taken. Techniques used in this process include confidence intervals, hypothesis testing, and experimental design. For example, a chemical manufacturer might be interested in determining the effect of temperature on the yield of a new manufacturing process. Because of variation in yields, a confidence interval might be constructed to quantify the uncertainty of sample data. In a controlled experiment, the manufacturer might test the hypothesis that the temperature has an effect on the yield against the alternative hypothesis that temperature has no effect. If the temperature is, in fact, a critical variable, steps will be required to maintain the temperature at the proper level and to draw inferences as to whether the process remains under control, based on samples taken from it. Experimental design is important for helping to understand the effects of process factors on output quality and for optimizing systems.

The final component in statistical methodology is **predictive statistics**, the purpose of which is to develop predictions of future values based on historical data. Correlation analysis and regression analysis are two useful techniques. Frequently, these techniques can clarify the characteristics of a process as well as predict future results. For example, in quality assurance, correlation is frequently used in test instrument calibration studies. In such studies, an instrument is used to measure a standard test sample that has known characteristics. The actual results are compared to standard results, and adjustments are made to compensate for errors.

Microsoft Excel provides a variety of functions and data analysis tools for performing statistical calculations. The *Data Analysis ToolPak* is especially useful (unfortunately, it is currently not available in the Apple Macintosh® [Mac] versions of Excel). To view a list of available analysis tools in Excel, click on *Data Analysis* in the *Analysis* group under the *Data* tab in the Excel 2010 menu bar. If this is not present, then you must install the add-ins. To install them in Excel 2010, click the *File* tab and then *Options* in the left column. Choose *Add-Ins* from the left column. At the bottom of the dialog, make sure *Excel Add-Ins* is selected in the *Manage:* box and click *Go*. In the *Add-Ins* dialog, if *Analysis Toolpak* and *Analysis Toolpak VBA* are not checked, simply check the boxes and click *OK*. You will not have to repeat this procedure every time you run Excel in the future.

Sampling

Sampling forms the basis for statistical applications. Many types of sampling schemes exist. The following are some of the most common:

1. *Simple Random Sampling:* Every item in the population has an equal probability of being selected.
2. *Stratified Sampling:* The population is partitioned into groups, or strata, and a sample is selected from each group.
3. *Systematic Sampling:* Every *n*th (4th, 5th, etc.) item is selected.
4. *Cluster Sampling:* A population is partitioned into groups (clusters) and a sample of clusters is selected. Either all elements in the chosen clusters are included in the sample or a random sample is taken from each of them.
5. *Judgment Sampling:* Expert opinion is used to determine the sample.

A good sampling plan should select a sample at the lowest cost that will provide the best possible representation of the population, consistent with the objectives of precision and reliability that have been determined for the study.

Simple random sampling is the most common type of sampling procedure and forms the basis for most scientific statistical surveys, such as auditing and market research, and is a useful tool for quality assurance studies. Most statistical procedures depend on taking random samples. If random samples are not used, bias may be introduced. For instance, if the items are rolled in coils, sampling only from the exposed end of the coil can easily result in bias if the production process that produced the coils varies over time. Simple random sampling is generally used to estimate population parameters such as means, proportions, and variances. To use simple random sampling effectively, you must also determine the appropriate sample size.

Any sampling procedure can result in two types of errors: **sampling error** and **systematic error**. Sampling error occurs naturally and results from the fact that a sample may not always be representative of the population, no matter how carefully it is selected. The only way to reduce sampling error is to take a larger sample from the population. Systematic errors, however, usually result from poor sample design and can be reduced or eliminated by careful planning of the sampling study.

Descriptive Statistics

A **population** is a complete set or collection of objects of interest; a **sample** is a subset of objects taken from the population. Descriptive statistics summarize the numerical characteristics of populations or samples. The most important types of descriptive statistics and formulas are summarized below.

Measures of Location   The mean of a population is denoted by the Greek letter μ, and the mean of a sample is denoted by $\bar{x}$. If a population consists of N observations $x_1, x_2, ..., x_N$, the population mean, μ is calculated as:

$$\mu = \frac{\sum_{i=1}^{N} x_i}{N} \tag{6.14}$$

The mean of a sample of n observations, $x_1, x_2, ..., x_n$, denoted by "x-bar" is calculated as:

$$\bar{x} = \frac{\sum_{i=1}^{n} x_i}{n} \tag{6.15}$$

We may calculate the mean in Excel using the function AVERAGE(*data range*).

The **median** specifies the middle value (or 50th percentile) when the data are arranged from smallest to largest. Half the data are below the median, and half the data are above it. For an odd number of observations, the median is the middle of the sorted numbers. For an even number of observations, the median is the mean of the two middle numbers. We may find the median using the Excel function MEDIAN(*data range*).

The **mode** is the observation that occurs most frequently. The mode is most useful for data sets that consist of a relatively small number of unique values. For data sets that have few repeating values, the mode does not provide much practical value. In Excel 2010, you can use the function MODE.SNGL(*data range*) or MODE.MULT(*data range*) to identify a single mode or multiple modes in the data.

Measures of Dispersion   The **range** is the simplest measure of dispersion and is computed as the difference between the maximum value and the minimum value in the data set. Although Excel does not provide a function for the range, it can be computed easily by the formula =MAX(*data range*) – MIN(*data range*).

The **variance** is a measure of dispersion that depends on *all* the data. The larger the variance, the more the data are "spread out" from the mean, and the more variability one can expect in the observations. The formula for the variance of a population is:

$$\sigma^2 = \frac{\sum_{i=1}^{N} (x_i - \mu)^2}{N} \tag{6.16}$$

where x_i is the value of the ith item, N is the number of items in the population, and μ is the population mean. Essentially, the variance is the average of the squared deviations of the observations from the mean. The variance of a sample is calculated using the formula:

$$s^2 = \frac{\sum_{i=1}^{n} (x_i - \bar{x})^2}{n - 1} \tag{6.17}$$

where n is the number of items in the sample, and $\bar{x}$ is the sample mean. The Excel 2010 function VAR.S(*data range*) may be used to compute the sample variance, s^2, while the Excel function VAR.P(*data range*) is used to compute the variance of a population, σ^2.

The **standard deviation** is the square root of the variance. For a population, the standard deviation is computed as:

$$\sigma = \sqrt{\frac{\sum_{i=1}^{N} (x_i - \mu)^2}{N}} \tag{6.18}$$

and for samples, it is:

$$s = \sqrt{\frac{\sum_{i=1}^{n} (x_i - \bar{x})^2}{n - 1}} \tag{6.19}$$

The Excel 2010 function STDEV.P(*data range*) calculates the standard deviation for a population (σ); the function STDEV.S(*data range*) calculates it for a sample (s).

EXAMPLE 6.9

Calculating Basic Statistical Measures

The times required for 30 housekeeping workers to each clean one room at Stayside Hotels are given below:

16, 13, 12, 14, 10, 12, 14, 10, 15, 17, 13, 9, 16, 13, 18, 10, 17, 12, 13, 17, 9, 18, 12, 11, 14, 15, 9, 12, 8, 15

Using Excel functions, calculate the mean, median, mode, range, sample variance, and sample standard deviation. The results are shown in Figure 6.10, which is available on the Excel spreadsheet *Example 6.9.xlsx* and can be found on the Student Companion Site.

The Proportion   In a customer satisfaction survey, for example, we might collect data on gender, education, income categories, job status, and so on; or we might record the results of functional testing of a product as pass or fail. Such data are called categorical data and are not numerical. Thus, statistics such as means and variances are not appropriate. Instead, we are generally interested in the fraction of data that have a certain characteristic, for example, the fraction of respondents that are female or male. The formal statistical measure is called the **proportion**, usually denoted as p. Proportions are key descriptive statistics for categorical data, such as defects or errors. If the data are stored on an Excel worksheet, we may use the Excel COUNTIF(*range, criteria*) function to find the number of cells within a range that meet a specified criteria and then compute the proportion as a ratio of the count to the total number of observations.

FIGURE 6.10
Using Excel to
Calculate Basic
Statistical Measures

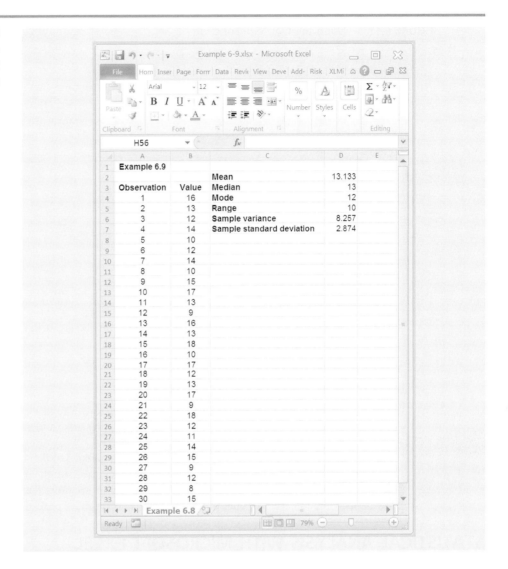

EXAMPLE 6.10

Computing a Proportion

The Excel spreadsheet *Example 6.10.xlsx*, shown in Figure 6.11 and available on the Student Companion Site, provides a sample of 100 items that were inspected after a production operation. Each of these were recorded as either "good" or "defective." To count the number of good and defective items, we use the formulas =COUNTIF(A3:J12, "Good") and =COUNTIF(A3:J12, "Defective") in cells A15 and B15, respectively. Therefore, the proportion of defective items is 25/100 or 0.25.

Measures of Shape   **Skewness** describes the lack of symmetry of data. The **coefficient of skewness (CS)** measures the degree of asymmetry of observations around the mean. If CS is positive, the distribution of values is positively skewed; if negative, it is negatively skewed. The closer CS is to zero, the less the degree of skewness. A coefficient

FIGURE 6.11 Using the COUNTIF Function

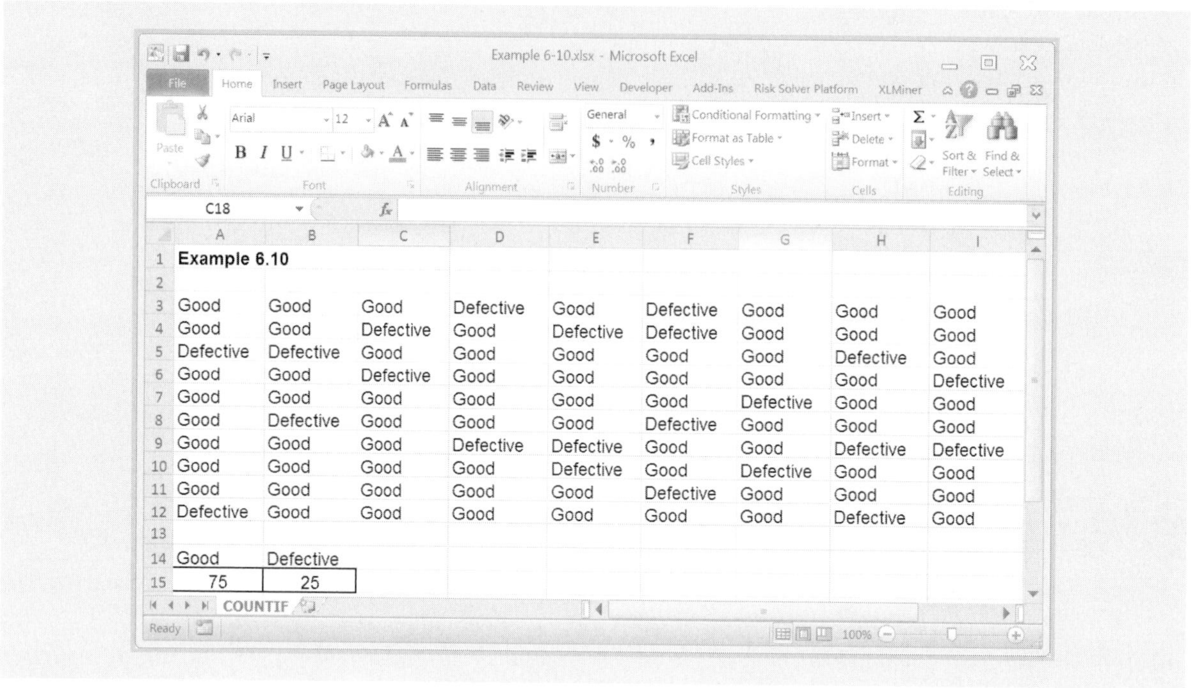

	A	B	C	D	E	F	G	H	I
1	**Example 6.10**								
2									
3	Good	Good	Good	Defective	Good	Defective	Good	Good	Good
4	Good	Good	Defective	Good	Defective	Defective	Good	Good	Good
5	Defective	Defective	Good	Good	Good	Good	Good	Defective	Good
6	Good	Good	Defective	Good	Good	Good	Good	Good	Defective
7	Good	Good	Good	Good	Good	Good	Defective	Good	Good
8	Good	Defective	Good	Good	Good	Defective	Good	Good	Good
9	Good	Good	Good	Defective	Defective	Good	Good	Defective	Defective
10	Good	Good	Good	Good	Defective	Good	Defective	Good	Good
11	Good	Good	Good	Good	Good	Defective	Good	Good	Good
12	Defective	Good	Good	Good	Good	Good	Good	Defective	Good
13									
14	Good	Defective							
15	75	25							

of skewness greater than 1 or less than −1 suggests a high degree of skewness. A value between 0.5 and 1 or between −0.5 and −1 represents moderate skewness. Coefficients between 0.5 and −0.5 indicate relative symmetry.

Kurtosis refers to the peakedness (i.e., high, narrow) or flatness (i.e., short, flat-topped) of a histogram. The **coefficient of kurtosis** (**CK**) measures the degree of kurtosis of a population. Distributions with values of CK less than 3 are more flat with a wide degree of dispersion; those with values of CK greater than 3 are more peaked with less dispersion.

STATISTICAL ANALYSIS WITH MICROSOFT EXCEL

The Data Analysis Toolpak *is not available on Excel for the Mac. Some of these procedures are available in the free edition of* StatPlus:mac LE *(http://www.analystsoft.com). A more complete version,* StatPlus:mac Pro, *can also be purchased. However, there are some significant differences between this software and the Data Analysis Toolpak.*

The *Data Analysis Toolpak* in Microsoft Excel for Windows provides many procedures for conducting statistical analyses that only require you to point to data or enter data into a dialog; the tools perform the calculations and display the results. Two of the most useful Excel tools for statistical analysis are the *Descriptive Statistics* and *Histogram* tools.

The Excel Descriptive Statistics Tool

The Excel *Descriptive Statistics* tool is a convenient way of obtaining basic summary measures for sample data. Click on *Data Analysis* under the *Data* tab in the Excel menu bar. Select *Descriptive Statistics* from the list of tools. The *Descriptive Statistics* dialog shown in Figure 6.12 will appear. You need only enter the range of the data, which must be in a *single row or*

FIGURE 6.12
Excel *Descriptive Statistics* Dialog

column. If the data are in multiple columns, the tool treats each row or column as a separate data set, depending on which you specify. This means that if you have a single data set arranged in a matrix format, you would have to stack the data in a single column before applying the *Descriptive Statistics* tool. Check the box *Labels in First Row* if labels are included in the input range. You may choose to save the results in the current worksheet or in a new one. For basic summary statistics, check the box *Summary statistics*; you need not check any others. The tool provides the basic statistical measures of location, dispersion, and shape, as well as the *standard error*, which is the standard deviation divided by the number of observations (*Count*). The standard error will be discussed later in this chapter.

EXAMPLE 6.11

Using the Excel Descriptive Statistics Tool

The Excel file *U-Bolt Data.xlsx,* available on the Student Companion Site, contains a sample of 120 measurements of a critical dimension of U-bolts (U-bolts are used in automotive assembly). In the dialog in Figure 6.12, provide the input range of the data (check the *Labels in First Row* box if you include the column header in the input range); also check the *Summary Statistics* box. Figure 6.13 shows the output from the *Descriptive Statistics* tool for these measurements. We see that the mean is 10.7171, the median is 10.7, and the (sample) standard deviation is 0.0868. The distribution is symmetric as indicated the skewness value that is close to zero.

The Excel Histogram Tool

A **frequency distribution** is a table that shows the number of observations in each of several nonoverlapping groups. A graphical depiction of a frequency distribution for numerical data in the form of a column chart is called a **histogram**. Frequency

FIGURE 6.13
Descriptive Statistics
for U-Bolt
Measurements

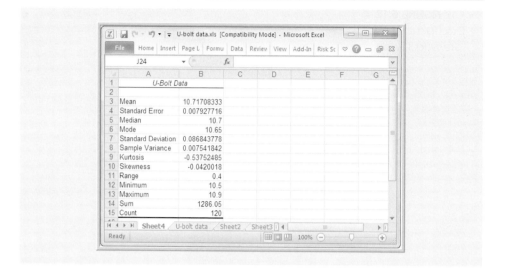

distributions and histograms can be created using the *Data Analysis Toolpak* in Excel. To do this, click the *Data Analysis* tools button in the *Analysis* group under the *Data* tab in the Excel menu bar and select *Histogram* from the list. In the dialog box (see Figure 6.14), specify the *Input Range* corresponding to the data. If you include the column header, then also check the *Labels* box so Excel knows that the range contains a label. The *Bin Range* defines the groups used for the frequency distribution. If you do not specify a *Bin Range,* Excel will automatically determine bin values for the frequency distribution and histogram, which often results in a rather poor choice.

If you have discrete values, set up a column of these values in your spreadsheet for the bin range and specify this range in the *Bin Range* field. For numerical data that have

FIGURE 6.14
Excel *Histogram*
Dialog

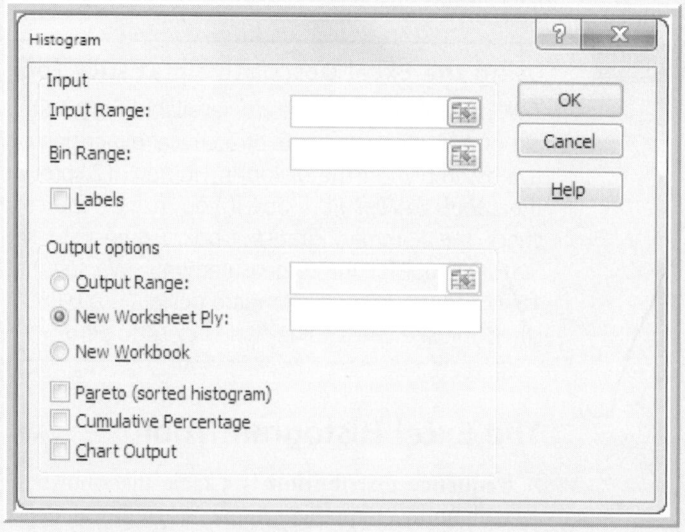

a many different discrete values with little repetition or are continuous, define bins by specifying

1. the number of bins,
2. the width of each bin, and
3. the upper and lower limits of each bin.

It is important to remember that the bins may not overlap so that each value is counted in exactly one group.

You should define the bins after examining the range of the data. Generally, you should choose between 5 to 15 bins, and the range of each should be of equal width. Sometimes you need to experiment to find the best number of bins that provide a useful visualization of the data. Choose the lower limit of the first bin (LL) as a whole number smaller than the minimum data value, and the upper limit of the last bin (UL) as a whole number larger than the maximum data value. Generally, it makes sense to choose nice, round whole numbers. Then you may calculate the group width as

$$\text{Group width} = (\text{UL} - \text{LL})/\text{Number of Groups} \qquad (6.20)$$

Check the *Chart Output* box to display a histogram in addition to the frequency distribution.

EXAMPLE 6.12

Using the Excel Histogram Tool

We will construct a frequency distribution and histogram for the U-bolt data using Excel's Histogram tool. Because the minimum value (from Figure 6.13) is 10.5 and the maximum value is 10.9, we chose the upper limit of the bins from 10.50 to 10.90 in increments of 0.05. Figure 6.15 shows the frequency distribution and histogram generated. We will use these results in another example later in this chapter.

FIGURE 6.15
Histogram for
U-Bolt
Measurements

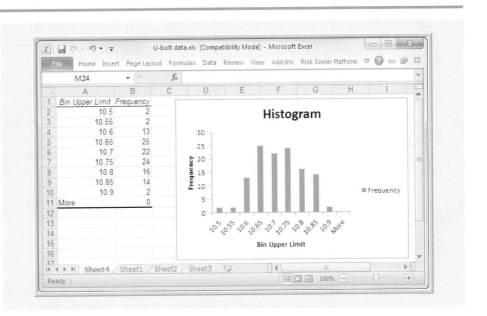

FIGURE 6.16   Frequency Distribution and Histogram Excel Template

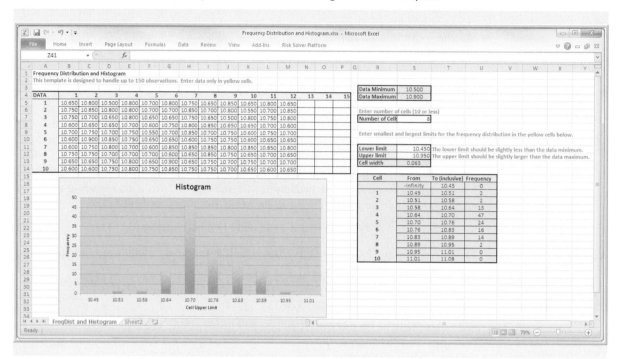

Frequency Distribution and Histogram Spreadsheet Template

One of the major disadvantages of the *Histogram* tool and most Excel *Data Analysis* procedures is that the results are not dynamically linked to the data. If you change the data or wish to use a different number of cells, you must run the tool again. As an alternative, we have created a simple spreadsheet template, *Frequency Distribution and Histogram.xlsx*, which allows you to create frequency distributions and histograms for up to 150 observations and experiment with different numbers of cells. This is shown in Figure 6.16 for the U-bolt data and is available on the Student Companion Site. Simply enter the data in the data matrix and also enter the number of cells and lower and upper limits for the histogram in the yellow cells in column S. The spreadsheet will automatically adjust the frequency distribution and histogram.

STATISTICAL INFERENCE

Statistical inference is concerned with drawing conclusions about populations based on sample data. To be able to make probability statements about the relationship between sample statistics and population parameters and draw inferences, we first need to understand sampling distributions.

Sampling Distributions

Sample statistics such as $\bar{x}$, s, and p are random variables that have their own probability distribution, mean, and variance. Thus, different samples will produce different estimates of the population parameters. These probability distributions are called sampling distributions. A **sampling distribution** is the distribution of a statistic for all possible samples of a fixed size. In quality, the sampling distributions of $\bar{x}$ and p are of the most interest.

Let us first consider the sampling distributions of $\bar{x}$. When using simple random sampling, the expected value of $\bar{x}$ is the population mean μ. The standard deviation of $\bar{x}$ (often called the **standard error of the mean**) is given by the formula

$$\sigma_{\bar{x}} = \frac{\sigma}{\sqrt{n}} \quad \text{for infinite populations or sampling with replacement from an infinite population} \tag{6.21}$$

$$\sigma_{\bar{x}} = \sqrt{\frac{N-n}{N-1}} \frac{\sigma}{\sqrt{n}} \quad \text{for finite populations} \tag{6.22}$$

When $n/N \leq 0.05$, $\sigma_{\bar{x}} = \sigma/\sqrt{n}$ provides a good approximation for finite populations.

We also need to characterize the probability distribution of $\bar{x}$. If the true population distribution is unknown, the Central Limit Theorem (CLT) can provide some useful insights:

If simple random samples of size n are taken from any population having a mean μ and a standard deviation of σ, the probability distribution of the sample mean approaches a normal distribution with mean μ and standard deviation (standard error) $\sigma_{\bar{x}} = \frac{\sigma}{\sqrt{n}}$ as n becomes very large. In more precise mathematical terms: As $n \to \infty$ the distribution of the random variable $z = (\bar{x} - \mu)/(\sigma/\sqrt{n})$ approaches that of a standard normal distribution.

The power of the central limit theorem can be seen through computer simulation using the *Quality Gamebox* software.[5] Figure 6.17 shows the results of sampling from a triangular

---

FIGURE 6.17   Illustration of the Central Limit Theorem

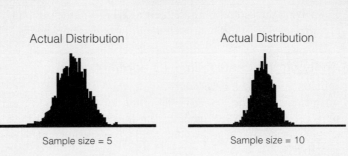

distribution for sample sizes of 1, 2, 5, and 10. For samples as small as five, the sampling distribution begins to develop into the symmetric bell-shaped form of a normal distribution. Also observe that the variance decreases as the sample size increases. The approximation to a normal distribution can be assumed for sample sizes of 30 or more. If the population is *known* to be normal, the sampling distribution of $\bar{x}$ is normal for any sample size.

EXAMPLE 6.13

Using the Sampling Distribution of the Mean

The mean length of shafts produced on a lathe has historically been 50 inches, with a standard deviation of 0.12 inch. If a sample of 36 shafts is taken, what is the probability that the sample mean would be greater than 50.04 inches?

The sampling distribution of the mean is approximately normal with mean 50 and standard error of $0.12/\sqrt{36} = 0.02$. Thus,

$$z = \frac{\bar{x} - \mu}{\sigma/\sqrt{n}} = \frac{50.04 - 50}{0.12/\sqrt{36}} = 2.0$$

The z-value of 2.0 yields the cumulative probability $P(z < 2.0) = P(\bar{x} < 50.04) = 0.9772$. This may also be found using the Excel function NORM.DIST(50.04,50,0.02,TRUE). Therefore, $P(z > 2.0) = P(\bar{x} > 50.04) = 1 - 0.9772 = 0.0228$. Thus, the probability that the mean of a sample of 36 items is greater than 50.04 inches is only 0.0228. The applicability of sampling distributions to statistical quality is that "shifts" in the population mean can quickly be detected using small representative samples to monitor the process.

Similarly, if a sample size of 64 is used, the standard error of the sampling distribution is $0.12/\sqrt{64} = 0.015$ and

$$z = \frac{\bar{x} - \mu}{\sigma/\sqrt{n}} = \frac{50.04 - 50}{0.015} = 2.67$$

and $P(z > 2.67) = P(\bar{x} > 50.04) = 0.0038$. As the sample size increases, it is less likely that a mean value of at least 50.04 will be observed purely by chance.

Next, consider the sampling distribution of p, the sample proportion. The expected value of p is π, the population proportion. The standard deviation of p is

$$s_p = \sqrt{\frac{\pi(1 - \pi)}{n}} \tag{6.23}$$

for infinite populations. For finite populations, or when $n/N \geq 0.05$, modify s_p by

$$s_p = \sqrt{\frac{N - n}{N - 1}}\sqrt{\frac{\pi(1 - \pi)}{n}} \tag{6.24}$$

In applying the central limit theorem (CLT) to p, the sampling distribution of p can be approximated by a normal distribution for large sample sizes.

EXAMPLE 6.14

Applying the Central Limit Theorem

Fabulous Flavors, Inc. produces soft drink flavorings and has historical data on process performance. Specifically, data collected over a long period of time shows that, on average, 15 percent of the batches produced did not meet specifications. If 35 batches are tested, what is the probability that 9 or fewer batches will be rejected?

The sampling distribution of p has a mean of $\pi = 0.15$ and a standard deviation

$$s_p = \sqrt{\frac{\pi(1-\pi)}{n}} = \sqrt{\frac{(0.15)(0.85)}{35}} = 0.06$$

The sample proportion is $p = 9/35 = 0.25714$. Using the Central Limit Theorem to assume normality because the sample size is relatively large, the probability of rejecting 9 or fewer batches can be found using the Excel function NORM.DIST(0.2574,0.15, 0.06,TRUE) = 0.963. We may calculate the exact probability using the binomial distribution function BINOM.DIST(9,35,0.15,TRUE) = 0.9708.

Confidence Intervals

A **confidence interval (CI)** is an interval estimate of a population parameter that also specifies the likelihood that the interval contains the true population parameter. This probability is called the *level of confidence*, denoted by $1 - \alpha$, and is usually expressed as a percentage. For example, we might state that "a 90 percent CI for the mean is 10 ± 2." The value 10 is the point estimate calculated from the sample data, and 2 can be thought of as a margin for error. Thus, the interval estimate is [8, 12]. However, this interval may or may not include the true population mean. If we take a different sample, we will most likely have a different point estimate, say 11.4, which results in the interval estimate [8.4, 12.4]. Again, this interval may or may not include the true population mean. If we chose 100 samples, leading to 100 different interval estimates, we would expect that 90 percent of them—the level of confidence—would contain the true population mean. We would say we are 90 percent confident that the interval we obtain from sample data contains the true population mean. Commonly used confidence levels are 90, 95, and 99 percent; the higher the confidence level, the more assurance we have that the interval contains the true population parameter. As the confidence level increases, the confidence interval becomes larger to provide higher levels of assurance.

Some common confidence intervals are

Confidence interval for the mean, standard deviation known, sample size $= n$:

$$\bar{x} \pm z_{\alpha/2}\sigma/\sqrt{n} \qquad (6.25)$$

Confidence interval for the mean, standard deviation unknown, sample size $= n$:

$$\bar{x} \pm t_{\alpha/2,\, n-1}\left(s/\sqrt{n}\right) \qquad (6.26)$$

Confidence interval for a proportion, sample size $= n$:

$$p \pm z_{\alpha/2}\sqrt{\frac{p(1-p)}{n}} \qquad (6.27)$$

The Student Companion Site provides an Excel workbook Confidence Intervals.xlsx with worksheet templates formulas (6.25) through (6.27).

Confidence intervals may be computed for other population parameters such as the variance and also for differences in means or proportions of two populations. Some advanced software packages and spreadsheet add-ins provide additional support. We encourage you to consult a comprehensive statistical reference.

EXAMPLE 6.15

Computing a Confidence Interval with a Known Population Standard Deviation

A laboratory in a hospital is required to ensure that the temperature in their sterilizer stays at an average of at least 100°C. Over an extended period of time, the population standard deviation has been shown to be stable at $\sigma = 0.5$. Find the 95 percent confidence interval for the population mean if a sample of 36 readings was taken, and the sample mean was found to be $\bar{x} = 100.3$.

Using formula (6.24), we compute the confidence interval as

$$\bar{x} \pm z\frac{\sigma}{\sqrt{n}} = 100.3 \pm 1.96\left(\frac{0.5}{\sqrt{36}}\right) = 100.3 \pm 0.1633 = 100.1367 \text{ to } 100.4633$$

This shows that the temperature of the sterilizer has a mean that exceeds 100°C and meets their requirements. Figure 6.18 shows the application of the Excel template *Population Mean Sigma Known* in the *Confidence Intervals* workbook.

EXAMPLE 6.16

Computing a Confidence Interval with an Unknown Population Standard Deviation

Suppose that for the same situation as in Example 6.15, the population standard deviation is unknown, and a sample of $n = 16$ was taken. The sample standard deviation was found to be $s = 0.7$. Find the 95 percent confidence interval for the population mean if the sample mean was found to be $\bar{x} = 100.3$.

Using formula (6.25), we compute the confidence interval as

$$\bar{x} \pm t\frac{s}{\sqrt{n}} = 100.3 \pm 2.131\left(\frac{0.7}{\sqrt{16}}\right) = 100.3 \pm 0.3730 = 99.9270 \text{ to } 100.6730$$

In this case, it would not be guaranteed that the temperature of the sterilizer would be expected to stay above 100 degrees C., with 95 percent confidence. Figure 6.19 shows the application of the Excel template *Population Mean Sigma Unknown* in the *Confidence Intervals* workbook.

FIGURE 6.18
Confidence Interval
Template for the
Population Mean,
Sigma Known

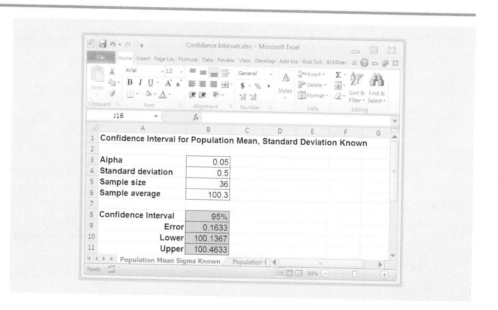

FIGURE 6.19
Confidence Interval
Template for the
Population Mean,
Sigma Unknown

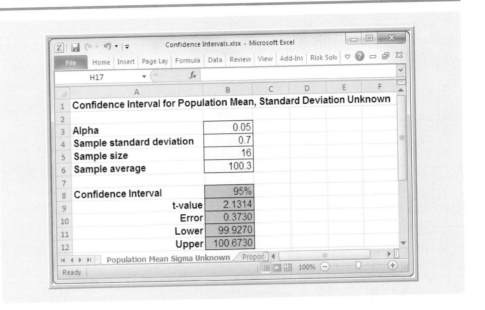

| EXAMPLE 6.17 | **Computing a Confidence Interval for a Proportion** |

A marketing research firm sampled the preferences of 200 potential buyers to determine if they would buy their client's e-reader or a rival brand. The sample showed that 42 percent of the potential customers preferred the client's brand. The client would like to be 99 percent confident of the percentage of customers who would purchase their brand. Formula (6.26) applies here. The confidence interval is

$$p \pm z\sqrt{\frac{p(1-p)}{n}} = 0.42 \pm 2.5758\sqrt{\frac{0.42(0.58)}{200}} = 0.42 \pm 0.0899 = 0.3301 \text{ to } 0.5099$$

This shows that the client can be 99 percent confident, based on this sample, that between 33 percent and 51 percent of the potential customers are likely to buy their e-reader. Figure 6.20 shows the application of the Excel template *Proportion* in the *Confidence Intervals* workbook.

Hypothesis Testing

Hypothesis testing involves drawing inferences about two contrasting propositions (hypotheses) relating to the value of a population parameter, one of which is assumed to be true in the absence of contradictory data (called the *null hypothesis*), and the other which must be true if the null hypothesis is rejected (called the *alternative hypothesis*). For instance, suppose that a company is testing a prototype process that is designed to reduce manufacturing cycle time. They can evaluate the proposed process by testing the null hypothesis that the mean cycle time of the prototype process is the same as the mean of the current process against the alternative hypothesis that the mean cycle time of the prototype process is different from the mean of the current process.

FIGURE 6.20
Confidence Interval
Template for the
Proportion

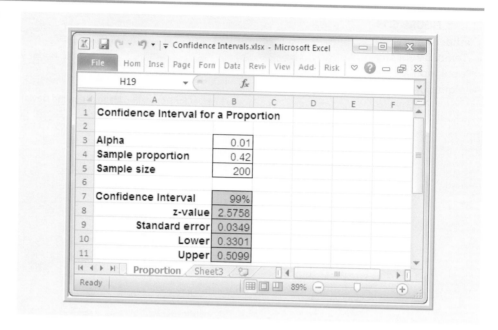

FIGURE 6.20
Confidence Interval
Template for the
Proportion

A hypothesis test involves the following steps:

1. Formulate the hypotheses to test.
2. Select a level of significance.
3. Determine a decision rule on which to base a conclusion.
4. Collect data and calculate a test statistic.
5. Apply the decision rule to the test statistic and draw a conclusion.

The *level of significance* (α) defines the risk that we are willing to take in making the incorrect conclusion that the alternative hypothesis is true when in fact the null hypothesis is true. Commonly used levels for α are 0.10, 0.05, and 0.01. The decision to reject or fail to reject H_0 is based comparing the value of the test statistic to a "critical value" from the sampling distribution of the test statistic based on the null hypothesis and the chosen level of significance. The sampling distribution of the test statistic is usually the normal distribution, *t*-distribution, or some other well-known distribution. For example, the test statistic for a one-sample test for the mean with an unknown population standard deviation is

$$t = \frac{\bar{x} - \mu_0}{s/\sqrt{n}} \tag{6.28}$$

where μ_0 is the hypothesized mean of the unknown population. The sampling distribution of this statistic has a t distribution with $n-1$ degrees of freedom. (For large samples, when n $\geq$ 30, a normal distribution is often used as an approximation.) As another example, the test statistic for a one-sample test for the proportion is

$$z = \frac{p - \pi_0}{\sqrt{\pi_0(1 - \pi_0)/n}} \tag{6.29}$$

where π_0 is the hypothesized population proportion. The sampling distribution of this statistic is a standard normal distribution. Test statistics for other types of tests may be found in comprehensive books on statistics.

The critical value divides the sampling distribution into two parts, a *rejection region* and a *nonrejection region*. If the null hypothesis is false, it is more likely that the test statistic will fall into the rejection region. If it does, we reject the null hypothesis; otherwise, we fail to reject it. The rejection region is chosen so that the probability of the test statistic falling into it if H_0 is true is the probability of a Type I error, α. For a one-tailed test, the rejection region is either in the upper or lower tail with probability α; for a two-tailed test, the rejection region is in both tails. Usually, each tail has an area of $\alpha/2$.

EXAMPLE 6.18

Conducting a Hypothesis Test for the Mean

A producer of computer-aided design software for the aerospace industry receives numerous calls for technical support. Tracking software is used to monitor response and resolution times. The company has a service standard of four days for the mean resolution time. However, the manager of the technical support group has been receiving some complaints of long resolution times. During one week, a sample of 44 customer calls resulted in a sample mean of 5.23 and standard deviation of 13.5. Even though the sample mean exceeds the four-day standard, does the manager have sufficient evidence to conclude that the mean service time exceeds four days, or is this simply a result of sampling error?

The hypothesis tested is

H_0: Mean response time ≤ 4

H_1: Mean response time > 4

The appropriate test statistic is formula (6.29) with $\mu_0 = 4$:

$$t = \frac{\bar{x} - 4}{s/\sqrt{n}}$$

Because this is a one-tailed test, the critical value is $t_{n-1,\ \alpha}$. Using a level of significance of 0.05, $t_{43,\ .05} = 1.6811$. Because this is an upper-tailed test, the decision rule is to reject H_0 if $t > 1.6811$. We compute the value of the test statistic as

$$t = \frac{\bar{x} - 4}{s/\sqrt{n}} = \frac{5.23 - 4}{13.5/\sqrt{44}} = \frac{1.24}{2.035} = 0.609$$

Therefore, we cannot reject the null hypothesis and the manager can conclude that there is insufficient statistical evidence that the mean response time exceeds 4. The Excel function T.INV(*probability, deg_freedom*) may be used to calculate the critical value. In this case, T.INV(0.05, 43) = 1.6811.

Because the sample size exceeds 30, we could have used the normal distribution instead of the t-distribution to find the critical value. In this case, NORM.S.INV(0.95) = 1.645, which closely approximates the true t-value.

An alternative approach to comparing a test statistic to a critical value in hypothesis testing is to find the probability of obtaining a test statistic value equal to or more extreme than that obtained from the sample data when the null hypothesis is true. This probability is commonly called a **p-value**, or **observed significance level**. To draw a conclusion, compare the p-value to the chosen level of significance α; whenever $p < \alpha$, reject the null hypothesis, otherwise fail to reject it. P-values make it easy to draw conclusions about hypothesis tests and are usually provided by statistical software.

Two-sample tests have wide applicability in quality to test differences between populations. However, the test statistics for two-sample tests are more complicated.

Fortunately, the Excel *Data Analysis Toolpak* has procedures for conducting several types of two-sample hypothesis tests. These are summarized below:

Type of Test	Excel Procedure
Two-sample test for means, σ^2 known	Excel *z*-test: Two-Sample for Means
Two-sample test for means, σ^2 unknown, unequal	Excel *t*-test: Two-Sample Assuming Unequal Variances
Two-sample test for means, σ^2 unknown, assumed equal	Excel *t*-test: Two-Sample Assuming Equal Variances
Paired two-sample test for means	Excel *t*-test: Paired Two-Sample for Means
Two-sample test for equality of variances	Excel *F*-test Two-Sample for Variances

---

EXAMPLE 6.19

Using Excel Hypothesis Testing Tools

A company's purchasing manager has observed some differences in the lead time for orders placed with two major suppliers, Bryant Products and Elgin Metals. A sample of orders (Figure 6.21) showed that the average lead time for Bryant Products was 7.00 days, while that for Elgin Metals was 4.92 days. Therefore, he would like to test the hypothesis

$$H_0: \mu_1 - \mu_2 \geq 0$$
$$H_1: \mu_1 - \mu_2 < 0$$

where μ_1 = mean lead time for Bryant Products and μ_2 = mean lead time for Elgin Metals. Rejecting the null hypothesis suggests that the lead time for Bryant Products is statistically better than Elgin Metals. However, if we cannot reject the null hypothesis, then even though the mean lead time for Elgin Metals is smaller, the difference would most likely be due to sampling error and we could not conclude that there is a statistically significant difference.

To conduct the hypothesis test for comparing the lead times, select *t-test: Two-Sample Assuming Unequal Variances* from the *Data Analysis* menu. The dialog is shown in Figure 6.22. The dialog prompts you for the range of the data for each variable, hypothesized mean difference, whether the ranges have labels, and the level of significance α. If you leave the box *Hypothesized Mean Difference* blank or enter zero, the test is for equality of means. In this example, the *Variable 1* range defines the lead times for Bryant Products, and the *Variable 2* range for Elgin Metals.

Figure 6.23 shows the results from the tool. The tool provides information for both one-tailed and two-tailed tests. Because this is a lower-tailed, one-tailed test, we need only use the one-tail information in the output. You must be *very careful* in interpreting the output information from these Excel tools and apply the following rules:

a. If the test statistic is negative, the one-tailed *p*-value is the correct *p*-value for a lower-tail test; however, for an upper-tail test, you must subtract this number from 1.0 to get the correct *p*-value.

b. If the test statistic is nonnegative (positive or zero), then the *p*-value in the output is the correct *p*-value for an upper tail test; but for a lower tail test, you must subtract this number from 1.0 to get the correct *p*-value.

c. For a lower tail test, you must change the sign of the one-tailed critical value.

For this example, *t Stat* is positive and we have a lower-tailed test; therefore using the rules, the correct *p*-value is calculated as $1 - 0.00166 = 0.99834$. Based on this alone, we

FIGURE 6.21 Supplier Lead Time Data (Excel file *Supplier Comparison.xlsx*)

Supplier	Order Date	Arrival Date	BP Lead Time		Supplier	Order Date	Arrival Date	EM Lead Time
Bryant Products	10/15/12	10/20/12	5		Elgin Metals	10/01/12	10/06/12	5
Bryant Products	10/20/12	10/27/12	7		Elgin Metals	10/03/12	10/08/12	5
Bryant Products	08/08/12	08/14/12	6		Elgin Metals	10/09/12	10/14/12	5
Bryant Products	09/01/12	09/10/12	9		Elgin Metals	10/07/12	10/12/12	5
Bryant Products	09/05/12	09/12/12	7		Elgin Metals	10/05/12	10/11/12	6
Bryant Products	10/25/12	11/03/12	9		Elgin Metals	10/15/12	10/20/12	5
Bryant Products	10/29/12	11/04/12	6		Elgin Metals	10/05/12	10/10/12	5
Bryant Products	10/10/12	10/17/12	7		Elgin Metals	09/25/12	09/30/12	5
			7.00		Elgin Metals	08/25/12	08/28/12	3
					Elgin Metals	09/05/12	09/09/12	4
					Elgin Metals	09/27/12	10/03/12	6
					Elgin Metals	10/25/12	10/30/12	5
					Elgin Metals	09/29/12	10/04/12	5
								4.92

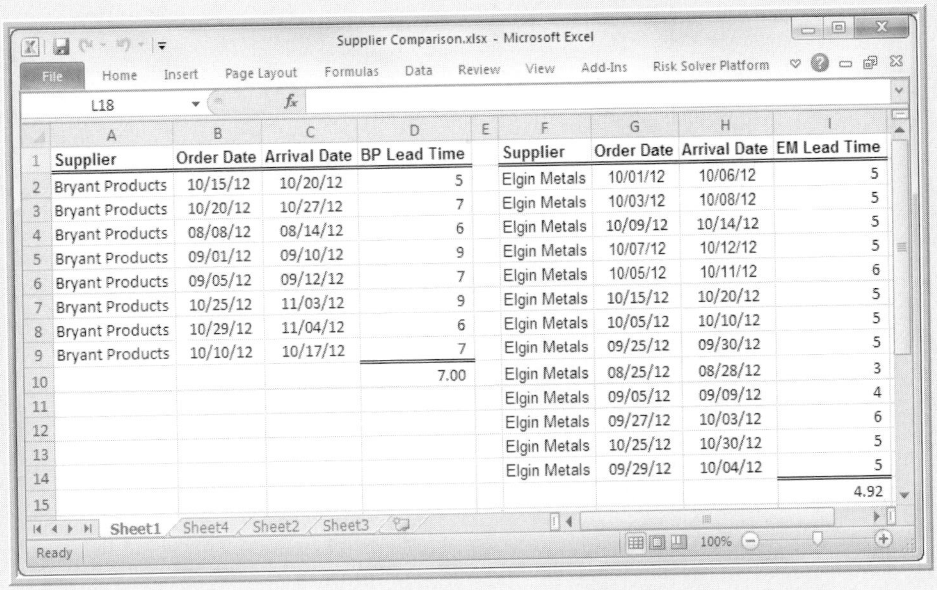

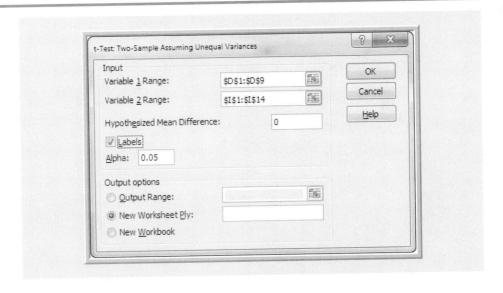

FIGURE 6.22
Excel t-Test Dialog

cannot reject the null hypothesis and must conclude that Bryant Products has a statistically higher average lead time than Elgin Metals. We may draw the same conclusion by comparing the value of *t Stat* with the critical value *t Critical one-tail*. Since this is a lower tail test, the correct value of *t Critical one-tail* should be negative, or – 1.812. Comparing this with the value of *t Stat*, we would only reject H_0 if *t Stat* < *t Critical one-tail*. Since *t Stat* is not less than *t Critical one-tail*, we do not reject the null hypothesis.

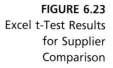

FIGURE 6.23

Excel t-Test Results for Supplier Comparison

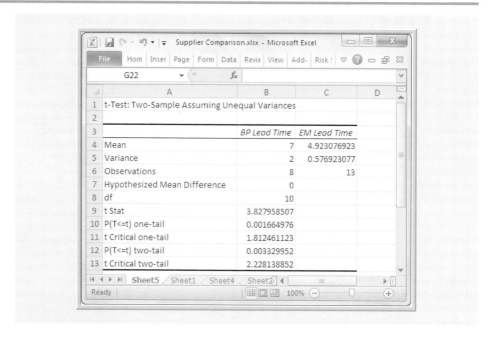

Analysis of Variance (ANOVA)

Analysis of Variance, or **ANOVA**, is a hypothesis-testing methodology for drawing conclusions about equality of means of multiple populations. In its simplest form—one-way ANOVA—we are interested in comparing means of observed responses of several different levels of a single factor. ANOVA tests the hypothesis that the means of all populations are equal against the alternative hypothesis that at least one mean differs from the others. To make this determination, ANOVA partitions the total variability of the data into two parts: the variation between groups and the variation within groups. If the total variation between groups is relatively small compared with the variation within groups, it suggests that the populations are essentially the same. A relatively large variation between groups, however, suggests that differences exist in the unknown population means. The variation in the data is computed as a sum of squared (SS) deviations from the appropriate sample mean, and scaled as a variance measure, or "mean square" (MS). By dividing the mean square between groups by the mean square within groups, an F statistic is computed. If this value is larger than a critical value, F_{crit}, then the data suggest that a difference in means exist.

Microsoft Excel provides a simple procedure to conduct a one-way ANOVA. Select *ANOVA: Single Factor* from the *Data Analysis* options. In the dialog box that pops up, enter the input range of the data in your spreadsheet and check whether it is stored in rows or columns.

EXAMPLE 6.20   Using the Excel ANOVA Tool

Megalife Batteries manufactures lithium batteries for notebook computers. The quality analyst for the company wants to test three battery designs to determine if one is better than the others as measured by the length of discharge time. The analyst wishes to test the hypothesis that the mean discharge time is the same for all designs versus the alternate hypothesis that at least one mean is different at a 0.05 significance level. The following values were obtained by testing 5 batteries for each design.

Process A	Process B	Process C
8.4	8.8	8.0
8.1	7.8	7.0
8.3	8.9	7.5
6.8	8.0	6.9
8.3	8.8	8.0

The Excel tool, ANOVA: *Single Factor* provides the results in Figure 6.24. Comparing the calculated $F = 3.631048$, with the critical value $F_{crit} = 3.885294$, we see that we cannot reject the hypothesis, and we must conclude that there is no significant difference between the three battery designs. Likewise, the *P-value* = 0.058461 is larger than the significance level of 0.05, which leads to the same conclusion. Even had ANOVA concluded that a difference in means exists, it would not tell us precisely which means differ from one another; other statistical tests are available to do this, but they are beyond the scope of this book.

Regression and Correlation

Regression analysis is a tool for building statistical models that characterize relationships between a dependent variable and one or more independent variables, all of which are numerical. A regression model that involves a single independent variable is called *simple regression*. A regression model that involves several independent variables is called *multiple regression*. Linear regression—which assumes a linear relationship between the independent and dependent variables—is the most common application. To verify linearity,

FIGURE 6.24
ANOVA Results using Excel ANOVA: Single Factor Tool

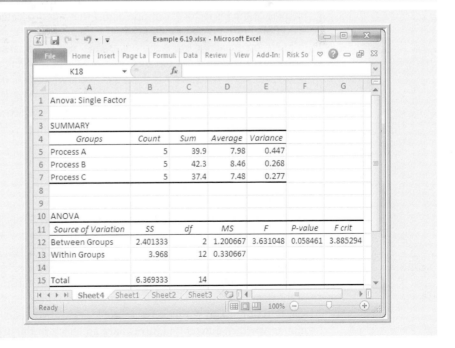

we recommend that you first plot the data on a scatter chart to determine if linear regression applies.

Correlation is a measure of a linear relationship between two variables, X and Y, and is measured by the (population) correlation coefficient. Correlation coefficients will range from -1 to $+1$. A correlation of 0 indicates that the two variables have no linear relationship to each other. Thus, if one changes, we cannot reasonably predict what the other variable might do by using a linear equation (we might, however, have a well-defined nonlinear relationship). A correlation coefficient of $+1$ indicates a perfect positive linear relationship; as one variable increases, the other will also increase. A correlation coefficient of -1 also shows a perfect linear relationship, except that as one variable increases, the other decreases. The square of the correlation coefficient, R^2, is called the *coefficient of determination*, and measures the proportion of the variation in the dependent variable that is explained by the independent variable(s).

Regression is a complex topic, and we assume that you have prior familiarity with the basic concepts and theory. Microsoft Excel has a *Data Analysis* tool for conducting simple or multiple linear regression. We will illustrate a simple application in quality.

EXAMPLE 6.21

Using the Excel Regression Tool

We will use a common issue in quality that we will discuss again in a later chapter—ensuring that instruments are properly calibrated. In principle, it is a simple matter to check calibration. One connects the instrument to a known source, such as an extremely accurate voltage generator to check a voltmeter, or a use precision gauge block with known dimensions to check a micrometer. A reading is then obtained to determine whether the instrument accurately measures the known variable. In practice, numerous sources of variation in the process may make calibration difficult.

The data in Figure 6.25 represent actual readings obtained from the calibration of a voltmeter versus the standard source readings from an accurate voltage generator. The source readings were purposely not set in even integer increments so as to minimize possible bias of the inspector taking the actual readings. To determine whether the instrument is accurate, we can develop a regression equation for the data. Using the *Regression* tool in Microsoft Excel, we input the data range and characteristics shown in Figure 6.26 and we obtain the results shown in Figure 6.27. The estimated regression equation is $Y = 0.0265 + 0.9914\,X$, where Y is the actual reading and X is the true voltage generated.

The value of R^2 is 0.9999, indicating an excellent fit. Note also that the value of the intercept is close to 0 and the slope is close to 1, which is where they should be. We would conclude that the instrument is in near perfect calibration, as the line fit plot in Figure 6.27 also indicates.

Design of Experiments

Design of experiments (DOE), developed by R. A. Fisher in England, dates back to the 1920s. A **designed experiment** is a test or series of tests that enables the experimenter to compare two or more methods to determine which is better or determine levels of controllable factors to optimize the yield of a process or minimize the variability of a response variable.[6] DOE differs from observational statistical studies in that the factors of interest are controlled by the experimenter, rather than simply observed through the selection of random samples. For example, a paint company might be interested in determining whether different additives have an effect on the drying time of paint in order to

FIGURE 6.25
Voltmeter
Calibration Data

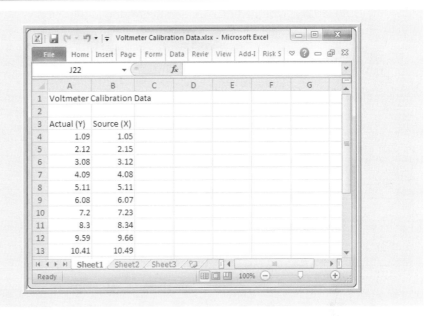

FIGURE 6.26
Regression Tool
Dialog

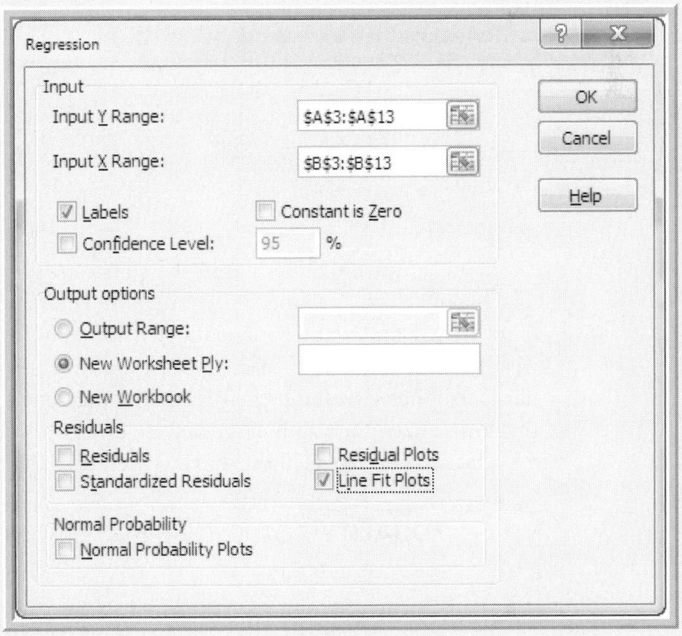

FIGURE 6.27 Voltmeter Calibration Regression Results

	A	B	C	D	E	F	G	H	I	J	K
1	SUMMARY OUTPUT										
2											
3	*Regression Statistics*										
4	Multiple R	0.999967043									
5	R Square	0.999934087									
6	Adjusted R Square	0.999925848									
7	Standard Error	0.027282724									
8	Observations	10									
9											
10	ANOVA										
11		*df*	*SS*	*MS*	*F*	*Significance F*					
12	Regression	1	90.33725522	90.337255	121364.43	5.1612E-18					
13	Residual	8	0.005954776	0.0007443							
14	Total	9	90.34321								
15											
16		*Coefficients*	*Standard Error*	*t Stat*	*P-value*	*Lower 95%*	*Upper 95%*	*Lower 95.0%*	*Upper 95.0%*		
17	Intercept	0.02648404	0.018447595	1.4356364	0.1890278	-0.01605619	0.0690243	-0.0160562	0.06902427		
18	Source (X)	0.991364042	0.002845689	348.37398	5.161E-18	0.98480187	0.9979262	0.98480187	0.99792621		
19											
20											
21											
22	RESIDUAL OUTPUT										
23											
24	*Observation*	*Predicted Actual (Y)*	*Residuals*								
25	1	1.067416284	0.022583716								
26	2	2.15791673	-0.03791673								
27	3	3.119539851	-0.039539851								
28	4	4.071249331	0.018750669								
29	5	5.092354294	0.017645706								
30	6	6.044063774	0.035936226								
31	7	7.194046063	0.005953937								
32	8	8.294460149	0.005539851								
33	9	9.603060685	-0.013060685								
34	10	10.42589284	-0.015892839								

select the additive that results in the shortest drying time. As another example, suppose that two machines produce the same part. The material used in processing can be loaded onto the machines either manually or with an automatic device. The experimenter might wish to determine whether the type of machine and the type of loading process affect the number of defectives and then select the machine type and loading process combination that minimizes the number of defectives. As a practical tool for quality improvement, experimental design methods have achieved considerable success in many industries.

 QUALITYSPOTLIGHT

Rich Products Corporation

Rich Products Corporation, set out to develop an all natural bread dough that would meet the same quality and taste standards as the company's popular conventional bread doughs.[7] Nearly all frozen bread dough products use chemicals like oxidizers, emulsifiers, and reducing agents to maintain strength after being frozen, thawed, and baked. The few frozen bread doughs that have been introduced with all natural ingredients have not been successful; consumers were not happy with product quality, and the doughs suffered from short frozen shelf life. A food scientist at the company identified a number of possible natural ingredients, and then used DOE to optimize the amount of each ingredient in order to meet specified requirements for flavor, appearance, and softness, among other qualities. Each sample was evaluated based on 10 different responses. Four of the responses were objective and included volume, length, the height of the bread after baking, and the width of the bread after baking. A panel of taste testers subjectively evaluated the other responses. They considered overall likability, crust flavor, crumb flavor, softness, cell size, and crumb density. Based on manufacturability and cost, he identified the best recipe formed the basis of the company's new line of bread doughs.

Historically, experimental design was not widely used in industrial quality improvement studies because engineers had trouble working with the large number of variables and their interactions on many different levels in industrial problems. However, improved computer software and the widespread application of Six Sigma have made experimental design an important tool for quality.

One of the most common types of experimental designs is called a **factorial experiment**. In a factorial experiment, all combinations of levels of each factor are considered. The simplest type of factorial experiment is one with two factors at two levels. This would result in $2^2 = 4$ possible combinations to test. In general, an experiment with m factors at k levels would have k^m combinations. Each combination of different levels of the factor is called a **treatment**. Often the factor levels are designated as "high" or "low." Thus in a 2^2 factorial experiment, we could designate the treatments as:

Treatment	Factor 1	Factor 2
A	Low	Low
B	High	Low
C	Low	High
D	High	High

Often, multiple observations are taken for each treatment combination to account for sampling error. Each combination should be performed in a random fashion to eliminate any potential systematic bias.

EXAMPLE 6.22

Calculating Main Effects in a DOE

Suppose that temperature and reaction time are identified as important factors in the yield of a chemical process. Currently the process operates at a temperature of 100°C and a 60-minute reaction time. In an effort to reduce costs and improve yield, the plant manager wants to determine if changing the temperature to 120°C and reaction time to 75 minutes will have any significant effect on the percent yield and, if so, to identify the best levels of these factors to optimize the yield.

For this experiment we have four different treatment combinations:

Treatment	Temperature	Time
A	100°C (low)	60 minutes (low)
B	120°C (high)	60 minutes (low)
C	100°C (low)	75 minutes (high)
D	120°C (high)	75 minutes (high)

For instance, treatment A corresponds to setting the temperature at 100° and the reaction time at 60 minutes.

The purpose of a factorial experiment is to estimate the effects of each factor and any possible interaction. A **main effect** measures the difference that a factor has on the response. For instance, what is the effect of increasing the temperature regardless of the value of the reaction time? Or, what is the effect of increasing the reaction time regardless of the temperature? These questions are answered easily by finding the differences of the averages at each level. A main effect is calculated as follows:

Main effect = (Average response at high level) − (Average response at low level) (6.30)

EXAMPLE 6.23

Calculating Main Effects in a DOE

Using the information from Example 6.22, suppose we obtained the following results (with two observations for each treatment):

Treatment	Temperature	Time	Yield (%)
A (low, low)	100°C	60 minutes	84
B (high, low)	120°C	60 minutes	90.5
C (low, high)	100°C	75 minutes	88.5
D (high, high)	120°C	75 minutes	81

The main effects are calculated as follows:

$$
\begin{aligned}
\text{Temperature main effect} &= (\text{Average yield at high level}) - (\text{Average yield at low level}) \\
&= (90.5 + 81)/2 - (84 + 88.5)/2 \\
&= 85.75 - 86.25 = -0.5 \text{ percent}
\end{aligned}
$$

$$
\begin{aligned}
\text{Reaction time main effect} &= (\text{Average yield at high level}) - (\text{Average yield at low level}) \\
&= (88.5 + 81)/2 - (84 + 90.5)/2 \\
&= 84.75 - 87.25 = -2.5 \text{ percent}
\end{aligned}
$$

From these results, we might conclude that increasing either the temperature or reaction time decreases the yield of the process and that increasing both from their low to high levels would decrease yield by 0.5 + 2.5 = 3.0 percent. However, we can add main effects in this fashion *only* if interactions are not present. An **interaction** is the effect of changing one factor has on the level of other factors. Interaction describes a dependency between one factor and the other. For example, increasing factor 1 when factor 2 is at the low level might result in an increase in the response variable; however, increasing factor 1 when factor 2 is at the high level might result in a decrease in the response variable. When no interaction exists, then we would see a similar change in the response when factor 1 is increased no matter what the level of factor 2.

We may quantify the interaction by taking the average of difference of the response (yield) when the factors are both at the high or low levels and subtracting the average difference of the response when the factors are at opposite levels:

Interaction effect = (Average response with both factors at the same level)
−(Average response with both factors at opposite levels) (6.31)

The closer this quantity is to zero, the smaller the interaction effect.

EXAMPLE 6.24

Calculating Interaction Effects in a DOE

In our example, we see that if the temperature is held constant at 100°, an increase in reaction time results in a higher yield. However, when the temperature is 120°, an increase in reaction time decreases the yield. The interaction between temperature and time is computed as:

$$\text{Temperature} \times \text{Time interaction} = (\text{Average yield, both factors at same level})$$
$$- (\text{Average yield, both factors at opposite levels})$$
$$= (84 + 81)/2 - (90.5 + 88.5)/2 = -7.0 \text{ percent}$$

In this case, a significant interaction is apparent. Interaction measures how much influence the reaction time has on temperature. For example, the main effect of temperature was found to be −0.5 percent. Because the interaction is −7.0 percent, the effect of temperature will vary from its average value of −0.5 percent by plus or minus −7 percent as the level of reaction time changes. Thus, if we examine the results where time is fixed at its high level (treatments B and D), the average difference in yield by increasing the temperature is 81 − 88.5 = −7.5 percent—that is, the main effect of −0.5 percent plus the interaction of −7.0 percent. If we look at the results where reaction time is fixed at its low level, the average difference in yield by increasing the temperature is 90.5 − 84 = 6.5 percent. This is the same as subtracting the interaction effect from the main effect—that is, −0.5 − (−7.0) = 6.5 percent. Our conclusion is that a combination of higher temperature and lower time appear to optimize the yield.

> *The Student Companion Site provides an Excel template, 2x2 Factorial Experiment.xlsx, for analyzing a 2^2 factorial experiment. The template also constructs a chart to illustrate the interaction effect.*

Figure 6.28 shows the results for the chemical process example we have been discussing. Each line of the interaction plot shows the response for Factor 1 when Factor 2 is held at either the low or high level. If the lines are nearly parallel, then no interaction exists. If the lines are somewhat, but not quite, parallel, then we have a mild interaction. If the lines have opposite slopes, then a strong interaction exists. In this case, we observe a strong interaction. When interactions are present, we *cannot* estimate response changes by simply adding main effects; the effect of one factor must be interpreted relative to levels of the other factor.

Factorial experiments can be applied to any number of factors and levels. For example, a 3-factor DOE with 2 levels would have $2^3 = 8$ treatments:

Treatment	Factor 1	Factor 2	Factor 3
A	Low	Low	Low
B	High	Low	Low
C	Low	High	Low
D	High	High	Low
E	Low	Low	High
F	Low	High	High
G	Low	High	High
H	High	High	High

Main effects and interactions are calculated in the same fashion using formulas (6.30) and (6.31). The Student Companion Site also has an Excel template for 2^3 factorial experiments (*2x3 Factorial Experiment.xlsx*).

FIGURE 6.28
Excel Template for Factorial Experiment

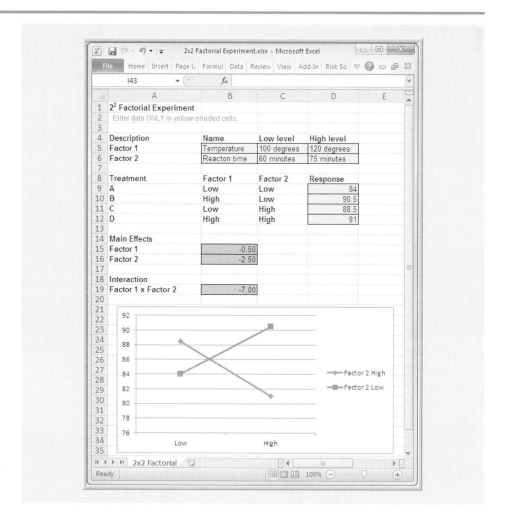

Classical design of experiments can require many, often costly, experimental runs to estimate all main effects and interactions. A Japanese engineer, Dr. Genichi Taguchi, proposed another approach to DOE. He developed an approach to designing experiments that focused on the critical factors while deemphasizing their interactions, which greatly reduced the number of required experiments. However, Taguchi's approach violates some traditional statistical principles and has been criticized by the statistical community.[8] To add to the shortcomings of his approach, Taguchi introduced some statistically invalid and misleading analyses, ignored modern graphical approaches to data analysis, and failed to advocate randomization in performing the experiments. Even though many of these issues are subject to debate, numerous companies have used Taguchi's approaches effectively.

SUMMARY OF KEY POINTS AND TERMINOLOGY

The Student Companion Site provides a summary of key concepts and terminology introduced in this chapter.

Improving Quality of a Wave Soldering Process Through Design of Experiments[9]

A Printed Circuit Assembly-Encoder (PCA-Encoder) is a critical component for the base carriage assembly for a printer. The PCA-Encoder is produced by putting the electronic components on printed circuit boards (panels) that contain eight small boards, and then soldering the components using a wave soldering process. Any defect in any of the solder joints will lead to the failure of the circuit. Thus, it is important to ensure that soldering is defect-free. Typical soldering defects are blowholes (insufficient solder) and bridges (solder between two joints). At a Hewlett-Packard India, Ltd., plant in Bangalore, India, a high level of soldering defects was observed, necessitating 100 percent inspection for all circuit boards. Any defects identified required manual rework, which consumed much time.

A study was undertaken to optimize the wave soldering process for reducing defects, thereby eliminating the inspection stage after the process. The quality engineers conducted a detailed study on the solder defects to understand what aspects of the wave soldering process might affect the resulting quality. These were identified as

1. Conveyor speed
2. Conveyor angle
3. Solder bath temperature
4. Solder wave height
5. Vibration of wave
6. Preheater temperature
7. Air knife
8. Acid number (solid content in the flux), which is difficult to control because of environmental conditions

The engineers decided to use experimental design because of the long time frame required to adjust process parameters by trial and error, and the lack of insight into the possible joint effects of different parameters. Based on discussions with technical personnel, seven factors at three levels were selected for the experiment, as shown in Table 6.1. Conveyor speed and conveyor angle were fixed. A full factorial experiment would take 1,458 trials to conduct, which was not deemed to be practical. From statistical theory in the design of experiments, the seven main

TABLE 6.1   Factors and Levels for Experimentation

Factor	Code	Level 1	Level 2	Level 3
Bath temperature (°C)	A	248[a]	252	
Wave height[b]	B	4.38	4.40[a]	4.42
Over heated preheater (OH-PH) (PH-1)	C	340	360[a]	380
Preheater-1 (PH-1) (°C)	D	340	360[a]	380
Preheater (PH-2) (°C)	E	340	360[a]	380
Air knife	F	0	3[a]	6
Omega[c]	G	0	2[a]	4

[a]Existing level.
[b]The wave height is measured as the rpm of the motor pumping the solder.
[c]Omega refers to the vibration of the solder wave.

effects could be estimated by conducting only 18 trials as shown in Table 6.2. The experimental outcomes (response) were the number of defective solder joints in a frame (352 joints). Each experiment was repeated three times.

Using analysis of variance, it was observed that bath temperature, wave height, and omega had a significant effect on the soldering defects. By setting the factors at the optimum levels identified through the experiments, the predicted defect level was 1,670 ppm as opposed to the current rate of more than 6,000 ppm. However, the predicted average and the result of a confirmatory experiment were not sufficient to eliminate inspection completely, so additional experimental designs were conducted to reduce defects.

TABLE 6.2   Data Corresponding to the First Experiment

Exp. No.	(1) Bath Temp. (°C)	(2) Wave Height	(3) OH-PH (°C)	(4) PH-2 (°C)	(5) PH-1 (°C)	(6) Air Knife	(7) Omega	Response 1	2	3
1	248	4.38	340	340	340	0	0	1	2	1
2	248	4.38	360	360	360	3	2	0	2	0
3	248	4.38	380	380	380	6	4	0	1	0
4	248	4.40	340	340	360	3	4	1	0	1
5	248	4.40	360	360	380	6	0	4	2	0
6	248	4.40	380	380	340	0	2	8	1	6
7	248	4.42	340	360	340	6	2	2	4	3
8	248	4.42	360	380	360	0	4	4	1	0
9	248	4.42	380	340	380	3	0	2	2	4
10	252	4.38	340	380	380	3	2	1	3	1
11	252	4.38	360	340	340	6	4	1	2	1
12	252	4.38	380	360	360	0	0	6	3	2
13	252	4.40	340	360	380	0	4	3	3	4
14	252	4.40	360	380	340	3	0	4	3	8
15	252	4.40	380	340	360	6	2	2	1	1
16	252	4.42	340	380	360	6	0	2	7	3
17	252	4.42	360	340	380	0	2	2	1	3
18	252	4.42	380	360	340	3	4	4	2	1

Source: Copyright 2000 From Quality Improvement Through Design of Experiments: A Case Study by Kalyan Kumar Chowdhury, E.V. Gigo, and R. Raghavan. Reproduced by permission of Taylor & Francis Group, LLC. (http://www.tandfonline.com).

FIGURE 6.29   Solder Defects After Experimental Design Optimization

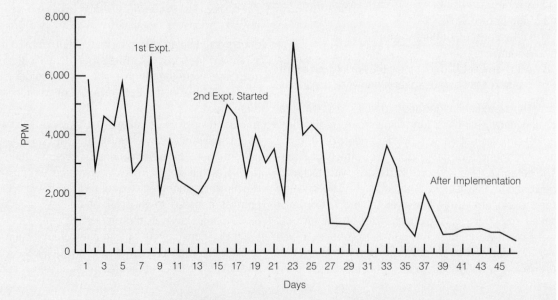

The next experiment considered the results of the first experiment and some of the uncontrollable factors. However, the different levels of the significant factors from the first experiment were selected in such a way that the new levels were allowed to vary around the optimum level of the first experiment. Based on the results of these additional experiments, new optimum levels of factors were identified and implemented with significant improvements. Figure 6.29 shows the parts per million level during the course of the experimentation, which took only 45 days.

Key Issues for Discussion

1. Why did the first experimental design not find the true optimum combination of factors to achieve the maximum reduction of defects?
2. What were some of the advantages of using experimental design over a traditional trial-and-error approach?

QUALITY *in* PRACTICE

Applying Statistical Analysis in a Six Sigma Project at GE Fanuc[10]

In mid-2002 a team at the GE Fanuc manufacturing plant in Charlottesville, Virginia, led by Six Sigma Black Belt Donald Splaun was given the go-ahead to investigate Black Belt Project #P52320. The objective of the project was to evaluate Printed Wire Board (PWB) Fabricated Board Finishes to determine if the high-priced nickel-gold (Ni-Au) finished boards that were being used were necessary as mounting platforms for fine pitch surface-mounted devices (SMDs) or for fine-pitched Ball Grid Array (BGA) electronic controller boards. SMDs are electronic components, such as microprocessors, that are placed on the top of electronic circuit boards (fabricated boards) and then have their electrical wire leads soldered into place. Fine pitch SMDs don't have much space between their electrical wire leads, making it difficult to put just the right amount of solder on them to make the proper electrical connect to the circuit boards on which they are mounted. The completed boards with all components properly mounted on them are then used in electrical assemblies to control the operations of industrial machinery.

Splaun had seven people on his analysis team, plus a financial representative to verify the dollar costs and savings; a Master Black Belt reviewer, who would evaluate the project to prevent obvious gaps in the analysis; and perhaps most importantly from a managerial standpoint, a Champion/Sponsor, who would ensure project visibility and that resources were allocated to complete the project. Team members and their job functions were:

Team Members, Titles, and Functions

Team Leader and Black Belt

Process engineer and fabricated board expert

Advanced manufacturing engineer responsible for SMD board assembly

Sourcing agent who purchases the boards

Test engineer who tests and evaluates boards

Producibility engineer who works with design teams

Production line operator who runs boards

Supplier quality analysis technician responsible for incoming board quality

Outside Resources

Financial representative to assist in cost calculations

Champion/Sponsor

Reviewer and Master Black Belt

The team developed their charter to define the problem and working relationships. The problem clearly and succinctly stated as: *GE Fanuc currently specifies Ni-Au on fine-pitch SMD and BGA boards. The purpose of this project is to evaluate if this specification is necessary.*

The team also identified tools and databases that were to be used in the study, not only to ensure that everyone was working from a common source, but also to take advantage of the training that had been provided to team members. The tools included two statistical/spreadsheet software packages

(Minitab and Excel) and a plant-wide integrated database (SAP) that contained information on board characteristics, usage, specifications, costs, and so on.

Based on a 29-step process flowchart, it was decided that the analysis would require the use of a moderately complex experimental design. This design was required to determine the effects of supplier differences and finishes, because relatively few defects were being observed in manufacturing the boards. Data would have to be gathered from the experiment and from supplier surveys to help the team track potential causes that could have a bearing on the functionality and cost of each of the alternative boards or board materials being considered.

The experiment was designed to sample and test 288 CX3A1 boards:

- 96 hot air solder leveled (HASL) boards, 32 from each supplier
- 96 nickel-gold (Ni-Au) boards, 32 from each supplier
- 96 silver (Ag) boards, 32 from each supplier and to evaluate three suppliers

The three suppliers were:

- Vendor G, Singapore/China (one or two GE Fanuc production suppliers)
- Vendor P, Taiwan/China (second major GE Fanuc supplier)
- Vendor D, USA (current prototype/fast turn supplier)

The team identified 13 characteristics (Xs, or independent variables) that were considered important to measure during the experiment for each of the three finish types (Ys, or dependent variables). The primary hypothesis was that no significant differences in numbers of defects would be incurred, regardless of finish. In addition, a hypothesis that no significant interaction effects existed between suppliers, coatings, and any of the 13 characteristics considered essential for quality board functioning was investigated. The data collection and analysis process consisted of eight carefully defined steps conducted over a six-day period, involving almost $37,500 worth of boards and hard-to-measure production delays while the test boards were run on what is normally high speed, highly automated production machines.

TABLE 6.3　　Typical ANOVA Output for Vendor and Finish Analysis

Solder Skips, Analysis All
Two-Way Analysis of Variance
Analysis of Variance for Wave Solder Skips

Source	DF	SS	MS	F	P
Vendors	2	36.55	18.27	15.27	0.000
Finish	2	16.44	8.22	6.87	0.001
Interaction	4	23.39	5.85	4.89	0.001
Error	279	333.94	1.20		
Total	287	410.32			

Process Variable Averages	
Manufacturers	**Mean Number of Defects**
Vendor C	0.03
Vendor D	0.80
Vendor G	0.06
Finish	
HASL	0.271
Ni-Au	0.021
Silver	0.604

After the data were collected, numerous ANOVA computer runs were made to pinpoint problem areas and test hypotheses. It was especially important to test the capabilities of each of the three types of board finishes to determine whether they were equivalent to the current, and very expensive, Ni-Au finished boards. It was also necessary to get some data to prove or disprove hypotheses about supplier capabilities as well. Table 6.3 shows a typical computer printout and analysis of one of the 13 variables that was tested, called "Wave Solder Skips."

Of 15 ANOVA analysis runs performed on the 13 experimental variables that were measured, eight showed no significance, primarily because those variables had zero defects. Other findings included:

- Ni-Au boards are not significantly different from or better than horizontally processed HASL or Silver Boards for fine pitch SMD processing, therefore the firm can save money by switching from Ni-Au to HASL or Silver.
- The company should not use Vendor D for production. Results and suggestions for improvement of their prototype quality should be discussed with them.
- Ni-Au is worse for wave soldering, based on a defect measure of "insufficient solder fill."

- Vendor G was found to have an issue with a defect measure of "GR False Failures" (to be reviewed with the supplier).
- The GE Fanuc PWB Fab Specifications should be changed to reflect these conclusions.

From these analyses, the summary conclusion was that GE Fanuc did not need nickel-gold boards for fine pitch SMD.

The estimated savings from this project ranged from 7.1 percent on two-layer boards to 22.8 percent on four-layer boards, with an average of 14.3 percent savings on these 89 board types, and total estimated savings of $190,000 per year.

Key Issues for Discussion

1. Why did the experimental design have to be so complex? Why were so many individuals involved in this project?
2. What might have been some contributing factors that caused the company to select the Ni-Au over the cheaper boards in the past?
3. For Table 6.3, what can you conclude, given the F values and the p-values in the table? What steps should the team take, regarding use of vendors and further testing for this particular independent variable?

REVIEW QUESTIONS

1. What is the science of statistics? Why is it important in quality management?
2. Explain the difference between an experiment, an outcome, and a sample space.
3. State the four rules for calculating probabilities of events.
4. Explain the multiplication rule of probability. How does independence of events affect the multiplication rule?
5. List the most important types of probability distributions used in quality management.
6. How do discrete probability distributions differ from continuous probability distributions?
7. List and explain the three basic elements of statistical methodology.
8. Describe the common types of sampling schemes.

9. What is the difference between sampling error and systematic error? Why are these important to understand?
10. Explain the difference between a population and a sample.
11. List the common types of statistical measures of location and explain how to compute them.
12. List the common types of statistical measures of dispersion and explain how to compute them.
13. Explain how to compute a proportion.
14. Explain the difference between the standard deviation and the standard error of the mean. How are they related?
15. State the meaning of the central limit theorem in your own words. How important is it to the development and use of statistical quality control techniques?

16. What are some of the descriptive statistical tools available in Microsoft Excel, and how can they be used?

17. What is a confidence interval? What value do they have?

18. Describe some applications of hypothesis testing that might be applied to the topics in Chapters 3, 4, and 5.

19. Explain the hypothesis that is tested in analysis of variance.

20. Describe some applications of regression and correlation that might be applied to the topics in Chapters 3, 4, and 5.

21. What is the purpose of design of experiments?

22. Describe a factorial experiment. Provide some examples of factorial experiments that you might use to solve some type of quality-related problem.

PROBLEMS

Note: Data sets for many problems in this chapter are available in the Excel workbook C06Data.xlsx on the Student Companion Site. Click on the appropriate worksheet tab as noted in the problem (e.g., Prob. 6-1) to access the data. In addition, the spreadsheet templates illustrated in the chapter are also available to aid in solving many of these problems.

1. A new production process at Fabulast, Inc. has two in-line stages. The probability of defective components being produced in stage 1 is 15 percent and 10 percent in stage 2. Assembled units that have defective components only from stage 1 OR only from stage 2 are considered repairable. However items that have defective components from both stage 1 and stage 2 (completely defective) must be scrapped.

    a. Use a probability tree diagram and calculate the probabilities that the Fabulast assembled units are: (i) defective in stage 1 and defective in stage 2 (are completely defective); (ii) defective in stage 1 and are not defective in stage 2 (called Repairable I); (iii) not defective in stage 1 but are defective in stage 2 (called Repairable II); and (iv) not defective in stage 1 and are not defective in stage 2 (completely good). What is the probability of producing repairable assembled units?

    b. Explain the results in terms of the multiplication and the addition rules for probability.

2. Auditors at the Numeros Verdes Partners, P.S.C. took a sample of 200 accounts payable bills, as shown in the table found in the Excel worksheet *Prob. 6-2* in the Excel workbook *C06Data.xlsx*.

    a. Find the proportion of the accounts payable in the sample that are classified as overdue by using the Excel COUNTIF function.

    b. If an auditor takes a random sample of only 10 accounts from this population, assuming that they follow a binomial distribution, what is the probability that: (i) exactly 5 bills will be overdue? (ii) 4 or fewer bills will be overdue? (iii) 6 or more bills will be overdue? Use the binomial probability distribution formula and verify your result using Excel *Binomial* spreadsheet template.

3. The Turkuman Rug Company buys medium grade carpet in 100-foot rolls. The average number of defects per roll is 1.8. Assuming that these data follow a Poisson distribution, use the *Poisson* spreadsheet template to answer the following questions.

    a. What is the probability of finding exactly 7 defects in a carpet roll chosen at random?

    b. What is the probability of finding 4 or fewer defects in a carpet roll?

4. Southwestern Punch was made by Frutayuda, Inc. and sold in 12-ounce cans to benefit victims of Hurricane Zero. The mean number of ounces placed in a can by an automatic fill pump is 11.7 with a standard deviation of 0.18 ounce. Assuming a normal distribution, determine the probability that the filling pump will cause an overflow in a can, that is, the probability that more than 12 ounces will be released by the pump and overflow the can.

5. Los Alamos Green Tea is sold in 500 milliliter bottles. The standard deviation for the filling process is 7 milliliters. What must the target mean for the process be to ensure that the probability of

overfilling more than 500 ml in a bottle is at most 1 percent?

6. Kiwi Oil is sold in 950 milliliter (ml) cans. The mean volume of oil placed in a can is 920 ml with a standard deviation of 12 ml. Assuming a normal distribution of the data, what is the probability that the filling machine will cause an overflow in a can, that is, the probability that more than 950 ml will be placed in the can?

7. Wayback Cleaning Co. has found that standard size offices have a standard deviation of 5 minutes for their cleaning time. The operations manager knows that 95 percent of the offices require more than 120 person-minutes to clean. However, she wishes to find out the average cleaning time for the offices. Can you calculate that for her?

8. The mean time to pour and process 5 cubic yards of concrete by the Piedra Cretebuilders Co. is 15.5 minutes. If 2 percent of the projects with 5 yards of concrete require more than 15.75 minutes, what is the standard deviation of the time for such projects?

9. The dimension of a machined part has a nominal specification of 11.9 cm. The process that produces the part can be controlled to have a mean value equal to this specification, but has a standard deviation of 0.05 cm. What is the probability that a part will have a dimension
   a. exceeding 12 cm?
   b. between 11.9 and 11.95 cm?
   c. less than 11.83 cm?

10. Genjeteye, Inc. makes aircraft engines. The mean time to failure has been found to be 100,000 hours and is exponentially distributed.
    a. What is the failure rate, λ, per hour?
    b. What is the cumulative probability of failure after 10,000 hours or fewer? Between 10,000 and 15,000 hours?
    c. If Genjeteye wishes to provide a warranty that no more than 5 percent of the units will fail, how many hours of operation without failure should the company guarantee?

11. Use the data for Twenty-first Century Laundry for the weights of loads of clothes processed through their washing department in a week. (See *Prob. 6-11* in *C06Data* workbook.)
    a. Apply the Excel *Descriptive Statistics* tool to compute the mean, standard deviation, and other relevant statistics, and interpret the results in a meaningful fashion.

b. Use the *Frequency Distribution and Histogram* Excel template to construct a frequency distribution and histogram for the data. From what type of distribution might you suspect the data are drawn? Experiment with the number of cells to create a visually appealing histogram and use the Excel *Histogram* tool to verify the results.

12. The times for carrying out a blood test at Rivervalley Labs for 100 tests, found in the *Prob. 6-12*, in the *C06Data* Excel workbook, were studied in order to better understand the process. Apply the *Descriptive Statistics* tool to compute summary statistics and explain the results. Also, construct a frequency distribution and histogram, for the data taken from set. From what type of distribution might you suspect the data are drawn?

13. The data for *Prob. 6-13* found in *C06Data* Excel workbook shows the weight of a set of castings (in kilograms) being made in the Fillmore Metalwork foundry. Construct an Excel spreadsheet to compute the mean and standard deviation using formulas (6.15) and (6.19). Verify your results using Excel functions.

14. A warehouse manager at Wherehousing, Inc. maintains a large inventory of video games. The company's database states that the mean value of the games in inventory is $50, with a standard deviation of $5. The manager is concerned about pilfering the more expensive games by the warehouse employees. She picked a random sample of 100 games and found the mean value to be $48.50. Assuming a normal distribution, what is the probability that the sample mean would be $48.50 or less if all the inventory can actually be accounted for? What conclusions would you reach?

15. The distribution center manager at Internet distributor CyberAuto Warehouse wants to find a confidence interval for the average time required for an associate to fill an order for shipment. A sample of 16 orders is taken and the mean time was found to be 8.5 minutes, with a standard deviation of 2.8 minutes. Compute 95 percent and 99 percent confidence intervals. Which one is larger? Explain why.

16. A new product is being tested by Zed Electronics to determine if it will continue to operate in a stable fashion under a variety of conditions. A sample of 400 items were tested, and 60 failed the test.

Determine a 90 percent confidence interval for the population proportion.

17. Tessler Electric utility requires service operators to answer telephone calls from customers in an average time of 0.1 minute or less. A sample of 25 actual operator times was drawn, and the results are given in the following table. In addition, operators are expected to determine customer needs and either respond to them or refer the customer to the proper department within 0.5 minute. Another sample of 25 times was taken for this job component and is also given in the table. If these variables can be considered to be independent, are the average times taken to perform each component statistically different from the standards?

Component	Mean Time	Standard Deviation
Answer	0.1023	0.0183
Service	0.5290	0.0902

18. A quality manager at Newvis Pharmaceutical Company is monitoring a process that fills vials with a liquid medication designed to prevent glaucoma in the eyes of the user. The company wants to ensure that each vial contains at least 60 mL (2.03 fluid oz.) of the product. A sample of 25 vials is tested, and a mean of 63 mL and a sample standard deviation of 10 mL are found. The quality manager wishes to test the null hypothesis that vials contain less than or equal to 60 mL using an $\alpha = 0.05$ significance level (rejecting this hypothesis provides evidence that the vials contain the required amount). Conduct the test and explain your results.

19. The quality manager at Newvis Pharmaceutical Company is certifying a new process that must produce 90 percent (or better) good product before certification can be completed. A sample of 49 containers from the process line are tested, and 87 percent are found to be good. Formulate the appropriate hypotheses and test them using an $\alpha = 0.05$ significance level. Explain your results.

20. Rabbitfoot Community Bank makes a large number of home equity loans each year. The vice president of loan administration wishes to determine if their time for paperwork processing is lower than the average time of their top competitor. A sample of 30 loans taken at Rabbitfoot Bank yielded a mean of 38.10 minutes and a standard deviation of

2.58 minutes (see the data in the *Ch06Data* Excel workbook). Data obtained from competitor of 36 applications indicates that the average time for processing an application is 39.48 minutes, with a standard deviation of 2.48 minutes.

a. Verify the calculation of the mean, standard deviation, and variance for each set of data using the *Descriptive Statistics* tool.

b. Test the null hypothesis that his bank's processing time is greater than or equal to the competitor's average, versus the alternative hypothesis that the bank's time is less than the competitor at the 5 percent significance level. Use the *z-Test: Two Sample Assuming Equal Variances* from the *Data Analysis* menu in Excel.

21. Softswift, a software developer, is trying to determine if any of three potential subcontractors has better programmers in order to outsource a development project. The three subcontractors agreed to test 5 programmers, using a standardized test provided by Softswift, as provided in the data in the *Ch06Data* Excel workbook. Use the single factor ANOVA Excel tool to determine if there is a significant difference between the scores of programmers at the three contractors at the 5 percent level.

22. At Rockglass, Inc. a kiln is used to bake ceramic pottery. The production manager wishes to determine the relationship between temperature and brittleness, so he takes measurements of the brittleness of test items versus the temperature of the oven. Use the Excel *Regression* tool to determine the regression equation and the R^2 value. Explain the output. If the oven is heated to 975°C, what would you predict that the brittleness measure will be?

23. The process engineer at Sival Electronics was trying to determine whether three suppliers would be equally capable of supplying the mounting boards for the new "gold plated" components that she was testing. The table found in the worksheet *Prob. 6-23* in the Excel workbook *C06Data* shows the coded defect levels for the suppliers, according to the finishes that were tested. Lower defect levels are preferable to higher levels. Using ANOVA, analyze these results. What conclusion can be reached?

24. A quality analyst at Paintfast Manufacturing Co. wants to determine if a new paint formulation,

used to paint parts for a customer's assembly operation will dry fast enough to meet the customer's needs. The customer would prefer to obtain a high level of "dryability" at low temperatures, even if it requires a higher level of drying agent. He hypothesizes that a high level of drying agent will result in high dryability, high temperature—alone—will result in a moderately high level of dryability, and low temperature or a low level of drying agent will result in a low level of dryability. He hopes that the main and interaction effects with the temperature, which is expensive (because an oven would need to be used), will be minimal. The data found in the worksheet *Prob. 6-24* in the Excel workbook *C06Data* were gathered in testing all combinations. What recommendation would you make?

25. The process engineer at Sival Electronics is also trying to determine whether a newer, more costly design involving a gold alloy in a computer chip is more effective than the present, less expensive silicon design. She wants to obtain an effective output voltage at both high and low temperatures, when tested with high and low signal strength. She hypothesizes that high signal strength will result in higher voltage output, low temperature will result in higher output, and the gold alloy will result in higher output than the silicon material. She hopes that the main and interaction effects with the expensive gold will be minimal. The data found in the worksheet *Prob. 6-25* in the Excel workbook *C06Data* were gathered in testing of all combinations. What recommendation would you make?

PROJECTS, ETC.

1. Devise an experiment similar to the battery performance test case (see the Battery Experiment case that follows) to test different levels of some factor and conduct a statistical analysis of the results. Write up your experiment and results in a report along with the conclusions that you reach from the analysis. You might wish to consult the following paper: "101 Ways to Design an Experiment, or Some Ideas About Teaching Design of Experiments" by William G. Hunter, Technical Report No. 413 dated June 1975 at http://curiouscat.com/bill/101doe.cfm for some ideas.

2. Using one sheet of paper, design and build a helicopter. Some methods of making a paper helicopter can be found at: http://www.exploratorium.edu/science_explorer/roto-copter.html and http://www.faa.gov/education/student_resources/kids_corner/ages_13/paper_helicopter/

   Use design of experiments to evaluate and identify the best design that keeps the helicopter airborne for as long as possible.

CASES

SIZZLEGRILL BURRITO HOUSE

Sizzlegrill Burrito House is a small regional chain of quick service restaurants in the Midwest. They specialize in four types of burritos: chicken, beef, pork, and a bean-based vegetarian item. The burritos are made-to-order, so customers can add rice, cheese, guacamole, tomato, lettuce, and salsa to fill out the wrap. The burrito is then placed in a paper wrapper to ensure ease of handling and sanitary delivery to the customer.

Lately, one of the store managers, Juan Niceley, has been hearing customer complaints, ranging from

such comments as: "The tortilla wrap (bread) is too thin, it's breaking"; or "The food is not hot"; "Every time I get a burrito it seems to be a different size"; and "I got the wrong ingredients on my burrito." Juan knew that he needed to systematically survey his customers. Many complaints were submitted through the corporate website. Juan's district manager was most concerned with the comment on size. To be competitive, it is important that customers receive consistent food and service.

TABLE 6.4 Customer Survey Questions	Was the menu easy to read?
	Was order prepared correctly?
	Was the food tasty?
	Was the food served hot?
	Were employees courteous and polite?
	Was the restaurant clean?
	In your opinion, did you receive a good value for the price you paid?
	What was your level of satisfaction?
	How likely are you to dine with us again?
	How likely are you to recommend us to your friends/family?
	How often do you eat at Sizzlegrill? First time, less than once/month, 1-3 times a month, weekly?
	What was the main ingredient in your burrito: chicken, beef, pork, beans?

Juan knew Professor Evalind at the local university, who taught an MBA class in quality management. He told Juan that he was always looking for projects for his student teams. Juan decided to ask the professor if he would have a team of students design a customer survey, instruct his workforce on how to weigh and record burrito weights, gather customer comments, analyze the data, and make recommendations on what should be done to improve the operations of Sizzlegrill Burrito House.

The student team developed a survey using the questions in Table 6.4, based on a 5-point Likert scale [5 = excellent, or strongly agree; 1 = poor or strongly disagree] for the first 10 questions. The last two questions were coded as a 1, 2, 3, or 4. They administered the questionnaire to 25 random customers and gathered data on 150 burrito weights in samples of 3, each. See spreadsheet Ch06-Sizzlegrill Case.xlsx for the data.

Discussion Questions

1. What conclusions do you reach when you calculate descriptive statistics for the answers to each of the survey questions in the database?

2. If you average the responses to the first seven questions by customer, how closely are those averages correlated to the satisfaction score? Include a scatter chart in your analysis.

3. Can the likelihood of the customer dining again at Sizzlegrill be predicted by using the satisfaction score and regression analysis? How good is that prediction likely to be, based on the R^2 value?

4. Analyze the data on burrito weights using descriptive statistical measures such as the mean and standard deviation, and tools such as a frequency distribution and histogram. What do your results tell you about the consistency of the food servings?

5. What recommendations for decision-making and improvement can you make to Juan Niceley?

BERTON CARD COMPANY[11]

The Berton Card Company (BCC) is a manufacturer of playing cards and novelty cards for consumers and entertainment businesses. Playing cards are produced to individual specifications, which include the customer requirements of colors and patterns, and other quality characteristics that affect durability, such as thickness, stiffness, and smoothness or roughness. The production process consists of producing the paper stock by gluing rolls of paper together, printing the ink patterns on the continuous roll of paper stock, applying a coating to the sheets, drying the paper stock, cutting them into 22" by 26" sheets that contain an entire deck of cards, and finally cutting the sheets into individual cards that are boxed and shipped.

Coatings are applied by metal rollers that press against the paper stock, one for the face side and one for the backs of the cards. Each roller has two pressure settings, one high, and one low. BCC has recently installed a new roller to apply the coating, but needs to find the best possible settings for the line speed and pressure.

Technicians designed a 2^3 factorial design for three factors (line speed, front face pressure, and back pressure) at two levels (low and high) as summarized in Table 6.5. Operators ran eight experiments -- one for each combination of these three factors.

Samples of five sheets for each experiment were taken to a laboratory and the surface roughness was measured using a special machine. The data in the Ch06-BCC Case.xlsx Excel workbook on the Student Companion Site provides measurements of the surface roughness from the five randomly-selected sheets for each experiment, A higher value indicates

TABLE 6.5   Factors and Levels for Experimentation

Factors	Low	High
Line speed	1000 ft/min	1150 ft/min
Pressure – Front (Face)	900 psi	1000 psi
Pressure – Back	765 psi	800 psi

a higher level of roughness. For this particular customer, the specifications are between 7.0 and 9.0. Using whatever statistical calculations and methods that you feel are appropriate, analyze these data and prepare a report summarizing your conclusions along with a recommendation for controlling the line speed and pressure of the roller. Be sure to include appropriate charts that help explain your findings.

THE BATTERY EXPERIMENT[12]

Many one-tenth scale remote control (RC) model car racing enthusiasts believe that spending more money on high-quality batteries, using expensive gold-plated connectors, and storing batteries at low temperatures will improve battery life performance in a race. To test this hypothesis, an electrical test circuit was constructed to measure battery discharge under different configurations. Each factor (battery type, connector type, and temperature) was evaluated at two levels, resulting in $2^3 = 8$ experimental conditions, shown in Table 6.6.

Model race car enthusiasts are also interested in determining whether any significant differences exist between various brands of batteries. Understanding possible differences in battery performance could be a first step in examining whether connection or temperature has an effect on performance. Table 6.7 shows discharge times for three different brands of batteries, gathered through a measurement process.

TABLE 6.6
Experimental
Design for
Testing Battery
Performance

Experimental Run	Battery Type	Connector Type	Battery Temperature	Discharge Time (minutes)
1	High cost	Gold-plated	Ambient	493
2	High cost	Gold-plated	Cold	490
3	High cost	Standard	Ambient	489
4	High cost	Standard	Cold	612
5	Low cost	Gold-plated	Ambient	94
6	Low cost	Gold-plated	Cold	75
7	Low cost	Standard	Ambient	93
8	Low cost	Standard	Cold	72

TABLE 6.7 Battery Discharge Time Data by Brand

Observation	Brand		
	A	**B**	**C**
1	493	108	94
2	490	95	75
3	489	115	93
4	612	82	72

Discussion Questions

1. Use the data in Table 6.6 to find the main effects, interactions, and interaction plots for the three factors (use the Excel template *2x3 Factorial Experiment.xlsx* on the Student Companion Site). Thoroughly explain your results.
2. Use the data in Table 6.7 and the Excel *Data Analysis* tool to conduct an ANOVA to determine whether a significant difference exists between battery types. Explain the ANOVA output and your conclusions.

NOTES

1. J. M. Juran and Frank M. Gryna, Jr., *Quality Planning and Analysis*, 2nd ed. (New York: McGraw-Hill, 1980), 35.
2. Scott M. Paton, "Juran: A Lifetime of Quality: An Exclusive Interview with a Quality Legend," *Quality Digest*, August 2002, 19–23.
3. Thomas Pyzdek, "Non-Normal Distributions in the Real World," *Quality Digest*, December 1999, 36–41.
4. Arne Buthmann, "Dealing with Non-normal Data," *isixsigma magazine*, May–June 2009, http://digital.isix-sigma-magazine.com.
5. Quality Gamebox is a product of PQ Systems; further information is available at http://www.pqsystems.com/products/sixsigma/QualityGamebox/QualityGamebox.php.
6. Johannes Ledolter, and Claude W. Burrill, *Statistical Quality Control* (New York: John Wiley & Sons, 1999).
7. Jerry Fineman, "A Formula For Flavor Company Uses Statistics to Improve Taste of Its Bread Dough," *Food*

Quality (June/July 2009), http://www.foodquality.com/details/article/807869/A_Formula_For_Flavor.html (accessed 10/15/2011).
8. Joseph J. Pignatiello, Jr., and John S. Ramberg, "The Top 10 Triumphs and Tragedies of Genichi Taguchi," presented at the 35th ASQC/ASA Fall Technical Conference, Lexington, KY, 1991.
9. Kalyan Kumar Chowdhury, E.V. Gigo, and R. Raghavan, "Quality Improvement Through Design of Experiments: A Case Study," *Quality Engineering* 12, no. 3 (2000), 4072416. Copyright 2000 by Marcel Dekker, Inc.
10. Courtesy of Donald B. Splaun, Jr., Manager, Advanced Manufacturing Technology, GE-Fanuc, Inc.
11. We greatly appreciate the contribution of one of our former students, Stephen Berton, in preparing this case.
12. Eric Wasiloff and Curtis Hargitt, "Using DOE to Determine AA Battery Life," *Quality Progress*, March 1999, 67–71. © 1999, American Society for Quality. Reprinted with permission.

Design for Quality and Product Excellence

Companies today face incredible pressures to continually improve the quality of their products while simultaneously reducing costs, to meet ever-increasing legal and environmental requirements, and to launch new products faster to meet changing consumer needs and remain competitive. The ability to achieve these goals depends on a large extent on product design (by which we also imply *redesign*). Better designs not only reduce costs, but improve quality. For example, simpler designs have fewer components, which mean fewer points of failure and less chance of assembly error.[1]

Despite remarkable advances in manufacturing and service technology, businesses and consumers are still plagued with product failures or service upsets. Consumers don't receive the products they ordered, or are given inaccurate information. Thousands of people die from medical errors each year. Software that control most modern products are prone to failure.[2] Most of these problems fundamentally result from poor design or inadequate design processes. In 2011, for example, a fatal train crash on a high-speed railway in China killed 39 people and injured 192. An initial investigation showed that design flaws in railway signal equipment led to the collision. After being struck by lightning, the signal system at a railway station failed to turn one of its green lights to red, leaving railway staff unaware of the stalled train and leading to the collision.[3]

Although we tend to equate product design with manufactured goods, it is important to realize that design processes apply to services as well. For example, Citibank once designed a new mortgage approval procedure that reduced turnaround times from 45 to less than 15 days; FedEx has consistently developed new variations of its package delivery services.[4] Effective design processes are vital to meeting customer requirements, achieving quality, and innovation, as the Quality Profiles in this chapter suggest. In this chapter, we introduce some of the more important practices and tools that support quality design efforts.

quality**profiles**

Spicer Driveshaft and Poudre Valley Health System

Spicer Driveshaft, a former division of Dana Corporation, now Torque Traction Technologies, Inc., is one of the largest manufacturers of driveshafts and related components for light, medium, heavy duty, and off-highway vehicles. (This profile describes some practices of the company when it received the Baldrige Award in 2000.)

Customer Platform Teams are one of the focal points for identifying customer requirements and building and maintaining new business, product offerings, and customer relationships. These teams include sales, engineering, quality, and warranty personnel who use a variety of formal and informal methods to listen and learn from customers. All senior leaders are involved in a two-phase strategic planning process that addresses long-term direction and short-term objectives, which are linked and aligned from headquarters to the individual manufacturing plants. A comprehensive diversity plan is used to help develop candidates for promotion from within the organization, improve community involvement efforts, and establish a mentoring program.

Over a three-year period, sales increased by nearly 10 percent; economic value added increased from $15 million to $35 million; inventory as a percentage of sales decreased from 6.8 percent to 6.3 percent; and working capital decreased from 13 percent to 10.2 percent of sales. Internal defect rates decreased more than 75 percent. Employees were encouraged to develop and implement changes and innovative ideas and evaluate their results. Ideas submitted by employees averaged about three per month, and almost 80 percent of their ideas were implemented. The employee turnover rate was below 1 percent, which was better than the best competitor; and the attendance rate consistently remained above 98 percent.

Poudre Valley Health System (PVHS) is a locally owned and private, not-for-profit health care organization serving residents of northern Colorado, Nebraska, and Wyoming. PVHS designs new services using the Voice-of-the-Customer (VOC) approach. During the planning of the system's newest hospital, the Medical Center of the Rockies (MCR), community VOC data led to improved emergency room layout, private patient rooms with spectacular mountain views and windows that open, healing gardens, and installation of family amenities such as showers and kitchens.

Partnering relationships help PVHS focus on the future and turn competitors into allies. After first establishing relationships with physicians, PVHS expanded its partner base to include entities such as home health agencies, a long-term care provider, community health organizations, and a health plan administrator—a partnership that saves local employers $5 million each year. A partnership with a community hospital in Scottsbluff, NE, led to the building of MCR, which opened in February 2007. PVHS's partners are driving innovation by designing and testing innovative systems and technologies to meet health care needs. For example, PVHS was among the first health systems in the nation to use a robotic-assisted surgery system in four medical specialty areas and among the first 24 health systems in the world to integrate medical imaging systems across service lines.

From design of new services to bedside care, PVHS uses interdisciplinary teams to meet patient needs. These teams demonstrate "the best collaboration of nurses and doctors, relative to any trauma program in the United States," according to a recent survey team by the American College of Surgeons. In 2008, the system's overall staff voluntary turnover rate decreased to 8 percent, well below that of competitors, and reached the Healthcare Human Resources Administration's top 10 percent performance level. The system's overall employee satisfaction ranks at the 97th percentile nationally, and *Modern Healthcare* magazine named PVHS as one of "America's 100 Best Places to Work in Healthcare" in 2008. PVH has been recognized as the nation's number one hospital for sustained nursing excellence by the American Nurses Association and the National Database of Nursing Quality Indicators (NDNQI). For five consecutive years, PVH has been one of seven U.S. hospitals to be named a Thomson 100 Top Hospital (for superior outcomes, patient safety, and operational and financial performance).

Source: Adapted from Malcolm Baldrige National Quality Award, Profiles of Winners, National Institute of Standards and Technology, Department of Commerce.

PRODUCT DEVELOPMENT

Most companies have some type of structured product development process. The typical product development process, shown in Figure 7.1, consists of six phases:

1. *Idea Generation*: New or redesigned product ideas should incorporate customer needs and expectations. However, true innovations often transcend customers' expressed desires, simply because customers may not know what they like until they have it (think iPhone or iPad). Thus, idea generation often focuses on exciters and delighters as described in the Kano model in Chapter 3.
2. *Preliminary Concept Development*: In this phase, new ideas are studied for feasibility, addressing such questions as: Will the product meet customers' requirements? Can it be manufactured economically with high quality? Objective criteria are required for measuring and testing the attributes associated with these questions.
3. *Product/Process Development*: If an idea survives the concept stage—and many do not—the actual design process begins by evaluating design alternatives and determining engineering specifications for all materials, components, and parts. This phase usually includes prototype testing, in which a model (real or simulated) is constructed to test the product's physical properties or use under actual operating conditions, as well as consumer reactions to the prototypes. Concurrently, companies develop, test, and standardize the processes that will be used in manufacturing the product or delivering the service, which include selecting the appropriate technology, materials, and suppliers and performing pilot runs to verify results.

FIGURE 7.1
Structured Product
Development
Process

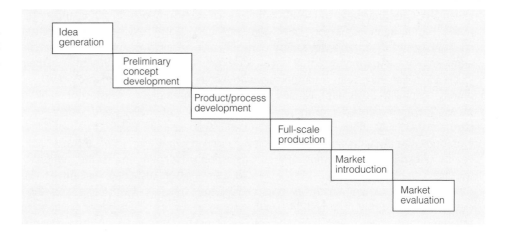

4. *Full-Scale Production*: Once the design is approved and the production process has been set up, the company releases the product to manufacturing or service delivery teams.
5. *Market Introduction*: The product is distributed to customers.
6. *Market Evaluation*: Deming and Juran both advocated an ongoing product development process that relies on market evaluation and customer feedback to initiate continuous improvements.

Many companies view customers and suppliers as significant partners in product development, and include them in planning and review meetings. Customer involvement enables them to integrate market evaluation throughout the process and early supplier involvement facilitates higher-quality purchased materials and components as well as improved supply chain management.

 QUALITYSPOTLIGHT

Caterpillar

Caterpillar implements its product development process using an approach called DMEDI (*define, measure, explore, design, implement*):

1. *Define Opportunities:* Understand the purpose of the process to be developed by goal statements, generation plans, and resource identification.
2. *Measure Customer Needs:* Understand the outputs required of the new process by examining customer needs and competitive analysis.
3. *Explore Design Concepts:* Use creative techniques to develop alternative concepts and evaluate those ideas by validating customer requirements.
4. *Develop Detailed Design:* Turn the concept into reality by the use of process and product designs, pilot programs, and testing.
5. *Implement Detailed Design:* Fully deploy the new process and assess its value against the desired outcome.

Concurrent Engineering

The importance of speed in product development cannot be overemphasized. To succeed in highly competitive markets, companies must churn out new products quickly. Nearly every industry is focused on reducing product development cycles. Whereas automakers once took as many as eight years to develop new models, most are now striving to do it within a year. Rapid product development demands the involvement and cooperation of many different functional groups within an organization, such as marketing, engineering, and manufacturing. Unfortunately, one of the most significant barriers to efficient product development is poor intra-organizational cooperation.

In many firms product development is accomplished in a serial fashion, as suggested in Figure 7.1. In the early stages of development, design engineers dominate the process. Later, the prototype is transferred to manufacturing for production. Finally, marketing and sales personnel are brought into the process. This approach has several disadvantages. First, product development time is long. Second, up to 90 percent of manufacturing costs may be committed before manufacturing engineers have any input to the design. Third, the final product may not be the best one for market conditions at the time of introduction.

Concurrent engineering is a process in which all major functions involved with bringing a product to market are continuously involved with product development from conception through sales. Such an approach not only helps achieve trouble-free introduction of products and services, but also results in improved quality, lower costs, and shorter product development cycles. Concurrent engineering involves multifunctional teams, usually consisting of 4 to 20 members and including every specialty in the company. The functions of such teams are to perform and coordinate the activities in the product development process simultaneously, rather than sequentially. For example, Boeing A&T has more than 100 integrated product teams (IPTs) that oversee the design, production, and delivery of the C-17 aircraft's more than 125,000 parts and supporting services. Developing a unique approach, AT&T established nine expert breakthrough teams—called Achieving Process Excellence Teams—that identify process improvements for developing and deploying products faster in the market. They establish standards, procedures, and training for cross-functional communication that prevents problems from occurring. At The Ritz-Carlton Hotel Company, customized hotel products and services, such as meetings and banquet events, receive the full attention of local hotel cross-functional teams. These teams involve all internal and external suppliers, verify production and delivery capabilities before each event, critique samples, and assess results.

Companies such as Apple and Jawbone (a producer of Bluetooth earpieces)—both on *Fast Company* magazine's list of the worlds 50 Most Innovative Companies—exploit concurrent engineering to achieve a competitive advantage.[5] Typical benefits of concurrent engineering include 30 to 70 percent less development time, 65 to 90 percent fewer engineering changes, 20 to 90 percent less time to market, 200 to 600 percent improvement in quality, 20 to 110 percent improvement in white collar productivity, and 20 to 120 percent higher return on assets.[6]

Design for Six Sigma

Design for Six Sigma (DFSS) represents a structured approach to product development and a set of tools and methodologies for ensuring that goods and services will meet customer needs and achieve performance objectives, and that the processes used to make and deliver them achieve high levels of quality. DFSS helps designers and engineers better translate customer requirements into design concepts, concepts into detailed designs, and detailed designs into well-manufactured goods or efficient services. Through good communication and early involvement in the product development process, this approach leads to reduced costs, better quality, and a better focus on the customer. DFSS is a complementary approach to Six Sigma methods for process improvement, which we will learn about in Chapter 9. Most tools used in DFSS have been around for some time; its uniqueness lies in the manner in which they are integrated into a formal methodology, driven by the Six Sigma philosophy, and with clear business objectives in mind.

DFSS consists of four principal activities:[7]

1. *Concept Development:* Concept development focuses on creating and developing a product idea and determining its functionality based upon customer requirements, technological capabilities, and economic realities.
2. *Detailed Design:* Detailed design focuses on developing specific requirements and design parameters such as specifications and tolerances to ensure that the product fulfills the functional requirements of the concept.
3. *Design Optimization:* Design optimization seeks to refine designs to identify and eliminate potential failures, achieve high reliability, and ensure that it can be easily manufactured, assembled, or delivered in an environmentally-responsible manner.
4. *Design Verification:* Design verification ensures that the quality level and reliability requirements of the product are achieved.

These activities are often incorporated into a process, known as **DMADV**, which stands for *define, measure, analyze, design,* and *verify. Define* focuses on identifying and understanding the market need or opportunity. *Measure* gathers the voice of the customer, identifies the vital characteristics that are most important to customers, and outlines the functional requirements of the product that will meet customer needs. *Analyze* is focused on concept development from engineering and aesthetic perspectives. This often includes the creation of drawings, virtual models, or simulations to develop and understand the functional characteristic of the product. *Design* focuses on developing detailed specifications, purchasing requirements, and so on, so that the concept can be produced. Finally, *Verify* involves prototype development, testing, and implementation planning for production.

General Electric was an early adopter of DFSS. For example, back in its 1998 annual report, GE stated that "Every new product and service in the future will be DFSS.... They were, in essence, designed by the customer, using all of the critical-to-quality performance features (CTQs) the customer wanted in the product and then subjecting these CTQs to the rigorous statistical Design for Six Sigma Process." One of the early applications of DFSS was at GE's Medical Systems Division. The Lightspeed Computed Tomography (CT) System was the first GE product to be completely designed and developed using DFSS. Lightspeed allows doctors to capture multiple images of a patient's anatomy simultaneously at a speed six times faster than traditional scanners. As a result, productivity doubled while the images had much higher quality.[8]

 QUALITYSPOTLIGHT

John Deere

John Deere Power Systems, headquartered in Waterloo, Iowa, designs and manufactures engines that meet stringent customer and regulatory standards. The company adopted DFSS in 2006 to help build its competitive position. In 2011, the Environmental Protection Agency (EPA) mandated extensive engine emission reductions, requiring them to emit 90 percent less particulate matter and 50 percent fewer nitrogen oxides. Meeting these standards requires more complex emission-control strategies and consequently, more technically-complex engines. DFSS has provided the company with an approach to finding design solutions in less time and with fewer resources, and helps them put systems in place as early as possible in the design and development process.[9]

The remainder of this chapter introduces various tools and approaches that support the four stages of DFSS.

CONCEPT DEVELOPMENT AND INNOVATION

Concept development is the process of applying scientific, engineering, and business knowledge to produce a basic functional design that meets both customer needs and manufacturing or service delivery requirements. Developing new concepts requires innovation and creativity.

Innovation involves the adoption of an idea, process, technology, product, or business model that is either new or new to its proposed application. The outcome of innovation is a discontinuous or breakthrough change and results in new and unique goods and services that delight customers and create competitive advantage. The Small Business Administration classifies innovations into four categories:

1. An entirely new category of product (for example, the iPod),
2. First of its type on the market in a product category already in existence (for example, the DVD player),
3. A significant improvement in existing technology (for example, the Blu-ray disc technology),
4. A modest improvement to an existing product (for example, the latest iPad).

Innovation has been the hallmark of Apple and the late Steve Jobs, whose inspiration was driven by simplicity, ease of use, using computers to do creative work, and making life easier.[10] A *BusinessWeek* poll observed that a large majority of senior executives indicated that innovation was one of their top three priorities, and that the speed of implementation and ability to coordinate processes required to bring an idea to market were the biggest obstacles to successful innovation.[11]

Innovation is built upon strong research and development (R&D) processes. Many larger firms have dedicated R&D functions. Government agencies also promote innovation. For example, the National Institute of Standards and Technology (NIST), an agency of the U.S. Department of Commerce, promotes U.S. innovation and industrial competitiveness by advancing measurement science, standards, and technology in ways that enhance economic security and improve our quality of life. NIST laboratories conduct research that advances the nation's technology infrastructure and is needed by U.S. industry to continually improve products and services; the Hollings Manufacturing Extension Partnership, a nationwide network of local centers offers technical and business assistance to smaller manufacturers; and the Technology Innovation Program provides cost-shared awards to industry, universities, and consortia for research on potentially revolutionary technologies that address critical national and societal needs.

Creativity is seeing things in new or novel ways. In Asian cultures, the concept of creativity has been said to translate as "dangerous opportunity." Many creativity tools, such as brainstorming and "brainwriting," its written counterpart, are designed to help

The creativity of the brilliant mathematician John Nash, whose life was profiled in the book and movie A Beautiful Mind, *was described by one of his colleagues in the following way: "Everyone else would climb a peak by looking for a path somewhere on the mountain. Nash would climb another mountain altogether and from a distant peak shine a searchlight back on the first peak."[12]*

change the context in which one views a problem or opportunity, thereby leading to fresh perspectives.

One creativity tool that finds extensive use in product design is **TRIZ**, which is a Russian acronym for the *Theory of Inventive Problem Solving*. TRIZ was developed by a Russian patent clerk who studied thousands of submissions, and observed patterns of innovation common to the evolution of scientific and technical advances. He recognized that these concepts could be taught, and he developed some 200 exercises to foster creative problem solving. TRIZ has been used by such companies as Samsung, Ford, Motorola, Procter & Gamble, 3M, Phillips, LG, and many others. It has been useful in increasing the yield of semiconductor factories, designing new motors for washing machines, and increasing the viewing angle of LCD televisions.[13]

The first question one must ask during concept development is: What is the product (good or service) intended to do? In Chapter 3, we stressed the importance of understanding the voice of the customer. It is the starting point for concept development. How the voice of the customer is translated into physical or operational specifications and production processes for a product or service can mean the difference between a successful product and an outright failure. Other design considerations include a product's weight, size, appearance, safety, life, serviceability, and maintainability. When decisions about these factors are dominated by engineering considerations rather than by customer requirements, poor designs that fail in the market are often the result.

After potential ideas have been identified, they are evaluated using cost/benefit analysis, risk analysis, and other techniques. Finally, the best concept is selected, often using some type of scoring matrix to weight the selection criteria.

 QUALITYSPOTLIGHT

Domino's Pizza

In late 2009, Domino's, the world's largest pizza delivery chain, announced it was changing every part of its core pizza—new crust, new cheese, and new sauce. "We've always been known as the 30-minute delivery guys," the president of the U.S. business said. "There's no reason we can't have the best pizza in the marketplace, too." For the new recipe, Domino's tested dozens of cheeses, 15 sauces and 50 crust-seasoning blends over two years. With the economic crisis and changing demographics and consumer tastes, the change was needed from a competitive standpoint. "We weren't winning against everyone on taste," stated Domino's chief marketing executive.[14]

DETAILED DESIGN

Conceptual designs must be translated into measurable technical requirements and, subsequently, into detailed design specifications. Detailed design focuses on establishing technical requirements and specifications, which represent the transition from a designer's concept to a producible design, while also ensuring that it can be produced economically, efficiently, and with high quality. Dr. Nam Suh from MIT developed a methodology called **axiomatic design**, based on the premise that good design is governed by laws similar to those in natural science. Two axioms (statements accepted as true without proof) govern the design process:

1. *Independence Axiom*: good design occurs when the functional requirements of the design are independent of one another
2. *Information Axiom*: good design corresponds to minimum complexity

These axioms guide the design process with the goal of creating the best possible product to achieve the desired functions. The method has been shown to reduce design time and achieve better designs and has been used successfully by many companies such as Ford Motor Company. The principles of axiomatic design help designers better apply tools such as TRIZ and quality function deployment, which we discuss next.

Quality Function Deployment

A major problem with the traditional product development process is that customers and engineers speak different languages. Technical requirements, sometimes called design characteristics, translate the voice of the customer into technical language that provides a basis for design specifications such as dimensions and tolerances. A customer might express a requirement for a car as "easy to start." The translation of this requirement into technical language might be "car will start within 10 seconds of continuous cranking." Or, a requirement that "soap leaves my skin feeling soft" demands translation into pH or hardness specifications for the bar of soap. Such specifications provide manufacturing with actionable information for designing and controlling processes.

A powerful tool for establishing technical design requirements that meet customer needs and deploying them in subsequent production activities is **quality function deployment (QFD)**. The term, which is a translation of the Japanese Kanji characters used to describe the process, can sound confusing. QFD is simply a planning process to guide the design, manufacturing, and marketing of goods by integrating the voice of the customer throughout the organization. Through QFD, every design, manufacturing, and control decision is made to meet the expressed needs of customers. QFD benefits companies through improved communication and teamwork between all constituencies in the value chain, such as between marketing and design, between design and manufacturing, and between manufacturing and quality control.

QFD originated in 1972 at Mitsubishi's Kobe shipyard site. Toyota began to develop the concept shortly thereafter, and has used it since 1977 with impressive results. Between January 1977 and October 1979, Toyota realized a 20 percent reduction in start-up costs on the launch of a new van. By 1982, start-up costs had fallen 38 percent from the 1977 baseline, and by 1984, were reduced by 61 percent. In addition, development time fell by one-third at the same time that quality improved.

Xerox and Ford initiated the use of QFD in the United States in 1986. (At that time, more than 50 percent of major Japanese companies were already using the approach.) Today, QFD is used successfully by manufacturers of automobiles, electronics, appliances, clothing, and construction equipment, by firms such as Mazda, Motorola, Xerox, IBM, Procter & Gamble, Hewlett-Packard, and AT&T. Two organizations, the American Supplier Institute, Inc., a nonprofit organization, and GOAL/QPC, a Massachusetts consulting firm, have publicized and developed the concept in the United States.

Under QFD, all operations of a company are driven by the voice of the customer, rather than by edicts of top management or the opinions or desires of design engineers. QFD departs from the traditional product planning process in which product concepts are originated by design teams or research and development groups, tested and refined, produced, and marketed. Often, a considerable amount of wasted effort and time is spent redesigning products and production systems until customer needs are met. If customer needs can be identified properly in the first place, then such wasteful effort is eliminated, which is the principal focus of QFD.

Product objectives are better understood and interpreted during the production process because all key design information is captured and synthesized. This approach helps to understand trade-offs in design, and promote consensus among managers. Use of QFD focuses on the drivers of customer satisfaction and dissatisfaction, making it a useful tool for competitive analysis of product quality by top management. Productivity as well as quality improvements generally result. Perhaps most significant, though, QFD reduces the time for new product development. QFD allows companies to simulate the effects of new design ideas and concepts. Through this benefit, companies can reduce product development time and bring new products into the market sooner, thus gaining competitive advantage.

QFD uses a set of linked matrixes to ensure that the voice of the customer is carried throughout the production/delivery process (see Figure 7.2). Because of the visual structure, these are called "houses of quality." The first house of quality relates the voice of the customer (customer requirements) to a product's overall technical requirements; the second relates technical requirements to component requirements; the third relates component requirements to process operations; and the final one relates process operations to quality control plans. In this fashion, every design and production decision, including the design of production processes and the choice of quality measurements, is traceable to the voice of the customer. If applied correctly, this process ensures that the resulting product meets customer needs. We will focus on the first matrix, the *customer requirement planning matrix* (commonly referred to as the **House of Quality**) shown in Figure 7.3.

Building the House of Quality consists of six basic steps:

1. Identify customer requirements.
2. Identify technical requirements.
3. Relate the customer requirements to the technical requirements.
4. Conduct an evaluation of competing products or services.
5. Evaluate technical requirements and develop targets.
6. Determine which technical requirements to deploy in the remainder of the production/delivery process.

FIGURE 7.2 The Four Linked Houses of Quality

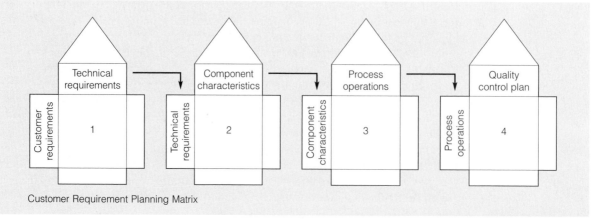

Customer Requirement Planning Matrix

FIGURE 7.3
The House of
Quality

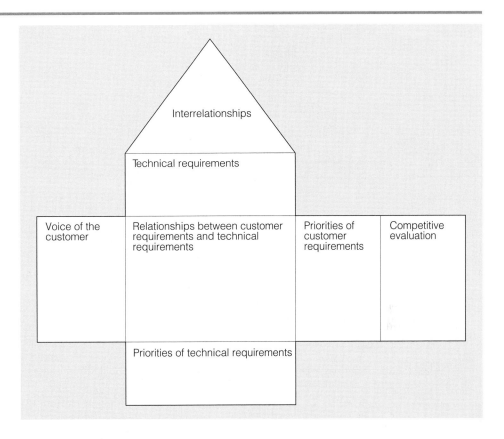

To illustrate the development of the House of Quality and the QFD process, the task of designing a new fitness center in a community with two other competing organizations is presented.

Step 1: Identify customer requirements. The voice of the customer is the primary input to the QFD process. As discussed in Chapter 3, many methods can be used to gather valid customer information. The most critical and most difficult step of the process is to capture the essence of the customer's needs and expectations. The customer's own words are vitally important in preventing misinterpretation by designers and engineers. Figure 7.4 shows the voice of the customer in the House of Quality for the fitness center, perhaps based on a telephone survey or focus groups. They are grouped into five categories: programs and activities, facilities, atmosphere, staff, and other. These groupings can easily be done using affinity diagrams, for example.

Step 2: List the technical requirements that provide the foundation for the product or service design. Technical requirements are measurable design characteristics that describe the customer requirements as expressed in the language of the designer or engineer. Essentially, they are the "hows" by which the company will respond to the "whats"—the customer requirements that will determine customer satisfaction or delight, often called *critical to quality* characteristics (CTQs). They must be measurable, because the output is controlled and compared to objective targets. For the fitness center, these requirements include the number and type of program offerings and equipment, times, staffing requirements, facility characteristics and maintenance, fee structure, and so on. Figure 7.5 adds this information to the House of Quality.

FIGURE 7.4   Voice of the Customer in the House of Quality (Step 1)

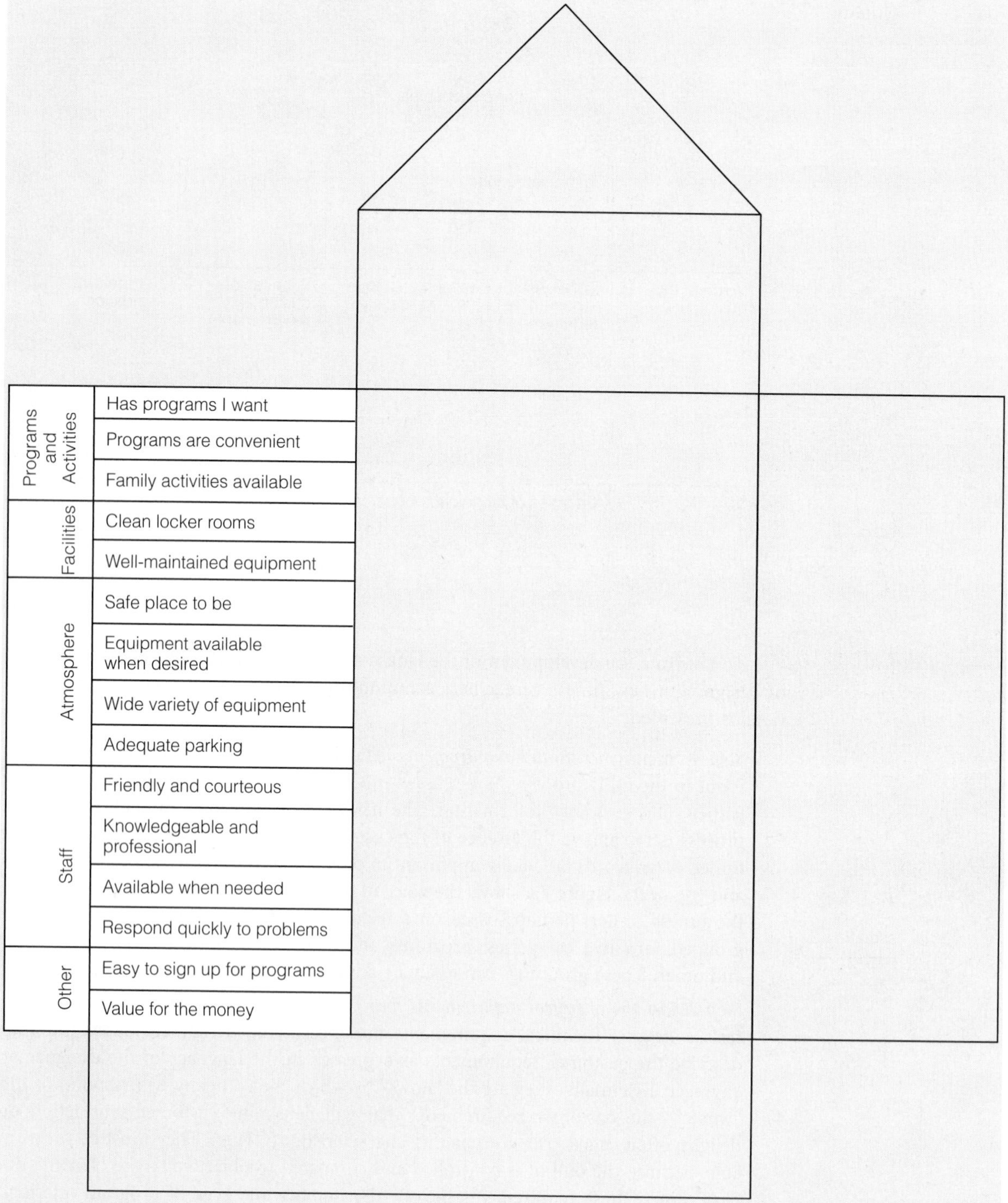

Programs and Activities	Has programs I want	
	Programs are convenient	
	Family activities available	
Facilities	Clean locker rooms	
	Well-maintained equipment	
Atmosphere	Safe place to be	
	Equipment available when desired	
	Wide variety of equipment	
	Adequate parking	
Staff	Friendly and courteous	
	Knowledgeable and professional	
	Available when needed	
	Respond quickly to problems	
Other	Easy to sign up for programs	
	Value for the money	

FIGURE 7.5   Technical Requirements in the House of Quality (Step 2)

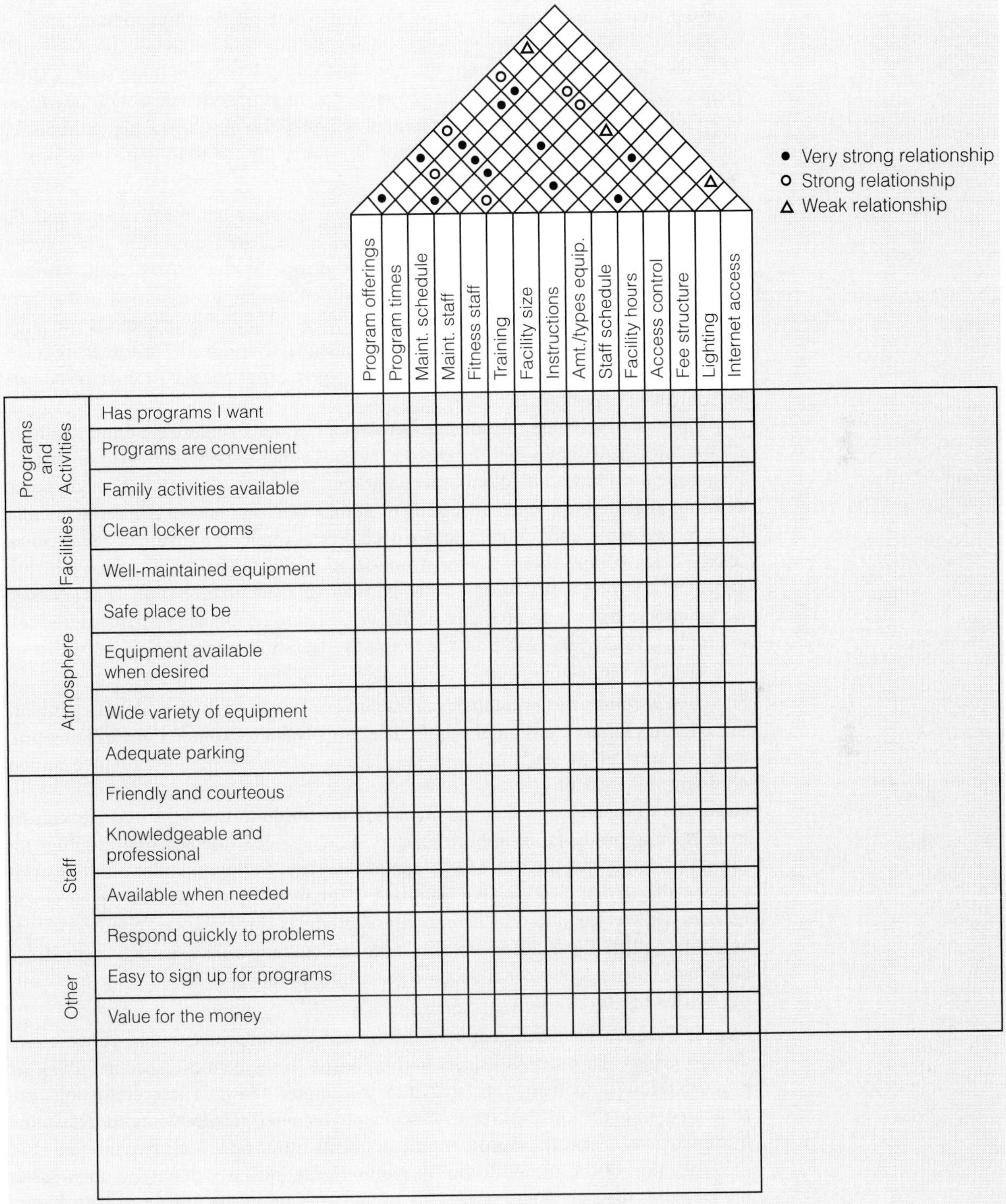

- Very strong relationship
- Strong relationship
- Weak relationship

		Program offerings	Program times	Maint. schedule	Maint. staff	Fitness staff	Training	Facility size	Instructions	Amt./types equip.	Staff schedule	Facility hours	Access control	Fee structure	Lighting	Internet access
Programs and Activities	Has programs I want															
	Programs are convenient															
	Family activities available															
Facilities	Clean locker rooms															
	Well-maintained equipment															
Atmosphere	Safe place to be															
	Equipment available when desired															
	Wide variety of equipment															
	Adequate parking															
Staff	Friendly and courteous															
	Knowledgeable and professional															
	Available when needed															
	Respond quickly to problems															
Other	Easy to sign up for programs															
	Value for the money															

The roof of the House of Quality shows the interrelationships between any pair of technical requirements. **Various symbols denote these relationships. A typical scheme uses the symbol ●** to denote a very strong relationship, O for a strong relationship, and Δ to denote a weak relationship. These relationships indicate answers to questions such as, "How does a change in a technical characteristic affect others?" For example, increasing program offerings will probably require more staff, a larger facility, expanded hours, and higher costs; hiring more maintenance staff, building a larger facility, and buying more equipment will probably result in a higher membership fee. Thus, design decisions cannot be viewed in isolation. This relationship matrix helps to evaluate trade-offs.

Step 3: Develop a relationship matrix between the customer requirements and the technical requirements. Customer requirements are listed down the left column; technical requirements are written across the top. In the matrix itself, symbols indicate the degree of relationship in a manner similar to that used in the roof of the House of Quality. The purpose of the relationship matrix is to show whether the final technical requirements adequately address customer requirements. This assessment is usually based on expert experience, customer responses, or controlled experiments.

The lack of a strong relationship between a customer requirement and any technical requirement shows that the customer needs either are not addressed or that the final design will have difficulty in meeting them. Similarly, if a technical requirement does not affect any customer requirement, it may be redundant or the designers may have missed some important customer need. For example, the customer requirement "clean locker rooms" bears a very strong relationship to the maintenance schedule and only a strong relationship to the number of maintenance staff. "Easy to sign up for programs" would probably bear a very strong relationship to Internet access and only a weak relationship to the hours the facility is open. Figure 7.6 shows an example of these relationships.

Step 4: Add competitor evaluation and key selling points. This step identifies importance ratings for each customer requirement and evaluates competitors' existing products or services for each of them (see Figure 7.7). Customer importance ratings represent the areas of greatest interest and highest expectations as expressed by the customer. Competitive evaluation highlights the absolute strengths and weaknesses in competing products. By using this step, designers can discover opportunities for improvement. It also links QFD to a company's strategic vision and indicates priorities for the design process. For example, if an important customer requirement receives a low evaluation on all competitors' products (for instance, "family activities available"), then by focusing on this need a company might gain a competitive advantage. Such requirements become key selling points and the basis for formulating marketing strategies.

Step 5: Evaluate technical requirements of competitive products and services and develop targets. This step is usually accomplished through intelligence gathering or product testing and then translated into measurable terms. These evaluations are compared with the competitive evaluation of customer requirements to determine inconsistencies between customer requirements and technical requirement but the evaluation of the related technical requirements indicates otherwise, then either the measures used are faulty or else the product has an image difference (either positive toward the competitor or negative toward the company's product), which

FIGURE 7.6   Relationship Matrix (Step 3)

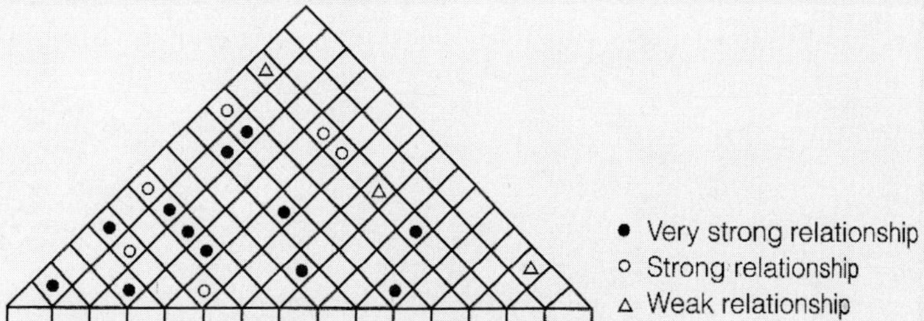

FIGURE 7.7 Competitive Evaluation (Step 4)

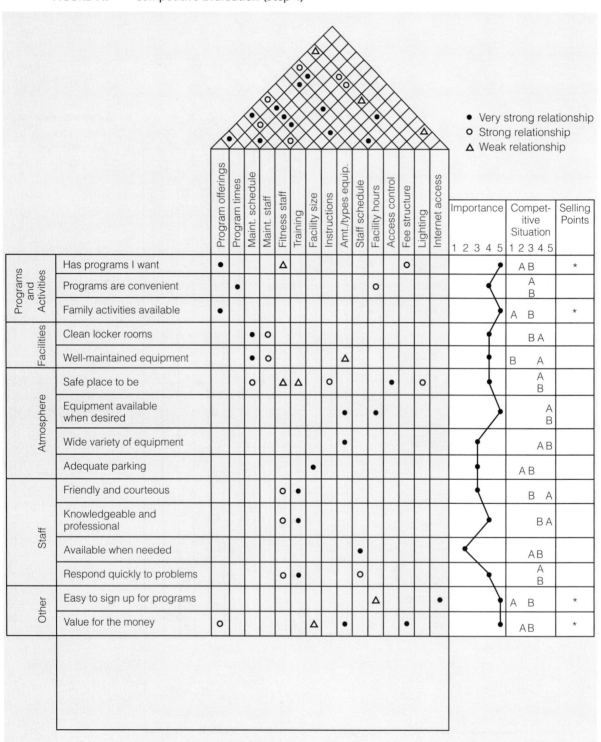

affects customer perceptions. On the basis of customer importance ratings and existing product strengths and weaknesses, targets for each technical requirement are set, as shown in Figure 7.8. For example, customers rated programs and family activities of high importance while competitive evaluation shows them to be quite low. Setting a higher target for these requirements will help to meet this critical need and be a source of competitive advantage.

Step 6: Select technical requirements and targets to be deployed in the remainder of the process. The technical requirements that have a strong relationship to customer needs, have poor competitive performance, or are strong selling points are identified during this step. These characteristics have the highest priority and need to be "deployed" throughout the remainder of the design and production process to maintain a responsiveness to the voice of the customer. Those characteristics not identified as critical do not need such rigorous attention. For example, program offerings, amount and types of equipment, facility hours, fee structure, and Internet access have been identified in Figure 7.8 as the key issues to address in designing the fitness center.

As we noted in discussing Figure 7.2, the House of Quality is linked to three other "houses," or planning matrixes, as part of the QFD process. The second house expands the overall design into more detailed component characteristics. In the fitness center example, for instance, we might develop more detailed customer and technical requirements for program offerings. The third house relates the component characteristics to key process operations, representing the transition from planning to execution. For the fitness center, this step might involve creating a project plan for selecting, designing, and evaluating programs. Key process operations are the basis for a quality control plan in the last house of quality. At this point, for example, the fitness center might design membership surveys for evaluating programs, checklists for maintenance, performance appraisal approaches for the staff, and measures of equipment failures and problems. These activities are what must be measured and evaluated on a continuous basis to ensure that processes continue to meet the important customer requirements defined in the first House of Quality.

Target and Tolerance Design

After basic technical requirements have been established, designers must set specific dimensional or operational targets and tolerances for critical manufacturing or service characteristics. These might be based on product functionality that reflects the voice of the customer or other considerations such as safety. For example, the National Highway Traffic Safety Administration dictates standards for motor vehicles, such as requiring two windshield wiper speeds, one of which must be faster than 45 cycles per minute and the other at least 15 cycles per minute slower than the faster speed but no slower than one cycle every three seconds.[15]

Manufacturing specifications consist of nominal dimensions and tolerances. **Nominal** refers to the ideal dimension or the target value that manufacturing seeks to meet; **tolerance** is the permissible variation, recognizing the difficulty of meeting a target consistently. Tolerances are necessary because not all parts can be produced exactly to nominal specifications because of natural variations (common causes) in production processes due to the "5 Ms": men and women, materials, machines, methods, and measurement.

FIGURE 7.8   Technical Requirements Evaluation, Targets, and Deployment (Steps 5 and 6)

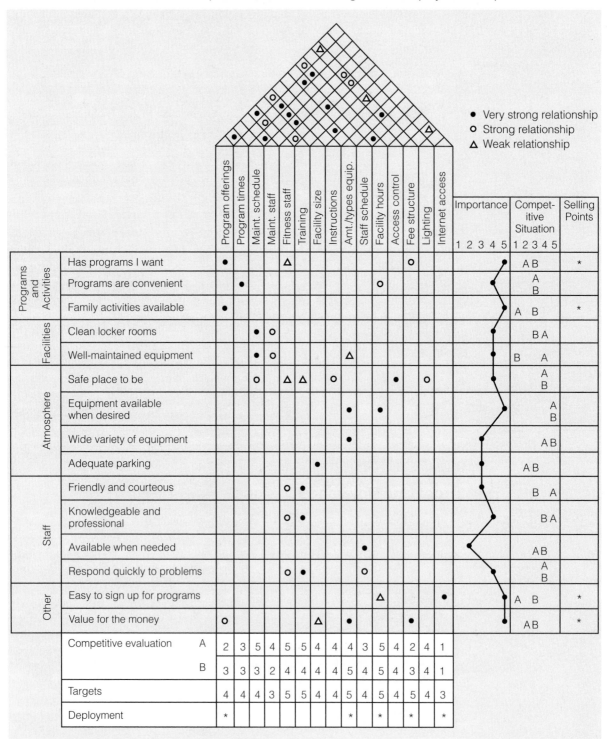

EXAMPLE 7.1

Nominal Dimensions and Tolerances

Consider a typical microprocessor. The drawing in Figure 7.9 shows some of the critical dimensions and tolerances for the microprocessor. The "ratio" notation (0.514/0.588) denotes the permissible range of the dimension. Unless otherwise stated, the nominal dimension is the midpoint. Thus, the specification of 0.514/0.588 may be interpreted as a nominal dimension of 0.551 with a tolerance of plus or minus 0.037. Usually, this is written as 0.551 ± 0.037. The manufacturing-based definition of quality conformance to specifications is based on such tolerances.

Although we will focus our attention on manufactured goods, similar considerations apply to services. At Starbucks, milk must be steamed to at least 150 degrees Fahrenheit but never more than 170 degrees, and every espresso shot must be pulled within 23 seconds of service or tossed.[16] Government regulations often determine specifications for food and pharmaceutical products. For example, the U.S. Food and Drug Administration (FDA) sets quality standards regarding the number of unsavory items that find their way into food products.[17] Packaged mushrooms are allowed to contain up to 20 maggots of any size per 100 grams of drained mushrooms or 15 grams of dried mushrooms, while 100 grams of peanut butter may have an average of 30 insect fragments and one rodent hair. (Need we say more?)

Tolerance design involves determining the permissible variation in a dimension. To design tolerances effectively, engineers must understand the necessary trade-offs. Narrow tolerances tend to raise manufacturing costs but they also increase the interchangeability of parts within the plant and in the field, product performance, durability, and appearance. Also, a tolerance reserve or factor of safety is needed to account for engineering uncertainty regarding the maximum variation allowable and compatibility with satisfactory product performance. Wide tolerances, on the other hand, increase material utilization, machine throughput, and labor productivity, but have a negative impact on product characteristics, as previously mentioned. Thus, factors operating to enlarge tolerances include production planning requirements; tool design, fabrication, and setup; tool adjustment and replacement; process yield; inspection and gauge control and maintenance; and labor and supervision requirements.

FIGURE 7.9
Microprocessor
Specifications

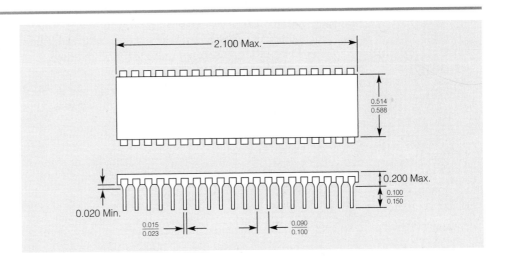

Traditionally, tolerances are set by convention rather than scientifically. A designer might use the tolerances specified on previous designs or base a design decision on judgment from past experience. Setting inappropriate tolerances can be costly. For instance, in one company, a bearing seat had to be machined on a large part, costing more than $1,000. Because of the precision tolerance specified by design engineers, one or two parts per month had to be scrapped when the tolerance was exceeded. A study revealed that the bearings being used did not require such precise tolerances. When the tolerance was relaxed, the problem disappeared. This one design change resulted in approximately $20,000 in savings per year.

Tolerance design often takes place in isolation, with inexperienced designers applying tolerances to parts or products while having little awareness of the capabilities of the production process to meet these design requirements. Even experienced designers may be hard-pressed to remain up-to-date on the capabilities of processes that involve constant equipment changes, shifting technology, and difficult-to-measure variations in methods at scores of plants located hundreds or thousands of miles away from a centralized product design department. It is important that design engineers understand the capability of processes to meet the specifications they set, particularly in a DFSS environment.

The Taguchi Loss Function

All too often, tolerance settings fail to account for the impact of variation on product functionality, manufacturability, or economic consequences. In a review of Audi's TT Coupe when it was first introduced, automobile columnist Alan Vonderhaar noted, "There was apparently some problem with the second-gear synchronizer, a device that is supposed to ease shifts. As a result, on full-power upshifts from first to second, I frequently got gear clashes." He observed others with the same problem, from reading Internet newsgroups and concluded, "It appears to be an issue that surfaces just now and again, here and there throughout the production mix, suggesting it may be a tolerance issue—sometimes the associated parts are close enough to specifications to get along well, other times they're at the outer ranges of manufacturing tolerance and cause problems."[18]

What Mr. Vonderhaar observed can be explained using the manufacturing-based definition of quality. For example, suppose that a specification for some quality characteristic is 0.500 ± 0.020. Using this definition, the actual value of the quality characteristic can fall anywhere in a range from 0.480 to 0.520. This approach assumes that the customer, either the consumer or the next department in the production process, would accept any value within the 0.480 to 0.520 range, but not be satisfied with a value outside this tolerance range (see Figure 7.10).

But what is the real difference between 0.479 and 0.481? The former would be considered as "out of specification" and either reworked or scrapped resulting in a monetary

FIGURE 7.10
Traditional Economic View of Conformance to Specifications

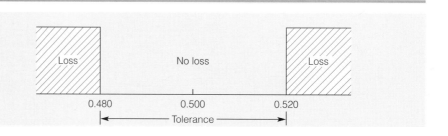

loss to the company, while the latter would be acceptable. Actually, the impact of either value on the performance characteristic of the product would be about the same. Neither value is close to the nominal specification 0.500, which is the ideal target value for the quality characteristic.

A Japanese engineer, Genichi Taguchi—whose philosophy was strongly advocated by Deming—maintained that this "goal-post" definition of quality is inherently flawed and explained the economic value of reducing variation and producing to the nominal specification. Taguchi suggests that no strict cut-off point divides good quality from poor quality, but that losses occur whenever there is a deviation from the nominal specification. The following case supports this notion.

The Japanese newspaper *Asahi Shimbum* published an example comparing the cost and quality of Sony televisions at two plants in Japan and San Diego.[19] The color density of all the units produced at the San Diego plant were within specifications, whereas some of those shipped from the Japanese plant were not (see Figure 7.11). However, the average loss per unit of the San Diego plant was $0.89 greater than that of the Japanese plant. This increased cost occurred because workers adjusted units that were out of specification at the San Diego plant, adding cost to the process. Furthermore, a unit adjusted to minimally meet specifications was more likely to generate customer complaints than a unit close to the original target value, therefore incurring higher field service costs. Figure 7.11 shows that fewer U.S.-produced sets met the target value for color density. The distribution of quality in the Japanese plant was more uniform around the target value, and though some units were out of specification, the total cost was less.

Taguchi measured quality as the variation from the target value of a design specification, and then translated that variation into an economic "loss function" that expresses the cost of variation in monetary terms. In mathematical terms, Taguchi assumes that losses can be approximated by a quadratic function so that larger deviations from target correspond to increasingly larger losses. For the case in which a specific target value, T, is determined to produce the optimum performance, and in which quality deteriorates as the actual value moves away from the target on either side (called "nominal is best"), the loss function is represented by

$$L(x) = k(x - T)^2 \qquad (7.1)$$

where x is any actual value of the quality characteristic and k is some constant. Thus, $(x - T)$ represents the deviation from the target, and the loss increases by the square of the deviation. This is called the **Taguchi loss function** and is illustrated in Figure 7.12.

The constant, k, is estimated by determining the cost associated with a certain deviation from the target, as the following example illustrates.

FIGURE 7.11
Variation in U.S.-Made versus Japanese-Made Television Components

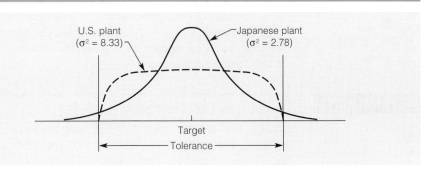

U.S. plant
($\sigma^2 = 8.33$)

Japanese plant
($\sigma^2 = 2.78$)

Target

Tolerance

FIGURE 7.12
Nominal-Is-Best Loss
Function

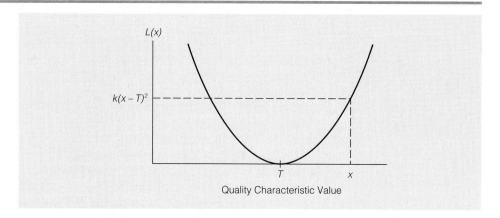

EXAMPLE 7.2

Finding a Taguchi Loss Function

Assume that a certain quality characteristic has a specification of 0.500 ± 0.020. An analysis of company records reveals that if the value of the quality characteristic exceeds the target of 0.500 by the tolerance of 0.020 on either side, the product is likely to require an adjustment during the warranty period and cost $50 for repair. Then, $50 = k (0.020)^2$ and $k = 50/0.0004 = 125{,}000$. Therefore, using formula (7.1), the loss function is

$$L(x) = \$125{,}000(x - T)^2$$

Thus, if the deviation is only 0.010, the loss is

$$L(0.010) = \$125{,}000(0.010)^2 = \$12.50$$

Not all quality characteristics have nominal targets with tolerances on either side. In some cases, such as impurities in a chemical process or fuel consumption, "smaller is better." In other cases, "larger is better" as with breaking strength or product life. The loss function for the smaller-is-better case is

$$L(x) = kx^2$$

and for the larger-is-better case is

$$L(x) = k(1/x^2)$$

These formulas can be applied in a manner similar to the previous example.

If the distribution of the variation about the target value is known, the average loss per unit can be computed by finding the expected value of the loss using routine expected value calculations.

EXAMPLE 7.3

Computing Expected Loss

Suppose that two processes, A and B, have the following distributions of a quality characteristic with specification 0.50 ± 0.02. In process A, the output of the process has dimensions ranging from 0.48 to 0.52, all of which are equally likely. For process B,

60 percent of the output is expected to have a value of 0.50, 15 percent has a value of 0.49, and so on, as shown in the table below:

Dimension	Process A Probability	Process B Probability
0.47	0	0.02
0.48	0.2	0.03
0.49	0.2	0.15
0.50	0.2	0.60
0.51	0.2	0.15
0.52	0.2	0.03
0.53	0	0.02

Notice that the output from process A is spread equally over the range from 0.48 to 0.52 and lies entirely within specifications. In process B, output is concentrated near the target value, but does not entirely lie within specifications.

Using the loss function $L(x) = \$125,000(x - 0.50)^2$, the expected loss for each process can be computed easily as shown below by multiplying the loss associated with each dimensional value by its probability and summing the total.

Dimension	Loss	Process A Probability	Weighted Loss	Process B Probability	Weighted Loss
0.47	$112.50	0	$0.00	0.02	$2.25
0.48	$50.00	0.2	$10.00	0.03	$1.50
0.49	$12.50	0.2	$2.50	0.15	$1.88
0.5	$0.00	0.2	$0.00	0.60	$0.00
0.51	$12.50	0.2	$2.50	0.15	$1.88
0.52	$50.00	0.2	$10.00	0.03	$1.50
0.53	$112.50	0	$0.00	0.02	$2.25
		Expected Loss	$25.00		$11.25

Clearly, process B incurs a smaller total expected loss even though some output falls outside specifications.

The expected loss, EL, can also be found using a simple formula that involves only the variance of the quality characteristic, σ^2 and the square of the deviation of the mean value from the nominal specification:

$$EL = k(\sigma^2 + D^2) \tag{7.2}$$

EXAMPLE 7.4

Applying the Expected Loss Formula

Using the data in Example 7.3, we may compute the variance of the quality characteristic using the following statistical formula for a discrete probability distribution:

$$Var[X] = \sum_{j=1}^{\infty} (x_j - E[X])^2 f(x_j) \tag{7.3}$$

Figure 7.13 shows a spreadsheet for calculating both the expected value and variance for each process, and then applying the expected loss formula (7.2), which may be found on the Student Companion Site. The Excel formula in cell B18, for example, is =B5*(B17+(B16-B4)). This results in the same values for the expected loss that we computed in Example 7.3.

FIGURE 7.13 Calculation of Expected Value, Variance, and Expected Loss *(Example 7.4.xlsx)*

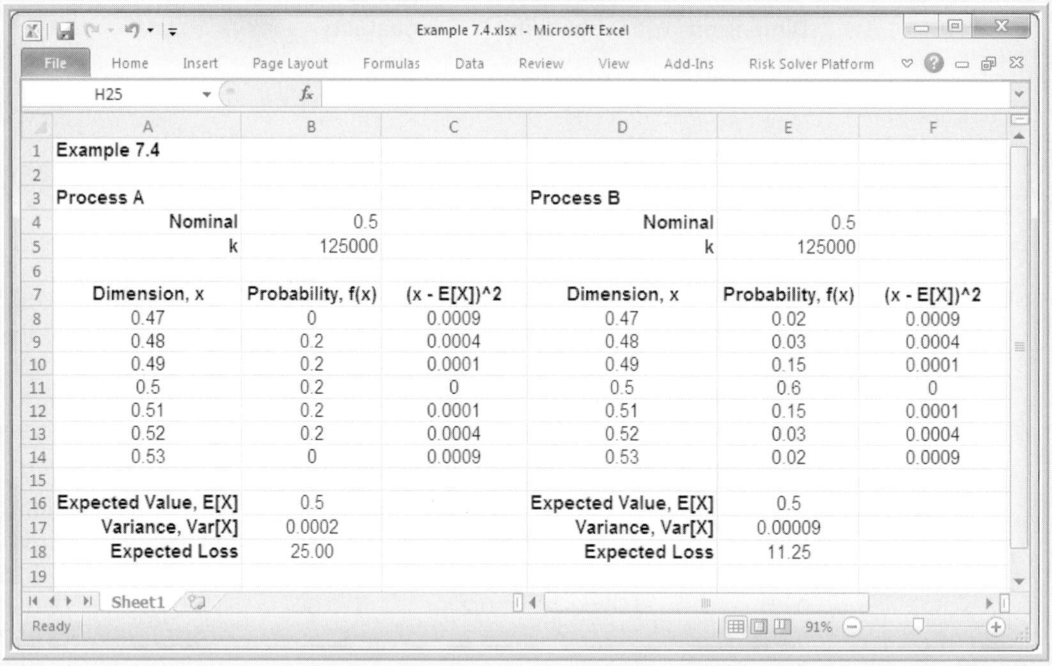

	A	B	C	D	E	F
1	Example 7.4					
2						
3	Process A			Process B		
4	Nominal	0.5		Nominal	0.5	
5	k	125000		k	125000	
6						
7	Dimension, x	Probability, f(x)	(x - E[X])^2	Dimension, x	Probability, f(x)	(x - E[X])^2
8	0.47	0	0.0009	0.47	0.02	0.0009
9	0.48	0.2	0.0004	0.48	0.03	0.0004
10	0.49	0.2	0.0001	0.49	0.15	0.0001
11	0.5	0.2	0	0.5	0.6	0
12	0.51	0.2	0.0001	0.51	0.15	0.0001
13	0.52	0.2	0.0004	0.52	0.03	0.0004
14	0.53	0	0.0009	0.53	0.02	0.0009
15						
16	Expected Value, E[X]	0.5		Expected Value, E[X]	0.5	
17	Variance, Var[X]	0.0002		Variance, Var[X]	0.00009	
18	Expected Loss	25.00		Expected Loss	11.25	
19						

To relate the expected loss formula to the Sony television example cited above, k was determined to be 0.16. Because the mean of both distributions of color density fell on the target value, $D^2 = 0$ for both the U.S. and the Japanese plants. However, the variance of the distributions differed. For the San Diego plant, $\sigma^2 = 8.33$ and for the Japanese plant, $\sigma^2 = 2.78$. Thus, the average loss per unit was computed to be 0.16 (8.33) = \$1.33 at the San Diego plant, and 0.16 (2.78) = \$0.44 at the Japanese plant, for a difference of \$0.89 per unit.

If the quality characteristic has a normal distribution or another distribution whose mean and variance is known, then the calculation of the expected loss is straightforward, as the following example illustrates.

EXAMPLE 7.5

Computing the Expected Loss with Known Process Characteristics

Suppose that a part has a specification of 0.6500 ± 0.0275, and the Taguchi loss function is found to be $L(x) = \$99{,}174\,(x - T)^2$. Assume that the process that produces the part is normally distributed with a mean of 0.6620 and standard deviation 0.0087. Then the variance is $(0.0087)^2 = 0.00007569$ and $D^2 = (0.6620 - 0.6500)^2 = 0.000144$. Therefore, the expected loss is

$$EL = 99{,}174(0.00007569 + 0.000144) = \$21.79 \text{ per unit}$$

Using the Taguchi Loss Function for Tolerance Design

The Taguchi loss function may be used to set tolerances in an economical fashion. The following example illustrates how to use it by applying break-even analysis.

EXAMPLE 7.6

Using the Loss Function and Breakeven Analysis for Tolerance Design

Cassette tapes are still used in some handheld recording devices and in less expensive portable musical instrument recording devices. The desired speed of a cassette tape is 1.875 inches per second. Any deviation from this value causes a change in pitch and tempo and thus poor sound quality. Suppose that adjusting the tape speed under warranty when a customer complains and returns a device costs a manufacturer $20. (This repair expense does not include other costs due to customer dissatisfaction and therefore is at best a lower bound on the actual loss.) At the factory, an adjustment can be made at a much lower cost of $5, which consists of the labor to test the unit and make the adjustment if needed. What should the tolerance be before an adjustment is made at the factory?

Based on past information, the company knows the average customer will return a player if the tape speed is off the target by at least 0.15 inch per second. Thus, $L(.15) =$ $20. The loss function constant is computed by solving $20 = k(0.15)^2$ for k, yielding $k = 888.9$. Therefore, the Taguchi loss function is $L(x) = 888.9(x - 1.875)^2$. For example, if the actual speed is 1.925 inches per second, the Taguchi loss function estimates that the loss will be $L(1.925) = 888.9(1.925 - 1.875)^2 = \$2.22$. Some, but not all, customers might perceive poor sound quality for this small of a deviation and return it for adjustment, so the average loss is smaller.

The table below shows the economic loss computed for tape speeds ranging from 1.725 to 2.025.

Tape speed, x	L(x)
1.725	$20.00
1.740	$16.20
1.755	$12.80
1.770	$9.80
1.785	$7.20
1.800	$5.00
1.815	$3.20
1.830	$1.80
1.845	$0.80
1.860	$0.20
1.875	$0.00
1.890	$0.20
1.905	$0.80
1.920	$1.80
1.935	$3.20
1.950	$5.00
1.965	$7.20
1.980	$9.80
1.995	$12.80
2.010	$16.20
2.025	$20.00

We may perform a simple breakeven analysis using the loss function to find economical design specifications. Using the data above, note that if the tape speed is less than 1.800 or greater than 1.950, the loss incurred by *not* adjusting the tape is greater than $5. Therefore it is more economical to inspect and adjust if the actual speed is outside of these limits. If the speed is greater than 1.800 or less than 1.950 (shaded values), then clearly it costs more to inspect and adjust than to simply ship the unit as is. Therefore, 1.800 and 1.950 and represents the economical design specifications.

DESIGN FOR RELIABILITY

Reliability—the ability of a product to perform as expected over time—is one of the principal dimensions of quality. As the overall quality of products continues to improve, consumers expect higher reliability with each purchase; they simply are not satisfied with products that fail unexpectedly. Reliability is an essential aspect of both product and process design. Sophisticated equipment used today in such areas as transportation (airplanes), communications (satellites), and medicine (pacemakers) requires high reliability. High reliability can also provide a competitive advantage for many consumer goods. Japanese automobiles gained large market shares primarily because of their high reliability, and current models typically dominate the *Consumer Reports* annual ranking for predicted reliability. However, domestic manufacturers have made significant improvements.[20] Likewise in manufacturing, the increased use of automation, complexity of machines, low profit margins, and time-based competitiveness make reliability in production processes a critical issue for survival of the business. However, the increased complexity of modern products makes high reliability more difficult to achieve.

Formally, **reliability** is defined as the probability that a product, piece of equipment, or system performs its intended function for a stated period of time under specified operating conditions. This definition has four important elements: probability, time, performance, and operating conditions.

1. First, reliability is defined as a *probability*, that is, a value between 0 and 1. Thus, it is a numerical measure with a precise meaning. Expressing reliability in this way provides a valid basis for comparison of different designs for products and systems. For example, a reliability of 0.97 indicates that, on average, 97 of 100 items will perform their function for a given period of time and under certain operating conditions. Often reliability is expressed as a percentage simply for descriptive purposes.

2. The second element of the definition is *time*. Clearly a device having a reliability of 0.97 for 1,000 hours of operation is inferior to one having the same reliability for 5,000 hours of operation, assuming that the mission of the device is long life.

3. *Performance* is the third element and refers to the objective for which the product or system was made. The term *failure* is used when expectations of performance of the intended function are not met. Two types of failures can occur: ***functional failure*** *at the start of product life due to manufacturing or material defects such as a missing connection or a faulty component*, and ***reliability failure*** *after some period of use*. Examples of reliability failures include the following: a device does not work at all (car will not start); the operation of a device is unstable (car idles rough); or the performance of a device deteriorates (shifting becomes difficult). Because the nature of failure in each of these cases is different, the failure must be clearly defined.

4. The final component of the reliability definition is *operating conditions*, which involves the type and amount of usage and the environment in which the product is used. Automobiles, for example, "must run in temperatures ranging from -70F in Barrow, AK to

130F in the Arizona desert. They have to work while driving over gravel roads or washboard concrete. Worse, they have to operate reliably, even when they are poorly maintained by owners who seem oblivious to their requirements."[21]

By defining a product's intended environment, performance characteristics, and lifetime, a manufacturer can design and conduct tests to measure the probability of product survival (or failure). The analysis of such tests enable better prediction of reliability and improved product and process designs. Reliability engineers distinguish between **inherent reliability**, which is the predicted reliability determined by the design of the product or process, and the **achieved reliability**, which is the actual reliability observed during use. Achieved reliability can be less than the inherent reliability due to the effects of the manufacturing process and the conditions of use.

Reliability testing can be expensive, so organizations usually maintain historical data on failure information and use them to calculate failure rates for new components or systems. In addition, various government and commercial sources of failure data are available; one is MIL-HDBK-217F, Reliability Prediction of Electronic Equipment, which provides failure rate data for electronic components used in military applications.

Mathematics of Reliability

In practice, reliability is determined by the number of failures per unit time during the duration under consideration (called the **failure rate,** λ). Some products must be scrapped and replaced upon failure; others can be repaired. For items that must be replaced when a failure occurs, the reciprocal of the failure rate (having dimensions of time units per failure) is called the **mean time to failure (MTTF)**. For repairable items, the **mean time between failures (MTBF)** is used.

We may compute the failure rate by testing or using a sample of items until all fail, recording the time of failure for each item, and use the following formulas:

$$\text{Failure rate} = \lambda = \frac{\text{Number of failures}}{\text{Total unit operating hours}} \quad (7.4)$$

or alternatively,

$$\lambda = \frac{\text{Number of failures}}{(\text{Units tested}) \times (\text{Number of hours tested})} \quad (7.5)$$

EXAMPLE 7.7   ### Computing a Failure Rate

Suppose that 10 units are tested over a 100-hour period. Four units failed with one unit each failing after 6, 35, 65, and 70 hours; the remaining 6 units performed satisfactorily until the end of the test. The total unit operating hours are

$$
\begin{aligned}
1 \times 6 &= 6 \\
1 \times 35 &= 35 \\
1 \times 65 &= 65 \\
1 \times 70 &= 70 \\
6 \times 100 &= \underline{600} \\
&\ 776
\end{aligned}
$$

Therefore, λ = (4 failures)/(776 unit operating hours) = 0.00515 failures per hour. In other words, on average in a one-hour period, about 0.5 percent of the units would be expected to fail. On the other hand, over a 100-hour period, about (0.00515)(100) = 0.515 or 51.5 percent of the units would be expected to fail. In the actual test, only 40 percent failed.

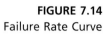

FIGURE 7.14

Failure Rate Curve

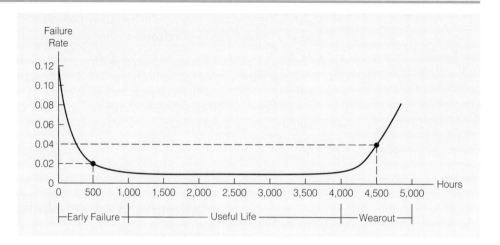

Many electronic components commonly exhibit a high, but decreasing, failure rate early in their lives (as evidenced by the steep slope of the curve), followed by a period of a relatively constant failure rate, and ending with an increasing failure rate. This is depicted in Figure 7.14, which is called a **product life characteristics curve**, and shows the instantaneous failure rate at any point in time. (This is often referred to as a "bathtub" curve for obvious reasons.) We see that the failure rate is rather high at the beginning of product life, then levels out over a long period of time and then eventually begins to increase. This is a typical phenomenon for electronic components such as semiconductors and consumer products such as light bulbs.

In Figure 7.14, three distinct time periods are evident: early failure (from 0 to about 1,000 hours), useful life (from 1,000 to 4,000 hours), and wearout period (after 4,000 hours). The first is the early failure period, sometimes called the **infant mortality period**. Weak components resulting from poor manufacturing or quality control procedures will often lead to a high rate of failure early in a product's life. This high rate usually cannot be detected through normal test procedures, particularly in electronic semiconductors. Such components or products should not be permitted to enter the marketplace. The second phase of the life characteristics curve describes the normal pattern of random failures during a product's useful life. This period usually has a low, relatively constant failure rate caused by uncontrollable factors, such as sudden and unexpected stresses due to complex interactions in materials or the environment. These factors are usually impossible to predict on an individual basis. However, the collective behavior of such failures can be modeled statistically. Finally, as age takes over, the wearout period begins, and the failure rate increases.

New car owners generally experience this phenomenon. During the first few months of ownership, owners may have to return their car to the dealer to remove the initial bugs caused by poor workmanship or manufacturing processes, electronic failures or rattles. Such defects are monitored by J. D. Power's Initial Quality metrics of which you are probably aware. During its prime lifetime, the car may have few failures; however, as parts begin to wear out, the number and rate of failures begin to increase until replacement becomes desirable.

Knowing the product life characteristics curve for a particular product helps engineers predict behavior and make decisions accordingly. For instance, if a manufacturer knows that the early failure period for a microprocessor is 600 hours, it can test the chip for 600 hours (or use techniques called accelerated life testing for shorter periods of time which we discuss later) before releasing the chip to the market.

Reliability is the probability that an item will *not* fail over a given period of time. We express this using the **reliability function, R(T)**, which characterizes the probability of survival to time T. It has the following properties:

1. $R(0) = 1$
2. As T becomes larger, R(T) is non-increasing
3. $R(T) = 1 - F(T)$, where F(T) is the cumulative probability distribution of failures

Thus, to tabulate a reliability function, we simply need to know the cumulative probability distribution of failures over time.

EXAMPLE 7.8

Computing a Reliability Function

Knowledge of a product's reliability function is useful in developing warranties. Consider a tire manufacturer who must determine a mileage warranty policy for a new line of tires. Suppose that the mean life of a tire is 50,000 miles with a standard deviation of 1500 miles and is normally distributed. We may use the cumulative normal distribution to calculate the reliability function. For example, the probability of a tire wearing out before 48,000 miles would be found using the Excel function = NORM.DIST(48000, 50000,1500,TRUE) = 0.0912.

Figure 7.15 shows a spreadsheet to calculate the probability of failure before x miles and the probability of survival; that is, the reliability function. For example, about 25 percent of tires are expected to last beyond 51,000 miles. If a 48,000-mile warranty is established, management can compute the expected cost of replacing about 9 percent of the tires. If a 45,000-mile warranty is made, then virtually no tires will be replaced. Of course, the warranty must balance cost with competitor offerings. Note that in this example, time is not measured chronologically, but in terms of product usage.

During the useful life of a product the failure rate is assumed to be constant. Mathematically, the probability of failure over time is often modeled by an exponential probability distribution. Not only is this mathematically justified, but it has been empirically validated for many observable phenomena, such as failures of light bulbs, electronic components, and repairable systems such as automobiles, computers, and industrial machinery.

If λ is the failure rate, the exponential probability density function of failures is

$$f(t) = \lambda e^{-\lambda t} \quad t \geq 0 \tag{7.6}$$

Thus, the probability of failure by time T is given by the cumulative distribution function

$$F(T) = 1 - e^{-\lambda T} \tag{7.7}$$

We can easily calculate the probability of failing during a time interval (t_1, t_2) as

$$F(t_2) - F(t_1) = e^{-\lambda(t_2 - t_1)} \tag{7.8}$$

Because reliability is the probability of *survival*, the reliability function is

$$R(T) = 1 - F(T) = e^{-\lambda T} \tag{7.9}$$

The simplicity of the exponential distribution makes it easy to use in reliability calculations.

FIGURE 7.15   Spreadsheet for Calculating a Reliability Function *(Example 7.8.xlsx)*

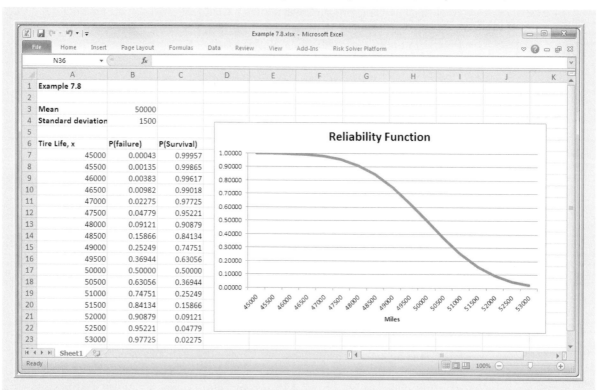

EXAMPLE 7.9

Exponential Reliability Function

Consider, for example, a component that has a reliability of 0.97 for 100 hours of normal use. We may determine the failure rate λ by solving the equation (7.9) for λ. Substituting R(100) = 0.97 and T = 100 into this equation yields

$$0.97 = e^{-\lambda(100)}$$
$$\ln 0.97 = -100\lambda$$
$$\lambda = -(\ln 0.97)/100$$
$$= 0.0304/100$$
$$\approx 0.0003 \text{ failures per hour}$$

Thus, the reliability function is $R(T) = e^{-0.0003T}$. We may tabulate this function and chart it on an Excel spreadsheet as shown in Figure 7.16. The cumulative fraction of items that are expected to survive after each 1000-hour period are shown in the figure.

Reliability engineers characterize the instantaneous failure rate over time by what is called the **hazard function**, which is computed as follows:

$$h(t) = f(t)/[1 - F(t)] = f(t)/R(t) \qquad (7.10)$$

The hazard function may be interpreted as the probability that an item that has not failed up to time t will fail immediately after time t. For the exponential distribution, the hazard function is as follows:

$$h(t) = \lambda e^{-\lambda t}/e^{-\lambda t} = \lambda \qquad (7.11)$$

FIGURE 7.16   Exponential Reliability Calculations and Reliability Function *(Example 7.9.xlsx)*

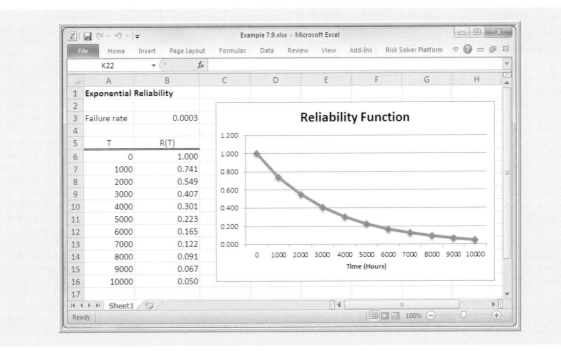

This simply states that the instantaneous failure rate is constant (for example, as assumed during the useful life period in Figure 7.14). Note, however, that the exponential distribution is not appropriate for characterizing the reliability over the entire lifetime of the product life characteristics curve in Figure 7.14 because the hazard function is not constant over the entire range, only during the useful life period.

The hazard function is useful for characterizing the failure rate curve when the distribution of failures is characterized by different probability distributions than the exponential (a topic beyond the scope of this book). More advanced books on reliability discuss this in more detail.

The reciprocal of the failure rate is often used in reliability computations. For nonrepairable items, $\theta = 1/\lambda$ is defined as the *mean time to failure* (MTTF). Thus, in the preceding example for $\lambda = 0.0003$ failure per hour, $\theta = 1/.0003 = 3,333$ hours. That is, one failure can be expected every 3,333 hours on the average. The probability distribution function of failures and the reliability function can be equivalently expressed using the MTTF as

$$F(T) = 1 - e^{-T/\theta} \tag{7.12}$$

and

$$R(T) = e^{-T/\theta} \tag{7.13}$$

For repairable items, θ is usually called the *mean time between failures* (MTBF). For example, suppose that a machine is operated for 10,000 hours and experiences four failures that are immediately repaired. The mean time between failures is $\theta = 10{,}000/4 = 2{,}500$ hours and the failure rate is

$$\lambda = 1/2{,}500 = 0.0004 \text{ failures per hour}$$

Using MTTF in Reliability Prediction

Suppose that an electronic component has a failure rate of $\lambda = 0.0001$ failure per hour. The MTTF is $\theta = 1/0.0001 = 10{,}000$ hours. The probability that the component will not fail in 15,000 hours can be found using formula (7.13):

$$R(15{,}000) = e^{-15{,}000/10{,}000}$$
$$= e^{-1.5}$$
$$= 0.223$$

System Reliability

Many systems are composed of individual components with known reliabilities. The reliability data of individual components can be used to predict the reliability of the system at the design stage. Systems of components may be configured in *series*, in *parallel*, or in some mixed combination. Block diagrams are useful ways to represent system configurations where blocks represent functional components or subsystems. Engineers can use reliability calculations to predict performance and evaluate alternative designs to optimize performance within cost, size, or other constraints.

We first consider a **series system**, illustrated in Figure 7.17. In a series system, all components must function or the system will fail. For example, inexpensive Christmas tree lights use a series system whereby if one light goes out, the entire string does. If the reliability of component i is R_i, the reliability of the system is the product of the individual reliabilities, that is

$$R_S = R_1 \, R_2 \, ... \, R_n \tag{7.14}$$

This equation is based on the multiplicative law of probability.

Computing Series System Reliability

Suppose that a personal computer system is composed of the processing unit, graphics board, and keyboard with reliabilities of 0.997, 0.980, and 0.975, respectively. Clearly if one component fails, the computer will not function correctly. Using formula (7.14), the reliability of the system is

$$R_S = (0.997)(0.980)(0.975) = 0.953$$

Note that when reliabilities are less than one, system reliability decreases as additional components are added in series. Thus, the more complex a series system is, the greater the chance of failure.

FIGURE 7.17
Series System

If the reliability of component i is exponential with failure rate λ_i, for example, $R_i = e^{-\lambda_i T}$, then the reliability of a series system is a simple formula:

$$
\begin{aligned}
R_S &= e^{-\lambda_1 T} e^{-\lambda_2 T} \cdots e^{-\lambda_n T} \\
&= e^{-\lambda_1 T - \lambda_2 T \cdots - \lambda_n T} \\
&= e^{-\left(\sum_{i=1}^{n} \lambda_i\right) T}
\end{aligned}
\tag{7.15}
$$

EXAMPLE 7.12

Series Reliability with Exponential Failure Rates

Suppose that a two-component series system has failure rates of 0.004 and 0.001 per hour. Then using formula (7.15), we have

$$
\begin{aligned}
R_S(T) &= e^{-(0.004 + 0.001)T} \\
&= e^{-0.005T}
\end{aligned}
$$

The probability of survival for 100 hours would be

$$
\begin{aligned}
R_S(100) &= e^{-0.005(100)} \\
&= e^{-0.5} \\
&= 0.6065
\end{aligned}
$$

Redundancy offers backup components that can be used when the failure of any one component in a system can cause a failure of the entire system. Redundant components can increase reliability dramatically. Redundancy is crucial to systems in which failures can be extremely costly, such as aircraft or satellite communications systems. For example, airplanes have dual ignition systems and two spark plugs in each cylinder and two magenetos that produce a charge for the spark plugs. Redundancy, however, increases the cost, size, and weight of the system. Redundant components are designed in a **parallel system** configuration as illustrated in Figure 7.18. In such a system, failure of an individual component is less critical than in series systems; the system will successfully operate as long as one component functions.

The reliability of the parallel system in Figure 7.18 is derived as follows. If $R_1, R_2, \ldots, R_n$ are the reliabilities of the individual components, the probabilities of failure are $1 - R_1$, $1 - R_2, \ldots, 1 - R_n$, respectively. Because the system fails only if each component fails, the

FIGURE 7.18
Parallel System

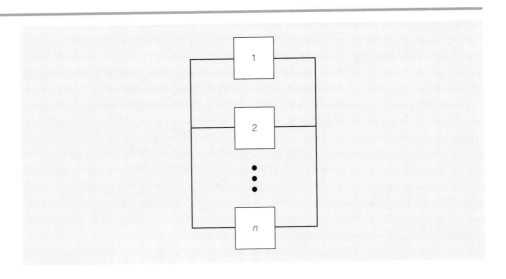

probability of system failure is $(1 - R_1)(1 - R_2) \cdots (1 - R_n)$. Hence, the system reliability is computed as

$$R_S = 1 - (1 - R_1)(1 - R_2) \cdots (1 - R_n) \tag{7.16}$$

If all components have identical reliabilities R, then

$$R_S = 1 - (1 - R)^n \tag{7.17}$$

EXAMPLE 7.13

Computing Parallel System Reliability

The computers on the space shuttle were designed with built-in redundancy in case of failure. Five computers were designed in parallel. Thus, for example, if the reliability of each is 0.99, using formula (7.17), the system reliability is

$$R_S = 1 - (1 - 0.99)^5 = 0.9999999999$$

If the reliabilities of the components of a parallel system are exponential, then simply replace R_i in formulas (7.15) or (7.16) with $R_i = e^{-\lambda_i T}$

EXAMPLE 7.14

Suppose that the failure rate for each component of a two component parallel system is 0.01. The reliability of the system is

$$R_S = 1 - (1 - e^{-0.01T})^2 = 2e^{-0.01T} - e^{-0.02T}$$

The probability than an individual component will survive 100 hours is $e^{-0.01(100)} = 0.3678$; however, the probability that the system will survive 100 hours is $2e^{-0.01(100)} - e^{-0.02(100)} = 2(.3678) - 0.1353 = 0.6003$.

Most systems are composed of combinations of series and parallel systems. To compute the reliability of such systems, decompose the system into smaller series and/or parallel subsets of component, compute the reliabilities of these subsets, and continue until you are left with a simple series or parallel system.

EXAMPLE 7.15

Computing the Reliability of Mixed Series and Parallel Systems

Consider the system shown in Figure 7.19(a). To determine the reliability of this system, first compute the reliability of the parallel subsystem for components B:

$$R_B = 1 - (1 - 0.9)^3 = 0.999$$

This is equivalent to replacing the three parallel components B with a single component B having a reliability of 0.999 in series with A, C, and D, as shown in Figure 7.19(b). Next, compute the reliability of this equivalent series system:

$$R_S = (0.99)(0.999)(0.96)(0.98) = 0.93$$

A second type of series-parallel arrangement is shown in Figure 7.20(a). System reliability is determined by first computing the reliabilities of the series systems ABC and DE:

$$R_{ABC} = (0.95)(0.98)(0.99) = 0.92169$$
$$R_{DE} = (0.99)(0.97) = 0.9603$$

The result is an equivalent parallel system shown in Figure 7.20(b). The system reliability is then computed as

$$R_S = 1 - (1 - 0.92169)(1 - 0.9603) = 0.9969$$

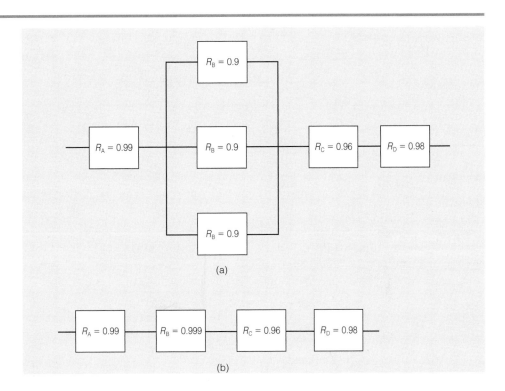

(a)

(b)

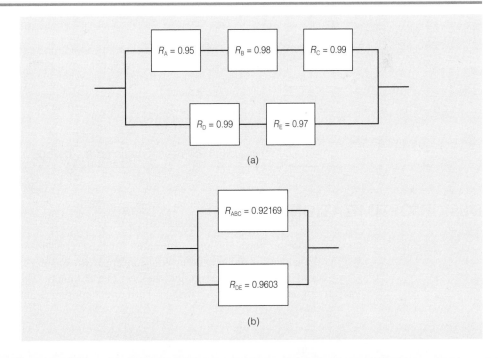

(a)

(b)

FIGURE 7.21
Three Alternate
Design
Configurations

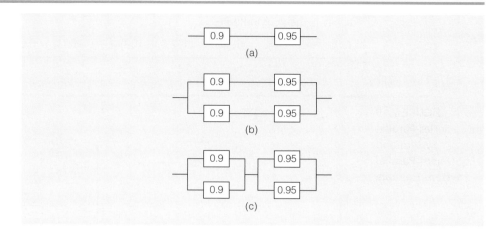

Reliability requirements are determined during the product design phase. The designer may use these techniques to determine the effects of adding redundancy, substituting different components, or reconfiguring the design.

EXAMPLE 7.16

Comparing the Reliability of Alternative Designs

A design requires two components, with reliabilities of 0.9 and 0.95 respectively, in series as shown in Figure 7.21(a). The reliability of this system is

$$R_S = (0.9)(0.95) = 0.855$$

To increase the reliability of this system, the designer is considering adding redundancy in one of two alternate design configurations as shown in Figure 7.21(b) and (c). The first alternate configuration has a redundant series system, while the second has individual redundant components in series. Which is the best?

Because the reliability of each series system in the first alternative is 0.855, we have a simple parallel system with reliability

$$R_S = 1 - (1 - 0.855)^2 = 1 - (0.145)^2 = .978975$$

To compute the reliability of the second alternative, first find the reliability of each equivalent parallel subsystem and then find the reliability of the resulting series system.

First parallel system: $R_S = 1 - (1 - 0.9)^2 = 0.99$

Second parallel system: $R_S = 1 - (1 - 0.95)^2 = 0.9975$

Series reliability: $R_S = (0.99)(0.9975) = 0.987525$

Therefore, the second alternative configuration is the best design.

DESIGN OPTIMIZATION

Designers of products and processes should make every effort to *optimize* their designs. A good analogy for understanding this concept is to consider the task of a major league baseball manager who must design the best player lineup. Although variation will be a factor among individuals as well as with the opposing team's defense, the manager would like to set the lineup that best plays to their strengths and overcomes their weaknesses. **Robust design** refers to designing goods and services that are insensitive to variation in manufacturing processes and when consumers use them. Robust design is facilitated by design of experiments (see Chapter 6) to identify optimal levels for nominal dimensions and other tools to minimize failures, reduce defects during the manufacturing process, facilitate assembly and disassembly (for both the manufacturer and the customer), and improve reliability.

In a celebrated case, Ina Tile Company, a Japanese ceramic tile manufacturer, had purchased a $2 million kiln from West Germany in 1953.[22] Tiles were stacked inside the kiln and baked. Tiles toward the outside of the stack tended to have a different average size and more variation in dimensions than those further inside the stack. The obvious cause was the uneven temperatures inside the kiln. Temperature was an uncontrollable factor. To try to eliminate the effects of temperature would require redesign of the kiln itself, a very costly alternative. A group of engineers, chemists, and others who were familiar with the manufacturing process brainstormed and identified seven major controllable variables that could affect the tile dimensions:

1. Limestone content
2. Fineness of additive
3. Content of agalmatolite
4. Type of agalmatolite
5. Raw material quantity
6. Content of waste return
7. Content of feldspar

The group designed and conducted an experiment using these factors. The experiment showed that the first factor, the limestone content, was the most significant factor; the other factors had smaller effects. By increasing the limestone content from 1 percent to 5 percent and choosing better levels for other factors, the percentage of size defects was reduced from 30 percent to less than 1 percent. Limestone was the cheapest material in the tile. In addition, the experiment revealed that a smaller amount of agalmatolite, the most expensive material in the tile, could be used without adversely affecting the tile dimension. This created a robust design that was insensitive to the uneven temperatures in the kiln, and was a breakthrough in the ceramic tile industry.

Design Failure Mode and Effects Analysis

Safety in consumer products represents a major issue in design, and certainly an important part of a company's public responsibilities. All parties responsible for design, manufacture, sales, and service of a defective product are now liable for damages. In a survey of more than 500 chief executives, more than one-third worked for firms that canceled the introduction of products because of liability concerns.

According to the theory of strict liability, anyone who sells a product that is defective or unreasonably dangerous is subject to liability for any physical harm caused to the user, the consumer, or the property of either.[23] This law applies when the seller is in the business of selling the product, and the product reaches the consumer without a substantial change in condition even if the seller exercised all possible care in the preparation and sale of the product. The principal issue is whether a defect, direct or indirect, exists. If the existence of a defect can be established, the manufacturer usually will be held liable. A plaintiff need prove only that (1) the product was defective,

(2) the defect was present when the product changed ownership, and (3) the defect resulted in injury. In 1997, Chrysler was ordered to pay $262.5 million in a case involving defective latches on minivans; thus, the economic consequences can be significant.

Attention to design quality can greatly reduce the possibility of product liability claims as well as provide supporting evidence in defense arguments. Liability makes documentation of quality assurance procedures a necessity. A firm should record all evidence that shows the designer established test and monitoring procedures of critical product characteristics. Feedback on test and inspection results along with corrective actions taken must also be documented. Even adequate packaging and handling procedures are not immune to examination in liability suits, because packaging is still within the manufacturer's span of control. Managers should address the following questions:[24]

- Is the product reasonably safe for the end user?
- What could possibly go wrong with it?
- Are any needed safety devices absent?
- What kind of warning labels or instructions should be included?
- What would attorneys call "reasonable foreseeable use"?
- What are some extreme climatic or environmental conditions for which the product should be tested?
- What similarities does the product have with others that may have encountered previous problems?

One tool for proactively addressing product risks is **design failure mode and effects analysis (DFMEA)**, often simply called *failure mode and effects analysis* (FMEA).[25] DFMEA was used by NASA in the 1960s and became popular in the automotive industry in the 1980s. Recently, it has found increasing application in health care. A Joint Commission for Accreditation of Healthcare Organizations standard lists DFMEA as a risk assessment tool, referring to it as "fault mode and effect analysis." The Institute for Healthcare Improvement defines FMEA as "a systematic, proactive method for evaluating a process to identify where and how it may fail and to assess the relative impact of different failures, in order to identify the parts of the process that are most in need of change."[26]

A DFMEA usually consists of specifying the following information for each design element or function:

- *Failure modes.* Ways in which each element or function can fail. This information generally takes some research and imagination. One way to start is with known failures that have occurred in the past. Documents such as quality and reliability reports, test results, and warranty reports provide useful information.
- *Effect of the failure on the customer.* Such as dissatisfaction, potential injury or other safety issue, downtime, repair requirements, and so on. Maintenance records, customer complaints, and warranty reports provide good sources of information. Consideration should be given to failures on the function of the end product, manufacturability in the next process, what the customer sees or experiences, and product safety.
- *Severity, likelihood of occurrence, and detection rating.* These are subjective ratings best done by a cross-functional team of experts. The severity rating is based on how serious the impact would be if the potential failure were to occur. Severity

FIGURE 7.22   Scoring Rubric for DFMEA Ratings

Rating	Severity	Occurrence	Detection
10	Hazardous or potentially life-threatening	Very high or almost certain probability of occurrence	Cannot detect or hidden defect
7–9	Serious impact on customer safety or satisfaction	High probability of occurrence	Low chance of detection
5–6	Major impact on customer satisfaction	Moderate probability of occurrence	Moderate chance of detection
2–4	Minor defect or customer inconvenience	Low probability of occurrence	High chance of detection
1	Little to no effect	Unlikely to occur	Will almost always be able to detect

might be measured on a scale of 1 to 10, where a "1" indicates that the failure is so minor that the customer probably would not notice it, and a "10" might mean that the customer might be endangered. The occurrence rating is based on the probability of the potential failure occurring. This might be based on service history or field performance and provides an indication of the significance of the failure. The detection rating is based on how easily the potential failure could be detected prior to occurrence. Figure 7.22 shows an example of a scoring rubric for these ratings. Based on these assessments, a risk priority number (RPN) is computed by multiplying the severity, occurrence, and detection ratings, resulting in a number from 1 to 1,000, which is used to identify critical failure modes that must be addressed. The lower the value, the lower the risk.

- *Potential causes of failure.* Often failure is the result of poor design. Design deficiencies can cause errors either in the field or in manufacturing and assembly. Identification of causes might require experimentation and rigorous analysis.
- *Corrective actions or controls.* These controls might include design changes, mistake proofing, better user instructions, management responsibilities, and target completion dates.

After a DFMEA is completed, the organization should take corrective and preventive action to avoid the potential failures in the design or process. Figure 7.23 shows an example in health care. The risk priority number is the product of the severity, likelihood of occurrence, and detection ratings, whose scales are shown in Figure 7.24.

Using DFMEA will not only improve product functionality and safety, but also reduce failure costs—particularly warranty costs, as well as decrease manufacturing and service delivery problems. It can also provide a defense against frivolous lawsuits. DFMEA should be conducted early in the design process to save costs and reduce cycle times, and provide a knowledge base to improve subsequent design efforts. This approach can also be used for processes to identify hazardous conditions that may endanger a worker or operational problems that can disrupt a production process and result in scrap, downtime, or other non-value-added costs.

FIGURE 7.23   Example of a DFMEA in Health Care

Description: Specimen collection/procession
Year(s): 2004
Location: Detroit

Process responsibility: Jane S.
Key date:

FMEA number: 2004-1
Prepared by: RDR Team
Revision date: 2/7/2005

Line No.	Process function/ requirements	Potential failure mode	Potential effect(s) of failure	Severity	Class	Potential cause(s)/ mechanism of failure	Occurrence	Current process controls	Detection	Risk priority number	Recommended action(s)	Responsibility and target completion date	Action taken	New severity	New occurrence	New detection	New risk priority number
1.	1.0 Take specimen	1.1 Put in wrong tub	1.1.1 Run wrong task	8		Inadvertent error	3		9	192	Organics tubes by color, implement "pull" system of inventory mgmt.	Betty L 12/2/2004	Recommended actions done	9	1	1	9
		1.2 Not refrigerated on time	1.2.1 Ruin specimen	8		Inadvertent error	6		9	288	Implement tracking log & use of alarms, audit chart daily for completion	Betty L 11/25/2004	Recommended actions done	9	2	2	36
		1.3 Not centrifuged on time	1.3.1 Ruin specimen	8		Inadvertent error	6		9	288	Implement tracking log & use of alarms, audit chart daily for completion	Betty L 11/15/2004	Recommended actions done	9	1	8	72
		1.4 Shortage of tubes	1.4.1 Rework another	4		Work load	7		7	196	Pull system of inventory management	Betty L 12/02/2004		4	3	7	94
2	2.0 Centrifuge it	2.1 Equipment failure	2.1.1 can't run test	4		Aged equipment	2		10	80	Add to PM log	Kaye P 12/01/2004		4	2	6	48
		2.2 Insufficient run time	2.2.1 specimen	6		Inadvertent error	4		9	216	Set alarm to warn, provide process definition on RASIC chart, implement verification and audit daily	Kaye P 10/30/2004	Recommended actions done	9	1	2	18
3	3.0 Store/ refrigerate it	3.1 No Temperature log	3.1.1 Uncertainty of specimen	8		No the moniater	3	Acquire thermometer	10	190	Audit temperature log each shift	Kaye P 11/07/2004					
		3.2 Temperature wrong	3.2.1 specimen tainted	8		Equipment failure	2		7	94	Add to PM log	Kaye P 10/30/2004		6	3	6	106
		3.3 Drop it	3.3.1 Ruin specimen	8		Inadvertent error	1		3	18	Work instruction	Kaye P 10/30/2004		6	2	6	72

FIGURE 7.24   Severity, Likelihood, and Detection Rating Scales

Severity Rating		Likelihood Detection of Rating				Occurrence Rating	
Rating	Criteria	Rating	Failure probability	IPTO*	IPMO**	Rating	Detection
10	Failure may seriously endanger patient.	10	Very high	>500	>500,000	10	Almost impossible
9	Failure involves regulatory noncompliance	9	Very high	333	333,333	9	Very remote
8	Failure causes patient high dissatisfaction.	8	High	125	125,000	8	Remote
7	Failure causes patient dissatisfaction	7	High	50	50,000	7	Very low
6	Failure causes disruption of patient ADL	6	Moderate	12.5	12,500	6	Low
5	Inconvenience for patient and multiple providers	5	Moderate	2.5	2,500	5	Moderate
4	Inconvenience at subsequent function; minor rework	4	Moderate	0.5	500	4	Moderately high
3	Slight inconvenience at next function; minor rework	3	Low	0.067	67	3	High
2	Slight inconvenience at delivery; minor rework	2	Very low	0.0067	7	2	Very high
1	Patient will probably not notice	1	Remote	0.00067	1	1	Almost certain

*Activities of daily living.

*Incident per thousand opportunities.
**Incident per million opportunities.

Source: Reprinted with permission form FMEA—"Something Old, Something New," *Quality Progress*, May 2005, pp. 90–93. Copyright © 2005 American Society for Quality. No further distribution allowed without permission.

Fault Tree Analysis

Fault Tree Analysis (FTA), sometimes called **cause and effect tree analysis**, is a method to describe combinations of conditions or events that can lead to a failure. In effect, it is a way to drill down and identify causes associated with failures and is a good complement to DFMEA. It is particularly useful for identifying failures that occur only as a result of multiple events occurring simultaneously. A cause and effect tree is composed of conditions or events connected by "and" gates and "or" gates as shown in Figure 7.25. An effect with an "and" gate occurs only if *all* of the causes below it occur; an effect with an "or" gate occurs whenever *any* of the causes occur.

Design for Manufacturability

Product design can significantly affect the cost of manufacturing (direct and indirect labor, materials, and overhead), redesign, warranty, and field repair; the efficiency by which the product can be manufactured, and the quality of the output. Designers must pay particular attention to cost, quality, and manufacturability in order to meet price targets that customers are willing to pay. A Samsung manager noted that 70 to 80 percent of quality, cost, and delivery time is determined in the initial design stages. This is one reason's for the company's obsession with reducing complexity early in the design cycle. As a result, Samsung has lower manufacturing costs, higher profit margins, quicker times to market, and more often than not, more innovative products than its competition.[27]

Simplifying designs can often improve both cost and quality. Mercedes-Benz, for example, saw its global leadership decline behind BMW and Lexus because of high costs and degrading quality. Although a technology leader, Mercedes' vehicles were packed with numerous electronic systems that need to be integrated and function seamlessly together, a very difficult task. Engineers typically designed new electronics for each model, adding to complexity and cost. One of the initiatives the company has undertaken to improve is to design less complex cars similar to what BMW did, for instance, using electronics architectures with common components that can be shared across

FIGURE 7.25
Example of a Cause
and Effect Tree

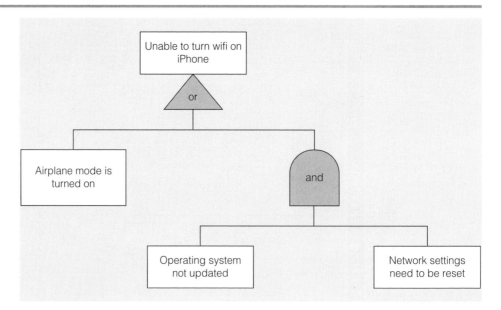

many models.[28] By cutting the number of parts, material costs generally go down, inventory levels fall, the number of suppliers shrinks, and production time can be shortened.

Many aspects of product design can adversely affect manufacturability and, hence, quality.[29] Some parts may be designed with features difficult to fabricate repeatedly or with unnecessarily tight tolerances. Some parts may lack details for self-alignment or features for correct insertion. In other cases, parts so fragile or so susceptible to corrosion or contamination may be damaged in shipping or by internal handling. Sometimes a design simply has more parts than are needed to perform the desired functions, which increases the chance of assembly error. Thus, problems of poor design may show up as errors, poor yield, damage, or functional failure in fabrication, assembly, test, transport, and end use.

Designs with numerous parts increase the incidence of part mix-ups, missing parts, and test failures. Parts that are similar but not identical create the possibility that an assembler will use the wrong part. Parts without details to prevent insertion in the wrong orientation lead to more frequent improper assembly. Complicated assembly steps or tricky joining processes can cause incorrect, incomplete, unreliable, or otherwise faulty assemblies. Finally, the designer's failure to consider conditions to which parts will be exposed during assembly such as temperature, humidity, vibration, static electricity, and dust, may result in failures during testing or use.

Design for manufacturability (DFM) is the process of designing a product for efficient production at the highest level of quality. DFM is typically integrated into standard design processes, but because of the need for highly-creative solutions, it might be addressed in specialized "think-tank" departments in a company. Samsung, for example, supports a Value Innovation Program (VIP) Center, which has been described as "an invitation-only, round-the-clock, assembly line for ideas and profits where Samsung's top researchers, engineers, and designers come to solve their grittiest problems."[30] Typical projects might involve reducing material costs on a new printer by 30 percent, or reducing the number of steps needed to manufacture a new camcorder by 25 percent. Texas Instruments locates its design centers strategically throughout its facilities. These centers offer expertise and systems with extensive capability for electrical and mechanical computer-aided design, system engineering, and manufacturing, and allow the evaluation of parts that have the best quality history, producibility, reliability, and other special engineering requirements.

DFM is intended to prevent product designs that simplify assembly operations but require more complex and expensive components, designs that simplify component manufacture while complicating the assembly process, and designs that are simple and inexpensive to produce but difficult or expensive to service or support. Table 7.1 summarizes important DFM guidelines that can improve quality and reduce costs. Many industries have developed more specific guidelines. For example, guidelines for designing printed circuit boards include:

- Placing all components on the topside of the board
- Grouping similar components whenever possible
- Maintaining a 0.60-inch clearance for insertable components

Design and Environmental Responsibility

Environmental concerns have an unprecedented impact on product and process designs. Hundreds of millions of home and office appliances are disposed of each year. The problem of what to do with obsolete computers is a growing design and technological waste

TABLE 7.1　Design Guidelines for Quality Assurance

Minimize Number of Parts

• Fewer parts and assembly drawings	→	Lower volume of drawings and instructions to control
• Less complicated assemblies	→	Lower assembly error rate
• Fewer parts to hold to required quality characteristics	→	Higher consistency of part quality
• Fewer parts to fail	→	Higher reliability

Minimize Number of Part Numbers

• Fewer variations of like parts	→	Lower assembly error rate

Design for Robustness (Taguchi method)

• Low sensitivity to component variability	→	Higher first-pass yield; less degradation of performance with time

Eliminate Adjustments

• No assembly adjustment errors	→	Higher first-pass yield
• Eliminates adjustable components with high failure rates	→	Lower failure rate

Make Assembly Easy and Foolproof

• Parts cannot be assembled wrong	→	Lower assembly error rate
• Obvious when parts are missing	→	Lower assembly error rate
• Assembly tooling designed into part	→	Lower assembly error rate
• Parts are self-securing	→	Lower assembly error rate
• No "force fitting" of parts	→	Less damage to parts; better serviceability

Use Repeatable, Well-Understood Processes

• Part quality easy to control	→	Higher part yield
• Assembly quality easy to control	→	Higher assembly yield

Choose Parts That Can Survive Process Operations

• Less damage to parts	→	Higher yield
• Less degradation of parts	→	Higher reliability

Design for Efficient and Adequate Testing

• Less mistaking "good" for "bad" product and vice versa	→	Truer assessment of quality; less unnecessary rework

Lay Out Parts for Reliable Process Completion

• Less damage to parts during handling and assembly	→	Higher yield; higher reliability

Eliminate Engineering Changes on Released Products

• Fewer errors due to changeovers and multiple revisions/versions	→	Lower assembly error rate

Source: Reprinted with permission from D. Daetz, "The Effect of Product Design on Product Quality and Product Cost," *Quality Progress* vol. 20, no. 6, pp. 63–67, June 1987. Copyright 1987 American Society for Quality. No further distribution allowed without permission.

problem today.[31] Pressures from environmental groups clamoring for "socially responsive" designs, states and municipalities that are running out of space for landfills, and consumers who want the most for their money all cause designers and managers to look carefully at the concept of **design-for-environment**, or **DFE**.[32] DFE is the explicit consideration of environmental concerns during the design of products and processes, and includes such practices as designing for recyclability and disassembly.

DFE offers the potential to create more desirable products at lower costs by reducing disposal and regulatory costs, increasing the end-of-life value of products, reducing material use, and minimizing liabilities. Recyclable products are designed to be taken apart and their components repaired, refurbished, melted down, or otherwise salvaged for reuse. For example, General Electric's plastics division, which serves the durable goods market, uses only thermoplastics in its products.[33] Unlike many other varieties of plastics, thermoplastics can be melted down and recast into other shapes and products, thus making them recyclable.

Many products are discarded simply because the cost of maintenance or repair is too high when compared with the cost of a new item. Now **design for disassembly** promises to bring back easy, affordable product repair. For example, Whirlpool Corporation is developing a new appliance designed for repairability, with its parts sorted for easy coding. Thus, repairability has the potential of pleasing customers, who would prefer to repair a product rather than discard it. At the same time, companies are challenged to consider fresh approaches to design that build both cost-effectiveness and quality into the product. For instance, even though it is more efficient to assemble an item using rivets instead of screws, this approach is contrary to a design-for-disassembly philosophy. An alternative might be an entirely new design that eliminates the need for fasteners in the first place.

Design for Excellence

Design for Excellence (DFX) is an emerging concept that includes many design-related initiatives such as concurrent engineering, design for manufacturability, design for assembly, design for environment, and other "design for" approaches.[34] DFX objectives include higher functional performance, physical performance, user friendliness, reliability and durability, maintainability and serviceability, safety, compatibility and upgradeability, environmental friendliness, and psychological characteristics. DFX represents a total approach to product development and design involves the following activities:

- Constantly thinking in terms of how one can design or manufacture products better, not just solving or preventing problems
- Focusing on "things done right" rather than "things gone wrong"
- Defining customer expectations and going beyond them, not just barely meeting them or just matching the competition
- Optimizing desirable features or results, not just incorporating them
- Minimizing the overall cost without compromising quality of function

DESIGN VERIFICATION

The final phase of DFSS is verification of product and process designs. Sometimes verification is required by government regulation or for legal concerns. For products, reliability testing provides a means for obtaining data about product performance as both a verification approach and a means for design improvement.

Design Reviews

One approach often used to facilitate product development is the **design review**. The purpose of a design review is to stimulate discussion, raise questions, and generate new ideas and solutions to help designers anticipate problems before they occur. Generally, a design review is conducted in three major stages: preliminary, intermediate, and final. The preliminary design review establishes early communication between marketing, engineering, manufacturing, and purchasing personnel and provides better coordination of their activities. It usually involves higher levels of management and concentrates on strategic issues in design that relate to customer requirements and thus the ultimate quality of the product. A preliminary design review evaluates such issues as the function of the product, conformance to customer's needs, completeness of specifications, manufacturing costs, and liability issues. Eastman Chemical reviews designs for safety, reliability, waste minimization, patent position, toxicity information, environmental risks, product disposal, and other customer needs. It also conducts a market analysis of key suppliers' abilities to manage costs, obtain materials, maintain production, and ship reliably. AT&T Transmission Systems has a new product introduction center that evaluates designs based on manufacturing capabilities, recognizing that good designs both reduce the risk of manufacturing defects and improve productivity.

After the design is well established, an intermediate review takes place to study the design in greater detail to identify potential problems and suggest corrective action. Personnel at lower levels of the organization are more heavily involved at this stage. Finally, just before release to production, a final review is held. Materials lists, drawings, and other detailed design information are studied with the purpose of preventing costly changes after production setup.

Reliability Testing

The reliability of a product is determined principally by the design and the reliability of the components of the product. However, reliability is such a complex issue that it cannot always be determined from theoretical analysis of the design alone. Hence, formal testing is necessary, which involves simulating environmental conditions to determine a product's performance, operating time, and mode of failure. Testing is useful for a variety of other reasons. Test data are often necessary for liability protection, as means for evaluating designs or vendor reliability, and in process planning and selection. Often, reliability test data are required in military contracts. Testing is necessary to evaluate warranties and to avoid high costs related to early field failure. Good testing leads to good reliability and hence good quality. Verizon Wireless advertises itself as being the "leader in network reliability." It has its engineers travel around the country in unmarked vehicles to make millions of voice calls and perform data tests on the network and those of competitors each year.

Product testing is performed by various methods. For example, Hewlett-Packard's popular HP-12c financial calculator, which is essentially unchanged since 1981 and still is a popular seller, undergoes a drop test in which engineers repeatedly drop it from desk height onto a hard floor. They also subject the keyboard to mechanical button-pushers to simulate the effects of 5 to 10 years of use.[35]

Semiconductors are the basic building blocks of numerous modern products such as MP3 players, automotive ignition systems, computers, and military weapons systems. Semiconductors have a small proportion of defects, called *latent defects*, which can cause them to fail during the first 1,000 hours of normal operation (the infant mortality period in Figure 7.14). After that, the failure rate stabilizes, perhaps for as long as 25 years, before beginning to rise again as components wear out. These infant mortalities can be as high as 10 percent in a new technology or as low as 0.01 percent in proven technologies. Thus, electronic components are often tested for the length of the infant mortality period prior to being placed into service to eliminate early functional failures. This is called **burn-in**. Studies and experience have demonstrated the economic advantages of burn-in. For example, a large-scale study of the effect of burn-in on enhancing reliability of memory chips was conducted in Europe. The failure rate without burn-in was 0.24 percent per thousand hours, whereas burn-in reduced the rate to 0.02 percent per thousand hours. When considering the cost of field service and warranty work, for instance, reduction of semiconductor failure rates in a large system by an order of magnitude translates roughly into an average of one repair call per year versus one repair call per month.

The purpose of *life testing*, that is, running devices until they fail, is to measure the distribution of failures to better understand and eliminate their causes. However, such testing can be expensive and time-consuming. For devices that have long natural lives, life testing is not practical. **Accelerated life testing** involves overstressing components to reduce the time to failure and find weaknesses. This form of testing might involve exposing integrated circuits to elevated temperatures or voltage in order to force latent defects to occur. For example, a device that might normally fail after 300 hours at 25°C might fail in less than 20 hours at 150°C. A more recent approach, called **highly accelerated life testing**, is focused on discovering latent defects that would not otherwise be found through conventional methods. For example, it might expose products to rapid, extreme temperature changes in temperature chambers that can move products between hot and cold zones to test thermal shock, or also extreme vibrations.[36]

SUMMARY OF KEY POINTS AND TERMINOLOGY

The Student Companion Site provides a summary of key concepts and terminology introduced in this chapter.

QUALITY *in* PRACTICE

Testing Audio Components at Shure, Inc.[37]

Shure Incorporated is a global, privately held company headquartered in Evanston, Illinois, with manufacturing facilities in Illinois, Texas, and Mexico, and sales offices in Germany and Hong Kong. Shure's mission is to deliver high-performing, quality, rugged and reliable audio products, and to provide superior customer service and support. Shure's philosophy is to be market-driven and customer-focused in their chosen markets. Each market segment has its own quality and reliability needs:

- Performance Audio: Musical performers and those who record and monitor their work on stage or in the studio. Anyone who has attended a rock concert can attest to the rough treatment microphones receive from the entertainers, some actually throwing them across the stage.

- Presentation and Installation Audio: Anywhere a sound system is installed, such as houses of worship, hotels, conference rooms, clubs, theaters, and auditoriums. Many users are unfamiliar with the acoustical characteristics of the equipment they are using and sound technicians are often not on site, so the equipment really needs to run by itself.
- Radio and TV: Broadcast industry both in studio and on location in the field. Technicians need to have total confidence in the equipment they are using on a live, remote broadcast, because they cannot go back and redo that on-the-spot interview.
- Consumer Market: Phonograph cartridges and low-cost microphones, including audiophiles, hip-hop DJs, and home recording. Scratch DJs literally take a record and pull it back and forth to the beat of a song, causing tremendous pressure on the phonograph stylus.
- Mobile Communications: Audio subsystems, such as hands-free cellular, within the automotive environment. Microphones need to perform in a variety of temperatures.

S. N. Shure began the company by launching a one-man operation in 1925 that sold radio parts kits. It was the microphone that marked the company's entry into manufacturing in 1932, and the microphone remains Shure's flagship product to this day. Because of its emphasis on engineering research, Shure products became known early on for their outstanding quality and durability. During World War II, Shure was awarded a U.S. government contract to provide microphones to the military, and needed to meet strict specifications for performance and ruggedness. Shure took the extra step to develop a rigorous in-house testing program that remains in place today.

In addition to microphones (both wired and wireless) and phonograph cartridges, Shure manufactures a number of other audio electronics products, including mixers, digital signal processors, personal monitoring systems, and digital feedback reducers. Shure's quality philosophy is reliability oriented. Products are tested for reliability well beyond the warranty period, with the goal of providing the customer long-term service and satisfaction. Testing is designed to simulate actual operating conditions. Shure has more than

80 test procedures in place. The following are a few examples:

- Microphone Drop Test: To determine whether a microphone is capable of dynamic shock stress. Initial performance data are taken on the mic. Then the mic is dropped numerous times onto a hardwood floor from a height of 6 feet at random angles. The mic is "talked out" after every two drops. After the drop tests, level and response are tested and compared to the initial data. Any unit not meeting original print specifications is considered a failure.
- Perspiration Test: To evaluate the corrosion resistance of painted/plated parts exposed to an acid solution simulating sweat. Parts are placed in a perspiration chamber that consists of a stand supporting the parts over a large glass jar containing acid solution. Parts are inspected daily for amounts of corrosion for a period of seven days. Parts are then compared to good control parts to determine amount of corrosion present.
- Cable and Cable Assembly Flex: To ensure that any cable that would normally be subjected to random twisting motion under tension will meet field requirements. Cable flex test equipment provides for two independent motions: rocking motion and rotation, and twisting motion and rotation. Cables not meeting flex life specification are considered a failure.
- Sequential Shipping: To evaluate the packaging effectiveness and mechanical integrity of the product under simulated shipping conditions. This test is used for all Shure products. Products packaged for shipping are given the following tests, in order: drop test, vibration test, and rough handling test. When the product is removed from its packaging, it must appear and operate as new. If appropriate, an electrical test is performed and compared to initial electrical test data.
- Cartridge Drop and Scrape Test: To determine ability of stylus to withstand accidental drops and side impacts. A cartridge mounted in a tone arm is dropped onto a moving record at least 100 times. The cartridge is scraped across a moving record 100 times. This test simulates and exceeds any abuse given to the cartridge and stylus in normal use.
- Temperature Storage: To determine ability to withstand extreme temperatures for extended

periods of time. Initial performance data are taken. For high temperature, the product is placed in a preheated high temperature chamber for seven days. The product is allowed to stabilize at room temperature for 24 hours and then the same performance data are taken. For low temperature, the product is placed in a low temperature chamber for seven days, allowed to stabilize to room temperature for 24 hours, and tested.

By performing these and other rigorous tests, Shure consistently meets its goal of exceeding customers' product performance and reliability expectations.

Key Issues for Discussion

1. Describe how the definition of reliability presented in this chapter applies to the performance tests described here. Do these tests measure inherent reliability or achieved reliability?

2. For the examples of product testing provided in this case, discuss what quality/reliability measurements might be taken and how the data might be analyzed. For example, are the measurements attributes or variables? Would they be analyzed using descriptive statistics, Pareto charts, and so on?

QUALITY *in* PRACTICE

Applying QFD in a Managed Care Organization[38]

Managed care was introduced in the United States nearly two decades ago as a means to maintain quality while managing costs. A managed care organization (MCO) contracts with physicians, hospitals, medical equipment companies, and home health agencies to provide services to its members (patients).

The MCO markets its services and actively enrolls people. Once enrolled, members receive a handbook that explains how they can access the services offered by the MCO and its affiliated providers. The member handbook has become a main source of information regarding an increasingly complex array of benefits offered by the thousands of MCOs. Designing the handbook and creating its content are, therefore, important components of any MCO's business strategy. Unfortunately, a member satisfaction survey indicated that members have a poor understanding of their benefits. When members are unable to understand their benefits, the MCOs' member services switchboards are inundated with calls, resulting in frustration and anger and further delaying patient access to the MCOs' services. The MCO receives an average of 3,000 calls per day, with each call lasting an average of 3.2 minutes. Approximately 50 percent of these calls involve issues discussed in the member handbook. The MCO also spends more than $250,000 per year in providing supplemental materials to its members as a result of inadequacies in the member handbook.

To improve the handbook and member satisfaction, QFD was used to redesign it. The input for the QFD process was obtained through a series of focus groups. A total of 131 MCO customers participated in six focus group sessions. Participants were selected based on two criteria:

1. They had to have been members of a competing MCO—whose member handbook was used for comparison—for at least two years prior to joining the MCO being studied.

2. They had to have been members of the MCO being studied for at least two consecutive years.

The focus group process was then administered in two stages:

Stage 1. Participants were provided with a copy of the company's member handbook and the competitor's member handbook. Even though the participants had all used the competitor's member handbook, it was necessary to provide them with copies to ensure a fair comparison. They were allowed to take both handbooks home for one week to look them over.

Stage 2. The groups were brought together for a follow-up session that focused on data collection.

Each session was facilitated by an independent researcher unaffiliated with the MCO, and each participant was provided lunch as a reward for participating in the study.

The six focus groups all followed these steps:

1. Determine customer requirements.
2. Measure the importance of the customer requirements.
3. Rate customer satisfaction with the company's current member handbook.
4. Rate satisfaction with the competitor's member handbook.
5. Develop a list of characteristics that are within the control of the company and could potentially improve the handbook. These characteristics are referred to as substitute quality characteristics.

The QFD process begins by capturing the voice of the customer or the customer requirements. The key customer requirements identified were ease of use, accuracy, timeliness, clarity, and consciousness. The technical requirements that describe how the organization will respond to each of the customer requirements were identified as follows:

- Font size
- Up-to-date information
- Use of pictures or illustrations
- Use of colors
- Glossary of terms
- Answers to frequently asked questions
- Expanded table of contents
- Offering the handbook in more than one language

After gathering the customer and technical requirements, the MCO determined there was a strong correlation between the substitute quality characteristic (technical requirement) of ease of use and the customer requirements of expanding the glossary of terms and the table of contents. Similarly, the following substitute quality characteristics had a moderate correlation with ease of use:

- Font size
- Use of pictures or illustrations
- Use of colors
- A question and answer section
- More language friendly

Providing updates had a weak correlation with ease of use.

The results of the MCO's QFD study resulted in the House of Quality shown in Figure 7.26. The numbers in the *Rate of Importance* column indicate the relative importance customers assigned to each requirement. The importance rating uses a numerical scale from 1 to 5, with 1 being low and 5 being high. Members were asked to use such a rating scale during the focus group sessions. Two customer requirements—ease of use and accuracy—were assigned high importance ratings of 4.5 and 5, respectively. The other three customer requirements—clarity, timeliness, and conciseness—received importance ratings of 3.8, 3.2, and 2.5, respectively.

The entries in the *Company Now* column indicate how customers rate the organization's performance with respect to their stated requirements. This rating is based on a numerical scale from 1 to 5, with 1 being poor and 5 being excellent. The entries in *Competitor X* column represent how the customers rate the chief competitor X with respect to their stated requirements. As is the case in the *Company Now* column, these ratings are based on a numerical scale from 1 to 5, with 1 being poor and 5 being excellent. According to this study, the chief competitor's handbook is outperforming the MCO's handbook in ease of use, accuracy, and clarity, as perceived by its customers. The *Plan* column indicates where the company wishes to be with respect to each of the quality requirements stated by its customers. The plan for each requirement is determined by examining the MCO's position in relation to its competitor(s) and its customers' rate of importance. It is also based on the organization's strategic plan.

After taking all things into account, the MCO's QFD team set a goal of achieving a performance rating of 4.5 for ease of use, 4.6 for accuracy, 3.8 for timeliness, 3.9 for clarity, and 4.1 for conciseness. The MCO expects to achieve these levels of performance the next time its customers are surveyed. The *Rate of Improvement* column contains the ratio of the company's goal compared to where the company is today. It is determined by dividing the value in the *Plan* column by the value in the *Company Now* column for each requirement. The *Absolute Quality Weight* is determined by multiplying the rate of importance by the rate of improvement. It is an attempt to assign a weighted rate to what the

FIGURE 7.26 House of Quality for the MCO Membership Handbook

Direction of improvement	
Maximize ↑	1
Target ×	0
Minimize ↓	−1

		1 Rate of importance	1 Font size	2 Updates	3 Photos or illustrations	4 Use of colors	5 Glossary of terms	6 Question and answer section	7 Table of contents	8 Laguage friendly	1 Competitive analysis	2 • Company now	3 • Competitor X	4 • Plan	5 • Rate of improvement	6 Absolute weight	7 Percentage of importance	Maximum = 29.5 Percentage of importance Minimum = 9.9	
Direction of improvement	1		↑	↑	↑	↑	↑	↑	↑	↑									
Ease of use	1	4.5	○	▽	○	○	●	○	●	○		3.2	4.3	4.5	1.4	6.3	25.2		1
Accuracy	2	5.0		●			▽	○		▽		3.1	4.1	4.6	1.5	7.4	29.5		2
Timeliness	3	3.2		●				▽				3.8	3.4	3.8	1.0	3.2	12.7		3
Clarity	4	3.8	▽	▽	○	▽	●	○	▽	○		2.6	3.7	3.9	1.5	5.7	22.7		4
Conciseness	5	2.5	▽		▽							4.1	3.3	4.1	1.0	2.5	9.9		5
Importance of the hows	1		108.1	427.9	153.4	98.2	460.0	244.7	249.1	173.0									
Percentage of importance of the hows	2		5.6	22.4	8.0	5.1	24.0	12.8	13.0	9.0									
Maximum = 24 Percentage of importance of the hows Minimum = 5.1	3																		
Competitive benchmarking results	4																		
• Company now	5		10	1	1	2	5	5	10	2									
• Competitor X	6		12	3	4	5	15	10	6	1									
• Plan	7		12	4	4	5	20	15	10	2									
			1	2	3	4	5	6	7	8									

Standard 9-3-1

Strong	●	9
Moderate	○	3
Weak	▽	1

Source: Reprinted with permission from Vincent Omachonu & Paul Barach, "QFD in a Managed Care Organization," *Quality Progress*, November 2005, pp. 36–41. Copyright © 2005 American Society for Quality. No further distribution without permission.

customer considers to be important and the goal (value established in the *Plan* column). The *Percentage of Importance* was determined by transforming each absolute weight value into a percentage of the total absolute weight value (25.1).

After thoroughly looking at what is important to the MCO's customers, the company's current performance, its chief competitor's current position, and the goal, the MCO determined that accuracy is the most important requirement driving customer satisfaction, with nearly 30 percent of the demanded weight.

The figures in the *Importance of the Hows* row represent the sum of the products of each column symbol value and the corresponding demanded weight. The two most important technical requirements were glossary of terms and updates, with totals of 460 and 427.9, respectively. Each entry in the *Percentage of Importance of the Hows* row is divided by the sum of all the entries in that row and multiplied by 100 to convert it into a percentage.

The *Company Now* row gives the values of the measurable technical requirements. The QFD team examined and analyzed the chief competitor's member handbook and interviewed the sales and marketing representatives of both companies to determine the values of the technical requirements for the chief competitors marketing representatives participated in this study. They were selected based on their knowledge of and experience working with the two companies. The competitor outperformed the MCO under study in all aspects of the technical requirements, except language friendliness and table of contents. The most aggressive plans were targeted at the two technical requirements with the highest totals: glossary of terms and updates. The plan values represent the design targets for the team's effort for the redesign of the MCO's member handbook.

Following the redesign of the member handbook, the volume of calls associated with the issues addressed in the handbook decreased from 3,000 calls per day to 1,900 (about a 35 percent reduction).

Member services telephone operators were able to attend to other important issues facing the members of the health plan. Besides increasing operational efficiency, this improvement enhanced member satisfaction and reduced employee frustration in having to repeatedly deal with these issues.

Key Issues for Discussion

1. Although this example of QFD involved the design of tangible items, why is it more difficult to implement in a service context as opposed to a pure manufacturing context?
2. Verify the calculations in the *Importance of the Hows* row and *Percentage of Importance of the Hows* row by showing the detailed calculations used to arrive at these figures.
3. What lessons can be learned and applied to other service organizations that seek to design or redesign their products and services?

REVIEW QUESTIONS

1. Describe the steps of the product design and development process.
2. Discuss the importance of and impediments to reducing the time for product development.
3. What is concurrent engineering? What benefits does it have?
4. What is Design for Six Sigma (DFSS)? Explain the four basic elements of DFSS and the various tools and methodologies that comprise this body of knowledge.
5. Explain concept development and innovation. Describe the importance of innovation and creativity in concept development.
6. What is the purpose of detailed design?
7. Explain the concept and the principal benefits of QFD.
8. Outline the process of building the House of Quality. What departments and functions within the company should be involved in each step of the process?
9. Explain and give an example of nominal specifications and tolerances in both manufacturing and service.
10. Explain the Taguchi loss function and how it is used in process and tolerance design.
11. Define reliability. Explain the definition thoroughly.
12. What is the difference between a functional failure and a reliability failure?
13. What is the difference between inherent reliability and achieved reliability?
14. What is the definition of failure rate? How is it measured?
15. Explain the product life characteristics curve and its implications for reliability and quality control.
16. What is a reliability function? Explain how to determine it.
17. Explain how to compute the reliability of series, parallel, and series-parallel systems.
18. What is robust design? Explain why it is important for both consumers and manufacturers.
19. What is design failure mode and effects analysis (DFMEA)? Provide a simple example illustrating the concept.
20. What is fault tree analysis? How does it differ from DFMEA?
21. How can product design affect manufacturability? Explain the concept and importance of design for manufacturability.

22. Summarize the key design practices for high quality in manufacturing and assembly.
23. Discuss environmental responsibility issues relating to product design facing businesses today.
24. Describe the basic approach to design for excellence.
25. Explain the purpose of design reviews and how they facilitate product development.
26. Describe different forms of product testing.

PROBLEMS

Note: Data sets for several problems are available in the Excel workbook C07Data in the Student Companion Site for this chapter. Click on the appropriate worksheet tab as noted in the problem (e.g., Prob. 7-5, etc.) to access the data.

1. A hospital developed a design process consisting of the following steps: Plan, Design, Measure, Assess, and Improve. Below is a list of specific activities that comprise these five steps in random order. Place the activities in the most appropriate order within the correct step of the design process.

   Pilot or test design

   Submit proposal

   Define measures to assess design performance

   Implement design

   Identify potential solutions to reduce out of control conditions

   Develop business plan

   Disseminate improvements throughout the organization

   Monitor process performance

   Select the best solution to improve control

   Identify out-of-control conditions

   Propose new concept

   Create design to meet requirements

   Identify new improvement opportunities

   Monitor the new process design

   Implement the best solution to improve control

   Verify proposal alignment with strategic objectives

   Establish design team

   Identify causes of out of control conditions

   Analyze causes

   Identify and validate customer requirements

   Identify and evaluate best practices

2. Newfonia, Inc. is working on a design for a new smart phone. Marketing staff conducted extensive surveys and focus groups with potential customers to determine the characteristics that the customers want and expect in a smart phone. Newfonia's studies have identified the most important customer expectations as
   - Initial cost
   - Reliability
   - Ease of use
   - Features
   - Operating cost
   - Compactness

   Develop a set of technical requirements to incorporate into the design of a House of Quality relationship matrix to assess how well your requirements address these expectations. Refine your design as necessary, based upon the initial assessment.

3. Newfonia, Inc. (Problem 2) faces three major competitors in this market: Oldphonia, Simphonia, and Colliefonia. It found that potential consumers placed the highest importance on reliability (measured by such things as freedom from operating system crashes and battery life), followed by compactness (weight/bulkiness), followed by flexibility (features, ease of use, and types of program modules available). The operating cost was only occasionally noted as an important attribute in the surveys. Studies of their products yielded the information shown in the table in the worksheet tab *Prob.7-3* in the Excel file *C07Data*. Results of the consumer panel ratings for these competitors are also shown in that spreadsheet. Using this information, modify and extend your House of Quality from Problem 2 and develop a deployment plan for the new smartphone. On what attributes should the company focus its marketing efforts?

4. Georgio's Giant Gyros conducted consumer surveys and focus groups concerning a new gyro sandwich design and the restaurant facility, and

identified the most important customer expectations (not in any order of priority) as:

- Tasty, attractive, moderately healthy food
- Speedy service
- An easy-to-read menu board
- Accurate order filling
- Perceived value

Develop only a set of technical requirements to incorporate into the design of the product and its delivery. Use a House of Quality relationship matrix to assess how well your requirements address these expectations. Include some technical dimensions that may be used to measure tasty, attractive, and "healthy" food; speedy service, acceptable menu boards, order accuracy, or perceived value. Refine your design as necessary based upon the initial assessment.

5. Georgio's Giant Gyros (Problem 4) acquired some additional information about product characteristics. It found that consumers placed the highest importance on taste appeal (especially flavor), followed by healthiness (measured by sodium content and calories), value, and service. The menu board and accurate order filling appeared to be less important attributes in the surveys. Georgio faces three major competitors in this market: Mario's, Gyroking, and Antonio's. Studies of their products yielded the information shown in the worksheet tab *Prob.7-5* in the Excel file *C07Data*. Results of the consumer panel ratings for each of these competitors can also be found there (a 1–5 scale, with 5 being the best). Using this information, modify and extend your House of Quality from Problem 4 and develop a deployment plan for a new gyro. Assume that a separate study will be made on the physical facilities and design of service delivery. On what product attributes should the company focus its marketing efforts?

6. A blueprint specification for the thickness of a refrigerator part at Refrigeria, Inc. is 0.300 ± 0.025 centimeters (cm). It costs \$25 to scrap a part that is outside the specifications. Determine the Taguchi loss function for this situation.

7. A team was formed to study the refrigerator part at Refrigeria, Inc. described in Problem 6. While continuing to work to find the root cause of scrap, they found a way to reduce the scrap cost to \$15 per part.
   a. Determine the Taguchi loss function for this situation.

   b. If the process deviation from target can be reduced to 0.015 cm, what is the Taguchi loss?

8. A specification for the length of an auto part at PartsDimensions, Inc. is 5.0 ± 0.10 centimeters (cm). It costs \$40 to scrap a part that is outside the specifications. Determine the Taguchi loss function for this situation.

9. A team was formed to study the auto part at PartsDimensions described in Problem 8. While continuing to work to find the root cause of scrap, the team found a way to reduce the scrap cost to \$20 per part.
   a. Determine the Taguchi loss function for this situation.

   b. If the process deviation from target can be reduced to 0.040 cm, what is the Taguchi loss?

10. Ruido Unlimited makes electronic soundboards for car stereos. Output voltage to a certain component on the board must be 12 ± 0.5 volts. Exceeding the limits results in an estimated loss of \$60. Determine the Taguchi loss function.

11. An electronic component at Eltcomp has a specification of 100 ± 0.4 ohms. Scrapping the component results in a \$81 loss.
    a. What is the value of k in the Taguchi loss function?

    b. If the process is centered on the target specification with a standard deviation of 0.2 ohm, what is the expected loss per unit?

12. An automatic cookie machine at AutoCM, Inc. must deposit a specified amount of 25 ± 0.3 grams (g) of dough for each cookie on a conveyor belt. It costs \$0.03 to scrap a defective cookie. A sample of 50 cookies was drawn from the production process, which has been determined to be approximately normally distributed, and the results, in grams, can be found in worksheet tab *Prob. 7-12* in the Excel file *C07Data*.
    a. What is the value of k in the Taguchi loss function?

    b. Determine how much the process varies from the target specification, based on the mean difference and standard deviation of the sample results. What is the expected loss per unit?

13. A computer chip designed by the MicroKeeb Co. has a specification for the distance between two adjacent pins of 2.000 ± 0.002 mm. The loss due to a defective chip is \$4. A sample of 25 chips was drawn from the production process and the

results, in millimeters , can be found in the worksheet tab *Prob. 7-13* in the Excel file *C07Data* file.

a. Compute the value of k in the Taguchi loss function.

b. What is the expected loss from this process based on the sample data?

14. In the production of Raphael Transformers, any output voltage that exceeds 120 ± 10 volts is unacceptable to the customer. Exceeding these limits results in an estimated loss of $200. However, the manufacturer can repair a defective unit by changing a resistor that costs $2.25.

a. Determine the Taguchi loss function.

b. Suppose the nominal specification is 120 volts. At what tolerance should the transformer be manufactured?

15. At Elektroparts Manufacturers' integrated circuit business, managers gathered data from a customer focus group and found that any output voltage that exceeds 55 ± 2.5 volts was unacceptable to the customer. Exceeding these limits results in an estimated loss of $75. However, the manufacturer can still adjust the voltage in the plant using a quick diagnostic test that costs $2.00.

a. Determine the Taguchi loss function.

b. Suppose the nominal specification remains at 55 volts. At what tolerance should the integrated circuit be manufactured?

16. Two processes, P and Q, are used by a supplier to produce the same component, Z, which is a critical part in the engine of the BearingPort 778 airplane. The specification for Z calls for a dimension of 0.24 mm ± 0.03. The probabilities of achieving the dimensions for each process based on their inherent variability are shown in the table found in the worksheet tab *Prob. 7-16* in the Excel file *C07Data*. If $k = 60,000$, what is the expected loss for each process? Which would be the best process to use, based on minimizing the expected loss?

17. The average time to handle a call in the Call-Nowait call processing center has a specification of 6 ± 1.25 minutes. The loss due to a mishandled call is $12. A sample of 25 calls was drawn from the process and the results, in minutes, can be found in the *C07Data* file for *Prob. 7-17*.

a. Compute the value of k in the Taguchi loss function.

b. What is the expected loss from this process based on the sample data?

18. Massive Corporation's tested five motors in a 900-hour test. Compute the failure rate if, three failed after 200, 475, and 750 hours and the other two ran for the full 900 hours each.

19. The life of a Supercellular phone battery is normally distributed with a mean of 950 days and standard deviation of 40 days. Using the Excel functions (see Chapter 6), determine the following:

a. What fraction of batteries is expected to survive beyond 1010 days?

b. What fraction will survive fewer than 900 days?

c. Draw a chart of the reliability function using Excel.

d. What length of warranty is needed so that no more than 10 percent of the batteries will be expected to fail during the warranty period?

20. Widetred, Inc. makes automobile tires that have a mean life of 60,000 miles with a standard deviation of 2,000 miles. Using Excel functions (see Chapter 6), determine the following:

a. What fraction of tires is expected to survive beyond 63,250 miles?

b. What fraction will survive fewer than 56,600 miles?

c. Draw a chart of the reliability function using Excel.

d. What length of warranty is needed so that no more than 5 percent of the tires will be expected to fail during the warranty period?

21. Livelong, Inc.'s computer monitors have a failure rate of $\lambda = 0.00095$ units per hour. Assuming an exponential distribution, what is the reliability function? What is the probability of failure within 5,000 hours? Calculate your answer using the appropriate mathematical formula and verify your result using Excel.

22. An electronic component in a satellite radio has failure rate of $\lambda = 0.000015$ units/hour. Find the mean time to failure (MTTF). What is the probability (assuming an exponential probability distribution) that the component will not have failed after 12,000 hours of operation? Calculate your answer using the appropriate mathematical formula and verify your result using Excel.

23. The MTBF of an integrated circuit made by Outer Limits, Inc. is 18,000 hours. Calculate the failure rate.

24. A manufacturer of MP3 players purchases major electronic components as modules. The reliabilities

of components differ by supplier (see the system diagram below). Suppose that the configuration of the major components is given by:

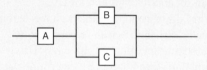

The components can be purchased from three different suppliers. The reliabilities of the components are as follows:

Component	Supplier 1	Supplier 2	Supplier 3
A	0.98	0.96	0.95
B	0.95	0.97	0.98
C	0.99	0.96	0.94

Transportation and purchasing considerations require that only one supplier be chosen. Which one should be selected if the radio is to have the highest possible reliability?

25. An electronic missile guidance system consists of Components A, B, C, and D, which have reliabilities of 0.98, 0.97, 0.91, and 0.99, respectively (see the following diagram).

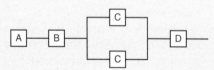

a. What is the reliability of the entire system?
b. Suppose the customer requires a reliability of at least 0.98. Try to find a configuration that meets this requirement using the minimum number of components.

26. Bestronics has a three-step process for processing customer sales. First, the cashier must look up the customer's loyalty card on the company's information system. Second, the cashier enters the transaction on the point-of-sale register. Third, the cashier processes the credit card through a verification system.

a. If the reliability of the information system is 0.998, the reliability of the point-of-sale register is 0.992 and the reliability of the credit card verification system is 0.978, what is the overall system reliability?
b. If the store manager wants to ensure at least a 98 percent system reliability, make a recommendation of how to do this.

27. Manuplex, Inc. has a complex manufacturing process, with three operations that are performed in series. Because of the nature of the process, machines frequently fall out of adjustment and must be repaired. To keep the system going, two identical machines are used at each stage; thus, if one fails, the other can be used while the first is repaired (see accompanying figure).

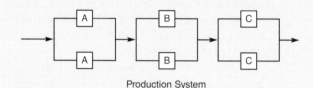

Production System

The reliabilities of the machines are as follows:

Machine	Reliability
A	0.85
B	0.92
C	0.90

a. Analyze the system reliability, assuming only one machine at each stage (all the backup machines are out of operation).
b. How much is the reliability improved by having two machines at each stage?

28. An automated production system at Autoprod, Inc. consists of three operations: turning, milling, and grinding. Individual parts are transferred from one operation to the next by a robot. Hence, if one machine or the robot fails, the process stops.

a. If the reliabilities of the robot, turning center, milling machine, and grinder are 0.994, 0.980, 0.95, and 0.88, respectively, what is the reliability of the system?
b. Suppose that two grinders are available so that the system does not stop if one fails. What is the reliability of the system?

29. CajaGigante, a large department store, has a very successful and profitable package-wrapping department. The department uses two complex bow-making machines that work inline to make the bows for the packages. There is one skilled operator who knows how to operate the machines. She had been very reliable, but recently has had increasing health problems which caused her to miss work about 10 percent of the time. Bow-making Machine 1 has a reliability of 0.97. Machine 2 has a reliability of 0.90.

a. What is the current reliability of the system, including the operator?

b. Management is considering either scrapping Machine 2 and replacing it with a new machine which has a reliability of 0.97 at a cost of $5,000, or training another operator to fill in when the first operator is absent at a cost of $5,100. The prospective trainee has an excellent attendance record and has only been absent 4 days out of 250 work days for the department, last year. Management estimates that profits from the department would increase by $6,000 per year, if the bow-making line operated at 100 percent of capacity. If management wants to pay off its investment in the first year, determine the expected net profit for each alternative, and recommend which one will be the most profitable to management.

30. National Partamiento installs and maintains thousands of refrigerators and other appliances in rental apartments across the country. They have conducted a short study of failure rates based on following the performance of 25,440 refrigerators that were installed during one month a year ago. The table found in the worksheet tab *Prob.7-30* in the Excel file *C07Data* on the Student Companion Site contains the data. The data show the number of failures of these 25,440 refrigerators each month over the past year.

a. Compute the average failure rate, λ. Is the failure rate relatively constant each month?

b. Use regression analysis to predict future failures. What is the predicted number of failures each month for the next two years (that is, through month 36)?

c. If the refrigerators are typically under a 36-month warranty, how many cumulative failures would be predicted in 36 months? What percentage of the total does this represent?

d. What are the strengths and limitations of using regression analysis in this situation?

PROJECTS, ETC.

1. Using whatever "market research" techniques are appropriate, define a set of customer attributes for
   a. Purchasing books at your college bookstore
   b. A college registration process
   c. A hotel room used for business
   d. A hotel room used for family leisure vacations
   For each case, determine a set of technical requirements and construct the relationship matrix for the House of Quality.

2. (This exercise would best be performed in a group.) Suppose that you were developing a small pizza restaurant with a dining area and local delivery. Develop a list of customer requirements and technical requirements and try to complete a House of Quality. What service standards might such an operation have?

3. Most children (and many adults) like to assemble and fly balsa-wood gliders. From your own experiences or from interviews with other students, define a set of customer requirements for a good glider. (Even better, buy one and test it to determine these requirements yourself.) If you were to design and manufacture such a product, how would you define a set of technical requirements for the design? Using your results, construct a relationship matrix for a House of Quality.

4. Fill in the following relationship matrix of a House of Quality for a screwdriver. By sampling your classmates, develop priorities for the customer attributes and use these and the relationships to identify key technical requirements to deploy.

	Price	Interchangeable bits	Steel shaft	Rubber grip	Ratchet capability	Plastic handle
Easy to use						
Does not rust						
Durable						
Comfortable						
Versatile						
Inexpensive						
Priority						

5. Prepare a full DFMEA for a casual dining restaurant. Consider failure modes that might occur both

in food preparation and in service. Clearly explain and justify your choices for the severity, likelihood, and detection ratings.

6. Investigate design-for-environment practices in some of your local industries. Describe company policies and the methods and techniques that they use to address environmental concerns in product design.

CASES

THE ELEVATOR DILEMMA

In a true story related by our colleague Professor James W. Dean, Jr., the general manager of an elevator company was frustrated with the lack of cooperation between the mechanical engineers who designed new elevators and the manufacturing engineers who determined how to produce them.[39] The mechanical engineers would often completely design a new elevator without consulting with the manufacturing engineers, and then expect the factory to somehow figure out how to build it. Often, the new products were difficult or nearly impossible to build, and their quality and cost suffered as a result. The designs were sent back to the mechanical engineers (often more than once) for engineering changes to improve their manufacturability, and customers sometimes waited for months for deliveries. The general manager believed that if the two groups of engineers would communicate early in the design process, many of the problems would be solved. At his wits' end, he found a large empty room in the plant and had both groups moved into it. The manager relaxed a bit, but a few weeks later he returned to a surprise. The two groups of engineers had finally learned to cooperate—by building a wall of bookcases and file cabinets right down the middle of the room, separating them from each other! What would you do in this situation and why?

APPLYING QUALITY FUNCTION DEPLOYMENT TO A UNIVERSITY SUPPORT SERVICE[40]

This case is based on an application of QFD at Tennessee Technological University to their Research Resources Center (RRC), an internal service system. Originally created as a support facility for faculty and student research, the RRC has grown to offer many more services, including test preparation, manuscript preparation, resumes, flyers, brochures, faxing, copying, typing, and computer applications. The RRC is staffed weekdays from 7:30 A.M. to 4:30 P.M. with highly experienced support personnel. Jody, the head coordinator of the RRC, is proficient in specialty computer applications. She has a workstation at her disposal loaded with word-processing, graphics, and desktop publishing software. Peripherals such as a laser printer, color printer, and a full-page scanner allow her to generate high-quality output. Candy specializes in word processing, and Marie specializes in copying, collating, and stapling or binding. All three are proficient in most of the RRC functions.

Jobs can be classified as student, teacher, or rush. Most jobs are single-task oriented and can be completed by one RRC professional. The professional may be dependent on student workers to process job orders accurately and place them in the appropriate incoming jobs bin. Some jobs, however, are dependent on the other employees' functions. For instance, Candy types the tests, and Marie makes the copies and packages the final product. In these instances, Marie functions as an internal customer. She becomes dependent on another professional employee to accomplish her job.

Students involved in scholarship and work study programs are also employed part time to support RRC personnel. The RRC, functioning as a unit of the College of Business, is bound by the same regulations as other university offices: It has little control over the student employment selection process.

The responsibilities of the students include taking work orders and assisting customers in low-tech functions, such as making copies and finding research materials. No formal training is provided. The student workers are briefly informed of the RRC's functions and told to be courteous to customers. When student workers have questions, they ask one of the professionals. The student workers are primarily used as an interface between RRC professionals and customers.

A security issue is associated with some of the documents that the RRC processes. Some faculty members choose to have the RRC type and print their tests. In these instances, student workers cannot be involved in any process related to the test. The order is taken by one of the professionals, the job is executed, and the final product is locked in a file cabinet in a room where student workers are not allowed. Additionally, some student documents may not be handled by student workers. Project papers submitted for typing

should not be viewed by a student worker who, by chance, may be in the same class and have the same assignment.

Because of limited space in the RRC, little distinction can be made between back office and front office. A counter is set up to the right of the door as customers walk in. All workers are stationed behind this counter. As customers need assistance, they are met at the counter by student workers who assist them. If a customer requires a job, then the appropriate work-order forms are filled out. During this time, the customer is in full view of the operations. Some frequent customers prefer to relay their job orders directly to the professionals. As a result of the customized nature of many of the jobs, this direct contact is sometimes appropriate. Some customers, however, prefer to do business with certain RRC representatives, which means that RRC professionals occasionally have to leave the work they are doing to serve the customer.

The area to the left of the counter is available for customer use (see Figure 7.27). Four large tables are

FIGURE 7.27   RRC Old Layout

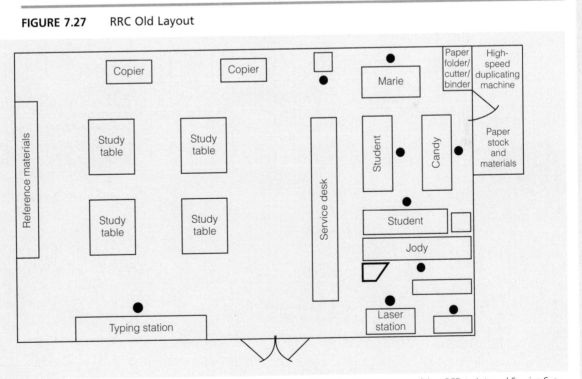

FIGURE 7.28   RRC House of Quality

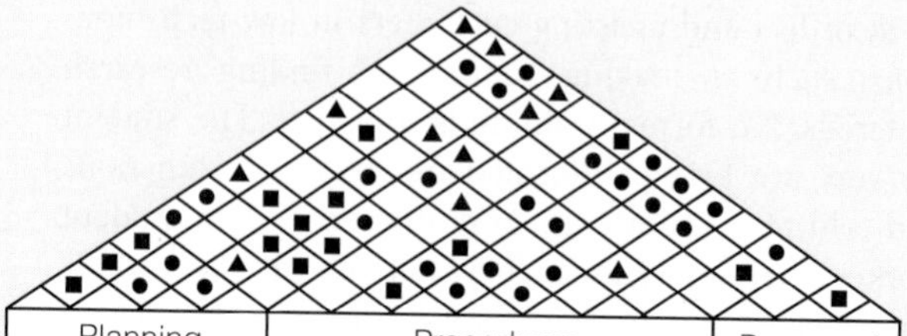

Legend: ■ Strong   ● Medium   ▲ Weak

What? Customer quality criteria — Primary	Secondary	Relative importance	Layout	Resources (equipment)	Resources (personnel)	System capacity	Housekeeping	Customer handling	Documents handling	Information handling	Nonroutine situations	Inventory	Job/personnel scheduling	Selection	Skills/training	Attitudes/morals
Reliability	Accuracy	5			■				■	■						
Reliability	Dependability	5		■	■					■	■	●	■		●	
Responsiveness	Willingness to help	4			■			■		●						■
Responsiveness	Prompt service	4	▲		■	■		■	■	■			●			■
Assurance	Knowledge and courtesy of employees	3			■			●			▲	■			●	●
Assurance	Ability to convey trust and assurance	3			●			●								●
Empathy	Caring of and attention to customers	2			●	■	▲	■			▲	■			■	■
Tangibles	Appearance of physical facility, equipment, personnel, and materials	1	●	■								▲	●			

Service facility facets — How?

Planning: Layout, Resources (equipment), Resources (personnel), System capacity
Procedures: Housekeeping, Customer handling, Documents handling, Information handling, Nonroutine situations, Inventory, Job/personnel scheduling
Personnel: Selection, Skills/training, Attitudes/morals

Source: Reprinted with permission from R. Nat Natarajan, Ralph E. Martz, and Kyouske Kurosaka, "Applying QFD to Internal Service System Design," *Quality Progress*, Vol. 31, No. 2, February 1999, pp. 65–70. Copyright © 1999 American Society for Quality. No further distribution without permission.

centrally located for faculty members and students to use for study purposes. The waiting area is merely the area between the counter and these tables. Service lines are not structured, and service personnel attempt to serve customers on a first-come, first-served basis. When customers have work orders that can be completed quickly, they may choose to wait at the counter. Occasionally, a queue develops in front of the service counter.

QFD was used to analyze where a concerted effort might increase the RRC's quality level as perceived by the customer. Customer requirements were grouped along the five dimensions of service quality (in rank order of importance): reliability, responsiveness, assurance, empathy, and tangibles. These categories were further broken down into secondary requirements as shown in the House of Quality (Figure 7.28).

Key Issues for Discussion

1. Do you agree with the relative importance of measures of the voice of the customer in Figure 7.28? Explain why these rankings are reasonable, or provide counterarguments for a different ranking.

2. Using the relative importance ratings of the customer attributes and setting a scale of 1 = weak, 3 = medium, and 5 = strong for the relationship matrix, compute a weighted score for each of the technical requirements in Figure 7.28. Do your scores support the conclusions of the study in terms of the key service components to deploy in the QFD process?

3. What conclusions can you reach in terms of the key service components to deploy in the QFD process? What other recommendations might you suggest based on the information provided in this case? Propose an improved layout of the RRC and justify your proposal.

BLACK ELK MEDICAL CENTER

Black Elk Medical Center (BEMC) is a quality-driven acute care hospital organization that includes three medical facilities that treat both inpatients and outpatients. BEMC has won numerous national and local quality awards. These included the J.D. Power awards in 2009 and 2011, First in Kentucky and Ohio in Hospital Quality Award by Anthem Insurance Co., and a listing as one of the Top Ten Hospitals. Black Elk's mission statement says: "We will strive for excellence in all services we provide compared to national standards."

In 2012, the Board of Trustees for Black Elk Medical Center set a goal to reduce the fall rate within the hospital nursing units below the national norm, defined by one national benchmark as 3.4 falls/1000 patient days. The current organizational fall rate for 2011 averaged 4.8 falls/1000 patient days and through first six months of 2012 average fall rate averaged 4.75 falls/1000 patient days. The fall rate at any health care institution is significant to elderly patients, and especially so to those that are 65 years of age and older. Many elderly patients fall, break a hip, or even die within one year of the fall. The Board set the fall reduction goal in conjunction with a new regulation, National Patient Safety Goal 9B, that stated that health care organizations must implement a fall reduction program and evaluate the effectiveness of the program no later than January 1, 2013.

Each health care organization was required to create or adopt a fall risk assessment process specific to the population served. The Joint Commission on Accreditation of Healthcare Organizations (JACHO) does not define a fall. Each health care organization must operationally define what they consider to be a fall, while meeting individual states' rules and regulations. The level of injury or type of injury must be tracked and documented to avoid counting near misses as falls. All age groups must be assessed for the risk of falling, not just the geriatric population. The health care organization also had to determine when the initial fall risk assessment was performed and the time frame for reassessments. Reassessments should be performed when a patient's condition changes, the patient is moved to another level of care, or when medications are ordered for the patient that would increase the risk of falling.

An 11-member interdisciplinary Fall Prevention Task Force was formed with representatives from Nursing, Facilities, Safety, Quality Management, Housekeeping, Plant Engineering, and Accreditation Services. The scope of the project was to assess the operations and environment at BEMC for actual or potential change to protect patients from accidental falls. The committee chair, Maureen Hebert, is the Long Term Care Administrator and has worked at Black Elk for over 18 years. Her responsibility includes providing patient care from acute care through a continuum of programs that include hospice, and long term care.

One of the first tasks was to perform an environmental assessment of all three acute care hospitals owned by Black Elk. The environment for each of the different nursing units is unique, which makes it more difficult to standardize and create hazard free environments. Task Force members visited each nursing unit and a patient room, which was invaluable for assessing risk factors and recommending or making appropriate changes. A standard checklist-style form was developed

FIGURE 7.29
Fall Checklist

FALL CHECKLIST (To be done on all falls)

1. Patient diagnosis: _____
2. Number of days patient in hospital: ___   Today's date: ___
3. Patients fall risk level on day of admission: ___ Fall risk level day of fall ___
4. Was there a STAR up if patient was a high fall risk: YES ___ NO ___ N/A ___
5. Was fall risk level on patients caremap: YES ___ NO ___
6. If patient was a high fall risk, was "safety" on caremap as a problem?
   YES ___ NO ___ N/A ___
7. Was there documentation on the PFER that the fall letter was given and reviewed with the patient and/or family? YES ___ NO ___
8. If patient was high fall risk, was Q2hr toileting documented
   YES ___ NO ___ N/A ___
9. Did patient have on "safety socks" YES ___ NO ___
10. If necessary; was a walker/cane at bedside YES ___ NO ___ N/A ___
11. Number of siderails up: ___
12. Was patient injured? YES ___ NO ___
13. Was patient in restraints? YES ___ NO ___
14. Was Bed Alarm in use? YES ___ NO ___
15. Was any family at bedside: YES ___ NO ___
16. What was patient's mental status? ___ Number of nurse assistants on ___
17. What was the patient to nurse ratio? ___ What shift did the fall occur on? ___
18. Brief description of what happened, and was it witnessed?

and helped to ensure a more thorough evaluation (see Figure 7.29).

Suppose that you were consulting for this organization. What would your next steps be? How would you use data gathered from the checklist? How would you design improved processes and systems to improve and control the incidence of falls, and to effectively and rapidly reduce the fall rate to be below 3.4 falls/1000 patient days?

NOTES

1. Steven H. Wildstrom, "Price Wars Power Up Quality," *BusinessWeek*, September 18, 1995, 26.
2. Peter Svensson, "It's Not Just Computers: Gadgets Crash," *Cincinnati Enquirer*, April 3, 2003, A3.
3. "Design Flaws Led to China Train Disaster," Xinhua Economic News Service, July 29, 2011.
4. Philip A. Himmelfarb, "Fast New-Product Development at Service Sector Companies," *Quality Digest*, April 1996, 41–44.
5. See Walter Isaacson's biography *Steve Jobs* and the March 2012 issue of *Fast Company* to read about how these companies have applied concurrent engineering.
6. Don Clausing and Bruce H. Simpson, "Quality by Design," *Quality Progress*, January 1990, 41–44.
7. C. M. Creveling, J. L. Slutsky, and D. Antis, Jr., *Design for Six Sigma in Technology and Product Development* (Upper Saddle River, NJ, Prentice Hall, 2003).
8. Charles Humber and Robert Launsby, "Straight Talk on DFSS," *Six Sigma Forum Magazine* 1, no. 4 (August 2002).
9. Kate Burrows, "Better by Design," *iSixSigma*, May/June 2011, 20–25.
10. Romain Moisecot, "Steve Jobs: a Biography," http://www.allaboutSteveJobs.com.
11. James R. Stevenson and Ali E. Kashef, "Newer, Better, Faster: How Six Sigma Boosts Innovation and Reinvention," *Quality Progress*, September 2008.
12. Sylvia Nasar, "What Makes Beautiful Minds," *Fast Company*, December 2004, 50–52.

13. Peter Lewis, "A Perpetual Crisis Machine," *Fortune*, September 19, 2005, 57–76.

14. Bruce Horovitz, "Domino's Pizza Delivers Change in Its Core Pizza Recipe," *USA Today*, December 16, 2009; Courtney Dentch, "Domino's Changing Recipe to Help Lift U.S. Sales," http://www.bloomberg.com.

15. Csaba Csere, "Rules and Regs: Why Do All Cars Do That?" Car and Driver, April 2012, p. 24.

16. Jennifer Reese, "Starbucks: Inside the Coffee Cult," *Fortune*, December 9, 1996, 190–200.

17. Susan Dillingham, "A Little Gross Stuff in Food Is OK by FDA," *Insight*, May 22, 1989, 25.

18. Alan Vonderhaar, "Audi's TT Coupe's Ever So Close," *Cincinnati Enquirer*, November 27, 1999, F1, F2.

19. April 17, 1979; cited in L. P. Sullivan, "Reducing Variability: A New Approach to Quality," *Quality Progress* 17, no. 7 (July 1984), 15–21. See http://www.asahi.com/english for current business and other news in Japan.

20. Chris Woodyard, "Japanese Makers Maintain Reign on Reliability," *USA Today*, October 24, 2008, 4B.

21. Charles J. Murray, "Eight Ways to Boost Product Reliability," *DesignNews*, November 23, 2009, http://www.designnews.com/document.asp?doc_id=228706 (accessed 10/22/11).

22. N. Raghu Kackar, "Off-Line Quality Control, Parameter Design, and the Taguchi Method," *Journal of Quality Technology* 17, no. 4 (October 1985), 176–188.

23. John H. Farrow, "Product Liability Requirements," *Quality Progress*, May 1980, 34–36; Mick Birmingham, "Product Liability: An Issue for Quality," *Quality*, February 1983, 41–42.

24. Randall Goodden, "Quality and Product Liability," *Quality Digest*, October 1995, 35–41.

25. R. Dan Reid, "FMEA—Something Old, Something New" *Quality Progress*, May 2005, 90–93.

26. "Failure Mode and Effects Analysis," Institute for Healthcare Improvement, 2004, p. 1.

27. Peter Lewis, "A Perpetual Crisis Machine," *Fortune*, September 19, 2005, 58–76.

28. Gail Edmondson, "Mercedes' New Boss Rolls Up His Sleeves," *BusinessWeek*, October 17, 2005, 56.

29. Adapted from Douglas Daetz, "The Effect of Product Design on Product Quality and Product Cost," *Quality Progress*, June 1987, 63–67. © 1987, Hewlett-Packard Co. All rights reserved. Reprinted with permission.

30. Lewis, "Perpetual Crisis Machine."

31. David Pescovitz, "Dumping Old Computers—Please Dispose of Properly," *Scientific American* 282, no. 2 (February 2000), 29; http://www.sciam.com/2000/0200issue/0200techbus2.html.

32. Early discussions of this topic can be found in Bruce Nussbaum and John Templeton, "Built to Last—Until It's Time to Take It Apart," *BusinessWeek*, September 17, 1990, 102–106. A more recent reference is Michael Lenox, Andrew King, and John Ehrenfeld, "An Assessment of Design-for-Environment Practices in Leading U.S. Electronics Firms," *Interfaces* 30, no. 3 (May/June 2000), 83–94.

33. Nussbaum and Templeton, "Built to Last."

34. Jui-Chin Jiang, Ming-Li Shiu and Mao-Hsiung Tu, "DFX and DFSS: How QFD Integrates Them," *Quality Progress*, October 2007; "A Smarter Way to Manufacture," *BusinessWeek*, April 30, 1990.

35. Svensson, "It's Not Just Computers."

36. Reliant Labs, www.reliantlabs.com.

37. Appreciation is expressed to Christine Schyvinck, VP Operations, Shure, Inc., for providing this case (October 2000).

38. Adapted from Vincent Omachonu and Paul Barach, "QFD in a Managed Care Organization," *Quality Progress*, November 2005, 36–41. © 2005, American Society for Quality. Reprinted with permission.

39. This story was first published in James W. Dean, Jr. and James R. Evans *Total Quality: Management, Organization, and Strategy*, Minneapolis/St. Paul: West Publishing Company, 1994, p. 143.

40. Adapted from R. Nat Natarajan, Ralph E. Martz, and Kyosuke Kurosaka, "Applying QFD to Internal Service System Design," *Quality Progress*, February 1999, 65–70. © 1999, American Society for Quality. Reprinted with permission.

Measuring and Controlling Quality

We introduced the concept of control in Chapter 5. Quality control seeks to ensure that processes perform in a stable and predictable fashion by identifying when corrective action is needed. Good data and measurement systems are the basis for effective quality control as well as for quality improvement. As one notable example, when Dr. Noriaki Kano of Japan consulted with Florida Power and

Light (FPL), the company told him that lightning was the principal cause of service interruptions. Kano asked why groundings or arresters had not prevented the interruptions; FPL replied that these would not work with Florida's severe lightning. Kano asked for the data to back up this conclusion, but FPL could not produce any. About 18 months later, when Kano next visited the company, they had collected data and found that interruptions occurred even when strong lightning was not present. In addition, they discovered that many utility poles did not have sufficient groundings, a situation they had not recognized until they collected the data.[1]

In this chapter, we describe ways to measure quality, evaluate measurement systems, assess conformance to specifications, and use statistical process control to monitor manufacturing and service processes.

quality**profiles**

MESA Products, Inc. and Operations Management International, Inc.

MESA Products, Inc. is a small, privately held business that designs, manufactures and installs cathodic protection systems that control the corrosion of metal surfaces in underground and submerged structures, such as pipelines and tanks. MESA assembles more than 75,000 magnesium anodes each year, a product line that accounts for 30 percent of the company's material revenues. Beginning in 2002, MESA was instrumental in identifying and addressing an industry-wide issue of poor-quality magnesium anodes. Working with its key suppliers, the company implemented a comprehensive quality assurance specification for product acceptance, resulting in a significant improvement in the quality of the company's anodes. MESA then mounted an industry-wide awareness campaign to alert manufacturers and end users about the issue. As a result, the quality of anodes throughout the industry has improved.

Since its inception from a one-man service company in 1979 to a workforce of 75, MESA's philosophy has been to provide its customers with a quality product and outstanding service at a fair price. To achieve this goal, MESA focuses on teamwork and shared goals that include continuous improvement, continued growth and long-term success. A variety of tools help to improve performance, including "lean" manufacturing to reduce waste, certification for international quality standards by the International Organization for Standardization (ISO), and the Baldrige principles of performance excellence. A monthly balanced report card helps the company to review its performance and find ways to improve. For example, the report card process showed that MESA was routinely missing a target of shipping products within three days due to a lack of available inventory. MESA constructed a 5,000-square foot covered storage area, improving inventory availability and greatly facilitating timely shipments. From 2000 until MESA received a Baldrige Award in 2007, the company's on-time shipping performance improved from 93 percent to 97 percent, error rates went down 50 percent, throughput time in the magnesium assembly area improved by 82 percent, and assembly time of instrumentation equipment improved by 60 percent.

Headquartered in Greenwood Village, Colorado, Operations Management International, Inc. (OMI), operates and maintains more than 160 public and private sector wastewater and water treatment facilities in 29 states and facilities in Brazil, Canada, Egypt, Israel, Malaysia, New Zealand, Philippines, and Thailand. OMI's primary services are processing raw wastewater to produce clean, environmentally safe effluent and processing raw groundwater and surface water to produce clean, safe drinking water. OMI's "E3" motto, "Exceed our customers' expectations, empower our employees, enhance the environment," is the foundation for its Quality as a Business Strategy leadership system. Key enablers are the company's Linkage of Process Model, which defines relationships among processes, and its Family of Measures, a balanced scorecard of 20 integrated metrics. These measures of operational performance correspond to OMI's four strategic objectives—customer focus, business growth, innovation, and market leadership.

Improvement initiatives in the company's strategic plan are selected and crafted so that each initiative contributes significantly to achieving one or more strategic objectives and key customer requirements.

In 2000, OMI had 26 improvement initiatives under way, each one assigned to a team led by a high-level executive. All teams write charters that state their purpose, objectives, and timeline for completion. A team charter also specifies which of OMI's more than 150 critical processes are involved, the metrics that will be used for evaluation, costs, required resources, and other information vital to the success of the initiative. Charters provide team members and company executives with the means for a quick and thorough analysis of progress toward planned goals. OMI received a 2000 Baldrige Award.

Source: Adapted from Malcolm Baldrige National Quality Award, Profiles of Winners, National Institute of Standards and Technology, Department of Commerce.

MEASUREMENT FOR QUALITY CONTROL

Measurement is the act of collecting data to quantify the values of product, service, process, and other business metrics. **Measures and indicators** refer to the numerical results obtained from measurement. For example, the presence or absence of cosmetic defects such as dents or scratches on a kitchen faucet might be assessed by visual inspection. A quality measurement that might be derived from such inspection is the percentage of faucets that have cosmetic defects. As another example, the diameters of machined ball bearings might be measured with a micrometer; some quality measurements might be the average diameter and the standard deviation of a sample of ball bearings. For services, examples of quality measurements would be the percentage of orders filled accurately and the time taken to fill and ship a customer's order. The term *indicator* is often used for measurements that are not a direct or exclusive measure of performance. For instance, though you cannot directly measure dissatisfaction, you can use the number of complaints or lost customers as indicators of dissatisfaction.

What makes a good measurement? Many organizations use the acronym *SMART* to characterize them: *simple, measurable, actionable, related* (to customer and operational requirements), and *timely*. Measurements should be easy and cost-effective to obtain. A measurement should be clear and unambiguous; for instance, when measuring "invoice errors," a precise definition of what is an error and what is not is needed. Does an error include an omission of information, wrong information, or misspelling? Good measures should provide actionable information; that is, information for making good decisions for process management. Thus, they should be taken at critical points in a process where value-adding activities occur. Measures should clearly relate to what is important to customers—both external and internal—and for running the business. Finally, measurements need to be made available and communicated to workers and managers when they need them.

EXAMPLE 8.1   Quality Measurements for a Pizza Fulfillment Process

Consider the process of placing and filling a pizza order. Customer expectations include a quick response and a fair price. The process that provides this service is shown in Figure 8.1. Some possible quality measurements include:

- *Number of pizzas, by type per hour.* If this number is high relative to the kitchen's capacity, then perhaps cooking time and/or preparation is being short-cut or delivery times are stretched out.
- *Order accuracy (as transmitted to the kitchen).* This measure can indicate a lack of attention or knowledge on the part of the order taker.

FIGURE 8.1 Example of a Pizza Ordering and Filling Process for Home Delivery

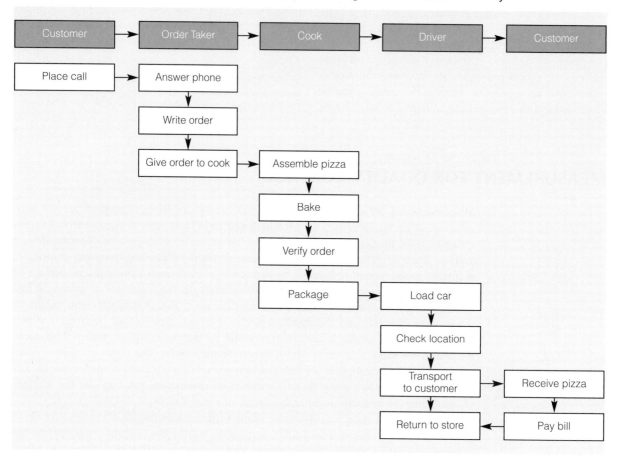

- *Number of pizzas rejected per number prepared.* A high number for this measure can indicate a lack of proper training of cooks, resulting in poor products and customer complaints.
- *Time to delivery.* This measure might indicate a problem within the restaurant or inadequate training of the driver. (Of course, as happened with Domino's Pizza, measuring delivery time could encourage drivers to drive too fast and lead to safety problems.)
- *Number of errors in collections.* Errors here can result in lost profits and higher prices.
- *Raw materials (dough, etc.) or finished pizzas inventory.* A high number might result in spoilage and excess costs. Low inventory might result in lost orders or excessive customer waiting time.

Notice that these measures—only a few among many possible measures—are related to customer expectations and business performance.

Many organizations use **dashboards**, which typically consist of a small set of measures (five or six) that provide a quick summary of process performance. This term stems from the analogy to an automobile's dashboard—a collection of indicators (speed, RPM, oil pressure, temperature, etc.) that summarize key performance measures. Dashboards often use graphs, charts, and other visual aids to communicate key measures and alert workers and managers when performance is not where it should be.

QUALITYSPOTLIGHT
Fluor Hanford

Fluor Hanford in Hanford, Washington, was the site of one of the world's largest environmental cleanup projects for nuclear waste after its nuclear reactors and plutonium processing facilities were decommissioned by the U.S. government. The company used a set of quality indicators to monitor performance during the cleanup project. These included first-aid case rates, safety inspection rates and scores, occurrence reports and near misses, employee safety-survey results and employee safety concerns. These leading indicators were combined with the existing lagging injury rates into a color-coded dashboard in which green indicated an improving trend or stable performance at an acceptable level, yellow indicated stable performance at an unacceptable level, and red indicated an adverse trend.[2]

Common Quality Measurements

Product and service quality measures focus on the outcomes of manufacturing and service processes. A **unit of work** is the output of a process or an individual process step. A unit of work might be a completed product ready to ship to a customer, a subassembly, an individual part produced on a machine, or a package to be delivered to a customer. A **nonconformance** is any defect or error associated with a unit of work. In manufacturing we often use the term **defect**, and in service applications, we generally use the term **error** to describe a nonconformance. A **nonconforming unit of work** is one that has one or more defects or errors.

Measures used in quality control fall into one of two categories. An **attribute measurement** characterizes the presence or absence of nonconformances in a unit of work, or the number of nonconformances in a unit of work. Attribute measurements often are collected by visual inspection and expressed as proportions and counts. The second type of quality measurement is called a **variable measurement**. Variable measurements apply to dimensional quantities such as length, weight, and time, or any value on a continuous scale of measurement. For example, we could determine whether a part meets a specification of 1.60 ± 0.01 inch (an attribute measurement), or measure and record the actual value of the diameter (a variable measurement). Variable measurements are generally expressed with statistical measures such as averages and standard deviations.

Collecting attribute data is usually easier than collecting variable data because the assessment can usually be done more quickly by a simple inspection or count, whereas variable data require the use of some type of measuring instrument. However, in a statistical sense, attributes measurement is less efficient than variables measurement; that is, attribute measurement requires a much larger sample size than variable measurement to obtain the same amount of statistical information. This difference can become significant when inspection of each item is time-consuming or expensive.

Table 8.1 provides some examples of attributes and variables measurements in services. Can you identify which are attribute and which are variable measurements? The most common quality characteristics in services, time (waiting time, service time,

TABLE 8.1
Quality
Measurements
in Service
Organizations

Organization	Quality Measure
Hospital	Lab test accuracy
	Insurance claim accuracy
	On-time delivery of meals and medication
Bank	Check-processing accuracy
Insurance company	Claims-processing response time
	Billing accuracy
Post office	Sorting accuracy
	Time of delivery
	Percentage of express mail delivered on time
Ambulance	Response time
Police department	Incidence of crime in a precinct
	Number of traffic citations
Hotel	Proportion of rooms satisfactorily cleaned
	Checkout time
	Number of complaints received
Transportation	Proportion of freight cars correctly routed
	Dollar amount of damage per claim
Auto service	Percentage of time work completed as promised
	Number of parts out of stock

delivery time) and number of nonconformances, can be measured rather easily. Insurance companies, for example, measure the time to complete different transactions such as new issues, claim payments, and cash surrenders. Time is easily measured by recording the starting time and finishing time of a transaction. Checklists can be used to record attribute data such as types of errors (wrong kind, wrong quantity, wrong delivery date, etc.). For example, a checklist for identifying nonconformances in pharmaceutical operations in a hospital might include the following questions:

- Are drug storage and preparation areas within the pharmacy under the supervision of a pharmacist?
- Are drugs requiring special storage conditions properly stored?
- Are drug emergency boxes inspected on a monthly basis?
- Is the drug emergency box record book filled out completely?

Even though human behavior is easily observable, the task of describing and classifying the observations is far more difficult. The major obstacle is developing operational definitions of behavioral characteristics such as courtesy, promptness, competency, and so on. Defining such quality characteristics is best done by comparing behavior against well-defined standards. For instance, a standard for "courtesy" might be to address the customer as "Mr." or "Ms." Failure to do so is an instance of a nonconformance. "Promptness" might be defined as greeting a customer within five seconds of entering the store, or answering letters within two days of receipt. These behaviors can easily be

---

FIGURE 8.2   Sample Hospital Staff Behavior Questions

Admissions
11. Altogether, how long did you have to wait to be admitted?
    More than 1 hour: _____ (1)   1 hour: _____ (2)   30 min.: _____ (3)   15 min.: _____ (4)
12. If you had to wait 30 minutes or longer before someone met with you, were you told why?
    YES: _____ (1)   NO: _____ (2)   Did not wait 30 minutes: _____ (3)

Nursing Staff
21. Did a nurse talk to you about the procedures for the day?
    Never: _____ (1)   Sometimes: _____ (2)   Often: _____ (3)   Always: _____ (4)
22. Were you on IV fluids?
    YES: _____ (1)   NO: _____ (2)
    A. If YES, did the IV fluids ever run out?
    YES: _____ (1)   NO: _____ (2)

Medical Staff
28. Did the doctor do what he/she told you he was going to do?
    Never: _____ (1)   Sometimes: _____ (2)   Often: _____ (3)   Always: _____ (4)

Housekeeping
36. Did the housekeeper come into your room at least once a day?
    YES: _____ (1)   NO: _____ (2)
39. Was the bathroom adequately supplied?
    Always: _____ (1)   Often: _____ (2)   Sometimes: _____ (3)   Never: _____ (4)

X-Ray
When you received services from the X-ray technician, were the procedures explained to you?
    Always: _____ (1)   Often: _____ (2)   Sometimes: _____ (3)   Never: _____ (4)

Food
34. Generally, were your meals served at the same time each day?
    Always: _____ (1)   Often: _____ (2)   Sometimes: _____ (3)   Never: _____ (4)

Source: Adapted from K. M. Casarreal, J. L. Mill, and M. A. Plant, "Improving Service Through Patient Surveys in a Multihospital Organization," Hospital & Health Services Administration, Health Administration Press, Ann Arbor, MI, March/April 1986, 41–52. © 1986, Foundation of the American College of Health Care Executives.

recorded and counted. Figure 8.2 shows some behavioral questions used in a patient survey by a group of Southern California hospitals.[3]

For attribute data, the two important quality measures are the **proportion nonconforming** and **nonconformances per unit**:

$$\text{Proportion nonconforming} = \frac{\text{Number of nonconforming units found}}{\text{Number of units inspected}} \quad (8.1)$$

$$\text{Nonconformances per unit (NPU)} = \frac{\text{Total number of nonconformances}}{\text{Number of units inspected}} \quad (8.2)$$

(In manufacturing it is common to use the terms "proportion defective" and "defects per unit, DPU, in these formulas.)

EXAMPLE 8.2

Computing Proportion Nonconforming and Nonconformances Per Unit

A hotel housekeeping manager inspects random samples of rooms each day to verify that they have been cleaned properly. The manager uses a checklist of 12 quality characteristics, such as "bed properly made," "shampoo bottles on sink," "garbage can empty," and so on. On a particular day, 35 rooms were inspected and 3 rooms were found to have nonconformances. One room had 1 nonconformance; the second had 3 nonconformances; and the third had 2 nonconformances. Using formula (8.1), the proportion of rooms that were nonconforming is calculated as 3/35 = 0.086. Using formula (8.2), the number of nonconformances per room is calculated as NPU = (1 + 3 + 2)/35 = 0.171. (Be careful in using these formulas. The number of nonconforming units is different than the number of nonconformances.)

Many manufacturing firms often classify defects into three categories:

1. *Critical Defect:* A critical defect is one that judgment and experience indicate will surely result in hazardous or unsafe conditions for individuals using, maintaining, or depending on the product and will prevent proper performance of the product.
2. *Major Defect:* A major defect is one not critical but likely to result in failure or to materially reduce the usability of the unit for its intended purpose.
3. *Minor Defect:* A minor defect is one not likely to materially reduce the usability of the item for its intended purpose, nor to have any bearing on the effective use or operation of the unit.[4]

Critical defects may lead to serious consequences or product liability suits; thus, they should be monitored and controlled for carefully. On the other hand, minor defects might not be monitored as closely, because they do not affect fitness for use. For many products, however, even minor defects can lead to customer dissatisfaction.

To account for the differences in severity, organizations often create a composite index in which major and critical defects are weighted more heavily than minor defects. For example, FedEx has an extensive quality measurement system that includes a composite measure, called the service quality indicator (SQI), which is a weighted sum of 10 factors that reflect customers' expectations of organizational performance. FedEx's SQI is shown in Table 8.2. Different weights reflect the importance of each failure; losing a package, for instance, is more serious than delivering it a few minutes late. The index is reported weekly and summarized on a monthly basis.

If NPU has been calculated and nonconformances occur randomly, we can estimate the number of units that have no nonconformances—called **throughput yield (TY)**—using the following formula:

$$TY = e^{-NPU} \tag{8.3}$$

EXAMPLE 8.3

Computing Throughput Yield

In Example 8.2 we inspected 35 units and found a total of 6 nonconformances. NPU = 0.171, and using formula (8.3), the throughput yield is

$$TY = e^{-0.171} = 0.843$$

That is, we can expect the about 84 percent of rooms to be free from any nonconformances, or equivalently, the proportion of nonconforming units to be 1 − 0.84 = 0.16. Note that this is not the same as we observed from the sample

	Error Type	Description	Weight
1.	*Complaints reopened*—customer complaints (on traces, invoices, missed pickups, etc.) reopened after an unsatisfactory resolution		3
2.	*Damaged packages*—packages with visible or concealed damage or spoilage due to weather or water damage, missed pickup, or late delivery		10
3.	*International*—a composite score of performance measures of international operations		
4.	*Invoice adjustments*—customer requests for credit or refunds for real or perceived failures		1
5.	*Late pickup stops*—packages that were picked up later than the stated pickup time		3
6.	*Lost packages*—claims for missing packages or with contents missing		10
7.	*Missed proof of delivery*—invoices that lack written proof of delivery information		1
8.	*Right date late*—delivery past promised time on the right day		1
9.	*Traces*—package status and proof of delivery requests not in the COSMOS IIB computer system (the FedEx "real time" tracking system)		3
10.	*Wrong day late*—delivery on the wrong day		5

TABLE 8.2
FedEx Service
Quality Indicator
and Factors

Source: Service Quality Indicators at FedEx (Internal company document).

data—we found the proportion of nonconforming rooms to be 0.086. The difference is due to statistical sampling error.

If a process consists of many steps, each step may create nonconformances, thus reducing the yield of the final output. One measure that is often used to evaluate the quality of the entire process is **rolled throughput yield (RTY)**. RTY is the proportion of conforming units that results from a series of process steps. Mathematically, it is the product of the yields from each process step.

EXAMPLE 8.4

Computing Rolled Throughput Yield

Suppose that a process consists of 3 steps. Each produces some nonconforming items. Step 1 has throughput yield of 97 percent; step 2, 95 percent; and step 3, 99 percent. The rolled throughput yield is computed as:

$$RTY = 0.97 \times 0.95 \times 0.99 = 0.912$$

Thus, only about 91 percent conforming output will be produced, or equivalently, the proportion nonconforming is $1 - 0.91 = 0.09$.

Nonconformances per unit is difficult to use when units of work display varying amounts of complexity. Two different processes might have significantly different numbers of opportunities for nonconformances, making appropriate comparisons difficult. An alternative measure that became popular with the emergence of Six Sigma is **defects per million opportunities (dpmo)**:

$$dpmo = (\text{Number of defects discovered})/\text{opportunities for error} \times 1,000,000 \qquad (8.4)$$

In services, the term often used as an analogy to dpmo is **errors per million opportunities (epmo).**

EXAMPLE 8.5

Computing DPMO/EPMO

Suppose that an airline wishes to measure the effectiveness of its baggage handling system. It might measure nonconformances per unit by calculating the number of lost bags per customer. However, customers may have different numbers of bags; thus the number of opportunities for error differs with each customer. Suppose that the average number of bags per customer is 1.6, and the airline recorded 3 lost bags for 8000 passengers in one month, then using formula (8.4) we have

$$\text{epmo} = 3/[(8,000)(1.6)] \times 1,000,000 = 234.375$$

The use of dpmo and epmo allows us to define quality broadly. In the airline case, a broad definition might mean every opportunity for a failure to meet customer expectations from initial ticketing until bags are retrieved (think back to the concept of moments of truth in Chapter 3, which could be used to define the number of opportunities for error).

Cost of Quality Measures

In most firms, cost accounting is an important function. All organizations measure and report costs as a basis for control and improvement; however, few explicitly measure the direct costs associated with quality. The concept of the **cost of quality (COQ)** emerged in the 1950s. Traditionally, the reporting of quality-related costs had been limited to inspection and testing; other costs were accumulated in overhead accounts. As managers began to define and isolate the full range of quality-related costs, a number of surprising facts emerged.[5] First, quality-related costs were much larger than previously reported, generally in the range of 20 to 40 percent of sales. Second, quality-related costs were not only related to manufacturing operations, but to ancillary services such as purchasing and customer service departments as well. Third, most of the costs resulted from poor quality and were avoidable. Finally, while the costs of poor quality were avoidable, no clear responsibility for action to reduce them was assigned, nor was any structured approach formulated to do so. As a result, many firms began to develop cost of quality programs. The "costs of quality"—or specifically, the costs of *poor* quality—are those costs associated with avoiding poor quality or those incurred as a result of poor quality.

Juran noted that workers and supervisors speak in the "language of things"—units, defects, and so on. Unfortunately, quality problems expressed as the number of defects typically have little impact on top managers who are generally more concerned with financial performance. But if the magnitude of quality problems can be translated into monetary terms, such as "How much would it cost us to run this business if there were no quality problems?" the eyes of upper managers are opened. Dollar figures can be added meaningfully across departments or products, and compared to other dollar measures. Middle managers, who must deal with workers and supervisors as well as top management, must have the ability to speak in both languages. Quality cost information serves a variety of other purposes, too. It helps management evaluate the relative importance of quality problems and thus identify major opportunities for cost reduction. It can aid in budgeting and cost control activities. Finally, it can serve as a scoreboard to evaluate the organization's success in achieving quality objectives.

To establish a cost of quality approach, one must identify the activities that generate cost, measure them, report them in a way that is meaningful to managers, and analyze them to identify areas for improvement. Quality costs can be organized into four major categories: prevention costs, appraisal costs, internal failure costs, and external failure costs.

Prevention costs are investments made to keep nonconforming products from occurring and reaching the customer, including the following specific costs:

- *Quality planning costs*, such as salaries of individuals associated with quality planning and problem-solving teams, the development of new procedures, new equipment design, and reliability studies
- *Process control costs*, which include costs spent on analyzing production processes and implementing process control plans
- *Information systems costs* expended to develop data requirements and measurements
- *Training and general management costs*, including internal and external training programs, clerical staff expenses, and miscellaneous supplies

Appraisal costs are those associated with efforts to ensure conformance to requirements, generally through measurement and analysis of data to detect nonconformances. Categories of appraisal costs include the following:

- *Test and inspection costs* associated with incoming materials, work-in-process, and finished goods, including equipment costs and salaries
- *Instrument maintenance costs* due to calibration and repair of measuring instruments
- *Process measurement and control costs*, which involve the time spent by workers to gather and analyze quality measurements

Internal failure costs are incurred as a result of unsatisfactory quality found before the delivery of a product to the customer; some examples include the following:

- *Scrap and rework costs*, including material, labor, and overhead
- *Costs of corrective action*, arising from time spent determining the causes of failure and correcting production problems
- *Downgrading costs*, such as revenue lost when selling a product at a lower price because it does not meet specifications
- *Process failures*, such as unplanned machine downtime or unplanned equipment repair

External failure costs occur after poor-quality products reach the customer, specifically:

- *Costs due to customer complaints and returns*, including rework on returned items, cancelled orders, and freight premiums
- *Product recall costs* and *warranty claims*, including the cost of repair or replacement as well as associated administrative costs
- *Product liability costs*, resulting from legal actions and settlements

Costs such as service effort, product design, remedial engineering effort, rework, in-process inspection, and engineering change losses must usually be estimated or collected through special efforts. Some costs due to external failure, such as customer dissatisfaction and future lost revenues, are impossible to estimate accurately. Although prevention costs are the most important, appraisal costs, internal failure, and external failure (in that order) are usually easier to collect. Typical accounting systems are not structured to capture cost-of-quality information. However, **activity-based costing**, which organizes information about the work activities such as moving, inspecting, receiving, shipping, and order processing that consume resources, facilitates the capture of quality costs.

A convenient way of reporting quality costs is through a breakdown by organizational function as shown in Figure 8.3. Such a report can be implemented easily on a spreadsheet. This matrix serves several purposes. First, it allows all departments to recognize their contributions to the cost of quality and participate in a cost of quality program. Second, it pinpoints areas of high quality cost and directs attention toward improvement efforts. For instance, if we rank internal failure costs from largest to smallest, chances are that 70 or 80 percent of all internal failure costs are due to only one or two manufacturing problems. Identifying these "vital few," as they are called, leads to corrective action that has a high return for a low dollar input. This technique, which we will study formally in a later chapter, is called *Pareto analysis*. Quality costs are also often reported as an *index*, that is, the ratio of the current value to a base period.

Experts estimate that 60 to 90 percent of total quality costs are the result of internal and external failure and are the responsibility of management. Managers typically react to high failure costs by increasing inspection. Such actions, however, only increase appraisal costs. The overall result is little, if any, improvement in overall quality or profitability. In practice, an increase in prevention usually generates larger savings in all other cost categories. In a typical scenario, the cost of replacing a poor-quality component in the field might be $500; the cost of replacement after assembly might be $50; the cost of testing and replacement during assembly might be $5; and the cost of changing

FIGURE 8.3 Cost of Quality Matrix

	Design	Purchasing	Production	...	Finance	...	Accounting	Totals

Prevention costs
  Quality planning
  Training
  ...								

Appraisal costs
  Test and inspection
  Instruments
  ...								

Internal failure costs
  Scrap
  Rework
  ...								

External failure costs
  Returns
  Recall costs
  ...								

Totals								

the design to avoid the problem might be only 50 cents. Thus, organizations should first attempt to reduce external failure costs to zero by investing in appraisal activities to discover the sources of internal failures and take corrective action. As quality improves, failure costs will decrease, and the amount of appraisal can be reduced with the shift of emphasis to prevention activities. However, because many organizations focus on the short term, they fail to understand that investment in prevention will reduce overall system costs.

The nature of quality costs differs between service and manufacturing organizations. External failure costs such as warranty claims and field support, are easy to identify in manufacturing. For a service, the primary external failure costs are those due to complaint-handling and lost customers, which are more difficult to quantify. Internal failure costs also tend to be much lower for service organizations with high customer contact, which have little opportunity to correct an error before it reaches the customer. By that time, the error becomes an external failure. In general, the intangible nature of output makes quality cost accounting for services difficult.

MEASUREMENT SYSTEM EVALUATION

Measuring quality characteristics generally requires the use of the human senses—seeing, hearing, feeling, tasting, and smelling—and the use of some type of instrument or gauge to measure the magnitude of the characteristic. Common types of measuring instruments used in manufacturing today fall into two categories: low-technology and high-technology. Low-technology instruments are primarily manual devices such as gages that have been available for many years; high-technology instruments describe those that depend on modern electronics, microprocessors, lasers, or advanced optics.

Observed variation in process output stems from the natural variation that occurs in the output itself as well as the measurement system. The measurement system includes the workers who take the measurements and the instruments they use. If there is little variation in the measurement system, then the observed measurements reflect the true variation in the process. However, if the variation in the measurement system is high, then it is difficult to separate the true variation in the process from the variation in the measurement system, resulting in misleading conclusions about quality. This can be summed up by the following equation, which states that the total observed variation in production output is the sum of the true process variation (which is what we actually want to measure) plus variation due to measurement:

$$\sigma^2_{\text{total}} = \sigma^2_{\text{process}} + \sigma^2_{\text{measurement}} \tag{8.5}$$

Thus, an objective of quality assurance is to minimize measurement error.

In many industries, in-process measures are collected through some type of manual inspection process. Processes that rely on visual interpretation of product characteristics or manual reading of gauges and instruments may encounter error rates of from 10 to 50 percent. These high rates occur for several reasons:

- *Complexity:* The number of defects caught by an inspector decreases with more parts and less orderly arrangement.
- *Defect Rate:* When the product defect rate is low, inspectors tend to miss more defects than when the defect rate is higher.

- *Inspection Rate:* The inspector's performance degrades rapidly as the inspection rate increases.[6]

These factors can be mitigated by using automated technology, or at the very least, minimizing the number of quality characteristics that must be inspected, reducing time pressures, using repeated inspections (if the same item is inspected by several people, a higher percentage of total defects will be caught), and improving the design of the workspace to facilitate the inspection task.

Metrology

Metrology is the science of measurement and is defined broadly as the collection of people, equipment, facilities, methods, and procedures used to assure the correctness or adequacy of measurements. Metrology is vital in our daily lives. Some examples include wondering whether you are getting a true gallon of gasoline at a gas station, whether the scanners at grocery stores are correctly reading the bar codes, if a box of cereal contains the amount stated on the package, or if the timers at a swim meet provide correct times.

Metrology is also vital to global competitiveness. In testifying before the U.S. Congress, the director of the Office of Standards Services at the National Institute of Standards and Technology noted that efficient national and international trade requires weights and measures organizations that assure uniform and accurate measures used in trade, national or regional measurement standards laboratories, standards development organizations, and accredited and internationally recognized calibration and testing laboratories.[7]

Measurements must be both accurate and precise. **Accuracy** is defined as the difference between the true value and the observed average of a measurement. Accuracy is measured as the amount of error in a measurement in proportion to the total size of the measurement. One measurement is more accurate than another if it has a smaller relative error. The lack of accuracy reflects a systematic bias in the measurement such as a gage that is not properly calibrated, worn, or used improperly by the worker. **Precision** is defined as the closeness of repeated measurements to each other. Precision, therefore, relates to the variance of repeated measurements. A measuring instrument with a low variance is more precise than another having a higher variance. Low precision is the result of random variation that is built into the instrument, such as friction among its parts. This random variation may be the result of a poor design or lack of maintenance.

EXAMPLE 8.6

Evaluating Accuracy and Precision

Suppose that two instruments measure a dimension whose true value is 0.250 inch. Instrument A may read 0.248 inch, whereas instrument B may read 0.259 inch. The relative error of instrument A is $(0.250 - 0.248)/0.250 = 0.8\%$; the relative error of instrument B is $(0.259 - 0.250)/0.250 = 3.6\%$. Thus, instrument A is more accurate than instrument B. Now suppose that each instrument is used to measure the dimension three times. Instrument A records values of 0.248, 0.246, and 0.251; instrument B records values of 0.259, 0.258, and 0.259. Instrument B is more precise than instrument A because its values are clustered closer together.

A measurement system may be precise but not necessarily accurate at the same time. The relationships between accuracy and precision are summarized in Figure 8.4.

FIGURE 8.4
Accuracy Versus
Precision

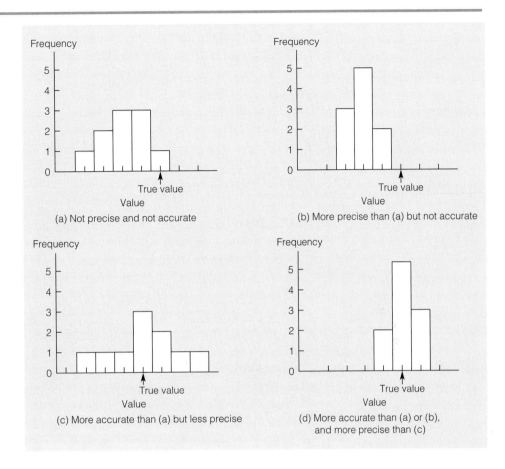

The figure illustrates four possible frequency distributions of 10 repeated measurements of some quality characteristic. In Figure 8.4(a), the average measurement is not close to the true value. Moreover, a wide range of values fall around the average. In this case, the measurement is neither accurate nor precise. In Figure 8.4(b), even though the average measurement is not close to the true value, the range of variation is small. Thus, the measurement is precise but not accurate. In Figures 8.4(c) and 8.4(d), the average value is close to the true value—that is, the measurement is accurate—but in 8.4(c) the distribution is widely dispersed and therefore not precise, whereas the measurement in 8.4(d) is both accurate and precise.

Calibration

When we take any measurement, we need to ensure that the instrument used is capable of making the correct measurement; for instance, that a scale accurately measures weight. According to *The Quality Calibration Handbook*, **calibration** is the process of verifying the capability and performance of an item of measuring and test equipment compared to traceable measurement standards.[8] Measurements made using uncalibrated or inadequately calibrated equipment can lead to erroneous and costly decisions. For example, suppose that an inspector has a micrometer that is reading 0.002 inch too low. When measurements are made close to the upper limit, parts that are as much as 0.002 inch over the maximum tolerance limit will be accepted as good, whereas those at the lower tolerance limit or that are as much as 0.002 inch above the limit will be rejected as nonconforming. This can lead to failure or unsatisfactory performance of the end product and unnecessary costs associated with scrapping good parts.

The federal government has many calibration requirements that cover such areas as the accuracy for radio transmitter frequencies, aircraft altimeters, and automobile speedometers. Measures taken to assess compliance with a regulatory requirement must be made with a calibrated instrument.[9] The National Institute of Standards and Technology (NIST) maintains national measurement standards and provides technical advice on making measurements consistent with national standards. NIST works with various metrology laboratories in industry and government to assure that measurements made by different people in different places yield the same results. Thus, the measurement of "voltage" or "resistance" in an electrical component has a precise and universal meaning. This process is accomplished in a hierarchical fashion. NIST calibrates the reference-level standards of those organizations requiring the highest level of accuracy. These organizations calibrate their own working-level standards and those of other metrology laboratories. These working-level standards are used to calibrate the measuring instruments used in the field. The usual recommendation is that equipment be calibrated against working-level standards that are 10 times as accurate as the equipment. When possible, at least a four-to-one accuracy ratio between the reference and working-level standards is desired—that is, the reference standards should be at least four times as accurate as the working-level standards.

Many government regulations and commercial contracts require regulated organizations or contractors to verify that the measurements they make are *traceable* to a reference standard. For example, world standards exist for length, mass, and time. For other types of measurement, such as chemical measurements, industry standards exist. Organizations must be able to support the claim of traceability by keeping records that their own measuring equipment has been calibrated by laboratories or testing facilities whose measurements can be related to appropriate standards, generally national or international standards, through an unbroken chain of comparison.[10] The purpose of requiring traceability is to ensure that measurements are accurate representations of the specific quantity subject to measurement, within the uncertainty of the measurement. Not only should there be an unbroken chain of comparisons, each measurement should be accompanied by a statement of uncertainty associated with the farthest link in the chain from NIST—that is, the last facility providing the measurement value. This accountability can be assured by purchasing an instrument that is certified against a higher level (traceable) standard or by contracting with a calibration agency that has such standards to certify the instrument.

Smaller precision-manufactured parts, tighter tolerances, and the need to measure and verify parts faster, more accurately, and with greater repeatability are driving developments in metrology systems and equipment. How to manufacture and measure these cost-effectively is a challenge for both machine tool and metrology equipment manufacturers. To meet the anticipated industry needs, equipment manufacturers are looking for ways to optimize the functionality of measurement and inspection equipment using a wide range of sensor and mechanical technologies to reduce inspection time and costs. Multisensor data-gathering systems are being developed that incorporate tactile, vision, and laser-scanner systems. As production technology evolves, so too will the capabilities of equipment to provide manufacturers with not only a means of inspection, but also valuable insights into the production process that will lead to higher quality at lower cost.[11]

Repeatability and Reproducibility Analysis

When a worker measures the same part multiple times, the results will usually show some variability. **Repeatability**, or **equipment variation (EV)**, is the variation in multiple measurements of a quality characteristic by an individual using the same instrument. Repeatability indicates how consistent a measuring instrument is. It is influenced by the condition of the measurement instrument, environmental conditions such as noise or lighting, the worker's health and eyesight, and the process used to take the measurement such as how a part is positioned in a gage. **Reproducibility**, or **appraiser variation (AV)**, is the variation when using the same measuring instrument by different individuals to measure the same parts. Reproducibility indicates how consistent workers are in using measurement instruments. It is influenced by the training of workers in the use of the instrument, clarity of the directions or procedures of the measurement process, calibration of gages between workers, gage maintenance, and worker health.

A **repeatability and reproducibility (R&R) study** is a study of variation in a measurement system using statistical analysis. An R&R study is conducted in the following manner.[12]

1. Select m operators and n parts. Typically at least 2 operators and 10 parts are chosen. Number the parts so that the numbers are not visible to the operators.
2. Calibrate the measuring instrument.
3. Let each operator measure each part in a random order and record the results. Repeat this procedure for a total of r trials. At least two trials must be used. Let M_{ijk} represent the kth measurement of operator i on part j.
4. Compute the average measurement for each operator:

$$\bar{x}_i = \left(\sum_j \sum_k M_{ijk} \right) / nr \tag{8.6}$$

The difference between the largest and smallest average is

$$\bar{x}_D = \max_i\{\bar{x}_i\} - \min_i\{\bar{x}_i\} \tag{8.7}$$

5. Compute the range for each part and each operator:

$$R_{ij} = \max_k\{M_{ijk}\} - \min_k\{M_{ijk}\} \tag{8.8}$$

These values show the variability of repeated measurements of the same part by the same operator. Next, compute the average range for each operator:

$$\bar{R}_i = \left(\sum_j R_{ij} \right) / n \tag{8.9}$$

The overall average range is then computed as

$$\bar{\bar{R}} = \left(\sum_i \bar{R}_i \right) / m \tag{8.10}$$

6. Calculate a "control limit" on the individual ranges R_{ij}:

$$\text{control limit} = D_4 \bar{\bar{R}} \tag{8.11}$$

where D_4 is a constant that depends on the sample size (number of trials, r) and can be found in Table 8.3 along with other constants used in the calculations. Any range

Number of Trials	D_4	K_1
2	3.27	4.56
3	2.58	3.05
Number of Operators		K_2
2		3.65
3		2.70
Number of Parts		K_3
2		3.65
3		2.70
4		2.30
5		2.08
6		1.93
7		1.82
8		1.74
9		1.67
10		1.62

value beyond this limit might result from some assignable cause, not random error. Possible causes should be investigated and, if found, corrected. The operator should repeat these measurements using the same part. If no assignable cause is found, these values should be discarded and all statistics in step 5 as well as the control limit should be recalculated.

Once these basic calculations are made, an analysis of repeatability and reproducibility can be performed. The repeatability, or equipment variation (EV) is computed as

$$EV = K_1\overline{\overline{R}} \tag{8.12}$$

Reproducibility, or operator (sometimes called appraisal) variation (AV), is computed as

$$AV = \sqrt{(K_2\overline{x}_D)^2 - (EV^2/nr)} \tag{8.13}$$

(If the value under the radical is negative, then AV defaults to zero.) The constants K_1 and K_2 depend on the number of trials and number of operators, respectively, and are given in Table (8.3). An overall measure of repeatability and reproducibility (R&R) is given by

$$R\&R = \sqrt{(EV)^2 + (AV)^2} \tag{8.14}$$

Part variation (PV) measures the variation among different parts. Part variation is determined by multiplying the range of part averages, R_p, by a constant K_3:

$$PV = R_pK_3 \tag{8.15}$$

The total variation, TV, is calculated as:

$$TV = \sqrt{R\&R^2 + PV^2} = \sqrt{EV^2 + AV^2 + PV^2} \tag{8.16}$$

A measurement system is adequate if R&R is low relative to the total variation, or equivalently, the part variation is much greater than the measurement system variation. The industry guides have historically expressed EV, AV, R&R, and PV as a percent of the total variation by dividing each by TV and multiplying by 100 as a means of evaluating measurement systems. That is,

$$\%EV = 100\,\frac{EV}{TV} \tag{8.17}$$

$$\%AV = 100\,\frac{AV}{TV} \tag{8.18}$$

$$\%R\&R = 100\,\frac{R\&R}{TV} \tag{8.19}$$

$$\%PV = 100\,\frac{PV}{TV} \tag{8.20}$$

From these calculations, experts suggest the following guidelines for evaluating EV, AV, and R&R measures:

- *Under 10 percent:* This rate is acceptable.
- *10 to 30 percent:* This rate may be acceptable based on the importance of the application, cost of the instrument, cost of repair, and so on.
- *Over 30 percent:* Generally, this rate is not acceptable. Every effort should be made to identify the problem and correct it.

Repeatability and reproducibility measures are also often expressed as a percentage of the tolerance of the quality characteristic being measured instead of the total variation; the same guidelines as above can be applied.

The Student Companion Site provides an easy-to-use Excel template, R&R.xlsx, for all the calculations we have described for an R&R study.

Note, however, that these percentages of EV, AV, and R&R will not add to 100 percent because standard deviations are not additive (variances, however, can be added). As a result, the industry-based calculations have been difficult for many practitioners to interpret and have been somewhat controversial.[13] The proper way to express the results as a percentage of the total is to use the ratio of variances from formula (8.16), that is,

$$EV\% \text{ of Total Variance} = 100\,\frac{EV^2}{TV^2} \tag{8.21}$$

$$AV\% \text{ of Total Variance} = 100\,\frac{AV^2}{TV^2} \tag{8.22}$$

$$R\&R\% \text{ of Total Variance} = 100\,\frac{R\&R^2}{TV^2} \tag{8.23}$$

$$PV\% \text{ of Total Variance} = 100\,\frac{PV^2}{TV^2} \tag{8.24}$$

For example, the variance of R&R is the sum of the variances of EV and AV; thus, $\frac{EV^2}{R\&R^2}$ yields the true proportion of the R&R variance resulting from equipment variation.

EXAMPLE 8.7	R&R Calculations

Suppose that a gauge used to measure the thickness of a gasket having a specification of 0.50 to 1.0 mm is to be evaluated. Ten parts have been selected for measurement by three operators. Each part is measured twice with the results as shown in the *Process Capability* spreadsheet template in Figure 8.5. (Slight rounding differences from manual calculations may be evident.)

The average measurement for each operator, $\bar{x}_i$, is

$$\bar{x}_1 = 0.830 \quad \bar{x}_2 = 0.774 \quad \bar{x}_3 = 0.829$$

Thus $\bar{x}_D = 0.830 - 0.774 = 0.056$. The average range for each operator is

$$\bar{R}_1 = 0.037 \quad \bar{R}_2 = 0.034 \quad \bar{R}_3 = 0.017$$

The overall average range is $\bar{\bar{R}} = (0.037 + 0.034 + 0.017)/3 = 0.0293$. From Table 8.3, $D_4 = 3.27$ because the two trials were conducted. Hence the control limit is

FIGURE 8.5   Gauge Repeatability and Reproducibility

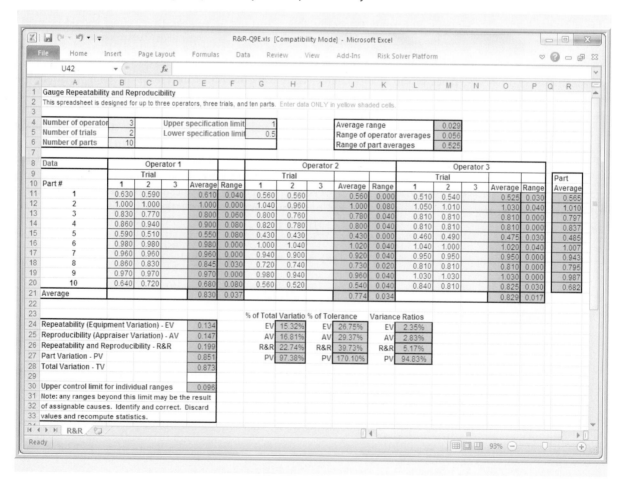

3.27(0.0293) = 0.096. Because all range values fall below this limit, no assignable causes of variation are suspected. Compute the repeatability and reproducibility measures:

$$EV = (4.56)(0.0293) = 0.134$$

$$AV = \sqrt{[(0.056)(2.70)]^2 - (0.134)^2/(10)(2)} = 0.147$$

$$R\&R = \sqrt{(0.134)^2 + (0.147)^2} = 0.199$$

$$PV = (0.525)(1.62) = 0.851$$

$$TV = \sqrt{(0.199)^2 + (0.851)^2} = 0.873$$

As a percent of total variation, the measurement system appears adequate, however, as a percent of tolerance, the equipment and operator variation are marginal and their combined R&R measure is at best marginal, suggesting that the variation should be reduced. However, the variance ratios from formulas (8.21) through (8.24) suggest that R&R is only 5.17 percent of the total variation; the rest is attributable to variation in parts. From this interpretation, the measurement system appears to be acceptable.

PROCESS CAPABILITY MEASUREMENT

Process capability is the ability of a process to produce output that conforms to specifications. To evaluate it, we need the specifications for the output, and statistical information about the actual process performance.

EXAMPLE 8.8

The Concept of Process Capability

Suppose that the inside diameter of a bushing that supports a steel shaft has a lower specification of 1.498 and upper specification of 1.510 inches. If the diameter is too small, it can be enlarged through a rework process. However if it is too large, the part must be scrapped. If the natural variation in the machining process results in diameters that typically range from 1.495 to 1.515 inches, we would say that the process is not capable of meeting the specifications. Management then faces three possible decisions: (1) measure each piece and either rework or scrap nonconforming parts, (2) develop a better process by investing in new technology, or (3) change the design specifications.

Understanding process capability is important for many reasons. For example, manufacturing may wish to determine a performance baseline for a process, to prioritize projects for quality improvement, or to provide statistical evidence of quality for customers; purchasing might conduct a study at a supplier plant to evaluate a new piece of equipment or to compare different suppliers; or engineering might conduct a study to evaluate new processes. Also, process capability should be carefully considered in determining design specifications, especially in a DFSS environment (see Chapter 7). Inexperienced designers often choose tolerances with little awareness of the capabilities of the production process to meet them.

A **process capability study** is a carefully planned study designed to yield specific information about the performance of a process under specified operating conditions. Typical questions that are asked in a process capability study include the following:

- Where is the process centered?
- How much variability exists in the process?

- Is the performance relative to specifications acceptable?
- What proportion of output will be expected to meet specifications?
- What factors contribute to variability?

The steps in a process capability study are similar to those of any systematic investigation and include the following:

1. Choose a representative machine or segment of the process.
2. Define the process conditions.
3. Select a representative operator.
4. Provide materials that are of standard grade, with sufficient materials for uninterrupted study.
5. Specify the gauging or measurement method to be used.
6. Collect the measurements and interpret the data.

To obtain useful statistical information, the sample size should be fairly large, generally at least 100.

Three types of studies are often conducted.

1. A *process characterization study* is designed to determine how a process performs under actual operating conditions, which may include both common and special causes of variation. It is typically performed over a moderate to long time interval to capture any and all variations that might occur.
2. A *peak performance study* determines how a process performs when only common causes of variation are present. Typically this is done over a short time interval under carefully-controlled conditions.
3. A *component variability study* assesses the relative contribution of different sources of total variation. A component variability study uses a designed experiment to evaluate the sources of variability.

The only information needed to conduct a process characterization study is the mean, standard deviation, and histogram of a sample of measurements. If the distribution is approximately normal, then we know that 99.73 percent of the observations will fall within three standard deviations from the mean. Thus, the natural variation of a process can be characterized as $\mu - 3\sigma$ and $\mu + 3\sigma$, where μ is the process average. Such a six standard deviation spread is commonly used as a measure of process variability.

EXAMPLE 8.9

Evaluating Process Capability

Let us consider the U-bolt data we introduced in Chapter 6 (which are available in the Excel file *U-Bolt Data* on the Student Companion Site). To recap, we saw that the mean dimension is $\bar{x} = 10.7171$, and the sample standard deviation $s = 0.0868$. The histogram suggested that the data are approximately normally distributed. Thus, nearly all U-bolt dimensions are expected to fall between $10.7171 + 3(0.868) = 10.4566$ and $10.7171 - 3(0.0868) = 10.9766$. These calculations tell the production manager that if the design specifications are between 10.55 and 10.90, then clearly the process will produce some nonconforming units.

We may use normal probability calculations as described in Chapter 6 to find the expected percentage of nonconforming U-bolts by computing the area under a normal distribution having a mean of 10.7171 and standard deviation 0.0868 to the left and right of these specifications, as illustrated in Figure 8.6. For example, the Excel function = NORM.DIST(10.55, 10.7171, 0.0868, TRUE) = 0.0271 calculates the proportion of output below the lower specification. Similarly, the Excel formula = 1 − NORM.DIST(10.90,

FIGURE 8.6
Probability of Non-
conforming Product
with Specifications
of 10.55 to 10.90

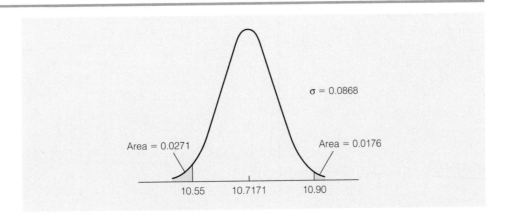

$\sigma = 0.0868$

Area = 0.0271

Area = 0.0176

10.55   10.7171   10.90

10.7171, 0.0868, TRUE) = 0.0176 is the probability of exceeding the upper specification. Therefore, the probability that a part will not meet specifications is 0.0271 + 0.0176 = 0.0447 or, expressed as a percentage, is 4.47 percent.

Not all process output will fit neatly into a normal distribution; however, one can usually obtain useful insights directly from the histogram. Figure 8.7 shows some typical examples of process variation histograms that might result from a capability study. Figure 8.7(a) shows an ideal situation in which the natural variation is well within the specified tolerance limits. In Figure 8.7(b), the variation and tolerance limits are about equal; any shift of the distribution will result in nonconformances. The histogram in 8.7(c) shows a distribution with a natural variation greater than the specification limits; in this case, the process is not capable of meeting specifications. The histograms in Figures 8.7(d), (e), and (f) correspond to those in Figures 8.7(a), (b), and (c), except that the process is off-center from the specified tolerance limits. The capability of each is the same as in Figures 8.7(a), (b), and (c), but the shift in the mean of the distribution results in a higher level of nonconformance. Thus, in Figure 8.7(d), the process is capable; it is simply not adjusted correctly to the center of the specifications. In Figure 8.7(g), the bimodal shape suggests that perhaps the data were drawn from two different machines or that two different materials or products were involved. The small distribution to the right in Figure 8.7(h) may be the result of including pieces from a trial setup run while the machine was being adjusted. The strange distribution in Figure 8.7(i) might be the result of the measurement process, such as inadequate gauging or rounding of data, and not inherent in the process itself. Finally, the truncated distribution in Figure 8.7(j) is generally the result of sorting nonconforming parts; one would expect a smoother tail of the distribution on the left.

To conduct a peak performance study, we must ensure that the variation in the process is due only to common causes and does not include any special causes. When the variation in the process is due to common causes alone, we say it is **in statistical control** (or simply, **in control**). When special causes are present, the process is said to be **out of control**. A practical definition of statistical control is that *both* the process averages and variances are constant over time.[14]

Process capability calculations make little sense if the process is not in statistical control because the data are confounded by special causes that do not represent the inherent capability of the process. Statistical process control techniques, which we

FIGURE 8.7
Examples of Process
Variation Histo-
grams and
Specifications

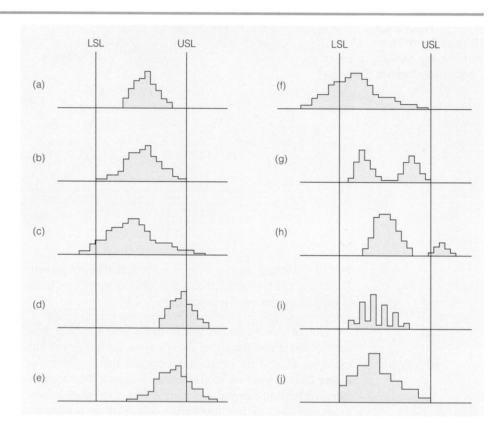

introduce later in this chapter, provide the means to determine whether a process is in control and to identify special causes before conducting a peak performance study. The following example illustrates these concepts.

EXAMPLE 8.10

Limitations of Histograms

Consider the data in Figure 8.8 (available in the Excel file *Quality Measurements* on the Student Companion Site), which shows measurements of a quality characteristic for 30 samples from a manufacturing process with specifications 0.75 ± 0.25 or LSL = 0.50 and USL = 1.00. Each row corresponds to a sample size of 5 taken every 15 minutes. The mean of each sample is also given in the last column. A frequency distribution and histogram of these data is shown in Figure 8.9. The data form a relatively symmetric distribution with a mean of 0.762 and standard deviation 0.0738. We see that the sample mean is close to the nominal specification of 0.75, and that most of the measurements fall between the specification limits. Thus, it appears that the process is at least marginally capable of meeting specifications.

How can we tell if any special causes are present? A histogram alone does not provide this information. However, if we plot the mean of each sample over time, we obtain the chart, commonly called a **run chart**, shown in Figure 8.10. This chart suggests that the mean changed around the time that sample 17 was taken. In fact, the process average for the first 16 samples is only 0.738, whereas the average for the remaining samples is 0.789. Therefore, although the overall average is close to the target specification, at no time was the actual process average centered near the target.

FIGURE 8.8
Thirty Samples of
Quality
Measurements

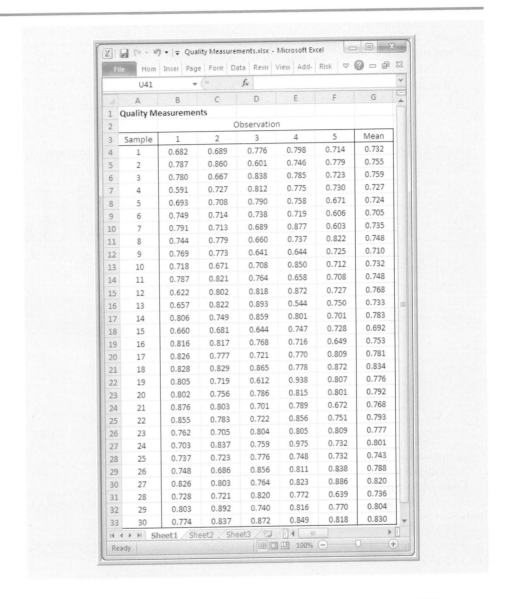

Sample	1	2	3	4	5	Mean
1	0.682	0.689	0.776	0.798	0.714	0.732
2	0.787	0.860	0.601	0.746	0.779	0.755
3	0.780	0.667	0.838	0.785	0.723	0.759
4	0.591	0.727	0.812	0.775	0.730	0.727
5	0.693	0.708	0.790	0.758	0.671	0.724
6	0.749	0.714	0.738	0.719	0.606	0.705
7	0.791	0.713	0.689	0.877	0.603	0.735
8	0.744	0.779	0.660	0.737	0.822	0.748
9	0.769	0.773	0.641	0.644	0.725	0.710
10	0.718	0.671	0.708	0.850	0.712	0.732
11	0.787	0.821	0.764	0.658	0.708	0.748
12	0.622	0.802	0.818	0.872	0.727	0.768
13	0.657	0.822	0.893	0.544	0.750	0.733
14	0.806	0.749	0.859	0.801	0.701	0.783
15	0.660	0.681	0.644	0.747	0.728	0.692
16	0.816	0.817	0.768	0.716	0.649	0.753
17	0.826	0.777	0.721	0.770	0.809	0.781
18	0.828	0.829	0.865	0.778	0.872	0.834
19	0.805	0.719	0.612	0.938	0.807	0.776
20	0.802	0.756	0.786	0.815	0.801	0.792
21	0.876	0.803	0.701	0.789	0.672	0.768
22	0.855	0.783	0.722	0.856	0.751	0.793
23	0.762	0.705	0.804	0.805	0.809	0.777
24	0.703	0.837	0.759	0.975	0.732	0.801
25	0.737	0.723	0.776	0.748	0.732	0.743
26	0.748	0.686	0.856	0.811	0.838	0.788
27	0.826	0.803	0.764	0.823	0.886	0.820
28	0.728	0.721	0.820	0.772	0.639	0.736
29	0.803	0.892	0.740	0.816	0.770	0.804
30	0.774	0.837	0.872	0.849	0.818	0.830

It is also important to understand that *control* and *capability* are two different concepts. A process may be capable or not capable, or in control or out of control, independently of each other. Clearly, we would like every process to be both capable and in
control. If a process is neither capable nor in control, we must first get it in a state of
control by removing special causes of variation, and then attack the common causes to
improve its capability. If a process is capable but not in control, we should work to get it
back in control.

Process Capability Indexes

Process capability is measured by computing numerical indexes. In Figure 8.7 we saw
that the distribution of process output can differ in both location and spread relative to
the specifications. The relationship between specifications and the natural variation of

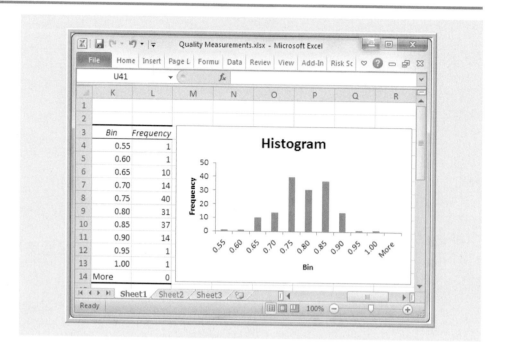

FIGURE 8.10
Chart of Sample
Means

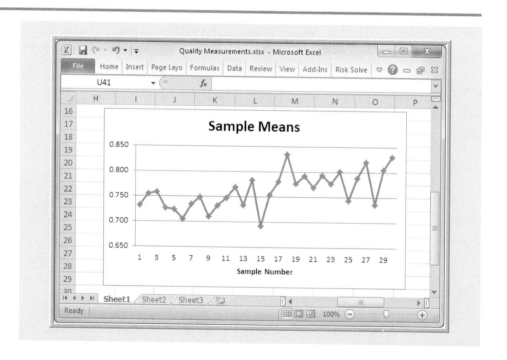

the process is often quantified by a measure known as the **process capability index**. In numerical terms, the formula is

$$C_p = \frac{\text{USL} - \text{LSL}}{6\sigma} \tag{8.25}$$

where

USL = upper specification limit

LSL = lower specification limit

σ = standard deviation of the process (or the sample standard deviation as an estimate)

A spreadsheet template, Process Capability.xlsx, is available on the Student Companion Site for computing process capability indexes and displaying a histogram of the data.

C_p is simply the ratio of the specification range to the process variation. If $C_p > 1$, then the process is capable of meeting specifications because the process variation is smaller than the specification range. If $C_p < 1$, then the process cannot produce 100 percent conforming output. This assumes that the process is centered in the specification range. C_p can be larger than 1.0 even if the process variation is well outside the specification range. To include information on process centering, one-sided indexes are often used. One-sided process capability indexes are as follows:

$$C_{pu} = \frac{\text{USL} - \mu}{3\sigma} \quad \text{(upper one-sided index)} \tag{8.26}$$

$$C_{pl} = \frac{\mu - \text{LSL}}{3\sigma} \quad \text{(lower one-sided index)} \tag{8.27}$$

$$C_{pk} = \min(C_{pl}, C_{pu}) \tag{8.28}$$

EXAMPLE 8.11   Calculating Process Capability Indexes

We will calculate the process capability indexes for the U-bolt data discussed in Example 8.9.

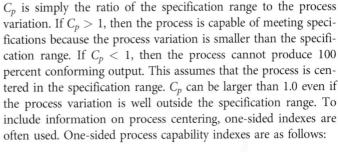

$$C_p = \frac{\text{USL} - \text{LSL}}{6\sigma} = \frac{10.90 - 10.55}{6(0.0868)} = 0.67$$

$$C_{pu} = \frac{\text{USL} - \mu}{3\sigma} = \frac{10.90 - 10.7171}{3(0.0868)} = 0.70$$

$$C_{pl} = \frac{\mu - \text{LSL}}{3\sigma} = \frac{10.7171 - 10.55}{3(0.0868)} = 0.64$$

$$C_{pk} = \min(C_{pl}, C_{pu}) = \min(0.064, 0.70) = 0.64$$

Thus, as we saw in Example 8.9, these indexes show that the process is not capable of producing to specifications. Figure 8.11 shows the results using the *Process Capability* spreadsheet template.

It is important to remember that C_p and C_{pk} are simply point estimates from some unknown distribution because they are based on samples. A confidence interval for C_{pk} can be expressed as:[15]

$$C_{pk} \pm z_{\alpha/2} \sqrt{\frac{1}{9n} + \frac{C_{pk}^2}{2n - 2}} \tag{8.29}$$

FIGURE 8.11 Process Capability Spreadsheet for Example 8.11

Example 8.11.xlsx - Microsoft Excel

Process Capability Analysis

This spreadsheet is designed to handle up to 150 observations. Enter data ONLY in yellow-shaded cells.

Nominal specification	10.70
Upper specification limit	10.90
Lower specification limit	10.55

DATA

	1	2	3	4	5	6	7	8	9	10	11	12	13	14	15
1	10.650	10.800	10.500	10.800	10.700	10.800	10.750	10.650	10.850	10.650	10.800	10.650			
2	10.750	10.850	10.800	10.800	10.700	10.700	10.850	10.700	10.800	10.550	10.700	10.850			
3	10.750	10.700	10.650	10.800	10.650	10.650	10.750	10.650	10.500	10.800	10.750	10.800			
4	10.600	10.650	10.650	10.700	10.600	10.750	10.800	10.850	10.650	10.650	10.700	10.600			
5	10.700	10.750	10.700	10.750	10.550	10.700	10.850	10.700	10.750	10.600	10.750	10.700			
6	10.600	10.900	10.850	10.750	10.650	10.650	10.600	10.750	10.750	10.600	10.650	10.650			
7	10.600	10.750	10.800	10.700	10.600	10.850	10.850	10.850	10.800	10.850	10.850	10.800			
8	10.750	10.750	10.700	10.700	10.700	10.600	10.650	10.850	10.750	10.650	10.700	10.650			
9	10.650	10.650	10.750	10.800	10.650	10.900	10.650	10.750	10.700	10.750	10.700	10.700			
10	10.600	10.600	10.750	10.800	10.750	10.850	10.750	10.750	10.700	10.650	10.600	10.650			

Process Capability Index Calculations

Average	10.7171
Standard deviation	0.0868

Cp	0.672
Cpl	0.641
Cpu	0.702
Cpk	0.641

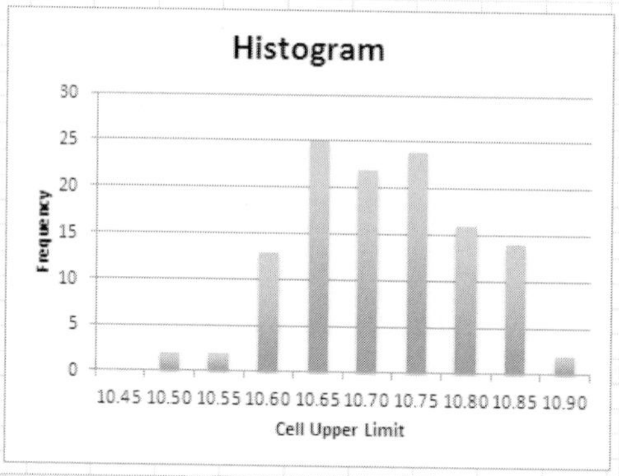

Process Capability

Ready

EXAMPLE 8.12 Computing a Confidence Interval for C_{pk}

To illustrate the use of the confidence interval formula (8.29) suppose the point estimate is 1.15 and the sample size $n = 45$. Using formula 8.29, a 95 percent confidence interval is (0.89, 1.41). Although 1.15 may seem good, it is quite possible that the true population parameter is less than one because of sampling error. If a sample size of 400 were used instead to obtain the same point estimate, the confidence interval would be (1.06, 1.24), providing a better indication that the capability is indeed good.

The process capability index can be used for setting objectives and improving processes, as the next example illustrates.

TABLE 8.4
Process Standard
Deviations

C_p	USL − LSL	6σ	σ
1.33	8	6	1
1.66	8	4.8	0.8
2.00	8	4	0.67
2.33	8	3.43	0.57

EXAMPLE 8.13

Using Process Capabiliy Indexes

Suppose that a quality manager in a firm has a process with a standard deviation of 1 and a specification range of 8. The value of C_p for this situation is 1.33. The manager realizes that the natural spread is within specifications at this time, but new contracts call for increasing the value of the capability index. Targets are set for increasing the index to 1.66 within three months, to 2.00 within six months, and to 2.33 within a year. Given that the specification range (USL − LSL) is held at the previous level of 8, the following Table 8.4 shows the required process standard deviation for each phase of the project. Operationally, this task involves reducing the variability in the process from a standard deviation of 1.000 to 0.444, which results in the desired increase of C_p from the current level of 1.33 to the final level of 2.33, which might be accomplished using process improvement and technology upgrades.

Some controversy exists over C_p and C_{pk} as measures of process capability, particularly with respect to the economic loss function philosophy of Taguchi.[16] For example, a process may have a high C_{pk} even when its mean is off target and close to the specification limits, as long as the process spread is small.[17] As a result, researchers have proposed alternative measures.

Process Performance Indexes

If a process may include special causes of variation, practitioners use alternative capability indexes, called **process performance indexes**: P_p, P_{pl}, P_{pu}, and P_{pk}. Mathematically, these are exactly the same as the process capability indexes C_p, C_{pl}, C_{pu}, and C_{pk}, but represent the actual, rather than ideal, performance in a noncontrolled environment. In reality, this makes little sense; many experts do not recommend this because it is important to control a process and remove special causes in order to achieve high levels of quality and customer satisfaction.

PRE-CONTROL[18]

In manufacturing operations such as machining, it is important to ensure that all parts are produced within specifications. **Pre-control** is a simple technique for ensuring that a process that has relatively good capability remains in control. The idea behind pre-control is to divide the tolerance range into zones by setting two *pre-control lines* halfway between the center of the specification and the upper and lower specification limits (see Figure 8.12). The center zone, called the *green zone*, comprises one-half of the total tolerance. Between the pre-control lines and the specification limits are the *yellow zones*. Outside the specification limits are the *red zones*.

FIGURE 8.12
Pre-Control Ranges

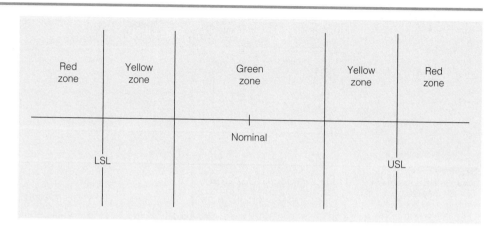

Pre-control is applied as follows. As a manufacturing run is initiated, five consecutive parts must fall within the green zone. If not, the production setup must be re-evaluated before the full production run can be started. Once regular operations commence, one part is sampled; if it falls within the green zone, production continues. However, if it falls in a yellow zone, then a second part is inspected. If the second part falls in the green zone, production can continue; if not, production should stop and the process should be investigated. If any part falls in a red zone, then action should be taken.

The rationale behind pre-control can be explained using basic statistical arguments. Suppose that the process capability is equal to the tolerance spread (see Figure 8.13). The area of each yellow zone is approximately 0.07, whereas that of the red zone is less than 0.01. The probability of two consecutive parts falling in a yellow zone is $(0.07)(0.07) = 0.0049$ if the process mean has not shifted. If $C_p > 1$, this probability is even less. Such an outcome would more than likely indicate a special cause. If both parts fall in the same yellow zone, you would conclude that the mean has shifted; if in different yellow zones, you would conclude that the variation has increased.

The frequency of sampling is often determined by dividing the time period between two successive out-of-control signals by six. Thus, if the process deteriorates, sampling frequency is increased; if it improves, the frequency is decreased.

FIGURE 8.13
Basis for Pre-Control
Rules

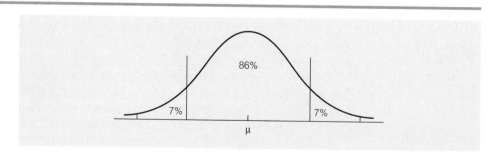

EXAMPLE 8.14

Applying Pre-Control

The force necessary to break a wire used in electrical circuitry has a specification of 3 gm–7 gm. Thus, the pre-control zones are

Range	Zone
<3	Red
3–4	Yellow
4–6	Green
6–7	Yellow
>7	Red

The following samples were collected:

Sample	First Measurement Value	Second Measurement Value
1	4.7	
2	4.5	
3	4.4	
4	4.2	
5	4.2	
6	4.0	
7	4.0	
8	3.7	3.6
9	6.5	3.5

For samples 1 through 7, the first measurement falls in the green zone; thus no further action need be taken. For sample 8, however, the first measurement falls in a yellow zone. The second measurement also falls in a yellow zone. The process should be stopped for investigation of a shift in the mean. At the next time of inspection, both pieces also fall in a yellow zone. In this case, the probable cause is a shift in variation. Again, the process should be stopped for investigation.

Pre-control should only be used when process capability is no greater than 88 percent of the tolerance, or equivalently, when C_p is at least 1.14. If the process mean tends to drift, then C_p should be higher. If managers or operators are interested in detecting process shifts even though the product output falls within specifications, pre-control should not be used because it will not detect such shifts. A more powerful approach for controlling processes is statistical process control, which we introduce next.

STATISTICAL PROCESS CONTROL

Statistical process control (SPC) is a methodology for monitoring a process to identify special causes of variation and signal the need to take corrective action. Many customers require their suppliers to provide evidence of statistical process control. Thus, SPC provides a means by which a firm may demonstrate its quality capability, an activity necessary for survival in today's highly competitive markets. SPC is particularly effective for companies in the early stages of quality assurance. SPC helps workers to know when to take action, and more importantly, when to leave a process alone.

SPC relies on control charts. A **control chart** is simply a run chart to which two horizontal lines, called **control limits** are added: the **upper control limit (UCL)** and **lower control limit (LCL)**, as illustrated in Figure 8.14. Control charts were first

FIGURE 8.14
Structure of a
Control Chart

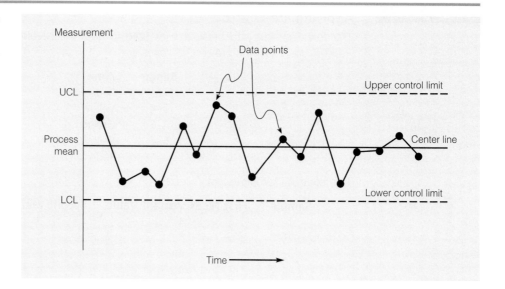

proposed by Walter Shewhart at Bell Laboratories in the 1920s and were strongly advocated by Deming. Control limits are chosen statistically to provide a high probability (generally greater than 0.99) that points will fall between these limits if the process is in control. Control limits make it easier to interpret patterns in a run chart and draw conclusions about the state of control. If special causes are present, the control chart will indicate them, and corrective action can be taken quickly. This will reduce the chances of producing nonconforming product.

Patterns in Control Charts

When a process is in statistical control, the points on a control chart fluctuate randomly between the control limits with no recognizable pattern. The following list provides a set of general rules for examining a control chart to determine whether the process is in control:

1. No points are outside control limits.
2. The number of points above and below the center line is about the same.
3. The points seem to fall randomly above and below the center line.
4. Most points, but not all, are near the center line, and only a few are close to the control limits.

The chart in Figure 8.15 illustrates a process in control. The underlying assumption behind these rules is that the distribution of sample means is normal. This assumption follows from the central limit theorem of statistics, which states that the distribution of sample means approaches a normal distribution as the sample size increases regardless of the original distribution. Of course, for small sample sizes, the distribution of the original data must be reasonably normal for this assumption to hold. The upper and lower control limits are computed to be three standard deviations from the overall mean. Thus, the probability that any sample mean falls outside the control limits is small. This probability is the origin of rule 1.

FIGURE 8.15   Example of a Process in Control

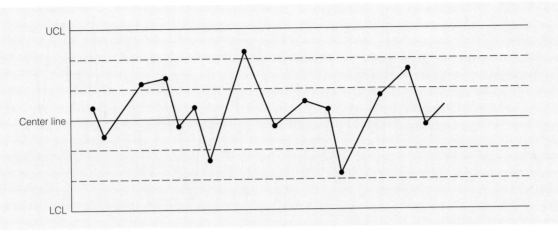

Because the normal distribution is symmetric, about the same number of points fall above as below the center line. Also, because the mean of the normal distribution is the median, about half the points fall on either side of the center line. Finally, about 68 percent of a normal distribution falls within one standard deviation of the mean; thus, most—but not all—points should be close to the center line. These characteristics will hold provided that the mean and variance of the original data have not changed during the time the data were collected; that is, the process is stable.

Several types of unusual patterns may arise in control charts.[19]

One Point Outside Control Limits   A single point outside the control limits is usually produced by a special cause. Once in a great while, however, such points are a normal part of the process and occur simply by chance. A common reason for a point falling outside a control limit is an error in the calculation of the control limits. You should always check your calculations whenever this occurs. Other possible causes are a sudden power surge, a broken tool, measurement error, or an incomplete or omitted operation in the process.

Sudden Shift in the Process Average   An unusual number of consecutive points falling on one side of the center line (see Figure 8.16) is usually an indication that the process average has suddenly shifted. Typical causes might be a new process operator, a new inspector, a new machine setting, or a change in the production setup or method.

Three rules of thumb are used for early detection of process shifts. A simple rule is that if eight consecutive points fall on one side of the center line, one could conclude that the mean has shifted. Second, divide the region between the center line and each control limit into three equal parts. Then if (1) two of three consecutive points fall in the outer one-third region between the center line and one of the control limits or (2) four out of five consecutive points fall within the outer two-thirds region, one would also conclude that the process has gone out of control. Examples are illustrated in Figure 8.17.

Cycles   Cycles are short, repeated patterns in the chart, alternating high peaks and low valleys (see Figure 8.18). These patterns are the result of special causes that come and go on a regular basis. They may result from operator rotation or fatigue at the end of a shift,

FIGURE 8.16
Shift in Process
Average

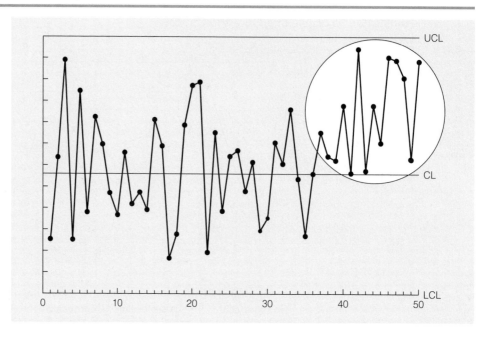

FIGURE 8.17 Indicators of Shifts

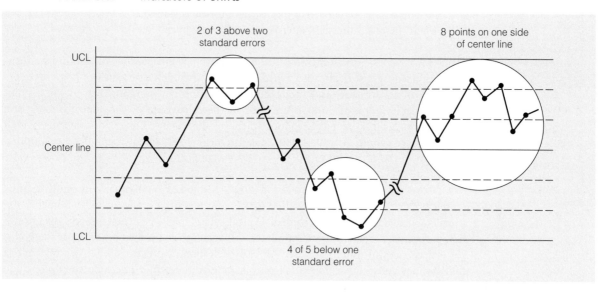

different gauges used by different inspectors, seasonal effects such as temperature or humidity, or differences between day and night shifts, or maintenance schedules.

Trends A trend is the result of some cause that gradually affects the measurement and causes the points on a control chart to gradually move up or down from the center line (see Figure 8.19). Trends may be the result of improving operator skills or fatigue, dirt or chip buildup in fixtures, tool wear, changes in temperature or humidity, or aging of equipment.

FIGURE 8.18
Cycles

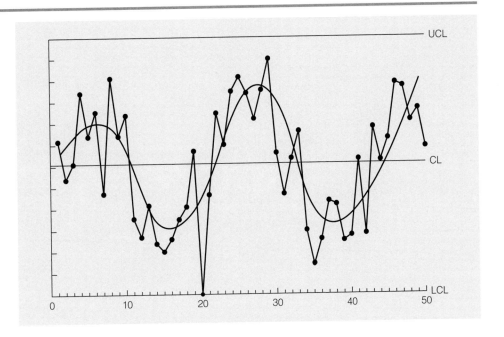

FIGURE 8.19
Trend

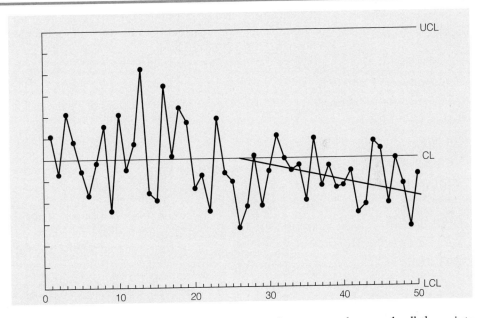

Hugging the Center Line   Hugging the center line occurs when nearly all the points fall close to the center line (see Figure 8.20). In the control chart, it appears that the control limits are too wide. An often-overlooked cause for this pattern is miscalculation of the control limits, perhaps by using the wrong factor from the table, or misplacing the decimal point in the computations. Otherwise, this usually occurs because each sample includes a mixture of data from two or more different processes. A histogram will generally show multiple distributions overlaid together. When this occurs, a separate chart should be constructed for each process.

FIGURE 8.20
Hugging the Center
Line

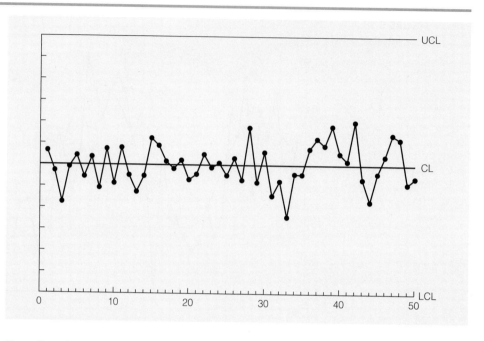

Hugging the Control Limits   This pattern shows up when many points are near the control limits with few in between (see Figure 8.21). This can result when each sample is taken from different process (but not mixed together) and plotted on the same chart.

Control charts are relatively simple to use. The following is a summary of the steps required to develop and use control charts.

To facilitate control chart calculations and to avoid the tedious task of either drawing control charts or constructing an Excel chart manually, we have created Excel 2010 templates for control charts discussed in this chapter, all of which may be found on the Student Companion Site. These templates include automatic calculation of statistics and control limits and the charts themselves (on separate tabs in the workbook).

1. Prepare
   a. Choose the variable or attribute measurement.
   b. Determine the basis, size, and frequency of sampling.
2. Collect data
   a. Record the sample observations.
   b. Calculate relevant statistics: averages, ranges, proportions, and so on.
   c. Plot the statistics on the chart(s).
3. Determine initial control limits
   a. Compute the upper and lower control limits.
   b. Draw the center line (average) and control limits on the chart.
4. Analyze the chart
   a. Determine if it is in control.
   b. Identify and eliminate out-of-control points and recompute control limits.
5. Use for ongoing control
   a. Continue collecting data and plotting on the chart(s).
   b. Stop the process when an out-of-control condition is identified and make necessary corrections or adjustments.

In the remainder of this chapter we discuss the construction, interpretation, and use of control charts following this methodology. Although many different charts are described, they differ only in the type of metric for which the chart is used; the basic approach described above applies to each of them.

FIGURE 8.21
Hugging the
Control Limits

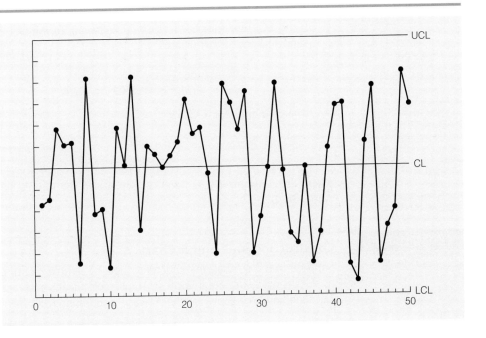

CONTROL CHARTS FOR VARIABLES DATA

The charts most commonly used for variables data are the $\bar{x}$-chart ("x-bar" chart) and
the R-chart (range chart). The $\bar{x}$-chart is used to monitor the centering of the process,
and the R-chart is used to monitor the variation in the process. The range is used as a
measure of variation primarily for convenience, particularly when workers on the factory
floor perform control chart calculations by hand, and works well for small samples. For
large samples and when data are analyzed on a computer, the standard deviation is
recommended; we will discuss this later.

Constructing $\bar{x}$- and R-Charts

The first step in developing $\bar{x}$- and R-charts is to gather k samples over a period of time,
each of size n. Usually, about $k = 25$ to 30 samples are collected. Samples sizes between
$n = 3$ and 10 are generally used, with 5 being the most common. For each sample i, the
mean (denoted x bar, $\bar{x}_i$) and the range (R_i) are computed. These values are then plotted
on their respective control charts. Next, the *overall mean* and *average range* calculations
are made. These values specify the center lines for the $\bar{x}$- and R-charts, respectively. The
overall mean (denoted as x *double bar*, $\bar{\bar{x}}$, and often called the *grand average* or *grand
mean*) is the average of the sample means:

$$\bar{\bar{x}} = \frac{\sum_{i=1}^{k} \bar{x}_i}{k} \tag{8.30}$$

The average range denoted as (R bar, $\bar{R}$) is similarly computed, using the formula:

$$\bar{R} = \frac{\sum_{i=1}^{k} R_i}{k} \tag{8.31}$$

The overall mean and average range are used to compute upper and lower control limits (UCL and LCL) for the charts using the following formulas.

Control Limits for R-Chart:

$$\text{LCL}_R = D_3 \overline{R}$$
$$\text{UCL}_R = D_4 \overline{R}$$

(8.32)

Control Limits for $\overline{x}$-Chart

$$\text{LCL}_{\overline{x}} = \overline{\overline{x}} + A_2 \overline{R}$$
$$\text{UCL}_{\overline{x}} = \overline{\overline{x}} - A_2 \overline{R}$$

(8.33)

where the constants D_3, D_4, and A_2 depend on the sample size n and can be found in Appendix B.

EXAMPLE 8.15

Constructing an $\overline{x}$ and R Chart

Suppose that a seatbelt manufacturer took 10 sample measurements of 7 buckle parts, as follows (all values are in inches). The sample means and ranges for each sample were calculated and are shown in the Average and Range rows below the samples.

					Samples					
DATA	1	2	3	4	5	6	7	8	9	10
1	2.3	2.5	2.6	2.4	2.4	2.6	2.5	2.5	2.4	2.6
2	2.7	2.5	2.5	2.6	2.6	2.4	2.6	2.7	2.6	2.7
3	2.6	2.6	2.6	2.5	2.5	2.6	2.7	2.5	2.5	2.5
4	2.6	2.4	2.7	2.5	2.5	2.7	2.5	2.5	2.4	2.5
5	2.4	2.7	2.6	2.6	2.5	2.5	2.7	2.4	2.5	2.6
6	2.5	2.5	2.5	2.6	2.5	2.7	2.3	2.6	2.6	2.6
7	2.4	2.6	2.5	2.5	2.4	2.4	2.5	2.6	2.7	2.6
Average	2.5	2.543	2.571	2.529	2.486	2.557	2.543	2.543	2.529	2.586
Range	0.4	0.3	0.2	0.2	0.2	0.3	0.4	0.3	0.3	0.2

The next step is to calculate the key statistics and trial control limits for the control charts. The overall mean is the sum of the sample averages divided by the number of samples (10), or equivalently, the average of the sample averages. The average range is the sum of the sample ranges divided by the number of samples, or, the average of the sample ranges. These can easily be found using the Excel AVERAGE function. The overall mean is $\overline{\overline{x}} = 2.539$, and the average range is $\overline{R} = 0.280$. You should verify these values.

Because the sample size is 7, the factors used in computing the control limits found in Appendix B are $A_2 = 0.419$, $D_4 = 1.924$ and $D_3 = 0.076$. Using the formulas for the control limits (8.32 and 8.33), we have

$$\text{LCL}_R = D_3 \overline{R} = 0.076(0.280) = 0.021$$
$$\text{UCL}_R = D_4 \overline{R} = 1.924(0.280) = 0.539$$
$$\text{LCL}_{\overline{x}} = \overline{\overline{x}} - A_2 \overline{R} = 2.539 - 0.419(0.280) = 2.422$$
$$\text{UCL}_{\overline{x}} = \overline{\overline{x}} + A_2 \overline{R} = 2.539 + 0.419(0.280) = 2.656$$

The control limits represent the range between which all points are expected to fall if the process is in statistical control. If any points fall outside the control limits or if any unusual patterns are observed, then special causes are most likely present. The process should be studied to determine the cause. The corresponding data points should be eliminated, and the overall mean, average range, and control limits should be recomputed.

In determining whether a process is in statistical control, the R-chart should be analyzed first. Because the control limits in the $\bar{x}$-chart depend on the average range, special causes in the R-chart may produce unusual patterns in the $\bar{x}$-chart, even when the centering of the process is in control.

Control limits are often confused with specification limits. Thus, control charts might mislead one into thinking that if all sample averages fall within the control limits, all output will be conforming. This is not true. A sample average may fall within the upper and lower control limits even though some of the individual observations are out of specification. Control limits are based on the sampling distribution of the mean; therefore, the standard error becomes smaller with increasing sample sizes and therefore, the larger the sample size, the narrower the control limits.

Process Monitoring and Control

After the final control limits are determined, the charts should be used to monitor performance, identify any special causes that might arise, and make corrections only as necessary. This should be done by the employees who run the process. In this way, they can react quickly to changes in the process and make adjustments immediately.

Improvements in conformance typically follow the introduction of control charts in any process, particularly when the process is labor intensive. Apparently, management involvement in employees' work often produces positive behavioral modifications (as first demonstrated in the famous Hawthorne studies at the Western Electric Company). Under such circumstances, and as good practice, control limits should be reevaluated periodically and revised as process improvements take place.

Estimating Process Capability

After a process has been brought to a state of statistical control by eliminating special causes of variation, the control chart statistics may be used to obtain a quick estimate of process capability. Under the normality assumption, the standard deviation of the original data can be estimated as:

$$\hat{\sigma} = \bar{R}/d_2 \qquad (8.34)$$

where d_2 is a constant that depends on the sample size and is also given in Appendix B. Using this along with the specifications, process capability indexes can easily be computed using formulas (8.25) through (8.28). However, this approach is not as accurate as computing the true standard deviation of the observations and we do not recommend it.

Case Study: La Ventana Window Company

The La Ventana Window Company (LVWC) manufactures original equipment and replacement windows for residential building and remodeling applications. LVWC landed a major contract as a supplier to Southwestern Vista Homes (SVH), a builder of residential communities in several major cities throughout the southwestern United States. Because of the large volume of demand, LVWC expanded its manufacturing operations to two shifts. Soon, they were working six days per week and hired additional workers and added on to their facility. The company based its manufacturing capability on its well-trained and dedicated employees, so it never felt the need to consider formal process control approaches. However, not long after La Ventana began shipping windows to Southwestern, it received some complaints about narrow, misfitting gaps between the upper and lower window sashes.

The plant manager suspected that the rapid expansion to a full two-shift operation, the pressures to produce higher volumes, and the push to meet just-in-time delivery requests were causing a breakdown in quality. He hired a quality consultant to train the shift supervisors and selected line workers in statistical process control methods.

As a trial project, the plant manager wants to evaluate the capability of a critical cutting operation that he suspects might be the source of the gap problem. The nominal specification for this cutting operation is 25.500 inches with a tolerance of 0.030 inch. Thus, the upper and lower specifications are LSL = 25.470 inch and USL = 25.530 inch. The consultant suggested inspecting five consecutive window panels in the middle of each shift over a 15-day period and recording the dimension of the cut. The worksheet *Case Data*, shown in Figure 8.22, in the Excel workbook *La Ventana Example*

FIGURE 8.22
La Ventana Case
Data

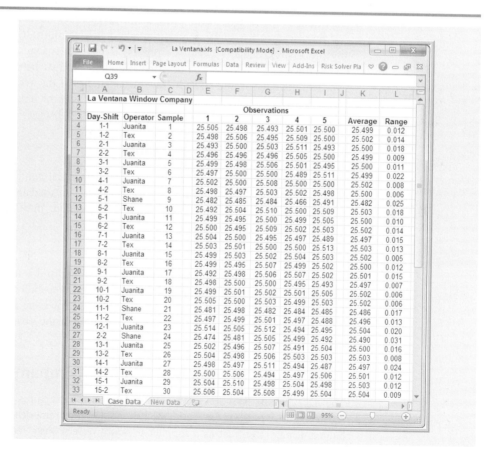

In using the control chart spreadsheet templates, please note the following:

- *You may need to rescale the vertical axis of the charts to eliminate blank space and make them more visually appealing. See the appropriate Excel help files for the version you are using. This is rarely necessary.*

- *When a sample is deleted from a data set in the templates, do not enter zero for the data; instead, leave the cells blank (just delete the data using the "delete" key). The charts are set up to interpolate between non-missing data points.*

- *When deleting sample data, be sure to update the number of samples used in the calculations to compute the statistics or the control charts will not display correctly.*

(available on the Student Companion Site) shows the results of the data collection, along with the sample averages and ranges. The overall mean is $\bar{\bar{x}} = 25.499$, and the average range is $\bar{R} = 0.14$.

Because the sample size is 5, the factors used in computing the control limits found in Appendix B are $A_2 = 0.577$ and $D_4 = 2.114$. (For sample sizes of 6 or less, factor $D_3 = 0$; therefore, the lower control limit on the range chart is zero.) Using formulas (8.32) and (8.33) for the control limits, we have

$$
\begin{aligned}
\text{LCL}_R &= D_3\bar{R} &&= 0 \\
\text{UCL}_R &= D_4\bar{R} = 2.114(0.0136) &&= 0.0288 \\
\text{LCL}_{\bar{x}} &= \bar{\bar{x}} - A_2\bar{R} = 25.499 - 0.577(0.014) &&= 25.491 \\
\text{UCL}_{\bar{x}} &= \bar{\bar{x}} + A_2\bar{R} = 25.499 + 0.577(0.014) &&= 25.507
\end{aligned}
$$

The spreadsheet for $\bar{x}$- and R-charts is the Excel template *Xbar&R.xlxs*. A portion of it for the La Ventana case data is shown in Figure 8.23. Figures 8.24 and 8.25 show the control charts.

Examining the range chart first, we see that sample 24 is clearly out of control. In the $\bar{x}$-chart, sample 24 is also outside the control limits, as are samples 9 and 21. If you look closely at the data, these samples have one characteristic in common: Shane was the operator during the time these samples were taken. In fact, these were the only times that Shane was running the process. On investigation, it was found that the regular operators, Juanita and Tex, were called away to troubleshoot a problem on another production line and replaced by Shane who usually works on the packaging line. Thus, we may attribute these anomalies to special causes of variation and should eliminate these from the control chart calculations.

After deleting the special cause samples from the data, the new charts appear to be in control as shown in Figures 8.26 and 8.27. Note that the control limits have changed somewhat; the new limits are:

$$
\begin{aligned}
\text{LCL}_R &= 0 \\
\text{UCL}_R &= 0.0262 \\
\text{LCL}_{\bar{x}} &= 25.494 \\
\text{UCL}_{\bar{x}} &= 25.508
\end{aligned}
$$

Now that statistical control has been established, process capability may be evaluated. Figure 8.28 shows the portion of the Excel template that calculates the process capability indexes. The Excel template calculates six times the standard deviation of the data as the process variation in cell R6. The process capability indexes suggest that as long as the process remains in control, process capability is quite good; $C_p = 1.875$, $C_{pk} = 1.833$, and the process average is close to the nominal specification, as suggested by C_{pu} and C_{pl}.

FIGURE 8.23 Portion of Excel Template *Xbar&R.xlxs* for La Ventana Case Data

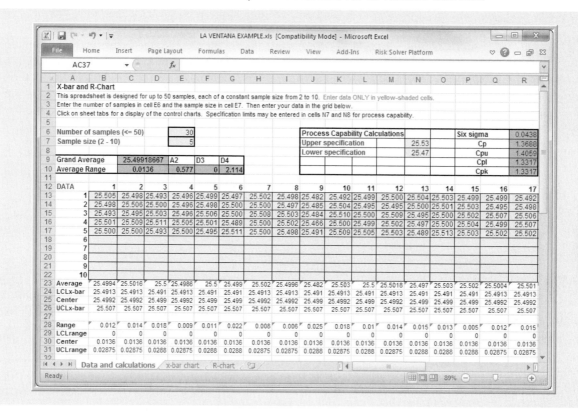

FIGURE 8.24 *R*-Chart for La Ventana Case

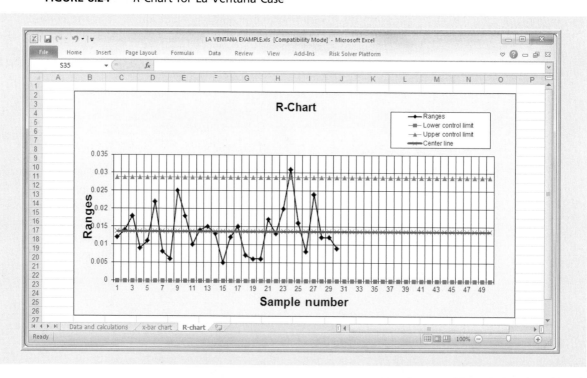

FIGURE 8.25 $\bar{x}$-Chart for La Ventana Case

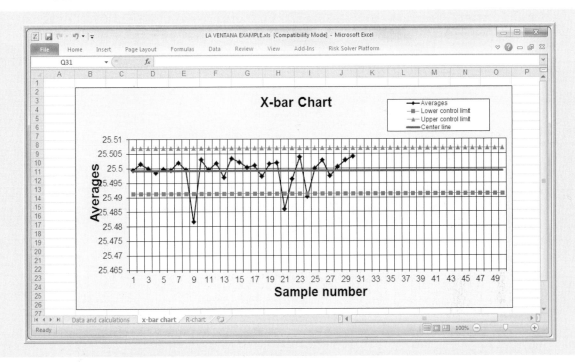

FIGURE 8.26   Revised *R*-Chart

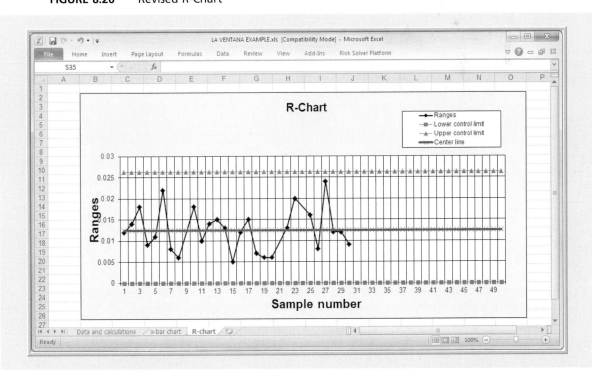

FIGURE 8.27   Revised $\bar{x}$-Chart

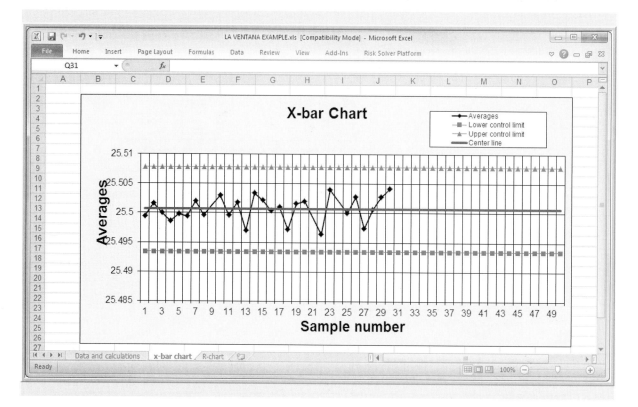

FIGURE 8.28
La Ventana Process
Capability Results

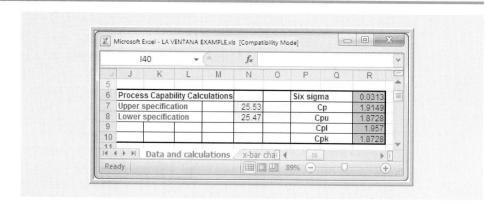

The revised control limits, after removing special causes, should be used for continuing monitoring of the process. For example, suppose that the company collected new production data over the next 10 shifts. These are shown in Figure 8.29 (and are labeled "Additional Data" on the worksheet in the *La Ventana* workbook). Figures 8.30 and 8.31

FIGURE 8.29
New Production
Data

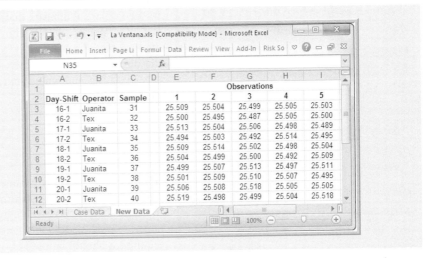

FIGURE 8.30   *R*-Chart with Additional Data

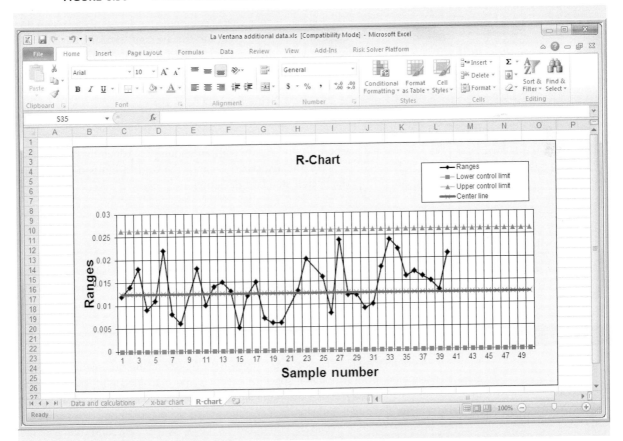

When adding additional data to the spreadsheet template but to maintain the established control limits, do not change the number of samples in cell E6 on which the control limits were based. Also, you must modify the formulas in cells C9 and C10 for the calculations of the grand average and average range to use only the column range of the original data so as not to change the calculated center lines or control limits. For the La Ventana example with additional data, change the formula in cell C9 from =SUMIF(B13:AY13,">-99999",B23:AY23)/$E$6 to =SUMIF(B13:AE13,">-99999", B23:AE23)/$E$6. We have bolded the changes; note that the range from column B through column AE includes the original 30 samples, not the additional data. Similarly, the formula for cell C10 should be changed from =SUMIF(B13:AY1, ">-99999",B28:AY28)/$E$6 to: =SUMIF(B13:AE13,">-99999", B28:AE28)/$E$6. The template will still chart all the data, but use control limits established from the first 30 samples.

show the R- and $\bar{x}$-charts with the new data (samples 31 to 40). In the R-chart, it appears that the variation has increased as the last nine points all fall above the mean. In the $\bar{x}$-chart, it appears that the average is going up, and sample 39 exceeds the upper control limit. Both of these indications suggest some special cause, and management should stop the process and investigate the cause.

$\bar{x}$- and s-Charts

A better alternative to the R-chart to monitor variation is to compute and plot the standard deviation s of each sample. The sample standard deviation is a more sensitive and better indicator of process variability than the range, especially for larger sample sizes. Thus, when tight control of variability is required, s should be used.

The sample standard deviation is computed as

$$s = \sqrt{\frac{\sum_{i=1}^{n} (x_i - \bar{x})^2}{n - 1}} \tag{8.35}$$

To construct an s-chart, compute the standard deviation for each sample. Next, compute the average standard deviation, $\bar{s}$, by averaging the sample standard deviations over all samples. Control limits for the s-chart are given by

$$\begin{aligned} \text{LCL}_s &= B_3\bar{s} \\ \text{UCL}_s &= B_4\bar{s} \end{aligned} \tag{8.36}$$

where B_3 and B_4 are constants found in Appendix B.

For the associated $\bar{x}$-chart, the control limits derived from the overall standard deviation are

$$\begin{aligned} \text{LCL}_{\bar{x}} &= \bar{\bar{x}} - A_3\bar{s} \\ \text{UCL}_{\bar{x}} &= \bar{\bar{x}} + A_3\bar{s} \end{aligned} \tag{8.37}$$

where A_3 is a constant found in Appendix B. Observe that the formulas for the control limits are equivalent to those for $\bar{x}$- and R-charts except that the constants differ.

EXAMPLE 8.16

Constructing an $\bar{x}$ and s Chart

Consider the data shown in Figure 8.32. These data represent measurements of deviations in millimeters from a nominal specification for some machined part; thus, a value of 1 indicates 1 millimeter above the nominal, and so on. Samples of size 10 are used; for each sample, the mean and standard deviation have been computed.

The average (overall) mean is computed to be $\bar{\bar{x}} = -0.164$, and the average standard deviation is $\bar{s} = 1.467$. For samples of size 10, $B_3 = 0.284$, $B_4 = 1.716$, and

FIGURE 8.31 $\bar{x}$-Chart with Additional Data

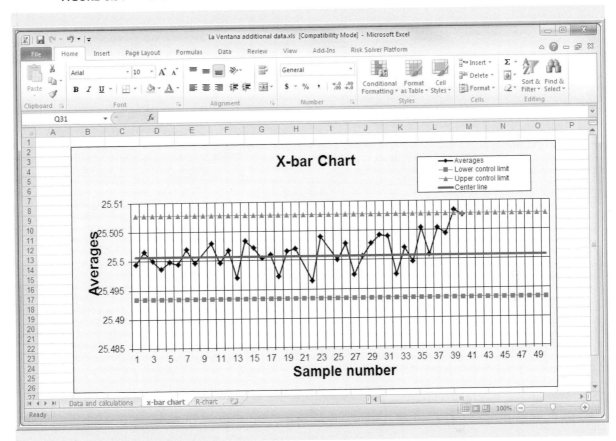

$A_3 = 0.975$. Using formulas (8.36) and (8.37), control limits for the s-chart and the $\bar{x}$-chart are:

$$\text{LCL}_s = B_3\bar{R} = 0.284(1.467) \qquad\qquad = 0.417$$
$$\text{UCL}_s = B_4\bar{R} = 1.716(1.467) \qquad\qquad = 2.518$$
$$\text{LCL}_{\bar{x}} = \bar{\bar{x}} - A_2\bar{R} = -1.64 - 0.975(1.467) = -1.59$$
$$\text{UCL}_{\bar{x}} = \bar{\bar{x}} + A_2\bar{R} = -1.64 + 0.975(1.467) = 1.267$$

The charts are shown in Figures 8.35 and 8.34. This evidence indicates the process is not in control, and an investigation as to the reasons for the variation in the $\bar{x}$-chart is warranted.

Charts for Individuals

In some situations, it may be inappropriate or undesirable to collect samples of multiple observations. For instance, in a chemical production process, sampling from a homogeneous mixture will result in little variation, except possibly from measurement error. In very low-volume production situations, a reasonable sample might cover a long period of time during which the process might have changed, thus not providing good information for control. In other situations, we might simply want to chart every observation, such as

FIGURE 8.32   Data and Calculations for Example 8.16 (Excel template *Xbar&S.xlsx*)

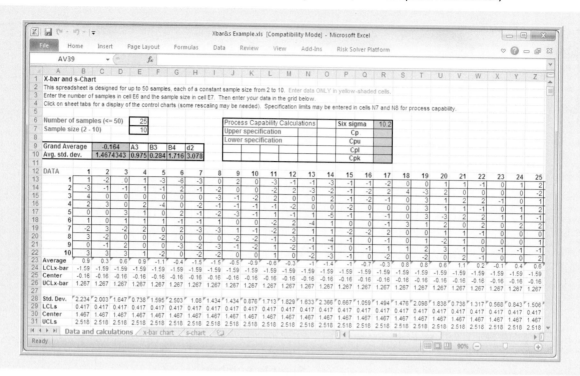

FIGURE 8.33   *s*-Chart for Example 8.16

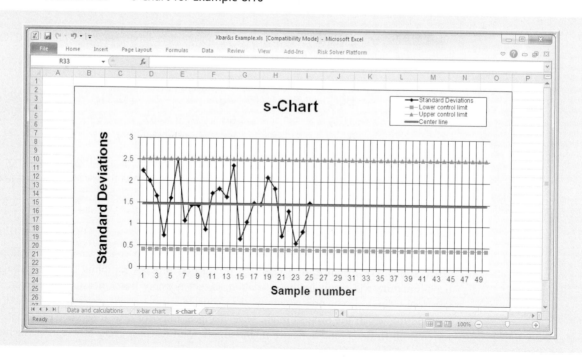

FIGURE 8.34 $\bar{x}$-chart for Example 8.16

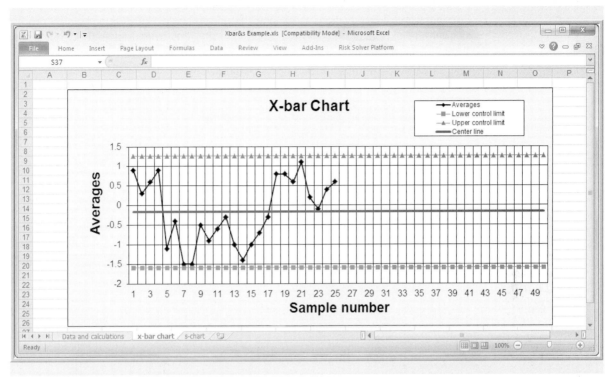

the waiting time of patients in an emergency room. With automated inspection for many manufacturing processes, the technology can easily collect quality data on every item produced. In all of these situations, the sample size for process control is $n = 1$, and a control chart for *individual measurements*—also called an *x-chart*—can be used.

With individual measurements, the process standard deviation can be estimated and 3σ control limits used. As shown earlier, $\bar{R}/d_2$ provides an estimate of the process standard deviation. Thus, an *x*-chart for individual measurements would have 3σ control limits defined by

$$\begin{aligned} \text{LCL}_x &= \bar{x} - 3\bar{R}/d_2 \\ \text{UCL}_x &= \bar{x} + 3\bar{R}/d_2 \end{aligned} \tag{8.38}$$

(Note that for a more precise calculation of control limits, we can replace $\bar{R}/d_2$ with the actual sample standard deviation computed from the data; however, these formulas have been traditionally used.)

Samples of size 1, however, do not furnish enough information for measuring process variability. One way of getting around this limitation is to use a moving average of the ranges, or a *moving range*, of n successive observations. For example, a moving range for $n = 2$ is computed by finding the absolute difference between two successive observations, a moving range for $n = 3$ is computed by finding the difference between the largest and smallest observations in groups of 3, and so on. The number of observations used in the moving range determines the constant d_2; hence, for $n = 2$, from Appendix B, $d_2 = 1.128$. The moving range chart has control limits defined by

$$\begin{aligned} \text{LCL}_R &= D_3\bar{R} \\ \text{UCL}_R &= D_4\bar{R} \end{aligned} \tag{8.39}$$

which is the same as in the ordinary range chart.

EXAMPLE 8.17

Constructing *x*- and *MR*-Charts

Consider a set of observations measuring the percentage of cobalt in a chemical process as given in Figure 8.35. The moving range with $n = 2$ is computed as shown by taking absolute values of successive ranges and using the constants in Appendix B. For example, the first moving range is the difference between the first two observations, or $|3.75 - 3.80| = 0.05$. The second moving range is computed as $|3.80 - 3.70| = 0.10$, and so on.

Using the formulas (8.36) and (8.37), we obtain:

$$LCL_R = D_3\overline{R} \qquad\qquad\qquad = 0$$
$$UCL_R = D_4\overline{R} = 3.267(0.352) \qquad = 1.15$$
$$LCL_x = \overline{x} - 3\frac{\overline{R}}{d_2} = 3.498 - 3\left(\frac{0.352}{1.128}\right) = 2.56$$

FIGURE 8.35

Data and Calculations for Example 8.17 (Excel template *X&MR.xlsx*)

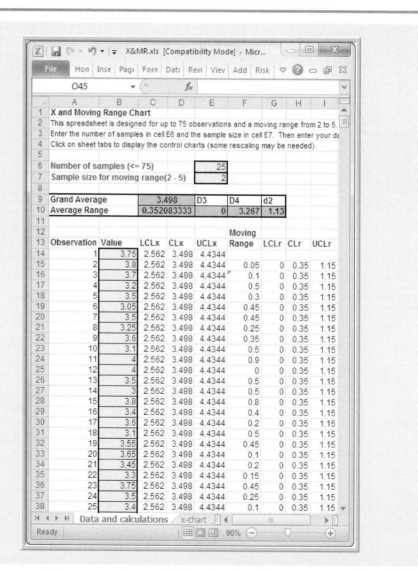

FIGURE 8.36   Moving Range Chart for Example 8.17

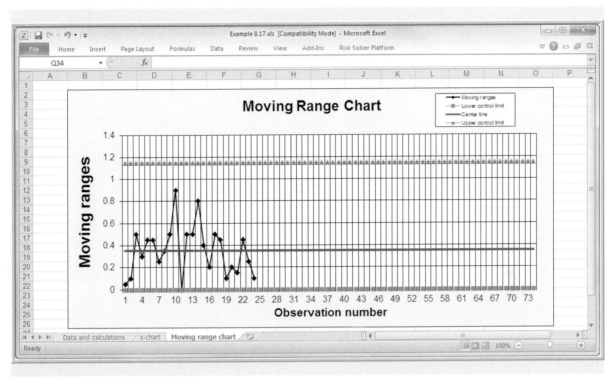

$$UCL_x = \bar{x} + 3\frac{\bar{R}}{d_2} = 3.498 + 3\left(\frac{0.352}{1.128}\right) = 4.43$$

The moving range chart shown in Figure 8.36 and the x-chart in Figure 8.37 indicate that the process is in control.

Some caution is necessary when interpreting patterns on the moving range chart. Points beyond control limits indicate assignable causes. Successive ranges, however, are correlated, and they may cause patterns or trends in the chart that are not indicative of out-of-control situations. On the x-chart, individual observations are assumed to be uncorrelated; hence, patterns and trends should be investigated. In addition, charts for individuals are less sensitive to many of the conditions that can be detected by $\bar{x}$- and R-charts; for example, the process must vary a lot before a shift in the mean is detected. Also, short cycles and trends may appear on these charts and not on an $\bar{x}$- or R-chart. Finally, the assumption of normality of observations is more critical than for $\bar{x}$- and R-charts; when the normality assumption does not hold, greater chance for error is present. One advantage of an x-chart is that we can draw specifications on the chart for a quick assessment of process capability.

CONTROL CHARTS FOR ATTRIBUTES DATA

Attribute data that can be observed and counted are useful in many practical situations as we discussed earlier in this chapter. Control charts that monitor the proportion of

FIGURE 8.37   Individuals (*x*) Chart for Example 8.17

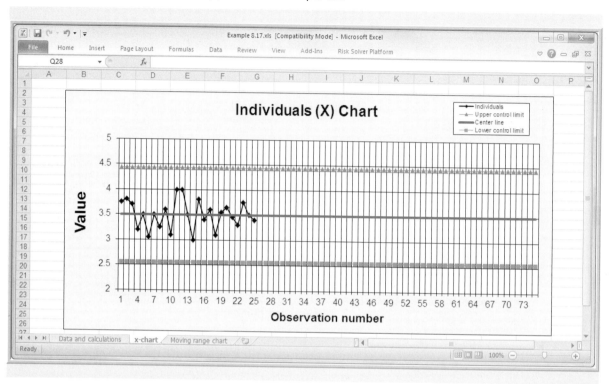

nonconforming units are called *p*-charts; those that monitor the number of nonconformances per unit are called *c*- and *u*-charts.

Fraction Nonconforming (*p*) Chart

A **p-chart** monitors the proportion, or fraction, of nonconforming units. As with variables data, a *p*-chart is constructed by first gathering 25 to 30 samples of the attribute being measured. The size of each sample should be large enough to have several nonconforming units. For example, if the probability of finding a nonconforming unit is only 0.05, then a sample of only 10 units would result in little measurable variation—about half the samples would only have about one nonconforming unit and half would not have any, because the expected number of nonconforming units is $10(0.05) = 0.05$. However, a sample size of 100 would have an expected value of 5 and would therefore show enough variation to use a control chart.

Let us suppose that *k* samples are chosen. Let y_i represent the number of nonconforming units in sample *i*, and n_i be the size of sample *i*. (In many cases, the size of each sample will be the same; however, each sample may have a different sample size.) The proportion nonconforming in sample *i* is $p_i = \dfrac{y_i}{n_i}$. The average proportion nonconforming $\bar{p}$ for the group of *k* samples is

$$\bar{p} = \frac{\sum y_i}{\sum n_i} \tag{8.40}$$

One would expect a high percentage of samples to have a fraction nonconforming within three standard deviations of $\bar{p}$. If the sample size is constant, an estimate of the standard deviation is given by

$$s_{\bar{p}} = \sqrt{\frac{\bar{p}(1-\bar{p})}{n}} \qquad (8.41)$$

Therefore, upper and lower control limits are given by

$$\begin{aligned} \text{LCL}_p &= \bar{p} - 3s_{\bar{p}} \\ \text{UCL}_p &= \bar{p} + 3s_{\bar{p}} \end{aligned} \qquad (8.42)$$

If LCL_p is less than zero, a value of zero is used.

Analysis of a p-chart is similar to that of an $\bar{x}$- or R-chart. However, a shift below the center line or a decreasing trend indicates an improvement and should be verified.

EXAMPLE 8.18

Constructing a p-Chart

The operators of automated sorting machines in a post office must read the ZIP code on a letter and divert the letter to the proper carrier route. Over one month's time, 25 samples of 100 letters were chosen, and the number of errors was recorded. In this example, the sample size is constant. This information is summarized in Figure 8.38. The fraction nonconforming is found by dividing the number of errors by 100. Using formula (8.40), the average fraction nonconforming, $\bar{p}$ is determined to be

$$\bar{p} = \frac{3 + 1 + \mathbf{0} + \cdots + 1}{25(100)} = 0.022$$

The standard deviation is computed using formula (8.41):

$$s_{\bar{p}} = \sqrt{\frac{0.022(1 - 0.022)}{100}} = 0.01467$$

Thus, using formulas (8.42), the control limits are

$$\begin{aligned} \text{UCL}_p &= 0.022 + 3(0.01467) = 0.066 \\ \text{LCL}_p &= 0.022 - 3(0.01467) = -0.022. \end{aligned}$$

Because this is negative, zero is used. The control chart for this example is shown in Figure 8.39. The sorting process appears to be in control. Any values found above the upper control limit or evidence of an upward trend might indicate the need for more experience or training of the operators.

---

p-Charts with Variable Sample Size

Often 100 percent inspection is performed on process output during fixed sampling periods; in these cases, the number of units produced in each sampling period will vary. When this occurs, the standard deviation will also vary for different sample sizes (note that the sample size is used in formula (8.41) to compute the standard deviation). Thus, control limits are given by

$$\bar{p} \pm 3\sqrt{\frac{\bar{p}(1-\bar{p})}{n_i}} \qquad (8.43)$$

In this case, the control limits will be different for different sample sizes.

FIGURE 8.38 Data and Calculations for Example 8.18 (Excel template *p-chart.xlsx*)

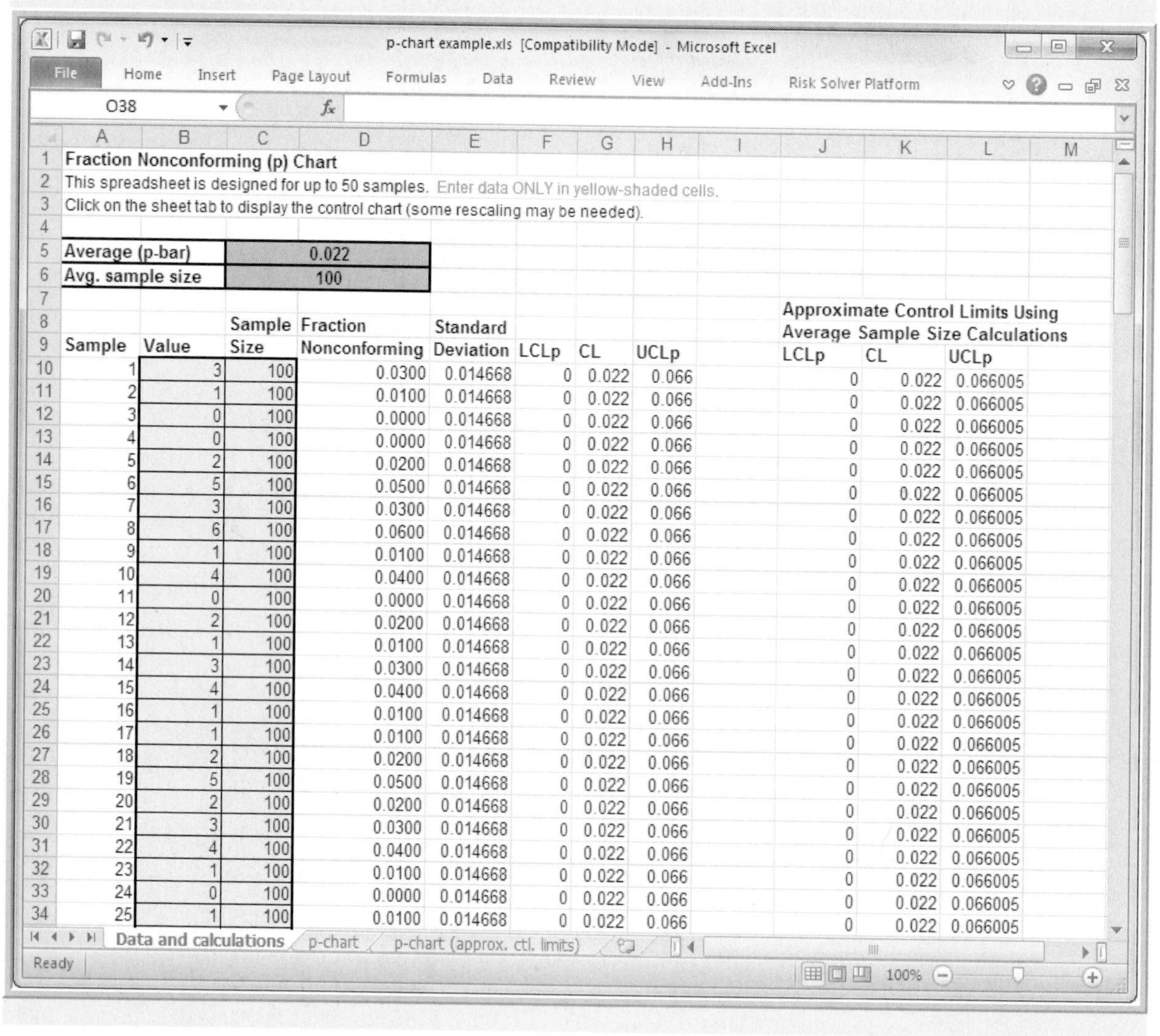

p-chart example.xls [Compatibility Mode] - Microsoft Excel

Fraction Nonconforming (p) Chart

This spreadsheet is designed for up to 50 samples. Enter data ONLY in yellow-shaded cells.

Click on the sheet tab to display the control chart (some rescaling may be needed).

Average (p-bar)	0.022
Avg. sample size	100

Sample	Value	Sample Size	Fraction Nonconforming	Standard Deviation	LCLp	CL	UCLp	Approximate Control Limits Using Average Sample Size Calculations LCLp	CL	UCLp
1	3	100	0.0300	0.014668	0	0.022	0.066	0	0.022	0.066005
2	1	100	0.0100	0.014668	0	0.022	0.066	0	0.022	0.066005
3	0	100	0.0000	0.014668	0	0.022	0.066	0	0.022	0.066005
4	0	100	0.0000	0.014668	0	0.022	0.066	0	0.022	0.066005
5	2	100	0.0200	0.014668	0	0.022	0.066	0	0.022	0.066005
6	5	100	0.0500	0.014668	0	0.022	0.066	0	0.022	0.066005
7	3	100	0.0300	0.014668	0	0.022	0.066	0	0.022	0.066005
8	6	100	0.0600	0.014668	0	0.022	0.066	0	0.022	0.066005
9	1	100	0.0100	0.014668	0	0.022	0.066	0	0.022	0.066005
10	4	100	0.0400	0.014668	0	0.022	0.066	0	0.022	0.066005
11	0	100	0.0000	0.014668	0	0.022	0.066	0	0.022	0.066005
12	2	100	0.0200	0.014668	0	0.022	0.066	0	0.022	0.066005
13	1	100	0.0100	0.014668	0	0.022	0.066	0	0.022	0.066005
14	3	100	0.0300	0.014668	0	0.022	0.066	0	0.022	0.066005
15	4	100	0.0400	0.014668	0	0.022	0.066	0	0.022	0.066005
16	1	100	0.0100	0.014668	0	0.022	0.066	0	0.022	0.066005
17	1	100	0.0100	0.014668	0	0.022	0.066	0	0.022	0.066005
18	2	100	0.0200	0.014668	0	0.022	0.066	0	0.022	0.066005
19	5	100	0.0500	0.014668	0	0.022	0.066	0	0.022	0.066005
20	2	100	0.0200	0.014668	0	0.022	0.066	0	0.022	0.066005
21	3	100	0.0300	0.014668	0	0.022	0.066	0	0.022	0.066005
22	4	100	0.0400	0.014668	0	0.022	0.066	0	0.022	0.066005
23	1	100	0.0100	0.014668	0	0.022	0.066	0	0.022	0.066005
24	0	100	0.0000	0.014668	0	0.022	0.066	0	0.022	0.066005
25	1	100	0.0100	0.014668	0	0.022	0.066	0	0.022	0.066005

Data and calculations / p-chart / p-chart (approx. ctl. limits)

EXAMPLE 8.19

Constructing a *p*-Chart With Variable Sample Sizes

The data given in Figure 8.40 represent 20 samples with varying sample sizes. The value of $\bar{p}$ is computed using formula (8.40) as

$$\bar{p} = \frac{18 + 20 + 14 + \cdots + 18}{137 + 158 + 92 + \cdots + 160} = \frac{271}{2{,}980} = 0.0909$$

Using formula (8.43), the control limits for sample 1 are

$$\text{LCL}_p = .0909 - 3\sqrt{\frac{.0909(1 - .0909)}{137}} = 0.017$$

$$\text{UCL}_p = .0909 + 3\sqrt{\frac{.0909(1 - .0909)}{137}} = 0.165$$

For the second sample, we would use 158 in the denominator of the standard deviation, and so on. The *p*-chart is shown in Figure 8.41. Note that points 13 and 15 are outside the control limits.

An alternative approach is to use the average sample size, $\bar{n}$, to compute *approximate* control limits by using the average sample size in the formula for the standard deviation. This results in control limits

$$\text{LCL}_p = \bar{p} - 3\sqrt{\frac{\bar{p}(1 - \bar{p})}{\bar{n}}}$$

$$\text{UCL}_p = \bar{p} + 3\sqrt{\frac{\bar{p}(1 - \bar{p})}{\bar{n}}}$$

(8.44)

EXAMPLE 8.20

Constructing a *p*-Chart Using Average Sample Size

For the data in Example 8.19, the average sample size is $\bar{n} = 2980/20 = 149$. Using this value in formulas (8.44), the lower control limit is 0.0202 and the upper control limit is 0.1616. However, this approach has several disadvantages. Because the control limits are only approximate, points that are actually out of control may not appear to be so on this chart. Second, runs or nonrandom patterns are difficult to interpret because the standard deviation differs between samples as a result of the variable sample sizes. Hence, this

---

FIGURE 8.39 *p*-Chart for Example 8.18

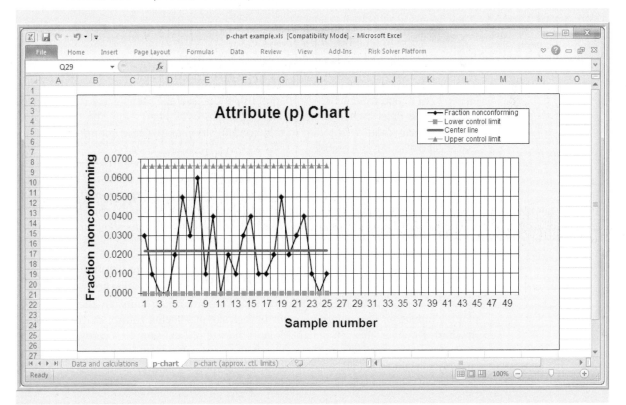

FIGURE 8.40 Data and Calculations for Example 8.19

Example 8.19.xls [Compatibility Mode] - Microsoft Excel

Fraction Nonconforming (p) Chart

This spreadsheet is designed for up to 50 samples. Enter data ONLY in yellow-shaded cells.

Click on the sheet tab to display the control chart (some rescaling may be needed).

Average (p-bar)	0.090939597
Avg. sample size	149

Sample	Value	Sample Size	Fraction Nonconforming	Standard Deviation	LCLp	CL	UCLp	Approximate Control Limits Using Average Sample Size Calculations LCLp	CL	UCLp
1	18	137	0.1314	0.024565	0.0172	0.091	0.1646	0.020275	0.09094	0.161604
2	20	158	0.1266	0.022874	0.0223	0.091	0.1596	0.020275	0.09094	0.161604
3	14	92	0.1522	0.029976	0.001	0.091	0.1809	0.020275	0.09094	0.161604
4	6	122	0.0492	0.026031	0.0128	0.091	0.169	0.020275	0.09094	0.161604
5	11	86	0.1279	0.031004	0	0.091	0.184	0.020275	0.09094	0.161604
6	22	187	0.1176	0.021026	0.0279	0.091	0.154	0.020275	0.09094	0.161604
7	6	156	0.0385	0.02302	0.0219	0.091	0.16	0.020275	0.09094	0.161604
8	9	117	0.0769	0.026582	0.0112	0.091	0.1707	0.020275	0.09094	0.161604
9	14	110	0.1273	0.027414	0.0087	0.091	0.1732	0.020275	0.09094	0.161604
10	12	142	0.0845	0.024128	0.0186	0.091	0.1633	0.020275	0.09094	0.161604
11	8	140	0.0571	0.0243	0.018	0.091	0.1638	0.020275	0.09094	0.161604
12	13	179	0.0726	0.02149	0.0265	0.091	0.1554	0.020275	0.09094	0.161604
13	5	196	0.0255	0.020537	0.0293	0.091	0.1526	0.020275	0.09094	0.161604
14	15	163	0.0920	0.022521	0.0234	0.091	0.1585	0.020275	0.09094	0.161604
15	25	140	0.1786	0.0243	0.018	0.091	0.1638	0.020275	0.09094	0.161604
16	12	135	0.0889	0.024746	0.0167	0.091	0.1652	0.020275	0.09094	0.161604
17	16	186	0.0860	0.021082	0.0277	0.091	0.1542	0.020275	0.09094	0.161604
18	12	193	0.0622	0.020696	0.0289	0.091	0.153	0.020275	0.09094	0.161604
19	15	181	0.0829	0.021371	0.0268	0.091	0.1551	0.020275	0.09094	0.161604
20	18	160	0.1125	0.022731	0.0227	0.091	0.1591	0.020275	0.09094	0.161604

Data and calculations / p-chart / p-chart (approx. ctl. limits)

approach should be used with caution. Figure 8.42 shows the control chart for this example with approximate control limits using the average sample size (this chart is shown in the Excel *p*-chart template on a separate worksheet). Note the difference in sample 13; this chart shows that it is in control, whereas the true control limits show that this point is out of control.

As a general guideline, use the average sample size method when the sample sizes fall within 25 percent of the average. For this example, 25 percent of 149 is 37.25. Thus, the average could be used for sample sizes between 112 and 186. This guideline would exclude samples 3, 6, 9, 11, 13, and 18, whose control limits should be computed exactly.

np-Charts for Number Nonconforming

Instead of using a chart for the proportion of nonconforming units, an alternative is to plot the *number of nonconforming units* in each sample. Such a control chart is called an ***np*-chart**. However, this can only be done if the size of each sample is constant. The *np*-chart is a useful alternative to the *p*-chart because it is often easier for workers to understand because they simply need to count the number of nonconforming units in each sample, thus eliminating the need to calculate proportions.

FIGURE 8.41   Variable Sample Size *p*-Chart for Example 8.19

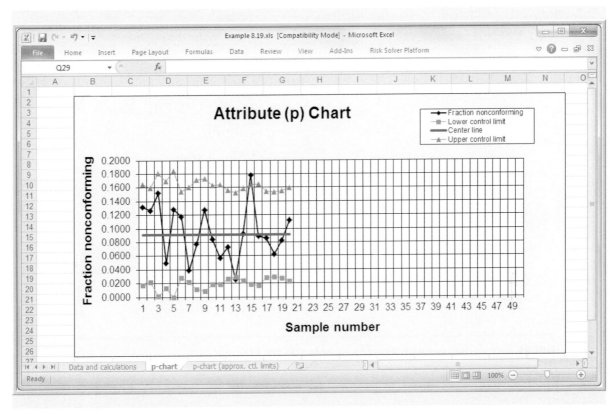

The center line is the average number of nonconforming items per sample and is denoted by $n\bar{p}$ which is calculated by taking k samples of size n, summing the number of nonconforming items y_i in each sample, and dividing by k. That is,

$$n\bar{p} = \frac{y_1 + y_2 + \cdots + y_k}{k} \tag{8.45}$$

An estimate of the standard deviation is

$$s_{n\bar{p}} = \sqrt{n\bar{p}(1 - \bar{p})} \tag{8.46}$$

where $\bar{p} = n\bar{p}/n$. The control limits are specified by

$$\text{LCL}_{n\bar{p}} = n\bar{p} - 3\sqrt{n\bar{p}(1 - \bar{p})}$$
$$\text{UCL}_{n\bar{p}} = n\bar{p} + 3\sqrt{n\bar{p}(1 - \bar{p})} \tag{8.47}$$

EXAMPLE 8.21   Constructing an *np*-Chart

We will illustrate an *np*-chart using the data for the post office example in Example 8.18. Figure 8.43 shows the data. The average number of errors per sample is found using formula (8.45):

$$n\bar{p} = \frac{3 + 1 + \cdots + 0 + 1}{25} = 2.2$$

To find the standard deviation, we first compute

$$\bar{p} = \frac{2.2}{100} = 0.022$$

Then, using formula (8.46), we have

$$s_{n\bar{p}} = \sqrt{2.2(1 - 0.022)}$$

$$= \sqrt{2.2(0.978)}$$

$$= \sqrt{2.1516} = 1.4668$$

The control limits are computed using formulas (8.47):

$$\text{UCL}_{n\bar{p}} = 2.2 + 3(1.4668) = 6.6$$

$$\text{LCL}_{n\bar{p}} = 2.2 - 3(1.4668) = -2.20$$

Because the lower control limit is less than zero, a value of 0 is used. The control chart for this example is given in Figure 8.44. Note that the control chart is identical to the one in Figure 8.39 except for the scale on the y-axis.

FIGURE 8.42   *p*-Chart with Average Sample Size for Example 8.20

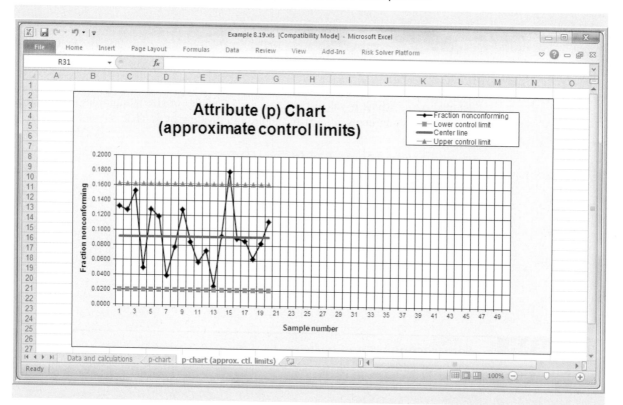

FIGURE 8.43
Data and Calculations for Example 8.21 (Excel template *np-Chart.xlsx*)

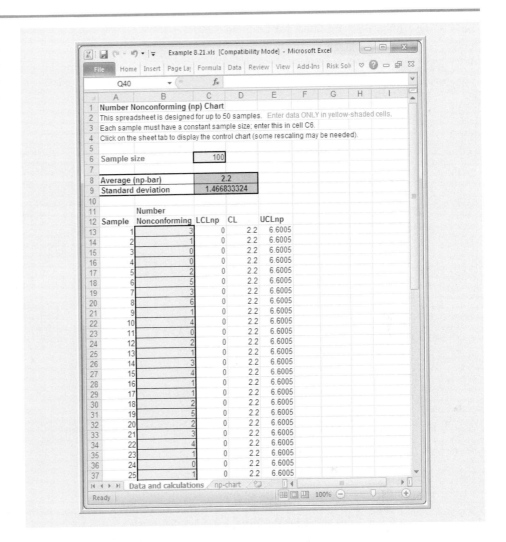

Charts for Nonconformances

Charts for nonconformances, called the **c-chart** and **u-chart,** are used for monitoring the number of nonconformances per unit. The key issue between these charts is that a c-chart applies when the number of opportunities for nonconformances in each sampling unit is constant, whereas the u-chart is used when the number of opportunities for nonconformances in each sampling unit is not constant. It is very important to clearly define the sampling unit.

The term "unit" can be interpreted broadly. For example, it may be a physical good such as a circuit board or a piece of fabric. Circuit boards may contain various defects, such as missing or bad solder connections, so we might monitor the number of defects per circuit board. If each circuit board is the same, then clearly the number of opportunities for nonconformances is the same for each unit and we would use a c-chart. Similarly, inspection of fabric made in a textile mill might identify various nonconformances such as pulls, discolorations, and so on. If each sample of fabric has the same area, then the number of opportunities for nonconformances is constant and we can chart the

FIGURE 8.44   *np*-Chart for Example 8.21

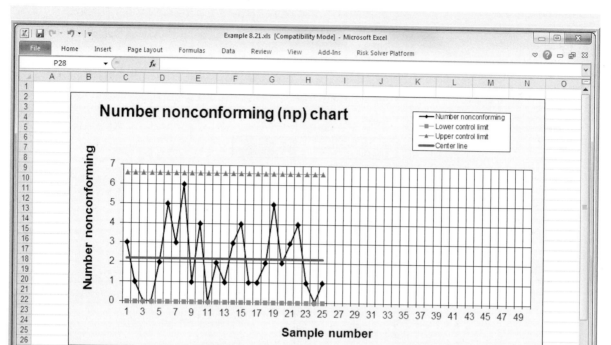

number of nonconformances per piece of fabric using a *c*-chart. However, if the fabric samples are of different sizes, then the number of opportunities for nonconformances is *not* constant; therefore, we must define a common unit of measure, such as nonconformances per square yard and use a *u*-chart. We might also define the sampling unit as a group larger than one, for example, 1000 circuit boards or 50 yards of fabric. Thus the measures would be the number of defects per 1000 circuit boards or the number of defects per 50 yards of fabric. These are simply differences in scale.

A "unit" need not be a physical good. For instance, consider a telemarketing firm that wants to track the number of calls needed to make one sale. In this case, the firm has no physical sampling unit. However, we could make an analogy using a "call" as a nonconformance, and the sampling unit being a successful sale. Because every sale is constant, we could use a *c*-chart. In contrast, suppose we tracked the number of calls made per day and the number of sales. The number of calls made per day would probably vary, so if we were interested in monitoring the number of sales made per call, we would use a *u*-chart. As another example, in administering daily drugs to patients, a hospital would be interested in monitoring the number of errors. Simply counting the number of errors per day (using a *c*-chart) would not be a good idea because the number of patients in the hospital change each day. A better measure would be the number of errors per patient using a *u*-chart. Both *c*- and *u*-charts find many useful applications in services.

c-Charts

To construct a c-chart, first collect $k = 25\text{-}30$ samples of constant size and record the number of nonconformances per sample. Define $c_i = $ number of nonconformances in sample i. Next, compute the average number of nonconformances per unit $\bar{c}$, which will be the center line for the c-chart. This is computed as:

$$\bar{c} = \frac{\sum c_i}{k} \tag{8.48}$$

A c-chart is based on the Poisson distribution, so the standard deviation is

$$s_c = \sqrt{\bar{c}} \tag{8.49}$$

Thus, control limits for the c-chart are given by

$$\begin{aligned} \mathrm{LCL}_c &= \bar{c} - 3\sqrt{\bar{c}} \\ \mathrm{UCL}_c &= \bar{c} + 3\sqrt{\bar{c}} \end{aligned} \tag{8.50}$$

EXAMPLE 8.22

Constructing a c-Chart

Figure 8.45 shows the number of machine failures over a 25-day period. The total number of failures is 45; therefore, the average number of failures per day, calculated using formula (8.48), is

$$\bar{c} = \frac{45}{25} = 1.8$$

Control limits for the c-chart are found using formulas (8.49) and (8.50):

$$\mathrm{LCL}_c = 1.8 - 3\sqrt{1.8} = -2.22, \text{ or zero}$$
$$\mathrm{UCL}_c = 1.8 + 3\sqrt{1.8} = 5.82$$

The chart is shown in Figure 8.46 and appears to be in control. Such a chart can be used for continued control or for monitoring the effectiveness of a process for improving machine reliability.

---

u-Charts

To construct a u-chart, first collect $k = 25\text{-}30$ samples and record the number of nonconformances in each sample (c_i) and the size of each sample or number of opportunities for nonconformances in each sample (n_i). Next, compute the average number of nonconformances per unit, $\bar{u}$, which will be the center line for the u-chart:

$$\bar{u} = \frac{c_1 + c_2 + \cdots + c_k}{n_1 + n_2 + \cdots + n_k} \tag{8.51}$$

The standard deviation of the ith sample is calculated as

$$s_u = \sqrt{\frac{\bar{u}}{n_i}} \tag{8.52}$$

Note that the standard deviation of each sample varies because the size of the sampling unit varies. This is similar to the p-chart with variable sample size. The control limits, based on three standard deviations around the mean, are

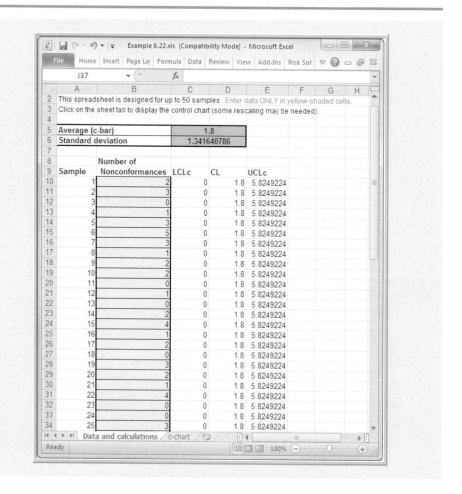

$$LCL_u = \bar{u} - 3\sqrt{\frac{\bar{u}}{n_i}}$$

$$UCL_u = \bar{u} + 3\sqrt{\frac{\bar{u}}{n_i}}$$ (8.53)

EXAMPLE 8.23

Constructing a *u*-Chart

Suppose that a catalog distributor ships a variety of orders each day. The packing slips often contain errors such as wrong purchase order numbers, wrong quantities, or incorrect sizes. Because the sample size varies each day in the following example, a *u*-chart is appropriate. Figure 8.47 shows the error data collected during August. Column B lists the number of nonconformances found among all packing slips (column C) each day. The average number of errors per slip, $\bar{u}$, is found using formula (8.51) by dividing the total number of errors (209) by the total number of packing slips (2,765):

$$\bar{u} = \frac{209}{2765} = 0.0756$$

Using formula (8.52), the standard deviation for a particular sample size n_i is therefore

$$s_u = \sqrt{\frac{0.0756}{n_i}}$$

The control limits for each sample are shown in the spreadsheet. As with a p-chart, individual control limits will vary with the sample size. The control chart is shown in Figure 8.48. One point (#2) appears to be out of control.

One application of c-charts and u-charts is in a quality rating system when defects or nonconformances are classified into categories and rated according to their severity as we discussed earlier in this chapter. For instance, a critical defect might be assigned a penalty value of 10; a major defect, 5; and a minor defect, 1. A weighted service quality rating scale would be another example. These ratings can be used as the basis for a c-chart that would monitor total penalties per day (assuming a constant number of units each day) or a u-chart that would monitor penalties per unit. Such charts are often used for internal quality control and as a means of rating suppliers.[20]

FIGURE 8.46 c-Chart for Example 8.22

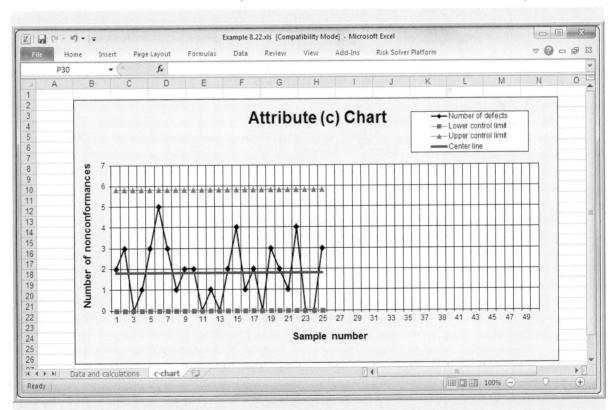

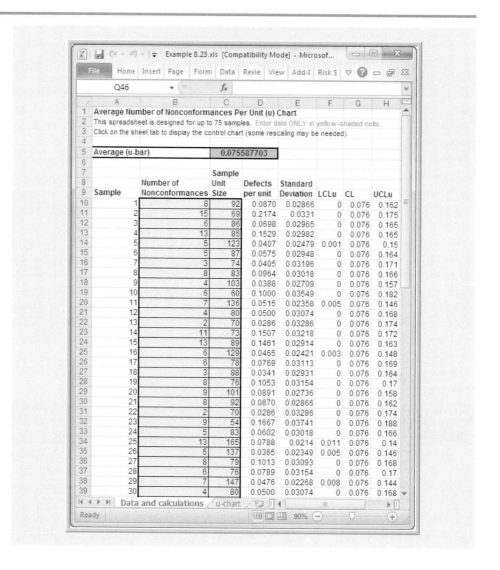

SUMMARY OF CONTROL CHART CONSTRUCTION

Table 8.5 summarizes the formulas used for constructing the different types of control charts discussed thus far. Figure 8.49 provides a summary of guidelines for chart selection.

A wide variety of commercial software is available to implement SPC. For example, one package is *CHARTrunner,* product of PQ Systems (http://www.pqsystems.com). *CHARTrunner* generates SPC charts and performs statistical analyses using data that are collected, stored, and managed by other applications such as Microsoft Access or Excel, SQL Server, Oracle, text files, and many others. It generates control charts, as well as histograms, process capability results, Pareto charts, scatter diagrams, and others; performs curve fitting and linear regression; and allows users to customize out-of-control tests, select colors for sigma zones, display multiple sets of control limits, and save charts

FIGURE 8.48   *u*-Chart for Example 8.23

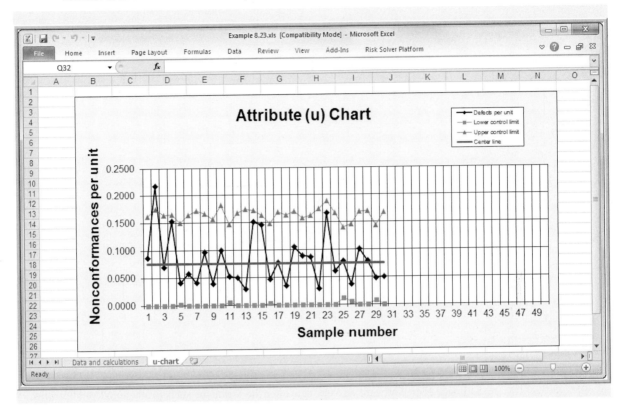

Type of Chart	LCL	CL	UCL
$\bar{x}$ (with R)	$\bar{\bar{x}} - A_2\bar{R}$	$\bar{\bar{x}}$	$\bar{\bar{x}} + A_2\bar{R}$
R	$D_3\bar{R}$	$\bar{R}$	$D_4\bar{R}$
p	$\bar{p} - 3\sqrt{\bar{p}(1-\bar{p})/n}$	$\bar{p}$	$\bar{p} + 3\sqrt{\bar{p}(1-\bar{p})/n}$
$\bar{x}$ (with s)	$\bar{\bar{x}} - A_3\bar{s}$	$\bar{\bar{x}}$	$\bar{\bar{x}} + A_3\bar{s}$
s	$B_3\bar{s}$	$\bar{s}$	$B_4\bar{s}$
x	$\bar{x} - 3\bar{R}/d_2$	$\bar{x}$	$\bar{x} + 3\bar{R}/d_2$
np	$n\bar{p} - 3\sqrt{n\bar{p}(1-\bar{p})}$	$n\bar{p}$	$n\bar{p} + 3\sqrt{n\bar{p}(1-\bar{p})}$
c	$\bar{c} - 3\sqrt{\bar{c}}$	$\bar{c}$	$\bar{c} + 3\sqrt{\bar{c}}$
u	$\bar{u} - 3\sqrt{\bar{u}/n_i}$	$\bar{u}$	$\bar{u} + 3\sqrt{\bar{u}/n_i}$

TABLE 8.5
Summary of
Control Chart
Formulas

FIGURE 8.49   Control Chart Selection

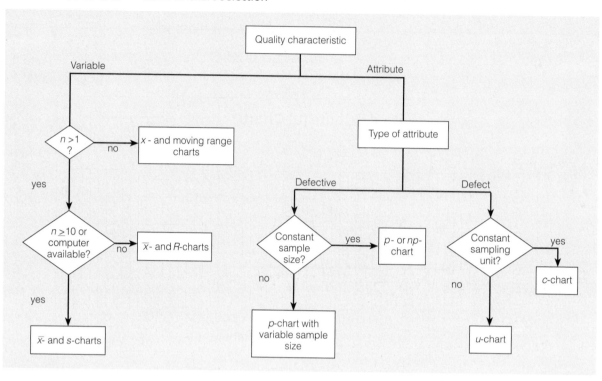

as image files. Software surveys can often be found in such professional publications as *Quality Digest* (http://www.qualitydigest.com).

IMPLEMENTING STATISTICAL PROCESS CONTROL

ISO 9000:2000 emphasizes the use of statistical methods.[21] For example, the standards require "applicable methods, including statistical techniques" be identified and used for monitoring and measuring products and processes, and that through monitoring and measurement, the organization can demonstrate the ability of processes to meet requirements and that product requirements have been met. A more recent ISO standard, 11462-1, provides guidance for organizations wishing to use SPC to meet these requirements. The standard addresses the following elements:

- *Definition of SPC goals.* Such goals might include reducing variation around target values and compensating for process variation to ensure product conformity, reducing costs, indicating how the process is likely to behave in the future, and quantifying process capability.
- *Conditions for a successful SPC system.* These conditions include integration with a formal quality management system, management support, use of information for data-driven decisions and management reviews, and ensuring the competence of those who will be using the tools.
- *Elements of the SPC system.* These address the processes an organization should implement and actions it should take to ensure that a successful SPC system includes both operational and support activities. These elements include a process documentation and control plan, definition of process targets and limits, data collection, measuring

equipment, data recording and analysis, process control, short- and long-term process capability assessment, communication of results, and process improvement implementation and project management activities. This standard can provide useful assistance for organizations that are beginning to develop a formal SPC approach.

When implementing SPC, practitioners must consider four issues: (1) the basis for sampling, (2) the sample size, (3) the frequency of sampling, and (4) the location of the control limits.

Basis for Sampling

The purpose of a control chart is to identify the variation in a system that may change over time. In determining the method of sampling, samples should be chosen to be as homogeneous as possible so that each sample reflects the system of common causes or assignable causes that may be present at that point in time. A good sampling method should have the property that, if special causes are present, the chance of observing differences between samples is high, whereas the chance of observing differences within a sample is low. Samples that satisfy these criteria are called **rational subgroups**. One approach to constructing rational subgroups is to use samples of consecutive measurements over a short period of time. Consecutive measurements minimize the chance of variability within the sample while allowing variation between samples to be detected.

Sample Size

The choice of sample size represents a trade-off between cost and information. Small sample sizes reduce costs associated with the time that workers must spend collecting data; however, they provide less statistical information. Large samples are more costly but allow smaller changes in process characteristics to be detected with higher probability. Figure 8.50 shows the probability of detecting a shift in the mean in the next sample (that is, the probability of seeing the next point outside the control limits when the process mean has shifted some number of standard deviations) as a function of the sample size for an $\bar{x}$-chart. For example, a sample size of 5 will allow you to detect a shift of 2 standard deviations approximately 95 percent of the time. If the process has shifted 1.5 standard deviations, a sample size of 5 provides only a 64 percent chance of detection. For a 95 percent chance of detecting such a shift, a sample of at least 10 is needed. To detect a one standard deviation shift, samples of size 20 are required. Therefore, the appropriate sample size depends on the process capability and the criticality of not letting a process drift too far. In addition, control limits are based on the assumption of a normal distribution of the sample means. If the underlying process is not normal, this assumption is can be violated for small samples so larger samples would be recommended.

For attributes data, too small a sample size can make a p-chart meaningless. Even though many guidelines such as "use at least 100 observations" have been suggested, the proper sample size should be determined statistically, particularly when the true portion of nonconformances is small. If p is small, n should be large enough to have a high probability of detecting at least one nonconformance. For example, if $p = 0.01$, then to have at least a 95 percent chance of finding at least one nonconformance, the sample size must be at least 300.

Sampling Frequency

The third design issue is the sampling frequency. Taking large samples on a frequent basis is desirable but clearly not economical. No hard-and-fast rules exist for the

FIGURE 8.50 Probability of Detecting a Shift in Mean

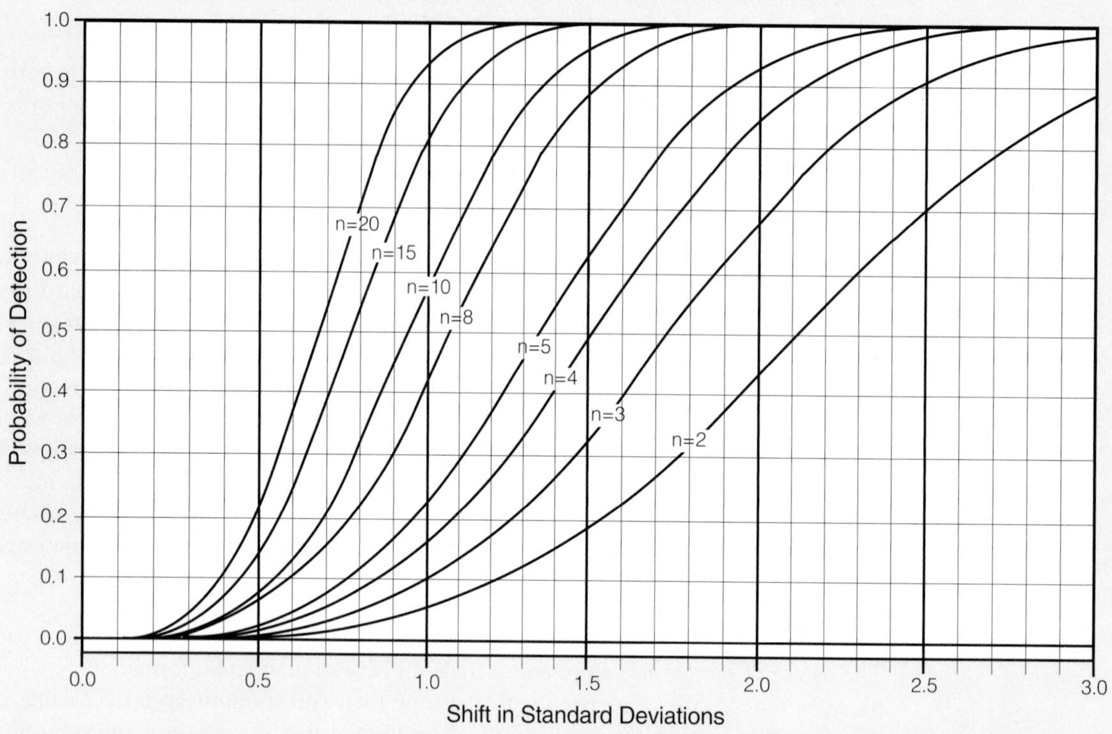

Source: Reprinted with permission from Lyle Dockendorf, "Choosing Appropriate Sample Subgroup Sizes for Control Charts," Quality Progress Vol. 25, no. 10, p. 160, October 1992. Copyright © 1992 American Society for Quality. No further distribution allowed without permission.

frequency of sampling. Samples should be close enough to provide an opportunity to detect changes in process characteristics as soon as possible and reduce the chances of producing a large amount of nonconforming output. However, they should not be so close that the cost of sampling outweighs the benefits that can be realized. This decision depends on the individual application and production volume.

Location of Control Limits

Control limits need not adhere to the statistical "3 standard errors about the mean" formulas. In some situations it may be desirable to use wider or narrower control limits to reduce the costs associated with drawing wrong conclusions. Two types of errors may occur in using control charts. The first occurs when an incorrect conclusion is reached that a *special cause is present when in fact one does not exist* and results in the cost of trying to find a nonexistent problem. The second occurs when *special causes are present but are not signaled in the control chart* because points fall within the control limits by chance. Because nonconforming products have a greater chance to be produced, a cost will eventually be incurred as a result.

Practical Guidelines

Much research has been performed on economic design of control charts.[22] Cost models attempt to find the best combination of design parameters (center line, control limits, sample size, and sampling interval) that minimize expected cost or maximize expected profit. As a practical matter, one often uses judgment about the nature of operations and the costs involved in making these decisions. Raymond Mayer suggests the following guidelines:[23]

1. If the cost of investigating an operation to identify the cause of an apparent out-of-control condition is high, wider control limits should be adopted. Conversely, if that cost is low, narrower limits should be selected.
2. If the cost of the defective output generated by an operation is substantial, narrower control limits should be used. Otherwise, wider limits should be selected.
3. If the cost both types of errors are significant, wide control limits should be chosen and a larger sample size should be used. Also, more frequent samples should be taken to reduce the duration of any out-of-control condition that might occur.
4. If past experience with an operation indicates that an out-of-control condition arises quite frequently, narrower control limits should be considered. In the event that the probability of an out-of-control condition is small, wider limits might be preferred.

SUMMARY OF KEY POINTS AND TERMINOLOGY

The Student Companion Site provides a summary of key concepts and terminology introduced in this chapter.

QUALITY *in* PRACTICE

Using a *u*-Chart in a Receiving Process

A distributor of electrical automation and power transmission products implemented a total quality program. One manager was eager to collect data about the organization's receiving process because of a decrease in the organization's on-time deliveries. The manager suspected that the data entry person in the purchasing department was not entering data in the computer in a timely fashion; consequently, packages could not be properly processed for subsequent shipping to the customer.

A preliminary analysis indicated that the manager's notion was inaccurate. In fact, the manager was able to see that the data entry person was doing an excellent job. The analysis showed that handling packages that were destined for a branch operation in the same fashion as other packages created significant delays. A simple process change of placing a branch designation letter in front of the purchase order number told the receiving clerk to place those packages on a separate skid for delivery to the branch.

However, this analysis revealed a variety of other problems. Generally, anywhere from 65 to 110 packing slips were processed each day. These were found to contain many errors in addition to the wrong destination designation that contributed to the delays.

Errors included

- Wrong purchase order
- Wrong quantity
- Purchase order not on the system
- Original order not on the system
- Parts do not match

- Purchase order was entered incorrectly
- Double shipment
- Wrong parts
- No purchase order

Many packing slips contained multiple errors. Table 8.6 shows the number of packing slips and

TABLE 8.6   Packing Slip Error Counts

Date	Packing Slips	Errors	Date	Packing Slips	Errors
21 Jan	87	15	4 Mar	92	8
22 Jan	79	13	5 Mar	69	13
23 Jan	92	23	6 Mar	86	6
24 Jan	84	3	9 Mar	85	13
27 Jan	73	7	10 Mar	101	5
28 Jan	67	11	11 Mar	87	5
29 Jan	73	8	12 Mar	71	3
30 Jan	91	8	13 Mar	83	8
31 Jan	94	11	16 Mar	103	4
3 Feb	83	12	17 Mar	82	6
4 Feb	89	12	18 Mar	90	7
5 Feb	88	6	19 Mar	80	4
6 Feb	69	11	20 Mar	70	4
7 Feb	74	8	23 Mar	73	11
10 Feb	67	4	24 Mar	89	13
11 Feb	83	10	25 Mar	91	6
12 Feb	79	8	26 Mar	78	6
13 Feb	75	8	27 Mar	88	6
14 Feb	69	3	30 Mar	76	8
17 Feb	87	8	31 Mar	101	9
18 Feb	99	13	1 Apr	92	8
19 Feb	101	13	2 Apr	70	2
20 Feb	76	7	3 Apr	72	11
21 Feb	90	4	6 Apr	83	5
24 Feb	92	7	7 Apr	69	6
25 Feb	80	4	8 Apr	79	3
26 Feb	81	5	9 Apr	79	8
27 Feb	105	8	10 Apr	76	6
28 Feb	80	8	13 Apr	92	7
2 Mar	82	5	14 Apr	80	4
3 Mar	75	3	15 Apr	78	8

FIGURE 8.51   *u*-Chart for Packing Slip Errors

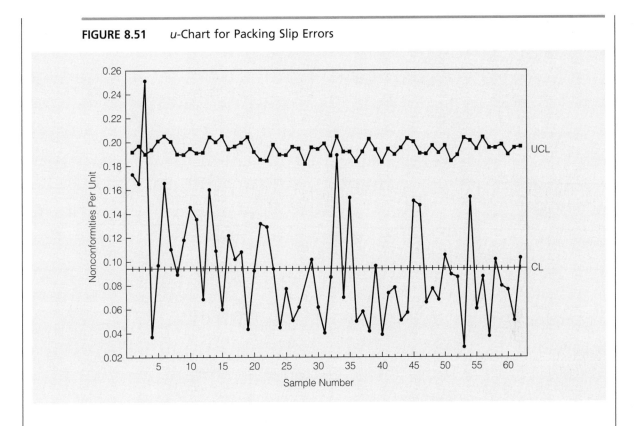

total errors identified. A *u*-chart was constructed for each day to track the number of packing slip errors—defects—found. A *u*-chart was used because the sample size varied each day. Thus, the statistic monitored was the number of errors per packing slip. Figure 8.51 shows the *u*-chart that was constructed for this period. (This change in the branch designation took place on January 24, resulting in significant improvement, as shown on the chart.)

Although the chart shows that the process is in control (since the branch designation change), the average error rate of more than 9 percent still was not considered acceptable. After consolidating the types of errors into five categories, a Pareto analysis was performed. This analysis showed the following:

Category	Percentage
Purchase order error	35
Quantity error	22
No purchase order on system	17
Original order not on system	16
Parts error	10

The analysis is illustrated in Figure 8.52.

The first two categories accounted for more than half of the errors. The remedy for these problems was to develop a training module on proper purchasing methods to ensure that vendors knew the correct information needed on the purchase orders. The third category—no purchase order on the computer system—caused receiving personnel to stage the orders until an investigation could find the necessary information. Because of this problem, the company realized it needed to revamp the original order-writing process. Specifically, both the order-writing and purchase order activities needed to be improved.

An analysis of the control chart shows that the average error rate has gradually improved. To a large extent, this improvement was due to the recognition of the problems and enhanced communication among the constituents. While the full training program had not been implemented at the time this case was written, the company believed that a significant reduction in the error rate would result once the training was completed.

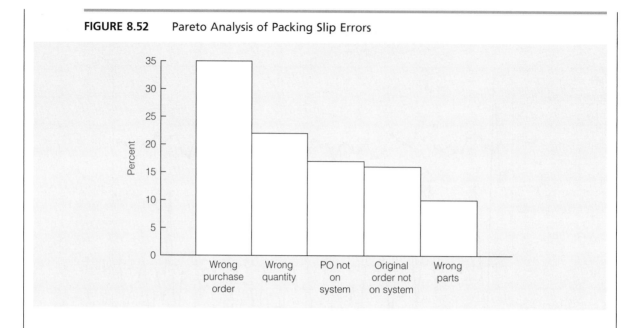

FIGURE 8.52   Pareto Analysis of Packing Slip Errors

Key Issues for Discussion

1. Verify the computation of the center line and control limits in Figure 8.51.

2. What information might a separate chart for each error category provide? Would you recommend spending the time and effort to make these additional computations?

QUALITY *in* PRACTICE

Applying SPC to Pharmaceutical Product Manufacturing[24]

A Midwest pharmaceutical company manufactures (in two stages) individual syringes with a self-contained, single dose of an injectable drug. In the first stage, sterile liquid drug is filled into glass syringes and sealed with a rubber stopper. The remaining stage involves insertion of the cartridge into plastic syringes and the electrical "tacking" of the containment cap at a precisely determined length of the syringe. A cap that is "tacked" at a shorter than desired length (less than 4.920 inches) leads to pressure on the cartridge stopper and, hence, partial or complete activation of the syringe. Such syringes must then be scrapped. If the cap is "tacked" at a longer than desired length (4.980 inches or longer), the tacking is incomplete or inadequate, which can lead to cap loss and potentially a cartridge loss in shipment and handling. Such

syringes can be reworked manually to attach the cap at a lower position. However, this process requires a 100 percent inspection of the tacked syringes and results in increased cost for the items. This final production step seemed to be producing more and more scrap and reworked syringes over successive weeks.

At this point, statistical consultants became involved in an attempt to solve this problem and recommended SPC for the purpose of improving the tacking operation. The length was targeted as a critical variable to be monitored by $\bar{x}$- and R-charts, which eventually led to identifying the root cause of the problem. The actual case history contains instances in which desired procedures were not always followed. As such, this case illustrates well the properties, problems, pitfalls, and peculiarities in applying such charts, as well as the necessity of having well-trained quality specialists involved.

Operators of the final stage of this syringe assembly process were trained in the basics of process capability studies and control charting techniques. In an attempt to judge the capability of the process, the responsible technician was called in to adjust the tacking machine and to position and secure it at what seemed to be its best possible position. Then, 35 consecutive observations were taken (see Table 8.7), and a capability study was undertaken. The process had a sample mean of $\bar{x} = 4.954$ inches, which was close to the nominal aim (or target) of 4.950 inches with a sample standard deviation of $s = 0.0083$ inches. Upper and lower specifications of 4.980 and 4.920 inches, respectively, gave an estimated $C_{pk} = 1.03$. Thus, it was determined that the

process was minimally capable and could indeed produce the length desired.

To establish the control charts, the operators then collected 15 samples each of size 5 taken every 15 minutes. The $\bar{x}$ and R-charts are shown in Figure 8.53. These charts show that the process is already out of statistical control in both charts. Proper application of SPC procedures would have indicated that special causes should be identified and new control limits constructed. Unfortunately, the operators from this shift did not plot these points but only used the control limits they obtained to evaluate future measurements. The operators from this first shift continued to collect samples of size 5 every 15 minutes, but due to their unfamiliarity with charting, they never plotted these 15 new points either. At 4:00 P.M. of the same day, a new shift arrived and operators did plot this second set of

TABLE 8.7   Initial 35 Consecutive Observations Taken for the Capability Study

4.95888	4.95533	4.94294	4.95422	4.96679	4.94487	4.95775	4.95710
4.96543	4.95603	4.95210	4.95311	4.95385	4.96014	4.95252	4.96633
4.96255	4.95287	4.93541	4.94840	4.96114	4.93901	4.95966	4.93667
4.95941	4.94539	4.96238	4.94337	4.95550	4.95482	4.96230	4.96175
4.96016	4.94626	4.95904					

Source: Adapted from LeRoy A. Franklin and Samar N. Mukherjee, "An SPC Case Study on Stabilizing Syringe Lengths," *Quality Engineering* 12, no. 1 (1999–2000), 65–71. Reprinted from Quality Engineering, courtesy of Marcel Dekker, Inc.

FIGURE 8.53   Initial $\bar{x}$- and R-Charts for the First 15 Samples

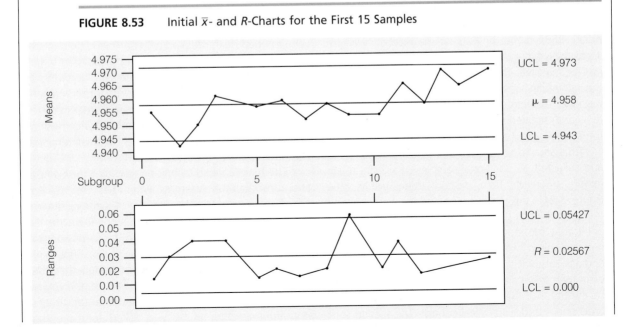

FIGURE 8.54 $\bar{x}$ and R-Charts, Next 17 Samples

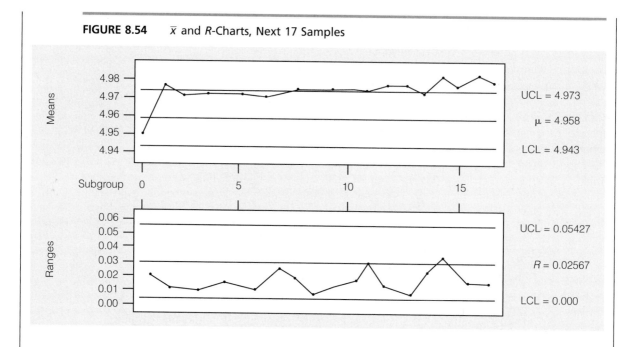

15 points using the control limits obtained from the first set of 15 points as shown in Figure 8.54. These charts show clearly that the centering was out of statistical control, with the average length far greater than desired. This conclusion was substantiated by operators noticing that the caps were not being tacked properly. The maintenance technician was immediately called in to adjust the machine properly.

After the first adjustment by the technician, the plot of the next sample taken 15 minutes later was already beyond the upper control limit for the $\bar{x}$- chart. Thus, the syringes were still too long, although the technician affirmed that he had set the height lower just 15 minutes earlier. The technician was recalled to readjust the machine. The second try was no better, and so the technician was called a third time to adjust the machine. This third try was successful in the sense that the length seemed to be reduced enough to have both the $\bar{x}$- and R-values inside their control limits.

This second shift operators continued sampling and collected 15 additional samples of size 5, at 15-minute intervals. They plotted these results (see Figure 8.54), but because no values were beyond the control limits, they took no action. It was at this point that the statistical consultants reviewed what had transpired. They not only determined that the original 15 points used to define the $\bar{x}$- and R-charts were themselves showing a process not under statistical control, but that the last 15 points also showed a process not under statistical control. The second shift

workers had failed to notice the string of 15 points of the $\bar{x}$-chart all above the center line and failed to conclude that the center was "not where you wanted it." If they had, they would have once again called the technician to adjust the machine to lower the length of the syringes.

Fortunately, however, the consultants examined the R-chart as well as the $\bar{x}$-chart. Again, the last 14 points of R were all on one side of the center line, indicating a lack of statistical control. Careful examination of both charts revealed that the points of R were below the center and were indicating that the overall variation had been reduced by what the maintenance technician had done. Yet, in reading the $\bar{x}$-chart (after examining the R-chart), the length of the syringes seemed to have increased. The consultants contacted both the operators and the technician in order to try to find out what had happened to cause this confusing "good and bad" thing to occur. The maintenance technician's story was most revealing.

The maintenance technician said that for his first two (unsuccessful) attempts when he was told to adjust the process center (length of syringe) down, he moved the height adjustment stop down on its threaded shaft. However, he found it was difficult to tighten the locknut for this adjustment stop. The third time (the successful one), being frustrated that the thread of the shaft was too battered at the lower end of the stud, he actually moved the adjustment stop up even though he was asked to make the

FIGURE 8.55 $\bar{x}$ and R-Charts for the Last 15 Samples

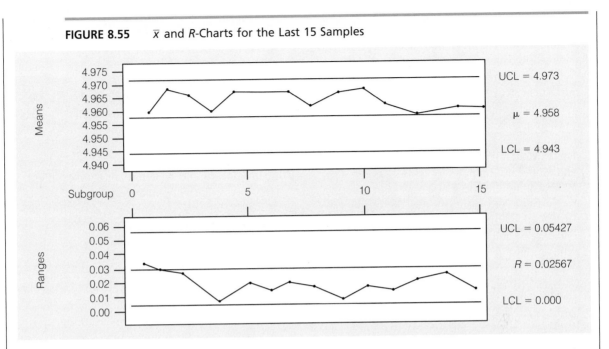

syringe lengths shorter. He thought this would result in still longer syringes being produced, but at least the locknut would hold. When he was told by the shift that the process was now producing the proper length syringes and that the operators were satisfied, he was mystified. He left wondering how a machine adjusted upward (toward longer lengths) could wind up producing shorter-length syringes!

The consultants realized the dramatic improvement (shortening) of the process variation told the important story. When the maintenance technician set the length of the adjustment cap where he was supposed to (lower), the threads were so worn as to make it impossible to hold the locknut in place. Thus, the vibration from the running machine (within about 15 minutes) loosened the locknut and adjustment cap quickly, resulting in drifts off center, producing syringes of erratic lengths. However, when the maintenance technician set the adjustment cap higher (which would make syringes longer), the threads there were good enough for the locknut to hold the cap in place. The lengths, indeed, were a little longer than what was targeted, but the variation had been so dramatically reduced that the overall effect was one of making acceptable syringes; that is, the syringes were a tiny bit longer than desired but very consistent in their length so no plotted points were beyond the upper control limit for the $\bar{x}$-chart.

The operators were satisfied with this situation because now the plotted points of the syringe lengths came under the upper control limit of the $\bar{x}$-chart, which convinced them that they were making syringes to the proper length. The consultants recommended to the managers that the threaded stud on which the adjustment stop moved be replaced. The repair work needed a special part that was fairly expensive and necessitated some downtime for the manufacturing process; nevertheless, on the strength of the control chart data and the explanation of the maintenance technician's and consultant's stories, the recommendation was implemented. Upon replacement of the threaded stud, waste and rework from the final step dropped to virtually zero over the period of many weeks.

Key Issues for Discussion

1. Using the data for the initial process capability study sample given in Table 8.7, compute the process capability indexes and construct a histogram for these data.
2. Explain why it was incorrect that the operators did not plot the initial data, find special causes, and compute new control limits. What might have happened had they done it correctly?
3. What lessons can be learned from this case?

REVIEW QUESTIONS

1. Define *measurement*, and explain the difference between measures and indicators.

2. What does the acronym SMART signify for measurement? Why are these characteristics important?

3. What is a dashboard and why is it valuable in quality control?

4. Explain the difference between a nonconformance and a nonconforming unit of work.

5. What is the difference between an attribute measurement and a variable measurement?

6. Explain the difference in measuring nonconformances per unit and defects per million opportunities (dpmo)? What advantages does dpmo have as a quality measure?

7. Why are cost of quality programs valuable to managers?

8. List and explain the four major categories of quality costs. Give examples of each.

9. Provide some examples of low-tech and high-tech measuring instruments used in quality control.

10. Explain the importance of formula (8.5):
$$\sigma^2_{total} = \sigma^2_{process} + \sigma^2_{measurement}$$

11. Describe the science of metrology.

12. What is the difference between accuracy and precision?

13. What is calibration and why is it important to a good quality control system?

14. Explain the difference between repeatability and reproducibility.

15. How is an R&R study performed? What is its purpose?

16. Explain the term *process capability*. How can process capability generally be improved?

17. What are the three major types of process capability studies? Describe the methodology of conducting a process capability study.

18. Define the process capability indexes, C_p, C_{pb}, and C_{pu}, and explain how they may be used to establish or improve quality policies in operating areas or with suppliers.

19. What does the term *in statistical control* mean?

20. How does a process performance index differ from a process capability index?

21. Explain how pre-control is applied. How does it differ from statistical process control?

22. Briefly describe the methodology of constructing and using control charts.

23. What does one look for in interpreting control charts? Explain what a control chart for a process in statistical control should look like, and the characteristics of out-of-control indicators.

24. Why is the *s*-chart sometimes used in place of the *R*-chart?

25. Describe some situations in which a chart for individual measurements would be used.

26. Does an *np*-chart provide any different information than a *p*-chart? Why would an *np*-chart be used?

27. Explain the difference between a *c*-chart and a *u*-chart.

28. What guidance does ISO standard 11462-1 provide for organizations wishing to use SPC?

29. Explain the concept of rational subgroups.

30. What trade-offs are involved in selecting the sample size for a control chart?

31. Explain the economic trade-offs to consider when determining the sampling frequency to use in a control chart.

PROBLEMS

Note: Data for many of the problems in this chapter can be found in the Excel workbook C08Data.xlsx on the Student Companion Site. Click on the appropriate worksheet tab as noted in the problem (e.g., Prob. 8-6, etc.) to access the data.

1. EL Specialty Manufacturing Company makes an artificial leather-like product for the fashion accessory market. The material is made in sheets and has the appearance of a thin rug. Each sheet is 36 inches wide and 100 feet long and is wound into a roll. The quality manager has requested that 100 rolls be inspected. Thirty-eight nonconformances were found.

a. Calculate the nonconformances per unit (NPU) and the throughput yield (TY).

b. If the production process consists of three steps, with step 1 having a TY of 83 percent; step 2, 90 percent; and step 3, 92 percent, what is the rolled throughput yield (RTY), and the proportion nonconforming?

2. Wellplace Insurance Company processes insurance policy applications in batches of 100. One day, they had 10 batches to process and, after inspection, it was found that 4 batches had nonconforming policies. One batch had 3 nonconformances, another had 5, another had 2, and another had 1 nonconformance. What were (a) the proportion nonconforming for each batch, (b) the nonconformances per unit (NPU), in total for the 10 batches, and (c) the total throughput yield (TY) for the 10 batches?

3. Flybynight Airlines measured their numbers of lost bags in one month and found that they had lost 130 bags for 10,000 customers. If the average number of bags per customer is 1.3, how many errors per million opportunities (epmo) does this represent? The worldwide rate of baggage mishandling reported by SITA (Société Internationale de Télécommunications Aéronautiques) in 2011 was 12.07 per 1,000 passengers. If the average number of checked bags per passenger is assumed to be 1.3, how many errors per million opportunities (epmo) does this represent? How does this compare with the rate for Flybynight—better or worse?

4. Broadwork Electronics manufactures 500,000 circuit boards per month. A random sample of 5,000 boards is inspected every week for five characteristics. During a recent week, two defects were found for one characteristic, and one defect each was found for the other four characteristics. If these inspections produced defect counts that were representative of the population, what are the dpmo's for the individual characteristics and what is the overall dpmo for the boards?

5. Analyze the cost data in the Excel workbook *C08Data.xlsx* for the Costcutin Co. What percent of sales are represented by each category of cost? What are the implications of these data for management?

6. Prepare a pie chart showing the different quality cost categories and percentages for the Great Press Printing Company. See the data for *Prob. 8-6* in the Excel workbook *C08Data.xlsx*.

7. Compute a labor cost base index for Miami Valley Aircraft Service Co. to analyze the quality cost information and prepare a memo to management explaining your conclusions. See the data for *Prob. 8-7* in the Excel workbook *C08Data.xlsx*. (See the file on Indexes on the Student Companion Site for an explanation.)

8. Repack Solutions, Inc. has a distribution center in Cincinnati where it receives and breaks down bulk orders from suppliers' factories and ships out products to retail customers. Prepare a pie or bar chart showing the different quality cost categories and percentages for the company's quality costs that were incurred over the past year. See the Excel workbook *C08Data.xlsx* for the data.

9. The Excel workbook *C08Data.xlsx* provides data on quality losses at Nosoco Paper Mill. Construct an appropriate Excel chart to analyze the data. What conclusions do you reach?

10. Stateside Metrology Repairs, Inc. has a thriving business repairing and upgrading high-technology measuring instruments. The costs of quality that they have collected over the past year can be found in the Excel workbook *C08Data.xlsx*. Use Pareto analysis to investigate their quality losses and to suggest which areas they should address first in an effort to improve their quality.

11. Use Pareto analysis to investigate the quality losses at Beechmount Software Corp. using the data for *Prob. 8-11* in the Excel workbook *C08Data.xlsx*. What conclusions do you reach?

12. A genetic researcher at GenLab, Ltd. is trying to test two laboratory thermometers (that can be read to 1/100,000th of a degree Celsius) for accuracy and precision. She measured 25 samples with each and obtained the results found in the *C08Data.xlsx* file for *Prob. 8-12* on the Student Companion Site for this chapter. The true temperature being measured is 0°C. Which instrument is more accurate? Which is more precise? Which is the better instrument?

13. Two scales at Aussieburgers, Ltd. were used to weigh the same 25 samples of hamburger patties for a fast-food restaurant in Australia. Results are shown in *C08Data.xlsx* file for *Prob.8-13* on the Student Companion Site for this chapter. The samples were weighed in grams, and the supplier has ensured that each patty weighs 114 grams.

Which scale is more accurate? Which is more precise? Which is the better scale?

14. A gauge repeatability and reproducibility study at NEW Gauge, Inc., collected the data for three operators, two trials, and eight parts, as found in the worksheet *Prob. 8-14* in the Excel file *C08Data.xlsx* on the Student Companion Site for this chapter. Analyze these data. The part specification is 1.5 ± 0.1 inches.

15. A gauge repeatability and reproducibility study at Frankford Brake Systems collected the data found in the worksheet *Prob. 8-15* in the Excel file *C08Data.xlsx* on the Student Companion Site for this chapter. Analyze these data. The part specification is 1.0 ± 0.06 mm.

16. A gauge repeatability and reproducibility study was made at Precision Parts, Inc., using three operators, taking three trials each on identical parts. The data that can be found in the worksheet tab *Prob. 8-16* in the Excel file *C08Data.xlsx* on the Student Companion Site for this chapter were collected. Do you see any problems after analyzing these data? What should be done? The part specification for the collar that was measured was 1.6 ± 0.2 inches.

17. A machining process at the Mach4 Tool Co. has a required dimension on a part of 0.575 ± 0.007 inch. Twenty-five parts each were measured as found in the worksheet tab *Prob. 8-17* in the Excel file *C08Data.xlsx* on the Student Companion Site website for this chapter. What is its capability for producing within acceptable limits?

18. Adjustments were made in the process at the Mach4 Tool Co. discussed in Problem 17 and 25 more samples were taken. The results are given in the worksheet tab *Prob. 8-18* in the Excel file *C08Data.xlsx* on the Student Companion Site for this chapter. What can you observe about the process? Is it now capable of producing within acceptable limits?

19. From the data for Kermit Theatrical Products, construct a histogram and estimate the process capability. If the specifications are 24 ± 0.03, estimate the percentage of parts that will be nonconforming. Finally, compute C_p, C_{pu}, and C_{pl}. Samples for 5 parts were taken as shown in the worksheet tab *Prob. 8-19* in the Excel file *C08Data.xlsx* on the Student Companion Site for this chapter.

20. Samples for three parts made at River City Parts Co. were taken as shown in the worksheet tab *Prob. 8-20* in the Excel file *C08Data.xlsx* on the Student Companion Site for this chapter. Data set 1 is for part 1, data set 2 is for part 2, and data set 3 is for part 3.
    a. Calculate the mean and standard deviations for each part and compare them to the following specification limits:

Part	Nominal	Tolerance
1	1.750	± 0.045
2	2.000	± 0.060
3	1.250	± 0.030

    b. Will the production process permit an acceptable fit of all parts into a slot with a specification of 5 ± 0.081 at least 99.73 percent of the time?

21. Suppose that a refrigeration process at Coolfoods, Ltd. Has a normally distributed output with a mean of 25.0 and a variance of 1.44.
    a. If the specifications are 25.0 ± 3.25, compute C_p, C_{pk}, and C_{pm}. Is the process capable and centered?
    b. Suppose the mean shifts to 23.0 but the variance remains unchanged. Recompute and interpret these process capability indexes.
    c. If the variance can be reduced to 40 percent of its original value, how do the process capability indices change (using the original mean of 25.0)?

22. River Bottom Fire Department is evaluating their response times in order to determine whether a new fire station is needed. Samples were taken for 30 random days from 6 stations. These data can be found in the worksheet *Prob. 8-22* in the *C08Data.xlsx* file.
    a. Using Microsoft Excel® or similar software with statistical capability, construct a histogram for these 180 individual readings.
    b. Construct a run chart for the sample means.
    c. Interpret what the data show. Does the process appear to be in control?

23. Palma State Bank is investigating the processing time for loan applications. Samples were taken for 25 random days from 5 branches. These data can be found in the worksheet *Prob. 8-23* in the *C08Data.xlsx* file on the Student Companion Site for this chapter.

a. Using Microsoft Excel® or similar software with statistical capability, construct a histogram for these 125 individual readings.

b. Construct a run chart for the sample means.

c. Interpret what the data show. Does the process appear to be in control?

24. Hawkeye Magnetronics makes induction meters used in vending machines to test the validity of coins. Their specifications require the induction reading capability of the meters to fall between 0.25 and 0.50 Tesla (T) units. Quality analysts took 3 random test readings of 30 meters, as found in the worksheet *Prob. 8-24* in the *C08Data.xlsx* file.

a. Using Microsoft Excel® or similar software with statistical capability, construct a histogram for these 90 individual readings.

b. Construct a run chart for the sample means.

c. Interpret what the data show. Does the process appear to be in control?

25. River Bottom Fire Department (Prob. 8-22) determined that they needed to adjust their data-gathering process for response time to eliminate bias. The times were expected to fall within 3.8 and 5.3 minutes. After doing so, they wanted to evaluate the process to determine whether or not it was under control. Thirty new samples were taken on 30 random days from 6 stations. These data can be found in the worksheet *Prob. 8-25* in the *C08Data.xlsx* file on the Student Companion Site for this chapter.

a. Compute the mean and range of each sample, calculate control limits, and plot them on $\bar{x}$ and R control charts.

b. Does the process appear to be in statistical control? Calculate descriptive statistics that may help you to determine the answer to this question. What evidence is there for your conclusion?

26. J. McWilliams Swim Club is trying to calibrate their chlorine pump to ensure that the right amount of chlorine (1.0–1.5 ppm of free chlorine) is mixed into the water. Thirty samples of 4 readings at random times during the week were taken. These data can be found in the worksheet *Prob. 8-26* in the *C08Data.xlsx* file.

a. Compute the mean and range of each sample, calculate control limits, and plot them on $\bar{x}$ and R control charts.

b. Does the process appear to be in statistical control? Calculate descriptive statistics that may help you to determine the answer to this question. What evidence is there for your conclusion?

27. Twenty-five samples of size 4 resulted in statistics of $\bar{\bar{x}} = 35.0$ minutes and $\bar{R} = 2.7$ minutes for the Turko Cleaning Company's average time to completely clean a rug. Compute control limits for $\bar{x}$ and R-charts and estimate the standard deviation of the process.

28. In testing the temperature in an analysis process in Hermitage DNA Labs, LLC, containing both positive and negative values, the data listed in the worksheet *Prob. 8-28* in the *C08Data.xlsx* file on the Student Companion Site for this chapter were obtained.

a. Compute the mean, standard deviation and other descriptive statistics for the data.

b. Construct $\bar{x}$ and R-charts for these data. Determine whether the process is in control. If not, eliminate any assignable causes and compute revised limits.

29. The data for 30 samples of three items each, from the study at Hawkeye Magnetronics (from *Prob. 8-24*, above), was further analyzed in an effort to use it for process control.

a. Compute the mean and range of each sample, calculate the control limits, and plot them on $\bar{x}$ and R control charts.

b. Does the process appear to be in statistical control? Why or why not?

30. The data in worksheet *Prob. 8-30* in the *C08Data.xlsx* file represent processing time values for 40 samples of size 4 that were taken from Rapid Check Kiters, Inc.'s check processing firm over a 20-hour period.

a. Compute the mean and standard deviation of all 40 samples for the sample data.

b. Calculate the control limits and construct the $\bar{x}$ and R-charts, using the first 20 samples. Is the process under control at that point?

c. Specifications for the process are 1.065 ± 0.14. If the process is under control, calculate the capability indexes based on the first 20 samples. *Cpu, Cpl, Cp,* and *Cpk* using the part of the $\bar{x}$ and R-charts Excel template that calculates the process capability. What do the indexes indicate?

d. After calculating the control limits, the last 20 samples were collected. When plotted using the control limits calculated earlier, does the process appear to be in statistical control? Why or why not? What should be done if it is not under control?

31. For each of the following control charts, assume that the process has been operating in statistical control for some time. What conclusions should the operators reach at this point?

32. PCDrives has a manufacturing process that is normally distributed and has the sample means and ranges for 15 samples of size 5, found in the worksheet *Prob. 8-32* in the *C08Data.xlsx* file on the Student Companion Site for this chapter. Note that only sample statistics have been given, instead of the raw data from the samples. Determine process capability limits by estimating the standard deviation using formula 8.34. If specifications are determined to be 70 ± 25, what percentage will be out of specification?

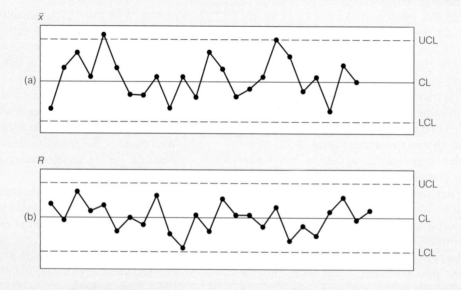

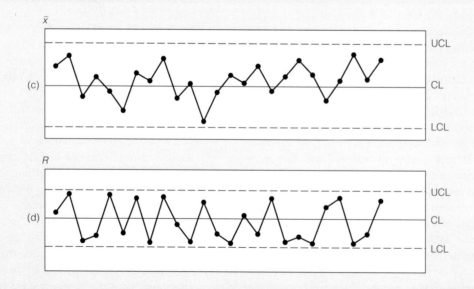

33. Constant Hope Hospital wants to set up a control chart for the time required to perform a critical step in gall bladder surgery. Use the data, consisting of 25 samples of size 4 found in the worksheet *Prob. 8-33* in the *C08Data.xlsx* file to construct $\bar{x}$- and *s*-charts. What conclusions do you reach concerning the state of the process? Is it under control? Why or why not?

34. Fujiyama Electronics needs to construct $\bar{x}$ and *s*-charts for circuit boards that are purchased from an outside supplier. A critical dimension is the distance between two holes on the board that are supposed to be 5 cm apart. Use the data, consisting of 30 samples of size 4 found in the worksheet *Prob. 8-34* in the *C08Data.xlsx* file. What conclusions do you reach concerning the state of the process? Is it under control? Why or why not?

35. El Toro Grande Restaurante advertises that customers will have their orders taken within three minutes after being seated. Management wants to monitor average times, as it is such an important guarantee for business. Construct $\bar{x}$ and *s*-charts for the data given in the worksheet *Prob. 8-35* in the *C08Data.xlsx* file on the Student Companion Site for this chapter.
    a. Compute the sample means and the average standard deviation, calculate the control limits, and plot them on control charts.
    b. Does the process appear to be in statistical control? Why or why not?
    c. Calculate the process capability statistics, using three minutes as the upper tolerance limit and zero as the lower tolerance limit. What recommendation would you make to management concerning the process, based on these findings?

36. An injection molding machine at the Moby Molding Co. used to make plastic bottles has four molding heads. The outside diameter of the bottle is an important measure of process performance. The table in the worksheet *Prob.8-36* in the *C08Data.xlsx* file shows the results of 30 samples in which the data are coded by subtracting the actual value from the nominal dimension. Construct $\bar{x}$ and *s*-charts charts and discuss the results.

37. Calculate the process capability statistics for the outside diameters of the bottles made on the injection molding machine at the Moby Molding Co. (from *Prob. 8-36*). Use 0.12 as the upper tolerance limit and −0.10 as the lower tolerance limit for this important measure of process performance. What recommendation would you make to management concerning the process, based on these findings?

38. Chief Henry Batter of the Gotham City Police Department is trying to reduce the time required to answer the phone at police headquarters (in fractions of a minute). The data in the worksheet for *Prob. 8-38* in the *C08Data.xlsx* file on the Student Companion Site for this chapter represent time in fractions of minutes for three individual readings taken at random for 25 days.
    a. Compute control limits for an *x*-chart (chart for individuals) using the statistic $\bar{R}/d2$, with a 3-period moving range, as an estimate of the standard deviation.
    b. Construct an *x*-chart for individuals, using the data. Interpret the results.

39. Charlie Plato owns Charlie's China Emporium, which sells inexpensive cups, dishes, and bric-a-brac in a seaside resort. She has three checkout stations, which she would like to test to see if they are under control and capable. She considers sales of $36.50 per hour, per station, to be a representative average. Consider the data for 75 individual results of sales dollars per hour, per unit, shown in the worksheet *Prob. 8-39* in the *C08Data.xlsx* file.
    a. Compute control limits for an *x*-chart (chart for individuals) using the statistic $\bar{R}/d2$ as an estimate of the standard deviation with a 3-period moving range.
    b. Construct an *x*-chart for individuals, using the data. Interpret the results.

40. Thirty samples of 75 items each were inspected at the Yummy Candy Company and 75 **items** were found to be defective. Compute control limits for a *p*-chart for this process.

41. Samples of packages orders were taken at the R.A. Treinta Package Co. to determine if the orders were prepared correctly. The percent defectives for each sample are given in the worksheet *Prob. 8-41* in the *C08Data.xlsx* file on the Student Companion Site for this chapter for 25 samples. Five hundred orders are inspected each day for each sample. Construct a *p*-chart and interpret the results.

42. One hundred insurance claim forms are inspected daily at Full Life Insurance Co. over 25 working days, and the number of forms with errors have been recorded in the worksheet *Prob. 8-42* in the

C08Data.xlsx file. Construct a *p*-chart. If any points occur outside the control limits, assume that assignable causes have been determined. Then construct a revised chart.

43. SpeedyNetService.com, an Internet service provider (ISP), is concerned that the level of access of customers is decreasing due to heavier use. The proportion of peak period time when a customer is likely to receive busy signals is considered a good measure of service level. The percentage of times a customer receives a busy signal during peak periods varies. Using a sampling process, the ISP set up control charts to monitor the service level, based on proportion of busy signals received. Construct the *p*-chart using on the sample data in the table in the worksheet *Prob.8-43* in the *C08Data.xlsx* file on the Student Companion Site for this chapter. What does the chart show? Is the service level good or bad, in your opinion?

44. Construct an *np*-chart using the data in *Prob.8-42*, the Full Life Insurance Co. What does the chart show?

45. Construct an *np*-chart using the data in *Prob. 8-45* in the *C08Data.xlsx* file on the Student Companion Site for this chapter from Delgado Manufacturing Co. What does the chart show?

46. Federal Scandex, Inc. uses a scanner on a conveyor line which scans 1,000 packages per hour. Packages which have defective labels or detectable damage to the package are automatically offloaded and hand-sorted by severity of defects, on a scale of 1-5. A minor defect is a 1, such as a single number missing from a zip code. A 3 would be a moderate defect, such as a missing addressee name or partially missing address. A 5 would be a critical defect, such as a severely damaged package or missing address label. Construct a *c*-chart for the 30 samples showing critical defects from the data

in the table in the worksheet *Prob. 8-46* in the *C08Data.xlsx* file and interpret the results.

47. FarmaSuitica, Inc., a mail-order prescription drug vendor, measured the number of defects per standard 200 line order being picked in their distribution center. Construct a *c*-chart for data in the table in the worksheet *Prob. 8-47* in the *C08Data.xlsx* file and interpret the results.

48. A quality consultant was asked to analyze the data from order errors at the Audubon Books, Inc., distribution center as shown in the table in the worksheet *Prob. 8-48* in the *C08Data.xlsx* file on the Student Companion Site for this chapter. The data represent a typical order processed in each month, and show the errors found in those orders. Any order can have errors due to a number of causes, e.g. wrong item, incorrect customer information, etc. Develop a run chart, a frequency histogram, and a *u*-chart for these data. What insights do you get from each chart? What would you advise the distribution center manager to do about the errors?

49. Top Billers processes bills for customers. Lately, they have been getting complaints of errors in the bills they have processed. Bills can contain errors due to a number of causes, such as incorrect amounts, wrong dates, wrong customer information, etc. The quality manager for Top Billers decides to sample one customer's batch of bills, per day, to determine the number and proportion of errors. Use the *u*-chart to analyze the data found in the table in the worksheet *Prob. 8-49* in the *C08Data.xlsx* file.

50. Determine, using Figure 8.50, the appropriate sample size for detecting:
    a. A 1-sigma shift in the mean with a 0.80 probability.
    b. A 2-sigma shift with 0.95 probability
    c. A 2.5-sigma shift with 0.90 probability

CASES

CONTROL OF TFE'S AT HALLENVALE HOSPITAL

The Joint Commission Accreditation of Health Care Organizations (JCAHO) monitors and evaluates health care providers according to strict standards and guidelines. Improvement in the quality of care is a principal concern. Hospitals are required to identify and monitor important quality indicators that affect

TABLE 8.8   Monthly Data on Infections After Surgery

Month	Surgeries	Infections	Percent	Month	Surgeries	Infections	Percent
1	208	1	0.48	19	187	1	0.53
2	225	3	1.33	20	252	2	0.79
3	201	3	1.49	21	201	1	0.50
4	236	1	0.42	22	226	0	0.00
5	220	3	1.36	23	222	2	0.90
6	244	1	0.41	24	212	2	0.94
7	247	1	0.40	25	219	1	0.46
8	245	1	0.41	26	223	2	0.90
9	250	1	0.40	27	191	1	0.52
10	227	0	0.00	28	222	0	0.00
11	234	2	0.85	29	231	3	1.30
12	227	4	1.76	30	239	1	0.42
13	213	2	0.94	31	217	2	0.92
14	212	1	0.47	32	241	1	0.41
15	193	2	1.04	33	220	3	1.36
16	182	0	0.00	34	278	1	0.36
17	240	1	0.71	35	255	3	1.18
18	230	1	0.43	36	225	1	0.44
					8,095	55	

patient care and establish "thresholds for evaluation" (TFEs), which are levels at which special investigation of problems should occur. TFEs provide a means of focusing attention on nonrandom errors (that is, special causes of variation). A logical way to set TFEs is through control charts.

Suppose that Hallenvale Hospital collects monthly data on the number of infections after surgeries. These data are shown in Table 8.8. Hospital administrators are concerned about whether the high percentages of infections (such as 1.76 percent in month 12) are caused by factors other than randomness.

Questions for Discussion

1. Using the data in Table 8.8, what is the average percentage of infections?
2. Construct an appropriate control chart, compute the upper and lower control limits, plot the data on a control chart, and determine if the process is in statistical control. Based on your analysis, what action, if any, should management take?
3. What TFE should management use to monitor future data?

MORELIA MORTGAGE COMPANY

The Morelia Mortgage Company (MMC) is a medium-sized mortgage lender that has continued to do well, despite the "meltdown" in the mortgage lending industry. Prior to the economic downturn, MMC was a principal supplier of lending services to Southwestern Desert Homes, a builder of residential communities in several major cities throughout the southwestern United States. Because it carefully selected clients who were able to make substantial down-payments for homes, and it avoided sub-prime or variable-rate mortgage lending, MMC has been shielded from the effects of "toxic mortgages" on its balance sheet. In fact, MMC expanded its mortgage refinancing and home remodeling credit operations to two shifts, as other lending company's ability to take on new clients contracted. Soon, they were working six days per week and hiring additional workers.

Not long after MMC began its second shift operations, it received some complaints about long mortgage processing times. This information alarmed Pete Purnell, CEO of Morelia Mortgage. He had retired early from a bank in a cold Midwestern city and decided that he wanted to relocate to the desert Southwest. He had hiked in the mountains and played golf during the first six months, but then realized that he needed more of a challenge than the recreational activities could provide. That was when he started Morelia Mortgage, using his experience in the mortgage and home loan business. MMC, under Pete's leadership, soon built a reputation as a high-quality, if somewhat conservative, lender. Among other things, the company was known for the capability of its well-trained and dedicated employees, who could generally complete the loan process in around 2–3 workdays. Thus, Pete never felt the need to consider formal process control approaches. Now many customers were complaining that it took a week or two to close on a loan, even with an excellent credit score. In view of the recent complaints, Pete suspected that the rapid expansion to a full two-shift operation, the pressures to produce higher volumes, and the push to meet requests from high-profit customers was causing a breakdown in their quality.

On the recommendation of the V.P. for loan processing, Pete hired a quality consultant to train the process managers and certain loan workers in statistical process control methods. As a trial project, one process manager wanted to evaluate the capability of a critical operation that she suspects might be a major source of the delays. The nominal specification for this processing operation is 15.5 hours with a tolerance of 5 hours. Thus,

the upper and lower specifications are LSL = 10.5 hours and USL = 20.5 hours. The consultant suggested inspecting five consecutive processing times, per loan worker, in the middle of each shift over a 15-day period and recording the completion times for loans that they had finished processing. The table in the worksheet *Morella Mortgage Case* in the workbook *C08CaseData* (available on the Student Companion Site), shows 15 days' data collected for each shift, by loan worker.

Assignment

1. Interpret the data in the *MMC Case* worksheet in the Excel workbook *C08CaseData* (available on the Student Companion Site), establish a state of statistical control, and evaluate the capability of the process to meet specifications. Consider the following questions: What do the initial control charts tell you? Do any out-of-control conditions exist? If the process is not in control, what might be the likely causes, based on the information that is available? What is the process capability? What do the process capability indexes tell the company? Is MMC facing a serious problem that it needs to address? How might the company eliminate the problems of slow loan processing?

2. The process manager who initiated the trial project implemented the recommendations that resulted from the initial study. Because of her success in using control charts, MMC made a decision to continue using them on that process. After establishing control, one additional sample was taken over the next 20 shifts, shown in second part of the table in the *MMC Case* worksheet. Evaluate whether the process remains in control, and suggest any actions that should be taken. Consider the following issues: Does any evidence suggest that the process has changed relative to the established control limits? If any out-of-control patterns are suspected, what might be the cause? What should the company investigate?

MONTVALLEY SHORT-HAUL LINES, INC.

Montvalley Short-Haul Lines, Inc. (MSL), is a small independently-owned narrow-gauge railway in Montana. It supplies contract transportation services to

many mining firms, hauling ore and mining equipment. One of its principal customers, Cranford Consolidated Products (CCP), is actively improving quality by using the Malcolm Baldrige Criteria. In an effort to improve supplier quality, Cranford mandated, last year, that all suppliers provide factual evidence of quality improvement efforts that lead to highly capable processes.

As part of its supplier development program, CCP held a seminar for all its suppliers to outline this initiative and provide initial assistance. The executive officers of MSL participated in this seminar and recognized that MSL was seriously lacking in its quality improvement efforts. More importantly, Jeff Blaine, who was the purchasing manager at CCP, told them privately that many errors had been found in MSL's shipping documents. CCP would not continue to tolerate this high number of errors; and if no improvements were made, it would seek transportation services elsewhere.

Rob Langford, president and CEO of MSL, was concerned. During an off-site meeting, he and other MSL executives developed a comprehensive blueprint to help MSL develop a total quality focus. One of the key objectives was to establish an SPC effort to gain control of key customer-focused processes and establish priorities for improvement.

The Billing Study After Process Improvement

In a good-faith attempt to respond to CCP's feedback, MSL turned its attention to its billing input errors and worked on them over the following six months. To gain some understanding of the situation, MSL conducted an initial (base case) study by sampling 20 bills of lading, each day, over a 20-day period. Initial results were dismal, with defective bills averaging a horrible 60 percent!

After process improvement and an intensive effort to train shipping clerks not to make errors, the company was ready to make another study to determine what progress had been made. The first set of tables in the *Montvalley Case-Initial* worksheet in the Excel workbook *C08CaseData* on the Student Companion Site shows the results of the initial study. The worksheet *Montvalley Case-Revised* shows the results of the second study, after improvements were made. Both studies revealed that field employees were correcting the errors as they found them. In both cases, rework was costing the company almost $2 per error, but the number of errors had been substantially reduced between the two studies. However, field employees still were not always catching the errors, which led to field service and other problems.

Discussion Questions

1. At this point, MSL is unsure of how to interpret these results. You have been hired as a consultant by the executive committee to analyze these data and provide additional recommendations for integrating SPC concepts into MSL's quality system. Using the results from the base case data, determine the performance, that is, the process capability, in a qualitative and quantitative sense, of the billing input. What is the average rate of defective bills? Is the process in control? What error rates might the company expect in the future? What general conclusions do you reach?

2. Perform the same statistical analysis with the second set of data. How do the results differ? What is the average rate of defective bills? Is the process in control? What error rates might the company expect in the future? What general conclusions do you reach?

The Billing Study, Part II

The revelations from the initial study had been startling. The results from the second study were encouraging, but not yet where the company wanted to be. Rob Montvalley personally led a group problem-solving session to address the root causes of the current error rate. During this session, the group members constructed a cause-and-effect diagram to help determine the causes of incorrect bills of lading.

Eight categories of causes were identified:

1. Incomplete shipper name or address
2. Incomplete consignee name or address
3. Missing container type
4. Incomplete description of freight
5. Weight not shown on bill of lading
6. Improper destination code
7. Incomplete loader's signature information
8. Inaccurate piece count

Using Deming's plan-do-study-act process, the group at Montvalley designed a plan to examine all bills of lading over a 25-day period and count the number of errors in each of these categories. They repeated the study six months later to determine what progress, if any, had been made in error reduction. The second table in the *Montvalley Case-Initial* worksheet and the second table in the worksheet *Montvalley Case-Revised* show the data for the distribution of billing errors for these studies. Rob thought that the *p*-chart developed in the first study and reapplied to the second study provided significant information about the process; however, he was curious to find out whether another method could tell them more about the nature of the defects they were encountering.

Discussion Questions (cont.)

3. After developing *p*-charts for the first and second studies, you decide to analyze the data to determine whether the system is in control by constructing another appropriate control chart (other than a *p*-chart) that could better tell you about the nature of the defects. You also decide that it would be wise to construct a Pareto diagram to gain additional insight into the problem, and suggest recommendations to reduce billing errors.

4. Complete your analysis by using the three charts from each of the two studies to advise Rob and his managers at Montvalley on the next steps. How do the results differ from the first to the second study? Is the process in control? What error categories have improved? Which ones might the company need to work on immediately in order to bring about further improvements? What general conclusions do you reach?

SKYHIGH AIRLINES

Skyhigh Airlines is a small regional airline that was started by Tex Weston in West Texas in the 1980s. Tex was the first regional airline CEO to come up with the idea of developing a strategic partnership with a major carrier, which provided stability and a guaranteed market. In turn, Skyhigh developed a reputation for high reliability, on-time arrivals and departures, and safety.

Like all domestic air carriers, Skyhigh's fleet must be certified by the Federal Aviation Agency (FAA), in order to fly domestic airline routes. Required avionic systems are on board all their airplanes, which must be inspected periodically, according to FAA regulations. An avionic system normally includes several electronic "boxes" containing components essential to safe navigation of the aircraft. Some of these boxes are located in the cockpit, whereas other parts of the system are located in the tail of the plane, with cables connecting the components. There are five components in the avionic system on the typical airplane in Skyhigh's fleet.

A critical avionics maintenance procedure at Skyhigh Airlines requires the assignment of five workers on each avionics crew for a full eight hours per day. All crew members are cross-trained and can work on any tasks necessary to complete the procedure. There are five tasks (A through E) that must be carried out

sequentially, in order to complete the procedure. Each task requires five labor hours to complete.

Because of tight spaces in the aircraft, only three people can work on task A at the same time, while the remaining two are idle; four people can work on task B, with one idle; all five people can work on task C at the same time; two people can work on task D, with three idle; and four people can work on task E, with one idle.

Assignment

Address the questions below, and after doing so, state the general conclusions you can reach, and what advice would you give to management in a brief report.

1. Because each task requires five person hours to complete, determine how much elapsed time will it take to complete the entire procedure, considering that work on the next task cannot begin until work on the previous task is completed?

2. What percent of time will be productive and what percent will be wasted on each task?

3. What is the rolled throughput yield (RTY) of the procedure?

4. If a tool could be developed which would allow all five workers to work on task D at the same time, how would that effect the RTY of the procedure?

NOTES

1. Noriaki Kano, "A Perspective on Quality Activities in American Firms," *California Management Review*, Spring 1993, 12–31.

2. Steven Prevette, "Applying Quality Methods Improves Safety at Nuclear Cleanup Site," *Quality Progress*, May 2010.

3. Adapted from K. M. Casarreal, J. I. Mills, and M. A. Plant, "Improving Service Through Patient Surveys in a Multihospital Organization," *Hospital & Health Services Administration*, Health Administration Press, Ann Arbor, MI (March/April 1986), 41–52. © 1986, Foundation of the American College of Health Care Executives.

4. Glenn E. Hayes and Harry G. Romig, *Modern Quality Control* (Encino, CA: Benziger, Bruce & Glencoe, Inc., 1977).

5. Frank M. Gryna, "Quality Costs," in *Juran's Quality Control Handbook*, 4th ed. (New York: McGraw-Hill, 1988).

6. Douglas H. Harris and Frederick B. Chaney, *Human Factors in Quality Assurance* (New York: John Wiley & Sons, Inc., 1969).

7. Statement made by Belinda Collins before the House Subcommittee on Technology, Committee on Science, June 29, 1995.

8. Jay Bucher, *The Quality Calibration Handbook*, ASQ Quality Press, 2007.

9. Jennifer Pollock, "Built to Last, and Last ..." *Fast Company*, May 2006, 83–84.

10. This section is adopted from NIST Calibration Services, available at http://www.nist.gov.

11. Jack Anderson, "The Future of Metrology," *Quality Digest*, January 31, 2008.

12. ASQC Automotive Division Statistical Process Control Manual (Milwaukee, WI: American Society for Quality Control, 1986).

13. Donald J. Wheeler, "Problems with Gauge R&R Studies," *Quality Digest*, January 13, 2011. http://www .qualitydigest.com/inside/quality-insider-column/problems -gauge-rr-studies.html.

14. Robert W. Hoyer and Wayne C. Ellis, "A Graphical Exploration of SPC, Part 1," *Quality Progress* 29, no. 5 (May 1996), 65–73.

15. Mark L. Crossley, "Size Matters. How Good Is Your C_{pk}, Really?" *Quality Digest*, May 2000, 71–72.

16. Paul F. McCoy, "Using Performance Indexes to Monitor Production Processes," *Quality Progress* 24, no. 2 (February 1991), 49–55; see also Fred A. Spring, "The Cpm Index," *Quality Progress* 24, no. 2 (February 1991), 57–61.

17. Helmut Schneider, James Pruett, and Cliff Lagrange, "Uses of Process Capability Indices in the Supplier Certification Process," *Quality Engineering* 8, no. 2 (1995–1996), 225–235.

18. See Robert W. Traver, "Pre-Control: A Good Alternative to x-R-Charts," *Quality Progress* 18, no. 9 (September 1985) for a more thorough discussion of pre-control.

19. This discussion is adapted from James R. Evans, *Statistical Process Control for Quality Improvement: A Training Guide to Learning SPC* (Englewood Cliffs, NJ: Prentice Hall, 1991). Reprinted with permission of Prentice Hall, Upper Saddle River, NJ.

20. H. F. Dodge and M. N. Torrey, "A Check Inspection and Demerit Weighting Plan," *Industrial Quality Control* 13, no. 1 (July 1956), 5–12.

21. John E. West, "Do You Know Your SPC?" *Quality Digest*, July 2001, 51–56.

22. D. C. Montgomery, "The Economic Design of Control Charts: A Review and Literature Survey," *Journal of Quality Technology* 12, no. 2 (1980), 75–87.

23. Raymond R. Mayer, "Selecting Control Limits," *Quality Progress* 16, no. 9 (1983), 24–26.

24. Adapted from LeRoy A. Franklin and Samar N. Mukherjee, "An SPC Case Study on Stabilizing Syringe Lengths," *Quality Engineering* 12, no. 1 (1999–2000), 65–71. Reprinted from Quality Engineering, courtesy of Marcel Dekker, Inc.

Process Improvement and Six Sigma

When former Cincinnati City Manager Valerie Lemmie started her job, she asked building inspectors whether the city had a "one-stop shop" for building permits. They said, "Sure. You stop here once, you stop there once, and you stop there once." What she found out was that a permit stops 473 times on its way from the initial application to the printer! After spending a week at City Hall and taking notes on every step of the process, a consultant hired to analyze the Department of Buildings and Inspections ended up with about 30 feet of flowcharts that depicted the building permit process. Although Ms. Lemmie conceded that improvement wouldn't be easy, an assistant noted that a lot of people wanted to know how they could do their jobs better. "They know everything that's wrong with it probably more than anyone else. And more than anyone else, they need to be part of the solution."[1]

Many years ago, Juran defined **breakthrough** as the accomplishment of any improvement that takes an organization to unprecedented levels of performance. Breakthrough attacks chronic losses or, in Deming's terminology, common causes of variation. Improving processes takes a lot of work, as organizations such as Iredell-Statesville Schools and Caterpillar Financial Services (see the Quality Profiles) certainly understand. Having the right tools is important and can make the task considerably easier. We introduced basic concepts of process improvement in Chapter 5. However, the focus in that chapter was on the philosophy of improvement in the broader context of process management. In this chapter, we focus on process improvement methodologies and tools, and how they provide the foundations for modern Six Sigma approaches.

quality**profiles**

Iredell-Statesville Schools and Caterpillar Financial Services Corporation

Iredell-Statesville Schools (I-SS) is a K–12 public school system located in southwestern North Carolina within a diverse community and economy. With a new vision to "improve student learning by igniting a passion for learning," I-SS senior leaders have moved the district from a "focus on teaching" to a "focus on learning." The Superintendent of Schools and the Senior Leadership Team use the I-SS Performance Excellence Model as the management approach to share and accomplish the district's vision. In the classroom, five key learning questions form the basis for action by focusing discussion and analysis on what students should know and be able to do:

1. "What do students need to know?"
2. "How will they learn it?"
3. "How will we know they have learned it?"
4. "What will we do if they have not learned it?" and
5. "What will we do if they already know it?"

When student performance does not meet targets, the gap is addressed through the systematic use of a Plan, Do, Study, Act (PDSA) cycle to identify and implement improvements. PDSA is also used throughout the school district in operational and support areas as well. Best practices are shared throughout the district, departments, and schools.

The system's results illustrate the impact of its focused efforts to improve student achievement. For example, I-SS has achieved 94 percent of its Adequate Yearly Progress goals and outperforms peer districts and the state in this No Child Left Behind measure.

The End-of-Grade (EOG) Reading Composite improved from 75 percent of students proficient to 90.6 percent proficiency in just six years. Also, I-SS closed the EOG reading proficiency gap between African-American children and all students from 23 percent to 12.3 percent. Cohort graduation rates (the percentage of ninth-grade students who graduate from high school four years later) increased steadily from 64 percent to 80.7 percent. Perhaps most impressive is the fact that although its per-pupil operations expenditures are among the lowest in North Carolina, I-SS ranked academically in the state's top 10 school systems.

With total U.S. assets exceeding $14 billion and managing more than 100,000 contracts monthly, Caterpillar Financial Services Corporation U.S. (CFSC) is the second-largest captive-equipment lender in the United States. With a U.S. workforce of nearly 750 employees, CFSC has more than $1 billion in revenues as the financial services business unit within Caterpillar Inc. True to its mission of "helping Caterpillar and our customers succeed through financial service excellence," CFSC maintains a constant focus on process improvement. Tools such as Six Sigma, help CFSC prioritize and manage projects, design products, and improve processes. Ninety-seven percent of employees are trained in Six Sigma procedures for designing new processes, called DMEDI (Define, Measure, Explore, Develop, Implement), and for improving existing ones, called DMAIC (Define, Measure, Analyze, Improve, Control). The teams that implement these procedures are comprised of specially trained employees called Black Belts, experts in the Six Sigma process and team facilitation; Green Belts, subject matter experts; and Yellow Belts, trained in basics of Six Sigma.

Handling over 100,000 contracts monthly and working with customers and equipment dealers who demand accurate, timely, complete, and responsive service have led CFSC to invest in leading-edge information-management systems and hardware. Investments in technology along with a continuing focus on excellence and process improvements are helping CFSC achieve its corporate vision: "to be a significant reason why customers select Caterpillar worldwide." Seventy-nine percent of customers considering the purchase of Cat equipment say that CFSC products and services favorably influenced their decision. Research also verified that CFSC exceeded customers' expectations twice as often as competitors. Satisfaction levels of performance exceed industry and ACSI (American Customer Satisfaction Index) world-class benchmarks. CFSC received a Baldrige Award in 2003.

Source: Malcolm Baldrige National Quality Award Winners' Profiles, U.S. Department of Commerce, National Institute of Standards and Technology.

PROCESS IMPROVEMENT METHODOLOGIES

Process improvement depends on the ability to effectively identify problems, develop good solutions, and implement them. A systematic, fact-based problem-solving approach is vital to accomplishing this. A structured problem-solving approach provides all employees with a common language and a set of tools to communicate with each other, particularly as members of cross-functional teams. It also ensures that solutions are developed objectively, rather than based on opinions or rash judgments.

Numerous methodologies for improvement have been proposed over the years, and different organizations use different approaches. Although each methodology is distinctive in its own right, they share many common themes:[2]

1. *Redefining and Analyzing the Problem:* Collect and organize information, analyze the data and underlying assumptions, and reexamine the problem for new perspectives, with the goal of achieving a workable problem definition.
2. *Generating Ideas:* "Brainstorm" to develop potential solutions.
3. *Evaluating and Selecting Ideas:* Determine whether the ideas have merit and will achieve the problem solver's goal.
4. *Implementing Ideas:* Sell the solution and gain acceptance by those who must use them.

We will review some of the more prominent approaches here.

The Deming Cycle

The **Deming cycle** is a simple adaptation of the scientific method for process improvement. In 1939, Walter Shewhart first introduced this as a three-step process of *specification, production,* and *inspection* for mass production that "constitute a dynamic scientific process of acquiring knowledge."[3] These steps correspond to the scientific method of hypothesizing, carrying out an experiment, and testing the hypothesis. Shewhart depicted this process graphically as a circle to convey the importance of continual improvement. Deming modified his idea and presented it during his seminars in Japan in 1950. The "Deming wheel" consisted of:

1. Design the product with appropriate tests.
2. Make the product and test in the production line and in the laboratory.
3. Sell the product.
4. Test the product in service and through market research. Find out what users think about it and why nonusers have not bought it.

Japanese executives adapted this into the PDCA cycle—*Plan* (design the product), *Do* (ensure that production makes the product as designed), *Check* (check sales/complaints and confirm whether the customer is satisfied), *Act* (use feedback to incorporate improvements in the next phase of planning). This became known as the *Deming cycle*; Deming reintroduced this during his management seminars in the 1980s and changed "Check" to "Study," calling it the PDSA cycle, which is illustrated in Figure 9.1. However, some organizations still use PDCA. For example, Mercy Health Systems, a 2007 Baldrige recipient, uses the Deming cycle as its process management framework as shown in Figure 9.2.

FIGURE 9.1
The Deming Cycle

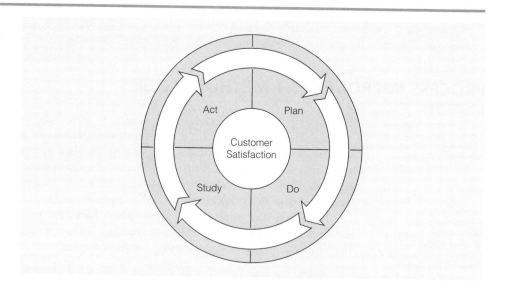

FIGURE 9.2
Mercy Health System Application of the Deming Cycle

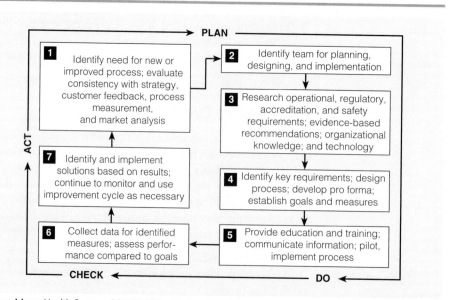

Source: Mercy Health Systems 2007 Baldrige National Quality Award application Summary. Reprinted with permission.

Over the years, PDSA evolved into a more general process for both short-term continuous improvement and long-term organizational learning, well beyond its original focus on product design, based on contributions and writings by several quality practitioners.[4] The fundamental premise of PDSA is that improvement comes from the application of knowledge.[5] This knowledge may be knowledge of engineering, management, or how a process operates that can make a job easier, more accurate, faster, less costly, safer, or better meet customer needs. Three fundamental questions to consider are:

- What are we trying to accomplish?
- What changes can we make that will result in improvement?
- How will we know that a change is an improvement?

Through a process of learning, knowledge is developed. From this perspective, many organizations use the Deming cycle as the basis for their organizational performance improvement activities.

PDSA provides a basic framework for developing, testing, and implementing changes to any process that will lead to improvement. The Plan stage consists of studying the current situation and describing the process (its inputs, outputs, customers, and suppliers); understanding customer expectations; gathering data; identifying problems; testing theories of causes; and developing solutions and action plans. In the Do stage, the plan is implemented on a trial basis, such as in a laboratory, pilot production process, or with a small group of customers, to evaluate a proposed solution and provide objective data. Data from the experiment are collected and documented. The Study stage determines whether the trial plan is working correctly by evaluating the results, recording the learning, and determining whether any further issues or opportunities need be addressed. Often, the first solution must be modified or scrapped. New solutions are proposed and evaluated by returning to the Do stage. In the last stage, Act, the improvements become standardized and the final plan is implemented as a "current best practice" and communicated throughout the organization. This process then leads back to the Plan stage for identification of other improvement opportunities. Table 9.1 summarizes the steps in the Deming Cycle in more detail.

The following example demonstrates how the Deming cycle can be applied in practice.

EXAMPLE 9.1   Applying the Deming Cycle

The co-owners of a diner decided to do something about the long lines that occurred every day in their place of business.[6] After discussions with their employees, several important facts came to light:

- Customers waited in line for up to 15 minutes.
- Usually, tables were available.
- Many of their customers were regulars.
- People taking orders and preparing food were getting in each other's way.

To measure the improvement that might result from any change they made, they decided to collect data on the number of customers in line, the number of empty tables, and the time until a customer received the food ordered.

In the Plan stage, the owners wanted to test a few changes. They decided on three changes:

1. Provide a way for customers to fax their orders in ahead of time (rent a fax machine for one month).

TABLE 9.1 Detailed Steps in the Deming Cycle

Plan

1. Define the process: its start, end, and what it does.
2. Describe the process: list the key tasks performed and sequence of steps, people involved, equipment used, environmental conditions, work methods, and materials used.
3. Describe the players: external and internal customers and suppliers, and process operators.
4. Define customer expectations: what the customer wants, when, and where, for both external and internal customers.
5. Determine what historical data are available on process performance, or what data need to be collected to better understand the process.
6. Describe the perceived problems associated with the process; for instance, failure to meet customer expectations, excessive variation, long cycle times, and so on.
7. Identify the primary causes of the problems and their impacts on process performance.
8. Develop potential changes or solutions to the process, and evaluate how these changes or solutions will address the primary causes.
9. Select the most promising solution(s).

Do

1. Conduct a pilot study or experiment to test the impact of the potential solution(s).
2. Identify measures to understand how any changes or solutions are successful in addressing the perceived problems.

Study

1. Examine the results of the pilot study or experiment.
2. Determine whether process performance has improved.
3. Identify further experimentation that may be necessary.

Act

1. Select the best change or solution.
2. Develop an implementation plan: what needs to be done, who should be involved, and when the plan should be accomplished.
3. Standardize the solution, for example, by writing new standard operating procedures.
4. Establish a process to monitor and control process performance.

Source: Adapted from *Small Business Guidebook to Quality Management*, Office of the Secretary of Defense, Quality Management Office, Washington, DC. Copyright © 1998.

2. Construct a preparation table in the kitchen with ample room for fax orders.
3. Devote one of their two cash registers to handling fax orders.

Both the length of the line and the number of empty tables were measured every 15 minutes during the lunch hour by one of the owners. In addition, when the 15-minute line check was done, the last person in line was noted, and the time until that person got served was measured.

In the Do phase, the owners observed the results of the three measures for three weeks. In the study phase, they detected several improvements. Time in line went down from 15 minutes to an average of 5 minutes. The line length was cut to a peak average of 12 people, and the number of empty tables decreased slightly. In the Act phase, the owners held a meeting with all employees to discuss the results. They decided to purchase a fax machine, prepare phone orders in the kitchen with the fax orders, and use both cash registers to handle walk-up and fax orders.

Creative Problem Solving

Solving quality problems often involves a high amount of creativity. **Creativity** is seeing things in new or novel ways. In the Toyota production system, which has become the benchmark for world-class efficiency, a key concept is *soikufu*—creative thinking or inventive ideas, which means capitalizing on worker suggestions. The chairman of Toyota once observed, "One of the features of Japanese workers is that they use their brains as well as their hands. Our workers provide 1.5 million suggestions a year, and 95 percent of them are put to practical use. There is an almost tangible concern for improvement in the air at Toyota."[7] Many creativity tools are designed to help you change the context in which you view a problem or opportunity, thereby leading to fresh perspectives.

While many creative ideas seemingly come at moments of inspiration, systematic approaches can refine your thinking and help prepare for those moments. An effective problem-solving process that can easily be adapted to quality improvement stems from creative problem-solving (CPS) concepts pioneered by Alex Osborn and refined by Sidney Parnes.[8]

This strategy consists of the following steps:

- Understanding the "mess"
- Finding facts
- Identifying specific problems
- Generating ideas
- Developing solutions
- Implementing solutions

The CPS literature provides many tools and approaches to facilitate each of these steps and develop more creative results.

Custom Improvement Methodologies

Numerous variations of the Deming Cycle and creative problem-solving process exist. For example, an approach used by some hospitals and the U.S. Coast Guard is known by the acronym FADE: *focus, analyze, develop,* and *execute.* In the Focus stage, a team selects the problem to be addressed and defines it, characterizing the current state of the process, why change is needed, what the desired result should be, and the benefits of achieving that result. In the Analyze stage, the team works to describe the process in detail, determine what data and information are needed, and develop a list of root causes for the problem. The Develop stage focuses on creating a solution and implementation plan along with documentation to explain and justify recommendations to management who must allocate the resources. Finally, in the Execute stage, the solution is implemented and a monitoring plan is established.

Process-improvement methodologies are often aligned with the unique organizational culture of many organizations. For example, Park Place Lexus, the first automobile dealership to receive the Baldrige Award, uses a process known as DRIVE—*Define* the problem, *Recognize* the cause, *Identify* the solution, *Verify* the actions, and *Evaluate* the results. Clearly this acronym has meaning for the organization and is easy for employees to remember.

Some organizations embed the Deming cycle within a broader framework. An example from a health care organization is shown in Figure 9.3. The left side of the figure incorporates the essential elements of CPS. Once a solution is proposed, the Deming

FIGURE 9.3
Incorporating the
Deming Cycle in a
Process Improve-
ment Model

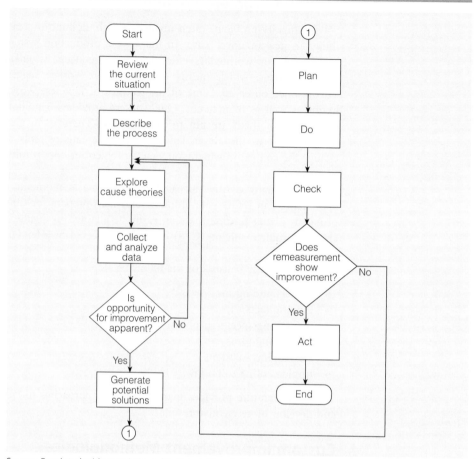

Source: Reprinted with permission of Bethesda Hospital, Inc., 619 Oak Street, Cincinnati, OH 45241.

cycle is then used to test and evaluate the solution prior to implementation. Not every approach is appropriate for all organizations; one must be chosen or designed to fit the organization's culture and people.

DMAIC

Perhaps the most widely-known process improvement methodology is DMAIC—*define, measure, analyze, improve,* and *control.* DMAIC is the process improvement approach used in Six Sigma, which we will discuss shortly. The following example shows how DMAIC was used at American Express to improve the number of customers who received renewal cards.[9] (In this example, data have been masked to protect confidentiality.)

- *Define and Measure:* On average in one year, American Express received 1,000 returned renewal cards each month. Of these renewals, 65 percent are due to the fact that the card members changed their addresses and did not tell the company. The U.S. Post Office calls these forwardable addresses. Amex does not currently notify a card member when they receive a returned plastic card.
- *Analyze:* Analysis of the data noted significant differences in the causes of returned plastics between product types. Optima, the revolving card product, had the highest

incidence of defects, but was not significantly different from other card types in the percentage of defects. Renewals had by far the highest defect rate among the three areas of replacement, renewal, and new accounts. After additional testing, returns with forwardable addresses were overwhelmingly the largest percentage and quantity of returns.

- *Improve*: An experimental pilot study was run on all renewal files issued, comparing records against the National Change of Address database. As a result, they were able to reduce the dpmo rate by 44.5 percent, from 13,500 to 6,036 defects per million opportunities. This action enabled over 1,200 card members who would not have automatically received their credit cards to receive them, increasing revenue and customer satisfaction.
- *Control*: Amex began tracking the proportion of returns over time as a means of monitoring the new process to ensure that it remains in control.

As you can see, DMAIC is not that much different from the other process improvement approaches we have discussed, and bears a close resemblance to the creative problem-solving process. Because of the popularity of Six Sigma and the fact that many organizations train their workforce to use DMAIC, we will use it as the basic framework for further discussion of process improvement tools and techniques. To understand DMAIC better, we introduce the Six Sigma philosophy next.

SIX SIGMA

Six Sigma has garnered a significant amount of attention and credibility because of its acceptance at such major firms as Allied Signal (now part of Honeywell) and General Electric. **Six Sigma** can be described as a business improvement approach that seeks to find and eliminate causes of defects and errors in manufacturing and service processes by focusing on outputs that are critical to customers and a clear financial return for the organization. The term **six sigma** is based on a statistical measure that equates to 3.4 or fewer errors or defects per million opportunities (dpmo) (this calculation was explained in Chapter 8). An ultimate stretch goal of all organizations that adopt a Six Sigma philosophy is to have all critical processes, regardless of functional area, at a six-sigma level of capability.

> *In this book we use "six sigma" to refer to the statistical measure and "Six Sigma" to refer to the management philosophy.*

Evolution of Six Sigma

Motorola pioneered the concept of Six Sigma as an approach to measuring product and service quality. The late Bill Smith, a reliability engineer at Motorola, is credited with originating the concept during the mid-1980s and selling it to Motorola's CEO, Robert Galvin. Smith noted that system failure rates were substantially higher than predicted by final product test, and suggested several causes, including higher system complexity that resulted in more opportunities for failure, and a fundamental flaw in traditional quality thinking. He concluded that a much higher level of internal quality was required and convinced Galvin of its importance.[10] As a result, Motorola set the following goal in 1987:

> *Improve product and services quality ten times by 1989, and at least one hundred fold by 1991. Achieve six-sigma capability by 1992. With a deep sense of urgency, spread dedication to quality to every facet of the corporation, and achieve a culture of continual improvement to assure total customer satisfaction. There is only one ultimate goal: zero defects—in everything we do.*

While Motorola initiated the concept, the efforts by General Electric, driven by former CEO Jack Welch, brought significant media attention to the concept and made Six Sigma a popular approach to quality improvement. In the mid-1990s, as quality emerged as a concern within GE, Welch invited Larry Bossidy, then CEO of Allied Signal who had phenomenal success with Six Sigma, to talk about it at a Corporate Executive Council meeting. The meeting caught the attention of GE managers and as Welch stated, "I went nuts about Six Sigma and launched it," calling it the most ambitious task the company had ever taken on.[11] To ensure success, GE changed its incentive compensation plan so that 60 percent of the bonus was based on financials and 40 percent on Six Sigma, and provided stock option grants to employees in Six Sigma training. In their first year, they trained 30,000 employees at a cost of $200 million and got back about $150 million in savings. From 1996 to 1997, GE increased the number of Six Sigma projects from 3,000 to 6,000 and achieved $320 million in productivity gains and profits. By 1998, the company had generated $750 million in Six Sigma savings over and above their investment, and would receive $1.5 billion in savings the next year.

GE had many early success stories. GE Capital, for example, fielded about 300,000 calls each year from mortgage customers who had to use voice mail or call back 24 percent of the time because employees were busy or unavailable. A Six Sigma team analyzed one branch that had a near perfect percentage of answered calls and applied their learning of their best practices to the other 41 branches, resulting in a 99.9 percent chance of customers getting a representative on the first try. A team at GE Plastics improved the quality of a product used in CD-ROMs and audio CDs from a 3.8 sigma level to 5.7 level and captured a significant amount of new business from Sony.[12] GE credits Six Sigma with a 10-fold increase in the life of CT scanner X-ray tubes, a 400 percent improvement in return on investment in its industrial diamond business, a 62 percent reduction in turnaround time at railcar repair shops, and $400 million in savings in its plastics business.[13]

After many years of implementation, Six Sigma became a vital part of GE's company culture. In fact, as GE continues to acquire new companies, integrating Six Sigma into different business cultures is a significant challenge. Six Sigma is a priority in acquisitions and is addressed early in the acquisition process. One of the key learnings GE discovered was that Six Sigma is not only for engineers. Welch observed the following:[14]

- Plant managers can use Six Sigma to reduce waste, improve product consistency, solve equipment problems, or create capacity.
- Human resource managers need it to reduce the cycle time for hiring employees.
- Regional sales managers can use it to improve forecast reliability, pricing strategies, or pricing variation.
- For that matter, plumbers, car mechanics, and gardeners can use it to better understand their customers' needs and tailor their service offerings to meet customers' wants.

Many other organizations such as Texas Instruments, Allied Signal (which merged with Honeywell), Boeing, 3M, Home Depot, Caterpillar, IBM, Xerox, Citibank, Raytheon, and the U.S. Air Force Air Combat Command have embraced Six Sigma and also report significant results. Between 1995 and the first quarter of 1997, Allied Signal reported cost savings exceeding $800 million from its Six Sigma initiative. Citibank groups reduced internal callbacks by 80 percent, credit processing time by 50 percent, and cycle times of processing statements from 28 days to 15 days.[15] Six Sigma has been applied in product development, new business acquisition, customer service, accounting, and many other business functions.

Principles of Six Sigma

Six Sigma began as a manufacturing focus to reduce defect levels to only a few parts per million. It evolved into a formal business strategy designed to accelerate improvements in every facet of an organization.[16] Six Sigma incorporates many traditional statistical methods and quality improvement and control tools that have found widespread application over the last century. However, the way it is practiced represents a significant departure from the "total quality management" practices of the 1970s and 1980s. The core philosophy of Six Sigma is based on the following concepts:[17]

1. Think in terms of key business processes and customer requirements with a clear focus on overall strategic objectives.
2. Focus on corporate sponsors responsible for championing projects, support team activities, help to overcome resistance to change, and obtain resources.
3. Emphasize such quantifiable measures as dpmo that can be applied to all parts of an organization: manufacturing, engineering, administrative, software, and so on.
4. Ensure that appropriate metrics are identified early in the process and that they focus on business results, thereby providing incentives and accountability.
5. Provide extensive training followed by project team deployment to improve profitability, reduce non-value-added activities, and achieve cycle time reduction.
6. Create highly qualified process improvement experts ("Green Belts," "Black Belts," and "Master Black Belts") who can apply improvement tools and lead teams.
7. Set stretch objectives for improvement.

As such, Six Sigma is quite different from the older TQM philosophy. Some of the contrasting features between TQM and Six Sigma include:

- TQM is based largely on worker empowerment and teams; Six Sigma is owned by business leader champions.
- TQM activities generally occur within a function, process, or individual workplace; Six Sigma projects are truly cross-functional.
- TQM training is generally limited to simple improvement tools and concepts; Six Sigma focuses on a more rigorous and advanced set of statistical methods and DMAIC methodology.
- TQM is focused on improvement with little financial accountability; Six Sigma requires a verifiable return on investment and focus on the bottom line.

In many ways, Six Sigma is the realization of many fundamental concepts of TQM, notably, the integration of human and process elements of improvement.[18] Human issues include management leadership, a sense of urgency, focus on results and customers, team processes, and culture change; process issues include the use of process management techniques, analysis of variation and statistical methods, a disciplined problem-solving approach, and management by fact. In addition, Six Sigma has elevated the importance of statistics and statistical thinking in quality improvement. Six Sigma's focus on measurable bottom-line results, a disciplined statistical approach to problem solving, rapid project completion, and organizational infrastructure makes it a powerful approach for improvement.

The Statistical Basis of 3.4 DPMO

As we noted earlier, six sigma represents a quality level of at most 3.4 defects per million opportunities, or 3.4 dpmo. Figure 9.4 explains the theoretical basis for this measure in

FIGURE 9.4

Theoretical Basis for
Six Sigma

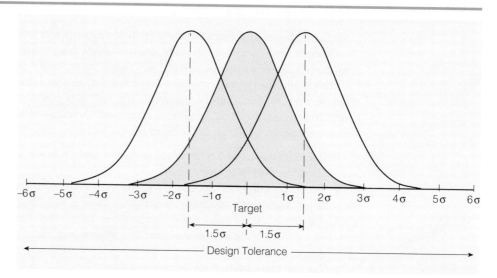

the context of traditional manufacturing specifications. The shaded distribution represents the natural variation of the process output. It is assumed to be normally distributed
and centered on the nominal (target) specification. Recall that nearly 100 percent of the
area under a normal distribution is within three standard deviations on either side of the
mean. We also assume that the design tolerance has a 12-standard deviation spread so
that the process capability index for the shaded distribution is $C_p = 2.0$, which represents
excellent capability.

Field failure data analyzed by Motorola discovered that Motorola's processes drifted
by an average of 1.5 standard deviations under normal control (the nonshaded distributions in Figure 9.4). As we noted in Chapter 8, many common statistical process control
plans use sample sizes that only allow detection of shifts of about two standard deviations. Thus, it would not be unusual for a process to drift this much and not be noticed.
The allowance of a shift in the distribution is important, because no process can be
maintained in perfect control. If we calculate the tail area of one of the shifted curves
beyond the specification limit (which is six standard deviations from the target—the
basis for the name "six sigma"), we obtain 0.0000034, or 3.4 parts per million. Thus, a
"six-sigma quality level" corresponds to a process variation equal to half of the design
tolerance while allowing the mean to shift as much as 1.5 standard deviations from the
target. In a similar fashion we could define "three-sigma quality," "four-sigma quality,"
and so on.

The easiest way to understand this is to think of the distance from the target to the
upper or lower specification (half the tolerance), measured in terms of standard deviations of the inherent variation, as the sigma level. A k-sigma quality level satisfies the
equation:

$$k \times \text{process standard deviation} = \text{tolerance range}/2 \tag{9.1}$$

In Figure 9.4, the process standard deviation is σ and the tolerance range is 12σ. Thus,
using Equation (9.1), we have

$$k \times \sigma = 12\sigma/2$$

Thus, $k = 6$ is the calculated sigma level.

| EXAMPLE 9.2 | ### Calculating the Sigma Level |

Suppose that the specification limits for some process are LSL = 0.02 and USL = 0.10, with the nominal specification being 0.06. Find the sigma level if the process standard deviation is 0.01. Using equation (9.1):

$$k \times 0.01 = (0.10 - 0.02)/2$$

or

$$k = 0.04/0.01 = 4$$

Therefore, this process operates at a 4-sigma level as long as it remains centered in the tolerance range (on 0.06) and the process mean does not drift by more than $1.5(0.01) = 0.015$.

The following Excel function can be used to calculate dpmo corresponding to the sigma level:

$$=(1-\text{NORM.DIST}(\textit{sigma level}, 1.5, 1, \text{TRUE})) * 1000000 \tag{9.2}$$

| EXAMPLE 9.3 | ### Calculating DPMO for a Sigma Level |

To verify the calculation of a six-sigma quality level using formula (9.2), we would find

$$=(1-\text{NORM.DIST}(6, 1.5, 1, \text{TRUE})) * 1000000 = 3.4 \text{ dpmo}$$

In Example 9.2, a four-sigma quality level corresponds to a dpmo value of

$$=(1-\text{NORM.DIST}(4, 1.5, 1, \text{TRUE})) * 1000000 = 6210 \text{ dpmo}$$

Using formula (9.2) we could tabulate dpmo for various sigma levels as shown in Table 9.2. You may use this table to estimate the value of dpmo for a given sigma level, or to estimate the sigma level for a given dpmo.

We may also compute the exact sigma level for a given value of dpmo using the following Excel function:

$$=\text{NORM.S.INV}(1 - \text{dpmo}/1000000) + 1.5 \tag{9.3}$$

TABLE 9.2
Tabulation of
dpmo for Different
Sigma Levels

Sigma Level	dpmo
3.0	66807.2
3.5	22750.1
4.0	6209.7
4.5	1349.9
5.0	232.6
5.5	31.7
6.0	3.4

EXAMPLE 9.4	Calculating the Sigma Level for DPMO

In Example 8.6 in Chapter 8, we calculated epmo for shipping orders as 35,256. Using Formula (9.3), =NORM.S.INV(1−35256/1000000) + 1.5, we find that this process is operating at a sigma level of 3.31.

The difference between a four- and six-sigma quality level can be surprising. Put in practical terms, if your cellular phone system operated at a four-sigma level, you would be without service for more than four hours each month, whereas at six sigma, it would only be about 9 seconds a month; a four-sigma process would result in one nonconforming package for every three truckloads, whereas a six-sigma process would have only one nonconforming package in more than 5,000 truckloads. And, if you play 100 rounds of golf each year, you would only miss one putt every 163 years at a six-sigma level!

All processes need not operate at a six-sigma level.[19] The appropriate level should depend on the strategic importance of the process and the cost of improvement relative to the benefit. It is generally easy to move from a two- or three-sigma level to a four-sigma level, but moving beyond that requires much more effort. As Table 9.2 shows, a change from three to four sigma represents about a 10-fold improvement in dpmo; from four to five sigma, a 30-fold improvement; and from five to six sigma, a 70-fold improvement—difficult challenges for any organization!

Although originally developed for manufacturing in the context of tolerance-based specifications, the Six Sigma concept has been operationalized to any process and has come to signify a generic quality level of at most 3.4 dpmo. At Motorola, for example, Six Sigma became part of the common language of all employees. To them, it means near perfection, even if they do not understand the statistical details. (Some tell their coworkers, "Have a six-sigma weekend!") Since stating its goal, Motorola has made great strides in meeting this goal, achieving six-sigma capability in many processes and 4- or 5-sigma levels in most others. Even in those departments that have reached the goal, Motorola employees continue their improvement efforts in order to reach the ultimate goal of zero defects.

IMPLEMENTING SIX SIGMA

The first step in using Six Sigma is to select an appropriate problem; however, not every problem can be addressed using Six Sigma methodology. According to Kepner and Tregoe, a **problem** is a deviation between what should be happening and what actually is happening that is important enough to make someone think the deviation ought to be corrected.[20] Research using more than a thousand applicable published cases suggests that virtually every instance of quality problem-solving falls into one of five categories:[21]

1. *Conformance problems*, which are characterized by unsatisfactory performance that causes customer dissatisfaction, such as high levels of defects, service failures, or customer complaints. The processes that create these results are typically well-specified and can be easily described.
2. *Efficiency problems*, which are characterized by unsatisfactory performance that causes dissatisfaction from the standpoint of noncustomer stakeholders, such as managers of financial or supply chain functions. Typical examples are high cost, excessive inventory, low productivity, and other process inefficiencies.
3. *Unstructured performance problems*, which are characterized by unsatisfactory performance by processes that are not well-specified or understood. For example, a

company might discover that employee turnover is much higher than desired or employee satisfaction is low. The factors that contribute to such results do not stem from processes that can easily be described.

4. *Product design problems*, which involve designing new products or redesigning existing products to better satisfy customer needs.

5. *Process design problems*, which involve designing new processes or substantially revising existing processes. These might include new factory processes to manufacture a new product line or designing a more flexible assembly line.

Each of these categories of problems requires different approaches and methodologies. Six Sigma methods are most applicable to conformance problems because the processes that create the problems can be easily identified, measured, analyzed, and changed. For efficiency problems, lean tools, which we discuss later in this chapter, are generally used. Unstructured performance problems require more creative approaches to solving them. For product design problems, special tools and methods are available, which we discussed in Chapter 7. Process design problems may require a combination of many of these approaches.

Project Management and Organization

Projects are the vehicles that are used to organize and to implement Six Sigma. Although projects are set up as temporary organization structures, their flexibility allows cross-functional teams to complete significant work in minimum time, if well managed. One of the challenges of implementing Six Sigma projects is to coordinate them with normal work activities. Some slack time, as well as physical and financial resources, must be allocated to project teams in order for them to achieve their objectives. Team members and project leaders cannot be expected to carry a full load of routine work and still participate fully and effectively on Six Sigma project teams.

Projects fail for a variety of reasons, including not adhering to schedules, poor planning, and "scope creep" when the nature of the project gradually loses its focus and becomes unwieldy, mismatching of skills, and insufficient knowledge transfer.[22] Being able to manage a large portfolio of projects, as would be found in Six Sigma environments, is vital to organizational success. The Project Management Body of Knowledge (PMBOK),[23] developed by the Project Management Institute, defines 69 tools that every project manager should master. Achieving professional certification in project management can significantly assist Six Sigma efforts.

Teams are vital to Six Sigma projects because of the interdisciplinary nature of such projects. Six Sigma projects require a diversity of skills that range from technical analysis, creative solution development, and implementation. Thus, Six Sigma teams not only address immediate problems, but also provide an environment for individual learning, management development, and career advancement. Six Sigma teams are comprised of several types of individuals:

- *Champions:* Senior-level managers who promote and lead the deployment of Six Sigma in a significant area of the business. Champions understand the philosophy of Six Sigma, select projects, set objectives, allocate resources, and select and mentor teams. Champions own Six Sigma projects and are responsible for their completion and results; typically they also own the process that the project is focused on improving. More importantly, champions work toward removing barriers—organizational, financial, personal—that might inhibit the successful implementation of a Six Sigma project.

- *Master Black Belts:* Full-time Six Sigma experts who are responsible for Six Sigma strategy, training, mentoring, deployment, and results. Master Black Belts are highly trained in how to use Six Sigma tools and methods and provide advanced technical expertise. They work across the organization to develop and coach teams, conduct training, and lead change, but are typically not members of Six Sigma project teams.

- *Black Belts:* Fully-trained Six Sigma experts with extensive technical training who perform much of the technical analysis required in Six Sigma projects, usually on a full-time basis. They have advanced knowledge of tools and DMAIC methods, and often act as project team leaders. They also mentor and develop Green Belts. Thus, Black Belts need good leadership and communication skills. As such, Black Belts are often targeted by the organization as future business leaders.

- *Green Belts:* Functional employees who are trained in introductory Six Sigma tools and methodology and work on projects on a part-time basis, assisting Black Belts while developing their own knowledge and expertise. Typically, one of the requirements for receiving a Green Belt designation is to successfully complete a Six Sigma project. Successful Green Belts are often promoted to Black Belts.

- *Team Members:* Individuals from various functional areas who support specific projects.

Green, Black, and Master Black Belts require a significant amount of training. Large companies such as Motorola, General Electric, and Johnson & Johnson train and certify their own employees at these levels. Professional and consulting organizations, such as the American Society for Quality and iSixSigma, also offer training and professional certification in Six Sigma at different belt levels. There is no universal body of knowledge or certification process recognized by all.

 QUALITYSPOTLIGHT

Bridgestone Americas, Inc.

Nashville-based Bridgestone Americas, Inc. was formed when Firestone Tire and Rubber Company was purchased by Bridgestone Corporation, a Japanese tire manufacturer, in 1988. Its main line of products is tires for automobiles, trucks, and other vehicles. Employees selected for the Belt program typically have high potential and are expected to move up in the company, have the ability to successfully complete appropriate Six Sigma training, and are expected to become Six Sigma champions when they move up in the organization. All belts are expected to integrate Six Sigma responsibilities into their everyday work. Bridgestone designed their own Black Belt training, consisting of a blend of online computerized group and individual work and traditional face-to-face classroom learning. Green Belt training also uses a blended learning model. They receive online training with content that is appropriate for Green Belts, with additional classroom training conducted on-site by the full-time company Black Belts.[24]

More than any other type of organizational structure, the Six Sigma team structure depends on cooperation, communication, and clarity. Experts suggest that 60 percent of failures of Six Sigma teams are due to failures in the "mechanics" of team operations, as opposed to poor project selection or improper use of tools.[25] Contributing factors include lack of application of meeting skills, improper use of agendas, failure to determine team member roles and responsibilities, lack of setting and keeping ground rules, and lack of appropriate facilitative behaviors. Many of these issues were discussed in Chapter 4.

Selecting Six Sigma Projects

There are two ways for an organization to generate Six Sigma projects: top-down and bottom-up.[26] Top-down projects generally are tied to business strategy and are aligned with customer needs. Their major weakness is that they are often too broad in scope to be completed in a timely manner. In addition, top managers may underestimate the cost and overestimate the capabilities of the team or teams to which the project is assigned. In a bottom-up approach, Black Belts (or Master Black Belts) choose the projects that are well-suited to the capabilities of teams. However, a major drawback of this approach is that the projects may not be tied closely to strategic concerns of top management, thus receiving little support and low recognition from the top. Perhaps the best way to ensure success is for executive champions, who understand the impact of projects from a strategic perspective, to work closely with the technical experts in choosing the most relevant projects that fit within the capabilities of Six Sigma teams.

A Six Sigma project might span an entire division or be as narrow as a single production operation. Factors that should be considered when selecting Six Sigma projects include the following:

- Financial return, as measured by costs associated with quality and process performance, and impacts on revenues and market share
- Impacts on customers and organizational effectiveness
- Probability of success
- Impact on employees
- Fit to strategy and competitive advantage

Six Sigma projects are driven by expected financial returns. Reducing costs associated with poor quality, such as scrap, rework, excessive cycle times, delays, and lost customers often provide an obvious justification for pursuing a project. Both Juran and Crosby strongly advocated translating tangibles such as defects, scrap, and lost customers into dollars to justify quality improvement projects. Traditionally, measuring reductions in quality-related costs through cost of quality analysis (see Chapter 8) was the principal method of documenting the benefits of improvement initiatives. However, this approach only focused on internal benefits. Six Sigma has placed more attention on external benefits related to increases in revenues associated with improved quality and customer satisfaction. The foundation for the approach stems from the model shown in Chapter 1 (Figure 1.3) relating quality and profitability, which proposes that quality improvement leads to financial returns through improvements in customer satisfaction and loyalty.

Balancing quality costs against expected revenue gains has become known as **return on quality (ROQ)**. ROQ is based on four main principles:[27]

- *Quality is an investment.* Thus, it is not fundamentally different from investing in equipment or buildings.
- *Quality efforts must be made financially accountable.* Because businesses evaluate other investments in this way, quality efforts should be subject to the same types of financial justification.
- *It is possible to spend too much on quality.* Customers might not be willing to pay the premiums associated with higher levels of quality, or the process improvement benefits might not justify the expense.
- *Not all quality expenditures are equally valid.* An improvement in product design or customer response might be much more important from a strategic point of view than improving the capability of a minor process in the manufacturing plant.

Sophisticated statistical methods are often used to estimate these effects and the financial implications.

One of the pitfalls experienced in organizations new to Six Sigma is a lack of ability of senior managers to estimate what the resources they allocate (or fail to allocate) to Six Sigma projects will "buy" in the way of bottom-line returns. Thus, it becomes important to be able to differentiate between, and to estimate fairly accurately, the differences in resources required to bring a $250,000 project versus a $50,000 project to a successful conclusion. Six Sigma projects should lead to improved customer satisfaction and organizational performance. Such improvements can lead directly to higher sales or market share, thus providing financial justification for selecting a project.

Projects chosen should have a high likelihood of success. Considerable risk comes in choosing problems that can best be compared with "solving world hunger." At the outset of a Six Sigma initiative, it is beneficial to pick the "low-hanging fruit"—projects that are easy to accomplish, or even can be completed by a single individual in order to show early successes. This visible success helps to build momentum and support for future projects. Studies show that many projects are significantly over budget, behind schedule, or do not result in desired outcomes.[28] This is why effective project management is essential for success.

Six Sigma projects should fit within the capabilities of the people and teams that work on them. Many indirect benefits accrue. The training received as Green or Black Belts improves employee and organizational knowledge, and participating in Six Sigma projects improves team and leadership skills. Six Sigma can motivate employees to innovate and improve their work environment, and ultimately their satisfaction on the job and personal self-esteem. Many projects offer opportunities to reduce frustration with inadequate work processes or to provide increased value to customers; these types of projects are certainly important candidates for selection.

Finally, Six Sigma projects should support the organization's vision and competitive strategy. At GE, for example, business goals work their way down the organization, helping employees to distinguish between projects that will not have a significant effect on business performance and those that do.[29]

Of course, most organizations probably have more opportunities for Six Sigma projects than available resources to do them. In many cases, project selection is often political in nature. Senior executives who champion Six Sigma projects might exercise political influence to get their pet projects recognized and accepted. However, taking a more objective viewpoint is more effective. Prioritizing and selecting projects using some rational criteria can contribute to greater effectiveness. Project steering committees that include at least a portion of the organization's senior leadership often guide these decisions. This group can act as a filter for the voices of both the external and internal customers in evaluating and prioritizing projects. At Xerox, the management teams identify Six Sigma projects based on customer experience improvement opportunities, alignment of strategic plans, ability to close business gaps, and key areas for process improvement. Potential projects are assessed based on their potential business impact and estimated effort; projects with relatively high benefits compared to effort requirements are the ones selected.[30]

Simple scoring models may be used to evaluate and prioritize potential projects. An example of a project selection matrix is shown in Figure 9.5. The top box shows the customer importance ratings on a set of key *critical to quality* (CTQ) characteristics using the scale at the bottom left. The numbers in the main table are based on the scale on the bottom right, and are determined by the steering committee. By multiplying these rankings by the customer importance ratings, we can arrive at a total score in the right-hand column (*Project ranking metric*). The higher the number, the more the project affects customer issues. This process takes the guesswork and opinions out of the project selection process and focuses on the important issues to the customer and the organization.

FIGURE 9.5
Example of a
Project Selection
Matrix

Customer Issues	Missing parts ordered	Late delivery	Damaged orders	Wrong orders	More parts than ordered	On hold too long
Customer importance	8	5	7	10	3	3

Project	Project ranking based on correlation to customer issues						Project ranking metric
Order fill process flow optimization	5	8	3	3	5	0	146
Replenishment cycle time reduction project	5	8	5	0	0	0	115
Customer service feedback reporting	5	3	3	8	0	5	171
Delivery vendor certification	0	10	8	0	0	0	106
IT upgrade process integration	7	5	0	8	8	3	194

Customer importance	Relationship to customer importance		Project rank	Relationship to customer issue
0	Not important		0	No correlation
3	Slightly important		3	Very little correlation
5	Important		5	Some correlation
8	Very important		8	High correlation
10	Critical		10	Complete correlation

Source: Reprinted with permission from William Michael Kelly, "Three Steps to Project Selection," *Six Sigma Forum Magazine* 2, no. 1 (November 2002), 29–32. © 2002, American Society for Quality.
No further distribution allowed without permission.

USING THE DMAIC PROCESS

To use the DMAIC process, one needs the ability to think critically about the goals and objectives of the Six Sigma project, ask pertinent questions, and apply various tools and techniques.

DMAIC Tools and Techniques

Most of the tools used in DMAIC have been around for a long time. For example, both Deming and Juran promoted using statistics and simple visual tools in quality improvement activities. However, tools used for quality improvement rarely went beyond basic statistics and simple visual tools. Early practitioners of Six Sigma recognized the power of advanced statistical methods such as design of experiments and took them beyond the realm of engineering. Thomas Pyzdek, a noted quality consultant, states that more than 400 tools are now available in the "TQM Toolbox."[31] Table 9.3 shows a brief list of the more common tools used in each step of DMAIC. We have discussed many of these tools in previous chapters; as we work through the steps of DMAIC, we will introduce additional tools as necessary.

Seven of these tools—flowcharts, check sheets, histograms, Pareto diagrams, cause-and-effect diagrams, run charts, and control charts are known as the **Seven QC** (quality control) **Tools**, and they have been used for decades to support quality improvement efforts. They are simple so that workers at all levels can use them easily. More significantly, they are all *visual*, which makes them easy to understand and interpret the data or information they convey, and facilitate communication among team members.

> *Although we view process improvement tools and techniques from the perspective of Six Sigma, it is important to understand that they are simply a collection of methods that have been used successfully in all types of quality management and improvement initiatives, including early TQM efforts and ISO 9000 initiatives.*

Toyota created a unique tool, called the **A3 Report**, to succinctly consolidate and visualize information for identifying and solving quality problems.[32] They exploit simplicity and visualization to facilitate process improvement. A3 reports are printed on a single sheet of 11-inch by-17-inch paper and contain text, pictures, diagrams, and charts, designed to enrich and clarify the problem and data. The reports are divided into seven sections (see Figure 9.6), which roughly follow the flow of the DMAIC process:

1. *Theme*, which succinctly states the problem being addressed.
2. *Background*, which contains a description of all pertinent information needed to understand the scope of the problem.
3. *Current condition*, which deals with developing an understanding of the process using a value-stream map.
4. *Cause analysis*, which focuses on determining the cause of the problem.
5. *Target condition*, which specifies possible improvement ideas that could solve the problem.

TABLE 9.3 Common Six Sigma Tools Used in DMAIC		
Define:	**Measure:**	
Project charter	Run charts	
Cost of quality analysis	Check sheets	
Pareto analysis	Descriptive statistics	
High level process mapping	Measurement system evaluation	
	Process capability analysis	
Analyze:	Benchmarking	
Scatter diagrams		
Detailed process mapping	**Improve:**	
Statistical inference	Design of experiments	
Cause-and-effect diagrams	Mistake proofing	
Failure mode and effects analysis	Lean production	
Root cause analysis	Deming cycle	
	Seven management and planning tools	
Control:		
Control charts		
Standard operating procedures		

FIGURE 9.6   Structure of Toyota A3 Report

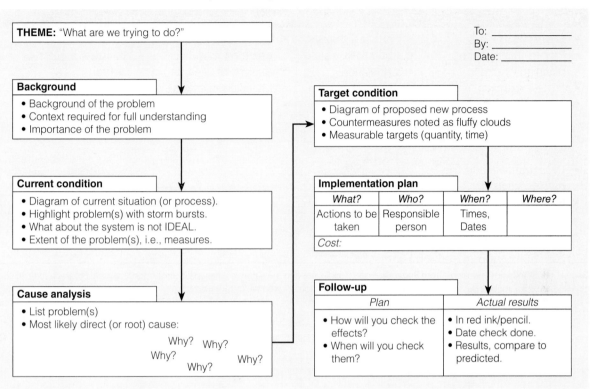

Source: http://www.coe.montana.edu/IE/faculty/sobek/a3/report.htm

6. *Implementation plan*, which identifies the steps that need to be accomplished in order to achieve the improvements.
7. *Follow-up*, which lists activities that will need to be completed after implementation along with the results of the implementation. It might also document obstacles encountered during implementation to provide a basis for learning.

These tools are integrated into standard Six Sigma curricula, which typically involve a blend of technical topics and project management and leadership topics. Table 9.4 shows a typical Six Sigma Black Belt training curriculum. The topics covered may be categorized into seven general groups:[33]

- *Elementary statistical tools* (basic statistics, statistical thinking, hypothesis testing, correlation, simple regression)
- *Advanced statistical tools* (design of experiments, analysis of variance, multiple regression)
- *Product design and reliability* (quality function deployment, failure mode, and effects analysis)
- *Measurement* (process capability, measurement systems analysis)
- *Process control* (control plans, statistical process control)
- *Process improvement* (process improvement planning, process mapping, mistake proofing)
- *Implementation and teamwork* (organizational effectiveness, team assessment, facilitation tools, team development)

TABLE 9.4   Six Sigma Black Belt Training

Week 1	Week 2	Week 3	Week 4
• Overview • Process improvement planning • Process mapping • Quality function deployment • Failure mode and effects analysis • Organizational effectiveness concepts • Basic statistics • Process capability • Measurement systems analysis	• Statistical thinking • Hypothesis testing • Correlation • Simple regression • Team assessment	• Design of experiments • Analysis of variance • Multiple regression • Facilitation tools	• Control plans • Statistical process control • Mistake-proofing • Team development

Source: Reprinted with permission from Roger W. Hoerl, "Six Sigma and the Future of the Quality Profession," *Quality Progress*, June 1998, 35–48. © 1998. American Society for Quality. No further distribution allowed without permission.

A more complete list of the "Six Sigma Body of Knowledge" can be found on the American Society for Quality's website, www.asq.org.

Define

After a Six Sigma project is selected, the first step is to clearly define the problem. This activity is significantly different from project selection. Project selection generally responds to symptoms of a problem and usually results in a rather vague problem statement. One must describe the problem in operational terms that facilitate further analysis. For example, a firm might have a history of poor reliability of electric motors it manufactures, resulting in a Six Sigma project to improve motor reliability. A preliminary investigation of warranty and field service repair data might suggest that the source of most problems was brush wear, and more specifically, suggest a problem with brush hardness variability. Thus, the problem might be defined as "reduce the variability of brush hardness." This process of drilling down to a more specific problem statement is sometimes called **project scoping**.

One useful tool to help identify the most important issue among a mess of symptoms is *Pareto analysis*. We used this concept in analyzing quality cost data in Chapter 8. Joseph Juran coined the term "the Pareto principle" and popularized it in 1950 after observing that a high proportion of quality issues resulted from only a few causes. He named this technique after Vilfredo Pareto (1848–1923), an Italian economist who determined that 85 percent of the wealth in Milan was owned by only 15 percent of the people. For instance, in analyzing costs in a paper mill, Juran found that 61 percent of total quality costs were attributable to one category—"broke," which is paper mill terminology for paper so defective that it is returned for reprocessing. In an analysis of 200 types of field failures of automotive engines, only five accounted for one-third of all failures; the top 25 accounted for two-thirds of the failures. In a textile mill, three of fifteen weavers were found to account for 74 percent of the defective cloth produced. Pareto analysis clearly separates the vital few from the trivial many and provides direction for selecting projects for improvement.

A **Pareto distribution** is one in which the characteristics observed are ordered from largest frequency to smallest. A **Pareto diagram** is a graphical description of a Pareto distribution. Figure 9.7 shows an example of a Pareto diagram that was used by a manufacturer of retaining rings and self-tightening hose clamps that was concerned about rising premium freight charges for shipping retaining rings.[34] The results were startling: The most frequent cause of higher freight charges was customer requests. The second largest contributor was the lack of available press machine time. These data helped to scope an improvement project to identify which customers consistently expedited their shipments and to work closely with them to find ways of reducing costs and improving the availability of press time.

Pareto diagrams help analysts to progressively focus in on the most appropriate problems. Figure 9.8 shows one example. At each step, the Pareto diagram stratifies the data to more detailed levels, eventually isolating the most significant issues.

Process mapping was introduced in Chapter 5, and is an important tool for DMAIC. In defining a problem, it is important to have a fundamental understanding of the process that drives the results. This is often done using a high-level process map called a **SIPOC diagram**. SIPOC stands for Suppliers-Inputs-Process-Outputs-Customers. SIPOC maps provide a broad overview of the key elements in the process and help to explain who is the process owner, how inputs are acquired, who the process serves, and how it adds value. Inputs are goods and services required by a process to generate its outputs. Outputs may be physical items, documentation, electronic information, and so on. Inputs are provided by suppliers, who may be external or internal to the organization (suppliers may also be customers, for example, in a product design process). Customers—the people, departments, or organizations that receive outputs— also can be external or internal to the organizations. Different outputs may have different customers. Figure 9.9 shows the general structure of a SIPOC diagram, and Figure 9.10 shows an example for a typical automobile manufacturing process.

FIGURE 9.7
Pareto Diagram of Customer Calls

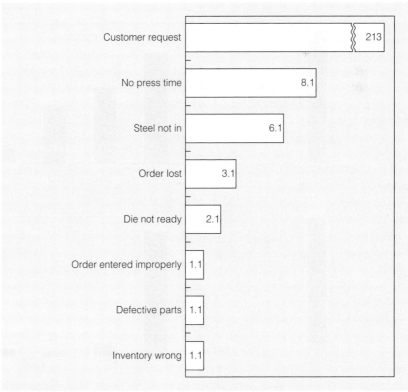

Source: Adapted from Bruce Rudin, "Simple Tools Solve Complex Problems." Reprinted with permission from Quality, April 1990, 50–51; a publication of Hitchcock Publishing, a Capital Cities/ABC, Inc.

FIGURE 9.8
Use of Pareto
Diagrams for
Progressive Analysis

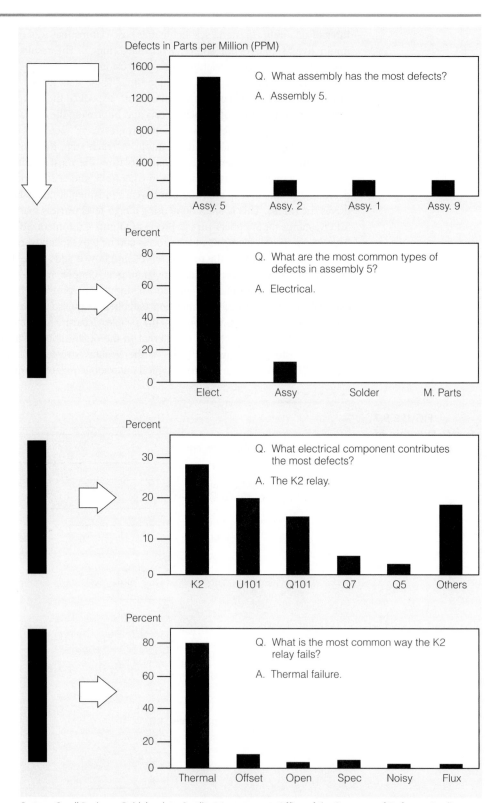

Source: *Small Business Guidebook to Quality Management*, Office of the Secretary of Defense, Quality Management Office, Washington, D.C.

FIGURE 9.9
General Structure of
a SIPOC Diagram

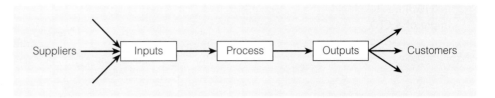

FIGURE 9.10
Example of a SIPOC
Diagram

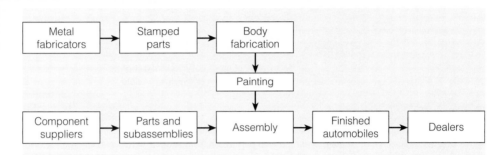

The Define phase should also address such project management issues as what will need to be done, by whom, and when. This is usually done in a formal project mission statement called a project charter. A **project charter** defines the project, its objectives, and deliverables, and represents a contract between the project team and the sponsor. A project charter will typically define the problem in a simple fashion, the project objective, the project team and sponsor, the customers and CTQs on which the project focuses, existing measures and performance benchmarks, expected benefits and financial justification, a project timeline, and the resources needed to carry out the project. Cost of quality analysis, which we discussed in Chapter 8, is often used to quantify the benefits of reducing defects or errors.

Measure

The measure phase of the DMAIC process focuses on understanding process performance and collecting the data necessary for analysis. Six Sigma uses the notion of a function in mathematics to portray the relationship between process performance and customer value: $Y = f(X)$, where Y is the set of CTQs and X represents the set of critical input variables that influence Y. For example, Y might represent the time to deliver bags from an airplane to baggage handling and the number of lost bags, X might include the number of baggage handlers, number of trucks, time they are dispatched, bar code scanning accuracy, and so on. Figure 9.11 shows a visual example of how one might "drill down" from Y to identify the critical X-factors; this structure is often called a **CTQ tree**. Understand these relationships also helps in defining the experiments that need to be conducted to confirm how input variables affect response variables. In addition, it sets the stage for the Control phase by defining those factors that requiring monitoring and control.

We discussed the foundations of measurement in Chapter 8. One must first ask some basic questions related to measurement:

- What questions are we trying to answer?
- What type of data will we need to answer the question?
- Where can we find the data?
- Who can provide the data?
- How can we collect the data with minimum effort and with minimum chance of error?

FIGURE 9.11

Example of a CTQ
Tree

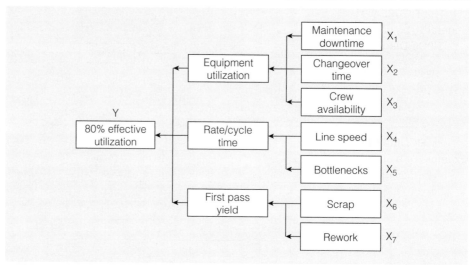

Source: Reprinted with permission from Thomas Bertels and George Patterson, "Selecting Six Sigma Projects that Matter," *Six Sigma Forum Magazine*, November 2003, pp. 13–15. Copyright © 2003 American Society for Quality. No further distribution allowed without permission.

It is also important to develop **operational definitions** for all performance measures that will be used. For example, what does it mean to have "on-time delivery"? Does it mean within one day of the promised time? One week? One hour? What is an error? Is it wrong information on an invoice, a typographical mistake, or either? Clearly, any data are meaningless unless they are well defined and understood without ambiguity.

The Juran Institute suggests 10 important considerations for data collection:

1. Formulate good questions that relate to the specific information needs of the project.
2. Use appropriate data analysis tools and be certain the necessary data are being collected.
3. Define comprehensive data collection points so that job flows suffer minimum interruption.
4. Select an unbiased collector who has the easiest and most immediate access to the relevant facts.
5. Understand the environment and make sure that data collectors have the proper experience.
6. Design simple data collection forms.
7. Prepare instructions for collecting the data.
8. Test the data collection forms and the instructions and make sure they are filled out properly.
9. Train the data collectors as to the purpose of the study, what the data will be used for, how to fill out the forms, and the importance of remaining unbiased.
10. Audit the data collection process and validate the results.[35]

These guidelines can greatly improve the process of uncovering relevant facts necessary to identify and solve problems.

Process capability analysis, along with basic statistical methods such as descriptive statistical measures, frequency distributions, and histograms, provide baseline measures to describe process performance. Benchmarking is often used to compare current performance to best-in-class performance to measure the potential for improvement. Measurement system analysis, which we discussed in Chapter 8, is vital to ensure that manufacturing-based data used in a Six Sigma project is valid and reliable.

Nearly any kind of form may be used to collect data. **Data sheets** use simple columnar or tabular forms to record data. However, to generate useful information from raw data, further processing generally is necessary. **Check sheets** are special types of data collection forms in which the results may be interpreted on the form directly without additional processing (see guideline #6 above). In manufacturing for example, check sheets similar to Figure 9.12 are designed to create a histogram of continuous measurements

FIGURE 9.12
Check Sheet for
Data Collection

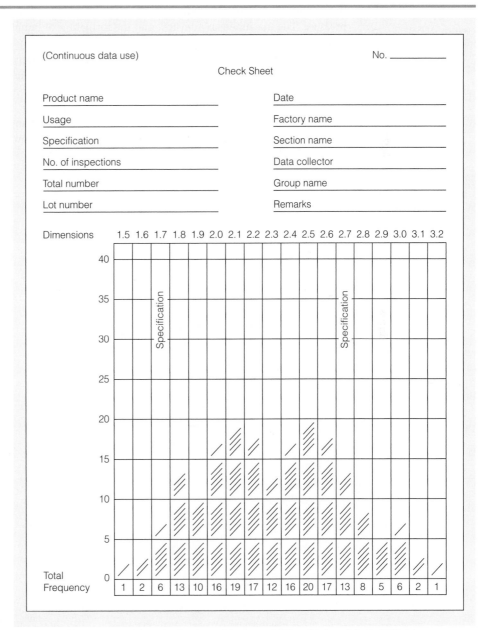

Source: K. Ishkawa ed., *Guide to Quality Control*, 2nd rev., 1982, p. 31 Copyright © 1982 Asian Productivity Organization, Tokyo. Reprinted by permission.

as they are collected. Such a check sheet can also include specification limits, making it easy to evaluate process capability and the percentage of nonconforming output.

A second type of check sheet for defective items is illustrated in Figure 9.13, which shows the type of defect and a tally in a resin production plant. Such a check sheet can be extended to include a time dimension so that data can be monitored and analyzed over time and trends and patterns, if any, can be detected.

Figure 9.14 shows an example of a defect location check sheet. Kaoru Ishikawa relates how this check sheet was used to eliminate bubbles in laminated automobile windshield glass.[36] The location and form of bubbles were indicated on the check sheet; most of the bubbles occurred on the right side. Upon investigation, workers discovered that the pressure applied in laminating was off balance—the right side was receiving less pressure. The machine was adjusted, and the formation of bubbles was eliminated almost completely.

Data such as production volume, cost, and customer satisfaction indexes are often plotted on a **run chart**, which displays the data over time. The vertical axis represents a measurement; the horizontal axis is the time scale. Run charts show how the data change over time; for example, if the average value of the measure is improving, staying the same, or getting worse, or if the variability in the data is changing. Run charts are also useful in the control stage of DMAIC to show the effects of process improvements.

FIGURE 9.13
Defective Item
Check Sheet

Check Sheet

Product:	Date:	
	Factory:	
Manufacturing stage: final insp.	Section:	
	Inspector's name:	
Type of defect: scar, incomplete, misshapen	Lot no.	
	Order no.	
Total no. inspected: 2530		

Remarks: all items inspected

Type	Check	Subtotal
Surface scars	//// //// //// //// //// //// //	32
Cracks	//// //// //// //// ///	23
Incomplete	//// //// //// //// //// //// //// //// //// ///	48
Misshapen	////	4
Others	//// ///	8
	Grand total	115
Total rejects	//// //// //// //// //// //// //// //// //// //// //// //// //// //// //// //// //// /	86

Source: K. Ishkawa ed., *Guide to Quality Control*, 2nd rev., 1982, p. 33. Copyright © 1982 Asian Productivity Organization, Tokyo. Reprinted by permission.

FIGURE 9.14
Defect Location
Check Sheet

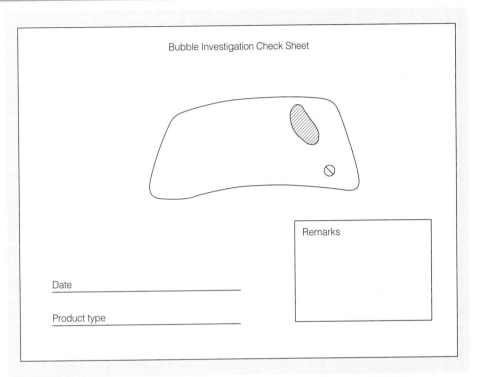

Source: K. Ishkawa ed., *Guide to Quality Control*, 2nd rev., 1982, p. 34. Copyright © 1982 Asian Productivity Organization, Tokyo. Reprinted by permission.

Analyze

A major flaw in many problem-solving approaches is a lack of emphasis on rigorous analysis. Too often, we want to jump to a solution without fully understanding the nature of the problem and identifying the source of the problem. Analyzing a problem starts with a fundamental understanding of the process; this is typically accomplished through detailed process mapping, expanding on the SIPOC diagram that is developed in the Define phase. Figure 9.15 shows a portion of a detailed process map for the marketing and sales department that was developed by a team in the Timber and Wood Products Division of Boise Cascade (now Boise) to improve a customer claims processing and tracking system that affected all areas and customers in its six divisions. The marketing and sales portion of the flowchart alone consisted of up to 20 separate tasks and seven decisions, which sometimes took months to complete. The team discovered that more than 70 steps were performed for each claim, most of which added no value to the settlement outcome. Their analysis helped them eliminate 70 percent of the steps for small claims in the original flowchart, as shown in Figure 9.16.

A special type of process map is a **value stream map**. The value stream refers to all activities involved in designing, producing, and delivering goods and services to customers. These activities include the flow of materials throughout the supply chain, transformation activities in the manufacturing or service delivery process, and the flow of information needed to support these activities. A value stream map shows the process flows in a manner similar to an ordinary process map; however, the difference lies in that value stream maps highlight value-added versus

FIGURE 9.15 Original Flowchart from the Marketing and Sales Department

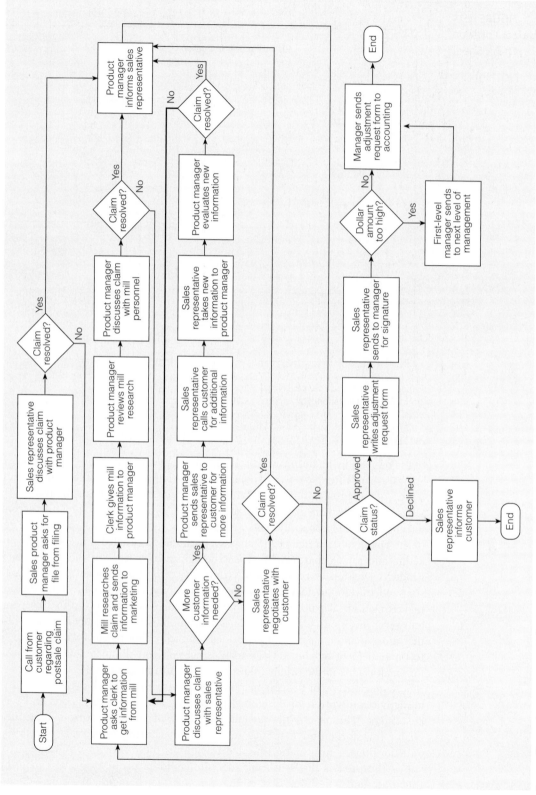

Source: Process Improvement at Boise Casade. Reprinted with permission.

FIGURE 9.16   New Small Adjustment Request Form Process Flowchart for Marketing and Sales
Department

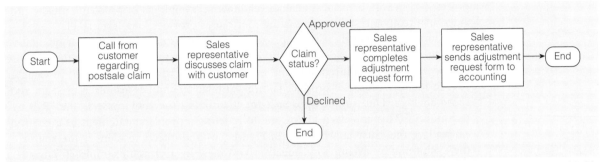

Source: Reprinted with permission from Lakshmi U. Tatikonda, "A Less Costly Billing Process," *Quality Progress*, January 2008, pp. 31–39.
Copyright © 2008 American Society for Quality. No further distribution allowed without permission.

non-value-added activities, and include times that activities take. This aspect allows
one to measure the impact of value-added and non-value-added activities on the
total lead time of the process, and compare this to the **takt time**—which is the ratio
of the available work time to the required production volume necessary to meet customer demand. If the value stream is faster than the takt time, it generally means that
waste in the form of overproduction is occurring; when it is less, the firm cannot
meet customer demand. Value stream maps might also include other information
such as machine uptime and reliability, process capacity, and size of batches moving
through the process. All this information provides a more factual basis for identifying
improvements in the Improve phase of DMAIC. Value stream maps are an important
tool in lean thinking that we discuss later in this chapter.

The Analyze phase of DMAIC focuses on *why* defects, errors, or excessive variation
occur, which often result from one or more of the following:

- A lack of knowledge about how a process works, which is particularly critical if dif-
  ferent people perform the process. Such lack of knowledge results in inconsistency
  and increased variation in outputs.
- A lack of knowledge about how a process *should* work, including understanding cus-
  tomer expectations and the goal of the process
- A lack of control of materials and equipment used in a process
- Inadvertent errors in performing work
- Waste and complexity, which manifest themselves in many ways, such as unneces-
  sary steps in a process and excess inventories
- Hasty design and production of parts and assemblies; poor design specifications;
  inadequate testing of incoming materials and prototypes
- Failure to understand the capability of a process to meet specifications
- Lack of training
- Poor instrument calibration and testing
- Inadequate environmental characteristics such as light, temperature, and noise

A quality problem can occur for a variety of reasons, such as materials, machines,
methods, people, and measurement. The goal of problem solving is to identify the fundamental causes of problems in order to correct them—the root causes. NCR Corporation

defines **root cause** as "that condition (or interrelated set of conditions) having allowed or caused a defect to occur, which once corrected properly, permanently prevents recurrence of the defect in the same, or subsequent, product or service generated by the process."[37] As with a medical analogy, eliminating symptoms of problems usually provides only temporary relief; eliminating root causes provides long-term relief.

Root cause analysis is an approach using statistical, quantitative, or qualitative tools to identify and understand the root cause. You might recall that the purpose of DFMEA (design failure mode and effects analysis), which we discussed in Chapter 7, is to identify causes of product failures. Similar techniques are often used for root cause analysis. One simple approach for identifying the root cause is the "5 Why" technique.[38] This approach forces one to redefine a problem statement as a chain of causes (see the cause analysis box in Figure 9.6) and effects to identify the source of the symptoms by asking why, ideally five times. In a classic example at Toyota, a machine failed because a fuse blew. Replacing the fuse would have been the obvious solution; however, this action would have only addressed the symptom of the real problem. Why did the fuse blow? Because the bearing did not have adequate lubrication. Why? Because the lubrication pump was not working properly. Why? Because the pump axle was worn. Why? Because sludge seeped into the pump axle, which was the root cause. Toyota attached a strainer to the lubricating pump to eliminate the sludge, thus correcting the problem of the machine failure.

A **cause-and-effect diagram** is a simple graphical method for presenting a chain of causes and effects and for sorting out causes and organizing relationships between variables. Cause-and-effect diagrams are useful in assisting teams to generate ideas for problem causes and, in turn, serves as a basis for identify solutions. Kaoru Ishikawa introduced the cause-and-effect diagram in Japan, so it is also called an Ishikawa diagram. The general structure of a cause-and-effect diagram is shown in Figure 9.17; because of its structure, it is also called a fishbone diagram. At the end of the horizontal line, a problem is listed. Each branch pointing into the main stem represents a possible cause. Branches pointing to the causes are contributors to those causes.

Cause-and-effect diagrams are constructed in a brainstorming type of atmosphere. Everyone can get involved and feel they are an important part of the problem-solving

FIGURE 9.17
General Structure of
Cause-and-Effect
Diagram

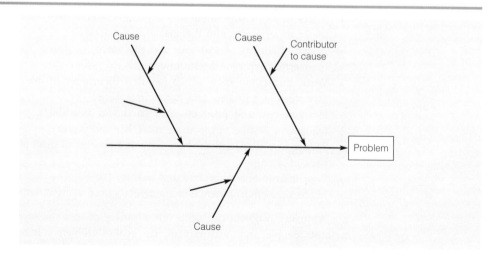

process. Usually small groups drawn from operations or management work with a trained and experienced facilitator. The facilitator guides attention to discussion of the problem and its causes, not opinions. As a group technique, the cause-and-effect method requires significant interaction between group members. The facilitator who listens carefully to the participants can capture the important ideas. A group can often be more effective by thinking of the problem broadly and considering environmental factors, political factors, employee issues, and even government policies, if appropriate.

In one case, a major hospital was concerned about the length of time required to get a patient from the emergency department to an inpatient bed. Significant delays appeared to be caused by beds not being available. A quality improvement team tackled this problem by developing a cause-and-effect diagram. They identified four major causes: environmental services, emergency department, medical/surgery unit, and admitting. Figure 9.18 shows the diagram with several potential causes in each category.

FIGURE 9.18   Cause-and-Effect Diagram for Hospital Emergency Admission Problem

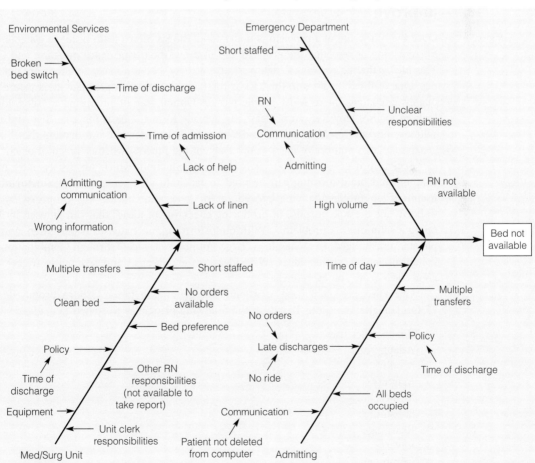

It served as a basis for further investigations of contributing factors and data analysis to find the root cause of the problem.

After potential variables are identified, experiments are often conducted to verify them. These experiments generally consist of formulating some hypothesis to investigate, collecting data, analyzing the data, and reaching a reasonable and statistically supportable conclusion. Statistical inference plays a critical role in this phase. It is one of the reasons why statistics is an important part of Six Sigma training. Other experiments might employ computer simulation techniques.

One tool that is often used to verify a potential cause-and-effect relationship is a scatter diagram. **Scatter diagrams** are the graphical component of regression analysis. Even though they do not provide rigorous statistical analysis, they often point to important relationships between variables, such as the percentage of an ingredient in an alloy and the hardness of the alloy. Typically, the variables in question represent possible causes and effects obtained from Ishikawa diagrams. For example, if a manufacturer suspects that the percentage of an ingredient in an alloy is causing quality problems in meeting hardness specifications, an employee group might collect data from samples on the amount of ingredient and hardness and plot the data on a scatter diagram.

Improve

Once the root cause of a problem is understood, the Six Sigma team needs to generate ideas for removing or resolving the problem and improve the performance measures and CTQs. This idea-gathering phase is a highly creative activity, because many solutions are not obvious. One of the difficulties in this task is the natural instinct to prejudge ideas before thoroughly evaluating them. Most people have a natural fear of proposing a "silly" idea or looking foolish. However, such ideas may actually form the basis for a creative and useful solution. Effective problem solvers must learn to defer judgment and develop the ability to generate a large number of ideas at this stage of the process, whether practical or not.

Several processes and tools such as lean production, which we discuss later in this chapter, and brainstorming can be used to facilitate idea generation. **Brainstorming**, a useful group problem-solving procedure for generating ideas, was proposed by Alex Osborn "for the sole purpose of producing checklists of ideas" that can be used in developing a solution to a problem.[39] With brainstorming, no criticism is permitted, and people are encouraged to generate a large number of ideas through combination and enhancement of existing ideas. Wild ideas are encouraged and frequently trigger other good ideas from somewhere else.

Checklists are often used as a guide for generating ideas. Osborn proposed about 75 fundamental questions based on the following principles to spawn new ideas:

- Put to other uses
- Adapt
- Modify
- Magnify
- Minify
- Substitute
- Rearrange
- Reverse
- Combine

By consciously trying to change an idea using these principles, one can generate many unusual and potentially valuable ideas. For example, the iPhone combined features of a phone with music playing and Internet capability, and the iPad substituted a virtual keyboard for a physical keyboard.

After a set of ideas have been proposed, it is necessary to evaluate them and select the most promising. Tools such as design of experiments and the Deming cycle are useful. This process includes confirming that the proposed solution will positively impact the key process variables and the CTQs, and identifying the maximum acceptable ranges of these variables. Improving a process should also include mistake-proofing, and poke-yoke (see Chapter 5) is often used as a final step in this process.

Problem solutions often entail technical or organizational changes. Often some sort of decision or scoring model is used to assess possible solutions against important criteria such as cost, time, quality improvement potential, resources required, effects on supervisors and workers, and barriers to implementation such as resistance to change or organizational culture. To implement a solution effectively, responsibility must be assigned to a person or a group who will follow through on what must be done as well as where, when, and how it will be done.

> *A set of tools that facilitate the implementation process is called the Seven Management and Planning Tools. These tools—affinity diagrams, interrelationship diagraphs, tree diagrams, matrix diagrams, matrix data analysis, process decision program charts, and arrow diagrams—are visual techniques that can help teams plan to implement an improvement. They will be explained and illustrated in Chapter 11.*

Control

The Control phase focuses on how to maintain the improvements, which includes putting tools in place to ensure that the key variables remain within the maximum acceptable ranges under the modified process. These improvements might include establishing the new standards and procedures, training the workforce, and instituting controls to make sure that improvements do not die over time. Controls might be as simple as using checklists or periodic status reviews to ensure that proper procedures are followed, or employing a control chart (see Chapter 8) or a run chart (a line chart of time series data without control limits) to monitor the performance of key measures.

LEAN TOOLS FOR PROCESS IMPROVEMENT

As we noted earlier in this chapter, Six Sigma is most applicable to attacking conformance problems. Efficiency problems, which are driven by metrics such as cycle time, cost, and throughput, require different improvement approaches. The approach most applicable to these types of problems is lean production. **Lean production** refers to approaches that originated at the Ford Motor Company in the early 1900s, but which were refined and modernized by the Toyota Motor Corporation later in the century. Lean approaches focus on the elimination of waste in all forms, including defects requiring rework, unnecessary processing steps, unnecessary movement of materials or people, waiting time, excess inventory, and overproduction. A simple way of defining it is "getting more done with less."[40] It involves identifying and eliminating non-value-added activities throughout the entire value chain to achieve faster customer response, reduced inventories, higher quality, and better human resources.

Lean production is facilitated by a focus on measurement and continuous improvement, cross-trained workers, flexible and increasingly automated equipment, efficient machine layout, rapid setup and changeover, just-in-time delivery and scheduling, realistic work standards, worker empowerment to perform inspections and take corrective action, supplier partnerships, and preventive maintenance. Some of the benefits claimed by proponents of lean production include the following:

- 60 percent reduction (or more) in cycle times
- 40 percent improvement in space utilization
- 25 percent greater throughput
- 50 percent reduction in work-in-process and finished goods inventories
- 50 percent improvement in quality
- 20 percent improvements in working capital and worker productivity

However, as one industry expert observed, it takes "an incredible amount of detailed planning, discipline, hard work, and painstaking attention to detail." Surveys have noted that midsized and large companies are likely to be familiar with lean principles and have systems in place; however, few small manufacturing shops have much familiarity with the principles. Thus, considerable opportunity exists for this important economic sector.

Some of the key tools used in lean production include:

- *The 5S's.* The 5S's are derived from Japanese terms: *seiri* (sort), *seiton* (set in order), *seiso* (shine), *seiketsu* (standardize), and *shitsuke* (sustain). They define a system for workplace organization and standardization. Sort refers to ensuring that each item in a workplace is in its proper place or identified as unnecessary and removed. Set in order means to arrange materials and equipment so that they are easy to find and use. Shine refers to a clean work area. Not only is this important for safety, but as a work area is cleaned, maintenance problems such as oil leaks can be identified before they cause greater problems. Standardize means to formalize procedures and practices to create consistency and ensure that all steps are performed correctly. Finally, sustain means to keep the process going through training, communication, and organizational structures.
- *Visual controls.* Visual controls are indicators for tools, parts, and production activities that are placed in plain sight of all workers so that everyone can understand the status of the system at a glance. Thus, if a machine goes down, or a part is defective or delayed, immediate action can be taken.
- *Efficient layout and standardized work.* The layout of equipment and processes is designed according to the best operational sequence, by physically linking and arranging machines and process steps most efficiently, often in a cellular arrangement. Standardizing the individual tasks by clearly specifying the proper method reduces wasted human movement and energy.
- *Pull production.* In this system (also known as *kanban* or *just-in-time*), upstream suppliers do not produce until the downstream customer signals a need for parts.
- *Single minute exchange of dies (SMED).* SMED refers to rapid changeover of tooling and fixtures in machine shops so that multiple products in smaller batches can be run on the same equipment. Reducing setup time adds value to the operation and facilitates smoother production flow.
- *Total productive maintenance.* Total productive maintenance is designed to ensure that equipment is operational and available when needed.
- *Source inspection.* Inspection and control by process operators guarantees that product passed on to the next production stage conforms to specifications.
- *Continuous improvement.* Continuous improvement provides the link to Six Sigma. In order to make lean production work, one must get to the root causes of problems and permanently remove them. Teamwork is an integral part of continuous improvement in lean environments. Many techniques that we discuss in subsequent chapters are used.

> ### **QUALITY**SPOTLIGHT
> *Sunset Manufacturing*
>
> Sunset Manufacturing, Inc., of Tualatin, Oregon, is a 35-person, family-owned machine shop.[41] Because of competitive pressures and a business downturn, Sunset began to look for ways to simplify operations and cut costs. They established a lean steering committee to coordinate and drive the process. The committee chartered a kaizen team to reduce setup time on vertical milling machines by 50 percent. The team used SMED and the 5S's approach as their basic tools. Several actions were taken, including (1) standardizing parts across milling machines, (2) reorganizing the tool room, (3) incorporating the SMED approach in machine setups, and (4) and implementing what was termed "dance cards," which gave operators the specific steps required for the SMED of various machines and products. The results were impressive. Tool preparation time dropped from an average of 30 minutes to less than 10 minutes, isolation and identification of worn tools was improved, safety enhancement and orderliness in the tool room due to 5S's application was apparent, and machine setup time was reduced from an average of 216 minutes to 36 minutes (an 86 percent improvement). Estimated savings were $33,000 per year, with an implementation cost of less than half of that amount. The net impact was to allow smaller lots to be run, a 75 percent reduction in setup scrap, emergence of a more competitive organization, and a morale boost for team members.

Lean tools can easily be applied to nonmanufacturing environments. Pure service firms such as banks, hospitals, and restaurants have benefited from lean principles. In these contexts, lean production is often called **lean enterprise**. For example, banks require quick response and efficiency to operate on low margins, making many of their processes, such as check sorting and mortgage approval, natural candidates for lean enterprise solutions. Handling of paper checks and credit card slips, for instance, involves a physical process not unlike an assembly line. The faster a bank moves checks through its system, the sooner it can collect its funds and the better its returns on invested capital.

One North American financial institution applied lean enterprise principles to check processing operations.[42] They followed one check as it made its way through the bank's systems, documenting the time spent in actual processing and in waiting, rework, and handling. They found that almost half of the bank's processing capacity was consumed by nonprocessing activities such as fixing jams and setting up machines. Further investigation revealed wide variations in productivity between individual operators on a single shift. When the work practices of the least and most productive operators were compared, it became evident that although all were engaged in the same task, differences in the way they performed it were creating huge swings in productivity.

To adopt a lean manufacturing approach, the bank first matched the flow of incoming checks to processing capacity. At the end of each business day, the check processing operation was swamped with more checks than it could handle; this bottleneck created the false impression that capacity was constrained. The bank applied just-in-time principles to the processing of incoming checks and spread the check flow evenly through the day. A second bottleneck occurred at the beginning of the day; standard practice dictated that all checks presented for morning processing were sorted three times. This process prevented the processing operation from handling the morning check volume in time to meet the account posting deadline. However, many of the checks did not need to be completed by the morning deadline, and once the sorting of these low-priority items was shifted to later in the day when volumes were lower, capacity increased by 122 percent.

By uncovering and freeing up "phantom" capacity that had previously been taken up by waiting time, maintenance, and rework, they could increase actual capacity by more than 25 percent without investing in additional equipment. The bank was able to both sell its services to other banks at an attractive price and to expand capacity during the most time-sensitive period of the day, when its services could be priced at a premium. In all, these one-off improvements resulted in a more than doubling of the margin contributed by the operation.

 QUALITYSPOTLIGHT

Metro Health Hospital

Metro Health Hospital in Grand Rapids, Michigan, has successfully applied lean principles in its pharmacy services.[43] The Metro pharmacy started with a modest goal of reducing the lead time for getting the first dose of a medication to a patient. The lead time was measured from the time an order arrived at the pharmacy to its delivery on the appropriate hospital floor. Using lean, the Metro pharmacy carefully laid out all the process steps involved in getting the first dose of the correct medication to the right patient. The pharmacy found that it had a 14-stage process with some unnecessary steps, resulting in a total lead time of 166 minutes. During the evaluation process, the pharmacy calculated that it took technicians an average of 1.5 minutes to locate a product. For a pharmacy operating around-the-clock and delivering more than 100,000 doses a month, time wasted in searching was costly to the organization. In fact, technicians were spending 77.4 percent of their time locating products; when a pharmacist needed a technician for clinical activities, the technician was usually off searching for a drug.

The lean teams outlined several non-value-added steps in the process, only one of which was out of the pharmacy's control (i.e., the time it took to transport the ordered medication, once filled, to the appropriate floor). Standardization was a key component of the redesign, especially with the process flow as it moved through the department. As a part of the standardization process, the pharmacy implemented two new counters: a "check" counter and a "to-go" counter. They put in a simple color system in which red indicated the check counter and green indicated the to-go counter. They decreased the number of distractions by implementing a "safe zone" where a pharmacist could check medications without being disturbed. Product no longer sits on the counter without a pharmacist knowing it's there, nor are there redundant steps between the delivery baskets and delivery carts. After the checkpoint, the medication automatically goes in the "to-go" area delivery bin. Overall, the pharmacy at Metro realized a 33-percent reduction in time to get medications to patients, and reduced the number of process steps from 14 to nine simply by removing non-value-added steps. Patients have experienced a 40 percent reduction in pharmacy-related medication errors, and the severity of those errors has decreased.

Lean Six Sigma

As organizations developed Six Sigma capabilities to address conformance problems, they began to realize that many important business problems fell into the category of efficiency problems and assigned these problems to Six Sigma belts and project teams. As a result, Six Sigma teams began to use tools of lean production to eliminate waste and non-value-added activities within processes. As the tools of Six Sigma and lean production merged, the concept of Lean Six Sigma (LSS) emerged, drawing upon the best practices of both approaches. **Lean Six Sigma** can be defined as an integrated improvement approach to improve goods and services and operations efficiency by reducing defects, variation, and waste.

Both Six Sigma and lean are driven by customer requirements, focus on real dollar savings, have the ability to make significant financial impacts on the organization, and can easily be used in non-manufacturing environments. Both exploit data and logical problem-solving analysis. For example, a cycle time reduction project might involve aspects of both. Lean tools might be applied to streamline an order entry process. This application leads to the discovery that significant rework occurs because of incorrect addresses, customer numbers, or shipping charges and results in high variation of processing time. Six Sigma tools might then be used to drill down to the root cause of the problems and identify a solution. An executive search firm, Avery Point Group, noted that more companies are looking for candidates who demonstrate a mix of lean and Six Sigma skills, even for companies that may not have a full-blown Six Sigma or lean deployment underway.[44]

 **QUALITY**SPOTLIGHT

Best Buy

Best Buy began to implement Lean Six Sigma in 2005 to focus on both creating efficiencies and enhancing the customer experience. They have trained over 500 Green Belts and have over 60 Black and Master Black Belts as part of an Enterprise Continuous Improvement Capability Team. One project involved the home installation process. The project was designed to improve the customer's experience during appliance installations. In one case, they determined that some dryer installations were unsuccessful because the customer did not own certain necessary components. The LSS team collaborated with product buyers and vendors to create bundled kits of necessary installation parts that are delivered to the point of installation. This not only improved customer satisfaction but also streamlined the process and eliminated wasted trips and rescheduling. Another project involved optimizing the assortment of products and inventory levels within stores of different revenue levels to best service unique segments of customers.[45]

Some differences clearly exist between lean production and Six Sigma. First, they attack different types of problems. Lean production addresses visible problems in processes, for example, inventory, material flow, and safety. Six Sigma is more concerned with less visible problems, for example, variation in performance. In essence, lean is focused on efficiency by reducing waste and improving process flow, whereas Six Sigma is focused on effectiveness by reducing errors and defects. Another difference is that lean tools are more intuitive and easier to apply by anybody in the workplace, whereas many Six Sigma tools require advanced training and expertise of Black Belt or Master Black Belt specialists (or consultant equivalents). For example, the concept of the 5S's is easier to grasp than statistical methods. Thus, organizations might be well-advised to start with basic lean principles and evolve toward more sophisticated Six Sigma approaches. However, it is important to integrate both approaches with a common goal—improving business results.

Lean Six Sigma in Services

Although Six Sigma and lean were developed in the manufacturing sector, it can easily be applied to a wide variety of transactional, administrative, and service areas.[46] In fact, it is generally agreed that 50 percent or more of the total savings opportunity in an organization lies outside of manufacturing. General Electric was one of the early organizations that understood that Six Sigma could be applied to any process that created defects, and introduced Six Sigma in GE Financial.

Services are generally driven by four key measures of performance:

- *Accuracy*, as measured by correct financial figures, completeness of information, or freedom from data errors
- *Cycle time*, which is a measure of how long it takes to do something, such as pay an invoice
- *Cost*, that is, the internal cost of process activities (in many cases, cost is largely determined by the accuracy and/or cycle time of the process; the longer it takes, and the more mistakes that have to be fixed, the higher the cost)
- *Customer satisfaction*, which is typically the primary measure of success

Thus, it is easy to see how LSS can provide substantial benefits to services. However, the unique characteristics of services often make opportunities difficult to identify, and projects more difficult to define. For example, the culture of services is such that service employees typically do not think in terms of processes, measurements, and data; processes are often invisible, complex, and not well defined or well documented; service work typically requires considerable human intervention; and similar service activities are often done in different ways.

Fortunately, important similarities exist between manufacturing and nonmanufacturing processes. First, both types of processes have "hidden factories," those places where the defective "product" is sent to be reworked or scrapped (revised, corrected, or discarded in nonmanufacturing terms). Find the hidden factory and you also find opportunities to improve the process. Performing manual account reconciliation in accounting, revising budgets repeatedly until management will accept them, and making repeat sales calls to customers because all the information requested by the customer was not available are all examples of the hidden factory.

We can cite numerous applications of LSS in services.

- At CNH Capital, a project was implemented to decrease asset management cycle time in posting repossessions to a bid list and remarketing website.[47] Cycle time was reduced 75 percent, from 40 days to 10 days, resulting in significant ongoing dollar savings.
- A facility management company had a high level of "days sales outstanding." Initially, they tried to fix this issue by reducing the term of days in its billing cycle, which, however, upset customers. Using LSS tools, they found that a large percentage of accounts with high days sales outstanding received invoices having numerous errors. After understanding the source of the errors and making process changes, the invoice process improved and days sales outstanding was reduced.
- At DuPont, a Six Sigma project was applied to improve cycle time for an employee's application for long-term disability benefits.[48]
- One large banking and financial services company, facing increasing customer dissatisfaction because of inefficiencies in international wire-transfer operations that increased the bank's costs—some of which were passed on to customers as transaction fees—applied LSS to redesign the process, greatly reducing errors, customer callbacks, transfer delays, and transfer fees. Transfer cycle time was reduced 46 percent and the cost-per-payment order was reduced by more than 50 percent, enabling the bank to waive its transaction fees and improve customer satisfaction.[49]
- LSS is widely used in health care, such as increasing capacity in the X-ray or surgical departments, reducing discharge delays, decreasing patient waiting time, reducing defects in billing or patient records, and so on.

- The city of Fort Wayne, Indiana applied LSS to pothole repair and permitting. Using simple tools, the time to fix potholes was reduced from as much as four days to four hours, and the time to issue a permit was cut from 50 days to around 12. In the first five years, the city completed 60 Six Sigma projects and saved $10 million.[50]

SUMMARY OF KEY POINTS AND TERMINOLOGY

The Student Companion Site provides a summary of key concepts and terminology introduced in this chapter.

QUALITY *in* PRACTICE

An Application of Six Sigma to Reduce Medical Errors[51]

Medication administration and laboratory processing/results reporting are examples of complex systems in health care that are known to be error prone. As described in the report of the National Academy of Sciences/Institute of Medicine, medication errors are a substantial source of preventable errors in hospitals, but result in part from poorly designed complex systems. At Froedtert Hospital in Milwaukee, Wisconsin, errors with IV medication drips and laboratory processing and results reporting were well documented. Additionally, errors in ordering, transporting, analyzing, and reporting clinical laboratory tests were known to be a significant source of error at the hospital. It is for these reasons that these two areas were targeted for initial study.

A consortium was created by four Milwaukee-based organizations committed to the development of an approach to reduce errors and improve patient safety. The consortium members include the Medical College of Wisconsin, Froedtert Memorial Lutheran Hospital, the American Society for Quality, and Secur-Trac, a company formed specifically to develop technologies to improve patient safety. The consortium is currently addressing three major efforts: (1) improved identification and reporting of health care errors, (2) deployment of the Six Sigma methodology to reduce errors, and (3) testing and implementation of technical solutions to improve patient safety. At the center of this approach is the effort to determine whether the Six Sigma error reduction methodology can be successfully applied in health care.

Using Six Sigma methods and selected statistical tools, Froedtert Hospital's processes for medication delivery were evaluated with the goal of designing an approach that would decrease the likelihood of errors. The design employed the classic Six Sigma process steps. A multidisciplinary group of physicians, nurses, pharmacists, and administrators identified medication delivery by continuous IV infusions as a process subject to substantial error. Continuous IV infusions are used in many clinical settings and errors can severely impact patient well-being. Initially, the focus was on five specific IV medications. Soon it was realized that the number was too small to permit quantification of error rates. The scope of the project was expanded to 22 medications delivered by continuous IV infusion. Team members developed a process map (flowchart) to delineate each step in the procedure for continuous IV medication infusion. The process map revealed nine steps: (1) physician order, (2) order review, (3) pharmacist order entry, (4) dose preparation, (5) dose dispensing, (6) infusion rate calculation, (7) IV pump setup, (8) pump programming, and (9) pump monitoring.

Each of the steps was subjected to a failure modes and effect analysis (FMEA—see Chapter 7) and scored on a scale of 1 to 10 for three categories: frequency of occurrence, detectability, and severity. The scores were multiplied together to yield a risk priority number (RPN) for each step. Eighteen months of retrospective medication error reports were reviewed to provide additional data for the RPN calculation. This review confirmed the

FMEA results that IV rate calculations and IV pump setup were the two most error-prone steps in the IV infusion process. Initial efforts to delineate and reduce errors focused on these two steps.

Because it was not known how often errors went unrecognized or unreported, an audit was conducted to determine whether the prescribed dose rate matched the actual infusion rate. Two weeks of audit data were collected and the resulting 124 data points were rated on a discrepancy scale of 1 to 3 (1 for a #1 mL/hr discrepancy, 2 for a 1–5 mL/hr discrepancy, 3 for a > 5mL/hr discrepancy). Ten of the audits were rated at level 2 and four were rated at level 3. Root cause analysis was employed to determine the cause of the discrepancies. Work was then begun to affect the accuracy of infusion rates.

Using Six Sigma methods and statistical tools, the team also examined the hospital's clinical laboratory process. Key elements in the acquisition, laboratory analysis, and reporting of patient specimens were identified. The steps included (1) physician order, (2) order entry, (3) matching the order to the patient, (4) collecting the specimen, (5) labeling the specimen, (6) transporting the specimen, (7) analyzing the specimen, (8) reporting the results, and (9) entering the results into the patient's chart. Each of these steps is subject to error. Applying Six Sigma analysis, the steps subject to the most errors were identified. These steps were: order entry by the unit clerical staff, transportation of the specimens to the lab, and analysis of specimens in the lab. To identify, define, and reduce these errors, a laboratory error reduction task force was established. It included members from administration, lab, nursing, clerical staff, information systems, and quality management. The task force first developed a process map so that all members could appreciate the complexity and vulnerability of the entire process. The process map provided the task force with the tools to analyze the clinical laboratory problem in depth. The FMEA technique was employed to arrive at a risk priority number (RPN) so that steps in the laboratory analysis process could be prioritized in terms of their vulnerability to error. Again, order entry, transportation, and analysis of specimens were identified. Statistical tools, including correlation and regression, analysis of variance, confidence intervals, and hypothesis testing, were employed to evaluate the laboratory process further.

The analysis of medication delivery by IV infusions served as a good example of deployment of Six Sigma methodology to reduce error and improve patient safety in a health care setting. Significant variability in the ordering and processing of IV drips was identified. Lack of standardization in many steps of the process posed the greatest risk for system failure. Those steps with the highest degree of variability and the greatest chance for error were

1. MD ordering practices (i.e., lack of standardization in medication description, dosage, concentration, etc.)
2. IV drip preparation (lack of standardization by pharmacy and nursing of IV bag concentrations)
3. RN labeling and documentation of IV concentrations

In these three areas, a multidisciplinary task force created standards to reduce variation. Specific interventions included implementation of standardized physician order sheets, a policy requiring preparation of all IV medications in a standard concentration, and use of color-coded labels when nonstandard concentrations were in use. Thirty days after implementation, measurable improvement was evident. Level 1 discrepancies fell from 47.4 percent to 14 percent. Level 2 discrepancies fell from 21.1 percent to 11.8 percent and level 3 discrepancies fell from 15.8 percent to 2.9 percent. Though far from achieving a six-sigma level of performance, substantial efforts continue to move toward that goal.

The laboratory project proved to be more complex. It was evident early on that the scope of this complex system was too broad for an initial effort. The project was broken down into smaller individual steps of the larger process. Once refocused, the appointed task force identified opportunities to reduce variation in select steps of the laboratory process. Alternate means of identifying specimens, changes in the approach to "point of care" laboratory analysis, decentralization of some laboratory tests, and a revised system to order and process stat lab tests was put into place. Effectiveness monitoring continues as does measurement of sustainable error reductions. These efforts marked the beginning of a long laboratory redesign process aimed at driving out error, reducing turnaround time, and improving patient safety.

Key Issues for Discussion

1. How did the team use process mapping as a key part of the Six Sigma process? What value did process mapping have?
2. Why were the teams and task forces multidisciplinary in nature? What benefits does this approach have?

Q QUALITY *in* PRACTICE

Applying Process Improvement Tools to an Order Fulfillment Process[52]

This case study involves a large automotive parts distribution center in Europe. Car dealerships and repair garages from several countries call in orders for replacement parts needed to repair various types of motor vehicles. When an order is received, the distribution center must quickly locate the requested parts and ship them to the repair facility. Time is of the essence because car owners typically become increasingly upset the longer their vehicles are out of service.

Because the distribution center was having trouble shipping orders on time, many of its customers were unhappy and threatening to switch to other part distributors. To appease these customers, the manager of the center promised all orders would be delivered within 24 hours or the customer would get the parts at no charge. The manager then assembled a team to discover ways to reduce order processing time so at least 98 percent of orders would meet the 24-hour deadline.

To better understand the situation, the team decided to draw a map showing how an order was received, filled, checked, packed, and finally shipped to the customer. After discussing the required steps and actually following an order from start to finish, the team created a flowchart of the entire order fulfillment process. The diagram, which is shown in Figure 9.19, identifies those activities the team had the power to change and, it was hoped, improve. This type of layout also encouraged every team member to focus on the big picture rather than on only the particular activity in which he or she worked.

To determine where the longest time delays were occurring, the team randomly chose 50 orders from those received during a one-week period. As members tracked these selected orders through the distribution center, they noted the time each entered and left the various activity areas appearing on the flowchart. To ensure these times were accurately and consistently recorded, the team designed the check sheet shown in Figure 9.20. One sheet was used per order, with the completion time for a given activity computed by subtracting its in time from its out time. For example, order XR-03018 began the "pack parts" activity at 2:16 P.M. and finished at 2:34 P.M. Therefore, the time to complete this particular activity was 18 minutes. At the end of the week, the average completion time for

FIGURE 9.19   Flowchart for the Order Fulfillment Process

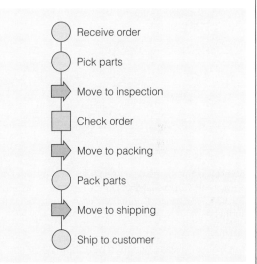

Receive order

Pick parts

Move to inspection

Check order

Move to packing

Pack parts

Move to shipping

Ship to customer

Source: Reprinted with permission from Davis R. Bothe, "Improve Service and Administration," *Quality Progress*, September 2003, pp. 53–57. Copyright © 2003. No further distribution allowed without permission.

FIGURE 9.20   Check Sheet for Recording Times

| Order # XR = 03018 Recorder   Robert |
| Date 16 Dec   Comments |

Activity	In	Out	Completion
Receive order	1:24	1:31	7
Pick parts	1:32	1:51	19
Move to inspection	1:52	2:03	11
Check order	2:04	2:10	6
Move to packing	2:11	2:15	4
Pack parts	2:16	2:34	18
Move to shipping	2:35	2:38	3

Source: Reprinted with permission from Davis R. Bothe, "Improve Service and Administration," *Quality Progress*, September 2003, pp. 53–57. Copyright © 2003 American Society for Quality. No further distribution allowed without permission.

FIGURE 9.21 Pareto Diagram for Average Time of Each Activity

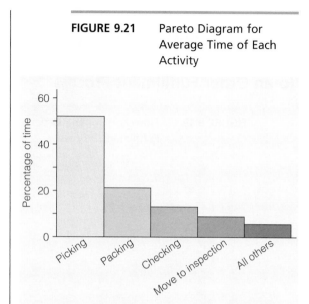

Source: Reprinted with permission from Davis R. Bothe, "Improve Service and Administration," *Quality Progress*, September 2003, pp. 53–57. Copyright © 2003 American Society for Quality. No further distribution allowed without permission.

FIGURE 9.22 Histogram of Picking Times

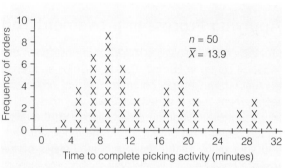

Source: Reprinted with permission from Davis R. Bothe, "Improve Service and Administration," *Quality Progress*, September, 2003, pp. 53–57. Copyright © 2003 American Society for Quality. No further distribution allowed without permission.

each activity was calculated by adding its 50 completion times—one for each of the 50 orders tracked—and dividing this total by 50. When these average times were analyzed with the Pareto diagram in Figure 9.21, picking time was identified as the largest contributor to order processing delays, representing about 52 percent of the total time needed to process an order.

Based on this new information, the team refined its original mission statement, "Reduce the time for processing an order," to the more specific, "Reduce the time for picking parts." With the scope of the search narrowed to just the picking operation, members invited some of the part pickers to join the team because these personnel were the local experts in picking parts and possessed the most knowledge about the function.

To provide a more detailed analysis of the picking operation, the 50 individual times recorded for picking orders (one from each of the 50 check sheets collected during the team's earlier study) were plotted on the histogram in Figure 9.22. The shape of the histogram—having three humps—was an initial surprise because it implied the existence of three distinct clusters of picking times. With this valuable clue in mind, the team now concentrated on what could be responsible for these three separate time groups.

During a brainstorming session, a part picker suggested the three humps of the histogram reflected the number of trips made to the parts storage area of the distribution center to complete an order. He explained that many orders were filled with just one trip, but two were sometimes required and, on occasion, even three. Thus, the left hump could consist of times an order was completed with only one trip, the middle could represent those requiring two, whereas the third could be those in which three trips were needed. By watching the part picking activity for two days, the team members could verify the part picker's theory was indeed correct.

Armed with this additional insight, the team brainstormed reasons multiple trips were needed to complete an order and then organized these ideas on the cause-and-effect diagram in Figure 9.23. After discussion, the team eventually decided that the push carts used by the part pickers to carry the parts were too small (see the equipment branch of Figure 9.23). When part pickers were gathering parts to fill a large order, the cart became full long before all the needed parts were gathered. The picker had to travel to the inspection area to empty the cart and make a return trip to the warehouse to retrieve the remainder of the order.

As a pilot study, a few wider push carts were ordered and put into service for a one-week trial run. Although more parts could fit into these new carts, the pickers complained they were so wide that two of them could not pass each other in the narrow aisles, causing traffic jams and thereby actually increasing picking times. The team then tried using longer carts, which were found to take care of both problems. By watching the part picking activity over the next several days, the

FIGURE 9.23   Cause-and-Effect Diagram of Potential Causes of Multiple Trips

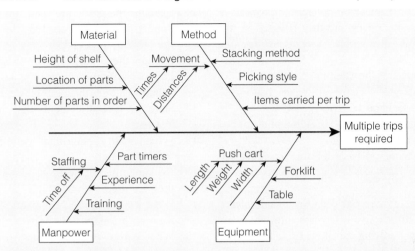

Source: Reprinted with permission from Davis R. Bothe, "Improve Service and Administration," *Quality Progress*, September 2003, pp. 53–57. Copyright © 2003 American Society for Quality. No further distribution allowed without permission.

team was able to verify the switch to longer carts greatly reduced the number of multiple trips needed. In fact, with the new push carts, a picker could often complete two small orders during the same trip.

To estimate the decrease in part picking time, the team constructed a histogram of 30 picking times associated with the longer carts (see Figure 9.24). This example has a unimodal distribution, with an average picking time of only 8.3 minutes vs. the original average of 13.9 minutes.

FIGURE 9.24   Histogram of Picking Times with Longer Carts

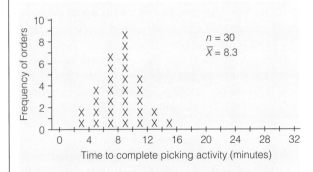

Source: Adapted from Davis R. Bothe, "Improve Services and Administration," *Quality Progress*, September 2003, pp. 53–57. Copyright 2003 American Society for Quality. Reprinted by permission.

Although a reduction of 5.6 minutes (13.9–8.3) per trip doesn't seem like much of a time savings, consider that on an eight-hour shift, a part picker spends about seven hours—420 minutes—actually gathering parts. Using the old push carts, a picker would complete an average of 30.2 orders (420/13.9) per shift. With the longer carts, that same picker could now complete 50.6 orders (420/8.3) per shift. This increase of 20.4 orders (50.6–30.2) per worker meant the four part pickers could fulfill an additional 81 orders (20.4 × 4) during their shift. Thus, the seemingly small reduction in average trip time translated into a fairly significant increase in the throughput of this bottleneck operation.

Key Issues for Discussion

1. Explain how the process the team followed might align with DMAIC, the Deming Cycle, and the creative problem-solving process.

2. What might the team do if the reduction in order processing time resulting from the introduction of the longer carts was not large enough to achieve the goal of having 98 percent of the orders meet the 24-hour deadline?

3. Suppose packing parts is now the activity responsible for the greatest delays in processing an order. How might this affect the project organization and next steps?

REVIEW QUESTIONS

1. Explain the four themes that different improvement methodologies share. How are they reflected in the Deming cycle, creative problem-solving process, and DMAIC?
2. Explain the steps of the Deming cycle.
3. What is Six Sigma? Briefly outline its history at Motorola and General Electric.
4. List the key principles of the Six Sigma philosophy. How does it differ from TQM?
5. Explain the theoretical basis for the six-sigma 3.4 dpmo measure. How does it relate to process capability concepts?
6. What is Kepner and Tregoe's definition of a problem?
7. List and explain the five categories into which all quality problem solving can be classified. Provide some quality-related examples in each category.
8. Explain the role of projects in Six Sigma. How are Six Sigma teams typically organized?
9. Explain the knowledge and management expertise that Green Belts, Black Belts, and Master Black Belts should have?
10. Discuss factors that should be considered when selecting Six Sigma projects.
11. Explain the structure and purpose of the A3 Report that Toyota created. How does it support the DMAIC process?
12. Explain the concept of Pareto analysis. How is a Pareto distribution created?
13. What is a SIPOC diagram? How is it used in DMAIC?
14. State the typical elements that make up a project charter.
15. What is an operational definition? Why is it important?
16. Explain different types of check sheets and how they are used.
17. What is a value stream map and how does it differ from an ordinary flowchart?
18. What is root cause analysis? Describe some tools that are useful in identifying a root cause.
19. Why is brainstorming an important tool in the Improvement phase of DMAIC?
20. Describe the key tools used in lean production.
21. How did Lean Six Sigma evolve? How does it differ from the original concept of Six Sigma?
22. Why is Lean Six Sigma especially useful in services? Cite some examples.

DISCUSSION QUESTIONS

1. The January 22, 2001, issue of *Fortune* contained an article "Why You Can Safely Ignore Six Sigma," that was highly critical of Six Sigma. Here are some of the criticisms levied against Six Sigma:
   a. The results often don't have any noticeable impact on company financial statements. Thus, Six Sigma success doesn't correlate to higher stock value. This criticism applies to 90 percent of the companies that implement Six Sigma.
   b. Only early adopters can benefit.
   c. Six Sigma focuses on defects, which are hard to objectively determine for service businesses.
   d. Six Sigma can't guarantee that your product will have a market.

   How would you respond to these statements?
2. Some of the key processes associated with business activities for a typical company include sales and marketing, supply chain management, managing information technology, and managing human resources. What types of Six Sigma projects might be considered in order to improve each of these activities?
3. Suggest a set of CTQs that might influence overall service satisfaction for service at an automobile dealership.
4. "Resistance to change" is a common theme in the behavioral sciences. What part do you believe that resistance to change plays in management's fostering of successful versus unsuccessful adoptions of Six Sigma approaches? What impact does workers' resistance or lack of resistance have?
5. List some of the common processes that a student performs. How can these processes be improved using a process improvement approach?
6. Discuss how DMAIC might be used in your personal life. For example, how could you use it if you wanted to lose weight or improve a skill such as playing a musical instrument?
7. Discuss what would be the most appropriate tool to use to attack each of these problems:
   a. A copy machine suffers frequent paper jams and users are often confused as to how to fix the problem.

b. The publication team for an engineering department wants to improve the accuracy of its user documentation but is unsure of why documents aren't error-free.

c. A rental car agency is getting numerous complaints about the length of time that customers have to wait to obtain a car. They need to get a better handle on the factors that relate to the wait time.

d. A kitchen in a restaurant always seems to be getting orders mixed up and plated incorrectly.

e. A local zoo wants to understand where its guests come from in order to better target marketing efforts.

f. A contracting agency wants to investigate why they had so many changes in their contracts. They believe that the number of changes may be related to the dollar value of the original contract or the days between the request for proposal and the contract award.

g. A travel agency is interested in gaining a better understanding of how call volume varies by time of year in order to adjust staffing schedules.

8. How can lean concepts be applied in a classroom?

9. The Six Sigma philosophy seeks to develop technical leadership through "Belt" training, then use it in team-based projects designed to improve processes. To what extent are these two concepts (technical experts versus team experts) at odds? What must be done to prevent them from blocking success in improvement projects?

10. How might a Six Sigma project be done to improve a registration process in a university? An admission process?

11. How can a manager effectively balance the key components of a Six Sigma implementation design related to who, what, where, when, why, and how it could be done?

12. In 1995, Jack Welch, who was then CEO of General Electric, sent a memo to his senior managers telling them that they would have to require every employee to have started Six Sigma training to be promoted. Furthermore, 40 percent of the managers' bonuses were to be tied to the successful introduction of Six Sigma. Do you believe that this directive was a motivational action, or did it violate W. Edwards Deming's maxim that managers and leaders must "cast out fear"? Why or why not?

13. A consultant told the story of two Six Sigma teams that made separate presentations on how they would improve processes in their own areas. At the end of the second presentation, the consultant asked a basic question that stopped both Black Belt team leaders in their tracks: "Haven't you both just proposed making improvements based on eliminating parts of processes in the other group's areas? It seems that the implementation costs in one area will cancel out the savings in the other area!" What had the Black Belts failed to recognize? What would you recommend to prevent this situation from happening in other organizations?

PROBLEMS

Note: *Data sets for many problems in this chapter are available in the Excel workbook C09Data.xlsx on the Student Companion Site. Click the appropriate worksheet tab as noted in the problem (e.g. Prob. 9-12, etc.) to access the data.*

1. Megasigma Corp. has a process they believe is operating near a six-sigma level and want to verify this. If the specification for a critical part in the process is 2.75 cm $\pm$ 0.05 and the standard deviation for the process is 0.02, at what sigma level is this process operating?

2. Neverflounder Fish Company advertises that 98.7 percent of their fish were caught within the past 36 hours and that all of their products are 100 percent fresh. How many dpmo does this claim represent? At what sigma level is this process operating?

3. During one month, MegaInvCo (MIC) processed 51,000 invoices for Alpha Corp., 49,000 for Beta Corp., and 25,000 for Gamma Corp. Of these, 510 of the Alpha, 525 of the Beta, and 480 of the Gamma invoices had to be reprocessed for errors. What is the overall defect rate and the sigma level for all of the combined batches? For each individual batch?

4. Expand Table 9.2 for sigma levels from 3.0 to 6.0 in increments of 0.1 on a spreadsheet. Construct a chart showing dpmo as a function of the sigma level.

5. Nanospark Electronics manufactures 100,000 circuit boards per month. A random sample of 1,000 boards is inspected every week for three characteristics. During a recent week, three defects were found for one

characteristic, and one defect each was found for the other two characteristics. If these inspections produced defect counts that were representative of the population, what is the overall sigma level for this process? What is the sigma level for the characteristic that showed three defects?

6. Verasource Microprocessor Corporation (VMC) sells 2,000 specialized microprocessor chips each month at a price of $1,500 each. Variable costs amount to $1,500,000, and fixed costs are $500,000. Currently the company has a defect rate of 8 percent (which are chips returned by customers, scrapped by VMC, and replaced). Note that the variable costs include the cost of producing the defective chips.
   a. What is the hidden cost to the company of making this rate of defectives instead of 2,000 good chips each month?
   b. Suppose a Six Sigma effort can reduce the defects to a six-sigma level (assume for simplicity that the defective rate is essentially zero). What is the impact on profitability?

7. A flowchart for a fast-food drive-through window is shown in Figure 9.25. Determine the important quality characteristics inherent in this process and suggest possible improvements.

8. The current process for fulfilling a room service request at the Luxmark hotel can be described as follows. After the tray is prepared at the room service station, the server proceeds to the room, knocks on the door, sets up the meal, has the customer sign the check, asks if anything else is needed, and then returns to the room service station.
   a. Draw a flowchart that describes this process.
   b. From the perspective of creating a high level of customer satisfaction from this experience, what improvements might you suggest to enhance this process? Think creatively!

9. Placewrite, Inc., an independent outplacement service, helps unemployed executives find jobs. One of the major activities of the service is preparing resumes. Three word processors work at the service typing resumes and cover letters. Together they handle about 120 individual clients. Turnaround time for typing is expected to be 24 hours. The word-processing operation begins with clients placing work in the assigned word processor's bin. When the word processor picks up the work (in batches), it is logged in using a time clock stamp, and the work is typed and printed. After the batch is completed, the word

FIGURE 9.25   Flowchart for a Fast-Food Drive-Through Window (Problem 7)

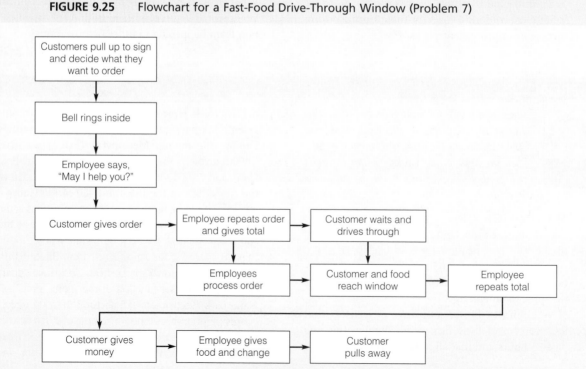

processor returns the work to the clients' bin, logs in the time delivered, and picks up new work. A supervisor tries to balance the workload for the three word processors. Lately, many of the clients have been complaining about errors in their documents—misspellings, missing lines, wrong formatting, and so on. The supervisor has told the word processors to be more careful, but the errors still persist.

  a. Develop a cause-and-effect diagram that might clarify the source of errors.
  b. What tools might the supervisor use to study ways to reduce the number of errors?

10. The maintenance of products such as aircraft engines is part of a complex supply chain. Distribution centers fulfill orders for spare parts to customers around the world and typically run on a 24/7 basis. Each day, as many as 4,000 different SKUs are shipped out and over 1,000 SKUs are received in inventory. It is critical that each order be 100 percent accurate. For example, orders that don't match the shipping list are returned to the distribution center because of customs regulations.

  a. If the distribution center has identified inaccurate shipments as a significant problem, explain how the DMAIC process might be applied.
  b. Develop a logical cause-and-effect diagram for the problem "inaccurate shipment."
  c. Think about how a process for fulfilling orders might work and create a process map (you might want to refer back to process design concepts in Chapter 7).

11. A catalog order-filling process at Cats Catalog Company for personalized printed products for pet owners can be described as follows:[53] Telephone orders are taken over a 12-hour period each day. Orders are collected from each person at the end of the day and checked for errors by the supervisor of the phone department, usually the following morning. The supervisor does not send each one-day batch of orders to the data processing department until after 1:00 P.M. In the next step—data processing—orders are invoiced in the one-day batches. Then they are printed and matched back to the original orders. At this point, if the order is from a new customer, it is sent to the person who did the customer verification and setup of new customer accounts. This process must be completed before the order can be invoiced. The next step—order verification and proofreading—occurs after invoicing is completed. The orders, with invoices attached, are given to a person who verifies that all required information is present and correct to permit typesetting. If the verifier has any questions, they are checked by computer or by calling the customer. Finally, the completed orders are sent to the typesetting department of the print shop.

  a. Develop a flowchart for this process.
  b. Identify opportunities for improving the quality of service in this situation.

12. A Six Sigma analyst at Lakerside United Bank suspected that errors in counting and manually strapping cash into bundles were related to the number of weeks that employees had been employed on that job. The data available in the worksheet Prob. 9-12 were gathered from the process. What do you conclude from your analysis? What do you recommend?

13. The times required for trainees in an electronics course at ElecktronTech to assemble a component used in a computer were measured. These are provided in the worksheet *Prob. 9-13*. Construct a histogram of the data. What recommendations for improvement would you give the course instructor?

14. The times required to prepare standard-size packages for shipping at Packman Shipping Company were measured. The packers were divided into two equal groups of 20 people, each, having similar experience in packing. These data are provided in the worksheet *Prob. 9-14*. Construct a scatter diagram for these data. What recommendations for improvement would you give the section leader, based on your findings?

15. A process at PrintHeads, Inc.'s largest facility is used to make plastic gears for a computer printer. The data found in the worksheet *Prob. 9-15* were gathered by a quality analyst. The gears were designed to be 3.75 ± 0.05 centimeters (cm) in diameter. Construct a histogram of the data. What can you observe about the shape of the distribution? What would you recommend to the production manager based on your analysis?

16. Deuce Printing Company realized that they were losing customers and orders due to various delays and errors. In order to get to the root cause of the problem, they decided to track problems that might be contributing to customer dissatisfaction. The list of the problems provided in worksheet *Prob. 9-16* shows their frequencies of occurrence over a six-month period. What technique might you use to graphically show the causes of customer dissatisfaction? What recommendations could you make to reduce errors and increase customer satisfaction?

17. In a DeltaWidgets, Inc. process, the production rate (parts/hour) was thought to affect the number of defectives found during a subsequent inspection. To test this theory, the production rate was varied and the numbers of defects were collected for the same batch sizes. The results can be found in the worksheet *Prob. 9-17*. Construct a scatter diagram for these data. What conclusions can you reach?

18. The number of defects found in 25 samples of 100 Buenosdientes Candy Company lemon drops taken on a daily basis from a production line over a five-week period is given in the worksheet *Prob. 9-18*.
    a. Compute dpmo and find the sigma level.
    b. Plot these data on a run chart. Can you identify any special causes?

    c. Plot the data on the appropriate control chart. Does this confirm your answer to part (b) or does it provide better information?

19. Analysis of customer complaints at the Lauren Elizabeth Apparel Company revealed errors in five categories, such as billing, shipping, etc. Data can be found in the worksheet *Prob. 9-19*. Construct a Pareto diagram for these data. What conclusions can you reach?

20. The Monterey Fiesta Mexican Restaurant is trying to determine whether sales of its popular Pan Con Mucho Sabor breadsticks are correlated with the sales of margaritas. It has data on sales of breadstick baskets and margaritas for 25 weeks, shown in the worksheet *Prob. 9-20*. Plot a scatter diagram and compute the correlation using Excel tools. What do your results indicate?

PROJECTS, ETC.

1. Three popular websites for Six Sigma are http://www.ge.com/sixsigma, http://www.isixsigma.com, and http://asq.org/sixsigma. Explore these sites and consider the following questions.
    a. How does GE use Six Sigma to enhance customer perception of its products and services?
    b. What is the apparent purpose of the isixsigma website?
    c. Who are the customers of the sixsigmaforum website?
    d. Do the three websites reach basic agreement about the concept of Six Sigma? How do they differ?

2. Identify an important problem around your school or in some related function, such as a student organization, and apply the DMAIC process to develop an improved solution. Use whatever process improvement tools are appropriate.

3. Find a local company that is using Six Sigma or lean principles. Write a case study of their

experiences, focusing on the challenges they faced during their implementation efforts.

4. Develop a flowchart of the process you use to study for an exam. How might you improve this process?

5. In small teams, develop cause-and-effect diagrams for the following problems:
    a. Poor exam grade
    b. No job offers
    c. Late for work or school

6. Search the Internet for websites that contain descriptions and examples of quality improvement methodologies. How do they compare with the ones described in this chapter?

7. Work with teachers at a local high school or grade school to identify some students who are having difficulties in school. Apply quality tools to help find the source of the problems and create an improvement plan.

CASES

LT, INC.[54]

LT, Inc. started as a small, family-owned company. For a long time, owners managed most of the operations, including billing, and customers were happy. Over time, the

company grew steadily and acquired plants in the United States and many other countries. Most of its operations were departmentalized, and the accounting systems varied among the many companies LT acquired. While LT successfully dealt with most of the problems caused by rapid growth, it remained unable to get a grip on billing errors. The customer service and billing departments were often flooded with complaints about erroneous bills.

The billing process at LT evolved over time, resulting in a lack of consistency among billing personnel. Customer order taking and billing procedures were confusing, inadequate and obsolete. Not all billing clerks had the same level of knowledge and training. A lack of documentation added to the confusion and

aggravated the situation. Billing personnel followed the policies and procedures they thought were reasonable and did things the way they felt was right.

To get a handle on its billing problem, LT appointed a Six Sigma team comprised of employees with various interdisciplinary backgrounds and expertise. The team discussed the problem, researched Six Sigma and lean tools and techniques, learned from other companies and consulted with experts in the field.

The first thing the team did was study the billing process and prepare a flowchart (see Figure 9.26). The

FIGURE 9.26
Flowchart of LT
Billing Process

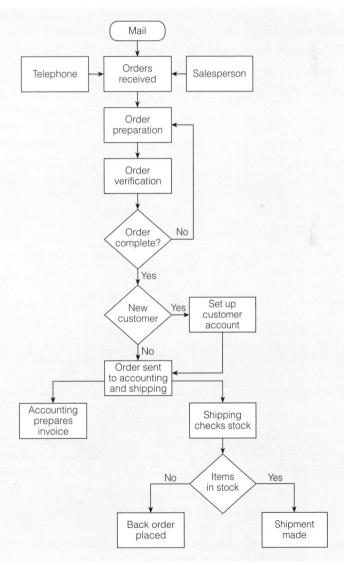

Source: Reprinted with permission from Lakshmi U. Tatikonda, "A Less Costly Billing Process," *Quality Progress*, January 2008, pp. 31–39. Copyright © 2008 American Society for Quality. No further distribution allowed without permission.

team then reviewed how billing errors were resolved. Most scenarios followed a similar path: A customer calls to inquire about a bill and listens to a pre-recorded message with menu options. The customer listens to several options that don't describe their particular problem and gets frustrated when the system only deals with select inquiries. After several minutes, the customer finally gets to speak to a customer service representative, but only after being put on hold or bounced from one representative to another, forcing the customer to repeat the problem several times. Finally, the customer is assured the problem will be corrected, only to have the next month bring the same bill, the same error, the same complaint, the same aggravation and, in the end, the loss of an annoyed customer.

A further study revealed many different types of billing errors:

- Bills with wrong prices and charges
- Bills sent to the wrong customer
- Bills sent to the wrong address
- Double billing and late billing
- Billing for unordered goods
- Billing for returned goods
- Billing before the goods were shipped

Using cause-and-effect diagrams, the Six Sigma team brainstormed potential causes and explored them in depth (see Figure 9.27). A Pareto analysis showed that 70 percent of the errors were due to an incorrect amount on the bill or billing for unordered goods.

To gain a better understanding of the sources of communication errors, the team members decided to walk through the billing activities. Customer orders arrived via mail, fax and phone. At each step, they were batched and queued for processing. The main steps included: order taking (folders made for each customer), order preparation (current and new customers sorted, information added), order pricing, shipping, and billing. Table 9.5 provides a detailed description of the activities.

Using the information provided, outline specific steps that you would recommend to improve the process. Include a list of performance metrics that you would recommend that the company monitor in the future to track the efficiency and effectiveness of the process. Summarize your results in a formal report the company's management.

FIGURE 9.27   Cause-and-Effect Diagram for Billing Errors

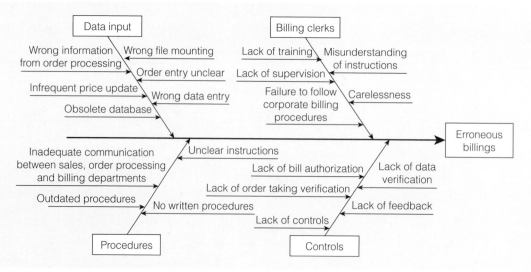

TABLE 9.5   Data and Activities Included in the Billing Process

Customer	Order Preparation	Billing
• Orders via mail, fax, phone, and e-mail. • Average daily orders: 200/day Central mailroom • Receive outside mail. • Sort according to departments. • Put in boxes. • Deliver to departments. • Stamp postage and send out-going mail. Order taking • Receive orders from customers and central mailroom, • Open customer mail orders. • Record customer phone orders on paper. • Sort all orders by customer name and stamp date. • Prepare folders with customer order information. • Move batch of customer orders to order preparation once a day. Credit check • Check customer credit once a week. • Add credit status to folders. • Sort customers according to acceptable and not acceptable credit. • Batch and move the sorted folders to billing.	• Receive folders with customer order information. • Sort folders according to new and current customers. • Send new customer folders to data processing. • Receive new customer folders from data processing. • Move customers order folders to order verification. • Receive folders from order verification. • Make two copies of customer order folders. • Send one copy of the order to shipping and one copy to billing. Data processing • Receive new customer folders from order taking. • Batch the folders, assign a customer number and create customer record. • Add new customer number and other information to customer folders. • Batch customer folders to order preparation once a day. Order verification • Receive customer order folders from order preparation. • Check stock availability. • Make price estimates. • Add price estimates to customer order folder. • Move the folders to order preparation once a day.	• Receive copy of customer order folders from order preparation. • Send new customer folders to credit check. • Receive customer folders from credit check with credit status. • Sort the customer folders according to acceptable and not acceptable credit. • Send the customer folders with not acceptable status back to order takers. • Send the acceptable customer folders to sales tax department. • Receive customer folders from sales tax. • Calculate the total amount (purchases, taxes) to bill. • Enter all the necessary data into computer and print invoices twice a month. • Address envelopes, fold, insert invoices and close. Move the envelopes to central mailroom twice a day. Shipping • Receive customer order folders from other preparation. • Pick and pack the items in the order. • Print and paste address labels on the boxes. • Ship the packages twice a day.

Source: Reprinted with permission from Lakshmi U. Tatikonda, "A Less Costly Billing Process," *Quality Progress*, January 2008, pp. 31–39. Copyright © 2008 American Society for Quality. No further distribution allowed without permission.

ROCKSTONE TIRES[55]

Rockstone makes tires for the automotive market. Employees noticed that there is a great deal of congestion at the shipping dock as pallets of material that had been picked in the warehouse were waiting to be moved by forklifts to outbound tractor-trailers. Warehouse stock-picking employees had to wait their turn, move the product onto the trucks, and return to a distant location in the warehouse to pick up another order to process.

You have been assigned as a Lean Six Sigma project manager to improve this process. Write a project charter and discuss what information you would need to collect in order to perform the improvement project. How might the DMAIC process be used to systematically tackle this project? Also, discuss what tools you would most likely use in the project.

JANSON MEDICAL CLINIC

The Janson Medical Clinic recently conducted a patient satisfaction survey of 100 patients. Using a scale of 1–5, with 1 being "very dissatisfied" and 5 being "very satisfied," the clinic compiled a check sheet for responses that were either 1 or 2, indicating dissatisfaction with the performance attributes. This check sheet is shown in Table 9.6.

Doctors have extremely busy schedules. They have surgeries to perform, and many are teaching faculty at the local medical school. Many surgeries are emergencies or take longer than expected, resulting in delays in getting back to the clinic.

In the clinic, one or two telephone receptionists answer calls for three different departments, which

include 20 or more doctors. Their job is basically to schedule appointments, provide directions, and transfer calls to the proper secretaries, which generally requires putting the patient on hold. Often, the receptionist must take a handwritten message and personally deliver it to the secretary because the secretary's phone line is busy. However, the receptionist cannot leave her desk without someone else to cover the phones.

A student intern examined the processes for answering phone calls and registering patients. The flowcharts she developed are shown in Figures 9.28 and 9.29.

TABLE 9.6   Check Sheet of Dissatisfied Responses

Making an Appointment
Ease of getting through on the phone—10
Friendliness of the telephone receptionist—5
Convenience of office hours—7
Ease of getting a convenient appointment—12

Check-in/Check-out
Courtesy and helpfulness of the receptionist—7
Amount of time to register—1
Length of wait to see a physician—13
Comfort of registration waiting area—4

Care and Treatment
Respect shown by nurses/assistants—0
Responsiveness to phone calls related to care—5
How well the physician listened—3
Respect shown by the physician—2
Confidence in the physician's ability—1
Explanation of medical condition and treatment—2

FIGURE 9.28   Current Process for Answering Phone Calls

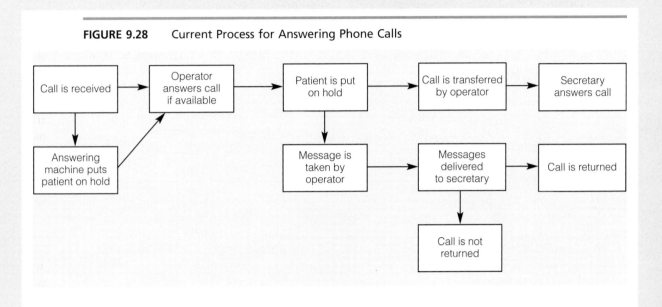

FIGURE 9.29   Current Patient Registration Process

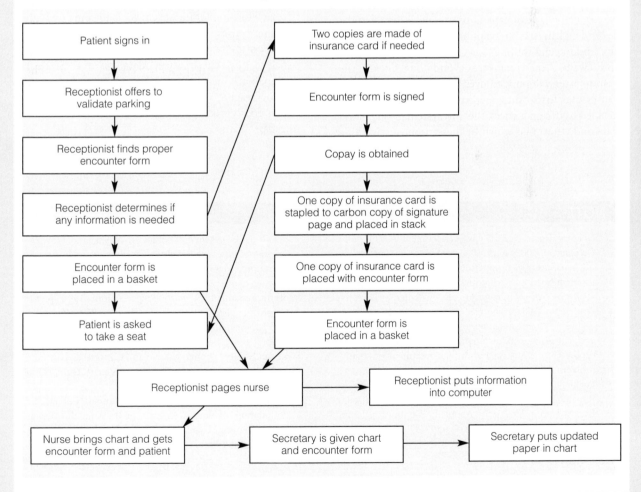

Discussion Questions

1. Construct a Pareto diagram for the causes of dissatisfaction. What conclusions do you reach?
2. Select the top three sources of patient dissatisfaction and propose cause-and-effect diagrams for the possible reasons behind them.
3. Propose some process improvements to the flow-charts in Figure 9.28 and develop redesigned processes along with new flowcharts. How will your suggestions address the sources of dissatisfaction in Table 9.6?

FREADILUNCH RESTAURANT

Fred Read, the owner of the Freadilunch (pronounced Freddylunch) Restaurant, a suburban, quick service restaurant, was concerned about the loss of several regular customers. He measured the number of empty lunch tables from 11 A.M. until 2 P.M. over a four-week period. To better understand the reasons for the loss of customers, long lines, and dissatisfied patrons, Fred talked to several regular customers. He found that they liked the food and atmosphere of the restaurant, but felt that there were opportunities for improvement based on the lack of capability to quickly handle take-out orders (they had to be phoned in, not faxed), excessive time spent waiting for tables, inefficient service, surly waiters on certain days, and long lines at the cash register. He puzzled over how to sort out possible causes that led to these perceived problems. Fred also decided to design a check sheet to systematically gather data and determine which of these problems were the most significant. (Data for the check sheet information gathered for "Vacant Tables" and for "Customer Concerns" can be found in the *Freadilunch 1* and *Freadilunch 2* tabs in the Excel workbook *C09Data.xlsx* on the Student Companion Site.)

Discussion Questions

1. Plot the average number of empty tables on a run chart, computing the average value (center line), but ignoring the control limits. What do these data show?
2. Use one or more of the seven Tools to come up with possible causes to explain customer dissatisfaction, based on the reasons described in the case.
3. Analyze the check sheet data on the Student Companion Site for this chapter. What conclusions do you reach?
4. What do you recommend that Fred do to overcome these problems?

NOTES

1. Gregory Korte, "473 Steps," *The Cincinnati Enquirer*, October 30, 2002, A1, A10.
2. A. VanGundy, "Comparing 'Little Known' Creative Problem-Solving Techniques," in *Creativity Week III, 1980 Proceedings* (Greensboro, NC: Center for Creative Leadership, 1981). The reader is also referred to James R. Evans, *Creative Thinking in the Decision and Management Sciences* (Cincinnati, OH: South-Western Publishing Co., 1991), for a thorough treatment of creative problem solving from business decision perspectives.
3. For the history of the evolution of the Deming Cycle, see Ronald D. Moen and Clifford L. Norman, "Circling Back: Clearing Up Myths About the Deming Cycle and Seeing How It Keeps Evolving," *Quality Progress*, November 2011, pp. 22–28.
4. See Ronald D. Moen, Thomas R. Nolan, and Lloyd P. Provost, *Improving Quality Through Planned Experimentation*, McGraw-Hill, 1991, p. 11; Gerald Langley, Kevin Nolan, and Thomas R. Nolan, "The Foundation of Improvement," *Quality Progress*, June 1994, p. 81; Gerald Langley, Kevin Nolan, Thomas R. Nolan, Clifford L. Norman, and Lloyd P. Provost, *The Improvement Guide*, Jossey-Bass, 1996, p. 10; and Gerald Langley, Kevin Nolan, Thomas R. Nolan, Clifford L. Norman, and Lloyd P. Provost, *The Improvement Guide*, 2nd ed., Jossey-Bass, 2009, p. 24.
5. Gerald Langley, Kevin Nolan, and Thomas Nolan, "The Foundation of Improvement," Sixth Annual International Deming User's Group Conference, Cincinnati, OH (August 1992).

6. Gerald Langley, Kevin Nolan and Thomas R. Nolan, "The Foundation of Improvement," *Quality Progress*, June 1994, p. 81.

7. Masaaki Imai, *Kaizen: The Key to Japan's Competitive Success* (New York: McGraw-Hill, 1986), 15.

8. A. F. Osborn, *Applied Imagination*, 3rd ed. (New York: Scribner's, 1963); S. J. Parnes, R. B. Noller, and A. M. Biondi (eds.), *Guide to Creative Action* (New York: Scribner's, 1977).

9. Reprinted with permission of Chris Bott, Elizabeth Keim, Sai Kim, and Lisa Palser, "Service Quality Six Sigma Case Studies," *ASQ's 54th Annual Congress Proceedings*, 2000, 225–231. No further distribution allowed without permission.

10. "Origin of Six Sigma: Designing for Performance Excellence," *Quality Digest*, (May 2000), 30; Harry Mikel and Richard Schroeder. *Six Sigma* (New York: Currency, 2000), 9–11.

11. Jack Welch, *Jack: Straight from the Gut* (New York: Warner Books, 2001), 329–330.

12. Jack Welch, ibid, 333–334.

13. "GE Reports Record Earnings with Six Sigma," *Quality Digest*, December 1999, 14.

14. Jack Welch, ibid, 329–330.

15. Rochelle Rucker, "Six Sigma at Citibank," *Quality Digest*, December 1999, 28–32.

16. Ronald D. Snee, "Why Should Statisticians Pay Attention to Six Sigma?" *Quality Progress*, September 1999, 100–103.

17. A composite of ideas suggested by Stanley A. Marash, "Six Sigma: Business Results Through Innovation," *ASQ's 54th Annual Quality Congress Proceedings*, 2000, 627–630; Dick Smith and Jerry Blakeslee, *Strategic Six Sigma: Best Practices from the Executive Suite* (New York: Wiley, 2002).

18. Ronald D. Snee, "Guest Editorial: Impact of Six Sigma on Quality Engineering," *Quality Engineering* 12, no. 3, 2000, ix–xiv.

19. Kervin Linderman, Roger G. Schroeder, Srilata Zaheer, and Adrian S. Choo, "Six Sigma: A Goal-Theoretic Perspective," *Journal of Operations Management* 21, (2003), 193–203.

20. Charles H. Kepner and Benjamin B. Tregoe, *The Rational Manager* (New York: McGraw-Hill, 1965).

21. Gerald F. Smith, "Too Many Types of Quality Problems," *Quality Progress*, April 2000, 43–49.

22. H. James Harrington, "Creating Organizational Excellence—Part Two," *Quality Digest*, February 2003, 14.

23. *A Guide to the Project Management Body of Knowledge* (PMBOK® Guide)—4th ed. (Newtown Square, PA: Project Management Institute), 2008.

24. Elaine Schmidt, "Where the Rubber Meets the Road," *iSixSigma Magazine*, May/June 2010, pp. 23–29.

25. George Eckes, *The Six Sigma Revolution* (New York: John Wiley & Sons, 2001), 251–254.

26. Donald P. Lynch, Suzanne Bertolino, and Elaine Cloutier, "How to Scope DMAIC Projects," *Quality Progress* 36, no. 1 (January 2003), 37–44.

27. R. T. Rust, A. J. Zahorik, and T. L. Keiningham, "Return on Quality (ROQ): Making Service Quality Financially Accountable," *Journal of Marketing* 59, no. 2 (April 1995), 58–70.

28. Jeffrey K. Pinto, "The Power of Project Management," *Industry Week*, August 18, 1997, 138–140.

29. "Six Sigma at GE-Lunar, Manufacturing and Technology Matters," Erdman Center for Manufacturing and Technology Management, University of Wisconsin-Madison School of Business, Fall/Winter 2002, 1–3.

30. Arthur Fornari and George Maszle, "Lean Six Sigma Leads Xerox," *Six Sigma Forum Magazine*, August 2004, 11–16.

31. Thomas Pyzdek, *The Six Sigma Handbook* (Tuscon, AZ: McGraw-Hill/Quality Publishing, 2001), 301.

32. Satya S. Chakravorty, "Process Improvement: Using Toyota's A3 Reports," *Quality Management Journal* 16, no. 4 (2009), pp. 7–26.

33. Roger W. Hoerl, "Six Sigma and the Future of the Quality Profession," *Quality Progress*, June 1998, 35–42. © 1998, American Society for Quality. Reprinted with permission.

34. Adapted from Bruce Rudin, "Simple Tools Solve Complex Problems." Reprinted with permission from Quality, April 1990, 50–51; a publication of Hitchcock Publishing, a Capital Cities/ABC, Inc.

35. "The Tools of Quality Part V: Check Sheets," *Quality Progress* 23, no. 10 (October 1990), 53.

36. Kaoru Ishikawa, *Guide to Quality Control*, 2nd rev. ed. (Tokyo: Asian Productivity Organization, 1986). Available from UNIPUB/Quality Resources, One Water Street, White Plains, NY 10601.

37. "NCR Corporation," in *Profiles in Quality* (Needham Heights, MA: Allyn and Bacon, 1991).

38. Howard H. Bailie, "Organize Your Thinking with a Why-Why Diagram," *Quality Progress* 18, no. 12 (December 1985), 22–24.

39. A. F. Osborn, *Applied Imagination*, 3rd ed. (New York: Scribners, 1963); S. J. Parnes, R. B. Noller, and A. M. Biondi (eds.), *Guide to Creative Action* (New York: Scribners, 1977).

40. Gary Conner, "Benefitting from Six Sigma," *Manufacturing Engineering*, February 2003, 53–59.

41. Gary Conner, "Benefitting from Six Sigma," *Manufacturing Engineering*, February 2003, 53–59.

42. Anthony R. Goland, John Hall, and Devereaux A. Clifford, "First National Toyota," *The McKinsey Quarterly* no. 4 (1998), 58–66.

43. Patricia Houghton, "Improving Pharmacy Service," *Quality Digest*, October 18, 2007.

44. "Study Shows Six Sigma, Lean Are Merging," *Industry Week*, March 7, 2008.

45. Kate Burrows, "Outside of the Box," *iSixSigma Magazine*, January/February 2011, pp. 22–30.

46. Soren Bisgaard, Roger W. Hoerl, and Ronald D. Snee, "Improving Business Processes with Six Sigma," *Proceedings of ASQ's 56th Annual Quality Congress*, 2002 (CD-ROM); Kennedy Smith, "Six Sigma for the Service Sector," *Quality Digest*, May 2003, 23–28.

47. Adapted from Elizabeth Keim, LouAnn Fox, and Julie S. Mazza, "Service Quality Six Sigma Case Studies," *Proceedings of the 54th Annual Quality Congress of the American Society for Quality*, 2000 (CD-ROM).

48. Lisa Palser, "Cycle Time Improvement for a Human Resources Process," *ASQ's 54th Annual Quality Congress Proceedings*, 2000 (CD-ROM).

49. Zachery Brice, "Six Sigma Sharpens Services," *Quality Digest*, May 2004, 37–42.

50. Laura Smith, "Six Sigma Goes to Washington," *Quality Digest*, May 2005, 20–24.

51. Reprinted with permission from Cathy Buck, "Application of Six Sigma to Reduce Medical Errors," *Proceedings of the 55th Annual Quality Congress of the American Society for Quality*, 2001 (CD-ROM). © 2001, American Society for Quality. No further reproduction allowed without permission.

52. Reprinted with permission from Davis R. Bothe, "Improve Service and Administration," *Quality Progress*, September 2003, 53–57. Copyright © 2003 American Society for Quality. No further distribution allowed without permission.

53. Adapted from Ronald G. Conant, "JIT in a Mail Order Operation Reduces Processing Time from Four Days to Four Hours," *Industrial Engineering* 20, no. 9 (September 1988), 34–37.

54. Reprinted with permission from Lakshmi U. Tatikonda, "A Less Costly Billing Process," *Quality Progress*, January 2008, 31–39. Copyright © 2008 American Society for Quality. No further distribution allowed without permission.

55. Inspired by a project described in Elaine Schmidt, "Where the Rubber Meets the Road," *iSixSigma Magazine*, May/June 2010, pp. 23–29.

PART 3

Beyond Quality Management: Managing for Performance Excellence

In Parts I and II of this book we established the principles of quality management and the tools and techniques by which quality of goods and services can be assured through design, control, and improvement. As the discipline of quality management matured, organizations discovered that the quality of management practices is as important to build and sustain a successful organization as the quality of its goods and services.

In Part III we focus on the organizational aspect of quality, which we called *performance excellence* in Chapter 1. The concept of performance excellence was created and promoted through the Baldrige Performance Excellence Program and its Criteria. Many of the principles of TQ that we discussed in previous chapters are embodied within the Criteria. However, the Criteria provide a much broader framework on which to improve all aspects of managing an organization, well beyond a focus on the quality goods and services.

From its inception in 1987 until 2012, the Baldrige program was administered through the National Institute of Standards and Technology, a division of the United States Department of Commerce. In 2012, the House Appropriations Committee of the U.S. Congress targeted dozens of federal programs for elimination to reduce the federal budget by at least $1.5 billion. Unfortunately, even though the portion of its budget that came from federal funding was miniscule (only $9.6 million), the Baldrige program was among them, and Congress approved the committee's recommendation.

The Baldrige program reacted quickly and began a transition to a sustainable, non-government-supported business model. (While it is unclear how this will be realized by the time this edition is published, you can search for "Baldrige transition" on the Internet to seek current information about it. The program's current website as of 2012, www.nist.gov/baldrige provides extensive information about the Baldrige program.) In April 2012, the Baldrige Foundation committed funds to sustain the program through the fiscal year 2015. The Baldrige program has had a substantial impact on organizations throughout the world, and we are confident that it will continue to lead in building performance excellence and providing organizational leaders with a roadmap to achieving high quality and outstanding results throughout their organizations.

Chapter 10 introduces the Baldrige Criteria for Performance Excellence as a framework for building and managing successful organizations and discusses its global influence. Chapter 11 focuses on performance excellence from a strategic perspective, how organizations design for performance excellence, and how they use strategic planning processes to focus on the future and build a sustainable organization. In Chapter 12, we learn how organizations measure organizational performance (beyond specific quality measurements that we introduced in Chapter 8) and manage information and knowledge. Chapter 13 discusses leadership—the driver of quality and performance excellence, and how organizations implement performance excellence practices. Finally, Chapter 14 focuses on building and sustaining performance excellence in organizations.

The Baldrige Framework for Performance Excellence

"There is no single more important job or initiative in this company than performance excellence." These are the words that Ronald L. Nelson, CEO of Avis Budget Group Inc. (ABG), chose when he addressed an assembly of ABG's top 70 senior executives, asking them to join him in leading every location, operation, and department down the road to performance excellence. Within a year performance excellence has become the way ABG does business, and has positioned the company to meet business challenges more effectively than ever before.[1]

The concept of performance excellence has its roots in the Malcolm Baldrige Award. Recognizing that U.S. productivity was declining, President Reagan signed legislation mandating a national study/conference on productivity in October 1982. The American Productivity and Quality Center (formerly the American Productivity Center) sponsored seven computer networking conferences in 1983 to prepare for an upcoming White House Conference on Productivity. The final report on these conferences recommended

The Deming Application Prize was instituted in 1951 by the Union of Japanese Scientists and Engineers (JUSE) in recognition and appreciation of W. Edwards Deming's achievements in statistical quality control and his friendship with the Japanese people. Details about the Deming Prize can be found at http://www.juse.or.jp/e/index .html.

that a National Quality Award, similar to the Deming Prize, which had been given in Japan since 1951, be awarded annually to those firms that successfully challenge and meet the award requirements. The Malcolm Baldrige National Quality Improvement Act was signed into law (Public Law 100-107) on August 20, 1987. The focus of the program was defined as follows:

- Helping to stimulate American companies to improve quality and productivity for the pride of recognition while obtaining a competitive edge through increased profits;
- Recognizing the achievements of those companies that improve the quality of their goods and services and providing an example to others;
- Establishing guidelines and criteria that can be used by business, industrial, governmental, and other enterprises in evaluating their own quality improvement efforts; and
- Providing specific guidance for other American enterprises that wish to learn how to manage for high quality by making available detailed information on how winning enterprises were able to change their cultures and achieve eminence.

The award was named The Malcolm Baldrige National Quality Award after President Reagan's Secretary of Commerce, who was killed in an accident shortly before the Senate acted on the legislation. Malcolm Baldrige was highly regarded by world leaders, having played a major role in carrying out the administration's trade policy, resolving technology transfer differences with China and India, and holding the first Cabinet-level talks with the Soviet Union in seven years, which paved the way for increased access for U.S. firms in the Soviet market. Initially, awards were established in the categories of manufacturing, small business, and service. Congress approved award categories in nonprofit education and health care in 1999. A final award category for other types of nonprofits was approved and implemented in 2007. This allowed virtually any organization to apply for the Award. Table 10.1 lists the recipients of the Award through 2012.

The award evolved into a comprehensive National Quality Program that, up until 2012 (see the introduction to Part III of this book), was funded primarily through a private foundation and administered through the National Institute of Standards and Technology in the Department of Commerce as a public–private partnership. In 2010, via an act of Congress, the Program changed its name to the Baldrige Performance Excellence Program, dropping the term "quality" to signify its broader mission: to improve the competitiveness and performance of U.S. organizations, rather than merely the improvement of quality, which many people associate primarily with goods and services. The award's name also changed to simply the Malcolm Baldrige Award, although the former name is often used.

In this chapter we introduce the award's Criteria for Performance Excellence, which establishes a framework for integrating total quality principles and practices in any organization. We also describe and contrast Baldrige with other quality and performance excellence awards and frameworks around the world.

TABLE 10.1   Malcolm Baldrige Award Recipients

Manufacturing
Motorola, Inc. (1988)
Westinghouse Commercial Nuclear Fuel Division (1988)
Xerox Corp. Business Products and Systems (1989)
Milliken & Co. (1989)
Cadillac Motor Car Division (1990)
IBM Rochester (1990)
Solectron Corp. (1991)
Zytec Corp. (now part of Artesyn Technologies) (1991)
AT&T Network Systems (now Lucent Technologies, Inc. Optical Networking Group) (1992)
Texas Instruments Defense Systems & Electronics Group (now part of Raytheon Systems Co.) (1992)
Eastman Chemical Co. (1993)
Armstrong World Industries Building Products Operations (1995)
Corning Telecommunications Products Division (1995)
ADAC Laboratories (1996)
3M Dental Products Division (1997)
Solectron Corp. (1997)
Boeing Airlift and Tanker Programs (1998)
Solar Turbines, Inc. (1998)
STMicroelectronics, Inc.–Region Americas (1999)
Dana Corporation–Spicer Driveshaft Division (now Torque Traction Technologies, Inc.) (2000)
KARLEE Company (2000)
Clarke American Checks, Inc. (2001)
Motorola, Inc. Commercial, Government and Industrial Solutions Sector (2002)
Medrad, Inc. (2003)
The Bama Companies, Inc. (2004)
Sunny Fresh Foods, Inc. (2005)
Cargill Corn Milling North America (2008)
Honeywell Federal Manufacturing & Technologies, LLC (2009)
MEDRAD (2010)
Nestlé Purina PetCare Co. (2010)
Lockheed Martin Missiles and Fire Control (2012)

Small Business
Globe Metallurgical, Inc. (1988)
Wallace Co., Inc. (1990)
Marlow Industries (1991)
Graniterock Co. (1992)
Ames Rubber Corp. (1993)
Wainwright Industries, Inc. (1994)
Custom Research, Inc. (1996)
Trident Precision Manufacturing, Inc. (1996)
Texas Nameplate Company, Inc. (1998)
Sunny Fresh Foods (1999)
Los Alamos National Bank (2000)
Stoner, Inc. (2003)
Texas Nameplate Company, Inc. (2004)

(continued)

TABLE 10.1   Malcolm Baldrige Award Recipients (*Continued*)

Park Place Lexus (2005)
MESA Products, Inc. (2006)
PRO-TEC Coating Company (2007)
MESA Products, Inc. (2012)

Service
Federal Express (FedEx) (1990)
AT&T Universal Card Services (now part of Citigroup) (1992)
The Ritz-Carlton Hotel Co. (now part of Marriott International) (1992)
AT&T Consumer Communication Services (now the Consumer Markets Division of AT&T) (1994)
Verizon Information Services (formerly GTE Directories, Inc.) (1994)
Dana Commercial Credit Corp. (1996)
Merrill Lynch Credit Corp. (1997)
Xerox Business Services (1997)
BI (1999)
The Ritz-Carlton Hotel Company, LLC (1999)
Operations Management International, Inc. (2000)
Pal's Sudden Service (2001)
Branch-Smith Printing Division (2002)
Boeing Aerospace Support (2003)
Caterpillar Financial Services (2003)
DynMcDermott Petroleum Operations (2005)
Premier Inc. (2006)
MidwayUSA (2009)
Freese and Nichols Inc. (2010)
K&N Management (2010)
Studer Group (2010)

Education
Chugach School District (2001)
Pearl River School District (2001)
University of Wisconsin–Stout (2001)
Community Consolidated School District #15, Palatine, IL (2003)
Robert W. Monfort College of Business (2004)
Richland College (2005)
Jenks Public Schools (2005)
Iredell-Statesville Schools (2008)
Montgomery County Public Schools (2010)

Health Care
SSM Health Care (2002)
Baptist Hospital, Inc., Pensacola, FL (2003)
Saint Luke's Hospital of Kansas City (2003)
Robert Wood Johnson University Hospital Hamilton (2004)
Bronson Methodist Hospital (2005)
North Mississippi Medical Center (2006)
Mercy Health System (2007)
Sharp HealthCare (2007)
Poudre Valley Health System (2008)

(*continued*)

TABLE 10.1   Malcolm Baldrige Award Recipients (*Continued*)

AtlantiCare (2009)
Heartland Health (2009)
Advocate Good Samaritan Hospital (2010)
Henry Ford Health System (2011)
Schneck Medical Center (2011)
Southcentral Foundation (2011)
North Mississippi Health Services (2012)

Nonprofit
City of Coral Springs (2007)
U.S. Army Armament Research, Development and Engineering Center (2007)
VA Cooperative Studies Program Clinical Research Pharmacy Coordinating Center (2009)
Concordia Publishing House (2011)
City of Irving (2012)

quality**profiles**

Heartland Health and the Cedar Foundation

Heartland Health (HH) is a not-for-profit, community-based integrated health system serving the residents of northwest Missouri, northeast Kansas, southeast Nebraska, and southwest Iowa. Their three-level Health Pyramid depicts the structure for HH's business entities. At the top is Heartland Regional Medical Center (HRMC), a 353-bed tertiary care hospital, and Heartland Clinic, a group practice of 107 physicians. In the middle is Community Health Improvement Solutions, which promotes individual health and provides disease management. At the bottom is Heartland Foundation, the organization's outreach arm to help build a healthier, more livable community. The Health Pyramid aligns all HH entities to further its mission to "improve the health of individuals and communities located in the Heartland region and provide the right care" and its vision to make the area "the best and safest place in America to receive health care and live a healthy and productive life."

Senior leaders use the framework of the Baldrige Criteria for Performance Excellence to take action on the organization's mission and strategic objectives. Among the tools used to achieve these objectives are an integrated, organization-wide strategic planning process, balanced scorecards, and a fully deployed workforce management system. The organization's strategic planning process ensures sustainability, allowing HH to anticipate health care industry changes in time for course corrections, as well as to plan for major capital, building, and strategic projects. The balanced scorecard aligns performance measures with organizational strategies. The *People Plan* ensures that every element of the caregiver (employee, volunteer, and health care practitioner) life cycle is carried out according to industry best practices and aligns with the HH mission, vision, and strategic framework. In 2009, HRMC received the Patient Safety Excellence Award from Healthgrades, an independent health care rating organization. Health-Grades presents this award to hospitals with overall patient safety records in the top 5 percent of the nation. HRMC is among 75 acute-care hospitals nationwide to receive the Superior Quality Merit Award from the 2009–2010 Hospital Value Index study by Data Advantage, LLC. In addition, the Commonwealth Fund, a nonprofit quality rating system, ranked HRMC the 19th-best hospital in the nation in 2009, based on measures of evidenced-based care, patient experience, readmission, mortality rates, and costs.

The Cedar Foundation is a leading voluntary organization in Northern Ireland and is a chief contributor to delivering services to disabled people including people with brain injury. The organization delivers its mission by living and upholding its Values of Respect for the Individual; Equality of Opportunity; Pursuit of

Excellence; Openness and Accountability; Teamwork and Partnership; and Commitment and Enthusiasm. In the 1990s, The Cedar Foundation went through a significant period of change in response to the changing expectations of disabled people and the sponsors. In order to respond to the changing market, the Foundation committed to a process of continuous improvement and the application of a range of quality management tools was central to the strategy. The organization adopted and has continued to use the Balanced Scorecard approach (see Chapter 8) to business planning. In 2005, ISO 9001:2000 registration was achieved by the whole organization. The Foundation was the first voluntary organization in Northern Ireland to use the European Federation for Quality Management (EFQM) Excellence Model, which is similar to the Baldrige Award, and was a 2007 EFQM Award winner.

The Cedar Foundation has derived significant benefits from its journey towards excellence; the organization has enjoyed substantial financial growth, more than doubling its customer and service base in the last 10 years. By applying quality standards, the Foundation is able to identify and embrace best practice, thereby delivering better quality services, which achieve better results for service users and higher levels of customer satisfaction. At every level of the organization there is a clear understanding of and commitment to the vision and mission, which translates into a focus on the achievement of defined results. Strong leadership within the Foundation ensures that leaders are accessible to all stakeholders. The Foundation's comprehensive process management system ensures the effective execution and implementation of policy and strategy. Processes are reviewed and improved against factual information. There has also been a significant impact on the Foundation's people; staffs are expressing high levels of satisfaction, turnover is reducing, and retention and absenteeism has improved.

Source for Heartland Health: Malcolm Baldrige Award Recipient Profiles, National Institute of Standards and Technology, U.S. Department of Commerce.

Source for The Cedar Foundation: EFQM 2007 Recognition Book (http://excellenceone.efqm.org/Default.aspx?tabid=381). Reprinted with permission.

THE CRITERIA FOR PERFORMANCE EXCELLENCE

The Baldrige Award examination is based upon a rigorous set of criteria, called the **Criteria for Performance Excellence**, designed to encourage companies to enhance their competitiveness through an aligned approach to organizational performance management that results in:

1. Delivery of ever-improving value to customers, resulting in improved marketplace success
2. Improvement of overall company performance and capabilities
3. Organizational and personal learning

The criteria consist of a hierarchical set of *categories*, *items*, and *areas to address*. The seven categories and a brief description of each are described next.

1. *Leadership*: As the first of the seven categories, it signifies the critical importance of leadership to business success. Item 1.1, Senior Leadership, examines the key aspects of senior leaders' responsibilities. It examines how senior leaders set and communicate the organization's vision and values and how they practice these values. It focuses on senior leaders' actions to create a sustainable, high-performing organization with a business, customer, and community focus. Item 1.2, Governance and Societal Responsibilities, examines key aspects of an organization's governance system, including leadership improvement. It also examines how an organization ensures that everyone in the organization behaves legally and ethically and how the organization fulfills its societal responsibilities and supports its key communities.

2. *Strategic Planning*: This category examines how an organization develops strategic objectives and action plans. Item 2.1, Strategy Development, examines how an organization determines its core competencies, strategic challenges, and strategic advantages and establishes its strategic objectives to address its challenges and leverage its advantages. The aim is to strengthen overall performance, competitiveness, and future success. Item 2.2, Strategy Implementation, examines how an organization converts strategic objectives into action plans to accomplish the objectives. It also examines how the organization assesses progress relative to these action plans. The aim is to ensure that strategies are successfully deployed for goal achievement.

3. *Customer Focus*: This category examines how an organization engages its customers for long-term marketplace success and builds a customer-focused culture. Item 3.1, Voice of the Customer, examines an organization's processes for listening to customers and determining their satisfaction and dissatisfaction. It also examines processes for using these data. The aim is to capture meaningful information in order to exceed customers' expectations. Item 3.2, Customer Engagement, examines an organization's processes for identifying and innovating product offerings that serve customers and markets; enabling customers to seek information and support; and using customer, market, and product offering information. The item also examines how the organization builds relationships with customers and manages complaints in order to retain customers and increase their engagement. The aim of these efforts is to improve marketing, build a more customer-focused culture, enhance customer loyalty, and identify opportunities for innovation.

4. *Measurement, Analysis, and Knowledge Management*: This category is positioned as the foundation for all other categories in the systems framework that underlies the Baldrige philosophy and provides a key feedback structure linking business results. Item 4.1, Measurement, Analysis, and Improvement of Organizational Performance, examines an organization's selection and use of data and information for performance measurement, analysis, and review in support of organizational planning and performance improvement. The item serves as a central collection and analysis point in an integrated performance measurement and management system that relies on financial and nonfinancial data and information. The aim of performance measurement, analysis, review, and improvement is to guide the organization's process management toward the achievement of key organizational results and strategic objectives, to anticipate and respond to rapid or unexpected organizational or external changes, and to identify best practices that may be shared. Item 4.2, Management of Information, Knowledge, and Information Technology, examines how the organization ensures the quality and availability of needed data, information, software, and hardware for its workforce, suppliers and partners, collaborators, and customers, normally and in the event of an emergency. It also examines how the organization builds and manages its knowledge assets. The aim is to improve organizational efficiency and effectiveness and to stimulate innovation.

5. *Workforce Focus*: This category examines how an organization builds an effective and supportive workforce environment. Item 5.1, Workforce Environment, examines an organization's workforce environment, workforce capability, and capacity needs, how it meets those needs to accomplish the work of the organization, and how it ensures a safe and supportive work climate. The aim is to build an effective environment for accomplishing work and for supporting the workforce. Item 5.2, Workforce Engagement, examines an organization's systems for engaging, developing, and assessing the engagement of its workforce, with the aim of enabling and

encouraging all members of the workforce to contribute effectively and to the best of their ability. These systems are intended to foster high performance, to address core competencies, and to help accomplish action plans and ensure organizational sustainability.

6. *Operations Focus:* This category examines how an organization designs, manages, and improves its work systems and work processes to deliver customer value and achieve organizational success and sustainability. Item 6.1, Work Systems, examines an organization's overall approach to work system design, management, and improvement, capitalizing on core competencies, with the aim of creating value for customers, preparing for potential emergencies, and achieving organizational success and sustainability. Item 6.2, Work Processes, examines the design, management, and improvement of key work processes, with the aim of creating value for customers, operating efficiently and effectively, and achieving organizational success and sustainability.

7. *Results:* The Results category provides a results focus that encompasses objective evaluation and customers' evaluation of an organization's product offerings, as well as evaluation of key processes and process improvement activities; customer-focused results; workforce results; governance, leadership system, and societal responsibility results; and overall financial and market performance. Through this focus, the criteria's purposes—superior value of offerings as viewed by customers and the marketplace; superior organizational performance as reflected in operational, workforce, legal, ethical, societal, and financial indicators; and organizational and personal learning—are maintained. Category 7 thus provides "real-time" information (measures of progress) for evaluation and improvement of processes and products, in alignment with overall organizational strategy.

The 2011–2012 criteria can be found in the Baldrige Materials folder on the Student Companion Site. We encourage you to read the entire document for clarifying notes and explanations. Also, slightly different versions of the criteria are written for education and health care, primarily to conform to unique language and practices in these sectors. Because the criteria are updated every other year, we suggest that you obtain the latest version from the Baldrige Performance Excellence Program website www.nist .gov/baldrige.

The seven categories form an integrated management system as illustrated in Figure 10.1. The umbrella over the seven categories reflect the fact that organizations must understand its competitive environment, organizational relationships, and strategic situation to develop and implement action plans as a basis for all key decisions. This is accomplished by developing an "organizational profile," which we will discuss in the next chapter. Leadership, Strategic Planning, and Customer Focus represent the "leadership triad," and suggest the importance of integrating these three functions from a strategic perspective to develop the organizational structure and plans to make and deliver goods and services. This leads to how work is executed: Workforce Focus and Operations Focus represent how the work in an organization is accomplished. Good execution leads to good Results. Finally, Measurement, Analysis, and Knowledge Management support the entire framework by providing the foundation for a fact-based system for analysis and improvement. In this fashion, the seven categories represent a logical approach to planning, executing, and reviewing performance that is reminiscent of the Deming cycle. Every activity performed in an organization falls somewhere in this framework.

Each category consists of several items (numbered 1.1, 1.2, 2.1, etc.) that focus on major requirements on which businesses should focus. Each item, in turn, consists of a small number of areas to address (e.g., 6.1a, 6.1b) that seek specific information on

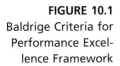

FIGURE 10.1
Baldrige Criteria for Performance Excellence Framework

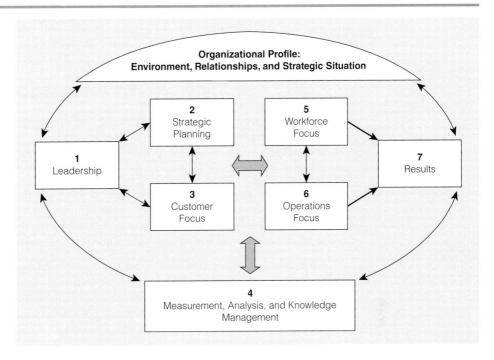

The "key practices for quality management" listed in tables for customer focus, workforce focus, and process focus in Chapters 3, 4, and 5 reflect the Baldrige Criteria requirements for categories 3, 5, and 6 respectively. We will address key practices for the remaining categories in the next three chapters.

approaches used to ensure and improve competitive performance, the deployment of these approaches, or results obtained from such deployment.

For example, the Leadership category in the 2011–2012 Baldrige Criteria consists of two examination items, with a total of five areas to address:

1.1 Senior Leadership
    a. Vision, Values, and Mission
    b. Communication and Organizational Performance

1.2 Governance and Societal Responsibilities
    a. Organizational Governance
    b. Legal and Ethical Behavior
    c. Societal Responsibilities and Support of Key Communities

The Vision, Values, and Mission area to address asks organizations to answer the following questions:

1. *Vision and Values*: How do senior leaders set your organizational vision and values? How do senior leaders deploy your organization's vision and values through your leadership system, to the workforce, to key suppliers and partners, and to customers and other stakeholders, as appropriate? How do senior leaders' personal actions reflect a commitment to the organization's values?

2. *Promoting Legal and Ethical Behavior*: How do senior leaders' actions demonstrate their commitment to legal and ethical behavior? How do they promote an organizational environment that requires it?

3. *Creating a Sustainable Organization*: How do senior leaders create a sustainable organization? How do senior leaders achieve the following:
   - create an environment for organizational performance improvement, the accomplishment of mission and strategic objectives, innovation, performance leadership, and organizational agility
   - create a workforce culture that delivers a consistently positive customer experience and fosters customer engagement
   - create an environment for organizational and workforce learning
   - develop and enhance their leadership skills
   - participate in organizational learning, succession planning and the development of future organizational leaders

To illustrate how an organization might address these questions, consider some of the information for the Leadership category provided by K&N Management (in their own words) in their Award Application Summary (available at the Baldrige website, www .nist.gov/baldrige) for the Vision and Values questions above.

K&N Management is passionate about guest delight and excellence, which is evident throughout our operation. The senior leadership team (SLT) consists of two owners and seven directors who are responsible for setting and deploying the vision and values of the organization. The mission, vision, and KBDs [key business drivers] were originally set by a group of senior leaders and managers as a result of a benchmarking visit to Pal's Sudden Service in 2002. Our vision reflects the passion for guest delight while our mission statement defines the role of each team member in achieving that vision. If team members guarantee that each guest is delighted, we will be recognized world-wide as being excellent in hospitality, processes, and performance. The core values were set by senior leaders with input from team members about what they felt was most fundamentally important about our culture. Our passion for guest delight is integrated into our values, which are thoroughly deployed throughout the organization.

Senior leaders refer to the mission, vision, values, and KBDs throughout key leadership process deployment, measurement, data analysis, evaluation, and performance improvement (Figure 10.2). The mission, vision, values, and KBDs are reviewed annually by the SLT during the strategic planning workshop to decide if any changes should be made.

Our commitment to excellence is evident in our people selection and development processes, concept design, and operational management. The mission, vision, values, and KBDs are first deployed through the Foundations session, then reinforced through training, shift meeting communication, and performance appraisals. The first flashcards in every set of training modules communicate the key elements of our culture to TMs [team members]. During Foundations, TMs receive a culture card that contains the mission, vision, values, KBDs, and the Building Blocks of FISH [a team member morale and motivation philosophy]

Our mission, vision, and values are deployed to key suppliers and guests in a variety of ways. The mission and vision are printed on all business cards. Our guests can easily view our mission, vision, values, and KBDs posted on the walls of our restaurants, the Mighty Fine website, and demonstrated through the attitudes of our team members. Our values are communicated to our key suppliers through a key vendor scorecard conducted annually by the executive director. The criteria of the scorecard essentially holds suppliers accountable to our product and delivery standards. We require our suppliers to provide us with product that meets our quality specifications at the scheduled delivery time in order for us to maintain our KBDs. Suppliers who do not meet the standards of the vendor scorecard are replaced. Figure 10.3 illustrates how senior leaders show their commitment to support the core values of the organization through personal action.[2]

FIGURE 10.2   K&N Management Leadership Performance Excellence Model

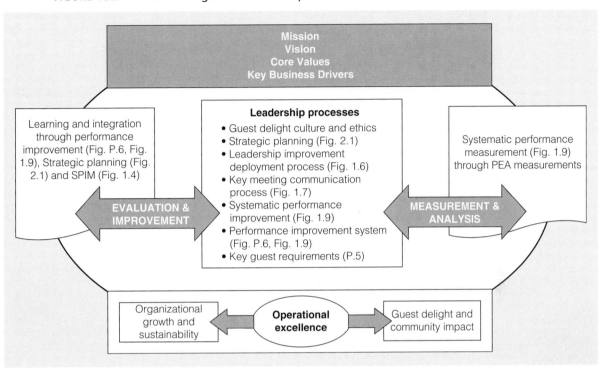

FIGURE 10.3   K&N Management Senior Leadership Support of Values

Value	Example of SLT Personal Action
Excellence	• One owner and two directors completed Quality-Texas Examiner training. • SLT lead the effort to apply Baldrige principles within K&N Management. • Benchmarking best practices inside and outside the hospitality industry. • Sharing process excellence and operational information with others.
Quality	• Facilities design • Product standards • Topgrading selection process • Cleanliness innovations (automatic hand wash sinks) • Resources allocated to keep managers on the front line for maximum guest accessibility.
Integrity	• Role model behavior • Team member comments • On-time payment to suppliers, banks, and team members
Relationships	• Team member picnic • Excellent benefits package • Team member awards • Community impact is the 2010 Yearly Focus • Team member contributions matched for Austin Habitat charity partner • Senior leaders donate time to community impact events

In the Baldrige Criteria, areas to address that request information on approach or deployment begin with the word *how*. This wording means that the organization should be able to describe methods, measures and evaluation, learning, and improvement factors in explaining their approach for meeting the criteria requirements. It also implies that these approaches are performed on a regular basis and embedded in the practices of the organization, and are not simply ad hoc ways of doing business.

One thing the criteria do not do is prescribe specific quality tools, techniques, technologies, systems, or starting points, nor are the criteria associated with any one quality philosophy. Companies are encouraged to develop and demonstrate creative, adaptive, and flexible approaches to meeting basic requirements. Many innovative approaches have been developed by Baldrige recipients and are now commonly used by many other organizations.

The Baldrige Criteria are based on a set of key principles, called the **Core Values and Concepts**:

- Visionary Leadership
- Customer-Driven Excellence
- Organizational and Personal Learning
- Valuing Workforce Members and Partners
- Agility
- Focus on the Future
- Managing for Innovation
- Management by Fact
- Societal Responsibility
- Focus on Results and Creating Value
- Systems Perspective

(They are described in detail in the Baldrige Criteria document.) These values are embedded throughout the criteria and in essence, provide a description of a culture of performance excellence. For example, if you review the criteria for Item 1.1, Senior Leadership, you can easily find direct or implied references to almost all of these values. The Core Values and Concepts represent the underlying philosophy of the criteria, similar to the principles of quality management we discussed in Chapter 2.

Criteria Evolution

As the important management practices of any organization should be, the criteria are evaluated and improved each year. Over the years, the criteria have been streamlined and simplified to make them more easily understood and useful to organizations of all types and sizes, and its content revised to reflect the most relevant business practices and contemporary organizational thinking. For example, the initial set of criteria in 1988 had 62 items with 278 areas to address. Refinements over the next decade made the criteria more generic and user-friendly, and by 1997, resulted in 20 items and 30 areas to address. In 1999, the criteria were reworded in a question format that managers can easily understand. Most significantly, the word "quality" was judiciously dropped in the mid-1990s. For example, prior to 1994, the Strategic Planning category was titled "Strategic Quality Planning." The change to "Strategic Planning" signifies that quality should be a part of an organization's overall business planning, not a separate activity. Throughout the document, the term *performance* has been substituted for *quality* as a conscious attempt to recognize that the principles of total quality are the foundation for a company's entire management system, not just the quality system.

To this end, the most significant changes in the criteria reflect the maturity of business practices and total quality approaches. The criteria evolved from an initial emphasis on product and service quality assurance to a broad focus on performance excellence in a global marketplace. In addition, criteria updates are designed to address emerging and relevant issues facing business. In 2003, for example, the criteria strengthened its emphasis on organizational governance and ethics in the wake of the various business scandals that emerged early in this century. In 2005, Baldrige introduced the concept of (**organizational**) **sustainability**—which refers to an organization's ability to address current business needs and to have the agility and strategic management to prepare successfully for the future, and to prepare for real-time or short-term emergencies—into the criteria. Recently, concepts of workforce and customer engagement have been integrated within the criteria, and questions addressing outsourcing decisions have been added.

The Baldrige Award Process

Organizations that apply for the Award submit a 50-page application responding to the questions in the criteria; the example from K&N Management that we discussed above was part of their application. The Baldrige Award evaluation and selection process is rigorous and designed to be objective and immune to political pressures. In the first stage, each application is thoroughly reviewed by approximately seven examiners chosen from among leading professionals in business, education, health care, and nonprofits (all of whom are volunteers). Examiners evaluate the applicant's response to each examination item, listing major "strengths" and "opportunities for improvement" relative to the criteria. Strengths demonstrate an effective and positive response to the criteria. Opportunities for improvement address deficiencies in responding to the criteria, but do not prescribe specific practices or examiners' opinions on what the company should be doing. Based on these comments, a percentage score from 0 percent to 100 percent in increments of 5 percent is given to each item in the criteria.

Each item in categories 1–6 focuses on some type of process ("How do you...?") and is evaluated on four factors: approach, deployment, learning, and integration. **Approach** refers to the methods used to accomplish the process, the appropriateness of the methods to the item requirements and the organization's operating environment, the effectiveness of the use of the methods, and the degree to which the approach is repeatable and based on reliable data and information (i.e., systematic). **Deployment** refers to the extent to which the approach is applied in addressing item requirements relevant and important to the organization, the approach is applied consistently, and the approach is used (executed) by all appropriate work units. **Learning** refers to refining the approach through cycles of evaluation and improvement, encouraging breakthrough change to the approach through innovation, and sharing refinements and innovations with other relevant work units and processes in the organization. **Integration** refers to the extent to which the approach is aligned with organizational needs identified in the Organizational Profile and other process items; measures, information, and improvement systems are complementary across processes and work units; and plans, processes, results, analyses, learning, and actions are harmonized across processes.

Category 7 addresses **results** —an organization's outputs and outcomes. The factors used to evaluate results include current performance levels; the rate and breadth of performance improvements; performance relative to appropriate comparisons and benchmarks; and the extent to which they address important customer, product, market, process, and action plan performance requirements. In addition, results must be valid indicators of future performance and should be harmonized across process and work units to support organization-wide goals.

The examiner team conducts a process in which they discuss variations in individual scores and comments, and arrive at a consensus for each item. A national Panel of Judges then selects the applicants that they believe have the potential to be a recipient for site visits. At this point, an examiner team visits the company for up to a week to verify information contained in the written application and resolve issues that are unclear. The judges use the site visit reports to recommend award recipients. All information is kept strictly confidential, and examiners and judges are bound by conflict of interest rules and a code of conduct. For instance, judges do not participate in discussions or vote on applications in which they have a competing or conflicting interest or in which they have a private or special interest, such as an employment or a client relationship, a financial interest, or a personal or family relationship.

All applicants receive a feedback report that critically evaluates the company's strengths and areas for improvement relative to the award criteria. The feedback report, frequently 30 or more pages in length, contains the evaluation team's response to the written application. It includes a distribution of numerical scores of all applicants and a scoring summary of the individual applicant. This feedback is one of the most valuable aspects of applying for the award.

Organizations that receive the Baldrige Award are highly-regarded role models for others. Characteristics that distinguish them from other organizations—even those that reach the site visit stage but are not selected for the Award—are:[3]

- *Achievement in Results*: These organizations achieved significant results across all areas: product (e.g., health care outcomes) and process, customers, workforce, leadership and governance, and financials and marketplace. Results were trended over time, and comparisons were made to benchmarks (top performance levels). Furthermore, results measured were critical to managing the organization and to making fact-based decisions and improvements.
- *Entrepreneurism and Innovation*: These organizations use innovative approaches to serve their customers' current needs and guide them with enticing products and services that address their not-yet-articulated needs. They provide products, services, and opportunities that lead their marketplace. They take intelligent risks to sustain themselves through challenging times and environments and achieve market leadership positions. They do not rely on past achievements or reputation. They are the organizations that ask "Why not?" rather than "Why?"
- *Agility*: These organizations are strategic in their decision making and in their ability to adjust strategy. When conditions change or are anticipated to change, they are ready to adapt, look for new markets, and adjust to sustain themselves and their stakeholders. Strategic plans do not sit on their shelves gathering dust, and these plans are developed with processes that cause and monitor execution. These organizations track the execution of their plans with metrics, and the ability to make change is part of the execution process.
- *Governance and Leadership Metrics*: These organizations have leadership and governance systems in place that provide them with sound guidance. They measure the performance of their leadership and governance teams—which is not common practice. They are good citizens of their communities and measure their social responsibility results. They understand the needs of their communities and provide resources of all types.
- *Work Systems and Work Processes*: This is probably the most challenging concept to master. These organizations understand their work. They know their core competencies. They make intelligent decisions on their staff-performed work processes, capitalize on their core competencies to decide on those processes, and execute

those processes well (with data to prove it). They know when to rely on suppliers and partners. They use these critical decisions to succeed in the marketplace, even when competitors do not.

Using the Baldrige Criteria

The Baldrige Award Criteria form a model for business excellence in any organization— manufacturing, service, health care, education, or not-for-profit; large or small; public or private. For example, although the legal profession in general has not adopted quality management practices, the Trial Division of Nationwide Insurance, which operates 56 law offices in 20 states, uses the Baldrige model as a key component of its business plan. Senior leaders introduced it to all of the company's managing trial attorneys and encouraged individual offices to apply for local or state Baldrige-based awards.[4] Many school districts now use the criteria, some states even mandate Baldrige assessment, and traditional accreditation bodies now allow Baldrige as an alternative means of preparing for accreditation. One large Chicago-area hospital applied for the Baldrige-based Lincoln Award for Excellence and prepared for its accreditation visit by JCAHO at the same time, recognizing the synergy and overlap of Baldrige principles and JCAHO standards.

 QUALITYSPOTLIGHT

Texas Instruments

The former Texas Instruments Defense Systems and Electronics Group (now part of Raytheon) used the criteria to provide focus and coherence to the activities across the corporation.[5] The company was able to tackle a part of total quality that previously had been unreachable: implementing quality efforts in staff, support, and nonmanufacturing areas. TI asked every business unit to prepare a mock award application as a way of measuring its progress. This task represented a radical change for some operations because, until that time, most staff functions were not required to measure their processes or their results. The Defense Systems & Electronics Group's self-assessment revealed that they were a long way from applying for and winning the Baldrige Award. But the group aggressively adopted the criteria as a blueprint for improving its business. Many executives did not believe that the criteria could be applied to defense contractors, but TI's experience clearly showed that it could.

Many small businesses (defined as those with 500 or fewer employees) believe that the Baldrige Criteria are too difficult to apply to their organizations because they cannot afford to implement the same types of practices as large companies. This assumption is simply not true, as many recipients have been small businesses, some with only about 50 employees. What is important, however, is whether the company is using appropriate mechanisms to address the criteria. For example, the ability to obtain customer and market knowledge through independent third party surveys, extensive interviews, and focus groups, which are common practices among large companies, may be limited by the resources of a small business. In a small company, the major source of customer and market knowledge may be personal sales contacts and field intelligence. Similarly, large corporations frequently have sophisticated computer/information systems for data management, while small businesses may perform data and information management with a combination of manual methods and personal computers. Also, systems for employee involvement and process management may rely heavily on informal verbal communication and less on formal written documentation. Thus, the size or nature of a business does not affect the appropriateness of the criteria, but rather the context in which the criteria are applied.

Many organizations use the Baldrige Criteria for self-assessment or internal recognition programs, even if they do not intend to apply for the award. The benefits of using the criteria for self-assessment include accelerating improvement efforts, energizing employees, and learning from feedback—particularly if external examiners are involved. For instance, Honeywell, Inc., uses it as a companywide framework for understanding, evaluating, and improving their business. Honeywell's mandate is to use the model for managing the business and engaging senior management in an annual assessment process. This framework is used by general managers to exchange information, ask for help, and learn from each other.[6] Even the U.S. Postal Service decided to use the Baldrige Criteria as a basis to reestablish a quality system by identifying the areas that need the most improvement and providing a baseline to track progress. Using the award criteria as a self-assessment tool provides an objective framework, sets a high standard, and compares units that have different systems or organizations.

The approaches used for self-assessment vary. They may include simple questionnaires developed from the criteria, for which answers are compiled and used as a basis for an improvement plan; facilitated assessments in which key business leaders gather together to examine their organization against the criteria; and full written "applications" that are evaluated by trained internal or external examiners.[7] Assessments are often linked to the organization's strategic planning process, which serves as a means of implementing the opportunities for improvement that are identified through the process.

In 2012, the Baldrige Performance Excellence Program announced the Baldrige Collaborative Assessment pilot project, which allows organizations to partner with examiner teams and collaboratively develop recommendations for performance improvement without requiring a written application or extensive preparation. The jointly constructed recommendations are prioritized and reviewed with the organization on the last day of a 4½-day site visit. A full written report detailing all recommendations will be provided after the visit. A benefit of this process is that the organization will achieve in-depth learning about the meaning, relevance, and applicability of the Baldrige Criteria.

> *The Baldrige Materials folder on the Student Companion Site contains a brochure entitled "Baldrige 20/20" that provides the case for why the Baldrige approach is valuable to any organization.*

Impacts of the Baldrige Program

An economic evaluation study of the Baldrige program by the U.S. Department of Commerce released in December 2011 estimated the net social value of the Baldrige Performance Excellence Program.[8] The study concluded that the benefit-to-cost ratio for the group of surveyed applicants was 820 to 1, supporting the belief that the program creates great value for the U.S. economy. More importantly, the program changed the way in which many organizations around the world manage their operations, and helped significantly to bring the principles of TQ into the daily culture of these organizations. The true benefactors are the customers and other stakeholders who received better products and services.

Many U.S. states have developed award programs similar to the Baldrige Award. State award programs generally are designed to promote an awareness of productivity and quality, foster an information exchange, encourage firms to adopt quality and productivity improvement strategies, recognize firms that have instituted successful strategies, provide role models for other businesses in the state, encourage new industry to locate in the state, and establish a quality-of-life culture that will benefit all residents of the state.[9] Each state is unique, however, and thus the specific objectives will vary. For instance, the primary objectives of Minnesota's quality award are to encourage all Minnesota organizations to examine their current state of quality and to become more involved in the movement toward continuous quality improvement, as well as to recognize outstanding quality achievements in the state. Missouri, on the other hand, has as its objectives to educate all Missourians in quality improvement, to foster the pursuit of quality in all aspects of Missouri life, and to recognize quality leadership. Other states, such as Tennessee and Ohio, use their award programs to provide developmental advice to organizations just starting on their quality journey. Jim Collins (author of *Good to Great: Why Some Companies Make the Leap … and Others Don't*) endorsed Baldrige with the following statement: "I see the Baldrige process as a powerful set of mechanisms for disciplined people engaged in disciplined thought and taking disciplined action to create great organizations that produce exceptional results."

> *Information and links to state award programs can be found at the Alliance for Performance Excellence website, http://www .baldrigepe.org/alliance/.*

Baldrige and the Deming Philosophy

It is no secret that W. Edwards Deming was not an advocate of the Baldrige Award.[10] (In contrast, Joseph Juran was highly influential in its development.) Deming viewed the Award as a competition, which was fundamentally at odds with his teachings. However, many of Deming's principles are reflected directly or in spirit within the criteria. In fact, Zytec (now a part of Artesyn Technologies), which implemented its total quality system around Deming's 14 Points, received a Baldrige Award. Below is a brief summary of how the Baldrige Criteria support Deming's 14 Points:

1. *Statement of Purpose*: Strategy development requires a mission and vision. Commitment to aims and purposes by senior leaders is specifically addressed in the Leadership category and in enhancing customer satisfaction and relationships.
2. *Learn the New Philosophy*: Communication of values, expectations, customer focus, and learning is a key area of the Senior Leadership item.
3. *Understand Inspection*: The Operations Focus category addresses the development of appropriate measurement plans. The criteria seek evidence of how a company aims to minimize the costs associated with inspection.
4. *End Price Tag Decisions*: This is implicitly addressed throughout the Operations Focus category and in the criteria's emphasis on overall performance and linkages among processes and results.
5. *Improve Constantly*: Continuous improvement through organizational and personal learning and innovation are core values of the criteria. Approaches to evaluation and improvement of key organizational processes are an important part of the Baldrige scoring guidelines.
6. *Institute Training*: Item 5.2, Workforce Engagement, recognizes the importance of workforce and leader development in meeting performance objectives.
7. *Teach and Institute Leadership*: Category 1 is devoted exclusively to leadership, and it is recognized as the principal driver of the management system in the Baldrige framework.
8. *Drive Out Fear and Innovate*: The Workforce Focus, Customer Focus, and Strategic Planning categories focus on work design, empowerment, and implementation issues that support this point.
9. *Optimize the Efforts of Teams and Staff*: The criteria have a significant focus on teamwork and collaboration between the organization and its customers, workforce, suppliers, and other collaborators.

10. *Eliminate Exhortations*: The criteria seek evidence on how an organization's performance management system supports high performance work. Clearly, such a system transcends exhortations and motivational approaches.
11. *Eliminate Quotas and MBO; Institute Improvement; and Understand Processes*: Two of the important Core Values are management by fact and focus on results and creating value, which support this point.
12. *Remove Barriers*: The Leadership and Workforce Focus categories support this goal.
13. *Encourage Education*: This is addressed directly in the Workforce Engagement item.
14. *Take Action*: This is the role of leadership, and is clearly addressed in the Leadership category.

The consistencies among Deming's 14 Points and the Baldrige Criteria attest to the universal nature of quality management principles.

INTERNATIONAL QUALITY AND PERFORMANCE EXCELLENCE PROGRAMS

The Baldrige Program has inspired many other awards and quality programs across the world.

European Quality Award

In October 1991, the European Foundation for Quality Management (EFQM) in partnership with the European Commission and the European Organization for Quality announced the creation of the European Quality Award (now called the European Excellence Award). EFQM was, and remains, a nonprofit organization. The award was designed to increase awareness throughout the European Community, and businesses in particular, of the growing importance of quality to their competitiveness in the increasingly global market and to their standards of life.

Figure 10.4 shows the integrated management framework for the European Excellence Award.[11] The model, which recognizes that there are many approaches to achieving sustainable excellence in all aspects of performance, is based on the following premise: *Excellent results with respect to Performance, Customers, People and Society are achieved through Leadership driving Policy and Strategy, that is delivered through People, Partnerships and Resources, and Processes*. Results are driven by "Enablers," the means by which an organization approaches its business responsibilities, and a foundation of innovation and learning. The categories are roughly equivalent to those in Baldrige. However, the results criteria of people satisfaction, customer satisfaction, impact on society, and business results are somewhat different.[12] The impact on society results category focuses on the perceptions of the company by the community at large and the company's approach to the quality of life, the environment, and the preservation of global resources. The European Excellence Award criteria place greater emphasis on this category than is placed on the public responsibility item in the Baldrige Award Criteria.

Like the Baldrige Core Values and Concepts, the EFQM framework is based on a set of "Fundamental Concepts of Excellence":

- *Results Orientation*: Excellence is achieving results that delight all the organization's stakeholders.
- *Customer Focus*: Excellence is creating sustainable customer value.

FIGURE 10.4   European Excellence Award Framework

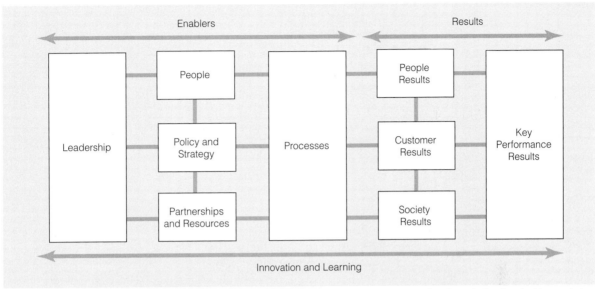

Source: Used with permission of EFQM. © EFQM, 1999. The EFQM Excellence Model is a registered trademark. Reprinted with permission.

- *Leadership and Constancy of Purpose:* Excellence is visionary and inspirational leadership, coupled with constancy of purpose.
- *Management by Processes and Facts:* Excellence is managing the organization through a set of interdependent and interrelated systems, processes and facts.
- *People Development and Involvement:* Excellence is maximizing the contribution of employees through their development and involvement.
- *Continuous Learning, Innovation, and Improvement:* Excellence is challenging the status quo and effecting change by utilizing learning to create innovation and improvement opportunities.
- *Partnership Development:* Excellence is developing and maintaining value-adding partnerships.
- *Corporate Social Responsibility:* Excellence is exceeding the minimum regulatory framework in which the organization operates and to strive to understand and respond to the expectations of their stakeholders in society.

EFQM has three recognition levels. The EFQM Excellence Award is the highest form of recognition, similar to Baldrige. Previous Award winners include BMW, TNT Express, Yell, Bosch, Nokia, Volvo, as well as smaller progressive organizations, such as St. Mary's College in Northern Ireland, Maxi Coco-Mat in Greece, and Schindlerhof Hotel in Germany. Two additional recognition levels have been added: (1) Recognized for Excellence, designed for organizations that are well along the journey to excellence, and (2) Committed to Excellence, for organizations that are at the beginning of the journey. Through the assessment process, these award levels provide feedback for further improvement.

Canadian Awards for Business Excellence

Canada's National Quality Institute (NQI) (http://www.nqi.ca) recognizes Canada's foremost achievers of excellence through the prestigious Canada Awards for Excellence. NQI is a nonprofit organization designed to stimulate and support quality-driven innovation within all Canadian enterprises and institutions, including business, government, education, and health care. The Canadian Awards for Business Excellence quality criteria are similar in structure to the Baldrige Award Criteria, with some key differences. Separate, but similar, criteria are used for business organizations, public sector organizations, and "healthy workplace" organizations. The major categories and items within each category are:

1. *Leadership:* Strategic direction, leadership involvement, and outcomes
2. *Customer Focus:* Voice of the customer, management of customer relationships, measurement, and outcomes
3. *Planning for Improvement:* Development and content of improvement plan, assessment, and outcomes
4. *People Focus:* Human resource planning, participatory environment, continuous learning environment, employee satisfaction, and outcomes
5. *Process Optimization:* Process definition, process control, process improvement, and outcomes
6. *Supplier Focus:* Partnering and outcomes

These categories seek similar information as the Baldrige Award Criteria. For example, the People Focus category examines the development of human resource planning and implementation and operation of a strategy for achieving excellence through people. It also examines the organization's efforts to foster and support an environment that encourages and enables people to reach their full potential. Recent recipients of Canada's top quality award include Delta Hotels Canada, Statistics Canada, The College of Physicians & Surgeons of Nova Scotia, College of Registered Nurses of Nova Scotia, Real Estate Board of Greater Vancouver, Toronto Transit Commission—Information Technology Services Department, and Ricoh Canada Inc.

Australian Business Excellence Award

The Australian Quality Awards (now called the Australian Business Awards) were developed independently from the MBNQA in 1988. The Awards were previously administered by the Australian Quality Awards Foundation, a subsidiary of the Australian Quality Council, a private, for-profit organization. In 2002, Standards Australia International [SAI] formally acquired a range of products and services previously owned by the Australian Quality Council [AQC]. SAI's Professional Services Division became the new home of the AQC and in recognition of the importance of business excellence to SAI, the division has been renamed Business Excellence Australia.

The Australian Business Excellence Prize is the preeminent award available for businesses in Australia. Only two organizations have achieved this level of excellence since the Awards' inception in 1988. In addition to the Australian Business Excellence Prize, four levels of awards are given:

1. *The Foundation in Business Excellence Level*—provides encouragement recognition for progress toward business excellence."
2. *The Bronze Award Level*—Bronze Award recipients will demonstrate Approach and Deployment that are well defined, planned, subject to review and show evidence of improvement over time.
3. *The Silver Award Level*—Organizations at this level should be able to demonstrate not only performance against the Framework at Bronze level, but also a philosophy of management that reflects the principles that underpin it and other Frameworks around the globe.

4. *The Gold Award Level*—Organizations at this level should meet Silver recognition plus be able to demonstrate superior performance in at least 5 of the Categories in the Framework and also have scored at least 50 percent in each Item.

The program also confers The Excellence Medal to the highest scoring applicant organization, and Category Awards to organizations that have achieved the highest evaluation score for that category, above the benchmark set for a given year.

The Business Excellence Award Framework is based on eight Principles: leadership, customers, systems thinking, people, information and knowledge, corporate and social responsibility, and sustainable results. The assessment criteria address leadership, strategy and planning, information and knowledge, people, customer focus, process management, improvement and innovation, and success and sustainability within the framework shown in Figure 10.5. In this model, leadership and customer and market focus are the drivers of the management system and enablers of performance. Strategy and planning, information and knowledge, and people are the key internal components of the management system. Quality of process management, improvement, and innovation are focused on how work is done to achieve the required results and obtain improvement. Success and sustainability is the outcome of the management system—a results category. As with Baldrige, the framework emphasizes the holistic and interconnected nature of the management process. The criteria are benchmarked with the Baldrige Criteria and the European Business Excellence Model. One of the distinctive aspects of Australia's program is solid union support.

Quality Awards in China

In 2001, the China Association for Quality (CAQ) introduced the National Quality Award, which it recently renamed the Performance Excellence Award. To facilitate the emerging economy of China, the Chinese government has issued new quality standards that became effective on January 1, 2005, which are designed to encourage China's thriving business sector to strive for better quality.[13] The award criteria are based on components of the Malcolm Baldrige National Quality Award, and are geared toward China's unique business environment—especially in improving business credibility, brand-building strategy and sustainable development. The Chinese government used

FIGURE 10.5
Australia Business
Excellence Award
Framework

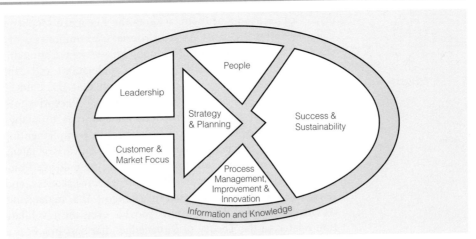

Source: Adapted from www.businessexcellenceaustralia.com/au.

Representatives of the Shanghai Academy of Quality Management, who helped write the country's new quality standard, and invited Baldrige Award winners to Shanghai to report on their processes. At the same time, they held many seminars to study Baldrige Criteria, learning to adapt those concepts to Chinese quality policy. Seventeen businesses have been awarded the Chinese National Quality Award during the first three years. Among them, Baosteel and Shanghai Dazhong Taxi won the World Class Organization Award and the Asia–Pacific Quality Award, in 2002 and 2004, respectively.

In 2004, Shenzhen became the first city to launch a local quality award, called the Mayor's Cup Quality Award. It is operated by the Shenzhen Bureau of Quality and Technical Supervision. The vice mayor leads an evaluation committee of local experts, which uses many of the Baldrige Criteria, including international best practices, social factors, and governmental strategic initiatives issued by Shenzhen government leaders.

At the end of 2006, more than 55 organizations had applied for the award, and six firms had won, including Huawei in 2004, one of the first winners (see the Quality in Practice feature in Chapter 1). The 3 million RMB ($387,000 U.S.) prize is the highest among quality awards in China and has encouraged many organizations to participate and share best practices. Other cities and provinces, including Shanghai, have now set up local governmental quality awards to promote quality management systems and share experiences in various industries. There are over 200 locally applied district awards.[14]

China has also begun to embrace Six Sigma.[15] For example, the Shanghai Association for Quality created the Six Sigma Excellent Organization Award in 2004 to recognize Chinese businesses for innovative and successful Six Sigma implementations. The first winners were Bao Shan Iron and Steel Co. Ltd., Shanghai Airlines Co. Ltd., Shanghai Turbine Generator Co. Ltd., Shanghai Jinting Automobile Harness Ltd., Shanghai Viva Ecology Electronics Technology Co. Ltd., Mettler-Toledo Instruments Co. Ltd. (Shanghai), Mettler-Toledo Instruments Weighing Equipment System Co. Ltd. (Changhzhou), and Ningbo Baoxin Stainless Steel Co. Ltd. Many enterprises report that the methodology solved problems they once thought were unsolvable. For example, winning company Baosteel decreased its oil consumption by a third after implementing Six Sigma.

Baldrige and National Culture

It is interesting to observe that although many countries substantially adopt the Baldrige Criteria, some of them, such as the European Quality Award framework or the Chinese National Quality Award Criteria, use components of the Baldrige Criteria, but customize them to reflect their unique business environment. Investigation of international cultural differences can help to understand and explain these differences. A recent study found support for the notion that the Baldrige award is better suited with some national cultures than with others.[16] Receptiveness to change differs greatly among cultures, suggesting the need for countries to adapt their quality award programs to local conditions to ensure effectively implementing them. Perhaps surprisingly, Baldrige is a better fit to the national culture of Japan than it is to the United States. Some of the reasons for this are that the Baldrige framework was initially influenced heavily by Japanese quality management practices, and that changes to the criteria over the years are focused on *changing* U.S. management culture, not reflecting its current practice. These results provide even more validation of Deming's observation related to the Theory of Knowledge, that best practices cannot be copied blindly, but must be understood and adapted intelligently. This is an important lesson for managing in today's global environment.

BALDRIGE, ISO 9000, AND SIX SIGMA

In Parts I and II of this book, we introduced ISO 9000 and Six Sigma, both of which are frameworks for quality management. A natural question that is often asked is how ISO 9000, Six Sigma, and Baldrige compare with one another. Although each of these frameworks is process-focused, data-based, and management-led, each offers a different emphasis in helping organizations improve performance and increase customer satisfaction. For example, Baldrige focuses on performance excellence for the entire organization in an overall management framework, identifying and tracking important organizational results; ISO focuses on product and service conformity for guaranteeing equity in the marketplace and concentrates on fixing quality system problems and product and service nonconformities; and Six Sigma focuses on measuring product quality and driving process improvement and cost savings throughout the organization.

Although the 2000 revision of ISO 9000 incorporated many of the Baldrige Criteria's original principles, it still is not a comprehensive business performance framework. Nevertheless, it is an excellent way to begin a quality journey. In fact, it provides more detailed guidance on process and product control than Baldrige, and provides systematic approaches to many of the Baldrige Criteria requirements in the Operations Focus category. Thus, for companies in the early stages of developing a quality program, the standards enforce the discipline of control that is necessary before they can seriously pursue continuous improvement. The requirements of periodic audits reinforce the stated quality system until it becomes ingrained in the company.

Six Sigma initiatives fulfill in part many of the elements of ISO 9000:2000, including the Quality Management System, Resource Management, Product Realization, and Measurement, Analysis, and Improvement sections of the standards.[17] For instance, Six Sigma helps to demonstrate management commitment through periodic review of Six Sigma plans and projects, providing champions to sponsor projects, providing training resources, and communicating progress and achievements.

Let us examine how ISO 9000 and Six Sigma compare with each of the Baldrige categories. Leadership underlies many of the requirements of ISO 9000:2000. The entire section on Management Responsibility is concerned with the role of leadership in driving a quality system. For example, the standards require that "Top management shall provide evidence of its commitment to the development and implementation of the quality management system and continually improving its effectiveness by a) communicating to the organization the importance of meeting customer as well as statutory and regulatory requirements, b) establishing the quality policy, c) ensuring that quality objectives are established, d) conducting management reviews, and e) ensuring the availability of resources." More specific responsibilities are spelled out in detail in other clauses of the standards.

Leadership is a fundamental value of Six Sigma. Driving organizational change to create and sustain a Six Sigma culture simply cannot be done without strong leadership. In other words, Six Sigma cannot be an add-on or a "flavor of the month." It must become the way business is done in organizations that adopt it.

ISO 9000 does not address strategic planning as broadly as in the Baldrige Criteria; however, the ISO 9000 standards do require that top management ensure that quality objectives are established at relevant functions and levels within the organization, that they be measurable and consistent with the quality policy, that planning be carried out in order to meet quality system requirements and the quality objectives, and that the integrity of the quality management system is maintained when changes are planned and implemented.

Six Sigma must be integrated into strategic planning processes in order to be effective. In many organizations there are three levels of strategy: corporate, strategic business unit

(SBU), and competitive.[18] At the corporate strategy level, the key question facing planners is, "How do we, as an organization, grow?" At the SBU or divisional level, the strategic question is, "Where does the organization focus its resources to enhance its value offering?" An organization's competitive strategy is its plan for enhancing its capacity to deliver value, thus increasing market share. Competitive strategy that focuses on value enhancement addresses key questions such as: "Where are the organization's best opportunities for widening a value advantage or closing a disadvantage? On what basis does the organization widen or close the value gap? How does the organization get its best return on investment for these efforts?" The competitive strategy level is where organizational strategy and Six Sigma must align, because it is at this level that the tools of Six Sigma can be most effectively applied. Effective competitive strategies are necessarily focused on value gaps and are either designed to extend value leadership or to close the gap with a value leader. In either case, the deployment of that strategy will require a focus on the organization's business processes. The tools of Six Sigma are particularly effective for improving business processes. The challenge lies in directing those tools toward improvements that will have a direct impact on value gaps. That requires aligning Six Sigma with the organization's competitive strategy.

Customer focus is a key requirement of ISO 9000:2000. For example, the Management Responsibility section states, "Top management shall ensure that customer requirements are determined and are met with the aim of enhancing customer satisfaction." This puts the responsibility for customer focus on senior leadership. In the Product Realization section, the standards require that the organization determine customer requirements, including delivery and postdelivery activities, and any requirements not stated by the customer but necessary for specified or intended use. In addition, the organization must establish procedures for communicating with customers about product information and other inquiries, and for obtaining feedback, including complaints. In the Measurement, Analysis, and Improvement sections, the standards require that the organization monitor customer perceptions as to whether the organization has met customer requirements; that is, customer satisfaction. Note that even though some basic customer-focused processes are required, the scope is not as broad as in Baldrige.

Customers are sometimes a "hidden" part of Six Sigma efforts, because the focus tends to be on the improvement projects and measurement issues. However, a focus on the customer is vital at every stage of Six Sigma projects. For instance, product design (and design of associated manufacturing or service delivery processes) will be far more successful if the "voice of the customer," is included. A fundamental aspect of Six Sigma methodology is identification of critical to quality (CTQ) characteristics that are vital to customer satisfaction. During the process of producing a product or service, it is important to gather information needed by internal customers for process control activities to ensure that the product is meeting the CTQs. If the CTQs are not being met, then the organization needs to develop a better measurement and control system.[19] Often, internal data that can improve control processes—such as whether materials arrived on time, how often an accounting report had incorrect data, or how many employees were absent from work—are kept in departmental records, where they are difficult to access. The solution may require a Six Sigma study to determine the types of data and information that are needed to provide necessary monitoring and control, and how the information gap (if one exists) can be closed. Finally, at the delivery stage, customer satisfaction measures can provide clear information about the success of Six Sigma efforts. In fact, many common Six Sigma projects revolve around developing appropriate customer satisfaction measurement processes, as well as trying to improve the design and delivery of CTQs identified through voice of the customer processes.

ISO 9000:2000 provides a basic framework for managing data and information. The document and data control requirements of ISO 9000 require organizations to define a process for ensuring that any critical information that is required for the performance of a business process is accurate, up-to-date, and effective for its intended purpose. Because ISO 9000 places an emphasis on processes that, in many cases are cross-functional, it forces companies to break down some of the organizational and functional silos that inhibit effective sharing of information.[20] The measurement, analysis, and improvement requirements of ISO 9000:2000 deal with the measurement of product and process characteristics, performance of the quality system, and search for continuous improvement, requiring that management make decisions based on analysis and trends of product and process performance indicators, internal auditing, and customer feedback. Specific requirements include the following:

- Establishing, planning, and implementing measurement, monitoring, and improvement activities
- Monitoring information about customer satisfaction as a performance metric
- Establishing measurement and monitoring methods to assure that product and process requirements are attained
- Acquiring and analyzing data to determine improvement effectiveness
- Promoting continuous improvement using auditing reports, data analysis, and management reviews

Using a balanced scorecard approach or the Baldrige measurement framework can clearly provide the foundation for meeting these requirements for firms that pursue ISO 9000.

Six Sigma emphasizes fact-based decisions and provides organizations with tools to generate measurable results from Six Sigma projects. Six Sigma methodology requires measuring and reporting performance goals, and using performance indicators to control and sustain improvements. Project selection is based on understanding the financial as well as the nonfinancial benefits to the organization, such as cost savings, increased sales, reduced cycle times, or improved customer satisfaction. Thus, measurements are vital in "selling" Six Sigma projects to top management. Six Sigma can have a significant impact on the cost of quality because of its focus on financial return; in fact, one survey observed that the top three measures used to quantify Six Sigma success are cost takeout, productivity, and revenue generation.[21] Many Six Sigma projects focus on reducing the costs of poor quality that result from low sigma levels of performance, and improved designs that will increase customer satisfaction and hence, revenue. The different categories of the cost of quality provide many opportunities for Six Sigma projects. For example, an organization might identify all costs that would vanish if sigma performance levels were increased. The list might include costs associated with credits given to customers because of late delivery, billing errors, scrap and rework, unplanned downtime, extra inventory to buffer against defects, errors in specifications and drawings, and accounts payable mistakes. Quantifying these costs establishes the justification for Six Sigma projects. Six Sigma projects can also be categorized in different levels, based upon their impact on results:[22]

1. Level 1 projects directly affect an organization's profit margin (projects have a clear, hard dollar impact on profitability).
2. Level 2 projects result in redeployment of resources inside an organization to increase operating efficiency or productivity.
3. Level 3 projects directly affect operations by avoiding expenditures or increasing the chances of obtaining higher future revenues.

Workforce focus in ISO 9000:2000 revolves primarily around training and the work environment, but does not address the subject as comprehensively as Baldrige does. The standards require that "Personnel performing work affecting product quality shall be competent on the basis of appropriate education, training, skills, and experience." The standards further require that organizations determine the level of competence that employees need, provide training or other means to ensure competency, evaluate the effectiveness of training or other actions taken, ensure that employees are aware of how their work contributes to quality objectives, and maintain appropriate records of education, training, and experience. The standards also address the work environment from the standpoint of providing buildings, workspace, utilities, equipment, and supporting services needed to achieve conformity to product requirements, as well as determining and managing the work environment, including safety, ergonomics, and environmental factors.

Workforce focus is essential to Six Sigma. We discussed the role of project teams in Six Sigma earlier in this chapter. One quality professional noted that "Six Sigma actually owes its success to all the quality efforts that have come before it, and teams are an integral part of Six Sigma implementation."[23] In addition to teams, selecting the right people to serve on teams, training and skill development, and reward and recognition approaches to drive behavior are vital to Six Sigma efforts. Six Sigma efforts often result in significant change recommendations to the organization; work processes change and employees need to do things differently. Understanding how changes affect people is a necessary issue that organizations must address after Six Sigma projects are completed; project champions, in particular, need to apply high-performance workforce principles to their organizations.

Many aspects of ISO 9000:2000 deal with operations focus activities such as process management. (In fact, the entire set of standards is focused on an organization's ability to understand, define, and document its processes.) For example, one of the requirements is that organizations plan and control the design and development of products and manage the interfaces between different groups involved in design and development to ensure effective communication and clear assignment of responsibility. The standards also address the management of inputs and outputs for design and development activities, and use of systematic reviews to evaluate the ability to meet requirements, identify any problems, and propose necessary actions; purchasing processes; control of production and service, including measurement and process validation; control of monitoring and measuring devices used to evaluate conformity; analysis and improvement; monitoring and measurement of quality management processes; and continual improvement, including preventive and corrective action. The standards require that an organization use its quality policy, objectives, audit results, data analysis, corrective and preventive actions, and management reviews to continually improve its quality management system's effectiveness.

Six Sigma is based on understanding and improving processes on a project-by-project basis. Two of the advantages of Six Sigma are that projects are clearly linked to strategic needs and organizational objectives, and that projects are managed under a common framework. This linkage enables projects to be timely and relevant, and ensures that controls are put in place to leverage the improvements that are identified. The Six Sigma team-project approach provides a natural fit with the requirements of product and process design, control, and improvement. A good system for process management is a prerequisite to Six Sigma. Obviously, to effectively design or improve a process you first need to understand it. If an organization does not have an ongoing system of process management, it will be quite difficult to implement Six Sigma. Some key processes that are necessary to implement Six Sigma include the following:

- Project selection and definition
- Financial review
- Training
- Leadership for project leaders

- Project leader mentoring
- Certification for Six Sigma specialists
- Project tracking and reporting
- Information management and dissemination

It is important to note that Six Sigma is not a substitute for continuous improvement.

Because of its reliance on specialists—the "Black Belts" who lead the high-profile projects—it becomes quite easy to ignore simple improvements that can be achieved at the process owner level. In fact, it can easily alienate process owners who, instead of seeking continuous improvements, leave them to the specialists. Thus, the objectives are somewhat different, yet both approaches can easily support one another. Process owners should be trained in Six Sigma methods and be involved in formal Six Sigma projects, but still have responsibility for continuous improvement on a daily basis.

Many organizations have successfully blended ISO 9000, Six Sigma, and/or Baldrige in their practices. For example, Honeywell Federal Manufacturing & Technologies uses all three. They use the metaphor of taking a journey to performance excellence. ISO 9000 is the driver's license; it provides the discipline and the rules to follow. Six Sigma is the car; the tool that gets you to your destination. Baldrige is the roadmap. All work harmoniously together.[24] The Veterans Affairs Cooperative Studies Program (VACSP) Clinical Research Pharmacy Coordinating Center, a 2009 Baldrige recipient, began using the Baldrige Criteria in 1996. Mark Jones, the assistant center director for technical operations, noted that receiving the Baldrige Award "tells us we're doing a good job…. We really have in place good procedures and processes." VACSP was also the first Veteran's Affairs agency to become ISO certified. This was important because the organization works with and ships products to numerous countries. Being certified requires performing internal audits, reflecting on what the organization is doing, and ensuring personnel are on the right course. The ISO-based quality management system provides synergies with its Baldrige-based performance excellence approaches.[25] Jack Swaim of Compaq Computer (now Hewlett-Packard), a former Baldrige examiner, observed that Six Sigma can provide the impetus for change, while Baldrige provides the keys to sustainability. He also suggests that pursuing Baldrige first can make it easier to implement Six Sigma. Six Sigma can lay the foundation for a broader Baldrige perspective; Cynthia Scribner at Raytheon notes that Six Sigma makes a great unifying story for a Baldrige application.

 QUALITYSPOTLIGHT

Baxter Healthcare International

One example of merging Baldrige with Six Sigma is Baxter Healthcare International.[26] The Business Excellence organization within Baxter is a small group of people focused on helping internal clients improve their operations. Specific areas of responsibility in Business Excellence include:

- The Baxter Award for Operational Excellence (an internal Baldrige Award)
- Deployment of the Baxter Integrated Management System (the Baldrige model)
- The Corporate Quality Manual
- The Baxter Quality Institute (an internal quality training group)
- The Quality Leadership Process (a method of deploying performance excellence in manufacturing)
- Lean Manufacturing Initiative
- Six Sigma Initiatives

They rolled all of these areas together into a unified service offering. For example, consider the following hypothetical scenario. The supply chain organization determined that their operating cost and cash flow contributions are not meeting the targets. Business Excellence would set out to help them in the following way. First, they work with members of the leadership team to develop an organizational profile of the supply chain organization. This initial assessment helps the team focus on who they are and what their specific challenges are. Next, they perform a simple Baldrige assessment online and then use the output to generate a feedback report of strengths and opportunities for improvement with strong emphasis on the integration of the model. Then they distill the feedback report down to 10–12 cross-cutting themes for the leadership team to focus on. These themes are built into an Excel spreadsheet for a "prioritization matrix" exercise, designed to identify the top two or three critical opportunities or issues that the group will focus on. Next, they bring in the Six Sigma approach and drill down into these opportunities to determine potential projects. When these projects have been identified and scoped sufficiently to make a decision to move forward, project charters are developed and assigned to Six Sigma specialists to implement them.

SUMMARY OF KEY POINTS AND TERMINOLOGY

A summary of key concepts and terminology introduced in this chapter may be found on The Student Companion Site.

QUALITY *in* PRACTICE

Leveraging Baldrige at AtlantiCare[27]

New Jersey-based health care provider AtlantiCare was one of five Baldrige award recipients for 2009. Although the organization didn't implement the Baldrige Criteria until the new millennium, its culture was rooted in quality well before that. In the 1990s, it built its operations around the concept that patients are the center of everything, and it also employed a total quality management philosophy that gave it the necessary tools to create sustainable improvements in customer service and adopted the plan-do-check-act cycle. Then, in 2000, it began implementing the Baldrige Criteria to push its performance levels to new heights.

In 2006, AtlantiCare crafted its first national application but failed to receive a site visit. The next year, however, resulted in a site visit, providing a measure of encouragement and an expectation of disappointment. "You don't know how much work you

have to do, but we knew we were not Baldrige worthy when we had our first site visit," said AtlantiCare President and CEO David Tilton. "We knew we could be a lot better." Another site visit in 2008 further drove home the fact the organization was making progress, a feeling borne out by its triumph a year later.

At orientation, new employees get a crash course in AtlantiCare's improvement methods, as well as a performance excellence framework it calls the 5Bs—a program with the aim of making the organization the best in five areas: quality, customer service, people and workplace, growth and financial performance. As employees ascend the organization's ranks, the emphasis on improvement follows. At the managerial level, AtlantiCare requires attendance at an educational program outlining how to use the Baldrige framework to enhance performance and foster innovation. That gives managers the tools they need to operate within a leadership environment referred to by the organization as the tight-loose-tight process (TLT). The strategy refers to the level of autonomy and authority given to those below the top management level. By loosening the reins, AtlantiCare empowers its employees in individual business units to customize the means by which they meet high-level goals, thus creating a more agile organization.

Along with setting targets, the business units establish annual action plans and identify key measurements to help them identify when they've met their targets. Each action plan set by the business units relates to the nine strategic challenges AtlantiCare identified as keys to organizational success:

Health care delivery

- Engaging physicians in new models of collaboration and partnership.
- Creating sustainable growth outside of the primary service area.
- Identifying and prioritizing health care service opportunities for investment and recruitment.

Health engagement

- Developing new business and care models to support and grow primary care.
- Identifying and improving critical success factors for community health and wellness.

Health information

- Increasing quality of care through clinical communication and transparency.
- Using technology to improve patient safety and clinical quality.

Operational

- Recruiting, training and retaining a highly skilled workforce.
- Succeeding in an environment of decreasing reimbursement and access to capital, and a growing uninsured population.

In another effort to overcome those challenges, AtlantiCare rolls several voice of the customer activities into its planning processes. By collecting web-user data, analyzing call center trends, and conducting focus groups, the organization evaluates and improves customer access. The most visible example of the benefits of this focus is the Access Center, which AtlantiCare established in 2006 after focus group research revealed a customer base frustrated with its access to and navigation of an often-convoluted health care system. The toll-free physician and event scheduling line tracks customers' requests and needs. These efforts resulted in increased customer satisfaction, higher market share, and increased revenues. The organization is in the top 10 percent for CMS patient-care measurements related to congestive heart failure, acute myocardial infarction and pneumonia. The Home Health Division was awarded HomeCare Elite status by OCS Inc., which delivers performance improvement benchmarking measures to home health and hospice providers. The title,—based on quality outcomes, quality improvement, and financial performance,—puts AtlantiCare in the top 100 of 8,222 organizations in the United States. Results for effectiveness of treatment in behavioral health consistently surpass the Mental Health Corp. of America's benchmark and include a 2009 result that is 16 percent above the benchmark.

The numbers back up AtlantiCare's wholehearted embrace of the Baldrige Criteria, but its belief in the program goes beyond measurables and the award that followed. Despite competing in the highly competitive health care industry, AtlantiCare established a series of Baldrige Sharing Days for any organization that wants to travel the same road to improvement. "We believe a commitment to quality and continuous improvement is imperative in the health care field. Part of our responsibility as a recipient of the Baldrige award is to share our performance excellence strategies and practices with other organizations. We humbly look forward to serving as mentors and role models for those who wish to join us on our quality journey."

Key Issues for Discussion

1. How might the different categories of the Baldrige Criteria relate to the strategic challenges that AtlantiCare faced? Specifically, clearly explain how effective approaches to the questions in the Criteria will help address these challenges.
2. What lessons can other organizations learn from AtlantiCare's experience?

QUALITY *in* PRACTICE

Branch-Smith Printing Division's Baldrige Journey[28]

Note: *This Quality in Practice feature provides some good insights into the nature of feedback that Baldrige examiners provide as part of the formal Award assessment process. Normally, such feedback is not publicly disseminated; however, the feedback was provided by Mr. David Branch to one of the authors for a research study cited in the endnote.*

Located in Fort Worth, Texas, Branch-Smith Printing Division (BSPD)—one of two divisions of Branch-Smith, Inc.—is a fourth-generation, family-owned business founded in 1910 by Aaron Smith. Employing under 100 full-time employees, Branch-Smith Printing specializes in providing a wide range of turnkey services to its customers—including designing, printing, binding and mailing—related to sheet-fed printing of multipage bound materials. Products include publications, magazines, catalogues, directories and books.

BSPD's Baldrige journey began in 1992 as David Branch, President and CEO, recognized the need to move the business forward from a typical small company paternalistic culture that was characterized by activities rather than processes, and reacting to problems, to a more "professionalized" business built around documented procedures, repeatable operations, regular evaluation and improvement, and a fully integrated management system. Part of this motivation was to capitalize on the manufacturing industry focus on quality that was prevalent during the early 1990s. BSPD became involved with a consortium of businesses that were organized by Marlow Industries (a previous Baldrige recipient) and a consultant, Warren Hogan. They developed a two-year training curriculum on performance excellence topics, such as customer satisfaction, strategic planning, measurement—essentially the key elements of the Baldrige Criteria.

In 1994, BSPD developed a quality plan and began an internal Baldrige assessment process. The most significant opportunity for improvement they recognized was to improve in the process management area. As a result BSPD embarked on achieving ISO 9000 certification. In January of 1996, they became the first American independent printing company to be certified. Around the same time, Quality Texas, the state

equivalent of the Baldrige program, was gaining momentum. Like many state programs, Quality Texas designed multiple award levels that are designed to assess the degree to which an organization has developed and deployed sound, balanced approaches resulting in improved performance levels and trends. These differ by the size of the application required, whether a site visit is made to the organization, and whether scoring is performed by the examiners. In all cases, however, a feedback report is provided to the applicant. BSPD applied for a Level 2 award in 1995; the next year, David Branch became an examiner. Using the Quality Texas feedback as well as the experience of participating in site visits, David gained considerable insight into how to apply the Baldrige Criteria to his company. Among these insights were the importance of aligned goals and a solid quality information database with cascaded metrics from the top down to work groups. The database became the foundation on which strategic planning, leadership accountability, and management review activities drove the business. This led to the beginnings of an integrated performance excellence model called Innovating Excellence™ that became fully deployed in 2001.

BSPD applied again for developmental feedback from the Texas Quality Award program in 1998. BSPD then applied for the top-level award in 1999 and received the Texas Quality Award (now called the Texas Award for Performance Excellence). The feedback at that time noted that

> [The scoring] range is indicative of organizations that have effective approaches and good results in most categories, but deployment in some key areas is still too new to demonstrate results. Further deployment measures and results are needed to demonstrate integration, continuity, and maturity.

Thus, while further refinements were identified at the state level, BSPD's overall approaches merited a high level of recognition of achievement.

Over the next three years, BSPD applied for the Baldrige Award. In 2000, the company did not receive a site visit. Although the examiners recognized that the company had some key strengths and outstanding practices, for example:

Branch-Smith Printing Division uses a fact-based systematic planning process throughout the organization, from setting its overall organization direction to details such as determining its recognition and reward system. Branch-Smith Printing Division collects inputs, either directly or indirectly, from customers, employees, suppliers, peer groups within the industry, professional organizations, and benchmark organizations outside of the industry. Senior leaders use that information to set short-range and longer-range objectives that align with each of its four major goals. Employee teams create action plans to meet those goals and objectives. Branch-Smith Printing Division has an extensive system for collecting performance data in its Quality Improvement Database (QID) for daily monitoring of performance, for monthly analysis and review, for creating new action plans to address processes falling short of performance goals, and for annual strategic planning. This systematic approach is a key factor in the division's success in meeting the requirements of its customers.

They also pointed to some weaknesses (opportunities for improvement), such as:

Branch-Smith Printing Division does not provide results information about several areas that seem important to its success. These areas include market share, the level of errors and the level of errors that reach customers, the effectiveness of its education and training programs, customer loyalty and referral, results measuring responsibility to the public other than VOC emissions, the effectiveness of its work system, the impact of supplier performance on Branch-Smith Printing Division's performance, and indicators that it is reaching its goal of continuously improving its quality systems. It also does not segment results by product, service, or employee groups.

and

Development of Branch-Smith Printing Division's design and delivery processes appears to focus on the availability of new technology to a greater degree than on changes in the marketplace. Branch-Smith Printing Division does not supply

evidence that it keeps abreast of changes in the marketplace with the same thoroughness that it keeps abreast of technological changes in the industry.

The examiner's feedback noted that

Branch-Smith Printing Division scored in band 3 (351–450) in the consensus review of written applications for the Malcolm Baldrige National Quality Award. Branch-Smith Printing Division demonstrates a systematic approach that is responsive to the basic purposes of most Items, but deployment in some key Areas to Address is still too early to demonstrate results. Early improvement trends in areas of importance to key organizational requirements are evident.

A significant reason why BSPD's results were lagging its approaches can be explained from a strategic perspective. As Mr. Branch explained, "we were using the Criteria to improve how we run the business, but we also had to make fundamental changes regarding what businesses we were in." In the late 1990s, BSPD recognized the need to change to digital printing technology in order to survive in the evolutionary and highly competitive printing industry. The high capital cost of this technology necessitated a new growth model to justify the investment. This led to changes in the products and services offered: an increased sales force; a new emphasis on customer service; and a better information system to manage complexity. As a result, it took several years before improved results—especially in the financial and customer areas—began to occur. During this transition, BSPD continued to use the Baldrige Criteria as a basis for refining its management systems.

In 2001, the company received a site visit but was not selected as an award recipient. The 2001 feedback stated:

Branch-Smith Printing Division scored in band 5 (551–650) in the consensus review of written applications for the Malcolm Baldrige National Quality Award. Although no rescoring is done at the site visit, the site visit findings would have resulted in a scoring increase in Category 6 and no change in Categories 1, 2, 3, 4, 5 and 7. An organization with this scoring profile typically demonstrates an effective, systematic approach responsive to many of the Areas to Address and to key organizational needs, with a fact-based evaluation and improvement process in place in key Areas. There are no major gaps in deployment, and a commitment exists to organizational learning and sharing. Improvement trends and/or good performance are reported for most areas of importance. Results address most key customer/ stakeholder and process requirements and demonstrate areas of strength.

Finally in 2002, BSPD received another site visit and was selected as a recipient of the Baldrige Award. The company made substantial progress in improving its approaches and results. For example, the weakness cited above in 2000 regarding the lack of staying abreast of changes in the marketplace was now cited as a strength:

Changes in customer requirements are incorporated into Branch-Smith Printing Division's design and production processes through the use of the PSI software, which uses estimate request forms to create job tickets. For the design phase, the Art and Electronic Prepress departments use proofing processes for this purpose as well. CSRs and sales personnel are responsible for ensuring that changes are incorporated into a customer's job ticket. The INC process is used to monitor

and track the costs associated with failing to keep customer requirements up to date when such errors occur.

In summary, the feedback noted:

The Site Visit Team found the descriptor for scoring band 6 (650–750) to be the most accurate overall for Branch-Smith Printing Division. An organization in this band typically demonstrates refined approaches, including key measures, good deployment, and very good results in most Areas. Organizational alignment, learning, and sharing are key management tools. Some outstanding activities and results address customer/stakeholder, process, and action plan requirements. The organization is an industry leader in some Areas.

BSPD clearly made substantial progress in its journey toward performance excellence, culminating in being recognized as a national role model.

Key Issues for Discussion

1. Identify what Baldrige Core Values and Concepts are reflected in the strength and opportunity for improvement comments cited in this case.
2. What value can you see in David Branch, the CEO, becoming an award examiner?

REVIEW QUESTIONS

1. Summarize the purposes of the Malcolm Baldrige National Quality Award.
2. Describe the key issues addressed in each of the seven categories of the Criteria for Performance Excellence.
3. Explain the logic of the Baldrige Criteria framework and why each element is important in any organization.
4. List the Baldrige Core Values and Concepts. Why do you think they are important for any organization to pursue?
5. What is organizational sustainability? Why is it vital to business success?
6. Describe the Baldrige Award process. How does it ensure that organizations are truly worthy of receiving the Award?
7. Explain the concepts of approach, deployment, learning, and integration in Baldrige assessment.
8. What are the characteristics that distinguish Baldrige Award recipients from other organizations?
9. Describe some approaches that organizations use to conduct Baldrige self-assessments.
10. What are some of the impacts that the Baldrige program has provided, both in the United States and around the world?
11. How does Baldrige support Deming's 14 Points?
12. Explain the differences between the Baldrige framework and the EFQM framework.
13. What is the role of national culture in adapting the Baldrige framework to a particular country?
14. What are the similarities and differences among Six Sigma, ISO 9000, and the Baldrige approaches?
15. Why can Baldrige, ISO 9000, and Six Sigma be used together in an organization?

DISCUSSION QUESTIONS

1. Do you believe that eliminating federal funding for the Baldrige Program was appropriate, given that it was originally established by an act of Congress? Critics have suggested that the loss of interest by manufacturing companies and the surge in health care applications has taken the program away from its roots. Do you agree or not?

2. Study the questions asked in the Baldrige Criteria. Select what you believe are the "top 10" most difficult questions for an organization to answer and justify your reasoning.

3. Refer to the example of how K&N Management addressed some of the questions in the Senior Leadership category of the Baldrige Criteria in this chapter. Explain what practices address each of the specific questions:
   a. How do senior leaders set your organization's vision and values?
   b. How do senior leaders deploy your organization's vision and values through your leadership system, to the workforce, to key suppliers and partners, and to customers and other stakeholders, as appropriate?
   c. How do senior leaders' actions reflect a commitment to the organization's values?

4. Discuss how the Baldrige Core Values and Concepts define a high performance culture. How might they be used as a starting point for self-assessment, without actually answering the formal questions in the Baldrige Criteria?

5. Create a matrix diagram in which each row is a category of the Baldrige Award criteria and four columns correspond to a level of organizational maturity with respect to quality:
   - Traditional management practices
   - Growing awareness of the importance of quality
   - Development of a solid quality management system
   - Outstanding, world-class management practice
     In each cell of the matrix, list two to five characteristics that you would expect to see for a company in each of the four situations for that criteria category. How might this matrix be used as a self-assessment tool to provide directions for improvement?

6. Examine the questions in the Baldrige Criteria and discuss which ones relate to the concept of organizational sustainability as defined in this chapter? Why is sustainability an important issue in business?

7. Discuss the implications of the Baldrige Criteria for e-commerce. What are the specific challenges that e-commerce companies face within each category of the criteria?

8. As we noted in the chapter, process items in the Baldrige Criteria are assessed on four dimensions: approach, deployment, learning, and integration. The following are opportunities for improvement that an examiner team identified in the Leadership Category for a Baldrige applicant. Discuss which of the four dimensions are implied in these comments (some may address more than one dimension).
   a. The applicant presents limited evidence of systematic evaluation and refinement of several key leadership approaches that may support operational excellence and enhance sustainability. These include approaches for innovation, performance leadership, creation of a workforce culture that delivers a consistently positive customer experience, and enhancement of leadership skills. Other examples are the Leadership Development Series, legal and ethical approaches, methods used to create a focus on action, and Legendary Service standards.
   b. A systematic process is not evident to create and balance value for the applicant's customers and stakeholders (regulators, shareholders, and the community). For example, the applicant does not describe the activities, people, and steps involved in the Leadership System and in aligning associates to customers through the Performance Management and Development Process.
   c. Several key leadership approaches do not appear to be fully deployed. For example, it is unclear how the Mission/Vision/Values (MVV) are deployed to key suppliers and partners; how development opportunities are deployed to all workforce members; and whether the MVV, service standard training, and legal and ethical requirements are deployed to support center employees (nearly 20 percent of the workforce).
   d. It is not evident that the applicant deploys its approaches to ethical behavior to interactions with customers, partners, suppliers, and other stakeholders. For example, the applicant describes only one approach focused on non-workforce stakeholders, and no enabling/monitoring processes appear to include them. This gap may be significant in light of the applicant's numerous supplier and partner relationships.

PROJECTS, ETC.

1. Visit the Baldrige Program website (http://www.nist.gov/baldrige) and write a report on the information that can be found there. (The link may have changed as Baldrige transitions from a government-sponsored program.)
2. Find the application summary for a recent Baldrige recipient on the Baldrige website, and identify at least one "role-model" practice in each of the first six categories. Justify why you choose consider them "role-model" practices.
3. For each numbered set of questions in Categories 1–6 of the Baldrige Criteria, determine whether each of the core values and concepts are reflected (a) strongly,

(b) moderately, or (c) little to not at all. Summarize your results in a matrix (rows represent core values and columns represent the item questions).
4. Select a category from the Baldrige Education Criteria found in the Baldrige Materials folder on the Student Companion Site, and interview your school administrators using the criteria questions as a basis for the interview. Write a report assessing your school against the criteria.
5. Does your state have a quality award program? If so, obtain some current information about the program and report on it. If not, try to find a neighboring state with an award program and report on it.

CASES

The Baldrige Materials Folder on the Student Companion Site contains a case study of a fictitious company, TriView National Bank (TNB). This case study was used to train national examiners in the award process (new case studies are prepared each year for examiner training). This case study will be used in the cases for this chapter.

TRIVIEW NATIONAL BANK—UNDERSTANDING KEY ORGANIZATIONAL FACTORS

Read the Organizational Profile, which is a description of the organizational environment, relationships, and challenges that impact the company's performance excellence approaches. In examining the scope of the first six categories (excluding Category 7, Results) in the 2011–2012 Baldrige Criteria, list the most relevant factors from the Organizational Profile that would affect your assessment of the management practices for this organization. For example, one of their strategic challenges is "Addressing the loss of public confidence in the financial industry in general and the impact this has had on customer confidence and expectations, particularly important in local community-focused banks

such as TNB." This would clearly relate to organizational governance in Item 1.2, and you would expect to see that their response to the questions in this item would address this issue. Similarly, in Figure P.1-1, TNB states that one of their core competencies is Operational Excellence: demonstrating process and performance discipline. If so, you would expect to see strong practices in Category 6, Operations Focus.

Your assignment is to compile a list of the most important factors from the Organizational Profile that would influence the responses to the questions in each of the first six categories, and explain why you believe they relate to the Baldrige Criteria questions.

TRIVIEW NATIONAL BANK—ASSESSING CUSTOMER FOCUS

In a typical Baldrige assessment, examiners identify strengths and opportunities for improvement based on an applicant's response to the Baldrige Criteria questions. Read the response to the Criteria questions

in Category 3, Customer Focus, for TNB. (You might wish to review Chapter 3 to refresh your thinking about customer-focused practices). Identify what you believe are the most important strengths and opportunities for improvement that TNB has in this category. To do this, carefully compare their response

to the Criteria questions (be sure to read the clarifying notes in the Criteria).

TRIVIEW NATIONAL BANK—ASSESSING WORKFORCE FOCUS

In a typical Baldrige assessment, examiners identify strengths and opportunities for improvement based on an applicant's response to the Baldrige Criteria questions. Read the response to the Criteria questions in Category 5, Workforce Focus, for TNB. (You might wish to review Chapter 4 to refresh your thinking about workforce-focused practices). Identify what you believe are the most important strengths and opportunities for improvement that TNB has in this category. To do this, carefully compare their response to the Criteria questions (be sure to read the clarifying notes in the Criteria).

NOTES

1. "Pursuing Performance Excellence at Avis Budget," *Quality Digest*, http://www.qualitydigest.com/print/8033 (accessed 4/6/12).

2. 2010 K&N Management Award Application Summary.

3. Harry Hertz, "Distinguishing 'Role Model' from 'Really Good.'" Insights on the Road to Performance Excellence, November/December 2011, http://www.nist.gov/baldrige/insights.cfm.

4. Nancy Blodgett, "Service Organizations Increasingly Adopt Baldrige Model," *Quality Progress*, December 1999, 74–78.

5. Adapted from Jerry R. Junkins, "Insights of a Baldrige Award Winner," *Quality Progress* 27, no. 3 (March 1994), 57–58. Used with permission of Texas Instruments.

6. Paul W. DeBaylo, "Ten Reasons Why the Baldrige Model Works," *Journal for Quality and Participation*, January/February 1999, 1–5.

7. DeBaylo, ibid.

8. Albert N. Link and John T. Scott, *Economic Evaluation of the Baldrige Performance Excellence Program*, Planning Report 11-2, National Institute of Standards and Technology, U.S. Department of Commerce, December 16, 2011.

9. Paul M. Bobrowski and John H. Bantham, "State Quality Initiatives: Mini-Baldrige to Baldrige Plus," *National Productivity Review* 13, no. 3 (Summer 1994), 423–438.

10. Letter from W. Edwards Deming, *Harvard Business Review*, January–February 1992, 134.

11. See the EFQM website for a brief history and explanation of the model, found at: http://ww1.efqm.org/en/Home/aboutEFQM/Ourmodels/TheEFQMExcellenceModel/tabid/170/Default.aspx (accessed 7/20/09).

12. B. Nakhai, and J. Neves, "The Deming, Baldrige, and European Quality Awards," *Quality Progress*, April 1994, 33–37.

13. "China Issues New Quality Standard," *Quality Digest*, December 2004, http://www.qualitydigest.com/dec04/news.shtml#3 (accessed 4/08/06).

14. Jack Pompeo "Living Inside China's Quality Revolution" *Quality Progress*, August 2007, 30–35.

15. "Chinese Businesses Receive Six Sigma Awards," *Quality Digest*, February 2005, http://www.qualitydigest.com/feb05/news.shtml (accessed 4/08/06).

16. Barbara B. Flynn and Brooke Saladin, "Relevance of Baldrige constructs in an international context: A study of national culture," *Journal of Operations Management*, 2005.

17. Ronald D. Snee and Roger W. Hoerl, *Leading Six Sigma* (Upper Saddle River, NJ: Prentice-Hall, 2002.

18. R. Eric Reidenbach and Reginald W. Goeke, "Six Sigma, Value, and Competitive Strategy," *Quality Progress*, July 2007, 45–49. Copyright © 2007 American Society for Quality. Reprinted with permission.

19. Mike Carnell, "Gathering Customer Feedback," *Quality Progress*, 36, no. 1 (January 2003), 60.

20. Chuck Cobb, "Knowledge Management and Quality Systems," *54th Annual Quality Congress Proceedings*, 2000, American Society for Quality, 276–287.

21. Brian Swayne and Brent Harder, "Where Has All the Magic Gone?" *Six Sigma Forum Magazine* 2, no. 3 (May 2003), 22–32.

22. George Byrne and Bob Norris, "Drive Baldrige Level Performance," *Six Sigma Forum Magazine* 2, no. 3 (May 2003), 13–21.

23. Nancy Page Cooper and Pat Noonan, "Do Teams and Six Sigma Go Together?" *Quality Progress*, June 2003, 25–28.

24. 2010 Quest for Excellence Video, National Institute of Standards and Technology, U.S. Department of Commerce.

25. Nicole Adrian, "Trial and No Error: Veterans Affairs Clinical Studies Center Has the Right Tools, Processes in Place." *Quality Progress*, January 2011, pp. 46–51.

26. The authors are grateful to Joe Sener, VP Business Excellence for Baxter International, for providing this information.

27. Brett Krzykowski, "Jersey Score," *Quality Progress*, September 2010, pp. 29–33.

28. Adapted from James R. Evans, "Organizational Learning for Performance Excellence: A Study of Branch-Smith Printing Division," *Total Quality Management & Business Excellence* 21, no. 3 (2010), pp. 225–243.

Strategy and Performance Excellence

In the executive suite at Best Buy's Minneapolis headquarters can be found a mock "retail hospital"—including a row of beds in which effigies of retailers like Kmart and Woolworth lie with their corporate logos propped up on pillows and awful financial results displayed on bedside charts.[1] A sign nearby reads: THIS IS WHERE COMPANIES GO WHEN THEIR STRATEGIES GET SICK. This provides a constant reminder that organizational success requires a clear, actionable, and effective strategy that must be kept current and fluid.

The concept of strategy holds different meanings for different people. One characterization of strategy is:

A strategy is a pattern or plan that integrates an organization's major goals, policies, and action sequences into a cohesive whole. A well-formulated strategy helps to marshal and allocate an organization's resources into a unique and viable posture based on its relative internal competencies and shortcomings, anticipated changes in the environment, and contingent moves by intelligent opponents.[2]

Essentially, **strategy** is the pattern of decisions that determines and reveals an organization's goals, policies, and plans to meet the needs of its stakeholders. **Strategic planning** is the process of envisioning the organization's future and developing the necessary goals, objectives, and action plans to achieve that future. A strategy provides a roadmap to achieve a vision of what the organization should and could be three, five, or more years in the future. A good example that illustrates the scope of strategic planning is Cargill Corn Milling.[3] The company asks key questions in four areas:

1. Where to Play—Which customers? Which segments? Which geographies? Which products? Where on the value chain?
2. How to Play—How much focus on each decision of where to play versus the other? What degree of strategic alliance at each step of the value chain? What value proposition to each customer segment?
3. What resources are needed to play—What capabilities do we need? What processes do we need? What is the ideal organizational structure? What skills do we need?
4. When to play—When is the right time to make our move?

A good strategy should build a competitive posture that is so strong in selective ways that the organization can achieve its goals despite unforeseeable external forces. For many firms, quality and performance excellence are essential elements of business strategy, as we saw in the case about Xerox in Chapter 1.

The Baldrige Criteria maintain a strong focus on strategic thinking and organizational sustainability and reflect much of Deming's philosophy regarding the need to plan for the long term. Pursuit of sustainable growth and market leadership requires a strong future orientation and a willingness to make long-term commitments to key stakeholders—customers, workforce, suppliers, partners, stockholders, the public, and the community. Thus, a focus on both customer- and stakeholder-driven quality and operational performance excellence, as opposed to simply financial and marketing goals, is essential to an effective strategy. To be competitive and profitable, an organization must focus on the drivers of customer satisfaction, customer retention, and market share; and build operational capability, including speed, responsiveness, and flexibility, to contribute to short- and longer-term productivity growth and cost/price competitiveness. Strategic planning also provides a framework for improvement and organizational learning. A key role of strategic planning is to align work processes and learning initiatives with an organization's strategic directions, thereby ensuring that improvement and learning prepare for and reinforce organizational priorities.

Organizations must also take a broad strategic focus in designing the organization and its work systems, and leveraging its core competencies—the things it does best. These include decisions regarding design of the organizational structure and leadership system, the structure of the supply chain, and outsourcing decisions. Table 11.1 summarizes key practices that organizations must address to achieve a strategic focus on performance excellence. The Quality Profiles highlight two organizations whose strategic focus has been vital to their success. We will expand upon these themes in the remainder of this chapter.

TABLE 11.1   Key Practices for a Strategic Focus on Performance Excellence

- Understand the organization's operating environment and its key relationships with customers, suppliers, partners, and stakeholders.
- Understand the competitive environment, the principal factors that determine success, the organization's core competencies, and strategic challenges—business, operational, and human resource-related— associated with organizational sustainability.
- Gather and analyze relevant data and information pertaining to such factors as the organization's strengths, weaknesses, opportunities, and threats; emerging trends in technology, markets, customer preferences, competitions, and the regulatory environment; long-term organizational sustainability; and the ability to execute strategic plans.
- Develop and refine a systematic approach for conducting strategic planning and setting strategic objectives, including identifying blind spots, leveraging strengths, and addressing challenges over appropriate time horizons.
- Develop and align short-term action plans with long-term strategic objectives, ensure adequate resources and the ability to sustain outcomes, assess financial and other risks associated with the plans, and communicate them throughout the organization.
- Derive human resource plans required to accomplish longer-term strategic objectives and shorter-term action plans that address the potential impacts on the workforce and potential changes to workforce capability and capacity needs.
- Identify key measures or indicators for tracking progress on action plans, ensure that the measurement system reinforces organizational alignment, and project performance of these key measures compared with competitors or comparable organizations to identify gaps and opportunities.
- Determine the organization's core competencies, and understand how they relate to the mission, competitive environment, and strategic objectives.
- View the work performed within the organization as a system, and make rational decisions about the mix of internal and external work processes that can best achieve the organization's mission.

quality**profiles**

Freese and Nichols, Inc. and Premier, Inc.

Freese and Nichols is a Texas-based multidiscipline consulting firm that offers services in engineering, architecture, environmental science, planning, construction services, and program management. Freese and Nichols has a strong ability to build long-term client relationships. Consistent with the long-term client relationships, the firm adheres to a Hedgehog Concept (a term coined by business author Jim Collins—the single thing that the organization aims to do well): *Be the very best at client service, resulting in long-term mutually beneficial relationships.*

Freese and Nichols has a comprehensive, year-long strategic planning process to identify key focus area indicators, critical actions, and balanced scorecard measures. Participants in the planning process represent all areas of the organization, including a management-level Futures Committee charged with examining trends and changes likely to affect the firm in 5 to 15 years. Freese and Nichols also uses a "catch-ball" process to cascade plans to divisions, groups, and individuals to ensure that resources are committed and agreed-upon strategies are implemented. As a result,

Freese and Nichols has built long-term client relationships, retaining 42 percent of its key accounts for more than 30 years and 71 percent for more than 10 years. Freese and Nichols also builds a sustainable organization through growth in retained earnings and use of restricted funds that support key business needs as well as growth strategies during a time of economic crisis.

Serving 1,700 hospitals and more than 43,000 other health care sites, Premier Inc. is the largest health care alliance in the United States dedicated to improving patient outcomes while safely reducing the cost of care. Premier's three business units provide the following services: group purchasing and supply chain management, insurance and risk management, and informatics and performance improvement tools.

Premier's "Big Hairy Audacious Goal" is for its member hospitals to deliver the best, most cost-effective care in the nation and for the alliance to have a major influence on reshaping health care. The success of this strategy is evident:

- Hospitals that make up the Premier alliance have validated more than $2.5 billion in savings over the past three years achieved through cooperative purchasing and participation in Premier's other services.
- Premier's customer satisfaction levels of over 90 percent significantly exceed industry benchmarks.
- Premier is partnering with the Centers for Medicare and Medicaid Services (CMS) in a voluntary national demonstration project aimed at improving the quality of inpatient health care. Through the Premier Hospital Quality Incentive Demonstration, CMS is rewarding top performing hospitals for high quality care by increasing their payments for Medicare patients. The results show that participating hospitals have shown dramatic improvements in quality and performance.
- Operating margins grew from 35 percent in 2003 to 50 percent in 2006 and exceeded that of Premier's largest competitor in all years, while operating expenses have remained well below those of that competitor.

Premier has taken a leadership role in promoting best practices in ethical conduct, transparency, and accountability within its own organization and throughout the industry. In 1998, Premier instituted a Corporate Values Program and an employee Values Conference at which employees and senior leaders meet together to discuss Premier's Core Values—focus on people, integrity, passion for performance, and innovation. The company's customers, who are also its owners, work closely with Premier and its employees to achieve their mutual goals. All of Premier's owners and other customers have ready access to the company's information, staff, resources, and services, particularly through Premier's field staff and its customer solution centers.

Source: Adapted from Malcolm Baldrige National Quality Award Profiles of Winners, National Institute of Standards and Technology, Department of Commerce.

THE SCOPE OF STRATEGIC PLANNING

Developing and implementing a strategy requires a robust and effective strategic planning and action plan deployment process. An effective strategic planning process requires that executives and managers understand the short- and longer-term factors that affect the organization and its marketplace, such as customers' expectations, new business and partnering opportunities, workforce development and hiring needs, the increasingly global marketplace, technological developments, e-commerce, changes in customer and market segments, evolving regulatory requirements, changes in community and societal expectations and needs, and strategic moves by competitors. However, while many organizations are quite proficient at strategic planning, executing plans is often a significant challenge. This is especially true in changing markets that require agility and preparation for unexpected change, such as disruptive technologies that can upset an otherwise fast-paced but more predictable marketplace.

Strategy Development Processes

The goal of **strategy development** is envisioning the future for purposes of decision making and resource allocation. One characterization of strategy development is

> .... *capturing what the manager learns from all sources (both soft insights from his or her personal experiences and the experiences of others throughout the organization and the hard data from market research and the like) and then synthesizing that learning into a vision of the direction that the business should pursue.*[4]

Effective strategy development requires a systematic process that involves participation by all necessary stakeholders, ensures that relevant and important data and information are captured and analyzed, addresses both short- and long-term time horizons, addresses key strategic challenges, and leads to innovation and sustainability. In many organizations, strategy development is nothing more than a group of managers sitting around in a room and proposing ideas. Clearly this is not an effective approach. Using a systematic process helps to optimize the use of resources, ensure the availability of trained employees, and ensure bridging between short- and longer-term requirements that may entail capital expenditures or supplier development, for example. Caterpillar Financial Services Corporation uses a structured six-step strategic planning process that yields both a one-year tactical plan and a four-year strategic plan. The process starts with an annual retreat where strategic direction is revised by the top senior leaders, followed by a four-month strategy development period; an annual leadership conference where the top 45 leaders and managers develop preliminary division strategies and support department requirements; a cycle for developing action plans and goals for divisions, support departments, and Six Sigma projects; a plan review and resource allocation step; and, the final step of developing unit action plans/goals and individual employee performance and development plans.

Although specific approaches vary from one organization to another, all generally follow the basic model that Eastman Chemical Company uses as shown in Figure 11.1. This model begins with gathering critical information about the organization and its environment, developing a strategy, translating that strategy into specific action plans or projects, and reviewing performance for improvement opportunities. In some organizations, strategic planning might involve participation by key suppliers, distributors, partners, and customers. It is not unusual for customers and suppliers to be involved in strategic planning efforts because of their importance in the supply chain and their knowledge of markets and technology.

Figure 11.2 shows the strategic planning process for Park Place Lexus, which shows the alignment of action plans and goals throughout the organization, and which is supported by ongoing review and tracking. Good strategy development processes often include active participation of top management, employees, and customers or suppliers. Employees represent an important resource in strategic planning. Not only can the company capitalize on employee knowledge of customers and processes, but also employee involvement greatly enhances the effectiveness of strategy implementation. Such "bottom-up" planning facilitates better understanding and assessment of customer needs. At Solar Turbines, Inc., the strategy development process involves people from all parts of its worldwide organization, customers, and suppliers. Sales, marketing, service, engineering, and manufacturing people in functional and cross-functional teams perform information gathering, analysis, and conclusions. This information is carried forward to the leadership system committees and the Operations Council where it is integrated and synthesized into strategies and critical success factor goals.

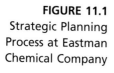

FIGURE 11.1
Strategic Planning
Process at Eastman
Chemical Company

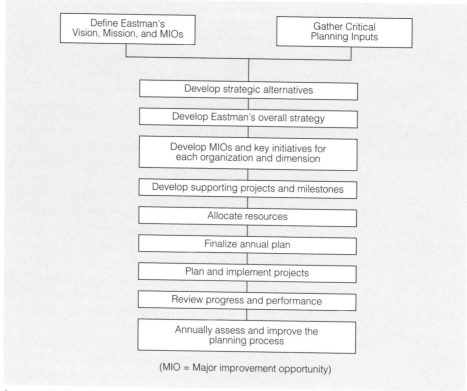

Source: Used with permission of Eastman Chemical Company.

FIGURE 11.2   Strategic Planning Process at Park Place Lexus

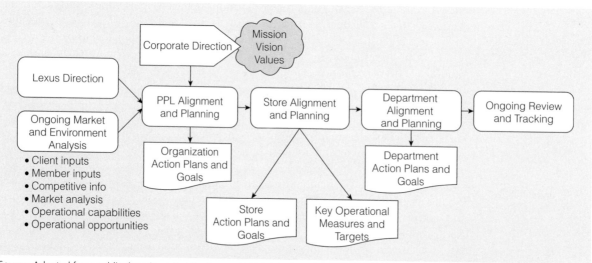

Source: Adapted from public domain material—*Source:* 2005 Malcolm Baldrige Application Summary, NIST U.S. Department of Commerce. Courtesy Park Place Lexus.

An organization cannot make good strategic decisions without a solid understanding of its internal and external environments. Yet, you would be amazed at how few senior executives truly grasp these characteristics and their impact on strategic decisions. Many strategic planning processes begin with the organization's leaders first exploring and agreeing upon (or reaffirming) the mission, vision, and guiding principles of the organization, which form the foundation for the strategic plan.

The **mission** of a firm defines its reason for existence; it answers the question "Why are we in business?" A mission statement might include a definition of products and services the organization provides, technologies used to provide these products and services, types of markets, important customer needs, and distinctive competencies or the expertise that sets the firm apart from others. For example, the mission of Freese and Nichols, Inc. and Premier, Inc. are, respectively, *Innovative approaches … practical results … outstanding service*, and *To improve the health of communities.*

A firm's mission guides the development of strategies by different groups within the firm. It establishes the context within which daily operating decisions are made and sets limits on available strategic options. In addition, it governs the trade-offs among the various performance measures and between short- and long-term goals. Finally, it can inspire employees to focus their efforts toward the overall purpose of the organization.

The **vision** describes where the organization is headed and what it intends to be; it is a statement of the future that would not happen by itself. The vision articulates the basic characteristics that shape the organization's view of the future and its strategy. A vision should be brief, focused, clear, and inspirational to an organization's employees. It should be linked to customers' needs and convey a general strategy for achieving the mission. For example, Premier's vision is stated as its "Big Hairy Audacious Goal"— *Premier's Owners will be the leading health care systems in their markets, and, with them, Premier will be a major influence in reshaping health care.* Freese and Nichols' vision statement is to *Be the firm of choice for clients and employees.*

A vision must be consistent with the culture and values of the organization—often called **guiding principles**—which are often stated formally to provide guidance to all employees and leaders in the organization, and are reinforced through conscious and subconscious behavior at all levels of the organization. The guiding principles of Freese and Nichols are:

- *We are ethical*
- *We deliver quality*
- *We are responsive*
- *We add value*
- *We improve continuously*

- *We are innovative*
- *We develop professionally*
- *We respect others*
- *We give back to our communities*

For Premier, the core values are

- *Integrity of the individual and the enterprise.*
- *A **passion for performance** and a bias for action, creating real value for all stakeholders, and leading the pace.*
- *Innovation: Seeking breakthrough opportunities, taking risks, and initiating meaningful change.*
- *Focus on people: Showing concern and respect for all with whom we work, building collaborative relationships with the community, our customers, co-workers, and business associates.*

The mission, vision, and guiding principles serve as the foundation for strategic planning. Top management and others who lead, especially the CEO, must articulate them. They also have to be transmitted, practiced, and reinforced through symbolic and real action before they become "real" to the employees and the people, groups, and organizations in the external environment that do business with the firm.

Although an organization's mission, vision, and values rarely change, the environment in which the organization exists usually does. Thus, strategy development requires an **environmental assessment** of key factors, which typically include:

- The organization's strengths, weaknesses, opportunities, and threats (SWOT)
- Early indications of major shifts in technology, markets, customer preferences, competition, or the regulatory environment
- Long-term organizational sustainability, including needed core competencies, and projections of future performance and competitors' or comparable organizations' future performance
- The ability to execute the strategic plan

A SWOT analysis should address all factors that are key to an organization's future success, and might include customer and market needs, expectations, and opportunities; opportunities for innovation and role model performance; core competencies; competitive environment and performance relative to competitors and comparable organizations; product life cycles; technological and other key innovations or changes that might affect products, services, and operations; human and other resource needs; ability to capitalize on diversity; opportunities to redirect resources to higher-priority products, services, or areas; financial, societal, ethical, regulatory, technological, security, and other potential risks; ability to prevent and respond to emergencies, including natural or other disasters; changes in the national or global economy; partner and supply chain needs, strengths, and weaknesses; and other factors unique to the organization. Solar Turbines, Inc., for instance, looks at six external factors that affect its business: customer needs and wants, market trends and opportunities, industry trends, competitive dynamics, governmental and regulatory issues, and technological innovations that can change the nature of products and services. The ability to execute a strategic plan should address how the organization is capable of mobilizing the necessary resources and knowledge and should also address how the organization might react to circumstances that require a shift in plans and rapid execution of new or changed plans.

> *The Organizational Profile is also the starting point for conducting a self-assessment using the Baldrige Criteria or writing a Baldrige application. It helps to identify potential gaps in key information and focus on key performance requirements and results. It is used by the examiners and judges in application review and the site visit to understand the organization and what it considers important relative the Criteria questions.*

The Baldrige Organizational Profile

The Baldrige Criteria provides a list of key questions called the **Organizational Profile**, which helps an organization summarize the elements of an environmental assessment. The Organizational Profile provides a frame of reference to help an organization better understand the internal and external factors that shape its operating environment, and set the context for strategic planning. The Organizational Profile addresses the basic characteristics of the organization, organizational relationships, the competitive environment, the advantages an organization has and the challenges that it faces, and its approach to performance improvement. These questions are shown in Table 11.2.

Why are they important? The Organizational Profile helps an organization better understand the context in which it operates; the key requirements for current and future business

TABLE 11.2   Baldrige Organizational Profile Questions

1. Organizational Description
   a. Organizational Environment
      (1) *Product Offerings* What are your organization's main product offerings? What is the relative importance of each to your organizational success? What mechanisms do you use to deliver your products?
      (2) *Vision and Mission* What are the distinctive characteristics of your organizational culture? What are your stated purpose, vision, values, and mission? What are your organization's core competencies and their relationship to your mission?
      (3) *Workforce Profile* What is your workforce profile? What are your workforce or employee groups and segments? What are their education levels? What are the key elements that engage them in accomplishing your mission and vision? What are your organization's workforce and job diversity, organized bargaining units, key workforce benefits, and special health and safety requirements?
      (4) *Assets* What are your major facilities, technologies, and equipment?
      (5) *Regulatory Requirements* What is the regulatory environment under which your organization operates? What are the applicable occupational health and safety regulations; accreditation, certification, or registration requirements; industry standards; and environmental, financial, and product regulations?
   b. Organizational Relationships
      (1) *Organizational Structure* What are your organizational structure and governance system? What are the reporting relationships among your governance board, senior leaders, and parent organization, as appropriate?
      (2) *Customers and Stakeholders* What are your key market segments, customer groups, and stakeholder groups, as appropriate? What are their key requirements and expectations for your products, customer support services, and operations? What are the differences in these requirements and expectations among market segments, customer groups, and stakeholder groups?
      (3) *Suppliers and Partners* What are your key types of suppliers, partners, and collaborators? What role do these suppliers, partners, and collaborators play in the production and delivery of your key products and customer support services? What are your key mechanisms for communicating with suppliers, partners, and collaborators? What role, if any, do these organizations play in implementing innovations in your organization? What are your key supply-chain requirements?

2. Organizational Situation
   a. Competitive Environment
      (1) *Competitive Position* What is your competitive position? What are your relative size and growth in your industry or markets served? What are the numbers and types of competitors for your organization?
      (2) *Competitiveness Changes* What are any key changes taking place that affect your competitive situation, including opportunities for innovation and collaboration, as appropriate?
      (3) *Comparative Data* What are your key available sources of comparative and competitive data from within your industry? What are your key available sources of comparative data from outside your industry? What limitations, if any, affect your ability to obtain these data?
   b. Strategic Context
      (1) What are your key business, operational, societal responsibility, and human resource strategic challenges and advantages?
   c. Performance Improvement System
      (1) What are the key elements of your performance improvement system, including your evaluation, organizational learning, and innovation processes?

success and organizational sustainability; and the needs, opportunities, and constraints placed on the organization's management systems. This helps to better focus strategic thinking within the organization. For example, knowledge of an organization's strengths, vulnerabilities, and opportunities for both improvement and growth helps an organization to identify those products, service and program offerings, processes, competencies, and performance attributes that are unique; those that set it apart from other organizations; and those that help to sustain a competitive advantage.

The first set of questions, under the heading "Organizational Description," help to provide a clear understanding of what the organization is all about. These include questions about the organization's product offerings, vision and mission, workforce profile, assets, regulatory requirements, organizational structure, customers and stakeholders, and suppliers and partners. Consider the Workforce Profile questions. Most organizations have a very diverse workforce from the perspective of job descriptions and responsibilities. In a manufacturing firm, for example, the workforce might be comprised of skilled labor, white-collar knowledge workers, and different levels of management; a health care system has physicians, nurses, general labor, managers, and so on. Some groups may be unionized and others not. Each of these groups may differ in terms of their requirements for training and safety, compensation and rewards, and motivation, for instance. This can impact the strategic decisions that the organization makes. Similarly, the mix of facilities, technologies, and equipment used in operations may limit strategic choices and affect how key processes are managed. Finally, the regulatory environment in which an organization operates places specific requirements on the organization. Understanding this environment is vital to making effective operational and strategic decisions. Further, it allows one to identify whether the organization is merely complying with the minimum requirements of applicable laws, regulations, and standards of practice or exceeding them, a hallmark of leading organizations.

The remaining questions under the heading "Organizational Situation" address the competitive environment, strategic context—specifically key strategic challenges and advantages—and the performance improvement system. The term **strategic challenges** refers to those pressures that exert a decisive influence on an organization's likelihood of future success. Strategic challenges frequently are driven by an organization's future competitive position relative to other providers of similar products or services. They might include operational costs (e.g., materials, labor, or geographic location); expanding or decreasing markets; mergers or acquisitions both by the organization and by its competitors; economic conditions, including fluctuating demand and local and global economic downturns; the cyclical nature of the industry; the introduction of new or substitute products or services; rapid technological changes; or new competitors entering the market. In addition, an organization may face challenges related to the recruitment, hiring, and retention of a qualified workforce. For example, like most health care organizations today, North Mississippi Medical Center faces strategic challenges such as shortages of health care providers and unique challenges in their community such as a high poverty level, poor health status, and lack of health care insurance. Their most significant strategic challenges are organized by their five critical success factors:[5]

PEOPLE—Maintain and enhance our employees' satisfaction, skills, and engagement. Recruit and retain skilled staff. Develop staff and physician leaders.

SERVICE—Increase our patients' and physicians' satisfaction. Enhance our patient–customer loyalty.

QUALITY—Provide high level, evidence-based, quality care and maintain patient safety.

FINANCIAL—Generate the financial resources necessary to support the organization in an environment of reimbursement pressures and increasing charity care.

GROWTH—Continue to expand in areas consistent with our Mission.

A particularly significant challenge that some organizations face is being unprepared for a disruptive technology that threatens its competitive position or its marketplace. In the past, such technologies have included personal computers replacing typewriters, cell phones challenging land lines and pay phones, fax machines capturing business from overnight delivery services, and e-mail challenging all other means of correspondence. Today, organizations need to be scanning the environment inside and outside their immediate industry to detect such challenges at the earliest possible point in time.

One of the many issues facing organizations today is how to manage, use, evaluate, and share their ever-increasing organizational knowledge. Leading organizations already benefit from the knowledge assets of their workforce, customers, suppliers, collaborators, and partners, who together drive organizational learning and improve performance. To leverage this knowledge, organizations need a performance improvement approach that can systematically drive organizational change. Overall approaches to performance improvement might include implementing a Lean Enterprise System, applying Six Sigma, using the ISO 9000:2000 or Baldrige frameworks, or employing other improvement approaches that we discussed in previous chapters.

Developing Strategies

Information from an environmental assessment is usually analyzed using various types of forecasts, projections, options, scenarios, or other approaches. Strategic planning teams use the results of these analyses to develop strategies, objectives, and action plans that address strategic challenges and opportunities and balance the needs of all stakeholders. **Strategies** are broad statements that set the direction for the organization to take in realizing its mission and vision. **Strategic objectives** are what an organization must change or improve to remain or become competitive. **Action plans** are things that an organization must do to achieve its strategic objectives.

A strategy might be directed toward becoming a preferred supplier, a low-cost producer, a market innovator, or a high-end or customized service provider. Strategic objectives set an organization's longer-term directions and guide resource allocation decisions. They are typically focused externally and relate to customer, market, product, service, or technological opportunities and challenges. For example, a strategic objective for a supplier in a highly competitive industry might be to develop and maintain a price leadership position. Action plans include details of resource commitments and time horizons for accomplishment. For the supplier seeking to develop a price leadership position, action plans might include the design of efficient processes and creation of an accounting system that tracks activity-level costs. Action plans form the basis for effective implementation, or what is called *deployment*, of a strategy.

Strategy Deployment

Strategy deployment involves developing specific action plans to achieve strategic objectives, ensuring that adequate financial and other resources are available to accomplish the action plans, developing contingencies should circumstances require a shift in plans and rapid execution of new plans, aligning work unit, supplier, or partner activities as necessary, and identifying performance measures for tracking progress. Essentially, strategy deployment links the planners (who focus on "doing the right thing") with the doers (whose focus is on "doing things right"). At The Ritz-Carlton, teams at all levels—corporate, management, and employee—set objectives and devise action plans. Each hotel designates a quality leader who serves as a resource and advisor to teams for developing and implementing plans.

Action plan development represents the critical stage in planning when strategic objectives and goals are made specific so that effective, organization-wide understanding and deployment are possible. Action plans typically include details of resource commitments and time horizons for their accomplishment. Deployment also might require specialized training for some employees or recruitment of personnel. An example of a strategic objective for a supplier in a highly competitive industry might be to develop and maintain a price leadership position. Action plans could entail designing efficient processes and creating an accounting system that tracks activity-level costs, aligned for the organization as a whole. Deployment requirements might include work unit and team training in setting priorities based on costs and benefits. Organizational-level analysis and review likely would emphasize productivity growth, cost control, and quality.

Many organizations simply do a poor job of deployment, despite having elegant and comprehensive strategy development approaches. Poor deployment often results from one of three reasons:[6]

1. *Lack of alignment across the organization.* Good deployment aligns resources and policies. For example, a strategic objective of increasing the number of patents generated might require hiring more engineers, developing a creativity training program, and changing its financial incentive approaches. Organizational goals should be linked, or aligned, with division, department, team, and individual goals. Everyone should be able to answer the question: What does strategy mean in terms that I can act on?

2. *Misallocation of resources.* Good strategic planning dedicates resources to making improvements or changes in those areas that are critical to an organization's strategic advantage. Spreading resources too thin to make a real difference in key areas of the business or allocating them to projects that have no real impact on strategy is ineffective.

3. *Insufficient operational measures.* Organizations need appropriate measurement systems at the operational level to track progress and know if action plans are really accomplishing their objectives. These measurement systems often include projections into the future based on accomplishment of action plans and might also compare to competitors' projections. Measures and indicators of projected performance might include changes resulting from new ventures; organizational acquisitions or mergers; new value creation; market entry and shifts; new legislative mandates, legal requirements, or industry standards; and significant anticipated innovations in products, services, and technology. Projections of key performance measures and comparisons with competitors, benchmarks, and past performance help an organization evaluate its performance in achieving its objectives, strategies, and ultimately, its vision. Organizations might use a variety of modeling, scenario, or other techniques and judgments to project the competitive environment. MEDRAD, for example, aligns strategic directions through a corporate scorecard, which measures performance on five short- and long-term goals: (1) exceed the financial objectives; (2) grow the company; (3) improve quality and productivity; (4) improve customer satisfaction; and (5) improve employee growth and satisfaction.

Many examples of effective deployment can be found among Baldrige recipients. SSM Health Care identified three specific action plans during one year to help meet its strategic objective of "Exceptional patient, employee, and physician satisfaction": improve patient satisfaction with pain management, implement Nursing Shared Accountability model, and increase diversity representation within leadership. Key indicators to track the success of these actions plans, such as nurse turnover rate and the number of minorities in managerial professional ranks, were developed and monitored. Communication ensures that strategies will be deployed effectively at the "three levels of quality"—the organization level, process level, and individual job level. At BI, the Strategic Business and Quality Plan (SBQP) is communicated to all BI leaders and then all vice presidents facilitate division planning with their teams. The result is a divisional SBQP with measurable objectives and action plans, which is communicated to all associates within the division. Each director, regional sales manager, and team leader then facilitates a planning session with his or her individual team, which results in a department, region, or team plan with objectives and action plans of its own. The Strategic Planning Team meets quarterly to report progress of each action plan against its timeline and reviews results measurements against corporate objectives.

Hoshin Kanri (Policy Deployment)

The traditional approach to deploying strategy has been top-down. However, taking a total quality perspective, subordinates are both customers and suppliers, and therefore their input and involvement is necessary. An iterative process in which senior management asks what lower levels of the organization can do, what they need, and what conflicts may arise can avoid many of the implementation problems that managers typically face.

Japanese firms introduced a deployment process known as **hoshin kanri**, or *hoshin planning*. In the United States, this process is often referred to as **policy deployment**, or *management by planning*. Many organizations, notably Florida Power and Light, Hewlett-Packard, and AT&T among many others, have adopted this process. The literal Japanese translation of hoshin kanri is "pointing direction."[7] The idea is to point, or align, the entire organization in a common direction. Florida Power and Light defines policy deployment as "the executive deployment of selected policy-driven priorities and the necessary resources to achieve performance breakthroughs." Hewlett-Packard calls it "a process for annual planning and implementation which focuses on areas needing significant improvement." AT&T's definition is "an organization-wide and customer-focused management approach aimed at planning and executing breakthrough improvements in business performance." Regardless of the particular definition, policy deployment emphasizes organization-wide planning and setting of priorities, provides resources to meet objectives, and measures performance as a basis for improving performance. Policy deployment is essentially a quality-based approach to executing a strategy by ensuring that all employees understand the business direction and are working according to a plan to make the vision a reality.

M. Imai provides an example of policy deployment:

> To illustrate the need for policy deployment, let us consider the following case: The president of an airline company proclaims that he believes in safety and that his corporate goal is to make sure that safety is maintained throughout the company. This proclamation is prominently featured in the company's quarterly report and its advertising. Let us further suppose that the department managers also swear a firm belief in safety. The catering manager says he believes in safety. The pilots say they believe in safety. The flight crews say they believe in safety. Everyone in the company practices safety. True? Or might everyone simply be paying lip service to the idea of safety?

On the other hand, if the president states that safety is company policy and works with his division managers to develop a plan for safety that defines their responsibilities, everyone will have a very specific subject to discuss. Safety will become a real concern. For the manager in charge of catering services, safety might mean maintaining the quality of food to avoid customer dissatisfaction or illness.

In that case, how does he ensure that the food is of top quality? What sorts of control points and checkpoints does he establish? How does he ensure that there is no deterioration of food quality in flight? Who checks the temperature of the refrigerators or the condition of the oven while the plane is in the air?

Only when safety is translated into specific actions with specific control and checkpoints established for each employee's job might safety be said to have been truly deployed as a policy. Policy deployment calls for everyone to interpret policy in light of his own responsibilities and for everyone to work out criteria to check his success in carrying out the policy.[8]

Figure 11.3 provides a simplified description of the policy deployment process.[9] With policy deployment, top management is responsible for developing and

FIGURE 11.3
The Policy Deployment Process

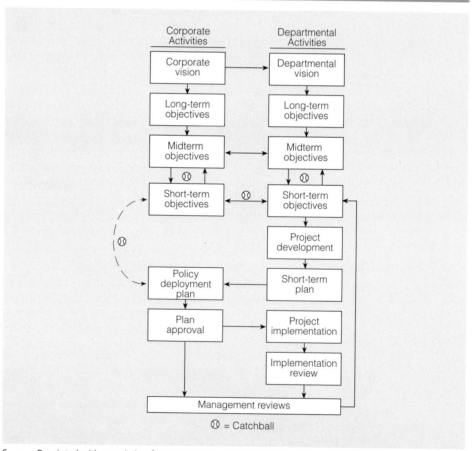

Source: Reprinted with permission from Kersi F. Munshi, "Policy Deployment: A Key to Long-Term TQM Success," *ASQC Quality Congress Transactions* (Boston, 1993), pp. 236–244. Copyright © 1993. No further distribution allowed without permission.

communicating a vision, then building organization-wide commitment to its achievement.[10] The long-term strategic plan forms the basis for shorter-term planning. This vision is deployed through the development and execution of annual objectives and plans. All levels of employees actively participate in generating strategy and action plans to attain the vision. At each level, progressively more detailed and concrete means to accomplish the objectives are determined. Objectives should be challenging, but people should feel that they are attainable. To this end, middle management negotiates with senior management regarding the objectives that will achieve the strategies, and what process changes and resources might be required to achieve those objectives. Middle management then negotiates with the implementation teams the final short-term objectives and the performance measures that are used to indicate progress toward accomplishing the objectives.

Management reviews at specific checkpoints ensure the effectiveness of individual elements of the strategy. The implementation teams are empowered to manage actions and schedule their activities. Periodic reviews (monthly or quarterly) track progress and diagnose problems. Management may modify objectives on the basis of these reviews, as evidenced by the feedback loop in the figure. Top management evaluates results as well as the deployment process itself through annual reviews, which serve as a basis for the next planning cycle.

Note, however, that top management does not develop action plans; it sets overall guidelines and strategies. Departments and functional units develop specific implementation plans. Hence, the process in Figure 11.3 includes both corporate and departmental activities. In practice, policy deployment entails a high degree of detail, including the anticipation of possible problems during implementation. The emphasis is on the improvement of the process, as opposed to a results-only orientation.

The negotiation process is called *catchball* (represented by the baseball symbol in Figure 11.3). Leaders communicate midterm objectives and measures to middle managers who develop short-term objectives and recommend necessary resources, targets, and roles/responsibilities. These issues are discussed and debated until agreement is reached. The objectives then cascade to lower levels of the organization where short-term plans are developed. Catchball is an up, down, and sideways communication process as opposed to an autocratic, top-down management style. It marshals the collective expertise of the whole organization and results in realistic and achievable objectives that do not conflict. In the spirit of Deming, the process focuses on optimizing the system rather than on individual goals and objectives. Clearly, this process can only occur in a culture that nourishes open communication.

Linking Human Resource Plans and Business Strategy

Whenever an organization seeks to do something different, people are invariably impacted. Thus, it is important to consider organizational change and plan for necessary human resource changes that may be needed. These changes might include redesigning the work organization, increasing empowerment, establishing new training initiatives, or modifying compensation and incentive approaches. For example, to address a national nursing shortage, Baptist Hospital's strategy for nurse recruitment and retention required numerous human resource changes, such as revamping the clinical ladder program, pay adjustments to recruit graduate nurses, increasing the number of scholarships to nursing students, and involving experienced nurses to speak to high school students to raise interest in the field. Motorola's Commercial, Government, and

Industrial Solutions Sector ties the following human resource plans into its strategic planning process: breakthrough changes in work design, team member development, education, and training; compensation, recognition, and benefits; and human resources needs identification and recruitment. When GE decided to adopt a Six Sigma framework for the organization, it was necessary to train 12,000 black-belt leaders to implement the plan. Incentives for project champions in upper management were restructured to account for 40 percent of their bonuses.[11]

Strategic human resource plans often include one or more of the following:

- Redesign of the work organization to increase empowerment and decision-making or team-based participation;
- Initiatives for promoting greater labor/management cooperation, such as union partnerships;
- Initiatives to foster knowledge sharing and organizational learning; and
- Partnerships with educational institutions to help ensure the future supply of well-prepared employees.

Whatever the choices, it is vital that they support the organization's overall strategy. For example, suppose that a firm identifies its critical success factors as customer satisfaction, employee satisfaction, market growth, and world-class performance. Each critical success factor will have one or more strategic objectives defined through the firm's strategic planning process. Because successful accomplishment of these strategic objectives will depend on execution by the firm's workforce, it is important that key human resource plans, such as enhancing skills, knowledge, and motivation, be identified to support these strategic objectives. Without proper alignment, the work that people do can be focused in an entirely different direction than the organization intends to go. Some generic examples are shown in Table 11.3.

TABLE 11.3   Alignment of Human Resource Plans with Critical Success Factors and Strategic Objectives

Critical Success Factor and Strategic Objectives	Human Resource Plans
Customer Satisfaction	
Strengthen customer relationships by improving responsiveness	Implement new training program for front-line staff
Employee Satisfaction	
Encourage employee development and career planning to capitalize on workforce diversity	Develop, implement, and deliver online training courses
	Require leadership rotation in team projects
Market Growth	
Pursue new and expanded market opportunities	Actively participate on marketing teams to determine HR requirements
	Develop a hiring plan for new product development and marketing initiatives
World Class Performance	
Improve process quality	Support Six Sigma training initiatives
Reduce costs to world-class benchmark levels	Develop lean expertise throughout the workforce

THE SEVEN MANAGEMENT AND PLANNING TOOLS

Managers may use a variety of tools and techniques, known as the **Seven Management and Planning Tools**, to implement policy deployment.

1. *Affinity Diagram*: A tool for organizing a large number of ideas, opinions, and facts relating to a broad problem or subject area
2. *Interrelationship Digraph*: A tool for identifying and exploring causal relationships among related concepts or ideas
3. *Tree Diagram*: A tool to map out the paths and tasks necessary to complete a specific project or reach a specified goal
4. *Matrix Diagram*: "Spreadsheets" that graphically display relationships between ideas, activities, or other dimensions in such a way as to provide logical connecting points between each item
5. *Matrix Data Analysis*: A tool to take data and arrange them to display quantitative relationships among variables to make them more easily understood and analyzed
6. *Process Decision Program Chart*: A method for mapping out every conceivable event and contingency that can occur when moving from a problem statement to possible solutions
7. *Arrow Diagrams*: A tool for sequencing and scheduling project tasks

These tools are particularly useful in structuring unstructured ideas, making strategic plans, and organizing and controlling large, complex projects. Thus, they can benefit all employees involved in quality planning and implementation.

The Seven Management and Planning Tools had their roots in post—World War II operations research developments in the United States, but were combined and refined by several Japanese companies over the past several decades as part of their planning processes. They were popularized in the United States by the consulting firm GOAL/QPC, and have been used by a number of firms since 1984 to improve their quality planning and improvement efforts. Many organizations formally integrated these tools into policy deployment activities. The following example illustrates how they can be used in strategic planning and deployment.

Using the Seven Management and Planning Tools for Strategic Planning

MicroTech is a hypothetical high-technology consumer electronics company. Micro-Tech's mission is *to design and manufacture miniature electronics products utilizing radio frequency technologies, digital signal processing technologies, and state-of-the-art surface mount manufacturing techniques.*

Affinity Diagram   The affinity diagram is a tool for organizing a large number of ideas, opinions, and facts relating to a broad problem or subject area. In developing a vision statement, for example, senior management might conduct a brainstorming session to develop a list of ideas to incorporate into the vision. This list might include

low product maintenance
satisfied employees
courteous order entry
low price
quick delivery
growth in shareholder value
teamwork
responsive technical support
personal employee growth

low production costs
innovative product features
high return on investment
constant technology innovation
high quality
motivated employees
unique products
small, lightweight designs

FIGURE 11.4
Affinity Diagram for
MicroTech

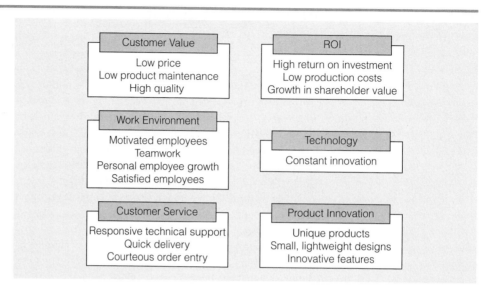

Once a large number of ideas have been generated, they can be grouped according to their "affinity" or relationship to each other. An affinity diagram for the preceding list is shown in Figure 11.4.

> *Affinity diagrams were introduced in Chapter 3 as a means of analyzing voice of the customer information.*

Interrelationship Digraph An interrelationship digraph identifies and explores causal relationships among related concepts or ideas. It shows that every idea can be logically linked with more than one other idea at a time, and allows for "lateral thinking" rather than "linear thinking." This technique is often used after the affinity diagram had clarified issues and problems. Figure 11.5 shows an example of how the key strategic factors for MicroTech relate to one another. The elements having the most net outward-pointing arrows (number out minus number in) represent the primary drivers of the company's vision: in this case, work environment and customer service. As a result, MicroTech might develop the following vision statement:

> *We will provide exceptional value to our customers in terms of cost-effective products and services of the highest quality, leading to superior value to our shareholders. We*

FIGURE 11.5
Interrelationship
Digraph of Micro-
Tech's Strategic
Factors

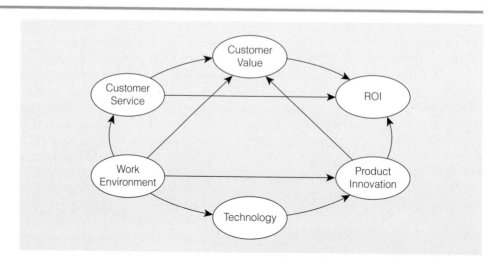

will provide a supportive work environment that promotes personal growth and the pursuit of excellence and allows each employee to achieve his or her full potential. We are committed to advancing the state-of-the-art in electronics miniaturization and related technologies and to developing market opportunities that are built upon our unique technical expertise.

Tree Diagram   A tree diagram maps out the paths and tasks necessary to complete a specific project or reach a specified goal. Thus, the planner uses this technique to seek answers to such questions as "What sequence of tasks will address the issue?" or "What factors contribute to the existence of the key problem?"

A tree diagram brings the issues and problems revealed by the affinity diagram and the interrelationship digraph down to the operational planning stage. A clear statement specifies problem or process. From this general statement, a team can be established to recommend steps to solve the problem or implement the plan. The "product" produced by this group would be a tree diagram with activities and perhaps recommendations for timing the activities. Figure 11.6 shows an example of how a tree diagram can be used to map out key goals and strategies for MicroTech.

Matrix Diagram   Matrix diagrams are "spreadsheets" that graphically display relationships between ideas, activities, or other dimensions in such a way as to provide logical connecting points between each item. A matrix diagram is one of the most versatile tools in quality planning. One example is shown in Figure 11.7. Here, we have listed the three principal goals articulated in MicroTech's vision statement along the rows, and the key strategies along the columns. Typically, symbols such as ●, O, and Δ are used to denote strong, medium, and weak relationships. Matrix diagrams provide a picture of how well two sets of objects or issues are related, and can identify missing pieces in the thought process. For instance, a row without many relationships might indicate that the actions proposed will not meet the company's goals. In Figure 11.7, we see that focused attention to these three strategies should meet MicroTech's goals. Other matrices might relate short-term plans to medium-term objectives, or individual actions to short-term plans. These visual depictions can help managers set priorities on plans and actions.

> *Matrix diagrams are fundamental tools in Quality Function Deployment that we discussed in Chapter 7.*

Matrix Data Analysis   Matrix data analysis takes data and arranges them to display quantitative relationships among variables to make them more easily understood and analyzed. In its original form used in Japan, matrix data analysis is a rigorous, statistically based "factor analysis" technique. Many feel that this method, while worthwhile for many applications, is too quantitative to be used on a daily basis and have developed alternative tools that are easier to understand and implement. Some of these alternatives are similar to decision analysis matrixes that you may have studied in a quantitative methods course.

A small example of matrix data analysis is shown in Figure 11.8. In this example, MicroTech market researchers determined that the four most important consumer requirements are price, reliability, delivery, and technical support. Through market research, an importance weighting was developed for each. They also determined numerical ratings for the company and their best competitor. Such an analysis provides information as to which actions the company should deploy to better meet key customer requirements. In this example, reliability is the highest in importance, and MicroTech has a narrow lead over its best competitor; thus, they should continue to strive for improving product reliability. Also, technical support is of relatively high importance,

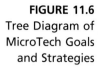

FIGURE 11.6
Tree Diagram of
MicroTech Goals
and Strategies

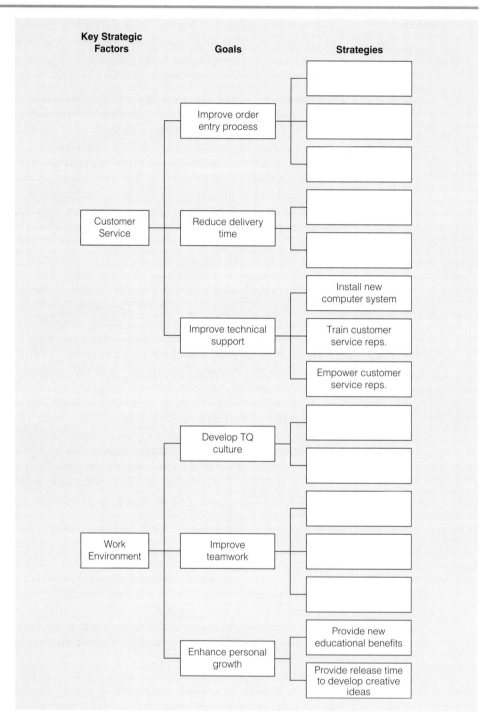

FIGURE 11.7 Matrix Diagram for MicroTech's Goals and Strategies

Goals \ Actions	Improve Work Environment	Improve Manufacturing Technology	Develop New Products
Cost Effectiveness	●	○	
High Quality	●	●	
Shareholder Value		△	●

● = Strong relationship
○ = Medium relationship
△ = Weak relationship

FIGURE 11.8 Matrix Data Analysis of Customer Requirements for MicroTech

Requirement	Importance Weight	Best Competitor Evaluation	MicroTech Evaluation	Difference
Price	.2	6	8	+2
Reliability	.4	7	8	+1
Delivery	.1	8	5	−3
Technical support	.3	7	5	−2

*MicroTech Evaluation—Best Competitor Evaluation

but MicroTech is perceived to be inferior to its best competitor in this category. Thus, improving the quality of support services should be a major objective.

Process Decision Program Chart A process decision program chart (PDPC) is a method for mapping out every conceivable event and contingency that can occur when moving from a problem statement to possible solutions. A PDPC takes each branch of a tree diagram, anticipates possible problems, and provides countermeasures that will (1) prevent the deviation from occurring, or (2) be in place if the deviation does occur. Figure 11.9 shows one example for implementing a strategy to educate and train all employees to use a new computer system.

Arrow Diagram For years, construction planners have used arrow diagrams to sequence and schedule project tasks. Arrow diagramming has also been taught extensively in quantitative methods, operations management, and other business and engineering courses in the United States for a number of years. Unfortunately, its use has generally been confined to technical experts. Adding arrow diagramming to the "quality toolbox" has made it more widely available to general managers and other non-technical personnel. Figure 11.10 shows an example. Time estimates can easily be added to each activity in order to schedule and control the project.

FIGURE 11.9
A Process Decision
Program Chart

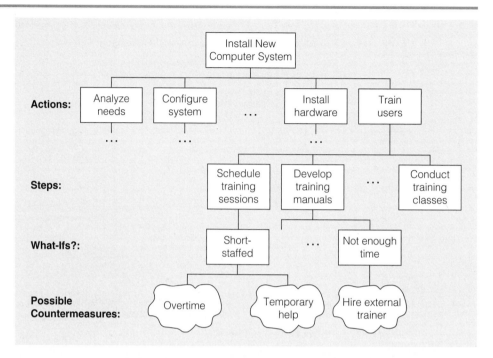

FIGURE 11.10
An Arrow Diagram
for Project Planning

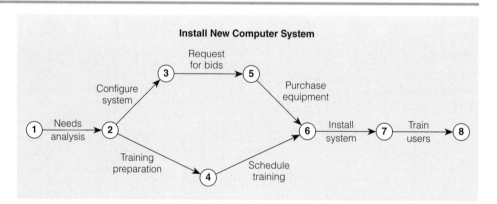

ORGANIZATIONAL DESIGN FOR PERFORMANCE EXCELLENCE

The effectiveness of an organization depends in part on its **organizational structure**—
the clarification of authority, responsibility, reporting lines, and performance standards
among individuals at each level of the organization. It is also true that effective strategy
deployment is dependent upon, and tends to shape, organizational structure because the
organizational structure must be aligned with and support the accomplishment of strategic initiatives. Thus, organizational design is an important strategic decision.

Traditional organizations tend to develop structures that help them to maintain stability. They tend to be highly structured, both in terms of rules and regulations, as well
as the height of the "corporate ladder," sometimes with seven or more layers of managers
between the CEO and the first-line worker. In contrast, organizations in the rapidly

changing environments characteristic of modern organizations have to build flexibility into their organization structures. Hence, they tend to have fewer written rules and regulations and flatter organizational structures.

Several factors having to do with the context of the organization affect how work is organized. They include the following:[12]

1. *Operational and organizational guidelines.* Standard practices that have developed over the firm's history often dictate how an organization organizes and operates.
2. *Management style.* The management team operates in a manner unique to a given organization. For example, management style might be formal or informal, or democratic or autocratic. If the organization operates in a highly structured, formal atmosphere, organizing a quality effort around informal meetings would probably meet with little success.
3. *Customer influences.* Customers, particularly governmental agencies, may require formal specifications or administrative controls. Thus, the organization needs to understand and respond to these requirements.
4. *Size.* Large organizations have the ability to maintain formal systems and records, whereas smaller ones may not.
5. *Diversity and complexity of product line.* An organization suitable for the manufacture of a small number of highly sophisticated products may differ dramatically from an organization that produces a high volume of standard goods.
6. *Stability of the product line.* Stable product lines generate economies of scale that influence supervision, corrective action, and other quality-related issues. Frequent changes in products necessitate more control and commensurate changes to the quality system.
7. *Financial stability.* Quality managers need to recognize that their efforts must fit within the overall budget of the firm.
8. *Availability of personnel.* The lack of certain skills may require other personnel, such as supervisors, to assume duties they ordinarily would not be assigned.

An organization chart shows the *apparent structure* of the formal organization. However, some organizations refuse to be tied down by a conventional organization chart, even to the extent that employees make a running joke of titles. Although many different organizational structures exist, most are variations or combinations of three basic types: (1) the line organization, (2) the line and staff organization, and (3) the matrix organization.

 QUALITYSPOTLIGHT

Semco S/A

Semco S/A, an unconventional manufacturer of industrial equipment (mixers, washers, air conditioners, bakery plant units) located in São Paulo, Brazil, has what is called a "circular" organization chart with four concentric circles. They avoid the use of the term *levels.* The titles that go with these are Counselors (CEO and the equivalent of vice presidents), Partners (business unit heads), Coordinators (supervisory specialists and functional leaders), and Associates (everyone else). If anyone desires, he or she can think up a title for external use that describes his or her area or job responsibility. As owner and CEO Ricardo Semler explains:

> *Consistent with this philosophy, when a promotion takes place now at Semco we simply supply blank business cards and tell the newly elevated individual: "Think of a title that signals externally your area of operation and responsibility and have it printed." If the person likes "Procurement Manager," fine. If he wants something more elegant, he can print up cards saying, "First Pharaoh in Charge of Royal Supplies." Whatever he wants. But inside the company, there are only four options. (Anyway, almost all choose to print only their name.)[13]*

The line organization is a functional form, with departments that are responsible for marketing, finance, and operations. In the traditional organization, the quality department ("Quality Control," "Quality Assurance," or some similar name) is generally distinct from other departments. In a TQ organization, the role of quality should be invisible in the organization chart, because quality planning and assurance are part of the responsibility of each operating manager and employee at every level. In theory, this organizational form could exist in a fairly large organization if all employees were thoroughly indoctrinated in the philosophy of quality and could be counted on to place quality as the top priority in all aspects of their daily work. In practice, this particular structure is not generally successful except when used in small firms. One example is Texas Nameplate Company, which trained all of its approximately 50 employees in quality management and assurance and effectively eliminated a formal quality control function.

The line and staff organization is the most prevalent type of structure for medium-sized to large firms. In such organizations, line departments carry out the functions of marketing, finance, and production for the organization. Staff personnel, including quality managers and technical specialists, assist the line managers in carrying out their jobs by providing technical assistance and advice. Variations on the basic line and staff organization can include geographic or customer organizations. In this traditional form of organization structure, instead of technical experts who assist line managers and workers in attaining quality, quality managers and inspectors may take on the role of guardians of quality. This guardian-type role also happens when the quality assurance function is placed too low in the organization or when pressure from higher levels of the organization forces quality inspectors to ease up on quality so that more products can be shipped. The major cause of this problem is too much responsibility with insufficient authority.

The matrix-type organization was developed for use in situations where large, complex projects are designed and carried out, such as defense weapons systems or large construction projects. Firms that do such work have a basic need to develop an organizational structure that will permit the efficient use of human resources while maintaining control over the many facets of the project being developed. In a matrix-type organization, each project has a project manager and each department that is providing personnel to work on the various projects has a technical or administrative manager. Thus, a quality assurance technician might be assigned to the quality assurance department for technical and administrative activities but would be attached to Project A for day-to-day job assignments. The technician would report to the project manager of Project A and to his or her "technical boss" in the quality assurance department. When Project A is completed, the technician might be reassigned to Project B under a new project manager. He or she would still be reporting to the "technical boss" in quality assurance, however.

The matrix type of organization for project work has a number of advantages. It generally improves the coordination of complex project work as well as improving the efficiency of personnel use. Its major drawback is that it requires split loyalty for people who report to two supervisors. This division of loyalty can be especially troublesome or even dangerous in a quality assurance area. For example, in a nuclear power plant project, a project manager who is under pressure to complete a project by a certain deadline might try to influence quality assurance personnel to take shortcuts in completing the inspection phase of the project. The quality manager, who might be hundreds of miles away from the site, would often not have the influence over the inspectors that the project manager would have. One example that revolves around customer teams is shown in Figure 11.11. Such an organizational structure would be appropriate for a marketing research firm, for instance, which may work with a small number of large corporate

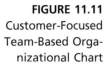

FIGURE 11.11
Customer-Focused
Team-Based Orga-
nizational Chart

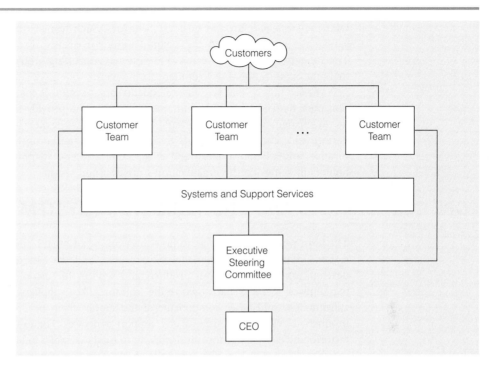

FIGURE 11.12
Cross-Functional
Team-Based Orga-
nizational Chart

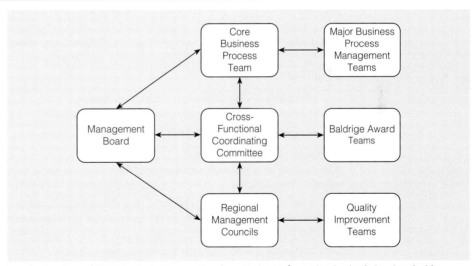

Source: Courtesy of GTE Directories Corporation (now Verizon Information Services). Reprinted with permission.

clients. Another example is shown in Figure 11.12. In this example, the management board leads the quality effort, meeting twice each month to discuss and review management and quality issues. Quality is implemented through various teams: core business process team, cross-functional coordinating committee, regional management councils, major business process management teams, Baldrige Award teams, and quality improvement teams. The regional management councils identify and address key regional issues;

the cross-functional coordinating committee reviews major proposals for consistency with the strategic plan and business priorities. Such team-based organization structures spread the ownership and the accountability for quality throughout the organization. The "quality department" serves as an internal consulting group, providing advice, training, and organizational development to the teams.

We see that a "one-size-fits-all" quality organization is inappropriate. The organization must be tailored to reflect unique differences and provide the flexibility and the ability to change. What is important, however, is that senior leaders drive quality and performance excellence concepts throughout the organization through effective communication and as role models, and ensure that strategic planning focuses all key stakeholders in achieving the organization's mission and vision.

CORE COMPETENCIES AND STRATEGIC WORK SYSTEM DESIGN

The term **work systems** refers to how the work of an organization is accomplished. Work systems coordinate the internal work processes and the external resources necessary to develop, produce, and deliver products and services to customers and to succeed in the marketplace. Work systems involve the workforce, key suppliers and partners, contractors, collaborators, and other components of the supply chain needed to produce and deliver products, services, and business and support processes. For example, Henry Ford's early factories did everything from steel-making to final assembly; today's automobile companies are characterized by complex networks of suppliers that are much more decentralized.

Decisions about work systems are strategic. These decisions involve protecting and capitalizing on core competencies and deciding what should be procured or produced outside the organization in order to be efficient and sustainable in the marketplace. **Core competencies** refer to an organization's areas of greatest expertise that provide a sustainable competitive advantage in the marketplace or service environment.

Gary Hamel and C.K. Prahalad suggested that a core competency meets three conditions:[14]

1. It contributes significantly to customer benefits.
2. It provides access to many products and markets.
3. It is difficult for competitors to imitate.

Core competencies may involve technology expertise, unique service offerings, a marketplace niche, or a particular business acumen (e.g., business acquisitions). Some examples of core competencies might be quality and productivity practices (e.g., Toyota), superior customer relationship management (e.g. Nordstrom), innovation in design and new product development (e.g., Apple), supply chain management (e.g., Dell), or marketing/branding expertise (e.g., Procter & Gamble). An organization needs to understand its core competencies and how they support the organization's mission, enable it to compete against its competitors, and help drive strategic objectives and action plans.

 QUALITYSPOTLIGHT
Mercy Health System

Mercy Health System's (MHS) core competencies are stated as 1) partnering with physicians to create and maintain an effective integrated health care delivery system; and 2) engaging employees and physicians using the Servant Leadership Philosophy and the Culture of Excellence model, which provide a balanced approach to patient-focused care. The integrated delivery system model has enabled growth and diversification of business lines, supporting the ability to effectively coordinate quality health care delivery across the continuum of care and supporting the mission, "to provide exceptional health-care services resulting in healing in the broadest sense." Partnering with physicians supports a collaborative focus on quality health care and information sharing across the organization's core services. The integrated delivery model supports coordinated transitions between departments, providers, and care settings to ensure efficient, effective, and patient-focused care. Through the use of the Servant Leadership Philosophy, leaders provide excellent service to partners, and partners provide excellent service to customers. Applying this philosophy, leaders are facilitators whose role is to serve those who provide value to patients. Caregivers provide patient-focused care by offering consideration for personal preferences, cultural traditions and family situations, and involving patients and their loved ones in care decisions to support healing in the broadest sense. These competencies drive action plans designed to achieve MHS's visionary strategic goals.[15]

Some contemporary theories suggest that business activities that do not comprise an organization's core competency should be outsourced. **Outsourcing** refers to the practice of transferring the operations of a business function to an outside supplier. Many organizations have done this; for example, outsourcing design, manufacturing, or assembly; information technology operations; human resource management; or customer service support operations. Much outsourcing is done through offshoring, in which the outsourced function is relegated to foreign shores. The opposite of outsourcing is **vertical integration**, by which certain business functions are acquired and consolidated within a firm. For example, a firm may purchase a key supplier to strengthen its value chain.

Because outsourcing can have significant impacts on an organization's work system effectiveness, it must be dealt with strategically. Outsourcing key activities that are highly interdependent with technologies that impact the overall performance of a product can lead to failure to adequately meet customer needs, and make it more difficult to deal with systems integration issues for complex products such as automobiles.[16]

The decision to outsource or vertically integrate should be examined relative to all factors that can affect organizational performance. In many cases, the decision is based solely on costs without considering the impact on other business priorities such as quality and customer satisfaction or risks associated with protecting intellectual property. For instance, the toy industry faced serious issues with toxic chemicals found in toys manufactured in China. Dell had moved a customer call center to India to lower costs, but later closed that center and moved it back to the United States because of dissatisfaction with the level of technical support that customers were receiving. In addition to cost, the impact of outsourcing on product and service quality should be examined. For example, one might ask: Does the outsourcing effort meet an individual function's goals including maintaining internal service quality? Does extensive use of outsourcing across numerous functions affect the general level of internal service within an organization? Can outsourcing suppliers meet service, productivity, and quality goals?[17]

QUALITYSPOTLIGHT

The City of Coral Springs, Florida

The City of Coral Springs, Florida, bases decisions to operate a process with internal resources on two criteria: whether the process is a key work process and whether an external resource can do it cheaper while sustaining quality standards. Key work processes are central to public trust and therefore are operated with internal resources. The

City needs to directly manage these areas to monitor the quality of outputs on a daily basis and to have the agility needed to adapt to changing customer requirements and civic emergencies. Occasionally, processes that are not fundamental to local government are subject to an RFP (request for proposal) process to determine if City staff can perform the function better and at a lower cost than the private sector. Fleet maintenance, operation of the Tennis Center, and water billing are examples of functions assessed through an RFP process. External resources are used for the operation of the Center for the Arts because a company called Professional Facilities Management can take advantage of economies of scale (they run several facilities in Florida) to get better prices on shows; Waste Management provides trash removal and recycling services for many south Florida municipalities; Charter School USA uses one management staff for several facilities and specializes in customer-driven education.[18]

SUMMARY OF KEY POINTS AND TERMINOLOGY

The Student Companion Site provides a summary of key concepts and terminology introduced in this chapter.

QUALITY in PRACTICE

Integrating Six Sigma with Strategic Planning at Cigna[19]

At Cigna Corp., a 28,000-employee provider of employee health care and related insurance benefits, the vice president of Six Sigma business excellence is just two levels below the CEO on the organizational chart. The woman who holds this title, reports directly to a member of the corporation's management team. This simple fact helps to explain the rapid growth, holistic use, and impressive results of Six Sigma at Cigna.

Cigna has five strategic imperatives:

1. Establish a meaningful cost advantage relative to the competition.
2. Help improve the health and well-being of members and the people Cigna insures.
3. Bring innovative products and services to market.
4. Become the partner of choice to its customers.
5. Create a winning environment in the organization.

Strategic planning is an absolute necessity in a company like Cigna that competes in a tough, volatile marketplace. Six Sigma is viewed as a means to execute the strategic plan effectively and to do so in a way that enhances quality, reduces costs and makes the company a stronger competitor. Executives and managers learn the basics of Six Sigma, lean tools, continuous improvement and the basics of design for Six Sigma (which we learned about in in chapters 7 and 9.). Managers also learn what behaviors are required to ensure the following:

- There is continuous improvement.
- The right projects are selected with the right people to lead them.
- There is ongoing assessment of projects.
- People have time to serve on projects.
- Managers ask the right questions during each phase of a project.

Strategic planning has become increasingly important as Six Sigma has matured at Cigna. When Six Sigma was launched at Cigna, leadership made it clear the approach would be holistic and would not just focus on productivity improvement, but would require behavioral changes and a focus on customers. Figure 11.13 shows the conceptualization of how Six Sigma supports a strategic focus at Cigna. One project involved one of Cigna's largest clients, which was dissatisfied with errors

FIGURE 11.13   Cigna's Holistic Six Sigma Model

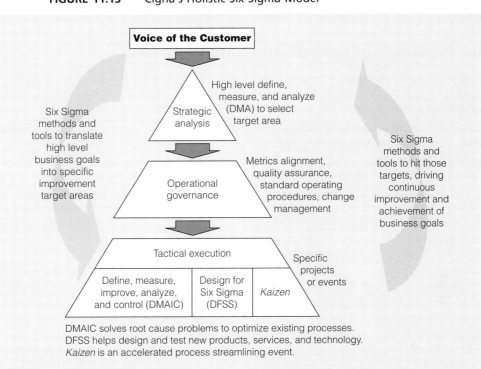

Source: Reprinted with permission from Susan E. Daniels, "Six Sigma at Cigna," *Quality Progress*, pp. 43–48, May 2007. Copyright © 2007 American Society for Quality. No further distribution allowed without permission.

and how long it was taking to pay claims accurately. This customer got its own Six Sigma professionals to work with Cigna. The Six Sigma project exceeded the customers' expectations from both timeliness and quality standpoints. In fact, the customer was so satisfied, it gave Cigna additional business.

Cigna looks at the cost of doing nothing differently, figures how much improvement it can make, and then comes up with a dollar differential. A 0.1 percent improvement can save millions. While initial concentration was on efforts that would bring quick and significant results, Six Sigma at Cigna has matured, and it has increasingly focused on impacting goals of the most strategic importance to the organization. The challenges of the huge cost of care and quality of care facing the U.S. health care industry have led Cigna managers to wonder whether they could extend its improvement methodology to the industry as a whole to address some of the key challenges in the U.S. health care marketplace, including:

- A shift away from cost based models of health care toward a value based system
- Medical care cost inflation

- Demographic changes that necessitate the need for more care availability
- Inconsistent quality of care
- The growing number of Americans who use emergency rooms for primary care because they lack health insurance
- Rising consumer expectations fueled by greater transparency of quality

As one of them noted, "Six Sigma is about quality, continuous improvement, and sustained excellence—all of which should be basic to the mission of every organization that's in the business of providing access to health care."

Key Issues for Discussion

1. Suggest how Six Sigma might be used to help Cigna address its five strategic imperatives? Is their approach consistent with the discussion of Six Sigma and competitive strategy at the end of this chapter?
2. Can you think of specific types of Six Sigma projects that might support Cigna's strategic imperatives?

QUALITY *in* PRACTICE

Strategic Planning at Branch-Smith Printing Division[20]

Branch-Smith, Inc., is a fourth-generation family business founded by Aaron Smith in 1910. The Branch-Smith Printing Division in Ft. Worth, Texas, has only 70 full-time employees and specializes in creating multi-page, bound materials with services ranging from design to mailing for specialty customers. The company produces publications, magazines, catalogs, directories, and books, as well as some general commercial printing, typically in quantities generally less than 20,000. It offers a complete array of turnkey services to customers, including design, image scanning, electronic and conventional prepress work, printing, binding, and mailing/delivery.

Within the Printing Division, the context of the business is set through their Vision Statement: *"Market Leading Business Results through an Expert Team providing Turnkey Solutions to Customer Partners."* This vision expresses the desire to produce strong and sustainable results through balanced performance improvement. It creates success for long-term customers and rewards for their employees who bring solutions to bear on our opportunities. The mission is stated as: *"The mission of the Branch-Smith Printing Division is to provide expert solutions for publishers."* This purpose guides Branch-Smith Printing in meeting customers' needs on its own terms. Publishers work with them because Branch-Smith focuses on serving publishers' niche requirements for printing as well as offering the vertically integrated value-added services that result in lower costs, reduced cycle times, and on-time delivery. An important component of the solution is easy accessibility for the customer, and timely and appropriate information. It is also expressed in its Quality Policy, which states: *"Branch-Smith Printing will seek to continuously improve results for all stakeholders through the application of its Innovating Excellence Process."*

The printing industry is very competitive with numerous companies seeking market share. Branch-Smith Printing stands out among competitors based on its approach for identifying and serving a specific niche, focusing on development of long-term relationships, partnering with suppliers, and involvement in standard defining industry associations. To ensure a competitive position, it focuses on serving a select market niche that most other printers have difficulty serving well. Many competitors focus on attracting jobs with greater quantity outputs because of the limitations of their equipment. They charge much higher prices for the shorter runs, thus giving Branch-Smith an advantage in this market. Its equipment and technologies are directed to cost-effectively serve this niche through sheet-fed press versus the popular web printing. This technology allows for faster changeovers from one type of print to another and process automation offers cost savings.

Although Branch-Smith is a small family business, they engage in a formal planning process annually with monthly updates during management reviews. The process is built around a continuous learning cycle that begins with lessons learned from previous years to determine and implement improvements. The strategic planning process (SPP) is a key tool the company uses to visualize the ideal future and create strategies and plans to achieve it, and to incorporate improvement opportunities into prioritized action plans. Strategic planning occurs formally each year with updates and tracking conducted monthly during management reviews. Ongoing updates throughout the year allow the company to correct direction or to proactively respond to risks and opportunities.

Figure 11.14 represents the full strategic planning, deployment, and review process. A month prior to strategic planning, assignments are made to PLT members to research information needed for strategic decision making. The assignment list includes 28 specific areas for understanding organizational and supplier/partner capabilities, market conditions, stakeholder input and requirements, competitive information, industry issues, and risks. Branch-Smith gathers information through a customer survey, lost revenues, and complaints to identify customer needs and their importance, trends and directions of the printing industry, and market requirements from industry association networking. Involvement in professional associations provides industry knowledge and benchmarks concerning customer needs and competitor actions,

FIGURE 11.14   Branch-Smith Strategic Planning Process

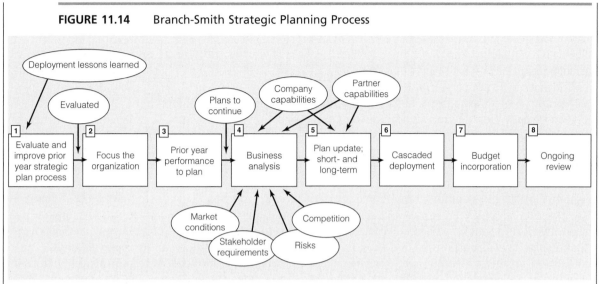

Source: Branch-Smith Printing, Strategic Planning Process. Courtesy of David Branch, President. This excerpt is reprinted with the understanding that the material herein included is historically accurate but is not in practice today.

including emerging tools and competitors. Trade magazines and discussions with key suppliers provide additional input about customer needs, competitor directions, and supplier capabilities. Trends and directions in technology and other environmental changes are also identified through involvement with trade associations and external benchmarking groups, and through general understanding of the business climate gained through newspapers, journals, and periodicals.

One important source of information for strategic planning regarding human resource needs and capability is an annual employee survey. Human resource and operational capabilities are identified through review of aggregate measures of performance and productivity, which are enhanced with feedback from scheduled ISO audits that identify processes in need of improvement. Primary inputs on process efficiency and capability come from in-process productivity measures, revenue lost due to complaints, and other measures, which include spoilage cost, frequency, and reason. These measures are recorded daily through electronic, shop-floor data collection. Strategic partnerships with key suppliers help to gather information about availability of materials and supplier growth plans to help determine their capability to meet Branch-Smith's changing needs. Finally, part of the annual operational review involves understanding suppliers' current financial position and trends in

profitability and utilization, which is compared to external economic conditions to identify areas of potential risk and opportunity over the short- and longer-term.

The formal planning activity is conducted during the fall of each year by the Print Leadership Team (PLT) through a series of meetings on and off site. Step 1 of Figure 11.14 ensures that lessons learned and improvement cycles are built into the SPP. The PLT analyzes the effectiveness of the overall planning and deployment process to determine and implement improvements. The effectiveness of the leadership system is also evaluated and areas for improvement for the coming year are determined. These improvements are documented as potential actions for the strategic plan. In Step 2, the company reviews its vision, mission, and values to ensure they still reflect the current environment. Next, management reviews and revises objectives, which are intended to communicate to employees and all stakeholders what the company expects to accomplish in the next three to five years.

In Step 3, the company conducts an operational review to analyze the results of the organization's key performance measures for the prior year. They then review and incorporate information into the plan from annual Baldrige-based self-evaluation or from external review feedback. This analysis provides an understanding of key strengths and weaknesses for the SWOT (strengths, weaknesses, opportunities, and threats) analysis in Step 5. Step 4 involves a business analysis to evaluate the external environment to forecast changing trends and gain market requirements. PLT members bring forward defined inputs, including literature and studies for scanning the environment and identifying new opportunities for products, services, competitive advantage, marketing, and technology approaches. From the review of this information, the PLT develops a list of potential opportunities and threats for each environmental element. In Step 5, a SWOT analysis is conducted based upon the issues identified in Steps 1, 3, and 4. SWOT elements are used to identify and prioritize key areas to address.

Based upon the SWOT review, the PLT develops short- and longer-term strategies and actions to move the company toward its vision and objectives. They add in action plans that are still in process from the prior year to allow them to also be prioritized, set appropriate measures and goals for objectives and strategies, and sort and prioritize the action plans. Action plans are assigned to PLT members to develop (or update) steps, timelines, resources, costs, and measures of success. These plans are then entered into the Quality Improvement Database (QID) for review and tracking. A final balancing meeting is held to review the plan as a whole and make needed adjustments to timing of plans and financial and human resource requirements to balance the plan to resource constraints. In Step 6, the company creates documents and methods to support deployment of the plan.

Results of strategic planning are first communicated to employees through a deployment meeting. Leaders, with their departmental teams or other appropriate members, then discuss the plans during follow-up sessions. Teams and individuals update goals and mission statements for their departments that support the division plans, thus aligning actions, measures, and goals throughout the organization. Other stakeholders receive a variety of communications to detail our plans and strategies for informational and planning purposes. For example, a supplier appreciation luncheon is held to provide a more direct opportunity to present plans to key supplier partners and receive feedback on plans and needs. In Step 7, financial resource requirements to accomplish the action plans are rationalized into short- and longer-term budget projections. Then, in Step 8, ongoing tracking of action plans is conducted through monthly management review of overall progress to plans and key measures. Throughout the year as needed, the strategic plan is updated with new or modified action plans to reflect the changes to the environment.

Key Issues for Discussion

1. Compare Branch-Smith's approach to the generic strategic planning process described in this chapter. What are some of its unique features?

2. Branch-Smith's current objectives are "1) To continuously improve business results through a process improvement focus, partnership with our suppliers, and strong financial performance. 2) To become the partner of choice for our customers through: a targeted marketing plan, excellent execution to customer requirements, and relationship development. To become the partner of choice, our value package must be continually improved. 3) To become the employer of choice through: a caring, involved culture; continually improving training systems; providing growth opportunities; and industry leading compensation, benefits, and reward and recognition systems. We extend the same quality environment to coworkers as we extend to customers." How do these objectives address the strategic challenges cited in the case? What types of activities might the company deploy to achieve these objectives?

Source: Branch-Smith Printing, Strategic Planning Process. Courtesy of David Branch, President. This excerpt is reprinted with the understanding that the material herein included is historically accurate but is not in practice today.

REVIEW QUESTIONS

1. What is a strategy? What does a good strategy provide for an organization?

2. Why is strategic planning important for all organizations?

3. Summarize the key practices for a strategic focus on performance excellence.

4. Explain the elements of a typical strategic planning process.

5. Define mission, vision, and guiding principles. What is the purpose of each?

6. What factors are examined in an environmental assessment?

7. What is the purpose of the Baldrige Organizational Profile? Summarize the information contained in the Organizational Profile. Why is knowing this information important?

8. What are strategic challenges? Why is it important to understand them in strategic planning?

9. Explain the difference between strategies, strategic objectives, and action plans.

10. What is strategy deployment? How does it differ from strategy development?

11. Explain the concept of hoshin kanri and provide a simplified description of this process.

12. How does catchball play an important role in policy deployment?

13. Why is it important to address human resource plans in strategic planning?

14. List and explain the seven management and planning tools.

15. Describe the key contextual factors that affect organizational structure. What implications do they have for quality?

16. Describe the types of organizational structure commonly used. What are the advantages or disadvantages of each?

17. What types of organizational structures are common in TQ-based organizations today?

18. What are core competencies? Why is it important to understand them?

19. Explain the strategic role of work systems design. How should outsourcing and vertical integration decisions be made from a strategic context?

DISCUSSION QUESTIONS

1. The Johnson & Johnson credo was written in 1943 by its chairman Robert Wood Johnson: "We believe our first responsibility is to the doctors, nurses, and patients, to mothers and fathers, and all others who use our products and services. In meeting their needs, everything we do must be of high quality." What would you expect to see in Johnson & Johnson's strategic planning approaches that reflect this philosophy?

2. Examine the following mission statements. Do you think they have a true purpose or are they merely cosmetic devices because someone felt that no major organization can be seen without one?[21]

   a. Our single focus will continue to be helping customers all over the world succeed in their businesses. When we do that—when we make them winners—then employees, dealers, and stockholders win as well.

   b. XYZ strives to understand and fulfill the needs of all our customers by providing the highest level of reliability and service at all times.

   c. XYZ creates value by providing transportation-related products and services with superior quality, safety, and environmental care to demanding customers in selected segments.

   d. We are dedicated to being the world's best at bringing people together—giving them easy access to each other and to the information and services they want and need—anytime, anywhere.

   e. To serve the most vulnerable.

3. Try to match the following companies with their actual mission statement in question 2. Could you think of more appropriate mission statements for any of these organizations?

   a. Volvo

   b. AT&T

   c. The International Red Cross

   d. Caterpillar

   e. DHL Worldwide Express

4. Contrast the following vision statements in terms of their usefulness to an organization.

   a. To become the industry leader and achieve superior growth and market share.

   b. To become the best-managed electric utility in the United States and an excellent company overall and be recognized as such.

   c. Being the best at everything we do, exceeding customer expectations; growing our business to increase its value to customers, employees, shareowners, and communities in which we work.

5. Propose three applications for each of the seven management and planning tools discussed in the chapter. You might consider some applications

around school, such as in the classroom, studying for exams, and so on.

6. What are the core competencies of your school, college, or university? How are they leveraged from a strategic perspective?

7. Discuss how each of the Baldrige Core Values and Concepts (see Chapter 10) are reflected in each item of the Baldrige criteria for Strategic Planning (i.e.,

Item 2.1 Strategy Development, and Item 2.2 Strategy Deployment): customer-driven excellence, visionary leadership, organizational and personal learning, valuing employees and partners, agility, managing for innovation, focus on the future, management by fact, social responsibility, focus on results and creating value, and systems perspective.

PROJECTS, ETC.

1. Use the Baldrige Organizational Profile questions to prepare an organizational profile for your college or a local organization that would be willing to provide you with the information. Use the format of the TriView Bank case study in the Baldrige Materials folder on Student Companion Site as a guide for writing the profile.

2. Interview managers at some local organizations to determine whether they have well-defined missions, visions, and guiding principles. If they do, how are these translated into strategy? If not, what steps should they take?

3. Find several examples of mission and vision statements for *Fortune* 500 companies. Critique these statements with respect to their usefulness, relevance to the organization, and ability to inspire and motivate employees.

4. Does your university or college have a mission and strategy? How might policy deployment be used in a university setting? Discuss with a senior executive administrator at your college or university

(such as the VP of administration or the VP of academic affairs/provost) how policy deployment is, or might be, done.

5. Research the strategic planning practices of recent Baldrige Award winners. Discuss different approaches that these firms use and why they seem appropriate for their organizations. How do they reflect the leading practices described in this chapter?

6. In your role as a student, develop your own statements of mission, vision, and guiding principles. How would you create a strategy to achieve your mission and vision?

7. Compare the organizational structures of several manufacturing or service firms. What differences are reflected in their quality approaches and results?

8. Try to identify and contrast the core competencies of two different organizations within the same industry, such as Dell and Apple, Toyota and General Motors, or Sears and Walmart, for example. Does your research suggest that these competencies are reflected in their supply chain or strategic directions?

CASES

A STRATEGIC BOTTLENECK[22] _____

An international bottle manufacturer produces glass containers for customers that include condiment producers, breweries, and wineries. The growing demand for plastic containers, and a history of higher production costs due to high scrap and return rates drove the business to focus its improvement efforts on cost and customer performance. However, the unique characteristics of the bottle manufacturing process and the way in which the company measured and motivated its workforce's performance made these improvements difficult to accomplish.

Bottle plants are traditionally organized around two primary functions: forming and selecting. Forming is where raw materials are melted in furnaces and molten glass is cut and formed by fast-moving, noisy, and dangerous machines that turn out thousands of bottles each minute. The workforce is primarily older males. In the selecting department, the work is relatively quiet and clean. The majority of workers are female, and the work is focused on spotting and removing bottles that fail to meet height, weight, dimension, centricity, and thickness specifications.

The principal performance measure in the forming department is the pack-to-melt ratio, calculated by dividing the total weight of bottles shipped by the total weight of the raw materials used. Individual and team performance goals are typically tied to this measure. The focus is on throughput and getting the highest percentage of produced bottles packed and shipped to customers. In the selecting department, customer satisfaction is the key measure of work performance, and compensation is based on how much product is accepted by the customer. As you can imagine, relations between the two departments were quite strained.

To achieve its strategic goals of lower cost and improved customer performance, what could this company do to align the goals of the forming and selecting departments?

CLIFTON METAL WORKS[23]

Clifton Metal Works (CMW) was founded in the mid-1940s by Donald Chalmer in a 3,000-square-foot building with nine people as a small family business to produce custom machined parts. In the 1960s, as business grew, the company expanded its facilities and its capability to develop its own tooling patterns, eventually moving into a 40,000-square-foot building.

However, as technology advanced, small family businesses like CMW met stiff competition. To survive, the company knew it had to listen more to its customers. From surveys and focus groups, the firm discovered that customers were not happy with the quality of the products they had been receiving. In 1985, CMW made a commitment to quality by hiring a quality assurance manager, Paul Levitt. Driven by the Deming philosophy, the company developed a variety of quality approaches and eventually became ISO 9000 certified in 1998. CMW made some substantial improvements in the quality of its products, particularly reducing scrap and reject rates. Paul worked closely with the factory workers directly responsible for the products, asking them what they needed to get the job done and ensuring management commitment to provide the necessary resources. For example, CMW invested in computer-based statistical process control technology, which enabled workers to monitor their processes and adjust them as needed. The success of this project led the company to empower employees to control many other aspects of the system.

Business remained steady, but after hearing presentations from some Baldrige winners, Chalmer realized that a lot more could be done. In 2005, he hired a senior executive for performance excellence, James Hubbard. Hubbard saw an opportunity to change the company's culture and introduce many Baldrige principles he had learned in his previous job at a manufacturing firm that had applied the Baldrige criteria for many years. One of the first things he did was to review the current mission statement, which had remained relatively untouched since 1985:

> Our mission at CMW is to improve the return on investment. We can accomplish this by changing attitudes and incorporating a quality/team environment. This will improve the quality of our products, enhance our productivity (which in turn will allow us to quote competitive prices), and elevate our service and response level to our customers. There are several factors which make positive change imperative.
>
> The standards for competitive levels of quality and service are becoming more demanding. The emergence of the "World Market" has brought on new challenges. We are in a low-growth, mature market. In order for CMW to improve return on investment, we must develop a strategy to improve quality and responsiveness in all areas of the company. We need to have all employees recognize the importance of product quality and service and move toward more favorable pricing. We need to change thinking throughout the organization to get employees involved, to encourage teamwork, to develop a more flexible workforce and adaptable organization. We need to instill pride in the workplace and the product.
>
> We believe that we can best achieve the desired future state by study of and adherence to the teachings of W. Edwards Deming.

Hubbard did not feel that this mission statement provided a clear and vivid direction, especially in the twenty-first century. Consequently, he set up a planning retreat for senior management (including Chalmer) to develop a new strategic vision.

Discussion Questions

1. Comment on the current mission statement. Does it provide the strategic direction necessary for success for this company?

2. How can the mission statement be improved? Suggest a better statement of mission, vision, and guiding principles.

TRIVIEW BANK—CORE COMPETENCIES AND WORK SYSTEMS DESIGN

The complete TriView Bank case study, a fictitious example of a Baldrige application, can be found in the Baldrige Materials folder on Student Companion Site. If you have not read the Organizational Profile, please do so first. Read the information provided in Item 6.1a(1) of the case study; these responses address the Baldrige Criteria questions:

How do you design and innovate your overall work systems? How do you capitalize on your core competencies? How do you decide which processes within your overall work systems will be internal to your organization (your key work processes) and which will use external resources?

How would you assess the company's approaches used to address these questions? Are they effective? Does Tri-View appear to understand its core competencies and how they support the organization's mission, enable it to compete against its competitors, and help drive strategic objectives and action plans? Can you identify any opportunities for improvement?

TRIVIEW BANK—STRATEGIC PLANNING

The complete TriView Bank case study, a fictitious example of a Baldrige application, can be found in the Baldrige Materials folder on Student Companion Site. If you have not read the Organizational Profile, please do so first. What factors in the Organizational Profile would be most important in evaluating their strategic planning and deployment approaches? Examine their response in Category 2 to the 2011–2012 Baldrige Criteria questions for this category). What are their strengths? What are their weaknesses and opportunities for improvement? What specific advice, including useful tools and techniques that might help them, would you suggest?

NOTES

1. Matthew Boyle, "Best Buy's Giant Gamble," *Fortune*, April 3, 2006, 69–75.

2. James Brian Quinn, *Strategies for Change: Logical Incrementalism* (Homewood, IL: Richard D. Irwin, 1980).

3. Cargill Corn Milling 2009 Baldrige Application Summary. http://www.nist.gov/baldrige.

4. Henry Mintzberg, "The Fall and Rise of Strategic Planning," *Harvard Business Review*, January–February 1994, 107–114.

5. 2007 North Mississippi Medical Center Malcolm Baldrige Application Summary.

6. Victor Cvascella, "Effective Strategic Planning," *Quality Progress*, November 2002, 62–67.

7. Bob King, *Hoshin Planning: The Developmental Approach* (Methuen, MA: GOAL/QPC, 1989).

8. M. Imai, *Kaizen: The Key to Japan's Competitive Success* (New York: McGraw-Hill, 1986), 144–145.

9. Adapted from Kersi F. Munshi, "Policy Deployment: A Key to Long-Term TQM Success," *ASQC Quality Congress Transactions* (Boston, 1993), 236–244.

10. The Ernst & Young Quality Improvement Consulting Group, *Total Quality: An Executive's Guide for the 1990s* (Homewood, IL: Dow Jones–Irwin, 1990).

11. Noel Tichy and Nancy Cardwell, *The Cycle of Leadership* (New York: HarperCollins, 2002), 185; and James M. Lucas. "The Essential Six Sigma," *Quality Progress* (January 2002), p. 28.

12. Kermit F. Wasmuth, "Organization and Planning," in Loren Walsh, Ralph Wurster, and Raymond J. Kimber

(eds.), *Quality Management Handbook* (Wheaton, IL: Hitchcock Publishing Company, 1986), 9–34.

13. Ricardo Simler, *Maverick* (New York: Warner Books, 1993), 196.

14. Gary Hamel and C. K. Prahalad, "The Core Competence of the Corporation," *Harvard Business Review* 68, no. 3 (May–June 1990), pp. 79–93.

15. Adapted from Mercy Health System Malcolm Baldrige 2007 National Quality Program Application.

16. Francesco Zirpoli and Markus C. Becker, "What Happens When You Outsource Too Much?" *MIT Sloan Management Review*, Winter 2011, pp. 59–64.

17. Jerry H. Seibert and William A. Schiemann, "Reversing Course? Survey Sheds Light on Pitfalls of Outsourcing," *Quality Progress*, July 2011, pp. 36–43.

18. Adapted from: Malcolm Baldridge Award application, printed courtesy of Liz Kolodney, Director of Communications and Marketing, City of Coral Springs, Florida.

19. Reprinted with permission from Susan E. Daniels, "Six Sigma at Cigna," *Quality Progress*, May 2007, pp. 43–48. Copyright © 2007 American Society for Quality. No further distribution allowed without permission.

20. Branch-Smith Printing, Application Summary, 2002. Courtesy of David Branch, President.

21. "Missions for All Seasons," *Across the Board*, April, 2000, 12.

22. Adapted material—Reprinted with permission from Victor Cascella, "Effective Strategic Planning," *Quality Progress*, November 2002, pp. 62–67. Copyright © 2002 American Society for Quality. No further distribution allowed without permission.

23. This fictitious case stems from ideas suggested by the author's former students John P. Rosiello and David Seilkop.

Measurement and Knowledge Management for Performance Excellence

In the early 1990s, Boeing's assembly lines were morasses of inefficiency. A manual numbering system dating back to World War II bomber days was used to keep track of an airplane's four million parts and 170 miles of wiring; changing a part on a 737's landing gear meant renumbering 464 pages of drawings. Factory floors were covered with huge tubs of spare parts worth millions of dollars. In an attempt to grab market share from rival Airbus, the company discounted planes deeply and was buried by an onslaught of orders. The attempt to double production rates, coupled with implementation of a new production control system, resulted in Boeing being forced to shut down its 737 and 747 lines for 27 days in October 1997, leading to a $178 million loss and a shakeup of top management. Much of the blame was focused on Boeing's financial practices and lack of real-time data. With a new CFO and finance team, the company created a "control panel" of vital measures such as material costs, inventory turns, overtime, and defects using a color-coded spreadsheet. For the first time, Boeing was able to generate a series of bar charts showing which of its programs were creating value and which were destroying it.

The results were eye-opening; not only did they help improve operations, but they also helped formulate a growth plan. As one manager noted, "The data will set you free."[1]

We introduced the importance of measurement in quality control in Chapter 8; however, measurement goes well beyond product quality and is vital to managing all aspects of an organization. The Baldrige framework we introduced in Chapter 10 establishes measurement and knowledge management as the foundation of performance excellence. Measurements and indicators provide a scorecard of business performance that can be used at all levels of the organization. This chapter focuses on the design and use of measurement and knowledge management systems to guide an organization toward the achievement of high performance and meeting its strategic objectives. Table 12.1 summarizes key measurement and knowledge management practices. The Quality Profiles describe two organizations that have exploited these practices to their advantage.

TABLE 12.1   Key Measurement and Knowledge Management Practices
for Performance Excellence

- Select, collect, align, and integrate data and information for tracking daily operations and for tracking overall organizational performance, including progress relative to strategic objectives and action plans, and using data and information to support organizational decision making and innovation.
- Select and ensure the effective use of comparative data and information.
- Review organizational performance and capabilities using effective methods of analysis to assess organizational success, competitive performance, and progress relative to strategic objectives and action plans, and using these reviews to assess the organization's ability to respond rapidly to changing organizational needs and challenges.
- Use organizational review findings to share lessons learned and best practices across the organization, project future performance, and develop priorities for continuous improvement and innovation.
- Ensure that data and information are accurate, reliable, timely, secure, and confidential.
- Make needed data and information available and accessible to the workforce, suppliers, partners, collaborators, and customers as needed.
- Manage organizational knowledge to accomplish the collection and transfer of workforce knowledge; the transfer of knowledge from and to customers and other stakeholders; rapid identification, sharing, and implementation of best practices; and the assembly and transfer of relevant knowledge for use in strategic planning.
- Ensure that hardware and software are reliable, secure, and user-friendly, and that information systems support the continued availability of data and information in the event of an emergency.

---

quality**profiles**

Wainwright Industries, Inc. and Baptist Hospital, Inc.

Wainwright Industries, Inc., headquartered in St. Peters, Missouri, is a small, family-owned business that manufactures stamped and machined parts for U.S. and foreign customers in the automotive, aerospace, home security, and information-processing industries. Craftsmanship, teamwork, and innovation have been commitments at Wainwright since its inception in 1947. Delivering products and services of unequaled quality that generate total customer satisfaction is Wainwright's principal objective.

Wainwright Industries aligns the company's business objectives with customers' critical success factors: price, line defects, delivery, and partnership. This alignment process prompted the development of five key strategic indicator categories: safety, internal customer satisfaction, external customer satisfaction, defect rate, and business performance. Within each category, Wainwright developed specific indicators and goals. For instance, for external customer satisfaction, they measure a satisfaction index and compile complaints each month; for business performance, they track sales, capital expenditure, and market share for drawn housings.

Wainwright constantly looks for ways to improve, searching inside and outside the organization for ideas and examples on how to streamline processes, cut delivery times, make training programs more effective, or enhance any other facet of its customer-focused operations. Its empowered workforce provides a rich source of ideas; each associate averages more than one implemented improvement per week. Ninety-five percent of all purchase orders are processed within 24 hours. The lead time for making one of Wainwright's principal products—drawn housings for electric motors—was reduced to 15 minutes from its former level of 8.75 days.

Baptist Hospital, Inc. (BHI) is a subsidiary of Baptist Health Care with about 2,252 employees and includes two hospitals and an ambulatory care complex that delivers an array of outpatient and diagnostic services. Continuous improvement is an important aspect of BHI's culture, driven by peer, employee, physician, and patient surveys, as well as Baldrige-based processes to gather information and identify opportunities for improvement.

BHI uses a variety of listening and learning approaches to determine customer needs, including surveys and Customer Value Analysis to determine patient loyalty attributes. Information gathered from the listening and learning activities is collected and analyzed using a customer relationship management database to identify the key requirements for each customer group and as input into strategic planning, service design and FOCUS-PDCA (a performance improvement process). BHI's information and knowledge management systems enable it to collect and integrate data from clinical systems, employees, patients, financial systems, decision support systems, and physicians for tracking overall organizational performance and for identifying opportunities for improvement. BHI has developed CARE (Clinical Accountability Report of Excellence) and BAR (Budget Accountability Report) reports, which allow it to aggregate and compare clinical quality improvement results, customer satisfaction data, financial information, and trends. Reports are generated to support organizational performance and learning, clinical outcomes improvement, team activities, and continuous improvement.

Overall satisfaction for inpatients, outpatients, ambulatory surgery, and home health care for services provided by BHI has been consistently near the 99th percentile of the national Press Ganey survey each quarter.

Source: Malcolm Baldrige National Quality Award, Profiles of Winners, National Institute of Standards and Technology, Department of Commerce.

THE VALUE AND SCOPE OF PERFORMANCE MEASUREMENT

Considerable value lies in using objective data to support strategic planning and daily operating decisions. Osborne and Gaebler make three insightful observations:

1. If you don't measure results, you can't tell success from failure.
2. If you can't see success, you can't reward it—and if you can't reward success, you are probably rewarding failure.
3. If you can't recognize failure, you can't correct it.[2]

Despite the fact that more than half of the workforce in the United States is engaged in the generation, processing, or dissemination of data and/or information, many organizations do a poor job of systematically collecting appropriate data, getting it to the right people, and analyzing it properly. Organizations ignore measurement for a variety of reasons: They don't know what to measure; they don't want to spend the time or effort to do it; they don't see the value of measurement; or they are afraid to uncover problems.

Organizations need good measures for three reasons:[3]

1. To lead the entire organization in a particular direction; that is, to drive strategies and organizational change.
2. To manage the resources needed to travel in this direction by evaluating the effectiveness of action plans.
3. To operate the processes that make the organization work and continuously improve.

A supply of consistent, accurate, and timely data across all functional areas of business provides real-time information for the evaluation, control, and improvement of processes, products, and services to meet both business objectives and rapidly changing customer needs. Effective information systems provide the right information to the right people at the right time. As a result, individuals in manufacturing can have input on product design and sales; designers can obtain immediate feedback about manufacturing and financial implications of decisions; and everyone can share information for solving problems. Empowered individuals with the right information can make more timely decisions and can take action to better serve customers.

Although Deming believed in using data as a basis for problem solving, he was highly critical of overemphasizing measurement. He often stated that the most important figures, such as the value of a loyal customer, are unknown and unknowable. However, as our understanding of measurement and the use of technology to support it has improved, many "intangibles" that were once thought to be impossible to measure can be measured economically.[4] Measurement-managed organizations are more likely to be in the top third of their industry financially, complete organizational changes more successfully, reach clear agreement on strategy among senior managers, enjoy favorable levels of cooperation and teamwork among management, undertake greater self-monitoring of performance by employees, and have a greater willingness by employees to take risks.[5]

The Balanced Scorecard

Robert Kaplan and David Norton pose the following scenario:[6]

Imagine entering the cockpit of a modern jet airplane and seeing only a single instrument there. How would you feel about boarding the plane after the following conversation with the pilot?

Q: *I'm surprised to see you operating the plane with only a single instrument. What does it measure?*
A: *Airspeed. I'm really working on airspeed this flight.*
Q: *That's good. Airspeed certainly seems important. But what about altitude? Wouldn't an altimeter be helpful?*
A: *I worked on altitude for the last few flights and I've gotten pretty good at it. Now I have to concentrate on proper airspeed.*
Q: *But I notice you don't even have a fuel gauge. Wouldn't that be useful?*
A: *You're right; fuel is significant, but I can't concentrate on doing too many things well at the same time. So on this flight I'm focusing on airspeed. Once I get to be excellent at airspeed, as well as altitude, I intend to concentrate on fuel consumption on the next set of flights.*

Clearly, you would be a bit uneasy about taking this flight. However, the analogy with business is not that far-fetched. Many organizations still manage by concentrating primarily on financial measures, such as return on investment, earnings per share, direct labor efficiency, and machine utilization.[7] Unfortunately, many of these indicators stress quantity over quality.[8] They reward the wrong behavior; lack predictive power; do not capture key business changes until it is too late; reflect functions, not cross-functional processes; and give inadequate consideration to difficult-to-quantify resources such as intellectual capital.[9] For example, financial measures reflect past decisions; they do not focus on factors that create value and predict financial success. Measurements such as direct labor efficiency promote building unnecessary inventory and lead to over-control of direct labor, thus preventing workers from assuming responsibility for process control and from focusing on process improvement. An emphasis on machine utilization encourages having fewer, but larger, general-purpose machines, which results in more complex material flows and increased inventory and throughput time. To achieve a high level of performance excellence requires a much broader set of performance measures that are aligned to an organization's strategy; this became known as the **balanced scorecard**. The purpose of the balanced scorecard is "to translate strategy into measures that uniquely communicate your vision to the organization."

The balanced scorecard consists of four perspectives:

- *Financial Perspective:* Measures the ultimate results that the business provides to its shareholders. They include profitability, revenue growth, return on investment, economic value added (EVA), and shareholder value.
- *Internal Perspective:* Focuses attention on the performance of the key internal processes that drive the business. They include such measures as quality levels, productivity, cycle time, and cost.
- *Customer Perspective:* Focuses on customer needs and satisfaction as well as market share. This includes service levels, satisfaction ratings, and repeat business.
- *Innovation and Learning Perspective:* Directs attention to the basis of a future success—the organization's people and infrastructure. Key measures might include intellectual assets, employee satisfaction, market innovation, and skills development.

Art Schneiderman at Analog Devices first developed the concept of a balanced scorecard in 1987. Analog Devices established and openly published a set of nonfinancial performance goals as part of its five-year strategic plan. A one-page summary that combined these performance goals with the key financial goals was originally referred to as the "Quarterly Performance Audit," but quickly became known as the "Scorecard." Robert Kaplan and David Norton of the Harvard Business School studied Analog Devices and promoted the concept of the balanced scorecard in several Harvard Business Review articles and books. You might wish to visit Schneiderman's website, http://www.schneiderman.com for many interesting papers about the history, design, and use of balanced scorecards and other aspects of performance measurement.

Organizations need to know what is happening now and what might happen in the future. A good balanced scorecard contains both leading and lagging measures and indicators. **Lagging measures** (outcomes) tell what has happened; **leading measures** (performance drivers) predict what will happen. For example, customer survey results about recent transactions might be a leading indicator for customer retention (a lagging indicator); employee satisfaction might be a leading indicator for turnover, and so on. For example, Pearl River School District uses a modified balanced scorecard that

FIGURE 12.1   Pearl River School District Balanced Scorecard

Strategic Objectives	Lag Indicators (long-term)	Lead Indicators (predictive)
Academic Performance		
Academic Achievement	Regents Diploma Rate	Achievement on 4th and 8th grade NYS exams
		CTPIII Reading and Math Achievement
College Admissions	AP Participation Rate	Special Education Opportunity
	AP Performance Rate	Passing rate on Regents exams
		SAT I and II Participation Rate
		Scholar Athlete Teams
Perception		
Parent/Community Satisfaction	Maintain 2:1 Plurality on Budget Votes	Stakeholder Satisfaction Surveys
		Adult Education Enrollment
	Market Share	Student Satisfaction Surveys
		Prospective Homeowner Requests
		New Resident Survey
Fiscal Stability		
Cost-Effective Fiscal Management	Contain Per-Pupil Expenditure	Reduce Costs in Noninstructional Areas

Source: Reprinted with permission of Pearl River School District.

includes leading and lagging indicators relative to strategic objectives under each of its three district goals (Figure 12.1). Lagging indicators represent long-term results and leading indicators are either short-term or line-of-sight predictors for lagging indicators. For example, stakeholder satisfaction rates are key factors in the level of support the district can expect in their annual budget vote. The fourth and eighth grade New York State exams are designed to be predictors of student success on the Regents examinations.

Leading and lagging measures and indicators can help to establish cause-and-effect relationships across perspectives. Figure 12.2 shows the causal relationships among the key measures in IBM Rochester's balanced scorecard. This model suggests that improving internal capabilities such as people skills, product/service quality, and products and channels, will lead to improved customer satisfaction and loyalty, which in turn, lead to improved financial and market share performance. Understanding such relationships is important in using data and information for strategic and operational decisions.

Kaplan and Norton's balanced scorecard is only one version of performance measurement systems that have emerged as organizations recognized the need for a broad set of performance measures that provide a comprehensive view of business performance. For instance, Raytheon's version defines customer, shareholder, process, and people perspectives. The Baldrige Criteria provides an alternative perspective.

FIGURE 12.2   Causal Relationships Among Categories of IBM Rochester's Balanced Scorecard

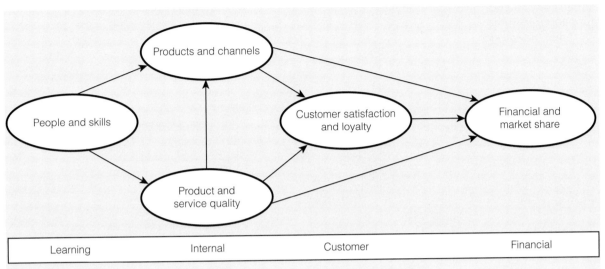

Source: Reprinted with permission of IBM Rochester, MN.

Performance Measurement in the Baldrige Criteria

Category 7 (Results) of the Baldrige Criteria for Performance Excellence groups performance measures into five sets:

- Product and process outcomes
- Customer-focused outcomes
- Workforce-focused outcomes
- Leadership and governance outcomes
- Financial and market outcomes

These categories are summarized in Figure 12.3, along with examples of measures in each category. This set is quite similar to the balanced scorecard, and in fact, any measure in the balanced scorecard can easily be assigned to one of these categories. We will briefly discuss each of these categories. As we describe specific examples, note that the specific measures an organization chooses are tied to the key factors that make it competitive in its industry.

Product Outcomes   Measures and indicators of product and service performance that have strong correlation with customer satisfaction and decisions relative to future purchases and relationships are important for organizations to track. They might include internal quality measurements, field performance of products, defect levels, service errors, response times, data collected from customers or third parties on ease of use or other attributes, and customer surveys on product and service performance. STMicroelectronics, for example, tracks the number of nonconforming production lots, which play a significant role in complaints received by their customers. They also track different measures for different customer segments. For instance, the telecommunications industry has a very short cycle-to-market requirement; key measures that address this factor are delivery time, flexibility, response delay, early warning, quality/reliability, and response quality.

FIGURE 12.3
Organizational Performance Measures and Indicators

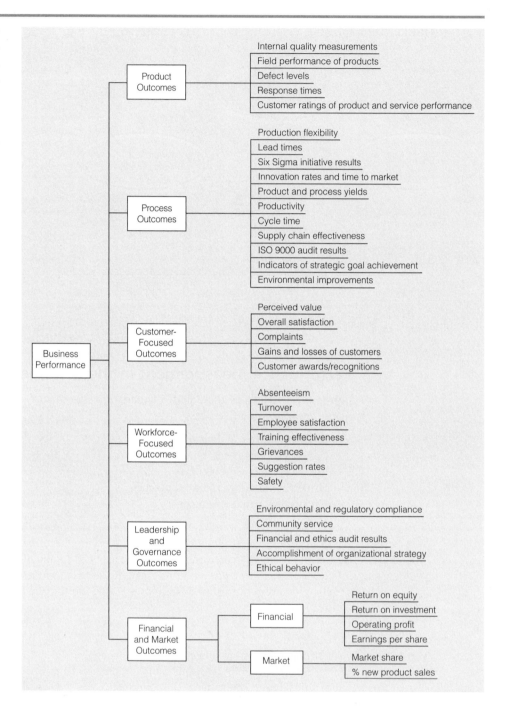

Business Performance

Product Outcomes
- Internal quality measurements
- Field performance of products
- Defect levels
- Response times
- Customer ratings of product and service performance

Process Outcomes
- Production flexibility
- Lead times
- Six Sigma initiative results
- Innovation rates and time to market
- Product and process yields
- Productivity
- Cycle time
- Supply chain effectiveness
- ISO 9000 audit results
- Indicators of strategic goal achievement
- Environmental improvements

Customer-Focused Outcomes
- Perceived value
- Overall satisfaction
- Complaints
- Gains and losses of customers
- Customer awards/recognitions

Workforce-Focused Outcomes
- Absenteeism
- Turnover
- Employee satisfaction
- Training effectiveness
- Grievances
- Suggestion rates
- Safety

Leadership and Governance Outcomes
- Environmental and regulatory compliance
- Community service
- Financial and ethics audit results
- Accomplishment of organizational strategy
- Ethical behavior

Financial and Market Outcomes
- Financial
  - Return on equity
  - Return on investment
  - Operating profit
  - Earnings per share
- Market
  - Market share
  - % new product sales

Process Outcomes   Measures and indicators of process effectiveness and efficiency might include work system performance that demonstrates improved cost savings or higher productivity by using internal and/or external resources; reduced emission levels, waste stream reductions, by-product use, and recycling; internal responsiveness indicators, such as cycle times, production flexibility, lead times, set-up times, and time to market; and improved performance of administrative and other support functions. They also might include business-specific indicators, such as innovation rates and increased use of product and process yields, Six Sigma initiative results, and acceptable product performance at the time of delivery; supply chain indicators, such as reductions in inventory and incoming inspections, increases in quality and productivity, improvements in electronic data exchange, and reductions in supply chain management costs; and third-party assessment results, such as ISO 9001 audits.

Boeing A&T, for instance, tracks the mean time between corrective maintenance of its aircraft; increasing this time indicates improved quality of the aircraft systems. Other examples are reduced emission levels and waste stream reductions, Six Sigma initiative results, and ISO 9000 assessment audits. STMicroelectronics tracks key indicators of strategic goal achievement, such as R&D investment and number of patents granted. American Express analysts monitor telephone conversations for politeness, tone of voice, accuracy of the transaction, and other customer service aspects. Comparisons between judgments of the analysts and judgments of customers in post-transaction interviews determine the relevance of specific internal measurements. Because of the importance of hiring skilled people, The Ritz-Carlton embarked on a major project to improve the cycle time from when a potential new-hire walks in the door until a job offer is tendered; it became one of their key measures in this category. With the increased focus on supply chain management, many organizations are now reviewing cost savings; total supply chain management costs; reductions in inventory and cycle time; and indicators of better communication, such as those achieved via electronic commerce. Solar Turbines, for example, monitors supplier lead times for two critical components—forgings and castings.

Customer-Focused Outcomes   Relevant measures and indicators of an organization's performance as viewed by customers include direct measures of customer satisfaction and dissatisfaction, customer retention, gains and losses of customers and customer accounts, customer complaints, and warranty claims. Other indicators of customer satisfaction include measures of perceived value, loyalty, positive referral, and customer relationship building. Service quality measures often revolve around the dimensions of reliability, assurance, tangibles, empathy, and responsiveness that we discussed in Chapter 3. As an example, 3M's automotive trades business has as its direct customers automotive distributors, while end users are the secondary group. Service quality and cycle times are key satisfaction measures for distributors, while product quality is the principal satisfaction indicator for end users. 3M's measurements include the following:

- In-stock service levels
- On-time delivery
- Order completeness
- Emergency response time
- Ease of dealing with supplier
- Ease of contact with customer service department
- Complaint handling
- Accuracy of shipment
- Order cycle time
- Product quality and performance[10]

Workforce-Focused Outcomes   Workforce-focused outcomes show how well the organization has created and maintained a productive, engaging, and caring work environment. One outcome measure might be increased workforce retention resulting from a peer recognition program or the number of promotions that have resulted from the organization's leadership development program. Other examples include safety, absenteeism, turnover, training effectiveness, engagement, and employee satisfaction. Texas Nameplate Company measures the percent of net earnings for its risk-based compensation (gain sharing) program, because it significantly impacts employee productivity, motivation, and satisfaction. Because of the important relationship that Boeing Airlift and Tanker Programs has with its unions, A&T tracks grievance backlog reduction as a way of quantifying improving relationships. The Ritz-Carlton tracks percent turnover closely, because this measure is a key indicator of employee satisfaction and the effectiveness of their selection and training processes.

Leadership and Governance Outcomes   With an increased focus on issues of governance, ethics, and leadership accountability, it is important for organizations to practice and demonstrate high standards of overall conduct. Relevant performance measures can help organizations monitor these issues. They might include measures of regulatory/ legal compliance, results of oversight audits, and financial and ethics review results. Leadership outcomes also include measures of social responsibility and community service, such as volunteer hours and presentations to educational or civic groups, and outcomes that relate to accomplishment of organizational strategy and action plans. Measuring progress in accomplishing their strategic objectives is also a key challenge. Frequently, these progress measures can be determined by first defining the results that would indicate end-goal success in achieving the strategic objective and then using that end goal to define intermediate measures.

Financial and Market Outcomes   Financial measures are generally tracked by senior leadership to gauge overall organizational performance and are often used to determine incentive compensation for senior executives. Measures of financial performance might include revenue, return on equity, return on investment, operating profit, pretax profit margin, asset utilization, earnings per share, and other liquidity measures. In a capital-intensive industry such as airplane production, key financial measures at Boeing Airlift and Tanker Programs are return on sales, return on net assets, and net asset turnover. The Ritz-Carlton Hotel Company, on the other hand, monitors earnings before taxes, depreciation, and amortization, administrative costs, and gross profit among its key financial indicators. A useful financial performance indicator is the cost of quality, which we discussed in Chapter 8. It is one of Solar Turbine's key measures.

Marketplace performance indicators could include market share, measures of business growth, new product and geographic markets entered, and percentage of new product sales as appropriate. In a commodity market in which Sunny Fresh Foods competes, its performance drivers include their share of the U.S. market and total pounds of egg products sold. In the highly competitive semiconductor industry, STMicroelectronics looks not only at sales growth, but at differentiated product sales.

DESIGNING EFFECTIVE PERFORMANCE MEASUREMENT SYSTEMS

The purposes of a performance measurement system include the following:

- Providing a perspective of the past, present, and future
- Identifying trends and progress
- Facilitating understanding of cause-and-effect relationships

- Providing direction and support for continuous improvement
- Allowing performance comparison to benchmarks

In addition, they should be intelligible to a majority of employees, provide real-time information for decisions, and support personal and organizational learning. Balanced scorecards often fail for a variety of reasons, including not identifying the real drivers of customer satisfaction; not defining measures appropriately to focus attention on the areas having the greatest impact on organizational performance; negotiating goals rather than basing them on customer requirements, process limitations, and improvement capabilities; or not linking nonfinancial and financial results in a quantitative fashion.[11] Thus, organizations must carefully design their performance measurement systems.

Selecting Performance Measures

An organization must align its measurement system to its vision and strategy and select meaningful measurements. Many organizations make two fundamental mistakes: (1) not measuring key characteristics critical to organizational performance or customer behavior, and (2) taking irrelevant or inappropriate measurements. In the first case, the organization often fails to meet customer expectations or performance goals. In the second, the organization cannot isolate the meaningful data and usually wastes considerable time and resources. Measurement systems often become unwieldy simply because of the lack of monitoring and assessment. Most measures have probably been around for a long time, and few managers can probably say where, when, and why they were developed. In most cases, somebody just decided they were good to have. When Ford studied Mazda's management approaches, former CEO Donald Peterson observed, "Perhaps, most important, Mazda had been able to identify the types of information and records that were truly useful. It didn't bother with any other data. [At Ford] we were burdened with mountains of useless data and stifled by far too many levels of control over them."[12]

Mark Graham Brown suggests some practical guidelines for designing a performance measurement system:[13]

- Fewer is better. Concentrate on measuring the vital few key variables rather than the trivial many.
- Measures should be linked to the factors needed for success, namely, the key business drivers.
- Measures should include a mix of past, present, and future to ensure that the organization is concerned with all three perspectives.
- Measures should be based around the needs of customers, shareholders, and other key stakeholders.
- Measures should start at the top and flow down to all levels of employees in the organization.
- Measures should be changed or at least adjusted as the environment and strategy changes.

Leading organizations select appropriate measures and indicators using well-defined criteria. IBM Rochester, for example, asks the following questions:

- Does the measurement support our mission?
- Will the measurement be used to manage change?
- Is it important to our customers?
- Is it effective in measuring performance?

- Is it effective in forecasting results?
- Is it easy to understand/simple?
- Are the data easy/cost-efficient to collect?
- Does the measurement have validity, integrity, and timeliness?
- Does the measure have an owner?

Boeing A&T uses five criteria to select data: important to customers, effective in measuring performance, effective in forecasting results, actionable, and easily collected with integrity. As another example, Clarke American structures its performance measurements along two dimensions: how they are used—to either *change the business* or *run the business*—and whether they are predictive (leading) or diagnostic (lagging). "Change the business" measures are those most critical to the achievement of strategic objectives and evaluate organizational performance, such as total order cycle time and implemented ideas. "Run the business" measures are those used for daily operations and include measures of accuracy, responsiveness, and timeliness for deliveries.

Linking Measures to Strategy

Kaplan and Norton note that inappropriate measures lead to actions incongruent with strategies, even if they are well formulated and communicated, while appropriate measures lead to attainment of strategic goals and impact the goals and strategies needed to achieve them. A balanced scorecard approach helps in identifying the right measures by aligning them with the organization's vision and strategy. With a balanced scorecard, organizations have a means of setting targets and allocating resources for short-term planning, communicating strategies, aligning departmental and personal goals to strategies, linking rewards to performance, and supplying feedback for organizational learning.

Effective performance measures that are aligned with business strategy should be driven by internal and external factors that shape an organization's operating environment. These factors are reflected in the Baldrige Organizational Profile that we described in Chapter 11 (see Table 11.2). In particular, performance measures should strongly align with the principal factors that determine competitive success and the strategic challenges the organization faces. For example, the First National Bank of Chicago asked its customers what they considered as good-quality features of a product and the delivery of those features.[14] Responses included timeliness, accuracy, operations efficiency, economics, and customer responsiveness. These responses initiated the development of performance indicators such as lockbox processing time, bill keying accuracy, customer service inquiry resolution time, and money transfer timeliness. A computer software company might not need to collect extensive data on environmental quality issues, whereas a chemical company certainly would. A pizza franchise that delivers bulk orders to fraternities and parties around a college campus would have a different set of performance measures and indicators than one in a quiet suburban residential neighborhood. Thus, an organization first needs to fully understand its internal capabilities and external environment.

Measures should logically be tied to key business drivers. MBNA, the Wilmington, Delaware, credit card company that markets custom cards to "affinity groups" such as professional associations, universities, and sports team fans, views speed of service as one of its key business drivers. Thus, it measures the time to process customer address changes, the percentage of times phones are picked up within two rings, and the times taken to transfer calls from the switchboard.[15] Armstrong Building Products Operations identified five components of value that drive its business strategy: customer satisfaction, sales growth, operating profit, asset management, and high-performance organization.

Each of these components is supported by key measurements and analysis approaches. For example, product quality, a key driver of customer satisfaction, is measured by dimensions and squareness, fire performance, acoustics and color, dimensional stability, competitor product quality analysis, and claims. Likewise, service quality is measured by on-time delivery and missed-item promises, pricing and billing, and information support for customers. Another key business driver, operating profit, is measured by process effectiveness, units per employee, scrap and downtime, and cost of quality. Organizational performance measures include recordable injury rate, number of improvements/work orders, percentage of employees recognized, gainsharing savings, and employee satisfaction trends and turnover rate.

Key performance measures should be aligned with strategies and action plans. Setting targets for each measure provides the basis for strategy deployment as discussed in Chapter 11. Mercy Health System has a formal performance measurement system that is shown in Figure 12.4. System measures are driven by strategic objectives and action plans and aligned with departmental measures. The Information Management Advisory Committee ensures proper infrastructure and technology are in place for gathering, reporting, analyzing, and integrating data and information. The Process Improvement process further ensures data integration through the committee reporting structure.

Aligning Strategic and Process-Level Measurements[16]

It is possible that all work processes could be meeting their requirements while the organization is not achieving its longer-term goals. Thus, aligning strategic and process-level measurements is vital to a high-performing organization, and can be viewed as an approach for strategy deployment (see Chapter 11). Figure 12.5 illustrates how goals and measures might be aligned for a hypothetical retail manufacturer. Alignment might even go further, down to the team and individual levels. Note that alignment is tied fundamentally to the performance goals; the measures support goal attainment. The organization does not have to have one set of performance measures that everyone produces and reports, but rather, measures are used where they are most appropriate. Production line data, for example, might be reviewed only at the line level for daily operations control, while some data might be integrated at the next level for process improvement. Information that supports review of organizational-level performance is passed on to the corporate level.

Enterprise Resource Planning (ERP) systems are software packages that integrate organizational information systems and provide an infrastructure for managing information across the enterprise.[17] They integrate key aspects of a business—accounting, customer relationship management, supply chain management, manufacturing, sales, and human resources—into a unified information system, and provide timely analysis and reporting of sales, customer, inventory, manufacturing, human resource, and accounting data. The three most prominent vendors for ERP software are SAP, Oracle, and People-Soft. For example, when a salesperson fills an order, the system can check the customer's credit and their own manufacturing capacity, record the order, schedule the shipment, log the order on the production schedule, order parts from suppliers, and update financial and accounting records. ERP systems allow organizations to share databases in a networking environment and store and process key data in a unique database, and distribute it to a large group of users. Typical ERP applications span financial, human resource, operations and supply chain, and sales and marketing data. Many ERP systems now offer performance measurement system modules that are focused on helping manage the wide scope of data that are collected in the system.

FIGURE 12.4
Mercy Health Sys-
tem Performance
Measurement
Process

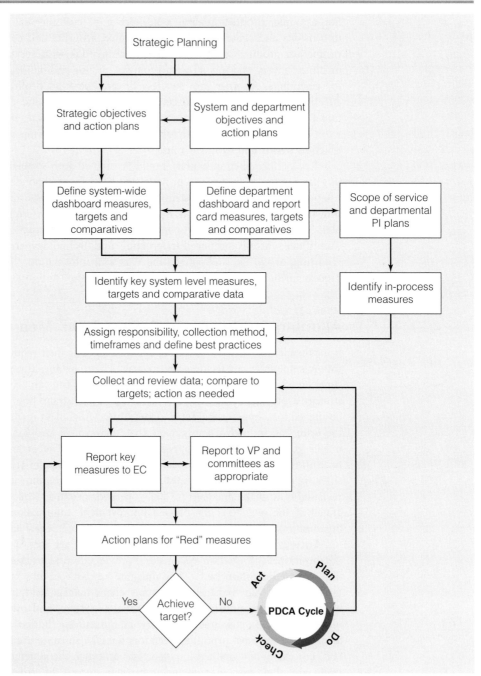

Source: Mercy Health System Malcolm Baldrige National Quality Award Application Summary, 2007.
Reprinted with permission.

FIGURE 12.5   An Example of Aligning Strategic and Process-Level Performance Measures

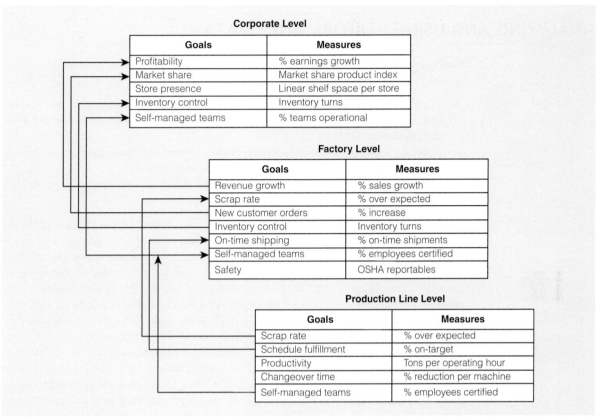

Source: R. I. Wise, "A Method for Aligning Process-Level and Strategy-Level Performance Metrics," *The Quality Management Forum*, 25, no. 1, pp. 4–6, (Spring 1999), Copyright © 1999 American Society for Quality, 11th Annual Quality Management Conference. Reprinted with permission.

Auditing the Measurement System

As the business environment changes, old measures can become obsolete or new measures might be needed. An outdated measurement system wastes resources, hinders strategic deployment, and often rewards the wrong behaviors. Thus, a periodic audit of an organization's measurement system is important.[18] Such an audit should examine whether the measures are aligned with the organization's goals, whether the right balance between leading and lagging measures and between operational and strategic measures has been struck, and whether any gaps, blind spots, or potential conflicts exist in the measurement system. Information gathered from an environmental assessment in the strategic planning process (see Chapter 11) can help to understand the changes in the business environment that may influence the measurement system. To help identify whether a measure should be deleted, one can simply ask, "What happens if we stop measuring?" As one consultant suggests, "If it does not help, it probably hurts." Measures in different functional departments often conflict with one another; for instance, faster customer service versus low inventory levels. What is more important is how the measures align with customer needs and requirements. Finally, it is vital to consider if measures drive the right behaviors and outcomes and whether any unintended consequences may result from them.

ANALYZING AND USING PERFORMANCE DATA

Analysis refers to an examination of facts and data to provide a basis for effective decisions. Examples of possible analyses include the following:

- Examining trends and changes in measures and indicators using charts and graphs
- Calculating a variety of statistical measures such as means, proportions, and standard deviations
- Applying sophisticated statistical tools such as correlation and regression analysis to help understand relationships among different measures
- Comparing results relative to other business units, competitors, or best-in-class benchmarks

At a basic level, measures should be charted over time to show levels, trends, and variation. Pal's Sudden Service uses an automated data collection, integration, and analysis system, SysDine, to generate store-level and companywide reports on sales, customer count, product mix, ideal food and material cost, and turnover rates, and also has an automated correlation routine available for analyzing key data to support organizational performance reviews and strategic planning. As a result, they are able to identify how changes in one performance area affect all other areas, make accurate performance projections, and understand how to optimize their management system.

Some organizations use creative ways to convey information to facilitate understanding and decision making. At Mercy Health System, for example, the Dashboard Alert System color codes each dashboard indicator relative to progress made toward targets: green (99 percent of target or higher); yellow (94–98 percent of target); and red (93 percent or less of target). Red dashboard measures prompt 90-day Dashboard Alert action plans and the Executive Council mobilizes Performance Improvement teams or the Leadership Group to redirect resources toward underperforming areas. Green indicators showing sustained success assist in identifying areas for best practice.

As we noted in our discussion of the balanced scorecard, managers must also understand the linkages between key measures of business performance. Examples of such analyses are:

- How product and service quality improvement correlates with key customer indicators such as customer satisfaction, customer retention, and market share
- Financial benefits derived from improvements in employee safety, absenteeism, and turnover
- Benefits and costs associated with education and training
- Relationships between product and service quality, operational performance indicators, and overall financial performance
- Profit impacts of customer satisfaction and retention
- Market share changes as a result of changes in customer satisfaction
- Impacts of employee satisfaction on customer satisfaction

Interlinking is the term that describes the quantitative modeling of cause-and-effect relationships between performance measures, such as the customer satisfaction and product quality or employee performance.[19] For example, the controls group of Johnson Controls Inc. examined the relationship between satisfaction levels and contract renewal rates. They found that 91 percent of contract renewals came from customers who were either satisfied or very satisfied, and customers who gave a "not satisfied" rating had a much higher defection rate. By examining the data, they found that a one percentage point increase in the overall satisfaction score was worth $13 million in service contract renewals annually. As a result, Johnson Controls made improving customer satisfaction a key strategic initiative.[20]

 QUALITYSPOTLIGHT
IBM Rochester

A study performed by IBM Rochester offers a compelling example of interlinking.[21] IBM's AS/400 Division in Rochester, Minnesota, winner of the 1990 Baldrige Award, struggled with understanding which factors have the greatest impact on overall business performance. IBM initiated a study to determine whether any relationships existed among the numerous measurements such as market share, overall customer satisfaction, employee morale, job satisfaction, warranty costs, inventory costs, product scrap, and productivity. Using 10 years of data, the researchers identified a strong correlation among market share, customer satisfaction, productivity, warranty cost, and employee satisfaction. Figure 12.6 shows a model that describes the cause-and-effect relationship among the key factors (those with a correlation factor equal to or greater than 0.7 are shown). This model suggests that to improve employee satisfaction, a manager must focus on improving job satisfaction, satisfaction with management, and satisfaction with having the right skills for the job. To improve job satisfaction, a manager must focus on improving satisfaction with management and satisfaction with having the right skills for the job. Improving satisfaction with having the right skills for the job will improve employee satisfaction and job satisfaction and will positively impact productivity, market share, and customer satisfaction. Improving employee satisfaction will directly impact productivity and customer satisfaction and will decrease warranty costs. Decreasing warranty costs will directly impact customer satisfaction and market share. Improving customer satisfaction will directly impact market share.

FIGURE 12.6   The Relationship Between Market Share, Customer Satisfaction, Productivity, Cost of Quality, and Employee Satisfaction

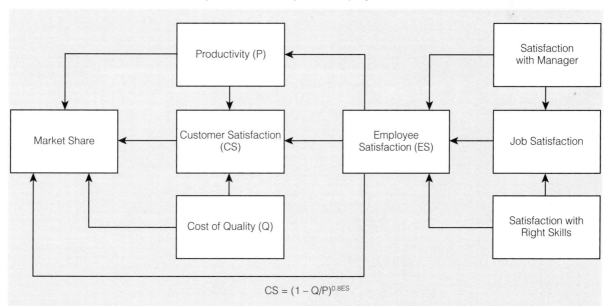

$$CS = (1 - Q/P)^{0.8ES}$$

Interlinking models do not have to be based on sophisticated statistical and computer models. Ames Rubber Corporation found that simple charts help to understand important correlations among measures that impact business decisions and strategy. It discovered that internal yields increase as employee turnover decreases, and that lost time accidents decrease with increasing training hours, leading to new initiatives for training and HR policies. North Mississippi Medical Center (NMMC) developed an innovative format for presenting the relationships between process and outcome measures, allowing clear understanding of cause-and-effect relationships. For example, Figure 12.7 shows that improvements in various in-process interventions for acute myocardial infarction (heart attack) patients result in improved outcomes.

Strong analytical capability supports good analysis. For example, Fuji-Xerox, a Japanese subsidiary of Xerox, uses a variety of statistical techniques such as regression and analysis of variance to develop mathematical models relating such factors as copy quality, machine malfunctions, and maintenance time to customer satisfaction results. Correlation analysis of product and service performance and customer indicators is a critical management tool for defining and focusing on key quality and customer requirements, identifying product and service differentiators in the marketplace, and determining cause-effect relationships between product and service attributes and measures of customer satisfaction and loyalty, as well as positive referrals. Caterpillar uses correlation analyses for its scoring and credit decision models to predict profitability, and segmentation analysis to compare satisfaction of origination processes versus termination processes, success in meeting varying requirements of differing industries, or describing employee salary ranges by job category.

The capabilities of today's spreadsheet and database software, such as Microsoft Excel and Access, make analysis simple to do by nearly any employee. Also, some evidence suggests that organizations that use more sophisticated statistical tools for analysis tend to have better business results. The fact that effective analysis requires more advanced statistical thinking might explain the lack of good approaches in most organizations. Thus, organizations are advised to develop improved statistical expertise among their employees, which is one of the key benefits of Six Sigma.

Business analytics technology such as data mining is improving organizational ability to develop good information. **Data mining** is the process of searching large databases

FIGURE 12.7
Example of NMMC
Process-Outcome
Linkages

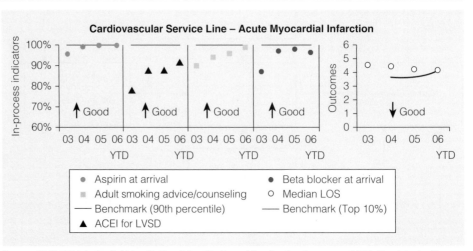

Source: NMMC Malcolm Baldrige National Quality Award Application Summary, 2007. Reprinted with permission.

to find hidden patterns in data, using analytical approaches and technologies such as cluster analysis, neural networks, and fuzzy logic. Data mining computer programs can sort through millions of pieces of information and identify subtle correlations between many variables, which is far more than the human mind is capable of doing. For example, data mining might discover that a particular supplier has a higher defect rate on parts costing less than $5, or that consumers who purchase a backup disk drive also tend to purchase a software utility package. Using data mining, MCI developed a set of 22 detailed and highly secret statistical profiles to identify potential customers who might leave for a rival company.[22] Data mining is relatively inexpensive and can provide new competitive knowledge. However, it requires clean data, even though it establishes correlations among variables, it cannot necessarily establish cause and effect. Also, it can easily lead to useless insights or overlook insights that are important. Nevertheless, the technology holds considerable promise.

The Role of Comparative Data

Comparative data refer to industry averages, competitor performance, world-class benchmarks, or performance measures of other organizations with similar product offerings. The use of comparative data is important to all organizations. Comparative data are needed because an organization needs to know where it stands relative to competitors and to best practices; comparative information and information obtained from benchmarking often provide the impetus for significant ("breakthrough") improvement or change; and comparing performance information frequently leads to a better understanding of processes and their performance. Looking at data without a basis for comparison can easily lead to a false sense of achievement. For example, a performance measure may be improving, but at a rate slower than its competition. Without that information, it would be difficult for an organization to recognize the need for further improvements or an accelerated pace of change to close the gap.

The effective selection and use of comparative data require the determination of needs and priorities, criteria for seeking appropriate sources for comparisons—from within and outside an organization's industry and markets, and the use of data and information to set stretch goals and to promote breakthrough improvements in areas most critical to the organization's competitive strategy.

Comparative data may be obtained in many ways and include third-party surveys and benchmarking approaches. The Ritz-Carlton Hotel Company, for instance, uses ratings and awards from travel industry publications and sales force reports to assess its competitive status. Boeing A&T seeks information from three sources:

1. *Best-in-Boeing:* High-performing processes identified through various company-level councils
2. *Best-in-Industry:* Organizations identified through various benchmarking centers, the International Benchmarking Clearinghouse, and their internal Business Environmental Assessment group
3. *World Class:* Leading-edge organizations, winners of national awards, or those cited by customers, suppliers, and industry experts

Figure 12.8 shows an example from Mercy Hospital in Janesville, Wisconsin. The average length of stay performance is compared to other hospitals in the state, a specific peer group of hospitals, and a best practice (BP) benchmark for a competitor. A good source of comparative benchmarks is often the performance of Baldrige recipients.

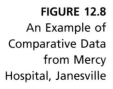

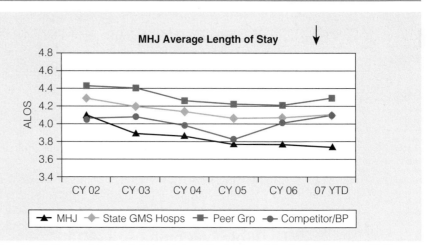

Source: Mercy Health Systems Malcolm Baldrige National Quality Award Application Summary, 2007.

Performance Review

The analysis of data provides the foundation for management review. Managers review performance results for several reasons:

- To assess organizational success and performance relative to competitors
- To understand how well progress on strategic objectives and action plans is being achieved
- To identify priorities for improvement and opportunities for innovation for products, services, and processes

Performance reviews are usually conducted on a daily or weekly basis for short-term control decisions, and periodically throughout the year for longer-term decisions and improvement. Figure 12.9 shows a summary of the performance reviews by which organizational decision-making and innovation are achieved at PRO-TEC Coating Company. Decisions regarding breakthrough innovations are decided at meetings with "change-the-business" aspects to them (Monday-Wednesday-Friday morning meeting, Departmental, and Management Committee and Leadership meetings). At the lower levels of the organization, PRO-TEC expects individual Associates and workgroups to review operational "run-the-business" metrics and provide most of the ideas for continuous improvement.

At Mercy Health System, senior leaders participate in performance review as members of interdisciplinary committees.[23] Standing system-wide committees, such as the Quality Council, Safety Committee, Information Management Advisory Committee, and Pharmacy and Therapeutics Committee, review in-process, trended performance, and create action plans to achieve goals. Key performance indicators are compared to best-practice measures during analysis to assess organizational success and competitive performance. Data summaries are integrated and reported to appropriate committees, company leadership, and physicians. MHS uses the results of organizational performance reviews to evaluate achievement of system-wide goals, on both an annual and ongoing basis. During the Strategic Planning Process and budgeting process, the Executive Committee identifies opportunities and priorities for improving key processes, sets targets for organizational performance, and defines system-level action plans to achieve those targets.

FIGURE 12.9   Performance Review Summary at PRO-TEC Coating Company

	Operational	Mon.-Wed.-Fri.	Departmental	Monthly	Others
Who	Value creation personnel	Value creation personnel, support processes	Each department personnel	Leadership Team and stakeholders	PRO-TEC Mgmt. Committee, Leadership Team (strategic planning), Departmental planning
When	Daily	3 times weekly	1–2 per month	Monthly	3 times a year, annual
What	Run Balanced Scorecard (BSC)—quality, volume, uptime	Run BSC—Interdepartmental cooperative efforts, corrective actions; Change BSC—current issues driving change	Run BSC—review projects, departmental issues, plan versus actual; Change BSC—support of tactical and strategic planning	Run BSC—review departmental performance, action items	Run BSC—review company performance; Change BSC—develop change strategy for long-term viability (update Change BSC)
Analysis	Trending, process logs	Review of operations, pareto, correlation, statistical	Statistical, uptime metrics, correlation, pareto	Statistical, uptime metrics, correlation, pareto	Roll-up of measures done at lower levels
Decisions made	Production, operational, equipment	Safety, business direction, operational	Innovation	Resourcing	Strategic planning, Change BSC items

Source: PRO-TEC Malcolm Baldrige Application Summary, 2007. Reprinted with permission.

MANAGING INFORMATION RESOURCES

Simply collecting data is not enough. Organizations must ensure that both data and information and the hardware and software systems that process them are reliable, accurate, user-friendly, and secure, and that data and information are available to all who need them in a timely fashion.

The familiar computer cliché, "Garbage in, garbage out," applies equally well to organizational performance data. Any measurement is subject to error, and hence the credibility of data can be suspect. Measurement reliability in manufacturing demands careful attention to metrology, the science of measurement. This topic was discussed in Chapter 8. A useful approach to ensuring data reliability is for internal cross-functional teams or external auditors to conduct periodic audits of the processes used to collect the data. Standardized forms, clear instructions, and adequate training lead to more consistent performance in data collection. An AT&T division, for example, used standard data entry templates and procedures to facilitate the consistency and uniform editing of manually input data. Data collected automatically from interfaces with other systems use standard record formats and edits, and are reconciled at each handoff. Also, a central data dictionary defined critical data elements according to source, meaning, format, and valid content of each. AT&T followed stringent guidelines and standards for developing, maintaining, documenting, and managing data systems.

Like any business process, information creation should be managed with total quality principles.[24] The quality of information can be improved by capturing data only once, and as close to the origin of the data as possible; eliminating human error by capturing data electronically where possible; using a single database whenever feasible; eliminating all unnecessary handling of data by intermediaries, such as data entry clerks; placing accountability on the creators of data and information; ensuring proper training; and defining targets and measures of data quality. Maintaining computer systems, backing up databases, and building error-checking capabilities into software provides added measures for ensuring data and information validity and availability. Frequent computer crashes or network problems can wreak havoc on operations and customer responsiveness.

An organization's efforts are wasted if collected data are not available to the right employees when needed. A customer service representative who tells a customer that he or she needs to find some information and will call back the next day cannot satisfy that customer in a timely fashion. At Milliken, all databases, including product specifications, process data, supplier data, customer requirements, and environmental data are available to every associate throughout the computer network. Electronic charts displayed throughout the plant and in business support departments show key quality measures and trends. Data accessibility empowers employees and encourages their participation in quality improvement efforts. Wainwright Industries posts all business information—quality, customer satisfaction, and financial performance—in a room accessible to all employees, customers, suppliers, and visitors. Organizations that share results often exhibit better performance because information provides the basis for better decisions, and employees understand why certain decisions are made. Figure 12.10 shows how a wide variety of data is made accessible to all stakeholders at Pearl River School

FIGURE 12.10   Data Accessibility at Pearl River School District

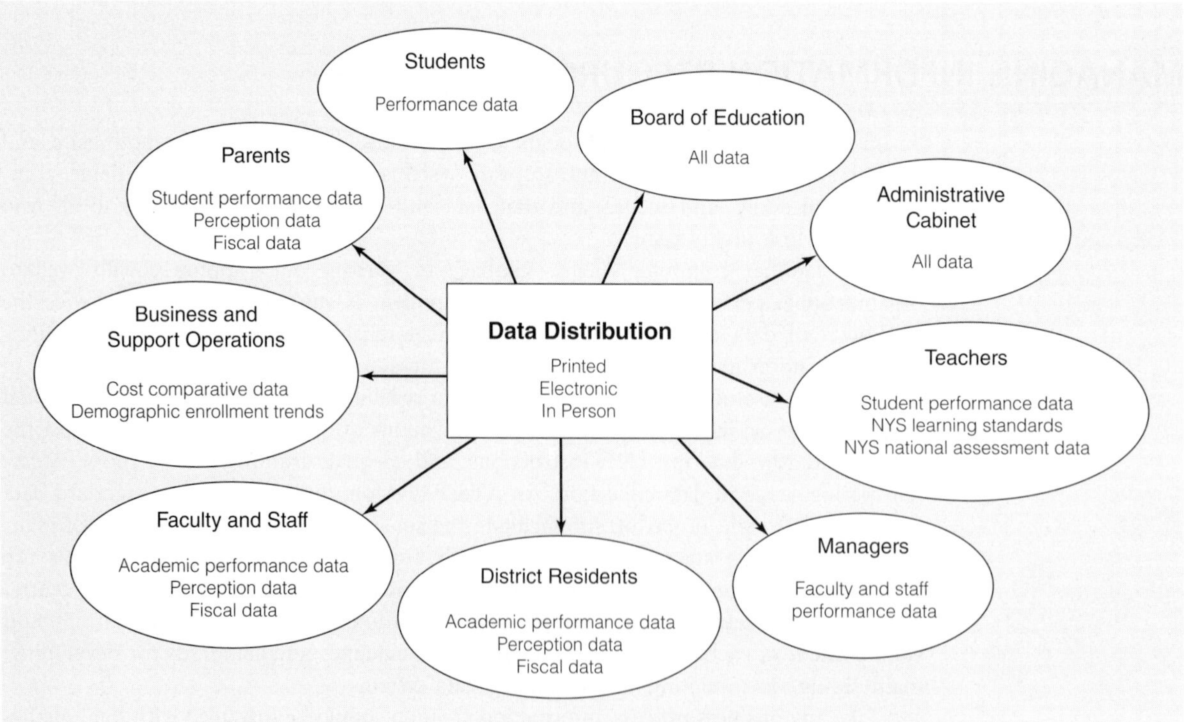

Source: Pearl River School District Malcolm Baldrige Application Summary, 2001. Reprinted with permission.

District. Sharing data is becoming increasingly important in business networks and supply chains.

Modern information technology plays a critical role in data accessibility. Many organizations have state-of-the-art online computer networks supplemented by local processing capabilities. Prudential Insurance Company agents take portable computers to customer's homes or places of business.[25] This practice reduces the time needed to answer a client's questions and increases the accuracy and reliability of the answers. Sales and service offices are connected electronically. Each can obtain information about the current status of contracts being serviced by another office, and thus can be of assistance to customers who contact them directly. They can also electronically forward requests for action to the appropriate office. The Hospital Information System (HIS) at Baptist Hospital is used to gather, connect, and integrate data from clinical systems, employees, patients, financial systems, decision support systems, and physicians. The HIS is accessed through mobile terminals, through the Medical Information Data Access System for physicians, and through kiosks located throughout the organization.

The reliability of hardware and software is crucial to ensure the integrity of performance measurement systems. At Branch-Smith Printing, server uptime is protected with redundant power supplies and hard drives. Two servers have two identical mirrored drives so that if a device on the primary fails, they can remove one of the drives and install it in the sister machine, and have the server operating again in just minutes. At Motorola, special interest groups or technical advisory boards and working groups have been formed across the corporation to involve users in establishing and updating desktop hardware and software standards to reduce costs, ensure reliability, and improve ease of use.

Confidentiality and security are critical in managing data, particularly with the increasing use of electronic data transfer. Using firewalls to prevent external systems attacks and passwords to ensure that only authorized users have access to sensitive data such as customer records and financial information are vital in an information management system. At Clarke American, for instance, when an associate leaves the company, the Termination Identification Process System (TIPS) automatically notifies Systems Assurance to remove access to all facilities and systems.

Finally, data and information must be kept current. Antiquated measurements lead to poor decisions. Leading organizations continually improve their performance measurement systems, staying abreast of new techniques. They conduct ongoing review and update their sources and uses of data, shorten the cycle time from data gathering to access, and broaden access to everyone who requires data for management and improvement. For example, ADAC Laboratories hosted quarterly "measurement summits" that included representatives from all departments to review the types of data collected according to three criteria: whether the data support key business drivers; address one of the "five evils"—waste, defects, delays, accidents, or mistakes; or support objective analysis for improvement. Teams at Corning TPD brainstorm and research new measurements, consult with experts, and test the measurements for three to six months before full implementation.

KNOWLEDGE MANAGEMENT

One Hewlett-Packard manager noted, "The fundamental building material of a modern corporation is knowledge." Process improvement requires new knowledge to result in better processes and procedures. Increasing the knowledge of the organization, both in an individual sense as well as for the organization as a whole, is the essence of learning and ties closely to Deming's concept of the theory of knowledge (see Chapter 2).

H. James Harrington observed, "All organizations have it, but most don't know what they know, don't use what they do know, and don't reuse the knowledge they have." Knowledge assets have become more important than financial and physical assets in many organizations. For example, Skandia, a large Swedish financial services company, internally audits its intellectual capital every year for inclusion in its annual report.

Chevron CEO Kenneth Derr has stated:

Of all the initiatives we've taken at Chevron … few have been as important or as rewarding as our efforts to build a learning organization by sharing and managing knowledge throughout our company. In fact, I believe this priority was one of the keys to reducing our operating costs by more than $2 billion per year … over the last seven years.[26]

Unfortunately, as compared with money, labor, and capital equipment, knowledge is probably the most difficult to manage. It can easily be lost if information is not documented or when individuals are promoted or leave the organization. Knowledge is perishable and if it is not renewed and replenished, it becomes worthless.

Knowledge assets refer to the accumulated intellectual resources that an organization possesses, including information, ideas, learning, understanding, memory, insights, cognitive and technical skills, and capabilities. Knowledge assets consist of two types: explicit knowledge and tacit knowledge. **Explicit knowledge** includes information stored in documents or other forms of media such as databases, policies and procedures, and technical drawings. Explicit knowledge is easily captured, stored, and disseminated using computer technology (think Google!). **Tacit knowledge** is information that is formed around intangible factors resulting from an organization's or individual's experience, and is content-specific. Intellectual assets such as patents, software, or a unique understanding of customer requirements that differentiates an organization from its competitors are some examples, as are knowledge resulting from research or job experience, cross-functional teamwork, or after action reviews. These two aspects represent the "know-how" that an organization has available to use, invest, and grow. Customers, suppliers, and partners may also hold key knowledge assets.

Knowledge management involves the process of identifying, capturing, organizing, and using knowledge assets to create and sustain competitive advantage. A knowledge management system allows intangible information to be managed as an organizational asset in a manner similar to tangible assets. A benchmarking study co-sponsored by the American Productivity and Quality Center reported that 79 percent of managers from the 70 responding companies felt that managing organizational knowledge is central to the organization's strategy, but 59 percent stated that their firm was performing this management function poorly or not at all.[27] Also, 88 percent believed that a climate of openness and trust is important for knowledge sharing, but 32 percent of the respondents believed that their organization did not have such a climate. In many organizations, the gap was attributed to a lack of commitment to knowledge management on the part of top managers.

Managing information and knowledge can require a significant commitment of resources as the sources of information grow dramatically each year. Information from internal operations, from the Internet, and from business-to-business (B2B) and business-to-consumer (B2C) communications challenges organizational abilities to provide the information that people need to do their work, keep current, and improve. Clarke American, for example, has an automated information collection and distribution system that provides a central repository for information for partners, customers, and associates. Caterpillar Financial Services Corporation manages organizational knowledge through several mechanisms, including e-mail; an Intranet; shared network drives; public folders which store knowledge by subject, department, and other customized formats; Caterpillar's Knowledge Network which is a web-based tool that provides for collaboration at many levels; and a searchable database called eTracker, which captures learning from over 1,000 Six Sigma projects. Best practices are identified through annual state quality conferences, the Quest for Excellence conference, which features recipients of the Baldrige Award, and Peer Learning Network meetings.

An effective knowledge management system should include the following:

- A way of capturing and organizing explicit as well as tacit knowledge of how the business operates, including an understanding of how current business processes function
- A systems-approach to management that facilitates assimilation of new knowledge into the business system and is oriented toward continuous improvement/ innovation
- A common framework for managing knowledge and some way of validating and synthesizing new knowledge as it is acquired
- A culture and values that support collaborative sharing of knowledge across functions and encourages full participation of all employees in the process[28]

Knowledge Transfer

The transfer of knowledge within organizations and the identification and sharing of best practices often set high-performing organizations apart from the rest. Many organizations perform similar activities at different locations or by different people. For example, consider a sales organization with district managers spread out over the country, or a clinical research organization that performs research studies for drug companies in a project environment, or a school district with teachers teaching the same subjects at different locations throughout the district. Suppose that an individual develops an innovative practice. How is this knowledge shared among others performing similar jobs? In many organizations, the answer is that knowledge is probably never shared.

High-performance organizations use many different mechanisms to share and transfer knowledge. For example, Premier, Inc. uses a team-oriented approach to transfer knowledge, which is accomplished using various tools, technologies, and processes to fill needs or gaps identified through proactive research. Teams use standardized tools for collection and transfer, which occurs regularly to support continuous cycles of improvement. Methods for collecting and transferring knowledge include large group meetings, work groups, surveys/market, publications, technology systems that are available 24/7, and functions to answer questions at any time. Special activities within key events (e.g., Values Conferences, Breakthroughs Conferences, as well as project team and staff meetings) include the transfer of best practices among employees and customers.[29]

The ability to identify and transfer best practices within the organization is sometimes called **internal benchmarking**. In this area, the most mature organizations may falter, even those that are adept at benchmarking other organizations. The American Productivity and Quality Center (APQC) noted that executives have long felt frustrated by their inability to identify or transfer outstanding practices from one location or function to another. They know that some facilities have superior practices and processes, yet operating units continue to reinvent or ignore solutions and repeat mistakes.[30] Research identified three categories of barriers:

1. Lack of motivation to adopt the practice
2. Inadequate information about how to adapt the practice and make it work

3. Lack of "absorptive capacity," the resources and skill to make and manage the change

APQC suggests that although most people have a natural desire to learn and share their knowledge, organizations have a variety of logistical, structural, and cultural hurdles to overcome, including the following:

- Organizational structures that promote "silo" thinking in which locations, divisions, and functions focus on maximizing their own accomplishments and rewards, or, as Deming called it, "suboptimization"
- A culture that values personal technical expertise and knowledge creation over knowledge sharing
- The lack of contact, relationships, and common perspectives among people who don't work side by side
- An overreliance on transmitting "explicit" rather than "tacit" information—the information that people need to implement a practice that cannot be codified or written down
- Not allowing or rewarding people for taking the time to learn and share and help each other outside of their own small corporate village

Internal benchmarking requires a process: first, identifying and collecting internal knowledge and best practices; second, sharing and understanding those practices; and third, adapting and applying them to new situations and bringing them up to best-practice performance levels. Technology, culture, leadership, and measurement are enablers that can help or hinder the process. Many organizations create internal databases by which employees can share their practices and knowledge. For example, Texas Instruments has a Best Practices Knowledgebase delivered via Lotus Notes, Intranet, and TI's network systems. Information is often organized around business core and support processes. Cultural issues include how to motivate and reward people for sharing best practices and establishing a supportive culture. As with any TQ effort, senior leadership must take an active role by tying initiatives to the organization's vision and strategy, communicating success stories at executive meetings, removing implementation barriers, reinforcing and rewarding positive behaviors, leading by example, and communicating the importance of best-practice sharing with all employees. Finally, measuring the frequency of use and satisfaction with best-practice databases, linking practices to financial and customer satisfaction, focusing on cycle time to implement best practices, and measuring the growth of virtual teams that share information are ways in which the organization can monitor the effectiveness of their approaches.

One example of an internal best-practice learning process is Royal Mail, the largest business unit within the Post Office Group in the United Kingdom (UK), which handles an average of 64 million letters per day using approximately 160,000 people at 1,900 operational sites throughout the UK.[31] Each potential good practice (a term used to recognize that a practice may not be the best, but is good enough to provide significant performance gains) requires formalized documentation that includes a description of the practice; names and telephone numbers of the contacts; date; process diagram; description of the major steps, who performs them, and what is needed to do the work; implementation resources; and risks and barriers. These good practice descriptions are scrutinized by a panel for evaluation of their potential for transferability to other parts of the business. The panel characterizes the good practice as either mandatory, where all units and staff are required to adopt it, or recommended, where application is optional, depending on local conditions. Royal Mail uses six measurements for evaluating its approach:

1. The number of potential national good practices reaching national process groups
2. The proportion of national good practices becoming confirmed good practices
3. The extent of implementation
4. The cycle time from first submission to entry in the national database
5. The benefit gained compared to the anticipated benefit
6. Satisfaction from members of the national and business unit process groups

Organizations such as Raytheon and Texas Instruments are beginning to exploit the concept of **rapid knowledge transfer (RKT)**.[32] Rapid knowledge transfer involves the discovery, learning, creation, and reuse of knowledge that eventually becomes intellectual capital—knowledge that can be converted into value and profits. Four global phenomena have increased the importance of RKT in organizations:

1. Driven by high-speed bandwidth, PC microchip improvements, digital technology, and the growth of the Internet, speed has become critical to every facet of business, giving an edge to organizations that rapidly transfer knowledge. These gains in speed have turned knowledge transfer into a race.
2. Intellectual capital (IC) has become a prominent concept that now overshadows physical capital. Knowledge is the main ingredient of IC, and human capital—the tacit knowledge in the minds of employees consisting of know-how, experiences, skills, and creativity—is the source of it all and must be nurtured and protected.
3. The upcoming record retirement of 77 million baby boomers, born between 1946 and 1964, will account for huge losses of vital tacit knowledge. The first group turned 65 in 2011. By 2030, the 65-plus segment will account for about 20 percent of the U.S. population—double what it was in 2000. When these workers retire, they will take their tacit knowledge with them. Why not capture and transfer the most vital knowledge before it is lost?
4. A growing reservoir of proven, valuable, and profitable best-practice business knowledge is currently available for transfer, and most of it is free. The worldwide quality and productivity improvement revolution has produced business excellence models that replicate successes, including the Baldrige criteria, the EFQM European Award, the Shingo Prize for Excellence in Manufacturing, ISO 9000, Lean, and Six Sigma.

A knowledge-enabled culture is created when an organization employs a system of aligned human resource policies, tactics, processes, and practices that ensure knowledge is created, captured, used, and reused to achieve superior organizational results as a sustainable advantage. RKT combines knowledge management and systematic improvement in an integrated process framework that consists of a knowledge-enabled culture and four key steps (see Figure 12.11):

1. Search for and import best practices
2. Learn, understand, and share
3. Create intellectual capital
4. Convert knowledge into value and profits

RKT has proven capable of replicating the successes of Baldrige winning organizations such as Texas Instruments (TI) at other geographical locations inside and outside of TI.

FIGURE 12.11   Rapid Knowledge Transfer Framework

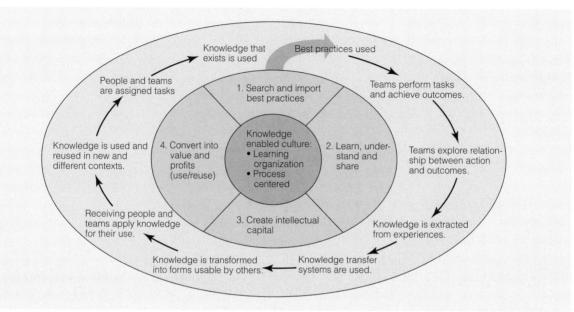

Source: Reprinted with permission from Michael J. English and William H. Baker, Jr. "Rapid Knowledge Transfer: The Key to Success," *Quality Progress*, February 2006, pp. 41–48. Copyright © 2006 American Society for Quality. No further distribution allowed without permission.

SUMMARY OF KEY POINTS AND TERMINOLOGY

The Student Companion Site provides a summary of key concepts and terminology introduced in this chapter.

QUALITY *in* PRACTICE

Using the Balanced Scorecard at the United States Postal Service[33]

The U.S. Postal Service (USPS) employs roughly 700,000 workers, with a fleet of over 200,000 vehicles driven about a billion miles a year to deliver more than 206 billion pieces of mail to over 142 million delivery points. It operates one of the largest facilities networks in the nation, with about 38,000 retail offices. Like most organizations, the Postal Service has multiple stakeholders. However, the scope and scale of postal operations makes balancing the interests of its stakeholders somewhat more complex, especially as there are no direct "shareholders" that command precedence in determining organizational priorities. As a public institution, the Postal Service has numerous responsibilities and accountabilities not shared by typical private sector organizations.

The Postal Service had traditionally been able to depend on the growth of the economy to drive mail volume and revenue increases in a protected environment. By the late 1980s it was becoming clear that this planning assumption could no longer be taken for granted. The Postal Service had fairly sophisticated operational planning, and in fact successfully deployed a massive automation program (Corporate Automation Plan) to reduce the number of manual processes in mail processing. The Postal Service also developed a rigorous financial planning process, including rate case and capital investment planning, but something more was needed because service performance and customer satisfaction were declining.

Anticipating the need for substantial change, the Board of Governors appointed Marvin Runyon as the nation's 70th postmaster general in July 1992. Formerly a senior executive with Ford Motor Company, and the first president and CEO of Nissan America, Runyon had successfully applied quality management principles. He established a quality group at the senior management level of the Postal Service.

Runyon began an assessment of the Postal Service in 1993 using the Baldrige criteria. The results of that process led to the creation of what was called CustomerPerfect!, now known simply as the management cycle. One of the critical features that emerged was the development of strategic goal areas of emphasis called "voices": Voice of the Customer, Voice of the Employee, and Voice of the Business. This was the beginning of the balanced scorecard approach in the Postal Service and served as a major focal point toward developing a quality approach. A senior management committee was established to set goals and improvement targets, and to develop specific performance indicators and measurement systems.

One of the first areas of emphasis was the "Voice of the Employee," which focused on providing a safe and secure workplace in response to instances of violence and poor employee relations. A second major initiative, the "Voice of the Business," focused on the "Breakthrough Productivity Initiative," while the third area, the "Voice of the Customer," focused on providing timely, reliable delivery. In their balanced scorecard work, Kaplan and Norton advocated a well-connected mapping that leads from an organization's main strategy to the four perspectives of the balanced scorecard: Financial, Customer Satisfaction, Internal Process, and Learning and Growth. Each element works to support the strategic objectives in a linked process. Learning and Growth ("Voice of the Employee" in postal terms) supports improved Internal

Processes ("Voice of the Business"), which support Customer Satisfaction ("Voice of the Customer"). Customer satisfaction leads to the desired financial outcome, which in the case of the Postal Service is sufficient revenue to support the universal delivery service mission.

Most organizations adapt the balanced scorecard to their own conditions, which is why it is difficult to assess the effectiveness of the approach across organizations. At USPS, they were responding to performance gaps in three specific and critical areas. One of the critical areas that needed improvement in the labor-intensive Postal Service was the workplace environment (Voice of the Employee). A strategic goal was established and indicators were developed to measure annual improvements. The primary indicators of performance in this category of the scorecard were safety, based on the requirements of the Occupational Safety and Health Administration, and employee satisfaction. Employee satisfaction is measured by a survey of all employees that is conducted annually but can be tracked monthly by each unit. The Voice of the Business was separated into two areas—one represented by a productivity measure and the other by a revenue generation measure. The last major area of strategic emphasis, "Voice of the Customer," is owned by the chief marketing officer in partnership with the chief operating officer. The primary indicator was a set of delivery service measurement systems.

The organization's efforts were focused on achieving specific, measurable results in each area. A balanced scorecard was constructed, as shown in Figure 12.12. As demonstrated by the arrows, there is an implied alignment from the performance-driven culture reflected in human capital improvements, to operational efficiency, to improvements in customer satisfaction, all of which will improve financial stability. The Postal Service drove the concept throughout the organization by deploying specific goals relevant to the functional and operational units involved.

The Postal Service developed a rigorous performance review process tied to achieving the targets set. Ann Wright, then-manager of performance assessment, stated, "USPS has developed a National Performance Assessment (NPA) system, which provides detailed measures for each of the corporate-level indicators, that provides a line-of-sight link to unit and individual performance down to the frontline supervisor. These are consistent across operating areas and job categories within the operating units. Each of

FIGURE 12.12
U.S. Postal Service's Balanced Scorecard

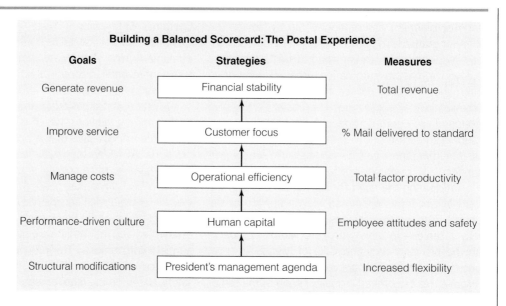

the indicators is objective and measurable, and focuses on results or outcomes rather than activities or processes." Individual and unit performance within organizations are driven, in large part, by the focus given to specific activities and by the incentives associated with achievement of the specific goals. The NPA system provides a systematic approach more akin to the private sector, and, in fact, the Postal Service has been a forerunner of "pay-for-performance" approaches now being implemented elsewhere in the federal government.

The results of these initiatives have delivered impressive results. The Postal Service has improved its performance on those measures assessing a safe and secure environment. USPS has been recognized as one of the best places for minorities to work. The Postal Service's implementation of the REDRESS (Resolve Employment Disputes Reach Equitable Solutions Swiftly) program has received national recognition. The USPS Occupational Safety and Health Administration OSHA Illness and Injury rate improved to 6.3 in 2004 from 8.7 in 2000. The results of the annual employee satisfaction survey, expressed as an index for six key questions (where a larger index indicates improvement), have advanced from 57.5 in 2000 to 62.1 in 2004. The improvements in the workplace, along with aggressive implementation of automation and other management investments, have led to a remarkable growth in postal productivity that has outpaced the growth of productivity in the U.S.

economy. The result is that the Postal Service is delivering more mail to more places, with fewer employees. Postal delivery service also has improved significantly. First-class mail performance has improved to over 95 percent of overnight mail being delivered on time, with improvements in other categories of first-class mail.

One way to summarize the effectiveness of the postal implementation of the balanced scorecard approach is to refer to the assessment of the American Society for Quality in their annual American Customer Service Index, where they described the Postal Service in their 2004 survey as "the most improved organization" since the comparative measurement program began in 1994. In an overall comparison to industry ratings of customer satisfaction, the Postal Service ranked above the Transportation, Telecommunications, and Utilities averages, and about equaled the Services industry.

Key Issues for Discussion

1. Explain how the Voice of the Employee supports improved internal processes (Voice of the Business), and how the Voice of the Business supports customer satisfaction (Voice of the Customer).

2. While Figure 12.12 shows only representative measures associated with the balanced scorecard, suggest some other measures that might be included, using your knowledge of postal operations.

QUALITY *in* PRACTICE

Knowledge Management at ConocoPhillips[34]

ConocoPhillips is an integrated energy company engaged in four core businesses:

1. petroleum exploration and production;
2. midstream natural gas processes and marketing;
3. petroleum refining, marketing, supply, and transportation; and
4. chemicals production and distribution.

Since 1999, ConocoPhillips has evolved through acquisitions involving more than 12 companies. The current organization employs almost 30,000 people worldwide and is known for its technological expertise in areas such as reservoir management and exploration, 3-D seismic technology, high-grade petroleum coke upgrading, and sulfur removal.

The main motivations behind ConocoPhillips' introduction of knowledge sharing in 2004 were to promote functional excellence, better leverage knowledge across the organization, and ensure that the next generation of technicians and engineers has access to the critical knowledge they need to do their jobs. In addition, a large percentage of ConocoPhillips' technical work force is either retirement-eligible or will become so in the next five years. These highly experienced employees possess valuable business knowledge that the organization needs to capture.

Knowledge sharing at ConocoPhillips is based on the FAST (Find, Ask, Share, Trust) model:

- *FIND*—the ability to locate trusted, validated content,
- *ASK*—peer Q&A and problem solving through discussion forums,
- *SHARE*—expertise location, and
- *TRUST*—strong global relationships on which employees can depend.

Figure 12.13 describes the organization's knowledge architecture. The Knowledge Management (KM) approach centers on 140 networks of excellence (i.e., virtual communities of practice) aligned with business functions. Each network has a Web-based portal that includes:

- a discussion board where members can post technical questions and answers,

- a knowledge library that houses content and reference materials, and
- expertise location tools for members seeking people with specific knowledge.

In addition to the network-based tools, the organization maintains an enterprise-wide wiki for technical knowledge. Networks are built in SharePoint, and the wiki is built in MediaWiki.

Knowledge sharing at ConocoPhillips is structured as a three-tiered support model:

1. the knowledge sharing team is responsible for enterprise KM process, tools, and templates,
2. IT partners provide infrastructure support and some SharePoint site maintenance, and
3. external consultants maintain SharePoint sites and provide customization and KM expertise.

The knowledge sharing team is responsible for overseeing networks of excellence. Formed in 2006, the team comprises seven full-time equivalent (FTE) employees led by a director of knowledge sharing. The director reports to the senior vice president of planning and strategy, who is a member of the executive team and reports to the chairman and CEO. A separate, 30-person knowledge sharing leadership team made up of functional leaders sets direction and strategy for KM.

Funding for networks is allocated to business streams. Some networks receive corporate seed money to get started, but funding is expected eventually to be distributed across relevant business units. The knowledge sharing team has a budget for technology platforms, but costs associated with network staffing and time are allocated to the business units. Senior executives support KM through participation in knowledge sharing leadership team meetings, communications, and appeals for employees to include KM goals in their individual commitments each year.

ConocoPhillips evaluates its networks of excellence using health checks that pinpoint strengths and areas for improvement within each network. It also assesses the maturity of each network on a six-point scale. Other measures include adoption/utilization data and success stories submitted by employees. The success story program is described in detail in the next section.

FIGURE 12.13 Knowledge Architecture Model at ConocoPhillips

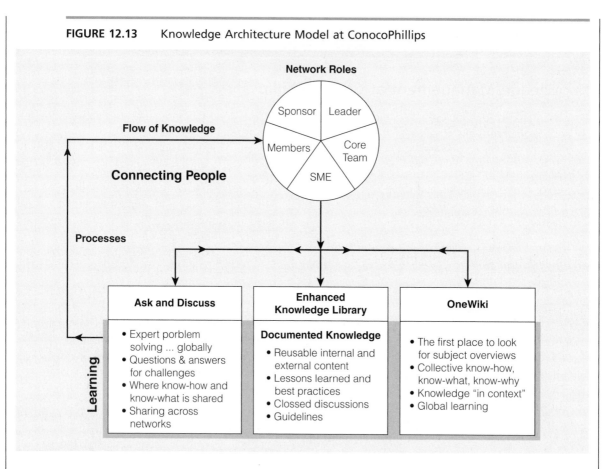

Assessing the financial impact of KM is important to most organizations, but ConocoPhillips tracks impact and return on investment in a unique way. Employees are encouraged to submit success stories based on their experiences using the networks of excellence. As part of the submission process, they are asked to provide details on measurable gains, such as cost savings, reduced cycle times, safety and environmental improvements, and other tangible business benefits. Each success story includes a benefits summary that leadership must certify as accurate before it is published.

Key Issues for Discussion

1. Explain how is the knowledge-sharing approach shown in the Figure 12.13 Knowledge Architecture Model is aligned with Conoco-Phillips' strategic motivation for knowledge management.
2. How does Conoco Phillips provide support for its KM system in the form of personnel and budget?
3. Explain the unique approach that Conoco-Phillips took to assess the financial impact of KM.

REVIEW QUESTIONS

1. Summarize the measurement and knowledge management practices for performance excellence.
2. Explain the importance of performance measurement in organizations.
3. What is the balanced scorecard? Describe its four components.
4. Explain the difference between leading and lagging measures. How are they used within a balanced scorecard?
5. What are the five groups of results measures in the Malcolm Baldrige Criteria? Provide examples of measurements and indicators in each group.

6. Describe the issues that organizations must consider in selecting measures and indicators.
7. What two fundamental mistakes do organizations frequently make about measurement?
8. How should performance measures be linked to strategy?
9. What is the role of enterprise resource planning (ERP) in performance measurement?
10. Why is it important to conduct periodic audits of a measurement system? What are some key questions to consider?
11. Describe ways by which data can be analyzed to generate useful managerial information.
12. What is interlinking? Provide an example.
13. What is the role of comparative data in a performance measurement system?
14. Why should managers review performance results?
15. Describe some important issues related to managing information resources.
16. Why is knowledge management important in modern organizations?
17. What are knowledge assets? Explain the difference between explicit knowledge and tacit knowledge.
18. What are some ways of transferring knowledge within organizations?

DISCUSSION QUESTIONS

1. What types of measurements, either formal or informal, do you use to manage your personal life? How might your personal measurement system be improved using the principles discussed in this chapter?
2. Under which perspective of the balanced scorecard would you classify each of the following measurements?
   a. On-time delivery to customers
   b. Time to develop the next generation of products
   c. Manufacturing yield
   d. Engineering efficiency
   e. Quarterly sales growth
   f. Percent of products that equal 70 percent of sales
   g. Cash flow
   h. Number of customer partnerships
   i. Increase in market share
   j. Unit cost of products
3. How might a SWOT (strengths, weaknesses, opportunities, and threats) analysis be of use for identifying measures in a balanced scorecard? What types of questions might you ask?
4. Many "course and instructor evaluation" systems consist of inappropriate or ineffective measurements. Discuss how the principles in this chapter can be used to develop an effective measurement system for instructor performance.
5. How can measurement be used to control and improve the daily operations of your college or university? You might conduct some research to understand what measures your school uses.

6. What types of performance measurements might be used by a fraternity or student organization?
7. In making cheese, companies test milk for somatic cell count to prevent diseases. They also test for bacteria to determine how clean the milk is, and perform a freezing-point test to see whether the milk was diluted with water (milk with water in it freezes at a lower temperature, which increases production costs because all the excess water must be extracted). Final cheese products are subjected to tests for weight, presence of foreign elements or chemicals, and for taste and smell. What customer-related measures might interlink with these internal measures?
8. What information would you need to fully answer the questions that IBM Rochester uses for selecting measures and indicators:
   • Does the measurement support our mission?
   • Will the measurement be used to manage change?
   • Is it important to our customers?
   • Is it effective in measuring performance?
   • Is it effective in forecasting results?
   • Is it easy to understand/simple?
   • Are the data easy/cost-efficient to collect?
   • Does the measurement have validity, integrity, and timeliness?
   • Does the measure have an owner?
      Where would you get this information?
9. Using information you learned in prior courses in statistics or quantitative methods, discuss some analytical approaches that organizations can use for analyzing performance data.

10. A large hospital identified the following strategic priorities:
    - Patient accessibility
    - Patient safety
    - Clinical excellence
    - Few hassles for patients and families
    - Workforce well-being

    - Family-centered care
    - Operational efficiency

    Suggest some measures that link to these strategic priorities. You might wish to do some research on how hospitals measure patient safety and clinical excellence.

PROJECTS, ETC.

1. Interview managers at a local airline, hospital, governmental agency, or police department to determine what types of performance measures or indicators they use. Can you construct a balanced scorecard for them?

2. Many restaurants and hotels use "tabletop" customer satisfaction surveys. Find several of these from local businesses. What internal performance indicators might be good leading indicators for the customer satisfaction items in the surveys?

3. Interview managers at a local company to identify the key factors that drive their business. What performance measures or indicators does the company use? Are these indicators consistent with their business factors?

4. Interview managers at a local company to determine which, if any, of the leading practices described in this chapter they follow. What advice would you give them?

CASES

COYOTE COMMUNITY COLLEGE

Coyote Community College (a fictitious entity) is a comprehensive, two-year public college that serves and strengthens the greater Albuquerque, New Mexico, community by providing postsecondary education and learning opportunities to all who want to identify and develop their abilities and interests. Since 1968, Coyote's programs and services have been providing accessible, affordable, high-quality higher education opportunities in a learning environment that encourages challenging, innovative teaching methods and delivery systems that enhance student learning. Coyote is a commuter college with a main campus in downtown Albuquerque and two branch campuses: one located in Bernalillo, 20 miles north of Albuquerque, and the other in Armijo, southeast of downtown Albuquerque. The campus in Albuquerque accounts for 44 percent of Coyote's enrollment, the Bernalillo campus accounts for 25 percent, and the Armijo campus accounts for 31 percent.

Coyote's innovative, community-centered educational programs are designed to meet a variety of academic, career, and personal educational goals. Program offerings fall into one of three general areas: (1) General Education, University Transfer Education, and Developmental Education; (2) Workforce Development, Certificate Programs, and Continuing Education; and (3) Community Education and Outreach. The majority of these programs lead to the award of diplomas, degrees, or certificates. Coyote also provides high-quality student support services and resources in collaboration with community agencies to enable students to formulate their goals and pursue them realistically. These services include academic and occupational counseling, job and educational placement services, assistance in obtaining financial aid, and special needs programs.

Programs and offerings in the area of General Education, University Transfer Education, and Developmental Education enable students to achieve academic and personal goals, enter the job market, or, in some cases, to successfully transfer to four-year colleges and universities. Coyote offers Associate of Arts (AA) degrees in liberal arts, business administration, education, hotel and restaurant management, computer science, pre-engineering, and biological sciences. AA degrees are intended for students transferring to four-year colleges and universities such that no remedial coursework is required upon transfer. Occupational programs in technical, vocational, and paraprofessional fields lead to an Associate of Science (AS) degree or a certificate. Occupational programs also provide retraining and upgrading of skills in these fields so that students are qualified to meet current needs of the labor market. AS degrees are generally not intended for transfer to four-year institutions. Students who do transfer with AS degrees are required to take additional remedial courses as required by each specific degree program. Students may select from 30 occupational programs, including computer technology, computer applications, day care management, nursing, retailing, computer-aided design/computer-aided manufacturing (CAD/CAM), graphic design technology, biotechnology, heating-ventilating-air conditioning (HVAC), hydrological technology, and contract administration.

In the area of Developmental Education, Coyote offers General Education Development (GED) preparation courses, courses in English as a Second Language (ESL), and strong remedial courses in math, reading, and writing. Sixty percent of all Coyote students enrolled in traditional college courses enroll in at least one remedial course, and 15 percent enroll in an ESL course.

In the area of Workforce Development, Certificate Programs, and Continuing Education, Coyote provides custom-designed, on-site training courses and services that meet the needs of local businesses. In partnership with several local employers, Coyote offers contract training for computer networking technicians, water management specialists, office managers, contract administrators, and prison guards. Coyote also offers intensive ESL and remedial English and math courses under contract. In addition, Coyote offers a wide variety of short-term certification courses, such as Network Administrator, Network Engineer, Advanced Office Automation, Systems Engineer, Quality Auditor, Purchasing Manager, and Certified Nursing Assistant, to the general public and by contract. Continuing Education programs address those students who wish to improve professional skills, acquire new skills, or expand their fields of knowledge and general interest.

In the area of Community Education and Outreach, Coyote provides programs and community services that offer multicultural, recreational, and community development activities to meet the needs of lifelong learners. These activities, which include a Women in Transition program, the Coyote Cultural Center, an Elder Learning Center, and a day care center, also encourage the use of community college facilities and services by all citizens of the community for educational and cultural purposes.

Students at Coyote are divided among (1) those enrolled in traditional college credit degree curricula, (2) those enrolled in noncredit contract training and in short-term certificate courses, and (3) those involved in the community outreach programs. Because of demands placed on their resources and time by employers, family, and others, students tend to pursue the education intermittently, and approximately 75 percent of students attend part-time.

Coyote employs 280 full-time faculty, 830 adjunct (part-time) faculty, 40 administrators, and 150 support staff. The faculty are members of the National Education Association union. Fifty percent of full-time faculty hold a master's degree, 40 percent hold doctoral degrees, and 10 percent hold bachelor's degrees. Adjunct faculty, many of whom are working in the field in which they teach, hold at least a bachelor's degree. Seventy-five percent of the administrators hold a master's degree or higher.

Although Coyote's primary stakeholders are its students, key stakeholders also include college faculty and staff, four-year colleges and universities to which Coyote's students transfer, local employers, the New Mexico State Board of Community Colleges, Coyote's Board of Governors (BOG), and the surrounding community at large, including local taxpayers. The requirements of the primary stakeholders are shown in Figure 12.14.

Coyote's oversight body is the BOG. The members of Coyote's BOG are elected by voters in seven geographical districts within the two-county region the college serves. Funding for programs and for most construction and equipment comes from a property tax levy in the two-county region and annual appropriations by the New Mexico legislature. Coyote's BOG approves spending over $50,000, intergovernmental agreements, bond spending, building improvements, and construction. The BOG also provides continuous evaluation and assessment of Coyote's policies, procedures, and practices to ensure that the college is fulfilling its mission and achieving its purposes. In addition, Coyote has a private nonprofit foundation for private contributions, which are increasing every year.

FIGURE 12.14   Stakeholders and Requirements

Stakeholder	Requirements
Students	Acquisition of needed skills and knowledge, learning skill development, accessibility, flexibility in scheduling, affordability, increased capacity for self-directed learning, responsive services, effective curriculum
Faculty/Staff	Receive professional development, feedback, support, recognition
Four-year colleges and universities	Strong student academic foundations compatible with higher learning
Employers	Current/future employees' acquisition of needed skills/ knowledge/attitude, cost-efficient learning, innovative problem-solving and team skills, leadership skills, computer proficiency, professional proficiency
SBCC and BOG	Return for dollar
Taxpayers and community	Fulfillment of education needs that are not met by other institutions, support to region/state, efficient expenditure of funding

Coyote is accredited by the North Central Association of Colleges and Schools (NCACS), and 12 individual programs are certified or accredited by other appropriate organizations. Coyote was reviewed by the NCACS in 1998 and is scheduled for another review in 2008. Coyote is also responsive to a variety of federal, state, and local regulations, including the Occupational Safety and Health Administration (OSHA) requirements, Environmental Protection Agency (EPA) regulations, federal and state financial aid regulations, and affirmative action guidelines. Coyote complies with the Americans with Disabilities Act (ADA). Coyote is also proud of its partnerships with the colleges and universities to which the majority of its credit students transfer. Faculty members from these universities serve on Coyote's Curriculum Advisory Teams. In addition, articulation agreements with all four-year institutions in the region are in place for all of Coyote's university transfer programs (AA degrees), as well as for more than 50 percent of the occupational degree programs.

A key differentiator of online programs offered by out-of-state colleges is convenience. Students can attend online courses any time of the day or night to accommodate their busy and sometimes changing schedules. Coyote is responding to this need by developing both online and video-based programs. In addition, Coyote's key differentiator is that it focuses on preparing graduates to be successful in the local community. Input of local employers in the planning process, new program design, and student internships enables Coyote's graduates to find desirable jobs in the local community more easily and to succeed at those jobs. Coyote's growing, individualized, technology-based delivery of educational programs with related support services (individualized program design and certification), which is targeted to employed adult students with needs for specific skill development, is another important competitive advantage. Planning is focused on providing learning excellence through use of state-of-the-art learning technologies to expand the off-campus student population while retaining the current levels of on-campus students.

The principal factors that determine competitive success include accessibility, flexibility in scheduling, affordability, ability to offer high value at a low cost, the effectiveness of the curriculum, the time to complete programs, and the range of programs offered. Dr. Gayle Brooks, who previously served as Deputy Provost at McMoto Industrial University, was selected as Coyote's president in 1992, with a mandate to reverse a six-year-long trend of declining enrollment and diminishing student success. In the last eight years, Coyote has shown steady increases in enrollment and in student success as judged by student employment rates and acceptance rates by four-year colleges and universities. The foundation of this turnaround was the establishment of a common mission, vision, and values. These provide continuing direction for the college and drive specific goals to stretch Coyote's capabilities. In 1994, under the direction of Dr. Brooks, Coyote developed and adopted LEARN, a three-point philosophy of education. These points are:

- *Learning Excellence:* All aspects of the education process are learner-centered, and the needs of the learner are paramount. Recognition of the diversity of learning styles and rates of learning is fundamental. Technology is used as a tool to facilitate learning.
- *Assessment:* Assessment of learning is ongoing for both learners and learning facilitators. Technology is a tool to facilitate the assessment of processes associated with learning.
- *Recognizing Needs:* It is imperative to identify and respond to the needs of all of Coyote's stakeholders. Needs vary by stakeholder, as shown in Figure 12.14.

As a result of implementing LEARN, Coyote recently identified the following three key technology-based strategies designed to improve student learning and meet learner requirements. Each of these strategies is currently at different levels of implementation within the college:

1. *Incorporation of technologies into the traditional classroom.* In order to enhance student learning, instructors are being encouraged to incorporate multimedia into traditional delivery techniques.

2. *Technology mediation allowing individually paced learning.* Computer-based instruction allows learners to begin precisely at their current level of knowledge and progress through structured materials at their own pace. Monthly start dates of sequenced courses allow students to proceed to the next course when ready, with no delays or potential loss of learning due to waiting.

3. *Distance learning delivery methods.* A variety of technologies allow Coyote to meet learner needs. An interactive video system (teleclasses) ties the three campuses together to decrease the need for students to drive from one campus to another. This system also allows Coyote to offer some traditionally low enrollment courses that meet specific student needs, including upper-level foreign language and math classes. Online courses offered via the Internet and video-based courses (telecourses) offered via cable television and video cassette checkout will meet the needs of students with difficult schedules and geographic constraints.

The leadership at Coyote wants to develop a balanced scorecard. To customize it for the educational environment, they renamed the categories as

1. Funder/Financial Perspective
2. Student/Participant Perspective
3. Internal Process Perspective
4. Innovation and Resource Perspective

Based on the description of this college and its environment, what specific types of measures should they include in each of these perspectives of the balanced scorecard? How would they be measured?

TRIVIEW BANK: IDENTIFYING KEY PERFORMANCE MEASURES

The complete TriView Bank case study, a fictitious example of a Baldrige application, can be found in the Baldrige Materials folder on the Student Companion Site. Review the Organizational Profile and then the response to Category 7 of the Baldrige criteria (Results). After carefully analyzing the measures used in tracking their performance results in comparison with their vital organizational factors and strategic challenges, identify gaps in their performance measurement system. For example, what other measures might be relevant to managing their business that they have not reported? Are all measures reported appropriately segmented (for instance, by location, type of employee, type of customer, and so on)? Summarize your findings as a consultant to the organization in a well-written report to the company president.

TRIVIEW BANK: MEASUREMENT, ANALYSIS, AND KNOWLEDGE MANAGEMENT

The complete TriView Bank case study, a fictitious example of a Baldrige application, can be found in the Baldrige Materials folder on the Student Companion Site. If you have not read the Organizational Profile yet, please do so first. Examine their response to Category 4 in the context of the practices described in this chapter (you need not consider the actual Baldrige criteria for this activity). What are their strengths? What are their weaknesses and opportunities for improvement? What specific advice, including useful tools and techniques that might help them, would you suggest?

NOTES

1. Jerry Useem, "Boeing Versus Boeing," *Fortune*, October 2, 2000, 148–160.
2. D. Osborne and T. Gaebler, *Reinventing Government: How the Entrepreneurial Spirit Is Transforming the Public Sector* (Reading, MA: Addison-Wesley Publishing Co., 1992).
3. Kicab Casteñeda-Méndez, "Performance Measurement in Health Care," *Quality Digest*, May 1999, 33–36.
4. Douglas W. Hubbard, *How to Measure Anything*, Hoboken, NJ: John Wiley & Sons, 2007.
5. Laura Struebing, "Measuring for Excellence," *Quality Progress*, December 1996, 25–28.
6. Robert S. Kaplan and David P. Norton, *The Balanced Scorecard* (Boston, MA: Harvard Business School Press, 1996), 1.
7. Robert S. Kaplan and David P. Norton, "The Balanced Scorecard—Measures That Drive Performance," *Harvard Business Review*, January/February 1992, 71–79. © 1992 by the President and Fellows of Harvard College; all rights reserved.
8. Ernest C. Huge, "Measuring and Rewarding Performance," in Ernst & Young Quality Consulting Group, *Total Quality: An Executive's Guide for the 1990s* (Homewood IL: Irwin, 1990).
9. New Corporate Performance Measures, A Research Report, Report Number 1118-95-RR, New York: The Conference Board, 1995.
10. John Geanuracos and Ian Meiklejohn, *Performance Measurement: The New Agenda; Using Non-Financial Indicators to Improve Profitability* (London: Business Intelligence, 1993).
11. Arthur M. Schneiderman, "Why Balanced Scorecards Fail," *Journal of Strategic Performance Measurement* 3, no. 1 (January 1999), 6–11.
12. Blan Godfrey, "Future Trends: Expansion of Quality Management Concepts, Methods, and Tools to All Industries," *Quality Observer* 6, no. 9 (September 1997) 40–43, 46.

13. Mark Graham Brown, *Keeping Score: Using the Right Metrics to Drive World-Class Performance* (New York: Quality Resources, 1996).
14. "First National Bank of Chicago," *Profiles in Quality* (Boston, MA: Allyn and Bacon, 1991).
15. Justin Martin, "Are You as Good as You Think You Are?" *Fortune*, September 30, 1996, 142–152.
16. Robert I. Wise, "A Method for Aligning Process Level and Strategy Level Performance Metrics," American Society for Quality, 11th Annual Quality Management Conference.
17. Marcelo Telles de Menezes and Roberto Antonio Martins, "Performance Measurement After ERP Implementation: Some Empirical Evidences," *Proceedings*, Third World Congress on Intelligent Manufacturing Processes & Systems, Cambridge, MA, June 2000, 146–151.
18. Thomas Bertels, "The Art of Measuring What Matters," *iSixSigma Magazine*, November/December 2010, 36–38.
19. David A. Collier, *The Service/Quality Solution* (Milwaukee, WI: ASQC Quality Press, and Burr Ridge, IL: Richard D. Irwin, 1994).
20. Steve Hoisington and Earl Naumann, "The Loyalty Elephant," *Quality Progress*, February 2003, pp. 33–41.
21. Reprinted with permission from Steven H. Hoisington and Tse-Hsi Huang, "Customer Satisfaction and Market Share: An Empirical Case Study of IBM's AS/400 Division," in Earl Naumann and Steven H. Hoisington (eds.), *Customer-Centered Six Sigma*. Copyright © 2001 American Society for Quality, Quality Press, Milwaukee, WI. No further distribution allowed without permission.
22. "Coaxing Meaning Out of Raw Data," *Business Week*, February 3, 1997, 134–138.
23. Mercy Health System 2007 Malcolm Baldrige National Quality Program Application.
24. Larry English, "Data Quality: Meeting Customer Needs," *Data Management Review*, November 1996, 44–51, 86.
25. Ethan I. Davis, "Quality Service at The Prudential," in Jay W. Spechler, *When America Does It Right* (Norcross,

GA: Industrial Engineering and Management Press, 1988), 224–232.

26. Comment made at the Knowledge Management World Summit, San Francisco, January 11, 1999; cited in R. Sabherwal and S. Sabherwal, "Knowledge Management Using Information Technology: Determinants of Short-Term Impact on Firm Value," *Decision Sciences* 36, no. 4 (2005), pp. 531–567.

27. Robert J. Heibeler, "Benchmarking Knowledge Management," *Strategy and Leadership* 24, no. 2 (March/April, 1996), as cited in Verna Allee, *The Knowledge Evolution: Expanding Organizational Intelligence* (Boston: Butterworth-Heinemann, 1997), 8.

28. Chuck Cobb, "Knowledge Management and Quality Systems," The 54th Annual Quality Congress *Proceedings*, 2000, American Society for Quality, 276–287.

29. 2007 Premier Baldrige Application Summary.

30. Carla O'Dell and C. Jackson Grayson, "Identifying and Transferring Internal Best Practices," APQC White Paper, 2000; http://www.apqc.org/free/whitepapers/cmifwp/index.htm.

31. Mohamed Zairi and John Whymark, "The Transfer of Best Practices: How to Build a Culture of Benchmarking and Continuous Learning—Part 1," *Benchmarking: An International Journal* 7, no. 1 (2000), 62–78.

32. This discussion is adapted from Michael J. English and William H. Baker, Jr. "Rapid Knowledge Transfer: The Key to Success," *Quality Progress*, February 2006, pp. 41–48.

33. Adapted from Nicholas J. Mathys and Kenneth R. Thompson, "Using the Balanced Scorecard: Lessons Learned from the U.S. Postal Service and the Defense Finance and Accounting Service."

34. Research provided by APQC, the international resource for benchmarks and best practices, © 2012 APQC. All rights reserved.

Leadership for Performance Excellence

Although Hyundai Motor Co. dominated the Korean car market in its early days, it had a poor reputation for quality overseas, with doors that didn't fit properly, frames that rattled, and engines that delivered puny acceleration. And the company was losing money. When Chung Mong Koo became CEO in 1999, he visited Hyundai's plant at Ulsan. To the shock of his employees, who had rarely set eyes on a CEO, Chung strode onto the factory floor and demanded a peek under the hood of a Sonata sedan. He didn't like what he saw: loose wires, tangled hoses, bolts painted four different colors—the kind of sloppiness you'd never see in a Japanese car. On the spot, he instructed the plant chief to paint all bolts and screws black and ordered workers not to release a car unless all was orderly under the hood. "You've got to get back to basics. The only way we can survive is to raise our quality to Toyota's level," he fumed. In addition to investing heavily in research and development, he created a quality control czar, who studied quality manuals of U.S. and Japanese automakers and developed one for the company, making it clear who is responsible for each manufacturing step, what outcome is required, and who checks and confirms performance levels. The next year, U.S. sales rose by 42 percent, and Hyundai is now recognized as one of the leading auto companies in the world.[1]

As this example suggests, achieving quality and performance excellence in an organization requires strong and committed leadership. Nevertheless, a codirector of the Juran Center for Leadership in Quality at the University of Minnesota observed:

- Despite substantial efforts, only a few U.S. organizations have reached world-class excellence.
- Even fewer companies have sustained such excellence during changes in leadership.
- Most corporate quality failures rest with leadership.[2]

Clearly, leadership is not an easy task.

Leadership was prominent in Deming's 14 Points, as well as the philosophies of Juran and Crosby. Several of Deming's 14 Points address leadership issues; for instance:

Point 1. Create and publish to all employees a statement of the aims and purposes of the company or other organization. The management must demonstrate constantly their commitment to this statement.

Point 7. Teach and institute leadership.

Point 12. Remove barriers that rob people of pride of workmanship.

Point 14. Take action to accomplish the transformation.

Leadership is also the first category in the Baldrige framework, signifying its importance in driving quality and performance excellence throughout an organization.

As one professional observed, managers manage for the present; leaders lead for the future. Effective leadership demands continual learning and adaption to the changing global business landscape. An important element of organizational sustainability is ensuring future leadership; thus the development of future leaders and a formal succession plan are vital. A 2011 survey of CEOs sponsored by The Conference Board identified talent as one of the most pressing leadership challenges.[3] The top two global strategies for addressing this challenge were to improve leadership development programs to grow talent internally and to enhance the effectiveness of the senior management team.

In this chapter, we focus on the role of leadership for guiding organizations through the process of creating a culture for performance excellence.

quality**profiles**

The Studer Group and Saint Luke's Hospital of Kansas City

Founded in 1999, the Studer Group is a private, for-profit health care consulting firm providing coaching, teaching, and evidenced-based tools and tactics to health care organizations and rural hospitals throughout the United States. Studer Group's senior leadership has embedded Evidence-Based Leadership (EBL) within the organization to provide the framework for its internal operations. Employing EBL processes supported by Studer's Leader Evaluation Manager™ software (which tracks goals and their achievement) and other leadership approaches, senior leaders have aligned goals, behaviors, and processes to achieve transparent communication, high performance, and workforce engagement.

Senior leaders have created a culture at Studer Group that is values-driven, transparent, and fosters passion for making a difference. This is accomplished through personal modeling of values, coupled with specific "must have" tactics for selecting, engaging, empowering, and retaining workforce members. Studer Group integrates its customer support system with its employee performance management processes to create a culture focused on a positive customer experience. The firm models the Evidence-Based Leadership service excellence it teaches and identifies its key support mechanism as "people interacting with people."

To support its key local community and the health care industry, Studer Group disseminates much of its evidence-based knowledge without charge to local organizations and the entire care community. Additionally, Studer Group offers in-kind donations of free coaching and training to local nonprofit organizations, as well as sponsorships and monetary grants for attendance at its conferences. The company's monetary and in-kind charitable donations amount to 5.1 to 6.9 percent of its net income. With a focus on financial sustainability, Studer Group's revenues have grown more than 30 percent annually since 2001, exceeding the Association of Management Consulting Firms (AMCF) average of 10 percent annual growth.

Saint Luke's Hospital (SLH) is the largest hospital in the Kansas City, Mo., metropolitan area. It is a not-for-profit comprehensive teaching and referral health care organization that provides 24-hour coverage in every health care discipline. SLH is driven by its vision, "The Best Place to Get Care, The Best Place to Give Care," and its core values of Quality/Excellence, Customer Focus, Resource Management, and Teamwork. Saint Luke's "Leadership for Performance Excellence + Model" captures all of the elements that drive its focus on performance improvement and excellence, including the strategic planning and performance

management process, process improvement model, and a commitment to excellence assessment model based on the seven Baldrige performance excellence categories. Saint Luke's vision, mission, core values, and strategy sit at the top of the model and influence all of the organization's plans and processes. A robust strategic planning approach consists of three phases and seven steps that integrate direction setting, strategy development and deployment, financial planning, and plan management. At a series of retreats, the leadership team develops strategy and uses a 90-day action planning process to deploy the strategy to all departments. The balanced scorecard process produces a measurement system that aligns all departments with the strategy and ensures the proper focus in key performance areas throughout the organization.

To ensure that everyone is in tune with the hospital's focus, all employees take part in the Performance Management Process. The process helps employees develop action plans and goals that are aligned with the organization's strategy and core values and identify personal commitments which contribute to SLH's values. An independent study by the National Research Corporation shows that patients believe SLH delivers the best quality health care and has the best doctors and the best nurses of the 21 facilities in the market area.

Sources: Baldrige Award Profiles of Winners, National Institute of Standards and Technology, Department of Commerce.

LEADERSHIP COMPETENCIES AND PRACTICES

Leadership is the ability to positively influence people and systems under one's authority so as to have a meaningful impact and achieve important results.

The Human Development and Leadership Division of the American Society for Quality has summarized six competencies for leadership based on more than 50 authors' thoughts on leadership.[4] These are:

- *Navigator*: Creates shared meaning and provides direction towards a vision, mission, goal or end-result. This competency may entail risk taking and requires constant evaluation of the operating environment to ensure progress in the appropriate direction is achieved.
- *Communicator*: Effectively listens and articulates messages to provide shared meaning. This competency involves the creation of an environment that reduces barriers and fosters open, honest and honorable communication.
- *Mentor*: Provides others with a role to guide their actions. This competency requires the development of personal relationships that help others develop trust, integrity, and ethical decision-making.

- *Learner*: Continuously develops personal knowledge, skills, and abilities through formal study, experience, reflection, and recreation.
- *Builder*: Shapes processes and structures to allow for the achievement of goals and outcomes. This competency also entails assuming responsibility for ensuring necessary resources are available and the evaluation of processes to ensure effective resource use.
- *Motivator*: Influences others to take action in a desirable manner. This competency also includes the evaluation of people's actions to ensure they are performing consistently with the mission, goal, or end-result.

A collection of personal leadership characteristics underlie these six competencies:

1. *Accountability:* Taking responsibility for the organization, community, or self that the leader serves. This provides the means for measuring performance and dealing with performance that is not good.
2. *Courage:* The mental or moral strength to venture, persevere, and withstand danger, fear, or difficulty with a firmness of mind and will, allowing leaders to navigate into the unknown.
3. *Humility:* What gives excellent leaders their ability to mentor, communicate, and learn, and understand that they are servants of those that follow.
4. *Integrity:* The ability to discern what is right from wrong and commit to the right path.
5. *Creativity:* The ability to see possibilities, horizons, and futures that don't yet exist, enabling the leader to help create a shared vision.
6. *Perseverance:* Sticking to a task or purpose, no matter how hard or troublesome. This is vital to overcoming obstacles and motivating subordinates.
7. *Well-Being:* The ability to stay healthy in both work and play, demonstrating the importance of being ready to implement leadership competencies when needed.

These characteristics provide the foundation for exercising the competencies. Many notable leaders, from presidents to CEOs, have exhibited these characteristics.

 QUALITYSPOTLIGHT

Baptist Hospital, Inc.

Baptist Hospital, Inc. (BHI) is part of the Baptist Health Care System in Florida. Senior leaders set a vision of becoming the best health system in America, and decided to rebuild the organization by engaging its staff and listening to its patients. One of their first actions was to create a flat, fluid, and open leadership system based on communication. Under this new system, staff are not just encouraged, they are expected to contact anyone in the organization, including the president, at any time to discuss work issues and improvement opportunities. To reinforce this message, the president established an "open-door" office that has a large glass window facing the busiest part of the hospital. Senior leaders also serve as role models and are personally engaged in creating a "no secrets" environment through activities such as the Daily Line-up, in which all leaders and employees gather at each shift to review information in the *Baptist Daily*, and quarterly around-the-clock employee forums. They are also accountable for organizational performance through a "No Excuses" policy.[5]

These leadership competencies are reflected in the Leadership category of the Baldrige criteria, which are summarized in Table 13.1. These practices are accomplished in many ways. For instance, CEOs often lead quality training sessions, serve on quality improvement teams, work on projects that do not usually require top-level input, and personally visit customers. Senior managers at the former Texas Instruments Defense Systems & Electronics Group, for example, led 150 of 1,900 cross-functional teams. In small businesses, such as

TABLE 13.1   Key Practices for Performance Excellence Leadership

- Set organizational vision and values and deploy them through the organization's leadership system, to the workforce, to key suppliers and partners, and to customers and other stakeholders as appropriate.
- Demonstrate a commitment to organizational values through personal actions.
- Promote an organizational environment that fosters, requires, and leads to legal and ethical behavior.
- Foster a sustainable organization by creating (1) an environment for organizational performance improvement, the accomplishment of the organization's mission and strategic objectives, innovation, competitive or role-model performance leadership, and organizational agility; (2) an environment for organizational and workforce learning; (3) a culture that fosters customer engagement; and developing and enhancing leadership skills and developing future organizational leaders.
- Communicate with and engage the entire workforce by encouraging frank, two-way communication throughout the organization, communicating key decisions, and taking an active role in reward and recognition programs to reinforce high performance and a customer and business focus.
- Create a focus on action to accomplish the organization's objectives, improve performance, and attain the organization's vision.
- Create and balance value for customers and other stakeholders in their organizational performance expectations.
- Maintain an effective governance system that provides for accountability for management's actions, transparency, and protection of stakeholder and stockholder interests.
- Evaluate performance of senior leadership and use performance reviews to improve personal leadership effectiveness.
- Actively support and strengthen key communities such as charitable organizations, education, and others.

Marlow Industries, CEO and president Raymond Marlow chairs the TQM Council and has daily responsibility for quality-related matters. To help accomplish its goals, General Electric redefined its promotion standards around quality. In the new standards, managers are not considered for promotions, and face dismissal, unless they visibly demonstrate support for the company's Six Sigma quality strategy.[6]

Successful leaders continually promote their vision throughout the organization using many forms of communication: personal interaction, talks, newsletters, seminars, e-mail, and video. For example, senior leaders communicate Medrad's values, direction, and expectations to all employees through the President's monthly highlights, a memorandum that summarizes trends and performance on each of the five goals listed above and provides special recognition for teams and individuals. Other key communication methods include Quarterly Business Reviews (QBR), Quarterly Management Interaction (QMI) sessions, Quality Forums, advisory board and function leadership, cross-functional team participation, staff meetings, the performance management system, participation in training for new and existing employees, and the annual "all-employee" meetings.

At Park Place Lexus, a Baldrige recipient, senior leaders receive feedback through employee surveys, committee findings, self-assessments, external consultant input, and Organizational Excellence department input, and use it to create training and development plans such as better business skills or team building.

Strategic Leadership

Providing a motivating environment in which work can take place in a productive and meaningful way and assuring that performance excellence is continuously pursued are the essential tasks of organizational leaders. Thus, strategy and leadership are closely linked. For a strategy to be successful, senior leaders must have extensive involvement in the planning process, create an environment for competitive success and performance leadership, and guide the design of the work and leadership systems that will ensure that the strategy is carried out.

Management theorists and practitioners have long recognized the differences between the work of senior leaders and those who perform supervisory roles at the operating levels. Senior leaders must think globally, while acting locally (in both a geographic and conceptual sense). This has been driven by the explosion in knowledge and complexity in the global business environment. In a study conducted by International Consortium for Executive Development Research,[7] 1,450 executives from 12 global companies were asked the question: "What are the key competencies that will emerge as critical for leadership effectiveness in the next three years?" Among 45 competencies that were suggested, the top one was: "articulate a tangible vision, values, and strategy." This was followed closely by "be a catalyst/manager of strategic change" and "get results—manage strategy to action."

These perspectives have led to the concept of **strategic leadership**, which can be defined as "a person's ability to anticipate, envision, maintain flexibility, think strategically, and work with others to initiate changes that will create a viable future for the organization, and its competitive advantage to the organization in this way."[8] Activities that strategic leaders perform generally include creating and communicating a vision of the future, sustaining an effective organization culture, making strategic decisions, developing key competencies and responsibilities, managing multiple constituencies, selecting and developing the next generation of leaders, and infusing ethical value systems into an organization's culture. Effective strategic leaders also have the capability to create and maintain what is termed absorptive capacity (the ability for an organization to learn) and adaptive capacity (the ability of an organization to change) in order to deal with increasingly hyper-turbulent environments.[9] Such leaders must also exhibit managerial wisdom, with the ability to perceive variation in their environment and understand the social actors and their relationship in the system.

Strategic leadership can also be viewed from three levels. For instance, senior leaders are involved in vision and strategy formulation, mid-level leaders develop executable action plans and projects that best use an organization's resources, and supervisory leaders ensure that these action plans are deployed throughout the organization so that essential tasks and projects may be accomplished in support of the strategic vision.[10]

The concept of strategic leadership has moved leadership perspectives away from the solitary "great leader" paradigm toward a team- and system-based "great group" concept.[11] Thus, the characteristics of effective strategic leadership include

- Serving as both leaders and team members;
- Demonstrating the importance of integrity through actions rather than simply articulating it;
- Thinking in terms of processes rather than outcomes;
- Leveraging the collective knowledge of everyone in the organization;
- Designing work that reflects relationships rather than the organizational hierarchy;
- Anticipating environmental change rather than reacting to it;
- Viewing employees as organizational citizens rather than resources; and
- Operating with a global mindset rather than a domestic mindset.

Many of these notions of strategic leadership are reflected in the Baldrige criteria, which recognize the value of strategic leadership in driving performance excellence.

Leadership Systems

The ability to successfully perform the activities listed in Table 13.1 requires an effective leadership system. The **leadership system** refers to how leadership is exercised, formally and informally, throughout an organization. These elements include how key decisions are made, communicated, and carried out at all levels. The leadership system includes structures and mechanisms for making decisions, selection and development of leaders and managers, and reinforcement of values, directions, and performance expectations. It builds loyalties and teamwork based upon shared values, encourages initiative and risk taking, and subordinates organization to purpose and function. An effective leadership system also includes mechanisms for leaders' self-examination and improvement.

To illustrate these themes, we highlight the leadership system at Stoner Incorporated, a very small chemical specialty manufacturing and sales company with fewer than 50 employees. Stoner has a six-member senior leadership team empowered by the owner to manage and lead the company. The leadership team created and refined the Stoner Excellence System to define and communicate to all team members how the business is run. This is depicted by the diagram in Figure 13.1. The system is based on Leadership, Strategy, and Process, which are combined with an Assess/Improve/Implement continuous improvement approach. Stakeholder value is at the center of the system to characterize the main focus on the customer. Stoner's leadership approach is built on (1) leadership at all levels, (2) worker leaders, and (3) strong fundamental leadership skills based on Stephen Covey's Seven Habits of Highly Effective People.

The use of steering teams of senior managers is prevalent in many leadership systems. Such teams assume many responsibilities such as incorporating total quality principles into the company's strategic planning process and coordinating the overall effort. At AT&T, the steering team is characterized by several essential elements.[12]

- *Leadership*: Promoting and articulating the quality vision, communicating responsibilities and expectations for management action, aligning the business management process with the quality approach, maintaining high visibility for commitment and involvement, and ensuring that business-wide support is available in the form of education, consulting, methods, and tools.
- *Planning*: Planning strategic quality goals, understanding basic customer needs and business capabilities, developing long-term goals and near-term priorities, formulating human resource goals and policies, understanding employees' perceptions about quality and work, ensuring that all employees have the opportunity and skills to participate, and aligning reward and recognition systems to support the quality approach.
- *Implementation*: Forming key business process teams, chartering teams to manage and improve these processes, reviewing improvement plans, providing resources for improvement, enlisting all managers in the process, reviewing quality plans of major organizational units, and working with suppliers and business partners in joint quality planning.
- *Review*: Tracking progress through customer satisfaction and internal measures of quality, monitoring progress in attaining improvement objectives, celebrating successes, improving the quality system through auditing and identifying improvement opportunities, planning improvements, and validating the impact of improvements.

FIGURE 13.1 Stoner Business Excellence System

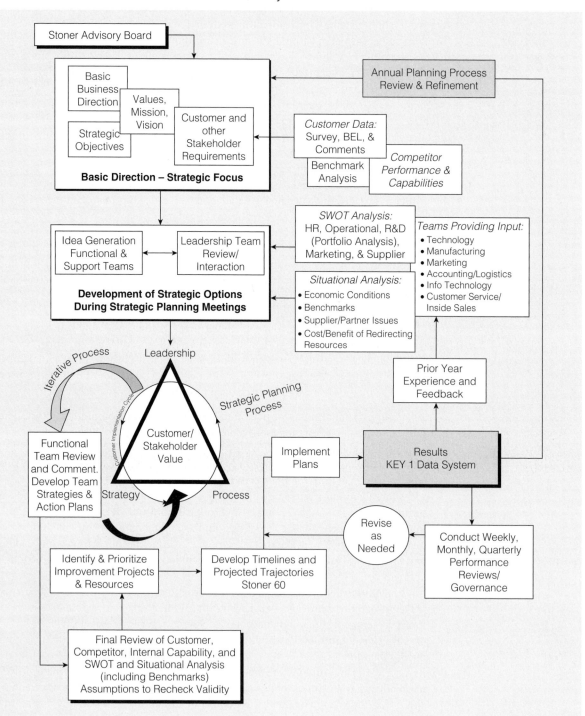

Source: Malcolm Baldridge National Quality Award Application Summary, 2005. Reprinted with permission of Stoner, Inc., www.moreshine.com.

LEADERSHIP THEORY AND PRACTICE

To understand how leadership is developed and practiced, it is important to understand its theoretical foundations. The purpose of leadership theories is to explain differences in leadership styles and contexts. Dozens of leadership theories have been derived from literally thousands of leadership studies. Unlike some areas of quality management that are only a few decades old, leadership theories can often be traced back 50–75 years or more.

Many leadership theories of the twentieth century are extensions or modifications of the work of Max Weber, a German lawyer, politician, historian, political economist, and sociologist.[13] Weber classified the way leaders exercise authority into three patterns:

- Rational-legal leadership, which is established by policies, rules, and laws. An example is government officials who legislate, execute, and enforce regulations.
- Traditional leadership, which extends from customs, habits, and social structures, and often involves the passing of position and power from one generation to the next, such as in monarchies or family-owned businesses.
- Charismatic leadership, which is based on an individual's ability to inspire others and usually is tied to that person's personal characteristics.

A comprehensive review of leadership theories is well beyond the scope of this text. However, the theories are quite important within the context of quality and performance excellence; therefore, we provide a brief summary of the most popular leadership approaches and discuss their implications for performance excellence. Table 13.2 summarizes some of the key theories that have influenced today's leadership styles.

TABLE 13.2   Classification of Leadership Theories[14]

Leadership Theory	Pioneer/Developer	Type of Theory
"Great man" model	Ralph Stogdill	Trait
Ohio State Studies	E. A. Fleishman, E. F. Harris et al.	Leader behavior
Michigan Studies	Rensis Likert	
Theory X-Theory Y model	Douglas MacGregor	
Managerial Grid model	Robert Blake; Jane S. Mouton	
Leadership effectiveness model	Fred E. Fiedler	Contingency (situational)
Supervisory contingency decision model	V. H. Vroom & P. W.Yetton V. H. Vroom and A. G. Jago	
Situational	Hersey and Blanchard	
Managerial roles	Henry Mintzberg	Role approach
Leader-Member Exchange	George Graen et al.	Emerging theories
Charismatic theory	R. J. House; J. A. Conger	
Transformational theory	James M. Burns; N. M. Tichy and D. O. Ulrich; B. M. Bass	
Substitutes for leadership	Jon P. Howell et al.	
Emotional intelligence	Daniel Goleman et al.	

Despite this extensive body of research, the precise nature of leadership and its relationship to key variables such as subordinate satisfaction, commitment, and performance is still uncertain. As Fred Luthans observed, "It does remain pretty much of a 'black box' or unexplainable concept."[15]

Because many of the traditional and contingency leadership theories are developed more fully in principles of management and organizational behavior courses, their characteristics will not be explored in detail here. Instead, we will focus on characteristics of the "emerging" leadership theories that are generating active discussion in academic settings and are being applied in practice today.

Contemporary and Emerging Leadership Theories

Emerging leadership theories build on or enlarge traditional theory by attempting to answer questions raised, but not answered, by earlier approaches. Many of the theories we classify as "emerging" were proposed in the 1970s and 1980s and have been around for many years, but are still considered "emerging" because of the difficulty that researchers encounter in testing social science theories. It often takes decades to establish empirical evidence as to a theory's value; for example, theories of team participation that originated in the 1930s were not researched adequately until the 1950s, and for the most part, have only recently found substantial application in practice.[16]

Situational Leadership   Situational leadership, one of the better-known contingency theories of leadership offers important insights into the interaction between subordinate ability and leadership style and is taught in many executive management seminars. The theory was initially introduced in 1969 and revised in 1977 by Hersey and Blanchard. The major proposition of situational leadership theory is that the effectiveness of task and relationship-oriented leadership behaviors depends upon the maturity of a leader's subordinates. It suggests that the key contingency factor affecting leaders' choice of leadership style is the task-related maturity of the subordinates. Subordinate maturity is defined in terms of the ability of subordinates to accept responsibility for their own task-related behavior. The theory classifies leader behaviors into the two broad classes of task-oriented and relationship-oriented behaviors.[17]

According to situational leadership, leadership styles might vary from one person to another, depending on the "readiness" of subordinates, which is characterized by their skills and abilities to perform the work, and their confidence, commitment, and motivation to do it. The model defines four levels of follower maturity (readiness):

1. Unable and unwilling
2. Unable but willing
3. Able but unwilling
4. Able and willing

Blanchard and Hersey defined four leadership styles that best address these four levels of maturity (readiness):

1. *Directing.* In this style of leadership, managers define tasks and roles, and closely supervise work. Communication is generally one way—top down. This style of leader-initiated "task-oriented" behavior applies best to followers who lack the skills and knowledge to perform a job and lack confidence or commitment to their work (unable and unwilling). Little time or effort is spent on developing relationships with followers.

2. *Coaching.* In this style, leaders set the overall approach and direction but work with subordinates and allow them to manage the details. Leaders might need to provide some direction, based on experience (a task-oriented behavior), or support (relationship-oriented behavior) to individual followers having the drive and motivation to do a good job, but who might lack some experience or skills (unable but willing).

3. *Supporting.* Here, leaders allocate tasks and set direction, but the subordinate has full control over the performance of the work. These individuals do not need much supervision or direction (task-oriented behavior), but may require leadership to assist them in building motivation and confidence (relationship-oriented behavior), particularly if the task is new (able but unwilling).

4. *Delegating.* In this style, subordinates can do their work with little supervision or support (minimal task-oriented behavior). Once the work is delegated, leaders take a hands-off approach (minimal relationship-oriented behavior), except when asked to provide assistance by the subordinate. The followers can work on a project by themselves with little supervision or support (able and willing).

A leader might also apply different styles to the same person at different times. This can be difficult, as many leaders seem to be more comfortable in one style. However, the choice should not be driven by personal preference, but rather the needs of the subordinates. In fully empowered TQ organizations and those with strong self-directed teams, you would probably find the delegating style to be most prevalent. However, when introducing new skills, such as Six Sigma, into an organization, it may be necessary to provide more direct control, coaching, or support while individuals are learning and practicing new skills or are transitioning into new job responsibilities. As managers work with different individuals in different stages of careers and maturity, it is their responsibility to adapt the leadership style to the individual and the situation.[18]

Although situational leadership theory is often used in practice, it has been criticized on both theoretical and methodological grounds, including ambiguity, a lack of consistency and incompleteness, as well as mixed empirical validation.[19] One author summarizes the controversy and contributions of situational leadership as follows:

> *A few studies found support for the proposition that more directive supervision is needed for subordinates who have low ability and confidence. However, there was little evidence that using the contingent pattern of task and relations behavior prescribed by the theory will make leaders more effective ... Despite its deficiencies, the theory has made some positive contributions to our understanding of dyadic leadership. One contribution was the emphasis on flexible adaptive behavior, which has become a central tenet of some recent theory and research.*[20]

According to the various contemporary leadership theories developed over the last 20 or 30 years, leadership effectiveness can be improved with the correct mix of the leader's style of management, the characteristics of those who are led, and the situation. Two of the most popular are transactional and transformational theory.

Transactional Leadership Theory assumes that certain leaders may develop the ability to inspire their subordinates to exert extraordinary efforts to achieve organizational goals, through behaviors that may include contingent rewards, and active and passive management by exception. Contingent reward behavior includes clarification of the work required to obtain rewards to influence motivation. Passive management by exception includes use of contingent punishments and other corrective actions in response to deviations from acceptable performance standards. Active management by exception is defined in terms of looking for mistakes and enforcing rules to avoid mistakes.

Transformational Leadership Theory was first developed by James M. Burns, and later extended by Bernard M. Bass and his colleagues.[21] According to this theory, leaders adopt many of the behaviors discussed earlier in this chapter: idealized influence, individualized consideration, inspirational motivation, and intellectual stimulation.[22] Leaders who take on a transformational style have a long-term perspective, focus on customers, promote a shared vision and values, work to stimulate their organizations intellectually, invest in training, take some risks, and treat employees as individuals.

Bass differentiated transformational from transactional leadership behavior, stating: "Transformational leaders have greater interest in continuous organizational change and improvement transcending or aligning self-interests for the longer-range greater good of the organization and its members. This is in contrast to transactional leaders, who are more focused on the satisfaction of self-interests and the maintenance of the organization's status quo."[23] In practice, however, it is often difficult to distinguish between the two theories, and research has discovered that they are distinct, but related processes. While transactional leaders may increase follower motivation and performance more than transactional leaders, effective leaders use a combination of both types, depending on the situation.[24]

Transformational leadership is more aligned with organizational change required by total quality and Baldrige-like performance excellence models. The CEOs and executive team members of nearly every Baldrige Award recipient have generally modeled this leadership behavior, and some empirical evidence found in research suggests that transformational leadership behavior is strongly correlated with lower turnover, higher productivity and quality, and higher employee satisfaction than other approaches. However, not all managers in TQ organizations need be transformational leaders. An organization pursuing TQ needs both those who establish visions and those who are effective at the day-to-day (transactional) tasks needed to achieve them.[25] In fact, Avolio and Bass extended the concept of transformational leadership by developing a hybrid of transactional and transformational leadership, which they labeled the Full Range of Leadership™ approach.[26] They noted that "Transformational leadership adds to transactional leadership in its effects on follower satisfaction and performance. Transformational leadership does not replace transactional leadership...Transactional leadership, particularly contingent rewards, provides a broad basis for leadership, but a greater amount of effort, innovation, effectiveness, risk taking, and satisfaction can be achieved by transactional leadership if it is augmented by transformational leadership."

An interesting study of patient safety in hospitals lends credibility to the role of transformational leadership in quality and performance excellence.[27] Creating a culture that supports patient safety is likely to require significant organizational change within a hospital. The study proposed that transformational leadership drives a culture of patient safety, patient safety initiatives, and positive outcomes. Using data collected from 371 hospitals, the study provided empirical evidence that improving patient safety begins at the top of the organization with a hospital CEO who possesses a transformational leadership style, and it demonstrated that this leadership style is directly related to a culture of safety within the hospital, which is tied to the successful implementation of patient safety initiatives and ultimately to improved patient safety outcomes.

The **Substitutes for Leadership theory** takes the intriguing view that in many organizations, if characteristics of subordinates (team members), the nature of the tasks that they perform, and the guidance and incentives provided by the organization are aligned, then formal leadership tends to be unproductive or counterproductive.[28] It is suggested that this leadership approach may be useful in cases of low leadership effectiveness where the leader cannot be removed for various political or other reasons (the owner's incompetent son or daughter is the "leader"), or where team member training or competence is especially high (a surgical team), or where the situation is particularly dynamic (battling oil well fires in the desert). In such situations, self-management, professional education, or even computer technology can be developed or built in to substitute for leadership. The implication for a TQ-focused organization is that each situation calls for just the right amount of leadership (not too much and not too little) in order to attain high-quality results.

Emotional Intelligence theory emerged from the observation that too much reliance had been placed on the rational side of leadership in research studies. This theory is based on five "emotional intelligence" components: (1) self-awareness, (2) self-regulation, (3) motivation, (4) empathy, and (5) social skill.[29] The theory argues that expectations for emotional intelligence are generally not captured in performance evaluation systems, but that the self-management (components 1 through 3) and interpersonal skills (components 4 and 5) represented by the five components are as essential for executive-level leaders as "traditional" intelligence (measured by IQ tests) and technical competence. The significance of emotional intelligence for effective total quality lies in translating the "vision" of an integrated leadership system and long-range planning process into action. Without credible self-management, represented by the first three components, it will be difficult for subordinates within the organization to "buy into" the vision of the leader. Without mature empathy and social skills, represented by the last two components, it will be difficult for the leader to work effectively with customers, suppliers, and others outside the organization in order to build rapport needed for long-term enterprise effectiveness, which is critical for a TQ-focused organization.

By examining characteristics of several of these leadership theories, we can see how they are applied in practice (see the Quality Spotlight about The Ritz-Carlton).

 QUALITYSPOTLIGHT

The Ritz-Carlton Hotel Company, LLC

Horst Schulze, the retired CEO of The Ritz-Carlton, and his senior leadership team take care that leaders' judgments on how to deal with subordinates in a specific situation are based on positive attributions (attribution theory). The assumption of worker competency is a given at Ritz-Carlton, even extending to the company motto of "We are ladies and gentlemen serving ladies and gentlemen."

Aspects of Transformational Leadership theory are evident during the new hotel start-up process, when senior leaders are visible, doing what transformational leaders do. These activities include taking a long-term perspective, focusing on customers, promoting a shared vision and values, working to stimulate their organizations intellectually, investing in training, taking some risks, and treating employees as individuals.

Can it be that The Ritz-Carlton's staff is expected to be like a team of oil-well firefighters? The Substitutes for Leadership theory provides some support for this notion. As outlined earlier, if characteristics of subordinates (team members), the nature of the tasks that they perform, and the guidance and incentives provided by the organization are aligned, then formal leadership tends to be unproductive or counterproductive. The Ritz-Carlton's leadership model incorporates a high level of team member training (focusing on the Gold Standards) and competence (often seen in highly professional jobs, such as surgical teams), and the situation is often very dynamic. Thus, workers must often be self-led. They "substitute for leadership" and are empowered to take action without waiting for supervisory approval.

By empowering employees as leaders at every level, The Ritz-Carlton provides an environment that will lead to the development and use of greater emotional intelligence, as outlined in Emotional Intelligence theory. Thus, the employee–guest interface and relationship management approaches that The Ritz-Carlton teaches every employee, provide interpersonal skills and supplement self-management. The components of emotionally intelligent leaders—self-awareness, self-regulation, motivation, empathy, and social skill—are regularly seen in employees' ability to be self-managed (components 1 through 3) and in their use of interpersonal skills (components 4 and 5).

New Perspectives on the Practice of Leadership[30]

The Center for Creative Leadership (CCL) has been studying the "changing nature of leadership" (CNL). CNL studies have engaged survey, interactive classroom, archival, and competitive benchmarking research. Subjects in the studies were U.S. and international top and middle managers, many of whom participated in CCL's widely-respected leadership training sessions. Two aspects of the research stand out—evidence that in an increasingly complex and chaotic business environment, critical leadership skills are trending away from "hard" analysis to "soft," collaborative ones, and that academic research journal articles are not mirroring that trend.

The research classified the types of challenges facing present and future management into three categories—technical, adaptive, and critical. Technical challenges were those that leaders and their organizations had faced in the past and built competence in solving. Adaptive challenges were those where current leadership skills had to be extended and adapted to new environments. Critical leadership skills were those required to meet discontinuous or crisis conditions, never before faced by the leader or the organization.

The research suggests that leadership skills will have to change from:

- A position to a process
- A functional orientation to a boundary-less orientation
- A focus at the top to a focus throughout the organization
- Independent decision making to interdependent decision making
- Developing via individual competencies to developing via groups and networks
- Power resulting from position to power resulting from knowledge
- Competition to collaboration
- Logical and rational to feeling and emotional
- Staying the course strategy to emergent/flexible strategy
- Selling opinions to inquiring for buy-in

Many of these changes are already evident in many organizations, particularly those that embrace quality principles, except for possibly feeling/emotional, as this conflicts with the management by fact philosophy of quality management. In the future, respondents believe organizations will continue to move towards viewing leadership as a process that happens throughout the organization through interdependent decision-making, and that organizations should continue to seek more of a balance between developing leadership through individual competencies and groups/network competencies, and between a functional versus a boundary-less orientation.

LEADERSHIP, GOVERNANCE, AND SOCIETAL RESPONSIBILITIES

An important aspect of an organization's leadership is its responsibility to the public and practice of good citizenship. General Electric's CEO Jeffrey Immelt noted, "Good leaders give back.... It's up to us to use our platform to be a good citizen. Because not only is it a nice thing to do, it's a business imperative."[31] **Corporate social responsibility (CSR)** is the "responsibility of enterprises for their impacts on society."[32] CSR implies that organizations must behave ethically and be sensitive of social, cultural, economic, and environmental issues. This includes compliance with legal and ethical standards, corporate governance, and protection of public health, safety, and environmental protection. These factors are becoming increasingly important to the workforce, to customers, and even to investors. CSR has become a strategic imperative and a competitive or marketplace necessity, particularly in the wake of corporate scandals that have occurred. Evidence suggests a positive relationship between CSR and business performance.[33] An ethical business environment creates trust from customers and employees, resulting in higher customer satisfaction, stronger employee commitment, and improved quality, all of which lead to higher profits.

The International Organization for Standardization has developed a voluntary social responsibility standard, *ISO 26000:2010 – Guidance on social responsibility*, attesting to the importance of this issue.[34] The standard provides guidance on

- concepts, terms and definitions related to social responsibility;
- the background, trends and characteristics of social responsibility;
- principles and practices relating to social responsibility;
- the core subjects and issues of social responsibility;
- integrating, implementing and promoting socially responsible behavior throughout the organization and, through its policies and practices, within its sphere of influence;
- identifying and engaging with stakeholders; and
- communicating commitments, performance and other information related to social responsibility.

The standard broadens awareness of CSR; assists organizations in addressing their social responsibilities while respecting cultural, societal, environmental and legal differences, and economic development conditions; provides practical guidance to operationalize social responsibility practices, and emphasizes performance results and improvement.

CSR has been prominent in the Baldrige Criteria since its inception.[35] In the initial 1988 Criteria, public responsibility was focused narrowly on mechanisms used for external communication of information concerning corporate support of quality assurance or improvement activities outside the company. Over the next several years, this item was expanded to include how the company extended its quality leadership to the external community and integrated its responsibilities to the public for health, safety, environmental protection, and ethical business practice into its quality policies and activities. This included how the company promoted quality awareness and sharing with external groups; how the company encouraged employee leadership and involvement in quality activities of external organizations; how the company defined and set quality improvement goals, indicators used to monitor quality, and progress reviews.

When the Baldrige Program first articulated its Core Values and Concepts in the 1992 criteria, one of the initial 10 core values was Public Responsibility:

A company's customer requirements and quality system objectives should address areas of corporate citizenship and responsibility. These include business ethics, public health and safety, environment, and sharing of quality-related information in the company's business and geographic communities. Health, safety, and environmental considerations need to take into account the life cycle of products and services and include factors such as waste generation. Quality planning in such cases should address adverse contingencies that may arise throughout the life cycle of production, distribution, and use of products. Plans should include problem avoidance and company response if avoidance fails, including how to maintain public trust and confidence. Inclusion of public responsibility areas within a quality system means not only meeting all local, state, and federal legal and regulatory requirements, but also treating these and related requirements as areas for continuous improvement. In addition, companies should support—within reasonable limits of their resources—national, industry, trade, and community activities to share nonproprietary quality-related information.

In 1993, the core value introduced the notion of treating local, state, and federal legal and regulatory requirements as areas for continuous improvement "beyond mere compliance." It also expanded on the notion of corporate citizenship, stating: "Corporate citizenship refers to leadership and support—within reasonable limits of a company's resources—of publicly important purposes, including the above-mentioned areas of corporate responsibility. Such purposes might include education, resource conservation, community services, improving industry and business practices, and sharing of nonproprietary quality-related information." This was further expanded upon in 1994 and 1995 with the additional statements "Leadership as a corporate citizen entails influencing other organizations, private and public, to partner for these purposes. For example, individual companies could lead efforts to help define the obligations of their industry to its communities."

In 2000, a significant revision was made to this core value:

An organization's leadership needs to stress its responsibilities to the public and needs to practice good citizenship. These responsibilities refer to basic expectations of your organization—business ethics and protection of public health, safety and the environment. Health, safety, and the environment include your organization's operations as well as the life cycles of your products and services. Also organizations need to emphasize resource conservation and waste reduction at the source. Planning should anticipate adverse impacts from production, distribution, transportation, use, and disposal of your products. Plans should seek to prevent problems, to provide a forthright response if problems occur, and to make available information and support needed to maintain public awareness, safety, and confidence. For many organizations, the product design stage is critical from the point of view of public responsibility. Design decisions impact your production process and the content of municipal and industrial wastes. Effective design strategies should anticipate growing environmental demands and related factors. Organizations should not only meet all local, state, and federal laws and regulatory requirements, they should treat these and related requirements as opportunities for continuous improvement "beyond mere compliance." This requires the use of appropriate measures in managing performance. Practicing good citizenship refers to leadership and support—within the limits of your organization's resources—of publicly important purposes. Such purposes might include improving education, health care in the community, environmental excellence, resource conservation, community service, industry and business

> *Item 1.2 in the Leadership category of the Baldrige Criteria is focused exclusively on CSR as well as organizational governance. The item addresses an organization's governance system; performance evaluation; legal, regulatory, and ethical behavior; societal well-being; and community support.*

practices, and sharing non-proprietary information. Leadership as a corporate citizen also entails influencing other organizations, private and public, to partner for these purposes. For example your organization could lead efforts to help define the obligations of your industry to its communities.

In 2003, the core value was renamed "Social Responsibility," and more recently, "Societal Responsibility."

Organizational Governance

Senior management is responsible for creating an environment in which employees' decisions and actions and stakeholder interactions conform to the organization's moral and professional principles. Senior leaders must build stakeholders' and employees' trust in the governance of their organizations and ensure legal compliance and ethical behavior. For any organization, large or small, public or private, ethics should mean going beyond profit or loss considerations, beyond simply distributing a code of conduct, to creating an organizational culture that values sound governance, transparency, integrity, and social responsibility.

SSM Health Care, for example, implemented a system-wide organizational ethics effort called the Corporate Responsibility Process (CRP). The CRP aligns with the elements of the national Office of Inspector General's model compliance plan, but goes beyond compliance to ensure that corporate values are reflected in all work processes. Employees, physicians, volunteers, and suppliers can use a confidential help line to raise questions, and any reported issues are investigated and acted upon. KPMG identified the CRP as a best practice nationwide. At MEDRAD, a Code of Conduct defines ethical behavior in all transactions and interactions and has been deployed to all employees worldwide as well as to MEDRAD's suppliers. Code of Conduct training is part of the company's employee orientation program, and the training is reinforced through a quarterly Code of Conduct Challenge distributed by e-mail to all employees. In addition, MEDRAD has an anonymous ethics hotline and e-mail address, a Business Ethics Committee, and a Legal Advisory Board.

An important aspect of any leadership system is **governance**, which refers to the system of management and controls exercised in the stewardship of an organization. Corporate charters, bylaws, and policies document the rights and responsibilities of owners/shareholders, board of directors, and the CEO, and describe how the organization is managed to ensure accountability, transparency of operations, and fair treatment of all stakeholders. Governance processes may include approving strategic direction, monitoring and evaluating CEO performance, succession planning, financial auditing, executive compensation, disclosure, and shareholder reporting. Effective governance processes can mitigate the types of problems manifested by stock manipulations, financial misreporting, and corporate and personal greed that have occurred in the past. In fact, evidence indicates that good governance and integrity are important ingredients for success; for example, organizations with the best corporate governance practices have also generally outperformed the major stock indexes.

The Public Company Accounting Reform and Investor Protection Act of 2002, commonly known as the *Sarbanes-Oxley Act*, was passed as a result of the corporate financial scandals at firms such as Enron. As a result of the legislation, all publicly-traded companies are required to submit an annual report of the effectiveness of their internal accounting controls to the SEC. The Sarbanes-Oxley Act imposes criminal and civil penalties for noncompliance, and requires certification of internal auditing, and increased financial disclosure.

In 2002, about the same time the Sarbanes-Oxley legislation was passed, The Business Roundtable, a respected group of CEO's from many of the *Fortune* 500 corporations, developed a set of Principles of Corporate Governance to provide guidelines for compliance.[36] These principles describe the responsibilities of the board of directors in overseeing senior managers and the ethical operation of the company, of management to operate in an effective and ethical manner, of producing fair and timely financial disclosures, of using an independent auditing firm to audit financial statements, of the independent accounting firm to avoid conflicts of interest and work in accordance with Generally Accepted Auditing Standards, of dealing with employees in a fair and equitable manner, of the board to respond to shareholders' concerns, and of the corporation to deal with all its stakeholders in a fair and equitable manner.

As one example, Caterpillar Financial Services Corporation (CFSC) has established strong internal financial control mechanisms. Segregation of duties and authorities prevents abuse, and systems are audited internally and externally. CFSC's Business Excellence Council monitors portfolio quality, and, as an issuer of publicly traded debt, CFSC's financial and portfolio practices and results are evaluated and made public by external rating agencies and analysts. The Caterpillar Executive Office and Audit Committee of the Board of Directors provide oversight to CFSC. Although not required by law, Caterpillar also established share ownership requirements for recipients of stock option grants more than a decade ago, and shareholders approve all equity programs.

Societal Responsibilities

An important aspect of CSR is safety in product design and manufacturing. Planning activities such as product design should anticipate adverse impacts from production, distribution, transportation, use, and disposal of a company's products to protect the welfare of consumers and society. Another responsibility is the management and security of sensitive information. For example, State Farm Insurance put in place physical, electronic, and organizational safeguards to protect customer information. They continually review their policies and practices, monitor computer networks, and test the strength of security in order to help ensure the safety of customer information. Finally, organizations have a responsibility to protect the environment. Research has suggested that superior environmental performance and superior quality are complementary. Firms that improve quality in goods and services can easily transfer their knowledge and learning to environmental processes. In addition, there is evidence that achieving superior environmental performance can be a significant driver of higher quality.[37]

At Solar Turbines, a wholly-owned subsidiary of Caterpillar Inc. and the world's largest supplier of mid-range industrial gas turbine systems, its Social Responsibility Core Business Principle and Environmental, Health, and Safety Policy guide the company's responsibility and citizenship actions. Solar's environmental health and safety strategy for its internal operation is to surpass compliance and strive for industry leadership. Products and services must comply with local, state, and federal standards in each locale as well as country-specific and governing body standards for emissions and effluent discharge. Solar's strategy has yielded significant reduction in the use of hazardous raw materials and production of hazardous waste, increased recycling and reuse, improved energy efficiency, and reduced water consumption. Solar and one of its key suppliers partnered with Cal-Poly State University to establish a Vibration and Rotor Dynamics Laboratory. Organizations should not only meet all local, state, and federal laws and regulatory requirements, but should treat these as opportunities for continuous improvement beyond mere compliance.

Practicing good citizenship refers to leadership and support—within the limits of an organization's resources—of publicly important purposes, including improving education, community health, environmental excellence, resource conservation, community service, and professional practices. It also entails leading efforts to help define the obligations of the industry to its communities. For example, Consolidated School District 15 supports the community in a variety of ways. It is one of the largest contributors to the local United Way, with contributions increasing by more than 50 percent from 1998–1999 to 2002–2003; it established the Al Hoover/PTA Health fund, which partners with local health providers to serve D15 students who otherwise would be unable to obtain needed medical care; and its administrators contribute more than 1,500 volunteer hours on 48 local committees. In addition, D15 has established numerous community service opportunities for its students, such as providing labor to repair homeless shelters, donating clothing and books to needy families, making quilts for children in hospitals, and supporting food drives.[38]

Many businesses partner with educational institutions for mutual benefit. Businesses bring to schools, colleges, and universities sound quality operational practices and processes, leadership and management skills and training, volunteers as mentors and tutors, and school-to-work opportunities. In return, the education community supplies businesses with potential employees who not only have traditional skills associated with academic subjects, but also have the new basic skills, such as problem solving, critical thinking, decision making, teaming, and creativity. By recognizing the business community as an important customer, business needs are factored into curriculum, and the end product, the graduate, is better prepared to enter the employment world.

SUMMARY OF KEY POINTS AND TERMINOLOGY

The Student Companion Site provides a summary of key concepts and terminology introduced in this chapter.

QUALITY *in* PRACTICE

Leadership at Advocate Good Samaritan Hospital[39]

Advocate Good Samaritan Hospital (GSAM), a part of Advocate Health Care located in Downer's Grove, Illinois (a suburb of Chicago), is an acute-care medical facility that, since its opening in 1976, has grown from a mid-size community hospital to a nationally recognized leader in health care. However, it was not always nationally-recognized. In 2004, Good Samaritan was true to its name—a "good," but not "great," hospital. Quality was generally perceived as good, but nursing care was seen as uneven; associate satisfaction was pretty good but not exceptional, physician satisfaction was mixed, and patient satisfaction was at best mediocre; technology and facilities were

increasingly falling behind other hospitals; and it was struggling financially in a highly competitive market. Its leadership was determined to achieve, sustain, and redefine health care excellence, so it embarked on an organizational transformation to take the organization "from Good to Great (G2G)" The rationale for doing this was:

- To make good on its mission to be "a place of healing,"
- To create a framework for inspiring and integrating its efforts to build loyal relationships and provide great care, and

- To differentiate itself and ensure future success by becoming the best place for physicians to practice, associates to work, and patients to receive care.

The first steps that Good Samaritan took included

1. Establishing an inspiring vision: *To provide an exceptional patient experience marked by superior health outcomes, service, and value.*
2. Enrolling leaders in the vision.
3. Creating alignment, ownership, and transparency to support the vision. Quoting Ghandi, the president recognized that "you must be the change you want to see in the world." He recognized that transforming an organization cannot be delegated. Leadership needed to create a sense of urgency, explain the "why," and overcommunicate by a factor of 10.

By 2006, the G2G journey had achieved some breakthrough results in patient satisfaction and clinical measures, and had spawned leading-edge innovations in health care. However, key questions remained: How would they ensure long-term sustainability? How would they create a legacy for the future? How could they hardwire best practices? How could they achieve repeatable excellence? Their response was to become a process-driven organization by embracing the Baldrige Criteria. The next major step was to establish a systematic leadership process, Good Samaritan Leadership System (GSLS), which is illustrated in Figure 13.2. The boxes represent the process steps, and the arrows represent the leadership behaviors needed to ensure that the steps are accomplished.

The GSLS ensures that all leaders at every level of the organization understand what is expected of them. Patients and stakeholders are at the center of the Leadership System. Driven by their Mission, Values, and Philosophy, all leaders must understand stakeholder requirements. At the organizational level, these requirements are determined in the Strategic Planning

FIGURE 13.2   Good Samaritan Leadership System

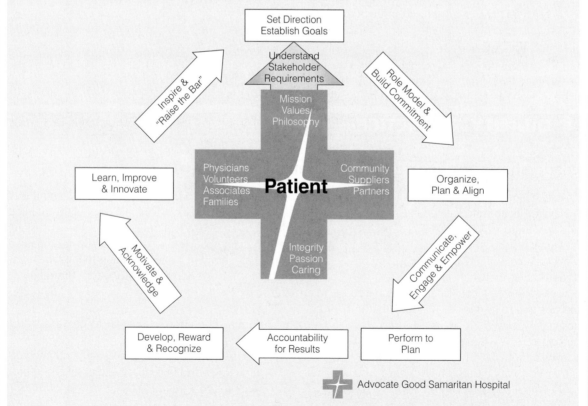

Process and used to set direction and establish and cascade goals. Action plans to achieve the goals are created, aligned, and communicated to engage the workforce. Goals and in-process measures are systematically reviewed and course corrections are made as necessary to ensure performance to plan. This focus on performance creates a rhythm of accountability and leads to subsequent associate development through the Capability Determination/Workforce Learning and Development System and reward and recognition of high performance. Development and recognition ensures that associates feel acknowledged and motivated. Stretch goals established in the SPP and a discomfort with the status quo prompts associates to learn, improve, and innovate through the Performance Improvement System. As leaders review annual performance, scan the environment, and recast organizational challenges, communication mechanisms are used to inspire and raise the bar.

GSAM has a systematic eight-step governance process that cascades guidance from the Advocate Health Care Governing Board and Senior Leadership to the GSAM Governing Council/Senior Leadership Team and to all associates. Guidelines and procedures at all organizational levels ensure that the overall intent of governance is achieved and tracked through measures and goals. The process ensures transparency and equity for all stakeholders via Governing Council committee oversight, independent audits and through the diverse composition of the board. Annual review of metrics, the mission, vision and philosophy, and Standards of Behaviors ensures accountability and compliance.

GSAM also uses multiple stakeholder and community listening posts as inputs into the strategic planning process to address the societal well being of the community. GSAM considers environmental impact on the community. GSAM's Green Team implements multiple strategies to conserve energy and recycle materials to ensure protection of the environment. In keeping with their mission, GSAM also views societal well-being and community health as providing care for those without the ability to pay. In addition, GSAM actively participates in Access DuPage, an innovative community health approach through which GSAM primary care physicians and specialists provide care to the uninsured population, and GSAM provides all diagnostic tests and treatment without charge. Community fairs, screenings, immunizations, a hospital food pantry for associates, and financial/in-kind gifts also support environmental, social, and economic systems. GSAM contributes to improving their communities by all executive team members having multiple involvements on local boards; as well as the professional nursing staff, medical staff, and other members of the workforce actively participating in numerous service and professional organizations.

Market share has risen; patient satisfaction has exceeded the 90th percentile nationally for multiple segments, and physician and associate satisfaction reached the 97th percentile. The Delta Group ranked GSAM #1 in Illinois and #4 in the US for overall hospital care in 2010, one of 2011's top 50 cardiovascular care hospitals by Thomson Reuters, and at the 100th percentile for patient safety by Thomson Reuters in 2010.

Key Issues for Discussion
1. How does GSAM reflect the concept of strategic leadership?
2. What leadership behaviors, practices, and theories are evident in this example?
3. How does the GSAM Leadership System model align with the Baldrige Criteria framework? State specific items in the criteria that are evident in this model.

QUALITY *in* PRACTICE

Leadership Changes at Alcoa[40]

Alcoa, ranked as the 79th largest firm in the 2005 *Fortune* 500, employs approximately 129,000 people worldwide and had 2004 annual sales of $23.96 billion. Alcoa has been known for progressive, innovative management. It treats its employees well, tries to avoid layoffs and plant closures unless forced to make changes as a result of continued negative results, and has unions at only about 15 of its 47 locations. Nevertheless, at Alcoa's industrial magnesium plant in Addy, Washington, a crisis of epic proportions rocked the plant and rattled the company, leading to some key leadership changes that ultimately resulted in dramatic improvements in safety, productivity, and profits.

At the time of this case (in the late 1980s) the plant was facing two severe problems: an unacceptable rate of serious injuries that averaged 12.8 per year, and five years of unprofitable operations. No clear, easily-implemented solutions were apparent for the first problem, but corporate management had suggested that layoffs of 100 or more employees were all but inevitable in order to stem the tide of red ink. Operating statistics bore out the depth and breadth of the problem. Prices of magnesium had dropped, and units selling for $1.45 on the open market cost $1.48 to make at Alcoa's plant. Quality control was below what was needed to counteract market forces, with magnesium recovery at only 72 percent of the raw material being processed.

The apparent causes of plant problems consisted of a complex mix of lack of accountability, poor quality control, inadequate leadership, and low morale, especially among hourly employees. Corporate management stressed safety above all, and profitability second. The death of an employee, who was related to seven other employees, and the unacceptable financial losses led senior corporate management to decide that a change in plant management was essential. Don Simonic, a former college football coach, with Alcoa experience, was tapped for the job of plant manager. His turnaround team members included the then-personnel manager, Tom McCombs, and outside consultants Robert and Patricia Crosby. If the new leadership team could not turn the plant around, plant closure or sell-off were the only remaining options.

Since its construction, the plant had been designed with an open-systems, team-based culture, adapted from socio-technical systems theory. It was structured similar to the way that Procter and Gamble had set up its soap plants, and was considered a leading-edge organizational design. The process for producing the industrial magnesium was highly advanced and technical, and the innovative work team structure seemed to fit the technical systems characteristics. The plant attracted visitors from inside and outside the company who wanted to benchmark the operation and talk to team members. The organizational structure included:

- Autonomous, self-directed teams with no immediate supervisors. Teams were responsible for their own work areas.
- Hourly employee leadership that consisted of a team coordinator, safety person, training person, and team resource (internal facilitator) on each team.
- Supervisors, called shift coordinators, with four or five teams reporting to them, who were connected to the team coordinators. Shift coordinators generally stayed at arm's length, because if they intervened in team operations, they would get in trouble. The teams would say, "Leave us alone. We know what we're doing." If they didn't intervene, upper management would say that the teams weren't doing what they should be. The supervisors were caught in the middle.

Employees were empowered, but unable to face critical decisions that needed to be made to stem the crisis. The Crosbys identified lack of clarity in decision making and authority as the main culprit in the plant's environment. The new leadership model, conceived by the Crosbys and the plant leaders, involved major changes in goal-setting and decision-making practices. It required:

- New clarity in goal-setting.
- A consultative, instead of a pure consensus approach to decision making.
- Coming to grips with the need to cut costs pragmatically.

As the turnaround proceeded, Simonic decided that cutting staff was essential to meeting the new goals. First, all temporary and contract workers were laid off. As leaders were explaining the facts that had led to a decision to lay off an additional 100 workers, an hourly worker revealed a breakthrough that his team had made to significantly reduce the downtime required to turn a magnesium smelting furnace around. This process involved switching over to a new crucible once the other was filled (a form of the Japanese manufacturing technique called SMED—single minute exchange of dies). The new team approach required more labor, but cut the downtime from the usual one-and-a-half-hour turnaround time to just one hour. Simonic called off the impending layoffs. When the new process was implemented on all nine furnaces in the plant, the savings reached $10 million. This was more than the wages of the 100 employees, who were allowed to keep their jobs.

Simonic held strategic meetings where he engaged salaried and non-salaried employees in intensive dialogue. His objective was to align all parts of the system, clarify who would be making what decisions, explain how decisions could be influenced, and communicate why decisions were made. Simonic then set the goals. Simonic made clear statements like, "These are the goals. You and all our employees have firsthand knowledge of how things work around here. I don't care how you get there. I will support you in making choices about how to get there. And, if you can't get there, I will step in and decide how we will get there." McCombs, the personnel manager, remembered how they developed a matrix reflecting what kind of decisions team members and supervisors would make. Supervisors would still retain authority over all decisions, if needed. Before Simonic's arrival, decisions had been made largely by consensus.

As a result of this process, one person was made responsible for every project or task, known as single-point accountability. This proved to be a critical change that was used instead of the consensus (team) approach, which was previously the only way to perform projects. McCombs and Simonic believed that for single-point accountability to succeed, it was necessary to establish the "by whens"—when particular tasks would be accomplished. After making clear to the teams and employees what was expected, they started achieving goals better.

Eighteen months after Alcoa's brought Simonic in as plant manager, the change efforts had produced

impressive results: Unit costs had been reduced from $1.48 to $1.18, recovery of magnesium increased by 5 percentage points (worth $1.3 million per point), and the serious-injury frequency fell from 12.8 to 6.3 per year. Although positive signs appeared throughout the process, the incident in which the layoffs were averted proved to be the most critical, because employees subsequently had taken responsibility for applying their own creativity to meeting plant goals. Over the next two years, the plant became the lowest-cost producer in the world, and shortly afterward had boosted productivity by 72 percent. The president of Alcoa even asked all of the plant managers to visit the site and learn from Addy's turnaround.

One decision-making technique that was practiced at Addy and several other Alcoa plants was consultative decision-making, where the manager makes the final decision but consults with the team first. For example, McCombs recalls an incident requiring disciplinary action on several teams: "The teams would have 24 hours to give their recommendations to management on how the discipline should be handled-up to and including termination- and management would administer the discipline. At least 95 percent of the time we took the team's recommendation and moved on," says McCombs.

The consultative method was also used to make hiring decisions. For example, the boundaries laid out for a team might concern Alcoa's desire to hire minorities. Typically, "the team would present their selection of who to hire to the manager, and often they would do such a good job the decision was just "'rubber-stamped,'" explains McCombs.

Another successful approach was called the "cadre." During the turnaround, Simonic and the Crosbys would work with the cadre, a group of key people, chosen from a vertical slice of the employees, who engaged in two specific roles: (1) observing and evaluating the change process as it played out while (2) simultaneously participating in the process. The cadre became a skilled resource for the plant on leadership development, change management, conflict management, quality, and work processes.

In reflecting on Simonic's impact on the organization, McCombs noted: "Don had a dynamic personality and was very charismatic. He possessed a very strong leadership style and was very clear. But you also must work with the intact families in the organization—one of Simonic's own beliefs. That's where change happens—in the small groups. You must work with that supervisor and that crew and get them aligned with the organization and work out any conflict." According to McCombs, Simonic was guided by four clear principles: "Leaders have to lead, make decisions, have a clear vision, and set direction. Once leaders set direction and get a breakthrough goal in mind that people can rally around, then people can tell the leader how they are going to get it done. A leader shouldn't tell how to do it, but he or she needs to set that direction. And that's what Simonic did very well," insists McCombs.

Unfortunately, Addy didn't sustain the momentum of the turnaround. In 1992, Simonic and McCombs left to help turn around other Alcoa plants. Corporate management continued to reduce the workforce. They eliminated all the department heads and everybody ended up reporting to the shift supervisor or plant manager. This caused lack of clarity about leadership and authority in decision making all over again, and as McCombs explained, "They stripped away the leadership that could have supported the change efforts afterwards."

Perhaps because of the previous successes and the skills gained in the previous turnaround, Crosby believed that the second recovery that occurred some time after Simonic and McCombs left was going to be much easier. The plant appeared to be back on track and headed for success again, but the fortunes of business intervened. There was another drop in the price of magnesium, and the Addy plant lost its competitive edge. In fall of 2001, the plant was closed down and approximately 350 employees lost their jobs.

Key Issues for Discussion

1. From a strategic management standpoint, why do you think that corporate management at Alcoa delayed taking action for five years as the plant continued to lose money and deteriorate in other operational measures?

2. What type of leadership style did Simonic seem to follow? Does it fit any of the leadership theories that were developed in the chapter?

3. How easy or difficult would it be for other organizations to duplicate the leadership style of Simonic and the organizational systems practiced at Addy, prior to, and after Simonic's tenure?

REVIEW QUESTIONS

1. Define leadership. Why is it necessary for a culture of performance excellence?

2. List and explain the key competencies and personal characteristics that strong leaders possess.

3. Summarize the key leadership practices for performance excellence.

4. What is strategic leadership? How does it differ from the common concept of leadership?

5. Explain the concept of a leadership system. What elements should an effective leadership system have?

6. What is the role of steering teams in many leadership systems?

7. How do emerging leadership theories differ from traditional theories? Summarize them and their importance in leadership for performance excellence.

8. How does transactional leadership theory differ from transformational leadership theory? Why is transformational leadership more relevant to quality and performance excellence?

9. What is corporate social responsibility and why is it important for organizations?

10. How does the ISO 26000:2010 standard guide organizations in CSR?

11. Explain how CSR is reflected in the Baldrige Criteria.

12. What is governance? Why is it important that organizations have a strong governance system?

13. State some examples of how organizations address societal responsibilities.

DISCUSSION QUESTIONS

1. We emphasized that leadership is the "driver" of a total quality system. What does this statement imply and what implications does it have for future CEOs? Middle managers? Supervisors?

2. Provide examples from your own experiences in which leaders (not necessarily managers—consider academic unit heads, presidents of student organizations, and even family members) exhibited one or

more of the six key leadership competencies described in this chapter. What impacts did these competencies have on the organization?

3. Explain how leaders can demonstrate each of the seven personal leadership characteristics cited in this chapter.

4. State some examples in which leaders you have worked for exhibited some of the leading practices described in this chapter. Can you provide examples for which they have not?

5. You have undoubtedly seen a flock of geese flying overhead. How do the following behaviors of this species provide insight about leadership?
   a. As each bird flaps its wings, it creates uplift for the bird behind. By using a "V" formation, the whole flock adds 71 percent more flying range than if each bird flew alone.
   b. Whenever one falls out of formation, it suddenly feels the resistance of trying to fly alone, and quickly gets back into formation to take advantage of the lifting power of the birds immediately in front.
   c. When the lead bird gets tired, it rotates back into formation and another flies at the point position.
   d. The birds in formation honk from behind to encourage those up front to maintain their speed.
   e. When one gets sick or wounded or shot down, two birds drop out of formation and follow their fellow member down to help or provide protection. They stay with this member of the flock until it can fly again or dies. Then they launch out on their own, with another formation or to catch up with their own flock.

PROJECTS, ETC.

1. Using the information in this chapter, design a questionnaire that might be used to understand leadership effectiveness in an organization.

2. Interview someone you know about the leadership characteristics of their supervisor. What leadership style does he or she appear to reflect?

3. Joseph Conklin proposes 10 questions for self-examination to help you understand your capacity for leadership.[41] Answer the following questions, and discuss why they are important for leadership.
   a. How much do I like my job?
   b. How often do I have to repeat myself?
   c. How do I respond to failure?
   d. How well do I put up with second guessing?
   e. How early do I ask questions when making a decision?
   f. How often do I say "thank you"?
   g. Do I tend to favor a loose or strict interpretation of the rules?
   h. Can I tell an obstacle from an excuse?
   i. Is respect enough?
   j. Have I dispensed with feeling indispensable?

4. Conduct some research to explain the traditional theories of leadership in Table 13.2 and their implications for quality and performance excellence.

CASES

JOHNSON PHARMACEUTICALS[42]

Johnson Pharmaceuticals is a large manufacturer that was highly motivated to meet quality challenges. It implemented an ISO 9000–compatible quality system to ensure not only FDA compliance requirements, but also customer satisfaction. As the manufacturing plants of the organization were audited by the internal audit division, it became apparent that some plants were meeting the challenge, while others continued to struggle in both the quality and the regulatory aspects of production. This fact was evident in the reports of internal findings and in FDA inspection reports.

For the most part, the manufacturing plants share consistent resources and face similar environments. All were issued the responsibility of meeting the expectations of the quality system through the same mechanism. All understood the consequence of not conforming, that is, of jeopardizing their manufacturing license as bound by the consent decree. The issue then became why some plants could successfully design and implement the requirements of the quality system, whereas others could not and still cannot.

Although the plants are similar in many ways, they differ in terms of leadership, as each plant has its own CEO. The CEO, as the leader of his or her plant, has the responsibility of ensuring the successful implementation of a quality system. The plants also differ in their organizational members, those who are to be led by the CEO. The relationship between the leader and the organizational members is critical to a plant's ability to implement an effective quality system, with effectiveness being a measure of how successfully a plant can comply with FDA regulations and internal quality standards.

Both plants have a similar culture that can be best described as conserving, reflecting a level of rigidity in response to the external environment, but demonstrating organizational commitment. The strategy used by the leader in Plant A was a combination of moderate to high amounts of structuring actions, with high to moderate amounts of inspiring actions, whereas the strategy used by Plant B's CEO was a combination of moderate to low amounts of structuring actions, with moderate to high amounts of inspiring actions.

Discussion Questions

1. What type of situational leadership style did the CEO of each plant demonstrate?
2. Which of these styles was more appropriate in view of the Situational Leadership model? Why?
3. Would it be surprising to find out that Plant A was more successful in achieving the goals of the quality system?

TRIVIEW BANK—LEADERSHIP

The complete TriView Bank case study, a fictitious example of a Baldrige application, can be found in the Baldrige Materials folder on the Student Companion Site. If you have not read the Organizational Profile yet, please do so first. What factors in the Organizational Profile would be most important in evaluating their leadership approaches? Examine their response in Category 1 to the 2011–2012 Baldrige Criteria questions for this category. What are their strengths? What opportunities for improvement can you identify? What specific advice, including useful tools and techniques that might help them, would you suggest?

NOTES

1. "Hyundai Gets Hot," *Business Week*, December 17, 2001, 84–85; J.D. Power and Associates, "The Power Report, Special Power Report on Hyundai," June 2004; "Hyundai: Kissing Clunkers Goodbye," *Business Week*, May 17, 2004, 45.
2. Debbie Phillips-Donaldson, "On Leadership," *Quality Progress*, August 2002.
3. *Answering the 2011 CEO Challenge: Accelerating Growth through Quality*, The Conference Board, CP-031, June 2011, http://www.conferenceboard.org.
4. Rudolph C. Hirzel, "Leadership Characteristics for Quality Performance," *Quality Management Forum* 30, no. 1 (winter 2004), 3–4.
5. 2003 Baldrige Award Profiles of Winners, National Institute of Standards and Technology, U.S. Department of Commerce.
6. Robert Slater, *Jack Welch and the GE Way* (New York: McGraw-Hill, 1999), 219.
7. Michael Hitt and Duane Ireland, "Achieving and Maintaining Strategic Competitiveness in the 21st Century: The Role of Strategic Leadership," *Academy of Management Executive* 19, no. 4 (November 2005), 63 (reprinted from February 1999).
8. Meryl Davids, "Where Style Meets Substance," *Journal of Business Strategy* 16, no. 1 (January/February 1995), 49.
9. Kimberly B. Boal and Robert Hooiberg, "Strategic Leadership Research: Moving On," *Leadership Quarterly* 11, no. 4 (2000), 516–518.
10. Mike Freeman with Benjamin B. Tregoe, *The Art and Discipline of Strategic Leadership* (New York: McGraw-Hill, 2003), 22–23.
11. Hitt and Ireland, pp. 65–67.

12. AT&T Quality Steering Committee, *Leading the Quality Initiative*, AT&T Bell Laboratories, 1990, 13–14.

13. Cited in Deborah Hopen, "The Changing Role and Practices of Successful Leaders," *Journal for Quality & Participation*, April 2010, 4–9.

14. The following references provided additional information about each of the leadership theories cited in Table 13.2. "Great man" model: R. M. Stogdill, *Handbook of Leadership* (New York: The Free Press, 1974); Ohio State Studies: E. A. Fleishman and E. F. Harris, "Patterns of Leadership Behavior Related to Employee Grievances and Turnover," *Personnel Psychology* 15 (1962), 43–56; Michigan Studies: Rensis Likert, *The Human Organization: Its Management and Value* (New York: McGraw-Hill, 1967); Theory X – Theory Y Model: Douglas McGregor, *The Human Side of Enterprise* (New York: McGraw-Hill, 1960); Managerial Grid model: R. R. Blake and J. S. Mouton, *The Managerial Grid* (Houston: Gulf Publishing, 1965); Leadership effectiveness model: Frederick E. Fiedler, *A Theory of Leadership Effectiveness* (New York: McGraw-Hill, 1967); Supervisory contingency decision model: V. H. Vroom and A. G. Jago, *The New Leadership* (Englewood Cliffs, NJ: Prentice-Hall, 1988); Managerial roles: Henry Mintzberg, *Mintzberg on Management: Inside Our Strange World of Organizations* (New York: The Free Press, 1989). Also, *The Nature of Managerial Work* (New York: Harper & Row, 1973); "The Manager's Job: Folklore and Fact," *Harvard Business Review* (July/August 1975); Leader-Member exchange: Graen, G. B., & Uhl-Bien, M. (1995). Relationship-based approach to leadership: "Development of Leader-Member Exchange (LMX) Theory of Leadership over 25 Years: Applying a Multi-Level Multi-Domain Perspective: Special Issue: Leadership: The Multiple-Level Approaches (Part 1)," *Leadership Quarterly*, 6, 219–247; Charismatic theory: R. J. House, "A 1976 Theory of Charismatic Leadership" in J. G. Hunt and L. L. Larson (Eds.) *Leadership: The Cutting Edge* (Carbondale, IL: Southern Illinois University Press, 1977), 189–207. Also, J. A. Conger, *The Charismatic Leader: Behind the Mystique of Exceptional Leadership* (San Francisco: Jossey-Bass, 1989); *Transformational theory*: op. cit. James M. Burns; N. M. Tichy and D. O. Ulrich, etc.; *Substitutes for leadership*: op. cit. Jon P. Howell, David E. Bowen, Peter W. Dorfman, Steven Kerr, Phillip M. Podsakoff; *Emotional Intelligence*: op. cit. Daniel Goleman.

15. http://www.referenceforbusiness.com/management/Int-Loc/Leadership-Theories-and-Studies.html. This and all documents under and extending from the group Encyclopedia of Management—Int-Loc are Copyright © 2006 by Thomson Gale, a part of the Thomson Corporation (accessed 2/17/06).

16. Bass, Bernard M. and Bruce J. Avolio, *Improving Organizational Effectiveness through Transformational Leadership*, Thousand Oaks, CA: Sage Publications (1994) 2.

17. http://www.referenceforbusiness.com/management/Int-Loc/Leadership-Theories-and-Studies.html. Encyclopedia of Management—Int-Loc are Copyright © 2006 by Thomson Gale, a part of the Thomson Corporation (accessed 2/17/06).

18. For further discussion of this model, see Richard A. Grover and H. Fred Walker, "Changing from Production to Quality: Application of the Situational Leadership and Transtheoretical Change Models," *Quality Management Journal* 10, no. 3 (2003), pp. 8–24; and Gary Yukl. *Leadership in Organizations*, 6th ed. (Upper Saddle River, NJ: Prentice-Hall, 2006), pp. 223–224.

19. Claude F. Graeff. Evolution Of Situational Leadership Theory: A Critical Review, *Leadership Quarterly*, Summer 1997, Vol. 8, No. 2; Warren Blank, John R. Weitzel, Stephen G. Green. A Test of the Situational Leadership Theory, *Personnel Psychology*, Autumn 1990, Vol. 43, Issue 3.

20. Gary Yukl. *Leadership in Organizations*, 6th Ed., Upper Saddle River, NJ: Prentice-Hall, 2006, 224–225.

21. The term *transformational leadership* has been attributed to James M. Burns. See his book, *Leadership* (New York: Harper & Row, 1978). Other sources are N. M. Tichy and D. O. Ulrich, "The Leadership Challenge: A Call for the Transformational Leader," *Sloan Management Review* 26 (1984), 59–68; N. M. Tichy and M. A. Devanna, *The Transformational Leader* (New York: John Wiley & Sons, 1986); B. M. Bass, *Leadership and Performance Beyond Expectations* (New York: The Free Press, 1985).

22. B. M. Bass. *A New Paradigm of Leadership: An Inquiry into Transformational Leadership*, Alexandria, VA: US Army Research Institute for Behavioral and Social Sciences (1996), cited in Yukl, *Leadership in Organizations*, 263.

23. Bruce J. Avolio and Bernad M. Bass, *Developing Potential Across a Full Range of Leadership* (2002), 117–118.

24. Yukl, *Leadership in Organizations* (citing Bass, 1985), p. 262.

25. Philip Atkinson, "Leadership, Total Quality and Cultural Change," *Management Services*, June 1991, pp. 16–19.

26. Bruce J. Avolio and Bernad M. Bass, *Developing Potential Across a Full Range of Leadership* (2002), p. 6.

27. Kathleen L. McFadden, Stephanie C. Henagan, and Charles R. Gowen III, "The Patient Safety Chain: Transformational Leadership's Effect on Patient Safety Culture, Initiatives, and Outcomes," *Journal of Operations Management* 27, no. 5 (October 2009), pp. 390–404.

28. Jon P. Howell, David E. Bowen, Peter W. Dorfman, Steven Kerr, and Phillip M. Podsakoff, "Substitutes for Leadership: Effective Alternatives for Ineffective Leadership," *Organizational Dynamics*, Summer 1990. Also see Steve Kerr and John Jermier, "Substitutes for Leadership: Their Meaning and Measurement," *Organizational Behavior and Human Performance*, December 1978; and Jon P. Howell, Peter W. Dorfman, and Steven Kerr,

"Moderator Variables in Leadership Research," *Academy of Management Review*, January 1986.

29. Daniel Goleman, "What Makes a Leader?" *Harvard Business Review*, November–December, 1998, 93–102; and Daniel Goleman, *Working with Emotional Intelligence* (New York: Bantam Books, 1998).

30. http://www.ccl.org/leadership/pdf/research/Nature Leadership.pdf (accessed 2/9/06); André Martin. *2005 Changing Nature of Leadership Report*. Center for Creative Leadership, 2005.

31. Marc Gunther, "Money and Morals at GE," *Fortune*, November 15, 2004, 176–182.

32. This definition was put forth by the European Commission as noted in http://europa.eu/rapid/pressReleases Action.do?reference=MEMO/11/730 (accessed 4/4/12).

33. Bjorn Andersen, "A Framework for Business Ethics," *Quality Progress*, March 2000, 22–28.

34. ISO 26000:2010 Abstract, http://www.iso.org.

35. A review of management theories and their relationships with CSR and the Baldrige Criteria can be found in Jessica Foote, Nolan Gaffney, and James R. Evans, "Corporate Social Responsibility: Implications for Performance Excellence," *Total Quality Management & Business Excellence* 21, no. 8 (August 2010), pp. 799–812.

36. n.a. The Business Roundtable. *Principles of Corporate Governance* (May 2002, revised in November 2005), http://www.businessroundtable.org/pdf/Corporate GovPrinciples.pdf (accessed 3/2/06).

37. Frits K. Pil and Sandra Rothenberg, "Environmental Performance as a Driver of Superior Quality," *Production and Operations Management* 12, no. 3 (2003), 404–415.

38. Consolidated School District 15, Malcolm Baldrige National Quality Award Application Summary, 2003.

39. Adapted from Advocate Good Samaritan Hospital Baldrige Award Application Summary, http://www.nist .gov/baldrige; and David S. Fox, "Leadership: Our Strategic Advantage," PowerPoint presentation at the 2011 Quest for Excellence conference, Washington, D.C.

40. Adapted from Sara R. Olberding, "Turnaround Drama Instills Leadership," *Journal for Quality and Participation*, Jan/Feb 1998. Source: http://www.findarticles.com/

41. Joe Conklin, "What It Takes to Be a Leader," *Quality Progress*, November 2001, 83.

42. Adapted from Lisa Walters, "Leading for Quality: The Implications of Situational Leadership," *Quality Management Journal* 8, no. 4 (October 2001), pp. 48–63.

Building and Sustaining Quality and Performance Excellence

The sparkly smiley-face stickers and pink crayons in first-grade teacher Carly Laurent's classroom at Washington Elementary School in Mt. Lebanon, PA, don't look as if they came from organizations that practice total quality and performance excellence. They are being used that way, however, as part of the same "continuous improvement" management model used by many organizations run by adults. At Washington Elementary, the "workers" are the pint-sized pupils, the end products are better spelling, reading, and math scores, and the day-to-day management techniques might sound a little different than those used in the corporate world. "All right, sweet pea, let's look at your spelling test," Ms. Laurent says to six-year-old Tiausa Brown, who gets a high-five and an "awesome" for her perfect score of 10 out of 10. Tiausa then places a smiley sticker to mark her score on a class graph of the test performance and, after conferring with a classmate, uses a pink crayon to fill in a bar graph in her personal data binder. After all of her pupils receive their scores and chart their progress in their binders, Ms. Laurent calls the class together to compare this week's spelling performance (all 8s, 9s, and 10s) to the previous week's (some 5s and 6s). They also discuss what worked well (spelling in their heads, practicing in the car) and what could be done differently to improve next time (checking their work, decorating the bathroom with words on Post-it notes). "What we try to do in an educational setting is apply the theory from the boardroom, the central office, down to the individual student, where even kindergartners are saying, 'Can I be better tomorrow than I am today?'" said an associate superintendent in Cedar Rapids, IA. After the continuous improvement plan was implemented in Cedar Rapids in 2004, fifth-graders increased their math proficiency by 6.9 percent by the time they reached eighth grade. Reading groups increased 9.6 percent over the same period.[1]

Quality and performance excellence can be applied in many types of organizations, as the example of Washington Elementary School shows (the Quality Profiles in this chapter highlight two other nontraditional examples). This example also suggests that creating a culture for quality and performance excellence is not difficult. Nevertheless, many organizations fail to implement quality and performance excellence initiatives successfully. Many that do find it only temporary; they fail to sustain it for the long run. Building and sustaining performance excellence requires effective leadership, a commitment to change and long-term **sustainability** (the ability to address current needs and have the agility and management skills and structure to prepare successfully for the future), the adoption of sound practices and implementation strategies, and continual organizational learning.

The motivation to adopt a performance excellence philosophy usually stems from one of two basic reasons—either a firm reacts to competition that poses a threat to its survival, or it recognizes that performance excellence practices represent an opportunity to improve and grow the business. No matter what the reason, building quality and performance excellence into an organization requires change, and change has always been a stumbling block for organizations. Researchers have noted that upwards of 70 percent of all change initiatives fail. The philosophies, tools, and frameworks that we discussed in the previous thirteen chapters are readily available to every organization; they just need to implement them. As we emphasized in the previous chapter, leadership is critical; but just as important is a solid understanding of culture, organizational change, learning, and self-assessment. In this final chapter we address these issues, which any organization must deal with in order to go from "good to great," or to simply improve and become more competitive.

quality**profiles**

Montgomery County Public Schools and the City of Coral Springs

Montgomery County Public Schools (MCPS) is Maryland's largest school district and the 16th-largest school district in the nation. Located in suburban Washington, D.C., MCPS serves an extremely diverse community, with its more than 144,000 students coming from 164 countries and speaking 184 languages. MCPS comprehensive reform efforts are guided by the district's strategic plan, Our Call to Action: Pursuit of Excellence (OCA). The plan incorporates five strategic goals, clearly defines the key performance measures

and action plans, and provides alignment throughout the district. Senior leaders engage in extensive outreach with partners, customers, and the community to solicit shared concerns and expectations that are codified in the OCA. The OCA then is deployed throughout the organization. The OCA is aligned with the Maryland State Board of Education's Bridge to Excellence Master Plan and federal requirements. Cascading downward, each office, department, and school has developed related improvement plans with performance measures for evaluating the proper courses of action, all of which are aligned with OCA. The systematic alignment of the district's strategic plan has a direct impact on MCPS's ability to fulfill its core competencies of developing and implementing a rigorous instructional program that is responsive to the needs of the individual student.

MCPS "reverse engineered" the education process by starting with the goal of college and career readiness, and then identifying the knowledge and skills needed for students to reach that target. The result is The Seven Keys to College Readiness, a pathway of seven measurable academic goals, from kindergarten through high school, that are deployed throughout the school system. The Seven Keys constitute a college-readiness trajectory in which each key builds on the previous one. MCPS students achieve at high levels on state assessments and are narrowing racial and socioeconomic achievement gaps. For instance, in middle school reading, MCPS has narrowed the achievement gap between its African American and white students by 13 percentage points in the five years from 2006 to 2010. Graduation rates and parent satisfaction are far above national comparative averages.

During the 1980s, Coral Springs, Florida, was one of the fastest growing cities in the nation and now is home to about 132,000 people. In 1993, the City of Coral Springs began its journey to be a high-performing "municipal corporation," a city government following a corporate management model. The city's organizational culture is reflected in its four core values: *customer focus*—demonstrate a passion for customer service; *leadership*—establish an inspiring vision that creates a government that works better and costs less; *empowered employees*—empower the people closest to the customer to continuously improve the organization's quality and services;

and *continuous improvement*—commit every day, in every way to getting better and better.

The city's strategic plan, which is reviewed and updated annually, represents a shared vision for the future of the community and spells out its priorities: customer-involved government; financial health and economic development; excellence in education; neighborhood and environmental vitality; youth development and family values; strength in diversity; and traffic, mobility, and connectivity. The strategic planning process has been cited by a number of organizations, including the American Productivity and Quality Center, as a "best practice."

A number of mechanisms make it as convenient as possible for customers to get information on services, conduct business, and communicate with city officials and employees. They include the city's website, podcasts and streaming video, e-mail, the CityHelpDesk (automated comment and complaint system), and the City Hall in the Mall, which offers services such as paying cable and water bills and applying for a passport and permits.

The city's flat organizational structure, training, and recognition encourage employees to be innovative in addressing customer concerns and make on-the-spot improvements. Teams of employees from across the organization work together to solve problems and review processes, promoting cooperation and driving organizational innovation. For the past 10 years, more than 90 percent of employees have been satisfied with their jobs and are willing to recommend the city as a place to work, outperforming a comparison group of federal government employees. The City of Coral Springs was the first state or local government agency to receive the Baldrige Award.

Source: Baldrige Award Recipient Profiles, National Institute of Standards and Technology, U.S. Department of Commerce.

ORGANIZATIONAL CULTURE AND CHANGE

For quality and performance excellence to truly succeed in an organization, it must define and drive the culture of the organization. **Culture** (specifically, *corporate culture*) is an organization's value system and its collection of guiding principles. Culture is an important factor for sustainability and long-term success of any organization. Strong corporate cultures are evident in firms such as Disney, Procter & Gamble, and IBM. A survey conducted by the Wyatt Company, a Washington, D.C., consulting firm, found that the barriers to change cited most often were employee resistance and "dysfunctional corporate culture"—one whose shared values and behavior are at odds with its long-term health.[2] An example of a dysfunctional culture is a high-tech company that stresses individual rewards while innovation depends on teamwork.

Culture is driven by leadership.[3] In an entrepreneurial venture, for instance, the founder's behavior is often reflected in the behavior of the organization's workforce. During the formative years, the leader's behavior and personality are showcased to the employees through day-to-day interactions. For example, one entrepreneur might establish a culture based on the timely delivery of products and honoring of promises to clients. Another might be more tolerant of delays in client deliveries, and be sending a dubious message to the workforce that negatively influences the firm's performance. Such values eventually can become the values of the workforce.

As the firm grows, the process of creating and disseminating the desired culture tends to become increasingly difficult because the entrepreneur is no longer involved in the day-to-day activities of the organization. At this stage, it becomes necessary to formally define the firm's cultural values and the behavior expected from the workforce. This is typically done through organizational policies and practices.[4] For example, cultural values are often seen in the mission and vision statements of organizations as we saw in Chapter 11. It is not unusual to see statements such as, "We will continuously strive to improve the level of quality in all our products" or "Teamwork is essential to our mutual success" in corporate mission and vision statements.

Culture is a powerful influence on behavior because it is shared widely and because it operates without being talked about, and indeed, often without being thought of. Therefore, organizations that believe in the principles of performance excellence are more likely to implement the practices successfully. Conversely, actions set culture in motion. As performance excellence practices are used routinely within an organization, its people learn to believe in the underlying principles of total quality, and cultural changes can occur.

Changing Organizational Culture

It is important to differentiate between organizational changes resulting from strategy development and implementation (i.e., "strategic change"), and organizational changes resulting from operational assessment activities (i.e., "process change").[5] Strategic change stems from strategic objectives, which are generally externally focused and relate to significant customer, market, product/service, or technological opportunities and challenges. An organization must change these aspects to remain or become competitive. Strategic change is broad in scope, is driven by environmental forces, and is tied closely to the organization's ability to achieve its goals. Some examples are General Electric's implementation of Six Sigma throughout the corporation, and Hewlett-Packard's decision to merge with Compaq. In contrast, process change deals with the operations of an organization. Some examples of process change are a healthcare organization that discovered weaknesses in the organization's ability to collect and analyze information, followed by a $50 million information system upgrade; or an AT&T division that found that many employees did not recall the division's strategic vision, which prompted managers to increase meetings and interactions with employees to improve communication.

Although change to a business process tends to have lasting effects, the change tends to be narrow in scope. Unlike strategic change, which motivates organization-wide changes in behavior, process change is often confined to a particular unit, division, or function of the organization. For example, changing an organization's process for

TABLE 14.1   Strategic versus Process Change

	Strategic Change	**Process Change**
Theme of change	Shift in organizational direction	Adjustment of organizational processes
Driving force	Usually environmental forces—market, rival, technological change	Usually internal—"How can we better align our processes?"
Typical antecedent	Strategic planning process	Self-assessment of management system
How much of the organization changes?	Typically widespread	Often narrow—divisional or functional
Examples	Entering new markets Seeking low-cost position Mergers and acquisitions	Improving information systems Establishing hiring guidelines Developing improved customer satisfaction measures

Adapted from Matthew W. Ford and James R. Evans, "Baldrige Assessment and Organizational Learning: The Need For Change Management," *Quality Management Journal*, 8, 3, 2001, 9–25.

measuring customer satisfaction usually requires substantive adjustment to a limited number of functional areas, such as marketing or information systems. In Table 14.1, we describe the characteristics of strategic change in contrast with process change. Strategic changes are the ones that impact culture the most rapidly. However, an accumulation of continuously improving process changes can also lead to a positive and sustainable culture change.

When organizations contemplate change, some tough questions must be answered: Why is the change necessary? What will it do to my organization (department, job)? What problems will I encounter? And perhaps the most important one—What's in it for me? Change makes people uncomfortable, thus managing change is seldom pleasant.[6] Managing change usually requires a well-defined process, just like any other business process. Thinking of change management as a process helps to define the steps necessary to achieve the desired outcomes. It also forces the organization to think of its employees as customers who will be affected by the change. Most change processes include three basic stages. The first stage involves questioning the organization's current state and dislodging accepted patterns of behavior. The second stage is a state of flux, where new approaches are developed to replace suspended old activities. The final period consists of institutionalizing the new behaviors and attitudes. American Express, for example, views its change process as consisting of five steps:[7]

1. *Scope the Change:* Why are we doing this?
2. *Create a Vision:* What will the change look like?
3. *Drive Commitment:* What needs to happen to make the change work?
4. *Accelerate the Transition:* How are we going to manage the effort on an ongoing basis?
5. *Sustain Momentum:* What have we learned and how can we leverage it?

The first question an organization must ask is "Why change?" Most firms—even Baldrige Award recipients—have changed their cultures because of threats to their survival. Xerox, for example, watched its market share fall from 80 percent to 13 percent in a little more than a decade (see the *Quality in Practice* feature in Chapter 1); and Boeing Airlift and Tanker Programs was on the verge of having its contract with the

U.S. government canceled. Although not facing dire crises, perceived future threats were the impetus for FedEx, Solectron, and Wainwright Industries. When faced with a threat to survival, an organization implements change more quickly and smoothly. However, an organization will generally have more difficulty in gaining support for any significant change when not facing a crisis. This reluctance is a reflection of the attitude "If it ain't broke, don't fix it." Unfortunately, complacency today often leads to crises tomorrow. Leaders with foresight view change as a way to get better and to maintain or enhance existing market leadership positions. In such cases, one might even attempt to manufacture a crisis mentality to effect change.[8]

In many situations, middle managers recognize the need for change, but gaining commitment from top executives is not easy. As one quality director noted, "It's a hard sell if management is not predisposed." Dale Crownover, CEO of Texas Nameplate Company, believes the best way to sell quality to top executives is to show them where money is being lost due to absenteeism, downtime, not having procedures in place, lack of job descriptions, and poor training. Demonstrating the return on investment is a powerful motivator.

Management must understand what needs to change. A culture of performance excellence is very different from a traditional management culture. Many traditional practices stem from the fundamental structure of U.S. business, which derives from the Adam Smith principles of division of labor in the eighteenth century and their reinforcement during Frederick Taylor's scientific management era.[9] These include autocratic leadership, internal competition, functional silos, and rigid procedures. Although they were quite appropriate in their time and contributed to past economic success, those practices no longer suffice. A culture of performance excellence can be summarized as follows:[10]

- A premium is placed on excellence in performance—obtaining desired behaviors and results. That is, there is a clear focus on results that support the organization's mission, vision, and strategic objectives.
- Organizations acknowledge that their success is contingent upon the successful performance of their employees. People are the most important driver of performance.
- Strategic outcomes drive the work. There is clear alignment at the organizational, process, and individual levels.
- Management is strongly committed to creating conditions and consequences that support and sustain strong performance. Finally, leadership is vital to success.

To drive change, organizations must change behavior as well as policies and procedures. Juran and others suggest that an organization must foster five key behaviors to develop a positive quality culture:[11]

1. It must create and maintain an awareness of quality by disseminating results throughout the organization.
2. It must provide evidence of management leadership, such as serving on a quality council, providing resources, or championing quality projects (Six Sigma, for example).
3. It must encourage self-development and empowerment through the design of jobs, use of empowered teams, and personal commitment to quality.
4. It must provide opportunities for employee participation to inspire action, such as improvement teams, product design reviews, or Six Sigma training.
5. It must provide recognition and rewards, including public acknowledgment for good performance as well as tangible benefits.

It is interesting to note that these suggestions generally revolve around people, and as we have emphasized, people are the most important element in a successful organization.

All employees play a critical role in achieving performance excellence. We have discussed extensively the role of senior leadership in the previous chapter. Middle managers provide the leadership by which the vision of senior management is translated into the operations of the organization. Middle management has been tagged by many as a direct obstacle to creating a supportive environment for performance excellence.[12] Because of their position in the organization, middle managers have been accused of feeding territorial competition and stifling information flow. They have also been blamed for not developing or preparing employees for change. Unwilling to take initiatives that contribute to continuous improvement, middle managers appear to be threatened by continuous improvement efforts. Often, they are left out of the equation, with attention being paid to top management and the front-line workforce. However, middle management's role in creating and sustaining a culture of performance excellence is critical. Middle managers improve the operational processes that are the foundation of customer satisfaction. They can make or break cooperation and teamwork; and they are the principal means by which the remaining workforce prepares for change.

Middle managers must exhibit behaviors that are supportive of performance excellence, as they act as role models for first-level managers and employees. Such behaviors include listening to employees as customers, creating a positive work environment, being role models for first-level managers and supervisors, implementing quality improvements enthusiastically, challenging people to develop new ideas and reach their potential, encouraging supervisors to empower their people, setting challenging goals and providing positive feedback, and following through on promises. These changes are often difficult for many middle managers to accept.

In the end, the workforce delivers quality and, for a performance excellence strategy to succeed, must be granted not only empowerment, but ownership. Ownership goes beyond empowerment; it gives the employee the right to have a voice in deciding what needs to be done and how to do it.[13] At Westinghouse, workers defined ownership as "taking personal responsibility for our jobs ... for assuring that we meet or exceed our customers' standards and our own. We believe that ownership is a state of mind and heart that is characterized by a personal and emotional commitment to approach every decision and task with the confidence and leadership of an owner." Self-managed teams, discussed in Chapter 4, represent one form of ownership.

Organizational policies and procedures such as reward systems often must be adjusted for the new culture to take hold. For instance, customer service representatives in many firms are rewarded for the speed with which they process calls, rather than for how completely they satisfy the customers who call. Unless this type of reward system is changed, management's pleas to increase customer satisfaction will fall upon deaf ears.

QUALITYSPOTLIGHT

Wainwright Industries

One powerful example of cultural change is the case of Wainwright Industries.[14] During the 1970s and 1980s, Wainwright lost millions of dollars in sales; operations slowed to three days a week; tensions grew between employees and management. Recognizing that the problem lay with management, the CEO made some radical changes. Workers were called "associates" and everyone was put on salary. Associates are paid even if they miss work and still receive time-and-a-half for overtime. The company has maintained better than 99 percent attendance since this change. Managers shed their white shirts and ties, and everyone from the CEO down wears a common uniform, embroidered with the label Team Wainwright. A team of associates developed a profit-sharing plan, whereby everyone receives the same bonus every six months. Everyone has access to the privately held company's financial records. In addition, all reserved parking spaces were removed; walls—including those for the CEO's office—were replaced with glass. Customers, both external and internal, are treated as partners, with extensive communication. The most striking example occurred when one worker admitted having accidentally damaged some equipment, even though most workers were afraid to report such incidents. The CEO called a plant-wide meeting and explained what had happened. Then he called the man up, shook his hand, and thanked him for reporting the accident. Reporting of accidents increased from zero to 90 percent, along with suggestions on how to prevent them. As we elsewhere in this book, Wainwright's culture can be summed up as a *sincere belief and trust in people.*

Barriers to Change

Numerous barriers exist to successfully transform organizations to a sustained culture of performance excellence. Understanding these barriers can help significantly in managing change processes. One reason for failure of quality initiatives is a lack of what Deming called "constancy of purpose" in his original version of the 14 Points. The people who implement quality initiatives often have conflicting goals and priorities and simply do not follow through with the initiative. In most cases, this is a failure to understand the benefits that can result. A new CEO may ignore or dismantle a successful quality initiative. Such behaviors can cause an incredible amount of cynicism on the part of the workforce who lose their motivation to participate.

Another reason for failure is the lack of a holistic systems perspective—one of the Core Values and Concepts of the Baldrige criteria. Many approaches to "implementing quality" are one-dimensional and are consequently prone to failure. For example, some firms might emphasize the use of Six Sigma, but may only deploy them in a narrow part of the organization, such as manufacturing. These firms will see some improvement, but because the entire organization is not involved success will be limited. Others might focus on reducing defects in production and customer service but ignore product design and customer relationship management processes. Achieving performance excellence requires a comprehensive effort that encompasses all of the elements discussed in this book and span across "three levels of quality" — individual, process, and organization. Even though it is easy to focus on process improvement, it is certainly more difficult to establish cross-functional cooperation and to build the entire organization around a framework such as Baldrige.

Perhaps the most significant failure encountered in most organizations is a lack of alignment and integration with the organizational system. The Baldrige criteria emphasize these concepts. **Alignment** refers to consistency of plans, processes, information, resource decisions, actions, results, and analyses to support key organization-wide goals. Effective alignment requires common understanding of purposes and goals and use of complementary measures and information for planning, tracking, analysis, and improvement at each of the three levels of quality. **Integration** refers to the harmonization of plans, processes, information, resource decisions, actions, results, and analyses to support key organization-wide goals. Integration goes beyond alignment and is achieved when the individual components of a performance management system operate as a fully interconnected unit.

A well-aligned organization has its processes focused on achieving a shared vision and strategy. Aligning the organization is a challenging task that is accomplished through a sound strategy and effective deployment.

STRATEGIES FOR QUALITY AND PERFORMANCE EXCELLENCE

Organizations can take many routes to quality and performance excellence, but none of them represents the "one best way." Many organizations use only ISO 9000; some use Six Sigma; and others use Baldrige. Many organizations integrate Baldrige, ISO 9000, and Six Sigma in some way (typically this occurs as the organization matures and grows).[15] For example, the performance improvement system at Mesa Products, Inc. is embedded and managed through its quality management system (QMS), primarily through ISO 9001 certification. The company uses several improvement processes built around methods such as the plan-do-check-act (PDCA) cycle, lean and Six Sigma's define, measure, analyze, improve, and control strategy. The ISO 9001 based QMS combines with the Baldrige criteria at Mesa to bind business processes in an integrated, aligned direction, resulting in performance excellence (see Figure 14.1).

Joshua Hammond of the American Quality Foundation urges business leaders in the United States to develop quality and performance excellence approaches that maximize their own strengths. A successful strategy needs to fit within the existing organization culture and capabilities, which is the reason the Baldrige Award criteria are nonprescriptive. One study of Baldrige Award recipients concluded that each has a unique "quality engine" that drives their culture and organizational processes.[16] Some examples are summarized in Table 14.2. This table does not suggest that all other aspects of performance excellence are ignored; they are not. The quality engine simply customizes the quality effort to the organizational culture and provides focus. Whatever approach or combination of approaches an organization uses should make the most sense—and work—in the organization.

Best Practices

Best practices are simply those that are recognized by the business community (and often verified through some type of research) to lead to successful performance. Such organizations

---

FIGURE 14.1
Mesa's Quality
Management
System

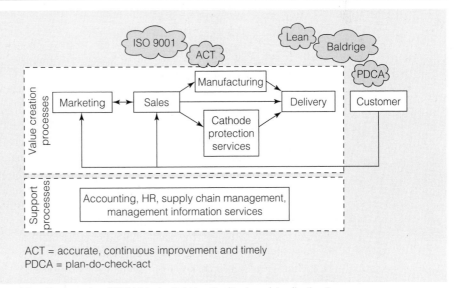

ACT = accurate, continuous improvement and timely
PDCA = plan-do-check-act

Source: Mesa Products, Inc. 2006 Malcolm Baldrige Quality Award Application Summary.

TABLE 14.2 Some Examples of Quality Engines

Organization	Quality Engine	Focus
Pal's Sudden Service	Process focus	Everything—from new product introduction to hiring to work systems—viewed as process that affects customer satisfaction.
Clarke American Checks	Strategic planning	Involving all stakeholders in a "First in Service" strategy focused on running and changing the business
Sharp Health Care	Customer focus	The Sharp Experience aimed at transforming the health care experience
North Mississippi Medical Center	Measurement and knowledge management	Award-winning management information system and electronic medical records
PRO-TEC Coating Co.	Workforce engagement	Safety as a first priority; leadership and communication throughout the organization
MESA Products	Technology	Manufacturing equipment and design center unique to the industry

as Disney, Microsoft, and many Baldrige winners have recognized best practices that are adopted by other organizations. Incorporating best practices into an organization is an important strategy for building quality and performance excellence capabilities.

Research performed by H. James Harrington with Ernst & Young and the American Quality Foundation, called the International Quality Study (IQS), suggested that trying to implement all the best practices of world-class organizations may not be a good strategy.[17] In fact, implementing the wrong practices can actually hurt the organization. The study indicated that only five best practices are "universal," and the chances are only 5 percent that they may not improve performance. They are:

1. Cycle-time analysis
2. Process value analysis
3. Process simplification
4. Strategic planning
5. Formal supplier certification programs

Beyond these five, best practices depend on an organization's current level of performance. That is, organizations must build their capability slowly and methodically. For example, organizations starting out on the road to performance excellence can reap the highest benefits by concentrating on fundamentals. These fundamentals include departmental and cross-functional teamwork, training in customer relationships, problem solving and suggestion systems, using internal customer complaint systems for new product and service ideas, emphasizing cost reduction when acquiring new technology, using customer satisfaction measures in strategic planning, increased training for all levels of employees, and focusing quality strategy on "building it in" and "inspecting it in." Once these fundamentals are in place, they can move on to practices such as department-level improvement teams, training employees in problem solving and other specialized topics, listening to supplier suggestions about new products, emphasizing the role of enforcement for quality assurance, making regular and consistent measurements of progress and sharing quality performance information with middle management, and emphasizing quality as a key to an organization's reputation. Finally, organizations that have a solid quality system in place can gain the most from providing customer-relationship training for new employees, emphasizing quality and teamwork for senior management assessment, encouraging widespread participation in quality meetings among non-management employees, using world-class benchmarking, communicating strategic plans to customers and suppliers, conducting after-sales service to build customer loyalty, and emphasizing competitor-comparison measures and customer satisfaction measures when developing plans. The study also showed that certain practices could have a negative impact on performance if applied inappropriately. For example, organizations at the early stages of the quality journey do not benefit from process benchmarking while those that have solid systems in place attain no benefit from increased training.

Strangely, the IQS Best Practices Report was interpreted by some news media as a criticism of the quality management philosophies that were advocated at that time.[18] They translated the report as simply saying that many quality practices are a waste of time and ineffective. On the contrary, the results were the first significant effort to develop a prescriptive theory (back to Deming again) of implementing quality and performance excellence, rather than relying on intuition and anecdotal evidence.

Impatient managers often seek immediate results by adopting off-the-shelf quality programs and practices, or by imitating other successful organizations. In most cases, this approach is setting themselves up for failure. Best practices, cannot be blindly benchmarked and adopted. Unfortunately, many organizations seek the magic quick fix for quality. In a famous anecdote, a person once wrote a letter to W. Edwards Deming and asked for the formula to quality improvement, offering to pay whatever price Deming required. This led to what has become one Deming's most famous quotes: "There is no instant pudding." We have seen similar behavior with Six Sigma. Many firms rushed to benchmark GE. However, GE already had a culture of quality improvement and extensive experience when Six Sigma began. The other firms were unable to copy the GE Method without the GE culture.

Rather, organizations advance in stages along a learning curve in their development of a quality culture and must carefully design their programs to optimize its effect. A good example is the Toyota Production System. It has never been a secret, yet many companies have tried and failed to duplicate it. Toyota's approach can be summarized as follows:

- They stayed the course and developed, implemented, and tweaked that system until it fit the organization like a glove.
- They did not spend their time looking for a prefabricated answer to all their problems that might or might not work in their organization.
- They took the time to understand their organization and their business and created a system that delivered the things they knew would make them a force in their industry.

As one professional observed: "The closest we will come to a silver bullet is innovative leadership. Courageous leaders have vision, take time to comprehend their own organizations, and create an indigenous strategy to fit their organization."[19]

Principles for Effective Implementation

No matter what approach an organization chooses, it must employ some basic principles to be implemented successfully. Lessons learned in implementing Six Sigma provide key insights that can apply to implementing any type of quality and performance excellence initiative. Principles for effective implementation of Six Sigma that have been cited are:[20]

- *Committed leadership from top management.* Managers at GE participate in hands-on approaches such as personally spending time in every Six Sigma training wave, speaking to and answering questions from students, dropping in (usually unannounced) on weekly and monthly Six Sigma reviews, and making site visits at the manufacturing and call-taking operations to observe firsthand the degree to which Six Sigma in ingrained in the culture.

- *Integration with existing initiatives, business strategy, and performance measurement.* Six Sigma should have a clear justification in terms of an organization's mission and strategic direction. However, with its focus on customers and the bottom line, this integration usually is not too difficult. At companies like GE and Allied Signal, Six Sigma has been extended to all areas of the company, such as product development and financial services. For example, GE first identifies all critical customer performance features and subjects them to a rigorous statistical design process, thus designing products for Six Sigma levels.

- *Process thinking.* As one of the foundation principles of total quality, a process focus is, not surprisingly, a necessary prerequisite. Mapping business processes is one of the key activities in Six Sigma efforts, as is a disciplined approach to the information gathering, analysis, and problem solving.

- *Disciplined customer and market intelligence gathering.* The ultimate goal is to improve those characteristics that are most important to customers; thus knowledge of customer needs is vital. Approaches that we discussed in Chapter 3 are essential to help focus Six Sigma projects on customers.

- *A bottom-line orientation.* Six Sigma projects must produce real savings or revenues in both the short term and long term. Most Six Sigma projects are designed to be completed within three to six months. GE has a financial analyst certify the results of every project.

- *Leadership in the trenches.* Within GE, Six Sigma includes a diverse population of technical and nontechnical people, managers, and others from key business areas who work together as a team to attack a problem using the DMAIC approach. All employees participate, not just those that hold the "belts."

- *Training.* Six Sigma organizations train nearly everyone in rigorous statistical and problem-solving tools. GE's Green Belt training is delivered to all GE employees and is available in strategic locations across the world. It is typically rolled out over a four-month period and is scheduled to help facilitate the trainee in leading a "Green Belt project" to not only yield savings but also practice in a real-life situation what is being learned in the training.

- *Continuous reinforcement and rewards.* Six Sigma organizations have significantly changed performance measurement and reward systems. At GE, 40 percent of executive incentives are tied to Six Sigma goals and progress. Before any savings are credited to an individual, the Black Belt overseeing the project must show that the problems are fixed permanently. All employees, even executives, who want to be considered for promotion must be trained in Six Sigma and complete a project. Some organizations also pool the savings at the business unit level and share the savings with the Six Sigma team members.

These principles are also reflected in the Baldrige model. For example, Baldrige stresses the importance of leadership; alignment of processes with strategic objectives, challenges and advantages, and with performance measures; process thinking; customer knowledge; a focus on results; and effective workforce management practices such as training and rewards and recognition.

THE JOURNEY TOWARD PERFORMANCE EXCELLENCE

Sustaining performance excellence requires the ability to overcome barriers and frustration, to view performance excellence as a journey, not an end, and the ability to develop into a "learning organization." Successful organizations realize that quality and performance excellence is a never-ending journey. As an old Chinese proverb says, a journey begins with a single step. Getting started often seems easy by comparison with sustaining a performance excellence focus. Numerous organizational barriers and challenges get in the way. New efforts usually begin with much enthusiasm, in part because of the sheer novelty of the effort. After awhile, reality sets in and doubts surface. Real problems develop as early supporters begin to question the process. At this point, the organization can resign itself to inevitable failure or persist and seek to overcome the obstacles.

The Life Cycle of Quality Initiatives

To help understand these issues, it is useful to recognize that quality initiatives—as well as most any business initiative—follow a natural life cycle.[21] Leonard and McAdam suggest that understanding the life cycle "provides a strategic mechanism to chart and sustain quality while proactively countering shortcomings of its implementation, such as stagnation and limited application, which can ultimately result in failure." The six stages of a quality life cycle are

1. *Adoption:* The implementation stage of a new quality initiative.
2. *Regeneration:* When a new quality initiative is used in conjunction with an existing one to generate new energy and impact
3. *Energizing:* When an existing quality initiative is refocused and given new resources
4. *Maturation:* When quality is strategically aligned and deployed across the organization
5. *Limitation or stagnation:* When quality has not been strategically driven or aligned
6. *Decline:* When the initiative has had a limited impact, is failing, and is awaiting termination

The following example serves to illustrate the implications of this life cycle model.

One organization began adopting quality by introducing team building and establishing problem-solving teams. However, after four years the quality management initiative failed. Initial training had been limited, and implementation was unfocused and not directly related to the strategic objectives of the organization. As a result, the new teamwork approach came as a culture shock to the organization, and its quality initiative began a decline. The organization was determined to continue with quality management and subsequently adopted a second initiative. This involved new training and teams provided with improvement kits based on problem solving tools and techniques. In addition, senior management focused on the coordination of improvement efforts with strong links to the organization's strategic goals. Structured performance assessments monitored progress. The quality manager cited "management commitment and leadership from the top" as the key to its successful second quality initiative. The quality life cycle of this second initiative reflects its progress from adoption to maturity. This approach created strong quality dynamics, which achieved strategic alignment and deployment throughout the organization. From this example, we observe two things:

1. Awareness that separate initiatives create a cumulative impact leads to an appreciation that selection of new quality initiatives must be based on where an organization is in the quality life cycle.

2. Understanding that the quality life cycle elements enable an organization to apply energizing or regenerating actions proactively to successfully sustain its quality journey.

An awareness of such impacts on the dynamics of quality, in particular on the characteristics of the quality life cycle, provides the capability to sustain successful quality management by strategically adopting responses based on energizing and regenerating elements.

In studying Baldrige recipients in the health care sector, a group of former Baldrige examiners and judges proposed a similar model that describes the Baldrige journey, shown in Figure 14.2.[22] At Stage 0, organizations opt to wait for mandates and regulations, and they implement change when required to maintain compliance. While they may experience occasional "random acts of improvement," there is no overarching impetus to drive the organization to higher levels of performance. In Stage 1, organizations commit to a proactive approach to improvement. Initial steps tend to include learning and implementing quality improvement tools and methods. Often this project-focused phase brings new capabilities to execute initiatives that change routine practices and processes for the better. However, organizations at this stage typically reach a plateau. Leaders became frustrated with the overall impact of their continuous improvement efforts and the pace of change. For most of these organizations, projects succeed often enough, but the overall culture does not change and system-wide performance excellence is elusive. Visionary leaders recognize the inherent limitations of a project-based approach to performance improvement: slow pace of change, incremental gains, and depleted organizational energy. They seek an approach to build system integration across silos and departments in order to create a high-performance, results-oriented culture throughout their organizations.

FIGURE 14.2
Baldrige Roadmap to Performance Excellence

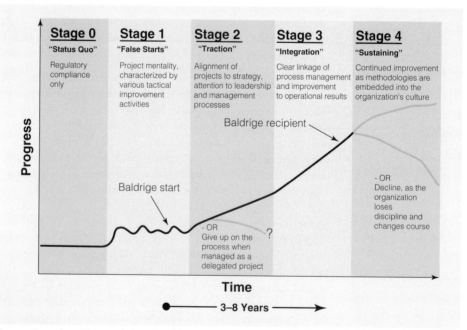

Source: Reproduced by permission of Kathleen J. Goonan, Joseph A. Muzikowski, and Patricia K. Stoltz, MD, Journey to Excellence: How Baldrige Health Care Leaders Succeed. (Milwaukee: ASQ Quality Press, 2009). To order this book, visit ASQ at http://www.asq.org/quality-press.

When senior leaders became personally and actively engaged with the criteria and feedback—whether through simply answering the questions, conducting a self-assessment, or writing an application for a state or national award program—they begin to experience traction on their organizational transformation strategies (Stage 2). This phase marks the transition from the singular focus on change through projects, however well executed, to systematic evaluation and improvement of leadership approaches. Projects become more focused and aligned to organizational strategy while leadership and management processes receive attention as well, shoring up capability to spread improvements and hardwire sustainability. As organizations become more skillful at these approaches, integration (Stage 3) begins to occur. Approaches and processes of leadership, such as values deployment and culture building, begin to link and align with strategic planning and action planning, scorecards and dashboards, job descriptions and performance review methods, and other operational processes. Nonaligned improvement initiatives are dropped or postponed as focused effort replaces frenetic activity. The Integration phase is characterized by action on the feedback, usually by incorporating it into the strategic planning process.

Finally, the Sustaining stage (Stage 4) can result in two outcomes: continued improvement or decline as organizations lose focus or become distracted. While Baldrige Award recognition might appear to carry with it the potential for loss of momentum, many organizations renew their commitment to achieving even higher levels of performance. This may occur through continuing annual participation in a Baldrige-based award process, or through internal assessment processes, often as a first step in annual strategic planning.

One example that reflects this roadmap is St. Luke's Hospital, which began its journey around 1988.[23] Key organizational milestones are summarized below:

1988–1991:
- Limited focus Patient Care Committee to a broader organizational quality assurance concept
- Hierarchal nursing governance to a shared governance model
- Decreased focus on the "bad apple" to process improvement activities
- Specialty-specific committees reconfigured to organizational cross-functional multidisciplinary teams

1992–1993:
- Development of an organization-wide customer satisfaction research program
- Individual care plans to formal clinical care pathways
- Cultural shift to organizational empowerment
- Board, medical staff, and administration retreat to implement Total Quality Management

1994:
- Organizational learning in statistical process control techniques
- Patient focused work redesign initiated
- Adopted Baldrige framework
- Participated on health care criteria design team for Missouri Quality Award

1995–1996:
- Embraced corporate culture of external performance review
- Received Missouri Quality Award (MQA)
- Began voluntarily reporting outcome data to the community

- Shared best practices across Missouri
- Used MQA feedback to improve performance

1997–1999:
- Deployed "Commitment to Excellence" initiative: an internal Baldrige-based assessment
- Received second Missouri Quality Award
- Quality was elevated to vice president status
- Restructured metrics architecture and developed Balanced Scorecard

2000–2001
- Used 1999 Baldrige and MQA feedback to improve organizational processes and share best practices
- Prepared internal Baldrige assessment and had it scored externally
- Focused on multiple action-oriented process teams
- Medical staff and senior leaders joined to drive organizational performance via Performance Improvement Steering Committee (PISC)

2002:
- Received third Missouri Quality Award
- Site visit by MBNQA
- Third refinement of the Balanced Scorecard
- Deployed 90-Day Action Planning Process

2003:
- Began preparation to achieve Nursing Magnet designation
- Created the role of Chief Learning Officer
- Developed and deployed process level scorecards in key areas
- Selected as a Malcolm Baldrige National Quality Award recipient

As you can clearly see, such a journey takes persistence and commitment. Implementing Baldrige requires repetitive cycles of self-assessment, priority-setting, action planning to address gaps and opportunities for improvement, and reflection of results, all driven by an organization's vision, strategic challenges, and capabilities.

Organizational Learning

Organizations are dynamic entities. Managers must consider the dynamic component in order to deal with instability in the environment, imperfect plans, the need for innovation, and the common human desire for variety and change. Sustainability requires continual learning, which we introduced in Chapter 5. Therefore, both the culture and the organizational structure should be designed to support the established direction in which the organization is moving, and modified whenever that direction changes significantly. Managers, especially those who do not understand the nature of leadership, are often hesitant to make needed organizational changes as the organization grows, even when the need for change becomes obvious. This need to change is embodied in a concept called the *learning organization*.

Learning organizations have become skilled in creating, acquiring, and transferring knowledge and in modifying the behavior of their employees and other contributors to their enterprises. A good example of a learning organization (and a learning individual!) is General Electric and its former CEO Jack Welch. In his first letter to GE shareholders in 1981, he noted, "This commitment to the utmost in quality and personal excellence is our surest path to continued business success. Quality is our best assurance of customer allegiance. It is our strongest defense against foreign competition and the only path to sustained growth and earnings." Welch's approach to business improvement has gone through three cycles of learning:

1. In the first cycle (early 1980s to late 1980s), he focused GE on the elimination of variety in its portfolio of businesses by reducing the nonperforming business units as judged by market performance. The elimination of unprofitable businesses permitted a better use of working capital. However, only so much gain can result from trimming the organization or eliminating bureaucracy, which led to the next phase of learning.

2. During the late 1980s to mid-1990s, he focused the company on simplifying and eliminating non-value-added activities through creative efforts of teams using Work-Outs and the Change Action Process (later renamed the Change Acceleration Process). Work-Out is a tool for involving all people from all ranks, levels, and functions of the organization in problem solving and improvement. Work-Out demolished the artificial barriers and walls within the organization and fostered the idea of "boundary-less learning."

3. Throughout his learning journey, Welch challenged his people to keep looking for creative ways to apply new learning from any source to improve the business. In 1995, Welch discovered Six Sigma and studied its implementation at both Motorola and Allied Signal. This phase of discovery focused on the elimination of variation from already lean business operations to drive gains in productivity and financial performance with a better focus on the customer.

Welch's process for continuous learning led to the discovery that business must simplify first, then automate best practices that have been designed for robust performance in the face of variation in business conditions. As Welch noted, "It is this passion for learning and sharing that forms the basis for the unrelenting optimism with which we view the future, and for the conviction that our greatest days lie ahead." The emphasis on quality and improvement through Six Sigma has been continued by Jeffrey Immelt, who succeeded Jack Welch as CEO at GE in 2001. Immelt's "Letter to Stakeholders" in the 2004 annual report stated:

> We have a new area of focus that we call **Lean Six Sigma**. We have leveraged Lean manufacturing's classic tools for reducing cycle time with the problem-solving capability of Six Sigma. In the last two years, Transportation improved inventory turns from seven to nine, and Advanced Materials improved receivables by six turns. We achieved $2.7 billion of improvements in working capital in 2003–04 and intend to continue this progress.
>
> We have a broad operating initiative called **Simplification**. We are targeting a reduction in "non-growth cost" of $3 billion over three years. We are measuring reductions in legal entities, headquarters, "rooftops," computer systems … anything that is not directly linked with customer satisfaction and growth. We are creating "Centers of Excellence" to share best practices and reduce cost.[24]

The 2007 annual report describes the results of a new initiative called "Growth as a Process," and its approaches to operational excellence that include using Lean Six Sigma, quality, and simplification to enhance value.

A major benefit of Baldrige is that it naturally provides a framework for organizational learning and, therefore, helps to enhance and sustain an organization, no matter what its current level of maturity. For example, the requirement of Performance

Analysis and Review in Category 4 focuses organizations to provide a picture of their "state of health" and examine how well they are currently performing and also how well they are moving toward the future. This review capitalizes on the information generated from the measurement and analysis of business results and is intended to provide a reliable means to guide both improvement and change at the strategic planning level.

The key to developing learning organizations is effective leadership (see Chapter 13). Researchers have suggested that both transactional and transformational leadership support organizational learning; in times of change, organizational learning benefits more from transformational leadership while in times of stability, organizational learning processes serve to refresh and reinforce current learning—a task best suited to transactional leadership. The ideal leader needs to identify and exercise the leadership behaviors appropriate to the circumstances.[25]

Learning organizations have to become good at performing five main activities, including systematic problem solving, experimentation with new approaches, learning from their own experiences and history, learning from the experiences and best practices of others, and transferring knowledge quickly and efficiently throughout the organization.[26] Virtually all of these skills are central to the philosophy of performance excellence. For example, systematic problem solving is reflected in Six Sigma and other improvement methodologies; experimentation is the basis for Deming's plan-do-study-act cycle; learning from experiences and history is often termed Santayana review[27] and is basic to Deming's philosophy; learning from the experiences and best practices of others is reflected in benchmarking practices; and transferring knowledge quickly and efficiently throughout the organization is the basis for modern knowledge management practices that we discussed in Chapter 12.

Cole has called for "continuous innovation" as an evolutionary step for extending "continuous improvement."[28] He pointed out that market pressures for better and cheaper products, delivered faster to the marketplace than ever before, require a new strategy that he advocates as a "probe and learn" process. Probe-and-learn is described as a non-linear, discontinuous, experimental, back-and-forth process that is needed in order to develop products and services to compete in the existing turbulent business environment. It requires methods such as rapid prototyping, beta testing with intentional generation of errors if they contribute to learning, learning from failure (and successes), and rapidly making decisions through peer and customer review.

You need only go back to the relationship between quality and profitability (Figure 1.3 in Chapter 1) to understand the importance of continuous innovation. From this argument, it is evident that the need for innovation has been known all along; however, most quality efforts (TQM, ISO 9000, Six Sigma, for example) have focused mainly on the quality of conformance rather than innovative design. Businesses are now closing the loop on a more complete performance excellence system with increasing emphasis on design and innovation.

Leaders in twenty-first-century organizations are finding that not only must they create learning organizations, but they must also create teaching organizations. For example, GE developed the concept of the virtuous teaching cycle (VTC) that guides their entire leadership development process, of which the Six Sigma approach is a vital part. The VTC includes some of the following concepts and assumptions, as well as others:[29]

- Leadership at all levels [as opposed to leadership at the top]
- Teamwork [as opposed to passive-aggressive behavior]
- Teachable point of view (TPOV) throughout [as opposed to a rigid, top-down process]

- Organizational knowledge grows [as opposed to organizational knowledge being depleted]
- Boundarylessness [as opposed to a boundary-laden, turf-oriented organization]

Self-Assessment

One way for organizations to build organizational learning is to conduct self-assessments of where it stands relative to best practices and key requirements. **Self-assessment** is the holistic evaluation of processes and performance.[30] It helps managers answer essential questions such as "How are we doing?," "What are our strengths?," and "What areas require improvement?" The *self* part of the term means that it should be conducted internally rather than simply relying on an external consultant, which promotes greater involvement of the organization's people, yielding a higher level of understanding and buy-in.

Self-assessment should identify both strengths and opportunities for improvement, creating a basis for evolving toward higher levels of performance. Thus, a major objective of most self-assessment projects is the improvement of organizational processes based on opportunities identified by the evaluation. At a minimum, a self-assessment should address the following:

- *Management involvement and leadership.* To what extent are all levels of management involved?
- *Product and process design.* Do products meet customer needs? Are products designed for easy manufacturability?
- *Product control.* Is a strong product control system in place that concentrates on defect prevention before the fact, rather than defect removal after the product is made?
- *Customer and supplier communications.* Does everyone understand who the customer is? To what extent do customers and suppliers communicate with each other?
- *Quality improvement.* Is a quality improvement plan in place? What results have been achieved?
- *Employee participation.* Are all employees actively involved in quality improvement?
- *Education and training.* What is done to ensure that everyone understands his or her job and has the necessary skills? Are employees trained in quality improvement techniques?
- *Quality information.* How is feedback on quality results collected and used?

Many self-assessment instruments that provide a picture of the state of quality in an organization are available. The Baldrige Program provides two simple instruments called *Are We Making Progress?* (one for employees and one for leaders). They provide a way of capturing the voice of the employee and the perspective of leadership to develop baseline measurements of an organization's progress using the Baldrige criteria. The *Are We Making Progress?* surveys are available in the Baldrige Materials folder on the Student Companion Site. Most self-administered surveys, however, can only provide a rudimentary assessment of an organization's strengths and weaknesses. The most complete way to assess the level of performance excellence maturity in an organization is to evaluate its practices and results against the Baldrige criteria by using trained internal or external examiners, or by actually applying for the Baldrige or a similar state award and receiving comprehensive examiner feedback. Of course, many organizations, especially smaller ones, that are just starting on a quality journey should begin with the basics, for example, a well-documented and consistent quality assurance system such as ISO 9000.

Assessment findings often identify specific processes and activities that require extensive modification.[31] A Baldrige assessment, for example, might find that the organization lacks a systematic approach for determining customer satisfaction relative to its competitors. A number of actions might be taken to address this opportunity. The organization might consider instituting a competitive analysis program, sponsoring an industry-wide customer satisfaction research program, benchmarking best-in-class organizations, or undertaking some other initiatives to improve its intelligence gathering practices. Although interventions of such scope commonly involve many employees, involvement of senior management in direction setting, resource provision, and subsequent monitoring is usually necessary for effective implementation.

Because the Baldrige process is based on self-assessment against the criteria, it is not surprising that some of the best examples of learning organizations are Baldrige winners. In pursuing their improvement efforts that eventually led to the award, they have continually and systematically translated the examiner feedback into improvements in their management practices. A vice president at Texas Instruments Defense Systems & Electronics (DS&E) Group noted that "participating in the Baldrige Award process energized improvement efforts."[32] By 1997, just before its purchase by Raytheon, DS&E had reduced the number of in-process defects to one-tenth of what they were at the time it won the Baldrige. Production processes that took four weeks several years before were reduced to one week, with 20 to 30 percent less cost. As another example, the superintendent of Iredell-Statesville Schools, a 2008 recipient, noted "The big [opportunity for improvement provided by the Baldrige feedback report] that kept us from achieving recognition in 2007 was that we had a well-deployed Baldrige criteria at the classroom level, but were so focused on meeting the requirements of the No Child Left Behind Act in student learning that we missed opportunities for improvement on the operation side, for example, in maintenance, transportation, and child nutrition. We were using Deming's plan-do-study-act cycles, and once we got into the operation side of the house we found all kinds of expenses that could be reduced, with the savings then used in the academic side of the house. So, it was a great feedback report. It gave us the impetus to go to the next level."[33]

Although some research suggests a positive relationship between the conduct of self-assessment and performance outcomes, other evidence suggests that many organizations derive little benefit from conducting self-assessment and achieve few of the process improvements suggested by self-study. It is not uncommon for organizations to spend considerable time and effort on assessing their organizations, only to seemingly ignore the results.[34] This lack of follow-through might seem a bit surprising: Why would organizations take the time to conduct a self-assessment and then not follow up on the results? After all, improvement opportunities usually offer significant gains in organizational effectiveness and competitive performance. Some managers may not follow up because they truly do not sense a problem—despite information suggesting otherwise. Often, however, managers get the message but choose not to respond. Many managers react negatively or by denial: "These are wrong," "This is not how it is here," and "These [examiners] missed the boat" are often heard. Such remarks are particularly likely when the report suggested that the organization was a less-than-stellar performer in areas perceived as strengths by senior managers.

Other managers may not know what to do with the information. Managers possessing little understanding of how the organization operates may not know which levers to pull in order to effect change or simply do it to appease their superiors. Typical comments include, "There's some good stuff here, but I have no idea where to go from here," and "It's hard for me to understand how to turn this [assessment report] into action." After reading his copy of the feedback report, the head of one manufacturing company manager muttered, "Well, we've satisfied [the boss's demand for conducting the self-assessment] for another year. Now we can put this all away and get back to business."

Managers must take a positive approach to self-assessment findings, no matter how unpleasant they might appear—"OK, what should we do to improve these areas?" Positive reactions often reinforce long-held but suppressed views about how the organization functioned. For example, at a meeting where results were being presented to the top management team, the chief engineering manager, upon hearing of low evaluations related to the organization's communications processes, exclaimed, "I've been telling you guys this for years! Maybe now you'll believe me that we need to do something."

Following up requires senior leaders to engage in two types of activities: action planning and subsequently tracking implementation progress. The action plan identifies particular activities necessary to address the improvement opportunities. Effective action plans share some common characteristics. First, key actions to address the opportunities must be identified. A meeting to discuss the findings with key employees is often an excellent way to begin. Once identified, action plans should be documented and the who, what, when, where, and how of each action item specified. A draft version of the action plan should be communicated to inform those directly affected and gain their cooperation. Finally, the action plan should be reviewed to ensure that it effectively addresses the key opportunities identified by the self-assessment findings.

Many managers consider their job finished when action plans are set in motion. However, planned changes are rarely implemented as initially intended. Moreover, people responsible for implementing the plans may need to use encouragement or involvement in order to effectively execute their portions of the intended change. Change implementation demands a second component of effective follow-up—tracking the progress of action plan execution—to provide managers with crucial feedback on whether the intervention is effective.

To leverage self-assessment findings, managers must do four things:

1. *Prepare to be humbled.* "Humbling" is a word we often hear from managers who have recently digested assessment findings. Many of them have trouble believing that the performance levels of the organization are as low as they appear. Managers can temper their expectations by learning about the self-assessment activities and experiences of other organizations. Hearing it from peers, through phone calls to colleagues, and attending conferences, permit managers to learn firsthand about the self-assessment experiences of others.

2. *Talk though the findings.* Follow-up can be enhanced when the top management team discusses the self-assessment findings. Discussing the issues, concerns, and ideas can generate greater shared perspective among executives and improve consensus.

3. *Recognize institutional influences.* Managers should be sensitive to the institutional forces working on their self-assessment activities, such as pressures from customers. Institutional influence can be covertly transmitted through the literature, presentations, and conversation that managers encounter. During the planning phase of the assessment, frank discussion about the environmental motivators of the project can sensitize managers to these outside influences.

4. *Grind out the follow-up.* Even though follow-up activities may not be as exciting as plotting competitive strategy or entertaining customers, they provide infrastructure for realizing the process improvements possible from self-assessment.

Challenges in Small Organizations and Nonprofits

Small organizations and nonprofits have generally been slow to adopt quality initiatives. In most cases, this lag is a result of a lack of understanding and knowledge of what needs to be done and how to do it, because managers are wrapped up in entrepreneurial activities that typically focus on sales strategies and market growth, day-to-day cash flow problems, and routine fire fighting. In addition, these organizations often lack the resources needed to establish and maintain more formal quality systems. However, in viewing the three core principles of TQ, a focus on customers is clearly vital to small enterprises; the company president or founder is often the principal contact with key customers and knows them intimately. Most small businesses live or die from their customer relationship practices, but the other two TQ principles—employee engagement and teamwork, and a process focus and continuous improvement—are generally not well addressed. Small business executives, especially in family-owned enterprises, often have a "command-and-control" attitude that dominates decision-making, leaving little discretion and empowerment to employees. In addition, processes tend to be highly unstructured and not based on adequate data and information. Simply getting by each day often takes precedence over long-term planning and improvement activities.

Many other characteristics of small firms adversely affect the implementation of TQ principles. These characteristics include the following:[35]

- The lack of market clout, which may impact a small firm's ability to get suppliers involved in quality efforts
- Not recognizing the importance of human resource management strategies in quality, and therefore experiencing lower levels of employee empowerment, involvement, and quality-related training
- Lack of professional management expertise and the short-term focus, which often results in inadequate allocation of resources to TQ efforts
- Lower technical knowledge and expertise, making it difficult for smaller firms to effectively use quality tools and improvement techniques
- The informal nature of communication and lack of structured information systems, which inhibit implementation

Nevertheless, many successful small businesses have shown that quality initiatives can be successfully accomplished. Small businesses often come to this conclusion as they grow or face critical market challenges; they simply cannot afford to be managed as they were in the past, and require a more systematic process-oriented infrastructure. Perhaps the most important factor in successful quality initiatives in small businesses is the recognition by the CEO or president that a quality focus can be beneficial and lead to achieving organizational goals.

 QUALITYSPOTLIGHT

Texas Nameplate

Texas Nameplate Company, Inc. (TNC) manufactures and sells identification and information labels that are affixed to refrigerators, oil-field equipment, high-pressure valves, trucks, computer equipment, and other products made by more than a thousand customers throughout the United States and in nine foreign countries. With less than 50 employees, it was the smallest company to receive a Baldrige Award, which it did twice, in 1998 and again in 2004. Their quality journey began when a large customer threatened to cut them off if they did not begin applying quality control tools. However, it was the persistence of TNC's president, Dale Crownover, who made the difference and kept faith in his people. Not only did Crownover begin training his people, but he instituted profit-sharing and gainsharing incentives, along with higher-than-industry-average pay scales, to reinforce the workforce's commitment to quality and foster company loyalty. Customer contact employees are empowered to resolve customer complaints without consulting management, and production workers are responsible for tailoring processes to optimize contributions to company goals and to meet team-set standards.

To help workers identify opportunities for improvement, each process at TNC is mapped using a flow chart. The average employee receives 75 hours of training in the first two years, much of it delivered on a just-in-time basis. About one in 10 workers is a multipurpose employee, trained in three or more jobs, allowing them to be moved to any area of the company that needs assistance to meet fluctuating customer and market demands. As a result of these efforts, the company disbanded its quality control department, replaced it with a cross-functional team, and made quality the responsibility of all employees. Defects fell from 2.4 percent to less than 1 percent, employee turnover improved, and market share increased by 45 percent in just three years. Was it hard? In one interview, Crownover stated, "Yeah, it was hard. The last five years of my life doing this was very hard. But let me tell you about the first five years I was president of this company. We had legal issues, EEOC, customer complaints, people quitting … that was hard!"

Similar comments hold true for nonprofits, who, unlike their business counterparts, are not driven by the bottom line (although tight budgets can certainly be a driving factor in pursuing quality) and whose managers often lack the business acumen and technical expertise needed to make an organizational transformation. Little literature exists on how to apply quality principles to not-for-profits, and employees use a "language" different from business, making it challenging for them to translate business concepts into meaningful applications. Among the key challenges that not-for-profits face are overcoming the fear of change, changing the mindset that not-for-profits are different and cannot effectively apply quality principles, identifying a vision and customers, understanding work processes, dealing with limited resources, and understanding relationships with government and large corporations.[36] However, numerous not-for-profit organizations are adopting TQ principles because of their impact on the public and society—their major customers and stakeholders. The United Way of America, for example, began recognizing United Way organizations for quality achievements in 1994.

The American Red Cross launched a multiyear, multimillion-dollar quality effort to enhance organizational effectiveness and improve its process of collecting, testing, and distributing blood. Their focus is to drive any variability, deviation, or error down to zero using initiatives such as the following:

- New technologies to reduce the potential for human error
- Restructuring and increasing the level of quality assurance staff
- Creating a more streamlined and comprehensive training system

- Reengineering the core manufacturing processes to make them more efficient and simplified so as to reduce and prevent errors
- Investing in facilities to enable more efficient and effective adoption of new technology[37]

Expansion of the Baldrige Award to all types of nonprofits in 2007 has spawned more interest in quality and performance excellence among these organizations.

A VIEW TOWARD THE FUTURE

As we end this book, it is a good exercise to try to look into the future and think about how things will be. In reflecting on quality in the previous century, A.V. Feigenbaum and Donald S. Feigenbaum observed:

> [Quality] has become one of the twentieth century's most important management ideas. It has exorcised the traditional business and graduate management school notion that a company's success means making products and offering services quicker and cheaper, selling them hard and providing a product service net to try to catch those that don't work well. It has replaced this notion with the business principle that making products better is the best way to make them quicker and cheaper and that what is done to make quality better anywhere in an organization makes it better everywhere in the organization.[38]

What the future will hold is never predictable. We face a serious challenge in sustaining the principles of quality amidst the continuing emergence of short-lived management fads, changing leadership driven by pressures of the stock market, e-commerce, and a myriad of other factors. In 2000, the American Society for Quality invited 21 individuals to provide comments on quality in the twenty-first century.[39] Although over a decade old, we cite a sample of those comments, and invite you to reflect on what they mean for you as you continue your education and embark on your future careers.

> *"Those who understand that quality is derived from effectively managing systems will provide leadership in the new millennium. How many CEOs do you know who arise from the ranks of quality? Few, if any. Yet, I believe tomorrow's business leaders will have deep roots in quality and advanced understanding of how it nourishes their organizations' broader management systems."—Alexander Chong*

> *"The new millennium presents us with some fundamental challenges:*
> - *Altered labor markets with higher skill levels, a greater gender balance, and increasing diversity.*
> - *Competitive demands for continuous improvement, customer responsiveness, and levels of business excellence that are not price prohibitive.*
>
> *These can only be met through an emphasis on quality with equality."—Eileen Drew*

> *"The twenty-first century will see leading edge companies apply to information the quality principles successfully applied to manufacturing. This will usher in the next economic revolution—the 'realized' Information Age, created by applying information quality management to information and knowledge processes."—Larry P. English*

"Quality is necessary for public education to thrive in the future. We have a moral imperative to use quality to make a difference in the lives of our children."—Diane Rivers

"The quality perspective will shape the redefinition of the role of government. This new role will mean serving as a facilitator of relationships and innovative partnerships across all sectors, with less focus on direct delivery of service. Those who understand this context will thrive."—Tina Sung

Finally, Miles Maguire, former Editor of *Quality Progress* noted:

In the first 10 seconds of the new century ... the world will witness the birth of 44 infants ... by the time a year has passed almost 140 million children will have been born ... Consider all the new technologies and products and concepts and ideologies that have taken hold in the last decade: flip phones, fax machines, hiphop, SUVs, global markets, cyberschooling, eco-tourism, eco-terrorism, extreme sports, e-commerce, gene therapy, streaming media, and digital encryption—to name just a few. And now consider how the next decade, the first 1 percent of the new millennium, will bring at least as great a proliferation of ideas, innovations, and improvements. These developments will set a higher standard of expectations, creating a marketplace with a dizzying diversity of demands that can scarcely be imagined. What will the voice of the twenty-first century customer be telling us? We'll have to listen carefully to find out.[40]

SUMMARY OF KEY POINTS AND TERMINOLOGY

The Student Companion Site provides a summary of key concepts and terminology introduced in this chapter.

QUALITY *in* PRACTICE

Merging Divergent Quality Systems at Honeywell[41]

AlliedSignal and Honeywell each had years invested in their quality management systems (QMSs) when they merged in 1999 into Honeywell International. AlliedSignal was a leading supporter of, and participant in, the Six Sigma movement. By the time of the merger, AlliedSignal was five years into its Six Sigma program, which was key to the company's effort to capture growth and productivity opportunities more rapidly and efficiently. Meanwhile, Honeywell had developed its own Baldrige-based QMS—the Honeywell Quality Value (HQV) program. The merger between Allied-Signal and Honeywell required merging and reshaping these two diverse approaches, which was renamed Six Sigma Plus. Six Sigma Plus combines the characteristics of the former AlliedSignal's Six Sigma program and the former Honeywell's HQV method, including lean enterprise, a lean manufacturing component; and activity-based management (ABM), which aids in analyzing customer profitability and targeting future costs for new product development.

Key to making Six Sigma Plus universal in each of Honeywell International's businesses was committing to a strategy of approaching every improvement project with the same logical method, the DMAIC process. Their leadership criteria were also logical and rigorous. Candidates for Six Sigma Plus leadership positions were expected to possess an aptitude for learning, the ability to lead, the ability to mentor others, and the desire to continue to progress through the organization.

Honeywell International's CEO Michael R. Bonsignore made clear the future of Six Sigma at the new company: "As a new organization, our challenge is to continue the performance improvements of our predecessors, delight customers, and achieve aggressive growth. Six Sigma Plus will drive growth and productivity by energizing all of Honeywell International's 120,000 employees worldwide—providing the skills and tools to create more value for our customers, improve our processes, and capitalize on the power of the Internet through e-business. I am determined to make it a way of life at Honeywell International."

Edward M. Romanoff, Honeywell International's communications director for Six Sigma Plus and productivity, stated: "Lean helps us to reengineer a process to focus only on customer value-added elements. ABM helps us to understand the profitability of our products and services and to tailor our business models appropriately. The HQV process is being streamlined, timed to affect our annual operating plans, and geared to help our businesses prioritize remedial process improvements that affect customers and the financial well-being of the business. These two pieces—Six Sigma and HQV—come together nicely in that the latter provides the framework for how one should run a business in total, and Six Sigma gives you the quantitative specifics of what and how to improve."

"The Baldrige criteria might mandate that a company measure a given product's performance from a customer's perspective," explains Ray Stark, VP of Six Sigma and Productivity. "And if no such reporting mechanism existed, the Baldrige examiner would suggest that best-performing companies have this kind of system and that your company should put one in place. With a Six Sigma QMS, we would not only say you should put something in place, but we would give you the specific measurements that would help you understand the capability of the product. And it would be done in a way that would allow you to index its quality against a yardstick that we call Six Sigma."

Being able to effectively use Stark's yardstick meant training. Employees of the former AlliedSignal needed to learn about the HQV elements added to their Six Sigma program to create Six Sigma Plus, but the bigger challenge was training employees of the former Honeywell in Six Sigma methodology, a program that had not been developed or implemented there.

But "training" didn't accurately characterize Honeywell International's project based educational system. "Our program is not about training, it's about learning," explains Romonoff. "You can put people in a classroom and give them statistical training. You can give them hypothetical examples to make your point and people do learn, some faster than others. But the part that's unique here is that people come into this mentored environment with a project beforehand. It's something that they or their business particularly needs done. And they're given that project and asked to go and learn about these tools and how they can apply them to get a desired result or 'outcome.' It's very much results-orientated." Management expects this newly gained knowledge to trickle down the corporate structure as soon as the training is completed. Employees who complete the program are expected to go back to their business and complete two to three Six Sigma projects per year. Additionally, they are to mentor as many as 10 groups of employees a year in their Six Sigma Plus learning curve.

"So if that's 10 teams at 10 people each, you've got 100 employees that can be potentially impacted by this one individual," explains Stark. "So it's very important that these people have the team-dynamic skills to deal with different types of people, behaviors and situations. At the end of the day, what we want is at least a simple understanding of the applications of these tools by every employee."

Honeywell International employees who become skilled in Six Sigma Plus tools can earn certification in the following core areas of proficiency:

- Green Belt—A person with working knowledge of Six Sigma Plus methodology and tools, who has completed training and a project to drive high-impact business results.
- Black Belt—A highly skilled Six Sigma Plus expert who has completed four weeks of classroom

learning and, over the course of four to six months, demonstrated mastery of the tools through the completion of a major process improvement project.

- Master Black Belt—The Six Sigma Plus expert most highly skilled in the methodologies of variation reduction. After a year-long, project-based certification program, Master Black Belts train and mentor Black Belts, help select and lead high-value projects, maintain the integrity of the sigma measurements, and develop and revise Six Sigma Plus learning materials.

- Lean Expert—A person who has completed four weeks of lean training and one or more projects that have demonstrated significant, auditable business results and the appropriate application of Six Sigma Plus lean tools.

- Lean Master—A person highly skilled in implementing lean principles and lean tool utilization in diverse business environments. Certification involves one year of intense study and practice in advanced lean tools, teaching, and mentoring.

- ABM Expert—A person who has demonstrated proficiency in activity-based management (ABM) through a business application involving product costing, process costing, or customer profitability analysis. Certification involves attending an ABM training course, defining a meaningful project, displaying knowledge of the ABM tools, and using the data for key decision making. ABM experts frequently link Six Sigma Plus tools to projected and actual financial results.

- ABM Master—A person who has the skills of an expert plus the ability to develop and deliver ABM learning courses. Certification typically takes one year and involves demonstrating the use of ABM data for multiple purposes with repeatable and sustainable results. ABM Masters are proficient in the use of advanced cost management tools and have the ability to tailor cost data and analysis to a business's vision and strategy.

- TPM Expert—A person who applies total productive maintenance (TPM) and reliability methodologies and tools to assist or lead teams in optimizing asset capacity-productivity at minimum life cycle cost. A TPM Expert is responsible for determining critical equipment and measuring its overall effectiveness, thus enabling growth and productivity through optimum asset utilization.

- TPM Master—A highly skilled individual experienced in the use of TPM and reliability tools and methodologies. TPM Masters' responsibilities include assisting leadership in identifying high–leverage asset improvement opportunities; leading critical, high-leverage improvement projects in a business; and leading cultural paradigm shifts from reactive to proactive asset management.

This commitment to training and expansion of Six Sigma Plus around the world has paid significant dividends. One of Honeywell's European divisions, Aerospace Services, merged activity-based management and lean manufacturing techniques at its Raunheim, Germany, facility. The site repairs auxiliary power units, propulsion engines, and components that provide air conditioning and other power-related features aboard aircraft. The site impressed customers over a recent two-year period with a 43 percent reduction in component repair time. It helped Honeywell achieve a $47 million increase in revenue and was a major factor in $900,000 worth of productivity improvements. An Industrial Control team developed a reliable, cost-effective family of chips and assembled components for the burgeoning data communications market. As a result, Industrial Control achieved a 500 percent increase in revenue growth, resulting in a year-over-year increase in operating profits of several million dollars. Cycle time was reduced 35 percent, and yields increased from 75 percent to 93 percent.

Key Issues for Discussion

1. Trace the development of Six Sigma, the Honeywell Quality Value (HQV) program, and Six Sigma Plus, before and after the AlliedSignal and Honeywell merger. What role did the corporate culture of each organization play in the results from the Six Sigma Plus initiative?

2. How does top management show its support of Six Sigma Plus? Do you believe that an adequate structure exists to continue building and sustaining the quality effort at Honeywell for the foreseeable future?

3. What are the unique features of Six Sigma Plus that are not part of the standard Six Sigma process discussed in earlier chapters?

QUALITY in PRACTICE

Integrating Quality Frameworks at Veridian Homes[42]

Veridian Homes began in June 2003, when Don Simon Homes and Midland Builders, two of Wisconsin's oldest home builders, merged. The family owned and operated company dedicated itself to quality home building, community involvement and environmental stewardship. With 100 employees, Veridian Homes now builds 500 single-family and condominium homes each year in Madison, WI, and the surrounding area. The company has found the use of several quality methods, including a Baldrige self assessment system, is critical to the success of the company's improvement initiatives. Using best quality practices to increase customer focus and satisfaction, it has improved productivity while reducing impact on the environment.

The goal at Veridian Homes is to promote, educate on, and coordinate quality throughout the company. Specifically, the structure and systems employed to achieve this goal, from a strategic and operational mindset, include the National Housing Quality Award (NHQA), Baldrige Award self assessment, builder certification and Six Sigma. The NHQA program is based on the Baldrige award, and provides applicants expert evaluation and feedback on their organizations' quality management practices. Unlike the Baldrige award, however, the NHQA process includes a third-party survey of the applicants' customers on their satisfaction with their homes and the home building process. The NHQA also includes a self-assessment, which helps identify opportunities for improvement (OFIs) and allows these efforts to be strategically implemented.

Self-assessments are conducted annually using Baldrige Express, an employee survey based on the Baldrige criteria. The National Council for Performance Excellence offers Baldrige Express surveys in association with state quality award organizations.

Employees rate the company on a Likert scale in each criterion and can provide detailed comments on strengths, weaknesses and OFIs. A report provides a detailed analysis for management to conduct annual measuring and monitoring and to identify and prioritize weaknesses. Veridian uses this analysis to drive its annual strategic planning process (SPP), placing Baldrige at the heart of the organizational strategy formation cycle (see Figure 14.3). Strategic goals are linked to each employee via the performance planning and development (PPD) process. This process helps an employee understand his or her role, priorities, resources, accomplishments and professional development as they relate to the company's vision, mission, strategic drivers and departmental strategic goals. The employees also take part in a profit sharing program, motivating and rewarding employees based on measured and sustained improvements in cost, quality, cycle times, customer service and profits.

In fall 2004, Veridian Homes earned NAHBRC builder certification status for quality and safety management systems. The certification, based on ISO 9000, is third-party audited and included Veridian's construction, sales and customer relations departments. Since earning certification, the land development, purchasing, estimating and design departments have been incorporated into the certification. Veridian has also expanded its management system to include an environmental management system that focuses on improving activities such as erosion control and recycling. This has formed an integrated quality, environmental, health and safety (QEHS) management system, which provides a tactical level methodology to structure, document, disseminate, implement and manage Veridian's QEHS requirements.

Veridian uses various improvement tools and techniques to support quality implementation. On the Veridian intranet, which is available to all employees, a quality toolbox provides templates, PowerPoint based training, videos and other materials covering topics such as trade partner certification, builder certification, NHQA criteria, Baldrige criteria; Six Sigma methodology, and other improvement tools and techniques.

Veridian uses numerous cross-functional improvement teams. Each team has a team leader, facilitator and sponsor, and the company has one Six Sigma Black Belt and two Green Belts to provide support and expertise. The construction and customer relations departments have launched 10 improvement teams focusing on issues raised through warranty and customer feedback and directly linked to the strategy for the operations department.

FIGURE 14.3   Strategic Planning Cycle Driven by Baldrige Assessment

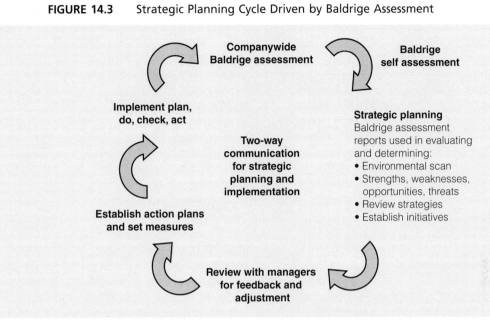

Source: Reprinted with permission from Denis Leonard, "Building Quality at Veridian Homes," *Quality Progress*, October 2006, pp. 49–54. Copyright © 2006 American Society for Quality. No further distribution allowed without permission.

Veridian's green building practices address the corporate social responsibility aspect of quality management and are reflected in the leadership criteria of the NHQA and the Baldrige award. In Wisconsin, green building practices are certified by Green Built Homes through the Wisconsin Environmental Initiative. Green Built certified builders undergo reviews of building plans, specifications and on-site visits to ensure the criteria are met. The criteria cover waste reduction, recycling and disposal of materials, energy efficient insulation and air sealing, storm water management and water conservation, landscape conservation, energy efficient mechanical systems, and use of recycled materials and energy efficient materials and construction products.

Veridian's quality initiatives have resulted in several performance improvements, including:

- Model homes sold cycle times reduced from 32 to 15 days.
- Drafting time on models reduced by more than an hour.
- Estimating time on model homes reduced by 32 percent.
- Material variance (difference between ordered and required, perhaps due to damage on site) down by 20 percent for lumber, 24 percent for siding and 38 percent for trim.

- Paperwork processing reduced by 208 hours per year, with a total estimated savings across Veridian of $200,000 through performance increases by implementing a production scheduler software system called Builder MT.
- Person hours down by 200 per year through escrow and warranty process improvements.
- Defects cut in half by using 10 defect reduction teams in cooperation with trade partners.

In national surveys conducted by NRS Corp., a consulting firm that specializes in research for the home building industry, Veridian customer satisfaction measures are consistently in the top 10 percent of the 333 builders reviewed. Satisfaction with Veridian's warranty is in the top 5 percent of all builders on the 30-day customer satisfaction survey and is in the top 15 percent of all builders on the annual customer satisfaction survey.

Key Issues for Discussion

1. What tools and approaches has Veridian used to integrate quality throughout the organization?
2. How have NHQA certification, the Baldrige process, and the Green Built certification process contributed to efficiency and cost effectiveness for Veridian?

REVIEW QUESTIONS

1. What is culture? How are cultural values reflected in organizations?
2. Explain the difference between strategic change and process change.
3. Describe questions that organizations must ask and steps they must take in change management processes.
4. Discuss the role of middle management and the workforce in achieving quality and performance excellence.
5. What lessons can be learned from Wainwright Industries about changing an organization's culture?
6. What are common barriers to change?
7. Define the terms alignment and integration. Why are they important?
8. Why is it important to customize performance excellence approaches to each organization?
9. What are best practices? What are the major conclusions and implications of the Best Practices report of Ernst & Young and the American Quality

Foundation? How do they relate to Deming's philosophy?
10. List the important principles for successfully implementing performance excellence approaches.
11. Describe the typical life cycle of a quality initiative and the Baldrige "Roadmap." Why are they important for senior leaders to understand?
12. Explain the notion of a learning organization. How does the Baldrige criteria provide a framework for organizational learning?
13. What is self-assessment? Why is it valuable? What issues should self-assessment address?
14. Why is follow-up important as a part of self-assessment processes? What two key activities should comprise follow-up? What advice should managers heed to leverage self-assessment?
15. Why have small businesses and not-for-profits been slow to adopt quality initiatives?
16. What must small businesses and not-for-profits do to successfully establish a total quality focus?

DISCUSSION QUESTIONS

1. We noted that creating a culture for quality and performance excellence is not rocket science. Summarize, in your own words, a simple explanation of what senior leaders need to do to accomplish it.
2. What might the term dysfunctional corporate culture mean? What implications does it have regarding quality?
3. What might be the value of creating a crisis mentality in an organization in order to motivate the need for improvement?

4. How would you describe the culture of your college or university?
5. Discuss how the Baldrige framework promotes alignment and integration.
6. What might the learning organization concept mean to a college or university?
7. What is your opinion on the future of quality? Do you agree with the comments made in the concluding section of this chapter? Why or why not?

PROJECTS, ETC.

1. Examine some corporate websites and comment on the cultural values that are reflected by the information you find. How important do these organizations view quality to their success?
2. Talk to individuals that you know from some local organizations (companies, schools, government agencies) about the organization's commitment to

quality and performance excellence principles. What factors do they attribute to either the success or failure of their organization's approaches?
3. Read the application summary for a recent Baldrige recipient (which can be found on the Baldrige website) and try to characterize what "quality engine" drives the organization.

4. Interview your fellow students to identify a set of "best learning practices." Develop a plan for sharing these throughout your school.
5. Find an organization that has implemented ISO 9000, Baldrige, or Six Sigma. Prepare a report on the implementation issues and challenges that the organization faced. How did they address them, and what was the result of their efforts?
6. Develop a hierarchy of the questions within the Baldrige Award criteria that would guide an organization starting to pursue performance excellence toward world-class performance. In other words, what key issues within the criteria would be more appropriate for organizations just starting out to concentrate on, and how should they progress toward fully meeting the Baldrige criteria?
7. Talk to a local not-for-profit organization manager or small business owner about quality. How aware are they of quality principles and tools? What challenges do they see in trying to build quality into their organizations?

CASES

DISTINGUISHED AD AGENCY[43]

Distinguished Ad Agency (DAA) had been in business for about 10 years. It had a strong regional reputation, and counted divisions of five *Fortune* 500 firms among its clients. Manuel Novedad, cofounder and president, had built the firm on a foundation of client focus, adherence to a quality system, and rapid response.

One of their largest customers, a *Fortune* 500 consumer products company, required compliance to jointly developed protocols and a mature quality management system, but not to registration under ISO. A documented system was in place, and Novedad chaired an active steering committee. Members were department heads, including the quality manager, and the union president. System upgrades were made on a routine basis. However, this valued customer, Megaproducts, Incorporated, had missed a scheduled launch date for a new, potentially important mega-product because of miscommunications with DAA's project team and faulty ad copy, which had to be revised after being sent to the printer. These problems could have been prevented if DAA's protocols had been followed and required quality checks had been performed.

Time was a factor because noncompliant product had been reaching the customer despite DAA's assurances that protocols were being followed. Much of the documentation had been written by the quality manager and edited by the president. Review by managers and supervisors, who were asked to implement applicable elements in their departments, was minimal. Consequently, many of the procedures and instructions did not reflect work realities. They depicted an ideal and were ultimately challenged as supervisors and process operators tried to implement them. But, since the clock was ticking and Megaproducts was threatening to cancel orders, implementation proceeded with promises of a complete quality management system revision once improvements were in place.

Making the quality system operable was chaotic. Managers, not wanting to appear unsure of their changed responsibilities and authority, clung to the status quo. Training—when done—focused on lower level employees, which left supervisors without a good understanding of new requirements. They were caught saying one thing but doing another. Interfaces between departments and individuals, although described in an organizational chart and statements of authority and responsibility, were not truly functional. System workflow faltered because new relationships and interdependencies encountered old departmental barriers. Audit reports and corrective actions languished because the president periodically overrode the quality manager's authority, fearing delivery promises might be compromised. However, early implementation steps were handled well. Gaps and shortfalls were identified, and proposed solutions recommended. But, because of time, it was assumed that acceptance and adoption would be automatic. Steering committee members rationalized that everyone knew what needed to be done because solution finding had been such a fervent effort. However, like many improvement projects, concluding steps were inadequately thought through and poorly managed. Proposed solutions were not completely integrated into daily activities.

Eventually the Steering Committee realized that they lacked a comprehensive plan that would make system changes truly operational. The Committee understood that this created indecision at supervisory levels, plus inadequate coordination and dissatisfaction by those trying to make the changes workable. They saw that first-line design project managers, writers, and artists were trying to maintain a sense of order and get their work done by falling back on customary routines. Amazingly, their "stopgap" actions allowed them to get some of the Mega-products projects back on schedule, but they realized that they must go back to the drawing board to develop a comprehensive plan. Time was running out.

Discussion Questions

1. What mistakes did Novedad and the Steering Committee make in the initial development of the protocols and documentation and the early implementation stage?
2. What were the early indications that the system was not working as planned, and why were they ignored? Why weren't improvement efforts more effective?
3. Now that Novedad and the Steering Committee have received their "wake-up" call, what steps should be taken to revise and implement an improved, workable quality management system?

THE PARABLE OF THE GREEN LAWN[44]

A new housing development has lots of packed earth and weeds, but no grass. Two neighbors make a wager on who will be the first to have a lush lawn. Mr. Fast N. Furious knows that a lawn will not grow without grass seed, so he immediately buys the most expensive seed he can find because everyone knows that quality improves with price. Besides, he'll recover the cost of the seed through his wager. Next, he stands knee-deep in his weeds and tosses the seed around his yard. Confident that he has a head start on his neighbor, who is not making much visible progress, he begins his next project.

Ms. Slo N. Steady, having grown up in the country, proceeds to clear the lot, till the soil, and even alter the slope of the terrain to provide better drainage. She checks the soil's pH, applies weed killer and fertilizer, and then distributes the grass seed evenly with a spreader. She applies a mulch cover and waters the lawn appropriately. She finishes several days after her neighbor, who asks if she would like to concede defeat. After all, he does have some blades of grass poking up already.

Mr. Furious is encouraged by the few clumps of grass that sprout. While these small, green islands are better developed than Ms. Steady's fledgling lawn, bare spots and weeds surround them. If he maintains these footholds, he reasons, they should spread to the rest of the yard. He notices that his neighbor's lawn is more uniform and is really starting to grow. He attributes this progress to the Steady children, who water the lawn each evening. Not wanting to appear to be imitating his neighbor, Mr. Furious instructs his children to water his lawn at noon.

The noon watering proves to be detrimental, so he decides to fertilize the remaining patches of grass. Because he wants to make up for the losses the noon watering caused, he applies the fertilizer at twice the recommended application rate. Most of the patches of grass that escape being burned by the fertilizer, however, are eventually choked out by the weeds.

After winning the wager with Mr. Furious, Ms. Steady lounges on the deck enjoying her new grill, which she paid for with the money from the wager. Her lawn requires minimal maintenance, so she is free to attend to the landscaping. The combination of the lawn and landscaping also results in an award from a neighborhood committee that determines that her lawn is a true showplace. Mr. Furious still labors on his lawn. He blames the poor performance on his children's inability to properly water the lawn, nonconforming grass seed, insufficient sunlight, and poor soil. He claims that his neighbor has an unfair advantage and her success is based on conditions unique to her plot of land. He views the loss as grossly unfair; after all, he spends more time and money on his lawn than Ms. Steady does.

He continues to complain about how expensive the seed is and how much time he spends moving the sprinkler around to the few remaining clumps of grass that continue to grow. But Mr. Furious thinks that things will be better for him next year, because he plans to install an automatic sprinkler system and make a double-or-nothing wager with Ms. Steady.

Discussion Questions

1. Within the context of the continual struggles to create a "world-class" lawn and "world-class" business, draw analogies between the events when total quality is implemented.

2. Specifically, translate the problems described here into business language. What are the implementation barriers to achieving total quality?

THE YELLOW BRICK ROAD TO QUALITY[45]

In the film *The Wizard of Oz*, Dorothy learned many lessons. Surprisingly, managers can learn a lot also. For each of the following summaries of scenes in the film, discuss the lessons that organizations can learn in pursuing change and a TQ culture.

1. Dorothy was not happy with the world as she knew it. A tornado came along and transported her to the Land of Oz. Dorothy's house was dropped by the tornado on the Wicked Witch of the East, killing the witch. "Ding, dong, the witch is dead!" rang throughout Munchkinland, but Dorothy had enraged the dead witch's sister. Dorothy only temporarily lost her home support provided by family back in Kansas. All is not good, however, in the Land of Oz. Dorothy's problem is to find her way home to Kansas. Her call to action was precipitated by a crisis—the tornado that transported her to an alien land.

2. In the throes of a Kansas tornado, Dorothy is transported to an unfamiliar land. Immediately, she realizes her world is different and the processes and people she encounters are different, yet bear some similarity to her Kansas existence. She is lost and confused and uncertain about the next steps to take. She realizes she is in a changed state—the Land of Oz—and must devise a plan to get home.

3. Dorothy is a hero for killing the Wicked Witch of the East. Glinda, the Good Witch, sends Dorothy on her way to meet the Wizard of Oz who will help her get back to Kansas. The Wicked Witch of the West tries to get Dorothy's newly acquired ruby slippers, but to no avail. Dorothy and Toto leave for Oz via the Yellow Brick Road. Along the way, they are joined by Scarecrow, Tin Man, and Lion. Through their teamwork, they provide mutual support to endure the vexing journey. They overcome many risks and barriers, including the sleeping poppy field, flying monkeys, and a haunted forest on the way to Oz.

4. Dorothy and her entourage finally reach Oz and meet the Wizard. Rather than instantly granting their wishes, the Wizard gives them an assignment—to obtain the Wicked Witch's broom. They depart for the West.

5. Charged with the task of obtaining the broom, Dorothy and company experience several encounters with near disaster, including Dorothy's incarceration in the witch's castle while an hourglass counts the time to her death. In a struggle to extinguish the Scarecrow's fire (incited by the Wicked Witch), Dorothy tosses a bucket of water, some of which hits the Witch and melts her. Dorothy is rewarded with the broomstick and returns to Oz.

6. Returning to Oz, the group talks with the Wizard, expecting him to help Dorothy return to Kansas. After defrocking the Wizard, they find out he does not know how. The Wizard tries to use a hot air balloon to return and accidentally leaves Dorothy and Toto behind upon takeoff. Glinda arrives and helps Dorothy realize she can return to Kansas on her own with the help of the ruby slippers.

7. Dorothy awakens from her dream and experiences a new understanding and appreciation for her home and family in Kansas. "Oh, Auntie Em, there's no place like home."

Discussion Questions

1. In examining the process that Dorothy used to manage the development and implementation of this project, what factors contributed to her success?

2. Try to develop a model in the form of a flowchart that characterizes an effective change process based on this case.

NOTES

1. "Continuous Improvement Making Inroads in the Classroom," *Pittsburgh Post-Gazette (PA)*, February 18, 2008.

2. Thomas A. Stewart, "Rate Your Readiness to Change," *Fortune*, February 7, 1994, 106–110.

3. Savio Capelossi Filho, "Creating and Preserving a Business Culture," *Quality Progress*, August 2007, 36–41.

4. James R. Evans and Matthew W. Ford, "Value-Driven Quality," *Quality Management Journal*, 4, no. 4 (1997), 19–31.

5. Matthew W. Ford and James R. Evans, "Baldrige Assessment and Organizational Learning: The Need for Change Management," *Quality Management Journal*, 8, no. 3 (2001), 9–25.

6. Much of this section and Table 14.1 are adapted from Matthew W. Ford and James R. Evans, "Baldrige Assessment and Organizational Learning: The Need for Change Management," *Quality Management Journal*, 8, no. 3 (2001), 9–25.

7. Janet Young, "Driving Performance Results at American Express," *Six Sigma Forum Magazine* 1, no. 1 (November 2001), 19–27.

8. Brian Dumaine, "Times Are Good? Create a Crisis," *Fortune*, June 28, 1993, 123–130.

9. Paul R. Keck, "Why Quality Fails," *Quality Digest*, November 1995, 53–55.

10. Julia Graham, "Developing a Performance-Based Culture," *Journal for Quality and Participation*, Spring 2004, 4–8.

11. Joseph M. Juran and A. Blanton Godfrey (eds.), *Juran's Quality Handbook*, 5th ed. (New York: McGraw-Hill, 1999); and Frank M. Gryna, *Quality Planning and Analysis*, 4th ed. (New York: McGraw-Hill, 2001). This concept is summarized in Mary Anne Watson and Frank M. Gryna "Quality Culture in Small Business: Four Case Studies," *Quality Progress*, January 2001, 41–48.

12. Mark Samuel, "Catalysts for Change," *TQM Magazine* 2, no. 4 (1992), 198–202.

13. James H. Davis, *Who Owns Your Quality Program? Lessons from Baldrige Award Winners* (New York: Coopers & Lybrand, undated).

14. Gregory P. Smith, "A Change in Culture Brings Dramatic Quality Improvements," *Quality Observer*, January 1997, 14–15, 37.

15. Susan E. Daniels, "From One-Man Show to Baldrige Recipient," *Quality Progress*, July 2007, 50–55.

16. Davis, *Who Owns Your Quality Program? in Lessons from Baldrige Award Winners* (New York: Coopers & Lybrand, undated).

17. "Special Report: Quality," *Business Week*, November 30, 1992, 66–75; and H. James Harrington, "The Fallacy of Universal Best Practices," Report TR 97-003, Ernst & Young, 1997.

18. Cyndee Miller, "TQM's Value Criticized in New Report," *Marketing News*, 1992; Gilbert Fuchsberg, "'Total Quality' Is Termed Only Partial Success," *Wall Street Journal*, October 1, 1992, B1, B7.

19. Mike Carnell, "Forget Silver Bullets and Instant Pudding," *Quality Progress*, January 2008, 72–73.

20. Source: Reprinted with permission of Jerome A. Blakeslee Jr., "Implementing the Six Sigma Solution," *Quality Progress*, July 1999, 77–85. Copyright © 1999 American Society for Quality. No further distribution allowed without permission.

21. This discussion and examples are adapted from Denis Leonard and Rodney McAdam, "Quality's Six Life Cycle Stages," *Quality Progress*, August 2003, 50–55.

22. Kathleen J. Goonan, Joseph Muzikowski, and Patricia K. Stoltz, "Journey to Excellence: Healthcare Baldrige Leaders Speak Out," *Quality in Healthcare*, American Society for Quality publication, January 2009, pp. 11–15, www.asq.org/qhc. Copyright © 2009 American Society for Quality. Reprinted with permission.

23. Adapted from presentation notes at the 2004 Baldrige National Quality Program Quest for Excellence XVI conference.

24. Letter to Stakeholders p. 4; source: http://www.ge.com/ar2004/letter3.jsp (accessed 3/03/06).

25. Dusya Vera and Mary Crossan, "Strategic Leadership and Organizational Learning," *Academy of Management Review* 29, no. 2 (2004), pp. 222–240.

26. David A. Garvin, *Learning in Action: A Guide to Putting the Learning Organization to Work* (Boston: Harvard Business School Press, 2000), 11.

27. This term was coined by Joseph Juran in *Juran on Quality by Design* (New York: The Free Press, 1992), 409–413. It refers to the remark made by philosopher George Santayana: "Those who cannot remember the past are condemned to repeat it."

28. Robert Cole, "From Continuous Improvement to Continuous Innovation," *Quality Management Journal* 8, no. 4 (2001), pp. 7–21.

29. Sim B. Sitkin, Kathleen M. Sutcliffe, and Roger G. Schroeder. "Distinguishing Control from Learning in Total Quality Management: A Contingency Perspective," *Academy of Management Review* 19, no. 3 (1994), 537–564.

30. Matthew W. Ford and James R. Evans, "Models for Organizational Self Assessment," *Business Horizons*, November–December 2002, 25–32.

31. Many examples of these interventions and of management's involvement in them have been documented in the popular literature. See, for example, D. H. Myers,

and J. Heller, "The Dual Role of AT&T's Self-Assessment Process," *Quality Progress*, January 1995, 79–83; D. Zaremba, and T. Crew, "Increasing Involvement in Self-Assessment: The Royal Mail Approach," *TQM Magazine*, February 1995, 29–32; and M. Blazey, "Insights into Organizational Self-Assessments," *Quality Progress*, October 1998, 47–52.

32. Ann B. Rich, "Continuous Improvement: The Key to Success," *Quality Progress* 30, no. 6 (June 1997).

33. "Speaking About the Baldrige: Terry Holliday Interview," *Quality Digest*, January 2009, 6.

34. Matthew W. Ford and James R. Evans, "Managing Organizational Self-Assessment: Follow-up and Its Influencing Factors," Working Paper, College of Business, Northern Kentucky University and College of Business, University of Cincinnati. See also Matthew W. Ford, "A Model of Change Process and Its Use in Self Assessment," Doctoral Dissertation, University of Cincinnati, 2000.

35. S. L. Ahire and D. Y. Golhar, "Quality Management in Large vs. Small Firms," *Journal of Small Business Management* 34, no. 2 (1996), 1–13.

36. Madhav N. Sinha "Helping Those Who Help Others," *Quality Progress*, July 1997; and Renee Oosterhoff Cox, "Quality in Nonprofits: No Longer Uncharted Territory," *Quality Progress*, October 1999, 57–61.

37. Kennedy Smith, "American Red Cross Undergoes Quality Transfusion," *Quality Digest*, March 2003, 6–7.

38. A.V. Feigenbaum and Donald S. Feigenbaum, "New Quality for the 21st Century," *Quality Progress*, December 1999, 27–31.

39. Reprinted with permission from "21 Voices for the 21st Century," *Quality Progress*, January 2000, 31–39, 41. © 2000 American Society for Quality. No further distribution allowed without permission.

40. Miles Maguire, "The Voice of the 21st Century Customer," *Quality Progress*, January 2000, 41.

41. Republished with permission of Quality Digest, from Robert Green, "Dedicated Teams Successfully Merge Two Divergent Quality Systems," *Quality Progress*, December 2000, pp. 24–28. Copyright © 2000; permission conveyed through Copyright Clearance Center, Inc.

42. Adapted from Denis Leonard, "Building Quality at Veridian Homes," *Quality Progress*, October 2006, 49–54.

43. This case was inspired by the article by John R. Schultz, "Eight Steps to Sustain Change," *Quality Progress*, November 2007, 25–31.

44. Reproduced with permission from James A. Alloway, Jr., "Laying Groundwork for Total Quality," *Quality Progress*, 27, no. 1 (January 1994), 65–67. © 1994 American Society for Quality. No further distribution allowed without permission.

45. David M. Lyth and Larry A Mallak, "'We're Not in Kansas Anymore, Toto' or Quality Lessons from the Land of Oz," *Quality Engineering* 10, no. 30 (1998), 579–588.

Appendices

Tables

TABLE 1   **Cumulative Probabilities for the Standard Normal Distribution**

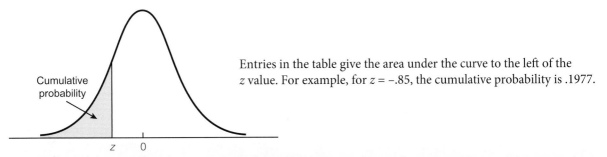

Entries in the table give the area under the curve to the left of the z value. For example, for $z = -.85$, the cumulative probability is .1977.

z	.00	.01	.02	.03	.04	.05	.06	.07	.08	.09
−3.0	.0013	.0013	.0013	.0012	.0012	.0011	.0011	.0011	.0010	.0010
−2.9	.0019	.0018	.0018	.0017	.0016	.0016	.0015	.0015	.0014	.0014
−2.8	.0026	.0025	.0024	.0023	.0023	.0022	.0021	.0021	.0020	.0019
−2.7	.0035	.0034	.0033	.0032	.0031	.0030	.0029	.0028	.0027	.0026
−2.6	.0047	.0045	.0044	.0043	.0041	.0040	.0039	.0038	.0037	.0036
−2.5	.0062	.0060	.0059	.0057	.0055	.0054	.0052	.0051	.0049	.0048
−2.4	.0082	.0080	.0078	.0075	.0073	.0071	.0069	.0068	.0066	.0064
−2.3	.0107	.0104	.0102	.0099	.0096	.0094	.0091	.0089	.0087	.0084
−2.2	.0139	.0136	.0132	.0129	.0125	.0122	.0119	.0116	.0113	.0110
−2.1	.0179	.0174	.0170	.0166	.0162	.0158	.0154	.0150	.0146	.0143
−2.0	.0228	.0222	.0217	.0212	.0207	.0202	.0197	.0192	.0188	.0183
−1.9	.0287	.0281	.0274	.0268	.0262	.0256	.0250	.0244	.0239	.0233
−1.8	.0359	.0351	.0344	.0336	.0329	.0322	.0314	.0307	.0301	.0294
−1.7	.0446	.0436	.0427	.0418	.0409	.0401	.0392	.0384	.0375	.0367
−1.6	.0548	.0537	.0526	.0516	.0505	.0495	.0485	.0475	.0465	.0455
−1.5	.0668	.0655	.0643	.0630	.0618	.0606	.0594	.0582	.0571	.0559
−1.4	.0808	.0793	.0778	.0764	.0749	.0735	.0721	.0708	.0694	.0681
−1.3	.0968	.0951	.0934	.0918	.0901	.0885	.0869	.0853	.0838	.0823
−1.2	.1151	.1131	.1112	.1093	.1075	.1056	.1038	.1020	.1003	.0985
−1.1	.1357	.1335	.1314	.1292	.1271	.1251	.1230	.1210	.1190	.1170
−1.0	.1587	.1562	.1539	.1515	.1492	.1469	.1446	.1423	.1401	.1379
−.9	.1841	.1814	.1788	.1762	.1736	.1711	.1685	.1660	.1635	.1611
−.8	.2119	.2090	.2061	.2033	.2005	.1977	.1949	.1922	.1894	.1867
−.7	.2420	.2389	.2358	.2327	.2296	.2266	.2236	.2206	.2177	.2148
−.6	.2743	.2709	.2676	.2643	.2611	.2578	.2546	.2514	.2483	.2451
−.5	.3085	.3050	.3015	.2981	.2946	.2912	.2877	.2843	.2810	.2776
−.4	.3446	.3409	.3372	.3336	.3300	.3264	.3228	.3192	.3156	.3121
−.3	.3821	.3783	.3745	.3707	.3669	.3632	.3594	.3557	.3520	.3483
−.2	.4207	.4168	.4129	.4090	.4052	.4013	.3974	.3936	.3897	.3859
−.1	.4602	.4562	.4522	.4483	.4443	.4404	.4364	.4325	.4286	.4247
−.0	.5000	.4960	.4920	.4880	.4840	.4801	.4761	.4721	.4681	.4641

TABLE 1   Cumulative Probabilities for the Standard Normal Distribution *(Continued)*

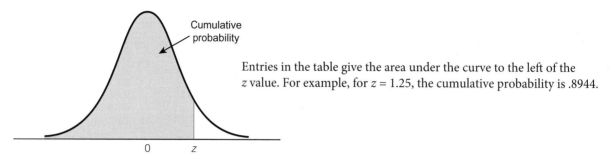

Entries in the table give the area under the curve to the left of the z value. For example, for $z = 1.25$, the cumulative probability is .8944.

z	.00	.01	.02	.03	.04	.05	.06	.07	.08	.09
.0	.5000	.5040	.5080	.5120	.5160	.5199	.5239	.5279	.5319	.5359
.1	.5398	.5438	.5478	.5517	.5557	.5596	.5636	.5675	.5714	.5753
.2	.5793	.5832	.5871	.5910	.5948	.5987	.6026	.6064	.6103	.6141
.3	.6179	.6217	.6255	.6293	.6331	.6368	.6406	.6443	.6480	.6517
.4	.6554	.6591	.6628	.6664	.6700	.6736	.6772	.6808	.6844	.6879
.5	.6915	.6950	.6985	.7019	.7054	.7088	.7123	.7157	.7190	.7224
.6	.7257	.7291	.7324	.7357	.7389	.7422	.7454	.7486	.7517	.7549
.7	.7580	.7611	.7642	.7673	.7704	.7734	.7764	.7794	.7823	.7852
.8	.7881	.7910	.7939	.7967	.7995	.8023	.8051	.8078	.8106	.8133
.9	.8159	.8186	.8212	.8238	.8264	.8289	.8315	.8340	.8365	.8389
1.0	.8413	.8438	.8461	.8485	.8508	.8531	.8554	.8577	.8599	.8621
1.1	.8643	.8665	.8686	.8708	.8729	.8749	.8770	.8790	.8810	.8830
1.2	.8849	.8869	.8888	.8907	.8925	.8944	.8962	.8980	.8997	.9015
1.3	.9032	.9049	.9066	.9082	.9099	.9115	.9131	.9147	.9162	.9177
1.4	.9192	.9207	.9222	.9236	.9251	.9265	.9279	.9292	.9306	.9319
1.5	.9332	.9345	.9357	.9370	.9382	.9394	.9406	.9418	.9429	.9441
1.6	.9452	.9463	.9474	.9484	.9495	.9505	.9515	.9525	.9535	.9545
1.7	.9554	.9564	.9573	.9582	.9591	.9599	.9608	.9616	.9625	.9633
1.8	.9641	.9649	.9656	.9664	.9671	.9678	.9686	.9693	.9699	.9706
1.9	.9713	.9719	.9726	.9732	.9738	.9744	.9750	.9756	.9761	.9767
2.0	.9772	.9778	.9783	.9788	.9793	.9798	.9803	.9808	.9812	.9817
2.1	.9821	.9826	.9830	.9834	.9838	.9842	.9846	.9850	.9854	.9857
2.2	.9861	.9864	.9868	.9871	.9875	.9878	.9881	.9884	.9887	.9890
2.3	.9893	.9896	.9898	.9901	.9904	.9906	.9909	.9911	.9913	.9916
2.4	.9918	.9920	.9922	.9925	.9927	.9929	.9931	.9932	.9934	.9936
2.5	.9938	.9940	.9941	.9943	.9945	.9946	.9948	.9949	.9951	.9952
2.6	.9953	.9955	.9956	.9957	.9959	.9960	.9961	.9962	.9963	.9964
2.7	.9965	.9966	.9967	.9968	.9969	.9970	.9971	.9972	.9973	.9974
2.8	.9974	.9975	.9976	.9977	.9977	.9978	.9979	.9979	.9980	.9981
2.9	.9981	.9982	.9982	.9983	.9984	.9984	.9985	.9985	.9986	.9986
3.0	.9987	.9987	.9987	.9988	.9988	.9989	.9989	.9989	.9990	.9990

Factors for Control Charts

	x-Charts				s-Charts				R-Charts					
n	A	A_2	A_3	c_4	B_3	B_4	B_5	B_6	d_2	d_3	D_1	D_2	D_3	D_4
2	2.121	1.880	2.659	0.7979	0	3.267	0	2.606	1.128	0.853	0	3.686	0	3.267
3	1.732	1.023	1.954	0.8862	0	2.568	0	2.276	1.693	0.888	0	4.358	0	2.574
4	1.500	0.729	1.628	0.9213	0	2.266	0	2.088	2.059	0.880	0	4.698	0	2.282
5	1.342	0.577	1.427	0.9400	0	2.089	0	1.964	2.326	0.864	0	4.918	0	2.114
6	1.225	0.483	1.287	0.9515	0.030	1.970	0.029	1.874	2.534	0.848	0	5.078	0	2.004
7	1.134	0.419	1.182	0.9594	0.118	1.882	0.113	1.806	2.704	0.833	0.204	5.204	0.076	1.924
8	1.061	0.373	1.099	0.9650	0.185	1.815	0.179	1.751	2.847	0.820	0.388	5.306	0.136	1.864
9	1.000	0.337	1.032	0.969	0.239	1.761	0.232	1.707	2.970	0.808	0.547	5.393	0.184	1.816
10	0.949	0.308	0.975	0.9727	0.284	1.716	0.276	1.669	3.078	0.797	0.687	5.469	0.223	1.777
11	0.905	0.285	0.927	0.9754	0.321	1.679	0.313	1.637	3.173	0.787	0.811	5.535	0.256	1.744
12	0.866	0.266	0.886	0.9776	0.354	1.646	0.346	1.610	3.258	0.778	0.922	5.594	0.283	1.717
13	0.832	0.249	0.850	0.9794	0.382	1.618	0.374	1.585	3.336	0.770	1.025	5.647	0.307	1.693
14	0.802	0.235	0.817	0.9810	0.406	1.594	0.399	1.563	3.407	0.763	1.118	5.696	0.328	1.672
15	0.775	0.223	0.789	0.9823	0.428	1.572	0.421	1.544	3.472	0.756	1.203	5.741	0.347	1.653
16	0.750	0.212	0.763	0.9835	0.448	1.552	0.440	1.526	3.532	0.750	1.282	5.782	0.363	1.637
17	0.728	0.203	0.739	0.9845	0.466	1.534	0.458	1.511	3.588	0.744	1.356	5.820	0.378	1.622
18	0.707	0.194	0.718	0.9854	0.482	1.518	0.475	1.496	3.640	0.739	1.424	5.856	0.391	1.608
19	0.688	0.187	0.698	0.9862	0.497	1.503	0.490	1.483	3.689	0.734	1.487	5.891	0.403	1.597
20	0.671	0.180	0.680	0.9869	0.510	1.490	0.504	1.470	3.735	0.729	1.549	5.921	0.415	1.585
21	0.655	0.173	0.663	0.9876	0.523	1.477	0.516	1.459	3.778	0.724	1.605	5.951	0.425	1.575
22	0.640	0.167	0.647	0.9882	0.534	1.466	0.528	1.448	3.819	0.720	1.659	5.979	0.434	1.566
23	0.626	0.162	0.633	0.9887	0.545	1.455	0.539	1.438	3.858	0.716	1.710	6.006	0.443	1.557
24	0.612	0.157	0.619	0.9892	0.555	1.445	0.549	1.429	3.895	0.712	1.759	6.031	0.451	1.548
25	0.600	0.153	0.606	0.9896	0.565	1.435	0.559	1.420	3.931	0.708	1.806	6.056	0.459	1.541

Source: Adapted from Table 27 of ASTM STP 15D ASTM *Manual on Presentation of Data and Control Chart Analysis.* © 1976 American Society for Testing and Materials, Philadelphia, PA.

Random Digits

63271	59986	71744	51102	15141	80714	58683	93108	13554	79945
88547	09896	95436	79115	08303	01041	20030	63754	08459	28364
55957	57243	83865	09911	19761	66535	40102	26646	60147	15702
46276	87453	44790	67122	45573	84358	21625	16999	13385	22782
55363	07449	34835	15290	76616	67191	12777	21861	68689	03263
69393	92785	49902	58447	42048	30378	87618	26933	40640	16281
13186	29431	88190	04588	38733	81290	89541	70290	40113	08243
17726	28652	56836	78351	47327	18518	92222	55201	27340	10493
36520	64465	05550	30157	82242	29520	69753	72602	23756	54935
81628	36100	39254	56835	37636	02421	98063	89641	64953	99337
84649	48968	75215	75498	49539	74240	03466	49292	36401	45525
63291	11618	12613	75055	43915	26488	41116	64531	56827	30825
70502	53225	03655	05915	37140	57051	48393	91322	25653	06543
06426	24771	59935	49801	11082	66762	94477	02494	88215	27191
20711	55609	29430	70165	45406	78484	31639	52009	18873	96927
41990	70538	77191	25860	55204	73417	83920	69468	74972	38712
72452	36618	76298	26678	89334	33938	95567	29380	75906	91807
37042	40318	57099	10528	09925	89773	41335	96244	29002	46453
53766	52875	15987	46962	67342	77592	57651	95508	80033	69828
90585	58955	53122	16025	84299	53310	67380	84249	25348	04332
32001	96293	37203	64516	51530	37069	40261	61374	05815	06714
62606	64324	46354	72157	67248	20135	49804	09226	64419	29457
10078	28073	85389	50324	14500	15562	64165	06125	71353	77669
91561	46145	24177	15294	10061	98124	75732	00815	83452	97355
13091	98112	53959	79607	52244	63303	10413	63839	74762	50289
73864	83014	72457	22682	03033	61714	88173	90835	00634	85169
66668	25467	48894	51043	02365	91726	09365	63167	95264	45643
84745	41042	29493	01836	09044	51926	43630	63470	76508	14194
48068	26805	94595	47907	13357	38412	33318	26098	82782	42851
54310	96175	97594	88616	42035	38093	36745	56702	40644	83514
14877	33095	10924	58013	61439	21882	42059	24177	58739	60170
78295	23179	02771	43464	59061	71411	05697	67194	30495	21157
67524	02865	39593	54278	04237	92441	26602	63835	38032	94770
58268	57219	68124	73455	83236	08710	04284	55005	84171	42596
97158	28672	50685	01181	24262	19427	52106	34308	73685	74246
04230	16831	69085	30802	65559	09205	71829	06489	85650	38707
94879	56606	30401	02602	57658	70091	54986	41394	60437	03195
71446	15232	66715	26385	91518	70566	02888	79941	39684	54315
32886	05644	79316	09819	00813	88407	17461	73925	53037	91904
62048	33711	25290	21526	02223	75947	66466	06232	10913	75336

Source: Reprinted from page 44 of *A Million Digits With 100,000 Normal Deviates,* by the Rand Corporation. New York: The Free Press, 1955. © 1955 by The Rand Corporation. Used by permission.

Bibliography

Ahmed, Pervaiz K. and Mohammed Rafiq. "Integrated Benchmarking: A Holistic Examination of Select Techniques for Benchmarking Analysis." *Benchmarking for Quality Management & Technology* 5, 3 (1998): 225–242.

Allen, Derek R. and Morris Wolburn. *Linking Customer and Employee Satisfaction to the Bottom Line.* Milwaukee, WI: ASQ Quality Press, 2002.

Alukal, George, and Anthony Manos. "Lean Manufacturing." *The Quality Management Forum* 28, 3 (Summer 2002): 4–7.

American National Standard, Definitions, Symbols, Formulas, and Tables for Control Charts. ANSI/ASQC A1-1987. American Society for Quality Control, 310 W. Wisconsin Ave., Milwaukee, WI 53203.

American National Standard: Guide to Inspection Planning, ANSI/ASQC E-2-1984. Milwaukee, WI: American Society for Quality Control, 1984.

Andersen, Bjorn, and Tom Fagerhaug. *Performance Management Explained: Designing and Implementing Your State-of-the-Art System.* Milwuakee, WI: American Society for Quality, 2002.

Andersen, Bjorn. *Business Process Improvement Toolbox.* Milwaukee, WI: ASQ Quality Press, 1999.

AT&T Quality Steering Committee. *Achieving Customer Satisfaction.* Quality Technology Center, AT&T Bell Laboratories, 1990.

AT&T Quality Steering Committee. *Batting 1000: Using Baldrige Feedback to Improve Your Business.* AT&T Bell Laboratories, 1992.

AT&T Quality Steering Committee. *Policy Deployment.* AT&T Bell Laboratories, 1992.

AT&T Quality Steering Committee. *Process Quality Management & Improvement Guidelines.* AT&T Bell Laboratories, 1987.

AT&T Quality Steering Committee. *Process Quality Management & Improvement.* Quality Technology Center, AT&T Bell Laboratories, 1987.

Badracco, Joseph L. *Leading Quietly.* Boston: Harvard Business School Press, 2002.

Bauer, John E., Grace L. Duffy, and Russell T. Wescott (eds.). *The Quality Improvement Handbook.* Milwaukee, WI: ASQ Quality Press, 2002.

Bennis, Warren G., and Robert J. Thomas. *Geeks and Geezers.* Boston: Harvard Business School Press, 2002.

Bennis, Warren, Grechen M. Spreitzer, and Thomas G. Cummings (eds.). *The Future of Leadership: Today's Top Leadership Thinkers Speak to Tomorrow's Leaders.* San Francisco: Jossey-Bass, 2001.

Bens, Ingrid. *Facilitation at a Glance!* Cincinnati: AQP, 1999.

Berry, Leonard L., Valarie A. Zeithaml, and A. Parasuraman. "Five Imperatives for Improving Service Quality." *Sloan Management Review* (Summer 1990): 29–38.

Blackburn, Richard, and Benjamin Rosen. "Total Quality and Human Resources Management: Lessons Learned from Baldrige Award-Winning Companies." *Academy of Management Executive* 7, 3 (1993): 49–66.

Blanchard, Ken. *The Heart of a Leader: Insights on the Art of Influence.* Tulsa, OK: Honor Books, 1999.

Boser, Robert B., and Cheryl L. Christ. "Whys, Whens, and Hows of Conducting a Process Capability Study." Presentation at the ASQC/ASA 35th Annual Fall Technical Conference, Lexington, Kentucky, 1991.

Bossidy, Larry, Ram Charan, and Charles Burch. *Execution: The Discipline of Getting Things Done.* New York: Crown Books—Random House, 2002.

Box, G. E. P., and S. Bisgaard. "The Scientific Context of Quality Improvement." *Quality Progress* 20, 6, June 1987: 54–61.

Brager, Joan. "The Customer-Focused Quality Leader." *Quality Progress* 25, 5, May 1992, 51–53.

Brassard, Michael, and Diane Ritter. *The Memory Jogger II*. Methuen, MA: GOAL/QPC, 1994.

Brassard, Michael. *The Memory Jogger Plus+*. Methuen, MA: GOAL/QPC, 1989.

Breyfogle, Forrest W. III. *Implementing Six Sigma*, 2nd ed. New York: John Wiley & Sons, 2003.

Breyfogle, Forrest W. *Integrated Enterprise Excellence—Vol. 3*. Austin, TX: Citius Publishing, 2008.

Breyfogle, Forrest W., III, James M. Cupello, and Becki Meadows. *Managing Six Sigma*. New York: Wiley-Interscience, 2001.

Brocka, Bruce, and M. Suzanne Brocka. *Quality Management: Implementing the Best Ideas of the Masters*. Homewood, IL: Business One Irwin, 1992.

Brown, Bradford S. "Control Charts: The Promise and the Performance." Presentation at the ASQC/ASA 35th Annual Fall Technical Conference, Lexington, Kentucky, 1991.

Brown, Mark Graham. *Baldrige Award-Winning Quality: How to Interpret the Baldrige Criteria for Performance Excellence*, 17th ed. Milwaukee: ASQ Quality Press, 2008.

Brown, Mark Graham. *Winning Score: How to Design and Implement Organizational Scorecards*. New York: Productivity Press, 2007.

Brown, Mark Graham. *Keeping Score: Using the Right Metrics to Drive World-Class Performance*. New York: Quality Resources, 2006.

Brue, Greg. *Six Sigma for Managers*. New York, McGraw-Hill, 2002.

Buckingham, Marcus, and Curt Coffman. *First, Break All the Rules: What the World's Greatest Managers Do Differently*. New York: Simon and Schuster, 1999.

Burke, Charles J. "10 Steps to Best-Practices Benchmarking." *Quality Digest*, February 1996, 23–28.

Burns, T., and G. M. Stalker. *The Management of Innovation*. London: Tavistock, 1961.

Bush, David, and Kevin Dooley. "The Deming Prize and the Baldrige Award: How They Compare." *Quality Progress* 22, 1, January 1989, 28–30.

Byrne, John. *Chainsaw: The Notorious Career of Al Dunlop in the Age of Profit-at-Any-Price*. New York: HarperBusiness, 2002.

Camison, Cesar. "Total Quality Management and Cultural Change: A Model of Organizational Development." *International Journal of Technology Management* 16, 4–6 (1998): 479.

Camp, Robert C. *Business Process Benchmarking: Finding and Implementing Best Practices*. Milwaukee, WI: ASQC Quality Press, 1995.

Carr, Maureen P., Francis W. Jackson, and Diane Cesarone. *The Crosswalk: Joint Commission Standards and Baldrige Criteria*. Oakbrook Terrace, IL: Joint Commission on Accreditation of Healthcare Organizations, 1997.

Case, Kenneth E., and Lynn L. Jones. *Profit Through Quality: Quality Assurance Programs for Manufacturers*. Norcross, GA: American Institute of Industrial Engineers, 1978.

Chatfield, Christopher. *Statistics for Technology: A Course in Applied Statistics*, 3rd ed. (Revised) New York: CRC Press, 1983.

Christison, William L. "Financial Information Is Key to Empowerment." *Quality Progress* 27, 7, July 1994, 47–48.

Cole, Robert E. "Corporate Strategy—Learning from the Quality Movement: What Did and Didn't Happen, and Why?" *California Management Review* 41, 1 (1998): 43.

Collins, James. *Good to Great: Why Some Companies Make the Leap … And Others Don't*. New York: HarperCollins, 2001.

Conger, J., and R. Kanugo. "Toward a Behavioral Theory of Charismatic Leadership in Organizational Settings." *Academy of Management Review*, October 1987: 637–647.

Conti, Tito. "Stakeholder-Based Strategies to Enhance Corporate Performance." *Denver, CO: Proceedings: Annual Quality Congress*, May 2002, 373–381.

Cooper, Robin, and Robert S. Kaplan. *The Design of Cost Management Systems: Text, Cases, and Readings*. New York: Prentice Hall, 1991.

Cullen, Thomas Patrick. *Managing Service Quality in the Hospitality Industry*. Ithaca, NY: Hotel School, Cornell University, 2000.

Cupello, James M. "A New Paradigm for Measuring TQM Progress." *Quality Progress* 27, 5, May 1994, 79–82.

DeCarly, Neil J., and W. Kent Sterett. "History of the Malcolm Baldrige Award." *Quality Progress* 23, 3, March 1990, 21–27.

Deming, W. Edwards. *Out of the Crisis*. Cambridge, MA: MIT Press, 2000.

Deming, W. Edwards. *The New Economics for Industry, Government, Education*, 2nd ed. Cambridge, MA: MIT Press, 2000.

DeToro, Irving, and Thomas McCabe. "How to Stay Flexible and Elude Fads." *Quality Progress*, March 1997, 55–60.

Donnell, Augustus, and Margaret Dellinger. *Analyzing Business Process Data: The Looking Glass*. AT&T Bell Laboratories, 1990.

Duncan, Acheson J. *Quality Control and Industrial Statistics*, 5th ed. Homewood, IL: Richard D. Irwin, 1986.

Duncan, W. Jack, and Joseph G. Van Matre. "The Gospel According to Deming: Is It Really New?" *Business Horizons*, July–August 1990, 3–9.

Dychtwald, Ken, Tamara J. Erickson, Robert Morison. *Workforce Crisis: How to Beat the Coming Shortage of Skills and Talent*. Cambridge, MA: Harvard Business School Press, 2006.

Easton, George S., and Sherry L. Jarrell. "The Effects of Total Quality Management on Organizational Performance: An Empirical Investigation." *The Journal of Business* 71, 2 (1998): 253.

Eckes, George. *The Six Sigma Revolution*. New York: John Wiley & Sons, 2001.

Emery, F. E., E. L. Trist, and J. Woodward. *Management and Technology*. London: Her Majesty's Stationery Office, 1958.

Eure, Rob. "E-Commerce (A Special Report): The Classroom—On the Job; Corporate E-Learning Makes Training Available Anytime, Anywhere." *The Wall Street Journal*, March 12, 2001, R33.

Evans, James R. *Quality and Performance Excellence: Management, Organization, and Strategy*, 5th ed. Cincinnati: Cengage Learning, 2008.

Evans, James R., and David L. Olson. *Introduction to Simulation and Risk Analysis*. Upper Saddle River, NJ: Prentice Hall, 2002.

Fitzsimmons, James A., and Mona J. Fitzsimmons. *New Service Development: Creating Memorable Experiences*. Thousand Oaks, CA: Sage Publications, 2000.

Ford, Matthew W. and James R. Evans. "Baldrige Assessment and Organizational Learning: The Need for Change Management." *Quality Management Journal* 8, 3, July 2001, 9–25.

Franz, Douglas. "To Put G. E. Online Meant Putting a Dozen Industries Online." *New York Times*, March 29, 2000.

Freund, Richard A. "Definitions and Basic Quality Concepts." *Journal of Quality Technology*, January 1985: 50–56.

Galford, Robert, Laurie Broedling, Edward G. Lawler, III, Tim Riley, et al. "Why Doesn't This HR Department Get Any Respect?" *Harvard Business Review* 76, 2, March/April 1998: 24–40.

Gantenbein, Douglas, and Marcia Stepanek. "Kaiser Takes the Cybercure." *Business Week*, February 7, 2000.

Garvin, David A. *Managing Quality*. New York: The Free Press, 1988.

George, Michael L. *Lean Six Sigma: Combining Six Sigma Quality with Lean Speed*. New York: McGraw-Hill, 2002.

Gitlow, H., S. Gitlow, A. Oppenheim, and R. Oppenheim. *Tools and Methods for the Improvement of Quality*. Homewood, IL: Irwin, 1989.

Godfrey, Blan. "Future Trends: Expansion of Quality Management Concepts, Methods and Tools to All Industries." *Quality Observer* 6, 9, September 1997, 40–43, 46.

Goetsch, David L., and Stanley B. Davis. *Understanding and Implementing ISO 9000:2000*. Upper Saddle River, NJ: Prentice Hall, 2002.

Goonan, Kathleen J., Joseph A. Muzikowski, and Particia K. Stoltz, *Journey to Excellence: How Baldrige Health Care Leaders Succeed*, Milwaukee, WI: ASQ Quality Press, 2009.

Grant, Eugene, L., and Richard S. Leavenworth. *Statistical Quality Control*, 7th ed. New York: McGraw-Hill, 1996.

Great Performances! AT&T Bell Laboratories, 1991.

Griffin, Ricky W., and Gregory Moorhead. *Organizational Behavior: Managing People and Organizations*, 9th ed. Mason, OH: Cengage Learning, 2010.

Griffith, Gary. *Quality Technician's Handbook*, 5th ed. New York: Prentice Hall, 2002.

Gryna, Frank M. *Work Overload: Redesigning Jobs to Minimize Stress and Burnout*. Milwaukee: ASQ Quality Press, 2004.

Gunter, Bert. "Process Capability Studies Part I: What Is a Process Capability Study?" *Quality Progress* 24, 2, February 1991, 97–99.

Haavind, Robert. *The Road to the Baldrige Award*. Boston: Butterworth-Heinemann, 1992.

Hackman, J. Richard. *Leading Teams: Setting the Stage for Great Performance*. Boston: Harvard Business School Press, 2002.

Hallowell, Roger. *Virtuous Cycles: Improving Service and Lowering Costs in E-Commerce*. Boston: Division of Research, Harvard Business School, 2001.

Harrington, H. James, and Kerim Tumay. *Simulation Modeling Methods*. New York: McGraw-Hill, 2000.

Harry, Mikel J. "Framework for Business Leadership." *Quality Progress*, April 2000.

Harry, Mikel J. *The Vision of Six Sigma: A Roadmap for Breakthrough*. Phoenix, AZ: Tri Star Publishing, 1997.

Hart, Christopher W. L., and Christopher E. Bogan. *The Baldrige*. New York: McGraw-Hill, 1992.

Hayes, Bob E. *Measuring Customer Satisfaction: Development and Use of Questionnaires*, 2nd ed. Milwaukee, WI: ASQC Quality Press, 1997.

Hayes, Glenn E. "Quality: Quandary and Quest." *Quality* 22, 7, July 1983, 18.

Henriques, Diana B., and Jacques Steinberg. "Right Answer, Wrong Score: Test Flaws Take Toll." *New York Times*, May 20, 2001; and Diana B. Henriques and Jacques Steinberg. "When a Test Fails the Schools, Careers and Reputations Suffer." *New York Times*, May 21, 2001. Source: http://deming.eng.clemson.edu/pub/psci/psn/inthe newsarchive.htm#2 (accessed June 24, 2009).

Herzberg, Frederick. "One More Time: How Do You Motivate Employees?" *Harvard Business Review* 46, (January/February 1968: 53–62.

Herzberg, Frederick. *Work and the Nature of Man*. Cleveland, OH: World, 1966.

Hesselbein, Frances, Marshall Goldsmith, and Richard Beckhard (eds.). *The Leader of the Future: New Visions, Strategies, and Practices for the next Era*. San Francisco: Jossey-Bass, Publishers, 1996.

Hiam, Alexander. *Closing the Quality Gap: Lessons from America's Leading Companies*. Englewood Cliffs, NJ: Prentice-Hall, 1992.

Hoerl, Roger W. "Six Sigma and the Future of the Quality Profession." *Quality Progress*, June 1998.

Hoffman, K. Douglas, and John E. G. Bateson. *Essentials of Services Marketing*. Fort Worth: Harcourt College Publishers, 2002.

Hradesky, John L. *Productivity and Quality Improvement*. New York: McGraw-Hill, 1988.

Hunt, V. Daniel. *Managing for Quality: Integrating Quality and Business Strategy*. Homewood, IL: Business One Irwin, 1993.

Hurley, Heather. "Cycle-Time Reduction: Your Key to a Better Bottom Line." *Quality Digest*, April 1996, 28–32.

Hutton, David W. *From Baldrige to the Bottom Line: A Road Map for Organizational Change and Improvement*. Milwaukee: ASQ Quality Press, 2000.

Janda, Swinder, Phillip J. Trocchia, and Kevin P. Gwinner. "Consumer Perceptions of Internet Retail

Service Quality." *International Journal of Service Industry Management* 13, 5 (2002): 412–431.

Johnston, Robert. "The Determinants of Service Quality: Satisfiers and Dissatisfiers." *International Journal of Service Industry Management* 6, 5 (1995): 53.

Jugulum, Rajesh, and Philip Samuel. *Design for Lean Six Sigma* Hoboken, NJ: John Wiley & Sons, 2008.

Juran, J. M. *Juran on Quality by Design*. New York: The Free Press, 1992.

Juran, J. M. "Product Quality—A Prescription for the West." *Management Review*, June–July 1981.

Juran, J. M. "The Quality Trilogy." *Quality Progress* 19, August 1986, 19–24.

Juran, J. M., Editor, *A Historyof Managing for Quality*. Milwaukee, WI: ASQ Quality Press, 1995.

Kanfer, Ruth. "Motivation Theory in Industrial and Organizational Psychology." In Marvin D. Dunnette and Leaeta M. Hough (eds.). *Handbook of Industrial and Organizational Psychology*, 2nd ed., vol. 1. Palo Alto, CA: Consulting Psychologists Press, Inc., 1990, 75–170.

Kaplan, Robert S., and David P. Norton. *The Balanced Scorecard*. Boston: Harvard Business School Press, 1996.

Kaplan, Robert S., and David P. Norton. *The Strategy-Focused Organization: How Balanced Scorecard Companies Thrive in the New Business Environment*. Boston: Harvard Business School Press, 2000.

Katzenbach, Jon R. *Teams at the Top*. Boston: Harvard Business School Press, 1998.

Katzenbach, Jon R. and Douglas K. Smith. *The Wisdom of Teams*. New York: HarperBusiness, 2003.

Kenyon, David A. "Strategic Planning with the Hoshin Process." *Quality Digest*, May 1997, 55–63.

Kern, Jill P., John J. Riley, and Louis N. Jones (eds.). *Human Resources Management*. Quality and Reliability Series, sponsored by the ASQC Human Resources Division. New York: Marcel Dekker, Inc., and Milwaukee: ASQC Quality Press, 1987.

Kets de Vries, Manfred F.R. and Elizabeth Florent-Treacy, The New Global Leaders: Richard Branson, Percy Barnevik, and David Simon, pp. xiii–xiv, 40, 56–57. Copyright © 1999 Josey Bass, an Imprint of John Wiley & Sons, Inc. Reprinted by permission.

King, Carol A. "Service Quality Assurance Is Different." *Quality Progress* 18, 6, June 1985, 14–18.

Kivenko, Ken. "Improve Performance by Driving Out Fear." *Quality Progress* 27, 10, October 1994, 77–79.

Kloppenborg, Timpthy J. and Joseph A. Petrick, *Managing Project Quality*. Vienna, VA: Management Concepts, 2003.

Kouzes, James M., and Barry Z. Posner. *The Leadership Challenge*, 3rd ed. San Francisco: Jossey-Bass, 2002.

Kyrillidou, Martha, and Fred M. Heath. *Measuring Service Quality*. Champaign, IL: University of Illinois Graduate School of Library and Information Science, 2001.

Lapin, Lawrence L. *Statistics for Modern Business Decisions*, 4th ed. San Diego: Harcourt Brace Jovanovich, Inc., 1987.

Lawrence, P. R., and J. W. Lorsch. *Organization and Environment*. Boston: Harvard University, Division of Research, Graduate School of Business Administration, 1967.

Ledolter, J., and A. Swersey. "An Evaluation of Pre-Control." *Journal of Quality Technology* 29, 2, April 1997, 163–171.

Levy, Steven. *Insanely Great: The Life and Times of Macintosh: the Computer That Changed Everything*. New York: Viking, 1994.

Lewin, Kurt. *A Dynamic Theory of Personality*. New York: McGraw-Hill, 1935.

Lindsay, William M., and Joseph A. Petrick. *Total Quality and Organization Development*. Boca Raton, FL: CRC/St. Lucie Press, 1997.

Lloyd's Register Quality Assurance, Ltd. *Getting the Most from ISO 9000*. 1999.

Locke, E. A., and G. P. Latham. *Goal Setting: A Motivational Technique that Works!* Englewood Cliffs, NJ: Prentice Hall, 1984.

Lowe, J. *Jack Welch Speaks*. New York: John Wiley & Sons, 1998.

Lowenthal, Jeffrey N. *Six Sigma Project Management: A Pocket Guide*. Milwaukee, WI: ASQ Quality Press, 2001.

Malcolm Baldrige National Quality Award. *2009-10 Criteria for Performance Excellence*. National

Institute of Standards and Technology, U.S. Department of Commerce.

Mayo, Elton. *The Human Problems of Industrial Civilization*. Cambridge, MA: Harvard Graduate School of Business, 1946.

Medina-Borja, Alexandra, and Konstantinos Triantis. "A Methodology to Evaluate Outcome Performance in Social Services and Government Agencies." *Proceedings* 55th Annual Quality Congress, May 2001, 707–719.

Melan, Eugene H. *Process Management: A Systems Approach to Total Quality*. Portland, OR: Productivity Press, 1995.

Messmer, Max. "Rightsizing, Not Downsizing: How to Maintain Quality Through Strategic Staffing." *Industry Week*, August 3, 1993, 23–26.

Michelli, Joseph A. *The New Gold Standard*, New York: McGraw-Hill, 2008.

Miller, Ken. *The Change Agent's Guide to Radical Improvement*. Milwaukee: ASQ Quality Press, 2002.

Miner, John B. *Theories of Organizational Behavior*. Hinsdale, IL: Dryden Press, 1980.

Mittal, Banwari, and Jagdish N. Sheth. *Value Space: Winning the Battle for Market Leadership: Lessons from the World's Most Admired Companies*. New York: McGraw-Hill, 2001.

Mohrman, Susan Albers, Ramkrishnan V. Tenkasi, Edward E. Lawler, III, and Gerald E. Ledford, Jr. "Total Quality Management: Practice and Outcomes in the Largest U.S. Firms." *Employee Relations* 17, 3 (1995): 26–41.

Montgomery, D. C. *Introduction to Statistical Quality Control*, 4th ed. New York: John Wiley & Sons, 2000.

Morgan, Ronald B., and Jacke E. Smith. *Staffing the New Workplace: Selecting and Promoting for Quality Improvement*. Milwaukee, WI: ASQ Press, 1996.

Neely, Andrew, Chris Adams, and Mike Kennerley. *The Performance Prism: The Scorecard for Measuring and Managing Business Success*. New York: Financial Times-Prentice Hall, 2002. Performance Measurement Association. http://www.performanceportal.org.

Nelson, Lloyd S. "Control Charts for Individual Measurements." *Journal of Quality Technology* 14, 3, July 1982, 172–173.

Nemiro, Jill, Michael M. Beyerlein, Lori Bradley, Susan Beyerlein (eds.) *The Handbook of High Performance Virtual Teams: A Toolkit for Collaborating Across Boundaries*. San Francisco: Jossey-Bass John Wiley & Sons, 2008.

Nogami, Glenda Y. "Eight Points for More Useful Surveys." *Quality Progress* 29, 10, October 1996, 93–96.

O'Dell, Karla, and C. Jackson Grayson, Jr. *If Only We Knew What We Know*. New York: Free Press, 1999.

Ohio Quality and Productivity Forum Roundtable. "Deming's Point Four: A Study." *Quality Progress* 21, 12, December 1988, 31–35.

Olian, Judy D., and Sara L. Rynes. "Making Total Quality Work: Aligning Organizational Processes, Performance Measures, and Stakeholders." *Human Resource Management* (Fall 1991) 303–333.

Ouelette, Steven M., and Michael V. Petrovich. "Daily Management and Six Sigma: Maximizing Your Returns." *Proceedings* ASQ 56th Annual Quality Congress, 2002.

Page, Harold S. "A Quality Strategy for the '80s." *Quality Progress* 16, 11, November 1983, 16–21.

Palmer, Brian, and Mike Ziemlanski. "Tapping Into People." *Quality Progress*, April 2000, 74–79.

Pande, Peter S., Robert P. Neuman, and Roland R. Cavanagh. *The Six Sigma Way Team Fieldbook: An Implementation Guide for Process Improvement Teams*. New York: McGraw-Hill Trade, 2001.

Parry, Pam. "Sears Delivers a Better QMS." *Quality Digest*, April 2006, 22–27.

Petrick, Joseph A., and Diana Furr. *Total Quality in Managing Human Resources*. Boca Raton, FL: CRC/St. Lucie Press, 1995.

Porter, Lyman W., Gregory A. Bigley, and Richard M. Steers. *Motivation and Work Behavior*, 7th ed. New York: McGraw-Hill, 2003.

Powell, Cash, Jr. "Empowerment, the Stake in the Ground for ABS." *Target*, January/February 1992.

Profiles of Malcolm Baldrige Award Winners. Boston: Allyn & Bacon, 1992.

Pyzdek, Thomas, *The Six Sigma Handbook*. New York: McGraw-Hill, 2003.

Pyzdek, Thomas. "Six Sigma Is Primarily a Management Program." *Quality Digest*, June 1999, 26.

Pyzdek, Thomas. *Pyzdek's Guide to SPC, Volume Two—Applications and Special Topics*. Milwaukee, WI: ASQ Quality Press, 1992.

Raju, P. S., and Subhash C. Lonial. "The Impact of Quality Context and Market Orientation on Organizational Performance in a Service Environment." *Journal of Service Research* 4, 2 (2001): 140–154.

Raturi, A., and D. McCutcheon. "An Epistemological Framework for Quality Management," working paper. Cincinnati, OH: University of Cincinnati, Department of Quantitative Analysis and Information Systems, March 1990.

Reilly, Norman B. *The Team Based Product Development Guidebook*. Milwaukee, WI: ASQ Quality Press, 1999.

Reimann, Curt W. "The Baldrige Award: Leading the Way in Quality Initiatives." *Quality Progress* 22, 7, July 1989, 35–39.

Reis, Dayr, Pahl, Joy, and Kuffel, Thomas. "Learning to Compete Through Quality." *The Quality Observer*, January 1997, 10–24.

Rice, George O. "Metrology." In Loren Walsh, Ralph Wurster, and Raymond J. Kimber (eds.). *Quality Management Handbook*. New York: Marcel Dekker, 1986, 517–530.

Robbins, C. L., and W. A. Robbins. "What Nurse Managers Should Know about Sampling Techniques." *Nursing Management* 20, 6, June 1989: 46–48.

Rosander, A. C. *Applications of Quality Control in the Service Industries*. New York: Marcel Dekker and ASQ Quality Press, 1985.

Rosander, A. C. *The Quest for Quality in Services*. Milwaukee, WI: ASQC Quality Press, 1989.

Rosenberg, Jarrett. "Five Myths about Customer Satisfaction." *Quality Progress* 29, 12, December 1996, 57–60.

Rosenfeld, Manny. "Only the Questions That Are Asked Can Be Answered." *Quality Progress*, April 1994, 71–73.

Rubinstein, Sidney P. "Quality and Democracy in the Workplace." *Quality Progress* 21, 4, April 1988, 25–28.

Rue, L. W., and L. Byars. *Management Skills and Applications*, 12th ed. New York: McGraw-Hill/Irwin, 2008.

Rust, Roland T., Christine Moorman, and Peter R. Dickson. *Getting Returns from Service Quality: Is the Conventional Wisdom Wrong?* Cambridge, MA: Marketing Science Institute, 2000.

Sample, Steven B. *The Contrarian's Guide to Leadership*. San Francisco: Jossey-Bass, 2001.

Sanes, Christina. "Customer Complaints = Golden Opportunities." *Transactions* 1993 ASQC Quality Congress, Boston, 45–51.

Scherkenbach, William W. *Deming's Road to Continual Improvement*. Knoxville, TN: SPC Press, 1991.

Schlesinger, Leonard A. "'Hardwiring' an Organization's Service Performance" Managing *Service Quality* 13, 1 (2003): 6–9.

Schmidt, Warren H., and Jerome P. Finnigan. *A Race Without a Finish Line*. San Francisco: Jossey-Bass Publishers, 1992.

Schneiderman, Arthur M. "Are There Limits to TQM?" *Strategy & Business* 11 (Second Quarter 1998): 35.

Schneiderman, Arthur M. "Why Balanced Scorecards Fail!" *Journal of Strategic Performance Measurement*, January 1999: 6.

Schneiderman, Arthur M. "Measurement, the Bridge between the Hard and Soft Sides." *Journal of Strategic Performance Measurement* 2, 2, April/May 1998: 14.

Scholtes, Peter R. "Communities as Systems." *Proceedings* ASQC 50th Annual Quality Congress (1996): 258–265.

Scholtes, P. R. *The Team Handbook*, 2nd ed. Madison, WI: Joiner Associates, 1996.

Semerad, James M. "Create a New Learning Environment." *APICS—The Performance Advantage*, April 1993, 34–37.

Sherman, Strat. "Stretch Goals: The Dark Side of Asking for Miracles." *Fortune*, November 13, 1995, 231–232.

Silverman, Lori with Annabeth L. Propst. *Critical SHIFT: The Future of Quality in Organizational Performance.* Milwaukee: ASQ Quality Press, 1999.

Simmons, David E., Mark A. Shadur, and Arthur P. Preston. "Integrating TQM and HRM." *Employee Relations* 17, 3 (1995): 75–86.

Smergut, Peter. "Total Quality Management and the Not-for-Profit." *Administration in Social Work,* 22, 3 (1998): 75.

Smith, Douglas K. and Robert C. Alexander. *Fumbling the Future: How Xerox Invented, Then Ignored the First Personal Computer.* New York: William Morrow and Co., 1988.

Snape, Ed, Adrian Wilkinson, Mick Marchington, and Ted Redman. "Managing Human Resources for TQM: Possibilites and Pitfalls." *Employee Relations* 17, 3 (1995), 42–51.

Snell, Scott A., and James W. Dean. "Integrated Manufacturing and Human Resource Management: A Human Capital Perspective." *Academy of Management Journal* 35, 3 (1992): 467–504.

Squires, Frank H. "What Do Quality Control Charts Control?" *Quality,* November 1982, 63.

St. Lawrence, Dennis, and Bob Stinnett. "Powerful Planning with Simple Techniques." *Quality Progress* 27, 7, July 1994, 57–64.

Stamatis, D. H. *Six Sigma and Beyond: Foundations of Excellent Performance.* Boca Raton, FL: St. Lucie/CRC Press, 2002.

Stewart, Thomas. *The Wealth of Knowledge.* New York: Currency, 2001.

Sutcliffe, Kathleen, Sim Sitkin, and Larry Browning. "Tailoring process management to situational requirements: Beyond the control and exploration dichotomy." from Robert E. Cole and W. Richard Scott [Eds.]. *The quality movement and organization theory.* Thousand Oaks, Calif.: Sage Publishing, 2000.

Taylor, Frederick W. *The Principles of Scientific Management.* New York: Harper & Row, 1911.

Taylor, Glenn L., and Martha N. Morgan. "The Reverse Appraisal: A Tool for Leadership Development" *Quality Progress* 28, 12, December 1995, 81–87.

Tedaldi, Michael, Fred Seaglione, and Vincent Russotti. *A Beginner's Guide to Quality in Manufacturing.* Milwaukee, WI: ASQC Quality Press, 1992.

Tedesco, Frank M. "Building Quality Goals into the Business Plan." *The Total Quality Review* 4, 1, March/April 1994: 31–34.

The Inc Team. *The Team Memory Jogger.* Madison, WI: Brian Joyner and Associates, Goal/QPC, 1995.

Tichy, Noel M., Andrew McGill, Andrew R. McGill (eds.). *The Ethical Challenge: How to Build Honest Business Leaders.* New York: John Wiley and Sons, 2003.

Tichy, Noel, and Eli Cohen. "The Teaching Organization." *Training and Development,* July 1998.

Tomas, Sam. "Six Sigma: Motorola's Quest for Zero Defects." *APICS, The Performance Advantage,* July 1991, 36–41.

Tomas, Sam. "What Is Motorola's Six Sigma Product Quality?" *American Production and Inventory Control Society 1990 Conference Proceedings.* Falls Church, VA: APICS, 27–31.

Tomas, Sam. "What Is Motorola's Six Sigma Product Quality?" *American Production and Inventory Control Society 1990 Conference Proceedings.* Falls Church, VA: APICS: 27–31.

U.S. Department of Commerce and Booz-Allen & Hamilton, Inc. "Total Quality Management (TQM): Implementer's Workshop." May 1990.

Van der Wiele, Ton, Alan Brown, Robert Millen, and Daniel Whelan. "Improvement in Organizational Performance and Self-Assessment Practices by Selected American Firms." *Quality Management Journal* 7, 4, October 2000, 8–22.

Van Gigch, John P. "Quality—Producer and Consumer Views." *Quality Progress* 10, 4, April 1977, 30–33.

Vance, Lonnie C. "A Bibliography of Statistical Quality Control Chart Techniques, 1970–1980." *Journal of Quality Technology* 15, 12, April 1983.

Wachniak, Ray. "World-Class Quality: An American Response to the Challenge." In M. Sepehri (ed.), *Quest for Quality: Managing the Total System.* Norcross, GA: Institute of Industrial Engineers, 1987.

Wadsworth, Harrison M., Kenneth S. Stephens, and A. Blanton Godfrey. *Modern Methods for Quality Control and Improvement*, 2nd ed. New York: John Wiley & Sons, 2002.

Waldman, David A. "A Theoretical Consideration of Leadership and Total Quality Management." *Leadership Quarterly* 4 (1993): 65–79.

Walton, Richard E. "From Control to Commitment in the Workplace." *Harvard Business Review* 63, 2, March/April 1985, 77–85.

Watson, Gregory H. Design for Six Sigma, Salem, NH: GOAL/QPC, 2005.

Watson, Gregory H. "Peter F. Drucker: Delivering Value to Customers." *Quality Progress* 35, 5, May 2002.

Welch, Jack, and John Byrne. *Jack: Straight from the Gut*. New York: Warner Books, 2001.

Welch, Jack, Rik Kirkland, and Geoffrey Colvin. "Jack: The Exit Interview." *Fortune*, September 17, 2001.

Whiteley, Richard C. *The Customer-Driven Company*. Reading, MA: Addison-Wesley, 1991.

Wilkerson, David, and Clifton Cooksey. *Customer Service Measurement*. Arlington, VA: Coopers & Lybrand, 1994.

Wong, Amy, and Amrik Sohal. "Customers' Perspectives on Service Quality and Relationship Quality in Retail Encounters." *Managing Service Quality* 12, 6, 2002: 424–433.

Yakhou, Mehenna, and Boubekeur Rahali. "Integration of Business Functions: Roles of Cross-Functional Information Systems." *APICS—The Performance Advantage* 2, 12, December 1992: 35–37.

Yee, William, and Ed Musselwhite. "Living TQM With Workforce 2000." *Transactions* 1993 ASQC Quality Congress. Boston, 141–146.

Zeithaml, A. Parasuraman, and Leonard L. Berry. *Delivering Quality Service*. New York: The Free Press, 1990.

Zemke, Ron. "The Emerging Art of Service Management." *Training* 29, January 1992: 36–42.

Zimmerman, Richard E., Linda Steinmann, and Vince Schueler. "Designing Customer Surveys That Work." *Quality Digest*, October 1996, 22–28.

Zubairi, Mazhar M. "Statistical Process Control Management Issues." 1985 IIE Fall Conference Proceedings. Reprinted in Mehran Sepehri (ed.), *Quest for Quality: Managing the Total System*. Norcross, GA: Industrial Engineering & Management Press, 1987.

Index

E

X

Gap
GE Fanuc
General Electric
General Foods
General Mills
General Motors
General Systems Company
Golden Plaza Hotel, San Francisco
Gold Star Chili, Inc.
Graniterock Company

Harley-Davidson, Inc.
Harley Owners Group
Heartland Regional Medical Center (HRMC)
Hennes & Mauritz
Hershey Foods Corporation
Hewitt
Hewlett-Packard
Hillerich & Bradsby Co.
Hilton Hotels Corp.
Home Depot
Honda
Honeywell International
Huawei Technologies
Hyundai Motor Company

IBM Credit Corporation
International Organization for Standardization
International Telephone and Telegraph

Jenks Public Schools
Johnson Controls, Inc.
Johnson & Johnson
Joint Commission on Accreditation of Healthcare
    Organizations
Jostens
Juran Institute

Kaizen Institute
KARLEE Company
Kenneth W. Monfort College of Business
K&N Management, Inc.
Kodak

L. L. Bean
Lands' End
LaRosa's Inc.
Levi Strauss
Lexus automobiles

Macy's Department Store
Magnivision
Maguire Miles
Managed Care Organization (MCO)

Marlow Industries
Mary Kay Cosmetics
MasteryWorks Inc.
Mazda
MCI
Medical College of Wisconsin
Medrad
Mercedes-Benz
Merrill Lynch Credit Corporation
MESA Products, Inc.
Mesa Products, Inc.
Microsoft
Midland Builders
MidwayUSA
Milliken
Mitsubishi
Motorola, Inc.

NASA
Nashua Corporation
National Academy of Sciences/Institute
    of Medicine
National Cash Register Company
National Council for Performance Excellence
National Housing Quality Award (NHQA)
National Institute of Standards and Technology
National Quality Institute
Nationwide Insurance
Naval Air Systems Command
Nestlé Purina PetCare Company
Netflix
Nissan Motor Car Company Limited
Nissan Motor Company Ltd.
Nordam Europe, Ltd.
Nucor Corporation

Occupational Safety and Health Administration
Operations Management International, Inc.
Oracle

Pal's Sudden Service
Park Place Lexus
Pearl River School District
Performance Improvement Steering Committee
    (PISC)
Philip Crosby Associates
PIMS Associates
Press Ganey Associates
Procter & Gamble

QuEST Forum

Rath & Strong
Raytheon

continued on next page